WORLD EXPLORERS
and
DISCOVERERS

WORLD EXPLORERS
and
DISCOVERERS

Editor
Richard E. Bohlander

Consultants

John L. Allen
Professor of Geography
University of Connecticut

Sanford H. Bederman
Professor of Geography
Georgia State University

Theodore N. Foss
Assistant Director,
Center for East Asian Studies
Stanford University

Edward J. Goodman
Professor Emeritus of History
Xavier University

Barry M. Gough
Professor of History
Wilfrid Laurier University

William C. Wonders
Professor Emeritus of
Geography
University of Alberta

DA CAPO PRESS • NEW YORK

Library of Congress Cataloging-in-Publication Data

World explorers and discoverers / editor, Richard E. Bohlander; consultants, John L. Allen . . .
    [et al.].—1st Da Capo Press ed.
        p.   cm.
    Originally published: New York: Macmillan, c1992.
    Includes bibliographical references and index.
    ISBN 0-306-80824-2 (alk. paper)
    1. Explorers—Biography—Dictionaries. I. Bohlander, Richard E.
[G200.W67 1998]
910′.922—dc21   97-41566
                                                                               CIP

First Da Capo Press edition 1998

This Da Capo Press paperback edition of *World Explorers and Discoverers* is an unabridged
republication of the edition first published in New York in 1992. It is reprinted by arrangement
with Macmillan Library Reference, a division of Simon and Schuster, Inc.

Published by Da Capo Press, Inc.
A Subsidiary of Plenum Publishing Corporation
233 Spring Street, New York, N.Y. 10013

CONTENTS

Preface   ix

Biographical Profiles

CONTENTS

CONTENTS

PREFACE

World Explorers and Discoverers is a biographical dictionary containing profiles of 313 of the most significant men and women in the history of world exploration. Intended for a wide range of readers, the articles describe the lives of these individuals, both famous and obscure, with an emphasis on their activities and contributions as explorers. As a group, their lives are characterized by the boldness, courage, and strength of character required of those who go where few—or none—have gone before. Their pioneering accomplishments were often achieved in dramatic fashion, frequently in the face of hunger, disease, mutiny, impenetrable terrain, public indifference, or other severe hardships.

The subjects of the profiles were selected by a board of distinguished editorial consultants, historians, and geographers known for their work in the field of the history of discovery. Their primary intent was to choose those explorers judged to be the most important in history. These six experts applied individual criteria in making these difficult determinations of relative historic importance. Their consensus choices constitute the table of contents of *World Explorers and Discoverers*.

Excluded from consideration were people known primarily for their pioneering efforts in the fields of space exploration, aviation, and mountaineering, activities that are sometimes viewed in the general context of world exploration. A handful of figures, however, have been included not for their accomplishments as explorers, but for their critical contributions to the field of exploration in other roles. These fall into three primary categories: geographers (such as PTOLEMY) whose work profoundly affected the history of exploration, inventors (such as JOHN HARRISON) whose new technologies changed the course of such history, and chroniclers (such as RICHARD HAKLUYT) whose writings not only recorded the history of discovery but shaped it by virtue of their own influence.

The length of the profiles, and therefore their scope, varies markedly, from as few as 450 words to as many as 4,000. Like the content determinations, these lengths have been chosen with an eye toward the historic importance of an individual's contributions as an explorer.

The profiles aim to provide the reader with the outlines of the explorer's life, character, and primary achievements. While biographical, they are intended to deal at least as much with the historic significance and context of the exploration as with the bare facts of that work. This is especially true of the longer profiles, which have the more important explorers as their subjects. Wherever possible, current interpretations of history regarding specific explorers and their achievements are discussed. For example, the great and ongoing debate over the site of landfall is examined in the profile on CHRISTOPHER COLUMBUS.

The biographical entries are arranged alphabetically by last name. When more than one form or spelling of an individual's name is known, the editors chose to use what they judged to be the best original form, unless an alternative is so commonly known as to be preferred, as with FERDINAND MAGELLAN, for example. Alternative name forms and spellings are shown parenthetically at the beginning of a profile. Where useful to the reader, these alternative forms appear in the main alphabetical listing with a reference to the form by which the subject is actually listed.

Each profile begins with a headnote listing the explorer's name (last name first), followed by nationality, date and place of birth, date and place of death, and a brief statement of the subject's primary accomplishments. Nationalities are listed as the best modern equivalent that fairly represents the various shifting realities of history. Thus the famous Venetian explorer MARCO POLO is listed as Italian, and so on. To simplify geographic identification, places of birth and death are recorded by their modern names, with historic names occasionally shown parenthetically when necessary for clarity. Places of birth and death may be assumed to lie within the native country implied by the listed nationality, unless noted otherwise.

Within the profiles, several devices have been used to aid the reader's understanding of the material. Initial references to an individual profiled elsewhere in *World Explorers and Discoverers* appear in SMALL-CAPITAL letters. This device is meant to help the reader trace interrelated developments and themes in the history of exploration and discovery. In addition, certain geographic and technical terms related to exploration appear in *italics* at the first instance of their use within a given profile. These are discussed at greater length in a glossary of terms at the back of this book. Finally, suggested reading notes appear at the conclusion of the book's forty longest profiles. These sources have been chosen for their authoritativeness, the likelihood of their general availability, and, where possible, a reading level appropriate for high school students. (A more comprehensive bibliography of both general and specific works related to exploration appears at the back of this book.)

Every effort has been made to ensure that the numerous place name references within the text are accurate and consistent. Nevertheless, readers should be aware that over the course of the history of exploration both nomenclature and spelling of place names have shifted frequently, as a result of time and history and of the inconsistent manner in which they have been recorded. For the sake of comprehension,

the editors have used the following general rules in reporting place names within the profiles. First, where place names other than current ones were in common use at the time of a particular exploration, the contemporary names are given first, with the best modern equivalents noted (usually parenthetically) at first use. Thus MARCO POLO is described as having traveled to and written of "Cathay (present-day China)," and so on. Second, both historic and modern name forms have been standardized as much as possible, despite the proliferation of alternative forms and spellings—especially of historic forms—in the various source materials. Wherever possible, name forms that appear most frequently in the literature have been chosen over other possibilities, and the listing of alternative names and spellings has been kept to the minimum required for comprehension.

Following the profiles are four appendixes (in order): the glossary of terms, mentioned above; a list of profiled explorers categorized by nationality; a similar list broken down according to broad geographic areas of exploration; and a bibliography of works related to the history of exploration and discovery. These are followed by a general subject index to the book.

The efforts of many people are responsible for bringing this book to fruition, most notably the consultants listed on its title page. Their numerous contributions in shaping and refining the work throughout its development were fundamental.

The credit for creating the original profiles constituting *World Explorers and Discoverers* goes to a talented group of writers: Linda Barrett, Loretta Bolger, Cathie Cush, Joseph Gregory, Galen Guengerich, William E. Klein, Lois Markham, and Donna L. Singer. The value of their original contributions cannot be overstated.

In addition, thanks are due five people for their contributions: Cheryl Mannes, for photo research and acquisition; Gyula Pauer, director of the University of Kentucky Cartography Lab, and lab assistant Jerri Williams, for original maps illustrating routes of exploration; and Linda Biemiller and Laura Daly, for copyediting.

The editor is particularly grateful to his colleagues at Visual Education Corporation: Richard Lidz and Paula McGuire, for their original conception of this work; Amy Lewis, for research; Dale Anderson, for his suggestions, support, and encouragement; Susan Tatiner, for coordination of all copyediting; Cindy Feldner, for her patient and expert inputting and proofreading of the manuscript; and especially Denise Wilkinson, who as assistant editor made a wide array of editorial and organizational contributions throughout the course of this work's development.

The editor extends his deepest personal appreciation to the reference division of Macmillan Publishing Company, which commissioned this work. Thanks are particularly due to Philip Friedman, president and publisher, whose support has been unqualified from the start and from whose insight and guidance this book has benefited immeasurably.

—Richard E. Bohlander
Princeton, New Jersey

BIOGRAPHICAL PROFILES

• Abruzzi, Luigi Amedeo, Duke of the

Italian
b January 29, 1873; Madrid, Spain
d March 18, 1933; near Mogadishu, Somalia
Led expedition to North Pole; first to ascend Mount St. Elias

An accomplished mountaineer who had several first ascents to his credit, Luigi Amedeo Abruzzi, a member of the royal house of Savoy, was also the leader of the Italian expedition to the North Pole in 1899. Though a severe case of frostbite prevented him from making the final dash to the pole, the expedition succeeded in reaching a record-high latitude (86°34′ North) under the second in command, Captain Umberto Cagni.

Abruzzi's ship, the *Stella Polare*, sailed from Christiania (present-day Oslo) on June 12, 1899, with all of the equipment recommended by the Arctic explorer FRIDTJOF NANSEN. Abruzzi's plan was to have the expedition follow the route north of Franz Josef Land that Nansen had pioneered from his ship the *Fram* four years earlier. The expedition wintered on Rudolph Island and set off in three parties in mid-February. After realizing that the **sledges** were badly overloaded, Cagni returned to base, reorganized, and set off again on March 10. Progress northward was very slow, and there was a considerable drift to the west. On April 25, 1900, the party hoisted the Italian flag at their northernmost point. The trip home was very difficult

due to the breakup of the ice and the drift. One of the supply parties was lost, but Cagni's lead party made it back to base on June 21. This was the first time a Mediterranean power had made history in the Arctic.

Vice Admiral Abruzzi was destined to play a major role in World War I as commander of the Italian naval forces in the Adriatic. After the war he took an important part in the Italian occupation of Somaliland. But it was his career as a mountain climber that made him world famous. Two years before the dash to the pole, he had been the first to ascend Mount St. Elias in Alaska. In 1906 he climbed the highest peaks of the Ruwenzori Range lying between Uganda and present-day Zaire. Three years later, he was in the Himalayas, where he ascended the peak called K2 beyond the 20,000-foot mark and Bride Peak up to 24,600 feet. His accounts of the ascents of Mount St. Elias and Mount Ruwenzori were translated into English early in the century.

• Acuña, Cristóbal de

Spanish
b 1597?; Burgos
d 1676; Lima, Peru
Produced earliest published account of Amazon River

An established rector of the college at Cuenca (in modern Ecuador), Father Cristóbal de Acuña suddenly found himself part of an extraordinary journey down the Amazon from Peru to Pará (present-day Belém), Brazil, in 1639. His journal of this journey, which is the earliest published narrative about the Amazon, details aspects of the great river, its tributaries, the various Indian tribes that lived along its banks, and the geographical features of the Amazon River valley.

Acuña was born in the city of Burgos in northern Spain around 1597; the exact date of his birth is unknown. Information about his life, except for the Amazon adventure, is very sketchy. Specifics about his childhood, education, and religious training are unavailable, but he apparently received the extensive training required to become a Jesuit missionary. Acuña arrived in Peru sometime in the 1620s and was appointed rector of the college at Cuenca, then part of Peru.

When the Portuguese captain PEDRO DE TEIXEIRA arrived in Quito in 1638 after his successful navigation up the Amazon from Pará, Spanish officials realized that they had better learn more about the Amazon in order to protect their Peruvian empire and their claim to the Amazon, as assigned by the **Treaty of Tordesillas**. After much discussion, the king of Spain ordered that a Spaniard accompany Teixeira on his return journey and give a detailed report to the king and the **Council of the Indies**. The governor of Quito, Don Juan Vásquez de Acuña, volunteered to make the trip, but his brother, Father Cristóbal de Acuña, was chosen instead. Father Acuña was instructed to "describe, with clearness, the distance in leagues, the provinces, tribes of Indians, rivers, and districts. . . ."

The Teixeira expedition left Quito on February 16, 1639, and traveled down the Napo River toward the Amazon. Acuña first noted the network of tributaries that fed into the Amazon from the upper Amazon Valley, permitting access to the Amazon from Peru and New Granada (modern Colombia) and permitting transport from these regions directly to the Atlantic Ocean. Traveling next down the Marañón River (the upper Amazon), Acuña was particularly impressed by the Agua Indians, whom he described as the "most intelligent and best governed of any tribe on the river."

His first sight of the Amazon proper inspired Acuña to exclaim that it was "the largest and most celebrated river in the world." As the expedition proceeded down the river, Acuña's near-poetic descriptions created a picture of the Amazon area as a Garden of Eden. He wrote, "The river is full of fish, the forests with game, the air of birds, the trees are covered with fruit . . . ," and he recommended that the Spanish authorities pursue cultivation of the resources he encountered along the river's banks—timber, cacao, tobacco, and sugarcane. He envisioned a shipbuilding industry using lumber from the forests, medicinal drugs being developed from materials known to the Indians, and tobacco and sugar plantations. Not only the natural resources but also the climate found favor with Acuña: he asserted that the "heat does not molest and cold does not fatigue."

Acuña viewed everything in a positive light, from the land to the people who inhabited it. He carefully documented more than 150 Indian nations, describing their customs, languages, trading practices, and wars with one another. He was particularly interested in the turtle roundups the Indians held. Captured turtles were kept in wooden holding tanks until the Indians needed them for food. Acuña recorded that turtle eggs were "almost as good as hen's eggs, though harder of digestion." Acuña also noted with interest the unusual Indian method of fishing by beating the water with poisonous vines, which stuns the fish and brings them floating to the surface.

While Acuña was impressed with the extensive trading systems of the Indians through which a tribe like the Omagua could trade their cotton work for the Curucirari's polychrome pottery, he was distressed by the constant tribal wars. However, he looked at these wars philosophically, stating that they were "the drain provided for so great a multitude, without which the entire land would not be large enough to contain them."

Acuña reserved his one negative reaction during the journey for the Portuguese practice of slaving along the river. Slave raids had made the tribes so terrified of Europeans that the Indians either fled inland as the expedition passed or were overly hospitable and obsequious. The slavers followed the practice of erecting crosses in the Indian villages as magic symbols to be paid for with captives. Because of the trickery involved, Acuña refused to erect any crosses. Once, at the mouth of the Río Negro, when the Portuguese soldiers wanted to go on a slave raid upstream, Acuña and the other Jesuits made such strenuous objections that Teixeira agreed to forgo the raid and continue down the Amazon.

Acuña noted the interesting sight of the black waters from the Negro mixing with the browner flow of the Amazon at the convergence of these two rivers. Two of the most interesting scientific accounts in Acuña's journal are the first recorded descriptions to reach Europe of a manatee and of what is now called an electric eel. In Acuña's words, the manatee "has hair all over its body, not very long, like soft bristles, and the animal moves in the water with short fins, which in the form of paddles, serve as propellers." The electric eel "is like a conger eel. It has the peculiarity that, when alive, whoever touches it trembles all over his body, while closer contact produces a feeling like the cold shiverings of **ague**; which ceases the moment he withdraws his hand."

Proceeding downriver, the expedition landed on the island of Tupinambarana, just beyond the mouth of the Madeira River, to get food. There they encountered the Tupinambá Indians who had migrated some 3,500 miles in order to escape the Portuguese invasions of Brazil. Acuña described these Indians as "noble-hearted" and very hospitable. From them he heard the legend of the Amazons (a civilization of women warriors), as well as a retelling of the legends of a land of giants, tribes of pygmies, and men whose feet were turned backwards—tales that had already been recounted to the priest by other tribes. He neither evaluated nor judged these stories but simply recorded them as recited, concluding that "time will discover the truth."

When the expedition reached Pará on December 16, 1639, Acuña immediately wrote to the king of Spain recommending that Spain act quickly to occupy "Amazonia." He suggested that the river would provide a well-protected route to transport riches from Peru and that occupation of the area would stop the English, Dutch, and Portuguese from encroaching on lands belonging to Spain. He also urged the monarch to stop the Indian wars and to support a plan to convert the Indians, since he felt they would "make good Christians." However, when Acuña reached Spain to present his report in person, the political climate was changing. By the time his journal, the *New Discovery of the Great River of the Amazons*, was published in 1641, Spain had already lost her claim to the Amazon. The Portuguese monarchy had been restored, and Teixeira had successfully extended Portuguese control over the Amazon region.

Disheartened, Acuña returned to Peru to take up religious duties, the nature of which is unknown. He died in Lima in 1676. Though Spain did not profit from the account of Acuña's journey, the world was given its first detailed record of the Amazon and its myriad Indian tribes by a man who was the first to see the infinite possibilities of the vast region's natural resources.

· Akeley, Delia Denning

American
b December 5, 1875; Beaver Dam, Wisconsin
d May 22, 1970; Daytona Beach, Florida
Explored Africa, collecting plant and animal
   specimens for museums

Through her travels and research, Delia Denning Akeley linked the world of equatorial Africa with museum visitors in Chicago, Manhattan, Brooklyn, and Newark. She made her first trip to Africa in 1905 to help her husband, Carl F. Akeley, collect animals for a new exhibit at the Field Museum of Natural History in Chicago. Over the next twenty years, she returned to Africa a number of times on her own, both to collect plant and animal specimens and to study the people of the Congo. Through numerous writings and lectures, she opened the wonders of exotic Africa to an eager American public.

Little is known about Delia Denning's early life, but she met Akeley when he was working as a sculptor at the Milwaukee Art Museum. She helped him prepare realistic animal exhibits for various museums. They were married in 1902, shortly after he was offered a job by the Field Museum in Chicago. He became famous for the lifelike animals and realistic backgrounds in his exhibits. With Delia as his assistant, Akeley went to Kenya in 1905 to collect specimens for a new exhibit.

During their eighteen months in East Africa, Delia shot two elephants—a major achievement for a beginner—and collected numerous other animals and birds. She also fell in love with Africa, a passion that deepened when the Akeleys returned in 1909 to collect elephants for the American Museum of Natural History in

Delia Denning Akeley (right), with Dr. George P. Englehardt. UPI/Bettmann.

New York. Carl spent much of this trip either sick or injured, but Delia carried on their work. In the process, she developed an interest in animal behavior and proved to be an astute observer of the human-like behavior of baboon families.

After helping with the war effort in both England and France during World War I, Delia returned to the United States. Soon thereafter, Carl traveled to Africa with another woman, whom he subsequently married after he and Delia were divorced in 1923. He died in Africa in 1926, and his will, written in 1921, left everything to his second wife, MARY LEE JOBE AKELEY. Delia's contributions to his earlier work were subsequently ignored.

Meanwhile, Delia Akeley had received a commission of her own from the Brooklyn Museum of Arts and Sciences to collect specimens for an exhibit. She went to Kenya and traveled up the Tana River with five canoes and a crew of native porters. After ten weeks on the river, she crossed the Somalia desert, then turned south to Meru, Kenya, from which she sent her completed collection to America.

Akeley was now free to pursue a plan to find and study a primitive African tribe. She set out for the Belgian Congo (now Zaire) looking for the Pygmies, a small-statured tribe said to make their home in the Ituri Forest. After a grueling journey, she found the Pygmies and lived with them for several months. She had expected to find them stunted by malnutrition, but, although small, they were happy, healthy, and well-nourished. They allowed her to participate in their hunting, and she taught them how to jump rope—or vines, as it happened.

When Akeley left the Congo, she returned to the United States and wrote two books and numerous articles about her adventures in Africa. A final trip to the Congo was terminated prematurely due to torrential rains.

• Akeley, Mary Lee Jobe

American
b January 29, 1878; Tappan, Ohio
d July 19, 1966; Stonington, Connecticut
Explored Africa and Canada

Mary Lee Jobe Akeley is best known for bringing public attention to the natural wonders of Africa

Mary Lee Jobe Akeley. UPI/Bettmann.

leave of absence from Hunter College in 1909 to join an expedition in British Columbia. The month-long trip whetted her appetite for exploration, and she made a series of return trips to the Canadian northwest during the following decade to study the region's Indian tribes and vegetation. She also earned fame as a mountain climber in the Canadian Rockies and later had a mountain named after her. When she married explorer Carl Akeley in 1924, she turned her attention to his primary interest—African exploration.

Determined to create a Great African Hall within New York's Museum of Natural History, Carl Akeley led a 1926 trip to collect plants and wildlife specimens and to study gorillas in the Belgian Congo. Late that year he died of a fever, and his widow continued his mission in the country's Parc National, completing the study of gorillas and collecting additional specimens needed for the museum exhibit. She also explored Tanganyika, Kenya, and the Congo, mapping out many unfamiliar areas, and studied the languages and cultures of native tribes. Returning to New York in 1927, she became a consultant on the African Hall project and gathered additional materials for the exhibit on a 1935 trip to Southern Rhodesia and Portuguese East Africa. For her work on behalf of the museum, she became known as the woman who "brought the jungle to Central Park West" (Central Park West is the museum's New York City location).

In the years between her first two trips to Africa, Akeley traveled to Belgium to report on the outcome of the Belgian Congo expedition and to receive the Cross of the Knight from King Albert in recognition of her work. She then took part in that country's effort to enlarge its African colony's national park and to preserve the area's large primates. Through her numerous books and photographs, she became one of the leading spokespersons in the growing movement to preserve the native cultures of Africa and to protect its wildlife from extinction. Her final trip to Africa was in 1952, when she surveyed the Congo's wildlife preserves and parks on behalf of the Belgian government and visited the park she had helped to enlarge. Reclusive in her later years, Akeley retired to her vacation home in Mystic, Connecticut.

through her exploration, writing, and photography. She also explored extensively in the Canadian northwest before traveling to the Belgian Congo (now Zaire) as part of her husband's expedition to study gorillas there. Upon his death, she took his place as leader, concluded the gorilla study, and went on to explore uncharted areas of the Congo, Kenya, and Tanganyika. Her pictures and writings highlighted the beauty of Africa's wildlife and landscapes and emphasized the importance of preserving its native cultures.

Born and educated in Ohio, Akeley pursued graduate study at Bryn Mawr. After several years of study and teaching, she requested a

Alaminos, Antón de

Spanish
b 1478?; Palos de Moguer, Huelva
d ?
Explored Gulf of Mexico

As a young boy, Antón de Alaminos had the privilege of sailing with CHRISTOPHER COLUMBUS on Columbus's second voyage to the New World in 1493. He then served as chief pilot for JUAN PONCE DE LEÓN's Florida expedition, for two expeditions to the Yucatán peninsula, and for HERNÁN CORTÉS's epic journey to conquer the Aztec empire in 1518. Finally, in partnership with ALONSO ALVAREZ DE PINEDA, he explored Mexique Bay (present-day Gulf of Mexico) in search of a passage to the South Sea (Pacific Ocean).

Aliminos was born in Palos de Moguer in the province of Huelva in Spain; his exact birthdate is unknown. He was probably born about 1478, but no later than 1480, as he was listed as being in his early teens when he sailed with Columbus in 1493. No known records mention him during the twenty years that passed after that voyage; he next appears in the records as chief pilot when Ponce de León discovered Florida in 1513.

He next sailed with Francisco Fernández de Córdoba in 1517, ostensibly to obtain slaves in the Bahamas; however, Alaminos persuaded the commander to sail west in search of rumored lands of wealth. Reaching the Yucatán peninsula near modern Cape Catoche, Alaminos expertly navigated the coral and limestone shoreline with its many lagoons and sandbars, sailing as far west as Petouchán (present-day Champotón). Returning to Cuba by way of Florida, Fernández de Córdoba and Alaminos were wounded in skirmishes with Indians along the southwest coast of Florida when they landed to obtain food.

With interest piqued by Alaminos's tales of Mayan temples and gold, another expedition led by Juan de Grijalva and piloted by Alaminos left Cuba in 1518 for the Yucatán. They discovered the island of Cozumel and explored the mouth of the Tabasco River (now the Grijalva), reaching a point north of the Pánuco River before returning. By this time Alaminos was considered Spain's best navigator in the Caribbean and was chosen as Cortés's chief pilot for the expedition to explore Mexico, which also took place in 1518.

While Cortés penetrated the interior of Mexico, Alaminos went to Jamaica, where he received support for a venture to explore Mexique Bay for a possible passage to the South Sea. With Alvarez de Pineda he sailed around the Gulf of Mexico, along the western coast of Florida, past the delta of the Mississippi River, and finally along the shores of what is now Texas. At a place called Chila near the mouth of the Pánuco River, the expedition group fought the Aztecs. Pineda and many others were killed, flayed, and eaten by the Aztecs. Alaminos managed to escape to Vera Cruz with one ship.

The remainder of Alaminos's life is shrouded in uncertainty, though he did pilot a ship loaded with gold from Mexico to Spain for Cortés in about 1520. The date and place of his death are unknown.

Albuquerque, Afonso de

Portuguese
b 1453; Alhandra, near Lisbon
d December 15, 1515; at sea off Goa, India
Consolidated Portuguese power in Orient

Afonso de Albuquerque was a charming **courtier**, a ruthless warrior, and perhaps the most able naval strategist of his day. As the second governor of Portugal's tenuously held colonies in India, he realized that the future of Lisbon's power in the East hung on its ability to establish and maintain a series of strategic maritime bases in the Arabian Sea and along the Malabar Coast of southwestern India. Using the Indian seaport city of Goa as a base, Albuquerque conquered Malacca, a nautical gateway to China located on the Malay Peninsula, and harassed and intimidated Portugal's European rivals and Islamic enemies in the Indian Ocean. His shrewd alliances and calculated military gambles enabled Portugal to dominate the lucrative Asian spice trade and made the tiny country one of the wealthiest nations of sixteenth-century Europe.

Albuquerque was born in 1453 in Alhandra, near Lisbon, to a wealthy military family with close ties to the Portuguese throne. As a young soldier, he fought Portugal's Islamic enemies in Morocco and Tangier. After ten years in North Africa, he returned to the court of Manuel I,

Afonso de Albuquerque. The Bettmann Archive.

the dynamic monarch who would lead Portugal to glory and wealth in the East.

During the sixteenth century, the Asian spice trade was immensely profitable and fiercely competitive. The powerful Islamic kingdoms of the Middle East had closed off the traditional overland trade routes to the Europeans, who vied among themselves to dominate the sea-lanes to the Orient. Since VASCO DA GAMA had first returned from India in 1499, the Portuguese had set up a series of trading "factories" along the Malabar Coast. Many Indian rulers were hostile to the interlopers, however. Moving quickly to consolidate his growing empire, Manuel sent a naval squadron commanded by Albuquerque to India in 1503 with orders to secure trade routes around the horn of Africa and into the Indian Ocean. A shrewd diplomat, Albuquerque was able to win the support of the raja of Cochin, who permitted him to build the first Portuguese fortress in Asia on the southwestern coast of India.

Albuquerque returned to Lisbon in July 1504. The following year, Manuel named Dom Francisco de Almeida viceroy of India. With a force of twenty-two ships and 2,500 men, Almeida set up a government in Cochin and took control of Ceylon (now Sri Lanka). Meanwhile, in April 1506, Albuquerque led a naval expedition aimed at cutting off Arab access to India. The Portuguese built a fort on the island of Socotra in the Gulf of Aden. In August 1507 they fought for and captured the city of Hormuz, which commands the entrance to the strategically important Persian Gulf. Here Albuquerque showed the savagery that made the Portuguese hated and feared in the East. Female prisoners had their noses and ears cut off; males, their noses and right hands.

In 1509 Albuquerque succeeded Almeida as governor-general of the East Indies. Realizing that Portugal's main trading centers on India's Malabar Coast lacked good harbors, he decided to capture the port of Goa. With a force of twenty-three ships and the aid of powerful Indian **corsairs**, the Portuguese waged a bitter struggle with Goa's Muslim defenders. In March 1510 they entered the city but were forced out by the Muslims a few months later. Finally, in November they made an all-out assault, overwhelmed the walls, and slaughtered the defenders. To ensure the permanence of their victory, Albuquerque ordered his men to marry the massacred Muslims' widows and produce Christian children loyal to Lisbon. By securing Goa, Albuquerque gained the support of the region's Hindu princes, who used the Portuguese as allies against their Muslim rivals.

At this point, Albuquerque was able to expand his power base to Southeast Asia. In July 1511 his fleet took the city of Malacca on the Malay Peninsula, thus gaining control of the strategic straits leading to China. But the Muslim threat was not completely crushed. Albuquerque returned to Goa to find the city under attack. Once again he fought off the Muslim offensive, then sailed for the Red Sea. But the Portuguese forces were spread too thin; Socotra had to be abandoned. Fighting at Hormuz flared intermittently. On an expedition there in 1515, Albuquerque fell ill. On December 15 he died aboard ship off Goa.

Albuquerque was a brilliant admiral who made the most of his limited resources. Inevitably, though, the tiny country of Portugal was not able to hold on to its huge gains. By the end of the sixteenth century, Portuguese influence in the Orient had waned.

Alexander the Great

Greek
b 356 B.C.; northern Greece (Pella)
d June 13, 323 B.C.; near Hilla, Iraq (Babylon)
Explored and conquered most of ancient world

One of the greatest generals in history, Alexander the Great conquered a great portion of Europe, Asia, and Africa before he was thirty. A man of profound intellectual curiosity, he led an international army through Persia (now Iran) to what are now southern Russia, Pakistan, and India—regions that no European had ever fully explored. Although cruel in war, Alexander had the wisdom to transcend the beliefs of his teacher, the great philosopher Aristotle, who thought Greece's enemies should be enslaved. Alexander generally extended the olive branch of peace to the peoples he conquered, building more than seventy cities and bringing

A bust of Alexander the Great. Alinari/Art Resource Center.

Hellenic culture to Asia. But his successors lacked his charisma and vision. Shortly after he died in his thirty-third year, his empire collapsed.

Alexander was born in 356 B.C. at Pella, the son of King Philip II of Macedonia and Queen Olympias. While still a child, his parents divorced, and Alexander and his mother were forced to flee the court. He later reconciled with his father and fought with him in battles to unify the Greeks and lead them against their common enemy, the Persians. When Philip was assassinatcd in 336 B.C., the youthful Alexander acted quickly to gain power, executing those he believed responsible for his father's death, as well as anyone who challenged his authority.

As a teenager, Alexander had been tutored by Aristotle, who inspired his interest in literature, philosophy, and exploration. At the age of twenty-one, assured of his throne, the new king was determined to realize his father's ambition to break the Persian empire. In the spring of 334 B.C., at the head of an army of 35,000, he set out to conquer eastern regions. Pausing at the ruins of Troy, Alexander visited the supposed grave of Achilles, whom he claimed as an ancestor. Then he moved south, retaking Persian-occupied cities along the Aegean coast of modern Turkey. Crossing into what is now Syria, he defeated the armies of King Darius III at the Battle of Issus but failed to capture the Persian king himself.

The city of Tyre (in what is now Lebanon), Persia's main port on the Mediterranean, put up a stubborn resistance through the winter of 332 B.C. In July 332 the Greeks attacked, devastating the city and selling its women and children into slavery. The victory made Alexander the master of the Mediterranean. In November 332 B.C. he reached Egypt, where he was crowned pharaoh and founded the city of Alexandria. In the spring of 331 B.C. he returned to Tyre, then headed north, pursuing Darius to the plains of Gaugamela (in present-day Iraq), near the biblical city of Nineveh, where the Persians suffered their greatest defeat of the war. Once again, Darius escaped, but Alexander had penetrated into the heart of the Persian Empire. He marched in triumph into the great city of Persepolis, then occupied the Persian capital of Ecbatana (near modern Hamadān, Iran). In July 330 B.C. Darius was murdered by Bessus, a Persian general whom Alexander later defeated and executed. By then the ruler

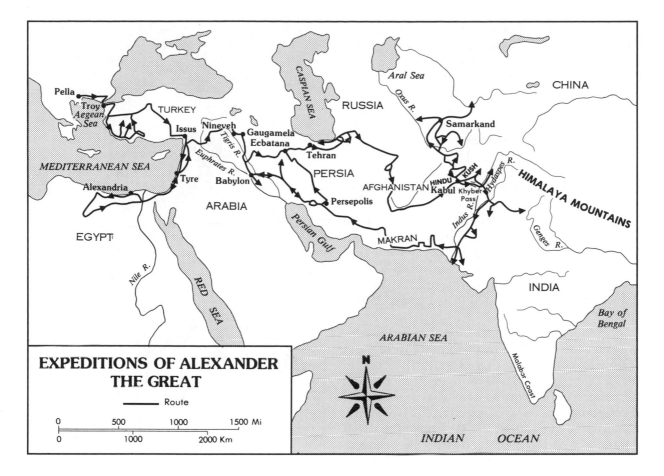

EXPEDITIONS OF ALEXANDER THE GREAT

—— Route

0   500   1000   1500 Mi

0   1000   2000 Km

of Persia, Alexander headed an army of more than 200,000.

For two years Alexander remained in central Asia, roaming eastward from what is now the Iranian capital of Tehran through present-day Afghanistan and Soviet Turkistan. Although tempted to explore the Caspian Sea, whose size was unknown, he decided instead to lead his army across the Hindu Kush through the Khyber Pass into India. In the summer of 327 B.C., his forces reached the northern part of the Indus River. Marching across the Punjab—the edge of the world known to the West, which even the Persians had not crossed—Alexander defeated the army of Porus, the local ruler, on the east bank of the Hydaspes River (a tributary of the Indus now called the Jhelum).

Hearing rumors of another great river farther east (most certainly the Ganges), Alexander was determined to push farther into India, resolved to find the great sea that ancient Europeans believed surrounded the dry lands of the earth. But his weary troops refused to go any further.

It was just as well, for Alexander and his contemporaries had no idea that the Asian steppes (arid plains) and Indian subcontinent stretched toward the vast kingdom of China. Alexander then ordered a Cretan general named NEARCHUS to build a fleet, planning to sail down the Hydaspes to the Indus. Believing that the great Indian river was a source of the Nile, he thought it would eventually lead his army back to the Mediterranean. When the local people shattered this illusion by telling him that a great sea— the Indian Ocean—lay to the south, Alexander decided to explore it, still convinced that it would take him back to Egypt.

Loading part of his army onto boats, Alexander marched with the rest along the riverbank, battling hostile tribesmen. The army's thousand-mile journey to the Indus River Delta, where the river flows into the Arabian Sea, took nine months. There Alexander split his soldiers into three groups. The sick and wounded were ordered to march back to Persia. Nearchus was to take the fleet and head west along the coast, exploring the Arabian Sea and the Persian Gulf. Alexander's army was to march along the shore, providing the fleet with supplies.

In September 325 B.C. the fleet set sail. The plan was a disaster. During its 130-day voyage, Nearchus's fleet met Alexander's army only once. Food and water were scarce along the barren coast. Many died before the fleet reached the mouth of the Euphrates River in Persia. Meanwhile, the rough terrain forced Alexander's army to march inland. This trek was also disastrous. Crossing the Makran desert in present-day Pakistan, the troops found little food or water, and many died from hunger and thirst. Eventually, they picked up a caravan route that led back to Persepolis and then to the city of Susa in what is now southwestern Iran. Alexander's army had marched more than 25,000 miles.

Alexander's days of exploration—and conquest—were over. His last two years were spent trying to consolidate his empire. In order to meld the best of Greek and Eastern culture, he conceived a plan to create a master race through intermarriage, ordering his Greek officers to take Persian wives. He himself married a daughter of Darius. Meanwhile, he began to show signs of megalomania, claiming himself a son of the gods blessed with divine powers. In the spring of 323 B.C., after a long drinking bout, he fell ill. On June 13 he died, possibly of malaria. His empire, split by squabbling generals, soon broke apart. Nevertheless, Alexander's achievements were great. His extensive travels and associated conquests had united the known world from Gibraltar to the Punjab and planted the seeds for greater trade and cultural interaction throughout the world.

al-Idrīsī. See **Idrīsī, al-**.

• Almagro, Diego de

Spanish
b 1474?; Almagro, Estremadura
d July, 1538; near Cuzco, Peru
Explored Chile by land

Diego de Almagro became an explorer and **conquistador** at the age of fifty. He then spent several years taking part in one of the greatest adventures in the history of exploration—which

Diego de Almagro. The Bettmann Archive.

was also one of the most infamous and brutal subjugations of a native population. From 1524 to 1534, in partnership with FRANCISCO PIZARRO, Almagro explored what is now Peru and discovered and conquered its great Inca civilization. After that he led the first European exploration of present-day Chile by land, enduring great hardships in his futile quest for more gold.

An illegitimate child, Diego de Almagro was probably born in the town of Almagro in the Estremadura region of Spain in about 1474. He spent the first forty years of his life in relative obscurity. Primarily a wandering adventurer during his years in Spain, he once murdered a man in a brawl. He traveled to the New World in 1514 with Pedro Arias de Ávila (Pedrarias), who was the new governor of Darién (in present-day Colombia). In 1524 he became a business partner with Francisco Pizarro and a wealthy priest, Hernando de Luque, pursuing ventures in mining, agriculture, and the slave trade.

The partners received a license to search for the rumored empire of the Incas, called Birú, believed to be a land of incredible wealth. Their first two expeditions along the western coast of South America failed, but they were not uneventful. Almagro lost an eye and several fingers in an Indian battle in 1525 during the first expedition. Having acquired a new royal commission for the Peruvian conquest in 1529—plus the personal right to a lion's share of the spoils this time—Pizarro embarked on another expedition in 1531. Though angered by Pizarro's duplicity, Almagro was mollified by the promise of future honors and riches. He stayed behind to gather recruits and supplies and joined Pizarro's forces at Cajamarca, Peru, in 1533. Their combined forces, already joined by those of HERNANDO DE SOTO, marched 750 miles from Cajamarca to Cuzco, the Inca capital. After the capture of the city, Almagro was named governor of Cuzco by Pizarro.

In 1534 the king of Spain appointed Almagro **adelantado** of New Toledo (present-day Chile), which extended some 200 **leagues** south from Pizarro's province of New Castile (present-day Peru). When conflict arose over whether Cuzco was within the boundaries of New Toledo or New Castile, Pizarro cleverly averted war by encouraging Almagro to explore the lands he was authorized to "discover, conquer, and settle" along the South Sea (Pacific Ocean).

Thus, Almagro left Cuzco on July 3, 1535, with 750 Spaniards and 12,000 Indians to explore New Toledo in the hope of finding a rich civilization like that of the Incas. Following the route used by the Incas, the expedition skirted the southwest shore of Lake Titicaca (on the modern Peru-Bolivia border) and wintered in the Salta Valley. Almagro had by this point already lost 150 soldiers, 10,000 Indians, and 30 horses due to his foolish decision to begin the march in winter.

When the journey resumed, the expedition crossed through parts of modern Bolivia and Argentina and made an arduous trek across the Andes via the San Francisco Pass. They then proceeded south, passing through the Copiapó Valley, on the plain of northern Chile, into the Aconcagua Valley, and then to present-day Santiago. Father Cristobál de Molina, a priest who was the scribe on the expedition, recorded many instances of brutality and gruesome acts against the Indians encountered and captured on the march. As an example, when one of the Indians, who were chained together, died, his head was cut off so his body could be removed without undoing the chains.

Discouraged and disillusioned after months of exploration during which they found no great treasures, the exploration party headed back to Cuzco. Following a coastal route north, they became the first Europeans to cross the forbidding 600-mile-long Atacama Desert in northern Chile.

Finding Cuzco under siege by the Inca leader Manco, Almagro defeated him and claimed the city. This action brought on a conquistadorial war between Almagro and Pizarro, who was supported by his three half brothers. Almagro defeated one Pizarro army at the Abancay River, but he was subsequently defeated and captured by Hernando Pizarro at the battle of Las Salinas (near Cuzco). After a farcical trial, Almagro was beheaded in July 1538. His son later avenged his death by murdering Francisco Pizarro.

Though he became wealthy, powerful, and famous for his part in the conquest of Peru, it is for his remarkable expedition through Chile that Diego de Almagro has earned a place among the explorers of the world. A contemporary description summarizes his personality and his achievements: he was "a man of short stature, with ugly features, but of great courage and endurance. . . . A great part of the discovery of these kingdoms [New Castile and New Toledo] was due to him."

Alvarado, Pedro de

Spanish
b 1485?; Badajoz, Estremadura
d June 29, 1541; Jalisco, Mexico
Explored Guatemala, El Salvador, Mexico, and Ecuador

From his first expedition to the Yucatán peninsula in Mexico in 1518 under the command of Juan de Grijalva, Pedro de Alvarado continually sought unknown regions to explore. He was chief lieutenant to HERNÁN CORTÉS from 1520 to 1521, during the conquest of Mexico. Then from 1523 to 1526, as a **conquistador** in his own right, he led a successful expedition to explore and conquer Guatemala and El Salvador. In 1533 he mounted an expedition to the province of Quito (present-day Ecuador) after hearing of FRANCISCO PIZARRO's discovery of the fabulous Inca empire. Expeditions Alvarado planned to explore the East Indies in 1540 and to search in North America for the legendary cities of Cíbola in 1541 never materialized.

ALVARADO, PEDRO DE

Pedro de Alvarado. The Granger Collection.

Born in Badajoz in the Spanish province of Estremadura about 1485, Alvarado spent his early life in relative obscurity. Nothing is known of him until 1510, when he landed in the West Indies with his four brothers. For the next eight years he helped to run a plantation on Santo Domingo (in the present-day Dominican Republic). Then, in 1518, he was named a commander of one of the ships in the expedition of Juan de Grijalva to explore the Yucatán peninsula of Mexico.

Having earned a reputation for courage, impetuousness, and cruelty, Alvarado next aligned himself with Cortés, who was commissioned to explore Mexico further. Alvarado quickly became second-in-command during the ensuing conquest of the Aztec empire. While Cortés was repulsing a challenge to his power by PÁNFILO DE NARVÁEZ, Alvarado was left in charge of Tenochtitlán, the conquered Aztec capital. There he tried to stop the Aztec practice of human sacrifice and in the ensuing struggle killed 200 Aztec nobles. When Cortés returned to the capital, he was forced to retreat from the city due to the consequences of Alvarado's actions.

By 1523, however, Cortés was in total control

of Mexico, and Alvarado was authorized to explore and conquer Central America. He proved to be a strong, forthright, and gifted leader on this expedition, earning the allegiance of his men and the respect of the Indians he conquered. Details of the expedition come primarily from two surviving letters from Alvarado sent to Cortés dated April 10 and July 28, 1524.

Traveling south along the western coast of Mexico, Alvarado reached Tehuantepac in Oaxaca province without much trouble. From there on, however, he had to fight Indians constantly as he progressed through Chiapas province and into Guatemala (although Indian resistance was curbed somewhat by an epidemic of smallpox that preceded the Spanish force). The force crossed "two rivers with very steep, rocky banks" and climbed a mountain pass which led to the great interior plateau of Guatemala. Alvarado described the scenery as "magnificent," and he counted sixteen volcanic peaks in a column along the Pacific, reaching to the frontier of El Salvador. He occupied the abandoned Indian city of Quezaltenango and repulsed a subsequent Indian attack. During the remainder of his march through Guatemala he made clever use of a war between the two major Indian tribes by allying himself with the Cakchiquel Indians in their fight against the Quiché.

By autumn Alvarado had reached the city of Tecpán, defeated the chiefs of Atitlán on the south shore of Lake Atitlán, and had begun to build the first capital of Guatemala at the site of present-day Guatemala City. Alvarado's conquest then continued into present-day El Salvador, which he penetrated as far south as Cuzcaclan, capital city of the Pipiles Indians (near present-day San Salvador).

In 1526 he returned to Spain where he was named captain general and governor of Guatemala and El Salvador. He successfully defended himself against charges of misconduct brought before the **Council of the Indies** in 1527, as well as against subsequent charges raised when he returned to Mexico City in 1528.

In 1533 Alvarado embarked on an expedition to the province of Quito in hopes of finding great wealth as Pizarro had done. He landed at Portoviejo (in present-day Ecuador) on February 25, 1534, and plunged into the interior, moving through jungles where the humidity rusted the weapons and armor. He penetrated the Andes by climbing one of the highest passes between the peaks of Chimborazo and Carituairazo, encountering bitter cold and difficult breathing due to volcanic ash from the eruption of the nearby volcano Cotopaxi. Men and horses that fell behind in the heavy snow froze to death where they stood. When he reached Quito, Alvarado found that the land had already been claimed by Pizarro and his partner DIEGO DE ALMAGRO. However, Almagro paid Alvarado 100,000 gold pesos in exchange for what remained of his army and equipment in order to avoid a conquistadorial war.

After returning to Guatemala, Alvarado planned an expedition to the Spice Islands in 1540; however, he was persuaded by the viceroy of New Spain (present-day Mexico), Antonio de Mendoza, to postpone that venture and instead lead an expedition to search for the legendary golden cities of Cíbola. The expedition reached New Spain in time to help quell an Indian revolt called the Mixtón War, but Alvarado did not get the chance to search for the golden cities. He was killed at Jalisco on June 29, 1541, when a rearing horse fell on him.

- Alvares (Alvarez), Francisco

Portuguese
b 1465?
d 1541 or 1542; Rome, Italy
Explored Ethiopia

A Roman Catholic priest, Francisco Alvares served as chaplain of a 1515 expedition to Abyssinia (now known as Ethiopia). A participant in Portugal's large-scale quest for the kingdom of Prester John, the mythical Christian king of Africa and Asia, Alvares remained in Abyssinia for six years trying to locate and establish relations with the nonexistent kingdom. The book Alvares wrote about his journey, widely circulated in Europe, provided a fascinated public with its first insight into the customs, society, and political structure of the Abyssinian people.

Alvares initially served under Duarte Galvão, who was commissioned by the Portuguese court to establish diplomatic ties with Abyssinia and seek access to Prester John (for a more complete discussion of Prester John, see PÊRO DA COVILHÃ). Galvão died en route, however, in 1517, on the island of Kameran in the Red Sea. Rodrigo de Lima then took command, reaching Massawa, on the southern coast of the Red Sea, in 1520 and leading the expedition on its final leg south.

The same year, the party arrived at the court of Lebna Dengel, the emperor of Abyssinia.

While Alvares could not fulfill his appointed role as liaison to the fabled Christian kingdom, he encountered an ally of a different sort in Pêro da Covilhã, a fellow countryman who had been missing for nearly three decades. The one-time explorer had been held hostage in Abyssinia since his arrival but had thrived there and become an expert on the native culture. Alvares's talent for observation and investigation, coupled with the information he gained from Covilhã, enabled him to write a comprehensive account of the Abyssinian land and people upon his return to Portugal in 1527. Translated into several languages, *True Information on the Countries of Prester John of the Indies* made Alvares famous in Europe. It is considered especially valuable because it preserved a detailed history of an empire that was soon to be destroyed by Muslim invaders.

Five years after his return to Portugal, Alvares traveled to Italy to deliver letters from the Abyssinian emperor to Pope Clement VII. He remained in Rome for nearly a decade until his death, which came a year or two after the publication of his book.

- Alvarez de Pineda, Alonso

Spanish?
b ?
d 1520; Pánuco River, Mexico
Explored Gulf of Mexico and made first sighting of Mississippi River by European

In 1519, in the service of the governor of Jamaica, Alonso Alvarez de Pineda embarked on a voyage of exploration that spanned a huge arc from the southern tip of Florida along the Gulf Coast to what is now Veracruz, Mexico. In the course of his voyage, Alvarez de Pineda proved conclusively that Florida was not an island, as had been believed up to that time. He also became the first European to see the mouth of the Mississippi River.

Nothing is known of Alvarez de Pineda before his historic voyage. Efforts to trace his origins have turned up no evidence in the archives of Spain, leading some historians to conclude that either he was not Spanish or he was an exile. While Alvarez de Pineda's background is ob-

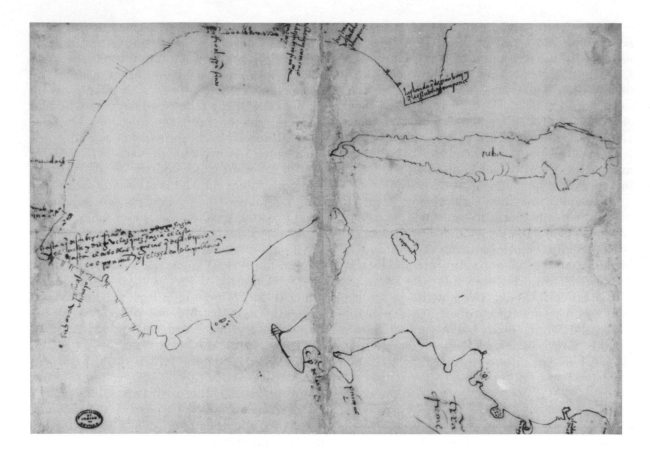

A sketch of the coastline of the Gulf of Mexico resulting from the voyage of Alonso Alvarez de Pineda. Archivo General de Indias, Seville.

scure, the purposes behind his historic voyage are clear. Governor Francisco de Garay of Jamaica had become a rich man in the New World, but he had also incurred serious debts and by 1519 was in need of a new source of income. Garay knew that the discovery of new lands would in all probability yield new wealth. He may also have had in mind tapping into the known wealth of Mexico, which HERNÁN CORTÉS was soon to conquer.

Sometime prior to March 1519 Garay received permission to arm four ships for a probe of the mainland coast. His stated purpose was to search between the area discovered by JUAN PONCE DE LEÓN (Florida) and the northernmost point reached by Juan de Grijalva (what is now east-central Mexico) for a strait connecting the Gulf of Mexico with the South Sea (Pacific Ocean) discovered by VASCO NUÑEZ DE BALBOA.

In March 1519, Alvarez de Pineda set sail from Jamaica in command of Garay's four armed ships and a party of approximately 270.

The explorers sailed through the Yucatán Channel between Mexico and Cuba and proceeded north until they sighted the mainland near the tip of Florida. They then turned east hoping to find the channel that separated the mainland from the "island" discovered by Ponce de León. Finding no such channel—thus dispelling the notion that Florida was an island—the pilots wanted to run up the east coast of Florida but were prevented from doing so by wind and currents.

After the ships reversed directions, Alvarez de Pineda guided them along the Gulf Coast until they reached the vicinity of present-day Veracruz, Mexico. Along the way, On June 2, 1519, the feast day of the Holy Spirit, the expedition observed the heavy outflow of the Mississippi River, and Alvarez de Pineda accordingly named the river Rio del Espiritu Santo. He also made note of it on his map of the voyage, which was preserved in the official Spanish decree summarizing the voyage.

As he sailed along the Gulf Coast, he observed "a very good land"—peaceful and healthful. The soil yielded a variety of fruits and other foodstuffs, and Alvarez de Pineda was certain that the rivers contained fine gold, since the Indians wore gold jewelry "in their nostrils, on their ear lobes, and on other parts of their body." The Indians appeared to him to be friendly.

Eventually they came to Villa Rica de Vera Cruz (modern-day Veracruz, Mexico), where Cortés was preparing to launch his attack on the Aztec empire. Four men were sent ashore to inform Cortés that Alvarez de Pineda intended to found a settlement at a location he had discovered north of present-day Nautla, Mexico. Unhappy with the incursion on his lucrative territory but preoccupied with military matters, Cortés seized the four messengers—and then two others who were sent to fetch them—but let Alvarez de Pineda's ships sail north to the mouth of the Pánuco River, where they had previously received a friendly reception from the Huastec Indians. When they reached the river again, they sailed up it about 20 miles, observing forty Indian villages. After about forty days on the river, the expedition returned to Jamaica in late fall of 1519.

Upon their return, they presented Governor Garay with a map that showed the Gulf of Mexico in relatively accurate proportions. The map and information about the expedition were sent to officials in Spain, who granted Garay the authority to settle the land discovered by Alvarez de Pineda and named the region Amichel. Long before the official decree arrived, however, Garay had sent out a party to settle near the Pánuco River. In fact, some historians believe that Alvarez de Pineda did not return to Jamaica with the original expedition but instead stayed at the river to found his settlement. If this is not the case, then he was certainly sent back to the Pánuco soon after the expedition returned to Jamaica. However, early in 1520, the region's once friendly Huastecs became hostile and killed all of the Spanish party's horses and all but sixty of its several hundred original members. Alvarez de Pineda died in the fighting.

Although no firsthand evidence remains of the character of Alonso Alvarez de Pineda, what is known suggests a careful explorer who documented his discoveries with accurate maps, a canny explorer who wisely avoided getting too close to Cortés, and a courageous explorer who stood by his men to the end. His single voyage of discovery contributed greatly to European knowledge of the New World, determining that Florida was not an island and bringing the continent's mightiest river to the attention of Europeans.

Amundsen, Roald Engelbregt Gravning

Norwegian
b July 16, 1872; Borge, near Oslo
d June 1928; near Spitsbergen
Navigated Northwest Passage; attained South Pole; explored Arctic and Antarctic by sea, land, and air

Taking advantage of unusually warm Arctic weather, Roald Engelbregt Gravning Amundsen launched his exploring career in 1903 with a stunning success: the first successful navigation by ship of the Northwest Passage, an accomplishment that had until that time eluded a host of explorers over hundreds of years. Made possible by channels that remained clear of ice until winter, the historic journey was nevertheless full of nerve-racking hazards made worse by the haunting memories of repeated tragedy that clung to the narrow sounds and channels of the passage. There could have been few moments when Amundsen did not think of the horrible fate of his boyhood hero, Sir JOHN FRANKLIN, whose ship had been entombed by the ice on the same route only a half-century earlier. By the end of the most harrowing part of the passage, when he kept a sleepless three-week vigil on the watch for shallow reefs and ice snares, Amundsen, according to his own testimony, had visibly aged thirty years.

This was to be only the first of the many ordeals and near escapes of a life devoted to polar exploration. Amundsen later added both the South Pole and the Northeast Passage to his accomplishments, as well as a pioneering Arctic airplane flight and the crossing of the polar basin by **dirigible**. He was the grand old man of the polar seas, a rugged vagabond (sometimes called the last Viking) who could not resist the chance to test his endurance and cunning at the extremes of the world.

Amundsen was born into a middle-class Norwegian family that had its paternal roots in a small fishing village on an island at the entrance to Oslo Fjord. His father and uncles had prospered in the shipping business, keeping their ties to the sea but living the life of the urban bourgeoisie in Oslo. The only chance the young Amundsen had to face the natural elements came when his family spent holidays on a farm they owned.

After his father died, Amundsen tried to oblige his mother's desire for him to become a doctor, but he seems not to have been cut out for it. When he was fifteen he read the works of the British explorer John Franklin "with a fervid fascination which has shaped the whole course of my life." It was the vivid tale of Franklin's first expedition to the shores of the Arctic Ocean, full of sensational suffering, that most affected him: "A strange ambition burned within me to endure those same sufferings." As long as his mother lived (until he was twenty-one), he stayed in school, but his passion to break away from the dull routines of civilized life interfered seriously with his studies. By the time he quit medical school, he was on the verge of failing.

His first adventure after declaring his intention to become an Arctic explorer brought him more suffering than he could possibly have imagined. Without any of the careful advance preparations that would become characteristic of his later explorations, he headed off with his brother in an attempt to cross the Norwegian plateau in the dead of winter. With only a small amount of food, two sleeping bags, and no tent, the two were soon starving and freezing. One night Amundsen burrowed into the snow to sleep. Then the weather changed, and the surrounding snow turned into "a ghastly coffin of ice." It took his brother three hours to chip him free. By the end of the ordeal, the young masochists had achieved the desired effect: "Our scraggly beards had grown, our eyes were gaunt and hollow, our cheeks were sunken, and the ruddy glow of [skin] color had changed to a ghastly greenish yellow."

Amundsen called this a training exercise, but it was more of a rite of passage marking his escape from bourgeois Norwegian society. His next break was to sign on as a common sailor aboard a ship that frequented Arctic waters. He sailed for three summers (1894–96) until he qualified as mate. At the age of twenty-five he was appointed first mate of the Belgian Antarctic Expedition (1897–99). Though the venture was a dismal failure, it was a remarkable triumph for Amundsen. After the *Belgica*, unequipped for winter, became caught in an ice field near Graham Land, the expedition's situation worsened through the failure of the commanding officers to provide fresh meat for the crew. As a result, both the officers and crew developed **scurvy**, and command fell to Amundsen. He and the ship's physician, Dr. FREDERICK COOK, proceeded to save the expedition, first by nursing everyone back to health, then by maneuvering the ship out of the ice the next spring.

When he returned to Norway, Amundsen received his skipper's license and began preparing for his great journey through the Northwest Passage (for a more complete discussion, see MARTIN FROBISHER). He had thoroughly studied previous British attempts at the passage and learned from FRANCIS LEOPOLD MCCLINTOCK's account that the best chance for success lay in the route Franklin had taken, with one exception. Rather than follow the main pack ice west of King William Island, Amundsen intended to follow the more frequently ice-free waters to the east of King William Island until reaching the continental coast. Amundsen's own improvement on this plan—aside from the lucky occurrence of warmer weather—was to use a small yacht powered by a diesel engine, the diesel being a new invention. He took his plan to the recognized dean of polar exploration, FRIDTJOF NANSEN, for his approval and was gratified to receive encouragement.

Since all of the territory through which he would be traveling was already well charted, and since no one imagined that these waters would ever yield a viable commercial waterway, the proposed expedition looked more like a journalistic stunt than a serious attempt to explore. Amundsen, like the American polar explorer ROBERT PEARY, was first and foremost an adventurer, and after the fact a journalist who made a living from publishing contracts and speaking engagements. In the early twentieth century, however, Norway's mass media was not ready to fund such activities, so Amundsen had to develop a scientific rationale for his proposals. "Otherwise," he admitted, "I should not be taken seriously and would not get backing."

Although he had no interest in science (scientists were a part of the dull world he wanted to break away from), Amundsen studied magnetism for a year with George von Neumayer, an expert on the subject. Von Neumayer was excited about the idea of gathering fresh data on the North Magnetic Pole to supplement the seventy-year-old findings of Sir JAMES CLARK ROSS (who located it on Boothia Peninsula), and this objective became Amundsen's official purpose. With this stated intention, he collected funds from learned societies and private patrons of science in the winter and spring of 1902–1903.

In the end, however, even though he did spend a year collecting data near the magnetic pole, he never took time to analyze it, nor to present it to the scientific community in any form. His scientific program was simply a method of obtaining money. Apparently, most of Norway's scientists quickly saw through his ruse, so he did not collect enough money to cover debts incurred while setting up his expedition. Rather than declare bankruptcy and have his yacht seized, he simply took off in the middle of the night—just before one of his creditors was to arrive. The escape from the law was thrilling to Amundsen: "When dawn arose on our truculent creditor, we were safely out on the open main, seven as light-hearted pirates as ever flew the black flag. . . ."

It was midnight, June 16, 1903, when the *Gjoa* sneaked out of Oslo. The seven members of the party organized themselves as a little republic, with Amundsen acting as president rather than dictator. There was none of the traditional strict naval discipline, which represented the kind of life they were all escaping. "Good work," Amundsen said, "can be done without the fear of the law." Though the *Gjoa* was heavily loaded, they made good progress

The *Gjoa*. Library of Congress.

and by mid-August were off the coast of northern Greenland, where they met fellow explorer KNUD RASMUSSEN and the rest of the Danish Literary Greenland Expedition. Amundsen's party picked up their supplies from a depot set up earlier and went on their way again.

By August 22, they were at Franklin's camp in Erebus Bay off Barrow Strait in the Canadian Arctic. After lingering over the remains of his hero's camp, Amundsen set off and soon reached the point in Franklin Strait beyond which no one had sailed since Franklin himself. At that point, sea swells indicated open water ahead. The party pressed on, hopeful that the channels would stay clear. Then in early September they were grounded and their ship nearly wrecked. Finally, all obstacles were overcome, and they reached their winter harbor on the south coast of King William Island. After two winters spent making observations and trading with local **Inuit** people, Amundsen sailed again in August 1905. The shallow, meandering channel of Simpson Strait between King William Island and the Adelaide Peninsula was the scene of Amundsen's worrying three-week ordeal. But on August 27 a ship that had come east from the Bering Strait sailed into sight. They knew they had done it.

Unfortunately, the ice closed in too fast for them to make it west to the Pacific that year. After another year in the Arctic, the expedition arrived in San Francisco in October 1906. Amundsen had managed earlier to hike overland from the Arctic coast to a telegraph station on the Yukon River to announce his achievement in advance, so a celebration was already organized when the *Gjoa* sailed into San Francisco Bay. When Amundsen finally arrived in Norway, instead of being arrested for skipping out on his creditors, he was given a hero's welcome.

Amundsen was now famous enough to raise money for his next feat—being the first to attain the North Pole—by drifting with the polar ice pack. This technique had been tried first by Nansen on the *Fram*. Amundsen was going to use the *Fram* again, trying a different route. But while preparations were under way, Peary made public his own plans to conquer the pole and subsequently announced its attainment on April 6, 1909.

Amundsen immediately decided on an attempt on the South Pole, also as yet unattained. He was worried, however, that if ROBERT FALCON

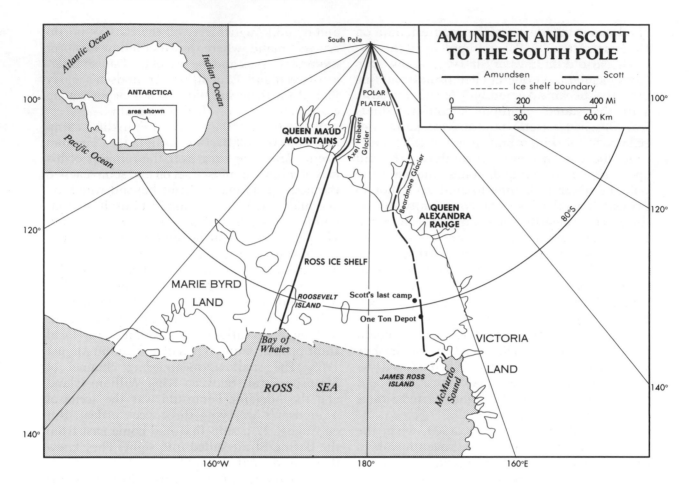

scott, who was known to be planning a dash to the southern pole himself, got wind of his plans, the British explorer would hasten his own preparations. So instead of announcing his new plan, Amundsen lied about his intentions, claiming that he was still planning to undertake a drift across the polar basin. In the meantime, he built a prefabricated house to serve as a base on the coast of Antarctica and purchased 100 Greenland dogs. On August 9, 1910, the *Fram* left Oslo bound for Alaska via Cape Horn—or so everyone thought. At Madeira, an island off the coast of Spain, Amundsen announced his real plan to his crew and to the world at large. His crew was enthusiastically in favor. To them, a quick dash to the South Pole, no matter how arduous, was bound to be an improvement over a three-year drift in a boat. Scott, on the other hand, was upset to be undercut in such a deceitful way and hurried his own preparations for what was now a race.

Etiquette (never Amundsen's strong point) aside, however, the plan Amundsen adopted was brilliant and its execution stunning. By studying the charts of the Ross Ice Shelf that Scott and his colleague ERNEST HENRY SHACKLETON had recently made, and comparing them to those of James Clark Ross, made seventy years earlier, Amundsen noticed that a portion of the shelf's eastern edge had not receded as had the rest of it. He correctly deduced that this section of the ice barrier lay on top of land rather than floating on water, as others thought. (The American explorer RICHARD BYRD later confirmed this fact with soundings.) Amundsen reasoned that if he camped there, in the Bay of Whales, he would have a base 69 miles closer to the pole than Scott's land base on James Ross Island. If he had been wrong, his camp could have dropped off the floating ice into the sea at any time.

There was another risk involved. Scott knew that his route had the advantage of a low pass onto the polar plateau (which Shackleton had discovered), but Amundsen had no idea what he would find between the Ross Ice Shelf and the plateau. As a consequence, he would not be able to plan his exact route and might even have ended up facing an impenetrable wall of mountains.

The risks paid off. After spending the winter laying depots along the proposed route over the ice shelf (using a carefully devised system of markers), Amundsen set off with four **sledges**, four human companions, and thirteen dogs on October 19, 1911. He had only limited experience sledging, but Helmer Hanssen, who led the team, was a virtuoso. Amundsen's schedule was almost perfectly adhered to as a result of the efficient use of dogs, though his party encountered a variety of dangerous conditions. On the ice shelf, bottomless crevasses often threatened the party, and some of the steep glaciers were especially rough going. But the polar plateau was reached in early December, and from then on the conditions were relatively easy by Antarctica's severe standards.

Part of the plan, which Amundsen derived from Nansen, concerned the fact that fewer dogs were needed to pull the sledges as food was consumed. The remaining food, however, would still have to be divided among all of the dogs. Amundsen could significantly increase the party's range if the unneeded dogs were shot even after having relied on them for weeks. Amundsen winced at the seemingly inhumane notion but adhered to the plan in the name of practicality—another reason he was not popular in some circles.

After shooting the unnecessary dogs at their camp at the base of the plateau—a spot they dubbed The Butcher Shop—the famished explorers dropped all former scruples and joined the remaining dogs in feasting on the carcasses. "But on this first evening," Amundsen explained, "we put a restraint on ourselves; we thought we could not fall upon our four-footed friends and devour them before they had had time to grow cold. . . ." Thus replenished, the team went on to reach the highest point of the plateau (11,024 feet) on December 6 and the pole itself on December 14. Still attached to the republican principle, Amundsen insisted that all five join in planting the Norwegian flag. "Five weather-beaten, frostbitten fists they were that grasped the pole," he reported, "raised the waving flag in the air, and planted it as the first at the geographical South Pole." After circling the area to be certain of covering the exact position of the pole, Amundsen left a letter for Scott to carry back to Norway's King Haakon VII in case the Norwegian team should not make it—a letter later found on Scott's frozen corpse. The team then began the descent of the plateau. All went well and the base camp was reached on January 11, 1912. The group had covered 1,860 miles in ninety-nine days.

Amundsen returned to Norway secretly so he could quickly write his book about the successful expedition in privacy and then move on to his next exploration. He was once again bankrupt, but a wealthy Norwegian living in Argentina assisted him financially. Amundsen then returned to his plan to drift across the polar basin, but World War I broke out before he could implement it.

Roald Amundsen. Mansell Collection.

He then decided to take advantage of the war by buying Norwegian ships and selling them at a profit to the Allies. With this new influx of funds, he had the *Maud* built especially for a polar-drift voyage like that of Nansen's *Fram.* Before the war had ended, Amundsen set off, in July 1918, for a successful crossing of the Northeast Passage (1918–20) prior to his planned drift toward the pole. Ice, however, stranded him for two winters before the *Maud* could reach the Bering Strait (during which time he was injured by a fall and seriously mauled by a bear), and he abandoned the attempt. Once again Amundsen's creditors demanded their money. He did get help from the Norwegian government in 1922, but postwar deflation soon reduced the value of the government's grant. As optimistic as he was naive about money, Amundsen again spent beyond his limits.

While the *Maud* was waiting in Seattle to proceed north to begin its polar drift, Amundsen had become excited about the possibility of using airplanes to explore the Arctic. He bought a Junker airplane and brought it aboard the *Maud* in Seattle, with the idea of later flying it from Point Barrow, Alaska, to Spitsbergen across the Arctic Ocean. While the *Maud* headed for the Bering Strait in the summer of 1922, Amundsen decided to leave Captain Wisting in command while he accompanied the Junker to Point Barrow aboard a merchant ship. The *Maud* began her drift but was soon repossessed by her creditors. Meanwhile, after several delays, the Junker was set to go in May 1923, but was then damaged in a trial run.

At this point, Amundsen's finances reached a serious crisis. On top of his usual problems, his involvement with an American promoter put him in real trouble. The Norwegian press attacked him, and even his brother gave up on him.

Trying to make up for some of his financial losses by hitting the lucrative American lecture tour, he began to despair when even this failed to bring in sufficient money. In his own words, he was "nearer to black despair than ever before in the fifty-four years of my life." While Amundsen was sitting in a hotel room wondering how he was going to pay his bill, the phone rang. It was the American LINCOLN ELLSWORTH, a college dropout and son of a millionaire, who was desperately searching for something to do with his life. Ellsworth said he would supply the money to bail out Amundsen (assuming his father would give it to him—which he did) in exchange for a share in the command of a flight to the North Pole. So began a great cooperative venture of polar aviation. "I was delighted," wrote Amundsen. "The gloom of the past year rolled away, and even the horrors of my business experience faded into forgetfulness in the activities of preparation."

The flight of 1925 was a great success, not because it achieved its goal of reaching the North Pole from Svalbard (it did not), but because it showed that despite his troubles, Amundsen was still as clever and resourceful as ever. The resulting drama of the two planes going down in the ice so near the pole, followed by the heroic effort to get the one working but overloaded plane back in the air, captivated the world.

Following fast on this success was the 1926 flight of the dirigible *Norge* across the Arctic Ocean from Svalbard to Alaska, a spectacular achievement in the history of exploration and transportation technology. Once again Amundsen was at the center of world attention, as the public followed the story of the beautiful dirigible floating over the polar ocean, bejeweled and at times dangerously weighted by a blanket of ice.

Unfortunately, by the end of the journey, Amundsen was furious with the aircraft's Italian designer and pilot, UMBERTO NOBILE. In his autobiography, which appeared soon after the flight, Amundsen launched into a lengthy attack. However well founded his complaints, they seemed meanspirited to most readers. He also added attacks on his brother, the famous Arctic explorer VILHJALMUR STEFANSSON, many of his long-term associates, and British people in general. Rather than the grand old man that he could have appeared, he came off as an egotistical, paranoid crank.

It was a strange, ironic tragedy that righted the public perception of this unusual man who had so often combined reckless passions with careful strategies. Nobile's dirigible had gone down while on its way back from the pole in 1928, a redundant mission Nobile had undertaken merely to clear his name in the face of Amundsen's smears. When he heard of it, Amundsen cast aside all of his animosity and without hesitation boarded a plane to join in the dangerous search. Although Nobile was ultimately rescued, Amundsen's plane went down and his body slipped unseen to the depths of the Arctic Ocean.

SUGGESTED READING: Roald Amundsen, *My Life as an Explorer* (Doubleday, Doran & Co., 1928); Gerald Bowman, *Men of Antarctica* (Fleet, 1958); Roland Huntford, *Scott and Amundsen* (Atheneum, 1984); Theodore K. Mason, *Two Against the Ice: Amundsen and Ellsworth* (Dodd, Mead & Co., 1982); J. Gordon Naeth, *To the Ends of the Earth: The Explorations of Roald Amundsen* (Harper & Row, 1962); L. H. Neatby, *Conquest of the Last Frontier* (Ohio University Press, 1966); Charles Turley, *Roald Amundsen Explorer* (Methuen, 1935).

• Andrée, Salomon August

Swedish
b October 18, 1854; Grenna
d 1897?; White Island, Svalbard
Attempted balloon flight to North Pole

Salomon August Andrée was last seen in July 1897 as his balloon, the *Ornen* (*Eagle*), drifted northward off the coast of Spitsbergen Island

Salomon August Andrée. Library of Congress.

(now part of Svalbard) seeking the North Pole. It was not until August 6, 1930, that the fate of the Andrée Polar Expedition became known from the remains and well-preserved records found at the site of its final camp on White Island, east of Spitsbergen.

Born in 1854 in Grenna, Sweden, one of seven children of an apothecary, Andrée exhibited an early interest in science. In 1869 he entered the Royal Institute of Technology in Stockholm, where he passed his final examinations in 1873. He then spent two years as a draftsman and designer in Stockholm.

In 1876 he went to America to visit the centennial exposition in Philadelphia and, while there, to consult John Wise, an experienced aeronaut who taught Andrée the basics of ballooning. Andrée had first caught his enthusiasm for ballooning by reading C. F. E. Bjørling's *Laws of the Wind*.

Returning to Sweden, Andrée was granted an assistantship at the Royal Institute of Technology. In 1882 he was appointed to make aero-electrical observations at the Swedish station at Spitsbergen in an international scientific investigation of the two polar regions. In 1885 he was appointed to the government patent office, where he became chief engineer.

Eight years later, Andrée received a grant to buy a balloon, the *Svea*, in which he made nine ascents and carried out a variety of scientific investigations. In February 1895, in an address at the Academy of Sciences, he announced a plan to balloon to the North Pole, a point that had not yet been reached by any means. His careful studies of geography, winds, and equipment included plans for an adjustable sail and devices that would make the balloon somewhat capable of being steered. Alfred Nobel, the inventor of dynamite and later the donor of the prizes in his name, was one of Andrée's financial backers.

The ascent of his new balloon, the *Ornen*, took place on July 11, 1896, from the coast of Spitsbergen Island. Andrée, the photographer and scientist Nils Strindberg, and the engineer Knut Fraenkel were on board. An initial mishap caused the important drag lines to be left behind. What happened from that point on remained a mystery for more than thirty years.

The records found in 1930, however, meticulously documented the rest of the *Ornen*'s flight, which lasted three days. Then, frost-laden and stymied by lack of sufficient wind, the balloon had been forced to land on ice floes some 325 miles northeast of its takeoff point.

Traveling southward by sledge, the three had to deal with heavy loads of equipment, shifting ice, polar bears, and ever-increasing cold. They had covered 200 miles when they reached White Island, Svalbard, in the first week of October. How much longer they managed to survive will never be known. Strindberg had been buried, but Andrée's and Fraenkel's bodies were found in the tent, probably victims of carbon monoxide poisoning from their kerosene stove. Their journals, photographs, and equipment, however, bore moving witness to a courageous and difficult Arctic journey.

Baron George Anson. National Maritime Museum, Greenwich.

• Anson, George

English
b April 23, 1697; Shrughborough Park,
  Staffordshire
d June 6, 1762; Moor Park, Hertfordshire
Circumnavigated; reformed British navy

Baron George Anson, first lord of the Admiralty, circumnavigated the globe (1740–44) and subsequently made sweeping changes in British naval administration. It is largely thanks to his influence that Captain JAMES COOK was given his first opportunity to explore the Pacific Ocean.

Anson was born in Staffordshire on April 23, 1697, to William Anson and Isabelle Carrier, the sister-in-law of Lord Chancellor Macclesfield. Anson went to sea with the navy in 1712 at the age of fifteen. He was made a lieutenant in four years and by 1723 had attained the rank of captain. Over the next sixteen years he would take his ships the *Scarborough* (1724–30), the *Squirrel* (1733–35), and the *Centurion* (1735–39) to the New World in order to protect British interests from Spanish attack, primarily along the southeast coast of North America.

On September 18, 1740, Anson left Spithead, England, with six ships bound for the west coast of South America, where he was to raid Spanish settlements. Three of his vessels were lost before they could round Cape Horn; shipwrecks and **scurvy** combined to cut his forces nearly in half. (Among those shipwrecked was young JOHN BYRON, who would circle the world in 1764.) Many of the lost crewmen were Chelsea pensioners (navy retirees) who had been drafted by naval press-gangs that were authorized to force men into service. During this era, roughly a third of the men in the British navy were originally mustered by these gangs.

Undaunted by his losses, Anson continued his voyage. When he reached the west coast of South America, he captured the town of Paita, on the Peruvian coast, inflicting extensive damage to Spanish shipping in the region.

With his own ships damaged, Anson consolidated their crews into a single vessel and sailed west to Tinian, in the western Pacific, where they rested briefly. Anson and his crew eventually reached Macao in November 1742. The following summer, on June 20, 1743, he captured the treasure-laden Spanish **galleon** *Nuestra Señora de Covadonga* as it sailed between the Philippines and Spanish settlements in the New

World carrying £400,000 in coins and ingot. In all, Anson sold some thirty-two wagonloads of Spanish booty to the Chinese at Macao before his departure for home. On June 15, 1744, he arrived back in England by way of the Cape of Good Hope, a rich man for life.

The same determination Anson showed on this difficult four-year journey was demonstrated again and again as he went on to create the "new" British navy. In the mid-eighteenth century the navy was corrupt and poorly managed. In fact, in 1745 Anson refused the rank of rear admiral and nearly resigned when the navy would not confirm a captain's commission for one of his men. Later that year, the duke of Bedford invited Anson to join the British Admiralty as rear admiral under Lord Sandwich.

Under Anson's able administration, the navy dockyards were improved and fleets were inspected regularly. To reduce corruption, Anson oversaw the navy's accounts, regulated its promotion system, and established the Navy Discipline Act. Due to these reforms, Captain James Cook, a navy man, was chosen to lead the *Endeavour* expedition to the Pacific in 1768 instead of the wealthy civilian ALEXANDER DALRYMPLE. Anson thus initiated Cook's brilliant accomplishments in the Pacific.

Anson went back to active duty, commanding the Channel fleet against the French in 1747. After his victory off Cape Finisterre, he was made vice admiral and given the title of baron. His work as a naval administrator continued. In 1755 he established the corps of marines.

Anson's four-year voyage around the world was the last of Britain's semipiratical raids into the Pacific. It was also instrumental in awakening that country's interests in the distant ocean. In 1748 Anson published a best-selling authorized account of his expedition, *A voyage round the World in the Years 1740–44 to the South Seas.* A French translation was published in 1751.

When Anson died at Moor Park, Hertfordshire, on June 6, 1762, he was a full admiral and first lord of the Admiralty. More a man of action than of words, he changed the British navy, raising it to new levels of respectability and professionalism.

Anza, Juan Bautista de

Spanish
b 1735 or 1736; Fronteras, Mexico
d December 19, 1788; Arizpe, Mexico
Established Sonora-California trail

Often called the last **conquistador**, Colonel Juan Bautista de Anza was a new breed of Spanish explorer, born in the New World and dedicated to defending the frontier of New Spain (present-day Mexico) from foreign invasion and hostile Indians and to blazing new trails connecting all the territories of the far-flung empire. He established the land route from Sonora, Mexico, to upper California (now the state of California), as well as the Santa Fe–Sonora Trail. In 1775 he led a group of colonists to reinforce the presidio (a fortified settlement) at Monterey, California, and to create a new settlement on San Francisco Bay.

Juan Bautista de Anza was born at the presidio of Fronteras in the Sonora province of New Spain, just a few miles south of modern Douglas, Arizona. Historians are undecided whether he was born in 1735 or 1736 (he was baptized on July 7, 1736). Little is known of his early years until 1752, when he enlisted as a volunteer in the Fronteras presidio army. By 1760 he had earned the rank of captain and was commander of the presidio of Tubac (south of modern Tucson), making him a part of the aristocracy. During the next decade he led many successful campaigns against the Apache Indians.

By 1770 the Spanish settlements in upper California were in trouble, threatened by the Russians pushing south from Alaska and by their own inability to get needed supplies quickly by sea. Anza volunteered to open a land route from Sonora to upper California at his own expense, reviving a plan that his father had proposed some thirty years earlier. Receiving permission from the viceroy of New Spain and the king of Spain, Anza left Tubac on January 8, 1774, with thirty-four men, including Father FRANCISCO GARCÉS. Circling south through the Altar River valley, they then headed north to the Gila River and followed it to its convergence with the Colorado. Here Anza befriended the Yuma Indians, and his report emphasized the importance of maintaining good relations with them since they controlled the important lower Colorado River area.

After crossing the Colorado, the expedition promptly got lost in the desert west of the river. Returning to Yuma territory, Anza and his party began again, this time circling the desert to the southwest and passing through the Cocopah Mountains near modern Signal Mountain. Heading northwest, he traveled along the western slope of the San Jacinto Mountains until he reached the San Gabriel mission (between the San Gabriel and Los Angeles rivers), where he left reinforcements. He then traveled north to the mission at Monterey, which he also fortified. Upon his return to Sonora, he was promoted to lieutenant colonel, chosen to lead colonists to upper California, and charged with exploring San Francisco Bay to find a site for a presidio.

The colonizing expedition left Tubac on October 23, 1775, with 240 colonists, 165 pack animals, 340 horses, and a herd of 300 cattle. Heading north, they traveled down the Santa Cruz River to the Gila, then down the Gila to the Colorado. Here Anza divided the expedition into three groups for the march across the Yuma Desert, each traveling a day apart, in order to give the few watering holes time to replenish themselves. Traveling during the winter, the group endured rain, snow, and freezing temperatures, and many of the livestock died. After one storm Anza wrote that it was followed "with an earthquake which lasted four minutes." En route to San Gabriel mission only one woman died (in childbirth), and three healthy infants were born. Anza led the colonists to Monterey, then pushed on to San Francisco Bay. In exploring the Bay area, Anza discovered the Guadalupe River and a spring he called Los Dolores Laguna. At the mouth of San Francisco Bay he selected a white cliff at the narrowest point (modern Fort Point) as a good location for a presidio and fort.

This difficult, multifaceted expedition exemplified what an outstanding leader Anza was. Anza helped his group overcome many obstacles as they made their way; for example, he forded the Colorado River without mishap, found watering holes in the desert, wisely provided his party with rest when needed, directed the herding of the animals through desert and mountain passes, and generally kept up morale.

Upon his return Anza was promoted to colonel and appointed governor of New Mexico on August 24, 1777. He did an excellent job in this office, bringing peace to the northern frontier by subduing the Apaches and Comanches. He went on several exploratory journeys during his ten years in New Mexico, the most important of which occurred in 1780 when he scouted a trail from Santa Fe via the Rio Grande to Arizpe in Sonora. He briefly lost his governorship after a 1781 Yuma uprising for which he was unfairly blamed. In 1786 he requested a transfer to a more healthful climate and was appointed commander of the presidio at Tubac on October 1, 1788. However, he died shortly after the appointment, on December 19, 1788, in Arizpe.

Juan Bautista de Anza, one of the foremost frontier commanders and governors, established important routes connecting the heart of New Spain with its outposts in California. On his journeys he kept detailed diaries on the nature of the landscape, water supply, mining possibilities, and Indian tribes—information that proved invaluable in later exploration and colonization efforts. Though an "Anza Myth" that surfaced in 1903 romanticized him as the founder of the city of San Francisco, he only explored the Bay area and selected a good location for settlement. The city's actual site, though within that general area, was chosen later. However, descendants of some of the settlers he brought to the Bay area in 1775 reside in San Francisco today.

Ashley, William Henry

American
b 1778?; Powhatan, Virginia
d March 26, 1838; Cooper County, Missouri
Explored Green River

At heart a businessman and politician rather than an explorer, William Henry Ashley organized the Rocky Mountain Fur Company to reap profits from the relatively untapped beaver sources in the mountains of the American West. Nonetheless, the explorations of Ashley's mountain men were instrumental in opening up the West to future waves of settlers. Ashley himself made only one journey of exploration. From 1824 to 1825, he crossed the Great Plains and the Rocky Mountains to deliver supplies to his trappers and then sought out the Green River, following it south through much of what is now eastern Utah.

Ashley migrated west to Missouri in 1805

and soon became involved in a profitable munitions business and then in real estate ventures in St. Louis. Around 1822 he and his partner, Andrew Henry, formed a fur trading company and advertised for "enterprising young men" to go into the wilderness. The people he attracted, among them JEDEDIAH SMITH, would come to form a virtual hall of fame of western explorers.

In the spring of 1823, Ashley led a party up the Missouri River on the route west that had been established by MERIWETHER LEWIS and WILLIAM CLARK almost twenty years before. However, near what is now the border between North and South Dakota, the party was attacked by hostile Arikara Indians. The Arikara were attempting to close off the Missouri to travel in order to establish a stranglehold on the role of middleman in all trade with the Indian tribes of the upper Missouri. Twelve of Ashley's group were killed in the fighting, and the others had to turn back. When a militia of some 1,000 men subsequently failed to subdue the Arikara, Ashley was forced to rethink his plans. Heavily in debt and desperate not to miss a trapping season, he decided to send his trappers overland to the Rockies.

Two parties set out, one led by Andrew Henry and the other by Jed Smith. A year later, four men from Smith's party limped into St. Louis with a mixture of good and bad news. The good news was that Smith had discovered rich fur trapping territory around a river they called Seedskeedee (or "Prairie Hen"; later named the Green River). The bad news was that the men were in dire need of supplies.

Ashley immediately decided to lead a relief expedition himself, although he was at least equally motivated by the news of good fur trapping. Early in November 1824, he left Fort Atkinson, near the confluence of the Missouri and Platte rivers, to follow the Platte west. Across the prairies and into the mountains in the dead of winter Ashley marched with his band of twenty-five men, fifty pack horses, and several wagons, facing constant extreme cold. After some profitable trapping in the Medicine Bow Mountains in what is now southern Wyoming, they crossed the range and then moved west and south until they reached the Green River on April 15.

Ashley then split his twenty-five men into four groups. Three were sent in different directions to trap beaver and were instructed to meet 50 miles down the Green River on or before July 10. This was to become the first rendezvous of American trappers, a practice that soon became a tradition—a sort of annual meeting of mountain men and their suppliers where trappers forsook their normally solitary existences and gathered for a few weeks of communal drinking, gambling, and story swapping.

Ashley took the fourth group with him and headed south on the Green River, hoping to locate a river that would lead farther west. Traveling in buffalo-skin boats, Ashley's party made its way down the turbulent river, where steep canyons alternated with short stretches of lush meadows. Ashley described part of the trip as follows:

> As we passed along between these . . . walls, which in a great degree excluded from us the rays of heaven . . . I was forcibly struck with the gloom which spread over the countenances of my men. They seemed to anticipate . . . a dreadful termination of our voyage, and I must confess that I partook in some degree of what I supposed to be their feelings, for things around us had truly an awful appearance.

Ashley was not just imagining his men's fear. They had all heard tales of an immense whirlpool ahead that would suck everything into the center of the earth. And while the danger might have been somewhat exaggerated, the party did indeed encounter large whirlpools. Ashley, who could not swim, narrowly avoided capsizing his boat at one point. According to legend, he was saved by a mountain man named Jim Beckwourth. Still the men continued on, but on May 16 they met up with two trappers from a party out of the south (from Taos, in present-day New Mexico), who informed them that further south there were no beaver and hunting was poor. Duly warned, Ashley turned back, having traveled for thirty-one days on the Green and reached what is now northeastern Utah.

The first rendezvous was a great success; Ashley collected enough furs to pay off his debts and make himself a wealthy man. With furs in hand, he headed back east over a northern route—north along the Bighorn River to the Yellowstone River to the Missouri River and then southeast back to St. Louis.

The next year, Ashley again went west for the rendezvous, which this time took place in Cache Valley near the Great Salt Lake. There he sold his business to Jed Smith and two of Smith's partners, then returned east to pursue—not entirely successfully—his interest in politics.

Ashley's contributions to the exploration of the American West include not only his own exploration of the Green River but the myriad achievements of the men he outfitted and sent into the wilderness to trap furs. Among their major contributions were the rediscovery of the South Pass through the Rockies (in present-day Wyoming)—which was to become a primary entryway to the West—and the discovery and exploration of the Great Salt Lake. Ashley's commercial zeal for the riches of the West had a direct impact on the major westward migration that followed shortly after the explorations carried out by Ashley and his trappers.

ash-Sharīf al-Idrīsī. See **Idrīsi, al-**.

John James Audubon. American Museum of Natural History.

Audubon, John James (Jean-Jacques)

French
b April 26, 1785; Les Cayes, Haiti
d January 27, 1851; New York, New York
Studied and drew birds of North America

Artist and ornithologist John James Audubon undertook his explorations of North America primarily to observe birds in the wild, to collect bird skins for use in his drawings, and to look for new species. While Audubon was usually at least one step behind the trailblazers of the North American continent, this in no way detracts from the immensity of his real achievement, which was to provide a stunning record of the birds of his adopted homeland in their natural settings.

The son of a French merchant, planter, and slave dealer and his **creole** mistress, Audubon was born on his father's plantation in what is now Haiti. Within the year his mother died, and when Audubon was four years old, his father took him and his half sister to France, where his father's wife adopted them as her own children. By the age of 15, Audubon had discovered the interest in drawing and natural history that would form the basis for his life's work, and he began a series of drawings of French birds.

In 1803, Audubon left France for an estate that his father had bought in Pennsylvania, where he began his study of American birds. He conducted the first banding experiment on an American wild bird when he tied silver threads around the legs of some young peewees and noted the return of two of them to the same location the next year.

Audubon married in 1808 and spent the next twelve years mainly in Kentucky pursuing a variety of halfhearted and futile business ventures in an attempt to support his family while still indulging his passion for drawing birds. In 1820, while serving as a taxidermist at the Western Museum in Cincinnati, Ohio, Audubon hit upon the idea that was to dominate the rest of his life. He decided to publish a comprehensive collection of life-size drawings of American birds in their natural habitats. The same year he undertook his first expedition in pursuit of this goal: a flatboat trip down the Ohio and Mississippi rivers to New Orleans.

Failing to find a publisher for his drawings in the United States, Audubon traveled in 1826 to England and Scotland, where his work was received more favorably. In Scotland, he and an engraver developed a plan to sell full-size reproductions of his paintings on a subscription basis. From 1826 to 1838, Audubon divided his time between business trips to England and Scotland and birding explorations in North America.

Early in 1832, he made two trips to Florida to observe birds. The first trip was a difficult journey on the St. Johns River that yielded few bird specimens. Insects, on the other hand, were so thick that they extinguished Audubon's candle as he tried to write in his journal. A boat trip along Florida's east coast as far as Key West was more successful. Though disappointed that he found only two new species, Audubon acquired 1,000 specimens and made many drawings.

In the summer of 1833, Audubon organized an expedition north to the rugged coast of Labrador, where he hoped to discover new species and to study the summer plumage and breeding habits of water birds that summered there. Again he found few new species. He complained greatly of the cold and the mosquitoes and later wrote of the "wonderful dreariness of the country."

Spring of 1837 found Audubon traveling south again, this time to the newly established Republic of Texas, where, in addition to studying birds, he and his party met with its president, Sam Houston. Audubon failed to identify any new species of birds on this trip, but he did learn much about the habits of birds west of the Mississippi River.

Despite the difficulties he had encountered, his project was finally completed in 1838 when the last of the 435 plates of *Birds of America* were published. Audubon immediately began work on a companion series, *Quadrupeds of North America*. In March of 1843 he undertook an eight-month trip up the Missouri River to collect specimens for this work. He also wanted to find new bird species for additional plates he hoped to add to a miniature edition of *Birds of America*. At the end of the eight months, he had not reached his goal—the Rocky Mountains—but he had traveled throughout the regions of the upper Missouri and the Yellowstone rivers.

Audubon spent the rest of his life on the Hudson River estate he had purchased in 1841. He died there in 1851.

Audubon has been portrayed as a backwoodsman, an explorer, and a conservationist. In reality, he was none of these. However, he was the foremost student and artist of North American birds in his lifetime and perhaps ever. Although he never ventured into uncharted territory, Audubon added significantly to the store of information about the natural history of the North American continent, leaving an enduring artistic record of his contributions.

Back, George

English
b November 2, 1796; Stockport, Cheshire
d June 23, 1878; London
Explored central Canadian Arctic

According to one source, Admiral Sir George Back was "in bravery, intelligence, and love of adventure . . . the very model of an English sailor." During his various adventures in the North American Arctic he covered more than 10,000 miles by foot and canoe alone. He was crucially involved in Sir JOHN FRANKLIN's first three Arctic ventures; his prodigious efforts on Franklin's first overland expedition of 1819–22 to the Arctic coast saved the party from starvation. A talented artist, he illustrated his published account of his greatest feat of exploration, the descent of the Great Fish (now Back) River running from near the east end of Canada's Great Slave Lake to Chantrey Inlet on the Arctic coast (1833–35). While his final Arctic mission (1836–37), undertaken to chart the coast between the western end of Fury and Hecla Strait and Turnagain Point, was a failure, his cool command of the H.M.S. *Terror* when it was beset by ice in northern Hudson Bay won the admiration of all. On his return, he was awarded the Royal Geographical Society's highest honors, and in 1839 he was knighted.

Back's "training" for exploration consisted of an odd mixture of grueling naval battles, imprisonment by the French (during which time he studied mathematics, French, and drawing), and—during an interlude away from the navy—the study of art in Naples. He was also talented in languages and picked up a variety of Native American dialects.

Back's most significant contribution to discovery resulted not from the thirst for fame so common among explorers but from a desire to save the apparently lost expedition of British explorer John Ross. When Ross turned up unexpectedly, Back decided nevertheless to explore what was then the Great Fish River to its mouth, and he succeeded in doing so despite enormous obstacles.

Eleven years of arduous Arctic travel finally took its toll on Back, and for six years after his return to England in 1837 he was essentially an invalid. He nevertheless survived to old age, served on the Arctic Council of the Admiralty, and as a very old man was appointed to unveil the Franklin monument in Westminster Abbey—a ceremony of great emotion marking the passing of the major era of Arctic exploration.

• Baffin, William

English
b 1584?; London?
d January 23, 1622; Qeshm, Iran
Explored Greenland and attempted Northwest
Passage

William Baffin ranks with JOHN DAVIS as a brilliant scientific navigator of the Arctic during the Age of Discovery. He explored and charted the bay and eastern coast of the large island north of Davis Strait, both of which now bear his name. Though he wrote a detailed account of the expedition he piloted to the farthest north point of Baffin Bay in 1616, SAMUEL PURCHAS, the editor of his papers, was extremely careless with the text and left out the map altogether. These lapses led later geographers to doubt Baffin's story. In 1635 LUKE FOXE published a map incorporating the bay described by Baffin, but later maps simply left the area blank. It was not until Captain John Ross rediscovered the bay in 1818 that Baffin received full credit.

The real impact of Baffin's most important voyage of discovery was felt immediately by those who were in a position to care—the merchants desiring a Northwest Passage (for a more complete discussion, see MARTIN FROBISHER)—for he had come back with the news that there was no such passage out of the bay. In this he was technically incorrect, since there was a way out through Lancaster Sound, as WILLIAM PARRY was to discover two centuries later. But ice robbed this Arctic route of commercial viability and made it extremely dangerous. These waters were to prove alluring to fame seekers, scientists, and hardy adventurers who simply wanted to know what was there, but they were useless to commerce. Baffin did the merchants a great service by turning away from them so early.

Nothing is known of Baffin's early life. He first appears in the records as Captain James Hall's pilot on a voyage to Greenland in 1612. This mission ended in tragedy when **Inuits** attacked and killed Hall, who had been there on an earlier Danish expedition that had treated the Inuit badly. While there, Baffin became the first navigator to attempt to determine the longitude at sea by observing the moon's culmination, though his results were too crude to be useful. After writing up his account of this voyage, Baffin joined the English Muscovy Company as pilot aboard several successful whaling expeditions to Spitsbergen (now part of Svalbard), further honing his skills as an Arctic navigator.

In 1615 Baffin piloted the *Discovery* (HENRY HUDSON's ship) under Captain ROBERT BYLOT on the Northwest Passage Company's mission to explore the waters northwest of the Hudson Strait. (Baffin's measurements of latitude and notes on the tides were so accurate as to impress Parry in 1821, by which time instruments were much more precise. It was Parry who named Baffin Island.) Baffin's readings of the tides suggested that there was no passage to the north. He also tried a new method of reading longitude by measuring lunar distance from the sun, a method suggested but not tried by German mathematicians of the sixteenth century.

The next year Baffin piloted the *Discovery* for Bylot on the voyage up Baffin Bay to Smith Sound. When his passage was blocked by ice, he decided, like John Davis before him, to attempt the route from the Pacific; however, he had no better luck getting close enough to test the theory. Sailing from England as master's mate aboard the *Anne Royal*, an East India Company ship, Baffin reached Surat, India, in September 1617. The company ship then headed for the Red Sea to establish trade, and there Baffin was kept busy charting the waters. The next year he did the same in the Persian Gulf. He returned to England with the *Anne Royal* in 1619, having apparently given up the idea of reaching the North Pacific.

In 1620 Baffin boarded the *London* as master with the same captain, Andrew Shilling, but now with a fleet of four ships. The expedition returned to the Middle East and fought a combined fleet of two Portuguese and two Dutch ships at the entrance to the Persian Gulf, where Captain Shilling was killed. Captain Blyth took over and the fleet soon aided the shah of Persia (now Iran) in driving the Portuguese from the Strait of Hormuz.

Ever the scientist, Baffin was killed during a skirmish while on shore near the castle of Qeshm, near Hormuz. He had taken his mathematical instruments to determine the height and distance of the castle walls, so that the British guns could be precisely aimed. This was no doubt an unnecessary procedure, and the castle was taken without the help of the readings.

In the midst of gunfire, no less than in dangerous ice floes, Baffin was always observing, measuring, and taking notes. His readings of latitude were always near perfect, while his attempts to determine longitude without a **chronometer** have been deemed ingenious by modern experts. The same curiosity and passion for accuracy contributed valuable information in several areas. Without his readings of magnetic variation all over the world, for instance, the first magnetic chart could not have been constructed as early as it was (1701). If his editor, Purchas, had been as careful, there would never have been any doubt about the magnitude of his accomplishments.

Samuel White Baker. The Bettmann Archive.

• Baker, Samuel White

English
b June 8, 1821; London
d December 30, 1893; Devonshire
Explored Nile and Lake Albert

An explorer of the Nile River, Sir Samuel White Baker is noted for his efforts to establish British colonies in Africa and to abolish slavery in the Sudan. He and his second wife, Florence Ninian von Sass Baker, are known together for sailing up the White Nile in an attempt to discover its source. While they failed to earn this distinction, they investigated several of the river's tributaries and discovered Lake Albert and its cataracts (a waterfall or steep rapids). Baker also led a four-year mission to extend Egyptian control to the upper Nile region and wrote extensively about both his explorations and the horrors of the slave trading he encountered.

Born to an affluent family, Baker was educated in Germany and as a youth acquired a taste for travel, hunting, and adventure. Married to a minister's daughter when in his early twenties, he managed his father's plantations on the island of Mauritius, in the Indian Ocean, before developing a successful agricultural concern of his own in present-day Sri Lanka. After approximately ten years abroad, Baker and his wife, Henrietta, returned to England, where she soon died of typhus, in 1855. The young widower spent the next several years visiting Asia Minor, Crimea, and the Balkans, and in 1860 he married a Hungarian woman fifteen years his junior. Florence Baker shared her energetic husband's love of adventure, and they were still newly married when they decided to undertake an expedition together into Central Africa to seek the source of the Nile.

The Bakers went to Cairo in 1861 and from there traveled south on the Nile to Berber (in the Sudan), learning Arabic as they went. They explored the river and its tributaries at a leisurely pace during the first year, a luxury they could afford since they had ample funds and were independent travelers rather than commissioned explorers. When they continued south to Khartoum, however, their venture took on a new urgency as they learned that the Royal Geographical Society of England needed their help. The Bakers were asked to organize a relief expedition to Gondokoro, in the Sudan, to locate JOHN HANNING SPEKE and JAMES AUGUSTUS GRANT, an exploration team under the society's sponsorship. Unaccounted for since the previous year, the two men were rumored to have died during their search for the Nile's source, and the society designated the Bakers to complete this task if necessary. Accepting eagerly, the Bakers spent six months organizing the expedition before setting out in December 1862 on the 1,000-mile journey southward. They arrived at Gondokoro nearly six weeks later and within two weeks were joined there by the missing explorers. Relieved to find the pair unharmed, though exhausted, Baker was nevertheless disappointed to learn that Speke and Grant had already solved the riddle of the Nile's source. As a consolation, the explorers told the Bakers about the portion of the Nile outlet they had left unexplored, including a lake said to be linked to the system.

Armed with a map of the Speke-Grant route, the Bakers proceeded south in March 1863 and reluctantly joined a slave trader's caravan in order to be granted passage. They were allowed to pass through the kingdom of Bunyoro (in what is now Uganda), despite the hostility they aroused, and arrived at the unknown lake's eastern shore a year after their departure. Baker renamed the Luta N'zige (as it was known locally) Lake Albert, in honor of Queen Victoria's late consort. Past the Nile's entry into the lake, they also discovered the Murchison Falls (now Kabalega Falls), named for the president of the Royal Geographical Society. Baker was awarded the society's gold medal for his accomplishments and also was honored with knighthood in 1866. During the same year, he published a book about the couple's travels, entitled *The Albert N'yanza, Great Basin of the Nile, and Explorations of the Nile Sources,* and in 1868 he released a second book, *Exploration of the Nile Tributaries.*

Baker's opportunity for a second major expedition came the following year, while he and his wife were in Egypt for the dedication ceremony for the opening of the Suez Canal. Viceroy Ismail of Egypt offered Baker a four-year appointment as leader of an expedition to expand Egyptian rule along the White Nile to Lake Victoria. Baker had traveled this route on his previous expedition from Khartoum to Lake Albert, and he was familiar with the squalor of the region as well as the treachery of its native tribes. However, his love of adventure, coupled with his strong desire to help Ismail stamp out the area's slave trade, prompted him to accept the appointment. Accorded the title of governor-general of the region, known as Equatoria province, and outfitted with a force of 1,200, Baker embarked on the colonization mission the same year.

Baker's journey as far as Gondokoro, through the river's near-impenetrable swamps, took an entire year. As he continued south, he found that conditions had worsened during his absence. The attractive western countryside had deteriorated into a wilderness, slave traders had become more prevalent and powerful, and the hostility of the region's native tribes toward outsiders had intensified.

Baker established a number of military stations during 1871, gaining the confidence of some of the native tribes to whom he offered the protection of the Egyptian empire. Other native chiefs, along with the area slave traders, were outraged at his interference. He became increasingly aggressive in his use of military force to quell these uprisings, and he further alienated many of the tribes by commandeering their supplies for his troops.

Among Baker's most strenuous opponents was the ruler of the Bunyoro kingdom, whose father and predecessor had extorted most of Baker's possessions during his first expedition in return for granting him access to the lake district. Baker and his troops were forced to fight the people of Bunyoro. Although the territory was nominally annexed to Ismail's empire after Baker's victory, Egypt's hold on the area was tenuous.

Baker's effort to abolish the slave trading of the province was not successful. Not only had the traders become near-dictators in many areas, but they incited the native tribes to undermine the work of the governor-general. Moreover, in many cases Egyptian officials placed in charge of military settlements took over the local slave trade following Baker's return to England in 1873.

Baker is credited, nevertheless, with leading the first important initiative to combat the area's slave trade as well as establishing Egyptian military posts as far south as Fatiko (in present-day Uganda). His experiences on the continent, as well as his writings, made him a leading expert on Africa and, until his death, England's foremost authority on the Nile River.

· Balboa, Vasco Nuñez de

Spanish
b 1475; Jerez de los Caballeros, Badajoz
d January 21, 1519; Acla, Panama
Discovered Pacific Ocean

Vasco Nuñez de Balboa founded the Spanish town of Darién (in present-day Colombia) and explored the surrounding area. Then, based on information obtained from Indians and acting on his own initiative and without any official authority, he led the historic expedition of 1513 that resulted in the discovery of the Pacific Ocean by Europeans.

Vasco Nuñez de Balboa. Library of Congress.

Balboa was born in 1475 to an impoverished noble family in Jerez de los Caballeros in the Spanish province of Badajoz. Little is known about his youth, except that he served for some period of time as a page to the Lord of Moguer. In 1501 he sailed for Hispaniola (the island now occupied by Haiti and the Dominican Republic) with RODRIGO DE BASTIDAS, a wealthy retired mariner and merchant, and JUAN DE LA COSA, an experienced cartographer and explorer. Enroute the expedition crossed the Gulf of Urabá (on the coast of modern Colombia); it was there that Balboa first saw the mainland of Panama and the attractive Indian village of Darién.

Upon arrival in Hispaniola, Balboa settled down as a planter; however, lacking the aptitude for such a life, he soon amassed large debts that he could not hope to pay. To escape his creditors, he concealed himself and his dog Leoncico in a huge cask that was then smuggled aboard a ship carrying supplies for the Spanish colony at San Sebastián on the Gulf of Urabá. During a stop at Cartagena (in what is now Colombia), a **brigantine** arrived under the command of FRANCISCO PIZARRO, who had been left in San Sebastián by ALONSO DE OJEDA as Ojeda's lieutenant. Pizarro related that all members of the colony, except his crew, had perished as a result of Indian attacks and disease. The commander of the supply ship, Martín Fernández de Enciso, nevertheless decided to proceed to San Sebastián and persuaded Pizarro to sail with him. Enciso's ship was wrecked entering the harbor, however, and all livestock and supplies aboard were lost. The crew was rescued by Pizarro's brigantine. When the Spaniards landed they found San Sebastián in ashes.

Balboa, who had by then been accepted as a member of Enciso's crew, gained attention at this point by describing the Indian village he had seen at Darién while sailing with Bastidas and La Cosa. A decision was made to proceed to Darién, where the Spaniards subsequently subdued the Indians and found plentiful food supplies, cotton, and various treasures. The Spaniards set up headquarters for future operations. Balboa then officially founded the town of Santa María la Antigua del Darién on the Darién River and promptly proceeded with plans to take control of the colony.

Enciso had proved to be an arbitrary leader, and Balboa arranged for his downfall by convincing the Spanish colonists that Enciso had no official authority in Darién. Enciso was forced to return to Spain to seek redress through King Ferdinand. Diego de Nicuesa, the newly appointed governor of Darién, then arrived to resolve the situation, but due to Balboa's influence the colonists rejected him. Thus, Balboa indirectly eliminated the only two people with the status required to assume official power in Darién. The Spaniards then picked Balboa and a man named Zamudio to rule them as *alcaldes* (mayors). However, it was not long before Balboa eliminated the threat of Zamudio by persuading him to take some gold to Spain and to defend Balboa there against any charges made by Enciso.

Balboa ruled wisely for two years and demonstrated a gift for making friends with the surrounding Indians. Indians who remained antagonistic, however, were subdued and their villages looted; Balboa amassed a fortune in gold and jewels pursuing these policies. From many Indians Balboa heard stories of the "Great Waters" beyond the mountains, and one Indian alluded to a land of great wealth—Birú (Peru)—that lay to the south of those waters. Convinced that a great sea did exist, he wrote to King Ferdinand and audaciously requested 1,000 men for an expedition of discovery. Before Balboa received his answer, he learned that the king was going to order him back to Spain to answer for his treatment of Enciso and Nicuesa. Realizing that he must move rapidly, Balboa mounted the expedition on his own.

The expeditionary force sailed from Darién on September 1, 1513, in one brigantine and ten **pirogues**, with 190 Spaniards, more than 800 Indians, and several dogs, including Balboa's Leoncico. They dropped anchor near Acla in San Blas at a spot that was, unknown to Balboa, the narrowest point in the Isthmus of Panama—a serendipitous choice. Balboa made an alliance with the local *cacique* (chief), Careta, who presented the Spaniard with a daughter to be his bride. Leaving the vessels in the care of about half of his men, Balboa started his trek south across the isthmus with the remainder.

After three days of extremely difficult going in the hot, humid climate, encumbered with heavy armor and weapons, and traveling over some of the most impenetrable terrain in the world, the group reached a deserted Indian village. Since it was necessary to obtain new guides for the remainder of the trip to the sea,

Balboa located and befriended the Indians who had vacated the village. Their chief was so impressed that he pointed out a ridge from which the "Great Waters" could be seen and supplied the needed guides.

Travel was no easier as they resumed their march; it took four days to go about 30 miles. In the Sierra de Quareca they encountered hostile Indians who were defeated after a violent battle. Many of the Indians were captured and tortured, and their village looted, bringing substantial treasure to the Spanish. Pushing across the last mountain barrier, the party reached a small plateau near a crest of the mountain range. On September 27, 1513, Balboa climbed alone to the top and from that vantage point, gazing past the intervening rocks and vegetation, became the first European to see the vast expanse of the Pacific Ocean from North America. When the rest of the party joined him, the Te Deum (a hymn of praise) was chanted and a cross was erected, and Balboa took possession of the ocean, its islands, and all the surrounding lands for Spain. He called the ocean the Mar del Sur (South Sea).

The expedition group partially descended the western slope of the mountain and subdued some Indians; the Spaniards then spent several days in the Indian village. Balboa sent out three separate parties to determine the best route to the actual shore of the ocean; his friend Pizarro commanded one of these groups. The chosen route was then followed to the ocean's edge, where Balboa, with drawn sword and carrying the banner of Castile and Aragon, waded into the water and claimed the ocean and all adjacent lands for his king and queen.

Although it took a different route, the return trip was as arduous as the outgoing one had been. The successful explorers nearly died of hunger because they were overloaded with plunder in preference to provisions. This situation was aggravated when they surprised and captured a powerful chief called Tubanama (from whose name the term Panama may have evolved), for whose release they collected a huge ransom. Balboa contracted a fever and had to be carried into Darién when they arrived on January 18, 1514, approximately 4½ months after their departure.

During Balboa's absence, King Ferdinand had appointed Pedro Arias de Ávila (known as Pedrarias) to supercede him as the head of government in Darién. Balboa gave an account of his expedition of discovery to Pedrarias. When asked if it was true that his dog, Leoncico, was receiving the same share of all booty as a soldier, Balboa confirmed this arrangement, saying that the troops had agreed to it because they estimated the dog was worth several fighting men.

Pedrarias proved to be inept in his position of authority and was envious of Balboa, whose popularity he tried to undermine constantly. During a lull in the tensions between the two, Balboa embarked on a bold venture—actually building ships on the shores of the Pacific for further exploration of its coastal areas. He formed the Company of the Southern Sea with financial support from his friend, Hernando de Aguilar, and was successful in assembling two brigantines on the west coast of Panama. Although the herculean task of transporting the necessary ship components over the mountains and through the jungles was relegated to Indian slaves—hundreds of whom died—the Spaniards claimed credit for the feat. One Spanish writer stated: "None but Spaniards could ever have conceived or persisted in such an undertaking, and no commander in the New World but Vasco Nuñez could have conducted it to a successful issue."

Upon completion of the brigantines Balboa immediately mounted an expedition, setting sail in the two vessels for the Pearl Islands in the present-day Gulf of Panama. When he left the islands, he headed south, but the winds became unfavorable. He decided to go back to the coast and build two more ships before starting another major mission.

In the interim, Pedrarias had become convinced that Balboa was plotting to establish an independent government on the west coast of Panama. Pedrarias sent a message to Balboa asking him to come to Darién, ostensibly for discussions but with the intent of arresting him immediately upon arrival. Fearing that he might not come, the governor then ordered Pizarro to assemble a force, proceed to the Pacific coast, and arrest him. Balboa met his former lieutenant enroute and offered no resistance. Upon reaching Darién, he was brought to trial and, with pressure from Pedrarias, convicted of planning treason. Although sentiment among the townspeople was highly supportive of the popular hero, he was sentenced to be beheaded immediately. Balboa was executed on January 21, 1514, in the town he had founded and made famous in the world of his time.

Vasco Nuñez de Balboa, though always loyal to Spain, was an intrepid, brash, and innovative explorer who often set his own expeditionary objectives and managed his own financing. Although the area he explored was relatively small, it included some of the most forbidding terrain in the world. His discovery of the Pacific Ocean stands out in the annals of history as a tremendous feat.

SUGGESTED READING: Charles L. G. Anderson, *Life and Letters of Vasco Nuñez de Balboa* (Fleming H. Revell Co., 1941); Jean Descola, *The Conquistadors,* trans. by Malcolm Barnes (Augustus M. Kelley, 1970); Kathleen Romoli, *Balboa of Darien: Discoverer of the Pacific* (Doubleday, 1953).

• Banks, Joseph

English
b February 15, 1743; London
d June 19, 1820; London
Accompanied James Cook on his first circumnavigation

Sir Joseph Banks sponsored a team of naturalists, including himself, on Captain JAMES COOK's first circumnavigation and exploration of the South Pacific. The team brought back thousands of specimens, drawings, and descriptions

Sir Joseph Banks. Bibliothèque Nationale, Paris.

BANKS, JOSEPH

of exotic plant and animal life from Tierra del Fuego, Tahiti, New Holland (now Australia), and the Great Barrier Reef, which became the foundation of the British Museum's natural history collection. Banks's great success on the *Endeavour* voyage paved the way for other naturalists, including CHARLES DARWIN, to take part in such expeditions as a matter of course.

Born into a well-to-do family in 1743, Banks was educated at the finest schools—Harrow, Eton, and Oxford—where he developed a strong interest in botany and the natural sciences. When he was just fifteen he took part in a collecting expedition to Newfoundland. He nearly died of a fever on the voyage, but the herbarium he created with the specimens gathered is today in the British Museum.

Upon the death of his father, a Lincolnshire doctor, in 1761, Banks inherited an income of £6,000 a year—certainly enough to allow him the leisure to pursue his interests in the natural sciences. In 1768, at the age of twenty-five, he convinced the British government to allow him to join Lieutenant James Cook on an expedition to the Pacific Ocean to chart the passing of Venus across the sun. Banks contributed £10,000 to sponsor the voyage and paid his own expenses as well as those of his entourage of artists and assistants. No team had ever been better equipped to do the job of collecting and preserving specimens at sea. In addition to a natural history library, they had, an associate of Banks wrote, "all sorts of machines for catching and preserving insects, all kinds of nets, trawls, drags, and hooks for coral fishing, they even have a curious contrivance of a telescope by which, put into water, you can see the bottom at great depth."

The *Endeavour* left England in August 1768. Banks and his team spent the long days at sea dragging nets through the water, then cataloging their finds. The ship reached Tierra del Fuego at the southern tip of South America in December, and a team went ashore to study alpine plant life. There two of Banks's servants froze to death.

Tahiti, their next stop, was much more hospitable. Banks learned to speak the language and set himself up as liaison with the natives, often handing out generous gifts. He was a sharp observer of the island culture, and his journal records the first description of surfing ever to reach Europe, as well as numerous other details of the islanders' daily life, including how they made fishhooks of bone and nets of jungle vine. In order to study the Tahitians, Banks stripped and blackened himself with charcoal and water; however, the islanders seemed to accept him without this disguise. Banks circumnavigated the island with Cook, visiting burial grounds no white man had ever seen. He even succumbed to the native practice of tattooing, possibly beginning the sailors' tradition of decorating their bodies in this way. And, like so many other Europeans who visited Tahiti, he was no stranger to the charms of the native women, particularly one he called Queen Obarea.

New Zealand, Australia's east coast, and the Great Barrier Reef—the *Endeavour*'s next stops—provided more opportunities to add to Banks's exhaustive specimen collection, although Australia's spear-throwing **aborigines** were not nearly as hospitable as the people of Tahiti. Near present-day Sydney, Australia, the naturalists found a spot so full of plant life they named it Botany Bay, and Banks became the first European to describe the beast that the natives called a kangaroo. Later in life Banks would recommend Botany Bay as the site for a new British penal colony.

Collecting activities were limited by native hostility in New Guinea and by an outbreak of dysentery among the crew on the island of Java (in present-day Indonesia). Still, by the end of the three-year voyage, Banks and his team had collected specimens of more than 1,000 plants, 500 fish, 500 bird skins and countless insects, shells, coral, and rocks, in addition to cultural artifacts, cloth, and carvings. They had drawn the eyes of the scientific community to the Pacific.

Banks was tremendously well received upon his return to England in 1771. In fact, the public considered the voyage to be his, rather than Cook's, success, and the naturalist was much in demand in the best social circles. King George III requested an interview, and Oxford awarded him an honorary degree. However, he did take some barbs from satirists who criticized his participation in the perceived promiscuity of Tahitian society.

The following year, Cook was to sail again, and Banks planned to accompany him. However, Banks's team had grown from eight to fifteen, including several musicians. When Cook's ship, the *Resolution*, was refitted to accommodate the group, it could no longer sail safely; so the extra cabin structure was removed at Cook's request, and Banks was asked to limit his entourage. Rather than give up his horn players, Banks angrily withdrew from Cook's expedition and set up a private, yearlong journey to the Hebrides and Iceland.

Despite Banks's withdrawal from Cook's second expedition, the young naturalist and the captain had developed a friendship, which they maintained through correspondence. Cook continued to bring Banks specimens, and Banks persuaded the Royal Society to strike a commemorative medal upon Cook's death.

When Cook brought Omai, a Tahitian native, to England from his second voyage, Banks took the young man under his wing, dressed him in the finest clothes, and introduced him to London society, even taking him on grouse-hunting trips to Yorkshire. Omai returned to the Pacific with Cook in 1777.

In 1776 Banks moved from his home on London's New Burlington Street to Soho Square and married a woman sixteen years his junior. The following year, he was named president of the Royal Society, an influential post he would hold for the next forty-two years. In that capacity he was responsible for promoting many new expeditions, including that of WILLIAM BLIGH, who was sent to Tahiti to bring back breadfruit trees for cultivation in the West Indies. A generous man of broad interests, Banks also sponsored such explorers as MUNGO PARK in Africa and MATTHEW FLINDERS in Australia. He served as royal adviser for London's Kew Gardens and was instrumental in establishing botanical gardens in Jamaica, St. Vincent, and Ceylon (now Sri Lanka). He also placed his personal libraries and collections at the disposal of researchers.

Banks remained active in natural history circles despite crippling gout that required him to be carried in a chair the last fifteen years of his life. He died childless in London in 1820 at the age of seventy-seven, and a statue in his honor was raised at the Natural History Museum in London. A heavily edited version of the journal he kept on the *Endeavour* voyage was published after his death.

Barbosa, Duarte

Portuguese
b 1480?; Portugal
d June 6, 1521; Cebu, Philippines
Explored Indian Ocean; sailed with Magellan
** in service of Spain**

Duarte Barbosa was already an experienced and knowledgeable seaman when he set sail from Spain with FERDINAND MAGELLAN's fleet of five ships in 1519. The great navigator's kin by marriage, Barbosa would prove to be one of Magellan's most loyal supporters on a historic voyage that was fraught with mutiny and discontent.

Barbosa was born in Portugal about the same time as his countryman Magellan. He is believed to have been the son of Diogo Barbosa, who served the Spanish government as an administrator in Seville, but at least one account suggests that the younger Barbosa may have been Diogo's nephew instead. When Magellan first arrived in Spain in 1517, he lived in the Barbosa household, eventually marrying Diogo's daughter, Beatriz.

By the early years of the sixteenth century Duarte Barbosa was lured to the sea, as were so many Portuguese youths of the time. His travels took him to the Cape of Good Hope and the east coast of Africa, as well as to Arabia and what is now Iran. Barbosa helped to establish important trade connections at Aden and Hormuz. He continued to India, where he traveled extensively both on land, particularly in the western part of the country, and through the adjacent seas as far east as Sumatra (in what is now Indonesia). It is likely that Barbosa first met Magellan in India, for Magellan was traveling with Francisco de Almeida, Portuguese viceroy of India, from 1504 to 1512.

Barbosa returned to Lisbon, Portugal, and by 1516 he had published his experiences in *The Book of Duarte Barbosa*. Eager to continue his explorations, he met with a cool reception at the Portuguese court. Unlike his predecessor, Prince Henry the Navigator, King Manuel I had little enthusiasm for the sea. Frustrated, Barbosa headed to Seville, the capital of Spain. Before settling in Spain, however, Barbosa visited Pôrto, a haven for discontented sailors in northern Portugal. There he met Magellan and easily interested him in heading an expedition to the Spice Islands (now the Moluccas) by way of South America. Together they left Pôrto on October 12, 1517.

Spain's King Charles I eagerly backed the voyage, and Barbosa set sail with Magellan in September 1519. The friction between the Spanish and Portuguese members of the crew was tremendous, and troubles began almost immediately. Barbosa proved his loyalty to Magellan many times, most notably on April 2, 1520. It was Easter night, and the ships were on the southern coast of South America, at San Julián, when thirty crewmen attempted a revolt. Barbosa and his handpicked crew easily recaptured the vessel that had been taken. For his role in thwarting the mutiny, he was given command of the *Victoria*, which would be the only ship to complete the circumnavigation.

Although little is written about Barbosa's character, it is reasonable to assume that he was a natural leader who also felt comfortable supporting his superiors. He was strong enough to survive the mental as well as the physical rigors of this daring and difficult voyage that entailed sailing into unknown waters without seeing land for months and eating rats and leather when the ship's stores were exhausted. It is known that Barbosa was a skilled seaman who knew the eastern waters well. At any rate, Barbosa and his countryman Juan Serrano were elected cocommanders of the expedition upon Magellan's death in the Philippines in April 1521. But Barbosa would not survive his fallen in-law for long.

Barbosa's death on the island of Cebu in the Philippines on June 6, 1521, was a result of treachery. The raja of Cebu invited Barbosa and twenty-six crewmen to a banquet on shore. Barbosa not only attended against Serrano's advice but prevailed on Serrano to go with him. At the banquet, all the mariners except Serrano and an interpreter were ambushed and killed, and their bodies were thrown into the sea. Serrano was put naked in chains, and his shipmates left him on the island to die.

Barents, Willem

Dutch
b 1550?; Terschelling Island
d June 20, 1597; Barents Sea
Explored Northeast Passage, discovered
**   Spitsbergen, and wintered in Arctic**

While his compatriots were discovering Australia and laying the foundations for a rich trade with the East Indies, Willem Barents, a seaman from Amsterdam, made three attempts to reach Cathay (now China) by sailing north of Europe. None of the expeditions made it significantly farther than the previous English missions in search of a Northeast Passage. On his third voyage, while proceeding to Novaya Zemlya, an island between the Kara Sea and the sea later named after him, he finally made good on his backers' investment by discovering the Spitsbergen group of islands (part of present-day Svalbard). This region soon became a rich source of profits in whale, seal, and walrus for both the Dutch and the English.

According to the great nineteenth-century Swedish explorer of these waters, NILS ADOLF ERIK NORDENSKIÖLD, a little perseverance against the ice in the channels south of Novaya Zemlya might have resulted in Barents's penetrating to the inhabited regions of Russia on the Obi and Yenisei rivers. This would have resulted in the early establishment of heavy trade between Europe and Middle Asia. Already the Dutchman Oliver Brunel had reached the great Obi by land, so Barents must have realized this

Willem Barents. The Bettman Archive.

possibility. On the first Barents expedition, two of the ships actually did penetrate into the Kara Sea, going as far as the Kara River and turning back, sure that they had discovered the passage to Cathay. Ice conditions were much worse the next year, however. After failing to penetrate the straits, the Dutch never tried again.

What prevented Barents from attempting the straits on his third voyage was his belief that ice formed only along the shore and not on the open polar sea. If he could get well out into the sea above Novaya Zemlya, he and his scientific adviser, the Reverend Peter Plancius, evidently believed the expedition would have clear water to Cathay. Trade with the people on the Obi River region must have seemed uninteresting by comparison.

On the first expedition of 1594, while the *Swan* and the *Mercury* made the promising voyage through Pet Strait (named after the English explorer Arthur Pet, whose sailing directions Barents had translated) into the Kara Sea, Barents pursued the fruitless northern route to Cape Nassau on Novaya Zemlya, where he was stopped by ice. The organizers of the second expedition, acting on the expectation that the southern route would prove successful, fitted out seven ships from four Dutch ports and filled them with goods to be traded in the Orient. This voyage, like the first backed by the public purse, proved a total failure when it hit the ice-clogged strait on August 19, 1595. The States General then voted to waste no more funds on exploring this route. Undeterred—in fact, encouraged by the visionary Plancius—Barents convinced the merchants of Amsterdam to try once more.

On this final voyage Barents was the pilot of a ship commanded by Jacob van Heemskerck. Another ship was commanded by Jan Cornelius Rijp. On June 9, 1596, both ships discovered Bear Island, to the south of the Svalbard **archipelago**, and on June 19 they discovered the island of Spitsbergen itself, which they thought was Greenland.

The two captains then disagreed about the best course and separated. Rijp sailed north briefly before heading back to Holland. Barents headed east to Novaya Zemlya and on August 21 reached a point at 76° North latitude that he aptly called Ice Haven. It was here on August 26 that the ship was beset by gathering ice. The crew was forced to abandon it and stayed the winter. With only the bleak example of HUGH WILLOUGHBY's fatal winter of 1553–54 before them, the crew must have assumed their chances for survival were slender; but they faced their fate with remarkable good humor and determination, later impressing the whole of Europe with their story.

Conditions were not as bad as they had been for Willoughby, since Barents and his crew had ship timbers and driftwood sufficient to construct a cabin and to provide fuel for fire throughout the winter. Foxes were plentiful enough in the area to provide the party with enough protein to fight off disease. Polar bears were also present (to the point of being a nuisance), but an early, bad experience with one meal of bear meat discouraged them from making use of this source of food.

Two of the seventeen men died during the winter, probably from **scurvy**, but the rest stayed healthy enough to plan their escape in the summer. Determined to learn from their experience, they took careful astronomical and geographical observations, which the surviving crew member Gerrit de Veer later reported to a fascinated Europe.

When summer came, Barents and his crew found that their ship was no longer seaworthy, and was in any case submerged and frozen in. Their only recourse was to take the two small boats remaining. Before putting to sea on June 13, 1597, Captain Heemskerck drew up two accounts of their hardships, one for each boat. Barents, weak from scurvy, wrote his own account and placed it in the cabin's chimney, where it was found 278 years later.

After many difficulties negotiating the ice-clogged seas, the two small boats made it after eighty days to a Dutch trading settlement on the mainland, where they met Captain Rijp, who took them home. Barents, however, had died on the seventh day of the ordeal of rowing and sailing over 1,600 miles.

It was 274 years until anyone else rounded the point off Novaya Zemlya where the Barents party had wintered. In 1871 the Norwegian whaling captain Elling Carlsen came across the driftwood house, which had been only slightly disturbed by scavenging animals. Until then, the Barents saga, with all of its "great cold, povertie, miserie and griefe," had discouraged the world from seeking wealth and adventure in these waters.

It was the promise of scientific discovery that finally lured Nordenskiöld back to the quest for the Northeast Passage in 1878. As for the Dutch, when Heemskerck returned home in 1597, they no longer had much need of a northern route to Cathay. They had just defeated the Spanish, so there were no obstacles to pursuing the southern trade route to the Indies. From time to time during the next 250 years some hardy adventurer would try the passage, but none had any better luck than Barents.

• Barrow, John

English
b June 19, 1764; Ulverston, Lancashire
d November 23, 1848; London
Founded Royal Geographical Society

As a young man, John Barrow displayed a diligence and sense of adventure that would enable him to make significant contributions to world exploration later in his life. At the age of fourteen, he was hired to work in a Liverpool iron foundry. Within a year, he was hard at work as a crewman aboard a whaling ship in the Arctic Ocean, an experience that spurred his interest in Arctic exploration. Barrow was also the first person to make a balloon flight in England (with the pioneer Italian balloonist Lunardi). These early events shaped the interests of the man who would later, as the secretary of the Admiralty, dedicate his life to the advancement of polar exploration by sea and to the founding of the Royal Geographical Society.

Barrow's route to the position of secretary of the Admiralty had stops in China and Africa. He served as a tutor to the son of Sir George Leonard Staunton, the chief assistant of Lord Macartney. When Macartney became ambassador to China in 1792, Barrow was invited to accompany him as his scientific adviser. In this position, Barrow's far-reaching observations and writings helped forge a new vision of the culture and history of China. When Macartney was subsequently appointed governor of Cape Province in South Africa, he took Barrow along as a member of the embassy staff, a post Barrow filled with distinction. In 1803 Barrow returned to England and was appointed permanent secretary to the Admiralty, a position he occupied for almost forty years.

The end of the Napoleonic Wars in 1815 released a large number of highly skilled naval officers from their wartime duties, and Secretary Barrow had both the authority and the inclination to employ many of them to make a series of expeditions to the Arctic. His book, *A Chronological History of Voyages into the Arctic Regions*, set the agenda for a systematic, scientific investigation of the region in search of a Northwest Passage to Asia (for a more complete discussion, see MARTIN FROBISHER). Even though none of the expeditions Barrow directed would find such a passage, the importance of their geographic findings and his key role in this monumental undertaking resulted in the naming of the Barrow Strait (in northern Canada) and Cape Barrow in his honor.

In 1830, along with six others, Barrow further advanced the cause of organized geographical research and exploration by founding the Royal Geographical Society. Primarily Barrow's brainchild, the Society would become the world's foremost independent sponsor of exploration, backing a host of history's most significant explorers and expeditions.

• Barth, Heinrich

German
b February 16, 1821; Hamburg
d November 25, 1865; Berlin
Explored North and Central Africa

Considered one of the leading African explorers and scholars, Heinrich Barth traveled in the Sahara and the Sudan for more than five years and provided a wealth of information about those areas through his writing and mapmaking. Much of the interior territory he visited was previously unknown to Europeans, and Barth's knowledge of geography, history, and archaeology enabled him to make important observations about these lands and their inhabitants. He explored extensively around Lake Chad, discovered the upper Benue River, and spent considerable time in the cities of Kano and Timbuktu (in modern Nigeria and Mali, respectively). (For a map of his route, see GUSTAV NACHTIGAL.) An accomplished linguist, Barth compiled vocabularies for approximately forty native dialects he encountered in the Lake Chad region. Fascinated with the continent, the aloof young professor developed an improbable degree of rapport with its native people and prolonged his stay to the point that his fellow Euro-

Heinrich Barth.   Royal Geographical Society.

peans suspected he had died and began printing his obituary. Barth's account of his 10,000-mile journey, published upon his return to Europe, was underappreciated at first but has since been recognized as an invaluable contribution to the field of African exploration and study.

The son of a prosperous, self-made merchant, Barth became obsessed in childhood with the desire to impress his mother by becoming more successful than his father. To that end, he studied avidly, both in school and on his own, and shunned all social activities in favor of concentrating on his science, geography, and language books. Consequently he became a loner, a condition that persisted throughout his college years. He excelled in his study of archaeology, geography, and history at the University of Berlin, where he failed again to acquire any social skills.

Hoping to remedy this situation, his father sent him on a lengthy tour of London, Paris, and the Mediterranean countries. Barth enjoyed North Africa in particular and was intrigued with the idea of exploring the lands that lay beyond Africa's coast. Nevertheless, he returned to Berlin after three years and took a teaching position at his alma mater. He spent the summer of 1849 teaching a course in the geology of North Africa, but his chronic inability to relate to people made him unpopular with both his students and his colleagues, and his course was canceled. While he was still trying to recover from this trauma, he suffered a second disappointment when the woman he had been courting abruptly ended their relationship. Barth's dejection proved to be short-lived, however, because the same batch of mail that contained his sweetheart's letter also included an invitation to join an expedition into the African interior. Overjoyed, the twenty-eight-year-old scholar accepted immediately, and two months later he returned to North Africa.

The English Mixed Scientific and Commercial Expedition, sponsored by the British government, enlisted Barth on the recommendation forwarded by his former teacher, geographer Karl Ritter, through the Prussian ambassador to England. The expedition leader, former missionary James Richardson, had already traveled some 700 miles south of Tripoli to Ghāt (in what is now Libya). Richardson's second trip was to cover more than twice that distance and take a more scientific approach to exploration. In addition to promoting commerce in the Sahara and attempting to abolish its slave trade, the 1850 expedition was intended to gather historical and scientific data about the region. Also joining the party was a German geologist named Adolf Overweg. The trio departed from Tripoli in March 1850 and traveled south toward the city of Kano in present-day Nigeria.

With the party taking a direct route some 500 miles south into the desert region of Libya, Barth recorded his first significant findings before they reached Murzuch. He found evidence that a Roman settlement had once existed along a dry river valley and, as he came closer to Murzuch, located fields of Roman ruins and graves. In the mountainous desert south of Murzuch, he discovered a series of rock paintings made by various civilizations from the Stone Age to around the first century A.D. The first group of paintings depicted tropical animals such as elephants and ostriches; later illustrations showed cattle and horses, and still later ones depicted camels. From Barth's account of this artwork, historians were later able to chronicle the once-fertile land's gradual deterioration into a desert.

Even at this early stage of the trip, Barth and Richardson had developed a mutual dislike, and Overweg had cast his support with Barth. While the two Germans officially remained with the expedition and were somewhat dependent on Richardson's experience and diplomatic connections, they rode and camped separately from their leader as they continued south. Barth left the party on several occasions, either alone or in the company of Overweg, to explore independently. One of these trips—to the allegedly haunted Mount Idinen outside Ghāt—nearly cost Barth his life. Separated from Overweg and their servants while climbing the barren, shadeless mountain, Barth was trapped there overnight and almost died before he was rescued. At one desperate point, he became so thirsty that he sucked blood from his own veins.

The violent Tuareg natives of the region also posed a hazard to the travelers, who were continually threatened with attack as they made their way to Ghāt and on toward the Aïr Mountains. By the summer, however, they had reached a truce with the Tuareg and were allowed safe passage. Barth then left his companions and visited Agadès, where he was an honored guest at the coronation of the new sultan. He spent several weeks investigating the ancient town and befriending its citizens. They came to refer to him as Abd-el-Kerim, meaning "servant of God."

Barth rejoined Richardson and Overweg in October, in the Tintellust oasis of the Aïr Mountains, and within three months they all parted company to pursue three separate paths to Lake Chad. They agreed to meet in Kuka (now Kukawa, Nigeria), near the lake's western shore, but the reunion of the three explorers was never to take place. Malaria would claim Richardson's life shortly before the others arrived at the city.

From Aïr, Barth rapidly traveled some 375 miles south to Kano within three weeks and reached the scenic, prosperous city in February 1851. Although his resources were quickly dwindling, he shrewdly offered expensive gifts to the province's chief officials and was rewarded with their full hospitality during his month-long stay. Again he made a thorough study of the society and geography of the area, as well as laying the groundwork for trade agreements that held enormous profit potential for Europe.

In early March he headed east to Bornu, and a short time before he reached the appointed rendezvous spot, the capital city of Kuka, messengers notified him of Richardson's death. Despite their differences, Barth was saddened by the news and stopped to pay tribute at the Englishman's grave site before continuing to Kuka in early April.

Barth's newly developed diplomatic graces earned him a warm welcome from Sultan Omar of Bornu, who gave him access to the entire territory and provided guides for the explorer's travels around Lake Chad. Thrilled by the sight of the large freshwater lake, Barth nevertheless decided to leave the task of investigating its banks to Overweg, who reached Kuka a few weeks after his colleague. Meanwhile, Barth went south to Yola, where he discovered the upper reaches of the Benue River in mid-June. He also confirmed that this body of water was not directly linked to Lake Chad but emptied into the Niger River to the west. Journeying east, he then explored the Shari River and established its connection to Lake Chad. Nearly out of funds at this point, he wrote to his sponsors in London to ask for money so he could continue traveling east to Zanzibar. Instead, the funds that arrived were accompanied by instructions to proceed west to Timbuktu. Barth and Overweg were preparing for this journey when Overweg, who had been recovering from malaria since his arrival in Kuka, suffered a relapse and died on September 27, 1852. Still grieving over the loss of his friend, Barth left the following year on a westward trip that was to be long and treacherous.

Leaving Bornu and proceeding west across the plains toward Sokoto, Barth eventually lost the protection of Sultan Omar and became prey to the marauders and warlike tribes of the region. He arrived in Sokoto, near the northern border of present-day Nigeria, in March 1853 and continued to cross unfamiliar territory. To survive, he kept his six-man force in a constant state of watchfulness, and he once simulated a late-night attack as an object lesson. In addition, he assumed the pose of a holy man on a mission to deliver religious books to the sheik of Timbuktu, and his guise was convincing enough that some native inhabitants mistook him for the Messiah. Barth reached Say, on the banks of the Niger, in June and traveled north to Timbuktu, arriving on September 7, 1853. Although in Europe it was still thought to be an opulent and beautiful city, Timbuktu in reality was at this time a drab community whose citizens hated strangers and suspected the inquisitive Barth of being a spy. He credited the Colt six-shooter he brandished with ensuring his safety, noting that the people in Timbuktu were in awe of the newly invented pistol.

Permitted to leave Timbuktu in May 1854, Barth traveled back toward Kuka, receiving a warm welcome en route from the various native tribes he had befriended. They also brought the news that in Europe he was rumored to be dead and that an explorer named Eduard Vogel had been sent to discover his fate. The two explorers met in the Bundi jungle in November and visited Kuka together before the exhausted Barth finally returned north to Tripoli in August 1855 and departed for Europe, having spent nearly six years in the African interior.

On his arrival in London the following month, Barth again became a reserved loner even as he was being honored for his achievements. He earned the Patron's Medal of the Royal Geographical Society in 1856 and spent three years writing a comprehensive account of his experiences. The five-volume publication got a lukewarm reception from Barth's contemporaries, many of whom considered his work credible but dull. Only in retrospect would it become prized for its abundance of useful facts and telling observations as well as for its detailed maps and drawings. Barth returned to Germany, where he was welcomed back to the University of Berlin as a geography professor in 1863. Barth remained disappointed at the public's lack of appreciation, and he did not live long enough to see opinions toward him change. He died at age forty-four of a stomach ailment he had developed during his travels.

SUGGESTED READINGS: Brian Gardner, *The Quest for Timbuctoo* (Harcourt Brace, 1968); Robert I. Rotberg, *Africa and its Explorers* (Harvard University Press, 1970).

• Bartram, John

American
b March 23, 1699; near Darby, Pennsylvania
d September 22, 1777; Kingsessing,
    Pennsylvania
Studied plants of eastern North America

John Bartram has been called the first native American botanist. In his passion for collecting and distributing new plants, he traveled over much of eastern North America. From 1765 to 1766, he and his son William made a journey through the Carolinas, Georgia, and Florida, in which they explored and prepared a map of the San Juan (now St. Johns) River.

Bartram was an unschooled farm boy when he first developed an interest in plants. Later on, he traveled to Philadelphia to purchase books on the subject and taught himself the science of botany. In 1728, he bought property 3 miles from Philadelphia on the banks of the Schuylkill River, established a botanical garden, and conducted experiments in creating new forms of plants (hybrids) from established species. George Washington and Benjamin Franklin often relaxed and conversed in Bartram's garden.

In 1738 Bartram made the first of his many botanical journeys around America. He traveled to Williamsburg, Virginia, up the James River, and across the Blue Ridge Mountains—in all a journey of over 1,000 miles—in five weeks. Later he traveled north to Lake Ontario, publishing the journals of his trip in 1751. In 1755 he was in the Catskill Mountains of New York, in 1760 he visited the Carolinas, and in 1761 he journeyed to the frontier fort at what is now Pittsburgh.

Bartram traveled at his own expense, and he was therefore both gratified and relieved when an English friend managed to have him appointed to the position of botanist to King George III of England with an annual salary of fifty pounds. Thus, it was in the service of the British that he set sail in 1765 for Charleston, South Carolina, where he joined his son William. Father and son spent two months exploring the Carolinas before picking up a wilderness trail that took them through Georgia. The going was rough, as shown in this excerpt that retains Bartram's unique spelling: "Travailed 30 miles over many bay and cypress swamps. . . . [T]his day's rideing was very bad thro bay swamps, tupelos . . . and cypress in deep water. . . . [D]ined by a swamp on bread and pomgranite." Another time they "lodged in ye woods under a pine amongst ye palmetoes and near a pond and musketoes." Eventually the Bartrams reached Florida, with its lush landscapes and exotic flowers. From the Spanish city of Saint Augustine, they traveled to Picatola and purchased a canoe for exploring what is now the St. Johns River. After charting the river and describing in detail its natural life—trees, flowers, fruits, birds, fish, and minerals—Bartram reluctantly returned home in the spring of 1766. This was his last great expedition.

While some explorers went in search of new territory, John Bartram investigated the plants that were native to the lands in which he traveled. Motivated by a desire for knowledge, he once suggested the need for a westward journey of exploration to his friend Benjamin Franklin, who in turn proposed the idea to Thomas Jefferson. Jefferson's eventual instructions to MERIWETHER LEWIS and WILLIAM CLARK are very similar to the outlines that Bartram proposed to Franklin much earlier. Thus, to Bartram's other credits might be added his inspiration of the Lewis and Clark expedition.

• Bastidas, Rodrigo de

Spanish
b 1460?; Triana, Seville
d 1526; Caribbean Sea
Explored coasts of Colombia and Panama

After achieving status as a wealthy merchant, retired mariner Rodrigo de Bastidas was motivated to explore by the profits others had made in the New World. In concert with the great cartographer JUAN DE LA COSA, Bastidas explored most of the coastline of present-day Colombia in 1501 and was the first European to reach Central America. Later, in 1524, he founded the present-day city of Santa Marta on the coast of Colombia.

Bastidas was born around 1460 in Triana, Spain; the exact date of his birth is unknown. At the time he received a royal commission for exploration (in 1500), Bastidas had already had a career as a mariner and merchant. The commission authorized Bastidas to discover any islands and new lands in "Tierra-firme" (South America) that would not encroach upon lands discovered by CHRISTOPHER COLUMBUS or territory belonging to Portugal. Forming a limited partnership with La Cosa, he sailed in late February 1501 following the route established by Columbus. On this voyage a new island was sighted (either modern Barbados or Grenada), which Bastidas called Isla Verde (Green Island) because of its lush vegetation. Upon reaching Trinidad the party sailed west to the Guajira Peninsula of present-day Colombia. Past the mouth of the Magdalena River the explorers discovered a bay, which Bastidas named Cartagena. After trading with the friendly Sinu (or Zenu) Indians, they proceeded to the Gulf of Urabá, then sailed along the coast of what is now Panama at least as far as modern Carreto, and perhaps to Cape San Blas. Thus, Bastidas led the first expedition to reach Central America. After being forced to turn back because *teredos* (shipworms) were destroying the ships, the expedition was shipwrecked on the southwest coast of Hispaniola (the island now occupied by Haiti and the Dominican Republic). Bastidas and La Cosa walked to the capital carrying a treasure of gold and pearls and were arrested for trading infringement. Later released, they returned to Spain in 1504.

Bastidas was named **adelantado** in 1504 and was given a lifetime annuity on income from the lands he discovered. In 1524 he was granted a license to start a colony on the **Spanish Main**. After recruiting 500 colonists in Hispaniola, he sailed in May 1526 and founded the city of Santa Marta on the coast of Colombia on July 25. Unlike most Spanish explorers, Bastidas protected the Indians near his colony from enslavement and encouraged the colonists to do their own manual labor. A rebellion of many colonists, coupled with an epidemic of dysentery that also struck Bastidas, forced Bastidas to set out to seek help at Hispaniola near the end of 1526. Twelve days out to sea he died.

• Bates, Henry Walter

English
b February 8, 1825; Leicester
d February 16, 1892; London
Explored upper Amazon River basin

Henry Walter Bates, perhaps the foremost authority of his day on Coleoptera (the insect order of beetles and weevils), accompanied his friend and fellow naturalist ALFRED RUSSEL WALLACE on an expedition to the Amazon river basin in Brazil in 1848. Bates remained in South America for almost eleven years, exploring the upper Amazon, observing its Indian cultures, collecting a wide variety of natural specimens, discovering thousands of new insect species, and de-

Henry Walter Bates.   Royal Geographical Society.

veloping the scientific theory now known as Batesian mimicry. After returning to England, Bates wrote *The Naturalist on the River Amazon* (1863), one of the finest and most popular travel books of the nineteenth century.

Born at Leicester in 1825, Bates had little formal education. His father, a manufacturer, wanted him to go into business and to that end apprenticed him to a hosiery maker. After working long hours during the day, Bates attended evening classes at the Mechanics Institute in Leicester. He read constantly, and his growing interest in zoology led him to roam the countryside collecting specimens whenever he got the chance. When he was just eighteen years old, Bates had a scientific paper on beetles published in the first issue of the *Zoologist*. He was also quite a linguist, mastering Greek, Latin, and French while attending night school and then teaching himself Portuguese and German later on in South America.

The turning point in Bates's life occurred in 1844 when he met Alfred Russel Wallace, who came to Leicester as a schoolmaster. The two men became fast friends and often went exploring together in the nearby countryside, collect-

ing specimens of insects, birds, and butterflies. Sharing an enthusiasm for natural history, they developed a friendship that would dramatically change their lives. When Wallace proposed that they journey to South America to explore the Amazon river basin, Bates saw a chance to make science and the study of nature his vocation rather than just a hobby.

Bates and Wallace arrived at Pará (present-day Belém), Brazil, near the mouth of the Amazon, on May 28, 1848. Together they explored the regions along the Tocantins and part of the Río Negro. The naturalists then decided to separate for a time in order to expand the area of exploration. Bates went to Caripí, 23 miles from Pará. He remained there from December 7, 1848, to February 12, 1849, collecting specimens of such creatures as anteaters and bats. After returning to Pará, Bates departed upriver on a schooner for Óbidos on September 5, 1849. At Óbidos he studied insect life and spider monkeys before rejoining Wallace farther upriver at Barra do Río Negro (present-day Manaus) on January 22, 1850. Situated at the confluence of the Río Negro and the upper Amazon, the town and its surrounding region was a naturalist's paradise.

When the two friends separated again, Bates decided to explore the upper Amazon, concentrating on the Solimões and Tapajós river basins. He spent the next 7½ years in these regions, focusing his attention primarily on insect life. Of the 14,500 specimens he collected during this time, 8,000 were previously unknown to science, including more than 500 species of butterflies alone.

While exploring in the Solimões area, Bates headquartered at the town of Ega (now Tefé) at the foot of the Andes. In 1851 he journeyed from Ega to Santarém (at the mouth of the Tapajós), making this his base of exploration for the next 3½ years. In 1855 he returned to Ega and made several lengthy excursions (as long as 400 miles) over the next three years. In 1856, for example, he traveled 250 miles to Turnaltins, an Indian settlement, where he collected specimens of insects, monkeys, and birds. An excursion to São Paulo de Olivença, some 260 miles from Ega, resulted in a five-month stay, during which he collected specimens from nature and observed the way of life of the region's Indians.

Though Bates was sometimes discouraged by his poor financial condition, his deteriorating health (the result of overwork and poor diet), and loneliness, his love of discovery and collecting always renewed his spirit. In his words: "The exquisite pleasure of finding another new species . . . supports one against everything."

Though he wanted to go up the Amazon as far as the Andes, Bates only reached Fonte Boa (about 66° West latitude). An attack of the **ague**, combined with his already failing health, forced him to leave for England on June 2, 1859.

From his explorations along the upper Amazon, Bates brought back to England an invaluable specimen collection and a great deal of geographical and scientific information. His experiences there also helped him to formulate the theory of mimicry in nature based on his observations of insects, particularly butterflies. Simply put, the principle of mimicry is that an unprotected species that is scarce and palatable to its predators will assume the appearance, either in shape or color, of a more abundant and unpalatable species, thus escaping the attention of predators. Though the principle of mimicry was later developed more fully by other scientists, Bates is recognized as being the first one to formalize the theory.

Once back in England, Bates served for twenty-eight years as assistant secretary of the Royal Geographical Society. During that time he edited the *Journals* and *Proceedings* of the Society and wrote his travel narratives. He received many honors, such as election to the presidency of the Entomological Society of London. Perhaps the honor that best reflects the importance of his explorations and discoveries, however, was the Order of the Rose, bestowed on Bates by the emperor of Brazil for the naturalist's outstanding work in that country. This distinction was rarely accorded to foreigners.

Today, Bates's home in England is administered by the National Trust and is open to visitors. Displayed there are examples of his many scientific writings, as well as thousands of the biological specimens that he brought back from Brazil.

Battūta, Ibn. See **Ibn Battūta.**

Baudin, Nicolas

French
b 1754; Île de Ré
d September 16, 1803; Port Louis, Mauritius
Explored coastline of Australia

Frenchman Nicolas Baudin commanded what was perhaps the most ill-fated, yet most scientifically successful, exploration ever of the coast of New Holland (now Australia). Although some of his survey work covered ground already mapped by rival British explorer MATTHEW FLINDERS, Baudin oversaw a team of naturalists that sent more than 10,000 plant and animal specimens back to France, including 2,500 new species.

After first serving in the merchant marine, Baudin joined the French navy in 1786. Long interested in natural history, he was no stranger to scientific exploration and spent twelve years in the service of the Austrian archduke Franz Josef. From 1793 to 1795 he collected specimens from China, the Sunda Isles, India, and the Antilles for the French Museum of Natural History. From 1796 to 1798 he explored South America, returning with dried plants, seeds, and more than 200 cases full of live shrubs. Both the Institut de France and the French emperor Napoleon backed his subsequent proposal for a major expedition in the South Pacific but limited his exploration to the shores of New Holland. He was to determine whether western Australia was separated from the British New South Wales by a strait, and if so, to claim the west for France.

Baudin left Le Havre, France, with two ships, *Géographe* and *Naturaliste*, on October 19, 1800. With him was a well-equipped team of twenty-four scientists, only six of whom would complete the journey. After a five-month voyage to Île de France (present-day Mauritius), some forty crewmen, officers, and scientists put ashore there and refused to go farther, because they were either physically ill or sick of Baudin's authoritarian command.

The two ships reached southwestern Australia on May 27, 1801, and shortly after were separated in a storm. Baudin explored from Cape Leeuwin to Geographe Bay, while Emmanuel Hamelin, captain of the *Naturaliste*, charted from Geographe Bay to south of the Swan River and Rottnest Island. The ships met again at Timor in September, where they dropped off members of the crew suffering from **scurvy**, then sailed for Van Diemen's Land (now Tasmania). Along the way, Baudin mapped Norfolk and Oyster bays, and the Freycinet Peninsula, and determined that the Tasman Peninsula was not an island. All along, he gave French names to the features he explored.

The southern summer of 1801–1802 was especially difficult, with little fresh food or water. There were deaths nearly every day. Still, Baudin pushed on, relentless and seemingly without mercy for his suffering crew.

In early 1802 he explored the Tasmanian rain forest. By April, half the crew was too sick to work the ship. When the *Géographe* reached Sydney, a **sloop** had to be sent to bring the weakened men to shore. Baudin remained in the port until November 1802, then continued to explore the coast of what is now Victoria, Australia, this time under the watchful eyes of the British.

In June 1803 Hamelin took the *Naturaliste* back to France, while Baudin explored Kangaroo Island, Cape Denial, and Cape Adieu, then sailed north to Timor. From there he wanted to sail east to the Torres Strait, but ill health—his own and the crew's—would not permit it. Instead, Baudin sailed west for Île de France on July 7. He died there in September. The expedition was completed by Louis de Freycinet, who had been lieutenant commander of the *Naturaliste*. He arrived at L'Orient, France, on March 25, 1804, as commander of the *Casuarina*, a vessel that had been acquired during the course of the expedition.

Bautista de Anza, Juan. See **Anza, Juan Bautista de.**

Belalcázar, Sebastián de. See **Benalcázar, Sebastián de.**

• Bell, Gertrude Margaret Lowthian

English
b July 14, 1868; Washington, Durham
d July 12, 1926; Baghdad, Iraq
Traveled in Arabian peninsula

Gertrude Bell's early exposure to the mysteries of Persia (now Iran) came while her uncle was

Gertrude Bell. Royal Geographical Society.

a minister in the British embassy in Tehran late in the nineteenth century. She relished the beauty of the Persian language, and her descriptions of the landscape made Persia seem like paradise. One day she traveled with a friend from the hill station of Gulahek through cool meadows and mountain trails near Tehran, an experience she later described in these words:

> We rode up and up the gorge; at the bottom there were regiments of tall single hollyhocks growing by the side of the torrent, yellow, pink and red, and battalions of willows climbing up the rocky side; but these were left behind and still we went up through absolute desolation until after about an hour's climb we came out on to the top of the shoulder and suddenly worlds upon unknown worlds lay before us. . . . It was very wonderful in that great bare silence watching the shadows of the mountains creeping over the plain below, eating up first the green villages, then Teheran and at last the far hill beyond.

Bell's captivation with the unknown worlds beyond that hill in the distance took her across

Arabia, and she became a recognized expert on the history and customs of the Middle East. In later years, she served as a British official in Baghdad, where her knowledge gave her considerable influence over British policies in the region.

Gertrude Bell's intellectual promise became apparent when she completed a natural history degree at Oxford University in less time than was normally required. In 1892, at the age of twenty-three, she made her first trip to Persia, "the place I have always longed to see," she wrote in a letter to a friend. She quickly became fluent in Persian and began to read and translate Persian poetry. Her translation of the poems of a fourteenth-century Sufi poet, published in 1897, was regarded by many as the finest rendering of any Persian poet in English.

After a six-month voyage around the world in 1897, Bell returned to the Middle East to visit Jerusalem and Moab, the desert region east of the Dead Sea. There she found the ruins of the Persian palace at Mashetta: "The beauty of it all was quite past words. It's a thing one will never forget as long as one lives." After trekking through the heart of the Druze country of Syria and enduring the hardships of a slow caravan journey to Palmyra, Syria, Bell left the Middle East and spent several summers climbing in the French Alps. But her interest in the culture and history of the Middle East continued to grow, and between 1900 and 1914 she made a number of journeys to explore the region.

In 1905 Bell embarked on her first major expedition into the desert, which she later described in her book *Syria: The Desert and the Sown*. As the first European woman to travel in some parts of the Syrian desert, she was accorded the respect usually reserved for male visitors; although she occasionally was taken to the harems to talk to the women, the Arab sheiks insisted that she visit and dine with the men. By 1907, this adventurous Englishwoman, who seemingly enjoyed the risk of attack by a bedouin raiding party, had become a celebrated traveler. Her search for archaeological records that would expand her knowledge of the region's history took her across northern Syria and into Asia Minor. In Constantinople (now Istanbul, Turkey), she studied ruins from early Byzantine civilizations, then continued through other deserts in the east, searching for new archaeological sites.

In 1913 Bell began what was to be her last major desert expedition. She traveled to Damascus, Syria, where she purchased twenty camels and hired three camel drivers and two other servants. Her departure for Hā'il (in what is now central Saudi Arabia) was made with the utmost secrecy because she feared that the British and Turkish authorities controlling the region would not permit her to lead an expedition into an area where bedouin raids were common. She began her journey without incident but was soon stopped by an Ottoman governor, who allowed her to continue only after she gave him a letter releasing him from any responsibility should anything happen to her. His concern was well founded, for her caravan was held up by a bedouin sheik while crossing the southwest corner of the Nafud Desert. When Bell tried to appease him with presents, the sheik suggested to her drivers and servants that they murder her and share the plunder. Fortunately for Bell, her party remained loyal, and the caravan was eventually allowed to proceed to Hā'il. The situation there was little better. The amir was away with his army fighting against tribes to the north, and Bell, suspected of being a spy, was placed under house arrest at the bidding of his grandmother. She waited until the amir's chief eunuch abruptly gave her permission to leave Hā'il. After a day spent photographing the city, she proceeded across the desert to Baghdad, which she reached in late March 1914.

Soon after World War I broke out in 1914, Bell was sent to Cairo to work for the Arab bureau of the British military intelligence. Eventually, after a stint in Basra (in what is now Iraq), Bell was transferred to Baghdad, where she became Oriental secretary in the British High Commission when Iraq became independent under British mandate in 1921. In later years, Bell was appointed the first director of Iraqi antiquities and actively promoted the building of a national museum in Baghdad. Six years after her death in 1926, money left in Bell's will was used to establish the British School of Archaeology in Iraq.

Belleborne (Bellesborne), Jean Nicolett de. See **Nicolett de Belleborne, Jean.**

Bellingshausen, Fabian Gottlieb von

Russian
b September 9, 1778; Saaremaa, Estonia
d January 13, 1852; Kronshlot
Circumnavigated Antarctica

Following in the wake of Captain JAMES COOK, the Russian admiral Fabian Gottlieb von Bellingshausen circumnavigated Antarctica, finished the charting of several islands begun by Cook, and discovered a great deal of new land, both on the continent and off its shore. Since he sailed close to continental glaciers several times and noted their enormity and unbroken extent, geographers have wondered why he did not claim to have discovered the continent. His failure to do so has left the question of Antarctica's discovery somewhat clouded and opened the issue to rival claimants.

Bellingshausen was born into an aristocratic German family, but at the age of ten he joined the Russian navy. Eight years later, in 1797,

Fabian Gottlieb von Bellingshausen. National Library of Australia.

he graduated from the naval academy at Kronstadt (present-day Kronshlot) and was commissioned an officer. He started his career as a fifth lieutenant on the circumnavigation of the *Nadezhda* under ADAM IVAN VON KRUSENSTERN from 1803 to 1806, and on his return was promoted to captain lieutenant. When Czar Alexander I chose him to lead the first Russian expedition to Antarctica in 1819, he was commanding a **frigate** in the Black Sea on surveying duties.

Besides making a wide variety of scientific observations, Bellingshausen was instructed to search for harbors that Russian ships might be able to use on transoceanic voyages. The *Vostok* and the *Mirny* sailed from Russia on July 17, 1819, and arrived at South Georgia Island in late December of the same year. Bellingshausen surveyed the southern coast, then moved on to clarify the nature of what James Cook called Sandwich Land. He found it to be a group of islands unconnected to Antarctica. Moving east around the continent, often breaking south of the Antarctic Circle, he continued adding precision to Cook's work but also discovered new land. On January 28, 1820, he discovered the coast that the Norwegians later called Queen Maud Land. He continued along the coast almost as far as Enderby Land, then headed north for the winter. The following spring (November 1820), he returned south and in January 1821 penetrated what is now the Bellingshausen Sea to discover Peter I Island and then Alexander Island off to its east. On his voyage back to Russia, he proved that New Shetland (now the South Shetland Islands) was not connected to the Antarctic continent.

Bellingshausen returned to Kronstadt on August 5, 1821, and continued to build on his achievements in the Russian navy. In 1828 he was promoted to vice admiral and given command of the Baltic fleet in the war against the Turks. In 1843 he achieved the rank of admiral.

Benalcázar (Belalcázar), Sebastián de

Spanish
b 1495?; Belalcázar, Córdoba
d April 1551; Cartagena, Colombia
Explored parts of Ecuador, Peru, and Colombia

Insatiable greed and personal ambition motivated Don Sebastián de Benalcázar to pursue exploration and conquest in the New World during the sixteenth century. With FRANCISCO PIZARRO, Benalcázar participated in the conquest of Peru and personally led the assault on the Inca city of Quito in modern Ecuador. He also founded the modern Ecuadorean cities of Guayaquil and Riobamba and then, in 1536, pushed farther north, exploring a large area of modern Colombia and founding the modern cities of Popayán and Cali. Rumors of a land of wealth to the northeast prompted Benalcázar to lead an expedition into the interior of Colombia, where he found that GONZALO JIMÉNEZ DE QUESADA had already conquered the rich Chibcha Indians.

Sebastián de Benalcázar was born Sebastián Moyano in about 1495 in Belalcázar, located in the Spanish province of Córdoba. Though Moyano was his real name, he became known by the name of his hometown. Not much is known of his early life except that he came from a humble background and did not learn to read. He went to the West Indies while in his mid-twenties (sometime between 1507 and 1511) and by 1522 was listed as an **encomendero** in what is now Panama. He fought with Francisco Fernández de Córdoba during the conquest of present-day Nicaragua and Honduras from 1524 to 1527. In 1527 he was listed as one of the founders of the city of Léon in Nicaragua and became *alcalde* (mayor) of the colony.

In 1532 Benalcázar arrived in Peru to help his friends, Francisco Pizarro and DIEGO DE ALMAGRO, conquer the Incas. As captain of the Spanish horsemen he played a major role in the conquest of Cajamarca and received a share of the vast Inca riches. Pizarro appointed him commander of the coastal city of San Miguel de Piura, a position that gave him considerable independence and power but removed him from the main thrust of conquest that moved on to Cuzco.

When the Inca general Rumiñavi led a revolt in Quito in 1534, Pizarro authorized Benalcázar to conquer the city. Departing Piura in February 1534, Benalcázar crossed the barren coastal plain of northern Peru and entered the hills on the main Inca highway. Along the route he recruited some of the Cañari Indians, who hated the Incas. Upon reaching Tumibamba (modern Cuenca, Ecuador), he was forced to fight the Incas, on a mountain pass made slippery by moss-covered boulders, on May 3, 1534 (the Battle of Teocajas). The Incas failed to stop the Spanish, and Benalcázar pushed onward, fighting constantly while marching through Andean valleys. When he arrived at Quito on June 22, 1534, he found that the city had been evacuated and burned. After seizing possession of the city, Benalcázar repulsed a surprise Inca attack, uncovered the city's hidden gold and silver, and reestablished Quito under Spanish control. He then subjugated the Indians surrounding the city, often slaughtering women and children and torturing their leaders in his efforts to locate more treasure. Benalcázar next pushed into the southern highlands of Ecuador and founded the city of Riobamba. Returning to the coast, he founded the port of Guayaquil.

Starting in 1536, Benalcázar led expeditions in search of the fabled lands of the golden man, and it was probably he who coined the name "**El Dorado**" to refer to this legend. When he left Quito in 1536 Benalcázar headed north, crossing rugged terrain into what is now Colombia. Proceeding along the Cauca River valley, he subdued the Popayán Indians and founded the cities of Popayán (1536) and Cali (1537). Then, in 1538, he led an expedition into the heartland of Colombia, still searching for the elusive El Dorado. Passing over the Continental Divide in Colombia's Cordillera Central, he discovered the sources of the upper Magdalena River and moved down the river valley for eight months (during which he lost twenty men from poison dart attacks by the Pijáo Indians). One soldier said the march was filled with "bad mountains, bad roads, and bad Indians." Reaching the plateau of Bogotá, he found that Jiménez de Quesada was already in control of the emerald-rich Chibcha Indian realm. The arrival of another claimant, NIKOLAUS FEDERMANN, led the three **conquistadores** to return to Spain to have the king resolve their claims. The king named Benalcázar captain general and **adelantado** of the province of Popayán (comprising the territory from Quito north to Cartagena, in modern Colombia).

Benalcázar returned to Popayán from Spain in 1541 and supported the royalists during the Peruvian Civil Wars (1541–46). In 1541 he killed Jorge Robeldo, who had encroached on his domain while he was away. As a result of the political pressure exerted by Robeldo's widow, Benalcázar was eventually arrested and condemned for the murder. In April of 1551, on his way to Spain to plead his case, he died at Cartagena, Colombia.

Bennett, Floyd

American
b October 25, 1890; Warrensburg, New York
d April 25, 1928; Québec, Canada
Piloted Richard Byrd's plane over North Pole

Both a pilot and an expert mechanic, Floyd Bennett was Admiral RICHARD BYRD's indispensable assistant from 1925 until his early death in 1928. The two were the first to fly over the North Pole.

Bennett worked as an automobile mechanic before joining the navy in 1917. He learned airplane mechanics and flying while at the Hampton Roads and Pensacola Naval Aviation bases. He was serving on the U.S.S. *Richmond* when Byrd first recruited him. Bennett then joined Byrd on DONALD BAXTER MAC MILLAN's 1925 Arctic expedition to Greenland and Ellesmere Island, which entailed more than 2,000 miles of flying.

The next year, on May 9, Bennett and Byrd undertook the first flight over the North Pole. They left from Kings Bay, Svalbard, on the Fokker trimotor *Josephine Ford*, and aside from an oil leak in the starboard engine, which luckily stopped on its own, they experienced no difficulty returning. The 1,360-mile round-trip took 15½ hours. Bennett received the congressional Medal of Honor for his part in this flight.

The pair immediately began preparations for flying across the Atlantic with the first passenger-carrying aircraft. They used a Fokker trimotor once again, but during a test flight, with Fokker himself at the controls, they discovered it was nose heavy. All survived the crash landing, but Bennett was too seriously injured to make the subsequent crossing, which began on June 29, 1927.

In 1928 Byrd made Bennett his second-in-command for an expedition to the South Pole. While preparations were still under way, Bennett, still weak from the crash, flew to rescue two German pilots who had crashed in the St. Lawrence River after a transatlantic flight. This effort, made in the wet cold of early spring, gave rise to a fatal case of pneumonia. When Byrd later reached the South Pole aboard the *Floyd Bennett*, he attached the American flag to a stone from Bennett's grave and dropped it to the earth below.

Bering, Vitus Jonassen

Danish
b August 12, 1681; Horsens, Denmark
d December 6, 1741; Bering Island, Soviet Union
Commanded first European crossing from Siberia to west coast of North America (Alaska)

One of the hundreds of western Europeans recruited by the government of Czar Peter the Great to modernize Russia, Captain Commander Vitus Jonassen Bering carried out the czar's plan to determine whether Siberia was linked to America by land or separated from it by a strait. His job was more an administrative nightmare and physical marathon than an opportunity to make brilliant geographic discoveries, but his expeditions to the northern Pacific did help pave the way for the expansion

Vitus Jonassen Bering. The Granger Collection.

of the Russian fur trade into North America. Even if SEMYON IVANOV DEZHNEV preceded him through the Bering Strait, Bering deserves significant credit for the nature and magnitude of his explorations.

Not much is known of Bering's life before he undertook the leadership of these important expeditions. He was invited to join the Russian navy as a sublieutenant in 1703, after having been to the East Indies. With the Russians, he served in campaigns in the Baltic, Black, and White seas, achieving the rank of captain second class in 1720. When in 1723 he applied for the rank of captain first class and was refused, he retired to an estate in Vyborg.

Bering had an accurate sense of his own worth, however, since within a year Admiral Apraksin had singled him out to lead the first of his great expeditions (at the rank of captain first class). With a hundred men under his command (and Lieutenants Martin Spanberg and ALEKSEI CHIRIKOV as his assistants), he left St. Petersburg on February 5, 1725, twelve days behind the vanguard. After the grueling trek across Siberia, in which the company grew by

the hundreds as it picked up laborers, he arrived at Okhotsk on the Siberian coast in July 1727. There he built the *Fortune*, which was used to shuttle supplies and men to Kamchatka, an operation completed with the help of the local Russian authorities on September 1. It took all fall and winter and half of the spring to cross the Kamchatka Peninsula, after which another ship, the *St. Gabriel*, was built. On July 13, 1728, 3½ years after leaving St. Petersburg, Bering was finally ready to embark by sea on his voyage of discovery. At this point, all that was left was to hug the shore and head northeast toward the far corner of Asia.

On August 11, Bering landed on an island he named after Saint Lawrence (still known by the same name, but now part of Alaska), and in two days he reached 65° North latitude, out of the sight of land. Chirikov argued that they should push on as the czar had ordered until either the shore turned east, indicating a land link between Asia and America, or they reached the Kolyma River, proving the existence of a strait. He wanted to pursue these possibilities even if it meant wintering in that

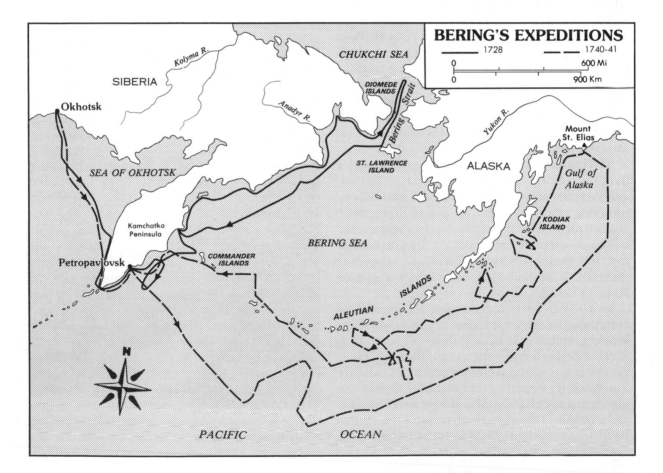

barren land. Spanberg, on the other hand, argued that they should turn back after only a few more days, since wintering so far north would be hazardous, and Bering agreed. After traversing the strait and reaching 67° North latitude on August 16, the *St. Gabriel* turned back. The next morning, the Diomede Islands were sighted. If it had been a clear day, Bering could have seen the westernmost point of North America, but fog shrouded the area and prevented him from making the otherwise easy discovery that he was in a narrow strait.

While wintering in Kamchatka, Bering heard from its residents that there was land nearby to the east. In the spring, on his way back to Okhotsk, Bering searched unsuccessfully for the islands that would eventually become the sight of his grave—what are now known as the Commander group.

Although Bering was personally satisfied of the existence of a strait separating the continents, the Russian public, on the whole, was not. When he reached St. Petersburg on March 1, 1730, he faced criticism for not following Chirikov's advice and rounding the cape. But the authorities, on the whole, were rightly impressed with his abilities as an organizer. When he suggested another, more ambitious effort to explore not only eastwards, where he was convinced America or some other landmass lay, but also the route from Siberia to Japan and the coast from the Ob River to the Lena, they responded in 1732 by vastly expanding the scope of the proposed mission to include an overland exploration of the entire north coast of Siberia. Bering was put in charge at the new rank of captain commander.

The Great Northern Expedition of 1733–42 was a vast undertaking involving thirteen ships and about 3,000 crew members. The mission included two landscape painters, five surveyors, and thirty scientists with their library of several hundred books and nine wagonloads of instruments. This time it took Bering eight years just to make it to Okhotsk. Not surprisingly, he was thoroughly exhausted when he set off from Kamchatka for Alaska on June 4, 1741.

After being separated from Chirikov's companion vessel in a storm, Bering in the *St. Peter* continued on to the Gulf of Alaska, sighting the Alaskan mainland, naming Mount St. Elias, and making brief landings throughout July. Ignoring the advice of his chief scientific officer, the German naturalist Georg Wilhelm Steller, to

winter in Alaska, Bering turned back while there was still time to reach Kamchatka, but storms made the journey difficult and finally blew the *St. Peter* to its winter harbor on present-day Bering Island in the Commander group, east of the Kamchatka Peninsula. There Bering joined the list of thirty killed by **scurvy** and exposure.

In the summer, the survivors built another boat from the remains of the *St. Peter* and made their way to Kamchatka, where they met Chirikov. He too had reached North America but was lucky enough to make it back to the Asian mainland before winter.

After his death, Bering was blamed by Steller for not allowing more than a few hours of scientific observation on the coast of Alaska. According to Steller, Bering "did not accept the least advice from me—he had too much regard for his own opinion. . . ." But Bering was under so many pressures by that time that it is not surprising he gave short shrift to the scientists. After a decade and a half of preparations, he had at last found an accessible part of North America rich in furs of all kinds, and, in his exhausted state, he no doubt hoped that this would satisfy the Russian authorities. Indeed, when word of the rich source of furs reached Russia, a steady stream of trappers began making their way to Alaska, thus paving the way for the first overseas expansion of the Russian Empire.

Bering's journeys were made arduous in part by the nature of the great Russian expansion to the Pacific. Each expedition had to originate at the western seat of the empire, St. Petersburg, radiate outward in symbolic advance, and return to report on its findings. If Czar Peter, who personally wrote the instructions for the first expedition just before he died, had simply wanted to have his eastern border expertly surveyed, he could have fitted out a ship from Archangel on Russia's northern coast to sail the Dutch route around Africa to the East Indies and then continue north past Japan. Instead he sent Bering on an exhausting land odyssey clear across northern Asia—more than three times the breadth of North America. This route had the double advantage of preventing outsiders from knowing exactly what the Russians were doing while also impressing upon the recently subjected natives of Siberia how powerful and technologically advanced was the distant government to which they paid taxes.

Bering thus had to cross four mountain chains, float down and fight his way up several rivers, and **portage** through near-Arctic conditions with snow deeper than the horses were high. All of this was done with enough equipment in tow to set up a boat-building factory on the Siberian coast to enable the actual sea voyage of discovery to take place. Before reaching the final stretch of water, Bering had to again portage across Kamchatka (a land already paying tribute to the czar and thus familiar to the Russians) and build another ship on the peninsula's eastern coast.

Bering's logistical problems of keeping these long-lasting expeditions on track, feeding and clothing the crew, preventing exhausted and homesick officers and workers from coming to blows or mutinying, and obtaining the cooperation of the freshly established local authorities were lost on his superiors. Few had been completely satisfied with the results of his first expedition, and the government continually sent him degrading, angry, and threatening dispatches when his second met with difficulties. The record makes clear that his spirit had long since been broken at the time of his death. Even upon sighting the shores of America, he remained sullen and worried, overwhelmed by anticipations of the next round of troubles.

Some historians (especially modern Soviets) diminish Bering's achievements by claiming that the Bering Strait had been navigated from the Chukchi Sea in the seventeenth century by the cossack (Russian frontiersman) Semyon Ivanov Dezhnev. But even if Dezhnev had preceded him, Bering deserves significant credit for the nature and magnitude of his explorations.

SUGGESTED READING: Raymond H. Fisher, *Bering's Voyages: Whither and Why* (University of Washington Press, 1977); F. A. Golder, *Russian Expansion on the Pacific, 1641–1850* (Peter Smith, 1960); Gerhard Friedrich Müller, *Bering's Voyages: The Reports from Russia*, trans. by Carol Urness (University of Alaska Press, 1986); Georg Wilhelm Steller, *Journal of a Voyage with Bering, 1741–1742*, trans. by Margritt A. Engel and O. W. Frost, ed. by O. W. Frost (Stanford University Press, 1988).

Bethencourt, Jean de

French
b 1360?; Normandy
d 1422; Grainville, Normandy
Explored Canary Islands (for Spain)

French nobleman Jean de Bethencourt is known for conquering the Canary Islands off the coast of Africa and claiming them for King Henry III of Spain. These islands eventually became a major provisioning port and jumping-off point for voyages to the Americas and beyond.

Bethencourt was born around 1360 to a noble family of Normandy. Considering his upbringing, it seemed only natural that he would join the court of French king Charles VI and hold high office there. While at the court, Bethencourt heard the tales of exploration and adventure that would inspire him to conquer the Canary Islands and convert its native people to Christianity.

Seven hundred miles south of Spain and 70 miles west of Morocco, the fourteen small islands that make up the Canaries may have been discovered by ancient Phoenician sailors; the Roman scholar Pliny mentions them in his writings. But in the late fourteenth century they were virtually unknown, visited only by a few merchants and Spanish pirates after brief occupations by the Genoese and Portuguese earlier in the century. The islands were populated by **aborigines**, called Canaries, who wore animal skins and woven grass garments.

At the turn of the century, Bethencourt put up his estates to raise money for an expedition. On May 1, 1402, he left La Rochelle, France, with two ships. In command of the second ship was Gadifer de La Salle. After quashing a threatened mutiny off the coast of Spain, Bethencourt reached the Canary Island known as Lanzarote in July and established himself there.

Bethencourt felt he had too few men to conquer the rest of the islands. He sought help in Castile, from Spanish king Henry III, a family friend. Bethencourt returned to the Canaries in 1404 with sovereign rights. In his absence, La Salle had conquered another island, Fuerteventura. With two islands under control, Bethencourt returned to Normandy in 1405 to gather colonists for the island of Hierro. On this journey he may have been the first European to sail past Cape Bojador, then considered the most distant navigable point on the west

African coast. He also was one of the first Europeans to capture African natives.

Retaining his royal title and rights to the colonies' profits, Bethencourt left government of the Canaries in the hands of his nephew, Maciot de Bethencourt, in December 1406 and returned to Normandy, where he spent the rest of his life. He wrote an account of his expeditions, which historians view with some skepticism. Bethencourt died in 1422 and was buried in the church of Grainville-la-Teinturière.

Bilot, Robert. See **Bylot, Robert.**

Hiram Bingham. Yale University Peabody Museum of Natural History.

• Bingham, Hiram

American
b November 19, 1875; Honolulu, Hawaii
d June 6, 1956; Washington, D.C.
Discovered Machu Picchu and Vitcos in Peru

Although over the years Hiram Bingham was a professor of Latin American history and geography at Yale University, a governor of Connecticut, and a United States senator, he always listed "explorer" as his primary occupation. From 1906 to 1915 Bingham made several expeditions to South America, where, in 1911, he discovered the ruins of the great Inca city of Machu Picchu as well as the ruins of Vitcos, the last capital of the Incas. For much of his life he tried to rooncile his family's expectation that he lead a religious life with his own adventurous nature and attraction to the material world. Consequently, Bingham was not only a man of conscience who felt his duty was to expand human knowledge, but also a man of great ambition—who loved to dance, attend parties, and fraternize with the rich and powerful.

Hiram Bingham was born on November 19, 1875, shortly after his missionary parents landed in Honolulu. He had an austere childhood, living in the shadow of the exploits of a father and grandfather who had sailed around Cape Horn to the then-remote Pacific Islands to serve as missionaries. In 1894 he entered Yale University, where he distinguished himself as a debater. At Yale he first felt the pull toward a more worldly life; however, upon graduation he dutifully returned to Hawaii to serve as pastor of the Palama Chapel in the slums of Honolulu.

The turning point in Bingham's life was when he fell in love with Alfreda Mitchell, who was vacationing in Hawaii with her wealthy family. Determined to get enough money to marry her, Bingham broke with the fundamentalist religious beliefs of his formative years, left his job as pastor, and went back to school, earning a master's degree in South American history from the University of California at Berkeley. After marrying Alfreda, he studied at Harvard University, where he earned his doctorate in 1905. He was hired as a preceptor at Princeton University. However, he soon became impatient with academic life and went on his first expedition (1906–1907) to trace Simon Bolívar's route across Venezuela and Colombia. Upon his return, Bingham was appointed lecturer at Yale, making full professor eight years later.

President THEODORE ROOSEVELT appointed

him a member of the U.S. delegation to the Pan-American Scientific Congress to be held in Santiago, Chile, in 1908. This opportunity permitted Bingham to explore the old Spanish trade route from Buenos Aires to Lima, with a detour to visit the ruins of Choqquequirau, previously thought to be the last capital of the Incas and **El Dorado**, the fabled city of gold. This encounter with Incan history changed the focus of Bingham's future explorations to a quest to find the last capital of the Incas.

In 1911 Bingham embarked on the most important expedition of his career, the Yale Peruvian Expedition. Its major objectives were to search for Inca ruins in the Urubamba valley in Peru and to climb and measure Mount Coropuna. On July 24, 1911, Bingham discovered the ruins of Machu Picchu, a terraced city perched on top of a sheer precipice 1,000 feet high, in an almost inaccessible corner of the Peruvian Andes. He reached the ruins by crawling on his hands and knees across a primitive bridge over dangerous rapids and climbing up the side of the mountain leading to Machu Picchu. Bingham photographed and recorded everything he saw, saying of his initial sight of the ruins: "I felt utterly alone. . . . Then I rounded a knoll and almost staggered at the sight I faced. Tier upon tier of Inca terraces rose like a giant flight of stairs. . . . Suddenly breathless with excitement, I forgot my fatigue and . . . I plunged once more into the damp undergrowth. . . ."

As spectacular as this city was, however, Bingham felt that it was not Vitcos, the lost capital of the Incas. With the help of a local guide he continued his search, arriving at a place called Nūsta Isppana which he believed to be Vitcos, the elusive last capital, because of the landmark large white rock over a spring and the temple ruins nearby. Later, on October 14, 1911, he reached the summit of the highest peak of the Coropuna Mountains, which did not prove to be the second highest peak in the Andean range as he had hoped.

Bingham made two other expeditions to Peru (1912 and 1914) under the auspices of Yale and the National Geographic Society, served in World War I, and then was elected governor of Connecticut in 1924. He resigned the governorship almost immediately in order to fill a vacancy in the United States Senate. He was elected to a full term as senator in 1926 and served until 1933. He died in Washington, D.C., on June 6, 1956.

There has been some question (especially in Peru) as to Bingham's claim to have discovered Machu Picchu in 1911, since he found the name "Lizarraga" and the date "1902" written in charcoal on a temple wall. However, since Augustine Lizarraga never reported his 1902 discovery of the ruins, Bingham is generally credited as the "scientific discoverer" of Machu Picchu. His precise geographical information about Machu Picchu and Vitcos added to the knowledge of the Incas and spurred renewed archaeological activity in both South and North America.

· Blaxland, Gregory

English
b June 27, 1778; Newington, Kent
d January 1853; North Parramatta, Australia
Explored Australia's Blue Mountains

Gregory Blaxland, one of the first freemen to emigrate to Australia, was also the first to find a way across the Blue Mountains, part of the Great Dividing Range that separates Australia's east coast from the rest of the continent. In so doing, he paved the way for other important explorations of the Australian interior.

Blaxland was born in England to a prosperous family and counted among his friends the influential naturalist Sir JOSEPH BANKS, who had explored Australia's Botany Bay with Captain JAMES COOK in 1770. It was Banks who first suggested the establishment of a British penal colony on the continent.

In 1805 Blaxland left Kent, England, for Australia, one of the few nonprisoners to emigrate there at that time. Pleased with his enterprise, the British Crown gave him 4,000 acres and forty convicts whom the government would feed and clothe for the first eighteen months while Blaxland established himself in New South Wales.

Blaxland set up a farm at the foot of the Blue Mountains northwest of present-day Sydney, but after a drought in 1813, he faced financial ruin. In May 1813 he and two other landowners, William Lawson and WILLIAM CHARLES WENTWORTH, set out to find—literally—greener pastures. They took with them an experienced bushman and three convict servants.

Others had tried unsuccessfully to cross the Blue Mountains by heading through the canyons running between their ridges. Blaxland and his band kept instead to the ridges themselves. The vistas from the heights were breathtaking, often taking in steep canyon walls and rushing waterfalls. Staying at such altitudes, Blaxland crossed the greater part of the range at the Nepean River.

On May 28, after about three weeks of hiking, the group reached Mount York, a few miles south of present-day Lithgow. Below them, the lush grasslands stretched for miles on either side of what is now called the Lett River, a tributary of the Nepean. They compared it to the biblical land of Canaan, and Blaxland said it had "enough grass to support the stock of this colony for thirty years."

In reality, what the group saw from the summit of Mount York was only an isolated fertile valley known today as the Bathurst Plains. They had gotten off the central mountain ridge and had not actually crossed the main range. Still, they had demonstrated a successful technique for crossing the mountains, and they convinced a growing colony that the continent west of the mountains was worth further exploration.

Blaxland published an account of the expedition in 1823. He spent his later life as a farmer, specializing in agricultural experimentation, including work in wine making and fertilization. In 1853, in a fit of severe depression, he hanged himself.

• Bligh, William

English
b September 9, 1754; Tyntan, Cornwall
d December 7, 1817; London
Charted northeast coast of Australia; explored South Pacific; commanded H.M.S. *Bounty*

One of the most controversial figures in the history of naval exploration, William Bligh is best known as the commander of H.M.S. *Bounty* who crossed almost 4,000 miles of open ocean in a small boat after his mutinous crew set him and nineteen loyal crew members adrift. A British naval officer, Bligh also was a skilled seaman and explorer who charted the northeast coast of New Holland (present-day Australia) and who introduced breadfruit to the West Indies for the purpose of providing a food source for the slave population there.

Born in Cornwall in 1754, Bligh showed early promise as a navigator and at the age of twenty-two was appointed master of Captain JAMES COOK's *Resolution* on Cook's third and final voyage. During the four-year expedition (1776–80), Bligh visited Tahiti, Christmas Island (now Kiritimati), the Sandwich Islands (now Hawaii), North America, and the Arctic Ocean, no doubt learning a great deal from the experienced and skillful Cook.

Upon his return, Bligh continued to advance his naval career, gaining some notice in 1782 for his part in a British expedition to rescue Gibraltar. In 1787, having been made lieutenant and given command of His Majesty's Armed Transport *Bounty*, Bligh was ordered to sail to Tahiti at the suggestion of Sir JOSEPH BANKS to obtain breadfruit for transplantation to the West Indies, where it was intended to serve as food for slaves. The 230-ton, three-masted ship had been refitted as a floating greenhouse.

The *Bounty* set sail from Portsmouth, England, on December 23, 1787, with a crew of only forty-four, including Fletcher Christian, master's mate and an old friend of Bligh's from the West India trade. Bligh was the only commissioned officer aboard. Rough weather, cramped quarters, and short supplies of poor food got the voyage off to a bad start. Bligh's strict discipline, changeable moods, and determination to round treacherous Cape Horn at the southern tip of South America in winter in order to make the voyage a circumnavigation did not endear him to his overworked and disgruntled crew. Bligh finally abandoned his plan, rounded Africa's Cape of Good Hope, and arrived in Tahiti on October 26, 1788.

Bligh and his crew spent five months in Tahiti—longer than any Europeans before them—waiting for the breadfruit seedlings to sprout. During this time many of the men formed strong attachments to the Tahitian women. Those bonds, and the appeal of the simple island lifestyle, probably were as much at the root of the coming mutiny as was Bligh's admittedly bad temper.

On April 5, 1789, the *Bounty* left Tahiti for the Friendly Islands (Tonga). Bligh was particu-

An artist's rendition of the mutiny on the *Bounty*. Peabody Museum of Salem.

larly frustrated by the crew's lack of discipline, and he punished transgressors by putting them in irons. He even accused Christian, whom he had earlier promoted to second in command, of stealing his coconuts. Christian, in turn, began planning his escape back to Tahiti. On April 28, off Tofua, one of the Friendly Islands, after a mutiny led by Christian, Bligh and nineteen "loyalists" were put on board a 23-foot launch and set adrift with some rations and a **chronometer**.

Skillful seaman that he was, Bligh navigated the small craft safely across some 3,618 nautical miles of open ocean from Tofua to the island of Timor in present-day Indonesia. Upon Bligh's rescue and return to England, an investigation was conducted, and the commander was acquitted of responsibility for the loss of the *Bounty* and deemed a hero.

The mutineers returned to Tahiti, where some were eventually taken prisoner by the H.M.S. *Pandora*. Christian, eleven other mutineers, and twelve Tahitian women continued on to remote Pitcairn Island, where to escape detection they burned the *Bounty*. When an American whaler visited Pitcairn in 1808, only one mutineer was still living. Five had died in violent quarrels over land and women, and the rest had died of natural causes. The descendants of the mutineers prospered, and by 1825 they had established a colony of sixty-five people.

Bligh repeated his Tahitian voyage in 1791, bringing breadfruit trees to Jamaica and taking time to chart Australia's northeast coast. He reported great changes on Tahiti since he and Cook had visited there fifteen years earlier. Venereal disease had become widespread, and the natives had taken to drinking and wearing dirty clothes left them by the sailors who by then called there frequently.

From 1795 until 1805 Bligh captained several vessels. He distinguished himself in two engagements in the Napoleonic Wars—at the Battle of Camperdown in 1797 and at the Battle of Copenhagen in 1801, receiving a personal commendation from Lord Horatio Nelson. But Bligh had not seen his last mutiny.

In 1805 he was named captain general and governor of New South Wales (now a province of Australia). Upon his arrival at the colony, he attempted to discipline an army that was more interested in profiteering than soldiering. After three years of Bligh's severe authority, the officers mutinied and imprisoned the governor until 1810, when he was recalled to England. The mutineers were court-martialed and dismissed from the service. Bligh was made rear admiral.

Bligh was promoted again, to vice admiral, in 1814. He died on December 7, 1817, in London, having lived a life of discipline, accomplishment, and controversy.

- Bodega y Quadra, Juan
Francisco de la

Spanish
b 1743; Lima, Peru
d March 26, 1794; Mexico City, Mexico
Explored northwest coast of North America

A Spanish naval officer, Juan Francisco de la Bodega y Quadra made two voyages of exploration along the Pacific coast of North America. In 1775 he reached as far north as latitude 58°30′, where he discovered and named Bucareli Sound. In 1779 he traveled as second-in-command on Ignacio de Arteaga's expedition, which reached Afognak Island, near present-day Kodiak, Alaska.

Along with five other young officers, Bodega was assigned in 1774 to the department of San Blas, on the west coast of New Spain (present-day Mexico), to participate in coastal explorations with the goal of strengthening Spanish control over the entire northwest coast of North America. When he was passed over for command of the 1775 expedition in favor of the younger BRUNO DE HEZETA (ostensibly because Hezeta had seniority; more likely because Bodega was a **creole**, born in Peru), Bodega volunteered to serve as second-in-command of the *Sonora*, a thirty-six-foot narrow-beamed vessel intended only for short trips to Baja California. The *Sonora*'s crew numbered seventeen in all, ten of whom had never before been to sea. Shortly after leaving San Blas, the captain of another vessel in the squadron exhibited signs of insanity, and the *Sonora*'s captain consequently was shifted to that vessel, leaving Bodega to command the *Sonora*.

Hezeta's instructions for the expedition were to sail as far as 65° North latitude, to avoid settlements of other nations, to go ashore and take possession wherever he could do so safely, to learn what the Indians offered in trade, and to establish friendly relations with them. On July 13, halfway up the coast of present-day Washington, the two vessels dropped anchor and Hezeta, not for the first time, tried to convince Bodega to return to San Blas rather than sail any farther with the light **schooner**. Bodega expressed his intention to continue. While they were there, somewhere near present-day Point Grenville, Washington, a band of Indians that had at first seemed friendly launched a vicious attack and killed several men sent ashore to retrieve fresh water. Bodega himself narrowly escaped the attack.

On July 29, Hezeta, with many of his men sick, expressed his intention to turn back soon, short of his objective. That night the *Sonora* became separated from Hezeta's ship. Most historians agree that Bodega intentionally lost contact with Hezeta, whom he viewed as being too timid. Bodega and his faithful pilot, Mourelle, felt honor-bound to follow their instructions and to sail as far north as they could in their small and fragile craft.

Though fresh water was low and food had to be rationed, the crew agreed to continue, and they sailed up the coast, landing on August 15 at 57° North latitude to take on water. They were on the coast of present-day Prince of Wales Island, at the southern tip of what is now Alaska. Bodega examined every inlet and bay in search of the Northwest Passage alleged to have been discovered near that latitude by one Bartholomew de Fonte in 1640. Failing to find such a passage (for a more complete discussion of the passage, see MARTIN FROBISHER), Bodega entered a calm bay whose mild temperature he attributed to the glowing volcanoes the sailors could see at night. After planting a cross and taking possession of the bay and naming it for the Mexican viceroy, Bucareli, Bodega sailed north again. On August 27, he reached his most northerly latitude—58°30′—and then was forced to turn south because five of his men were suffering from **scurvy**. By the time the *Sonora* reached Monterey Bay, California, on October 7, everyone on board was affected. Bodega and his crew were nursed back to health by the mission fathers there.

Bodega's next expedition north took place in 1779 when he served as second-in-command to Ignacio de Arteaga. The Spanish had learned that British Captain JAMES COOK was expected in the Northwest Pacific, and the purpose of the Arteaga expedition was both to warn Cook away from what Spain considered her territory and to determine how far Russia had extended its reach east from the Aleutian Islands. Arteaga was instructed to reach a latitude of 70° North if possible.

Leaving San Blas on February 11, 1779, the **frigates** arrived early in May at Bucareli Sound, which was considered a promising site for a naval base. After exploring the numerous channels in the area for over a month, the expedition continued north. A party went ashore to claim possession for Spain near the entrance to what is now Prince William Sound—the northernmost point ever claimed by Spain in North America. After another possession ceremony near the tip of the present-day Kenai Peninsula, the expedition sailed as far as Afognak Island, where heavy rains, seven deaths (from a variety of causes), and several cases of scurvy convinced them to begin their return voyage to San Blas.

Although Bodega's exploring days were over, he continued to serve Spain in North America. He was commander of the Nootka settlement (off the coast of present-day Vancouver Island) when Captain GEORGE VANCOUVER came in 1792 to reclaim a Britton's property that had been illegally seized by Spain. During his one summer at Nootka, Bodega oversaw an extensive exploration of the Strait of Juan de Fuca and the many inlets along the coast of what are now British Columbia and Alaska in search of a Northwest Passage. The resulting maps of these regions were the most complete to that time.

A gentleman, a friend to the Indians, and a lavish entertainer, Juan Francisco Bodega y Quadra was also a courageous explorer who faced grave dangers to carry out his orders. It was largely due to his bold explorations that Spain retained her hold on the coast of the Northwest as long as she did.

Benjamin Bonneville. Utah State Historical Society.

• Bonneville, Benjamin Louis Eulalie de

American
b April 14, 1796; Paris, France
d June 12, 1878; Fort Smith, Arkansas
Explored American West

From 1832 to 1835, Captain Benjamin Louis Eulalie de Bonneville ranged widely over the Rocky Mountains and beyond. Although he discovered no new territory, he added greatly to the United States government's knowledge of the land, its native peoples, and its natural history. Bonneville also directed JOSEPH REDDEFORD WALKER to make his historic journey to the Pacific coast and back, an exploration that contributed significantly to the opening of California to settlement.

After his family emigrated from France to the United States, Bonneville attended the U.S. Military Academy at West Point, graduating in 1815. During the next several years, he served at two frontier army posts in what are now Arkansas and Oklahoma. In 1830, having become interested in the fur trade, Bonneville requested a leave of absence to travel west and try his luck at trapping and trading furs. He easily obtained financial backing and, in 1832, led a well-supplied party of 110 men west.

Bonneville's true motives in going west are one of the unsolved mysteries of American history. While some historians maintain that he was interested only in the profits he could reap from the fur trade, others offer compelling evidence that he was singularly uninterested in profit. Proponents of the latter view suggest that Bonneville was actually spying for the United States government, emphasizing that much of the region he explored was also claimed by Great Britain. Supporters of the spying contention offer as evidence the fact that Bonneville had in his possession detailed instructions from the War Department on how he was to spend his leave of absence. (These instructions were much like those given by President Jefferson to MERIWETHER LEWIS and WILLIAM CLARK in 1803.) Bonneville was to explore the country to the Rocky Mountains and beyond, paying particular attention to the nature of the Indian tribes and the trade that might be carried on with them, as well as to the soil quality, mineral deposits, natural history, climate, geography, topography, and geology of the lands he explored. He was also to observe the number of warriors of each Indian tribe and their methods of making war. In short, Bonneville was to note anything and everything that might be of value to a government planning to encourage westward expansion.

On May 1, 1832, Bonneville led a caravan of wagons out of Fort Osage, Missouri, bound for the South Pass and the Green River, west of the Rockies. It was the first time that wagons were to cross the Continental Divide. Arriving at the Green River, Bonneville immediately built a fort as his permanent headquarters. Other trappers dubbed it "Bonneville's Folly" because it was too far north to be useful for trapping in winter—or even late fall and early spring. It was, however, a strategic location for keeping a watchful eye on comings and goings through various passes of the Rockies.

Through the winter of 1832–33 Bonneville and his men trapped the Salmon and Snake river valleys, with little success. In the summer of 1833, Bonneville made what is probably his greatest contribution to the exploration of the West by sending his field commander, Joseph Walker, with a party of forty to sixty to explore west of the Great Salt Lake. It is not clear whether Walker had specific orders to head for the Pacific coast of California, but that is where the expedition ended up. In the process of carrying out Bonneville's orders, Walker blazed the trail that would later be used by countless settlers to reach California.

Bonneville himself stayed in the Rockies, but his explorations added little new information to contemporary maps of the West. His movements, rather, support the theory that he was more interested in reconnaissance than anything else. In the winter of 1833 and fall of 1834, he made two separate forays to the Columbia River, presumably in an effort to learn more about the British presence in the Northwest. Both times he was repulsed by the British at Fort Walla Walla. He also sent a party into Crow territory in the northern Rockies to make con-

tact with the Indians, and just before leaving the West he made an extended tour of that region himself.

After three years in the Rockies, Bonneville returned east to learn that he had been discharged from the army for overstaying his leave of absence. A letter written in the interim, in which he had requested an extension, had apparently never arrived in Washington. The personal intervention of President Andrew Jackson led to his reinstatement. Bonneville later served in the Mexican War and was retired as a brigadier general.

Although Benjamin Bonneville failed to make a profit in his fur-trapping venture, his time in the West was well spent, especially that spent compiling two intelligence reports for the War Department. Though the second report was never received, the first minutely addressed each of the points he had been instructed to observe and was deemed one of the best intelligence reports ever received from the West.

Boone, Daniel

American
b November 2, 1734; Pennsylvania
d September 26, 1820; Missouri
Explored Kentucky

A skilled woodsman who was never happier than when he was alone in the wilderness, Daniel Boone may be the most famous pioneer America ever produced. Contrary to popular belief, however, he discovered neither Kentucky nor the Cumberland Gap (a mountain pass through the Appalachian Mountains). His great achievement, rather, was to blaze a trail (the Wilderness Road) through the Cumberland Gap that led settlers into the bluegrass region of central Kentucky.

Boone first heard tales of a fertile bluegrass region west of the Appalachian Mountains from fellow soldier John Finley during their brief stint in the French and Indian Wars (1754–63). In the winter of 1767–68, Boone made an unsuccessful attempt to reach bluegrass country from his home in Yadkin County, North Carolina. The next winter, Finley arrived in Yadkin County, and together they planned a spring expedition through the Cumberland Gap to Kentucky with four others. The group left North

Daniel Boone. Brown Bros.

the party were killed. Though Boone wanted to push on, the others convinced him to turn back.

In 1775, a land speculator named Judge Henderson bought land from the Cherokees through an illegal treaty. He hired Boone and twenty-eight others to mark a trail across Cherokee territory to Cumberland Gap and into Kentucky as far as the south bank of the Kentucky River. This was the famous Wilderness Road. On the south bank of the Kentucky, in what is now Madison County, Boone and his men built a few crude cabins that became the nucleus for Boonesborough, the first non-Indian settlement in Kentucky. He later found Kentucky too populated and moved on, first to what is now West Virginia and finally to Spanish territory in present-day Missouri, where he died in 1820.

Daniel Boone was a legend even in his own time, and some of the enduring myths about him have half-obscured his actual accomplishments. His courage and his love of the wilderness were unmatched, and it's doubtful that the first Kentucky settlements would have survived without him.

Carolina in May 1769 and camped the first summer by a small creek near the edge of the bluegrass plain. By day they hunted and explored; by night they read *Gulliver's Travels*.

Although most of the party had returned to North Carolina by the end of the year (one was killed by Indians), Boone stayed in Kentucky for two years, periodically joined by his brother, Squire Boone. During his time alone, Boone explored the Kentucky and Licking river valleys and followed the Ohio River as far as the falls near what is now Louisville. After two years in Kentucky, he packed up his furs and was headed home through the Cumberland Gap when a band of Cherokees stole his supplies and every fur that he had trapped during the two-year period.

Two years later, in 1773, Boone attempted to lead seven families, including his own, through the Cumberland Gap into Kentucky. They were stopped by an Indian ambush in which Boone's son and five other members of

---

• Borchgrevink, Carstens Egeberg

Norwegian
b December 1, 1864; Oslo
d April 21, 1934; Oslo
Explored Antarctica

In a period of four years (1895–99), Carstens Egeberg Borchgrevink went from being an obscure language teacher and surveyor in Australia to the leader of the first expedition to winter in Antarctica. In 1894 he quit his job to pursue his dream of going to Antarctica.

Borchgrevink first volunteered to serve on the *Antarctic*, a Norwegian ship under the command of Leonard Kristensen that was searching for new whaling waters. On January 24, 1895, the party landed on the shores of Antarctica, near Cape Adare in Victoria Land. They were the first humans recorded to have set foot on the continental mainland.

Thrilled at having discovered plants in this inhospitable terrain and excited about the prospect of returning to the same spot, which he judged to be an excellent harbor, the penniless Borchgrevink managed to raise money for a trip to the Sixth International Geophysical Congress in London in 1895. His enthusiasm was so infectious that, inexperienced and unknown as he was, his speech at the conference caused a sensation. Soon he was associating with the leading figures of the congress and sharing his plans for an expedition. But the president of the meeting, Sir Clements Markham, suddenly felt that his own plans for an Antarctic trip were being upstaged and decided to throw all of his considerable weight against the young enthusiast. Luckily, the newspaper publisher Sir George Newnes saw an opportunity for publicity and provided Borchgrevink with the money for the journey. Though the leader was Norwegian, the expedition is rated as British, having been financed and equipped in England, with most of the crew and staff British.

The *Southern Cross*, a converted 521-ton Norwegian sealing ship equipped with new engines, left Hobart, Tasmania, on December 19, 1898, and arrived off Cape Adare on February 17, 1899. A prefabricated house was put ashore in Robertson Bay. On March 1, the ship left a wintering party to its own devices in the land with the most severe climate in the world. The fact that they proved wintering on the Antarctic continent was physically possible was perhaps the most important result of the expedition. The staff, under the command of the thirty-four-year-old Borchgrevink, included an expert in magnetism, a meteorologist, and a naturalist from the British Museum, all of whom obtained useful scientific results. A **sledge** dog team under the care of two Finnish Lapps also came along. Borchgrevink ascended 3,700-foot Cape Adare that fall, and in the spring the area was fully explored and studied. When the ship arrived back in January 1900, further explorations were undertaken, and a sledge party was sent out across the Ross Ice Shelf, thus setting the stage for the explorations of ROBERT FALCON SCOTT and ERNEST SHACKLETON within the next decade.

• Bougainville, Louis-Antoine de

French
b November 12, 1729; Paris
d August 31, 1811; Paris
Circumnavigated; explored Pacific

Bougainville led the first French expedition (1767–69) to circumnavigate the world. It took

Louis-Antoine de Bougainville. Bettmann/Hulton.

place following the Seven Years' War (called the French and Indian War in America) at a time when France was exhausted and dispirited from the loss of its Canadian colonies and India to the British. The French sensed that their struggle for world power with the British would soon be renewed and sought ways to gain new territories ahead of their rival.

Born in Paris, the son of a lawyer, Bougainville first studied law, but his interests switched to mathematics and science. His treatise on integral calculus was published in 1754 and 1756 and earned him election to the British Royal Society.

In 1756, during the Seven Years' War, Bougainville went to Canada as military **aide-de-camp** to General Louis Joseph de Montcalm and supervised the evacuation of French troops after the fall of Quebec in 1759. Returning to France in 1760, he searched for a new way to serve his country.

He was attracted by the idea of exploring the Pacific Ocean and its undiscovered islands. As a step in this direction, he developed a plan to settle, at his own expense, the then-deserted Falkland Islands (or Malvinas) off the southeastern coast of South America. Bougainville reasoned that the islands were strategically positioned on the way to the Strait of Magellan and vital to a Pacific passage by unfriendly ships. King Louis XV approved his plan, and Bougainville established the colony in 1765 with Acadian, French-speaking families from what is now Nova Scotia and New Brunswick.

The British soon heard of the settlement and, claiming prior discovery of the island, sent a ship to establish a British colony on West Falkland. The Spanish let their French allies know they too were unhappy with the settlement of islands situated within the proclaimed bounds of the Spanish Empire. Reluctant to alienate the Spanish Bourbons and unwilling to confront the British again so soon, the French government asked Bougainville to give up the colony. In return, the Spanish refunded with interest the cost of the settlement. The British kept up an intermittent occupation until they abandoned the settlement in 1774.

For his part, the French king funded Bougain-

ville on a voyage through the Pacific and around the world. The two ships of the expedition set off from Nantes, France, for South America separately, one in late 1766, the other early in 1767. After formal ceremonies relinquishing the Falklands, they set sail from Rio de Janeiro in November 1767. Bougainville commanded the ships; with him as second-in-command was Pierre-Nicolas Duclos-Guyot, who had previously sailed to the Pacific coast of South America. Also included in the expedition were Philibert Commerson, botanist and naturalist, and Pierre-Antoine Véron, a young pilot and astronomer who was to determine accurate longitudes during the course of the voyage. Although he had no formal naval training, Bougainville had picked up considerable knowledge of navigation while crossing the Atlantic several times during the war in Canada.

The expedition took two months to navigate the treacherous Strait of Magellan at the southern tip of South America. Continuing northwest into the South Pacific, the ships went among the Tuamotu Islands in March 1768, where Bougainville recorded his first "Act of Possession."

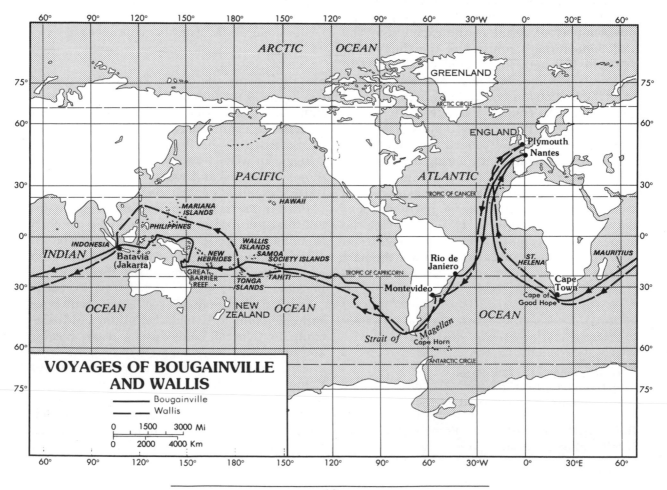

Experiencing foul weather, he then turned to the southeast. Bad luck continued as many of the sailors contracted **scurvy**. Then, in early April, they sailed along the east coast of Tahiti, found a safe opening through the reef, and anchored in Hitiaa Lagoon.

To the French explorers, Tahiti appeared a paradise. The natives were friendly and allowed a temporary sick camp to be set up. Although Bougainville understood from the Tahitians that he was not the first European to reach Tahiti, he nevertheless claimed possession of the island for France. He also took on board a Tahitian chief's son, Ahu-toru, who wanted to visit France. Bougainville was delighted to have a direct source of more information about Tahiti. He believed that Tahiti represented a place where human beings lived well in their natural state, a state that, according to the popular theory of the day in France, was by definition good until it was corrupted by civilization. After Ahu-toru described darker aspects of life on Tahiti, however, Bougainville modified his view. Nevertheless, when Ahu-toru later reached Paris, he became a sensation as a model for philosopher Jean-Jacques Rousseau's idea of the "noble savage."

After twelve days on Tahiti, the expedition sailed on through the Society Islands, Samoa, and the New Hebrides (now Vanuatu). Stores were low, and the sailors were now suffering from venereal disease as well as scurvy. (It was also around this time that the incidental discovery was made that Commerson's trusted servant, Jeanne Baret, was a woman dressed in men's clothing. Baret was surely the first female circumnavigator.)

Although Bougainville had the excuse of bringing his sailors relief from illness and starvation (by this time they were eating rats), he passed up the chance to claim Australia for France. Instead, he chose, as all earlier explorers had done, to veer north away from Queensland and the Great Barrier Reef with its dangerous breakers, fearing that his ships might founder in those waters.

As the ships headed northeast away from Australia, Bougainville was within sight of the Solomon Islands, discovered earlier but still uncharted. His account of the voyage established the certainty of their existence. Bougainville then headed for the Dutch East Indies, where, in October, the ships were at last able to replenish their stores at Buru Island and in Batavia (now Jakarta). In November the expedition finally touched French soil on Mauritius in the Indian Ocean. It arrived back in France in the spring of 1769 with a loss of only nine men (out of more than 200) in over two years, a remarkable achievement for the time.

Bougainville enjoyed great popular success. Though he had made few original discoveries, he brought back valuable information that laid the groundwork for later French voyages to the Pacific. Published in 1771, his *Voyage Around the World* was widely read.

In 1772 Bougainville became secretary to Louis XV and served as commodore of the French fleet in support of the American Revolution from 1779 to 1782. He escaped the massacres of Paris during the French Revolution and spent the remaining years of his life on his estate in Normandy doing scientific studies. Napoleon I made him senator, count, and member of the Legion of Honor.

The largest of the Solomon Islands and a strait in the New Hebrides today bear his name, as does the South American plant genus *Bougainvillaea*, which he introduced to Europe.

· Boyd, Louise Arner

American
b September 16, 1887; San Rafael, California
d September 14, 1972; San Francisco, California
Explored Greenland

Louise Arner Boyd was an heiress and socialite whose first summer cruise to the Arctic in 1924 on a Norwegian tourist boat turned her into a devoted and highly respected leader of seven expeditions to the far north. At first, her exploits, which included hunting polar bear and taking photographs on Franz Josef Land, were covered on the society page of her local newspaper. But as she developed more scientific interests and skill as a photographer and spent more and more of her fortune, she became a leading expert on the geography and natural history of Greenland.

Boyd was born, raised, and continued to live in an opulent San Rafael estate built by an ancestor who had struck it rich in the California gold rush. In 1920 she was left the sole surviving member of her family and succeeded her father as director of the Boyd Investment Company.

Louise Arner Boyd. UPI/Bettmann.

This put an enormous fortune at her disposal, but as yet she had no fixed idea about what to do with it. Then in 1924 the Norwegian cruise exposed her to what she described as "the Arctic lure."

After her sporting trip to Franz Josef Land in 1926, she had a chance to work with several "real" explorers, as she called them. She had intended to return to the hunt, but things changed as a result of the loss of UMBERTO NOBILE's **dirigible** *Italia* in 1928, followed by ROALD AMUNDSEN's plane crash during a rescue attempt of Nobile. She joined the international search for Amundsen, working closely with members of Amundsen's earlier expeditions for four months. By the time Amundsen was given up for dead, Boyd's new ambition to join the exotic and exclusive tribe of explorers had been shaped. Her resolve was strengthened when, in recognition of her brave work during the search, she was awarded Norway's Chevalier Cross of the Order of Saint Olav, the first foreign woman to be so honored, and France's Cross of the Legion of Honor.

In 1931 Boyd chartered the *Veslekari* for the first of four expeditions that undertook important studies in geography, botany, natural history, glaciology, magnetism, and ethnology in the interior of Franz Josef Fjord, East Green-

land. Meanwhile, she became an accomplished and prolific photographer. The director of the American Geographical Society, Dr. Isaiah Bowman, was so impressed by her efforts that he arranged for her future voyages to be sponsored by the organization.

Boyd's 1933 expedition visited the meteorological station at Jan Mayen Island and then conducted careful studies of Franz Josef and King Oscar fjords, out of which emerged the book *The Fiord Region of East Greenland* (1935). Two more trips to northeastern Greenland, in 1937 and 1938, provided the material for her book *The Coast of Northeast Greenland*. When she was preparing to publish this volume at the outset of World War II, the U.S. government advised her against it on the grounds that the region had become a strategically sensitive area. The War Department recruited her as a technical adviser and used her work in patrolling the region. (See ALFRED WEGENER for the Nazi use of the region.)

In 1955 Boyd chartered a plane and became the first woman to fly over the North Pole. After winning many honors, she became the first woman elected to the council of the American Geographical Society in 1960. Boyd is best remembered for her persistent work filling in the gaps left by others, for her exquisite photography, and for her ability (facilitated by her great wealth) to penetrate a world dominated by men.

Brandon, Saint. See **Brendan, Saint.**

· Brazza, Pierre-Paul-François-Camille Savorgnan de

Italian-French
b January 25, 1852; Rome
d September 14, 1905; Dakar, Senegal
Explored Central Africa

Considered the founder of French Equatorial Africa, Count Pierre Savorgnan de Brazza is known not only for his explorations but also for his promotion of the concept of expansion through treaties. A naturalized French citizen, Brazza competed on behalf of France in the nineteenth-century race among European countries to establish colonies in the African interior regions. He secured French control of a substan-

turn there for what Brazza correctly asserted was the purpose of colonization.

Brazza returned to Gabon in December 1879 and went up the Ogowe, stopping at the village of Mbe (now Brazzaville, Congo), on the bank of Stanley Pool. During his month-long stay, Brazza persuaded the Bateke ruler to put his ruler's mark on a contract placing his kingdom under the French flag and to let Brazza build a fort. The contract, or treaty, signed in October 1880 and ratified by France two years later, paved the way for French control of the Middle Congo, Chad, Gabon, and Ubangi-Shari (the present-day Central African Republic) through later expeditions overseen by Brazza. Appointed commissioner for the French Congo in 1886, he was discharged in 1898 after opposing the land rights granted to private firms. An investigation he undertook in 1905 uncovered abuses committed against local workers by corrupt concessionaires. He died the same year before reforms resulting from his efforts took place.

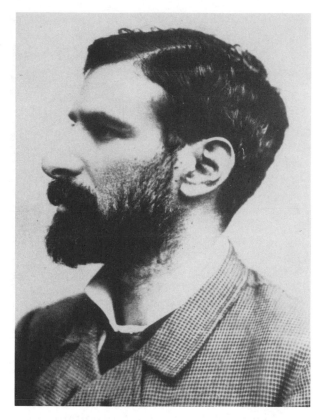

Savorgnan de Brazza. Collection Viollet.

tial amount of territory and negotiated treaties that led to the creation of the French Congo. Opposed to exploitation of the area's native inhabitants, he fought it strenuously but did not live long enough to see it eliminated.

Born into Italian nobility, Brazza studied at the naval academy of France and served in its navy during the Franco-Prussian War (1870–71), after which he became a naturalized citizen in 1874. While stationed on the coast of Gabon in the same year, he sought and received a paid leave to explore the Ogowe River the following year. He discovered the river's source and, aided by the friendly Bateke tribe, found the Alima River, a tributary that would have led him to the Congo (or Zaire) River if attacks by a cannibalistic tribe of the region had not forced him to retreat in early 1878. At the end of that year, outraged that HENRY MORTON STANLEY had succeeded in traveling down the Congo River, Brazza went back to France to seek funding for another journey. Dubious at first, officials consented to finance this trip to the Congo after learning that Belgium had hired Stanley to re-

Brendan (Brandon), Saint

Irish
b 484–89?; Tralee, County Kerry
d 577–83?
May have reached New World before Vikings

Saint Brendan was a historic figure whose name became associated with one or more legendary voyages described in ninth-century literature,

An illustration of St. Brendan's voyage. Library of Congress.

notably *Navigatio Sancti Brendani.* Some historians believe that Brendan, or other Irish explorers of his time, may have been the first to reach the New World.

Ordained in 512, Brendan was the abbot of the monastery at Clonfert in Galway, one of several he founded. According to the epic, he and seventeen other monks set out in a 30-foot-long curragh, a boat made of skins, in search of the mythical Saints' Promised Land, which they believed was somewhere in the Atlantic. On their journey they came to several islands, which may have been the Outer Hebrides and the Faeroes, and crossed a spot where the sea resembled a "thick, curdled mass." This may be history's first description of seaweed in the Sargasso Sea. Eventually they reached large, flat islands with clear water (possibly the Bahamas), where one monk was left behind as a missionary, and a "fragrant island of fountains," which may have been Jamaica. They sailed north to a large continent, then homeward. The tall crystal they saw covered with a silver veil may have been an iceberg.

"St. Brendan's Isle" remained on many maps until as late as 1759, although it was variously placed west of the Canaries, in the West Indies, near Ireland, and beyond Iceland. After centuries of searching, Christians finally gave up their quest for this mythical Eden as the known world expanded.

Known also as Brendan the Voyager, Saint Brendan is considered the patron saint of sailors.

• Bruce, James

Scottish
b December 14, 1730; Stirlingshire
d April 27, 1794; Stirlingshire
Explored Blue Nile

From the time he first arrived in Africa in 1763 on a diplomatic assignment, James Bruce had one principal ambition as an explorer—to travel to the Nile River and locate its source. He realized this goal (he believed) seven years later after a harrowing voyage up the Nile, across the desert, and through war-torn Abyssinia (modern Ethiopia) to the headwaters of the Blue Nile (which he wrongly construed to be the more major of the river's two primary tributar-

Sir James Bruce. National Galleries of Scotland.

ies). Elated by his success, he committed his adventures to writing in detailed, eloquent accounts that later filled five illustrated volumes.

Born to an upper-class Scottish family, Bruce studied both medicine and law before illness forced him to give up his academic work. Following his recovery, he met and married the daughter of a Scottish wine merchant and joined her family's business. His wife died of tuberculosis within a year of their marriage, however, and the twenty-three-year-old widower turned to travel for consolation. He visited Spain and Portugal and studied a number of languages, including Arabic. Four years later, in 1758, his father died, leaving him enough money to forgo a career and travel full time. He fought in the war against Spain in 1762 and then traveled to Africa where he was appointed British consul general to Algiers. When his two-year assignment ended, Bruce traveled along the Mediterranean coast of Africa to Egypt and made plans for his long-awaited expedition up the Blue Nile.

Bruce's journey began in 1768 from Cairo, taking a party of approximately twenty men up the river to Aswan and then east across the Eastern Desert to the Red Sea. His destination was Abyssinia, where he believed the source of the Blue Nile was located. While this eastern route was less direct, local authorities had advised him that it was less dangerous than a southern course through Sudan. Bruce traveled southeast across the Red Sea to Jidda, Arabia, and then recrossed the sea, south to Massawa. He and his party arrived at the Abyssinian capital of Gondar in February 1770, where he was granted the protection of the ruling emperor and **vizier**. War had broken out among the region's political factions, and Bruce took part in the royal army's battle campaign before completing the last leg of his trip. He finally reached Lake Tana, the source of the Blue Nile, in November 1770. Summing up his feelings, he wrote: "It is easier to guess than to describe the situation of my mind at that moment—standing in that spot which had baffled the genius, industry and inquiry of both ancients and moderns for the course of near three thousand years. . . . Though a mere private Briton, I triumphed here, in my own mind, over kings and their armies."

Bruce's joy was short-lived, he noted in his journal, in view of the grueling return trip that loomed ahead of him. He stayed another year in Abyssinia before setting out on his return. Traveling through Sudan this time, he suffered a twenty-day trip across the desert to Aswan before returning down the Nile to Cairo in early 1773.

On his arrival in Europe, Bruce's work elicited some praise in France, his first stop on the continent. Back in England, however, the public quickly became skeptical of his fantastic (although substantially truthful) accounts of his African adventures. These included tales of savage Abyssinian acts of war and one story of men slicing a sizable hunk of beefsteak from the flank of a live cow. The combination of Bruce's colorful stories and his own blustery, self-important nature attracted numerous critics, among them the influential Samuel Johnson. Johnson believed, and claimed publicly, that Bruce had fabricated his accounts, including his discovery of the source of the Blue Nile. Public opinion aligned with Johnson.

Frustrated and disgusted, Bruce returned to Kinnaird, his family estate in Scotland. There he married again, this time a woman twenty-four years younger than he. But this marriage was also to be brief. After being widowed again in 1785 at the age of fifty-four, Bruce spent his time compiling his journal writings and drawings into a five-volume book published in 1790.

Critics scorned the publication when it first appeared, although it later attained considerable popularity. Subsequent explorers validated much of Bruce's information about Africa, and his book eventually became highly respected for its colorful narration as well as the scientific and geographic data it contains.

Bruce died in 1794 as the result of a fall down the front staircase of his estate. Until the end, he remained unable to derive much satisfaction from his accomplishments due to the personal tragedies and professional disappointments that plagued him throughout his life.

Brulé, Etienne

French
b 1592?; Champigny-sur-Marne?
d June 1632?; Toanche (Huron country)
Explored Great Lakes, Susquehanna River, and Chesapeake Bay

Since Etienne Brulé produced no written record of his explorations, much of his life remains a mystery. What is clear is that he lived among the Huron Indians for many years, that he traveled the length of the Susquehanna River, and that in doing so he was probably the first European to set foot in what is now the state of Pennsylvania. The reports of his contemporaries suggest that he may also have been the first European to see four of the five Great Lakes.

In 1610, two years after arriving in Québec, Brulé was sent by the French explorer and colonizer SAMUEL DE CHAMPLAIN to live among the Indians and learn their language and customs. After a year with the Algonquins in the Ottawa River valley, he was reunited with Champlain, who recorded the meeting: "I also saw my French boy who came dressed like an Indian." This was only the beginning of Brulé's immersion in the Indian way of life.

Little is known of Brulé's travels between 1611 and 1615. Certain facts suggest that he stayed in Huron country, near Georgian Bay on the east side of Lake Huron. Thus he is credited with being the first European to see that lake.

In 1615 Brulé served as Champlain's interpreter on a trip to Huron country in search of new fur-trading alliances and new regions for colonization by the French. While Champlain and his Huron allies prepared to attack the Iroquois near Oneida Lake, Brulé went with a small party of Hurons to enlist the support of the Andastes, a tribe living somewhere between present-day Binghamton and Elmira, New York. (The journey took them around the western end of Lake Ontario, leading to the claim that Brulé was the first European to see that lake.)

Brulé and the Andastes arrived at the Iroquois village two days after Champlain and the Hurons had left the area as the result of a resounding defeat. Brulé then returned to the Andastes village near the headwaters of the Susquehanna River. Not one to remain idle, he soon set out unaccompanied on a journey of exploration, following the Susquehanna south. He eventually reached Chesapeake Bay and explored some of its many islands as well as the surrounding shores.

In his attempt to make his way back to Québec, Brulé was captured by Iroquois and tortured until an unexpected and violent thunderstorm convinced the Indians that it would be wise to treat their captive well.

Brulé reported his exploits to Champlain at their next meeting in 1618, and Champlain urged him to continue his explorations. Consequently, sometime around 1623 Brulé and another Frenchman named Grenolle explored the north shore of Lake Huron as far as Lake Superior. They may have penetrated Lake Superior as far as present-day Duluth.

In 1625, hearsay puts Brulé in the country of the Neutrals, Indians who lived near Lake Erie. If Brulé did in fact visit the Neutrals he was the first European to see Lake Erie.

When the English attacked Québec in 1629, Champlain's once-trusted interpreter put himself in their service, probably lured by the prospect of financial gain. After the English triumph, Brulé went back to Huron country, where sometime around 1632, for reasons never learned, his former friends and allies, the Hurons, killed—and ate—the man who had so successfully adopted their ways of life.

Bruni, Antoine Raymond Joseph de, Chevalier d'Entrecasteaux. See **Entrecasteaux, Antoine Raymond Joseph de Bruni, Chevalier d'**.

Burckhardt, Johann Ludwig (Jean-Louis; John Lewis)

Swiss
b November 24, 1784; Lausanne
d October 15, 1817; Cairo, Egypt
Explored Arabian Peninsula and East Africa

One of the earliest and most prominent scholarly explorers, Johann Ludwig Burckhardt made an extensive firsthand study of Muslim communities near the Red Sea. The first European to reach the ancient city of Petra (in present-day Jordan) since the Middle Ages, he also visited the famed cities of Mecca and Medina and the territory along the Nile River from Cairo to Nubia. His career was brief, owing to his death from dysentery at age thirty-two, and his five years of exploration yielded no geographical discoveries of consequence. Nevertheless, Burckhardt's copious and detailed accounts of his travels, published after his death, are held in high regard for the insight they provided into obscure areas of the Sudan and the secretive Muslim communities of the Arabian peninsula.

Johann Ludwig Burckhardt. Bibliotheque Nationale, Paris.

A member of an affluent family that was forced to leave Switzerland when the Bonapartists came into power, Burckhardt spent much of his youth in Germany. There he attended the universities of Leipzig and Göttingen, where he studied science and languages, excelling at both. In 1806 he went to England to seek employment and, intrigued with the idea of visiting exotic lands, applied to the Association for Promoting the Discovery of the Interior Parts of Africa (known as the African Association). Sir JOSEPH BANKS, founder of the organization, commissioned Burckhardt to explore the continent's northern interior, particularly the Niger River and the city of Timbuktu. Since this territory was dominated by Muslims, the novice explorer was assigned to study the Arabic language thoroughly before commencing his African travels.

Burckhardt's preparations went far beyond the directives of the African Association. Determined to be an effective explorer who could pose as a Muslim, the exacting and methodical young scholar spent more than four years in training. In England, he studied Arabic at Cambridge University, taking science courses there as well. He also researched the Arab mode of dress, practiced sleeping and walking barefoot outdoors for long periods, and limited his diet to the characteristic sparse Muslim fare of vegetables and water. In early 1809 he traveled to Syria, where he continued mastering the Arabic tongue, studying Muslim customs, and creating a suitable disguise for himself. Assuming the name Sheikh Ibrahim ibn Abdullah and an Arabian costume, he made three trial journeys in Syria before setting out for Egypt in June 1812.

The city of Cairo was intended to be a starting point for Burckhardt's lengthy trip southwest to investigate the Niger and visit Timbuktu. Instead, Cairo was to become his base for travel south on the Nile and southeast across the Red Sea into Arabia. Absorbed in his quest for further information about the Muslim culture, he delayed his original mission in favor of trying to penetrate some of the forbidden cities of Islam. Consequently, before going to Cairo, Burckhardt detoured to visit the almost impenetrable city of Petra, becoming the first modern European to give an account of this ancient community. Arriving in Cairo later that year, he could not locate a caravan heading west and instead opted to follow the Nile south.

Traveling by donkey, Burckhardt covered more than 1,000 miles before a group of native rebels blocked further passage to the south. It was on this expedition that he made one of his few actual discoveries, locating the temples of Ramses II at the village of Abu Simbel in southern Egypt, in March 1813. Carved into the side of a cliff in the thirteenth century B.C., the timeworn but still-impressive monuments had not been seen by European travelers since ancient times. In the region of Nubia, he also found many temples and remnants of villages. An extremely keen observer and a meticulous notetaker, Burckhardt provided insights into the history and geography of the near-forgotten region and its people. While he praised the Nubians on the whole, he was personally at risk since the region's moral code allowed robbers to prey on travelers—and to start digging the graves of those who refused to yield. Despite his reputation as serious-minded scholar, Burckhardt showed humor as well as bravado toward a would-be thief who dug his grave: "I alighted and, making another, told him that it was intended for his own sepulchre. . . . At this he began to laugh; we then mutually destroyed each other's labors."

Burckhardt was detained in the area for several months when he became ill and developed a problem with his eye. Recovered by March 1814, he took a caravan route south across the Nubian Desert and continued following the Nile to the towns of Berber, Shendi, and Sennar. Turning east, he then traveled to Suakin, on the coast of the Red Sea and, in the summer of 1814, ventured across the sea into Arabia, stopping first at the town of Jidda.

Notifying his sponsor in England of his intended detour, Burckhardt explained that it was a productive way to bide his time until the annual caravan departed west from Cairo to Fezzan in Libya. However, he was anxious to explore the Muslim region known as the Hejaz, whose legendary capital city of Mecca lay only a short distance from Jidda. Disguised as an Egyptian, he visited Mecca, as well as the holy city of Medina to the north, providing Europe with its most complete and reliable information to date about these forbidden cities and their inhabitants. Returning to Cairo the following year, he again departed for the east, to avoid a plague in Egypt. This time he traveled to the nearby Sinai Peninsula, studying the manuscripts in the monastery at Mount Sinai and tracing the adjacent coast of the Gulf of Aqaba.

Burckhardt returned to Cairo in 1816 after the two-month expedition and awaited a caravan that would take him west into the African interior. His uncertain health failed again, however, and he was forced to remain in Cairo. He died of dysentery the following year, as he was preparing to depart for Timbuktu; he was buried with Muslim rites as Sheikh Ibrahim ibn Abdullah.

While Burckhardt had not even begun the mission for which he had been engaged a decade earlier, the African Association was impressed with the body of work his journals represented. He had painstakingly recorded an enormous number of facts and observations about the terrain, meteorological conditions, and wildlife of the various regions through which he traveled, as well as documenting the customs and dialects of the people. Between 1819 and 1830, the African Association published his accounts in four separate books, entitled *Travels in Nubia*, *Travels in Syria*, *Travels in Arabia*, and *Notes on the Bedouins and Wahhabis*. Much of Burckhardt's writing was too dry and fact-laden to appeal to the average reader, but it held enormous importance for subsequent travelers and students of the areas he had explored.

· Burke, Robert O'Hara

Irish
b 1821; St. Clerans, County Galway
d June 28, 1861; Cooper's Creek, Queensland, Australia
Led Great Northern Exploration Expedition across Australia

One of Australia's best-known early explorers, Robert O'Hara Burke commanded perhaps the most tragic expedition in the continent's history. For this brave but inexperienced and impatient adventurer, his first major foray into the continent's barren interior would be his last.

Burke was born in Ireland and educated in Belgium, where he entered the service. At the age of twenty he joined the Austro-Hungarian army. He achieved the rank of captain before he left to join the Royal Irish Mounted Constabulary in 1848. In 1853 he emigrated to Tasmania but soon moved to Melbourne, Australia. He became a police sergeant in Melbourne and then a district inspector of police, supervising gold prospectors in the Orens and Beechworth diggings.

In 1860 Burke was selected to lead an expedition across the Australian continent from south to north. In 1858 JOHN MC DOUALL STUART had reached the interior on behalf of the government of South Australia, and the Royal Philosophical Society of Victoria was interested in establishing an overland telegraph route to northern Australia. Burke's was to be the best-outfitted, most expensive expedition of its day. Burke lacked many of the qualities that make a good leader. He was not a methodical planner, and he had no practical experience in the Australian bush.

Burke set out from Melbourne in a blaze of glory on August 21, 1860, with eighteen men, two dozen camels, twenty-eight horses, and twenty-one tons of provisions, including brandy for human consumption and rum for the expedition's camels. The camels, imported from India, were chosen because they could tolerate stony terrain and could travel for days without water. Three Pakistani camel drivers were brought to Australia to handle the animals.

Trouble started almost immediately—no doubt fueled by Burke's fiery temperament. By October, when the party reached Menindee on the Darling River some 400 miles from Melbourne, Burke's camel master and second in command, George Landells, quit and took the expedition's doctor with him. On October 19 Burke continued with a reduced party of six, leaving most staff and supplies behind at Menindee. On November 11, he reached Cooper's Creek, where he established another depot.

Originally Burke planned to stay at Cooper's Creek until a guide, William Wright, returned

Robert O'Hara Burke (left), with William Wills.
Australian Foreign Affairs and Trade Dept.

with the rest of the explorers and additional supplies, but his impatience got the best of him. Leaving William Brahe behind, Burke set off on December 16 with John King, Charles Gray, and WILLIAM JOHN WILLS, his new second in command. They took six camels, a horse, and provisions for twelve weeks. Brahe was told to wait three months for their return.

The crossing was brutal. The heat was a searing 140 degrees, and the men had little food. It was an exhausted band that reached the mouth of the Flinders River at the Gulf of Carpentaria on February 9, 1861, after two months of twelve-hour-long marches. The group never actually saw the ocean, as wide marshes stood between them and the shoreline, but they were close enough to know that it was there. They began their return journey almost immediately.

Their southern journey was as wet as their northward passage had been arid. Heavy rains and lightning storms made travel difficult. Once, they ran over a snake almost as large as a log; they killed it and ate it. Before their trek was over, they would be forced to eat two

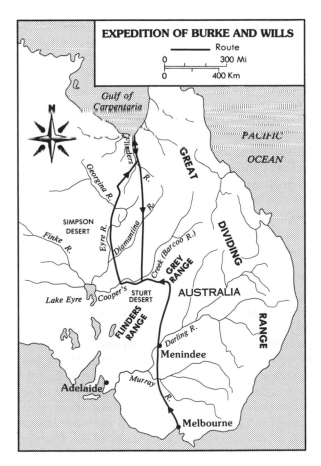

EXPEDITION OF BURKE AND WILLS

Route

0   300 Mi

0   400 Km

of their camels and then Burke's horse. Gray developed dysentery, although until he died of it two weeks later, the others in the party thought he was feigning illness. The day they spent burying him probably cost them their lives.

Burke finally arrived back at the Cooper's Creek depot on April 21, 1861, only to find it deserted. Brahe had left earlier that day, leaving them some provisions and a note with his intended route. At the time they arrived at Cooper's Creek, Brahe was only about 14 miles away. Wills and King wanted to try to follow Brahe, but Burke said that they would never catch up with him. Instead, he insisted on heading for Mount Hopeless, some 150 miles to the southwest, which was the nearest outpost of civilization. Wills was too young and inexperienced to stand up to Burke, and he and King consequently followed their stubborn and misguided leader.

The three headed southwest but wound up wandering in aimless circles. They were reduced to eating nardoo, a type of grass seed provided by the local **aborigines**, along with fish and rats. Each day the search for food became more difficult as the men grew progressively weaker.

In the meantime, Brahe finally met up with Wright, who had spent three months at Menindee instead of tracing his footsteps back to Cooper's Creek immediately as he had been ordered. The two returned to the Cooper's Creek depot on May 8, but they left it having again seen no sign of Burke or the others. Brahe apparently never bothered to see if the provisions he buried had been touched. Ironically, Burke was not far from the depot when Brahe and Wright were there, and Burke actually returned to Cooper's Creek on May 28.

Burke and Wills died of starvation within two days of each other at the end of June 1861. King survived thanks to the help of a group of aborigines, who cared for him until he was rescued on September 18 by a search party led by Alfred William Howitt.

Despite the tragic end to their story, the explorers, who had set out as heroes, had somehow achieved their primary goal. They had successfully crossed the inhospitable Australian continent, covering a distance of 1,500 miles in six months and establishing an overland route to the Gulf of Carpentaria. Although Burke was censured posthumously for his foolhardy actions, he and Wills today are recognized for their bravery on a memorial outside Melbourne's Parliament House.

· Burton, Richard Francis

English
b March 19, 1821; Torquay, Devonshire
d October 20, 1890; Trieste, Italy
Explored Africa and Asia; discovered Lake
**   Tanganyika**

Sir Richard Francis Burton was among the most notable and controversial figures involved in exploration during the nineteenth century. Credited with discovering Lake Tanganyika, he participated in two expeditions into East Africa to search for the source of the Nile River and later traveled through several areas of West Africa. His Asian journeys included visits to the Islamic holy cities of Mecca and Medina, strictly forbidden to Christians, in the guise of a Muslim pilgrim. A highly proficient observer and lin-

Captain Sir Richard Francis Burton. National Portrait Gallery, London.

guist, Burton amassed an enormous quantity of information about the lands and peoples he saw and was prodigal in sharing his findings and observations. He published more than fifty books during his lifetime, including poetry and translations of erotica and other classic works of Eastern culture, as well as original accounts of his travels. Many of his publications met with public and critical disapproval, due either to their shocking content or to the extreme racist attitudes they often betrayed. Nevertheless, the work of the bold, free-thinking Burton is widely respected today for the substantial knowledge it contributed to the field of African and Asian study.

The son of an English army colonel, Burton traveled through Europe with his family as a boy and even then showed signs of being a rebel. A chronic fighter, he did poorly in school and was given to recklessness. Dubbed ''Ruffian Dick'' while at Oxford, he cultivated what would be a lifelong interest in languages but was expelled for disobedience. He had learned six languages before he was eighteen, and he eventually mastered some twenty-five additional languages and dialects.

A love of travel and adventure prompted Burton to join the army of the East India Company at age twenty-one. During his seven-year stay in India he spent time in Sindh and Goa, conducting research on both places, as well as learning Arabic and ten other languages. He also published a report on homosexual brothels in the coastal town of Karachi, and the public outrage that ensued resulted in his being asked to leave India in 1849.

Still in the army, but on extended leave, he spent a year perfecting his study of Arabic. Burton, who was raised an Anglican, then began a lengthy courtship of the aristocratic Roman Catholic Isabel Arundell (whom he would eventually marry in 1861, despite the prevalence of anti-Catholic prejudice in nineteenth-century England). Fascinated by the famed Islamic holy cities of Mecca and Medina, he then laid plans to assume a disguise and penetrate these closely guarded communities of the Arabian peninsula. In 1853, after adopting Muslim clothing and darkening his complexion with henna, Burton spent several months in the cities posing as an Afghani doctor. He chronicled these experiences in an 1855 publication entitled *Personal Narrative of a Pilgrimage to Mecca and El Medina*, considered one of his better travel books.

The same year, he again donned a Muslim disguise and became the first European to visit the holy city of Harar in Ethiopia. This trip was part of an 1854 expedition with fellow army officer JOHN HANNING SPEKE to explore eastern Ethiopia and Somaliland (now known as Somalia) and to locate the source of the Nile River. An attack by Somalis at Berbera wounded both men in 1855, and they were forced to retreat from the country. Recovering from their injuries, the two soldiers traveled to the Black Sea and briefly fought in the Crimean War before returning to Africa in December 1856. This second expedition by Burton and Speke would prove more fruitful but would also result in a bitter feud between them.

Burton won the sponsorship of England's Royal Geographical Society for this mission and was appointed its leader. His assignment was to seek the origin of the White Nile, the Nile River's largest tributary, and to locate an unexplored body of water called the Sea of Ujiji (later known as Lake Tanganyika). Departing from coastal Zanzibar, the party traveled west

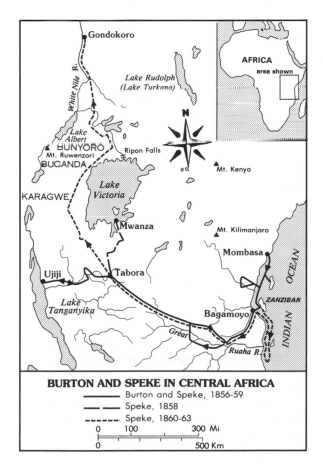

BURTON AND SPEKE IN CENTRAL AFRICA
———— Burton and Speke, 1856-59
— — Speke, 1858
- - - - Speke, 1860-63

0   100   300 Mi

0   500 Km

to Kazeh (now Tabora, Tanzania). By the time they reached the Sea of Ujiji in February 1858, Burton was suffering from malaria and Speke had been temporarily blinded by a tropical eye disease. They explored the lake only briefly before returning to Kazeh to recover from their ailments.

Recuperating more rapidly than Burton, Speke set out to locate a larger body of water rumored to lay northeast of the Sea of Ujiji. He found Lake Ukerewe in late July and renamed it Victoria Nyanza, or Lake Victoria, after his queen; he learned from local tribes and missionaries that a large river flowed from its north side. Correctly assuming that he had discovered the source of the Nile, the overjoyed explorer returned to Kazeh to share the news with his colleague. But the fiercely competitive Burton reacted with scorn, questioning the validity of his subordinate's claim and ridiculing his lack of proof.

Burton's animosity grew when Speke—contrary to his own stated intentions—returned to England ahead of his colleague to claim the discovery of the source of the Nile for himself. Burton was further incensed when Speke won financing from the Royal Geographical Society for additional exploration to confirm his self-proclaimed findings. Although Speke's subsequent three-year expedition with JAMES AUGUSTUS GRANT strengthened his credibility in England, Burton remained unconvinced. He demanded further proof that the Nile flowed from Lake Victoria, arguing that while Speke may have located cataracts (a waterfall or steep rapids) feeding a river, he could not claim that river to be the Nile without tracing its entire course to Gondokoro. The two rivals were scheduled to debate the issue publicly in September 1864, but Speke accidentally shot himself to death while hunting the day before the meeting.

In the interim, Burton had recuperated from the illness contracted in Africa while traveling across the United States in 1860. Studying the Mormon communities of Utah, he produced a book on the subject the following year. The newly married Burton then accepted the unimportant position as Her Majesty's consul to Fernando Póo (now Bioko) and the Bight of Biafra in West Africa. Stationed on the island of Fernando Póo, he found additional opportunities for exploration. With the Nile River dispute still in progress, Burton became embroiled in a bitter controversy over another alleged discovery.

In this case, however, Burton championed the explorer in question, PAUL BELLONI DU CHAILLU, whose 1861 account of observing gorillas in the highlands of West Africa came under sharp attack. Convinced that the French-American traveler was telling the truth, Burton spoke on his behalf at a heated public forum on the issue.

Inspired by Du Chaillu's report, Burton traveled to the Gabon eight months later and caught a brief glimpse of a gorilla. In the same region he investigated the cannibalistic Fang people, also known as Oahouins, and traveled to the estuary of the Congo (or Zaire) River. During his tenure on Fernando Póo, he was also the first European to climb Mount Cameroon; in addition, he went south to visit Angola, and explored the West African Gold Coast and western Nigeria. Part of his assignment as a diplomat was to discourage the rampant slave trading in Benin, and he tried to persuade Gelele, the local king, to withdraw from such trading. While Burton was not successful, he was able to study Gelele's realm and to produce a two-volume account of his observations. His West African experiences also resulted in an 1863 book about Nigeria and the Cameroons and another about his travels on the Gabon and the Congo, published fourteen years later.

Burton's next diplomatic assignment, in Santos, Brazil, allowed him to travel extensively in South America collecting information for a book on the Brazilian highlands, published in 1869. From his subsequent and admittedly favorite consul post, in Damascus, Syria, he researched and wrote books on Syria and Palestine. He also traveled far afield to Iceland, where he gathered material for a book published in 1877. From his final post in Trieste (in present-day Italy) where he was stationed for more than a decade until his death, Burton published a book about the peninsular region known as Istria (now part of Yugoslavia).

Among Burton's later travels were return visits to his original army post in India and to two of his former expedition sites. The latter trips, first to Arabia and later to Africa's Gold Coast with fellow explorer VERNEY LOVETT CAMERON, were unsuccessful efforts to locate gold.

Burton's long-term interest in erotica also continued to flourish. Turning his talent for languages to the field of literary translation, he was the first to publish English versions of Eastern erotica such as the *Kama Sutra* and *The Perfumed Garden*. He also published a seven-teen-volume translation of the *Arabian Nights* in its original (and sexually explicit) form. These publications horrified the prudish reading public of the Victorian era, including Burton's own wife, a pious Catholic. In fact, after his death in 1890, Isabel Burton destroyed those of his writings that she judged to be inappropriate.

Much of Burton's writing also offended the public on another count. Perhaps seeking to establish his own superiority, Burton wrote disparagingly about many of the native peoples he encountered in his travels. He continually belittled the appearance, habits, and religious beliefs of the African cultures, in particular. However, his writing also abounds with slurs toward various other groups, such as the Jews and the French.

Overall, his massive body of writing and translation is strikingly diverse in both its subject matter and the critical response it evoked. Some of his later travel books were considered relatively dull, for instance, while his poem on the ascetic philosophy of the Sufi cult was praised for its creativity. Among his most successful books was *The Lake Regions of Central Africa*, a two-volume account of the expedition that led to his greatest achievement as an explorer, the discovery of Lake Tanganyika.

SUGGESTED READINGS: Thomas J. Assad, *Three Victorian Travelers* (Routledge & Kegan Paul, 1964); Alfred Bercovici, *That Blackguard Burton!* (Bobbs-Merrill, 1962); Fawn M. Brodie, *The Devil Drives: A Life of Sir Richard Burton* (Norton, 1967); Fairfax Downey, *Burton, Arabian Nights Adventurer* (Charles Scribner's Sons, 1931); Byron Farwell, *Burton* (Holt, Rinehart, & Winston, 1963); Edward Rice, *Captain Sir Richard Francis Burton* (Charles Scribner's Sons, 1990); Hugh J. Schonfield, *Richard Burton, Explorer* (Herbert Joseph, 1936); Thomas Wright, *The Life of Sir Richard Burton* (Burt Franklin, 1968).

• Button, Thomas

Welsh
b ?; St. Lythans
d April 1634; Worlton
Attempted Northwest Passage; discovered
 Resolution, Coates, and Mansel islands

Admiral Sir Thomas Button had the disappointing job of discovering the west side of what is now Hudson Bay. This find dashed the hope that the great inland sea was part of the fabled Northwest Passage (for a more complete discussion, see MARTIN FROBISHER). Commanding the *Resolution* and the *Discovery*, Button carried the torch passed by HENRY HUDSON, who had been abandoned in the bay a year earlier by his mutinous crew. Brushing aside moral and legal niceties in their eagerness to find the passage, the "Governor and Company of the Merchants of London, Discoverers of the Northwest Passage," as the enterprise optimistically called itself, employed one of the mutineers, ROBERT BYLOT, as pilot. Though Hudson, his son, and loyal crew may well have been alive, the Button expedition made no effort to find them.

After losing five of his crew members in a skirmish with **Inuits** at Digges Island (at the northernmost tip of present-day Québec), Button moved into the bay, reaching its western shore on August 13, 1612. Button's expedition wintered at Port Nelson, where he kept his men in order with strict discipline. They were also involved in the planning process and became interested in all phases of their mission. Still, several died during the winter, and all were severely weakened.

In the summer of 1613, Button explored 600 miles of the west coast of the bay, leaving only the southwest side unexamined. He then headed back through the Hudson Strait, where he detected flood tides issuing from the northwest, indicating a passage in the direction of what would soon be called Foxe Channel, after its discoverer, LUKE FOXE.

Though he did not find a passage, he carefully explored an area rich in furs and future profit for the English. He continued a successful career in the navy, being appointed admiral of the king's ships on the coast of Ireland in 1618 and a member of the Council of War in 1624. His later years were clouded by the Admiralty's accusations of misconduct and failure to pay his pensions and allowances. He died peacefully at home in 1634.

---

* Bylot (Bilot), Robert

English
b ?
d ?
Attempted Northwest Passage

A highly resourceful natural leader who won the respect of all who dealt with him, Robert Bylot nevertheless tarnished his image forever when he joined the mutineers who left HENRY

HUDSON to die with eight others in Hudson Bay in 1611. This was not a heroic act by any standard. Bylot, however, not only escaped prosecution, but he was soon appointed captain of Hudson's former ship, the *Discovery*. With WILLIAM BAFFIN as his mate, he led two remarkable expeditions to seek the Northwest Passage (for a more complete discussion, see MARTIN FROBISHER). Whatever his actions in 1611, he was evidently deemed worthy of commanding two of the most important enterprises of those years.

That Hudson respected him is clear from the fact that Bylot was promoted from second to first mate after the original first mate, Robert Juet, was demoted—the action that pushed Juet toward mutiny. Bylot's reputation can be judged by the fact that the mutineers then chose him to captain the return voyage. They were right to do so: not only did he get the ship back to England with a weak and small crew of only seven, but he then won the confidence of the authorities, who might have otherwise hanged the lot.

Within a year, Bylot was back in Hudson Bay with Sir THOMAS BUTTON's expedition, which discovered the western shore of that great inland sea. In 1614 he was on board the *Discovery* again as William Gibbon's mate. This was the *Discovery*'s one mission to the Arctic with Bylot aboard that made no discoveries. For twenty weeks it lay trapped by ice off the coast of Labrador before returning home. Never missing a beat, Bylot returned as captain of the *Discovery* in 1615 and 1616, the two important voyages piloted by William Baffin.

Baffin has received all the credit for the discovery of Baffin Bay and the south coast of Baffin Island, as they later came to be called, but Bylot was the captain. He had been with the *Discovery* every year since Hudson's expedition left England in 1610. Unfortunately, there is no record of how he spent his later years or when he died.

---

* Byrd, Richard Evelyn

American
b October 25, 1888; Winchester, Virginia
d March 11, 1957; Boston, Massachusetts
Explored Arctic and Antarctica by plane; flew over both poles

Admiral Richard Evelyn Byrd ushered in the era of mechanized polar exploration that

Richard Evelyn Byrd. National Archives.

largely replaced the ancient **Inuit** methods of travel adopted by most successful polar explorers prior to Byrd. By using the airplane and the snow tractor—and equipping them with cameras and radio transmitters and receivers—Byrd put the most inaccessible places in the world, the polar regions, within relatively easy reach. Whereas ROBERT PEARY's successful attainment of the North Pole in 1909 required five weeks of grueling and treacherous travel by dog **sledge**, Byrd's 1926 round-trip from Svalbard took only 15½ hours. "To think," Byrd wrote in his log, "that men toiled for years over this ice, a few hard-won miles a day; and we travel luxuriously a hundred miles an hour. How motors have changed the burdens of man."

Byrd came from an upper-class Virginia family that gave him the resources to pursue his dreams. When he was only twelve he took a

trip around the world by himself. By the time he was fourteen he had decided that he would someday reach the North Pole. Athletically gifted, he broke his foot in three places while playing quarterback for the U.S. Naval Academy as a sophomore. Two years later, as captain of the gymnastic team, he crushed the same foot when he fell off the rings. When he fell on his foot once again while serving on the battleship *Wyoming*, his shattered ankle was set with a silver pin, but it never healed fully. Though often cited for bravery in the next few years, he was forced by the injury to retire from active service on March 15, 1916.

Byrd intended to go into the field of aeronautic exploration, but the United States was drifting into World War I and the navy needed instructors. After working as an inspector and instructor with the Rhode Island militia, he was given a command for a brief time. Then, when America declared war on Germany in 1917, Byrd took a desk job with the navy's Commission on Training Camps. Eager to see action, he soon convinced naval authorities to let him train as a pilot. He quickly showed his aptitude and was made an instructor at Pensacola, Florida.

When the NC-1, a flying boat, was under construction, Byrd developed its navigation system, using a drift indicator and inventing the Byrd Artificial Horizon Sextant (a navigational device that was still being used by the navy during World War II). On August 10, 1917, he went to Nova Scotia as a lieutenant commander to prepare a base for transatlantic flight for the NC-1, but the war ended before his work was completed.

For the next five years Byrd worked as a naval lobbyist in Congress, succeeding in getting a Department of Aeronautics set up under navy control. During this period, he barely escaped death aboard a **dirigible** that exploded outside London in 1921. His place on board had been given to someone else when his train arrived late on the day of the flight.

In 1925 Byrd headed the aeronautics division of a major Arctic expedition led by DONALD MAC MILLAN to northern Greenland. Despite only three days of flying, the trip did prove the suitability of planes for Arctic work. The next year he and FLOYD BENNETT flew to the North Pole from Svalbard in the trimotor Fokker *Josephine Ford*. They flew round-trip from Kings Bay on May 9, 1926, reaching the pole at 9:03 A.M. On the way to the pole, the plane's starboard engine developed an oil leak, and Bennett wanted to land to repair it. But Byrd wisely decided to keep going because of the hazards of landing on the rough ice. The two aviators were immensely relieved when the leak stopped on its own. Aside from the very real danger of mechanical failure in these early days of flight, there was the danger of running out of fuel in the event of a navigational error. This led the great Norwegian explorer ROALD AMUNDSEN, who was in Svalbard at the time of Byrd's flight preparing for his own Arctic flight aboard the dirigible *Norge*, to remark that "few more hazardous ventures have ever been undertaken in history."

Byrd next turned his attention to making the first transatlantic flight on a commercial-type aircraft, another Fokker trimotor. The *America* crashed on a test flight with Fokker himself at the controls, injuring everyone aboard (for once, Byrd's foot was spared, although Bennett's was crushed). Two months later, on June 29, the plane took off for Paris with a load of 15,000 pounds. Although Byrd's navigation was excellent, a malfunctioning steering compass caused

him to lose his bearings, and bad weather forced the plane to ditch in the ocean after it had successfully reached the continent. Having proved the feasibility of a transatlantic commercial flight, Byrd and his crew were given a hero's welcome in both Paris and New York.

Byrd then began preparations for the most massive assault on Antarctica yet launched. Close to a million dollars was spent in a privately sponsored expedition on the four ships, four planes, a wide variety of the most advanced photographic equipment, and supplies to support forty-two workers and ninety-four dogs in a small industrial village. In December 1928 the base, named Little America, was set up on the site of Amundsen's 1911 camp, at the Bay of Whales on the Ross Ice Shelf. From this spot several expeditions spread out to explore by plane and by sledge, but Byrd's main mission, the flight to the South Pole, took place on November 28 and 29, 1929, with the Norwegian-American explorer Bernt Balchen as pilot. Byrd's great fear was that the plane would not be able to rise high enough to make it over the "hump" in the Antarctic plateau that was

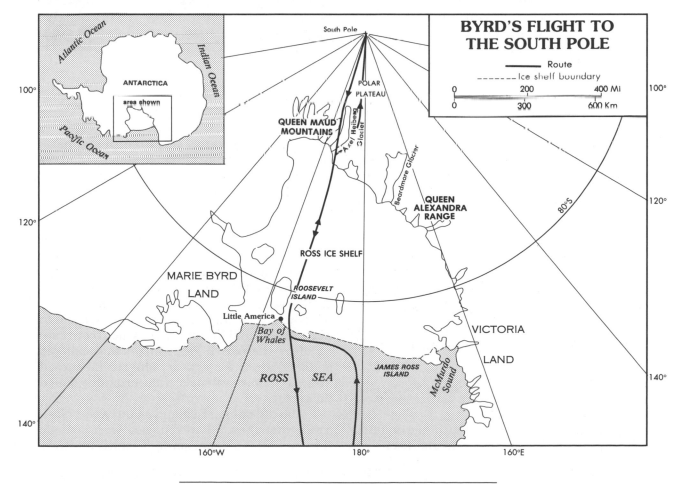

previously identified by Amundsen, but after some cargo was jettisoned the *Floyd Bennett* ascended to 10,500 feet and cleared the mountain pass.

When Byrd returned to the United States, the Great Depression was under way, and it was difficult to procure funds for a second trip. But with some economizing, a new fleet was prepared for his 1933–35 expedition, again, privately funded. This undertaking covered even more ground and recorded a great quantity of scientific data, but it was almost fatal for Byrd. Manning a scientific station alone during the winter of 1934, 125 miles from base camp, Byrd was overcome by carbon monoxide from a leaking stovepipe on May 31. He did not ask to be rescued, but his incoherent radio dispatches made it clear that something was seriously amiss. Still, he could not be rescued until August 10. He described his experience in *Alone* (1938), a surprisingly somber self-portrayal of a man who came to realize that his reasons for taking on the solitary burden were a "delusion" and a "dead end." He admitted that individuals like himself were merely "glamorous middlemen between theory and fact. . . ." He had nearly killed himself collecting a "tiny heap of data" in his lonely outpost, but he had no idea what theoretical significance the information had. He was "a fool, lost on a fool's errand. . . ."

He nevertheless continued working in Antarctica, leading the first officially sponsored American expedition in 1939 and the U.S. Operation High Jump in 1946 (with thirteen ships and 4,000 crew members). He played a key role in Operation Deepfreeze in 1955 and in the U.S. program for the International Geophysical Year of 1957. When Byrd died in his sleep in 1957, a year after his last flight over the South Pole, the world mourned the loss of its last great exploring hero.

• Byron, John

English
b November 8, 1723; Newstead Abbey, Nottinghamshire
d April 10, 1786; London
Circumnavigated; explored South Pacific and Falkland Islands

Commodore John Byron led one of the first British expeditions of discovery in the Pacific. In

John Byron. National Maritime Museum, Greenwich.

the course of his career he also explored parts of Patagonia, although unintentionally, and set a long-standing record for the fastest circumnavigation of the world.

Born November 8, 1723, at Newstead Abbey, John Byron was the second son of the fourth Baron Byron. He joined the navy as a youth and at seventeen served as a midshipman under GEORGE ANSON aboard the *Wager*, one of six ships on an expedition to raid Spanish settlements on the west coast of South America. In 1741 the *Wager* was shipwrecked on the Patagonian coast. Byron and his fellow crewmen were captured by the native Patagonians and suffered at their hands for a year, only to be turned over to Spanish officials, who promptly jailed them.

Byron did not see England again until 1745— a year after Anson had returned with a single ship and a king's ransom in Spanish treasure.

Upon his return, Byron published an account of his harrowing experience. Still, the trauma did not keep him from returning to the sea. In 1758 he distinguished himself in naval battles against France and was made commodore.

In the mid-eighteenth century both Britain and France looked to the sea as a source of prestige—as well as of new territories and new wealth. These lands were intended to provide both trade opportunities and strategic navigational way stations. Byron was put in command of an expedition to find and claim new lands in the South Atlantic between Africa's Cape of Good Hope and the South American Strait of Magellan. The elusive Pepys Island, a large and fertile landmass rumored to lie in the South Atlantic, was among his targets. Afterward, he was to explore the area of the California coast that Sir FRANCIS DRAKE had named New Albion in 1579 and to seek a Northwest Passage through Canada (for a more complete discussion of the passage, see MARTIN FROBISHER). A £20,000 prize awaited its successful discoverer.

On June 21, 1764, Byron left Plymouth Downs aboard the *Dolphin*, one of the first copper-sheathed **frigates**, along with the **sloop** *Tamar*. The crew was told that the expedition was headed to the East Indies. Only after the ships reached Rio de Janeiro did Byron tell them the truth, promising them double pay if they would stay on. The crew continued down the South American coast, staying at Port Desire in Patagonia for two weeks before heading south.

Pepys Island eluded him, but in early 1765 Byron reached the Falkland Islands and claimed them for England. Unknown to him, a French ship he had seen earlier in the Strait of Magellan had been that of the explorer LOUIS-ANTOINE DE BOUGAINVILLE, who had himself just established a French colony in the Falklands.

Entering the Pacific in April 1765, Byron tried to anchor at the Tuamotus, east of the Society Islands. When he could not, he named two of them the Disappointment Islands. He also named the islands now known as Takaroa and Takapoto for King George and named what is now Niukunau in the Gilbert Islands (present-day Kiribati) after himself. He then ignored his instructions. He did not attempt to explore the California coast; moreover, instead of sailing north to seek a Northwest Passage between the Atlantic and the Pacific as he was directed, Byron continued sailing west and reached Batavia (present-day Jakarta, Indonesia) in November 1765. Perhaps worried about the condition of his experimental copper-sheathed vessel, he sped toward Cape Town, South Africa, reaching it only three months later. On May 9, 1766, Byron and his crew returned to The Downs, England, having set a record for the fastest circumnavigation—less than two years. Unfortunately, that had not been his assignment, and his expedition was considered a failure.

The year following his return, Byron published his account of the voyage, and in 1769 he was named governor of Newfoundland. That was not the end of his naval career, however. In 1775, with trouble brewing in the North American colonies, Byron achieved the rank of rear admiral and three years later was promoted to vice admiral. In 1778, during the American Revolution, he took his fleet to the Americas to monitor the coastal movements of the French admiral Jean Baptiste Charles Henri Hector d'Estaing.

Byron often was plagued by foul weather at sea. In 1779, while conveying an army of reinforcements to help quiet the American rebellion, he encountered some of the worst storms ever recorded at sea. The incident earned him the nickname "Foul Weather Jack," and it may have been about him that his grandson, George Gordon Lord Byron, wrote in *Epistle to Augusta*:

A strange doom is the father's son's and past
Recalling as it lies beyond redress
Reversed for him our grandsire's fate of yore,
He had no rest at sea, nor I on shore.

Byron's adventures also inspired many episodes in his grandson's most famous work, *Don Juan*.

"Foul Weather Jack" was made commander in chief in the West Indies. In July 1779, the last campaign of his career was the indecisive Battle of Grenada, in which he faced the French admiral d'Estaing in the southern Windward Islands. Afterward he returned to England and retired. Byron died in London on April 10, 1786.

• Cabeza de Vaca, Álvar Núñez

Spanish
b 1490?; Jerez, Andalusia
d 1556; Seville?
Explored American Southwest and northern Mexico

Álvar Núñez Cabeza de Vaca's achievements as an explorer were unintended but far-reaching. As treasurer of an expedition commanded by PÁNFILO DE NARVÁEZ, he landed in Tampa Bay (in what is now Florida) in April 1528 with some 300 soldiers commissioned by the king of Spain to explore and conquer the unknown lands between Florida and Mexico. But poor planning, shipwreck, and savage fighting with the Indians turned the expedition into a rout. Narváez and his men were not heard of until eight years later when, in 1536, Cabeza de Vaca and three companions walked out of the deserts of northern Mexico, thus becoming the first Europeans to cross the North American continent from the Gulf of Mexico to the Gulf of California. (For a map of their route, see HERNANDO DE SOTO.) They were the only survivors of that unlucky band of would-be **conquistadores**. Their joint report and Cabeza de Vaca's personal account of his travels among the Indian tribes of the American Southwest proved the existence of a massive continent to the north of New Spain and inspired FRANCISCO VÁSQUEZ DE CORONADO, Hernando de Soto, and others to explore a land that had hitherto been known to Europe only in myth.

The details of Cabeza de Vaca's early life are sketchy. One of four children whose parents were both from distinguished military families, he followed the family calling as a young man. In 1511 he joined a military expedition sent by King Ferdinand II of Spain to aid Pope Julius II in the papacy's struggle against the French in Italy. Surviving the bloody defeat of the pope's allies at the Battle of Ravenna on April 11, 1512, he returned to Spain the following year. In 1520, Cabeza de Vaca fought under the duke of Medina Sidonia in a campaign to crush a rebellion in Seville. Later he fought against the French at Navarra. At some point he married, but his wife's name is not known. There is no record of their having children. Aside from these few details, the story of his early life has been lost to history.

Cabeza de Vaca was given a prominent post in the Narváez expedition, which sailed from Sanlúcar, Spain, on June 27, 1527, with five ships and about 600 men. Problems began almost as soon as the expedition arrived in the New World. At Santo Domingo (in the present-day Dominican Republic) about 140 men deserted, lured away by prospects of an easier life on the island. Narváez recruited more soldiers in Cuba, then sailed to Vera Cruz (in east-

ern Mexico). Meanwhile, Cabeza de Vaca, in command of two ships, was sent to Trinidad for more provisions. He was ashore with about thirty men when a hurricane struck; it wrecked both ships and drowned the sixty crew members left aboard. A few days later Narváez arrived as planned previously and picked up the survivors. In November the expedition sought winter refuge in the Spanish settlements along the Gulf of Mexico.

By the spring of 1528, Narváez had purchased two more vessels and set sail with a force that now numbered some 400 men. They sighted Florida on April 12. Two days later they landed on the shores of Tampa Bay and took formal possession of the land claimed earlier for Spain by JUAN PONCE DE LEÓN.

Provisions were already low, but the local Indians told them they would find food and much gold in a city called Apalachen in the north. At this point Narváez made a fatal error. Taking some 300 men, he set out for the city by foot, ordering his fleet to follow the unknown coastline to the north, where they were to rendezvous.

Hungry and harassed by hostile Indians, the soldiers trudged to Apalachen, near the present-day city of Tallahassee, where they found golden corn to eat but little else. The Spaniards moved on toward present-day St. Andrew Bay (near Panama City, Florida), looking for food and waiting for the ships, which never appeared. After searching for Narváez and his men for nearly a year, the ships had sailed back to New Spain.

As casualties to hunger, disease, and Indian arrows mounted, Narváez decided to build barges and head across the Gulf of Mexico to the Spanish settlement at Pánuco, north of Vera Cruz. It was approximately 600 miles away, much further than he realized. On September 22, at Bahia de Caballos, the Spaniards slaughtered and ate the last of their horses, then sailed west in five barges, hugging the coast. But the barges were barely seaworthy and were difficult to control. Narváez ordered each of the five crews to fend for itself, and they eventually drifted apart. Cabeza de Vaca later learned the fates of the various barges from Indians of the region. One barge, its crew weakened by hunger and thirst, put ashore and was attacked by Indians. Too weak to resist, all aboard were massacred. Another barge was stranded, and all aboard eventually starved to death. A third barge, commanded by Narváez, disappeared at sea.

The barge carrying Cabeza de Vaca was wrecked on present-day Galveston Island, Texas, in November 1528, not far from the only other remaining barge. There were now only about 90 men left of the original 300. The Spaniards were at first received hospitably by the Indians. But food was scarce, and in the unusually fierce winter that followed many Spaniards and Indians alike died from famine, disease, and the cold. Cabeza de Vaca fell ill. In the spring of 1529, when most of the other survivors left the region, he was too weak to travel and remained behind.

For the next five years Cabeza de Vaca lived among the Indians, first in semi-captivity and later as a wandering peddler, trading with various tribes along Galveston Bay and in the Texas interior. Many Indians believed that foreigners were great medicine men, and Cabeza de Vaca was said to have an amazing power to heal the sick, which may explain why the Indians allowed him to roam freely.

In the winter of 1534–35, at a place on the Colorado River of Texas, Cabeza de Vaca chanced upon the expedition's three other survi-

Cabeza de Vaca and companions bartering with Indians (undated engraving). The Bettmann Archive.

vors. Alonso Castillo Maldonado, Andres Dorantes, and the latter's Moorish slave Estéban (or Estebanico) were the last survivors of a group that had left Galveston Bay on foot in 1529 to follow the Gulf coast back to New Spain. The four men now resolved to try to get home again, this time by heading inland. Scholars differ on their exact route, but the four began their trek in August 1535 from a place near modern San Antonio, Texas, where the Indians gathered to harvest a type of prickly-pear cactus. Accompanied by Indian guides, they moved west without trouble, perhaps due to their reputation as great medicine men. From Texas they crossed into New Mexico and possibly into Arizona, then headed south through the Mexican province of Sonora toward the Gulf of California.

In the spring of 1536 the four, accompanied by a large party of Indians, encountered an amazed band of Spanish soldiers sent north on a slave-raiding expedition by Nuno de Guzmán, governor of the province of New Galicia. The soldiers wanted to enslave Cabeza de Vaca's Indian escort, but he objected so strongly that they desisted. (Indeed, his official complaints against the illegal trade in Indian slaves would later contribute to Guzmán's arrest for abuse of office.)

In July, Cabeza de Vaca and his companions reached Mexico City, where they were hailed as heroes. The three Spanish survivors submitted an account of their adventures, called the Joint Report, before Cabeza de Vaca left for Spain in 1537. His own account, published in 1542 under the title *Los Naufragios* (*The Shipwrecks*), is a more personal story of his years in the wilderness.

Back in Spain, Hernando de Soto asked Cabeza de Vaca to join an expedition to conquer Florida. He declined. But he had not completely lost his taste for adventure. In 1540 he accepted a post in Asunción (in present-day Paraguay) as governor of the Spanish settlements on the Río de la Plata. But just to get there he had to undertake a difficult four-month overland journey from Brazil, during which he probably became the first European to see Iguaçu Falls. Nearly 300 Spaniards plus an unknown number of Indians took part in this expedition. Only one person died, a remarkable achievement for the time and terrain.

The Paraguay post was to be his undoing.

In 1542 he organized and led an expeditionary party of 1,200 in a journey up the Paraguay River in search of gold, but thick forests forced him to return to Asunción. When he got there, he was deposed by his lieutenant governor and placed under arrest. The reasons for the coup are not clear. He may have clashed with subordinates, in part because he advocated a more humane policy toward the Indians. In 1545 he returned to Spain under arrest, charged with attempting to usurp royal authority. The case dragged on for six years. In the end he was found guilty and sentenced to banishment in Africa for eight years. But the crown intervened, allowed him to remain in Spain, and awarded him a pension. Little is known about his last years, which may have been spent in poverty. He died in 1556, probably in Seville.

John Cabot. Mary Evans Picture Library/Photo Researchers, Inc.

• Cabot (Gaboto; Caboto), John (Giovanni)

Italian
b 1450?; Genoa?
d 1499?
Made first North American landfall after the Norse (for England)

Having tried unsuccessfully to interest Spain and Portugal in supporting a transatlantic crossing, the Italian mariner John Cabot took his ideas to England, where they were well received. With the encouragement of King Henry VII, Cabot made two voyages of discovery to North America. Since neither he nor any of his crew kept a journal, the exact location of his first landfall in 1497 is not known for certain. In all probability, he reached some part of present-day Labrador, Newfoundland, or Nova Scotia, believing that he had landed on the northwest coast of China. Much confusion also surrounds his second voyage in 1498, with some sources claiming Cabot and his ships were lost at sea and others asserting that he completed a voyage down the coast of North America only to vanish into obscurity after his return to England.

Like most of the details of his life, the birthdate and birthplace of John Cabot are not known. Letters about Cabot refer to him as a Genoese like CHRISTOPHER COLUMBUS, but official records in Genoa make no reference to a Caboto family. Records do show a John Cabot who became a citizen of Venice in 1476, and since the requirement for citizenship was fifteen years of residence in the city, it is generally assumed that he was in Venice by 1461 or earlier.

Much later, when he resided in England, Cabot claimed that he had previously engaged in the spice trade and had traveled as far east as Mecca to obtain spices for trade in Europe. (In the days before refrigeration, spices were not a luxury but an absolute necessity for improving the unpleasant taste of spoiled meat.) He further reported that "when he asked those who brought them what was the place of origin of these spices, they answered that they did not know, but that other caravans came with this merchandise to their homes from distant countries, and these again said that the goods had been brought to them from other remote regions." Combining the information that spices were passed westward from one caravan to the next with knowing that the earth was round, Cabot reasoned that spices must originate so far east as to be reachable traveling west. Thus, he figured, a voyage west across the Atlantic Ocean should bring him to the origin of the spices. There is evidence that he had read MARCO POLO's account of his travels and subscribed to Polo's theory that all the spices and jewels of the world came from Cipangu (present-day Japan).

Whether Cabot developed the idea of sailing west in search of the Orient independently of Columbus is uncertain. There is some evidence that he was in Valencia, Spain, between 1490 and 1493 and thus could have witnessed Columbus's triumphant return from his first voyage to the Caribbean. In any case, Cabot added a new wrinkle to Columbus's ideas by suggesting that the voyage across the Atlantic Ocean could be made shorter by sailing at a more northerly latitude. (Since the earth's greatest circumference is at the equator, the farther north or south of the equator one gets, the smaller is the distance around the earth.)

Cabot took his idea about a shorter route to the Orient to both the Spanish and Portuguese courts, but neither chose to support him in a voyage of exploration. So the navigator moved his family to England. It had occurred to him that England—being at the very end of the spice route and therefore paying the highest prices for spices—would be most interested in a shorter route to the Indies that would reduce the cost of bringing spices to the tables of England.

Cabot chose to settle in the thriving port of Bristol on the west coast of England. It was a good choice for one seeking a shorter route to the land of spices. Some forty years earlier, a Robert Stormy, in an attempt to bypass the commercial middlemen of the trade, had sent two ships to the eastern Mediterranean to bring back spices. One was wrecked, and the other was destroyed by Genoese mariners who did not appreciate the attempt to deprive them of their customary middleman's profits. Thus Bristol had already evidenced an interest in acquiring spices more cheaply.

Well-to-do Bristol merchants would also be interested in a westward voyage because of their desire to develop new fishing grounds. For many years they had pursued this goal by searching for a legendary island called Hy-Brasil. Though no one had yet discovered such an island, it was shown on maps as being west of Ireland. Bristol sailors had more than once sought its allegedly rich fishing waters, and, according to reports, sometime prior to 1494 had reached a mainland, which may have been North America. Thus, in Bristol Cabot could hope to find not only interest in westward exploration but also the financial incentive for its support.

Nothing could happen, though, without the approval of the king. So Cabot presented his ideas to King Henry VII, who, eager to profit from new lands to the west as rival Spain was already doing, was more than receptive. On March 5, 1496, he granted John Cabot and his three sons letters patent, containing permission to sail under the flag of England to "discover and find whatsoever isles, countries, regions or provinces of heathens and infidels, in whatsoever part of the world they be, which before this time were unknown to Christians." Moreover, Cabot was empowered to govern such lands as the king's lieutenant, to "monopolize their produce," and to import it duty-free to England, with one-fifth of the proceeds going to the king. With the king's blessing, the Bristol merchants would finance the voyage.

Although Cabot was authorized to sail with five ships, he was able to obtain and find a crew for only one. Called the *Matthew*, it was about the same size as the *Niña*, Columbus's smallest ship. On May 20, 1497, John Cabot, probably accompanied by his son SEBASTIAN CABOT and with eighteen to twenty sailors, sailed west from Bristol. Two days later they departed Dursey Head, on the west coast of Ireland, and within thirty-three days had reached landfall in North America. (Although Cabot had traveled a much shorter distance than Columbus, his voyage took about the same amount of time because the winds in the northern latitudes were not as favorable as those Columbus had encountered.)

Cabot's method of navigation was known as latitude sailing; that is, he chose to sail at a specified latitude and maintained his course not only by keeping track of the North Star but also by using such instruments as a compass and **quadrant**, which would help him find the correct latitude if he were blown off course.

Though there is no way of telling exactly where in North America Cabot landed, a convincing case has been made for the northern peninsula of what is now Newfoundland, and specifically for modern Griquet Harbor, which has a latitude of 51°33' North—the same as Dursey Head, Ireland. Supporting this theory is the fact that Cabot reported a large island about 15 miles to the north of his landfall, which would correspond to modern-day Belle Isle. If Griquet Harbor was indeed Cabot's landfall, there is no small irony in the fact that it is located only about 5 miles as the crow flies

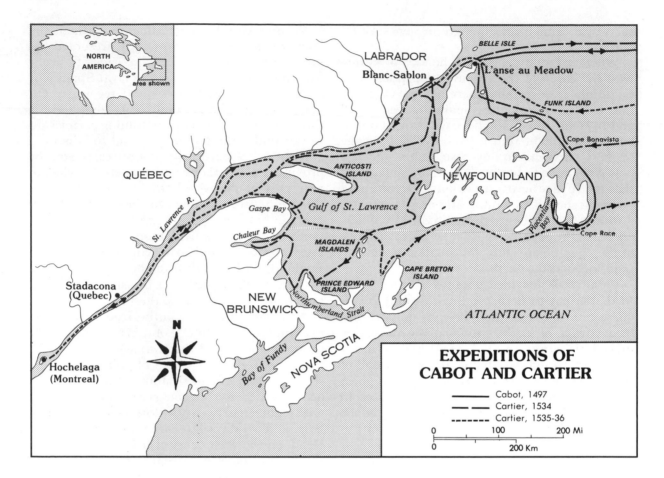

from present-day L'Anse au Meadow, thought by some historians to be the site of LEIF ERIKSON's Vinland almost 500 years earlier.

The most serious drawback to positively identifying Griquet Harbor as Cabot's landfall is that none of the secondhand reports of the voyage mentions ice or fog, which Cabot most surely would have encountered in northern Newfoundland in June. For this reason some historians have put his landfall further south, perhaps as far south as what is now Cape Breton Island, the northern part of Nova Scotia.

Though the exact spot Cabot landed remains a mystery, there is a fairly detailed description of the events attending landfall. After sighting land at 5 A.M., Cabot landed and formed a procession with his crew behind a ship's boy carrying a staff. Cabot took formal possession of the land for King Henry VII of England. They then raised the banners of Saint George (the patron saint of England) and Saint Mark (the patron saint of Venice).

Cabot and his men saw no people where they landed but they did see signs of life—snares, fishing nets, and a red stick with holes at both ends, which was probably a tool used for weaving the nets. A few years later, in 1501, Beothuk Indians kidnapped from the region by the Portuguese explorer Gaspar Corte Real had in their possession a broken gilt sword of Italian design and silver earrings made in Venice, which may have been left behind by Cabot's expedition.

For reasons not completely understood today, this landing was the only one made by Cabot and his men. Cabot himself said that he dared not let his men go further from the ship than the distance a crossbow could be shot because of the possibility of hostile native inhabitants. At least one historian has speculated that the Cabot party may have also been dissuaded from further land explorations by the vicious mosquitoes that plague Newfoundland at that time of year. For whatever reason, Cabot chose to spend the rest of his time sailing along the coast and observing the land from the relative safety of his ship.

Where Cabot and crew went is open to speculation. Historians who believe Cabot and his crew made landfall in northern Newfoundland surmise that they sailed down the east coast of Newfoundland and around what is now Cape Race, perhaps as far as present-day Placentia Bay, before turning around and sailing back to their first landfall, from which they headed east to England. Those who think Cabot landed further south than Newfoundland—whether it be Maine, Cape Breton Island, or southern Newfoundland—assume that he sailed north before turning east to retrace his way across the Atlantic.

Wherever they were, Cabot noted that fish were so plentiful that the sailors could let down weighted buckets and draw them up full of codfish. On the shore they observed tall trees that would make excellent masts, and what appeared to be cultivated fields, which may have been blueberry and other bushes. At one point they also saw two figures, one chasing the other, but whether the forms were human or animal, they could not tell.

Convinced that he had reached the northern shores of Asia—"the land of the Great Khan"—Cabot was ready to sail back to England to plan a larger expedition. After an easy fifteen-day crossing, the ship found itself off the coast of Brittany, France, and turned north to enter Bristol harbor in triumph on August 6.

Taking a map and a globe of his own making, Cabot lost no time in heading for London to inform the king of his accomplishments and future plans. Though Cabot had brought back neither spices nor jewels, he did bring the welcome news about the fishing prospects, as well as the false claim that the new land produced brazilwood and silk. Henry, generous with words but niggardly with money, was elated and immediately rewarded the explorer with a paltry ten pounds from the royal treasury and a yearly income of twenty pounds to be drawn from Bristol customs. A letter by a contemporary reports: "[Cabot] is called the Great Admiral and vast honour is paid to him and he goes dressed in silk, and these English run after him like mad."

Though Cabot was certain that he had landed on the northern coast of Asia, he also believed that the main part of his discovery was an island. (Avalon, the southeast peninsula of modern Newfoundland, could easily have appeared to be an island.) Thus, the king immediately dubbed the discovery New Isle, though by 1502 he was calling it "the newe founde lande," the name that has endured.

On Cabot's next trip, he planned to sail further southwest looking for Cipangu and its spices and jewels. Accordingly, on February 3, 1498, King Henry granted Cabot new letters patent for a second voyage. He was given permission to impress six English ships and enlist any English sailor who was willing to make the voyage. The king himself funded one ship, and the merchants of Bristol provided four more. The five set sail from Bristol early in May 1498.

What happened next is still a mystery. One source (Eden's *Treatyse of the Newe India*) says that the expedition sailed up the west coast of Greenland until it was stopped by huge icebergs; that Cabot then sailed south along the coast of Baffin Island, Labrador, Newfoundland, Nova Scotia, New England, and as far as Chesapeake Bay before provisions ran low; and that he had to return home empty-handed without having found the spices and jewels of Cipangu. Other historians speculate that this account has confused Cabot's second voyage with a voyage made much later by his son Sebastian when it had become clear that North America was not Asia and Sebastian was actually searching for the Northwest Passage to the Orient (for a more complete discussion of the passage, see MARTIN FROBISHER). Those who do not accept this account of John Cabot's second voyage maintain that after one ship had to turn back for unspecified reasons, the other four were never heard from again.

Whichever account is true, it is certain that Michaelmas (September 29) of 1498 was the last time Cabot's pension was collected from Bristol customs (whether by himself or by his wife is not clear) and that John Cabot drops out of sight of history that year. In part, he fell victim to the ego of his own son. Indeed, so effective was Sebastian (an explorer in his own right) at claiming his father's accomplishments as his own that it wasn't until the nineteenth century that history finally came to recognize John Cabot as the skilled navigator who undertook England's first voyage of exploration across the Atlantic.

Contemporary opinions of John Cabot mention that he was a most excellent mariner and a maker of maps and globes. Though he left no personal record of his voyages, the little that is known of him suggests a skillful navigator and a cautious explorer who would not unduly risk the lives of the small crew in his care. Though he believed to the end that he had discovered a water route to Asia, John Cabot had, in fact, discovered something far more valuable. His idea of crossing the Atlantic at a more northerly latitude than the route used by Columbus had not only given the English fertile new fishing grounds that forever ended their dependence on Iceland's dried fish, but even more significantly gave them their entrance and title to the large piece of North America that they eventually claimed.

SUGGESTED READING: Raymond Beazley, *John and Sebastian Cabot* (Burt Franklin, 1964); Editors of *American Heritage, Discoverers of the New World* (American Heritage, 1960); Henry Kurtz, *John and Sebastian Cabot* (Franklin Watts, 1973); Samuel Eliot Morison, *The European Discovery of America: The Northern Voyages* (Oxford University Press, 1971); Charles Norman, *Discoverers of America* (Crowell, 1968); Tee Loftin Snell, *The Wild Shores: America's Beginnings* (National Geographic, 1974); James A. Williamson, *The Cabot Voyages and Bristol Discovery Under Henry VII* (Hakluyt Society, 1962).

Sebastian Cabot. City of Bristol Museum.

Cabot, Sebastian (Gaboto, Sebastiano)

Italian
b 1476?; Venice
d 1557; London, England
Explored Río de la Plata (for Spain); reached mouth of Hudson Bay (for England)

One of the most accomplished cartographers of his time, Sebastian Cabot was the first explorer to search for the Northwest Passage to the Orient (for a more complete discussion of the passage, see MARTIN FROBISHER). On his English-sponsored expedition (1508–1509) he explored the coast of Labrador (previously discovered by his father, JOHN CABOT) and reached Hudson Bay. He subsequently organized three voyages for the purpose of finding a Northeast Passage to the Orient, one of which led to the development of trade between England and Russia. Cabot's most celebrated expedition, however, was under the auspices of Spain and led to a three-year exploration of the Río de la Plata, the Paraná River, and part of the Paraguay River (1526–29).

Born in Venice, Italy, about 1476, Sebastian Cabot was the son of the renowned navigator and explorer John Cabot. Little is known of his early life before the family moved to Bristol, England, sometime between 1490 and 1495. He most probably gained his knowledge of navigation, cartography, and **cosmography** from his father. He was nothing like his amiable father as a person, however. Vain and egotistical, Sebastian Cabot was prone to self-aggrandizement, even to the point of claiming some of his father's accomplishments as his own.

Questions exist as to whether Cabot went with his father on any expeditions, but he and his brothers are included by name in a license issued to John Cabot by King Henry VII in March 1496 to make a voyage of discovery across the Atlantic for England. It is likely, therefore, that he accompanied his father on the resultant 1497 expedition, the first journey across the North Atlantic since the voyages of the Vikings. On this voyage the Cabots sailed along the coast of Labrador, discovered Nova Scotia, and landed on Cape Breton Island (all in present-day eastern Canada).

Some disagreement also exists concerning the number of expeditions that Sebastian Cabot led himself, as well as the extent of his explorations. However, several historians list as his first voyage the expedition (1508–1509) to find a Northwest Passage to the Orient. Crossing the North Atlantic on a commission from the English Crown, he sailed northward along the coasts of Labrador and Newfoundland and through the Hudson Strait (between present-day Quebec and Baffin Island). When he reached the entrance to what is now Hudson Bay, Cabot mistakenly thought he had found a water passage leading to the Orient. The expedition may have penetrated as far north as Foxe Channel (between present-day Baffin Island and the Northwest Territories) before encountering dangerous chunks of floating ice and turning for home.

From 1509 to 1512 Cabot served as royal cartographer to the new English king, Henry VIII, and accompanied English forces in 1512 when they assisted Ferdinand of Aragon in his fight with France. Since Henry VIII was not as interested in exploration as was his predecessor, Cabot offered his services to the king of Spain. He spent most of the next thirty-five years in Spain, first as royal cartographer to King Ferdinand of Aragon, then as pilot major (from 1518) and member of the Spanish **Council of the Indies** under Holy Roman Emperor Charles V (King Charles I of Spain).

In 1526 Cabot was commissioned by the emperor to lead an expedition to seek the legendary lands of Tarshish, Ophir, and Cathay and "to barter and load his ships with gold, silver, [and] precious stones. . . ." Additional purposes of the voyage were to prove Cabot's theory that there was a shorter route to the Orient than that found by FERDINAND MAGELLAN, and to map the South American coast in more detail. The expedition left Sanlúcar de Barrameda, Spain, on April 3, 1526, with four ships and about 200 men. From the Cape Verde Islands Cabot followed a course toward Brazil, reaching the present-day port city of Recife on September 29, 1526. There he first heard stories of the "White King," a man who dressed like Europeans and ruled a kingdom of great wealth, including a mountain of silver. Sailing south along the coast of Brazil, Cabot landed on an island just north

of present-day Florianópolis, which he named Ilha de Santa Catarina in honor of his wife. Farther south, near present-day Lagoa dos Patos, he picked up two castaways from Alexio Garcia's ill-fated expedition. The castaways also claimed the existence of a rich civilization ruled by a white king, located somewhere north of present-day Paraguay. Motivated by the prospect of discovering great wealth, Cabot deviated from his original objectives in order to search for the land of the white king. When several of his officers objected, he simply marooned them.

Sailing farther south, he entered an estuary between present-day Uruguay and Argentina on February 21, 1527, and penetrated the interior of Argentina along a large river which he named the Río de la Plata (Silver River), after the silver pieces acquired from Indians along its shores. He mistakenly thought this silver was from a nearby source, although it had actually come from the great Inca civilization in Peru. Cabot next sailed up the Paraná River (in Argentina) to fifty miles above its confluence with the Paraguay River. On March 31, 1528, he began exploration of the Paraguay, reaching a point near what is now Asunción before he was forced to turn back due to food shortages and hostile Indian attacks.

Upon returning to the fort he had previously built on the Rio Carcarañá (a tributary of the Río de la Plata in Argentina), he heard from the Querandi Indians the legend of the "Enchanted City of the Caesars." According to this legend (which had many variations), the city was part of a wealthy, advanced, and idyllic civilization and was thought to exist somewhere in South America (most commonly it was held to be in Argentina or the Peruvian Andes). Cabot sent out an unsuccessful expedition in search of this city; he then encountered another explorer, Diego Garcia, and they joined forces to search for the legendary "White King." After several hostile Indian attacks, they retreated without reaching their goal. Finding that the fort had been destroyed and many members of its garrison cannibalized, and having nothing left to eat but seal meat, Cabot decided to return to Spain in November 1529.

When Cabot reached Spain in 1530 without the treasure from the Orient he was stripped of his rank and banished to Africa for two years for disobeying his original orders. Little is known of his life between 1533 and 1547, except that his rank as pilot major was restored at some point.

In 1547 Cabot returned to England at the invitation of King Edward VI and became a founder of the Company of Merchant Adventurers (the Muscovy Company), which was granted the right to discover and possess lands to the northeast, north, and northwest of England. As governor of the company from 1553 onward, Cabot organized three expeditions to find a Northeast Passage to the Orient. Though all three of the expeditions were unsuccessful in finding such a passage, one of them, RICHARD CHANCELLOR's expedition of 1553, discovered the White Sea in northern Russia and proceeded overland to Moscow. There Chancellor negotiated a favorable trade agreement between England and Russia.

Though Sebastian Cabot never achieved his major goal—to find a sea route to India in the Northern Hemisphere—he had become a major influence on the next generation of seamen by the time he died in London in 1557. His explorations of the Canadian coast and the interior of South America provided the stimulus for more comprehensive journeys; and his stories of the "White King" and the "Enchanted City of the Caesars" fired the imaginations of countless explorers up until the nineteenth century, inspiring them to risk everything to find the sources of these legends. His great map of the world, the *mappe-monde*, was a landmark in cartography and can be seen today at the Bibliotèque Nationale in Paris.

Caboto, Giovanni. See **Cabot, John.**

Caboto, Sebastiano. See **Cabot, Sebastian.**

• Cabral, Pedro Álvares

Portuguese
b 1467?; Belmonte, Castelo Branco
d 1520?; Santarém
Discovered Brazil

While leading a commercial expedition to India, Pedro Álvares Cabral discovered Brazil in 1500. Cabral was not on his plotted course for India, so it is still unknown for sure whether the discovery was accidental or intentional. Also somewhat debatable is whether Cabral was the first European to discover Brazil, but in the eyes of most historians he gets credit for the discovery because he found land that had not been discovered before. Cabral was also instrumental in setting up treaties to trade with the East after his commercial excursion to India got back on track.

Born on the family estate in Belmonte, Portugal, about 1467, Cabral grew up surrounded by wealth and power. His noble family was influential at the Portuguese court, and he served as a page to King John II. Little else is known of his life prior to 1499, except that he served in the council of King Manuel I and became a knight of the Order of Christ.

In 1499 Cabral was appointed chief captain of a fleet bound for the Malabar Coast of southern India to establish trading posts there. He set sail from the Tagus River in Lisbon on March 9, 1500, with thirteen ships and 1,000 men. Serving as one of Cabral's commanders on the voyage was BARTOLOMEU DIAS, the discoverer of the southern end of Africa. However, Cabral did not follow the west African coast as Dias had done but instead chose to follow the route to the East first charted by VASCO DA GAMA from 1497 to 1499.

After sighting the Canary Islands on March 18, and passing the Cape Verde Islands on March 22, Cabral headed south, switching then to a southwest direction to take advantage of the **trade winds**. When he reached the latitude of the Cape of Good Hope, he headed due east to approach the Cape. Wind and current pushed him farther west, however, and on April 22, 1500, land was sighted at 17° South latitude. The land sighted was the now-famous Mount Pascal in Brazil (some 200 miles south of the present-day city of Salvador). A ship was dispatched to Lisbon to report the discovery.

Cabral claimed the land for Portugal and named it Terra da Vera Cruz (Land of the True or Holy Cross) because it was discovered at Easter time and because the banner of the Order of Christ had a red cross on a white field. This name did not last, however, except in ecclesiastical writings. Once traders began cutting the brazilwood in this land for its red dye, they started calling the land Terra do Brazil. Thus, the name Brazil became popularly accepted.

Cabral explored about fifty miles of the Brazilian coast in about twelve days. He landed on an island in the inlet of Pôrto Seguro (present-day Baia Cabrália) just north of present-day Rio de Janeiro, planted a cross there, and celebrated mass. He encountered Indians, whom he described as "amiable and rustic" in a letter to King Manuel I. In the letter he also described the Indians' houses and commented on their use of decorative feathers.

Though no official log of Cabral's voyage exists, the letters he wrote to the king, as well as the eyewitness account of one of his crew, Pêro Vaz, contain some details of the exploration. One event they describe reveals Cabral's rather democratic approach to leadership. He asked the crew to vote on whether to send a ship to Lisbon with news of the discovery and whether to send Indians back to Portugal. The crew's decision was to dispatch the ship but not send the Indians.

While most historians believe that Cabral's discovery of Brazil was accidental, there are at least some who believe that he may have had secret orders to sail farther west purposely to determine if any land was at the extreme western part of the area given to Portugal under the **Treaty of Tordesillas**.

Cabral's right to claim Brazil as his discovery is also debatable as there were at least three other explorers with plausible claims. The expeditions of AMERIGO VESPUCCI, VICENTE YÁÑEZ PINZÓN, and Diego de Lepe sailed along the coastline of Brazil and made landfall prior to Cabral's voyage. However, these expeditions were primarily continuations of previous discoveries and explorations (primarily those of CHRISTOPHER COLUMBUS). Furthermore, they had only investigated the northern part of South America, reaching Brazil in the region of the Amazon River. Therefore, Cabral was the first to discover land where it was unexpected. Not everyone agrees that Cabral's claims are disputable: On the Cantion Chart of 1502 is recorded his discovery of Brazil, labeled "Terra da Vera Cruz" as he had named the land. And Brazilians today celebrate Cabral as the unquestionable and sole discoverer of their country.

As for Cabral, he appeared to be quite nonchalant about the discovery, spending very little time exploring the new land, preferring to get to India. Also, he was not sure whether this new land was a large land mass or simply an island, as indicated by one of his letters in which he refers to Brazil as "Ilha [island] da Vera Cruz" rather than Terra da Vera Cruz.

On May 2, 1500, Cabral's expedition resumed its voyage to the Cape of Good Hope. Disaster struck after three weeks at sea when four ships sank during a storm and the remaining ships were separated as they were buffeted around the Cape. After regrouping off Mozambique, the expedition reached Calicut on the Malabar Coast of India on September 13. Cabral set up a trading post, but the hostile Muslim population attacked the post, killing about fifty of the men garrisoned there. Cabral retaliated with a vengeance, burning Arab ships and punishing the entire town with an extended bombardment. Finally, he left Calicut and sailed down the Indian coast to Cochin and Cannanore, where he received a friendlier greeting. At these towns Cabral was successful in establishing trading posts and obtaining commercial treaties for Portugal.

Cabral returned to Lisbon in 1501, bringing back pearls, diamonds, porcelain, and the coveted spices of the East—pepper, ginger, cinnamon, and cloves, among others. The homecoming was not completely joyous, however, as there had been a tremendous loss of life, including that of Bartolomeu Dias, who had gone down with his ship off the Cape of Good Hope.

King Manuel I welcomed Cabral home, but the monarch and the explorer later seem to have disagreed because Vasco da Gama was chosen over Cabral to lead the next Indies expedition (1502–1503). Cabral left the court at this time and never returned. He married, had six children, and lived on his estate near Santarém on the Tagus River until his death in or about 1520.

Pedro Álvares Cabral is given much credit, not only for discovering Brazil but also for firmly establishing the sea route to India. He was the leader of the first successful commercial expedition to India and the first European to establish treaties to facilitate direct trade for the riches of the East. Today there are monuments in Rio de Janeiro and in Lisbon honoring him as the discoverer of Brazil, but in his own time he was recognized more for his trading ventures than for his discovery.

• Cabrillo, Juan Rodriguez (Cabrilho, João Rodrigues)

Portuguese
b 1498?
d January 3, 1543; San Miguel Island, California
Explored California and Central America (for Spain)

At the time of his death, Juan Rodriguez Cabrillo owned one of the richest estates in Central America and had been a soldier, sailor, shipbuilder, miner, explorer, and author at various times in his adventure-filled life. He not only explored the coast of California from 1542 to 1543 but also served under PÁNFILO DE NARVÁEZ during the exploration and conquest of Cuba (about 1518), aided HERNÁN CORTÉS in conquering the Aztec city of Tenochtitlán (present-day Mexico City) in 1521, and helped PEDRO DE ALVARADO explore and conquer present-day Honduras, Guatemala, and San Salvador (1523–35). Like most of the **conquistadores**, Cabrillo was motivated to explore the New World by the promise of great wealth—a promise fulfilled in the gold he found and mined in Cobán, Guatemala.

Cabrillo is a figure of some mystery; nothing certain is known of his parentage or the date and place of his birth. He was probably born around 1498, but no later than 1500, since he was reported to be in his early twenties when he left for Mexico in 1520. It is doubtful that he came from a noble family, but he earned the honor and privileges of an **encomendero** in both Cuba and Guatemala. Recently, some scholars have questioned Cabrillo's nationality, suggesting that he was Spanish and not a Portuguese in the service of Spain, as had been commonly accepted.

The first recorded information about Cabrillo concerns his military training in Cuba from 1510 to 1511. He distinguished himself as a soldier, crossbowman, and seaman during the conquest of Cuba and subsequently accompanied Narváez to Mexico when the latter was sent by the governor of Cuba to control the ambitious Cortés. After Narváez was defeated by Cortés, Cabrillo shifted his allegiance to the latter. Cabrillo directed the construction of thirteen **brigantines** for Cortés to use in mounting the final assault against the Aztec capital, Tenochtitlán. When the Aztecs were defeated on August 13, 1521, Cabrillo was wounded, but he recovered in time to accompany Francisco de Orozco on an expedition during which the city of Oaxaca was founded in late 1521.

In 1523 Cabrillo joined Pedro de Alvarado during his exploration and conquests throughout Central America. By 1532 Cabrillo was a registered citizen of Guatemala, living on an estate in Santiago with his Indian wife and children. Having acquired great wealth from gold mining, he went to Spain in 1532 to marry the sister of a friend. Upon his return in 1533, he was appointed an official of the port city of Iztapa, south of Santiago, and was commissioned to build an armada for Alvarado's planned expedition to the Moluccas (or Spice Islands). One of the ships he completed, the *San Salvador*, would later become the flagship for Cabrillo's California expedition.

In 1542 the viceroy of New Spain, Antonio de Mendoza, chose Cabrillo to lead an expedition along the Pacific coast by sea to the northern limits of New Spain to discover and claim new lands. Cabrillo departed from Navidad (present-day Acapulco) on June 27, 1542, with three ships and supplies to last two years. He sailed north, reaching Baja California by July 2. Although earlier expeditions had reached this point, Cabrillo made the first known European contact with the Indians of the area. By September 2 he found a sheltered bay further north that he named San Diego Bay after the smallest of his ships.

As the expedition proceeded north, every inlet and bay was explored and named. In October Cabrillo landed at Santa Barbara and traded with the friendly Chumash Indians. Sailing through the Santa Barbara Channel, he explored the group of islands off the coast, naming one San Salvador (present-day Santa Catalina) after his flagship and another Victoria (present-day San Clemente) after another of his ships.

Passing the entrance to San Francisco Bay, Cabrillo sailed up the coast some 50 more miles, reaching the Russian River before turning back to find a safe port in which to spend the winter. He did so on San Miguel Island in the Santa Barbara Channel. Here he broke his leg during an Indian attack and died from complications on January 3, 1543. Bartolomé Ferrera, named by Cabrillo as his successor, took the expedition as far as Oregon and returned to Mexico in April 1543.

Cabrillo's expedition marked the beginning of recorded history in California. His account of the journey (though not published until the nineteenth century) is the oldest written record of human activity on the west coast of the United States. Today he is remembered as the discoverer and explorer of the coast of California, and his name is found on schools, monuments, and roads throughout the state.

• Cadamosto, Alvise da (Ca' da Mosto, Alvise)

Italian
b 1432; Venice
d 1480?; Venice
Explored West African coast (for Portugal)

The Venetian Alvise da Cadamosto was among the first explorers to extend Europe's knowledge of the sea south beyond the shores of Spain and Portugal. Under the auspices of Portugal's famed Prince Henry the Navigator, Cadamosto explored the coastline of western Africa as far as modern-day Senegal and Gambia, and he may have discovered the Cape Verde Islands.

Born in 1432, as a young man Cadamosto left Italy for Flanders (a region that is now a part of Belgium and France) to join the sea trade and find wealth, knowledge, and fame. On August 8, 1454, he found himself aboard a **galley** bound for Flanders under the command of a fellow Venetian, Marco Zeno. When winds detained the ship off Portugal's Cape St. Vincent, Cadamosto had the opportunity to meet Prince Henry, who was in the nearby village of Reposeira. The great patron of exploration convinced Cadamosto to head a trading expedition for Portugal along the African coast.

Prince Henry outfitted Cadamosto in a ninety-ton **caravel**. In return, Cadamosto was to share half the profits of the voyage with the prince. The ship set sail on March 22, 1455, and within less than a week had touched at Madeira, where the Portuguese had established settlements and trading posts. Cadamosto then continued south to the Canary Islands, discovered earlier by JEAN DE BETHENCOURT. Although four of the islands had Christian settlements, the three largest were populated by indigenous people, called Canaries, who seemed to have no fixed religion. They wore goatskins or no clothing at all and painted their bodies with herbs.

For about a third of the journey from Cape Branco, south of the Canaries, to Arguin Island, where the Portuguese traded with Arabs, the caravel sailed out of sight of land, a daring feat at the time. Cadamosto continued along the African coast nearly 400 miles past Cape Branco to the Senegal River, which had been discovered earlier by Prince Henry's navigators. The Venetian spent about a month in the area in the company of Prince Budomel and his nephew Bisboror. At the marketplace Cadamosto marveled at the unfamiliar varieties of fruits, beans, herbs, and, especially, animal life. In addition to oxen, cows, and goats, Cadamosto saw lions, panthers, leopards, elephants, and exotic birds. In turn, he fascinated the Africans, who rubbed his hands with saliva to see if his "white paint" would come off. The Africans were equally amazed by the Europeans' "magic" bagpipes, although the cannons of the white men frightened them.

After leaving Senegal, Cadamosto's expedition joined with two other ships—another of Prince Henry's caravels and a ship under the Genoan Uso di Mare—to search for riches farther to the south. They found a river, the Joombas, some 60 miles below Cape Verde, but hostile native inhabitants prevented them from exploring it. When they reached the Gambia, they were able to travel upriver, but after one day the three boats were followed by canoes full of Africans in white garb with plumed headdresses and shields. Despite the Europeans' attempts to prove their peaceful intentions, a battle ensued. Although equipped with superior armaments, the Europeans tried merely to frighten the Africans rather than harm them.

The expedition returned to Portugal around 1456. Four years later, Cadamosto undertook another journey with di Mare. They set sail in three ships and went past the Canaries to Cape Branco and then on to the open sea, where a storm blew them off course for three days. On the third day they spotted two large and seemingly uninhabited islands, which they named Boavista and Santiago. These may have been the Cape Verde Islands, although some historians doubt that Cadamosto actually made this discovery.

Cadamosto and di Mare returned to the Gambia and sailed 10 miles upriver, where they encountered a group of Mandingos who offered to take the Europeans to meet Batti Mansa (King Batti). The travelers were received favorably by the king and traded goods for slaves and gold. They also traded for exotic animals, such as civet cats, baboons, and marmots, and for nuts, cotton, and ivory. The Mandingos gave Cadamosto an opportunity to try elephant meat, which he disliked, and showed him the "horsefish," or hippopotamus, as well as water serpents and large bats. After two weeks among the Mandingos, he traveled south for some 150 miles, passing Cape Roxo and exploring the mouths of five smaller rivers before returning to Portugal.

Of all those who sailed for Prince Henry, Alvise da Cadamosto was one of the most observant and articulate. His colorful account of his travels was published in Venice in 1507.

• Caillié (Caillé), René-Auguste

French
b November 19, 1799; Mauzé, Deux-Sèvres
d May 17, 1838; Mauzé, Deux-Sèvres
Explored Africa

René-Auguste Caillié was the first explorer to provide Europe with an eyewitness account of the land and people of Timbuktu. Long obsessed with seeing the legendary "Queen of the Desert," Caillié traveled thousands of miles across the Sudan and the Sahara despite bouts of severe illness and mounting hostility from native tribes. He made several attempts before gaining access to the forbidden city, and his return trip was as perilous as his entry. Although he was honored upon his return home, the French people grew increasingly scornful of his accounts of his journeys. Caillié died an embittered man before his information was validated by future exploration.

The son of a baker's assistant, Caillié was left on his own as a child after his mother died and his father went to prison. He left school to become an apprentice shoemaker, but he continued to read extensively and became fascinated by the tales of Africa, particularly of Timbuktu. At age sixteen, he left his village and took a job as a cabin boy on a ship headed for Africa. He arrived at Cape Verde (Africa's westernmost point) in July 1816 and deserted his ship to join an expedition up the Senegal River. He soon became gravely ill, however, and was sent back to France, where he remained for

René-Auguste Caillíe. Collection Viollet.

three years before attempting another trip. This second journey was also aborted by a serious illness, but a trip undertaken in 1824 would prove successful.

Caillié again began in Senegal but this time decided to prepare more intensively for his journey inland. He spent eight months living among the region's Arabic tribes, studying their dialects and customs, and then sought to raise money for his expedition. The French government denied his request, but a British colonial official gave him a job to help him finance his quest. A year later, in 1827, Caillié set out from Kakandé posing as an Egyptian Arab returning home by way of Timbuktu.

Fluent in the language and resembling the Arabs with his dark coloring, Caillié aroused little suspicion as he traveled to the upper Niger River with a small native caravan and crossed the previously uncharted mountains of Fouta Djallon. The difficult journey took a tremendous physical toll on him, however, and the pain of **scurvy** and fever immobilized him for days before he was able to continue. He reached Timbuktu in April 1828, almost exactly a year after his departure from Kakandé.

Caillié's elation at realizing his dream was tempered by two disappointing facts. Expecting to be the first European ever to see Timbuktu, he was disheartened to learn that ALEXANDER GORDON LAING had been in the city two years earlier (although the ill-fated Scottish explorer had been killed and never made it back to Europe). To Caillié's further chagrin, Timbuktu resembled neither the lively, affluent community recounted in Moorish history nor the lavish, exotic cities portrayed in the *Arabian Nights* stories. Instead, he noted in his journal, Timbuktu consisted of "badly built houses of clay" and streets that were "monotonous and melancholy like the desert." Nevertheless, he took detailed notes on the city and its inhabitants during his two-week visit, knowing that his account would be the first to reach Europe—if he could survive the 1,200-mile trip across the Western Sahara to Morocco.

Initially part of a huge caravan that included 600 camels, Caillié was able at first to ride across the desert until his fellow travelers gradually turned hostile toward him and began treating him like a slave. Forced to walk and physically abused by the others, he eventually struck out on his own and perilously made his way through the Moroccan territory forbidden to Christians. He arrived in Fès after about three months and sought aid from the French consul, who did not believe that the dark, emaciated stranger was French and refused to help him. Continuing north, he reached Tangier in August and found a sympathetic consul who arranged for his passage home.

Caillié received a hero's welcome on his return to France, earning a Legion of Honor knighthood and a 10,000-franc award from the Paris Geographical Society for being the first traveler to return from Timbuktu. Shortly after his three-volume journal of his trip was published, however, the tide of public opinion began to turn against him. Like Caillié, his readers had assumed that Timbuktu was a city of opulence and beauty, and they refused to accept his account of a drab, mediocre community. Citing his humble background and lack of scientific expertise, many cast aspersions on the accuracy of his reports, and some even accused him of fabricating the entire trip. Heartbroken, Caillié returned to his native village, where he lived until his death from tuberculosis. A decade later, the noted German explorer HEINRICH BARTH confirmed Caillié's findings and openly praised him as "one of the most reliable explorers of Africa."

Cam, Diego. See **Cão, Diogo.**

• Cameron, Verney Lovett

English
b July 1, 1844; Radipole, Dorset
d March 27, 1894; near Leighton Buzzard, Bedfordshire
Explored Central Africa

The first European to travel equatorial Africa from coast to coast, Verney Lovett Cameron explored Lake Tanganyika and located its outlet to a tributary of the Congo (or Zaire) River. Cameron led the 1872 expedition to locate missing explorer DAVID LIVINGSTONE in East Africa and, after learning of his death, recovered many

Verney Lovett Cameron. New York Public Library.

of Livingstone's papers and personal effects. He also became known for his strenuous opposition to the African slave trade and his efforts to promote development of commerce and a transportation system on the continent.

The son of a clergyman, Cameron left his village at the age of thirteen to join the British navy. He participated in the Abyssinia campaign of 1868 and the Royal Navy's antislavery patrols in Zanzibar. During his shore leaves, he spent considerable time in East Africa and became increasingly interested in exploring the interior of the continent. Cameron was twenty-eight when the Royal Geographical Society gave him his first opportunity to undertake a major expedition into Africa.

As leader of the Livingstone East Coast expedition, organized in 1872, Cameron was assigned to locate and assist the missing explorer. The party assembled in Zanzibar for the trip also included naval surgeon W. E. Dillon, army lieutenant Cecil Murphy, and Livingstone's nephew by marriage, Robert Moffat. They arrived in Bagamoyo, on the east coast of Africa, in February 1873 and departed for the interior the following month.

By the time the group reached Tabora (in present-day Tanzania) in August, Moffat had died of malaria, and the others were seriously ill. They were still in Tabora on October 20 when Cameron received a letter announcing that Livingstone had "died by disease beyond the country of Bisa." A few days later, Livingstone's servants arrived bearing his body, which they had pledged to return to England. Murphy and Dillon, believing their mission concluded, departed with Livingstone's caravan. But Cameron, determined to continue exploring Africa and to make a name for himself, proceeded to Ujiji on Lake Tanganyika and launched his own expedition, aided by the papers and equipment he had acquired from the Livingstone caravan.

At the southern end of Lake Tanganyika, Cameron identified the Lukuga River, a tributary of the Congo River, as the lake's outlet. From there he sailed north on the Lualaba, hoping it would lead to the Congo, but got only as far as Nyangwe (in what is now Zaire) before he was forced to abandon his plan to travel the length of the river. He was unable to obtain the equipment and local guides he needed, and settlers in Nyangwe warned him that warlike cannibals were preying on travelers along the river. Cameron was uncertain as to what course

to pursue next until Tippoo Tib, an Arab slave trader who had served as a guide to Livingstone, unexpectedly provided the solution.

Tippoo Tib, originally known as Hamed bin-Muhammad, called on Cameron in Nyangwe and, learning of the explorer's dilemma, suggested a westward journey that would lead to Angola on the Atlantic coast. Cameron agreed to this plan and also accepted the trader's offer to accompany Cameron's party as far as the Lomami River. The expedition left Nyangwe in August 1874, crossing the Congo River basin and arriving at the coastal village of Catumbela, north of Benguela, on November 7, 1875.

Having earned the distinction of being the first European to travel the width of tropical Africa from east to west, Cameron was acclaimed upon his return to England the following April. He received the Founder's Medal of the Royal Geographical Society, served as an English delegate to King Leopold II of Belgium's 1876 conference on Africa, and in 1877 published an account of his trip entitled *Across Africa*.

For the rest of his life, Cameron was an active spokesman on issues related to Africa and took part in several initiatives to develop commerce on the continent. He spoke publicly against the African slave trade and advocated constructing a railway that would run the length of the continent as well as an intercontinental rail link from Libya to Pakistan. Cameron returned to West Africa in 1883, accompanied by RICHARD FRANCIS BURTON, to study mining concessions, and the two explorers coauthored a book about the journey, *To the Gold Coast for Gold*, published the following year.

• Campbell, Robert

Scottish
b February 21, 1808; Glenlyon, Perth
d May 9, 1894; Manitoba, Canada
Explored headwaters of Yukon River

Fur trader Robert Campbell was one of the first explorers of the Yukon region of Canada. From 1834 to 1852, he explored many of the rivers in the most remote reaches of North America's far Northwest, including the headwaters of the Yukon River.

Campbell joined the Hudson's Bay Company

in 1830. In 1834, he was posted to the Mackenzie River territory to explore and build trading posts. He traveled up the Stikine River in 1837, and a year later built a post on Dease Lake, where, in his words, he passed "a winter of constant danger . . . and of much suffering from starvation. We were dependent for subsistence on what animals we could catch. . . . We were at one time obliged to eat our parchment windows, and our last meal before abandoning Dease Lake on 8th May, 1839, consisted of the lacing of our snow-shoes."

The following year, Campbell, with a party of seven men, explored the north branch of the Liard River and discovered a "beautiful lake," which he named Frances Lake, after the wife of Sir George Simpson of the Company. Leaving their canoe and proceeding on foot, they eventually came to the upper waters of a stream that flowed to the west, which Campbell named the Pelly after the governor of the Hudson's Bay Company. Campbell was later to discover that the Pelly is one of the main branches of the Yukon River and that the Yukon system is navigable for over 1,500 miles to its mouth in the Bering Sea.

After building a trading post at Frances Lake in 1842 (the Hudson's Bay Company's first post in today's Yukon), Campbell traveled down the river in a canoe in June 1843. Eventually he came to a place where another large river (the Lewes, or upper Yukon) joins the Pelly from the south to form the Yukon River proper. There a group of Wood Indians warned him that the Indians farther down the Yukon were numerous and ferocious. Campbell's companions were so alarmed by this information that he had to turn back.

In 1850 Campbell went down the Yukon to the mouth of one of its large northern tributaries, the Porcupine. He then ascended the Porcupine and crossed the mountains to the Mackenzie, which empties into the Arctic Ocean. After entering the lower Mackenzie he traveled up it to Fort Simpson, a major trading post west of Great Slave Lake. Campbell's discovery of the route between the Mackenzie, the Porcupine, and the Yukon rivers was a great boon to trade in the far reaches of the Northwest. Campbell left the Yukon territory in 1852, traveling south and east to Montréal—over 3,000 miles—on snowshoes.

Robert Campbell braved the cold and isolation of the far Northwest not only to further the business interests of the Hudson's Bay Company but also to increase the existing body of knowledge about one of the most remote regions on earth. Demonstrating remarkable courage and endurance, he thrived for eighteen years in that remote and harsh region.

Candish, Thomas. See **Cavendish, Thomas.**

Cano, Juan Sebastián del. See **Elcano, Juan Sebastián de.**

- ## Cão, Diogo (Cam, Diego)

  Portuguese
  b 1450; Trás-os-Montes
  d 1486; coast of Namibia?
  Explored coast of West Africa and discovered mouth of Congo (or Zaire) River

Portuguese navigator Diogo Cão discovered the lower course of the Congo River in 1482 and is responsible for giving both the river and its surrounding region the name Zaire. Considered one of the most capable seamen of his day, Cão was commissioned by King John II of Portugal to sail as far as possible down the Atlantic coast of Africa in search of a route around the continent to the Orient. Cão's first expedition, along some 800 miles of mostly unexplored coastline, took him to the mouth of the Congo and beyond. A second voyage, from which he apparently never returned, covered nearly twice this distance but still fell short of reaching the southern tip (present-day Cape of Good Hope) that would have led him around Africa.

Although he was knighted for his initial expedition and then touted by the Portuguese court as a born nobleman, Cão's roots were later traced to a common military family in the community of Villa Real. He joined the Portuguese navy as a youth, eventually becoming a captain, and distinguished himself in combat with **privateers** on the coast of West Africa. Cão was in his early thirties when his reputation as a courageous and talented seafarer brought him the opportunity to explore the continent's uncharted southern coastline.

Cão was the first explorer whom King John, eager to claim new territory, equipped with five-foot-high pillars to mark significant discoveries. Each of these limestone pillars, known as padrãos, was topped by a cross and inscribed with the names of the king and the expedition commander.

Setting sail from Portugal in June 1482, Cão traveled by way of the Canaries and the Gulf of Guinea. He proceeded against treacherous currents down the rugged coastline, 280 miles past the southernmost point previously explored, Cabo Santa Catarina (present-day Pointe Ste.-Catherine in Gabon). Late in the year, he reached the mouth of a large river and erected the first of King John's padrãos on the river's southern bank.

Convinced he had made an important discovery, Cão spent approximately a month near the river known to the native Bakongo people as Nzadi, meaning "the great water." Cão believed he might have found a strait leading to the kingdom of Prester John, the legendary immortal Christian priest with whom Portuguese rulers had long hoped to make contact (for a more complete discussion of Prester John, see PÊRO DA COVILHÃ). From the amicable Bakongo, through sketchy interpretations by Cão's Christianized Guinean slaves, the explorer learned that far upriver lay the royal city of the Mani Kongo, Lord of the Kongo. Hoping that this monarch would prove to be Prester John, Cão sent four of his slaves on a diplomatic mission to take gifts to the Mani Kongo while the rest of the expedition party continued south down the African coast.

Cão traveled at least as far as Cape St. Mary on the coast of Angola, approximately 500 miles south of the river mouth, where he put up a second padrão in August 1483. He then returned to the Congo, anxious to locate his slaves and learn the outcome of their meeting with the native king. When he reached the river mouth, however, Cão could find no trace of his men nor any explanation for their absence. Certain that the men were being held captive, Cão retaliated by kidnapping four of the Bakongo and sending word to the Mani Kongo that they would not be freed until Cão's men were released. Cão then departed for Lisbon with his hostages, assuring the Bakongo that he would return.

Upon his arrival in Portugal in April 1484, Cão was knighted for his accomplishments. King John, believing that the Bakongo might provide the key to locating Prester John, treated the captives as honored guests in his household. Royal cartographers designated the Bakongo territory and river as "Zaire," the garbled name reported by Cão, but also noted the word "Kongo" on maps. Confident that Cão had nearly circumnavigated Africa, the king opted to finance his second journey there rather than fund a westward voyage proposed by the then-unknown CHRISTOPHER COLUMBUS.

Cão left Portugal in late 1485 and returned to the Congo River to deliver his hostages, who were by then Portuguese-speaking Christians, and to ask for the release of his men. He also sailed about 100 miles upriver before the hazardous Crystal Mountain whitewater forced him to turn back. Resuming his journey down the coast, Cão reached Cape Negro in Angola and then Cape Cross in Namibia (at 22° South latitude), erecting the king's pillars at both sites. Cão's trail ends abruptly at this point, and his disappearance remains a mystery. Historians speculate that he may have been shipwrecked on Cape Cross or lost at sea en route back to Portugal. Since his Guinean slaves arrived safely in Lisbon, however, another theory is that Cão reached Portugal and then was executed by King John, who was angry that he had twice failed to circumnavigate Africa.

· Carpini, Giovanni de Plano (Johannes de; John de; John of Plano)

Italian
b 1180?; Umbria, near Perugia
d August 1, 1252; Italy?
Traveled across Europe and Asia to Mongol Empire

At the age of sixty-five, Giovanni de Plano Carpini was no stranger to long journeys. He had previously made lengthy trips from Italy to Spain in the south and to Scandinavia in the north on behalf of the Roman Catholic church's Franciscan order, in which he had been a friar for more than twenty-five years. But nothing Carpini had faced on his European excursions adequately prepared him for the rigors of the expedition he undertook in 1245: an embassy to the Mongols (or Tartars). Bearing a letter from the pope to "the King and Peoples of the Tartars"—no one in Europe knew who that was at the time—Carpini set out across Europe and

Asia into the heart of unknown Mongolia. (For a map of his route, see MARCO POLO.) By the time he returned 2½ years later, he had traveled over 15,000 miles and launched what would become medieval Europe's chief achievement in the field of exploration: the opening up of routes to the Far East. Carpini's subsequent description of Asia and the Mongols is one of the best provided by any medieval Christian writer.

Carpini was a contemporary and disciple of Saint Francis of Assisi, the influential reformer of medieval monasticism, and by 1220 had been ordained into the recently formed Franciscan order. He became a leading teacher in northern Europe and one of the Vatican's most able leaders, to whom Pope Innocent IV turned when world events demanded a papal mission to the Mongols in 1245. The pope's action was motivated by two events: the great Mongol invasion of eastern Europe in 1241, and the fall of Jerusalem and the Holy Land to the Muslim Saracens (nomadic tribes of the Arabian deserts). Before the Mongol expansion had reached Christian regions of Europe—lands that are now southern Russia, Poland, and Hungary—Innocent had thought that perhaps the Mongol invaders were Christians waging a holy war against Islam and could therefore be enlisted to help drive the Saracens out of the Holy Land. Stories from pilgrims and travelers about a Christian kingdom in Asia, ruled by the legendary Prester John (for a more complete discussion, see PÊRO DA COVILHÃ), had intrigued Europeans for many years. Every pope since the emergence of the Prester John tale had sought to locate this legendary Christian sovereign from the East. But if some of the Mongols were descendants of Prester John's followers, why would they invade Christendom? The pope decided to send an expedition to determine why the Mongols had invaded Europe and to assess the extent of the threat.

To increase the chances of a successful mission into the vast unknown regions to the east, Innocent IV took the expedient measure of sending two separate groups to the Great Khan, one led by Carpini, the other by Laurentius of Portugal, whose attempt ultimately failed. The pope's plea to the Mongol ruler was elegantly argued: since all the people, animals, and matter that make up the world "are united to each other as if by a natural association. . . . We are therefore greatly surprised that you, as We have learned, have attacked and cruelly destroyed many countries belonging to Christians and many other peoples." On Easter day 1245 Carpini and his companions left Lyon, France, the place to which the pope had fled from his enemy, Holy Roman Emperor Frederick II, and set out for the land of the Mongols.

The expedition first traveled to Prague (in present-day Czechoslovakia), where they were told to continue east into Poland. There they were to meet a Russian prince who would escort them to a place near the Volga River, where Batu, the Mongol conqueror of eastern Europe, was camped. After long weeks of winter travel, the party reached the city of Kiev (now in the Soviet Union), which had been almost completely destroyed by the Mongols. At Kiev, they met some Mongols who offered to take them on horseback directly to Batu. The pace of the journey increased dramatically, as Carpini explains: "We rode as fast as our horses could manage, and, since we were able to change horses nearly three or four times every day, we were in the saddle from early morning to the night, very often during the night as well." In spite of their rapid pace, they did not reach Batu's camp until the day before Easter, almost precisely a year after they had left Lyon.

Carpini's search for the Mongol leader had not ended, however, for Batu ordered the group to go on to Mongolia, where they could meet with the khan, Guyug. So the weary travelers mounted up once again and, accompanied by two Mongol escorts, followed the courier roads east toward the heart of Mongol territory, changing horses five to six times a day. They passed north of the Caspian and Aral seas, rode through a bitterly cold June snowstorm, then crossed "the true land of the Mongols . . . with all speed in three weeks." They arrived at Guyug's palace on July 22, just in time for the festive assembly for the election of the khagan (or "Khan of Khans"), which is why their escorts had been ordered to make all possible speed.

Carpini discovered that other ambassadors were present for the occasion: a Russian prince, two sons of the king of Georgia, a sultan sent by the caliph of Baghdad, and ten Saracen sultans—a total of more than 4,000 ambassadors, the imperial recorder informed Carpini. After Guyug had been installed as Great Khan, Carpini and the other official representatives were given an audience to present their messages. On the thirteenth of November, Guyug gave Carpini a response to the pope's letter and instructed him to begin his trip back to Rome.

Carpini later recounted, "We immediately set off on the journey home and traveled right through the winter. We often had to lie in snow in the wilderness. . . . For there were no trees there, only flat plains. When we awoke in the morning, we often found ourselves completely covered with snow which the wind had blown over us." On May 9, 1247, Carpini and his companions reached Batu's camp, and Carpini asked the Mongol conqueror if he had any response to Innocent IV. Batu replied that he had nothing to add to the message of the Great Khan. In his dealings with Batu, Carpini sensed discord between the conqueror and his new emperor, a fact that comforted worried European rulers. They hoped that if the Mongols were busy fighting among themselves, they would have little time for new conquests in Europe.

Carpini reached Lyon in November and made a full report to the pope. In his letter to the pope, Guyug claimed not to understand European distress over the Mongol invasion. Eastern Europe was given into the hands of the Mongols, according to Guyug, because its people "did not comply with the commandments of God and Genghis Khan, but rather, in their infamy, deliberately murdered Our ambassadors." What must the Europeans do to comply with the commandments? "Today you shall say from the depths of your heart: we wish to be Your subjects and give You some of our power"— not a concession the Europeans were likely to make.

While the expedition was not a political success, Carpini brought back valuable information about the Mongols and their lands. He wrote *History of the Mongols*, which contains detailed descriptions of the climate and physical features of the Mongol territories. He discussed the religion, history, and customs of the people, as well as the Mongols' political leaders and their tactics in battle, two issues of particular interest to European rulers. Carpini also wrote about the lands through which he and his companions traveled on their epic journey. His journey charted a course to the East soon followed by others, including Carpini's fellow Franciscan, WILLIAM OF RUBRUCK, who was the first to unravel the tangled story about Prester John and the Asian Christians.

Carteret, Philip

English
b January 22, 1733; Trinity Manor, Jersey
d July 21, 1796; Southampton, Hampshire
Discovered Pitcairn Island; circumnavigated twice

English naval officer and explorer Philip Carteret survived a harrowing thirty-one-month circumnavigation, during which he made several Pacific discoveries. While these were significant because they pointed the way for later explorers, they were generally overshadowed by those of his contemporaries, SAMUEL WALLIS and JAMES COOK.

Carteret was born in 1733 to a distinguished family at Trinity Manor on the island of Jersey. Befitting his status, he joined the navy as a young man in 1747. During the Seven Years' War against France, he served successfully in the English Channel and the Mediterranean, and in August 1758 he was made a second lieutenant.

One of the men Carteret had served under was JOHN BYRON. In 1764 Byron was leading an expedition on the **frigate** *Dolphin* and asked Carteret if he would serve as first lieutenant on the **sloop** *Tamar*, the *Dolphin*'s consort. Carteret accepted the post. During the course of Byron's two-year journey to the Falklands and several South Pacific isles, Carteret was promoted to first lieutenant on the *Dolphin*.

Byron's expedition wasn't considered a success, so when the *Dolphin* went to sea again in 1766, it was placed under the command of Samuel Wallis. This time the goal was to search for *Terra Australis Incognita*, the rumored but undiscovered Southern Continent, at the behest of the second earl of Egmont. (For a more complete discussion of *Terra Australis Incognita*, see ALEXANDER DALRYMPLE.) Carteret was to command the *Swallow*, a decrepit ship that was to be replaced when the expedition reached the Falklands. His disappointment in the vessel notwithstanding, Carteret sailed with Wallis from Plymouth on August 21, 1766.

When no new ship awaited Carteret in the Falklands, or anywhere else, he wanted to turn back. Wallis refused to allow it, and, to make sure that Carteret wouldn't try to return to England, he forced Carteret to take the *Swallow* in the lead as the two ships braved the Strait of Magellan. Weather and sea conditions were hostile, and it took four months to make the passage. Just before the vessels broke into the Pacific in April 1767, a strong wind forced Wallis's *Dolphin* into the lead and out of the strait well ahead of the *Swallow*. The two ships became separated.

Carteret pressed on as best he could, considering the condition of the ship and its **scurvy**-stricken crew. Now free of the *Dolphin*, Carteret could pick his own route, and he did so for the next two years.

Among Carteret's discoveries in the Pacific was the uninhabited Pitcairn Island, to which the *Bounty* mutineers would flee in 1790 (see WILLIAM BLIGH). He also rediscovered Santa Cruz and the Solomon Islands, which no European had seen since the sixteenth century, when they were first noted by ALVARO DE MENDAÑA DE NEHRA and PEDRO FERNANDEZ DE QUIRÓS. Carteret did not recognize, however, that these were the same islands that the earlier explorers had documented.

Sailing west from the Solomons, he reached New Britain, off the east coast of New Guinea. His explorations revealed that what was thought to be two islands actually were three. Carteret took possession of New Britain and discovered what he named the St. George Channel between it and an island to its north, which he named New Ireland. A second strait was found to separate New Ireland from yet another island, which he called New Hanover. Carteret named the strait after Byron and named a harbor on New Ireland in honor of himself. Carteret also named the Admiralty Islands, a group that Dutch navigator ABEL TASMAN had explored earlier. (The Admiralty Islands, along with New Britain, New Ireland, and New Hanover, are today part of the Bismarck Archipelago.)

By November 1767 Carteret reached Makassar (now Ujung Pandang) in the Celebes (present-day Sulawesi). He hoped to have the *Swallow* repaired there, but Dutch officials were unsympathetic to the Englishman's plight. Carteret continued west, finally reaching Batavia (now Jakarta, Indonesia) a year later, in November 1768. He spent four months there while the *Swallow* was repaired to face the journey home.

On February 19, 1769, en route from Batavia to England, he met a mysterious French mariner who said nothing about who he was or what he was doing on the high seas, but who had news of Wallis's *Dolphin*. It was French explorer LOUIS-ANTOINE DE BOUGAINVILLE, who was completing his own circumnavigation of the world. Carteret and the *Swallow* then sailed on, reaching Spithead, England, on March 20, 1769, after thirty-one months at sea. He had lost half his men.

Carteret was eventually given another command, that of the *Endymion* in 1779, a post he held for three years. Although he remained in the navy for the rest of his days, he never saw active duty after 1782. Made vice admiral in 1794, Carteret died in Southampton, Hampshire, on July 21, 1796, largely unrecognized by his country for his important work.

• Cartier, Jacques

French
b 1491; St.-Malo
d September 1, 1557; St.-Malo
Explored Gulf of St. Lawrence and St. Lawrence River

A master navigator and well-respected citizen of the port of St.-Malo in Brittany, Jacques Cartier led three early expeditions to North America. On the first (1534), he circumnavigated the Gulf of St. Lawrence without actually discovering the river. On the second voyage (1535), Cartier discovered the St. Lawrence River and explored it as far as present-day Montréal. His third voyage, an unsuccessful attempt to locate a mythical kingdom of great wealth and to establish a colony, added little new territory to Cartier's knowledge. (For a map of his routes, see JOHN CABOT.)

Little is known of Jacques Cartier's life before he made his 1534 voyage to North America. There has been speculation that he took part in GIOVANNI DA VERRAZANO's voyages to America in 1524 and 1528, based in part on Cartier's comparisons of the inhabitants and produce of Canada with those of Brazil and in part on the information that Cartier was absent from France during the time of Verrazano's expeditions. Evidence against this theory includes the fact that Cartier never mentions Verrazano's voyages in his writings and the fact that although he made comparisons between Canada and Brazil, he never mentioned the North American seaboard, which Verrazano also explored.

Nonetheless, Cartier was recommended to King Francis I of France by the abbot of Mont-Saint-Michel as someone who had voyaged to

Jacques Cartier. American Museum of Natural History.

Brazil and Newfoundland. The king was looking for an experienced sailor to mount an expedition to the North American coast. For some time France had been greedily eyeing the wealth that Spain and Portugal were bringing out of America. King Francis was eager to tap into the same source of riches. However, the **Treaty of Tordesillas**, a papal bull (decree) of 1494, had split the New World between Spain and Portugal, leaving other nations out in the cold. Finally in 1533 Francis convinced his friend Pope Clement VII to amend the decree so that it referred only to land that had already been discovered. From that year on, new discoveries could be claimed by the country that made them.

Thus it was that Cartier, with two ships and sixty-one men, set out from St.-Malo on April 20, 1534, with the twin goals of locating new sources of precious metals and of discovering a Northwest Passage to the Orient (for a more complete discussion of the passage, see MARTIN FROBISHER). Encountering fair weather all the way, the ships made an exceedingly easy Atlantic crossing in only twenty days and reached landfall at present-day Cape Bonavista, New-

foundland, on May 10. The island was a stopping-off place for French fishermen of the time and thus could have been known to Cartier through sailors' gossip.

In early May there was still so much ice in the water that, after making landfall, the ships had to sail southeast and put up at another harbor for repairs. On May 21, Cartier began sailing north again, stopping at what is now Funk Island to slaughter a large number of great auks (a type of sea bird) for food. Soon the ships entered the Strait of Belle Isle, the passageway into what was later to be called the Gulf of St. Lawrence.

Sailing along the rocky coast of Labrador, Cartier was unimpressed: "[O]n this entire northern coast I saw not one cartload of earth, though I landed in many places. Except for Blanc Sablon there is nothing but moss and stunted shrubs. To conclude, I am inclined to regard this land as the one God gave to Cain." Nor did the inhabitants he encountered excite any more enthusiasm: "The men are well enough formed but untamed and savage."

Weary of the bleak coast, Cartier turned back to the west coast of Newfoundland and sailed south. Reaching the southern end, he posited the existence of a channel "between Newfoundland and the Land of the Bretons" (present-day Nova Scotia), but for reasons never known he did not investigate the possibility. Instead he turned west, crossing to present-day Magdalen Islands, which he did not name, thinking them part of the mainland.

On June 29, the ships left the waters around the islands and traveled west all night, sighting present-day Prince Edward Island in the morning. This land, too, Cartier considered part of the mainland. Crossing Northumberland Strait, he sailed into what is now Miramichi Bay and then further north to Chaleur Bay. Cartier was more enthusiastic about this beautiful bay than about any other spot he discovered on this voyage, commenting on the warm air and water, the abundance of salmon, and the rich soil. As he sailed into the bay, the seemingly endless expanse of water ahead made him hopeful that he had discovered a strait that would lead to a passage to China.

On the north shore of Chaleur Bay, Cartier had his first encounter with the Micmac Indians. Their canoes surrounded his ships, and the Micmacs made "signs of joy and of wanting [their] friendship." Cartier was distrustful of these seemingly friendly overtures and had his men shoot small guns over the Micmacs' heads. Undiscouraged by this hostile response, the Micmacs returned the next day offering fur pelts for sale, and cordial trading ensued. Shortly afterward, Cartier's hopes of a passage to China were dashed when the party reached the end of the bay.

Traveling east and north, the expedition next explored Gaspé Bay at the tip of the Gaspé Peninsula. There they encountered about 200 Huron Indians with their chief, Donnaconna. It was a summer fishing party that had come down from what is now Québec to take advantage of the teeming waters. But Cartier didn't realize this and called them the "poorest people that can be in the world" because of their lack of material possessions. On July 24, the band of Frenchmen raised a thirty-foot cross on a high point at Gaspé Harbor. The cross was inscribed "Vive le Roi de France" ("Long live the King of France"). Despite the lack of translators, Donnaconna understood this to be a ceremony of possession. He quickly asserted his ownership of the land but was evidently appeased enough to agree to send his two sons, Domagaya and Taignoagny, to France to become interpreters, with the understanding that they would return the next year.

On July 25 Cartier set sail from Gaspé Harbor. The party explored present-day Anticosti Island and then by consensus decided to return to France. The master sailor Cartier returned to St.-Malo with both ships intact, having lost not one member of his crew.

Though he had not brought back gold or jewels or discovered a passage to the Orient, Cartier was given a hero's welcome in France. He had expanded his country's knowledge of North America, made valuable allies among the Hurons, and brought back two of them to train as interpreters. Within two months of Cartier's return, the king commissioned him to lead another expedition the following spring with the object of exploring beyond Terres Neufves (Newfoundland) to "discover certain faraway countries." This time Cartier was given three ships and 110 men.

The second expedition set sail on May 19, 1535, and unlike the first, ran into foul weather and winds. The Atlantic crossing took more than twice as long as the first. Landfall was made at Funk Island on July 7. This time there was no exploring the coasts of Newfoundland; in-

stead, the ships headed immediately for the Strait of Belle Isle and proceeded along the coast looking for the route inland. On August 10, the feast of Saint Lawrence, Cartier named a harbor after the saint. It was those who came after him who applied the same name to the gulf and the river he discovered.

Guided by Donnaconna's sons as interpreters, Cartier easily found the mouth of the river, which is 10 to 30 miles wide for a great distance from its mouth. They told him it was the route to Canada (meaning what is now the province of Québec). The waters, they told him, came from such a great distance that no one had ever seen their source. Cartier concluded that this was the passage to the Orient that he was seeking. Soon after entering the St. Lawrence, which Cartier always called la Grande Rivière, the party caught sight of a deep and rapid river coming in from the west, on the ships' righthand sides. This, the interpreters told them, was the way to the Saguenay, a kingdom of fabulous wealth, the search for which was to become the main purpose of Cartier's last voyage.

On September 8, they reached the village of Stadacona (the site of present-day Québec), and there were greeted by Donnaconna. The two interpreters, Donnaconna's sons, had promised to guide Cartier further inland to the village of Hochelaga (now Montréal), but they began to stall. Cartier eventually learned that Hochelaga's chief claimed dominion over Donnaconna, who preferred to keep his French allies near him to enhance his prestige. When Cartier expressed his intention to go to Hochelaga without the interpreters, Donnaconna tried subterfuge to keep the French at Stadacona. He had three medicine men dress up as devils with blackened faces and wearing long horns and dog skins. These "devils" warned the French that snow and ice upriver would cause the death of the entire crew if they insisted on going to Hochelaga. When the French laughed at the ruse, Donnaconna joined in the mirth as if he had intended a joke. Nonetheless, Cartier decided he would be better off without the chief's sons along on his trip to Hochelaga.

On September 19, one of Cartier's ships sailed up the river, arriving at Hochelaga on October 2. There, 1,000 Hurons came down to the shore to greet the Frenchmen and ply them with gifts, including cornbread, which the Indians threw into the longboats. They also brought their sick for Cartier to lay his hands on in healing. After an elaborate ceremony at the village's central plaza, the Frenchmen climbed the height that Cartier named Mont Réal (Mount Royal). There they caught sight of the rapids just beyond Hochelaga that made further travel up the St. Lawrence impossible except by canoe. Before Cartier left Hochelaga, the local Indians confirmed the stories about the land of Saguenay where there were precious metals and "bad people" who were armed and known to be tough fighters. They described the approach to Saguenay as being up the river (now the Ottawa) that stretched northwest from the St. Lawrence just to the west of Hochelaga.

Disappointed that his newly discovered passage to China was not navigable by his ships, Cartier returned to the mouth of the present-day St. Charles River and the port that he had named Ste.-Croix. There the sailors who had been left behind had built a fort on shore, where the entire party of Frenchmen spent the bitterly cold winter of 1535–36. Cartier used this time to make notes on the customs of the local Indians, including the first recorded mention of tobacco in northern North America.

From mid-November to mid-April the French ships lay frozen in the ice at the mouth of the St. Charles River while the sailors suffered through one of the coldest winters on record. To add to their misery, **scurvy** broke out among the crew, causing their legs to swell, gums to turn black, and teeth to fall out. Cartier wrote: "Out of the 110 men that we were, not ten were well enough to help the others, a thing pitiful to see." The crew was kept from what could have been total extinction by information they learned from Domagaya, who had recovered from the disease, about how to make an infusion from the bark and needles of the white cedar tree. In the end, all who took this cure recovered, leaving a crew of eighty-five.

Although relations with the Indians were strained, they had improved somewhat since the fall, and many of the long winter nights were spent listening to Donnaconna weave elaborate embroiderings on the tales his sons had told Cartier about the kingdom of Saguenay. He told not only of the gold and jewels but of white men like the Frenchmen who wore woolen garments, of creatures with only one leg, and of people who had no anuses and existed on a liquid diet. What Cartier never realized was that these Hurons not only were inveterate storytellers but also were eager to please their

guests by telling them whatever they might want to hear. Thus, when the Frenchmen's eyes lit up at the mention of gold, gold became even more prominent in the Hurons' stories.

Donnaconna was soon to regret his storytelling. Wanting King Francis I to hear about Saguenay directly from the Hurons, Cartier hatched a plan to seize Donnaconna, his sons the interpreters, and a few other important members of the tribe just before the French were to leave. The kidnapping was easily accomplished, and when Donnaconna's subjects raised a howling lamentation for their chief, Cartier promised to return him in ten or twelve months with gifts from the French king.

On May 6, 1536, Cartier set sail for France. On the return voyage he made two new discoveries. He now realized that the Magdalen Islands were not part of the mainland, and instead of traveling north to sail through the Strait of Belle Isle, he became the first Frenchman to navigate the strait between Newfoundland and what is now Cape Breton, Nova Scotia.

Back in France, Donnaconna and his elaborate tales of the kingdom of Saguenay were immensely popular at court, where the Huron leader was baptized and granted a pension. Noticing that the king was interested in spices as well as gold, Donnaconna further embroidered his earlier tales, adding cloves, nutmeg, and pepper, as well as oranges and pomegranates, to the products of Saguenay. Thus, a third voyage was assured as King Francis sought to tap into some of the wealth that he saw his country's rival, Spain, bringing out of America.

The goal of Cartier's third voyage, then, was the kingdom of Saguenay, but the expedition was delayed for five years. First, France's resources were tied up in one of its many wars with Spain. Then, after the war, preparations for the voyage took another three years, as Cartier had to assemble five ships and 1,000 people, including colonists, some of whom were drawn from the prisons of France.

In January 1541, when Cartier was nearing the end of his preparations for the expedition, the king abruptly and without warning placed Jean-François de la Rocque de Roberval at the head of the expedition and required all of the participants—including Cartier—to swear an oath of loyalty to Roberval. Cartier was still to be in charge of the navigation, but Roberval was clearly made his superior. Cartier's reaction to his demotion and the king's breach of faith was not recorded.

Cartier and his five ships left St.-Malo on May 23, 1541, with Roberval to follow as soon as he could get ready. On August 23, Cartier's party arrived in Stadacona, where Agona, who had taken Donnaconna's place, was not displeased to learn that his rival had died in France. What Cartier neglected to mention was that with the exception of one little girl, all the other Hurons who had been taken to France had also died. Instead, he informed the Hurons that the others were living the life of lords and didn't want to return. The lie stemmed from his intuition that the Hurons were not as friendly as they seemed.

The same sense of distrust probably occasioned Cartier's abandonment of the fort at Ste.-Croix for a new fortified settlement, called Charlesbourg-Royal, located at the mouth of a river 8 to 9 miles west of Stadacona. The convicts and other colonists stayed there, planted a garden, and began to collect "diamonds" (actually quartz) and "gold" (iron pyrite, or "fool's gold"), while Cartier and some others began their search for Saguenay.

Traveling west toward Hochelaga, they passed through the territory of Achelacy (whom Cartier had befriended on the previous voyage) and left with him two French youths to learn the language. Thus, Cartier established a tradition that SAMUEL DE CHAMPLAIN was to continue later of having French youths live among the Indians to learn their languages.

Just before reaching Hochelaga, the party encountered the first falls, which had blocked their way in 1535. Leaving their boats, they followed an Indian **portage** along the shore, which brought them to a friendly village called Tutonaguy. There Cartier acquired four guides to lead them to Saguenay. The guides took them to another village and drew a map with sticks showing the way to Saguenay, but they told Cartier that another series of falls blocked the way. For reasons unknown, they failed to tell him about the Ottawa River, which was also a supposed route to Saguenay. Perhaps they were trying to discourage him. If so, they succeeded; Cartier turned back. He had gotten as close to Saguenay as he ever would.

Returning to Charlesbourg-Royal, Cartier discovered that the Hurons had become openly hostile, as they inevitably did when they realized that visitors had come to stay. What actu-

ally happened throughout the long winter is not clear, as the one surviving record of the expedition ends with Cartier's return to Charlesbourg-Royal. From gossip picked up from French sailors, historians have surmised that the Indians attacked the settlement sporadically, killing about thirty-five Frenchmen over the winter. Scurvy broke out as well, but it was quickly cured by the method Cartier had learned on the previous voyage. There seems to have been an atmosphere of general depression and misery, compounded by the fact that Roberval had not appeared and Cartier did not know what to make of this.

In early June 1542, therefore, the French ships made their departure with all of the colonists aboard as well as barrels of what they thought were gold and silver and a basket of "jewels," all of which would turn out to be worthless. When Cartier reached the harbor of St. John's in Newfoundland at the end of June, he met up with Roberval and his three ships. Roberval ordered Cartier to turn around and go back to Stadacona. But Cartier, perhaps knowing that this would engender mutiny on the part of the disenchanted crew and colonists, perhaps eager to show his "valuables" to the king in person, slipped away at night and returned to St.-Malo in mid-October 1542.

Roberval went on to spend the winter in fortifications that he built near Stadacona and named France-Roy. In the spring of 1543 he too attempted to find Saguenay but like Cartier was stopped by the rapids past Hochelaga. He and his whole party were back in France by September 1543.

Strangely, Cartier's abandonment of Roberval, his superior, was not treated as desertion, and no dishonor was attached to it. As a reward for his efforts, the king gave him two of the ships from his expedition. The master sailor lived out the rest of his life in St.-Malo and his nearby estate, Limoïlou. He died at the age of sixty-six on September 1, 1557.

As for the mythical kingdom of Saguenay, it remained on maps for over a century and then disappeared. It had never existed, not even in Indian folklore. It was merely a collection of tall tales invented to amuse, and perhaps to fool, the greedy men predisposed to listen to such tales. As for the "riches" that Cartier brought back, they were eventually realized for the worthless rocks they were; their greatest contribution to France was an expression invoked for many years thereafter, "Voilà un diamant de Canada!" ("Behold, a Canadian diamond!"), which was used to refer to any worthless item originally perceived as being valuable.

A sailor par excellence, Jacques Cartier lost not one ship or crew member to mishaps at sea in his three voyages of discovery. He was a leader who maintained order and hope under the most difficult circumstances. His name is rightly remembered for the careful manner in which he conducted valuable exploration that added the Gulf of St. Lawrence and the St. Lawrence River to the world's maps and gave France an entry into the North American continent, an entry which it nevertheless declined to exploit for another half century.

SUGGESTED READING: Henry S. Burrage, ed., *Early English and French Voyages Chiefly from Hakluyt 1534–1608* (Barnes & Noble, 1934); Editors of *American Heritage, Discoverers of the New World* (American Heritage, 1960); Harold Lamb, *New Found World* (Doubleday, 1955); Samuel Eliot Morison, *The European Discovery of America* (Oxford University Press, 1971); David B. Quinn, *North America from Earliest Discovery to First Settlements* (Harper & Row, 1977).

Cavelier, René Robert, Sieur de La Salle.
See **La Salle, René Robert Cavelier, Sieur de.**

• Cavendish (Candish), Thomas

English
b 1560
d October 1592; at sea
Circumnavigated; discovered Port Desire, Argentina

English navigator Sir Thomas Cavendish headed the third expedition to circumnavigate the globe, after FERDINAND MAGELLAN and Sir FRANCIS DRAKE. He explored Patagonia, where he discovered Port Desire.

Born in 1560, Cavendish began his maritime career after leaving Corpus Christi College, Cambridge University, without a degree, to become a **courtier** and later a member of Parliament. His excessive life-style nearly ruined him financially, and he turned to the sea to make his living.

In 1585 Cavendish joined British admiral Sir Richard Grenville on a voyage to the colony of Virginia. When he returned to England, Cav-

endish began to plan his dream of duplicating Drake's great circumnavigation of 1577–80. On July 21, 1586, he set sail from Plymouth with 123 men in three ships, the *Desire*, the *Content*, and the *Gallant*. They sailed south down the west coast of Africa to Sierra Leone, then across to Cape Frio, Brazil, via the Cape Verde Islands. While exploring Patagonia, Cavendish made his major contribution: the discovery of Port Desire, named for his ship. This site would become a safe harbor for future sailors about to attempt to run the Strait of Magellan.

Cavendish and his crew continued south and then west through the Strait of Magellan and into the Pacific. Like Drake before and many English **buccaneers** to follow, they raided Spanish settlements as they made their way up the west coasts of South and Central America and Mexico. Cavendish also pillaged other vessels, among them the treasure **galleon** *Great St. Anne*, captured at Cape St. Lucas, Mexico, on November 14, 1587.

Cavendish and his men captured some nineteen vessels as they crossed the Pacific, by way of the Ladrone Islands (now the Marianas), the Philippines, Moluccas, Java, and around the Cape of Good Hope. When Cavendish's sole remaining ship, the 140-ton *Desire*, docked in England on September 9, 1588, after two years and fifty days at sea, her crew wore silk and her **topsail** was said to be of gold cloth.

In 1591 Cavendish, with financial troubles once again, decided to repeat his journey. He gathered five ships and set sail, only to die at sea in October 1592, somewhere in the South Atlantic.

• Chaillé-Long, Charles

American
b July 2, 1842; Somerset County, Maryland
d March 24, 1917; Virginia Beach, Virginia
Explored Nile region of Africa and discovered Lake Ibrahim (now Lake Kyoga)

In the late nineteenth century, Egypt attracted adventurous souls like a magnet. They came from every part of the world, hoping to find employment with either the Khedive Ismail, Egypt's ruler and the would-be conqueror of Central Africa, or with one of the expeditions setting out from Egypt for Africa's interior. The

Charles Chaillé-Long. Library of Congress.

American Charles Chaillé-Long had served as a captain in the Union army during the Civil War, but the war had not satisfied his zest for action, so he made his way to Egypt. In the years that followed, he carried out both diplomatic and geographic missions on behalf of the Egyptian government. He earned a reputation among his colleagues as a braggart and complainer, traits reflected in his subsequent writings, which consistently overstate the importance of his own discoveries.

War interrupted Chaillé-Long's education at Washington Academy in 1861. After the war, he traveled to Egypt, where he secured an appointment as a lieutenant colonel with the Egyptian army in 1869. Within five years, he was made chief of staff to General Charles "China" Gordon, who sent the American to reconnoiter the lightly explored lands south of the Sudan. Chaillé-Long's objective was twofold: to explore the geography of the region and, at the same time, to assess the land and its people with a view to future annexation by Egypt. In the course of his travels, Chaillé-Long conducted treaty negotiations with King Mutesa of Buganda (now part of Uganda) in Buganda's capital city of Rubaga. Chaillé-Long noted that Rubaga was a sizable settlement that covered the hills for several miles around and

included magnificent huts for housing visitors. He also noted a key military fact: Mutesa had 150,000 warriors under arms and a fleet of war canoes on Lake Victoria.

Chaillé-Long's geographical research in the lake regions of East Africa allowed him to plot the course of the upper reaches of the White Nile from its source as far as Karuma Falls in central Uganda, thus adding to the earlier reconnaissance by JOHN HANNING SPEKE. Along the way, he discovered Lake Ibrahim (now Kyoga)—an important find, but not worthy of Chaillé-Long's glorification of himself as a Nile explorer in his book on Uganda, *Naked Truths of Naked People*. The following year, 1875, Chaillé-Long traveled to the region dividing the watersheds of the Nile and Congo (or Zaire) rivers, adding to the geographical information gathered by earlier explorers. His travels and his subsequent work as a United States government official in Cairo and Korea are detailed at some length in his two-volume autobiography, *My Life in Four Continents*.

Chaillu, Paul Belloni Du. See **Du Chaillu, Paul Belloni.**

· Champlain, Samuel de

French
b 1567?; Brouage, Saintonge
d December 25, 1635; Québec, Canada
Explored and colonized eastern Canada

Adventurer, mapmaker, and leader of colonists, Samuel de Champlain devoted the last thirty years of his life to establishing the presence of France in the New World. Not only did he found France's first permanent colony in North America, he also explored the Atlantic coast as far south as Cape Cod and penetrated inland as far as Lake Huron. In addition, he was the first European to reach the lake to which he gave his name.

The son of a sea captain, Champlain was born some time around 1567 in Brouage, on the Bay of Biscay. He served King Henry IV, a Bourbon, during France's civil wars at the end of the sixteenth century and later joined a Spanish expedition to the West Indies in 1599. There he remained for two years during which time he observed that a canal might be built across the

Samuel de Champlain. Library of Congress.

After arriving in North America, he sailed up the St. Lawrence River with a small party to the Indian village of Tadoussac. From there he went 60 miles up the Saguenay River, surveyed the St.-Maurice River, and then traveled farther up the St. Lawrence as far as present-day Montréal. There the Indians told him of a lake to the west that was so large they were afraid to sail on it. Champlain thought this might be the Pacific Ocean, and his interest was piqued by the thought of a northern route to China. But the Lachine Rapids on the St. Lawrence just west of Montréal prevented him from exploring further.

Frustrated by his inability to pass beyond the rapids, Champlain formulated the theory that ensured the future success of French explorers in North America. He wrote: "He who would pass them [the rapids] must provide himself with the canoes of the savages, which a man can easily carry." With such canoes, "one may travel freely and quickly throughout the country. . . ."

On this first voyage, Champlain formed an alliance with the Algonquin Indians (later expanded to include the Montagnais and Hurons) against their common enemy, the Iroquois. Although the friendship of the Algonquins was valuable at the time, the long-term enmity of the Iroquois, who later allied themselves with the British, eventually would prove to be the downfall of the French in Canada.

Champlain returned to France to report his results, but he was back in North America in 1604 with a new fur-trading monopoly. This time he scouted the coast as far south as Cape Cod looking for a promising location for a settlement, finally choosing the east coast of the Bay of Fundy in the area the French called Acadie (also known as Acadia; now Nova Scotia). After two years, the trading monopoly was revoked by the king. With no financial support for the colony, Champlain and the other colonists were forced to return to France.

When a new monopoly was granted for a year, Champlain again made the trip across the Atlantic in 1608. This time he established a colony on the St. Lawrence River at a place the Indians called Kebec, "the narrowing of the waters." Champlain spelled it Québec. From there he hoped to resume his westward explorations begun in 1603.

In 1609 as he was about to set out for the west, a group of Algonquin and Huron Indians

Isthmus of Panama, thus anticipating the Panama Canal by about 300 years. Upon returning home, he wrote and illustrated a book about his experiences that was so impressive that King Henry made him royal geographer. But Champlain was not interested in a life of ease at the court, and he soon convinced his royal patron to let him join an expedition to North America.

At that time, France could not afford the expense of sending colonists to the New World. Yet the king was eager to establish France's presence there. The king's solution was to offer a monopoly in the fur trade to an individual or a company with the requirement that the fur-trading monopoly establish a French colony to be supported by the profits from the sale of fur.

In 1603 Champlain joined the party of the existing fur-trading monopoly as geographer.

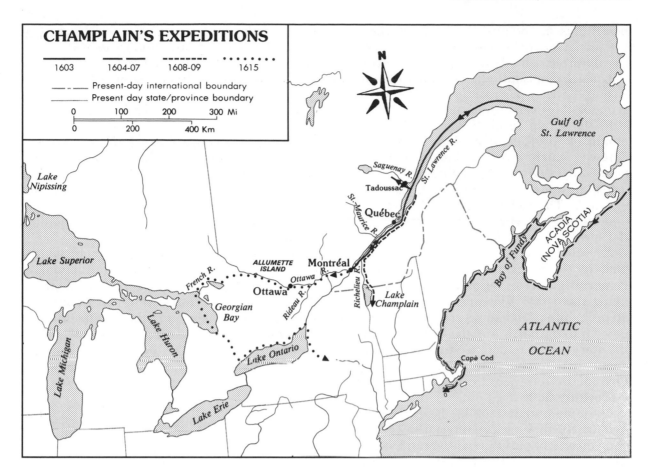

CHAMPLAIN'S EXPEDITIONS

came to Québec to ask his support for an attack on the Iroquois. He traveled south with them on what is now the Richelieu River toward the homeland of the Mohawk Iroquois. On the way they came upon the lake that now bears Champlain's name, which he described as having "many beautiful low islands covered with very fine woods and meadows with much wild fowl and animals to hunt."

When the Iroquois were finally encountered, Champlain's allies assembled around him. Marching toward the unsuspecting Iroquois, they suddenly stepped aside to reveal the fair-skinned stranger clad in gleaming steel armor and helmet. The sight surely awed the Iroquois, who were shocked further when Champlain raised his small musket and, with four shots, killed two chiefs and wounded another. The Iroquois scattered in dismay, while the Hurons rejoiced in their powerful new ally.

Champlain returned to New France from Iroquois country in 1610 and established a trading post at what is now Montréal in 1611. However, neither of these trips afforded him time for exploration. By this time the system of granting fur-trading monopolies had been abandoned, and there was competition for the Indians' furs. Champlain therefore spent much of his time consolidating his relationships with the Indians. However, like the true leader he was, Champlain had already established a means of continuing exploration even when he was not able to do it himself. Since 1610 he had been sending selected young men to live with the Indians in order to learn their ways and explore their lands. ETIENNE BRULÉ was one of these adventurers.

In 1613 Champlain was told by a **coureur de bois** named Vignau, who had lived among the Algonquins, that the Ottawa River had its source in a lake that emptied into a northern sea. Vignau claimed to have visited this sea and said it could be reached by a journey of seventeen days from Montréal.

Once again eager to pursue his interest in a water route to the Orient, Champlain made an arduous journey up the Ottawa River. The going was difficult, and the members of the party sometimes had to tie their canoes to their wrists and pull them over the rapids. Champlain nearly drowned doing this when he was knocked between two rocks with the towrope wound tightly around his hand. Later the party was plagued by mosquitoes, of which Champlain wrote: "[Their] pertinacity is so great that it is impossible to give any description of it." Later still, the group reached the waterfall at the mouth of the Rideau River near present-day Ottawa, which was also recorded by Champlain: "It falls with such impetuosity that it forms an archway nearly four hundred yards in width. The Indians, for the fun of it, pass underneath this without getting wet, except for the spray made by the falling water."

Eventually the party arrived at Allumette Island in the Ottawa River (near present-day Pembroke), only to be told by the Algonquins living there that Vignau's story was false. In all probability, Vignau was referring to Hudson Bay, far to the north, and the Algonquins denied the story out of reluctance to reveal too much about their territory. In disgust with Vignau, Champlain returned to Montréal just three weeks after he had set out.

Champlain undertook his last great journey into the North American interior in 1615. Traveling by way of the Ottawa River to Lake Nipissing and the French River, he eventually arrived at Georgian Bay on the east side of Lake Huron. Here were the villages of Champlain's Huron allies. The explorer declared it a "country so fine and fertile that it is a pleasure to travel about in it." But it was more than a pleasure, it was also business, and the route that Champlain used to get to the region became the fur traders' road west for several hundred years thereafter.

At Georgian Bay, Champlain and the Hurons prepared for a campaign against the Iroquois. While the interpreter Etienne Brulé went with a small group of Hurons to secure the help of the Andastes, Champlain and the main group of Hurons made their way south via the eastern end of Lake Ontario to the home of the Onondaga Iroquois southeast of Lake Ontario. There they mounted a chaotic and disastrous attack characterized by a total lack of discipline on the part of the Hurons. Even the firearms of the French could not save the day, and Champlain was wounded in the battle. He and his allies were forced to retreat before Brulé and the Andastes arrived. In the disgrace of defeat, the Hurons reneged on a promise to escort Champlain back to Montréal, and he was forced

to spend the winter with them near Lake Ontario. He took the opportunity to visit tribes and explore areas he had not seen before, returning to Montréal in the spring of 1616.

In 1616 Champlain returned to France once again, this time to have the king confirm his authority in Québec. The rest of the explorer's life was spent trying to make the colony prosperous and self-supporting. In 1629 Québec was captured by the British and Champlain was taken as a prisoner to England. When the city was returned to France by a treaty in 1633 Champlain returned to Québec, where he died on December 25, 1635.

Throughout years of neglect and official disinterest in the region, Samuel de Champlain persisted in his dream of establishing a strong French colony in North America. Despite his frustrations, he never lost his enthusiasm for exploration and his curiosity about what was around the next bend in the river. For his work in exploring, mapping, and settling, Champlain rightly deserves the title of Father of New France.

SUGGESTED READING: Editors of *American Heritage*, *Discoverers of the New World* (American Heritage, 1960); Samuel Eliot Morison, *Samuel de Champlain: Father of New France* (Little, Brown, 1972); Francis Parkman, *Pioneers of France in the New World* (Little, Brown, 1897); Reader's Digest Association, *Great Adventures That Changed Our World* (Reader's Digest Association, 1978).

• Chancellor, Richard

English
b ?
d November 10, 1556; Aberdour Bay, Scotland
Opened White Sea trade with Russia

Assigned to guide a small fleet eastward to China through the seas north of Europe (thus attempting what became known as the Northeast Passage), Richard Chancellor turned an impossible mission into a great success by discovering the northern sea route to Russia in 1553. This unanticipated result quickly led to a flourishing trade between the English Muscovy Company, established in 1555, and the land of Czar Ivan IV (the Terrible). The original mission was marked by tragedy, however, when a storm blew Chancellor's ship away from two accompanying ships, which were lost without Chancellor to guide them. Tragically, one of the first duties of the new Muscovy Company was to escort the two lost ships back to England after they were found by Russian fishermen with the frozen bodies of HUGH WILLOUGHBY and his crew still aboard.

This mission had originally been the brainchild of John Dudley, the duke of Northumberland, who was lord admiral under Henry VIII and subsequently a major force in the ruling council under the young and sickly Edward VI. In 1551 Northumberland gathered some 200 merchants into a new Company of Merchant Adventurers, with £6,000 capital and a royal charter granting exclusive rights to all northern trade routes. Their plan was to win the same kind of wealth that the Spanish and Portuguese had gained through their voyages of discovery in the south. SEBASTIAN CABOT was appointed governor of the organization, which later became known as the Muscovy Company. His first duty was to organize an expedition to Cathay (now China) via the northern coast of Europe and Asia. For this purpose, he fitted out three ships: the *Bona Esperanza*, captained by Willoughby; the *Edward Bonaventure*, captained by Chancellor; and the *Bona Confidentia*.

The ships left England on May 10, 1553, two months before Edward VI died and the duke of Northumberland was executed for opposing the new queen, Mary. With slightly different timing, this mission might never have set off. It was in mid-July that the gale separated Chancellor's ship from Willoughby and the other two ships off the coast of Finnmark (now northernmost Norway). Chancellor proceeded to the port of Vardø, the rendezvous point, but Willoughby never arrived. After waiting seven days, Chancellor proceeded to the White Sea, where he met Russians at Kholmogory on the Dvina River. The fishermen were "amazed with the strange greatnesse of his shippe," as the sixteenth-century account has it, and began to flee in terror. When Chancellor caught up with them, he "looked pleasantly upon them, comforting them by signs and gestures."

This made a good impression, and soon the Russians were freely supplying food and information. When Ivan the Terrible received word of the visitors sometime later, he invited them to Moscow at his expense. Russia was then reliant on the Hanseatic League (an alliance of north German merchants) for trade with the West, since its borders did not yet reach the Baltic Sea, so he welcomed the chance to open a new trade route. He sent letters with Chancellor to Edward VI, though Mary was by then queen, favoring the establishment of "free mart with all free liberties" to English merchants.

When Chancellor delivered the letters in 1554, Mary, with the blessings of her husband, King Phillip II of Spain, granted a new charter to Chancellor's company. The resulting Muscovy Company began the first phase of the global expansion of the British Empire.

Chancellor took the new sea–land route to Moscow with the *Edward Bonaventure* and the *Phillip and Mary* in October 1555 to establish English markets there. That accomplished, he left the Lapland coast the following July for England, with the first Russian ambassador to England on board. Off the coast of Scotland he ran into a storm that ended his good luck. The *Edward Bonaventure* was dashed against the shore and "split in pieces." Chancellor was killed, but the ambassador was one of the few survivors. He was taken hostage, however, by the Scots who saved him and was not released until February 1557. He was escorted to London by Muscovy Company merchants and reached London on March 20, a year after leaving Moscow.

The ensuing relations between England and Russia were excellent. Trade prospered, but the Muscovy Company continued to think of Russia as merely a stopping stone to the fabulous riches of China. In 1557 it sent ANTHONY JENKINSON inland on a remarkable voyage down the Volga to the Caspian Sea, where trade with Persia (now Iran) was established.

Meanwhile, two of Chancellor's crew, William Burrough and Arthur Pet, continued the search for a Northeast Passage, work which was to be continued by the Dutch explorer WILLEM BARENTS but not completed until the nineteenth century. What they discovered was enough for the time being—that a commercially viable route to Cathay through these frigid waters was very unlikely.

Chang Ch'ien. See **Zhang Qian.**

Chang K'ien. See **Zhang Qian.**

Charcot, Jean-Baptiste-Étienne-Auguste

French
b July 15, 1867; Neuilly-sur-Seine
d September 16, 1936; at sea off Iceland
Led two expeditions to Antarctica

Dr. Jean-Baptiste Charcot was the first French explorer to turn his attention to Antarctica since JULES DUMONT D'URVILLE'S major expedition (1838–40). In addition to his contributions to the geographical knowledge of the frozen continent, Charcot is credited with bringing some of the comforts of twentieth-century civilization to Antarctic exploration.

Charcot was born in France, son of the noted neurologist and pathologist Jean Martin Charcot. The younger Charcot studied medicine at the École Alsacienne and practiced neurology himself until 1898, when his interests turned to polar exploration.

In August 1903 Charcot left St.-Malo, France, aboard the 250-ton *Français*. He originally intended to come to the aid of Dr. Otto Nordenskiöld (nephew of NILS ADOLF ERIK NORDENSKIÖLD), whose vessel was floundering near the Antarctic Circle. By the time Charcot reached Argentina, the Swedish team had been rescued, so he continued to the western side of the Antarctic Peninsula. There, he wintered at Booth Island and charted the Palmer Archipelago in great detail. He also discovered the mountainous Loubet Coast of Graham Land and explored the area around Adelaide Island.

Charcot left Antarctica in 1905, returning in 1908 aboard his research vessel, the *Pourquoi Pas?* The French government and a French newspaper partially financed the project. On this two-year expedition Charcot lived in as much comfort as the bitterly cold continent would allow, bringing with him a library, fine wines, telephones, and electric lights. He used **sledges** to cross the frozen terrain and compared notes on their performance with the British explorer ROBERT FALCON SCOTT, a friendly rival. Charcot spent the winter at Petermann Island, charting the coast south to Alexander Island, discovering the Fallières Coast and Charcot Island. He published extensive reports on his scientific investigations and discoveries, as well as a book on CHRISTOPHER COLUMBUS.

At the conclusion of his second Antarctic expedition, Charcot continued his oceanographic studies in the North Atlantic, the Mediterranean, and the English Channel. World War I interrupted his research, and he served as an auxiliary lieutenant in the French navy until 1920. For the next sixteen years he made a research cruise every summer aboard the *Pourquoi Pas?* In 1936, while on an expedition to Greenland, the vessel capsized off Iceland, and Charcot and thirty-eight of his crew members drowned.

Jean-Baptiste Charcot. The Bettmann Archive.

Charlevoix, Pierre François Xavier de

French
b October 24, 1682; St. Quentin
d February 1, 1761; La Flèche
Traveled up St. Lawrence River to Great Lakes and down Mississippi River

A Jesuit priest of noble stock, Pierre François Xavier de Charlevoix journeyed to America to find out more about the location of the Western Sea, that elusive prize sought by so many sons of **New France**. In pursuit of information about the fabled inland sea that purportedly led to the Pacific Ocean, Charlevoix traveled around the Great Lakes and then down the Mississippi River. Upon returning to France, he wrote the first detailed and reasonably accurate descriptions of the eastern interior of America.

Charlevoix's first voyage to America took place in 1705 when, as a recently ordained deacon, he was sent to New France to teach in the Jesuit college at Québec. He returned to France in 1709, was ordained a priest in 1713, and continued his teaching career. In 1719, perhaps because of his earlier experience in New France, he was asked to recommend boundaries for Acadia, a region claimed by both France and England. While Charlevoix was still involved in this task, the regent of France asked him to travel again to New France to research the rumors of an inland sea that was said to give rise to rivers that emptied into the Pacific Ocean. Since his purpose was to be kept secret, Charlevoix traveled under the pretext of examining the Jesuit missions in the New World.

Arriving at Québec on September 23, 1720, Charlevoix was forced to winter there. When spring arrived, he departed for the West. From the beginning, he kept copious notes on everything he observed and experienced. After traveling up the St. Lawrence River, he canoed through the Great Lakes, describing the coastline, estimating distances, and verifying latitudes. His notes eventually led to the publication of more accurate maps of the Great Lakes area.

In the upper Great Lakes area, Charlevoix questioned everyone he met—missionaries, Indians, **voyageurs**, and officers—about the fabled Western Sea. The missionaries and officers could tell him nothing; the voyageurs and Indians made up stories, as was their custom when asked about matters of which they knew nothing. However, Charlevoix did learn about "a great river that flows westward and empties into the southern sea." In July, Charlevoix decided to travel down the Mississippi River, to continue his research in Louisiana, and then in the summer of 1722 to return north to the Lake Superior posts he had not yet visited.

Thus, on July 29, 1721, Charlevoix's party headed down the east side of Lake Michigan and into the St. Joseph River. Illness and bad weather kept him at Fort St. Joseph (probably located near what is now Niles, Michigan) for about a month, and he used his time there to study the Miami Indians. His chosen route then took him southwest down the Kankakee River to the Illinois River and then to the Mississippi.

Sandbanks and fallen trees on the Mississippi made travel in the party's dugout canoes difficult, and the weather was unexpectedly cold. After spending Christmas day in the small settlement of Natchez, Charlevoix and his group arrived in New Orleans on January 10, 1722. Even though the settlement at the time contained but "a hundred or so shacks," Charlevoix predicted that it would someday be "an opulent city."

Later the priest went as far as the mouth of the Mississippi and from there east to the settlement at Biloxi on the Gulf of Mexico. There he came down with jaundice and in a weakened condition decided he could not make the return trip up the Mississippi to fulfill his plan to visit Lake Superior. He attempted to return to Québec by ship, but after a shipwreck in which all aboard survived, the passengers and crew spent fifty days getting back to Biloxi on foot.

Charlevoix's next attempt to sail north was also thwarted: his ship took two months to get from Biloxi to St.-Domingue on Hispaniola (the island now occupied by Haiti and the Dominican Republic). When it reached the island at the end of September, Charlevoix decided it was too late in the year to go north to Québec and sailed instead for France, arriving on December 26, 1722, his North American odyssey at an end.

From the information he had gathered on his expedition, Charlevoix concluded that the Western Sea lay between 40° and 50° North latitude and that Indian tribes west of the Sioux probably lived near it. He was also convinced that rivers flowing westward would be found near the headwaters of the Missouri River. He consequently offered the French government two proposals for reaching the Western Sea. The first was to mount an expedition to travel up the Missouri River; the second was to send missionaries to the Sioux in the hopes that these missionaries would eventually make contact with the tribes west of the Sioux. Charlevoix preferred the former alternative, but the government favored the latter.

Although Father Pierre Charlevoix explored no new territory in North America and although his information on the Western Sea was erroneous (since such a sea did not exist), his contributions to the exploration of the continent were invaluable. The journal of his travels combines lively narration and finely observed details with scholarly documentation, making it an equal to the classics of historical literature.

Cheng Ho. See **Zheng He.**

Ch'ien, Chang. See **Zhang Qian.**

Chini (Chino; Chinus), Eusebio Francisco. See **Kino, Eusebio Francisco.**

• Chirikov, Aleksei

Russian
b 1703; ?
d November 1748; Moscow
Explored northern coast of Asia and southern coast of Alaska

Though second in command to VITUS BERING on the two great Kamchatka Expeditions of 1725–30 and 1733–41, Captain Commander Aleksei Chirikov was in charge of the vessel that first reached Alaska from Siberia, actually beating Bering by a day and a half in 1741. Many historians, especially Russians, have credited Chirikov with being the more capable leader. They point to the fact that in 1741 he successfully marshaled his crippled crew back to the Siberian mainland after making essentially the same discoveries as his less fortunate superior. They also suggest that Bering's first expedition would have gathered more valuable information had Chirikov's advice to proceed farther north along the Siberian coast been taken.

Whatever the case, it is worth remembering that the actual voyages of discovery by sea were minor affairs compared to the preceding efforts of both men to lead their huge, lumbering expeditions overland across Asia to its Pacific coast. Neither man seems to have been particularly jealous of the other. Both cooperated fully throughout their long ordeal, and both suffered enormously. Though Chirikov survived the trip back from the shores of Alaska, he contracted **scurvy** and never fully recovered, dying three years later at the age of forty-five.

Chirikov came to his job as Bering's principal aide by rising quickly through the ranks of the Russian navy. He graduated from the naval academy in 1721, was immediately appointed sublieutenant (skipping the rank of midshipman), and after a short stint at sea began teaching navigation at the academy. There he attracted the attention of the organizers of the Bering expedition, who made him, along with Martin Spanberg, second-in-command. Chirikov was remarkably coolheaded and dispassionate, even during the long and difficult second expedition when so many others broke down under the pressure. But his spirits finally flagged when his two landing parties were lost after the *St. Peter* reached Prince of Wales Island in southeastern Alaska in mid-July 1741, a month after his and Bering's ships became separated in a storm. The landing parties were apparently taken prisoner by the native people of Chicagof Island in what is now the Alexander Archipelago, though Chirikov could only guess their fate after both disappeared, the second party in search of the first. Their disappearance not only meant the loss of some twenty crew members with whom Chirikov had traveled for eight years, but the end of all land exploration (including landings for fresh water), since the ship's only boats had disappeared. Chirikov was consequently forced to head back to Siberia, passing the Kenai Peninsula and several of the Aleutian Islands, where he received some water (but not nearly enough) from a party of cautious Aleuts. By the time he reached Avatcha Bay on Kamchatka Peninsula on October 8, another twenty of his crew were dead from scurvy. As one contemporary pointed out, on this voyage Chirikov "had not less to suffer" than Bering.

After spending the winter recovering, Chirikov returned to sea to search for his missing leader, passing close by what is now Bering Island, where Bering had died earlier and where the remainder of his crew was preparing its escape. Chirikov intended to return to Alaska but was forced back to Avatcha by bad weather, getting no farther than Atka Island in the Aleutians. When he returned to St. Petersburg, he was promoted to captain commander. He spent his last days in Moscow.

Chouart, Médard, Sieur de Groseilliers. See **Groseilliers, Médard Chouart, Sieur de.**

Cintra, Pêro da. See **Sintra, Pedro de.**

Clapperton, Hugh

Scottish
b May 18, 1788; Annan, Dumfriesshire
d April 13, 1827; Sokoto, Nigeria
Explored West Africa

A member of the first European expedition known to reach Lake Chad, Hugh Clapperton explored extensively in the interior of West Africa, particularly along the Niger River. While he was only partially successful in his goal of tracing the path of the Niger, he uncovered significant information about the river's course. Initially given little credit for his accomplishments, Clapperton was eventually recognized not only for the accomplishments of his explorations but also for his outspoken opposition to the African slave trade.

One of twenty-one children fathered by a Dumfriesshire surgeon, Clapperton left home at age thirteen and took a job as a cabin boy on a trading ship. He later joined the British navy and had attained the rank of lieutenant by the time he was chosen for his first African expedition in 1820. The expedition group, led by Dr. Walter Oudney, was assigned by the British government to determine whether the Niger ran through Bornu (in present-day Nigeria). In 1821, Clapperton, Oudney, and the other members of the group reached Tripoli (in what is now Libya), where they were met by DIXON DENHAM, an army major who claimed he was to lead the expedition. Clapperton sided with Oudney in the resulting dispute, and the two went south to Murzuch in the Sahara desert and then to Bornu. Denham traveled separately.

Clapperton and Oudney reached Bornu in late 1822; they found Lake Chad within two months and learned there that the Niger ran south rather than east. Denham joined them in Bornu's capital city of Kuka (now Kukawa, Nigeria) and stayed there while the others trekked southwest toward Nupe to trace the Niger's path. Oudney became ill and died in early 1824, and Clapperton went west to Sokoto (in what is now northern Nigeria), where he met with its sultan, Bello. Clapperton and Bello had an amicable relationship despite Clapperton's objections to the local slave trade and Bello's ban on travel into Nupe on the grounds that it was unsafe. Clapperton returned to London in 1825 and arranged to have his journal published; he left for Africa again late that year.

In spite of poor health, Clapperton was determined to keep exploring the Niger and to petition Bello to give up slave trading. He and his servant, RICHARD LEMON LANDER, approached Sokoto from the south this time, via Yoruba and Kano. Clapperton died shortly after reaching Sokoto, however, and his account of the trip was later published by Lander.

Hugh Clapperton. Library of Congress.

Clark, William

American
b August 1, 1770; Caroline County, Virginia
d September 1, 1838; St. Louis, Missouri
With Meriwether Lewis, led major expedition
    exploring length of Missouri River and
    northwestern United States

The even-tempered William Clark was MERIWETHER LEWIS's able cocommander of the Corps of Discovery, better known as the Lewis and Clark expedition, which traversed and explored half of the North American continent. The expedition followed the Missouri River from its mouth (just north of St. Louis on the Mississippi

William Clark. Independence National Historical Park Collection.

River) to its source in the Rocky Mountains, crossed the mountains and followed the Columbia River to the Pacific coast, and then returned to Missouri by a similar route. (For a map, see LEWIS.)

Younger brother of Revolutionary War hero George Rogers Clark, William grew up hearing the tales of his brother's daring deeds. After the war, his family moved to Kentucky, and from 1789 to 1791 Clark participated in several skirmishes between the frontier settlers and Indians who were trying to protect their lands. In 1792, he was commissioned as lieutenant of infantry in the regular army. After four years of service under General "Mad Anthony" Wayne, Clark began to tire of military life. After resigning in 1796, he traveled widely until 1803, when he received a letter from Meriwether Lewis, who had served with him under General Wayne. Lewis wrote to invite him to serve as cocommander of the Corps of Discovery. The corps was to explore the western part of the continent acquired from France through the Louisiana Purchase just several months after

the creation of the corps by President Thomas Jefferson. Jefferson hoped Lewis and Clark could locate a practical water route to the Pacific coast and add to the geographic knowledge of the vast region.

While Lewis busied himself with preparations for scientific aspects of the journey, Clark put his affairs in order and then journeyed to St. Louis to meet up with Lewis. The expedition spent the winter in quarters nearby and on May 14, 1804, started up the Missouri. By October 27 they had navigated 1,600 miles of river to reach the Mandan villages first visited by LA VÉRENDRYE and his French-Canadian **voyageurs** in their search for the Western Sea. Near the Mandans, in what is now North Dakota, they built quarters and settled in to wait out the cold winter.

While in winter quarters, Lewis and Clark were approached by a Montréal fur trader, Toussaint Charbonneau, who wished to become part of the expedition. His pregnant wife, a Shoshone woman named Sacajawea, had been captured by Minetaree Indians and later sold to Charbonneau. Lewis and Clark could see immediately that Sacajawea would be invaluable both as an interpreter and as a symbol of the peaceful nature of the expedition (no war party ever traveled with a woman and child). Clark took a particular interest in Sacajawea's child, Jean-Baptiste Charbonneau, to whom he gave the affectionate nickname "Pomp." He also grew very fond of Sacajawea. (Later in his life he saw to the education of "Pomp" and other Charbonneau children.)

At the tender age of eight weeks, little "Pomp" was strapped to his mother's back to join the expedition as it set off west from the Mandan villages on April 9, 1805. As they worked their way along the upper Missouri, Clark and Lewis resumed their customary roles. While the moody and restless Lewis frequently took off on long inland explorations and hunting excursions, the sociable Clark stayed with the boats, surveying and making maps, writing journal entries, and enjoying the companionship of those in his party. The trip, while relatively easy at this point, was not without hazard. There were mild annoyances—squalls, head winds, and dust storms—and frequent meetings with grizzly bears, whose power to resist death when shot was a quality the hunters soon learned to respect. One evening a buffalo charged through the center of camp, barely avoiding crushing some sleeping explorers. Another time Clark himself narrowly escaped being bitten by a rattlesnake.

However, just below the Great Falls (in present-day Montana) the trip became more hazardous and uncomfortable as the river began to climb into the foothills of the Rockies. The water became shallower, the weather colder and rainy. The men were, in Clark's words, often "up to their armpits in the cold water, and sometimes walk[ed] for several yards over the sharp fragments of rocks." In spite of it all, they worked with "great patience and humour." The party took 12½ days to make an 18-mile **portage** around 10 miles of falls, all the while enduring oppressive heat punctuated by thunderstorms, hailstorms, and once even a tornado. With faces attacked by insects and moccasined feet tortured by prickly-pear thorns, the members of the party plodded on. By July 15 they were back on the Missouri again, but on July 25, after approximately 2,300 miles, the longest river in North America petered out into three source streams, which Lewis and Clark named after President Jefferson, Secretary of State Madison, and Secretary of the Treasury Gallatin.

By this time Sacajawea was beginning to recognize landmarks from her youth, but no Shoshones had yet appeared. While Lewis and a small party set off on foot, Clark, Sacajawea, and the rest of the expedition followed the Jefferson River. When they finally caught up with Lewis, on August 17, he had made contact with the Shoshones. Sacajawea began to "dance and show every mark of the most extravagant joy . . . suckling her fingers . . . to indicate that [the Indians] were of her native tribe." Taken to a council meeting, she immediately recognized the chief, Cameahwait, as her brother and embraced him.

Acquiring horses and a guide from the Shoshones, the party lost no time in moving on; Lewis and Clark knew they had far to go if they hoped to reach the Pacific coast before winter. The guide led them through the valley of the Salmon River, which was unnavigable, and into the Bitterroot Range of the Rocky Mountains. The next month was their most difficult yet as they were forced to hack their way through the wilderness. On September 16 snow fell, wiping out all signs of the trail. To add to their troubles, the expedition's hunters could not find enough game, and the members of the party began to grow thin and to suffer from dysentery (an acute intestinal disease) and **scurvy**.

At last they reached the friendly villages of the Nez Percés, where their Shoshone guide left them in the capable hands of two chiefs who volunteered to take them to the sea. On October 7, they started down the Clearwater River and entered the Snake River on October 10 and the Columbia River on October 16. The two Nez Percés and Sacajawea were guarantees of a friendly welcome at Indian villages along the way, and around evening campfires, Lewis and Clark entertained their Indian hosts with tobacco and violin music.

On October 22 the explorers came face to face with a second mountain range—the Cascades of what is now central Washington State—that had to be crossed before they could reach the Pacific. However, a difficult river pass through the Cascades was easily managed by the now thoroughly experienced rivermen, and by November 2 they had reached tidewater. Following the Columbia's tidal estuary to the sea, they finally caught sight of the Pacific on November 15. Soon they built their winter quarters, Fort Clatsop, near the site of present-day Astoria, Oregon. Pouring rains confined them to their quarters for most of the winter, and they spent the time eating, sleeping, and contemplating the sea, "more raging than Pacific."

When the weather cleared in March, the expedition retraced its route to the Bitterroot River valley, near modern-day Missoula, Montana. There they divided into two parties. While Lewis took an Indian shortcut to the Missouri and explored the Marias River—a northern tributary of the Missouri—Clark led the other group through Shoshone territory and down the Jefferson River to Three Forks. A few men continued on down the Missouri while Clark and the main body traveled overland south to the Yellowstone River and canoed down it to the Missouri.

Clark was reunited with Lewis on the Missouri near the mouth of the Yellowstone on August 12, and, two days later at the Mandan villages, Clark said good-bye to Sacajawea and her family. On September 23, 1806, the Corps of Discovery returned to St. Louis to the cheers of a welcoming crowd.

Immediately after the expedition, Clark devoted some attention to editing the several diaries that had been written during the journey, including his and Lewis's. Their account of the expedition, however, was not published until 1814. In the meantime, Clark was appointed brigadier general of militia and superintendent of Indian affairs for Louisiana (later Missouri) Territory. He served as governor of the territory, starting in 1813, and resided in St. Louis until his death in 1838.

William Clark and Meriwether Lewis were ideally suited to work together, being temperamental opposites who respected each other and always acted in harmony. Clark was the older of the two and the more experienced frontiersman. He was also a mapmaker and an artist, drawing birds, fish, and animals with great care and skill. The more even-tempered of the two, he contributed significantly to the harmonious nature of a difficult trek.

Although Lewis and Clark found no direct water route to the Pacific, the information they brought home was crucial in opening up the western North American continent to settlement. As a result of the expedition, the United States government acquired for the first time a measurement of the continent's width, a new understanding of the richness of the Western interior, and a legitimate claim to the Columbia River and the territory surrounding it. Lewis and Clark, guided by the wise instructions of President Jefferson, accomplished what no previous explorers had been able to. They focused attention on the land itself as a valuable commodity rather than a mere passageway to the Orient.

SUGGESTED READING: Ralph K. Andrist, *To the Pacific with Lewis and Clark* (American Heritage, 1967); John Bakeless, *Lewis and Clark: Partners in Discovery* (William Morrow, 1966); Rhoda Blumberg, *The Incredible Journey of Lewis and Clark* (Lothrop, 1987); Reader's Digest Association, *Great Adventures That Changed Our World* (Reader's Digest Association, 1978).

Claudius Ptolemaeus. See **Ptolemy.**

• Colter, John

American
b 1775?; Staunton, Virginia
d November 1813; near Missouri River
Explored uncharted territory in Wyoming, Montana, and Idaho

In the winter of 1807 and 1808, John Colter, who had been a member of the Lewis and Clark expedition, made an extraordinary circuit through land that is now Wyoming, Montana, and Idaho. Traveling alone, he spent several months in territory never before seen by a non-Indian. Among the wonders he viewed were the hot springs, boiling mudholes, and geysers in and near present-day Yellowstone National Park.

Little is known of John Colter's life before he joined the Corps of Discovery headed by MERIWETHER LEWIS and WILLIAM CLARK and participated in their historic voyage (1804–1806) up the Missouri River to its source in the Rocky Mountains and from there west to the shores of the Pacific Ocean. Lewis and Clark both mention Colter frequently in their journals, and the fact that he was singled out for some particularly dangerous missions attests to their confidence in him.

During its return trip to St. Louis in the summer of 1806, the Corps of Discovery met two fur trappers, Joseph Dickson and Forrest Hancock, who immediately realized what an advantage they would have in the wilderness if accompanied by a member of the expedition. They approached Colter, and he was granted permission to leave the expedition early, provided that no one else sought the same dispensation.

Over the next winter, Colter guided Dickson and Hancock around the valley of the Yellowstone River for a successful trapping season. The next spring Colter again started home. This time, at the mouth of the Platte River (near present-day Omaha, Nebraska), he met Manuel Lisa. Lisa was a bold, and generally disliked, entrepreneur who had recognized early the commercial implications of Lewis and Clark's explorations. In 1807 he had hired several former Corps members in order to establish a fur-trapping post somewhere up the Missouri. Lisa persuaded Colter to join them and head west again. At Colter's suggestion, Lisa built his fort and trading center where the Bighorn River flows into the Yellowstone in what is now eastern Montana. Lisa named it Fort Raymond, after his son.

While the others spent the winter of 1807–1808 trapping beaver, Colter embarked on what may rank as the most extraordinary solo exploration of North America ever undertaken by an American of European descent. Lisa had given him two objectives: to scout for new beaver territory and to encourage the Crows and other Indian tribes south and west of the Yellowstone to bring their furs to Fort Raymond. Based on his route, some historians believe that Colter was also looking for a way to hook up with the Spanish in the Southwest in order to engage them in fur trading.

Colter's trek took him over roughly 500 mountain miles in a mid-winter circuit through what is now Wyoming, Montana, and Idaho. Since he left no journals, the evidence of his route is scanty. Historians generally assume that he made a large figure eight to the south and west of Fort Raymond, traveling across the Bighorn basin to the Tetons and what is now Yellowstone Park. Although it is not definite in which direction he initially headed, it is generally assumed that when he left Fort Raymond he traveled west across the Pryor Mountains (a spur of the Bighorns) and then southwest across the Bighorn basin to the foot of the Absaroka Range on the eastern border of Yellowstone Park. He then turned southeast and followed the mountains to reach the Shoshone River. It was here that he saw the hot springs and geysers near what is now Yellowstone National Park. Still traveling south he skirted the Absarokas into the Wind River valley. Turning up the valley, he crossed into Jackson Hole and saw the magnificent sight of the Grand Tetons before him.

By this time, probably January, Colter had gone about as far from Fort Raymond as Indians were likely to consider bringing their furs, and his supplies must have been getting low. Nonetheless, he chose to press forward over the Tetons, probably on homemade snowshoes. (Interestingly, in 1931 a farmer plowing just inside the Idaho border on the western slope of Teton Pass unearthed a chunk of rock on one side of which was scratched "John Colter" and on the other, "1808." The etched notation is believed to be authentic.)

After crossing the Tetons, Colter turned south again, possibly still looking for Spanish settlements. Then he abruptly turned back and recrossed the Tetons, following them north back into modern Yellowstone National Park. Finally, he headed back in an easterly direction toward Fort Raymond.

After returning to the fort, Colter set out for the area in southwestern Montana where the Missouri River splits into three forks, named the Jefferson, the Madison, and the Gallatin by Lewis and Clark. There he was trapping beaver in October 1808 with one other man, John Potts,

keeping careful watch for the Blackfoot Indians, who were still looking to avenge two of their tribe killed in a skirmish with Meriwether Lewis in 1806. Potts and Colter were nevertheless taken by surprise by the Blackfoot Indians, and when Potts tried to defend himself, he was killed instantly. The Blackfoot Indians tormented Colter casually while they discussed the most entertaining way of putting him to death. Finally they asked him how good a runner he was. Colter, who was a swift runner, understood what they were up to and replied that he was as slow as a turtle. Stripped naked, he was given a thirty-second head start before the Blackfoot warriors took off after him. To their astonishment and chagrin, Colter quickly darted ahead and before long had outdistanced all but one of the Blackfoot Indians, who was gaining on him. Colter turned and, with exquisite timing, tripped his pursuer, wrested his spear away from him, and killed him. Colter then raced for the Jefferson Fork, jumped in the water and hid beneath a log jam of driftwood (or possibly a beaver lodge) while the angry Blackfoot Indians searched the shore for him. That night he swam 5 miles downstream in the frigid waters and then started running again. One hundred and fifty miles farther and a week or two later, he limped into Fort Raymond. His feet were torn to shreds by cactus thorns; he was naked and sunburned and covered by insect bites. He took a few weeks to regain his strength and then set out on another fur-trapping expedition.

After two more narrow escapes with the Blackfoot Indians, the last of which saw his five companions shot down around him, Colter made his way back to Fort Raymond early in 1810 and announced his retirement with these words: "If God will only forgive me this time and let me off I will leave the country . . . and be damned if I ever come into it again." He was true to his word. A few days later, he got into his canoe and paddled 2,000 miles to St. Louis, never to return to the Western wilderness again.

In St. Louis, he was well received by his former captain, William Clark, who added Colter's geographical information to a map he kept and added to as his former followers checked in with him to describe their own travels. This was the closest Colter came to providing a record of his extraordinary achievements. In general, he was given little credit for his trailblazing because he left neither charts nor journals of his travels. When he described some of the wonders he had seen to people in St. Louis, they found the idea of hot springs and geysers unfathomable and gave his discovery the mocking name "Colter's Hell."

John Colter was not only the archetypal American mountain man and trapper, he was possibly the finest expression of the type. Possessed of immense physical endurance, he also had the psychological stamina to exist alone in the wilderness for long periods. He was truly a trailblazer of the Rocky Mountain wilderness.

• Columbus, Christopher
(Colombo, Cristoforo; Colom, Cristovão; Colón, Cristóbal)

Italian
b August 25–October 31, 1451?; Genoa
d May 20, 1506; Valladolid, Spain
Discovered the Americas (for Spain)

The fundamental history lesson learned by students in the United States is that the Italian mariner Christopher Columbus, sailing under the auspices of the Spanish monarchs Ferdinand and Isabella, crossed the Atlantic Ocean in search of a shorter route to the Indies and discovered America on October 12, 1492. Through the centuries this momentous discovery has elicited continual inquiry into the explorer's precise route and the place where he first landed in what are now the Bahama Islands. During this first voyage Columbus also discovered several Bahama Islands, plus Cuba and Hispaniola (the island now occupied by Haiti and the Dominican Republic). On three subsequent voyages to the New World (1493, 1498, and 1502) he discovered what are now Puerto Rico, Jamaica, and various islands in the Leeward, Windward, and Virgin island chains; established the first European colony in the New World; and explored the coastlines of present-day Honduras, Nicaragua, Costa Rica, and Panama in search of a strait to the Asian mainland. Columbus's discoveries led directly to the exploration and consequent development of the Western Hemisphere by the countries of Western Europe.

In addition to inspiring intense investigation of his four voyages, Columbus himself has come under much personal scrutiny. His life is shrouded in mystery and controversy. The first item in question concerns where and when Christopher Columbus was born. Though it is generally accepted that he was born between August 25 and October 31, 1451, various other dates have been proposed, as early as 1435 and as late as 1460. His birthplace has variously been given as Genoa, the islands of Khíos or Majorca, Galicia, or any of several towns in Spain. The belief of some historians that Columbus was Spanish-born stems primarily from the fact that the forty surviving letters and documents with his authenticated signature are written in Spanish, as are most of the marginal notes in the books of his personal library, much of which has been preserved. However, Columbus stated that he was born in Genoa, and all chroniclers of his time, as well as many modern historians, refer to him as Genoese.

His heritage and educational background have ignited still more controversy. While many historians describe Columbus as the eldest of five children born to poor wool-weavers, some scholars argue that he was of higher birth, perhaps even descended from royalty. Support for this latter theory comes primarily from the fact that Columbus married a Portuguese noblewoman, an occurrence that would have been highly improbable if he had been a commoner. Scholars generally concede that he had little formal education, though he was quite knowledgeable regarding the scientific and philosophical concepts of his day. It is doubtful that he ever attended Italy's University of Pavia, as his son Fernando contended in his biography of his famous father. However, Columbus was a keen observer and extremely well-read, being particularly influenced by the works of Aristotle, the Scottish theologian Duns Scotus, and various Arab philosophers and astronomers, as well as by PTOLEMY's *Geographia* and MARCO POLO's *Travels*.

Evidence indicates that Columbus intentionally altered the facts of his personal background. Fernando even writes that his father purposely chose to conceal information about his birth and family. Scholars have speculated that this deliberate alteration may have been for political reasons; he may have fought against Spain at some time and prudently disguised it. Recently, it has been asserted that he was prompted to cloak his past because of Jewish heritage on one side of his family, a fact to be kept secret at a time when Jews were being expelled from Spain. Much circumstantial evidence has been gathered (notably by Jewish historian Simon Wiesenthal and Columbian scholar Salvador de Madariaga) to support this view. Whatever the reasons, little is known of Columbus's background and early life. It is generally accepted, however, that he went to sea at an early age with his brother Bartolomé, who was his closest friend and confidant throughout his life.

In 1476 Columbus traveled to Lisbon, Portugal, where there was an established Genoese population, including Bartolomé, a noted mapmaker by this time. The popular story of his arrival, as told by son Fernando, is that Columbus swam ashore after his ship sank during a sea battle. Between 1476 and 1485 he sailed with the Portuguese throughout the Mediterranean and in the Atlantic as far south as La Mina (present-day Elmina, Ghana) and as far north as England. That Columbus also made a voyage to Iceland in 1477 has received strong support by at least one contemporary Columbian scholar.

In 1479 Columbus married the Portuguese noblewoman Doná Felipa Perestrello e Moriz and established residence on one of the islands of Madeira (probably Porto Santo) where his son Diego was born in 1480. When his wife died, sometime between 1481 and 1485, he returned to Lisbon. As early as 1484 Columbus conceived a plan to sail west from the Canary Islands to reach the Indies (now the East Indies) and the island kingdom of Cipangu (modern Japan) thought to be located off the eastern coast of Asia. When King John II of Portugal rejected Columbus's "Enterprise of the Indies," the mariner decided to take his proposal to the Spanish monarchs. Accordingly, he traveled to Córdoba, Spain, in 1485. There he took a mistress, Beatriz Enríque de Arana, who bore him a son, Fernando, in 1488. He presented his plan to King Ferdinand and Queen Isabella on two different occasions, but both times a council of experts rejected his project, and his ideas were ridiculed by many at court. However, he received support from several powerful people, most notably Luis de Santangel, chancellor of the royal household of Aragon, and Prior Juan Perez, the queen's confessor. As a result, Isabella was convinced in 1491 to approve the project.

The primary purpose of Columbus's first voyage was to find a short route to the Indies by sailing west. A lucrative trading destination,

the Indies were reachable from Europe at that time only by sailing south and east around Africa's Cape of Good Hope, a long and dangerous route. The voyage's secondary goals were to convert any inhabitants of foreign lands to Christianity and to find gold. From the journal that Columbus kept on the voyage it is clear that he also expected to discover new lands and, in anticipation of doing so, had extracted a royal promise that he would be made governor and viceroy of all such lands, as well as "Admiral of the Ocean Sea" (with all titles to be hereditary). In addition, an underlying purpose throughout Columbus's life was to help form a new Christian Crusade for conquering the Holy Land, to be financed by any wealth gained from his ventures. That he was a devout Christian is evident in everything he did and wrote.

A crew and the necessary supplies were acquired in the town of Palos, where three ships were readied for the voyage. The flagship, the *Santa Maria*, was a three-masted, **square-rigged** cargo vessel that held forty sailors; the *Pinta* was a three-masted, square-rigged **caravel** carrying twenty-six and captained by MARTÍN ALONSO PINZÓN; and the *Niña* was a four-masted, **lateen-rigged** caravel carrying twenty-four and captained by Martín's brother VICENTE YÁÑEZ PINZÓN. On August 3, 1492, this small fleet left Palos but was forced to spend a month at the Canary Islands while the *Pinta*'s rudder was repaired and the *Niña* was converted to square-rigging to improve its sailing. The expedition finally departed the Canaries on September 6 on a voyage that would test Columbus's judgment, tenacity, diplomacy, and navigational skills.

Columbus navigated by the method known as dead reckoning (where a ship's route is recorded by using a compass, the speed through the water, and the direction and strength of the winds) and let the **trade winds** carry him south as he headed west. He accepted the prevailing idea of his day that the earth was round; the common belief that the earth was at that time thought to be flat is mythology. But he also accepted Greek mathematician and geographer Ptolemy's calculation of its size, consequently believing the sphere to be much smaller than it actually is. As a result, it took the ships longer to reach land (slightly over thirty-three days) than he had planned (twenty-one days), and he had to continually allay the fears of his mostly Spanish crew in order to prevent a mu-

Columbus's first fleet: (from left to right) the Santa Maria, the Pinta, and the Niña. The Bettmann Archive.

tiny. Wisely, he told them they had traveled fewer **leagues** than they actually had. He both understood and accepted their natural distrust of him as a foreigner.

The log of the voyage (actually BARTOLOMÉ DE LAS CASAS's abstract of the log; the original was lost) reveals that Columbus was a keen observer. It includes numerous references to a variety of natural phenomena, including weather conditions, water color, cloud formations, plants, and animals. He put his trust in the compass needle, which, he wrote, "always seeks the truth," and in his faith: "[W]ith God's help I shall persevere." Remarkably, though the 2,300-mile voyage was made during hurricane season, Columbus found the sea "like a river and the air sweet . . ."

On the night of October 11 Columbus thought he saw "a light to the west. It looked like a little wax candle bobbing up and down." Then, two hours after midnight on October 12, a seaman on the *Pinta*, Rodrigo de Triana, was the first to sight land—an island in the Bahamas. That morning Columbus went ashore, claimed the island for Spain—naming it San Salvador—and traded with its native people (he called them Indians, thinking mistakenly that he had reached one of the many islands off the coast of Asia, as described by Marco Polo).

Where exactly was this historic landfall, this island of San Salvador? No fewer than nine islands have been proposed as Columbus's first landfall in the Bahamas, including present-day Cat, Conception, Plana Cays, Mayaguana, East Caicos, Grand Turk, Egg, Watlings, and Samana Cay. Throughout much of the twentieth century, Watlings Island was generally accepted as the first landfall. In 1986 a team from the National Geographic Society concluded that Samana Cay was the landfall site, based upon geographical details in Columbus's log, archaeological evidence of the Arawak (or Lucayan or Taino) Indians he encountered, and the fact that from Samana Cay the route to Cuba is exactly as it was logged by Columbus. An equally thorough study published in 1991 concluded that the island of landfall was actually Grand Turk. Needless to say, questions remain as to these details of history; the broad facts, however, are well documented.

After trading glass beads with the islanders for parrots and "a kind of dry leaf" (tobacco), Columbus took six or seven Indians with him. He left the island on October 14, heading south to find a king reputed by the Arawaks to have much gold. He reached a second island, which he called Santa Maria de la Concepción (modern Crooked Island, by the 1986 reckoning; the Caicos Islands, by the 1991 plotting), then anchored at another island of unusual size, which he named Fernandina (modern Long Island or Mayaguana, by the respective studies). There he marveled at the many species of fish, the beautiful trees, and the temperate climate. De-

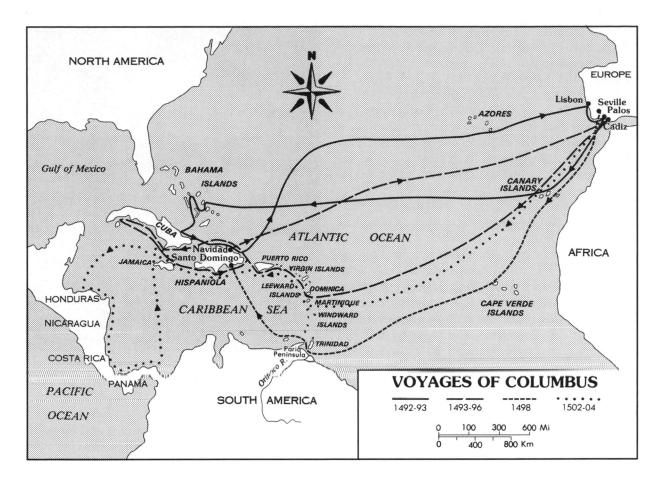

NORTH AMERICA

EUROPE

Lisbon
Seville
Palos
Cádiz

AZORES

Gulf of Mexico

BAHAMA
ISLANDS

ATLANTIC   OCEAN

CANARY
ISLANDS

AFRICA

CUBA

Navidad
Santo Domingo

PUERTO RICO
VIRGIN ISLANDS

JAMAICA

HISPANIOLA

LEEWARD
ISLANDS

DOMINICA

HONDURAS

CARIBBEAN   SEA

MARTINIQUE

WINDWARD
ISLANDS

CAPE VERDE
ISLANDS

NICARAGUA

COSTA RICA

PANAMA

PACIFIC

OCEAN

SOUTH   AMERICA

Paria
Peninsula

Orinoco R.

TRINIDAD

VOYAGES OF COLUMBUS

———	———	- - - - -	· · · · ·
1492-93	1493-96	1498	1502-04

0   100   300   600 Mi

0   400   800 Km

parting this island on October 17, he searched further for the land of the rich king, landing on an island he called Isabella (identified by the studies as Fortune Island and Great and Little Inagua, respectively). He then abandoned the search and headed west-southwest toward what is now Cuba. He reached it on October 28, first entering present-day Bahia de Bariay, then anchoring in present-day Bahia de Gibara. Traveling some 360 miles along the Cuban coast, he observed good harbors and made several more landings. There he first heard about the Caribs, Indians who ate human flesh, people the Arawaks called "cannibals."

On November 21, without permission from Columbus, Martín Alonso Pinzón took the *Pinta* to search for gold. The other ships sailed northeast by east, then reversed to a generally southeasterly course until they reached the island now called Hispaniola, making landfall at modern Môle St. Nicolas, Haiti. During the exploration of the Hispaniola coastline, the *Santa Maria* ran aground on December 24, and Columbus was forced to abandon it. A young Indian chief

of the island, Guacanaqari, sent people to help Columbus and his crew transfer supplies to the *Niña*, and the chief subsequently established a warm friendship with the admiral. Before leaving Hispaniola, Columbus founded the first European settlement in the Western Hemisphere since that of the Vikings; he called it La Villa de La Navidad (probably at what is now En Bas Saline, Haiti) and left roughly forty Spaniards behind to fortify it.

Reunited with the *Pinta*, Columbus sailed for Spain on January 16, 1493, having pardoned Pinzón for his desertion. On February 14 a severe storm separated the two ships, however, prompting Columbus to pledge to go on pilgrimages if God would rescue them. Columbus's superb navigation during this storm, as well as his earlier ability to adapt his navigation to the conditions posed by unfamiliar winds, coral reefs, and shallows encountered in the Bahamas, prompted Las Casas to write that "Christopher Columbus surpassed all his contemporaries in the art of navigation."

Preparations for a second voyage were

started almost immediately after his triumphant return to Spain. Columbus sailed again on September 25, 1493, this time from Cadiz with a much larger fleet of seventeen ships carrying 1,500 men—an indication that Ferdinand and Isabella were pleased with Columbus. The objectives for this voyage were to establish a permanent trading colony, to convert the Indians to Christianity, and to explore Cuba to determine if it was an island or part of the mainland.

The island now known as Dominica was sighted on November 3; from there Columbus sailed north and west, discovering and naming the Leeward Islands. He spent six days on the large island he called Santa Maria de Guadalupe (present-day Guadeloupe), then continued northwest, stopping at San Martin (modern Nevis). Sailing past the islands known today as St. Kitts, St. Eustatius, and Saba, he dropped anchor again on November 14 at a slipper-shaped island he named Santa Cruz (now known as St. Croix). Columbus next approached a series of islands that he named the Virgin Islands, then sailed to Hispaniola, where he found La Navidad in ruins and all the Spaniards left there the previous year killed. Abandoning this site, he established a new colony called Isabella farther east near the area of Cibao, where gold had been discovered. In 1494 he sent twelve ships back to Spain loaded with gold and requested additional supplies.

Meanwhile, Columbus explored Cibao and began erecting fortresses throughout Hispaniola. After restoring order at Isabella, he sailed for Cuba in April, spending six weeks picking his way among the small islands and dangerous shoals along its southern coast. On June 13 he reached the southernmost point of Cuba (Cape Cruz) and turned back, confident that Cuba was a peninsula of a continental mainland, which he believed to be Asia. After contending with strong head winds and currents while sailing eastward, he turned south from Cape Cruz and discovered the island now known as Jamaica. Increasingly bothered by arthritis, Columbus fell into a feverish stupor brought on by malaria and returned to Isabella in September. The colony was again in disorder, but fortunately his brother Bartolomé had arrived from Spain with supply ships and helped restore calm. Columbus lay ill at Isabella for five months, then decided to return to Spain to deal with charges being made against him by his enemies. Before

Christopher Columbus. Art Resource Center.

departing, he abandoned Isabella and founded the new colony of Santo Domingo, leaving Bartolomé in charge.

Upon reaching Spain, Columbus found that the king and queen still had confidence in him. They approved a third expedition to find the mainland that he reported lay south of the islands he had discovered. He departed from Seville in May 1498, after two years of preparation, with six ships. From the Canary Islands he sent three ships west to supply Hispaniola, while he directed the other three south to the Cape Verde Islands. Then, heading west, Columbus reached the island he named Trinidad on July 31 and sailed along its southern shore before turning north to sail along the Orinoco River delta of modern Venezuela. Seeing the fresh water flowing into the ocean from numerous tributaries of the Orinoco, Columbus deduced that he was sailing along the coastline of a continent. Though he wished to explore further in hopes of finding a strait that would lead to India and the Spice Islands (the present-day Moluccas), he decided to head for Hispaniola. On the way, however, he sailed through the Gulf of Paria and landed on the south coast of the Paria Peninsula (in present-day Venezuela); this was the first landfall by Europeans in South America.

When Columbus reached the colony of Santo Domingo, he had to quell a rebellion, which resulted in complaints being lodged against him. To investigate these allegations, the Spanish monarchs sent Francisco de Bobadilla, who was given the power to replace Columbus, if necessary. Consequently, on August 24, 1500, Columbus and Bartolomé were arrested and sent back to Spain for trial. Although they were ultimately absolved from any wrongdoing, they were not permitted to return to Hispaniola for a time.

Since Columbus's initial voyage, other explorers had made discoveries, and the idea was gaining acceptance that Columbus had not reached Asia, but a "New World." Eager to prove that he had in fact reached the Indies, Columbus petitioned Ferdinand and Isabella to allow another voyage to search for a strait that opened into the Indian Ocean. Authorization came in March 1502, and Columbus set sail on May 11 with four ships and 140 men, among them both his son Fernando and his brother Bartolomé, who commanded a ship.

Following the route of his second voyage, he sighted the island now called Martinique on June 15. Winding his way through the Leeward Islands, past present-day Puerto Rico to Hispaniola, Columbus was refused permission to land at Santo Domingo by the settlement's new governor, Nicolás de Ovando. Undeterred, he sailed west between Jamaica and Cuba, reaching modern Honduras in August. Though he tried to explore the Honduran coastline eastward, bad weather forced him to turn south, skirting the coasts of modern Nicaragua and Costa Rica in search of the hoped-for strait. When he reached what is now Panama, the Indians told him that he had reached a narrow isthmus between two seas. Columbus incorrectly concluded that this strip of land was the Malay Peninsula, and that China lay to its north while India was located across the sea on the other side. He postponed an attempt to prove this theory after discovering gold. He founded a settlement at Santa Maria de Belén in February 1503 but was forced to abandon it and set sail after hostilities with the Indians cost him one ship and the lives of ten crew members. After losing another ship during bad weather, he landed at St. Ann's Bay, Jamaica, because the remaining two ships were too damaged to make it to Hispaniola. Marooned, Columbus sent two canoes with twelve men and twenty Indians

to Santo Domingo for help in July 1503. By the time Ovando had them rescued in June 1504, there were about 100 survivors.

Exhausted, discouraged, and suffering from various ills (arthritis, and probably gout), Columbus returned to Spain in November 1504. He spent the rest of his life pursuing various legal claims against the Spanish Crown to settle grievances over titles and awards promised but not delivered to him. He died in Valladolid, Spain, on May 20, 1506, from "the gout, and by grief at seeing himself fallen from his high estate, as well as by other ills," according to Fernando's biography.

Ironically, little notice was taken of the death of the man who had opened the Americas to exploration and settlement by the powers of Europe. His fame had been overshadowed by that of AMERIGO VESPUCCI, who correctly declared that Columbus had discovered a New World. Whether the admiral clung to the end to his belief that he had reached Asia remains the subject of debate. In a letter written in 1500, Columbus succinctly stated his accomplishment: "[B]y the Divine Will, I have placed under the dominion of the King and Queen, our Sovereigns, a second world, through which Spain, which was reckoned a poor country, has become the richest." Some historians cite this reference to a "second world" along with a variety of additional evidence to suggest his understanding of the true nature of his discovery.

The final mystery of Christopher Columbus concerns the location of his remains, which were moved from Valladolid to Seville (1509) to Santo Domingo (1541–47) to Havana (1796) and back to Seville (1899). However, due to mix-ups, the remains of Columbus could be in Seville, Havana, or Santo Domingo today. In addition, there exist at least eight urns and vials that purportedly hold the ashes of Columbus, located in such far-flung places as Rome and New York City.

Finally, mention should be made of his relationship to the Indians he encountered on his voyages. Some historians have leveled accusations against him, charging that he encouraged slavery in the New World. He did promise to help the peaceful Indian tribes of Hispaniola and Cuba against the warlike, cannibalistic Indians of other islands, and he did enslave some of these Caribs. However, by the end of his second voyage, when many Indians had been enslaved by the settlers of Santo Domingo to dig for gold, Columbus had lost his power to control or even influence these events. His log of the first voyage is full of expressions of admiration and friendship for the Indians, as well as the certainty that they would make good Christians.

Not the least of the ironies attached to the discovery of America by Columbus is the fact that it was in no way a discovery. Both the North and South American continents—and the islands in between—were inhabited at the time by a wide variety of native peoples, some sophisticated culturally (notably the Aztecs and Incas), others primitive. Furthermore, Columbus was not even the first European to have reached this unknown hemisphere. Without question the Norse explorers LEIF ERIKSON and BJARNI HERJOLFSSON preceded him by roughly 500 years. But Europe took little or no notice of their discoveries in the long run. Columbus's first voyage, on the other hand, created great sustained excitement throughout Renaissance Europe, so much so that within a very brief time Europeans, motivated primarily by commercial incentives and empowered by superior technology, had transformed large portions of the New World and subjugated most of its native peoples. So complete was their "success" that the history of North and South America over the last 500 years is effectively the history of Europeans and their descendants.

Thus Columbus has over the years been given both credit and blame for everything that has happened in the Americas since 1492. No doubt he deserves some of both. But it is important to view his historic accomplishment for what it was—no more, and no less—and in the context in which it was made. Here was a sailor who dared to sail from the world he knew into a world he knew nothing of. He deserves all the credit for his success—however mixed its ultimate impact—and for the personal qualities that brought it about: bold imagination, stubborn perseverance, keen nautical skills, and unwavering leadership.

SUGGESTED READING: Fernando Colón, *The Life of the Admiral Christopher Columbus*, trans. by Benjamin Keen (Rutgers University Press, 1959); Robert H. Fuson, trans., *The Log of Christopher Columbus* (International Marine Publishing Co., 1987); Samuel Eliot Morison, *Admiral of the Ocean Sea* (Little, Brown & Co., 1942); Kirkpatrick Sale, *The Conquest of Paradise* (Knopf, 1990); John Boyd Thacher, *Christopher Columbus: His Life, His Work, His Remains*, 3 vols. (AMS Press, 1967); Paolo Emilio Taviani, *Christopher Columbus: The Grand Design* (Orbis Publishing, Ltd., 1985).

Conti, Nicolò de

Italian
b 1395?; Chioggia? (near Venice)
d 1469; Venice?
Traveled throughout southern Asia as merchant

The cause of world exploration has often been advanced by people whose motives were primarily religious. Such is the case with Nicolò de Conti's record of his extensive travels through southern Asia during the fifteenth century, even though his personal interests were mainly commercial. As Conti was passing through Egypt on his return trip to Italy, he was forced to renounce Catholicism and profess his faith in Islam in order to protect his wife and children, who were traveling with him. Once safely back in Italy, Conti sought absolution from the pope for his sin. The pope listened to Conti's plea, then promised him absolution if he would first give a detailed account of his entire trip to the papal secretary. His subsequent statement, since published in English as *India in the Fifteenth Century*, is a valuable record of the land and people of southern Asia during the Middle Ages.

Though born in Italy, as a young man Conti lived in the Syrian city of Damascus, where he worked as a merchant while learning Arabic. In 1414 Conti and 600 other merchants set off in a caravan to the East. They traveled along the Euphrates, through Baghdad (now in Iraq) to Basra, where they crossed the Persian Gulf to Hormuz. When Conti reached Calacatia, a port on the Indian Ocean, he remained long enough to learn the Persian language, then sailed with a group of merchants to the Indian state of Cambay. There Conti married an Indian woman and continued his travels south along the coast to Goa, where he turned inland to visit the kingdom of Deccan. (He is thought by some to have been the first European to enter the Indian interior.)

It is unclear whether Conti crossed to India's east coast by land or returned to Goa and sailed around the Indian peninsula. But in either case he visited Ceylon (now Sri Lanka), remained for a year, and became the first European to describe the cultivation of cinnamon there. Sailing east across the Bay of Bengal, Conti discovered cannibals on the Andaman Islands and reached the coast of Burma (now Myanmar). Turning northwest, he sailed up the Ganges River, the mouth of which was so broad he could see neither bank from midstream. Conti discovered what he described as "many renown cities unvisited" along the way, finally arriving at a place "where aloes, gold, silver, precious stones and pearls were to be found in abundance."

Conti's inland excursions in the Ganges delta and in Burma covered some of the same ground MARCO POLO had visited about 150 years earlier. Conti reported seeing tattooed men and elephant hunts, rhinoceroses and pythons. When he took to the sea once again, he sailed to Sumatra and Java (now in Indonesia), which some historians believe was the most distant place he visited. Although Conti found the inhabitants of these islands "more inhumane and cruel than any other people," he and his wife and children remained there for nine months. While there he visited the Banda Islands, the only place in the world where cloves were grown at that time, and an important source of nutmeg and other spices as well.

From Java, some scholars believe Conti sailed up the eastern coast of China as far as Nanking, while others contend that he began his homeward journey, traveling first to Ciampa (now Thailand) then on to Ceylon. All agree, however, that he made trading stops at Ceylon and along the Indian peninsula on his return trip, crossed the Arabian Sea to Aden, then sailed up the Red Sea to Jidda (in present-day Saudi Arabia). At Jidda, he and his family and their numerous servants disembarked and made their way overland to Cairo.

Cairo is probably where Conti was compelled to renounce his Catholic faith, but he endured much greater hardships there, as well. The papal scribe recorded it this way: "In this city he lost his wife, two children and all his servants, who died of the plague." From Cairo, Conti traveled to Mount Sinai before reaching Italy in 1444. The scribe described the end of Conti's epic adventure in simple words: "At last, as fortune would have it, after all his journeys by land and by sea, he arrived with his two surviving children at his native city of Venice."

Although Conti traveled almost as extensively as had Marco Polo, he was not afforded (as Polo had been) the protection of a powerful prince to reduce the dangers of his journey. That he survived his twenty-five-year odyssey at all was a remarkable achievement. But the fact that he did, and was called to give an account of his wanderings, helped fill in some of the blank spaces in Europe's maps of the East. Thirteen years after Conti returned to Venice, the great Italian cartographer Fra Mauro began to draw his map of the world. Without a doubt, many details supplied by Conti found their way onto Mauro's map.

Cooes, Bento de. See **Goes, Bento de.**

• Cook, Frederick Albert

American
b June 10, 1865; Hortonville, New York
d August 5, 1940; New Rochelle, New York
Explored Arctic and Antarctica; claimed to be
first to reach North Pole

In the fall of 1909 Dr. Frederick Albert Cook was cheered and honored all over the world as the first person to reach the North Pole. The American physician was—for the moment—the most famous explorer in the world as the result of this momentous achievement. Just fourteen years later, with his earlier claims of discovery effectively discredited by rival explorer ROBERT PEARY and his followers, Cook was convicted of mail fraud and sent to prison. His career was in shambles, his reputation ruined irretrievably. At his trial, the presiding judge shook his finger at the crumpled hero and admonished him: "Oh, God, Cook, haven't you any sense of decency at all. . . ." It was just another bizarre chapter in the story of the American physician and explorer's strange, checkered career.

Cook grew up surrounded by the wilderness of the Catskill Mountains of New York, where he learned to appreciate the beauty of nature and developed his capacity to struggle through difficult times. When Cook was only five, his father died. He subsequently worked as a farm laborer and in various other jobs to help support his family. When the Cooks moved to Brooklyn, he worked at a vegetable stand while attending night school. He then managed to work his way through the medical school of New York University by operating a milk delivery route in the early hours of every morning. In 1889 he mar-

Frederick Albert Cook. The Bettmann Archive.

ried Libby Forbes, who died in childbirth the next year.

After responding to an advertisement, Cook was hired by the Arctic explorer Robert Peary as surgeon and anthropologist for an expedition that crossed northern Greenland in 1891. In 1893 Cook led his own expedition to Greenland aboard the ship *Zeta*, and the next year returned aboard the *Miranda*. The *Miranda* was disabled by an iceberg, thus foiling Cook's chance to lead a significant scientific expedition. He then returned to medicine for three years, until in 1898 he sailed with the Belgian Antarctic Expedition as surgeon, photographer, and ethnologist. (The expedition's *Belgica* became the first ship to winter in Antarctica.) On this voyage, Cook worked with the Norwegian explorer ROALD AMUNDSEN, who developed a high opinion of the American. According to Amundsen, "the success of the whole Belgian expedition was due to" Cook.

In 1901 Cook agreed to sail north, at his own expense, with a relief expedition to treat Peary at Cape Sabine, Ellesmere Island, where he was

in poor health after having failed in his first attempt to reach the pole. Peary, a difficult man in the best of circumstances, did not take his failure easily, and Cook swore he would never work with him again.

While Peary continued trying to reach the North Pole, Cook remarried in 1902 and turned to a new venture. In 1903 he led an unsuccessful attempt to scale Alaska's Mount McKinley, then returned to the task in 1906. He and Edward M. Barrill claimed at that time to have reached the summit of McKinley, the highest mountain in North America at 20,391 feet above sea level. But this achievement was later questioned by Peary's supporters and is not generally believed today.

In 1907, while Peary was planning his final assault on the pole, Cook and a wealthy friend quickly put together a plan of their own. They hoped to claim for themselves the fame that was sure to come to whoever reached this important, though largely symbolic, unattained goal. If, in addition to seizing fame for himself, Cook could frustrate his rival Peary, for whom the pole was an obsession, so much the better.

The ship *John R. Bradley* dropped Cook and his supplies at Annoatok, 32 miles north of Etah, Greenland, on August 27, 1907, to prepare for his attempt. On February 19, 1908, Cook set off to cross Ellesmere Island with nine **Inuit** companions and 103 dogs. By March 18 he was prepared to head onto the frozen polar sea from the north coast of Axel Heiberg Island with only two of the Inuit guides. In addition to **sledges** and dogs, a collapsible canvas boat was used for crossing open leads (channels of water running through the ice pack). By his own claim, a month later, on April 21, 1908, he was at the pole, a year before Peary. Then began the treacherous journey back. After two months of travel, he was low on supplies by the time he reached land. He was also off course, nowhere near his supply depot. The three men then wintered in an ancient dugout on Jones Sound, living off the land using the traditional techniques of the Inuit. They finally returned to Annoatok on April 15, 1909.

Whether they reached the pole or not, their fourteen-month ordeal was a remarkable feat of survival that changed the way Cook saw the world. After so much time together in a cramped space, facing daily hardships and sharing the same experiences, fears, and hopes, the three men, once divided by huge cultural differences, "acquired unconsciously merged personalities," according to Cook. Back in civilization, they felt "exotic." "Henceforth we were native to Nowhere."

News of Cook's attainment of the pole did not reach Europe or the United States until September 1, 1909, just five days before Peary managed to communicate his own success. In the brief interim, Cook arrived in Copenhagen, Denmark, where he was received as a hero for his historic accomplishment. Within days, Peary had challenged Cook's claim, initiating a bitter—even vicious—five-year controversy, fanned by the rival newspapers supporting the vying explorers. In truth, there were holes and contradictions in the documentation offered by both explorers to support their respective claims. But by the outbreak of World War I in 1914, the majority of scholars—and the public—seemed to have judged Cook's to be the more suspect of the two accounts, for a variety of reasons, not the least of which were statements of contradiction from his two Inuit companions. Peary's claim, on the other hand, was supported by official U.S. bodies that had backed his expedition. As a result, Peary is today generally acknowledged to have reached the pole first, though supporters of Cook's claim recently renewed the controversy.

Cook persevered through it all, even after he had commonly become viewed as a liar of epic proportions. In 1915 he led an expedition around the world. He later made money in the oil business, which he used to found an oil exploration company in Texas. In this capacity, he was accused of selling worthless real estate, which led to his 1923 indictment and subsequent conviction for mail fraud. While serving time at Leavenworth Penitentiary, Cook was visited by his former colleague Amundsen, one of the few who stood by him. The Norwegian found Cook to be a different man, suggesting that "some physical misfortune had changed his personality."

In fact, Cook had held up well, considering what he had been through. He was still writing about his Arctic experiences, working as a doctor in the prison's hospital and editing its newspaper. Esteemed by both fellow prisoners and authorities, he was paroled in 1929. In May 1940 he suffered a serious stroke. Fifteen days later, he was granted an unconditional pardon by President Franklin D. Roosevelt. He died in August of that year, ending the life of one of the world's most colorful and contradictory explorers.

Cook, James

English
b October 27, 1728; Marton-in-Cleveland, Yorkshire
d February 14, 1779; Hawaii
Circumnavigated three times; explored North and South Pacific; discovered Hawaii

Captain James Cook is one of the outstanding figures in the history of exploration. Admired during his lifetime, he is noted for the contributions he made to the knowledge of the Pacific Ocean, its geography and **hydrography**, and its native peoples, as well as to the nature of maritime expeditions themselves. He not only delineated the boundaries of the Pacific Ocean, he conquered the traditional scourge of sailors, **scurvy**, and helped turn exploration into a science.

The eighteenth century's greatest explorer—the man who was considered a god by some native peoples of the Pacific—came from humble beginnings. He was born in a small Yorkshire village on October 27, 1728, the second of nine children of James Cook, a poor Scottish

James Cook. New York Public Library.

COOK, JAMES

farmer, and Grace Pace. At the age of thirteen he dropped out of school to help his father and, in 1742, became apprenticed to a grocer. Not long after, the future Captain Cook went to sea.

Cook began his career as a cabin boy aboard the *Freelove*, a collier, or coal ship, from the boatyard at Whitby. He learned to navigate in the rough Baltic and North seas and gained an appreciation for this sturdy type of vessel as well as for the seafaring life. Shipowner John Walker was about to promote him when talk spread of war against France and Germany. Cook enlisted in the Royal Navy in 1755 as an able-bodied seaman aboard the *Eagle*. Unusually astute and diligent for a sailor of his day, Cook worked his way up through the ranks quickly, making master in just four years. During the Seven Years' War he was given command of the *Mercury* and commissioned to chart Canada's St. Lawrence River. Thanks partly to his marking of the river's supposedly impassable channel, the British were able to capture Québec.

In 1762 Cook married Elizabeth Batts, of Shadwell, with whom he would have six children, despite his limited time at home over the next seventeen years. In fact, he soon was off again, this time to Newfoundland, Nova Scotia, and Labrador, where the navigational charts he drew proved invaluable to the fishermen of the Grand Banks. In 1766 Cook observed a solar eclipse and used it to pinpoint Newfoundland's longitude. This accomplishment was to bring him to the attention of the Royal Society and set the wheels of his first circumnavigation in motion.

The planet Venus was known to be making a transit of the sun in the summer of 1769, an occurrence that would be viewable from the South Pacific island of Tahiti. The Royal Society wanted to send an observer, and the Admiralty thought the required expedition would also offer an ideal opportunity to dispatch someone in search of *Terra Australis Incognita* (for a more complete discussion, see ALEXANDER DALRYMPLE). Cook seemed the obvious choice. He was placed in command of the *Endeavour* and given secret orders to seek out the great Southern Continent.

Endeavour sailed from Plymouth on August 26, 1768. Less than a hundred feet long, the ship carried a crew of ninety-four, including the naturalists JOSEPH BANKS and DANIEL CARL SOLANDER, artists, and an astronomer. The ship was a retrofitted Whitby collier, built not for

comfort but to take the sea at its worst. Quarters were close, but Cook, knowing the toll that disease could take on a journey of this length, insisted that the ship be kept clean. He also made sure that the crew got their fill of fresh vegetables and citrus fruits. Although by the end of the three-year journey, some thirty-eight crewmen would die, for the first time in the history of maritime exploration, not a single man was lost to scurvy. To encourage his men to eat the sauerkraut he brought along as a preventive, Cook had it served at the officers' table, and the crew soon began to request it for themselves.

Cook guided *Endeavour* across the Atlantic and around South America's Cape Horn, stopping at Tierra del Fuego and other South American sites along the way to collect biological specimens. On April 13, 1769, the ship anchored at Matavai Bay, on the northwest side of Tahiti. There Cook directed the construction of Fort Venus, which would serve as a base of operations during the crew's three-month stay. The time spent there was fruitful. With Banks and Solander, Cook explored the entire island. Although he chose not to participate in the feasts of love that the Tahitian women offered, he let his crew indulge themselves and even allowed the women to spend the night aboard ship. He observed island society closely, recording details of burial ceremonies, tattooing rituals, and other aspects of Tahitian life.

Cook's attitude toward his crew's social lives was neither prudish nor overly permissive. On board the ship and off, he maintained strict but fair discipline and rigorous but realistic work schedules. It could be said that he handled people as well as he handled ships—with a great deal of skill. Naturally, the relaxed Tahitian life-style held great appeal for the sailors, but with Cook in command, the disciplined shipboard life was not nearly as disagreeable as it might have been under a more tyrannical leader. Cook's down-to-earth temperament and evenhanded leadership help explain why he had to deal with only two would-be deserters when *Endeavour* set sail from Tahiti, rather than facing a mutiny, as WILLIAM BLIGH would under similar circumstances in 1789. Cook's style of leadership may also help explain why the crew was so willing to continue the expedition after leaving Tahiti, even though Cook could not reveal his mission.

With a Tahitian guide named Tupia, Cook sailed west to other islands (Huahiné, Otaha,

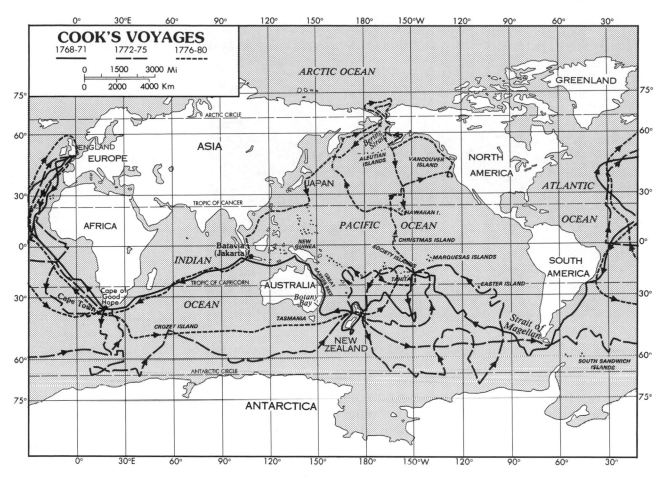

and Bora-Bora) in Tahiti's **archipelago**. He claimed the entire group for King George III and named them the Society Islands. From there he sailed south, and in October 1769 he rediscovered the islands that ABEL TASMAN had called Staaten Land (present-day New Zealand) in 1642. Cook spent several months circling the islands, proving that they were not, in fact, the tip of *Terra Australis Incognita*. The strait between the islands still bears his name. Cook and the naturalists explored the area in great detail, a difficult task considering that the islands' warlike and cannibalistic Maori people were not nearly as welcoming as the Tahitians had been.

Leaving New Zealand, Cook sailed west again, reaching the unexplored east coast of New Holland (present-day Australia) at a place the naturalists called Botany Bay because of the numerous plant species found there. After a week *Endeavour* headed north, as Cook guided the sturdy vessel through the maze of coral structures now known as the Great Barrier Reef.

Despite his navigation skills, the ship struck the reef and began to take on water through a gash in the hull. The incident could have been a disaster, but the level-headed Cook was able to direct his crew to keep the ship afloat, patch the hole, and get *Endeavour* to shore where it could be repaired permanently. (The spot where the ship put to shore is now known as Cooktown.) After a month, he continued north, charting some 2,000 miles of coastline before heading back to England by way of New Guinea, Batavia (present-day Jakarta, Indonesia), the Indian Ocean, and the Cape of Good Hope.

Cook reached home July 12, 1771; a year and a day later, he was on his way again. The issue of *Terra Australis Incognita* had not been laid to rest, and the Admiralty authorized a new expedition to search for the "missing" continent. This time Cook, commanding the *Resolution* and accompanied by the *Adventure*, sailed down the African coast and continued south from Cape Town, thereby becoming the first navigator to cross the Antarctic Circle. He con-

James Cook, leading a landing party. National Gallery of Victoria, Canberra.

tinued south until ice made passage impossible, then headed north, much to the crew's relief. In a dense fog the two ships became separated, but Cook had anticipated that possibility. The vessels met up three months later in New Zealand, as planned.

ALEXANDER DALRYMPLE, a self-proclaimed authority on *Terra Australis Incognita*, believed that this great postulated continent lay between New Zealand and Cape Horn, and so Cook planned to investigate that vast largely unknown stretch of the globe. He found only a few small islands. In August 1773 he returned to Tahiti for a month, then visited several other of the Society Islands, the Friendly (or Tonga) Islands, and New Zealand until the southern summer arrived and made another attempt at the lower latitudes possible.

In November 1774 Cook turned the *Resolution* south once more. The two ships had become separated again and, missing their rendezvous, the *Adventure* sailed back to England, returning almost a year before the *Resolution*. This was just as well. The *Adventure*'s commander did not insist that his crew eat fresh vegetables or sauerkraut; as a result, many became sick or died of scurvy. The men on Cook's boat, on the other hand, all remained healthy.

By December the *Resolution* was surrounded by icebergs, and Cook was suffering from gall bladder problems. One of the naturalists in the crew, JOHANN REINHOLD FORSTER, sacrificed his pet dog so the captain would have the meat he needed to regain his strength. Upon his recovery, Cook sailed north to warmer waters. To the dismay of the crew, who hoped to be headed for home, he took a southern course once again. This time the *Resolution* reached a latitude of 71°10' South before the pack ice became impassable. No one would surpass that latitude until 1841. Although on this voyage Cook would circumnavigate the South Pole and thereby rule out the existence of *Terra Australis Incognita*, he correctly suspected the existence of an antarctic continent. In his journal he wrote, "That there may be a continent or large tract of land near the Pole I will not deny; on the contrary I am of the opinion that there is, and it is probable that we have seen a part of it."

At that point, Cook could have turned the *Resolution* back to England, but he suspected that the Pacific still had more secrets to reveal. With the perilous antarctic waters behind them, the crew relished the opportunity to extend the voyage—another indication of the high regard in which they held their commander. In early March the *Resolution* reached Easter Island. It was their first landfall in four months.

Cook was the first European to visit Easter Island since Dutchman JACOB ROGGEVEEN had discovered it in 1722. Cook found the six or seven hundred inhabitants of this volcanic island to be friendly, although they stole nearly anything that they could carry. He also noted that they could easily converse with Oddidy, a Tahitian whom Cook was taking to England, leading Cook to surmise that many of the islanders of the South Pacific shared a common origin.

After three days on Easter Island, Cook went north to the Marquesas, another group of islands that Europeans had discovered earlier but that had not yet been charted. Cook added a fifth island in the group to the map, then sailed on to Tahiti, where he was a welcomed figure. Heading west, he charted and named the New Hebrides, New Caledonia, and Norfolk Island. He planned to journey home by way of Cape Horn, just in case he had missed something in his search for *Terra Australis Incognita*. He did not find it, but after he rounded the horn he did find and name South Georgia Island and the South Sandwich Islands.

Three years and eighteen days after leaving England, the *Resolution* returned, having completed a voyage of more than 70,000 miles. Cook had lost only four men—none to scurvy. Upon his return, Cook was elected to the Royal Society and promoted to captain in the navy. His report on scurvy and its prevention won him the Society's Copley Medal. He could have retired, and was given an honorary post; but the sea called and questions remained to be answered.

In February 1776 Cook began recruiting a crew for yet a third voyage, this time to seek out the Northwest Passage between the Atlantic and the Pacific. (For a more complete discussion of the Northwest Passage, see MARTIN FROBISHER.) The British Admiralty sent two expeditions to search for an Atlantic entrance near Baffin Bay; Cook was to sail north and east from the Bering Strait separating northeast Russia and Alaska. When the *Resolution* and the *Discovery* left Plymouth on July 12, 1776, they carried many faces that were familiar to Cook from his earlier ventures. Once again, Cook commanded the *Resolution*. With him as ship's master was a young sailor named William Bligh, who later commanded the *Bounty*.

The expedition sailed south to Cape Town in present-day South Africa, then ventured into the southern Indian Ocean to a group of rocky islands that had been noted by French explorers in 1772. Cook named two of the islands after Prince Edward and the others after their discoverers, Marion du Fresne and Julien-Marie Crozet (the present-day Crozet Islands). He continued eastward, sailing for nearly a month through a thick fog, until he reached Tasmania in January 1777. He anchored for four days at Adventure Bay, which he had named on the previous expedition, and recorded his observations of the "wretched" lives of the island's inhabitants.

In 1777 Cook made several stops in the South Seas—at New Zealand, Tahiti, the Friendly Islands, and at Palmerston and other islands between the Society and Friendly islands that are now known as the Cook Islands. Tensions were high during the few weeks he spent in New Zealand. The Maori tribesmen believed that Cook had come to avenge the deaths of the *Adventure*'s landing crew, who had been killed there—and likely eaten—during the previous expedition.

Cook spent most of the summer and fall as an honored guest in Polynesia, studying the customs of the island people and bringing them gifts of livestock from England. He was the first to note the concept of taboo (referring to the ritually forbidden) and looked with disgust on the practices of human sacrifice and cannibalism he saw even in Tahiti. He left the Society Islands in early December 1777 and sailed north.

On December 25 the crew landed on a deserted island just above the equator and christened it Christmas Island (now Kiritimati). On January 20, 1778, they reached a group of islands (present-day Hawaii) that Cook named after the earl of Sandwich. He visited the islands known today as Kauai, Oahu, Niihau, Lenai, Molokai and Tahura (or Kaula). Although some say the Sandwich Islands were explored by a sixteenth-century Spaniard, the islands did not appear on any maps and boasted no European settlements. Cook probably was the first European to discover them. On this first visit he stayed less than two weeks—long enough to become intrigued by the similarities between these people and those of Tahiti and the other Polynesian islands he had visited, and he wondered how the race had come to be so widespread. During their short stay, Cook and his crew, with their pale skin, huge ships, and strange equipment, made enough of an impression to merit mention in the islanders' oral histories.

The expedition spent the spring and summer

of 1778 charting the North American coast from what is now Oregon to the Bering Strait in search of the Northwest Passage. In bad weather, Cook missed the Strait of Juan de Fuca, between Vancouver Island and the North American mainland, and anchored his vessels in what is now Vancouver Island's Nootka Sound, where the ships were greeted by elaborately costumed Nootka Indians. With their headdresses, masks, and painted faces, the Nootkas did not resemble the Polynesians; but Cook noted, incorrectly, that they shared a penchant for cannibalism with other island peoples.

The two ships continued north and west, along the coasts of present-day Canada and southern Alaska. The farther west the coast led them, the less convinced Cook was that they would find a navigable northern passage between the Atlantic and the Pacific. He sailed along the Aleutian Islands, stopping at Unalaska Island, then into the Bering Sea. He forged north until ice blocked his way. On August 18, 1778, he found himself at 70°44' North, surrounded by ice floes, in a ship that was taking on water. Safety, he decided prudently, lay in the warmth of the south. He set his course for the Sandwich Islands for repairs, planning to renew his search for the Northwest Passage the following summer.

On his second trip to the Sandwich Islands, Cook discovered two more: Maui and Owhyhee (now the island of Hawaii). When he anchored in the latter's Kealakekua Bay, he was greeted by hordes of islanders bearing gifts. On that day, January 17, 1779, the navigator's precisely written journal ends. The events of the next few weeks, leading up to Cook's untimely death, were recorded only by his crew.

In the eyes of the Hawaiians, Cook was a supernatural being, a god come to earth by sailing into their sacred bay. The island chiefs feasted with him and called him "Orono" or "Lorono," the god of peace and prosperity. They looked on him with awe and, presumably, a bit of fear. After two weeks or so, Cook attempted to leave Hawaii, but bad weather forced him back into the bay.

Throughout his dealings with indigenous people of the various islands of the Pacific, Cook had handled even the most unpleasant encounters with discretion, diplomacy, and sensitivity to cultural differences. Thieves, common on all the islands, were punished, but not harshly, and Cook avoided the use of force whenever possible.

But on Hawaii, when islanders overran his ships and virtually attempted to take the boats apart, Cook allowed his men to display their weapons. Surprisingly, the Hawaiians were more startled than frightened, and the number of incidents increased. Cook decided that things had gone too far.

On the morning of February 14, 1779, a small English boat was missing. To ensure its return, Cook decided to bring a tribal chief on board and hold him until the boat was found. When Cook went ashore with the king, a great crowd gathered. Offshore, the British waited in armed longboats. Tensions rose on both sides. Some of the islanders made their way toward the British, and a crewman fired, killing an important chief. Ironically, when Cook turned his back on the islanders to order his men to hold their fire, the Hawaiians fell on him in a fury, stabbing him in the back, then hacking his body to pieces. Four of Cook's crewmen died with him.

Cook's death left the expedition in a state of shock. The crew went ashore and gathered as much of his remains as they could, then buried him at sea. Cook was fifty-one when he died. He left behind a widow and three of his six children.

On Cook's death, Charles Clerke, commander of the *Discovery*, took command of the expedition until his death from tuberculosis on August 22, 1779. He was succeeded by Lieutenant John Gore. The two ships sailed to eastern Russia, where they sent word of Cook's death back to England, then proceeded north to make another attempt to find the Northwest Passage. They were no more successful than Cook had been the year before and, after a stop on the Russian coast to repair ice damage, headed west to England in January 1780. They reached Stromness on August 22, 1780.

Cook's influence had been enormous. On his third journey he proved once again that long sea voyages need not be synonymous with illness and death. Between them the *Resolution* and the *Discovery* carried nearly 200 men; of the five lost to disease, three had been sick before they boarded the ships.

At one point in his life, Cook wrote that his ambition was "to go as far as it was possible for a man to go, and to make an exact recording of all that I saw." In so doing, he elevated exploration to a science. His navigational work in the northern Pacific not only disproved the existence of an easily navigable Northwest Passage, but opened up the northwest coast of North America to trade. In the South Pacific, he laid to rest the myth of *Terra Australis Incognita*, charted thousands of miles of unknown coastlines, and literally put dozens of islands on the map. And his journals from three voyages contained a wealth of observations on the people and customs of the Pacific island cultures. In the words of CHARLES DARWIN, Captain James Cook "added a hemisphere to the civilized world."

SUGGESTED READING: J. C. Beaglehole, *The Life of Captain James Cook* (Stanford University Press, 1974); J. C. Beaglehole, *The Voyages of Captain James Cook* (Hakluyt Society, University Press, 1955); A. Grenfell Price, ed., *The Explorations of Captain James Cook in the Pacific as Told by Selections of His Own Journals, 1768–1779* (Heritage, 1976); Alan Villiers, *Captain James Cook: A Definitive Biography* (Scribners, 1970); Oliver Warner, *Captain Cook and the South Pacific* (American Heritage, 1963); James A. Williamson, *Cook and the Opening of the Pacific* (Macmillan, 1948).

• Coronado, Francisco Vásquez de

Spanish
b 1510?; Salamanca
d 1554; Mexico City, Mexico
Explored southwestern United States

Francisco Vásquez de Coronado was the wealthy and respected governor of New Galicia in New Spain (present-day Mexico) when he left in 1540 on what would become an extraordinary expedition to find the seven cities of Cíbola and the fabled land of Quivira. His journey took him through present-day Arizona, New Mexico, Texas, and Oklahoma, and as far north as central Kansas. Although he failed to find the rumored civilizations, he explored a vast territory, penetrating farther north from New Spain than anyone had previously. Ironically, unknown to either man, at one point in 1541 Coronado was very close to the expedition of HERNANDO DE SOTO, which was marching through what is now eastern Oklahoma as it headed west from Florida. Together, these **conquistadores** explored a major portion of what is now the southern United States, helping to reveal the diversity—and immensity—of the North American continent.

Of noble lineage, Francisco Vásquez de Coronado was born at Salamanca in the Spanish

province of the same name, sometime around 1510. Although his family name was Vásquez, he has become known in history as Coronado through English misuse and misunderstanding of the Spanish naming system. Little is known of his early life until he came to New Spain in 1535 with the new viceroy, Antonio de Mendoza. He made a politically and personally brilliant marriage to Beatriz de Estrada, a wealthy heiress and cousin of King Charles I. In 1537 he gained fame for subduing miners who were revolting in Amatepeque (near modern Taxco, Mexico). His close friendship with Mendoza, as well as his successful exploits and royal connections, resulted in his appointment as governor of New Galicia (the modern Mexican states of Sinaloa and Nayarit) in 1538. In that capacity he was responsible for assisting in preparations for the expedition of Father MARCOS DE NIZA, who had been authorized by Viceroy Mendoza to explore the country north of the frontier of New Spain.

When Marcos returned from his journey with tales of the fabulously wealthy seven cities of Cíbola (which he claimed to have seen from a distance), the viceroy immediately made plans to find and conquer these cities to the north. To accomplish this task Mendoza chose Coronado, with Marcos to act as his guide.

During the first few weeks of 1540, Coronado assembled the various elements of the expedition at Compostela (in present-day Nayarit). In addition to the approximately 340 Spaniards, 300 Mexican Indian allies, and some 1,000 Indian and black slaves, he also took herds of cattle, sheep, swine, and goats to provide food. On February 23, 1540, this enormous expedition

Francisco Vásquez de Coronado, in a painting by N. C. Wyeth. The Bettmann Archive.

---

left Compostela and marched along the Gulf of California coast to Culiacán, which at that time was the farthest northwest of any European settlement in the New World.

By the time they reached Culiacán, Coronado was frustrated at the slow pace of such a large group. Among its many delays was the transporting of cattle one at a time, required across some rivers. Divesting himself of excess baggage, he selected 100 men and some Indians, equipped them for a rapid march, and headed up the Sonora River valley, leaving the main force to follow at a slower pace. Melchior Diaz was sent ahead to scout while Coronado proceeded up either the present-day Santa Cruz or San Pedro river valley into modern Arizona. Crossing what is now the Gila River, the expedition headed northeast across the present-day Fort Apache Indian Reservation, where many members of the party got quite sick from berries they ate. When Diaz rejoined the group, he brought disheartening news about what was thought to be the first city of Cíbola: all he had seen was an overcrowded village of huts.

Nevertheless, Coronado pushed ahead, crossing into modern New Mexico and reaching the Zuñi Indian **pueblo** of Hawikuh about July 4, 1540. What Marcos had described as a fabulous city turned out to be a collection of adobe and stone huts. At this point Marcos was sent back to Mexico City in disgrace. With his party's food supplies almost exhausted and morale at a low point, Coronado attacked the pueblo and secured it. He made it his headquarters, resting his men and dispatching Diaz to bring up the rest of the expedition. He then sent small parties to explore the other pueblos in the six-city Zuñi confederacy, which Marcos had mistakenly identified as the seven cities of Cíbola.

Next he sent a scouting party under Pedro de Tovar northwest, where it discovered seven Hopi Indian villages and learned of a great river farther west. Intrigued by this information, Coronado sent Garcia López de Cárdenas to search for this river. His journey stopped abruptly when he reached the Grand Canyon, where it was impossible to descend the steep canyon walls to the Colorado River below. However, Cárdenas and his men became the first Europeans to see the Grand Canyon, and their brief sighting constituted the first documented discovery of the Colorado River by Europeans.

Coronado also sent exploratory parties east, and one, under Hernando de Alvarado, found

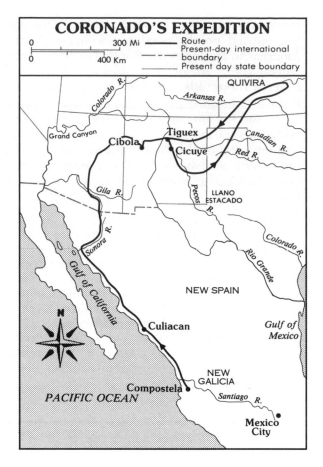

villages along the Rio Grande that were larger and could provide more food than the Zuñi pueblos. Coronado therefore established his winter quarters at the largest village, Tiguex (near modern Bernalillo, just north of Albuquerque, New Mexico). During the winter of 1540–41, the expedition endured severe weather and continual Indian attacks. Coronado finally brought the Indians under control by burning some captured Indians to death.

On one of his many forays from Tiguex, Coronado met a Plains Indian simply called "the Turk" who told him of a rich land to the northeast called Quivira. The Indian's vivid descriptions of fish as large as horses, gold jugs and bowls used for eating, and gold bells that hung on a great tree under which the ruler slept impressed Coronado. Not wishing to return to New Spain empty-handed after failing to find gold at "Cíbola," he decided to travel to Quivira in hopes of finding riches there.

Thus, on April 23, 1541, Coronado's expedition left Tiguex, with "the Turk" as their guide, and headed east to Cicuye (present-day Pecos,

New Mexico). Crossing the Pecos River, they marched across what they called the Llano Estacado (modern Staked Plain) of what is now the Texas Panhandle. The surviving journal of the expedition, written by Pedro de Castañeda, a private soldier who had joined the group at Culiacán, reveals that the men were amazed by the grassy prairie and the herds of bison, which they called "humpback oxen." He wrote, "The country is like a bowl, so that when a man sits down, the horizon surrounds him all around at the distance of a musket shot." They were disappointed, however, that the Indians they encountered, while giving them food, pottery, textiles, and some turquoise, had no gold or silver. Often the Indians fled from the advancing Spanish because they feared their horses (previously unknown in the Americas) and the wheels of their wagons.

After five weeks of wandering across Texas in an easterly direction, Coronado became suspicious of his guide's reliability. They had crossed the upper reaches of the present-day Colorado River of Texas and reached the headwaters of what is now the Nueces River. During that time the change in terrain, coupled with statements made by the region's Tejas Indians, convinced Coronado that "the Turk" was lying, perhaps trying to get them lost. "The Turk" finally confessed that he was in fact lying, for which he was eventually executed. With the food supply dwindling rapidly, Coronado sent most of the expedition back to Tiguex while he proceeded north with thirty horsemen, in the direction the local Indians had indicated that Quivira was located.

They traveled for forty-two days, following the compass needle north. They crossed the present-day Canadian River and rode through the westernmost part of modern Oklahoma before turning northeast. Reaching the Arkansas River in modern Kansas, they forded it near what is now Dodge City, then followed it downstream to the modern city of Great Bend. There they met some Quivira (later referred to as Wichita) Indians who guided them to a village near present-day Lindsborg, Kansas. What Coronado found was a series of Indian encampments characterized by thatched huts, rather than the prosperous civilization "the Turk" had described. In order to assure himself that he had investigated all possibilities for finding treasure, Coronado went on several forays into the surrounding regions. Although he perceived

the agricultural potential of the country, he concluded that the weather was too cold, the population too sparse, and the wealth far too meager to merit Spanish settlement. At this point he decided to rejoin the main force at Tiguex.

Some Quivira Indians acted as guides and took a much shorter route to Tiguex along part of what would become the Santa Fe Trail. Coronado spent the winter of 1541–42 there before starting back to New Spain. In December he was seriously injured when he fell from a horse.

In April 1542 the expedition began its long march home, traveling through the lands of the Zuñi confederacy and then through mountain passes to the Gulf of California. It was a terrible journey. The Spanish members of the party were ill-tempered, exhausted, and full of despair by this point, and they began deserting as soon as the first Spanish settlements were reached. By the time Coronado reached Mexico City to report to the viceroy, he had fewer than 100 men left. As Castañeda wrote, Coronado arrived "very sad and very weary, completely worn out and shame-faced." Viceroy Mendoza greeted him coolly but did not disavow him.

Although he had failed in his objectives, Coronado was allowed to continue to serve as governor of New Galicia until 1544. At that time he retired to Mexico City, where he continued in public service as a member of the municipal council. The single blemish on his distinguished career was an official inquiry, conducted in 1544–45, into his leadership on the expedition. He was accused of misconduct stemming from his execution of "the Turk" and his withdrawal from the explored lands. The *audiencia* (royal tribunal) of Mexico City completely exonerated him, and he lived the remainder of his years in peace, though in failing health. He never fully recovered from his injury, and he died in 1554 in Mexico City.

Coronado and his contemporaries may have thought of his expedition as a failure, but it was actually an extraordinary accomplishment. He revealed a vast geographical region to the eyes of the Spanish and expanded the boundaries of New Spain west to the mouth of the Colorado River and the Grand Canyon, east through the plains of Texas, and north to Kansas. The names of such places as the Coronado Mountains in Arizona, the Coronado State Monument in New Mexico, and Coronado City in Kansas are reminders of the impact of his achievement.

SUGGESTED READING: Herbert E. Bolton, *Coronado on the Turquoise Trail: Knight of Pueblos and Plains* (University of New Mexico, 1949); Castañeda, *The Journey of Coronado, 1540–1542*, trans. by George Parker Winship (Readex Microprint, 1966); Arthur Grove Day, *Coronado's Quest: The Discovery of the Southwestern States* (Greenwood, 1982); George Parker Winship, *The Coronado Expedition, 1540–1542* (Rio Grande Press, 1964).

• Cortés, Hernán (Hernando)

Spanish
b 1485; Medellín, Estremadura
d December 2, 1547; near Seville
Explored Mexico; conquered Aztec Empire

In many accounts of the conquest of Mexico, Hernán Cortés emerges as the epic hero, fighting righteously to bring Christianity and the benefits of Spanish rule to the New World. In actuality Cortés conquered the Aztec empire through a combination of trickery, bold tactical maneuvers, diplomacy, and sheer cruelty. Once he had captured the Aztec emperor Montezuma II and the capital of Tenochtitlán (modern Mexico City), he quickly brought all of Mexico—which he named New Spain—under Spanish control, establishing Mexico City as the headquarters for further Spanish expansion. He sent out expeditions to explore and conquer Central America and Baja California, and even attempted himself to start the first colony on the peninsula at La Paz Bay.

Hernán Cortés was born in 1485 in the town of Medellín in the Spanish region of Estremadura. His family was part of the lesser nobility. At age fourteen he went to the University of Salamanca to study law, but he returned home two years later for unknown reasons. He spent a couple of years indulging his high spirits and finally decided to pursue a life of adventure. In 1504 he sailed on a merchant ship bound for the New World and settled on Hispaniola (the island now occupied by Haiti and the Dominican Republic), becoming a public notary in the town of Azua. During the conquest of Cuba (1511–18) he served under the governor, Diego Velásquez, and eventually became a resident of Cuba, prospering as a miner and rancher.

Cortés's military skills, ingratiating personality, and ability to write good prose—and even verses "of some estimation"—quickly made him a favorite of Velásquez. As a result he was appointed treasury official and then *alcalde* (mayor) of Santiago de Cuba. However, two incidents ruptured the friendship between the two men. First, Cortés's flirtations with women led him into an affair with a noblewoman, Catalina Xuarez, whom he married only when pressured to do so. Second, his free spirit and unwillingness to submit to authority led to his being accused of trying to overthrow Velásquez, and although Cortés was pardoned, there was a tension in their relationship thereafter.

After hearing reports of the existence of gold and fabulous temples on the Yucatán Peninsula, as brought back by the expeditions of Hernández de Córdoba (1517) and Juan de Grijalva (1518), Velásquez named Cortés commander of an expedition to investigate these rich lands. Before Cortés could complete preparations for the journey, he heard that the governor was going to rescind his appointment. Therefore, on the night of November 18, 1518, Cortés quietly sailed out of port before the order could be delivered, obtaining additional supplies at the ports of Trinidad and Havana. His full complement included 780 soldiers, 100 sailors, 32 crossbowmen, 16 horses, 10 canoes, 4 falconers, and 13 **arquebuses**.

He first made land on the island of Cozumel (off the Yucatán coast), where he pulled down Indian idols erected there, subdued the Indians' resistance, and began the process of converting

Aztec emissaries meeting with Cortés. The Bettmann Archive.

them to Christianity. Like all **conquistadores**, Cortés explored in the name of "God and King." If the heathen Indians would not be converted, then they were destroyed as agents of the devil. At Cozumel he also found Jerónimo de Aguilar, who had been captured during an expedition eight years earlier; Aguilar joined Cortés as an interpreter, having learned the Mayan language from his captors.

Next, Cortés went to the coast of the modern Mexican state of Tabasco where he fought the local Indians, who fled at the sight of the horses, previously unknown in the Americas. Later a delegation of *caciques* (chiefs) brought food, gold, and young girls to gain Cortés's favor. Among the women was an Aztec noble named Malinche (or Malintzin), who became Cortés's interpreter, mistress, and one of the most influential members of his party. She was baptized and called Doña Marina by the Spaniards; her tact, linguistic ability, and skill at mediation would serve Cortés well during the conquest. Her importance was such that the Indians came to identify her and Cortés as one person, often calling him Malinche.

At sea again, Cortés moved north along the eastern coast of Mexico, landing at the harbor called San Juan de Ulúa. There he met with Montezuma's ambassador, who was sent to determine if the new arrivals were invaders or messengers of the great Aztec god Quetzalcoatl. Although the ambassador reported that the Spaniards were mortals, not gods, Montezuma vacillated, wondering if Cortés might be Quetzalcoatl himself. He then sent more emissaries bearing gifts of gold, hoping the Spanish would leave. At this point Cortés moved to legalize his position, since he had no real authority to conquer Mexico. He founded a town named Villa Rica de Vera Cruz (present-day Veracruz) and had himself named captain general of the new colony.

At Vera Cruz Cortés shaped the plans for his conquest. Careful and methodical, he paid close attention to details, yet could act on a moment's notice. For example, to ensure that none of his men would be tempted to return to Cuba, he destroyed all the ships. On the other hand, he fought beside his men and even helped carry dirt and stone to lay the foundations of Vera

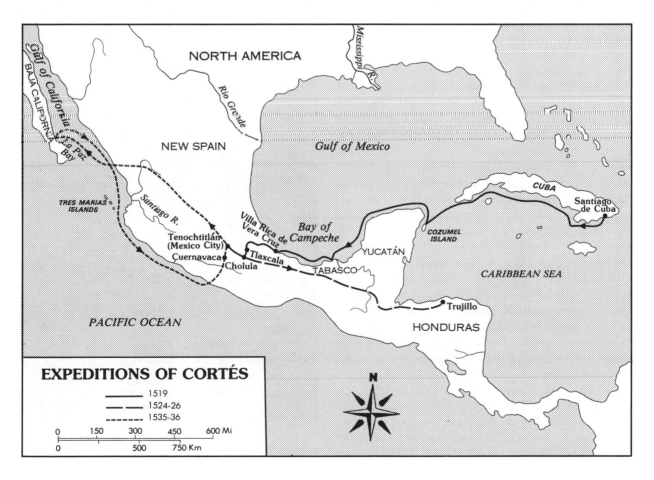

Cruz. Cortés planned that on his march inland he would subdue local Indian tribes, then persuade them to fight with him against the Aztecs. During his battles with the Aztecs, he would put these Indian allies in the front lines where they would suffer the most casualties.

On August 16, 1519, Cortés left Vera Cruz on his march inland to the Aztec capital of Tenochtitlán. The expedition moved from the hot, swampy coastal lands to the bleak plateau where the Tlaxcala Indians lived. After their defeat, the Tlaxcala became Cortés's strongest supporters. Next Cortés moved south to the holy city of Cholula where he tricked those sent to ambush him, then killed their leaders. He then headed west, reaching a point overlooking the Valley of Mexico from which he could see the center of the fabulous Aztec empire with its great cities and acres of cultivated land surrounded by lakes and volcanoes.

On their march through the valley, the Spaniards followed the southern borders of Lake Chalco, through irrigated fields to the great dike separating this lake from Lake Chimilco. They then went west on a narrow peninsula to another great dike or causeway leading directly through fortified portals and over a drawbridge into the great Aztec capital of Tenochtitlán. Cortés and his men were greeted with pomp by many Aztec chiefs, and finally by Montezuma himself. Although they were given a palace to stay in, the conquest was temporarily stymied. With the presence of the drawbridge, the Spanish realized they could be trapped in the city. Cortés therefore decided to take Montezuma captive. He arranged an audience with the emperor and, by threat of force tempered by promises of special treatment, coerced him into moving to the Spanish headquarters. By doing so Cortés had effectively gained control of the Aztec empire—though there would be later battles and an ongoing clash between the two cultures.

About this time Cortés had received word that PÁNFILO DE NARVÁEZ had landed at Vera Cruz with orders from Velásquez to relieve Cortés of his command. Cortés attacked Narváez by surprise one night after a storm, capturing Narváez and obtaining the allegiance of Narváez's men—thereby strengthening his own forces.

When Cortés returned to Tenochtitlán, he found the Aztecs on the verge of revolt. The Spaniards, under PEDRO DE ALVARADO, who had been left in command, had executed some of the Aztecs as a reprisal for their making human

sacrifices (of which there were tens of thousands annually). Cortés released some prisoners in an unsuccessful effort to appease the Aztecs and then had Montezuma appeal to them. But the emperor was stoned by his own people and later died from his injuries.

Cortés was forced to abandon the city. On the night of June 30, 1520—called the "Sorrowful Night" ("Nochetriste")—he fought his way out of the city in a battle that cost him half his men, all his horses, and most of the captured treasure. He retreated to Tlaxcala. All of his Indian allies deserted him except the Tlaxcalans. Meanwhile, smallpox was sweeping through Mexico, decimating the Indian population to the good fortune of the Spanish forces.

With characteristic resolve and ingenuity, Cortés had **brigantines** built by JUAN RODRIGUEZ CABRILLO, an expert shipbuilder from the Narváez force, for an assault on Tenochtitlán by water. The ships were disassembled and carried to the shores of Lake Texcoco, where they were reassembled. The Spanish attacked in May 1521

Hernán Cortés. Library of Congress.

and took the city on August 13, 1521, after heavy fighting.

In Spain, meanwhile, the stature of Cortés was being constantly undermined by Velásquez and the bishop of Burgos, who headed the colonial department of Spain. After considerable political maneuvering, King Charles I appointed a board to review the Cortés controversy. As a result, Cortés was completely exonerated of all charges, honored for his accomplishments, and, in late 1522, appointed governor, captain general, and chief justice of New Spain, with a liberal income and power to appoint all offices.

With his position secured, Cortés promptly initiated a program to build a new capital city and to expand his conquests in the New World. He selected as the site of the capital of New Spain the Aztec capital of Tenochtitlán, now to be called Mexico City. He ordered many expeditions, one of note sent to present-day Honduras under the command of Cristóbal de Olid. When Olid crossed into Honduras, he decided to assert his independence. In 1524 Cortés was forced to journey to Honduras to arrest him, but Olid had died by the time Cortés arrived.

During Cortés's absence from Mexico, however, his enemies were active, even reporting him dead. When Cortés finally returned to Mexico City, he had been superceded as governor. To seek amends, he sailed to Spain in 1528, where he was received with a tumultuous welcome from the people and honored by the king (who did not reinstate his governorship, however).

By 1530 Cortés was tired of life in Spain and returned to Mexico City, where more political intrigue led him to establish a home at Cuernavaca. In 1532 he financed an expedition that discovered the Tres Marías islands of the Pacific coast. Reports of a pearl-rich island, received from survivors of another expedition sponsored by Cortés, led him to mount his own expedition to find these islands. On April 18, 1535, he sailed with 170 men and three ships, landing at modern La Paz Bay on the eastern coast of Baja California. There he attempted to found a colony, but the scarcity of food and treasure forced him back to Mexico in 1536. In 1539, defying the orders of the viceroy of Mexico, Cortés sponsored another voyage of exploration to the Gulf of California, this one led by Francisco de Ulloa.

None of these expeditions were financially successful, however, and Cortés returned again

to Spain in 1540. He fought in a military campaign in Algeria in 1541, receiving no special honors. Deciding to return to Mexico, he first traveled to Seville; there he contracted dysentery and died on December 2, 1547.

An indefatigable, brilliant, and brutal conquistador, Hernán Cortés orchestrated the fall of the Aztec empire despite overwhelming odds. His explorations and colonizations were major steps in extending Spanish influence throughout Mexico and Central America.

SUGGESTED READING: Francisco Lopez de Gomara, *Cortes: The Life of the Conqueror by His Secretary*, trans. and ed. by Byrd Simpson (University of California Press, Berkeley, 1964); Salvador de Madariaga, *Hernan Cortes, Conqueror of Mexico* (University of Miami Press, 1967); Albert Marrin, *Aztecs and Spaniards: Cortes and the Conquest of Mexico* (Atheneum, 1986); Henry Morton Robinson, *Stout Cortes; A Biography of the Spanish Conquest* (Century, 1931).

Cosa, Juan de La. See **La Cosa, Juan de.**

· Cousteau, Jacques-Yves

French
b June 11, 1910; St. André-de-Cubzac
d June 25, 1997
Explores oceans of world as oceanographer and documentary filmmaker; coinvented scuba

Perhaps no name is as closely associated with modern oceanographic exploration as that of Captain Jacques-Yves Cousteau. As commander of the research vessel *Calypso*, Cousteau probably has done more than any single individual to bring the wonders of "Planet Ocean" and the underwater world to public attention through films, books, and television programs.

Born in France on June 11, 1910, Cousteau developed an early interest in the water. He learned to swim at the age of ten while at a Vermont summer camp, where he cleared the bottom of a shallow lake of branches and debris. During the early 1930s, as a young naval officer, Cousteau obtained his first pair of underwater goggles, which he used in the Mediterranean to see "a jungle of fish. That was like an electric shock. . . ." In 1943 Cousteau and engineer Emil Gagnan introduced the Aqua-lung, the first scuba (self-contained underwater breathing apparatus) unit. Using scuba gear, people

Jacques Cousteau. UPI/Bettmann.

could swim free beneath the sea for extended periods without cables, hoses, or bulky diving suits—something never before possible.

After World War II Cousteau organized a sea research company and, in 1950, acquired the ship *Calypso*. With his entire family, he sailed the world's oceans, capturing marine life on film. His underwater study of the Red Sea in 1951 was the first of its kind. Since then he and his crew have peered beneath most, if not all, of the world's oceans. Cousteau's Academy Award–winning 1956 documentary, *The Silent World*, was the first color underwater film to be shown to a general audience.

In the early 1960s Cousteau became intrigued by the possibility of living under water. His *Conshelf* project proved that this was technologically possible; Cousteau and four others lived in an underwater habitat for a month in 1963. The resulting film became a National Geographic Society television special and later a documentary series.

Cousteau cofounded the Cousteau Society (1974) and Fondation Cousteau (1981) to help carry out his goal of environmental education. In 1985, at the age of seventy-five, he began his most extensive expedition ever. Called "Rediscovery of the World," this major eight-year

research project is intended to answer questions about the health of the earth's waters.

- Covilhã (Covil; Covilham; Covilhão), Pêro da (Pedro de)

Portuguese
b 1460?; Beira
d 1526?; Abyssinia?
Explored India, Middle East, and Abyssinia

Pêro da Covilhã was one of the explorers commissioned by Portuguese rulers in the fifteenth century to sail to Africa for the combined purpose of seeking trade opportunities and making contact with Prester John, the legendary Christian king. Covilhã explored the trade centers of India, infiltrated the Islamic holy cities of Mecca and Medina, and finally traveled to Abyssinia (now Ethiopia), where he was given an official post but held captive for the remainder of his life.

As a youth, Covilhã went to Spain as a servant to the duke of Medina-Disonai and returned to Portugal to become a squire to King Alfonso V, accompanying the king when he claimed the Castilian throne. When Alfonso died, Covilhã became a squire to his successor, King John II, and served as John's messenger to Spain, also possibly working as a spy in North Africa. He was sent on two missions to North Africa, one posing as a merchant in order to win the friendship of the ruler of Tlemcen and another to purchase horses in Fès. Covilhã was chosen by King John in 1487 to travel to East Africa, where the kingdom of Prester John was believed to be located.

The legend of Prester John had been popular in Europe since the Crusades of the twelfth century. Depicted as a direct descendant of the Magi, he was said to rule over a wealthy and powerful Christian domain in the uncharted area beyond Persia (now Iran). Said to be immortal, owing to the "fountain of youth" located in his kingdom, Prester John was sought for centuries by Christian monarchs and religious leaders.

The story of a Christian kingdom somewhere in Asia or Africa probably had some basis in fact, since Christian missionaries are believed to have ventured into those regions during the time of the Crusades or earlier. A falsified letter to the emperor of Byzantium from Prester John fueled the legend considerably, especially after it reached the pope and the European monarchs. The author of the letter described a kingdom so prosperous that it boasted beds made of sapphires and tables of emeralds, as well as bountiful food supplies and powerful military forces. In the letter, Prester John is described as a protector of Christians everywhere and is said to "exceed in riches, virtue and power all creatures who dwell under heaven."

It was largely the ongoing search for Prester John that brought about Europe's discovery of the East. Although Europeans' perception of Prester John's wealth and power had become less grandiose by the fourteenth century, Prester John—or one of his descendants—was still sought as an important Christian ally against the Islamic world. King John also hoped that a relationship with Prester John might prove financially rewarding, leading him to the riches of the Indies.

At the time Covilhã left Portugal in May of 1487, Prester John was thought to reside in Abyssinia. Covilhã visited Barcelona and Naples before traveling to Alexandria, and posing as a Moorish merchant to protect himself in anti-Christian territory, joined a Muslim caravan headed for Cairo. He then sailed the Red Sea south to Aden and, in the company of Arab traders, proceeded to the Malabar Coast of India, the Persian Gulf, and Arabia. Still disguised, he gained access to the Islamic holy cities of Mecca and Medina, which were strictly forbidden to Christians, before returning to Cairo by way of the Arabian desert and the Red Sea.

By 1492 or 1493, Covilhã had surveyed many of the leading Eastern centers of commerce and collected information for a report to the king, which, among other things, included intelligence regarding India that would prove helpful to VASCO DA GAMA. Covilhã then began his search for Prester John in Abyssinia. Upon his arrival there, Emperor Eskender greeted him cordially and provided him with a house, servants, a harem, and a prestigious post as governor of one of the country's districts. The emperor then promptly barred Covilhã from leaving the country for the remainder of his life.

During Covilhã's absence, King John sent other explorers in search of Prester John, directing them to travel inland from Africa's west coast. The king also dispatched Christianized African slaves to various sites along the coastline and instructed them to travel inland bearing gifts for Prester John.

It was to be nearly thirty years before anything was learned of Covilhã's fate. The Portuguese king then sent an ambassador to Abyssinia. He arrived to find the elderly Covilhã a healthy, well cared for captive who showed little interest in leaving his African home. However, when the ambassador left the country in 1524, he took Covilhã's twenty-three-year-old son with him to be educated in Portugal. As late as 1526, Covilhã was reported to be alive and well at his home in Abyssinia.

da Gama, Vasco. See **Gama, Vasco da.**

• Dalrymple, Alexander

Scottish
b July 24, 1737; New Hailes, Midlothian
d June 19, 1808; London, England
Wrote *Account of the Discoveries Made in the South Pacific Previous to 1764*

A self-proclaimed authority on *Terra Australis Incognita*, Scottish aristocrat Alexander Dalrymple's book on this hypothetical continent sparked the Royal Society's interest in systematic exploration of the Pacific. A scholar, seaman, and geographer, Dalrymple was the first **hydrographer** to the Royal Navy.

Dalrymple was born in 1737 into the ancient and noble Scottish family that held the earldom of Stair. When he was a young man, his heroes were the great explorers CHRISTOPHER COLUMBUS and FERDINAND MAGELLAN, and so it was only natural that he pursue a career with the sea. He went to work as an administrator for the British East India Company in the Pacific and eventually became its staff hydrographer.

Dalrymple was a man of strong opinions who believed that his way was the only way. When he tactlessly suggested that the East India Company change its manner of operating, move its headquarters, and put him in charge, he was sent back to England instead. Health reasons (he suffered from gout) also contributed to his dismissal.

In his book, *An Historical Collection of the Several Voyages and Discoveries in the South Pacific Ocean,* Dalrymple expounded on the existence of *Terra Australis Incognita*, the great Southern Continent first postulated by the Roman astronomer and geographer PTOLEMY in the second century A.D. Ptolemy believed that land masses, not oceans, dominated the globe. His influential work, *Geography*, depicts a huge continent reaching from the part of Africa below the equator to the northeast corner of Asia and reduces the Indian Ocean and China Sea into enclosed seas, much like the Mediterranean. Many of his ideas about terra incognita (unknown land) were accepted in Europe until the early fifteenth century.

Explorations by the likes of BARTOLOMEU DIAS and Ferdinand Magellan proved that the Indian and Pacific oceans were not landlocked, and that Africa and South America were not part of a larger Southern Continent. But they did not disprove the existence of *Terra Australis Incognita;* they just ruled out its being in certain parts of the world. ABEL TASMAN's circumnavigation of Australia in 1642 proved that what the Dutch called the Great South Land was not part of *Terra Australis Incognita*, either, but the elusive continent merely was placed farther south by mapmakers.

Dalrymple was convinced that *Terra Australis Incognita* in fact existed, but that earlier explorers simply had missed this vast continent, which by the eighteenth century supposedly stretched from Chile to New Zealand. Logic, he said, dictated that the southern ocean must have a large land mass to counter that of Europe and Asia and thus balance the earth's motion, as the ancient Greeks had suggested. Explorers' reports of erratic winds in the Pacific were proof of the existence of a large land mass, he claimed. Like most mythical lands before it, *Terra Australis Incognita* was thought to be a vast and fertile land with a wealth of resources. Dalrymple was determined to be its discoverer. When he learned that the Admiralty planned an expedition in 1768 to find and claim the unknown land, he assumed himself to be the ideal commander.

Dalrymple was a fellow of the Royal Society, which, as a sponsor, asked him to take part in the expedition as a civilian observer. Command of the ship, however, was given to Captain JAMES COOK. In a fit of pique, Dalrymple refused to go at all. Cook's expedition disproved the continent's existence to everyone's satisfaction—except Dalrymple, who criticized the voyage,

claiming that Cook had discovered nothing that Dalrymple had not already documented.

Throughout his life, Dalrymple made a profession of charting winds and currents, and in 1795 he was named the first hydrographer to the Royal Navy. He died in 1808.

• Dampier, William Cecil

English
b 1652?; Yoevil, Somerset
d March 1715; England
Circumnavigated three times; discovered New Britain; explored Australia

Perhaps the best known of the seventeenth-century **buccaneers**, William Cecil Dampier was a skilled seaman and observer whose popular books helped focus the eyes of Europe on the Pacific. He circled the world three times, exploring the west coasts of Central and South America as well as Australia and New Zealand, and documenting currents, winds, flora, and fauna.

Dampier was born in a small village in Somerset, in southwest England, around 1652. He went to sea as a youth, working first in Newfoundland and then in the West Indies. In 1674 he joined a log-cutting camp on the Gulf of Mexico's Bay of Campeche, where he worked for four years until a hurricane destroyed most of the area's timber, leaving him penniless.

Ever the adventurer, Dampier joined a band of 336 buccaneers under John Coxon and Bartholomew Sharp. They crossed the Isthmus of Panama and raided villages along the west coast of South America. On April 17, 1681, Dampier and nearly fifty others set out to seek their own fortunes. He started a journal, which he maintained until he returned to Downs, England, ten years later. (For its protection, he carried the document in a hollow bamboo case sealed with wax.) In the interim, this "rolling stone" moved from ship to ship, from adventure to adventure, leading the pirate's life and learning as he went. He undertook pirating "more to indulge my curiosity than to get wealth." His travels took him from South America's Cape Horn north to Acapulco and west to the Juan Fernández and Galápagos islands. Unlike most buccaneers, he drank little and remained aloof from the rabble with whom he sailed.

In 1686 Dampier guided Captain Charles Swan's buccaneer ship *Cygnet* and another vessel from Cape Corrientes, Mexico, to Guam—some 7,300 miles—in fifty-one days, making landfall before provisions ran out. The ship continued on to the Philippines, where a mutinous crew left Swan behind, then sailed on to New Holland (present-day Australia), sighted on January 4, 1688. (Dampier's description of the **aborigines** encountered during his short stay in Australia may have been the basis for the Yahoos in Jonathan Swift's *Gulliver's Travels*.) Dampier left the *Cygnet* in the Nicobar Islands and roamed the waters of Southeast Asia for three years aboard various merchant ships.

Completing his westward circuit in 1691, Dampier returned to England with his journal, which now is housed in the British Library. When his first book, *A New Voyage Round the World,* was published in 1697, it became an immediate best-seller, going through four editions in two years. Other books followed, including *Discourse of Winds* and *Vindication.* JAMES COOK and other subsequent explorers were familiar

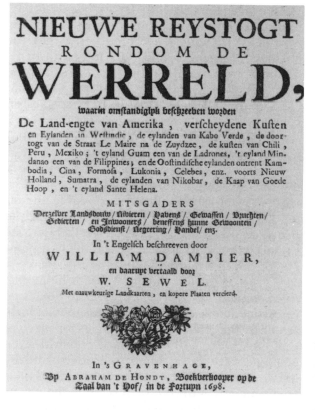

Frontispiece of a Dutch translation of Dampier's *New Voyage Around the World.* Library of Congress.

with and made use of his work, which included valuable geographical surveys and charts.

Dampier's reputation spread, and in 1698 his navigational skills earned him the command of the H.M.S. *Roebuck* on an Admiralty-sponsored expedition to search for *Terra Australis Incognita,* the unknown but postulated Southern Continent (for a more complete discussion, SEE ALEXANDER DALRYMPLE). Unfortunately, Dampier's expertise as a navigator and travel writer far outweighed his leadership skills. The ship was barely seaworthy, and Dampier slept with a gun at his side to protect himself from a mutinous crew who balked at taking orders from a pirate.

Dampier hoped to round Cape Horn and investigate the unexplored eastern coast of New Holland, but a delayed departure and the threat of bad weather forced him to take an eastward route. He explored New Holland's west and northwest coast and the **archipelago** that now bears his name. Northwest of New Guinea he discovered Nova Britannia (New Britain Island). On its return, the *Roebuck* foundered off Ascension Island in the South Atlantic; some weeks later, captain and crew were rescued by passing English merchant ships.

In 1699 Dampier was court-martialed—largely on the word of a few disgruntled crewmen—"for many irregularities and undue practices" and deemed "not a fit person to command any of Her Majesty's ships." Still, in 1702 he received a letter of marque, or license, and sponsors for a **privateering** expedition off South America. By this time, he seems to have lost his buccaneering touch, as he let several prizes slip by, including a coveted treasure **galleon** bound for Acapulco from Manila. His crew thought he was a coward. His letter of marque was stolen, and as a result, Dampier was thrown in a Dutch East Indies jail for piracy.

Dampier was eventually released and returned to England in 1707 and, a year later, joined Woodes Rogers's privateering expedition as pilot. For three years Rogers's ships, the *Duke* and *Duchess,* roamed the Pacific. When they reached the Juan Fernández Islands, they rescued the castaway Alexander Selkirk, who had been left ashore four years earlier during Dampier's previous voyage. The privateers were highly successful, and their piratical circumnavigation was profitable. After some years of litigation, Dampier received approximately

£1,500 for his efforts. He died in obscurity in 1715.

• Darwin, Charles Robert

English
b February 12, 1809; Shrewsbury
d April 19, 1882; Down, Kent
Explored South America and Pacific; developed theory of natural selection

Charles Darwin spent five years aboard the research vessel H.M.S. *Beagle* exploring the coast of South America and islands of the Pacific. His biological and geological discoveries led to his once-controversial but now widely accepted theory of evolution through natural selection, which he described in his book *The Origin of Species* (1859). The expedition also led Darwin to a new understanding of the earth's geological history.

Born on February 12, 1809, in Shrewsbury, England, to physician Robert Waring Darwin

Charles Robert Darwin. Popperfoto.

and Susannah Wedgewood, Darwin showed an early interest in natural science. By the age of eight he had begun collecting flowers, bugs, birds, rocks, and butterflies—pursuits of which his late grandfather, the poet and naturalist Erasmus Darwin, no doubt would have approved.

Darwin was an average student and left medical school at Edinburgh University because he disliked the sight of blood. While at Edinburgh he joined the Plinean Society, where he heard such speakers as the naturalist JOHN J. AUDUBON and the explorer-author Sir Walter Scott. In 1828 he entered Cambridge University to study for the Anglican ministry. Three years later, the twenty-two-year-old Darwin was just weeks shy of taking his holy orders when friend and professor John Stevens Henslow recommended him for an unpaid post as naturalist aboard the H.M.S. *Beagle* on an expedition to chart the coasts of South America. Darwin accepted the post. Later he would write: "The voyage of the *Beagle* has been by far the most important event in my life and has determined the whole of my existence."

The *Beagle* set sail on December 27, 1831, under the command of Captain ROBERT FITZROY, who held the widely accepted belief that the business of science—and thus the naturalist's findings—was to uphold the literal truth of the Old Testament. After all, every Christian "knew" that the world and all the species on it had been created in their current forms at 9 A.M. on Sunday, October 23, 4004 B.C., and that nature was static and unchanging.

Darwin collected specimens at sea using a tow net, working in spite of violent seasickness. He also went ashore whenever possible and often made long treks on foot, arranging for the *Beagle* to pick him up days or weeks later. He explored the high mountains and the vast pampas of South America, where he discovered a rare type of ostrich that now bears his name, *Rhea darwini*. He traveled upriver to points no European had seen before. He was particularly struck by the often violent struggles for survival that took place within the natural world, even among creatures as small as spiders, and by the relationships between the animals and their environment. With the help of an assistant, he collected and preserved numerous biological and geological specimens, and the cabin he shared with Fitzroy soon resembled a museum.

At Punta Alta, Argentina, in late 1832, Darwin

discovered the fossils that would set his ideas in motion. Influenced by the work of the geologist Charles Lyell and the naturalist Jean Lamarck, Darwin came to believe that the earth and the creatures on it were in a state of constant change. The remains of giant sloths and mastodons he found in Argentina resembled contemporary animals; and although he could not yet support his point, he had begun to doubt the commonly accepted explanation that the extinct species had not boarded Noah's ark in time to be saved from the Flood. Too many species had disappeared.

In 1834 Darwin spent six weeks high in the Andes, where he found fossilized seashells at 12,000-foot elevations some 700 miles from the Atlantic, and fossilized pine forests below them, leading him to the revolutionary notion that the mountains once were submerged and subsequently were thrust up from the seabed. If this were the case, he believed, these upheavals would have taken place over the course of millions of years.

The simultaneous eruption of three Andean volcanoes some 3,200 miles apart—Osorno, Aconcagua, and Cosigüina—in January 1835 supported his hypothesis. A month later, a major earthquake jolted south-central Chile. Darwin wrote that "the most remarkable effect of this earthquake was the permanent elevation of the land" by two or three feet. These incidents, along with his observations of marine fossils high in the mountains, convinced him of the earth's instability.

The idea that species evolve had been proposed before, most notably by Darwin's grandfather; however, the mechanism was unknown. Charles Darwin found the most convincing evidence to support this radical theory in the Galápagos, a group of Ecuadoran islands in the Pacific some 600 miles west of the mainland. Darwin visited several of these unpeopled lava islands over the course of more than a month late in 1835. He spent a week on James Island, where he made some of his most important observations. The island was populated by giant tortoises and by land and marine iguanas, which resembled prehistoric creatures.

While in the Galápagos, Darwin encountered more than a dozen species of finches. Although similar in appearance, each had a different beak uniquely adapted to the type of food available. Some beaks were delicate, while others were heavy enough to crush large, hard seeds. He found many other animal species that resembled South American species yet differed "by innumerable trifling details of structure," leading him to theorize that individuals best suited to a particular environment survive and reproduce, eventually evolving into new species, each descended from a common ancestor. These observations shaped Darwin's idea that species evolved through a process he named natural selection.

On October 20, 1835, the *Beagle* sailed west across the Pacific from the Galápagos, stopping at New Zealand, Australia, and many small islands. While visiting Tahiti in the Pacific and the Cocos (or Keeling) Islands in the Indian Ocean, Darwin studied the coral polyps on the surrounding reefs and took soundings along their slopes. Based on his findings, he theorized that large volcanic islands emerged from the sea a million years ago and that coral colonies had sprung up where the island met the water. Over hundreds of thousands of years, the islands sank back into the earth's crust, while the coral continued to build upward. Darwin's hypothesis of how these atolls were formed was not proven until the twentieth century.

By the time the expedition returned to England on October 2, 1836, Darwin was homesick, and he never returned to sea. He spent ten years cataloging his specimens and conducting research resulting from the *Beagle* expedition, and another eight studying a particular barnacle he had acquired while abroad. In 1839 he married his cousin Emma Wedgewood, with whom he had ten children. In 1842 the family moved to the village of Down, outside London, where he conducted research on sheep, pigs, goldfish, bees, and pigeons, as well as on plant life.

Darwin's conclusions shook his own religious convictions, and he probably could foresee public reaction to what would be considered his blasphemous claims concerning natural selection. It was not until 1858 that he presented a paper on evolution with ALFRED RUSSEL WALLACE, a fellow naturalist who independently had come to many of the same conclusions as Darwin. The following year Darwin published *The Origin of Species*. At first, the book was vehemently attacked, but it was later widely acclaimed and translated into almost every European language. Darwin published eight other major works, including *The Descent of Man*. Although his theories caused tremendous controversy, they have become accepted as the underpinnings of modern biological studies.

With the exception of seasickness and exhaustion after long forays into the mountains, Darwin was robust during the *Beagle* expedition, yet he never enjoyed good health after his return. This may have been psychosomatic or the result of mosquitolike bites suffered in South America. He died in Down on April 19, 1882, and is buried in Westminster Abbey.

SUGGESTED READING: Nora Barlow, ed., *Charles Darwin and the Voyage of the* Beagle (Philosophical Library, 1946); Charles Darwin, *The Origin of Species* (New American Library, 1986); Robert S. Hopkins, *Darwin's South America* (John Day, 1969); Alan Moorehead, *Darwin and the* Beagle, rev. ed. (Penguin, 1979).

• David-Neel, Alexandra

French
b October 24, 1868; St.-Mandé, suburb of Paris
d September 8, 1969; Digne, Provence
Explored Tibet, reaching Lhasa

Alexandra David-Neel is famous as the first Western woman (second Westerner) to enter the forbidden city of Lhasa, a place Tibetans considered so sacred that they warned foreigners who approached its gates to turn back on pain of death. Many famous travelers, including the great Swedish explorer SVEN ANDERS HEDIN, had tried but failed to penetrate Lhasa, the sanctuary of Tibet's spiritual leader, the Dalai Lama. When David-Neel, a fifty-five-year-old former opera singer and Oriental scholar, dressed as a Mongolian peasant to make the dangerous trek from China into Lhasa in 1924, she captured the imagination of the world. Her sudden fame was a fitting reward for long years of productive wandering in Asia.

From birth, David-Neel was a product of conflicting influences. Her father, Louis David, was from a well-to-do French Protestant family. A nephew of the painter Jacques-Louis David and a friend of the novelist Victor Hugo, he shared the political sympathies of both of these great artists and supported the revolution of 1848 against King Louis Philippe. When Napoleon III came to power, David fled to Brussels, where he met and married Alexandrine Borghmans, a Belgian of Dutch, Norwegian, and Siberian ancestry who was a devout Catholic and a mon-

archist. In 1867, under a general amnesty to political exiles, the couple returned to France, setting up house in the suburb of Saint-Mandé, where Alexandra was born.

Alexandra distinguished herself as a student and developed a keen interest in religion and a flair for independence. As a teenager, she liked to make unannounced trips alone to far-off places—traveling by train to Italy and by bicycle to Spain, for example. For a young, upper-class woman of that period this was scandalous behavior. During a trip to London in 1888 she became fascinated by the then-fashionable study of mysticism. At the age of twenty-one, eager to learn more about the religions of the East, she spent her entire inheritance on a trip to Ceylon (now Sri Lanka) and India.

Back in Europe, Alexandra studied music in Brussels and Paris. In 1893 she began working as an opera singer, pianist, and music director, first in the Orient, and later in the Mediterranean and North Africa. She also wrote essays on a wide range of topics—from politics, to women's rights, to Buddhism.

In 1900 she met Philippe Neel, a passionate man with an aristocratic background, who was chief engineer of a French railroad company, the Chemin de Fer d'Afrique. They married in Tunisia on August 4, 1904. Both were independent, free-spirited people. Their marriage was a difficult one, but it lasted nearly forty years. Philippe preferred to live in the West, but he gave his wife free reign to travel and funded many of her expeditions to the East. Even during her most trying times in Asia, Alexandra would write him whenever she could. When he died in 1941, she said that she had lost her greatest friend.

As her reputation as a writer grew, David-Neel began to give lectures all over Europe. In 1910 she finished a book on Buddhism, a religion that interested her more and more. In August 1911 she left her husband and sailed for India. Immersing herself in the study of the great religions of the East, she continued to write. She also became interested in photography and learned to speak many Asian languages.

In 1912 she traveled to the Himalayan kingdom of Sikkim on India's northeastern border. Befriended by the maharaja, she was presented to the Dalai Lama, who was in Sikkim after fleeing a Chinese invasion of Tibet. She lived for several months as a hermit in a mountain cave, then entered a Buddhist monastery, where she met the fifteen-year-old Aphur Yongden, who was to become her adopted son. Meanwhile, her reputation for holiness grew. Some natives believed she was actually a reincarnated goddess.

The British were less generous. Eager to keep foreigners out of Tibet, which they regarded as a strategic buffer state protecting their Indian empire, they were furious when they learned that the Frenchwoman had repeatedly crossed the border. Ordered out of India, David-Neel decided to return to Tibet via China. But first, accompanied by Yongden, she traveled to Burma (now Myanmar), Vietnam, Korea, and Japan. In October 1917 they arrived in Beijing. That winter, they began a 2,000-mile trek westward across China. It was a difficult, dangerous journey through a country riddled by banditry and civil war. In July 1918, after six months on the road, they reached Kumbum, the "Monastery of 10,000 Images," situated in disputed territory along the Chinese-Tibetan border. They based themselves there for more than three years, studying Buddhism, translating sacred texts, and making occasional trips into Mongolia and Tibet. Meanwhile, the political situation deteriorated throughout Asia. The Russian civil war spread to Mongolia. Fighting in China and along the Chinese-Tibetan border grew worse. In February 1921 David-Neel and Yongden left Kumbum. For nearly three years they wandered.

Finally, in October 1923, she and Yongden entered Tibet, determined to reach Lhasa. David-Neel's Tibetan was near-perfect by this time. She dyed her hair and her skin with ink and donned ragged peasant clothes. Traveling by night and sleeping by day, she and Yongden posed as a **lama** and his mother making a pilgrimage to Lhasa. The mountain passes were lonely, freezing, and treacherous. Thieves tried to rob them but were scared off when David-Neel fired her pistol. To fight the cold, they raised their body temperature through intense concentration, a technique that enabled Eastern holy men wearing even the flimsiest garments to stay warm. Food was scarce. On Christmas Day 1923 they rested in a freezing cave with nothing to eat but a soup made from boiling water and leather pieces cut from their shoes.

After four months of traveling, they caught sight of the highest point of Lhasa, the golden roof of the Potala, the Dalai Lama's palace. En-

Alexandra David-Neel, dressed as a Tibetan nun. UPI/Bettmann.

tering the city undetected, they roamed at will for the next two months, even visiting the Potala, which was open to pilgrims for the New Year festival. Then, quite by accident, they became witnesses in a domestic dispute that required a court hearing. Unwilling to risk exposure, they slipped out of the city and made their way to India. On May 10, 1925, David-Neel arrived in France.

The fact that others had been to Lhasa before her did not diminish David-Neel's resulting fame. France named her a **chevalier** of the Legion of Honor. The geographic societies of France and Belgium awarded her gold medals. (The British Royal Geographical Society did not, pointing out that her achievement was not a first and that the book she wrote about her trip did not contain a single map.) Her lectures were packed, and her books became best-sellers.

David-Neel's life as a traveler was far from over. In 1937, aided by a French government grant, she returned to China to continue her studies. As World War II enveloped the East, she moved to southeastern Tibet, then, in 1944, to Chengdu, China. After the war she returned to her home in Digne, a town in the Alps of

Provence. Yongden lived with her until he died in 1955.

David-Neel continued to write. When she died, at the age of 100, she had four major works in progress. Her intellectual voyages had made her one of the world's leading authorities on Tibetan Buddhism. Perhaps more than any of her contemporaries, she gave the West new insight into the spiritual world of Asia.

• Davis, John

English
b 1550?; Sandridge, Devonshire
d December 29 or 30, 1605; Bintang Island, near
Singapore
Attempted Northwest Passage and explored
Arctic

An expert navigator who invented the Davis **quadrant**, a device used for a century to determine latitude, John Davis in 1587 penetrated farther into the waters west of Greenland than Sir MARTIN FROBISHER had a decade earlier. But because neither Frobisher nor Davis was able to determine longitude precisely (something that could not be done without an accurate seagoing timepiece) and because both were misled by the faulty maps of Nicolo Zeno (see ANTONIO ZENO), they did not realize that their discoveries were contiguous (both thought Frobisher had been on the east coast of Greenland). Davis did, however, correctly chart the eastern shore of present-day Baffin Island, including Cumberland Sound. Davis left the area believing that a Northwest Passage was possible by that route, an idea that WILLIAM BAFFIN was soon to test.

Davis grew up in Devonshire and as a youth counted among his friends WALTER RALEIGH and HUMPHREY GILBERT. It was Gilbert's enthusiasm for the idea of the Northwest Passage (for a more complete discussion, see MARTIN FROBISHER) that eventually stimulated Davis on his own quest. After a fourteen-year stint at sea, Davis had become an accomplished and trusted captain and navigator ready to undertake the challenge of Arctic exploration.

Adrian Gilbert (Humphrey's brother) and Raleigh joined Davis in the 1580s in forming a company for carrying out the adventure. They planned it in consultation with John Dee, the mathematician and geographer, and Sir Francis Walsingham, Queen Elizabeth I's secretary of state. A wealthy merchant named William Sanderson, unsure of the chances for success but aware that Davis had a good reputation as a navigator who could bring home a profit, directed the preparations and handled the financing.

On June 7, 1585, Davis headed out to sea from Dartmouth with two small vessels, the fifty-ton *Sunshine* and the thirty-five-ton *Moonshine*. He sighted the east side of Greenland on July 20. After rounding the southern point of what he called the Land of Desolation, he anchored in a fjord that he named Gilbert Sound (now Godthaab Fjord). There he encountered **Inuits**, whom he enchanted with music from a quartet. Soon the fjord was swarming with kayaks, five of which Davis acquired in the ensuing trade. On August 1, the two ships crossed what is now Davis Strait and examined the entrance to Cumberland Sound (which Davis thought might be a strait), taking careful notes on the local vegetation and wildlife. By the time adverse winds and the advance of the season argued for their return, Davis was optimistic about finding a passage to the Orient.

A return expedition was dispatched the next year, with the same two ships being joined by the 120-ton *Mermaid* and a **pinnace**, the *North Star*. Since current theory suggested the existence of an open Arctic sea past the wall of ice encountered near the south coast of Greenland, two of the ships were sent to the east of Greenland to break though the wall. This proved impossible, and after visiting present-day Godthaab Fjord they returned to England.

Meanwhile, Davis took the *Mermaid* and the *Moonshine* to Godthaab Fjord, where remarkably friendly relations with the Inuits led to more trading and to soccer and wrestling matches. He also took careful ethnological notes, thus contributing to the growing body of European anthropological literature. Ever curious about natural history, he spent some time exploring the coast and the interior of Greenland before heading back to sea.

Much of the crew became skittish because of the heavy pack ice, and Davis responded in characteristically resourceful and humane fashion. Those whom he could inspire to press on stayed to explore in the *Moonshine*, while the bulk of the crew returned to England in the *Mermaid*. Not much progress was made, but a large catch of fish in Davis Strait helped defray at least some of the cost of the expedition, which was a hopeful sign to investors in Davis's next—and last—voyage to these waters.

This expedition started in 1587 with three vessels and ended with Davis and a small crew aboard the pinnace *Ellen*. He had once again inspired volunteers to push on no matter what the cost. He also ensured a profit by setting up a fishery off Godthaab Fjord with the other two ships.

The *Ellen* made its way up the coast of Greenland to a cliff at 72° North latitude, which Davis named Sanderson His Hope (present-day Upernavik, Greenland) after his chief financial backer. Prevented from further progress by ice floes and northerly winds, Davis then followed the ice pack south, barely escaping being frozen in with it. He explored the coast of Baffin Island, which both he and Frobisher had worked before, and was encouraged by the presence of strong currents at the opening of Frobisher's "Mistaken Strait" (although he did not realize that Frobisher had been there). This was the opening of Hudson Strait and seemed to Davis yet another possibility for a passage.

On his return to England, the outbreak of war with Spain prevented further attempts to navigate the passage until Baffin and Hudson could pursue Davis's leads some years later. Davis instead captained the *Black Dog* against the Spanish Armada in 1588. Then he was given the *Drake* to harass the Spanish fleet as a sort of government-sponsored pirate.

The riches he captured in these ventures allowed him to return to the search for the North west Passage, this time from the Pacific coast of North America. Unfortunately, his attempt as captain of the *Desire* to cross the Cape of Good Hope with the THOMAS CAVENDISH expedition of 1592 was a terrible failure, resulting in the loss of his fortune. On his return, he discovered the present-day Falkland Islands (or Malvinas), two years before Sir Richard Hawkins was to lay claim to them.

Though no longer wealthy, Davis still had an estate in Devonshire to which he could retire comfortably. There he composed two valuable works summing up his experience as a navigator and explorer, the *Seaman's Secret* and the *World's Hydrographical Description*. Davis also provided geographical data for the globe constructed by Emerie Mollineux in 1592, an object of considerable interest at a time when the outlines of the earth's land masses were finally beginning to take shape.

Retirement did not last long, and in 1596–97 he served with the earl of Essex in two naval expeditions. Then in 1598 he was employed by the Dutch to pilot their first voyage to the East Indies. Davis wrote the only surviving account of this difficult voyage, in which the chief was killed in a battle with Malaysians. With this experience under his belt, Davis was the obvious man to pilot the first voyage of the English East India Company in 1601–1603. On his final voyage, he piloted the ship of a rival group to the East Indies. In 1605 the ship was besieged by Japanese pirates off the coast of the Malay Peninsula. The pirates had actually boarded the ship peacefully and were having dinner with their English hosts when they unsheathed their swords. John Davis was one of the first killed. A brutal end, but the night was warm, the food was good, and riches were in sight—not the worst way for an Arctic explorer to breathe his last.

del Cano, Juan Sebastián. See **Elcano, Juan Sebastián de.**

De Long, George Washington

American
b August 22, 1844; New York City
d October 30, 1881; Lena River Delta, Siberia
Explored Russian and Alaskan Arctic;
attempted to reach North Pole

When Lieutenant Commander George Washington De Long of the U.S. Navy sailed through the Bering Strait in the summer of 1879, he intended to test the theory that the warm waters of the Pacific might cut a passage through the polar ice pack, perhaps all the way to the North Pole. Knowing that the results would be spectacular if the theory proved correct, the publisher of the *New York Herald*, Gordon Bennett, financed the operation in exchange for exclusive rights to the story. De Long kept his end of the bargain by keeping a daily record—right up to the day he died of starvation and exposure—but the resulting story was not at all what either man had expected.

Shortly after passing the Bering Strait, which separates Alaska and Siberia, De Long's *Jeannette* was caught in the ice pack near Herald Island on September 5, 1879. After drifting

George Washington De Long. U.S. Naval Institute.

years after the sinking of the *Jeannette*. There, halfway around the world from where it had been originally wrecked, the remains of the *Jeannette* washed ashore. This revealed for the first time the clockwise track of the polar ice pack, inspiring the subsequent drifting voyage of FRIDTJOF NANSEN.

· Denham, Dixon

English
b January 1, 1786; London
d May 8, 1828; Freetown, Sierra Leone
Explored West Africa

One of the first Europeans to reach Lake Chad, Major Dixon Denham was part of a team Britain sent to the interior of western Africa primarily to trace the course of the Niger River. Continually in conflict with other members of the expedition, Denham left and rejoined the party several times, independently exploring many of the small kingdoms and villages of Bornu (in what is now northern Nigeria). The initial acclaim he received for his explorations was later offset by substantial criticism when his published account of the trip failed to acknowledge the work of two colleagues.

A British army volunteer at the age of fifteen, Denham fought in the Peninsular War (in Spain and Portugal, 1808–14) before being accepted into the Royal Military College. Considered a gifted and courageous, although somewhat belligerent, officer, Denham had been promoted to the rank of major by the time he was chosen for the expedition into the African interior. Denham joined HUGH CLAPPERTON and Walter Oudney in Tripoli in North Africa in 1821, and quarreling broke out among the three men almost instantly. Both Denham and Oudney asserted that they had been named leader of the expedition. Denham consequently set out on his own and did not rejoin the others until 1822 in Murzuch in the Sahara, where he found that both Clapperton and Oudney had become ill.

When Clapperton and Oudney recovered, the trio continued south and reached the perimeter of Bornu by the end of the year. They arrived at Lake Chad, the first Europeans known to do so, in February 1823, and also reached Kuka (now Kukawa, Nigeria), the capital of Bornu, the same month. The hostility between Denham

northwest for twenty-one months, it was crushed and sunk by a sudden swell of pressure on June 13, 1881. De Long, who in 1873 had participated in the search for the missing Arctic explorer CHARLES FRANCIS HALL, and thirty-two crew members managed to escape to three open boats, which they then attached to runners for travel over the frozen sea. After a long and difficult haul over ice softened by the sun, they reached the New Siberian Islands at the end of July. Hoping to reach a Russian settlement on the mainland before winter, the party then crossed the open waters of the Laptev Sea but were separated in a storm. One boat was lost entirely, but the others landed successfully on the Lena River delta, where they became separated. From there the party led by George Melville, its chief engineer, made it to Yakutsk on December 30, 1881. Melville immediately set out to save De Long's team but found only two survivors. De Long had died over two months earlier at the age of thirty-seven.

The expedition would have been just another Arctic failure had it not been for a strange occurrence off the southwest coast of Greenland three

and the others persisted, however, and he avoided traveling with them whenever possible in favor of conducting his own explorations. When they found that the Niger flowed to the south, Oudney and Clapperton set out to trace it while Denham elected to stay in the area of Kuka. He spent considerable time visiting small communities in the area on the theory that his efforts would improve relations with the inhabitants.

After Oudney's death in 1824, Clapperton met Denham in Kuka and they returned to England together via Tripoli in 1825. Denham's *Narrative of Travels and Discoveries in Northern and Central Africa,* taking sole credit for all major achievements, was published in 1826. He went back to Africa that year with the title Superintendent of Liberated Africans and stayed there until his death in 1828.

D'Entrecasteaux, Antoine Raymond Joseph de Bruni, Chevalier. See **Entrecasteaux, Antoine Raymond Joseph de Bruni, Chevalier d'.**

de Soto, Hernando. See **Soto, Hernando de.**

• Dezhnev (Dezhnyov), Semyon Ivanov (Ivanovich)

Russian
b 1605; Veliki Ustyug
d 1672; Moscow
Sailed through Bering Strait (first to do so); explored Siberia

History, according to one dictionary, is a narrative of events, a chronological record of past occurrences. But unless the narratives that make up history are written down, they are often pushed aside by new events and lost, sometimes forever. In 1648 Semyon Dezhnev sailed out of the Kolyma River, along the Russian coast of the Arctic Ocean, and around the northeast corner of Asia. When he reached the mouth of the Anadyr River, the illiterate cossack (Russian soldier) had solved one of the remaining mysteries of the continents by discovering that Asia and North America were not connected. But no one kept records during Dezhnev's voyage, and news of his discovery did not quickly spread back to Europe from the distant outposts of maritime Siberia. Eighty

years later, VITUS BERING would sail into the same strait—which now bears his name—a fact announced to the world immediately upon his return to St. Petersburg in 1730. While Bering is well known to history, the scope of Dezhnev's achievement was not recognized for many years, and even today questions about it linger.

Information about Dezhnev's early years is sparse and uncertain, but he probably grew up in the northern part of European Russia. He somehow gained experience as a sailor, joined the Russian state service, and was sent to Siberia to collect tribute for the Russian czar from the Siberian people. Records indicate he was transferred from Yeniseisk to Yakutsk, then helped establish the first Russian outpost on the Kolyma River. Many Russian traders were drawn to the area as well, lured by reports of rivers farther to the east, where valuable sables, walrus, and silver were said to be abundant.

Interest in sending an expedition to explore the area east of the Kolyma grew quickly. The prospect of enormous financial gain was worth the risks and hardships of exploring this rugged region. Dezhnev was selected to lead an expedition east and made responsible for locating native people along the way who had not paid tribute to the czar. Dezhnev and about ninety explorers and traders set sail along the Arctic coast from the Kolyma River on June 20, 1648. They traveled in seven koches, ships whose hulls were designed to survive the pounding of the ice-filled Arctic Ocean. Even so, four ships had been lost by the time the small fleet sailed out of the Arctic and into what is now called the Bering Strait. By navigating the strait into the sea beyond (what is now called the Bering Sea), Dezhnev's expedition had established what was previously uncertain—that Asia and North America were separate continents. Little else is known about the actual voyage; the next time Dezhnev's party was sighted was on September 20, when they battled with the inhabitants of the Chukotski Peninsula. By then they had lost yet another ship, and their two remaining ships were wrecked shortly thereafter. Explorers who braved Arctic seas on subsequent expeditions found it difficult to believe that even three out of Dezhnev's seven ships had been able to navigate the Arctic Ocean successfully. Some suggested Dezhnev may have providentially chosen a year when the ice was less hazardous.

From the site of the wrecks, it took Dezhnev and his men about ten weeks to make their way overland to the mouth of the Anadyr River. There they built new boats and continued up the river to the region of the Anual people, where Dezhnev proceeded to carry out his assigned task. His standard method of collecting tribute left nothing to chance: he would subdue the people, by force if necessary, then take an assortment of hostages and hold them until appropriate tribute was presented. Dezhnev was also in an ideal situation to advance his own financial situation and often acquired furs and walrus ivory for himself in addition to those he collected for the state.

Dezhnev spent the next twelve years exploring and collecting tribute from people in the uncharted regions of Siberia, including along the Lena and the Yana rivers. In 1654 he asked to be relieved of his command, but five more years passed before his replacement arrived. Dezhnev returned to Irkutsk in 1661 laden with furs, silver, and more than two tons of walrus tusks. He gave a report on his mission, describing his hardships, wounds, debts, and expenditures in some detail—and then requested that he be paid the salary owed him for his nineteen years of service.

Dezhnev was eventually paid, but not before he made a trip to Moscow to present his case to the Siberian Department. He then returned to Yakutsk with his nephew and served as commandant on the Olenek River for several years. After a brief stint on the Vilyui River, he took charge of escorting a yearly sable shipment to Moscow in 1670. He arrived in Moscow after a two-year trip and died there later in 1672.

Bartolomeu Dias, as depicted on a Portuguese postage stamp issued in 1945. The Granger Collection.

• Dias (de Novaes), Bartolomeu (Diaz, Bartholomew)

Portuguese
b 1450?; Portugal
d May 24, 1500; at sea, off coast of South Africa
Explored African Congo; discovered Cape of
**   Good Hope; took part in discovery of Brazil**

Bartolomeu Dias was the first mariner to round Africa's Cape of Good Hope. Though his achievement came about virtually by accident, it opened up a much-hoped-for sea route to the Indies. On that voyage he added some 1,260 miles to the known coastline of Africa. (For a map, see VASCO DA GAMA.) He also later took part in the Portuguese discovery of Brazil, an expedition that proved to be his last.

Dias was born in Portugal sometime around 1450. Although his surname was a common one, some historians believe that Dias came from a long line of navigators that included Dinis Dias, who rounded Cape Verde in 1455, and João Dias, who rounded Cape Bojador with GIL EANNES in 1437.

In 1481 Bartolomeu Dias took part in an expedition along Africa's Gold Coast under Diogo d'Azambuja. In 1486 Dias was a cavalier in the household of Portugal's King John II and superintendent of the royal warehouse. That year he received an annuity of 6,000 *reis* (the former monetary unit of Portugal) for "services to come." The following year Dias was given command of three ships and sent to find the Prassum Promontorium, as the southernmost tip of Africa was called. Beyond it, he was to search for the legendary realm of Prester John, a Christian priest-king said to rule over great riches in the East (for a more complete discussion of Prester John, see PÊRO DA COVILHÃ). John II was eager to find a sea route to the Indies because turbulence in the Mongol Empire and wars against the Turks had closed overland trade routes to the Far East, and a Christian ally in those lands would be a great advantage.

Dias left Lisbon in July or August of 1487. Using a new technique, one of the three ships on the expedition was designated as a supply vessel, allowing the explorers to stay at sea longer. The supply ship was piloted by Dias's brother, Pedro. Dias took with him several African interpreters who had lived in Europe and could help establish trade with the native peoples they hoped to encounter.

The expedition sailed south for four months, stopping along the way to trade. The explorers passed the stone pillar left by DIOGO CÃO in what is now Namibia, which marked the southernmost point the Portuguese had reached thus far. As they continued south, Dias left his own pillars, including one of which fragments can still be seen at present-day Diaz Point (26°38' South latitude). By the end of December Dias's ships passed the Orange River just to the north of present-day South Africa.

Shortly after passing what Dias named Cape Voltas for its strong winds, at the southern bank of the Orange River, the ships encountered a terrible storm that blew them on a southerly course for the next thirteen days. When the wind finally abated, Dias sailed east, expecting to encounter Africa's west coast. When no land appeared, he turned north, eventually reaching Bahia dos Vaquieros (present-day Mossel Bay), roughly 200 miles east of the Cape of Good Hope, on February 3, 1488. It was obvious by the nature of the coast that they had once again found Africa, but the explorers did not realize that they had rounded the cape.

Dias spent little time at Bahia dos Vaquieros, for the Hottentot warriors he met there were not hospitable. They greeted the expedition by throwing stones, and Dias killed one of the warriors. Upon leaving the site, Dias sailed east to an island in Algoa Bay, which he named Santa Cruz. This was probably the first soil beyond the cape ever set foot upon by a European. Against his crew's protests, Dias continued sailing for a few more days until he reached a river that he named Rio de Infante in honor of the commander of his second ship. (This probably was what is now the Great Fish River.)

Dias would have gone on to look for a way to the Indies, but his crew begged him to turn around. He did so only after they signed sworn statements attesting to his skill as a navigator and a seaman. These documents were intended to support Dias should the king want to know why he had turned back before his mission was accomplished.

It was on the return journey that Dias spotted the much-looked-for cape as he sailed west. It was long told that Dias named it Cape Tormentoso in recognition of the storms he encountered there and that John II gave the piece of land the more appealing name it has today. However, modern historians credit Dias with naming it the Cape of Good Hope. Surprisingly, it is not the southernmost point of the African continent. That distinction belongs to Cape Agulhas, which lies roughly 160 miles east-southeast of the far more famous South African cape.

The rest of the return was mostly uneventful—with one exception. The supply ship had been left at Guinea, and when Dias found it, six of its nine crewmen were dead and all the provisions aboard had been looted. Dias reached the port of Lisbon in December 1488, sixteen months and seventeen days after he had left it.

At that time a little-known Italian navigator named CHRISTOPHER COLUMBUS was trying to persuade John II to finance an expedition to the Indies, which Columbus planned to reach by sailing west. The king might have been interested had Dias not been successful, but as it was, Columbus was required to look elsewhere for support.

Maps drawn by the Greek cartographer PTOLEMY had shown the Indian Ocean as a great landlocked sea, and land from the east reaching around and touching Africa's west coast. Reports from Dias's voyage, along with the letters of Pêro da Covilhã, who had reached the Indian Ocean overland by way of Cairo, dispelled that notion. Still, tensions with Spain and domestic problems kept the Portuguese from taking advantage of Dias's discoveries for ten years. Dias was not recognized as the hero of exploration that he was, and in 1494 he was appointed to oversee the construction and provisioning of a fleet of ships for an expedition to reach India by way of the Cape of Good Hope. The leader was to be Vasco da Gama, and Dias was to accompany the expedition as far as the Cape Verde Islands.

Dias was with Gama when the expedition set sail in 1497. When Dias reached the Cape Verde Islands, the new Portuguese king, Manuel I, ordered him to set up a trading post at Elmina on the African Gold Coast (in present-day Ghana). The venture apparently went well, and soon after King Manuel sent Dias to the east coast of Africa to establish trading at Sofala, a port opposite the island of Madagascar, in what is now Mozambique.

In March 1500, Dias embarked on his final voyage of discovery. He commanded a **caravel** in the thirteen-ship fleet of PEDRO ÁLVARES CABRAL, who was to repeat Gama's voyage. The expedition headed south from the Cape Verde Islands and crossed the equator. When the fleet hit the **trade winds**, Cabral veered to the west of the standard course to Africa. As a result, he made the first recorded European landing on the coast of Brazil on April 22, 1500, at what is now Pôrto Seguro.

After the expedition left Brazil, the explorers encountered a tremendous storm on May 24, 1500, possibly in the vicinity of the Cape of Good Hope. Four ships were lost, including the one Dias commanded, the storm "casting them into the abyss of that great ocean sea, . . . human bodies as food for the fish of those waters, which bodies we can believe were the first, since they were navigating in unknown regions."

d'Iberville, Pierre Le Moyne, Sieur. See **Iberville, Pierre Le Moyne, Sieur d'**.

• Doughty, Charles Montagu

English
b August 19, 1843; Leiston, Suffolk
d January 20, 1926; Sissinghurst, Kent
Wrote about his travels in Arabia

Charles Doughty's grave and aloof demeanor enshrouded an insatiable interest in the history and daily life of Arabia. Schooled in geology and literature at Cambridge University, Doughty lived for two years (1876–78) among

Charles Montagu Doughty. Library of Congress.

the bedouin, the nomadic tribes of the Arabian desert. He intended his account of the geography, geology, and anthropology of the region and its people to be more a monument to English prose than a collection of information. While his *Travels in Arabia Deserta* attracted little attention when it was published in 1888, it has since gained recognition as a masterpiece of travel writing.

Doughty's interest in Arabia stemmed from an early trip he made to Palestine and the Holy Land. After spending a year in Damascus (in present-day Syria) learning Arabic, he donned the garb of a Syrian Christian and joined a caravan bound for Mecca, traveling with the caravan as far as Madayin Salah (now in eastern Syria), where he had heard of monuments carved in a rock face. By the time the caravan had traveled to Mecca and back again, Doughty had gathered a sizable collection of facsimile rubbings from various tombs and monuments in the region. However, instead of returning to Damascus with the caravan, Doughty sent his rubbings to the British consul there and spent the next several months living with a bedouin family in the Arabian wilderness.

Doughty shared many hardships and adventures with his Muslim hosts, moving with the family as they sought fresh pasture for their camels. Each day he sat in a tent and diligently recorded details of bedouin household activities and daily life. Doughty and the bedouins wandered south through the hills and deserts of Arabia, until he decided to join a party headed for the black lava country of the Harra Plateau, an "iron wilderness" where Doughty found "a bare and black shining beach of heated volcanic stones."

After a period with the Moahib tribe, during which he discovered an unusual herd of dark gray gazelles, Doughty joined the Bishr tribe for a journey to Hā'il (now in Saudi Arabia). In the gardens of the prince of Hā'il's palace, Doughty saw a pair of oryx (a straight-horned species of antelope) and became the first person to report the species' existence to British scientists. Though by this time weary from months of hunger and fatigue, Doughty made his way to Khaibar to study Jewish antiquities located there. He also made stops in Anaiza, Taif, and Jidda (all now in Saudi Arabia) before returning to Damascus to collect his rubbings from the British consul. Doughty then proceeded to Naples, where he wrote his classic description of the land and people of the Arabian desert.

An astrolabe made for Drake. National Maritime Museum, Greenwich.

Drake, Francis

English
b 1540–42?; Tavistock, Devonshire
d January 28, 1596; at sea in West Indies
Circumnavigated; explored California coast

Sir Francis Drake was perhaps England's best-known and probably most successful pirate. His circumnavigation of 1577–80 helped break the Spanish and Portuguese monopoly on the high seas, and he was the first Englishman to explore the Pacific. Drake later led the defeat of the Spanish Armada in 1588, which marked the beginning of an era of British sea power.

Drake was born in the early 1540s in Devonshire to a large but poor family of tenant farmers. He was the oldest of twelve boys, most of whom eventually went to sea. When he was about seven, a violent pro-Catholic uprising forced his and other Protestant families in the area to flee for their safety. The Drakes first took shelter in Plymouth Sound, on an island now known as Drake's Island, and then at Kent, where Drake's father found work as a shipboard chaplain. This incident contributed to a lifelong hatred of Catholics that drove Drake throughout his career.

Drake was barely in his teens when he signed on as an apprentice aboard a coastal vessel, and he sharpened his piloting skills on voyages to France and the Netherlands. Drake inherited the ship when his master died, but he did not stay with it long. He wanted a taste of greater adventures, and so he approached John Hawkins, England's most successful merchant seaman and a wealthy relative. Hawkins first made Drake a purser (a sort of onboard record keeper) on a ship to Vizcaya in northern Spain, then sent him on a voyage to Guinea on the west coast of Africa. By the time Drake was twenty-two, Hawkins had made him captain of the *Judith*.

Hawkins had established a trade triangle between England, western Africa, and the West Indies, transporting African slaves to the New World in trade for goods, which he would then sell in England. On one such voyage in 1566, the Spanish attacked Hawkins's fleet at San Juan de Ulúa (near present-day Veracruz, Mexico), and only Drake's *Judith* and Hawkins's ship escaped. Drake became a hero, but the voyage was a financial disaster. Drake was to remedy that in the coming years.

In 1570, with a **privateering** commission from Queen Elizabeth I, Drake cruised the Panamanian coast, returning there again in 1572 with the *Pasha* and the *Swan* to pillage and plunder the **Spanish Main**. He captured enough gold and silver to make him a wealthy man. He sacked the village of Nombre de Dios in Panama, where Spain stored Peruvian gold, then crossed the Isthmus of Panama with the aid of descendants of escaped slaves (called Maroons or Cimmarrons). From atop a tree he glimpsed the Pacific and pledged to "sail an English ship in these seas."

Drake returned to Plymouth on August 9, 1573, and bought a house there. He purchased three ships and offered his services to the queen. Afraid of upsetting the delicate balance that had recently been achieved with Spain, Elizabeth I did not send Drake back to the West Indies but asked him to ferry troops to Ireland to support the earl of Essex. Drake did so, but in the meantime he proposed a voyage to the South Seas through the Strait of Magellan— something no Englishman had ever done.

As relations with Spain worsened, Elizabeth agreed to back Drake's expedition. He was ordered to set up English trading posts throughout the Pacific. His own plan was to attack Spanish settlements along the western coast of South America.

Drake gathered a crew of 166—primarily hardened seamen who could handle weapons as well as sail a ship. They were told the expedition was headed for trade in Alexandria, Egypt. Like the only circumnavigator before him, FERDINAND MAGELLAN, Drake took five ships, all well armed. They sailed from Plymouth on December 13, 1577.

When the expedition passed the Straits of Gibraltar and continued southwest toward the Cape Verde Islands, it became obvious that Egypt was not its true destination. Drake said little to the crew, but he enticed them with promises of great riches. To prove his point, he captured a Portuguese ship and its navigator, Nuño da Silva. The crew soon began to bicker over the pirated booty.

In early April 1578 Drake reached Brazil and

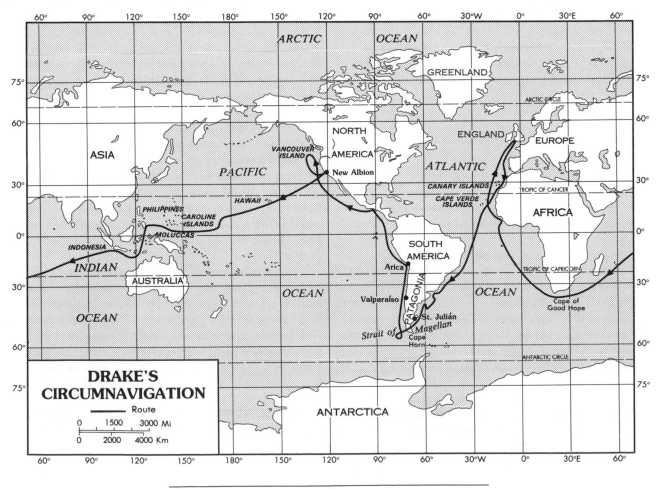

DRAKE'S CIRCUMNAVIGATION

Route

0   1500   3000 Mi

0   2000   4000 Km

sailed south along its coast. Some of the men were ill at ease, and their insecurities were fed by Thomas Doughty, a gentleman rather than a sailor, who knew Drake from the Ireland campaign. Other than Drake, Doughty and Captain John Winter were the only people aboard who knew the expedition's true purpose. Feeling self-important, Doughty often criticized Drake loudly. By the time the expedition reached Patagonia, Drake believed Doughty was trying to encourage a mutiny. At San Julián, where Magellan had executed two men in order to put down a mutiny nearly sixty years before, Drake had Doughty tried and beheaded.

When Drake reached the Strait of Magellan on August 21, 1578, he changed the name of his flagship from the *Pelican* to the *Golden Hind* in honor of one of his early patrons, whose coat of arms bore a deer. He scuttled two storeships to make it easier for the expedition to stay together; the three remaining vessels fought their way through the bitter winds and rain of the strait. Despite head winds that seemed to erase most of a day's progress, Drake reached the Pacific in only sixteen days (the same passage had taken Magellan more than a month). However, he lost one ship in a storm and was blown about a hundred miles south of Tierra del Fuego, inadvertently proving in the process that the land south of the strait was not a continent. In November, the *Elizabeth* returned to England; the *Golden Hind* was on its own.

Once in the Pacific, Drake set to raiding Spanish outposts in what are now Chile and Peru. At Valparaíso he captured the Spanish merchant ship *Capitana* and took another at Arica, up the coast. But word traveled fast that pirates were at large, and Drake soon found that most of the riches he hoped to take were no longer afloat but safely ashore under lock and key. Still, he captured some forty tons of gold and silver bullion (uncoined bars and ingots).

Drake sailed north along the coast, perhaps as far as what is now Vancouver Island, before turning south again. In June 1579 he found shelter briefly near present-day Coos Bay, Oregon. On June 17 he entered a bay (now called Drake's Bay) on the Pacific coast north of what is now San Francisco, performing much-needed repairs on the *Golden Hind*. He claimed the surrounding region for England and named it New Albion.

Drake's encounters with the area's Miwok Indians were, for the most part, friendly. When

Sir Francis Drake. The Bettmann Archive.

the Indians saw the Europeans building structures on the beach, they threatened the intruders with arrows, but Drake wisely did not overreact and was able to convince the Indians that he had come in peace. When the *Golden Hind* left Drake's Bay on July 23, 1579, Drake wrote that the Miwoks "took a sorrowful farewell of us."

For sixty-six days the voyagers saw no land. When they finally did come upon some islands, most likely in the Carolines, the native peoples were so aggressive in their attempts to steal things that Drake had to fire shots into the water to frighten them away. Eventually twenty islanders were killed.

Drake then visited Mindanao, a Muslim-controlled island in the present-day Philippines, then steered south in search of the Spice Islands (now the Moluccas). In this maze of unfamiliar islands, he relied on a local fisherman to guide him. The fisherman steered him to the island of Ternate (in present-day Indonesia), where the sultan received Drake well. Afterward, Drake spent a month in Celebes (now Sulawesi) repairing his heavily laden vessel. He could have extended his voyage by traveling to Cathay (China), but he chose not to risk his crew to a longer journey. Instead, after stops at Timor and Java (both in present-day Indonesia), Drake sailed for home in March 1580, rounding Africa's Cape of Good Hope in June with only fifty-seven crew members and three casks of water remaining. The *Golden Hind* reached England on September 26, 1580, after a journey of two years and ten months. Drake brought with him a treasure that today would be worth an estimated £10 million.

Still wary of starting trouble with Spain, Queen Elizabeth at first did not acknowledge Drake's accomplishment. However, in January 1581 she threw him a banquet aboard his ship, knighted him, and made plans to preserve the *Golden Hind.*

In 1581 Drake became mayor of Plymouth, a post he held for four years. His first wife died in 1583, and in 1585 he remarried. That year, as hostilities with Spain worsened, Drake went to sea again. His fleet attacked Vigo, Spain, then crossed the Atlantic. In the West Indies he took Cartagena (in present-day Colombia) and Santo Domingo (in the present-day Dominican Republic), then sailed north to capture St. Augustine, Florida. The voyage also took him to Fort Raleigh, in what is now North Carolina.

In 1587 Drake sailed to Lisbon, Portugal, with a fleet of thirty vessels and burned 10,000 tons of Spanish shipping in the Bay of Cádiz, "singeing the king of Spain's beard." This action likely delayed the attack of the Spanish Armada for a full year. As vice admiral under Lord Howard, Drake played an important role in the defeat of the Spanish Armada, which attacked England in 1588, and once again was proclaimed a hero.

The following year, a British attempt to restore Dom Antonio to the throne of Portugal was not successful, as Drake and the land commanders could not agree on strategy, and the mission was aborted. For some years afterward Drake remained in Plymouth.

Drake was called to sea again in 1595, once more with John Hawkins. The two were to capture Spanish settlements in the West Indies. Again, disagreements about tactics led to an unsuccessful mission that ultimately proved fatal to Drake. He contracted dysentery (an acute intestinal disorder) and died on January 28, 1596, off the coast of Panama.

At the time of his death, Drake was a figure of international importance. The very embodiment of the Elizabethan mariner, he was as beloved in his native England as he was feared throughout the rest of the world. Daring, bold, and ruthless, he inspired unwavering loyalty from his crews, despite his reputation as a strict disciplinarian. Even though he is best known for his military and privateering activities, his explorations, especially those of his important circumnavigatory voyage, were significant and wide-ranging.

SUGGESTED READING: J. H. Parry, *The Age of Reconnaissance* (The World Publishing Company, 1963); G. V. Scammell, *The World Encompassed: The First European Maritime Enterprises c. 800–1650* (University of California Press, 1981); Ralph T. Ward, *Pirates in History* (York Press, 1974); David Watkins Waters, *The Art of Navigation in England in Elizabethan and Early Stuart Times* (Yale University Press, 1958); James A. Williamson, *The Age of Drake* (Barnes & Noble, 1960); Derek Wilson, *The World Encompassed, Drake's Great Voyage 1577–1580* (Harper & Row, 1977).

• Drouillard, George

French-Canadian
b 1775?
d 1809; Three Forks, Montana
Explored Rocky Mountains

George Drouillard was one of only two civilians to accompany MERIWETHER LEWIS and WILLIAM CLARK for their entire journey up the Missouri River, west to the Pacific Ocean, and back again (1804–1806). After the expedition, Drouillard became a fur trapper and explored the basins of the Tongue, Bighorn, and Yellowstone rivers in what is now Wyoming and Montana, between 1807 and his death in 1809.

The son of a French-Canadian father and a Shawnee mother, Drouillard joined the Lewis and Clark expedition as a hunter and interpreter. He was recommended for his knowledge of Indians and their "hand talk," or sign language, and proved to be an invaluable and loyal member of the expedition.

Freshly returned from the Lewis and Clark expedition and eager for more adventure, Drouillard joined Manuel Lisa's Missouri Fur Company in 1807 and in April of that year headed up the Missouri with Lisa and a party of forty other trappers. In May one of the men deserted and Lisa ordered him brought back dead or alive. Drouillard caught up with the deserter and wounded him so severely that he died on the way to the nearest village. More than a year later, when Lisa and Drouillard returned to St. Louis, they were both tried for murder but were acquitted.

During the spring of 1808 Drouillard made two separate expeditions south from Manuel's fort at the juncture of the Yellowstone and Bighorn rivers. He was looking for two things: Indian villages where he could trade for furs, and Spanish settlements, which according to common erroneous beliefs of the day were relatively nearby. On his travels, Drouillard explored much of the river basins of the Yellowstone, Bighorn, and Tongue rivers. He drew a crude but accurate map of the regions, which he eventually presented to his former commander, William Clark.

Clark kept a map that he constantly revised as former associates checked in with him, and Drouillard's information filled in many of its holes concerning the Rocky Mountains. Unfortunately, Drouillard included two pieces of misinformation he had picked up from the Indians. Drouillard was predisposed to accept both bits of misinformation since they jibed with two basic ideas held by Lisa's mountain men. One was that all of the great western rivers had a common source, and the other was that the Spanish empire was but a twelve-day ride to the south of the Yellowstone River. Drouillard's rough map seemed to confirm both myths. His map indicated that Spanish settlements near the Colorado River and the Rio Grande were also relatively close to the upper Missouri and the Yellowstone. Clark's map consequently showed the same thing. The result was to eliminate from Clark's map much of the central Rockies. Since Clark was then governor of the whole Louisiana Territory, his map had a quasi-official status, meaning Drouillard's misinformation had a direct effect on the United States government's view of the West. It also had the inadvertent result of intensifying competition between Spanish and Americans for the Rocky Mountain region.

In fact, Drouillard narrowly missed discovering the true relationship of the Spanish settlements to the Rockies. For some unknown reason, he failed to make his way over the relatively low Owl Creek Mountains and into the Wind River valley of Wyoming. Had he done so, he would have probably discovered the South Pass. Crossing the pass would have led him to the Green River, an area frequented by Spanish traders from Taos. They could have given him a more accurate sense of the relatively great distance to Taos and other Spanish settlements in New Mexico. However, Drouillard did not find the South Pass, and his map remained seriously flawed.

Unfortunately, the mountain man was to have no further chance to explore the West. In the spring of 1809 he was trapping in the area of Three Forks when he was murdered and horribly mutilated by Blackfoot Indians.

Though Drouillard left no writings of his own, the surviving information about him suggests a man completely at home in the wild who was a steadfast supporter of his employers. He made invaluable early contributions to the Lewis and Clark expedition and then went on his own to explore and describe previously unknown regions of the American West.

Drygalski, Erich Dagobert von

German
b February 9, 1865; Kaliningrad, Soviet Union (formerly Königsberg, East Prussia)
d January 10, 1949; Munich
Explored Greenland and Antarctica

Dr. Erich Dagobert von Drygalski led two minor but not unimportant expeditions, the first, in 1891, to Qarajaks Isfjord, south of Umanak in West Greenland and the other, in 1901, to Antarctica on a three-year German expedition. Though a line of ice cliffs between 89° and 94° East longitude was named after King William II of Germany, the emperor was disappointed that nothing more spectacular was discovered. Antarctic work was thereafter discontinued by the Germans, while the expedition's ship, the *Gauss*, which had been specially built for polar work, was sold to Canada.

Drygalski published a general account of the Antarctic expedition in 1904. Departing from Kerguelen Island in the Indian Ocean on January 31, 1902, the *Gauss* headed south along the 90° East meridian. Soon after land was sighted, the ship was frozen in for the winter at 66°13′ South latitude, just north of the Antarctic Circle. **Sledge** parties reached an extinct volcano, which was named Gaussberg. This is part of the Gaussberg Ridge, extending out below sea level into the Indian Ocean past 80° South latitude. In February 1903 the ship was freed from the ice by laying ash on its surface, which collected the sun's radiation, helping to open a path to the open water.

From the point of view of scientific achievement, Drygalski's work was of the first rank. His publications from the early Greenland expedition won him a professorship in geography and geophysics at the University of Berlin in 1899. In 1906, after the *Gauss* expedition, he was appointed professor of geography in Munich. His own interests within the field of physical geography centered on the movement and effects of glaciers. His field work in this area took him to Spitsbergen (now part of Svalbard) in 1910 with Count Zeppelin, who was investigating possibilities for **dirigible** flights in the area. The team of scientists on the *Gauss* produced important results in many fields. Dr. Friedrich Bidlingmaier of Potsdam directed the work in meteorology and magnetism, and there were several other scientists in such fields as oceanography working full time for three years. It eventually took Drygalski a quarter of a century and twenty volumes to publish the results from his work in Antarctica.

· Du Chaillu, Paul Belloni

French-American
b July 31, 1835; Paris
d April 30, 1903; St. Petersburg, Russia
Explored Central Africa

An explorer of equatorial Africa, Paul Belloni Du Chaillu traced the courses of the Gabon and Ogowe rivers and traveled extensively in the interior forest areas of West Central Africa. He located Pygmies, native Africans of small stature, in the equatorial forest, and became the first modern European to see a live gorilla. The latter discovery made him famous, but his story was widely challenged by skeptics until a subsequent trip helped strengthen his credibility.

As a youth, Du Chaillu spent many years in coastal Gabon, West Africa, where his father was a trader of rubber and dyes. He worked at the trading post there for several years, became fascinated by the mysterious African interior, and decided to go to the United States to seek funding for an expedition. Within three years of his arrival in 1852, Du Chaillu had become an American citizen, studied natural

history as preparation for exploration, and won financing from the Philadelphia Academy of Natural Sciences.

Du Chaillu's four-year expedition took him from the coast of Gabon to the interior in a series of journeys on the Gabon, Ogowe, and Muni rivers. He collected a variety of plants and reported shooting thousands of animals, which he took back as specimens to America. His most dramatic discovery occurred in the interior highlands, where he encountered and shot a large male gorilla he was later to describe as "some hellish dream creature—a being of that hideous order, half-man, half-beast."

While missionaries had previously found skulls of gorillas in the area, Du Chaillu was the first European of his era to see the animal alive. He was celebrated on his return to the United States in 1859, and the publication of his colorful *Exploration and Adventures in Equatorial Africa* in 1861 added to his fame. Critics, however, challenged his claim, either citing his lack of scientific accuracy or bluntly calling him a liar.

Armed with additional training in science and photography, Du Chaillu returned to the equatorial forest in 1863. He encountered pygmies on this two-year trip and obtained both photographs and actual specimens of the gorilla, although the live animal he attempted to take back to England died en route. He published an account of this expedition, more scientifically oriented and less controversial than his previous book, in 1861 and then turned to writing children's books about Africa, for which he became well known and beloved as "Uncle Paul." In addition, he published two books about Scandinavia, which he visited several times, and spent two years in Russia before his death there in 1903.

· Dulhut (Du Lhut; Duluth),
Daniel Greysolon, Sieur

French
b 1639?; St.-Germain-Laval
d February 25, 1710; Montréal, Québec
Explored territory west of Lake Superior;
   sought Western Sea

Although Daniel Greysolon, Sieur Dulhut, is sometimes referred to as Duluth, he himself spelled his name Dulhut or Du Lhut. Dulhut's primary interest was in the land west of Lake Superior, and he spent much time there exploring and forging treaties among the Sioux, Chippewa, and other tribes of the region.

Born in France, Dulhut immigrated to present-day Canada, settling in Montréal in 1674. There he sought the friendship of Indians in order to learn more about the western lands. On September 1, 1678, he left Montréal with seven other Frenchmen and three Indian slaves to explore the upper Great Lakes region. After wintering at Sault Ste. Marie (a French fur-trading post located between Lake Huron and Lake Superior), the party pressed on past the western tip of Lake Superior. On July 2, 1679, he reached the great village of the Sioux on Lake Mille Lacs (southwest of the tip of Lake Superior). There he set up the arms of the French king. By September of the same year, he had concluded a peace treaty among the Sioux, the Chippewa, and other warring tribes.

Shortly after his arrival, Dulhut had sent three of his men west with a Sioux war party. They returned in the summer of 1680, bringing salt and the information that Indians had told them they were only a twenty-day journey from a sea whose water was not good to drink. This was probably Lake Winnipeg, but Dulhut understood it to be the Western Sea, a fabled inland sea believed to have its outlet in the Pacific Ocean.

In June 1680 Dulhut set out in search of this much-sought goal. However, on reaching the Mississippi River he learned of the capture of Father LOUIS HENNEPIN and his companions by a band of Sioux. He hurried to the priest's rescue and escorted the party back to Lake Michigan, displeased at the fragility of his treaty with the Sioux and consequently reluctant to push further west.

In spring of 1681 Dulhut returned to France to defend himself against charges that he had organized a group of unlicensed traders, as expressly forbidden by an edict of 1676. After clearing himself of these charges, he returned to the western Great Lakes region in 1683 with a three-year commission from the governor of **New France**. His aims were to control the Indians and to woo the tribes north of Lake Superior away from the English fur traders on Hudson Bay. Later, he supported military efforts to subdue the Iroquois. After his last campaign, Dulhut retired to Montréal, where he lived his last fifteen years quietly.

Respected by the French and Indians alike, Dulhut was regarded by his contemporaries as an honest man and a brave and loyal patriot. Although his tenure as an explorer was relatively brief, he was an important peacemaker between the French and the Indian tribes west of Lake Superior and in this sense opened up the west for future French explorers. The city of Duluth, Minnesota, named for him, is located at the site of one of his Indian councils.

Duluth, Daniel Greysolon, Sieur. See **Dulhut, Daniel Greysolon, Sieur.**

Dumont d'Urville, Jules-Sébastien-César

French
b May 23, 1790; Condé-sur-Noireau, Calvados
d May 8, 1842; near Meudon
Explored South Pacific Islands and Antarctica by sea

A French naval officer with a wide range of interests, Rear Admiral Jules-Sébastien-César Dumont d'Urville was mainly concerned with studying the geography, oceanography, and ethnology of the Pacific. It was only a short diversion into Antarctic exploration in 1840 that led to his discovery of Adélie Coast, which was later seen to be a part of the continental coast. He was searching for the South Magnetic Pole and was deeply disappointed to find land in his way. But his landing on an adjoining islet became the basis for France's formal claim to Antarctic territory in 1924, and its base of operations on that continent was consequently named in his honor.

Born the year after the French Revolution, Dumont d'Urville suffered the early loss of his father (who had been a judge before the revolution) and was raised by his mother and her brother, the Abbé de Croisilles. After failing the entrance examination for the École Polytechnique, he went off to sea in 1807 aboard the *Aquilon*. Later transferring to the naval base at Toulon, Dumont d'Urville studied a number of subjects, including entomology and five languages, though it is not clear how thoroughly he mastered any of them. Later he was often criticized for flaws in his scientific method, but certainly he was capable of making the sorts

Jules-Sébastien-César Dumont D'Urville. Library of Congress.

of observations and classifications required by the bulk of his fieldwork.

On an 1817 tour of duty in the Mediterranean, thanks to his familiarity with classical Greek culture, he noticed that a statue recently dug up on the Greek island of Melos was the Venus de Milo (one of the greatest works of classical art, now in the Louvre). His report on the matter led to its preservation and procurement by the French. For this he was made a member of the Legion of Honor and promoted. Then in 1822, while on the Duperrey expedition to the Pacific and around the world, his diligent effort in collecting plants led to his first published work on the flora of the Pacific islands.

On his return to France in 1825, he was promptly given command of Duperrey's former ship and promoted again. His commission was to study the **hydrography** of the Pacific **archi-pelago**, to make ethnological studies of its inhabitants, to acquire the usual collections of animate and inanimate natural specimens, and to inquire as to the fate of the expedition of French explorer JEAN FRANÇOIS DE GALAUP, COMTE DE LA PÉROUSE, which had vanished in the South Pacific some forty years earlier. Accordingly, he renamed his ship the *Astrolabe*, after one of La Pérouse's ships, and set sail on April 25, 1826. During this three-year voyage, several small islands were discovered, as well as what became known as Astrolabe Reef, off the island of Vatulele in Fiji. More importantly, Dumont d'Urville's thorough combing of the entire western Pacific led to a new general understanding of the distribution of land in the region, which appeared to be organized into three main island groups: Polynesia, Micronesia, and Melanesia. He also charted many previously unknown islands, collected thousands of valuable specimens, and established that La Pérouse's ships had run aground off Vanikoro in the Santa Cruz Islands.

Unfortunately, a third of his crew died of **scurvy** on this voyage—a poor record in the nineteenth century. In addition, some of his observations were questioned by the scientific community. As a result, Dumont d'Urville did not get a desired promotion until August 1829, and no new command followed. This gave him the leisure to compile his data and write his great *Voyage des découvertes autour du monde* (1832–34), which reestablished his reputation. After eight years without a command, during which time he became a founder of the Paris Geographical Society, he received a commission to return to the Pacific with the *Astrolabe* and the *Zélée*.

While the mission was being planned, King Louis Philippe himself suggested that an effort be made to penetrate the Weddell Sea in the Antarctic. After reading about the region, Dumont d'Urville became interested in the idea of locating the South Magnetic Pole. The three-year journey thus proceeded in three stages. First was the attack on the Weddell Sea via the Strait of Magellan, followed by a period of work in the Pacific, and then a quest for the South Magnetic Pole on the way back to France.

Leaving France on September 7, 1837, the ships arrived at the Antarctic ice in January 1838. They made little progress into the Weddell Sea but were able to survey land on its northern outskirts that had only been vaguely reported by commercial vessels (the tip of the Antarctic Peninsula and Joinville Island). After a year in the South Pacific, during which disease once again ravaged the crew, the *Astrolabe* headed for the pole, leaving the sick behind on the *Zélée* at Hobart, Tasmania. On January 19, 1840, the ice cliffs of Adélie Coast were sighted and a landing was made on an islet. The crew knew they were near the pole because the compass was spinning wildly, but a massive ice shelf, unbroken in either direction, blocked the way farther south. Upon returning to France, Dumont d'Urville was promoted to rear admiral, but before he could publish the results of the expedition, he and his wife and child were killed in a train accident.

d'Urville, Jules-Sébastien-César Dumont.
See **Dumont d'Urville, Jules-Sébastien-César.**

• **Duveyrier, Henri**

French
b February 28, 1840; Paris
d April 25, 1892; Sèvres
Explored Sahara Desert

Henri Duveyrier explored extensively in Africa's Sahara Desert and collected valuable information about its geography, archaeology, and culture. After living among and studying the Tuareg, the native people of the region, he became known as the leading authority on their language and customs. He was honored by the Paris Geographical Society while still in his teens and was an important official of that organization for most of his adult life. The information he gathered aided France's efforts to expand its colonial holdings in Africa.

Duveyrier's career began at age seventeen when he traveled to Algeria. He then studied Arabic and, under the guidance of his mentor, German explorer HEINRICH BARTH, made preparations for his first expedition. This journey through the northern Sahara, beginning in 1859, earned him the geographical society's gold medal at the age of nineteen. He continued traveling through the region for another two years, exploring the area south of the Atlas Mountains between Morocco and Tunisia and making detailed notes about its geography and geology as well as the culture and economy of its native tribes.

Nearly three years of travel in the Sahara seriously damaged Duveyrier's health, and he returned to France in 1861 to recuperate. In 1864, he published *Exploration of the Sahara: The Tuareg of the North*, a thorough and scientific account of his experiences that inspired a surge of enthusiasm for Saharan exploration. Convinced that the Sahara was ripe for development, Duveyrier continued to promote the colonization movement in France.

He later made several relatively brief trips to the Sahara, again studying the area south of the Atlas Mountains as well as exploring the salt lakes of Tunisia and Algeria. These journeys were chronicled in two later publications, one in 1881 on Tunisia and the other in 1884 about the Sanūsī Muslims. His published works served as references for subsequent travelers in North Africa. Though renowned as one of the foremost explorers of the Sahara, Duveyrier took his own life at age fifty-two.

• **Eannes (Eans), Gil**

Portuguese
b ?
d 1435?
Explored West African coast, passing Cape Bojador by sea

The commander of a landmark voyage in Portuguese exploration, Gil Eannes was the first to sail past Africa's Cape Bojador, thus carrying out Prince Henry the Navigator's order to "double the Cape." Eager to learn about as much of the West African coastline as possible, the prince had sent a number of previous navigators on this mission, all of whom had failed to pass the cape's treacherous reefs and shoals. Eannes, in rounding Cape Bojador, dispelled the widespread fears and myths of his day about what lay beyond it.

A squire raised in the prince's household, Eannes was given command of a ship in 1433 and told to sail around the cape and as far as possible down the west coast of Africa. Under pressure from his crew, however, he turned back at the Canary Islands and reported his failure to the court. Exasperated, Prince Henry told Eannes not to return until he had completed

ELCANO, JUAN SEBASTIÁN DE

his assignment. Setting out again in 1434, Eannes managed to negotiate the seas off the rough headland. Beyond the cape, which lies in present-day Western Sahara, the waters of the Atlantic were surprisingly calm, bearing no resemblance to the treacherous "Sea of Darkness" rumored for centuries to lie south of Bojador. He returned to the prince with the only vegetation he could find in the area as evidence, an herb called "roses of Santa Maria."

Delighted that Eannes had broken this important physical and psychological barrier, Henry assigned him to command one or two **caravels** and push farther down the coastline. Eannes departed in 1435, accompanied by Alfonso Goncalves Baldaya, and sailed approximately 200 miles past Cape Bojador before encountering evidence of human inhabitation. What became of Eannes from this point on is lost to history.

· Elcano, Juan Sebastián de
(Cano, Juan Sebastián del)

Spanish
b 1476?; Guetaria, Vizcaya
d August 4, 1526; at sea in the Pacific
Served as pilot on Magellan's circumnavigation

Juan Sebastián de Elcano, a Basque seaman, was one of only a handful who survived the circumnavigation begun by FERDINAND MAGELLAN. Elcano piloted the *Victoria* back to Spain in 1522, bringing with him spices, silks, and the revolutionary notion that travelers who sailed continuously west around the world lost a day by the time they arrived home. (For a map of the voyage, see MAGELLAN.)

Ironically, Elcano was not one of Magellan's strongest supporters. During the Easter Mutiny of 1520 at San Julián, on the South American coast of Patagonia, he sided with the Spanish captains who wanted to take three of the expedition's five vessels and return to Spain. For much of the rest of the trip he played an undistinguished role.

After the death in the Philippines of Magellan and then those of his immediate successors, DUARTE BARBOSA and Juan Serrano, command of the expedition changed from hand to hand. Elcano was made commander of the *Victoria* when the expedition reached Borneo. The ship was barely seaworthy.

With the advice of a captured Mindanaoan mariner, Elcano reached the Moluccas in November 1521. There he stocked the ship with cloves, gold, silks, sandalwood, cinnamon, wax, and provisions and headed homeward in February 1522. In an effort to avoid the hostile Portuguese, who controlled the ports in Indonesia, he sailed the tattered ship 10,000 miles without touching land, passing Africa's Cape of Good Hope on May 6. During the voyage a storm dismasted the ship, much of the food rotted, and **scurvy** struck the crew.

By their reckoning, the small remaining crew reached the Portuguese-controlled Cape Verde Islands on July 9, 1522, and put in at Santiago to get fresh water. There they realized they had lost a day, for it was July 10 in Santiago. (They had actually lost it gradually as they sailed west through each of the twenty-four now formally defined time zones of the world.) The Portuguese believed Elcano's fabricated story that they had been in America until one sailor mistakenly offered payment in spices. The Portuguese correctly surmised that the spices must have come from eastern seas, their area of monopoly. Elcano barely got the *Victoria* out of port before the Portuguese could attack.

Elcano reached Sanlúcar, Spain, on September 6, 1522, with seventeen other survivors, having completed the first successful circumnavigation of the world. He was in Seville two days later and was then summoned to Valladolid, where he received a life pension of 500 ducats and a patent of nobility. His coat of arms displayed cloves, cinnamon, and nutmeg, with a globe for a crest, and the motto *Primus circumdedesti me.* Elcano died four years later on an expedition to claim the Moluccas for Charles V.

· Ellsworth, Lincoln

American
b May 12, 1880; Chicago
d May 26, 1951; New York City
Flew airplanes over both polar regions (first to do so)

The son of a wealthy industrialist, Lincoln Ellsworth spent the first two-thirds of his life drifting aimlessly from adventure to adventure, following a succession of outdoor jobs, many of

Lincoln Ellsworth. UPI/Bettmann.

which were of the blue-collar variety. After flunking out of Yale University and dropping out of Columbia, he tried but failed to take a role in his father's coal-mining business. He was always at work, always doing something strenuous, but as late as 1925, when he was forty-five years old, he wrote that his father still considered him "his chief problem, the one sorrow and anxiety of his declining years."

It was then that he met ROALD AMUNDSEN, the discoverer of the South Pole (1911), who had recently fallen on financial hard times. Ellsworth convinced Amundsen that they could both go to his father to beg for money for an expedition to the North Pole. They succeeded in getting money for two Dornier-Wal seaplanes, an N-24 and an N-25, which they intended to land at the pole. Thus was born the daring Amundsen-Ellsworth Arctic flight that thrilled the world. And since the elder Ellsworth died while his son was flying north, so also began the unrestrained exploring career of Lincoln Ellsworth.

The two planes departed from Kings Bay, Spitsbergen, on May 21, 1925. After seven hours of flight, the N-25 lost an engine at 87°44' North latitude, forcing both planes to land in leads

(sections of open water) in the pack ice. This was treacherous enough, but to take off was nearly impossible. It took twenty-four days of hard work to clear a runway on the ice long enough for the N-24 (overburdened with both crews aboard) to take off. When the plane landed in Spitsbergen on June 15, Ellsworth was suddenly an Arctic hero. He and the rest of the crew had been within 156 miles of the North Pole.

In 1926 Amundsen, Ellsworth, and UMBERTO NOBILE crossed the Arctic Ocean aboard the **dirigible** *Norge*, using Ellsworth's funds. After Amundsen's death, Ellsworth joined Sir GEORGE HUBERT WILKINS's unsuccessful 1931 attempt to take the submarine *Nautilus* to the North Pole, once again providing financing. He then turned his attention to Antarctica. After two failed attempts, he succeeded in 1935 in flying 2,300 miles across the continent in the *Polar Star* with pilot Herbert Hollick-Kenyon. Ellsworth thus became the first aerial explorer to fly across both polar regions.

All told, Ellsworth claimed nearly 400,000 square miles of uncharted Antarctic territory for the United States. His accomplishments as an explorer were significant, due as much to his courage and energy as to the fortune with which he financed his expeditions.

Emin Pasha. See **Schnitzer, Eduard.**

- Entrecasteaux, Antoine Raymond Joseph de Bruni, Chevalier d'

French
b 1739; Chateau d'Entrecasteaux, Aix-en-Provence
d July 21, 1793; at sea near Java
Charted coasts of southern Australia and Tasmania

A career officer in the French navy, Antoine Raymond Joseph de Bruni, Chevalier d'Entrecasteaux, made his greatest contribution to the map of the South Pacific as it is known today on his final voyage—an unsuccessful search for the missing explorer JEAN LA PÉROUSE. Insufficient water supplies and the outbreak of the French Revolution made for a tense voyage, but

Entrecasteaux charted significant sections of coastline and his scientists identified numerous new species of plants and animals.

Entrecasteaux was born in 1739 on his family estate in southeastern France, northeast of Marseilles. His father presided over the provincial parliament. In 1755, at the age of fifteen, young Entrecasteaux joined the French marine guard under the bailiff of Suffren, a family relative, and soon distinguished himself at the Battle of Minorca off the Spanish coast. He worked his way up the ranks and in 1770 was promoted to lieutenant. In 1778 he distinguished himself again as a navigator and a tactician when he successfully guided a thirty-two-gun **frigate** from Marseilles, on the French coast, to the eastern Mediterranean, getting by two pirate ships that had outgunned him.

The following year Entrecasteaux was made assistant director of ports and arsenals; he later became director. After a nephew committed murder, Entrecasteaux asked to leave the service. Instead he was named commander of the French India Naval Station in 1785. As such, he sailed to China and other ports in the western Pacific. His next post, as governor of Île de France (present-day Mauritius) and Bourbon, found him in the Indian Ocean east of Madagascar, where he spent two years (1787–89).

In 1791 the French Assembly instructed Entrecasteaux to search for the explorer La Pérouse, who had not been heard from since February 1788, when his ships had left Botany Bay, New Holland (present-day Australia). Entrecasteaux was also to make detailed surveys of the coasts of New Holland and Van Diemen's Land (now Tasmania). His voyage was to take no more than three years.

Entrecasteaux was made rear admiral and given two 500-ton store ships, the *Recherche* and the *Espérance*, neither of which handled well. To add to the normal shipboard discomfort, France was on the eve of a revolution; consequently, tensions often ran high between the officers, most of whom were of noble birth, and the common sailors, who could not expect to achieve high rank no matter how well they performed.

The two ships left Brest on September 29, 1791, and sailed along the African coast. Trouble started almost immediately. The navigation took longer than expected, water supplies ran short, and maggots infested the food. When he reached Cape Town, South Africa, in January 1792, Entrecasteaux heard rumors that natives in the Admiralty Islands were seen wearing French uniforms. He decided to investigate.

By April 21, 1792, the ships had reached what is now Tasmania, where Entrecasteaux spent more than a month charting the coastline. He named the previously uncharted Recherche Bay, Bruny and D'Entrecasteaux islands, D'Entrecasteaux Channel, and the Huon River. Exploration on land also proved fruitful, and the ships' scientists identified three new species of eucalyptus tree and a kangaroo named *La Billardière thylogale* after the expedition naturalist.

Leaving Van Diemen's Land, the ships sailed along the western, reef-lined coast of New Caledonia and docked for a week at New Ireland. They reached the Admiralty Islands in late July 1792 but saw no French uniforms other than their own. When **scurvy** broke out among the crew, Entrecasteaux's party spent a month on Amboina, a Dutch East India Company settlement in the Moluccas. In October the expedition sailed again and by November reached a group of islands on the west coast of New Holland, christened the Recherche Archipelago. In mid-December Entrecasteaux and crew reached Nuyts Land, on New Holland's southwestern coast, which they explored carefully, and on January 21, 1793, they returned to Tasmania, anchoring in Recherche Bay.

The search for La Pérouse took them next to New Zealand—where they got food but no information—then on to New Caledonia, the Santa Cruz Islands, and the Solomons. By early July the crew was exhausted and Entrecasteaux himself suffered from scurvy and dysentery (an acute intestinal disorder). He called off the search and headed for Java (in present-day Indonesia) on July 9. Less than two weeks later, on July 21, 1793, he succumbed to his illnesses and was buried at sea off the coast of New Guinea. He died not knowing that he had been promoted to vice admiral.

The scurvy outbreak worsened and took sixty more sailors; dysentery killed six more. Not knowing that France and Holland were at war, the sailors headed for the Dutch port of Surabaja, on Java, which they reached October 9. The Dutch received them reluctantly. When the French received word of the full-scale revolution at home, many of the nobles on board were reluctant to return to France for fear of losing their lives. In the meantime, the Dutch kept the common-born French sailors prisoners.

Eventually two accounts of the expedition were published. The expedition's republican naturalist J. J. Houtou de La Billardière published his *Account of the Voyage in Search of La Pérouse* in 1799. Nine years later, Chevalier de Rossel, whose maps had been seized and copied by the British, published the official account.

· Eratosthenes

Greek
b 276 B.C.; Cyrene, Libya
d 192 B.C.; Alexandria, Egypt
Calculated circumference of earth (first to do so); developed system of grid lines for maps

The ancient Greeks are well known for their curiosity about both the physical world and the world of ideas. Eratosthenes, a mathematician and geographer, made important contributions to the knowledge of both these worlds. His intellectual achievements were substantial. In 255 B.C., he became director of the famous academy and library at Alexandria, Egypt. In that capacity, he developed a new calendar, composed poetry, and wrote essays on ethics and the theater. Eratosthenes' most lasting accomplishments, however, resulted from his use of mathematics and astronomy to describe the physical world. He devised a method for measuring the circumference of the earth, developed a system of parallel grid lines for use on a world map, and established that global circumnavigation might be possible. In light of his contributions to the exploration of the ancient world, Eratosthenes has been called the greatest of the ancient geographers.

Eratosthenes is best known for his calculation of the earth's circumference. Before his time, people had often wondered how large or small the earth was, but no one had discovered a method for measuring the distance around it. Eratosthenes' breakthrough involved observations at a deep well at Syene (now Aswan), Egypt, located about 500 miles southeast of Alexandria. He noted that the water at the bottom of the well reflected the sun at noon on the day of the summer solstice. This meant, Eratosthenes rightly observed, that the sun was precisely at its zenith. However, the same was not true at Alexandria; there, at noon on the

summer solstice, the sun's rays fell at an angle of slightly more than 7° from the absolute vertical.

Eratosthenes drew two conclusions from this difference in the angle of the sun's rays. First, if the sun's rays are almost parallel when they reach the earth at distant points, then, he inferred, the distance from the sun to the earth must be very great. Second, using the angle of 7.2° and an approximate measure of the distance between Syene and Alexandria, Eratosthenes calculated the circumference of the earth. His first conclusion was correct, and his second, which relied on travelers' estimates of the distance between the two cities, was remarkably accurate. He reported his calculations in stadia, a Greek unit of length. Historians disagree on how many feet equals one stadium. Thus Eratosthenes may have thought the circumference of the earth was as little as 24,985 miles or as much as 29,085 miles—surprisingly close to the actual distance of about 24,860 miles measured by modern astronomers thousands of years later.

Eratosthenes also developed a system of parallel grid lines that made it much easier to locate important places on a map of the world. His primary grid line running east-west was parallel to the modern equator, running through the island of Rhodes and the center of the Mediterranean. This line divided the inhabited world of his time into what he called a Northern Division and a Southern Division. At right angles to this line, he drew his primary grid line running north-south through the city of Alexandria. He added other parallel lines to the grid at irregular intervals, with each line running through a well-known location in the ancient world.

By the time Eratosthenes was finished with his grid, he had divided the sphere of the earth into sixty rectangular areas. Although they were not all the same shape or size, this network of parallel lines was a major advance in mapmaking. Eratosthenes himself knew that later explorers and cartographers would need to improve his grid system by adding more reference points and parallel lines, but he had established a basic scheme that geographers and cartographers would continue to refine in the future and use to this day.

Eratosthenes made one other significant contribution to the exploration of the earth. Before his time, people of the ancient world had often wondered what lay beyond the vast waters of the Atlantic Ocean to the west and the Indian Ocean to the east. Eratosthenes used his keen powers of observation and deduction to suggest a possible answer. He timed and measured the rise and fall of the tides in both the Atlantic and the Indian oceans. To his surprise, he found that the tidal pattern was similar in both places. This being so, he reasoned, they must both be part of one huge body of water, and a boat should be able to sail west into the Atlantic and, after circumnavigating the earth, return via the Indian Ocean. Once again, Eratosthenes was fundamentally correct, although his theory would wait many centuries before FERDINAND MAGELLAN and a group of courageous sailors would prove its truth in 1521.

· Erik (Eric) the Red

Norse
b 950?; Jaeren, near Stavanger
d 1001?; near modern Julianehåb, Greenland
Established first European settlement on Greenland

At a time when the Norse were expanding in all directions from their bases in Scandinavia (c. A.D. 760–1080), wreaking havoc in Europe as they skillfully exploited their mastery of the seas, Erik the Red, a Norse immigrant to Iceland, led a flotilla of peaceful settlers to the southern shores of Greenland. Since the island's native **Inuit** departed long before (probably because the climate had become too warm), this was one Norse migration that disturbed no one. A man capable of great violence (he was exiled from Iceland for murdering too many people), Erik's peaceful career as patriarch of the small community near present-day Julianehåb just west of Cape Farewell shows that the Norse were not just interested in blood and booty, but also in habitable land for peaceful settlement.

While Erik the Red was no doubt a competent sailor, able to follow a fixed latitude, his "discovery" of Greenland was not as remarkable as his role in promoting the settlement of the grassy shores of its southwestern fjords. Not only had previous sailors reported on Greenland (Gunnbjorn Ulf-Krakuson sighted it around A.D. 900), but the land itself is at times visible from the mountaintops near where Erik lived in Iceland. This westward move is important in the history of exploration because Greenland provided the platform from which Erik's son, LEIF ERIKSON, would reach the shores of North America (though it is now thought that BJARNI HERJOLFSSON preceded him).

In order to continue its Norse way of life, the colony traded extensively with Europe over the five centuries of its existence. This brought Europe into frequent contact with a world far beyond its early medieval boundaries. (It is known, for instance, that the duke of Burgundy paid a ransom in 1396 with "twelve Greenland falcons.") In addition, soon after the colony was established, it became converted to Christianity, tying it to the Mediterranean world of the popes as well as leading to the establishment of sixteen churches, a cathedral, and two monasteries in Greenland.

Erik was remembered and glorified for his role as founding father in two oral folk narratives that were written down in the thirteenth century: *The Saga of the Greenlanders* and *Erik the Red's Saga*. Various other sources corroborate the story; there is little doubt about his major activities. His own life exemplifies the kinds of pressures that resulted in the Norse migrations. As a boy, he was forced to leave Norway with his father, Thorvald, when a neighborhood quarrel ended in murder. After sailing west to Iceland, Erik and his father found that little good land was left for settlement, and they could do no better than to set up a farm on the rocky coast of northwesternmost Iceland. When Thorvald died, Erik managed to find better pastures to the south, but once again he began feuding violently with neighbors. After he killed two of them, Erik was banished from the district, then settled in the islands of Breidha Fjord. There he entered into a blood feud with his neighbors, killing at least two people.

The Icelanders finally had enough of Erik, and in A.D. 982 he was banished overseas for three years. With his family, followers, and slaves, he then determined to explore the land sighted by Gunnbjorn eighty years earlier. After a journey of some 450 miles along the sixty-fifth parallel, he came upon the inhospitable southeastern shore of Greenland. He proceeded south, rounded the cape, and discovered the "green land" he would explore for the next three years.

Returning to Iceland in 986 with a boatload of skins and sea ivory as proof of the land's riches, Erik soon convinced the crowded and hungry Icelanders to fit up a colonizing party of twenty-five ships to return. Because of shipwreck and forced returns, only fourteen of the ships made it to the final destination, but these contained enough people and supplies to set up a viable community, probably numbering around 400. Not much is known of Erik's role in formulating the constitution of the new community, but it is likely that this former outlaw became the "lawspeaker," playing a crucial role in setting up a republic along Icelandic lines. This Eastern Settlement community, as well as a smaller Western Settlement to its north near modern Godthaab, remained viable and independent until it granted sovereignty to the king of Norway in 1261. After that it began a steady decline, suffering from a change for the worse in climate (called the Little Ice Age) at the same time that it lost control over its destiny as a trading center. At the time of their greatest prosperity, the two settlements probably had about 2,000 people. By the time the region was visited by the British in the sixteenth century (see MARTIN FROBISHER and JOHN DAVIS), the cold had brought back the Inuit, but there was no trace of the descendants of Erik the Red.

- Erikson (Ericsson; Ericson; Eiriksson), Leif (Leifr)

Norse
b 980?
d 1020?; Greenland?
Explored coast of North America

From his father's settlement in Greenland, Leif Erikson set out on a journey of exploration that took him to three different places along the coast of North America. The last of these he named Vinland after the abundance of wild grapes he found there. Because of the scantiness of the existing evidence, opinions differ as to the locations of his landings. Wherever his landfall was, Erikson generally gets credit for being the first European to set foot in America.

Much of the confusion about Erikson's landfalls results from the fact that his travels were known through Norse Icelandic oral tradition before being written down. Erikson's adven-

tures were first recorded in writing in two sagas with significant differences. Recent scholarship suggests that *The Saga of the Greenlanders* may be the more reliable source because it was written about A.D. 1200 and thus predates *The Saga of Eric the Red* by fifty to seventy-five years.

The older saga describes Erikson as a "big, strapping fellow, handsome to look at, thoughtful and temperate in all things." He was raised in Greenland, where his father, ERIK THE RED, settled after being banned from the Norwegian colony of Iceland. In 999 or 1000, when Erikson was about twenty years old, he set out for Norway. Declining to sail by way of Iceland, he set his course directly for Norway, thus becoming the first person known to history to make a nonstop Atlantic crossing.

Back in Greenland, Erikson heard much talk of BJARNI HERJOLFSSON, who in 985 or 986 had mistakenly sailed past Greenland and reported sighting some new lands three distinct times. Being a businessman rather than an adventurer, Herjolfsson had not bothered to land, but he had reported that two of the lands he had sighted were wooded. This was exciting news to the Norse of Greenland, for no tree larger than a willow bush was to be found on their island, and they had only turf and driftwood to use for shelters and fires. The news that timber might be harvested relatively nearby was welcome.

In the summer of 1001 (possibly later), Erik-

An artist's rendering of Leif Erikson's vessel. The Bettmann Archive.

son bought Herjolfsson's boat and gathered a crew of thirty-five, including a German named Tyrker. Leif implored his father to come as well, and Erik finally agreed. However, when he was thrown by a horse on the day of departure, Erik claimed it was a sign he should not go, and the ship sailed without him.

Erikson attempted to retrace Herjolfsson's route in reverse, making his first landfall at the last of the three places Herjolfsson had seen before reaching Greenland. It was a region of flat ledges leading to icy mountains, and Erikson named it Helluland (Country of Flat Stones). Most, though not all, scholars agree that this was probably present-day Baffin Island, which lies directly west of Greenland. Seeing that this land contained no timber, Erikson sailed on to a flat wooded land with broad white beaches, which he named Markland (Land of Forests). This has been identified by some historians as a stretch of the Labrador coast. In spite of the timber, Erikson was not satisfied with Markland either.

Again Erikson and his crew took to the sea in their Viking ship, and after sailing for two doegr (a unit of measurement that is unknown, indicating either time or distance), they landed on an island to the north of a mainland. At low tide, their ship became beached, and rather than wait for the tide to come in, they ran up onto the shore and then, when the tide came in, towed the ship to shore. There, where a stream flowed out of a lake, they decided to spend the winter and built themselves large houses. This location was abundant with salmon and experienced no frost in winter, and the grass there did not wither much, meaning cattle could be left to graze outdoors all winter.

According to the saga, when they had finished building their houses, Erikson allowed the men to do some exploring. But, being a cautious leader, he divided them into two groups and sent out only one group each day, telling the members of the group to remain together and to return by nightfall. He himself went out on alternate days. One day, the group including Tyrker returned without the German; he had evidently strayed. Erikson led a search party that eventually found Tyrker, who was so excited that all he could do was roll his eyes and babble in German, a language no one else understood. Finally he managed to relate his exciting news in Norse: He had discovered grapes growing wild. Everyone was excited by this find. It meant they would have two profitable cargoes for their homeward journey: timber and grapes. In response to Tyrker's discovery, Erikson named the country Vinland.

When spring came, the adventurers loaded a small boat with grapes and the ship with timber. On the way back to Greenland, according to the saga, Erikson rescued fifteen sailors found shipwrecked on a reef. For this daring escapade he was given the nickname "Leif the Lucky."

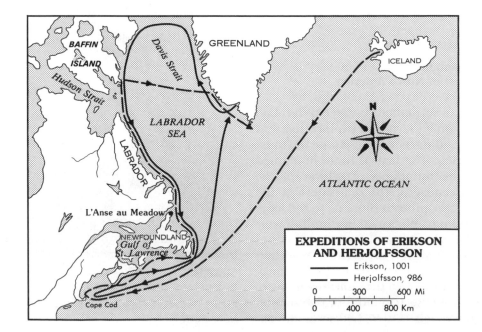

EXPEDITIONS OF ERIKSON
AND HERJOLFSSON
———— Erikson, 1001
— — — Herjolfsson, 986

0   300   600 Mi
0   400   800 Km

Erikson never saw Vinland again. The winter after his return to Greenland, his father died, leaving Erikson to administer his lands and the settlement as a whole. But he must have had plans to return to the new country, for whenever later expeditions to Vinland tried to buy his houses there, he always refused to sell, though he was generous in lending them out. One of these later expeditions was led by his brother Thorvald, who complained that Leif had been negligent in exploring. According to the saga, Thorvald was mortally wounded in a hostile encounter with the native inhabitants of Vinland, whom Leif and his party had never seen. Another later expedition, led by THORFINN KARLSEFNI, attempted to establish a colony in Vinland but was repulsed in hostile encounters with Vinland's indigenous people.

Of the three places Erikson landed, Vinland presents the greatest problems of identification. The scanty evidence that might help locate Vinland is confused and conflicting. The geographical landmarks mentioned in the sagas can be convincingly argued to represent either the northern tip of Newfoundland or the southern coast of Cape Cod, Massachusetts. Other evidence could also support either location, including the mention of self-sown wheat (which some scholars have identified as Lyme grass, which grows along shores from Iceland to Cape Cod) and the length of night and day in the wintertime, more equal than those of Iceland.

But the most compelling evidence is also the most confusing. Wild grapes no longer can be found in the climate of Newfoundland. Cape Cod is about as far north as grapes grow wild today. And it is mainly for this reason that scholars have placed Vinland anywhere from Cape Cod south to Florida. However, to assume that Erikson could have gone from the coast of Labrador, his most likely second landfall, to Cape Cod without noticing any other piece of land along the way stretches the imagination. Those who argue for Newfoundland, including the late historian Samuel Eliot Morison, suggest that the wild grapes of Vinland may actually have been red currants, gooseberries, or mountain cranberries from which wine could be made. They suggest that Erikson may have put the "Vin" in Vinland for the same reason that his father put the "Green" in Greenland—to entice future settlers. Other historians point to evidence that, during this period, Newfoundland's climate was considerably warmer than

it is now and thus could well have been conducive to the growth of grapes.

Aside from conjecture based on these details, there is some physical evidence of early Viking settlements in North America. In 1960 Norwegian archaeologist Helge Ingstad unearthed the foundations of two great houses in a spot called L'Anse au Meadow in northern Newfoundland, which may conceivably have been Erikson's settlement. Extensive digging has shown that the great houses were similar to Norse dwellings found in Greenland. But so far no one has been able to state definitively that they represent the Vinland settlement.

Leif Erikson was an ideal explorer. Boldly, he reached for distant, unknown territories, while at the same time leading his expedition so cautiously that he not only returned with all original hands but with fifteen rescued sailors as well. Whether or not the mystery of Vinland's location is ever solved, Erikson has earned a unique place in history as the first European explorer to set foot on the continent of North America, preceding Columbus and other followers by almost 500 years.

· Escalante, Silvestre Vélez de

Spanish
b 1751?; Santander Mountains
d ?
Explored American Southwest

Father Silvestre Vélez de Escalante made an incredible journey of some 1,500 miles in the American Southwest from 1776 to 1777, pushing northwest into unknown territory beyond the junction of the Gunnison and Uncompahgre rivers to the Great Salt Lake basin near Utah Lake. He was the first European to discover the only location at which the Colorado River could be crossed at that time; it was named the Crossing of the Fathers after Escalante and the other priest with him.

Born about 1751 in a small village in the Santander Mountains in Spain, Silvestre Vélez de Escalante came to New Spain (present-day Mexico) at an unrecorded age and for an unknown reason. At roughly the age of seventeen he entered the Convento Grande in Mexico City and was a practicing Franciscan friar at the Laguna Pueblo by 1774. In 1775 he moved to the mission at Zuñi Pueblo (in what is now New Mexico).

The reasons for Escalante's 1776 expedition are vague, though he did want to find a route from Santa Fe to Monterey in California and to convert Indians to Christianity along the way. Although Father Francisco Atanasio Dominguez was the expedition's religious leader and Miera y Pacheca was its civilian leader and map-maker, Escalante was the sustaining force of the expedition and kept its journal. Departing Santa Fe, New Mexico, on July 29, 1776, the group crossed the Rio Grande and headed northwest into modern Colorado. The travelers followed a series of canyons and high plateaus until they reached the junction of the Gunnison and Uncompahgre rivers at modern Delta, Colorado; from there they would travel into unknown land.

Heading northwest, they crossed the White River, reached another river that Escalante called San Buenaventura (now the Green River) at the site of present-day Dinosaur National Monument, and crossed into modern Utah. Hearing tales of a bearded Indian tribe that lived on the shores of an impassable river that flowed west, Escalante and his party pushed in that direction over the Utah Plateau and across the Wasatch Mountain divide. They entered the Great Salt Lake basin near Utah Lake, realizing this was the "river" the Indians had described. Avoiding the salt desert, they headed south, passing east of present-day Sevier Lake. When snow began to fall, they headed farther south and crossed what is now the Escalante Desert of southwest Utah, where they almost died of thirst and could find only dried seeds and sun-shriveled cactus to eat.

Reaching the vicinity of modern Zion National Park, the group crossed the Paria Plateau in what is now northern Arizona. Escalante and his party missed discovering the Grand Canyon when they headed east, but they did discover the only place at which the Colorado River could be crossed. Heading southeast through Zuñi Indian country, they reached Santa Fe on January 2, 1777. Nothing is really known of Escalante's life from this point on; even the date and place of his death are unknown.

The Spanish did not follow up with any explorations into the new areas Escalante had explored. It would be left for fur trappers in the next century to "rediscover" the lands of Utah.

Everest, George

English
b July 4, 1790; Gwernvale, Brecknockshire, Wales
d December 1, 1866; London
Surveyed India

One measure of Sir George Everest's great success in mapping the subcontinent of India is that the world's highest peak, Mount Everest, is named in his honor. Although he encountered considerable physical hardships, Everest successfully measured the meridian that passed from the Himalaya Mountains, through the center of India, to Cape Comorin. He also developed the gridiron system of triangulation, which he used to complete the long-distance trigonometric survey of central India. This survey forms the basis for the detailed mapping of India he supervised from 1830 to 1843.

Everest first encountered India's rugged mountains and broad plains in 1806 as a sixteen-year-old artillery cadet in the British army. In 1816, after two years of surveying the Indonesian island of Java, he was selected by the East India Company to help survey India. By 1818 he had become chief assistant to William Lambton, the founder and superintendent of the Great Trigonometrical Survey of India. When Lambton died in 1823, Everest succeeded him as superintendent. Seven years later, Everest was appointed to the additional position of surveyor general of India. From then until he retired in 1843, he was responsible for the immense task of mapping India.

Everest's achievements were made possible by the courage and innovation with which he responded to the many challenges he faced. He accepted physical danger as part of his work as a surveyor, but he could not climb each mountain peak in order to measure its height and fix its position. The jagged, snow-covered Himalayan peaks defied conventional means of measurement. So, using the great meridional arc as a foundation, Everest calculated a mathematical spheroid whose shape matched that of the land surface in India. He then used this spheroid to compute with considerable accuracy the positions and heights of the highest Himalayan mountain peaks—all without climbing them.

Eyre, Edward John

English
b August 5, 1815; Hornsea, Yorkshire
d November 30, 1901; Tavistock, England
Explored southern Australian deserts

Edward John Eyre, explorer and British colonial administrator, is remembered for the courage and bravery he demonstrated on his 1841 traverse of the arid Nullarbor Plain in South Australia. He made several forays into the continent's interior and is credited with proving the possibility of land communication between western and South Australia.

Eyre was born in 1815, the son of an English vicar who encouraged him for reasons of health to emigrate rather than enter military service. At the age of nineteen, Eyre went to Australia, where he managed sheep stations in the Hunter Valley near Canberra, New South Wales. He made several successful short journeys overlanding, or driving livestock from the farms to new settlements. In 1838 he settled in Adelaide, South Australia, on the east coast of the Great Australian Bight.

Edward John Eyre. Australian Foreign Affairs and Trade Dept.

From Adelaide, Eyre led two expeditions in search of new grazing lands and a possible route to western Australia. In May 1839 he followed the Flinders Range north to Mount Arden, then west across what is now the Eyre Peninsula on the west side of Spencer Gulf and on to Streaky Bay.

Eyre next planned to explore the central part of the continent and, if possible, to reach Port Essington on its north coast. In June 1840 he and seven others left Adelaide; a month later, they reached the muddy, salt-covered beds of Lake Torrens and what is now Lake Eyre. They attempted to cross the lakes but had to turn back after 6 miles, as the mud became deeper with every step they took. Believing the lakes an impassable barrier, Eyre was determined to "waste no more time or energy on so desolate and forbidding a region." The names he gave to the region's Mount Desolation and Mount Hopeless convey his discouragement.

Eyre began his best-known journey—an east-west crossing along the Great Australian Bight—on February 25, 1841. He left Fowler's Bay with his assistant, John Baxter, and three **aborigines** and headed west across the arid Nullarbor Plain. Eyre's journals tell of the oppressive heat as they trekked across the endless, treeless stretches of sand. He called the journey one of "perpetual and never-ceasing torment."

By March 2, the small party reached the westernmost watering hole. Continuing west, they survived only because the aborigines showed them how to find water in wells in the sand, holes in the rocks, and the roots of the gum scrub. In their desperation, they used sponges to collect dew. Near the site of the town that today bears his name, Eyre spent nearly three weeks digging six feet into the sand to get water. When rations ran low, he was forced to kill a horse and some sheep for food.

The harsh conditions kept tensions high, and on April 28, two of the aborigines murdered Baxter and deserted camp, taking most of the food and leaving Eyre alone in the wilderness with a young aboriginal boy named Wylie. Rain that fell a week later provided some relief, and when Eyre killed another one of the horses, Wylie ate more than six pounds of meat.

With winter coming on, the rains continued. On June 2, the pair reached a bay near Esperance, where a French whaler provided them with food and water. After a rest, Eyre moved on. When he reached his destination, Albany on King George Sound, on July 7, it was still raining.

Eyre's sponsors considered the expedition a failure because he could not successfully move livestock across the Nullarbor Plain. However, the Royal Geographical Society, in awarding Eyre a medal, recognized the remarkable courage and physical endurance it had taken to cross more than a thousand miles of desert without a single watercourse. The government of South Australia subsequently appointed him resident magistrate and protector of the aborigines on the Murray River.

Eyre returned to England in 1845, and in 1846 he was made lieutenant governor of the South Island of New Zealand under Sir George Grey. He later served as governor of Antigua and in 1864, after two years as acting governor of the island, was made governor of Jamaica. His severe reaction to a rebellion there in October 1865—in which he ordered some 400 executions—placed Eyre in the center of controversy, and he was recalled in July 1866. But the government could make no case against him, and Eyre was cleared in a civilian trial. He retired to Walreddon Manor with a colonial governor's pension in 1874. He died there in 1901, with his reputation as an explorer, at least, still untarnished.

Percy Harrison Fawcett. Popperfoto.

Fawcett, Percy Harrison

English
b 1867; Torquay
d May–June 1925?; Mato Grosso, Brazil
Explored interior of Mato Grosso and Bolivian boundary regions with Brazil, Paraguay, and Peru

Colonel Percy Harrison Fawcett began his career as a military surveyor and geographer and ended it searching for legendary lost cities deep in the interior of Brazil. From 1906 to 1912 he made official surveys of Bolivia's boundaries with Brazil, Paraguay, and Peru, exploring jungle regions south of the Amazon that were virtually unknown. Then, in April 1925, he left on a private expedition into the interior of Mato Grosso to find a "lost" city—and vanished without a trace.

Born in 1867 at Torquay, in southwestern England, Fawcett attended the Royal Military Academy at Woolwich and was commissioned in the Royal Artillery in 1886. He spent the next twenty years serving as a surveyor, geographer, and engineer with the army, traveling to such places as Ireland, Malta, and Ceylon. Then in 1906 he was commissioned by the Royal Geographical Society to survey the boundary region between Bolivia and Brazil.

Over the next fifteen years Fawcett made several official surveying expeditions as well as private explorations through jungle regions south of the Amazon, encountering hostile and, in some cases, cannibalistic Indians native to the area. During his survey of the Bolivia-Paraguay boundary he explored the Corumbá area of southern Brazil, and found the source of the Río Verde. Then, while making the survey of the Bolivia-Peru boundary (1910–12), he came into possession of a 150-year-old map which showed a lost, walled city (he named it "Z") located deep in the Brazilian state of Mato

Grosso. Also, Indians told him of another ruined city on the banks of a lake near a waterfall. Under the waterfall was the figure of a man carved in white rock which moved back and forth with the current. Fascinated by these romantic tales, Fawcett was determined to find the cities. His plans were delayed, however, by the advent of World War I, in which he served, earning the rank of army colonel.

Finally, Fawcett received financial backing from the North American Newspaper Alliance for his expedition in search of the lost cities. He left from Cuyabá, capital of Mato Grosso, on April 20, 1925, with his son Jack and a friend, heading northwest toward the area between the Xingu and São Francisco rivers in Brazil, where he believed the cities were located. A letter to his wife, dated May 29, 1925, from a place called Dead Horse Camp (named thus because his horse had died there in 1920), was the last communication received from the party. A 1928 search party could not find the members of the party or their remains; it has been widely assumed that Fawcett and the others were killed by Indians sometime after they left the camp. However, for many years rumors persisted of white men living deep in the Brazilian jungle with an Indian tribe.

- Federmann (Federman), Nikolaus (Nikolas, Nicolás)

German
b 1505?; Ulm
d 1542; Madrid, Spain
Explored interior of Venezuela

Nikolaus Federmann was a German **conquistador** who explored the interior of present-day Venezuela under the auspices of the Welsers, a powerful German banking family that had been given the right to govern the region by Holy Roman Emperor Charles V (King Charles I of Spain). On his most famous expedition in search of the fabled **El Dorado**, he spent almost three years traversing much of Venezuela and Colombia, arriving at the plateau of Bogatá only to find that GONZALO JIMÉNEZ DE QUESADA had already laid claim to the rich Chibcha Indian empire.

Nikolaus Federmann was born about 1505 in Ulm, Germany; the exact date of his birth is unknown. His life remains obscure until his arrival at Coro on the Gulf of Venezuela in 1530 as second-in-command of the German colony there. Hoping to capitalize on reports of riches in South America, the Welser banking house of Augsburg commissioned Federmann to explore the interior. He left Coro in 1531 and proceeded west along the Cojedes River to its confluence with the Portuguesa River. After exploring the **llanos** near the Portuguesa, he investigated the foothills of the Cordillera Mérida east of Lake Maracaibo before returning to Coro in 1532.

In 1533 Federmann joined an expedition under the command of Georg von Speier to find El Dorado, the fabled city of gold. However, disobeying orders, he broke away from the main force with 500 men to search on his own for the rich kingdom rumored to exist in the uplands of present-day Colombia. Heading southeast, Federmann crossed the Apure and Arauca rivers, ascended the Meta River, and crossed the floodplains of the Orinoco River. Reaching the upper Guaviare River (in Colombia), he made an incredible ascent of the Andes Mountains, despite constant harassment by Indians. At many points during the ascent the expedition's horses had to be hoisted by ropes.

By the time Federmann reached the plateau of Bogotá in 1539, only one-third of his force remained, starving and in tatters. When he arrived, however, he found Jiménez de Quesada already there. In the hope of avoiding a war over the region, Federmann was given gold, and his men were fed. Then Federmann, Jiménez de Quesada, and another claimant, SEBASTIÁN DE BENALCÁZAR, agreed jointly to travel to Spain to submit their various claims before the **Council of the Indies**. The council eventually ruled in favor of Spanish claims to the region, although neither Jiménez de Quesada or Benalcázar was appointed its governor.

Federmann received nothing for his accomplishment. In addition, he was deprived of his Venezuelan holdings by the Welser family, who also began legal proceedings against him. Federmann died in Madrid in 1542.

Fernandez de Quirós, Pedro. See **Quirós, Pedro Fernandez de.**

• Fitzroy (FitzRoy), Robert

English
b July 5, 1805; Suffolk
d April 30, 1865; Norwald, Surrey
Explored South America and Pacific, with
Charles Darwin, as captain of *Beagle*

Robert Fitzroy spent nearly ten years charting the coasts of South America. From 1831 to 1836, his best-known passenger was the naturalist CHARLES DARWIN, with whom the religious fundamentalist Fitzroy had many lively discussions concerning the origin of species.

Fitzroy was born at Ampton Hall, Suffolk, on July 5, 1805, to Lord Charles Fitzroy, a wealthy aristocrat, and the first marquess of Londonderry. In 1819 he entered the Royal Navy College and on September 7, 1824, was made lieutenant.

On November 13, 1828, upon the suicide of the captain, Commander Pringle Stokes of the *Beagle*, Fitzroy was appointed to fill the spot and to continue a survey of Patagonia and Tierra del Fuego, calling for the use of his additional skills as **hydrographer** and meteorologist. When he returned to England in 1830, Fitzroy brought back four native Fuegians. One died of smallpox; the surviving Fuegians were taught English culture and the Christian religion at

Fitzroy's expense. Fitzroy took them back to South America, hoping that they would spread Christianity among their countrymen. The experiment failed but was later taken up by missionaries.

From 1831 until 1836 Fitzroy charted the South American coasts with Darwin on board the *Beagle*. The two developed a strong friendship, despite their differing interpretations of the naturalist's findings. Darwin named a dolphin species after the commander, and Fitzroy christened Mount Darwin in Tierra del Fuego. Fitzroy was usually pleasant and courteous to all, although he once flew into a rage when Darwin disagreed with him over slavery and threatened to quit the expedition when the Admiralty would not support him when he purchased a second vessel, the *Adventure*. He was appeased when he sold the ship for a profit and was promoted to captain.

In 1837 Fitzroy received the Gold Medal of the Royal Geographical Society for his work. Two years later, he published *Voyage of the* Adventure *and the* Beagle. Other books followed, including a volume on meteorology in 1861 that advanced thinking in that field and established the basis for the storm-warning system in use today.

Fitzroy spent two years as a member of Parliament, then in 1843 was appointed governor

A painting of Fitzroy with his crew. National Maritime Museum, Greenwich.

and commander in chief of New Zealand. He arrived immediately after the Wairau massacre, a violent uprising against the British, and his sympathy toward the Maoris alienated the colonists. He was recalled in 1845.

In 1848 he was appointed acting superintendent of the dockyard at Woolwich and oversaw sea trials of the *Arrogant*, an early screw-driven **frigate**. In 1850 he retired for health and personal reasons. He was made a fellow of the Royal Society in 1851 and became head of the meteorological department of the Board of Trade in 1854.

Fitzroy married, but his wife and eldest daughter died in 1852. An embittered man, he took his own life on April 30, 1865, two years after achieving the rank of vice admiral.

• Flinders, Matthew

English
b March 16, 1774; Donnington, Lincolnshire
d July 19, 1814; London
Circumnavigated Australia (first to do so);
    charted its coast

Matthew Flinders. National Maritime Museum, Greenwich.

Considered among the world's most accomplished navigators and **hydrographers**, Matthew Flinders provided the first comprehensive picture of the continent then known as *Terra Australis*. He not only filled in great gaps of knowledge about the coastline and waterways of present-day Australia, but he made advances in the science of navigation, and naturalists on his 1801–1803 expedition collected hundreds of new plant and animal specimens.

The son and grandson of surgeons, Flinders was expected to follow in their footsteps. Instead, with his sense of adventure stimulated by reading *Robinson Crusoe*, he joined the Royal Navy in 1789 at the age of fifteen. Early in his naval career he served under Captain WILLIAM BLIGH in the South Pacific and the West Indies (1791–92) and took part in the Battle of Brest on June 1, 1794, aboard the H.M.S. *Bellerophon*.

In 1795 Flinders sailed to the British colony of New South Wales on the Australian continent as a midshipman aboard the *Reliance*, with Governor John Hunter and the ship's surgeon, George Bass, with whom Flinders later shared many explorations. Upon their arrival in Sydney, Flinders joined Hunter in exploring the surrounding bays and later was commissioned to survey the Furneaux Islands north of Van Diemen's Land (now Tasmania). He was promoted to lieutenant and sent to join Bass, who was searching for a passage between Van Diemen's Land and the south coast of Terra Australis. The pair not only discovered Bass Strait, but they circumnavigated Van Diemen's Land, proving that it was an island.

Flinders returned to England in 1800 to obtain support for an exploration of the unknown coasts of Terra Australis. He got it from Sir JOSEPH BANKS, who had retained a strong interest in the continent ever since he had explored Botany Bay with Captain JAMES COOK some thirty years earlier.

Flinders was made captain of the **sloop** *Investigator* and given a crew of eighty-eight men, including officers and scientists. Among them were the naturalist Robert Brown and the artists Ferdinand Bauer and William Westall. The expedition left Spithead, England, on July 18, 1801, and after making supply stops at Madeira and Africa's Cape of Good Hope, reached Cape Leeuwin on the southwest coast of Australia on December 6.

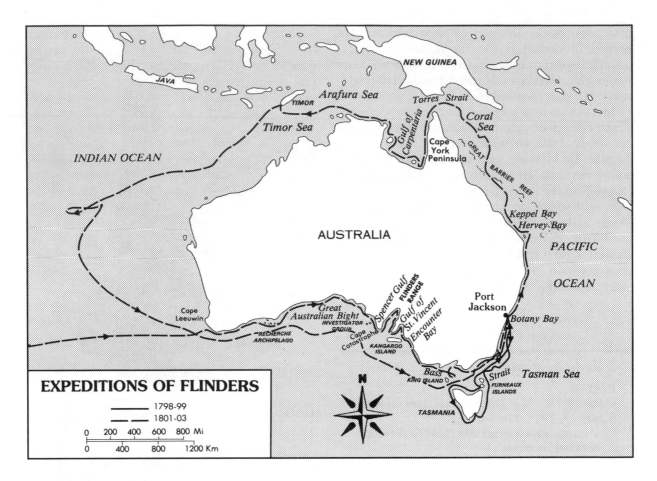

EXPEDITIONS OF FLINDERS

—————— 1798-99
— — — — 1801-03

0   200   400   600   800 Mi

0   400   800   1200 Km

Flinders spent nearly a month at nearby King George Sound. In mid-December he and his crew encountered a group of local **aborigines**, who had little interest in dealing with the Englishmen. At this spot Brown gathered specimens of 500 new species of flowers as well as of kangaroos, emus, snakes, lizards, and fish.

On January 3, 1802, Flinders sailed east along the southern coast. In the Recherche Archipelago Brown found ashy petrels and blue penguins, as well as a hundred new plants and a species of small kangaroo. In February the *Investigator* reached a group of islands that Flinders named after the ship. Today the largest of them bears the navigator's name. On February 21 a small crew went ashore in a longboat to search for water on the mainland near what is now Spencer Gulf. Neither the boat nor its crew was ever seen again; consequently, the fateful spot is now known as Cape Catastrophe.

Flinders sailed up Spencer Gulf for nearly 150 miles, where he observed a range of red clay mountains, one of which he named Mount Brown after the expedition's naturalist. To the east of Spencer Gulf, he explored the present-

day Gulf of St. Vincent and Kangaroo Island. There, starved for fresh meat, Flinders and the crew easily hunted down the strange, tame animals, which had never before seen human beings.

On April 8, Flinders met a rival explorer, the Frenchman NICOLAS BAUDIN, at what became known as Encounter Bay, near the Gulf of St. Vincent. Despite the fact that England and France were at war, the two navigators had an amiable exchange and breakfasted together before continuing on their respective ways. Ignoring earlier Dutch explorations, Baudin claimed that the French discovered much of the land west of Encounter Bay, a boast that Flinders set straight for the history books with his own publication. French place names were never to stick to the map of Australia.

In late April Flinders explored the Bass Strait and the northeast coast of present-day King Island, located between Australia and present-day Tasmania. When the scientists went ashore there, they found more plant species than anywhere else in their travels. They also encountered wallabies and wombats and nearly uncountable flocks of short-tailed shearwaters, a species of waterfowl.

In May Flinders reached Port Jackson (near present-day Sydney). He dined with Philip Gidley King, the governor of New South Wales. King offered him a small **brig**, a crew of convicts, and two aboriginal interpreters for the remainder of his journey. Before sailing north on July 22, Flinders sent many specimen cases to London and left numerous living plants with the governor.

Flinders next explored Hervey and Keppel bays, and a group of seventy small islands near the latter. In mid-August he reached the Great Barrier Reef, the world's largest coral reef. Despite the danger to the ship, Flinders examined the reef carefully and may have been the first to understand that the elaborate, mazelike structure was formed by the calcified outer skeletons of coral polyps. During this period he also became one of the first navigators to recognize and take into account the effect of a ship's iron fittings on its compass bearings. When Flinders's small brig tore her keel on the reef, the wounded vessel was forced to return to Port Jackson. Flinders continued north with the *Investigator*, however, sailing some 500 miles inside the reef before he was able to find a safe channel back to the open sea.

Having completed his journey northward along Australia's east coast, Flinders reached the Cape York Peninsula and sailed through Torres Strait between Australia and New Guinea and into what is now the Gulf of Carpentaria. From November 1802 until March 1803 he explored the gulf coast and the islands along it. The aboriginal inhabitants of northern Australia at times seemed friendly, yet on one occasion they attacked a landing party and on another took Brown's musket.

At the end of March the *Investigator* touched at Timor (in present-day Indonesia), then rounded the west and southern coasts of Australia, completing Flinders's circumnavigation and returning to Port Jackson on June 9, 1803. It was the end of an important voyage through which Flinders surveyed and charted the entire, and largely unknown, continent. He had literally put Australia "on the map" and had done so to a surprisingly accurate degree.

En route to England as a passenger on board the H.M.S. *Porpoise*, Flinders was shipwrecked on a reef and, in the course of two weeks, rowed nearly 700 miles back to Port Jackson for help.

Governor King then gave him the **schooner** *Cumberland*, and after arranging for the rescue of the shipwreck victims, Flinders made his way west across the Indian Ocean.

Unfortunately, the schooner was barely seaworthy, rations were low, and his crew was ailing. Rather than try for the Cape of Good Hope, Flinders landed at Île de France (now Mauritius) and asked for help. Unbeknownst to him, relations between England and France had worsened in the interim, and Flinders was taken prisoner as a spy on December 17, 1803. He was not released until June 13, 1810.

Flinders arrived in England on October 24, his health and spirit broken. Upon his return, he conducted experiments on the magnetism of ships for the Admiralty.

Flinders spent his last days preparing his account of his voyage, despite the fact that many of his papers had been confiscated in Île de France. *A Voyage to Terra Australis* was published July 19, 1814, the same day Flinders, the father of Australian hydrography, died. His exploration of the coast had been so thorough that it was said he left nothing for his followers to do.

• Forster, Johann Georg Adam

German
b November 27, 1754; Nassenhuben, Prussia, near Gdańsk, Poland
d January 12, 1794; Paris, France
Assisted as naturalist on James Cook's second circumnavigation

As one of the naturalists on board the *Resolution*, Johann Georg Adam Forster contributed to the expanding knowledge of the natural history of the South Seas. His journal provided a general account of Captain JAMES COOK's second major expedition (1772–75).

Forster began his career as an explorer at an early age. He was born November 27, 1754, at Nassenhuben in Prussia near Danzig (present-day Gdańsk, Poland) to JOHANN REINHOLD FORSTER, a pastor and schoolteacher with an interest in the natural sciences. In 1765, at the age of eleven, the young Forster accompanied his father on his first expedition, an exploration of Russia aboard the *Volga*.

Young Forster, known as Georg, was only

The Forsters. Bibliothèque Nationale, Paris.

seventeen when he joined his father in 1772 on Cook's *Resolution* on a search for the great unknown Southern Continent, *Terra Australis Incognita*, which was postulated to lie in the South Pacific (for a more complete discussion, see ALEXANDER DALRYMPLE). Throughout the three-year voyage Forster proved to be an easygoing and likable shipmate—unlike his father, who apparently did not share his son's amiable personality. In addition, Georg Forster was a bright young man with a talent for draftsmanship.

During the voyage Forster kept a journal, which later would be the basis of his books about the expedition. Probably the youngest aboard the ship, he was particularly taken aback by the promiscuous behavior he witnessed in Tahiti. "The excesses of the night were incredible," he wrote, yet he lay the blame more on the English sailors than on the native women.

The allure of Tahitian life was not entirely lost on the young man, however. "A kind of happy uniformity runs through the whole life of the Tahitians. . . . Thus contented with their simple way of life, and placed in a delightful country, they are free from cares, and happy in their ignorance," he wrote. When the Irish sailor John Marra attempted to jump ship as the *Resolution* left Tahiti, Forster sympathized with him, noting that "still he must earn his subsistence in England at the expense of labour and in the sweat of his brow when this eldest curse of mankind is scarcely felt at Taheitee."

Although Forster was liked by all aboard the *Resolution*, after the ship returned to England in 1775, the young naturalist and diarist was to cause Cook some discomfort. Johann Reinhold Forster had quarreled with Cook and his shipmates throughout the voyage, and Cook, who stood to earn significant royalties from his own writings, prohibited the elder naturalist from publishing an account of the expedition. In 1777 Georg Forster published *A Voyage Round the World*, two volumes that were very well received. His book not only preceded Cook's official account by six weeks, cutting into Cook's royalties, but misrepresented his commander—some historians say to the point of being libelous. This negative portrayal, seemingly so out of character, may have been instigated by the elder Forster, who apparently had spent his generous expedition fee soon after his return to England and was therefore in need of money.

Following publication of his book, Georg Forster spent a year in Paris, then returned to Germany in 1779. The next year he took a post as professor of natural history at Kassel, where he remained for four years before moving to the university at Wilna. At Wilna he continued to teach natural history while studying for his degree in medicine. Four years later, in 1788, he accepted a position as librarian for the elector of Mayence (now Mainz), one of the German princes entitled to take part in choosing the Holy Roman Emperor.

Forster's work in natural history and philosophy had a great influence on the great German naturalist, traveler, and statesman Baron ALEXANDER VON HUMBOLDT. In 1790–91, Forster accompanied the young Humboldt on a trip to Belgium, Holland, England, and France.

Upon Forster's return home, he became active politically. The people of Mayence deputized him to petition the National Convention to attach the city to the French Republic, but the leaders of the French Revolution ignored his requests. In 1793 he was denounced as a traitor in Germany. He died in Paris the following year.

· Forster, Johann Reinhold

German
b October 22, 1729; Tczew, Poland (formerly Dirschau, Prussia)
d December 9, 1798; Halle, Germany
Served as naturalist on James Cook's second circumnavigation

Johann Reinhold Forster and his son JOHANN GEORG ADAM FORSTER are credited with the systematic botanical knowledge of the South Pacific gained from Captain JAMES COOK's second Pacific expedition (1772–75). Their broad-based approach to the natural sciences significantly expanded on the work done by Sir JOSEPH BANKS and Doctor DANIEL CARL SOLANDER on Cook's first voyage.

Little is written about Johann Reinhold Forster's early life. He was born in Prussia on October 22, 1729, and spent his early adulthood as a pastor and a schoolteacher. He took part in a scientific expedition aboard the *Volga* in 1765, but other than that, historian J. C. Beaglehole writes that Forster was "quite unused to the sea or sailors."

Forster moved to London in 1766 and by 1772 had published two widely read books on natural history—*Flora Americae septentrionalis* and *Novae species insectorum*—and had translated an account of LOUIS ANTOINE DE BOUGAINVILLE's circumnavigation aboard the *Boudeuse* and the *Étoile*.

In 1772 James Cook was to embark on a Pacific voyage—his second—this one intended to resolve the question of the existence of the hypothetical continent, *Terra Australis Incognita* (for a more complete discussion, see ALEXANDER DALRYMPLE). When the naturalist Banks withdrew from the expedition in a disagreement over accommodations, Forster was offered the handsome sum of £4,000 to fill the position of "a man of science" on Cook's ship, the *Resolution*. Forster accepted the post and brought his son along as his assistant. He also persuaded

Cook to hire Anders Sparrman, a student of the Swedish botanist Linnaeus (Carl von Linné); Forster would collaborate with Sparrman on many detailed investigations of flora and fauna.

By all accounts, Forster was miserable on the journey. One of his first actions on board the *Resolution* was to offer a £100 bribe to obtain the master's cabin. His bid was unsuccessful, as bunk assignments on official expeditions were inflexible. A seasick Forster reluctantly retired to his original cabin. Throughout the journey he was mean-spirited and quarrelsome, and found reason to argue with almost everyone on board.

Fortunately, Forster was not entirely without virtues. He was an extremely precise scientist with an endless sense of curiosity. Wherever the *Resolution* called, Forster added to the tremendous inventory of plant and animal life that Banks and Solander had begun on the previous journey. He was the first to describe the Australian sea lion, and in Tahiti he added a swallow, a curlew, a parrot, and numerous plants to the earlier naturalists' list of native species. When the ship reached Antarctic waters, Forster did not let his rheumatism stand in the way of science. He identified four penguin species as well as the snow petrel and giant fulmar.

Another major contribution was Forster's detailed anthropological study of native Pacific peoples. In this pioneer study he identified two distinct major groups, the Polynesians and the Melanesians, and subgroups within them. At least one specific incident indicates that perhaps Forster was not entirely at odds with his fellow humans. In February 1774 Cook fell ill with "a bilious colic" that kept him in his cabin and forced him to turn the ship over to his second in command. By most accounts he was near death. As the ship had been in Antarctic waters for some time, no fresh meat was on board. Forster sacrificed his favorite dog in hopes of helping Cook regain his strength. Within two weeks Cook had recovered.

Apparently Forster's gesture was not enough to overcome the animosity that had grown between him and the commander. When the *Resolution* returned to England in 1775, Cook forbade the naturalist to publish anything about the expedition. Forster eventually did issue several volumes, however. His *Description of Species of Plants Collected During the Voyage in the South Seas*, written in Latin, was published in Göttingen, Germany, in 1776. *Observations*

Made During a Voyage Round the World, which included anthropological, geographical, botanical, zoological, and oceanographical data, was published in London in 1778.

In 1780 Forster returned to Germany at the request of Frederick II, who offered him the post of professor of natural history at the university at Halle and named him director of botanical gardens. In 1787 he published a volume on discoveries and voyages in the north. Forster remained at Halle until his death in 1798.

• Foucauld, Charles-Eugene de

French
b September 15, 1858; Strasbourg
d December 1, 1916; Tamanrasset, Algeria
Explored Morocco

As a French soldier, Charles de Foucauld fell in love with the desolate beauty of North Africa. He later developed the belief that the French could prevail in the region only by making religion their weapon: "If we do not manage to make Frenchmen out of the natives, they will drive us from their land. The only way, however, of turning them into Frenchmen, is by making them Christians first." Although Foucauld subsequently lived in the desert for many years as a Trappist monk, he won no converts. As an explorer, he is known primarily for his reconnaissance of Morocco from 1883 to 1884.

Foucauld was born into a socially prominent French family, but his indolent performance in school did not meet the Foucauld family's high standards. At the age of twenty, he enrolled in a cavalry school, and in 1880 he was sent to Algeria with the Fourth Hussars. He saw little or no military action, but he became entranced by the desert and at age twenty-four resigned from the army and moved to Algiers.

Foucauld wanted to explore Morocco, a largely unknown region virtually closed to Europeans. He adopted the disguise of a Russian rabbi and, in the company of an authentic rabbi, set out in June 1883. His purpose was to describe the geography of the land in such detail that cartographers could draw maps from his report. He returned almost a year later with a wealth of material and, by 1888, had published his *Reconnaissance of Morocco* to widespread public acclaim. The Paris Geographical Society

Charles-Eugene de Foucauld. New York Public Library.

awarded him its gold medal for his achievement.

By 1890, Foucauld's interests had changed: he had experienced a religious awakening and decided to become a monk. He entered a Trappist monastery, took his vows in 1901, then asked permission to work in the French colonies of North Africa. After living as a hermit in Béni Abbès, Algeria, for two years, Foucauld agreed to travel with an old friend from cavalry school, now a divisional commander in the Camel Corps of the Sahara, to the Hoggar Mountains across Algeria's Tanezruft Desert. The expedition embarked from Béni Abbès in January 1904. Foucauld stopped for a time in Adrar, in order to learn the language of the Tuareg, the untamed robber-knights of the desert. He then continued across the desert to the Hoggar Mountains and the small village of Tamanrasset, which lay in the heart of the land of the Tuareg. He was attracted to the village and decided to make it his home. He became friends with the Tuareg ruler, who was so taken with the Frenchman that he moved his capital to Tamanrasset. Foucauld thus accomplished on his own one of the main goals of the French military: the pacification of the Tuareg.

Foucauld is known for his exploration of Morocco and for his great and useful friendship with the Tuareg people. Ironically, although he went to the Sahara as a missionary, he never won a single convert. Rather, he left his mark in a different way in the last eleven years of his life, during which he produced comprehensive geographical studies of the Sahara region—complete with proposed locations for future roads, railroads, and irrigation systems—and compiled a major dictionary of the Tuareg language. He died in 1916 at the hands of a band of Muslims under mysterious circumstances, perhaps because he was suspected of being a military spy for the French.

Foxe, Luke

English
b October 20, 1586; Hull, Humberside
d July 1635; Whitby, North Yorkshire
Explored Hudson Bay; discovered Foxe
Channel

A colorful character and enthusiastic chronicler of his own adventures in the Arctic, "Northwest" Foxe, as he called himself, filled in the gaps left by THOMAS BUTTON, WILLIAM BAFFIN, and ROBERT BYLOT in mapping the Hudson Bay area. By sailing the entire western coast of Hudson Bay and then heading north through Foxe Channel to what he called Northwest Foxe His Furthest, he determined that the passage was cut off by land to the west and by impenetrable ice to the north.

Foxe was an excellent navigator, "sea-bred from his boystime" by his father, a seaman based at Hull. After sailing extensively in the Mediterranean and Baltic seas, Foxe became a student of Arctic exploration. He had a great source of knowledge in his friend John Tappe, a bookseller who published navigational works. What he could not learn about the Arctic from books, he got firsthand. "At the returnes home of all ships from thence," he wrote, "I enquired of the masters, mates, and others that were that way imployed, whereby I gathered from reports

and discourse and manuscripts how farre they had proceeded." Much of this valuable material appears in the book he later wrote, setting the background to his own discoveries.

Perhaps while seeking advice on some navigational problem, Foxe got to know Henry Briggs, the great Oxford mathematician and astronomer. Briggs must have been impressed by Foxe's abilities, because he brought Foxe to the attention of a key member of the royal court.

Foxe was subsequently supplied by London merchants with the seventy-ton H.M.S. *Charles*, an old gunboat, and a crew of twenty-three for a voyage to Hudson Bay. The party left England on May 5, 1631, and landed at Frobisher Bay on June 20. They made their way through the Hudson Strait, then sailed south of Southampton Island as far as James Bay, thus passing Button's southernmost point and matching Hudson's. On the way, they crossed paths with a rival expedition sent out by merchants from Bristol, and Foxe dined with its captain, Thomas James.

While James stayed in the southern part of the bay and endured a terrible winter, Foxe went due north to explore the waters Baffin had found unpromising, where he discovered what became known as Foxe Channel between Southampton Island and southwest Baffin Island. Following the coast of Baffin Island, he reached his northernmost point on September 22.

Realizing that there was no passage through the ice, he turned back and proceeded on to England without losing a crew member. James followed the next year, virtually repeating Foxe's course.

Foxe had made it to Arctic waters after twenty-five years of trying, but the news he brought back was not the kind that would make him either rich or famous. He seems to have ended his days in penniless obscurity.

Francis Xavier, Saint. See **Xavier, Saint Francis.**

• Franklin, John

English
b April 16, 1786; Spilsby, Lincolnshire
d June 11, 1847; near King William Island,
   Northwest Territories, Canada
Explored Canadian Arctic

Though once acclaimed for his heroic exploits in the Arctic and knighted for his contributions to overland exploration, Rear Admiral Sir John Franklin is best known today for his spectacular blunders. On the first expedition under his command (1819–21), half of his party died tragically (and one man even resorted to cannibalism) primarily because Franklin could not bring himself to turn back toward safety when supplies ran low. On his last foray into the Arctic (1845–47), an attempt to navigate the final unknown stretch of the Northwest Passage, he and all 129 of his crew died after he tried to navigate an ice-clogged strait and his ship became trapped.

Franklin grew up only a few miles from the Lincolnshire coast but did not see the sea until he was twelve. His father thought his gentle nature suited him for the ministry, but as soon as he saw the waves of the North Sea, the boy was struck with an overwhelming desire to become a sailor. Two years later, he joined the Royal Navy as a first-class volunteer on board the H.M.S. *Polyphemus*. He soon saw action in the Battle of Copenhagen (1801). After this he served in various engagements, including the Battle of Trafalgar (1805), and worked his way up the ranks, until the defeat of Napoleon in 1815.

With an eye to making use of its forces during peacetime, the Admiralty took an interest in exploring the Arctic. Since many geographers of the time believed that the polar ice cap was actually an open sea, the navy decided to send an expedition from Spitsbergen (now part of Svalbard) eastward to the Bering Strait through the Arctic Ocean. Franklin, now a lieutenant, was appointed second-in-command to Captain David Buchan. They sailed on April 25, 1818, sent off by throngs of well-wishers. Their two ships, the *Dorothea* and the *Trent*, did not get far before encountering ice. The ships' crews were severely tested when a gale forced both to seek refuge in the ice pack. The waves hitting hard against the ice made for "a sublime and awful sight," according to crew member Frederick Beechey, but this did not deter Franklin from calmly steering the *Trent* to safety. Eventually, both ships became trapped in ice north of Spitsbergen for three weeks. When they were freed, Buchan admitted defeat and ordered their return to England.

After nineteen years in the navy, Franklin was already an experienced mariner at the age of thirty-three, one who had proved he could function brilliantly at sea. But the Admiralty decided to send him to a world neither he nor his superiors knew much about—the north coast of North America—in order to take up the old search for the Northwest Passage (for a more complete discussion, see MARTIN FROBISHER).

WILLIAM PARRY was assigned to search for a strait off Baffin Bay, while Franklin was given the daunting task of charting the Arctic coast of North America by foot and canoe from the Coppermine River east to a point where Parry might be able to meet up with him. Only one European, SAMUEL HEARNE, had ever made it to the mouth of the Coppermine. Despite Hearne's experience in overland travel, it had taken him three years of hazardous exploration before he finally latched onto an Indian party that could

Sir John Franklin. Library of Congress.

Franklin's *Erebus*, trapped in the ice near King William Sound. National Maritime Museum, Greenwich.

lead him to his destination. Franklin lacked Hearne's experience and knew it. In a letter home, he admitted that "we do not permit ourselves to indulge in sanguine hopes of success. . . ."

The expedition (from May 1819 to May 1822) would end in disaster, but not before Franklin managed to chart 550 miles of the Arctic coast east of the Coppermine, thus accomplishing his mission in roughly the same amount of time it took Hearne to do much less. Though critics have found fault with his methods, the public feted him upon his return. (More significantly, two members of the party, Dr. John Richardson and GEORGE BACK, volunteered for Franklin's next overland expedition.) Indeed, most of his mistakes resulted from attitudes that his compatriots admired, such as his refusal to allow officers to carry heavy loads or to hunt for food and his resolute desire to accomplish his mission, no matter what the danger. He also encountered problems beyond his power to solve, such as a dispute between two fur-trading companies that were supposed to coordinate supply efforts. The fact that everyone in his party nearly starved to death (nine actually did) and that one of the Canadian **voyageurs** cannibalized an English crew member and was in turn exe-cuted just made the tale more romantic to the English public.

Far from being deterred by the agonies of the first Arctic trip, Franklin was off on another in February 1825. This time he made sure the supplies were adequate and brought along light boats he had designed for improved river and coastal travel. When the party reached the mouth of the Mackenzie River, Franklin and Back turned west to explore the coast toward the Bering Strait, while Richardson's party turned east toward the Coppermine. Though Franklin got only halfway up the coast before the weather forced him back, he had established the southern contours of the Northwest Passage. On his return to England, he was knighted.

Prior to his last, fatal trip to the Arctic, Franklin commanded the **frigate** *Rainbow* on an 1830 Mediterranean tour. In 1837 he took his first and only civilian job as lieutenant governor of Van Diemen's Land (now Tasmania) off the coast of Australia, then a penal colony. Not used to dealing with the clever politicians of the colonial office, Franklin did his best to govern the strange mix of prisoners and free settlers fairly. In the process, however, he stepped on the toes of an ambitious colonial secretary and was fired in 1843.

This was a bad end for a hero, and Franklin's many navy friends sympathized. When he told the Admiralty that he wanted to lead the next expedition being planned to the Northwest Passage, no one could refuse him.

The expedition departed in 1845. After first trying to break through Wellington Channel to what he still thought was an open Arctic Sea, Franklin headed south through Peel Sound and Franklin Strait. Not knowing of the existence of ice-free Simpson Strait to the south of King William Island, he then sailed west of the island. Unfortunately, his ships, the *Erebus* and the *Terror*, fitted out with steam engines and screw propellers, were much too large and unwieldy to be useful in the ice-clogged waters. In September 1846 they became mired in the ice and never escaped. As the only surviving record (which was found later) indicates, Franklin died a year before his men abandoned ship to walk south, eventually to their deaths. Some of them made it as far as Simpson Strait, the final key to the Northwest Passage.

When no word of Franklin's expedition had been received in England by 1848, the Admiralty, under mounting pressure from the British public, sent out the first relief mission in search of the missing hero and his crew. For more than a decade, their mysterious disappearance, which obsessed the British public, spurred repeated rescue expeditions, sponsored both by the Admiralty and by Franklin's widow, Lady Jane Franklin. Finally, in 1859, after more than fifty missions had been sent to the Canadian Arctic, an expedition financed by Lady Jane and led by FRANCIS MC CLINTOCK discovered the graves and skeletons marking the site of the disaster on King William Island. Ironically, it was through these numerous relief missions that the Northwest Passage was finally charted, a fitting if somber tribute to the spirit of Sir John Franklin.

• Fraser, Simon

Canadian
b 1776; Bennington, Vermont
d April 19, 1862; St. Andrew's, Canada West
(Ontario)
Explored Fraser River to its mouth

A fur trader whose explorations were conducted in the service of his company's business, Simon

Simon Fraser. William L. Clements Library, University of Michigan.

Fraser spent the early years of the nineteenth century establishing the North West Company west of the Rocky Mountains. In 1808, he undertook a harrowing journey down the turbulent river that now bears his name to its mouth on the Pacific Ocean at present-day Vancouver, British Columbia.

Fraser's father fought with the British during the American Revolution and died a prisoner of war. After the war, Fraser's mother took the family to Canada, where Fraser was apprenticed to the North West Company at the age of sixteen. By 1802, he had been made a partner in the company, and in 1805 he was given the job of establishing trading posts on the western side of the Rocky Mountains.

The North West Company had been interested in this area ever since ALEXANDER MACKENZIE had crossed the mountains from the east in 1793. The company hoped to find two things west of the Rockies: new sources of furs and an easy route from the Pacific by which trade goods and supplies could be brought inland, thus avoiding the long and expensive journey overland from Montréal. Mackenzie had tried to follow the Fraser to the coast (although he thought he was on the Columbia), but when the Indians insisted the river was too rough beyond a certain point, he had turned back to take an overland route. Now the company wanted Fraser to try the river, although there was no hurry. Putting business first, Fraser spent from 1805 to 1808 in the area he named New Caledonia (now central British Columbia) establishing several trading posts, building up the business, and making plans.

Then big news came: United States president Thomas Jefferson had sent MERIWETHER LEWIS and WILLIAM CLARK up the Missouri River with instructions to find a route to the Pacific. Lewis and Clark had complied and were claiming much of the Northwest for the United States. Suddenly, there was great urgency for the Canadians to establish their hold on the Northwest, and Fraser was told to get himself down the Columbia (in reality the present-day Fraser) as quickly as possible.

Thus, on May 28, 1808, he set out from Fort George (present-day Prince George) near the juncture of the Fraser and Nechako rivers with a party of twenty-four men, including his trusted friend, John Stuart. Down the river as far as present-day Alexandria they were following the footsteps of Mackenzie. Fraser, seemingly due to a sense of competition with his forerunner, had several unkind things to say in his journal about Mackenzie's failure to observe certain obvious landmarks. Like Mackenzie, Fraser encountered Indians who gave discouraging reports about the prospects ahead, namely that the river was full of rapids and falls and enclosed by steep rocky cliffs that made **portaging** around the rapids dangerous, if not impossible. While Mackenzie had heeded such warnings, Fraser was determined to carry out his orders and pressed ahead. He and his party found the river every bit as bad as they had been warned. The canoes swirled through the rapids, often narrowly avoiding capsizing. But as terrifying as the rapids were, the men often chose them over the arduous and equally frightening task of hauling the canoes up sheer cliff walls.

Finally, on June 10, after sending men ahead to scout, Fraser became convinced that the Indians were right and the river was impassable. The primary goal of his journey had been achieved: He knew the river could not be used

for transporting goods. But Fraser had been ordered to get to the coast, and he would not rest until he had followed those orders. And so the members of his party concealed their canoes under some bushes and went ahead on foot, still following the river. This brought its own perils, as they often had to make their way by narrow and slippery paths worn into the cliffs by generations of sure-footed Indians accustomed from youth to treading these dangerous grounds.

Passing the mouth of another river, Fraser named it the Thompson after his fellow trader and explorer DAVID THOMPSON, whom Fraser believed was at that moment exploring its headwaters. In reality, Thompson was on the Columbia, doing what Fraser thought he himself was doing. (Ironically, Thompson never saw the river named for him.) Past the Thompson, the present-day Fraser in places became calmer and possible to navigate, but several sectors of hazardous rapids in the mountainous canyon downstream forced the party to take precarious tracks on the steep banks.

On July 2, the explorers reached a spot where the river divided into several channels, one of which they followed to a bay of the sea (the Strait of Georgia). Fraser was disappointed not to find open water. (Vancouver Island blocked their view of the open Pacific Ocean.) He was also discouraged when he took a latitude reading and discovered beyond a doubt that he was far north of where the Columbia was known to empty into the sea.

The Indians along most of their route had been friendly and helpful, but those on the coast were hostile. That fact together with a shortage of provisions caused the party to turn around and head back immediately. The first leg of the homeward journey was harrowing. Indians followed them, occasionally shooting arrows and dropping stones on them from the cliffs above. The men were half out of their minds with fright and some threatened to leave the group and try to return overland. Fraser knew this would be folly, so he convinced the whole group to take an oath to remain together. They did, and the party returned intact on August 6. While their journey to the sea had taken thirty-six days, their return journey, paddling upstream, had amazingly taken only thirty-seven.

Though Simon Fraser was himself disappointed in his failure to follow the Columbia to the ocean and thus claim the surrounding land for Great Britain, he had achieved a monumental undertaking, following the second great river of western Canada (after the Mackenzic) to its mouth. And he had done so under the most adverse conditions imaginable, a tribute to his courage, his dogged determination, his physical and mental endurance, and his leadership.

Frémont, John Charles

American
b January 21, 1813; Savannah, Georgia
d July 13, 1890; New York, New York
Surveyed and mapped American West

John Charles Frémont did more than any other explorer to popularize the American West and promote its attractions to potential settlers. Between 1842 and 1845 he made three highly publicized surveying expeditions in the West. Although he discovered no new territory during his travels, Frémont's work added significantly to the body of organized knowledge about the West.

John Charles Frémont. New York Public Library.

Frémont was the son of a French schoolteacher and a woman who had abandoned her elderly husband in Richmond, Virginia. Together the couple eloped to Savannah, Georgia, where John Charles was born in 1813. Talented, handsome, and strong-willed, he briefly attended Charleston College, from which he was expelled in 1831 for poor attendance. He next entered the navy, in which he taught mathematics, and then, in 1835, entered the service of the Topographical Corps of the United States Army, which had been created to survey and map the lesser known areas of the United States. In 1838 he was commissioned a second lieutenant. His first job was as assistant to Joseph Nicollet, one of the most highly respected topographers of the time, in an expedition to map the area between the upper Mississippi and Missouri rivers. The young Frémont later referred to his experiences with Nicollet as his "Yale College and Harvard."

Having returned to Washington, D.C., to help Nicollet prepare the report of the expedition, Frémont met and fell in love with Jessie Benton, the beautiful, intelligent, and strong-willed daughter of Senator Thomas Hart Benton of Missouri. When the senator refused to consider the penniless Frémont an acceptable suitor for his daughter, the two young people married secretly in 1841. Confronted with a fait accompli, the senator immediately put his new son-in-law to work for his own causes.

Benton was a strong supporter of the doctrine of Manifest Destiny, the belief that the United States had a right and an obligation to rule all of the land between the Atlantic and the Pacific oceans. At the time, Spanish Mexico was in firm control of both California and New Mexico, and the Oregon Territory was held jointly by the United States and Britain. However, Benton and other expansionists of the day were committed to wresting control of the West from Mexico and Britain. Realizing that their cause would be greatly aided by permanent American settlements in Oregon and California, the expansionists made the creation of such settlements their immediate priority. Frémont's role in this grand scheme was first to survey and map the unknown parts of the West so that Americans could emigrate more easily, and second to write glowingly of its attractions in order to attract settlers. The first of these tasks he performed competently; at the second—with the help of his talented wife—he excelled.

Frémont's first major expedition was a survey of the route from the Mississippi River to South Pass in the Rocky Mountains. (South Pass is a 20-mile-wide gap in the Rockies that allowed wagons to traverse the mountains.) This was the beginning of the Oregon Trail, the primary avenue of westward emigration at the time. On May 22, 1842, Frémont arrived in St. Louis to assemble his party. On the way west, he hired as a guide the famous mountain man Kit Carson, who was to be a lifelong friend and a guide on many of Frémont's expeditions. The party proceeded along the south fork of the Platte River to St. Vrain's Fort (in what is now Colorado) and then turned north to Fort Laramie (in present-day Wyoming). Ignoring rumors of hostile Indians, Frémont took his party west along the Sweetwater River and through South Pass. He then turned north to the Wind River Range. There he spied a peak that he concluded (wrongly) was the highest in the Rockies, and he decided he must climb it. Of the two eyewitness accounts of the event, the cartographer Preuss's is the less flattering, picturing a vain

and posturing Frémont barely making it to the top. Frémont's own account, on the other hand, is full of romantic bombast. The entire journey was characterized by such foolish romantic gestures, calculated more to excite admiration than to achieve lasting results. Running the canyons of the Sweetwater River, for example, Frémont lost all of the plant and mineral specimens his party had collected to that point.

Returning to Washington, Frémont went to work with Jessie to produce a masterpiece of exploration propaganda. Years later, one Joaquin Miller recalled how Frémont's report had affected him as an Ohio farm boy:

> I fancied I could see Frémont's men, hauling the cannon up the savage battlements of the Rocky Mountains, flags in the air, Frémont at the head, waving his sword, his horse neighing wildly in the mountain wind, with unknown and unnamed empires at every hand. . . . I was no longer a boy . . . now I began to be inflamed with a love for action, adventure, glory, and great deeds away out yonder under the path of the setting sun.

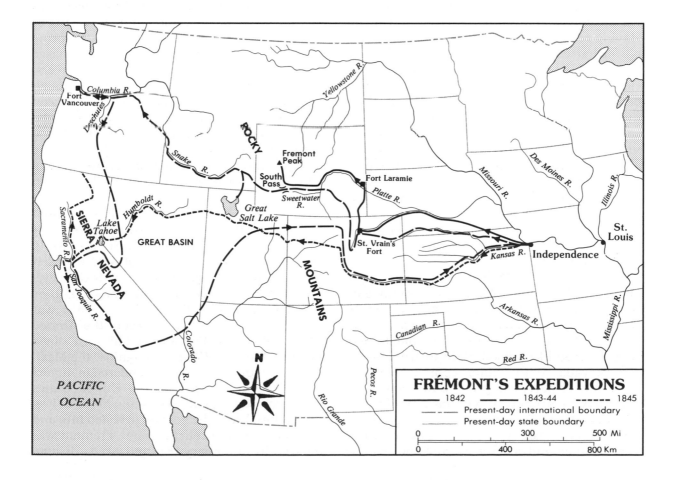

FRÉMONT'S EXPEDITIONS
——— 1842 ——— 1843-44 ------ 1845
––––– Present-day international boundary
––––– Present-day state boundary

In the spring of 1843, Frémont again headed west. This time his mission was to follow the Oregon Trail all the way to the Pacific Coast, carefully mapping it and laying out a road for emigrants. He was also instructed to gather details on the locations of campsites, wood, water, and Indian tribes and to collect information relevant to a series of proposed forts along the route. Leading a party of forty men, including Kit Carson, Frémont attempted to break a new trail by following the Kansas River rather than the Platte and crossing the mountains in what is now central Colorado. He then turned north and picked up the main trail at the Sweetwater River. On September 6, the party sighted the Great Salt Lake and, seemingly unaware that the lake had been thoroughly explored by mountain men, spent several days exploring its northern shore. Frémont's description of the area as a "bucolic region" well suited to settlement soon became instrumental in bringing Brigham Young and his band of Mormons into the area. Young was later to call Frémont's "bucolic" area a desert and to criticize his misrepresentation of the region.

From the Great Salt Lake Frémont proceeded via the Snake and Columbia rivers to Oregon. Having reached Fort Vancouver on the Columbia, he had completed his mission. But Frémont was not finished. On his own authority, he decided to march south to explore the country between Oregon and California and search for the Buenaventura, a mythical river that supposedly led to the Pacific. Although explorer BENJAMIN BONNEVILLE had already stated that the Buenaventura did not exist, it was still on the maps of the time. Frémont reasoned that if he could prove conclusively that there was no Buenaventura, there would be all the more reason for the United States to act quickly in assuming control of the Columbia River with its valuable outlet on the Pacific.

On November 25, 1843, he led his party south along the Deschutes River, and several days later the men arrived at the western rim of the Great Basin. Near Lake Tahoe (on what is now the Nevada-California border), Frémont found what seemed like a good place to cross the Sierra Nevada. With winter approaching, Frémont and his party trudged into the mountains. For thirty days they endured constant cold, hunger, and fatigue. Day after day, they broke trails through snowdrifts as deep as they were tall. Their Indian guides deserted, and one member of the party went mad from fear and exposure. But eventually Frémont led his men out of the mountains to Captain John Sutter's ranch on the American River. After resting there, the Frémont party followed the San Joaquin valley south and then crossed the mountains into the desert of the Great Basin (which Frémont was the first to formally identify and map), moving east over the trail established by JEDEDIAH SMITH and other mountain men ten years earlier. Near the Las Vegas meadows, they met JOSEPH REDDEFORD WALKER, who led them back east through some of the wildest and most barren country in North America. Back home, Frémont wrote another report of his travels, which also was received with wild enthusiasm.

In March 1845, Frémont was put in charge of another expedition. This time, he was to survey the Arkansas and Red rivers and to determine where they crossed the 100th degree of longitude, the supposed western border of the United States. A month after Frémont was given his assignment, the United States annexed the Republic of Texas, which had declared independence from Mexico just nine years earlier. The annexation had strong potential for precipitating war with Mexico, and Frémont seems to have plotted to be in the thick of things. Ignoring his orders and leaving someone else in charge of the project at the Red and Arkansas rivers, he blazed a new transcontinental route through the central Rockies and across the Great Basin to California. The presence of a band of armed Americans in Mexican territory was not taken lightly, and Frémont was ordered out of the province. After hoisting the American flag in a belligerent display, he retreated to the Oregon Territory.

A month later, he received a message from Washington, the contents of which have never been revealed. As a result, he hurried south to California, and when a group of American settlers declared independence from Mexico, Frémont supported them in what was later to be called the Bear Flag Revolt. Later, when war was officially declared between the United States and Mexico, Frémont and his men joined the army forces in California against the Mexicans. When the Mexicans surrendered in August 1846, General Kearney of the United States Army ordered Frémont to disband his unit. Frémont refused, and the general arrested him and sent him east for a court-martial. Frémont was found guilty in January 1848 and faced a dishonorable discharge. President Polk intervened and offered to let him stay in the army, but Frémont resigned, angered by the treatment he had received.

Frémont went on to make one more major expedition in the West as a civilian, but it was an unmitigated disaster. In 1848 he undertook a survey for Benton and others interested in promoting a transcontinental railroad. His task was to blaze a trail along the thirty-eighth parallel from St. Louis to San Francisco. Against all advice, Frémont decided to perform the survey and blaze the trail in mid-winter in order to prove the practicality of the route in any weather. In mid-December he headed into the heart of the San Juan Mountains in what is now southwest Colorado. With snow more than ten feet deep and temperatures as low as −20 degrees Fahrenheit, everyone suffered greatly. Ten members of the party died, and Frémont was forced to retreat to Taos, New Mexico. In typical fashion, he described the mission as a total success that proved the route was practical.

Frémont's later years were the antithesis of his early ones. Whereas success had previously clung to his every undertaking, in later life he became dogged by constant failure. Land he owned in California made him fabulously wealthy when gold was discovered there, but he then lost his fortune through mismanagement. He ran for president of the United States in 1856 on the ticket of the new Republican Party, but lost. During the Civil War he served the Union as a general until President Lincoln stripped him of his command. He died in poverty in 1890.

Whatever his late failures, John Charles Frémont played a major and vital role in the early expansion of the United States. Nicknamed "the Pathfinder," he mapped the route that eventually brought thousands of settlers to the West. Although many had contempt for his bombastic and self-important character, these traits were part of what enabled him to dream the dreams that brought him fame and glory and that led America westward.

SUGGESTED READING: Editors of Time-Life Books, *The Trailblazers* (Time-Life, 1973); Ferol Egan, *Frémont: Explorer for a Restless Nation* (Doubleday, 1977); Donald Jackson and Mary Lee Spence, eds., *The Expeditions of John Charles Frémont* (University of Illinois Press, 1970); Allan Nevins, *Frémont: Pathmarker of the West* (Ungar, 1955); Fredrika Shumway Smith, *Frémont: Soldier, Explorer, Statesman* (Rand McNally, 1966).

Frobisher, Martin

English
b 1540; Altofts, Yorkshire
d November 22, 1594; Plymouth
Discovered Frobisher Bay and Baffin Island

Sir Martin Frobisher was one of Queen Elizabeth I's most aggressive and enterprising **sea dogs**, feared by both the French and the Spanish for his **privateering**, and famous in English history for his crucial role in the battle against the Spanish Armada of 1588. His renown as an explorer derives from three expeditions to the waters of what is now northeastern Canada, where he attempted to find a northern passage to the Orient. Though his discoveries were promising enough to encourage later explorers to pursue his route to the Northwest Passage, his own backers became sidetracked by a tantalizing piece of fool's gold. Burdened by the task of directing the consequent mining operation, Frobisher never got the chance to discover that what he imagined to be an easy passage to China was merely a bay (now Frobisher Bay) of an island (present-day Baffin Island) at the beginning of a vast, ice-clogged **archipelago**. He was still far from the riches of China.

Frobisher was born to a Yorkshire family of gentry sometime around 1540. He went to sea in 1553 and did not return to play the role of the country gentleman until later in life, and then only briefly. His first trip was a hazardous but highly profitable commercial voyage—probably involving piracy—to Guinea (in West Africa) financed by London merchants and commanded by a Portuguese captain. Fewer than a third of the crew of 120 survived the heat and disease, but the conditions did not deter Frobisher from returning the following year. This time he survived a different sort of ordeal when he was captured by native Africans, then taken hostage by the Portuguese, who eventually released him.

Maturing as a mariner, he became a successful pirate, taking prizes from both the French and the Spanish. Occasionally he was arrested in England for these trade-disrupting activities, but he was never detained for long. This kind

Sir Martin Frobisher. Bodleian Library, Oxford.

declared this kind of business illegal, that Frobisher turned to less menacing affairs.

Apparently, while rubbing shoulders with the geographically savvy Portuguese on his early voyages, Frobisher had become fascinated with the idea of reaching the Orient via a Northwest Passage. He discussed the idea with the leading minds of England, including the mathematician John Dee. He may also have been influenced by Sir HUMPHREY GILBERT's *Discourse of a Discoverie for a New Passage to Cataia*, which circulated in manuscript for ten years before its publication in 1576. But this famous work of speculative geography, with its many arguments showing the probability of a passage above North America, mirroring the passage around South America at the Cape of Good Hope, merely restated ideas that were already common. It was an idea begging to be tested.

In fact, it had already been tested by JOHN CABOT, when he searched for a northwest passage at the end of the fifteenth century (though there is some doubt about where he landed). More recently, in 1534 the Frenchman JACQUES CARTIER had explored as far north on the American continent as the St. Lawrence River. By Frobisher's time, however, the true dimensions of North America were beginning to become clear, so that the passage to its north was no longer imagined to be short. It was also apparent that any passage would very likely extend into Arctic latitudes.

Geographers since PTOLEMY had believed that both the tropics and the Arctic regions were impossible to penetrate owing to extreme temperatures. But by Frobisher's time, successful voyages into the tropics had recently shattered that view of global climate. The theory developing in the sixteenth century was that the Arctic climate might be mild in the summer because of the continuous presence of the sun and that, in any case, the polar ocean—if there was one—would be too deep and agitated to freeze. This allowed for the hope that somewhere in the Arctic regions above North America there would be open sea.

The questions were, how far north was it and what would the ice conditions be? It was not until the nineteenth century that these questions were answered by Sir JOHN FRANKLIN (and by the search for him) and not until the twentieth that the passage was navigated by ROALD AMUNDSEN. Soon after Frobisher, however, JOHN DAVIS concluded that there could be no commer-

of terrorism was in fact useful to the English government in a period of growing hostility with Spain and unstable relations with France. In 1571 Queen Elizabeth rewarded his daring by providing him with a ship to serve in the government's campaign to subjugate Ireland. This did not stop his privateering, which he carried on as a kind of lucrative and dangerous sideline. It was only in 1573, after Elizabeth

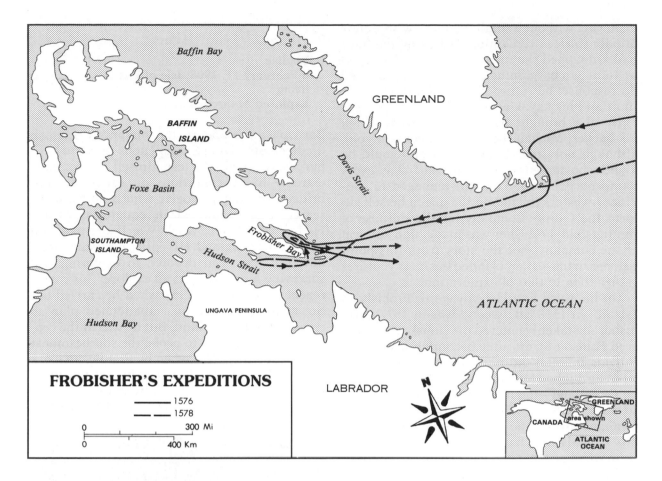

FROBISHER'S EXPEDITIONS

——— 1576
– – – 1578

0   300 Mi
0   400 Km

cially viable passage through the ice-clogged waters.

Frobisher's was the first well-documented attempt to try the northern waters west of Greenland for a Northwest Passage. The voyage's first leg, from England to Iceland, was difficult because land was out of sight for several days. West of Iceland, land is nearly always on the horizon, and the problem becomes maneuvering through the icebergs, fog, and ice floes, as well as the usual one of making it through storms. None of this proved too difficult for Frobisher, who made his way quickly back and forth to what is now Frobisher Bay on three separate occasions. The map he carried, however, was based on a misleading chart published by Nicolo Zeno in 1558 (see ANTONIO ZENO), and it created confusion in reporting his location to others.

After leaving the Shetland Islands in June 1576 with two ships, the *Gabriel* and the *Michael*, and a smaller **pinnace**, the Frobisher party soon ran into a storm in which the pinnace was lost. Soon afterward the remaining ships were separated and the *Michael* returned home,

turned back by heavy ice. With only eighteen crew members on the *Gabriel*, Frobisher pressed ahead until he reached the coast of Greenland, which he mistakenly identified as Zeno's imaginary "Frisland." After trying to land, he turned south to escape the fog and icebergs, only to hit a storm that turned the *Gabriel* on its side and filled it with water. Frobisher saved the day by cutting off the **mizzenmast**, an act that righted the ship.

After turning west again, the crew reached Frobisher Bay of present-day Baffin Island on August 11. Frobisher believed the large inlet was actually the start of a strait connecting the Atlantic with the Pacific. Soon he and his crew were in contact with the native **Inuit**, who warily engaged in some trading and eventually offered to guide the ship westward through the bay. Having lost two ships already, Frobisher was now about to lose the *Gabriel*'s boat along with five crew members. It is not clear from the records whether the sailors deserted or were somehow tricked into coming on shore by their prospective guides. In any case, they disappeared, and Frobisher felt he could not continue exploring without a small boat and with a crew of only thirteen remaining. Believing the Inuit had kidnapped the men, he in turn kidnapped an Inuit as a bargaining chip. When it produced no response, he returned to England with the Inuit and his kayak as a trophy.

He also brought back a heavy rock, which his backer, Michael Lok, took to contain gold, although only two assayers (testers) could be found who agreed. The queen's official assayers found no gold, but Lok still managed to convince investors (including the queen herself) to form the Cathay Company for the purpose of mining gold. Frobisher was made high admiral of the company, but the story from this point belongs to the history of failed business ventures rather than to that of exploration.

On his third and last voyage to Frobisher's "strait" in 1578 (the second was in 1577), Frobisher mistakenly entered previously undiscovered Hudson Strait after becoming lost in fog. But his mission did not allow him to explore what he dubbed Mistaken Strait. He also landed on Greenland—the first European known to do so since the Norse. There he found a settlement of abandoned tents, one of which contained a box of nails that had probably been salvaged from wreckage that had washed up on the coast.

The Cathay Company went bankrupt when the ore was finally found to contain no gold, so Frobisher turned again to privateering, first against the Dutch, then against the Spanish, in league with Sir FRANCIS DRAKE and under the protection of the English Crown. When these skirmishes escalated into war, the English navy had an exquisitely skilled sea dog in Martin Frobisher. Although he survived the battle with the Armada in 1588 (and was knighted for his brilliant work commanding the *Triumph*), he was mortally wounded six years later after heroically fighting off the Spanish at Brest, France.

SUGGESTED READING: William McFee, *Sir Martin Frobisher* (John Lane, The Bodley Head, 1928); Brendan Lehane, *The Northwest Passage* (Time-Life Books, 1981); Samuel Eliot Morison, *The European Discovery of America: The Northern Voyages*, A.D. *500–1600* (Oxford University Press, 1971); Frank Rasky, *The Polar Voyages* (McGraw-Hill Ryerson, 1976).

Fuchs, Vivian Ernest

English
b February 11, 1908; Isle of Wight
living
Explored Antarctica

Born on an island in the temperate English Channel, Sir Vivian Ernest Fuchs seems to have purposely sought to test himself in the most extreme living conditions on earth. A Cambridge-educated geologist whose doctoral research was conducted in equatorial Africa, Fuchs's work before World War II also took him to eastern Greenland. His entire postwar career, however, has been devoted to exploring and surveying Antarctica. As an explorer, his career reached a climax in 1957 when he carried out Sir ERNEST SHACKLETON's abandoned plan to cross Antarctica on land. But he was at the center of British efforts to probe the southernmost continent from 1947, when he first began work in the Falkland Islands, where he was the director of the Scientific Bureau from 1950 to 1955, until his retirement as director of the British

Sir Vivian Fuchs, upon his triumphant return to England from the Antarctic. UPI/Bettmann.

Antarctic Survey in 1973. The latter was a long-term effort involving over 1,200 people covering studies in biology, geology, mineralogy, glaciology, and meteorology.

Though Fuchs achieved Shackleton's basic plan, which was for one party to lay supply depots on a route to the pole from the Ross Ice Shelf while another proceeded to the pole from a base in the Weddell Sea, there was one major difference. Both explorers intended to use the best technology available, but the icebreakers, planes, snow tractors, heaters, and radios available to Fuchs—not to mention the comfortable American base at the pole itself—made his enterprise fundamentally different from anything Shackleton could have imagined in 1914. But then Shackleton had gone no farther than the Weddell Sea, where his wooden ship was crushed by the ice.

After nearly two years of advance work, Fuchs led his convoy of snow tractors from the Filchner Ice Shelf on November 24, 1957. The going was made slow by the unexpected depth of the sastrugi (ridges in the surface of the snow caused by the high winds). This led Sir EDMUND HILLARY, who had charge of the leg from McMurdo Sound, to panic and call for the postponement of Fuchs's final march from the pole to the Ross Sea. Fuchs, however, stuck to his plan, Hillary accepted the decision, and the two met at the pole on January 20, 1958. The rest of the 2,158-mile trip went off without a snag, and Fuchs reached Scott Base on March 2. He was knighted on his return to England.

Gaboto, Giovanni. See **Cabot, John.**

Gaboto, Sebastiano. See **Cabot, Sebastian.**

Galaup, Jean François de, Comte de La Pérouse. See **La Pérouse, Jean François de Galaup, Comte de.**

• Gama, Vasco da

Portuguese
b 1460?; Sines, Portugal
d December 24, 1524; Cochin, India
Explored Africa and India; opened up first European sea routes to East

When Vasco da Gama prepared to set sail for the Far East in the summer of 1497, many of

the people who came to bid his expedition farewell looked at his tiny fleet and despaired. Nine years earlier, two Portuguese **caravels** under the command of BARTOLOMEU DIAS had made a terrifying voyage around the horn of Africa, which they named the Cape of Good Hope. But when his fearful sailors had refused to go further, Dias was forced to turn back. Now, with four ships and approximately 170 men, Gama intended to build on Dias's accomplishment and press eastward—all the way to India. At the time, such a voyage was considered almost suicidal. But Gama's king, Manuel I, was determined to find a sea route that would give Portu-

Vasco da Gama. Museu Nacional de Arte Antiqua, Portugal.

gal access to the rich spices of the East. At the end of the fifteenth century, the Islamic nations of Asia Minor and Arabia controlled all the known overland and sea routes to Asia, and they had no love for Christian Europe. The only way to skirt their empire and reach India was to sail around Africa into the Indian Ocean. And no one in Europe knew how far that really was.

Even after he commissioned the expedition, Manuel acted as if he was not too optimistic that it would succeed. The quality of gifts chosen to be presented by Gama to the rulers of the East was poor, perhaps because the royal treasurers feared that the goods were likely to be lost at sea. Lisbon should have been less stingy, however. When the rajas of the Malabar Coast of southwest India saw what Gama had to offer, they were not impressed. Diplomatically, the expedition was to prove a failure. In almost every other respect, it was a resounding success. For the king of Portugal, who would become known to history as Manuel the Fortunate, the voyage was crucial in making his tiny nation into an international power. For Gama,

it brought wealth, influence, and a lasting place as one of the world's greatest maritime explorers.

Vasco da Gama was born about 1460 in Sines, a seaside town some 60 miles south of Lisbon. Little is known about his early life or his family, which was neither rich nor aristocratic but served with distinction in Portugal's wars against both its European and its Moorish enemies. The first mention of Vasco da Gama in contemporary records appears in 1492, when he received a government commission to seize French shipping in Portugal in retaliation for the confiscation of Portuguese property in France. Neither country wanted war, and the crisis was averted. Gama, who appears to have carried out his orders efficiently, is not mentioned anywhere again until his voyage to India.

Chroniclers differ on why he was chosen to head the important expedition. Some say his father, Estevao, was to command but died before the fleet was ready to sail. Others say the king chose him almost at random. In any event, Gama, a trained navigator and seaman, was given the job. His fleet consisted of two medium-

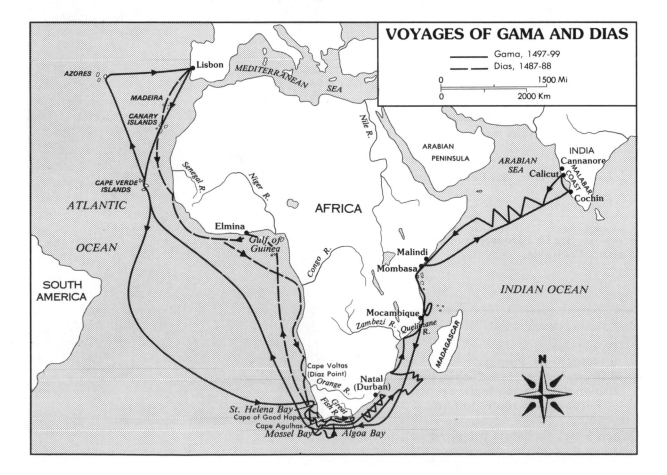

sized three-masted sailing ships—the flagship *São Gabriel* and the *São Rafael* (commanded by his brother Paul)—a smaller caravel called the *Berrio*, and an unnamed storeship. They were manned by experienced sailors, some of whom had accompanied Dias around the cape. The expedition also included interpreters (who spoke Arabic as well as Bantu dialects), a priest for each vessel, and several condemned criminals (who were to be assigned the dirtiest, most dangerous jobs).

On July 8, 1497, as the despairing onlookers commended the souls of Gama and his 170 men to God, the expedition set sail for Africa. The fleet reached the Canary Islands on July 15 and the Cape Verde Islands off the coast of northwest Africa on the twenty-sixth. There they rested for a week and repaired damage to the ships caused by foul weather. Then, on August 3, they set out for the unknown.

On the advice of Bartolomeu Dias, who had at first accompanied the expedition in a separate vessel bound for a Portuguese settlement on the African Gold Coast (in what is now Ghana), Gama avoided the continent's western coastline, with its dangerous offshore winds and currents. Instead, he bravely sailed into the unknown waters of the South Atlantic. As his ships crossed the Tropic of Capricorn, they were closer to Brazil than to Africa. Taking this circuitous route proved a wise choice, giving the fleet access to favorable winds and currents. In fact, the route pioneered by Gama was so efficient that it is still widely used by vessels sailing from Europe to Africa.

Nevertheless, sailing across the vast, unknown emptiness of the South Atlantic proved slow going. Days of torpid calm were punctuated with sudden, violent storms. Provisions ran low. Men began to sicken. The ships were out of the sight of land for ninety-six days, an unnerving amount of time in an era when most trade routes were rarely far from shore. Then, on November 7, the crews sighted the hills above St. Helena Bay in what is now South Africa.

There, Gama put ashore, pausing for a few days to clean the barnacles off the ships' hulls and to allow the crews to recuperate. The Portuguese traded trinkets for fresh food with the curious, seemingly friendly tribes of the area. Then one day, a sailor who had been invited to dine at a native village was seen running along the shore, pursued by an angry bushman.

He escaped, but in the skirmish that followed four Portuguese were wounded, including Gama, who was struck in the leg with an arrow. The reasons for the fight are not known, but it was an omen of future relations between Gama's crew and the people they were to encounter.

On November 16 Gama put to sea again. Battling head winds, the ships rounded the Cape of Good Hope four days later. On November 25 they anchored in present-day Mossel Bay, where they rested for the next thirteen days. There, for reasons that are not clear, Gama ordered the storeship destroyed, transferring provisions to the other vessels. (Historians speculate that the ship was dismantled because the Portuguese feared it would fall into the hands of an enemy.) The remaining ships set sail again on December 8, heading northeast. By late December they had passed what is now the Great Fish River that empties into Algoa Bay—the point where Dias and his men had turned back. Continuing along the coast, Gama put ashore on Christmas Day at a place he named Natal to commemorate Christ's nativity. Today the spot is the site of the South African port of Durban, in a province that still carries the name Gama gave to the region.

Proceeding north, the fleet reached the Quelimane River in what is now Mozambique on January 25, 1498. The people there were friendly, and Gama lingered for more than a month. After more than six months at sea, the mariners were weary, and many of them were sick with **scurvy**. During this brief respite, Paul da Gama won a reputation for kindness, generously sharing his personal medical supplies—an unusual act in an age of marked social indifferences between officers and men. But for many of the crew, his charity was to no avail. Historians are not certain how many died. All told, approximately two-thirds of those who sailed with Vasco da Gama did not return.

For the survivors, a major part of the great ordeal was over. They had conquered the South Atlantic and sailed through waters that Dias's men had been unwilling to explore. Now they were about to make their way northward along the East African coast toward territory that was relatively known. PÊRO DA COVILHÃ, a Portuguese explorer who had journeyed overland to India a decade earlier, had sent back reports that Arab vessels crossed the Indian Ocean and traded at Sofala and other African ports. He also wrote that he believed the land of Prester John, the legendary Christian king who ruled a fabulously wealthy kingdom somewhere in the East, lay in this region of Africa. Gama planned to sail along the coast and investigate these reports. His ships had already missed Sofala, which was south of Quelimane, but the ports of Moçambique (in present-day Mozambique) and Mombasa and Malindi (in modern Kenya) still lay ahead.

The three ships weighed anchor on February 28. On March 5 they sighted Moçambique. To this point they had passed along coastlands peopled by relatively unsophisticated tribesmen. Now they were entering a region of Arabic influence. At the time, the Arabs were undisputed masters of the Indian Ocean, waging a lucrative trade in slaves and other goods throughout the region. Therefore, in his relations with local populations who had had little if any previous contact with Europeans, Gama created the impression that he and his men were Muslims. At first, the Portuguese were courteously received by the local sultan. They tried to obtain all the information they could about inland Africa, its eastern coast, and the Arabian Sea. They were especially curious about the kingdom of Prester John. These inquiries made their hosts suspicious. Nevertheless, the sultan agreed to provide pilots to help them cross the Indian Ocean.

Then, by chance, the Portuguese encountered two Indian Christians, brought as captives from their native land. Noting the religious nature of the figureheads on the São Gabriel and the São Rafael, these Indians realized that the white mariners were fellow Christians. The sudden rapport between the Portuguese and the two slaves confirmed the Muslims' suspicions: the strange sailors were infidels. Fighting broke out between the local people and the Portuguese, perhaps because of religion, perhaps because the Portuguese seem to have behaved badly wherever they went.

On March 10 they were ordered to leave. Meanwhile, one of the native pilots deserted. The other was seized and held aboard ship while Gama, determined to capture the fugitive, took two boats and rowed toward shore. Suddenly, the Portuguese saw six boats loaded with heavily armed men bearing down on them, preparing to attack. Gama and his crewmen hurriedly returned to their vessels and sailed for the open sea. Over the next few days, though,

poor winds and currents forced them back toward shore. Low on water, they landed and became engaged in battle when they attempted to replenish their dwindling supply. In the skirmishing, several Muslims were killed, and the pilot who had escaped was recaptured. Finally, the winds improved and the ships were able to proceed up the coast.

The Muslim pilots were totally unreliable. When it became apparent that they were lying about the Portuguese fleet's location, Gama had them flogged. Another Arab, encountered in a dhow (a type of boat) at sea, was taken prisoner and tortured for information. But Gama's brutal methods would come back to haunt him. On April 7 his ships anchored in Mombasa, the finest harbor on the East African coast, where the local sheik gave him a friendly reception, sending a generous supply of fresh provisions. Gama remained suspicious. In return, he sent a string of coral beads, presented by two Portuguese convicts instead of the officers normally called for as a diplomatic courtesy. Nevertheless, the convicts were well treated. The next day, taking advantage of confusion created when two of the Portuguese vessels collided in the harbor, the two pilots jumped overboard and swam to safety. Enraged, Gama seized four Arabs who had been taken aboard earlier and ordered them to be tortured with "fire drops," a mixture of oil and resin brought to a boil and poured on their bare flesh. In excruciating pain, the hostages confessed that the sheik planned to attack. That night, Gama's watchmen saw Muslims swimming through the dark waters toward the São Rafael and the Berrio. The alarm was raised and the attackers beaten off. On the morning of April 13, the fleet fled.

Then Gama's luck began to improve. On the evening of April 14, he dropped anchor off Malindi, some 50 miles north of Mombasa. The local ruler, a rival of the sheik of Mombasa, saw the Portuguese as potential allies. He promised to provide a pilot to lead them across the Indian Ocean. In the Malindi harbor at the time were four merchant vessels from India, and there was much mutual curiosity between the Indians and the Portuguese. Curiously, the Indians, who were Hindus, thought the strange foreign men shared their religion. By the same token, the Europeans mistook the Indians for Christians. After a week of festivals and feasting, Gama grew impatient. He seized hostages and demanded that the sheik provide the pilot he had promised. His host proved as good as his word, providing an Arab named Ahmad ibn Majid, who was well acquainted with the sea route to India's Malabar Coast. On April 24 Gama's fleet left the shores of Africa, heading east. Twenty-three days later, they sighted land. On May 21 they anchored off Calicut.

The Malabar Coast was split into many petty states, both Muslim and Hindu. Calicut, one of the richest, was controlled by the Hindus. But the fifteenth-century spice trade was closely tied to the expansion of Islam. The Muslim traders, who had helped to spread their religion from the shores of Africa and India, were quick to see that the Portuguese threatened their monopoly. The ruler of Calicut, the zamorin or "Lord of the sea," was at first friendly to the mariners. Gama and his dirty, bearded crew, however, did not cut very impressive figures in this opulent court. The quality of goods the Portuguese offered to their hosts—cloth, hats, strings of coral, jars of honey—were regarded nearly as an insult by the zamorin's ministers.

Making matters worse, Gama was soon exposed as a liar. He had greatly exaggerated the size of his fleet, claiming that storms had separated his ships from many other Portuguese vessels. Arabian merchants, who had picked up intelligence about the Portuguese from their own vast commercial network, informed the zamorin that this claim was simply not true. News of the bad behavior of the Portuguese in Africa also filtered across the sea. To the officials and merchants of Calicut, Gama and his men seemed no better than pirates. Muslim intriguers offered the Hindus large bribes to destroy the Portuguese fleet.

Despite the tense situation, Gama managed to avoid disaster and even obtained a small store of spices to take back to Lisbon. In order to guarantee the safety of his men ashore, he took five hostages aboard his ships. At the end of August, having promised that they would one day return, the fleet set sail for home.

The return voyage was a nightmare. The ships battled the head winds of the Arabian Sea for three months. Scurvy killed thirty more of the crew. By the time the Portuguese reached Malindi on January 7, their three ships were dangerously undermanned. Gama ordered the São Rafael to be burned and its crew taken aboard the two other vessels. On March 10 the Berrio and the São Gabriel rounded the Cape of Good Hope. A month later, they were sepa-

rated in a fierce Atlantic storm. The São Gabriel, commanded by Gama, made it to the Cape Verde Islands. His brother Paul was close to death, perhaps from scurvy, and Gama sailed on to the Azores, stopping at the island of Terceira, where he hoped, vainly, that Paul would recover. Meanwhile, on July 10, 1499, two years and two days after its departure, the Berrio arrived in Lisbon. On September 9 Gama made a triumphal entry into the city. His voyage had set the stage for the rise of Portugal's empire. For Gama, the rewards were many—a lucrative annual pension, rich estates, and the title of dom (sir). The now-famous navigator apparently decided to settle down. Sometime between 1499 and 1502 he married Catarina d'Atayde, a noblewoman of whom little is known, who bore him six children.

Meanwhile, the Portuguese moved swiftly to consolidate their gains. In March 1500 Manuel commissioned PEDRO ÁLVARES CABRAL to lead a fleet of thirteen heavily armed ships back to India. Their outbound voyage was a disaster. An Atlantic storm swamped four of the ships, including one commanded by Bartolomeu Dias, drowning the crews. By the time the fleet reached Calicut, three other vessels had been lost. Cabral managed to ingratiate himself with the zamorin long enough to load his six remaining ships with cargoes of spices and other exotic goods; but he proved as high-handed as Gama in his treatment of the Muslims, and the general behavior of the Portuguese horrified Muslim and Hindu alike. Cabral established a trading "factory" or warehouse ashore. One day, without warning, the Indians attacked, killing fifty Europeans. In return, Cabral seized ten Muslim ships, appropriated their cargoes, and killed their crews. Then he sailed for home. The return voyage was uneventful. Although less than half the fleet made it back to Portugal, the expedition proved enormously profitable and was regarded as a great success. Many officials in Lisbon, however, felt that the Indians should be taught to respect the Portuguese. Gama was chosen as the perfect man to teach that lesson.

In February 1502 Gama, now known as Dom Vasco, Admiral of India, left Lisbon for India a second time, in command of a fleet that eventually comprised twenty ships. It was Portugal's largest, most heavily armed expedition to the East to date. Although its purpose was partially commercial, Gama had orders to punish the Africans and Indians who had been hostile to the Portuguese, to devastate Arab shipping, and to win control of the spice trade.

On the East African coast that summer, the Portuguese solidified their reputation for cruelty. On the island of Kilwa Kisiwani off what is now Tanzania, Gama exacted vengeance on the emir Ibrahim, who had been unfriendly to Cabral and had refused to accept Christianity. Gama threatened to kill the emir and burn his city if he did not pay a hefty ransom and swear allegiance to Lisbon. The emir complied.

Slowed by bad weather, the fleet sailed toward India, anchoring off Cannanore, where they lay in wait for Muslim ships. Their most infamous depredation was against the *Meri*, a merchant vessel carrying between 200 and 380 Muslim men, women, and children returning to India from a pilgrimage to Mecca. When confronted with the powerful Portuguese fleet, the sailors of the *Meri* realized that resistance was futile. They obeyed Gama's command to hand over their cargo. Then Gama ordered the Muslims down into the hold and set the *Meri* on fire. All aboard the vessel, with the exception of twenty small boys who had agreed to be converted to Christianity, died in the flames. This atrocity, perhaps Gama's most brutal, seems to have had no negative effect on the raja of Cannanore. He had been friendly to Gama on his first voyage and saw the Portuguese as allies against his rival, the zamorin of Calicut. When Gama arrived in Calicut, he demanded that the zamorin banish every Mohammedan from the city. To underscore his demands, Gama captured thirty-eight local fishermen, hanged them, dismembered the corpses, and threw them into the sea. The following day, his fleet bombarded the city. Leaving six ships to form a blockade, he sailed on to Cochin, where he concluded a trade agreement with the local raja. Meanwhile, an emissary from Calicut arrived, saying that the zamorin sought peace, but it was a trap. When Gama's ship anchored off Calicut, it was attacked but managed to fend off its assailants until additional Portuguese ships arrived to help. Returning to Cochin, Gama loaded his vessels with precious cargo. Then, on February 10, 1503, he sailed back to Calicut. Two days later, he engaged the Arab fleet. Though the Arabs fled, Gama gained no decisive victory. Now, with the holds of his ships full and the communities of the Malabar Coast more fearful than ever of Portuguese power, Gama

sailed for home. On October 11 he was back in Lisbon.

Gama had left a legacy of hate in India and Africa. In Portugal he was a hero and prepared to settle down to a life of luxury and ease. He returned to Sines, the village of his birth, but he quarreled with local religious authorities and was eventually ordered out of town. He also bickered with King Manuel. In 1519 the king had named him count of the city of Vidigueira. Gama seems to have been disappointed with the honor and, despite his achievements, fell from grace at court. In 1521 Manuel died and was succeeded by his eldest son, nineteen-year-old John III.

In 1524 King John sent Gama to India to rebuild morale and battle the corruption that had weakened Portugal's position there. In command of a fleet of fourteen ships, Gama left Lisbon for the last time on April 9, 1524. In early September, the fleet arrived on the Malabar Coast. Gama's reputation as a fierce disciplinarian preceded him, and his early efforts at reform were successful. But his administration did not last long. He fell ill and died on December 24, 1524.

Despite his ruthlessness and cruelty, Vasco da Gama's achievements were great. His courage, seamanship, and leadership were celebrated in *The Lusiads*, an epic poem of his exploits published in 1572 by Luiz de Camões. It is fitting that the story of his life would become one of his country's greatest literary classics, for he was, perhaps, its greatest explorer.

SUGGESTED READING: Richard Armstrong, *The History of Seafaring*, vol. 2, *The Discoverers* (Frederick A. Praeger, 1969); Henry H. Hart, *Sea Road to the Indies* (William Hodge, 1952); K. G. Jayne, *Vasco da Gama and His Successors* (Methuen, 1919).

• Garcés, Francisco Tomas Hermenegildo

Spanish
b 1741?; Aragon
d 1781; mouth of Gila River, Arizona
Explored southwestern United States

Fray (Father) Francisco Garcés explored the southwestern United States from southern Arizona to the Pacific Ocean, providing valuable knowledge of desert routes, mountain passes, and river courses for future use. With Captain JUAN BAUTISTA DE ANZA he established the first land route from Tubac, Arizona, to Monterey, California, thus creating a practical way for emigrants and traders to reach the Spanish outposts in California.

The exact date of Francisco Garcés' birth is not known, but from existing data it can be guessed to be around 1741. He came from Aragon, Spain, to Pimería Alta (what is now northwestern Mexico and southern Arizona) in 1768 to fill a vacancy created when the Jesuits were expelled. After rebuilding a plundered mission at San Xavier del Bac (near present-day Tucson, Arizona), he began his explorations in 1771. The Indians he befriended on his first journey referred to him as the "Old One," a term of respect, although he had barely turned thirty at the time.

On this initial trip Garcés headed north to the Gila River in Arizona, then west to the Colorado River. From the Yuma Indians he heard of other white men somewhere farther west. Deducing that it was the expedition of Don Gaspar de Portola and Father JUNÍPERO SERRA, which had started about two months earlier, he tried to make contact with them but got lost in the labyrinth of the Colorado River delta. After extricating himself, he pushed northwest and crossed the present-day Yuma and California deserts (first the present-day Mojave, then Death Valley) to the foot of the southern ridge of the Sierra Nevada. From there he could see two openings in the hazy blue mountains, which he felt might be passes through the mountains to the California missions. Fearing that he might not find water if he continued, Father Garcés returned to San Xavier del Bac.

Captain Juan Bautista de Anza, commandant of the presidio at Tubac (just south of San Xavier) and a close friend of Garcés, agreed that a route to Monterey in California should be sought by way of the openings Garcés had seen. After obtaining authorization from Antonio Bucareli, the viceroy of New Spain (present-day Mexico), Anza and Garcés left Tubac on January 8, 1774, with a party of about thirty-five men, a mule train, and cattle to slaughter for food. Garcés guided the expedition through the territory he had already covered and obtained the services of a Yuma Indian friend as guide for the remainder of the trip. The expedition party established a route from Tubac to Monterey without serious incidents.

In late October 1775, Garcés left Tubac again with Anza. They proceeded down the Santa Cruz and Gila rivers to the Colorado, where a cabin was erected at the site of modern-day Yuma, Arizona. Here Garcés and a companion remained and founded a mission among the Yuma Indians.

At the urging of the Spanish officials, Garcés then set out to open a route from New Mexico to the southern California missions. He traveled from the mouth of the Gila River up the Colorado River to present-day Needles, California. Then he crossed the Mojave Desert and arrived at the San Gabriel Mission near modern Los Angeles. Leaving the mission, Garcés headed north into the San Joaquin Valley, then returned to the Colorado River. He returned to the mission at San Xavier del Bac on July 2, 1776, after encountering some unfriendly Hopi Indians on the return journey.

Three years later Garcés returned to the mouth of the Gila River and helped found two missions among the Yumas. However, by 1781 the Indians had become dissatisfied, and they revolted, massacring Garcés, three of his companions, and some newly arrived settlers and soldiers.

Thus ended the career of one of the outstanding explorer-priests of the Southwest. Garcés' major contribution to exploration was the establishment of an overland route to link the Sonora province of New Spain and the Pimería Alta with the Spanish missions of upper California (what is now the state of California). Ironically, though he was killed by Indians, Garcés had maintained throughout his life a fine rapport with many Indian tribes and learned a great deal from them about the lands he explored. As a fellow priest said, "Father Garcés is so well fitted to get along with the Indians and go among them that he appears to be but an Indian himself. . . ."

Gilbert, Humphrey (Humfry)

English
b 1539?; Devon
d September 10, 1583; Atlantic Ocean
Led early expedition to Newfoundland

In the summer of 1583, Sir Humphrey Gilbert organized and led an expedition of five ships across the Atlantic in an attempt to establish a permanent British settlement on the Penobscot River (in present-day Maine). He landed first at Newfoundland, which he claimed for Great Britain, and then turned south. When one of his ships was wrecked near what is now Nova Scotia in late August, Gilbert was persuaded to return to England, vowing to return the next year to establish his colony. He died at sea on the return voyage.

A man of action—indeed of many actions—Sir Humphrey Gilbert was both a soldier (he was knighted for his part in the bloody crushing of an Irish rebellion in 1569) and a thinker. Among other ideas, he argued at court in 1566 for the existence of a Northwest (rather than northeast) Passage to the Orient (for a more complete discussion of the passage, see MARTIN FROBISHER). In 1576 he published a treatise argu-

Sir Humphrey Gilbert. The Bettmann Archive.

ing that British colonies should be established in the New World both for purposes of trade and in order to provide new job opportunities for unemployed Englishmen.

Since Gilbert was a favorite of Queen Elizabeth I, he took his ideas to court, where they were well received. On June 11, 1578, the queen granted him letters patent (what was later called a proprietary charter) allowing him to "discover, searche, finde out and viewe such remote heathen and barbarous landes countries and territories not actually possessed of any Christian prince or people." He was also granted the right to settle any lands between Labrador and Florida and to "take and surprise" any vessels trafficking in any harbor of the lands he settled.

Gilbert spent the summer of 1578 planning his voyage and trying to keep his destination secret from the Spanish, who would have loved to sabotage any English attempt to settle in the Americas. In fact, he succeeded so well in concealing his destination that even today historians are not sure where he intended to go. What is known is that an expedition of ten well-armed ships sailed out of Plymouth in November 1578 and that all of them had to turn back for various reasons before reaching North America. Thus Gilbert's first voyage, financed mostly with his own family's funds, was an utter failure.

Undaunted, he vowed to sail again. But in 1579 he was forbidden to do so after it was learned that some of his ships of the first expedition had engaged in piracy. In addition, he had to raise the money necessary for mounting his second expedition from outside sources. After trying without much success to sell his rights to the lands that he intended to settle, he ended up financing the second voyage with what remained of his own money and the additional backing of friends. This time his destination was not a secret. He intended to found a settlement near a city called Norumbega on the Penobscot River. In fact, Norumbega was a mythical city first reported by GIOVANNI DA VERRAZANO and JACQUES CARTIER. But Gilbert did not know that it did not exist.

Gilbert was delayed slightly when the queen forbade him to accompany his fleet, saying he was "a man of not good happ [luck] at sea." But when he argued with her, Elizabeth relented. On June 11, 1583, five ships carrying 260 men sailed from Plymouth Bay, taking the northern route across the Atlantic. They arrived on the Newfoundland coast July 30, and on August 5, 1583, at St. John's, Gilbert formally took possession of Newfoundland for the queen. (No one seems to have remembered that JOHN CABOT had already done this in 1497.) In the harbor as Gilbert took possession were fishing boats from Spain, Portugal, France, and England. But all was harmonious, and no one disputed Gilbert's right to promulgate laws and assign areas for the drying of fish. For two weeks Gilbert and his men feasted with the fishermen, sharing the meat the ships had brought and entertaining everyone with dancers who were aboard. As Gilbert was preparing to sail south, the captains of two of his ships pleaded sickness and refused to go farther, so only three ships sailed south on August 20. One was then wrecked in the shoals off Sable Island near Nova Scotia. Unfortunately, it was the ship carrying the metal samples mined in Newfoundland, which Gilbert hoped to use to persuade the queen to invest in another expedition.

The men on the two remaining ships were concerned about setting up a colony with winter coming on and persuaded Gilbert to turn back to England in the last days of August. On the return voyage, Gilbert remained aboard the smaller of the two boats even though it was overloaded with guns "for show" and thus was a risky vessel for an Atlantic crossing. North of the Azores, the ships ran into very rough weather, and on September 9, Gilbert's ship was nearly lost. However, later the same day, he was seen sitting on deck reading a book. He is said to have shouted to the other ship, "We are as near to heaven by sea as by land." It is assumed that he was reading Sir Thomas More's *Utopia*, which contains the passage, "The way to heaven out of all places is of like length and distance." Shortly after midnight, the lights of Gilbert's ship were seen no more; it had been presumably swallowed up by the sea with all on board lost.

Sir Humphrey Gilbert was a man of vision, one of the first Englishmen to see the importance of colonizing the New World for long-term as well as short-term profit. Unfortunately, he lacked the organizational skills to carry out his sound ideas. For example, both of his voyages started too late in the year to have any hope of establishing a viable colony before winter. Nonetheless, though he did not live to see his ideas reach fruition, Gilbert pointed the way

to New England and Virginia for British colonization. In fact, not long after his death, his half brother, Sir WALTER RALEIGH, took up the torch, sending the first British colonists to what is now North Carolina.

Giles, Ernest

Australian
b July 20, 1835; Bristol, England
d November 13, 1897; Coolgardie
Crossed Australia

An adventurer who loved exploration for its own sake, Ernest Giles made several forays into the interior of Australia and was the first to traverse the continent from east to west and back again. In so doing, he crossed two of the most inhospitable stretches of desert on earth.

Born in England in 1835, Giles was educated

ERNEST GILES,
The Australian Explorer, Born 1835.

Ernest Giles. Bettmann/Hulton.

at Christ's Hospital in London and joined his parents in Adelaide, in South Australia, in 1850. He spent several years working the gold fields and doing clerical jobs in Melbourne until 1861, when he was hired to seek out new grazing lands. For the next four years he surveyed lands past the Darling River.

In 1872 Giles and five others left the town of Charlotte Waters in an attempt to cross the continent along the overland telegraph line, intending to reach the Murchison River, 1,000 miles to the west. Although Giles did not meet his goal, he did discover the **monoliths** known as Mount Olga, a palm plant believed to be 2,000 years old, and the River Finke.

He tried again the following year with Alfred Gibson, an illiterate with no experience in the bush. Together they explored the desert west of the Petermann Range, but Gibson became lost in the sand (Giles subsequently named the desert after him). When Giles emerged from the desert bearing a forty-five-pound water keg that he had carried for 60 miles, he spotted a small, dying baby wallaby. He later wrote, "The instant I saw it, I pounced upon it and ate it, living, raw, dying—fur, skin, bones, skull and all."

In December 1873 John W. Lewis beat Giles to the west coast, and the following year John Forrest became the first to cross the continent from west to east. Nevertheless, Giles set out to cross the continent on May 6, 1875, with Henry Tietkins as his second in command; Saleh, an Afghani camel driver; an **aborigine** named Tommy; and twenty-two camels. The group left Port Augusta on Spencer Gulf and crossed the southern reaches of the Great Victoria Desert, reaching Perth in mid-November, having crossed 2,500 arid miles in five months. At one point, they crossed a stretch of 330 miles without water.

After a brief rest, Giles left Perth on January 13, 1876. The same team accompanied him, with the exception of Tietkins, who was replaced by Alec Ross. Their route took them north of their first crossing and across the Gibson Desert. Along the way they were attacked by hordes of flies and stinging ants, and Giles lost his sight. They finally reached the telegraph station at Peake on August 23, 1876. Of his feat, Giles wrote, "Exploration of a thousand miles of Australia is equal to ten thousand miles in any other part of the earth's surface, always excepting Arctic and Antarctic travel."

His accomplishment was recognized throughout the world, with the exception of his adopted homeland, where he was ignored because he had found no grazing lands. Giles died of pneumonia while working as a clerk in the gold fields in 1897.

• **Goes (Cooes), Bento de**

Italian
b 1562; San Miguel
d April 11, 1607; Jiuquan, China
Explored India and China; established that China and Cathay were same country

Bento de Goes was a restless adventurer, a one-time mercenary who became a Jesuit novitiate, an ambassador for the Mogul khan Akbar the Great, and an explorer of China. His five-year journey along MARCO POLO's route into China was motivated by two mysteries: the issue of the lost Asian Christians and the identity of the country of Cathay.

Bento de Goes was a traveler from the start. While still a very young man, he went to India as a mercenary. He became interested in the Society of Jesus, became a novitiate, then changed his mind and ran off to Hormuz, in the eastern Persian Gulf. Within several years, however, he decided to join the Jesuits as a lay brother and went to Lahore (now in Pakistan) with Jerome Xavier, great nephew of SAINT FRANCIS XAVIER, on the third Jesuit mission to the Moguls. There, the missionaries began to hear intriguing reports of Christian practices in western Tibet—perhaps these were the Christians led by the mythic Prester John (for a more complete discussion, see PÊRO DA COVILHÃ). Interest began to grow in sending an expedition to find these people and to solve the puzzle of whether the country called Cathay nearly 300 years earlier by Marco Polo was in fact China.

While he was in Lahore, Goes earned the confidence of Akbar the Great, the Mogul khan, who asked him to mediate a dispute between the Moguls and Portuguese settlers on the Deccan plateau of central India by meeting with the Portuguese viceroy at Goa. The efforts of Goes impressed the superior of the Jesuit mission at Goa, Father Pimenta, who was in charge of all the Asian Jesuit missions. As a result, Pimenta selected Goes to lead an expedition to central Asia to find the lost Christians and to settle the question of Cathay.

In 1602 Goes departed for Cathay, disguised as an Indian named Banda Abdullah, his prayer book wrapped carefully inside his turban. He was accompanied by two Greeks and an Armenian. This adventurous foursome traveled to Lahore and then to Kabul (in present-day Afghanistan), where the two Greeks quit the expedition. Undaunted, Goes continued east through what is now Afghanistan, across the desert to the frontiers of China. Along the way, he met a group of merchants from Cathay who said they knew MATTEO RICCI, a Jesuit missionary who had traveled to China with an earlier mission, and the merchants had papers in Portuguese from Ricci to prove it. This evidence enabled Goes to certify that Cathay and China were the same and that a large unknown area lay north of the known regions of India and China. He would discover nothing else, however, for he died of exhaustion in the Chinese frontier town of Suchow (present-day Jiuquan).

James Grant (right), with John Hanning Speke. Library of Congress.

• Grant, James Augustus

Scottish
b April 11, 1827; Nairn
d February 11, 1892; Nairn
Explored East Central Africa, searching for source of Nile

James Augustus Grant was second-in-command of the exploration team that discovered the source of the Nile River. Recruited for the second interior expedition of JOHN HANNING SPEKE, Grant was in charge of part of it for long periods when the group had to be divided. He is credited with collecting valuable data on the geography and cultures of East Africa and Uganda. After the sudden death of Speke, Grant undertook the task of defending the controversial findings of his friend and colleague.

Joining the British army while still in his teens, Grant served for eleven years in India, where he met and befriended Speke. After being discharged, Grant returned to England to recuperate from battle injuries suffered during the siege of Lucknow (India). Three years later he was invited to join Speke's expedition. The purpose of the expedition, sponsored by the Royal Geographical Society, was to obtain proof of Speke's theory (developed during his previous explorations with RICHARD FRANCIS BURTON) that Lake Victoria was the source of the Nile.

Traveling northwest from coastal Zanzibar, the team reached Tabora (in present-day Tanzania) in 1861 and proceeded north to circle the western perimeter of Lake Victoria. An infected leg forced Grant to remain nearby in Karagwe while his commander continued on to the Nile. Grant was not present, therefore, when Speke actually found the Nile's outlet from Lake Victoria in July 1862. He rejoined Speke at the Nile the following month, and they proceeded north, arriving in Gondokoro in the Sudan in February of 1863.

The two explorers earned lavish praise for their accomplishments when they returned to England, although their claim to have discovered the Nile's source was vehemently challenged by Speke's former collaborator Burton. Grant received a gold medal from the Royal Geographical Society and in 1864 published a comprehensive account of his travels entitled *A Walk Across Africa*. Grant became the expedition spokesman following the death of Speke in September 1864, and subsequent trips by other explorers ultimately validated Grant's position regarding the Nile's source. Grant was considered a leading Africanist, and he returned to the continent in 1868 for a year-long post with British military intelligence in Abyssinia (now Ethiopia). He was also an official British delegate to the international conference on Africa in Brussels in 1876 and served on the Royal Geographical Society's council for many years prior to his death in 1892.

Gray, Robert

**American
b May 10, 1755; Tiverton, Rhode Island
d Summer, 1806; at sea off east coast of United States
Explored northwest coast of North America, including Columbia River by ship; circumnavigated twice**

Between 1787 and 1793, Robert Gray made two trading voyages from Boston, Massachusetts, around Cape Horn to the Pacific Northwest and back by way of China. On his first voyage, he became the first American to circumnavigate the globe. On his second, he sailed his ship into the mouth of what became the Columbia River when he named it after his vessel.

Robert Gray. Oregon Historical Society.

After serving in the Continental Navy as a young man during the American Revolution, Gray joined a Massachusetts trading company. In 1787 six merchants agreed to outfit two ships for a voyage to the northwest coast of North America. The larger ship, *Columbia,* was captained by John Kendrick; Gray commanded the *Lady Washington.* Their object was to trade with the Indians of the northwest coast for highly desirable sea otter pelts and then to take the cargo of furs to China to trade them for tea. The tea, in turn, was to be sold at a profit back in Boston.

The two ships set off from Boston in the autumn of 1787 but became separated in heavy storms while rounding Cape Horn. Gray eventually landed in what is now Oregon for fresh water and for berries to fight the **scurvy** from which many of his men were suffering. He reached Nootka (an island off Vancouver Island that was the center of sea otter trading) in September 1788, eleven months after leaving Boston. Reunited by this time, Gray and Kendrick built huts on the shore and waited out the chilling rains of winter. In the spring Gray traded industriously for sea otter pelts, becoming more and more annoyed at Kendrick's lack of drive. Eventually Kendrick transferred command of the *Columbia* to Gray, and on July 30, 1789, Gray headed home by way of China. There he traded for tea, although not to his advantage, being new at the business. Nonetheless, Gray returned to Boston in triumph on August 10, 1790, having traveled almost 42,000 miles; he was the first American captain to sail his vessel around the world. While not lucrative in itself, his venture had revealed to Boston merchants a new source of riches.

After a scant month ashore while the *Columbia* was being refitted, Gray went to sea again in September 1790 and arrived at present-day Vancouver Island in June 1791. He was carrying a letter of instructions signed by both President George Washington and Secretary of State Thomas Jefferson that warned him not to enter any port held by the Spanish, who controlled the area, nor to trade in Spanish territory. Nootka, where Gray had traded two years before, was the scene of conflict between the Spanish and the British, and Gray, following his orders, steered clear of the profitable trading center. Instead, he traded at various points up and down the coast, reaching as far north as the large cluster of islands off what is now the southern tip of Alaska and as far south as present-day Oregon.

When winter approached, Gray dropped anchor 12 miles up Clayoquot Sound, not too far from Nootka, and built another ship, the *Adventure*, for use in trading the following spring. When spring arrived, the *Adventure* sailed north to trade, and Gray took the *Columbia* south. Competition among traders was keen, and Gray was looking for a new sound or river mouth where Indians unused to trade might accept lower prices for their furs. He was aware that several years earlier the Spaniard BRUNO DE HEZETA had noticed a major river but had been unable to get past the bar to explore it. Hezeta's discovery appeared on Spanish maps, and for seventeen years explorers had sought the river mouth in vain. Near the end of April, Gray found what he was looking for. At a latitude of 46°10' North he felt the strong currents and saw the churning water that are signs of a river mouth. However, those currents and the violent surf kept him from crossing the dangerous bar that led into the river. So on April 28, he sailed north and dropped anchor.

While Gray was contemplating his next move, two British ships under the command of GEORGE VANCOUVER approached the *Columbia*. Upon learning that it was commanded by Gray, Vancouver sent two of his crew to board the ship. Before leaving England for his surveying expedition of the Pacific coast of America, Vancouver had read a book by a Captain John Meares stating that Nootka Sound was not, as Captain JAMES COOK had claimed, situated off the mainland but rather was located off a large island (as it in fact is). As proof of his contention, Meares cited the claim of a Captain Robert Gray of Boston that he had sailed entirely around what is now called Vancouver Island, proving that it was not attached to the mainland.

Vancouver was eager to verify this report with its alleged author. Gray was astonished to learn of the fame he had attained through Meares's book but had to report that Meares's claim was completely false. Gray admitted that in 1789 he had sailed part way up the Strait of Juan de Fuca (between Vancouver Island and Washington), but finding the trading unsatisfactory, he had turned back. Modern historians suggest that Meares was probably not lying outright. One of Gray's crew members later reported that Gray had told Meares that he had sailed around the island and discovered the Northwest Passage because he knew Meares was fascinated with the quest for the passage and would pursue this lead, thus removing himself from the competition for sea otter pelts for a while (for a more complete discussion of the Northwest Passage, see MARTIN FROBISHER). Whether or not Gray had lied to Meares, he did have some exciting—and truthful—news to tell Vancouver's emissaries. Never one to keep a secret, he told them all about the river he had recently discovered. Surprisingly, they exhibited no interest in this information.

After the visit from Vancouver's ship, Gray sailed north and entered the harbor that now bears his name on the coast of present-day Washington. But, unable to forget the unmistakable signs of the mighty river that he had seen, he soon sailed south again. On the morning of May 11, 1792, Gray carefully guided the *Columbia* across the treacherous sand bar into "a large river of fresh water, up which we steered" and promptly named the river after his ship.

Gray sailed up the Columbia about 25 miles, but, although local Indians swarmed to the ship, trading was disappointing, and after about ten days, he left his great "discovery," never to return.

When the season's trading ended, Gray headed again for China and returned to Boston on July 20, 1793, having circumnavigated the globe for the second time. He married in 1794 and from then on confined his sailing to the Atlantic coast of America. He is presumed to have been buried at sea after dying of yellow fever in 1806.

Robert Gray's discovery of the Columbia River was of monumental importance to the history of the United States. Before Gray's explorations the Pacific Northwest was hotly disputed between Britain and Spain. Because of Gray—as well as MERIWETHER LEWIS and WILLIAM CLARK, who followed up Gray's discovery by approaching the Columbia from the east on foot in 1805—the United States ultimately had a strong claim to the Oregon Territory, from which the states of Oregon, Washington, and Idaho would eventually be carved.

Greysolon, Daniel, Sieur Dulhut. See **Dulhut, Daniel Greysolon, Sieur.**

Groseilliers, Médard Chouart, Sieur de

French
b 1621 or 1625?; Charly-Saint-Cyr
d 1696; Trois-Rivières, Québec
Opened up Hudson Bay to fur trade

A fur trader by profession, Médard Chouart, Sieur de Groseilliers, was also an entrepreneur who knew a good idea when he had one. From his travels around Lake Superior in search of beaver pelts, he eventually surmised that the best furs came from an area between Lake Superior and Hudson Bay. In partnership with his brother-in-law, PIERRE ESPRIT RADISSON, Groseilliers formulated the idea that gave rise to Britain's Hudson's Bay Company.

Médard Chouart arrived in **New France** in his late teens and by 1646 was serving as a lay assistant at a Jesuit mission to the Huron Indians near Georgian Bay. Having learned the Huron language, he soon gave up mission life for fur trading and eventually settled down on an estate near Trois-Rivières, Québec, which he named Groseilliers (Gooseberry Bushes) after his family's farm in France. In 1653 he married the widowed half-sister of Pierre Radisson. History does not comment on the success of the marriage, but the partnership of brothers-in-law seems to have been made in heaven. Radisson was the fast-talking promoter and salesman; Groseilliers was the steady organizer.

On a fur-trading expedition north of Lake Superior (and possibly to the upper reaches of the Mississippi River) between 1659 and 1660, Groseilliers and Radisson heard from the Indians of an area between Lake Superior and Hudson Bay that was rich in beaver. Returning to Québec from the trip laden with furs, the two were fined for trading without a license rather than praised for finding a new source of furs. Indignant at this treatment, the partners took their business and their ideas to England in 1666.

From 1668 to 1669 Groseilliers led a fur-trading expedition to Hudson Bay for England. The success of the undertaking was the impetus for the formation of the Hudson's Bay Company, which is still in existence.

Groseilliers worked for the Hudson's Bay Company until 1674, when he and Radisson switched their loyalties back to France. When France rewarded their fur-trading efforts in 1683 with high taxes, Groseilliers retired in disgust. He died at Trois-Rivières in 1696.

Although Radisson produced the written record of their exploits and received the lion's share of the publicity, historians agree that Groseilliers's contributions were equal to if not greater than those of his partner.

Hadley, John

English
b April 16, 1682; Hertfordshire
d February 14, 1744; East Barnet, Hertfordshire
Invented double-reflecting quadrant used to determine locations at sea

By the year A.D. 150, the Greeks—specifically ERATOSTHENES, HIPPARCHUS, and PTOLEMY—had developed and refined a system of latitude and longitude lines that could be used to locate places on the earth. The problem, of course, was that these lines were not on the earth's land and sea surfaces, but on maps. Over a thousand years passed before MARCO POLO reported that sailors in the Indian Ocean estimated their latitude and longitude by observing northern stars. John Hadley's eighteenth-century invention of the double-reflecting **quadrant**, a forerunner of the modern **sextant**, made it possible for sailors to measure their location much more precisely.

Hadley used his skill as a mathematician to further the cause of exploring both the heavens and the earth. He improved the reflecting telescope invented by Sir Isaac Newton, constructing in 1721 the first telescope powerful enough to be useful for astronomic observation. More important for explorers, he invented his quadrant in 1730. (Thomas Godfrey of Philadelphia invented a quadrant that same year, working independently.) Hadley's quadrant enabled mariners to measure the altitude above the horizon of the sun or a certain star. To use a quadrant, a navigator would sight a known celestial body along one of the instrument's sides. The angle of elevation above the horizon was indicated by a plumb line, which hung from the upper corner of the quadrant and crossed a curved arc marked in degrees. Consulting a star chart, the navigator then converted the degrees of their altitude above the horizon into degrees of latitude. For those times when fog or clouds obscured the horizon, Hadley attached a level to the quadrant, allowing accurate readings to be taken regardless of the weather.

Hadley's quadrant was a significant advance in navigational technology. But the constant motion of a ship at sea made it difficult to obtain accurate measurements. The sextant, a later, much-improved version of the quadrant, was easier to use and even more accurate. However, navigators were not able to calculate longitude with anywhere near the same precision until the invention of the first accurate **chronometer** by JOHN HARRISON. As a result, ships of Hadley's day often used his quadrant to sail first to the latitude of their destination, then east or west at that latitude until they made their desired landfall.

• Hakluyt, Richard

English
b 1552; London?
d November 23, 1616; London
Compiled accounts of great Elizabethan explorations

Richard Hakluyt never left Europe, but almost everything known of the great Elizabethan explorations is due to his painstaking efforts as an anthologist and geographer. He was a rigorous scientist and scholar in an age when many of his peers mixed fact with sensational fantasy in order to titillate a gullible readership ready to believe almost anything about the newly discovered lands across the seas. His efforts were by no means easy. Spain, England's great rival for control of the high seas, was protective of its new colonies and often reluctant to share information about them. Nevertheless, as chaplain to the English ambassador in Paris, Hakluyt functioned as a kind of intelligence officer, combining tact, diplomacy, and the persistence of a skilled reporter in obtaining firsthand information from voyagers fresh from the New World. His work had tremendous political influence in pushing his tiny island-nation toward overseas exploration and eventual empire. But his prose would prove even more enduring than the empire. His three-volume work, *The Principal Navigations, Voyages and Discoveries of the English Nation*, is still considered one of the classics of English literature.

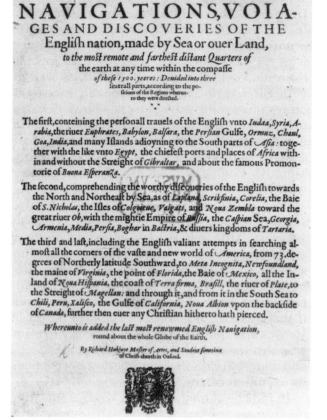

Title page of Hakluyt's *Voyages*, published in 1589. Hulton-Deutsch Collection.

Hakluyt was born in or near London in 1552 (the exact date is unknown) to a large, well-to-do family, possibly of Welsh origin. The Hakluyts had ties to English nobility and the emerging mercantile class. Hakluyt's father, Richard, was a London merchant. Of his mother, Margery, little is known. His father died in 1557 and his mother soon afterwards. Young Richard was placed under the protection of a cousin (some sources say uncle), also named Richard, a lawyer with a keen interest in geography. The young Hakluyt graduated from Oxford in 1574, earned a master's degree three years later, and was ordained in the Church of England. Although he would remain an active clergyman all his life, Hakluyt devoted himself primarily to geography. Indeed, he became the first academic to give formal lectures on the subject at Oxford.

As a young man, he corresponded with the

leading international authorities on geography, including Gerardus Mercator, the great Flemish cartographer, and Abraham Ortelius, the Dutchman who compiled the first modern atlas. In London, Hakluyt conversed regularly with prominent mariners. He was well acquainted with Sir FRANCIS DRAKE, who returned in 1580 from his voyage around the world, as well as with Sir MARTIN FROBISHER and Sir HUMPHREY GILBERT, seagoing adventurers who were eager to find a Northwest Passage through North America to the East. Hakluyt also kept close contact with the captains of Great Britain's Muscovy Company, which had begun trading with Russia.

Among his earliest literary work were two small volumes on the discoveries in North America. Although British efforts to discover a Northwest Passage were doomed to fail (for a more complete discussion, see Martin Frobisher), Hakluyt firmly believed that the continent must be explored for its own sake, even if there existed no easy sea route to the East. He was also quick to see that the secret to overseas wealth was not mining gold, as the Spanish had done, but establishing a network of colonies for commercial trade.

In 1582 he published *Divers Voyages Touching the Discovery of America*, in which he urged Britain to forcefully expand its interests in the New World. Two years later, at the insistence of Sir WALTER RALEIGH, he published a book privately, the *Discourse on Western Planting*, in which he urged the Crown to support overseas colonies.

In 1583 he was appointed chaplain to the British ambassador in Paris, Sir Edward Stafford. In this position he had much opportunity to learn about the explorations of other countries, particularly France, which, like England, had explored much of northern North America in its quest for a Northwest Passage. But Spain, not France, was Britain's great rival, and when war broke out with Spain, Hakluyt returned to England in 1588. That same year, Drake defeated the Spanish Armada off the English coast, putting an end to the threat of invasion and severely damaging Spain's naval power.

Hakluyt continued to work on his masterpiece, *The Principal Navigations, Voyages and Discoveries of the English Nation*, which he finished by 1600. By then an important influence at court, he was given a clergyman's post at Westminster, where he would be within easy reach of Queen Elizabeth I and her ministers.

He continued to collect and edit material on British voyages and the accounts of foreign travelers. He died on November 23, 1616, and was buried in an unmarked grave in London's Westminster Abbey, the honored resting place of so many of the great British writers.

Hall, Charles Francis

b 1821; Rochester, New Hampshire
d November 8, 1871; northwestern Greenland
Explored Canadian Arctic; attempted to reach North Pole

Inspired by the Arctic adventures of ELISHA KENT KANE, and convinced that he might still be able to find survivors of Sir JOHN FRANKLIN's lost expedition, Charles Francis Hall sold his small newspaper in 1859, left his family in Cincinnati, and arranged for a whaler to take him to the Arctic. Though he made important discoveries during his seventeen years (often alone) as a full-time Arctic explorer, it was his total immersion in **Inuit** life, made possible by his guides Tookolito and Ebierbing, that distinguished him and made his book, *Arctic Researches, and Life among the Esquimaux* (1864), of unique value.

It was Ebierbing's grandmother who led Hall to his first discovery when she told him a story about what he soon realized must have been the expedition of MARTIN FROBISHER to Baffin Island almost three centuries earlier. In the summer of 1861 the Inuit led Hall directly to the spot where Frobisher had set up his gold mine.

Unable to convince a whaler to take him to King William Island, the site of the Franklin disaster, Hall spent the next year seeking artifacts of the Frobisher expedition, amassing a valuable collection that has since mysteriously disappeared.

He returned home in 1862 and began planning a second expedition to King William Island. Impressed by the accuracy of the information the Inuit retained without the aid of writing, he was certain they would be able to describe the fate of Franklin's ships (the *Erebus* and *Terror*), point him to written records, and perhaps even lead him to survivors.

On his venture of 1864–69 he gathered both stories and artifacts from the Franklin expedition, but he found no written records and no sign of survivors. His romantic notion of the

Inuit was also shattered when he learned that one group had merely watched as the party of starving white men straggled slowly to their deaths.

Hall's last foray into the Arctic as captain of the government-funded *Polaris* was as remarkable for its achievements as for its problems. In August 1871 he sailed with a contentious crew up Smith Sound, which separates Greenland and Ellesmere Island, reaching 82°16′ North latitude on August 30. After a **sledge** journey to the end of the Greenland ice sheet, he discovered what became known as Hall Land, a green sweep of land full of wildlife. He then crossed Kennedy Channel and sledged north 200 miles farther than had Kane. When he returned to the ship, he fell ill and died within two weeks. (He may have been murdered, but the evidence is inconclusive.)

His crew immediately decided to return home, but in the summer the ice broke up so suddenly that half were stranded on the floe. Once again, it was the four Inuit members of the stranded party who made survival possible for the ten others by hunting, cooking, and building snow houses. When the world learned of their astounding 1,300-mile drift to Labrador, however, little attention was paid to the role of the Inuit. Today it is easier to see that Hall's expeditions achieved as much as they did only because he was wise enough to take advantage of the guidance so generously provided by his Inuit companions.

• Hanno

Carthaginian
b 500 B.C.?
d ?
Explored Africa

Hanno was the leader of a massive colonizing expedition that took thousands of Carthaginians to western Africa during the sixth century B.C. The only surviving account of the voyage contains factual errors about the areas explored, and historians have questioned both the accuracy of the incidents and the size of the expedition it recounts. Nevertheless, the report provides reliable evidence that Hanno and his people traveled a substantial portion of the western coastline, founded a number of communities there, and conducted some trading.

Apparently a prominent citizen of Carthage (an ancient Mediterranean civilization), Hanno is said to have led a sixty-vessel expedition of 30,000 men and women from that Phoenician colony to what is now Morocco, where several Carthaginian settlements had already been established. Rendered vulnerable by recent conflicts with the Greeks in nearby Sicily, the people of Carthage were eager to increase their land holdings along the coast. They also hoped to open up new trading opportunities.

Sailing through the Strait of Gibraltar, Hanno and his party established the city of Thymiaterion, later renamed Kenitra (in present-day Morocco), and built a temple at what later became known as Cape Meddouza. Among the five other communities founded in the area was the Carian Fortress, presumed to be the modern coastal community of Essaouira because of the archaeological remains discovered there. Farther south, the explorers established the community of Cerne, which served as a trading post and was apparently somewhat successful judging by contemporary reports of gold trading between Carthaginians and native inhabitants of the area. While it is not certain where Cerne was located, it is suspected to have been on modern Hern Island, at the mouth of the Río de Oro in Western Sahara.

Hanno and his people apparently explored south of Cerne, but the account of their travels becomes more unclear at this point. They may have proceeded to present-day Senegal—a river they observed was most likely the modern Senegal River—and on to present-day Guinea, or even farther, to Sierra Leone. Hanno and the Carthaginian travelers may even have ventured as far south as modern Cameroon, based on the streams of fire they reported seeing, which they described as a "Chariot of the Gods." If this fire came from a volcano, then the explorers had arrived either at Mount Cameroon or at Mount Kakoulima, farther up the coast in Guinea.

While some trade was conducted by Carthaginian settlers, none of their new colonies attained any lasting commercial importance. The Romans, who took control of that portion of coastal Africa after Carthage fell three centuries later, never conducted trade in the area, probably because it did not appear profitable.

The story of Hanno's expedition was immortalized in a manuscript translated from the

Punic to Greek in the tenth century A.D. and known as the "Periplus of Hannon." The voyage was confirmed by independent reports or references to Carthaginian exploration or trade on the western coast of Africa, such as an account written by HERODOTUS OF HALICARNASSUS that mentions gold trading between the Carthaginians and coastal tribes during that era. (However, some historians argue that no such voyage ever occurred.) The size of the expedition was never substantiated by any independent source and is suspected of being highly exaggerated. The number of settlements founded also remains uncertain since most are neither specified in more than one report nor verified by archaeological remains. Hanno's account also contains what appear to be inaccuracies, notably reporting the Lixus (now Larache) River as being to the south of Cape Meddouza. This confusion may be the result of difficulties with translation, although many historians suspect that some of the confusion was deliberate. They suggest that such misstatements are characteristic of the Carthaginians, who were somewhat paranoid and fiercely competitive in matters related to trade and therefore likely to publicize misleading information in order to confuse their rivals.

• Hargraves (Hargreaves),
Edward Hammond

English
b October 7, 1816; Gosport
d October 29, 1891; Sydney, Australia
Discovered gold in New South Wales, Australia

Edward Hammond Hargraves is credited with the discovery of gold along the Summerhill Creek in New South Wales, Australia. This event sparked a gold rush that tripled the continent's population to more than 1½ million people within a decade.

Hargraves was born in England in 1816. As a young man he joined the merchant marine and reached Australia at the age of sixteen. After a short stay on land, he returned to the sea on a ship headed for the Torres Strait, between Australia and New Guinea, to hunt tortoises for their shells.

The young seaman grew to be a big, burly man with a taste for adventure. In 1848, lured by the promise of gold, he left his home in New South Wales and headed for California. In his two years there, Hargraves convinced many fellow Australians to join him, despite the fact that he found no gold during his entire stay. Still, he *had* learned to use a pan and cradle to sift the river bottom for gold nuggets, and he suspected that he could put his skills to work back in Australia.

The quartz outcroppings and gullies of California gold country reminded Hargraves of the terrain he knew west of the Blue Mountains near Bathurst, northwest of Sydney. In 1850 he returned to Australia with his theory, but those he told laughed and "treated my views and opinions as those of a madman."

On February 12, 1851, Hargraves rode along the Summerhill Creek, a tributary of the Macquarie River, with John Lister, an innkeeper's son who served as a guide. Hargraves felt that he was "surrounded by gold"—and he was. Four of every five pans produced the shiny nuggets.

Back in Sydney, Hargraves offered to sell officials the location of Ophir, his goldfield, for £500, and in May the papers announced his find. By May 24, 1,000 prospectors worked the Summerhill Creek, and more men poured over the mountains every day. Lumps of gold worth £200 were common. In fact, so many people came to the region to seek their fortunes that labor became scarce and wages rose elsewhere in the country. Hargraves's discovery was followed by even richer finds in Victoria.

In 1855 Hargraves published *Australia and Its Gold Fields*. He was subsequently appointed commissioner of Crown Land and granted £10,000 by the legislature of New South Wales. He died in 1891, having opened the floodgates of Australian settlement with the magical lure of gold. His claim to be the first discoverer of gold in Australia is disputed. What is not in doubt is the impetus his find gave to the subsequent gold rush.

• Harrison, John

English
b March 1693; Foulby, Yorkshire
d March 24, 1776; London
Invented first accurate marine chronometer

John Harrison, the son of a Yorkshire carpenter, used his considerable mechanical skills and dogged persistence to overcome a major obstacle to world exploration. Over a period of thirty-five years, Harrison built a series of four increasingly accurate marine **chronometers**, the last of which enabled navigators to calculate their longitude to within 10 miles. For his efforts, Harrison was awarded a prize established by the British government to encourage development of an accurate means of finding longitude.

Determining longitude (the measure of east and west) at sea was always more difficult than finding latitude (the measure of north and south). JOHN HADLEY's double-reflecting **quadrant** of 1730, a prototype of the modern **sextant**, enabled navigators to accurately measure the angle of major celestial bodies above the horizon. With this information, they could determine, nearly exactly, their latitude. But to calculate longitude, navigators needed to know what time it was in Greenwich, England (the site of the Royal Observatory), when it was noon aboard ship. The difference in time would then tell them how far east or west they were of the prime meridian, the meridian of 0 degrees longitude passing through Greenwich. But the constant motion of a ship and the continual changes in temperature at sea made weight- or pendulum-driven clocks highly inaccurate. A series of maritime disasters prompted the British government in 1714 to offer a substantial reward of £20,000 to "such person who shall discover longitude at sea." The winner was required to determine the longitude of a ship within 34 miles at the end of a six-week voyage—dictating a timepiece accurate to within three seconds per day, better than the best pendulum clocks of the day.

Harrison began his work in 1728 and completed his first chronometer seven years later. It was not accurate enough to win the prize, however, so he returned to his workshop, supported by an interest-free loan from a famous London instrument maker. Twenty-seven years later, Harrison completed his famous No. 4 Timekeeper, which was found to have lost only 1¼ minutes of longitude after a nine-week voyage to Jamaica. Even though Harrison had fulfilled the requirements for the prize, political wrangling involving Sir Isaac Newton, then head of the Royal Society of London and an opponent of clock-based chronometers, delayed Harrison's receipt of all the money due him until 1774, twelve years after the Jamaica test. Nevertheless, Harrison had succeeded in developing an accurate instrument for determining longitude—a major advance in the history of maritime navigation. Captain JAMES COOK, who used a licensed copy of Harrison's prize-winning No. 4 on his second voyage (1772–75), called it "our never-failing guide" and "trusty friend." Both the original chronometer and Cook's copy are now located in the National Maritime Museum in Greenwich, England.

Hartog (Hartogzoon), Dirck (Dirk)

Dutch
b ?
d 1600s
Sighted western Australia

A navigator for the Dutch East India Company, Dirck Hartog was the first European to set foot on the west coast of Australia. It was a discovery made entirely by accident.

In the early years of the seventeenth century, navigators for the Dutch East India Company reached the Orient via the route established by the Portuguese. From the Cape of Good Hope at the southern tip of Africa, they would sail northeast to Madagascar, then past the Seychelles to the Maldives, off the coast of India. They would then sail east, skirting Sumatra, to their Indonesian outpost at Batavia (present-day Jakarta) on the island of Java. In 1611 the Dutch captain Hendrick Brouwer discovered that navigators could save time by sailing due east from Africa's cape for approximately 4,000 miles, then heading north to Java. This alternative route enabled ships to take advantage of the **westerlies** and the southeastern **trade winds**. Sometime after 1611 this became the standard route for the Dutch.

In January 1616 Hartog left Amsterdam with a Dutch East India Company ship, the *Eendracht*, bound for Bantam, a trading post on Java. By the end of August he reached the African cape and took an eastern heading. Like the others who followed Brouwer's route, Hartog could only estimate when to sail north, as early seventeenth-century navigators had no way to measure longitude. Hartog consequently sailed too far east, and, on October 25, 1616, he landed at what he described as "some islands" at a latitude of approximately 26° South.

Hartog came ashore on one of several islands that stretched across the mouth of a large and complex bay with a number of narrow capes. What he saw in the distance was the west coast of present-day Australia, on the far side of Shark Bay. He and three members of his crew spent three days on the island, which appeared to be uninhabited. Before they left, Hartog took a pewter plate and inscribed their names and the date of their visit, then nailed the plate to a post. (In 1697 another Dutch voyager, Willem de Vlamingh, found the plate while he was surveying Australia's west coast from the Swan River north to the North West Cape. It is now held by the Museum of Amsterdam.)

Hartog reached Java in December 1616 by way of Makassar (now Ujung Pandang) on the southwest coast of Celebes (in present-day Indonesia). To get there, it is assumed that he sailed north along the Australian coast to roughly 22° South latitude. Unfortunately, no journal of his voyage survived, and Hartog faded into virtual anonymity. However, soon after word of his discovery reached Java, the correspondence of the Dutch East India Company begins to refer to "Eendrachtsland," a name derived from that of Hartog's ship. On a company map drawn by Hessel Gerritz and dated 1627, this region stretched some 300 miles from what is now the North West Cape south to 28° South latitude just below Shark Bay. It is not known how much of this coast Hartog actually saw.

Following Hartog's discovery, the Dutch East India Company required that all Dutch ships sailing to the East Indies use Brouwer's route. As a result of this mandate, a number of navigators touched upon the shores of western Australia, most notably Frederik de Houtman, a senior officer with the company. Some believed that these explorers came upon the same stretches of coastline as Hartog had, but in those days measurement of latitude was imprecise at best. Also, reefs and shoals kept ships from coming too close to land. It was not until François Pelsaert's 1629 voyage that anyone would make a continuous journey along Australia's west coast to complete the map that was begun after Hartog's discovery.

He, Zheng. See **Zheng He.**

Hearne, Samuel

English
b 1745; London
d November 1792; London
Reached Arctic Ocean overland from Hudson Bay

After two unsuccessful attempts, Samuel Hearne accomplished one of the most remarkable overland journeys ever made in North America. On the third try, engaging a Chipewyan Indian named Matonabbee as his guide, Hearne spent eighteen months on a round-trip journey from what is now Churchill, Manitoba, on the western shore of Hudson Bay to the mouth of the Coppermine River on Coronation Gulf of the Arctic Ocean. In doing so, he became the first European to reach the Arctic Ocean by an overland route.

Samuel Hearne entered the Royal Navy at the age of twelve and served until 1763. Three years later he joined the Hudson's Bay Company, a band of adventurers and profit seekers licensed by the English Crown to develop the fur trade of Hudson Bay. For some time the

Samuel Hearne. Library of Congress.

company had been under attack for not fulfilling its charter commitment to explore as well as to trade. This pressure, coupled with rumors of rich copper mines in the remote northwest, prompted the company's directors to act.

In 1769 Hearne's superior, Moses Norton, recommended him to lead an overland expedition to discover the location of the rumored copper mines and to seek that elusive prize, the Northwest Passage to the Orient (for a more complete discussion of the passage, see MARTIN FROBISHER). Accordingly, Hearne set off from Fort Prince of Wales (now Churchill, Manitoba) on November 6, 1769, accompanied by two company servants and two Cree Indians. A group of Chipewyans, the hardy nomadic tribe that roamed the northern reaches of the continent, happened to depart at the same time. Three weeks later and 200 miles from the fort, the Chipewyans stole Hearne's food supply and departed, "making the woods ring with their laughter." Largely on the sheer strength of his will to survive, Hearne managed to bring his party back to the fort, arriving on December 11.

Within three months, the explorer was ready to try again. This time he spent nine months almost entirely in the barrens northwest of the fort, a desolate landscape that extends across the top of North America. At its southern end are evergreens and dwarf spruce, but to the north there is only gravelly soil amid spongy moss so difficult to walk on that explorer R. A. J. Phillips once said that doing so was like trying to wade through "porridge sown with razor blades."

Over this inhospitable terrain Hearne managed to make a huge figure eight reaching as far north as the lakes east of the Thelon River and as far west as Dubawnt Lake. There the explorer broke his **quadrant** and the next day had his gun and other possessions stolen by a group of Chipewyans who had attached themselves to his party. Lost and lacking supplies for the oncoming winter, Hearne trudged south for three days, desperately trying to keep himself from succumbing to the cold and starvation. Then on the horizon appeared salvation, a Chipewyan known as Matonabbee, of whom Hearne was later to say, "I have met with few Christians who possessed more good moral qualities, or fewer bad ones."

Matonabbee led Hearne back to Fort Prince of Wales and suggested that he serve as Hearne's guide in the future. After two weeks at the fort, Hearne slipped away and joined Matonabbee's extended family. Placing himself entirely in their hands, he traveled west and then north with them, following the caribou herds and feasting on such Indian delicacies as caribou stomachs and raw musk ox but declining to join the Chipewyans when they dined on the lice from their own heads. Hearne's survival of this difficult journey has been credited largely to his adoption of the Chipewyans' way of life and movement.

The group stayed within the forest belt as long as possible before striking off into the barrens. Eventually Matonabbee and Hearne left the main group of women and children behind and with a reduced band went on toward the Coppermine River. For this last leg of the journey, they were joined by a mysterious band of Indians who they eventually realized were bent on a massacre of the Indians' traditional **Inuit** enemies. Matonabbee's group was unwillingly drawn into this conflict, and on July 17 a brutal attack occurred at a spot Hearne subsequently named Bloody Falls. While Hearne stood by helpless to prevent the slaughter, one Inuit woman twined herself around his legs while her attackers plunged spears into her.

After this gruesome incident, the small remaining party proceeded to the copper mine, where four hours of searching produced only one sizable chunk of copper. Hearne's superiors, like so many Europeans in America, had fallen victim to the Indians' penchant for telling Europeans what they wanted to hear. The trek to the shore of the Arctic Ocean was no less disappointing. At the mouth of the Coppermine River on Coronation Gulf, Hearne realized that this was no Northwest Passage, since the Arctic Ocean was still frozen there in July.

Returning south, the party picked up the women and children and made its way across Point Lake and MacKay Lake into the forest, reaching the Great Slave Lake on December 24. Hearne and his group were back at Fort Prince of Wales on June 30, 1772, having been away eighteen months and twenty-three days.

Hearne served the Hudson's Bay Company for many more years, including a term as governor of Fort Prince of Wales, beginning in 1775. During the American Revolution, French troops under the command of JEAN FRANÇOIS DE GALAUP, COMTE DE LA PÉROUSE, attacked and captured the fort. Hearne—and his journals—were taken prisoner and sent to France. La Pérouse, already an accomplished geographer and soon to become a significant explorer himself, eventually arranged for Hearne's release on the condition that he publish his journals describing his travels. He returned to what is now Churchill in 1783, where he remained until ill health forced him to return to England in 1787. He died in London in 1792; his journals were published posthumously in 1795.

By his own account, Samuel Hearne's achievements fell mainly into the realm of disabusing people of mistaken notions. He showed that the company's scheme to establish copper mines in the north was founded on myth rather than reality, and he proved that there was no Northwest Passage through Hudson Bay. More lasting than what he did or did not discover was his detailed description of life among the Chipewyans under the extreme conditions of the northern barrens. His *Journey from Prince of Wales's Fort in Hudson's Bay to the Northern Ocean* is still considered a classic work in the literature of exploration.

Heçeta, Bruno de. See **Hezeta, Bruno de.**

Sven Hedin. Bettmann/Hulton.

• Hedin, Sven Anders

Swedish
b February 19, 1865; Stockholm
d November 26, 1952; Stockholm
Explored Central Asia (particularly Tibet and western China) and Middle East

Sven Anders Hedin was the man who quite literally put vast unknown regions of central Asia on the map. During more than forty years of travels, he systematically explored the far reaches of what is now Soviet and Chinese Turkistan; the barren, wild deserts of northwestern China and Mongolia; and the rugged Himalaya Mountains that girdle India, China, and Tibet. The breadth of his achievements is staggering: he was the first Westerner to find the sources of India's holy rivers, the Indus and the Brahmaputra; the first to chart vast stretches of the Takla Makan and Gobi deserts, where he uncovered ancient cities buried beneath the sands; and the first to locate Lop Nur, the fabled "Wandering Lake" of what is now China's northwest-

ern Xinjiang province. He was also the first to explore and map the unknown mountains between India and Tibet, now known as the Hedin transhimalayan range.

Hedin was born in Stockholm to a prominent family that traced its roots to the seventeenth century. Though not of royal blood, the Hedins were well acquainted with the royal house of Sweden. Hedin's father, Ludvig, was the official city architect of Stockholm, where two of his uncles held high posts in the civil service and a third, Svente Hedin, was a famous actor and friend of King Carl XI.

As a youth, Hedin showed a keen interest in geography and exploration. He was a good, well-rounded student with a yen for physical exercise, a penchant for sketching and mapmaking, and an ability to put whomever he was talking to at ease. At the age of twenty, he was hired as a private tutor to the son of a Swedish engineer living in the city of Baku on the Caspian Sea in what is now the Soviet Union. There he was able to put his gift for languages to good use, learning to speak Persian and Tartar as easily as he already spoke German, French, and English. When his year as a tutor ended, he traveled extensively throughout the kingdom of Persia.

Returning to Europe, Hedin attended Uppsala University in Sweden, then continued his studies in Germany, where he was befriended by Baron FERDINAND VON RICHTHOFEN, perhaps the greatest expert of the day on Asian geography. Hedin also published a book about his travels in the Middle East, the first of some thirty volumes he was to write.

In 1890 he was asked by the Swedish government to act as interpreter to a delegation of diplomats to the court of the shah of Persia in Tehran. When the brief mission ended, Hedin, who had attracted the favor of Sweden's King Oscar II, received government funding to explore central Asia. This, his first official expedition, took him to the cities of Tashkent, the capital of Russian Turkistan, and Samarkand, a major station on the ancient Silk Road mer-

chant route across Asia and the Middle East. Then, in a brutal winter trip, Hedin crossed the Pamir range between the Himalaya and Tian Shan mountains, reaching Kashi, the westernmost city of China. The trek produced no great discoveries, but it familiarized him with the merciless terrain and prepared him for the grueling trials that were to come.

Hedin returned to Europe in March 1891 to complete doctoral studies in Germany. Then, backed once more by a Swedish government grant, he set out on a journey that was to yield the first of his great discoveries. In late January 1894, Hedin departed Russian Turkistan with three servants to cross the Pamirs and return to Kashi. It was another bitter trek of several months over the "roof of the world." The mountain ice was treacherous, and the party almost got lost in the raging snow. But the trip won Hedin the respect of the Kirghiz tribesmen who were his guides. They admired the young Swede for his courage, humor, and generosity. They were also awed by the foreigner's unusual talents. Once across the mountains, the men took

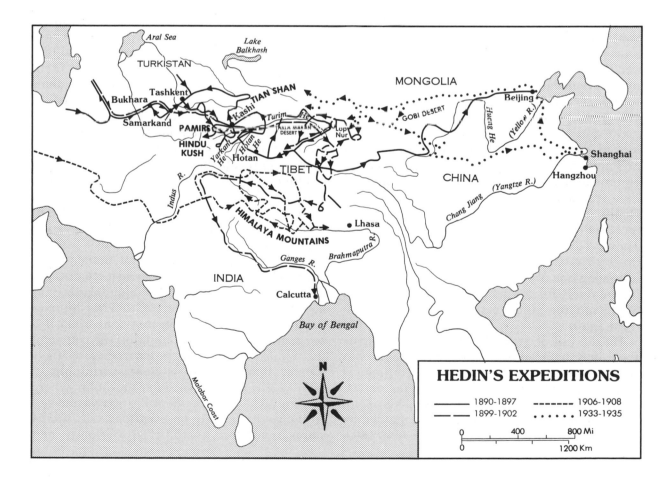

HEDIN'S EXPEDITIONS

——— 1890-1897   - - - - - - 1906-1908
— — — 1899-1902   · · · · · · 1933-1935

0   400   800 Mi
0   1200 Km

a rest on the Pamir plateau by the shores of Lake Karakul. Here, to their amazement and delight, Hedin built and sailed a small sailboat, the first they had ever seen.

Hedin had come determined to explore the Takla Makan Desert. Stretching through what is now China's Xinjiang province into Mongolia's Gobi Desert, the Takla Makan is girdled by three rivers: the Yarkant He in the west, the Hotan He, some 150 miles to the east, and the Tarim He to the north. At the end of the nineteenth century, the Western world knew little more about this arid region than it did when Marco Polo skirted its rim more than six centuries earlier. The people who lived along the Yarkant He told legends of great sandstorms that had buried ancient cities. They believed that the desert was an evil place, where malevolent spirits bewitched unwary travelers and led them to their deaths.

On April 10, 1895, Hedin left the banks of the Yarkant He accompanied by his three servants (Islam Bai, Kassim, and Mohammed Shah), a local guide called Yolchi, and several camels and other animals. As the party headed into the desert, tearful natives pleaded with them not to go. Within two weeks, the tiny caravan began to run out of water. By May 1 not a drop was left. The men slaughtered a sheep and tried to drink the animal's blood, which quickly congealed in the heat. The camels began to die. Men and animals drifted apart. Hedin and Kassim stayed together, crawling over great sand dunes toward the horizon and what looked like trees. They knew that any sign of greenery would mean that they were near the Hotan He. Their vision was not a mirage. When they reached the trees, Kassim collapsed, but Hedin struggled on and stumbled into the water. He drank deeply and then revived Kassim. They rested by the riverside and soon linked up with Islam Bai. He had saved himself by following one of the camels, which had headed instinctively for the nearest water. Mohammed Shah and the guide Yolchi were never heard from again.

By the fall of 1895, the survivors had made their way back to Kashi. Reprovisioned with supplies and new geological and meteorological instruments to replace those lost in the desert, Hedin was determined to get on with his exploration of the Tarim He basin. Accompanied by Islam Bai, Hedin set off again in December 1895, stopping first in the oasis city of Hotan. Not far from there they uncovered relics of a 2,000-year-old Chinese town. Then, following the Tarim He, Hedin eventually reached the shallow body of water called Lop Nur. By mapping ancient riverbeds, Hedin determined that this was the "Wandering Lake" referred to in ancient Chinese records. His calculation suggested that the changing physical geography of the region caused the lake to shift back and forth in the desert. Subsequent scientific investigation was to prove him correct.

By April 1896, the expedition was back in Hotan, having covered more than 1,200 miles. But Hedin had another great trek in mind; he was going overland to Beijing. Along the way he charted parts of northern Tibet and western China so remote that even tribes of the regions had no name for them. Heading on by camel through the southern part of the Gobi, Hedin made a triumphant entry into Beijing, capital of China. He had won the admiration of the Western world. (His faithful servant Islam Bai was not forgotten either—King Oscar awarded him a gold medal.)

In 1899 Hedin set out again for central Asia. First, he returned to western China to make additional surveys of the Tarim He basin. There his party unearthed the ancient city of Lou-lan, which had flourished 1,800 years earlier. Then, in 1901, Hedin disguised himself as a Mongolian monk and tried to enter the forbidden Tibetan city of Lhasa. But the ruse was discovered and officials of the Dalai Lama, the spiritual leader of Tibet, arrested Hedin and ordered him out of the country. Disappointed, he made his way to India and eventually back to Sweden.

Hedin was still to have one more great trek of discovery, which led him back to India in 1906 to explore the Himalayas. Much of the region had never been mapped, but it was believed to contain the sources of India's great rivers. The quest led him back and forth through the rugged mountains in India and Tibet that now bear his name—the Hedin Transhimalayas. He spent two years in that dangerous, frozen region, tracing and mapping the course of the Indus and Brahmaputra rivers to their sources. It was one of his greatest triumphs.

In 1908 Hedin returned to Stockholm, where he continued to write about his travels and scientific and political observations. He was a staunch admirer of Imperial Germany and wrote enthusiastic books about the kaiser's army on the Middle Eastern and Russian fronts during World War I.

In 1926 Hedin joined an expedition to central Asia sponsored by the German airline Lufthansa, which was interested in establishing an air route to China. Although the project faltered, the Chinese government asked Hedin to remain in Asia to make a detailed map of the old Silk Road. Although he was now nearing the age of seventy and China was torn by civil war, he completed the project in 1935 before returning to Sweden.

As a neutral country, Sweden did not take sides during World War II, but the Swedish government used Hedin as an unofficial ambassador to Berlin. Although he himself had some Jewish ancestry, Hedin kept ties with the Nazis, whom he supported because of their war against communist Russia. Through his influence, Hedin was able to save the lives of a few Jewish friends and Norwegian resistance fighters. However, his association with the Third Reich was a blot on his career. He died in Stockholm at the age of eighty-seven.

SUGGESTED READING: John Lennox Cook, *Six Great Travellers* (Hamish Hamilton, 1960); Sven Hedin, *My Life as an Explorer* (Garden City Publishing Co., 1925); George Kish, *To the Heart of Asia: The Life of Sven Hedin* (University of Michigan Press, 1984).

• Hennepin, Louis

Belgian
b May 12, 1626; Ath
d 1705?
Explored upper Mississippi River

Father Louis Hennepin was the first European to describe Niagara Falls in detail and to see the upper reaches of the Mississippi River. His claim to have traveled all the way to the mouth of the Mississippi before RENÉ ROBERT CAVELIER, SIEUR DE LA SALLE, is not generally accepted.

After serving numerous ministries in Europe, the Recollet friar Louis Hennepin was finally given an outlet for his missionary zeal and adventurous nature when King Louis XIV of France asked the Recollets to send five missionaries to **New France**. Hennepin was one of those chosen, and in 1676 he took up duties at a mis-

sion on Lake Ontario. In 1678 he was informed that he was to accompany La Salle on his explorations. On December 8, 1678, Hennepin, with an advance group that was instructed to build a fort and a ship on the Niagara River, reached Niagara Falls, which the priest described as "the most beautiful and altogether the most terrifying waterfall in the universe."

From August 7, 1679, to February 29, 1680, Hennepin traveled with La Salle. After the construction of Fort Crèvecoeur on the Illinois River, La Salle sent Hennepin and two others as an advance party to the Mississippi. Hennepin claimed that between February 29 and March 25 the three men canoed to the mouth of the Mississippi and that by April 10 they had returned—an altogether impossible feat given that it would have constituted a journey of more than 3,000 miles.

On April 11, the three men were captured by a Sioux war party in thirty-three canoes. Their lives were spared when they offered the calumet (peace pipe) and gifts. After traveling up the Mississippi, the party marched for five days to a Sioux village in the Thousand Lakes area of present-day Minnesota. During his captivity, Hennepin studied the customs and language of the Sioux.

In August 1680 the priest went with an Indian hunting expedition to the Wisconsin River. There he was discovered by the French explorer DANIEL GREYSOLON, SIEUR DULHUT, who demanded his release. The Frenchmen spent the winter at Michilimackinac (where Lake Michigan empties into Lake Huron) and in April 1681 set out for Québec. The same year Hennepin sailed for France, where he wrote a celebrated and exaggerated work about his travels. For reasons still unknown Hennepin fell into disgrace with church and political authorities. The last years of his life are unknown to history.

• Henson, Matthew Alexander

American
b August 8, 1866; Charles County, Maryland
d March 9, 1955; New York City
Explored Arctic with Robert Edwin Peary

Born into poverty and, as an African-American (of Ethiopian descent), destined to live the life

Matthew Alexander Henson. The Bettmann Archive.

of a second-class citizen in America, Matthew Alexander Henson began his professional relationship with ROBERT EDWIN PEARY as a valet while Peary was a surveyor for the U.S. Navy in Nicaragua. By the end of their twenty-three-year association, Henson had become the moving force behind the actual execution of Peary's historic polar expeditions. When Peary was asked by racist skeptics why he had taken a "Negro" to the North Pole rather than a "reliable witness," he acknowledged Henson's mastery of navigational techniques. He went on, however, to claim that Henson's racial inferiority prevented him from leading a supply party and that "reliable" whites therefore had to be used for this job. The fact that Henson knew navigational techniques and that Peary did not allow Henson to check his own latitude readings was never squarely faced by either Peary or his critics, who doubted his attainment of the pole.

In any case, the real reason Henson went to the pole in 1909 was stated clearly by DONALD MAC MILLAN, one of the whites who returned in a supply team before reaching the pole and who later became an explorer in his own right. Peary, he wrote, "never would have reached the Pole without Henson. Matt was of more real value than the combined services of all of us. With years of experience, an expert dog driver, a master mechanic, physically strong, most popular with the Eskimos, talking the language like a native, clean, full of grit, he went to the Pole because Peary couldn't get along without him."

Henson owed his escape from poverty and his general education to the master of the ship on which he served as cabin boy for five years. He was twenty-one and working in a clothing store when Peary first met him. Peary was looking for a servant to accompany him to Nicaragua, and the two immediately struck a deal. As Henson put it, "It was with the instinct of my race that I recognized in him the qualities that made me willing to engage in his service." Henson seems to have accepted the ruling ideology regarding race, claiming contentedness in his role as "the faithful and constant companion of the Caucasian. . . ." When he reached the pole with Peary and four **Inuit**, he felt proud that "it was I, a lowly member of my race, who had been chosen by fate to represent it, at this, almost the last of the world's great *work*."

Despite this attitude, Booker T. Washington believed Henson was an inspirational role model for America's blacks and wrote the introduction to Henson's account of the North Pole expedition. He no doubt believed that Henson's modest account of himself as a "splendid follower" gave every indication that, given the opportunity, he could have been a great leader.

But Henson's life after the North Pole trek was to afford no such opportunity—far from it. He worked in obscurity as a parking lot attendant in Brooklyn (for $16 a week) and later as a clerk at the New York customshouse (at a starting salary of $900 a year). His accomplishments as an explorer were virtually ignored until the late 1930s, when he was honored by the Explorers' Club of New York. He received a variety of additional honors late in his life, most notably the personal congratulations of President Eisenhower during a visit to the White House to celebrate the forty-fifth anniversary of the attainment of the North Pole. He died the next year, 1955, at the age of eighty-eight.

• Herbert, Walter William

English
b October 24, 1934; York
living
Crossed Arctic Ocean by dog sledge

Perhaps the most romantic of the twentieth-century polar explorers, Wally Herbert once admitted that he was born sixty or seventy years too late to make a fortune at his trade. He was referring to the large lecture fees and generous literary contracts awarded to Arctic explorers at the turn of the century, when the polar ice cap was still largely unknown and a source of great mystery. He was also betraying the obsession that drove him to cross the Arctic Ocean by dog **sledge** in 1968, the first surface crossing of its kind in history.

The story is a strange one, about a relatively uneducated drifter whose youthful work as a surveyor in the Antarctic under Sir VIVIAN FUCHS (1955–58) gave rise to his nearly maniacal pursuit to lead an Arctic expedition. His account of the Arctic journey is a peculiar mixture of modesty and self-aggrandizement that makes it clear that the plan would have gone nowhere without the generous patronage of Fuchs. He calls his journey "the culmination of four centuries of human endeavor," but at the same time describes the pitiful three-year campaign he waged from a small room in his parents' house to get the support he needed to do it. He wrote hundreds of letters to prominent people, applied without success to the Royal Geographical Society for aid, and borrowed money to live on. It was only when Fuchs put together a committee of supporters that the project became a viable possibility.

Herbert did possess the experience necessary to run an Arctic expedition. He was taught navigation by the British army, a skill he refined as a surveyor under Fuchs. He had also been a surveyor with the New Zealand Antarctic Expedition (1960–62) and had become an expert dog driver. In addition, he had the reasonable idea to take advantage of the drift of the polar pack, much as FRIDTJOF NANSEN had done with the *Fram*. The problem was that no one seemed to think there was much reason to travel across the Arctic Ocean by sledge when airplanes and **dirigibles** had already done so. While there was good reason to learn more about the Arctic

Ocean floor, submarines were by then addressing that need. As for observations of Arctic weather, the various floating observatories run by qualified scientists would have made Herbert's work redundant. In short, Herbert's plan was pure sport, which is why the Royal Geographical Society showed no interest. The parallel Herbert drew with Fuchs's transpolar crossing of Antarctica—a serious scientific undertaking, if also a bit sensational—was wishful thinking.

Still, if it had been the age of ROBERT PEARY, some newspaper publisher would have seized the chance to back Herbert in exchange for the publicity. In the age of astronauts, though, there was little interest in a man using antiquated techniques—and even then, backing himself up with airdrops of food and supplies—in order to cross a floating surface of ice. As Herbert later complained, the National Geographic Society did not even mention the feat in its magazine, much less offer support.

In addition to the support of Fuchs, Herbert was armed with his own stubborn persistence and powerful way with words. If anyone could convince private sponsors to back an old-fashioned plan of this sort, it was he. After five years of planning, he finally set off from Point Barrow, Alaska, on February 25, 1968 (the year Apollo 8 orbited the moon), with four companions on what he called the British Trans-Arctic Expedition. The North Pole was reached on April 5, 1969, and Svalbard on May 29, 1969 (two months before the American astronaut Neil Armstrong stepped onto the surface of the moon). Herbert's party had made the 3,600 route miles in sixteen months. His book describing the affair, *Across the Top of the World*, contains beautiful descriptions of the polar landscape and an admirably honest account of the troubles he endured to achieve his dream.

After 1969, Herbert continued working in the Arctic. In 1977 he led the first circumnavigation of Greenland by dog sledge and skin boat (made from animal hides), another remarkable achievement and one that would indeed have been widely heralded seventy years earlier.

In the 1980s, Herbert finally sat down to wrestle with the ghost of Peary, coming up with a fine book on both Peary and his archrival, Dr. FREDERICK COOK. In this "graceful, meticulous, superbly informed and gentlemanly effort" (as one reviewer called it), Herbert diagnoses Peary's major flaw: a pitiful clinging to the "delusion that fame is the proof of greatness." In the process, he argues convincingly that both Peary and Cook faked their claims to have reached the pole. If Herbert brings compassion and sense of fairness to the old controversy, it is perhaps because he himself has been through the same ring of fire and suffered similar delusions.

Herjolfsson (Herjulfson; Herjulfsson), Bjarni (Bjarne)

Norse
b ?
d ?
Sighted eastern coast of North America (first European to do so)

Sailing toward ERIK THE RED's Greenland settlements, Norseman Bjarni Herjolfsson is said to have been blown off course. He thus became the first European to sight the eastern coast of North America.

A prosperous shipowner, Herjolfsson made his living trading between Norway and the Norwegian colony of Iceland. Though he loved the sea, he made it a point to spend every other winter at his father's farm in Iceland. Near the end of summer in A.D. 986, he landed in Iceland only to discover that his father had emigrated farther west to Erik the Red's new colony in Greenland. Herjolfsson therefore convinced his crew to sail on with him to Greenland, though none of them had been there before. (For a map of their route, see LEIF ERIKSON.)

Immediately after leaving England, the voyagers were blown off course by stormy weather that lasted for several days. When the weather cleared, they were in sight of an unknown land, wooded and dotted with low hills. Having been told that Greenland was icy and mountainous, Herjolfsson knew that this land could not be his destination and ordered his crew to sail north. A second sighting of land revealed a landscape that was level and wooded; this, too, he knew could not be Greenland. Sailing on for three days, they came to a mountainous land covered with glaciers. From descriptions he had been given, Herjolfsson concluded that this also was not Greenland. Sailing with a southerly wind for four days, he and his crew finally reached Greenland and miraculously sailed into the fjord where his father, Herjolf, had established his home.

Because the evidence is scanty, scholars have been hard put to identify Herjolfsson's sightings with any certainty. The most commonly accepted theory is that the first land he sighted was part of Newfoundland, the second was the coast of Labrador, and the third was Baffin Island. But some historians place his first sighting as far south as Cape Cod. Wherever he was, Herjolfsson was likely the first European to see the eastern coast of North America. From him, Leif Erikson learned of the new lands to explore.

Hernández, Juan Josef Pérez. See **Pérez Hernández, Juan Josef.**

Herodotus of Halicarnassus

Greek
b 484 B.C.?; Bodrum, Turkey
d 420 B.C.?; near Corigliano Calabro, Italy
Traveled throughout Asia Minor, Mediterranean, and North Africa

Herodotus of Halicarnassus, whose *Histories* of the Greco-Persian wars is one of the great books of Western civilization, has been variously described as the "Father of History" and the "Father of Lies." A primary source of information about life in the ancient world, his writing is packed with detailed observations about the cultural traditions, religions, myths, and politics of the peoples he encountered during a lifetime of traveling. His journeys ranged from Babylon in ancient Persia (present-day Iran) to the deserts of Libya, from the Dnieper river basin on the northwestern shores of the Black Sea to the southern reaches of Egypt.

The physical world fascinated Herodotus. He theorized about the size of Africa, which he wrongly believed to be a part of continental Asia, and attempted unsuccessfully to trace the source of the Nile. Often inaccurate, his writing reflects the ignorance and superstition of the fifth century B.C. But the efforts of this pioneer historian, ethnographer, and geographer—one of the first scholars to employ firsthand investigation and research—are a landmark in human intellectual development.

The exact details of Herodotus's life are un-

A bust of Herodotus of Halicarnassus. The Bettmann Archive.

certain. Most of what is known about him today must be gleaned from the *Histories*, the only primary source concerning his life. Born about 484 B.C. in Halicarnassus, a Greek colony on what is now Turkey's Aegean coast, he probably came from a well-to-do family and was most certainly well educated. While still a young man, he was banished from Halicarnassus by Lygdamis, a tyrant who had suppressed the city's constitutional government and seized dictatorial powers. As an exile, Herodotus traveled

throughout the Ionian Islands in the Aegean Sea. He then returned to Halicarnassus to help overthrow Lygdamis and restore democracy. Though he could have settled in the city of his birth, Herodotus chose instead to continue his wanderings, a dangerous occupation in an age when frail **galleys** rarely left the sight of land and bands of cutthroat bandits haunted the roads. Herodotus, who may have spent as much as a third of his life traveling, was apparently undaunted by the dangers of the road. Modern scholars estimate that in crisscrossing the known world, he covered an estimated 1,700 miles from east to west and 1,600 miles from north to south.

The sequence of his travels is not clear, nor is their original purpose. Initially, he may have intended to build on the work of another geographer, Hecataeus of Miletus, who had written about the countries abutting the Mediterranean Sea. Some scholars speculate that Herodotus did not originally plan to chronicle the Greco-Persian War (which grew out of ancient rivalries between the two cultures and ended with a Greek victory in 478 B.C.). They point out, for example, that when he traveled to the Black Sea he made no effort to investigate the invasion route taken by Darius I, the Persian king whose army conquered the kingdom of Scythia in what is now Bulgaria and Romania. In later journeys, however, he made a point of describing battlefields in greater detail.

Herodotus's account of his trip to Egypt is his most thorough, taking up the entire second book of the *Histories*. In it, he speculated on the age of the pyramids, which many of his contemporaries believed had been built by the gods. But Herodotus dismissed that notion, arguing that they were obviously of human origin. He was also intrigued by the Nile and studied the various contemporary theories about its source. Though he traveled some 700 miles down the river to the sight of modern Aswan, he was unable to come up with a satisfactory theory of his own concerning the river's source. (In fact, the Nile's source would remain a mystery until the nineteenth-century discoveries by the English explorers RICHARD FRANCIS BURTON and JOHN HANNING SPEKE.)

In his work, Herodotus combined Asian mysticism with Greek rationality and a storyteller's appreciation of a tall tale. He reported, for example, that in Egypt a mare once gave birth to a rabbit, and that in the far reaches of western

Africa there lived headless creatures with eyes in their breasts. Although personally skeptical of stories, he felt duty-bound to report them, leaving it to the reader to decide if they were true.

Herodotus was a product of both the golden age of Athens and the mysticism of the East. He believed, for example, in the ability of the oracle of Delphi to foresee the future, but he also had a typically Greek faith in rationalism. He lived for a time in Athens, where he was influenced by the great playwrights Sophocles and Aeschylus, and where he may have held public readings of his work. Despite his work's many flaws, the fact that he is still read today confirms this ancient Greek as one of the great storytellers and travelers of any age.

• Heyerdahl, Thor

Norwegian
b October 6, 1914; Larvik, on Oslo Fjord
living
Sailed primitive vessels across Atlantic and
Pacific; wrote *Kon-Tiki* and *The Ra*
Expeditions

The anthropologist, author, and adventurer Thor Heyerdahl dedicated his career to proving that people of primitive cultures could have migrated across vast seas long before the Europeans did. To prove his controversial point, he made three voyages in replicas of the simple craft he believed were used by the earliest explorers of the seas.

Heyerdahl was born in Larvik, Norway, in 1914 to Thor Heyerdahl, Sr., a successful brewer and businessman, and the former Alison Lyng. Although both had children from previous marriages, young Heyerdahl was raised as an only child. He was particularly close to his mother and, according to a boyhood friend, spent more time daydreaming than socializing with his peers. He sometimes wrote stories about children who ran off to tropical islands, which is exactly what he would do someday.

As a youngster, he showed a talent for art and a strong interest in natural history. His specimen collection included starfish, shells, insects, and snakes. When he went to the hospital to have his appendix removed, he made the doctors promise to preserve the organ in alcohol

in order to add it to his collection. He built a small museum for his collections in the courtyard of his house and constructed a freshwater aquarium, as well. The Heyerdahl residence soon became something of an attraction in Larvik.

In 1933 Heyerdahl moved to Oslo, where he studied zoology at the university. He preferred field trips to lab work and added geography to his studies. He read everything he could on Polynesia and convinced his fiancée, Liv Coucheron Torp, to "go back to nature" with him in those South Pacific islands.

Heyerdahl wed Torp on December 24, 1936. The next day they boarded a train for France, then took an ocean liner to Tahiti, where they were quickly adopted by Chief Teriieroo. After they learned the island ways, the newlyweds took a **schooner** to the island of Fatu Hiva, where they were to remain for a year. They lived slightly apart from the hundred or so islanders; although they learned to eat raw fish, sea snails, and sea urchins, they soon longed for Norwegian sausage and other foods of their homeland. They were plagued by poisonous insects, disease-bearing mosquitoes, and open sores on their feet that the islanders called *fefe*. Bugs began to eat the couple's house, which the islanders had built of uncured green bamboo, rather than hardened, mature wood, thereby guaranteeing themselves repair work in the future. When the schooner came to retrieve them, the young couple was glad to get away. "There is no paradise to be found on earth today," Heyerdahl wrote upon his return to Norway in March 1938.

Although he collected specimens of fish and insects on Fatu Hiva, Heyerdahl's interests had turned from animals to people. Who had left the giant stone carvings he saw on the island, and who was the pale god they called Tiki? The islanders claimed that Tiki led their ancestors to the Marquesas from the east—what could only have been South America. When a farmer showed him photos from British Columbia of carvings resembling Tiki, Heyerdahl theorized that the Pacific was populated by two migrations: one from the Malay Peninsula by way of North America and Hawaii, and another from Peru. What's more, he postulated, the migrations from South America may have been led by early Europeans, who crossed the seas nearly a thousand years before CHRISTOPHER COLUMBUS and his contemporaries.

HEZETA, BRUNO DE

To prove that an early journey from the Americas to Polynesia was possible, Heyerdahl built a forty-five-foot-long raft out of balsa logs and bamboo. The raft was christened *Kon-Tiki* in honor of the pale, bearded god of the Polynesians. On April 28, 1947, Heyerdahl and a crew of five were towed out of the harbor at Callao, Peru, and set adrift. The winds and current carried them north along the South American coast, then turned them west just below the equator. They were followed by sharks and whales, and one night a rare deep-sea snake mackerel leaped aboard and wound up on a crewman's pillow. On August 6, having crossed some 4,300 miles of open ocean in 101 days, *Kon-Tiki* and its crew reached the Tuamotus.

Heyerdahl's account of the voyage, *Kon-Tiki*, was published in 1948, and his documentary film of the same name won an Academy Award in 1951. Two years later, he published the controversial *American Indians in the Pacific*, which challenged the accepted anthropological theory that the Pacific was peopled only from the west. In 1953 he found remains of Inca culture in the Galápagos Islands, and in 1955–56 he traveled to Easter Island to study the massive stone sculptures there.

Intrigued by the existence of pyramid-building technology in both the Middle East and South America, Heyerdahl organized the Ra expedition. In 1969 he and a crew of seven crossed the Atlantic from Morocco to Barbados in a papyrus-reed raft, *Ra II*, proving, he believed, that early Egyptians could have done the same.

Heyerdahl further proved the possibility of transmigration among primitive cultures by sailing through the Persian Gulf and around the Arabian Sea to Pakistan's Indus Valley. He and a crew of eleven covered 4,200 miles in four months in a sixty-foot boat made of reeds grown in the Tigris-Euphrates Valley of Asia Minor. The vessel was designed after those found on ancient Sumerian seals.

Some anthropologists and ethnologists reject Heyerdahl's theories, on the basis of language and on various other grounds. Still, the adventurer has won prestigious awards from the Swedish Society for Anthropology and Geography (1950), the Scottish Geographic Society (1950), and the French Société de Géographie (1950), plus the Gold Medal of Great Britain's Royal Geographical Society (1964) and the Lomonosov Medal from the Soviet Union (1962). He retired from his primitive voyaging in 1979,

stating that he had proved his point and that "the burden of proof now rests with those who claim the oceans were necessarily a factor in isolating civilizations."

· Hezeta (Heçeta), Bruno de
Spanish
b 1750?; Bilbao
d ?
Discovered mouth of Columbia River

In 1775 Spanish naval officer Bruno de Hezeta led a maritime expedition along the northwest coast of North America as far north as what is now Nootka Sound off Vancouver Island. On his return voyage he became the first European to observe the mouth of what is now the Columbia River.

In 1774 Hezeta arrived with five other young officers at San Blas, New Spain (present-day Mexico), the headquarters for Spanish naval operations in California. At the time, rumors abounded that Russia was expanding eastward from the present-day Aleutian Islands, and Spain was determined to counter Russian advances by establishing a presence on the northwest coast of the continent. Early in 1774 JUAN JOSEF PÉREZ HERNÁNDEZ had made an expedition northward from California but had failed to land or to take formal possession of any lands. So in 1775 Hezeta was put in charge of a new expedition with Pérez as second-in-command and JUAN FRANCISCO DE LA BODEGA Y QUADRA commanding the second of three ships. Hezeta's instructions were to reach a latitude of 65° North, avoid foreign settlements, go ashore and take possession wherever it was safe to do so, and establish friendly relations with the Indians wherever possible.

The expedition left San Blas on March 16, 1775. In northern California, Hezeta stopped in a bay and went ashore to take formal possession. By mid-July, he had reached the coast of what is now Washington and there performed another possession ceremony. By this time most of Hezeta's men were sick from **scurvy**, and he was already planning to turn back without reaching 65° North. Bodega, the bolder of the two, pressed on, with Hezeta sailing south on August 11 after reaching latitude 49° North near present-day Nootka Sound.

Although his instructions obligated him to follow the coast carefully on his return voyage, Hezeta passed the Strait of Juan de Fuca (between present-day Vancouver Island and Washington) without noticing it. A few days later, however, in the evening of August 17, Hezeta sighted a large bay between two promontories. The bay penetrated so far inland that it reached the horizon. Although Hezeta made several attempts to enter the bay, the current was so strong that he had to give up. He could not even land because his men were so weak from scurvy that he feared they would not be able to raise the anchor once it was dropped. Concluding that it must be the "mouth of some great river or of some passage to another sea," Hezeta named it Bay of the Assumption of Our Lady after a feast day celebrated on August 15. Thus, Hezeta was the first European to observe the mouth of what was later to be called the Columbia, one of North America's great rivers. Hezeta prepared a chart of the estuary on the basis of what he could see from outside the bay, and the bay later appeared on maps as "Entrada de Hezeta" (Hezeta's Entryway). Nonetheless, it was ignored by other explorers until seventeen years later when the American ROBERT GRAY managed to sail into the river.

Bruno de Hezeta was a cautious commander who chose to turn back rather than risk unknown seas with an ill crew. Though most of the glory from his expedition would in the end go to the more daring Bodega y Quadra, it was Hezeta who made the most significant discovery of the voyage.

Sir Edmund Percival Hillary. The Bettmann Archive.

• Hillary, Edmund Percival

New Zealander
b July 20, 1919; Auckland, North Island
living
Explored Antarctica and Himalaya Mountains

The explorer and adventurer Sir Edmund Hillary is best known as being part of the first team to reach the summit of Mount Everest—at the time considered the world's highest peak. He also led an important expedition to Antarctica in 1957. On January 4, 1958, Hillary became the first person since ROBERT FALCON SCOTT to reach the South Pole by an overland route.

Hillary was born in 1919 on New Zealand's North Island and raised on a small farm in the country village of Tuakau, about 40 miles south of Auckland. The second of three children, he was a good student who filled his time "with reading and dreaming. Books of adventure became my greatest support—Edgar Rice Burroughs, Rider Haggard, John Buchan. . . . In my imagination . . . I was always the hero."

Hillary got his first taste of real adventure when, at the age of twenty, he climbed Mount Oliver on New Zealand's South Island. A beekeeper by trade, he continued his mountaineering. In 1950 he climbed in the Austrian and Swiss Alps and in May 1951 made the first of many visits to the Himalayas. At the end of the summer, he was invited to join the British expedition to Mount Everest, which was already under way. But icefalls and avalanches thwarted this attempt to reach the summit.

Hillary returned to Everest in 1953 as part of a British team under Colonel John Hunt. On May 29 Hillary and Tenzing Norgay, a Nepalese Sherpa tribesman, became the first people ever to reach the mountain's summit. Queen Elizabeth II of England knighted Hillary for his achievement.

In 1955, while on a lecture tour of South Africa, Hillary was invited to lead an expedition to Antarctica. Dr. VIVIAN FUCHS wanted to cross the continent from the Weddell Sea to the Ross Sea via the South Pole, making scientific observations along the way. Hillary was asked to lead a supporting expedition, which was to establish a base on the Ross Sea, south of New Zealand, and set up supply depots toward the pole.

In the southern summer of 1955–56, Hillary accompanied Fuchs on an expedition to the Weddell Sea. They spent more than a month there with their ship trapped in pack ice before reaching the Filchner Ice Shelf, where they set up Fuchs's Shackleton Base.

Hillary returned to New Zealand in March and spent the next eight months lecturing and generating support for the expedition. On December 21, 1956, he boarded the vessel *Endeavor* bound for Antarctica. With him was a team that included three surveyors, two geologists, a meteorologist-biologist, three Royal New Zealand Air Force pilots, and five other scientists from the New Zealand International Geophysical Year party.

The expedition first established Scott Base on McMurdo Sound in the Ross Sea. By the end of January 1957, the first supply depot had been set up at the foot of Skelton Glacier, using planes to ferry in materials. Using dog teams, the group subsequently established a second depot on the polar plateau, some 290 miles from the base.

In March Hillary decided to do a trial tractor run and almost lost the tractor in a crevasse, a dangerous snow-covered fissure. When Hillary's team set out, they covered only 12 miles the first day. They eventually reached the hut of Dr. Edward Wilson, an early Antarctic explorer. After returning to base camp, they spent most of the winter customizing their tractors and other equipment to perform in deep snow and temperatures that sometimes reached −60 degrees Fahrenheit.

When the weather warmed, Hillary again began the push to establish supply depots closer to the pole. In all, five were set up. The last one, called Depot 700, was 500 miles from the pole. After some debate, Hillary became determined to reach the pole himself. On December 20, 1957, his team headed south from Depot 700.

For two tortuous weeks they traveled through soft snow, eventually dropping all supplies that were not essential. On January 4, 1958, Hillary reached the South Pole with only twenty extra gallons of fuel. Although his team did little research, they identified many of the crevasse areas and established a route from McMurdo Sound to the pole. Fuchs joined them there on January 20. Their return to Scott Base took two months, during which Fuchs performed a series of seismic measurements to determine the depth of the ice layer. The explorers left the continent on March 20.

In 1959 Hillary won *Argosy* magazine's Explorer of the Year Award. The following year he organized a Himalayan expedition to look for the legendary *yeti*, or abominable snowman. He returned to Antarctica in 1967 to climb Mount Herschel on the western shore of the Ross Sea. Next, with the same determination he demonstrated on his crossing to the pole, Hillary trekked over unstable sea ice and around crevasses for sixteen days to obtain rock samples from the north shore of Robertson Bay for Dr. Larry Harrington, who was studying continental drift.

Not content to rest, Hillary authored several books about his experiences in little-known parts of the world. At the end of his 1975 autobiography he wrote, "I can see a mighty river to challenge; a hospital to build; a peaceful mountain valley with an unknown pass to cross; an untouched Himalayan summit and a shattered Southern glacier—yes, there is plenty left to do."

· Hind, Henry Youle

Canadian
b June 1, 1823; Nottingham, England
d August 9, 1908; Windsor, Nova Scotia
Explored Canadian plains and Labrador

A professor of chemistry and geology at Trinity College, Toronto, Henry Youle Hind was a geologist on the Red River Exploring Expedition of 1857, which surveyed the territory between Lake Superior and the Selkirk (Red River) Settlement (present-day Winnipeg). In 1858 he headed the continuation of the expedition, which examined much of the territory bounded on the south by the Assiniboine and the Qu'Appelle rivers, on the north by the Saskatchewan, and on the east by Lake Winnipeg. Hind's conclusion—that the fertile Canadian plains could support thousands of emigrants—paved the way for the settlement of what were to become the Canadian provinces.

In 1857, the immense expanse of territory controlled by the Hudson's Bay Company fur-trading monopoly was unknown to anyone but the company's traders, who were not inclined to share their hard-won information with outsiders. However, the company's license was due to be renewed in 1859, and Canada and Britain were interested in opening the territory to settlement. In order to learn more about the nature of this region, the parliaments of Canada and Britain both organized explorations of the area. The stated purpose of the Canadian expedition was "to ascertain the practicability of establishing an emigrant route between Lake Superior and the Selkirk Settlement, and to acquire some knowledge of the natural capabilities and resources of the Valley of the Red River and the Saskatchewan."

The Canadian Red River Exploring Expedition of 1857 was nominally headed by George Gladman, a former official of the Hudson's Bay Company, but Henry Hind, its geologist, was in fact the guiding spirit of the party of forty-four. In 1858, Gladman's services were found to be an unnecessary expense, and Hind was put in charge of one-half of the expedition's continuation, which was to explore the Assiniboine and Saskatchewan rivers.

The difficulties experienced by Hind and his companions were mild compared to those of earlier explorers of the region. Occasionally they missed a meal, and the food was generally unappetizing. Like all canoe voyagers, they periodically encountered dangerous rapids on the rivers, and there was also the ever-present possibility of attack by hostile Indians. As it turned out, however, the expedition's most persistent and annoying attackers were mosquitoes and grasshoppers. In his report, Hind tells of spotting some large and luscious-looking raspberries that were unfortunately surrounded by a swarm of mosquitoes. Wrote Hind: "I offered the Cree guide a piece of tobacco for a tin cup full of the raspberries, he tried to win it, but after a short struggle with these terrible insects he rushed from the hillside and buried his face in the smoke of the fire we had lit in the hope of expelling them from the neighborhood of our camp." Hind also reported that the grasshoppers would "attack any substances presented to them, even such indigestible articles as leather, travelling bags, woollen garments, saddle girths, and harness. In a few minutes they ate the varnish from the leather case of a telescope I left on the ground in 1858, and so disfigured a valise that the owner who had seen it sound and untouched a few minutes before we stopped to camp, could not recognize it after it had lain ten minutes on the grass."

Despite the hardships, Hind seems to have enjoyed his task; and the conclusions he drew had far-ranging consequences. From direct observation and from talking with settlers who were already farming the land, Hind concluded that the prairies could provide a good living for many thousands of settlers. He even suggested a combined water and land route that could bring emigrants from Liverpool, England, to Fort Garry on the Red River in twenty-two days. His only significant error, in fact, was to underestimate the numbers of settlers the land could support. Influenced by the erroneous idea of a Great American Desert (first proposed by ZEBULON PIKE in 1810 and popularized by STEPHEN HARRIMAN LONG in 1823) dominating the heart of the continent and spilling over the border into the southernmost Canadian prairies (where it was known as the Palliser Triangle), Hind pointed out the greater agricultural potential of the parkland area of the Saskatchewan River valley farther north.

After the completion of the 1858 expedition, Hind wanted to go west again to finish his explorations of the South Saskatchewan River and to cross the Rockies. Failing to find financial support for this plan, he turned his attention to the East. In 1861 he explored the rivers of Labrador with his brother, an artist. In 1864 he made a geological survey of New Brunswick, and from 1869 to 1871 he examined gold fields in Nova Scotia. Later, while exploring northeastern Labrador, he discovered new cod-fishing grounds. By 1890 Hind's days in the field were over, and he became president of a church school in Nova Scotia.

Henry Youle Hind was of the second generation of explorers of North America. His thorough and careful examination of the land led him to conclusions that had lasting effects on Canada and its people.

· Hipparchus

Greek
b 165 b.c.?; Nicaea, now in Turkey
d 127 b.c.?
Refined Eratosthenes' grid system for maps

The ancient Greeks were attracted to the belief that the universe is a logical, orderly place. In fact, "cosmos," one of the words now used for the universe, is the Greek word meaning order, the opposite of chaos. The Greek astronomer Hipparchus was driven by this desire to describe the orderliness of the universe. He replaced ERATOSTHENES' irregular global grid system with a grid made up of lines occurring at even intervals. He also discovered an apparent variation over time in the measured positions of the stars, a phenomenon he called the procession of the equinoxes—the description still used by astronomers today. In addition, Hipparchus compiled a catalog of 850 stars, developed an early form of trigonometry, and computed the length of a year to within 6½ minutes. In light of his many achievements, Hipparchus is widely acknowledged to be the greatest of the ancient astronomers.

Hipparchus's insistence on order and balance in his explanation of the natural world is apparent in his description of the relative positions of the world's land and sea masses. In his view, each mass on the surface of the globe must be balanced by a similar mass in the opposite hemisphere. For example, Hipparchus believed the land masses in the Northern Hemisphere required equal land masses in the Southern Hemisphere to balance them.

His greatest influence on world exploration was his refinement of Eratosthenes' global grid system. Eratosthenes had divided the sphere of the earth into sixty rectangles, using lines perpendicular to primary north-south and east-west grid lines. Each of these lines passed through a prominent place in the ancient world. As a result, the areas on his map were not all the same size, although his network of parallel lines was still a major advance.

Hipparchus refined Eratosthenes' irregular grid system by using astronomical observation and applying rigorous mathematical principles. Many of the elements in Hipparchus's system were the result of his work on the trigonometry of the sphere. He divided the surface of the earth into 360 equal parts—the divisions that eventu-ally became the degrees used in modern geography. Furthermore, he stipulated that the location of all places on the earth should be specified by giving their longitude and latitude, a method also used by modern geographers. Hipparchus may not have actually originated the terms "latitude" and "longitude" (some think PTOLEMY did), but he is responsible for the system underlying the terms.

Unlike Eratosthenes, who set each grid line by its relation to a known place on earth, Hipparchus insisted that the lines be set in relation to celestial phenomena, which all places on earth had in common. For example, he proposed that the exact times when a solar eclipse began and ended at a given place on earth could be used to calculate its precise longitude (the east-west determination) of that place.

Earlier geographers had already used parallel lines to divide the earth into rudimentary latitude zones. According to their schemes, all the regions in a zone had the same length of longest day each year. So the latitude of a place (its north-south determination) could be calculated from the length of its longest day. Hipparchus refined this system as well, using the ratio of the longest day to the shortest day in a particular place to figure its latitude.

Hipparchus is perhaps best known for his discovery of a phenomenon he poetically described in the title of one of his books as "the procession of the equinoxes." Over time, astronomers had noticed an apparent shift in the measured positions of the stars. No one had been able to solve the puzzle until Hipparchus applied his considerable mathematical talents to the task. Perhaps, Hipparchus reasoned, it was not the stars that moved but rather the platform from which the stars are observed: the earth. By comparing his observations with those of earlier Babylonian astronomers, he correctly concluded that the earth wobbles slightly on its axis, thus explaining the observed shift of the stars.

Ho, Cheng. See **Zheng He.**

Hornemann, Friedrich Konrad

German
b September 1772; Hildesheim, Hanover
d February 1801?; Nigeria?
Explored North Africa

One of the earliest explorers of North Africa, Friedrich Konrad Hornemann was the first European to travel across the Sahara from Egypt and reach Hausaland (in what is now northern Nigeria). He explored southern Libya where, posing as an Arab, he visited the communities of Murzuch in the region of Fezzan. The substantial information he collected about the peoples of the Sahara and the Sudan was dispatched from Tripoli, but Hornemann never returned to Europe to take credit for his accomplishments. The fate he met in Africa remains a mystery.

Although he came from a long line of German clergy (and nearly completed his own theological studies), Hornemann was unable to resist pursuing his childhood dream of exploring Africa. On the eve of his final examinations in 1795, he left the seminary to apply for a commission as an explorer. The newly formed African Association of London (also known as the Society for Promoting the Discovery of the Interior Parts of Africa) accepted him on the condition that he learn the Arabic language. In September 1797 he was sent to Cairo with instructions to join a trading caravan that would take him southwest to the Hausa region.

Delayed by a plague that put Cairo under quarantine, he departed the following September with a caravan bound for Fezzan. He disguised himself as an Arab—perhaps the first of the many European explorers to do so—to avoid arousing suspicion and hostility. Accompanying a merchant caravan to the oases of Siwa and Aujila, he continued southwest to Temissa in Fezzan and arrived at Murzuch (in what is now southern Libya) in November. Hornemann spent six months in the city, at that time a lively trading community, and made a thorough study of its culture and economy, laying the groundwork for British commercial ventures there. He then decided to travel north to Tripoli (in present-day Libya) to send his journals to London, fearing that they would be lost forever if he failed to return from his planned trip south to the Niger River.

Hornemann's fears proved to be justified. After four months in Tripoli, he departed in December 1799 and was never heard from again. The African Association later learned that he had returned to Murzuch and may have even reached Timbuktu and Lake Chad. He is said to have died in Nigeria in February 1801, possibly of dysentery (an acute intestinal disease), although the British consul at Tripoli was told by another source that Hornemann had been seen in Nigeria in 1803.

Houghton, Daniel

Irish
b 1740?
d 1791; West Africa
Explored course of Niger River

In 1790 Daniel Houghton, a retired major in the English army, sailed from England to the mouth of the Gambia River on the west coast of Africa, intent on solving the riddle of the course of the Niger River. Some of Houghton's subsequent misadventures on his way to Timbuktu were well chronicled in reports sent back to England: the fire that destroyed most of his baggage, the gun accident that badly injured his arms and face, and the desertion of his interpreter, who took off with Houghton's horse and three of his five donkeys. But the mysterious circumstances surrounding his death remain a riddle. Some say he died of hunger; others think he was attacked by the Moors. However Houghton died, Scottish explorer MUNGO PARK, traveling through the same area several years later, determined that Houghton had managed to reach farther inland than any previous European on record.

Houghton spent part of his youth in Morocco and then a portion of his army career in the British consulate in Morocco and in a fort off the coast of Senegal. After he retired from the army, Houghton—perhaps impoverished by the financial demands of his large family—proposed to the African Association (also known as the Society for Promoting the Discovery of the Interior Parts of Africa) that they send him to explore the as-yet-undetermined course of the Niger River. He planned to travel east from the Atlantic coast of Africa as far as Timbuktu and Houssa, then return by way of the Sahara Desert, in order to report on the rise, course, and termination of the Niger and upon "the various nations that inhabit its borders." The Society agreed, and Houghton left England on October 16, 1790.

After his arrival on the west coast of Africa, Houghton followed the course of the Gambia River for several hundred miles, then prepared for a long overland trek by hiring a guide and purchasing a horse and five donkeys. Although he was well received by the rulers of the small kingdoms he passed through on his journey east, things soon began to go awry. He managed to foil a plot on his life by a group of river merchants who feared he might try to compete with them, but only because he had learned enough of the Mandingo language in his youth to understand a conversation he overheard by chance. When a hut next to the one in which Houghton was sleeping caught fire, his interpreter seized the opportunity to flee in the chaos with Houghton's horse and three of his donkeys.

In spite of these setbacks, it is known from his reports that Houghton doggedly continued to make his way toward Timbuktu. When he reached the land of the Moors, he bribed some merchants, offering them a gun and a little tobacco to escort him. Two days later, Houghton suspected he was being led in the wrong direction, but it was too late. The Moors robbed him of all his possessions and fled, leaving Houghton alone, perhaps to die of wounds he received from his former escorts, or possibly of starvation. Neither Houghton nor the journals containing his observations during his long journey were ever found. Nevertheless, prior to his death he managed to determine and accurately report that the course of the upper Niger River ran eastward, a fact previously unknown.

Hsüan-chuang. See **Xuan Zang.**

Hsüan-tsang. See **Xuan Zang.**

• Hudson, Henry

English
b ?
d 1611; Hudson Bay, Canada
Explored Arctic, eastern seaboard of North America, Hudson River, Hudson Bay

The English navigator Henry Hudson was possessed by the idea of finding a northern route from Europe to the Orient. In the attempt to do so, he made four voyages of discovery. The last two led him to North America, where he became the first European to sail up the Hudson River in what is now New York State and the first to enter Hudson Bay in northern Canada.

Nothing is known of Hudson's life until his final four years, when he stepped center stage in the annals of world discovery. It seems apparent that by 1607 he had established a reputation as a skilled navigator, for in that year the English Muscovy Company hired him to attempt to sail across the North Pole to China. Though no one knew for sure what the Pole was like in summer, respected geographers thought that its weather might well be warm enough to allow an open polar sea. If they proved wrong and polar passage was impossible, Hudson's orders were to proceed in an easterly direction until he reached China on the "warm sea."

Hudson, his young son John, and a crew of ten sailed out of Gravesend, England, in April 1607 in the ship *Hopewell*. Following the east coast of Greenland, they headed north until they were stopped by an ice barrier just ten degrees south of the Pole—farther north than any previous voyage had gone—proving that the pole remained frozen in summer. The *Hopewell* then turned east and proceeded to Spitsbergen, an island north of Norway. Confused by the inaccurate charts of the day as well as by storms, fog, and icebergs, Hudson turned back and reached England by mid-September. Though he had not found a Northeast Passage to the Orient, the voyage was considered a commercial success for opening up valuable whaling grounds off Spitsbergen to English ships.

In April 1608, the English Muscovy Company again sent Hudson out in search of a Northeast Passage to the Orient. This time he was to sail along the north coast of Russia through the Kara Sea to the Orient. The ship got as far as the island of Novaya Zemlya and then spent ten days trying to find a passage through the long barrier island. When this proved impossible, instead of going north or south of the island, Hudson turned back under threat of mutiny from his crew. Under pressure, he signed a certificate saying that he was returning of his own will, but the truth was the opposite. Hudson's capitulation to his crew established a dangerous precedent for his future voyages.

After two failures, the English Muscovy Company was not interested in sponsoring another

Henry Hudson and his party descending what is now the Hudson River. Library of Congress.

Hudson expedition. However, the Dutch East India Company was attracted by Hudson's growing reputation as a navigator of Arctic waters and in 1609 hired him to attempt once again to find a Northeast Passage to the Orient. As on the previous voyage, Hudson's mate on this voyage was Robert Juet, the only member of the expedition to keep a written record of it.

In a ship called the *Half Moon*, Hudson and a mixed crew of English and Dutch sailors proceeded up the coast of Norway and then turned east into the ice-laden waters of the Barents Sea. The frigid weather, thick fogs, and violent storms came as a shock to the Dutch sailors, who were accustomed to the tropical seas they sailed on the way to the East Indies. By May they were close to mutiny. As before, Hudson gave in to the crew's demands. This time he turned back before even reaching Novaya Zemlya.

Hudson himself may not have been entirely reluctant to turn back. In his possession were maps and letters from his friend Captain JOHN SMITH of the Jamestown colony in Virginia. Smith believed that a Northwest Passage to the Orient might well be found somewhere north of the Virginia colony, and Hudson was interested in trying out this theory (for a more complete discussion of the Northwest Passage, see MARTIN FROBISHER). So after the near-mutiny, he convinced the crew to change course to sail west across the Atlantic.

By mid-July they were off the coast of Maine. Sailing south, they reached the mouth of what is now Chesapeake Bay by mid-August. Strangely, Hudson made no attempt to reach his friend Smith at Jamestown, possibly because he was sailing under the flag of Holland rather than that of England. From the Chesapeake, he turned north to look for the passageway to the Pacific. The ship explored the mouth of Delaware Bay, but Hudson decided it was too full of shoals and sandbars to be the passage he was looking for. The expedition proceeded up the coast of present-day New Jersey and on September 2, 1609, found itself at the mouth of a huge open bay. It was the lower bay of today's New York harbor. (GIOVANNI DA VERRAZANO had sailed into this bay in 1524, but no one had followed up on his discovery.) From

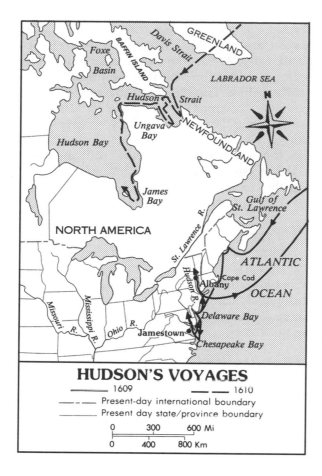

HUDSON'S VOYAGES
——— 1609 — — 1610
– – – Present-day international boundary
——— Present day state/province boundary

0	300	600 Mi
0	400	800 Km

anchor near what is now Albany and sent a boat upriver. His hopes were once again dashed when the boat returned with the news that the river soon became too shallow for the ship to pass. Clearly, this was not the desired Northwest Passage. Nonetheless, the voyage was far from a failure. Within a year the Dutch had colonized Manhattan and claimed the entire fertile Hudson River valley.

Hudson arrived in England in early November and sent a report to the Dutch East India Company in Amsterdam, planning to follow up with a trip there himself. However, the English authorities, impressed with what they heard of his voyage, refused to let him leave the country, and a group of wealthy merchants formed a private syndicate to finance the explorer's next expedition. On this voyage, his orders were to examine straits and inlets in the Canadian Arctic to see if "any passage might be found to the other ocean called the South Sea."

In a ship called the *Discovery*, Hudson, his son, and his crew sailed down the Thames. Aboard was a seaman name Abacuk Prickett, who recorded the details of the voyage in his journal, and Hudson's future nemesis, Robert Juet. The Atlantic crossing took ten weeks, an unusually long time, causing historians to speculate that there was friction among the crew early in the voyage. Prickett records that Juet

the strength of the current, Hudson realized that he must be at the mouth of some great river or strait. His hopes of a passage to the Orient mounted.

For several days the crew fished, took soundings, and explored the surrounding shores in haphazard fashion, impressed with the abundance of salmon, mullet, and rays and with the land surrounding the bay, which, according to Juet, was "as pleasant with grass and flowers and goodly trees as ever they had seen." They also encountered the local Indians, who came on board dressed in their finest garments of feathers and furs and with whom the crew traded for tobacco, beans, corn, and "great store of very good oysters, which we bought for trifles."

Eventually the *Half Moon* passed through the Narrows, entered the upper bay, and anchored off the coast of a densely forested island, which the Indians called Manna-hatta (present-day Manhattan). Then Hudson sailed north up the river which was to bear his name. On September 19, 150 miles up the river, Hudson dropped

Henry Hudson. The Bettmann Archive.

made fun of their "master's hope to see Bantam [Java] by Candlemasse [February 2]."

On June 25, the ship entered the strait that now carries Hudson's name and lies between Baffin Island and the northernmost reaches of Québec Province. It was early in the year to pass through the strait, which was still full of ice and fog. As the ship sailed back and forth between present-day Ungava Bay and Baffin Island, the crew was frightened by the bleak landscape, and a sense of unknown terrors prevailed. Like Hudson's previous crews, they defied Hudson and refused to go further. As before, he consulted with them and finally convinced them to proceed.

Avoiding the rocks near the shore, they pushed on against the current and the ice flowing from the west, which to Hudson was a clear indication of the nearness of the Pacific Ocean. Confident that his goal was within reach, Hudson turned south into Hudson Bay, only to have his hopes utterly dashed when he ran into the marshy and barren deltas of the south shore of James Bay, the southern extension of Hudson Bay. Unable to accept the fact that he had reached a dead end, Hudson sailed east and west, then north and south, aimlessly crossing James Bay for weeks, while his crew became increasingly concerned that their captain had lost his mind. When they finally expressed their doubts and fears, Hudson's response was to try his mate, Robert Juet, for "mutinous matters against the master," and replace him with ROBERT BYLOT.

Finally it became clear that Hudson intended to winter over in the bay. On November 1, the ship was beached on the south shore of James Bay and ten days later it became frozen in until spring. The winter was long and hard, and the ship's remaining provisions were barely adequate to keep the men alive. Added to the miseries of cold, wet, and hunger, **scurvy** broke out. When spring came, the men were so close to starvation that they went into the woods and foraged for frogs and lichen.

By June 12, 1611, the *Discovery* was able to set sail. But, with only two weeks' worth of provisions remaining, Hudson revealed his intention to continue the search for a passage to the Orient. The terrified crew were convinced they would not survive. Finally on June 22 or 23, mutiny broke out. It was led by Robert Juet and crew-member Henry Greene, who avowed he "would rather be hanged at home than starve abroad." The ringleaders imprisoned Hudson, his son, and six others in a **shallop** being towed by the ship, saying they were merely going to search the ship for food they believed Hudson was hoarding. Then they cut the shallop loose, leaving its occupants to a guaranteed death by starvation and exposure in the icy waters. Specific details about what happened to Hudson and the other abandoned men are unknown.

Henry Hudson was a skilled navigator who had the courage to dare much but whose personal qualities as a leader led him to failure. In just four years he added immensely to the world's store of geographic knowledge of areas as widespread and diverse as the Arctic Ocean and the fertile Hudson River valley. Although he is today remembered by the river, bay, and strait that bear his name, that memory is clouded by the tragic nature of his untimely death.

SUGGESTED READING: John Bartlet Brebner, *Explorers of North America 1492–1806* (World, 1955); *Great Adventures That Changed Our World* (Reader's Digest Association, 1978); Louis B. Wright and Elaine W. Fowler, eds., *West and By North: North America Seen Through the Eyes of Its Seafaring Discoverers* (Delacorte, 1971).

Huien-tsiang. See **Xuan Zang.**

• Humboldt, Alexander von

German
b September 14, 1769; Berlin
d May 6, 1859; Berlin
Explored South America and Mexico;
   discovered Humboldt current

A true Renaissance man, Baron Alexander von Humboldt was one of the greatest of the scientists who were both naturalists and explorers. During a five-year period (1800–1804) he covered over 6,000 miles throughout Peru, Ecuador, Venezuela, and Colombia, and also traveled extensively in Mexico, Cuba, and the United States. He explored remote rain forests and the great river system of Venezuela, climbing some of the highest volcanic mountains in the world, and he discovered the cold ocean current which bears his name. Unlike earlier explorers of South America, Humboldt had as his goal the

Alexander von Humboldt. American Philosophical Society.

educator) to be reared by their puritanical and aloof mother. To escape the constraints to his natural exuberance and vitality imposed in what he called the "Castle of Boredom," Humboldt explored the surrounding forests, collecting shells, rocks, and flowers. His interest in natural history earned him the nickname the "Little Apothecary." He also found escape in books, especially those about the explorations and discoveries of CHARLES-MARIE DE LA CONDAMINE, JAMES BRUCE, and Captain JAMES COOK.

He studied at the universities of Frankfurt and Ober (for six months in 1787) and Göttingen (for one year, 1789–90). The most important influence on Humboldt's future was naturalist and circumnavigator JOHANN GEORG ADAM FORSTER, with whom he became acquainted at Göttingen. It was from Forster that he learned about art and nature during a trip to England in 1790.

Humboldt next attended the School of Mines at Freiburg in Saxony (1791 92), where he taught himself chemistry and paleontology. He joined the school's mining department in 1792 and quickly rose to become chief inspector. While serving in this capacity he invented a safety lamp and a breathing apparatus for miners, revitalized the mines in Austria and Poland, and started a free mining school (with his own money) and a pension fund for miners.

By the age of twenty-seven, Humboldt was one of the most successful men in Prussia. A man with an amazing appetite for work and an encyclopedic knowledge of the world, he also enjoyed social gatherings and was described as being friendly, charismatic, and a witty conversationalist. He formed several intense friendships during his lifetime, but he never married and apparently never developed any permanent emotional ties.

When his mother died in 1796, Humboldt inherited a fortune, which freed him to pursue his two great loves—natural history and exploration. He resigned from his job in 1797 and planned two separate expeditions—one to Italy and one to Egypt—but was forced to abandon them both due to Napoleon's military activities. In 1799, he left with his friend, botanist Aimé Bonpland, to explore the interior of South America in order "to find out about the unity of nature."

They landed at Cumaná, Venezuela, and proceeded through the rain forest, stopping at Car-

acquisition of knowledge rather than material wealth. Toward that end he kept meticulous notebooks filled with statistics and measurements, maps, sketches, and observations. The information he gathered not only enriched the fields of geology, meteorology, zoology, botany, and ethnology but also provided the impetus for modern geophysics and the basis for a new approach to geography. Lionized during his lifetime as a great scientist and explorer, Humboldt was also a respected diplomat in service to the Prussian court and a successful author. He was equally at home discussing plant metamorphosis with Wolfgang von Goethe, the Mexican-American frontier with the American president Thomas Jefferson, or art with painter Gilbert Stuart.

Baron Friedrich Wilhelm Karl Heinrich Alexander von Humboldt was born on September 14, 1769, at the family estate, Schloss Tegal, 12 miles north of Berlin. His father, an officer in the Prussian army, died when Humboldt was nine, leaving him and his older brother Wilhelm (who would become a renowned statesman and

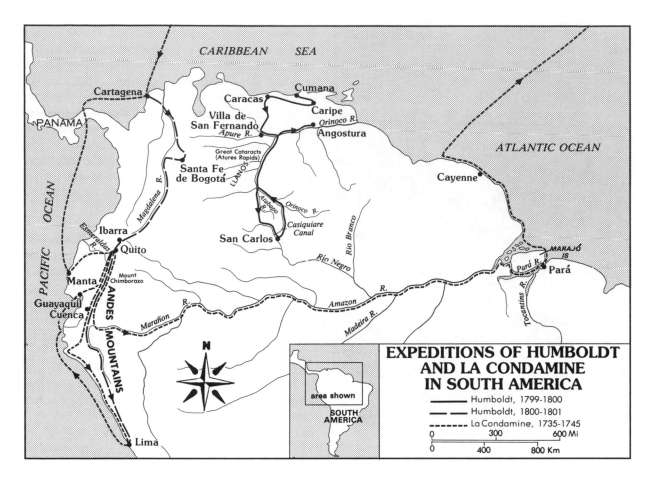

EXPEDITIONS OF HUMBOLDT AND LA CONDAMINE IN SOUTH AMERICA

——— Humboldt, 1799-1800
— — — Humboldt, 1800-1801
------- La Condamine, 1735-1745

ipe to study the Chayma Indians and collect plant specimens. They then journeyed on to Caracas. Leaving Caracas on February 7, 1800, they began the first scientific exploration of over 1,500 miles of virtually unknown land between the river basins of the Orinoco and the headwaters of the Amazon. Traveling at night to avoid the extreme heat, they first crossed the great **llanos**. Humboldt described it as a "vast and profound solitude" that "looked like an ocean covered with seaweed." When they reached the village of Villa de San Fernando, they traveled east on the Apure River until it connected with the Orinoco River, which they then followed south (upriver) to the Great Cataracts (present-day Atures and Maipures Rapids).

Although little was known of the Orinoco beyond this point, Humboldt and Bonpland plunged ahead to reach the upper Orinoco, find its source, and explore its tributaries. After battling the currents of the Orinoco, enduring endless downpours and "hands and faces swollen by mosquito bites," and living on bananas, water, and a little rice, they reached San Carlos on the Río Negro, at the border of Brazil and

Venezuela. (By this time Humboldt had accumulated a menagerie of twenty-five creatures, including a toucan, a macaw, seven parrots, and eight monkeys—all sharing the boat with the thirteen members of the expedition!)

On the return journey to the Caribbean coast of Venezuela, the members of the expedition endured even worse conditions as they traveled by way of the Casiquiare Canal. Besides having to cope with the devastating heat and a thick blanket of insects along the 200 miles of the Casiquiare, they also had to endure near starvation, eating ants and dry cacao to stay alive because they ran out of provisions. But however miserable the hardships, Humboldt achieved a main goal of his expedition: he proved that the Casiquiare Canal was a natural waterway connecting two large river systems, the Amazon and the Orinoco (it is the only such natural canal in the world). The expedition ended on June 13, 1800, at the mouth of the Orinoco in Angostura (present-day Ciudad Bolívar). Humboldt had measured the latitude and longitude of over fifty specific places, gathered data on climate and plant geography, and collected about 12,000 plant specimens, many of them new to science.

In late 1800 Humboldt embarked on a two-year expedition to the Andes mountains of Columbia, Ecuador, and Peru that would bring him international fame. He first traveled through 500 miles of uninhabited forests along Colombia's Magdalena River, then climbed 9,000 feet to the plateau of Bogotá. There he received a hero's welcome into the city of Santa Fe de Bogotá (the present-day capital of Colombia, Bogotá) and visited with the botanist José Celestino Mutis. Continuing the journey, the expedition went through a treacherous, snow-covered pass over the eastern end of the Andes, crossed the high desert region known as the Páramos of Pasto, and reached Quito, Ecuador. Humboldt spent six months exploring major volcanoes of the area, collecting data that would revolutionize the field of geology.

Humboldt's group then followed La Condamine's route from Quito to Peru. Humboldt stopped to climb Mount Chimborazo on June 23, 1802, making him the first person in history to climb to that height (20,702 feet above sea level, but short of its summit). Traveling south along the upper reaches of the Amazon toward Peru, the group crossed the magnetic equator. Humboldt's measurement of the earth's magnetic intensity at this place became the reference point for all geomagnetic measurements for the next fifty years. The expedition ended in Lima, Peru, on October 22, 1802. There Humboldt tried to determine the reason for the dry weather pattern along western South America. In the process he discovered the cold ocean current that flows north along the west coasts of Chile and Peru, which was named the Humboldt current in his honor.

Humboldt traveled on to Acapulco in March 1803. He spent the next year traveling around Mexico, researching its geography, economy, and politics, and compiling an authoritative map of the vice royalty. On March 7, 1804, he set sail from Veracruz for Havana, Cuba, in order to pick up his scientific collections being stored there and then to proceed home. However, he decided to make a detour to the United States for the express purpose of meeting President Thomas Jefferson, a man he much admired.

Arriving in Philadelphia in May of 1804, he was embraced by the scientific community. In Washington, D.C., he charmed everyone, prompting Dolley Madison to write, "He is the most polite, modest, well-informed, and interesting traveller we have ever met and is much pleased with America." He helped Jefferson determine the United States–Mexico border by loaning the president the detailed maps he had prepared. On June 30, 1804, Humboldt left for Bordeaux, France.

He lived in Paris for many years, devoting himself to the publication of the narratives of his expeditions. In 1827 he returned to Berlin, becoming an adviser to King Frederick William III of Prussia in 1830. He made one last expedition in 1829, spending nine months traversing Siberia on a mining survey for Czar Nicholas I of Russia. For the remaining years of his life Humboldt served as a diplomat and devoted his private time to writing his great work, the *Cosmos*, which he projected to be a comprehensive exposition of the physical world. When he died on May 6, 1859, he had completed five volumes of this monumental work.

Goethe called Humboldt a "true *cornu copiae* of natural science." He was indeed that—and much more. In the broadest sense, he opened up South America through the clear, detailed narratives of his expeditions, which offered a wealth of new information and insight. Today, Humboldt's memory is honored not only in South America and Berlin but also in Mexico City and Philadelphia, where statues of the great man have been erected. In addition, numerous cities and geographical features bear his name.

SUGGESTED READING: Douglas Botting, *Humboldt and Cosmos* (Harper & Row, 1973); Lotte Kellner, *Alexander von Humboldt* (Oxford University Press, 1963); Helmut de Terra, *Humboldt: The Life and Times of Alexander von Humboldt, 1769–1859* (Octagon Books, 1979); Victor Wolfgang von Hagen, *South America Called Them; Explorations of the Great Naturalists* (Knopf, 1945).

• Hume, Hamilton

Australian
b June 19, 1797; Parramatta, New South Wales
d April 19, 1873; Yass
Discovered Murray River; discovered Darling
River (with Charles Sturt)

The native-born Australian explorer Hamilton Hume is credited with making several major discoveries in the Yass Plains, Clyde River, Sydney, and Port Phillip Bay areas.

The son of Andrew Hume, a disreputable convict superintendent, Hamilton Hume was born near Sydney, New South Wales, in 1797 and began exploring south and west of Sydney at the age of seventeen. In the decade between 1814 and 1824, both on his own and as a government guide, he explored the Berrima and Bong Bong districts, the Sutton Forest, the Goulburn River, Lake Bathurst, Jervis Bay, the Yass Plains, and the Clyde River.

By the time he joined former merchant seaman William Hovell to explore the mountain ranges between Sydney and Port Phillip Bay in 1824, Hume was an experienced bushman. Hume, Hovell, and six convicts left Lake George and crossed the Murrumbidgee River on October 22 of that year on a raft consisting of their wagon and a tarpaulin. They next reached what later became known as the Murray River and named it the Hume River after the explorer's father, crossing it in another homemade craft.

Instead of following the southwestern course of the river, Hume and Hovell traveled due south. In the course of their journey, they used fallen trees to cross the Ovens and Goulburn rivers and found good grazing lands along the banks of the latter. Beyond it lay only scrubland full of leeches and razor grass. After surviving a brushfire, the explorers crossed the Great Dividing Range and reached the coast near Geelong on Port Phillip Bay on December 18. Hume and Hovell quarreled for most of the journey, largely because Hovell would not accept Hume's superior knowledge and experience in the bush. They continued to feud for the next fifty years.

In the southern summer of 1828–29 Hume joined Captain CHARLES STURT on an expedition across the Blue Mountains to explore the Macquarie Marshes. They reached the Darling River near present-day Burke, only to find that the river was too salty for drinking.

The government subsequently awarded Hume 1,200 acres of land in recognition of his discoveries. He retired to Yass, where he died in 1873.

Hamilton Hume. Australian Foreign Affairs and Trade Dept.

· Hunt, Wilson Price

American
b 1782?; Hopewell, New Jersey
d April 1842; St. Louis, Missouri
Blazed trail across Rocky Mountains south of
Lewis and Clark's route

In 1811, as a partner in John Jacob Astor's Pacific Fur Company, Wilson Price Hunt led the second great crossing of the Rocky Mountains, succeeding the 1804–1806 expedition of MERIWETHER LEWIS and WILLIAM CLARK. Although Hunt made at least one disastrous decision along the way, his expedition succeeded in discovering Union Pass (in what is now western Wyoming). A significant portion of the trail that Hunt blazed later became a part of the Oregon Trail.

Hunt moved from New Jersey to St. Louis in 1804 and for several years ran a general store there. In 1810 he joined up with businessman John Jacob Astor, whose intention was to exploit the fur trade west of the Rockies with a two-pronged attack. A ship carrying supplies was to be sent around South America's Cape Horn and north to the mouth of the Columbia River, where it would meet up with a party of fur trappers that had traveled overland from St. Louis. Astor put two men in charge of recruiting for the overland expedition. One was Canadian DONALD MC KENZIE, who had ten years of experience in the fur business; the other was Wilson Price Hunt, who had never been into the wilderness.

By the time Hunt and McKenzie had completed the difficult task of recruiting men for the trek to the Pacific, winter was coming on. Nonetheless, they started out from St. Louis, getting as far north on the Missouri River as what is now St. Joseph, Missouri, where they camped for the winter of 1810–11. While they were camped, Hunt received a letter from Astor putting him in full charge of the expedition. McKenzie was enraged.

In April 1811 the party set out, traveling up the Missouri as far as the Arikara Indian villages in present-day South Dakota. There, they spent close to three weeks trading for horses that would enable them to leave the river and travel overland in an attempt to avoid hostile Blackfoot Indians. In mid-July they set out across the plains into territory never before seen by non-Indians. They were awed—and intimidated—by the huge herds of buffalo, which could suddenly and unpredictably stampede. But the journey around the southern end of the Powder River basin passed uneventfully, and by mid-August they were in view of the Bighorn Mountains of what is now Wyoming.

At the Wind River in September, they found a way through the mountains at what is now called Union Pass. By September 26 the party had reached the Snake River, a tributary of the Columbia. There Hunt made the decision that turned the last part of the journey into a disaster. Despite warnings from local Indians who understood how treacherous the Snake could be, Hunt decided to turn loose all of the expedition's horses and take to the river in canoes. The French-Canadian **voyageurs** in the party were delighted—the decision put them back in their element—and they scoffed at the warnings of the Indians. For nine days, the canoes rushed down the Snake without problems. Then they reached the swirling waters they called Cauldron Linn (probably in what is now southern Idaho). There, a canoe was torn to pieces, and a man drowned.

For twelve days the party searched for a means of proceeding. Scouting ahead on the river, they found that it continued on its violent and treacherous course. At last they found a faint trail made by animals. Leaving behind valuable supplies in nine separate caches, the members of the party set out overland on November 9, each carrying his weapons and an equal share of the remaining food. In desperation they struggled through the bitter winter and rugged terrain toward the mouth of the Columbia. At times they divided into smaller groups, hoping to increase their chances of survival. Hunger reduced them to eating ground squirrels and beaver paws. A few men left the expedition to live among the Indians; several others became lost. But in the end the majority of the party staggered into Fort Astoria at the mouth of the Columbia. A party led by McKenzie arrived on January 18, 1812, and Hunt arrived with the main party about a month later.

From a business standpoint, Hunt's labors were for naught. The War of 1812 soon broke out between England and the United States, and during one of Hunt's absences from Astoria, his partners were persuaded by the presence of several heavily armed British ships to sell out to the Canadian North West Company. After two voyages to the Sandwich Islands (present-day Hawaii), Hunt left the Columbia River for the last time on April 3, 1814, returning to St. Louis, where he spent the rest of his life.

Despite the poor judgment sometimes exercised by Hunt on his transcontinental journey, it is generally considered to have been a success. Hunt discovered an important new route through the Rocky Mountains that opened up the Wind and Snake rivers to American trappers and the Oregon Territory to future settlement.

• Iberville, Pierre Le Moyne, Sieur d'

French-Canadian
b July 1661; Montréal
d July 1706; Havana, Cuba?
Explored lower Mississippi River and established French outposts on Gulf of Mexico

Pierre Le Moyne, Sieur d'Iberville, was more soldier than explorer. His efforts were largely

Pierre Le Moyne, Sieur d'Iberville. Louisiana State Museum.

directed toward expelling the English from North America or at least containing them along the Atlantic seaboard. To that end, he explored the Mississippi River north from the Gulf of Mexico and as well established three fortified posts on the gulf.

Born in **New France**, Iberville joined the French navy at the age of fourteen, but it was not until 1686 that he began his fighting career in North America. That year he and two of his brothers took part in an expedition against the English in James Bay, the southern extension of Hudson Bay. During this expedition, Iberville's reputation for bravery became firmly established. As leader of a French assault on Fort Moose, he found himself inside the fort and cut off from his troops when the English managed to close the gate behind him. Brandishing a pistol in one hand and a sword in the other, he held off the entire band of Englishmen until his men forced the gate open again.

When this campaign was successfully completed, Iberville was made governor of three Hudson Bay trading posts. From 1686 to 1697,

he traveled constantly among Hudson Bay, Québec, and France in a vain attempt to keep the English from reestablishing themselves in the bay.

Iberville also served in various other campaigns against the English, including one to Corlaer (present-day Schenectady, New York), in which the entire settlement was pillaged and burned and sixty inhabitants were massacred, and another against St. John's, the fortified English settlement in Newfoundland. After subduing St. John's, Iberville's forces destroyed thirty-six English hamlets and fisheries along the Newfoundland coast. As in all of his other campaigns against the English, Iberville's victories in Newfoundland were short-lived. As soon as he left, the English began rebuilding their settlements.

Iberville's 1697 campaign in Hudson Bay was his last in New France and, like all of the others, characterized by daring and swift attacks on his part. In one lively battle, Iberville, by his brilliant naval maneuvering, managed to sink one English ship and capture another without resistance. While a third fled, Iberville was forced to abandon his own sinking ship. Leading his men ashore, he commenced an attack on the strongest English fort. After five days of skirmishing, the English surrendered. Iberville soon departed for France, never to see Hudson Bay again.

Impressed with Iberville's exploits in the north, the French court decided he was just the person to establish a French presence in Louisiana, as SIEUR DE LA SALLE had tried but failed to do more than ten years before. Thus, in October 1698 Iberville sailed from Brest in order to find "the mouth [of the Mississippi], . . . select a good site which can be defended with few men, and . . . block entry to the river by other nations." He sailed first to St.-Domingue (present-day Santo Domingo, Dominican Republic), then north to Florida and along the gulf coast, passing the Spanish settlement at Pensacola. On March 2, 1699, the ship was driven by a storm into the delta of the Mississippi, but Iberville, although not sure he had the right river, sailed up it until he met Bayagoula Indians. Their chief appeared wearing a blue cloak that he had been given by La Salle's friend, Henri de Tonti, thirteen years earlier. Later Iberville's brother discovered a letter left for La Salle by Tonti. Convinced that he was on the Mississippi, Iberville turned back toward the delta, on the way exploring Lakes Maurepas and Pontchartrain.

After building a fort at Biloxi, Iberville sailed back to France, but he was ordered to return to Louisiana almost immediately in order to fortify the French presence in the region. This time he again traveled up the Mississippi, visiting the sun-worshipping Natchez Indians and their kin, the Taensas. On the way back down the Mississippi he built a wooden fort 40 miles from the mouth of the river. On a third expedition (1701) he built a fort at Mobile Bay.

This was the last of Iberville's activity in Louisiana. Ill health kept him in France for a time. By 1706 he was well enough to sail again for America with a squadron of twelve vessels whose purpose was to harass the English in the West Indies. After capturing the island of Nevis, however, Iberville died in Cuba where he had sailed presumably to sell a load of iron he had brought from France. After his death, Iberville's reputation suffered serious damage when he was deemed guilty of carrying merchandise, mainly iron, for illicit trade in the Caribbean.

Despite the cloud under which he died, Pierre Le Moyne, Sieur d'Iberville, has been called the first truly Canadian hero, not only because he was born in Canada but also because his character exhibited that toughness which the hard new land bred in its native sons. However self-motivated his exploits, Iberville's sincere devotion to France and his dedication to the task of driving the English out of North America were unquestionable.

· Ibn Battūta (Abū ʿAbd Allāh Muhammad ibn ʿAbd Allāh al-Lawātī at-Tanjī ibn Battūtah)

Arab
b February 24, 1304; Tangier, Morocco
d 1368 or 1369; Morocco
Traveled throughout Middle East, Asia, Europe, and Africa

I left Tangier, my city of birth, one Thursday [June 13, 1325], with the intention of making a pilgrimage to the Holy House [in Mecca] and of visiting the Tomb of the Prophet [in Medina]. . . .

So begins the chronicle of Ibn Battūta's twenty-six years of travel. His first two destinations revealed the religious orientation that would govern the course of his later travels. Ibn Battūta, a staunch Muslim, visited every major Islamic territory in the world except central Persia (now Iran), Armenia, and Georgia. By the time he died, his insatiable appetite for exploration had led him to traverse some 75,000 miles. The *Rihlah*, Ibn Battūta's chronicle of his wanderings, ranks as one of the most famous travel books in history. Ibn Battūta was without question the greatest Arab traveler of the medieval period.

Ibn Battūta was born in 1304 into a family with a long-standing tradition of service as Muslim judges. Although little is known of his early years, his family's position assures that he was well educated and widely read. When Ibn Battūta was twenty-one, he undertook the pilgrimage to Mecca and Medina referred to in the opening lines of his book. His journey had a dual purpose: to make the once-in-a-lifetime pilgrimage to Mecca (in what is now Saudi Arabia) required of all devout Muslims and to study with distinguished scholars from the East.

What was intended only as preliminary preparation for a career, however, became a career in itself. Ibn Battūta came to be ruled by a passion "to travel through the earth." The extent to which he achieved his goal reveals how strictly he observed his primary rule for travel: as much as possible, never pass a second time over any road. This rule suggests that Ibn Battūta traveled for the sheer joy of visiting new lands and learning about their native peoples. He took a particular interest in the sultans he met, and many of them generously rewarded his attention with contributions that enabled him to continue his journeys. Ibn Battūta was also curious about the many different religious brotherhoods he encountered. While these diverse elements animate the chronicle of the *Rihlah*, his narrative is especially valuable for its information on the history of Asia Minor, the area in which he traveled most intensively.

Indeed, Ibn Battūta did not even reach Mecca without first taking a thorough tour of Syria. He had traveled east from Tangier, along the Mediterranean to Cairo, where he boarded a boat for a trip down the Nile. He then went to the port of Aidhab, on the Red Sea. From there, he intended to sail across the Red Sea to Jidda (in present-day Saudi Arabia), but a regional war made the passage impossible and forced him to return to Cairo. On his way overland from Cairo to Mecca and Medina, he seized the opportunity to explore Syria (considerably to their north). In his book, Ibn Battūta implies that he may have already decided before leaving Egypt to visit all the countries in the world (excepting the Christian countries)—a decision that would account for his circuitous route between Cairo and Medina (in what is now Saudi Arabia).

Ibn Battūta remained in Mecca and Medina for a short time, then set out across the Arabian peninsula for Basra (now in Iraq). From Basra, he followed the Euphrates upriver to Baghdad, then proceeded along the Tigris River to Diyarbakir (now in Turkey), before returning to Mecca. He spent the next several years attending to his studies (probably law and religion) before his wanderlust compelled him to form an expedition to explore East Africa in 1330.

Ibn Battūta's expeditionary force in all likelihood included wives, children, and many servants. They sailed to the south end of the Red

Sea, where they had to wait for the storms of the southwest monsoon to subside and the gentle winds of the northwest monsoon to rise. When friendly winds came, they put to sea again, making stops along the eastern coast of Africa at Mombasa (now in Kenya) and Kilwa (now in Tanzania). Kilwa, Ibn Battūta reported, "is one of the most beautiful and well-built of all cities. It is built entirely of timber."

After sailing back up the African and Arabian coasts to the Persian Gulf, Ibn Battūta made his third pilgrimage to Mecca. He then decided to sail to India, where he had heard that the sultan showed great hospitality toward learned foreign travelers. Not content to sail down the Red Sea and across the Arabian Sea—he had passed that way before—Ibn Battūta sailed north, then crossed Asia Minor overland on his way to Sinop, a port on the Black Sea. From there, he journeyed to the Caucasus and was granted an audience by the khan of the Golden Horde. After an excursion up the frozen Volga River (in what is now the Soviet Union), Ibn Battūta made a detour to Constantinople (now

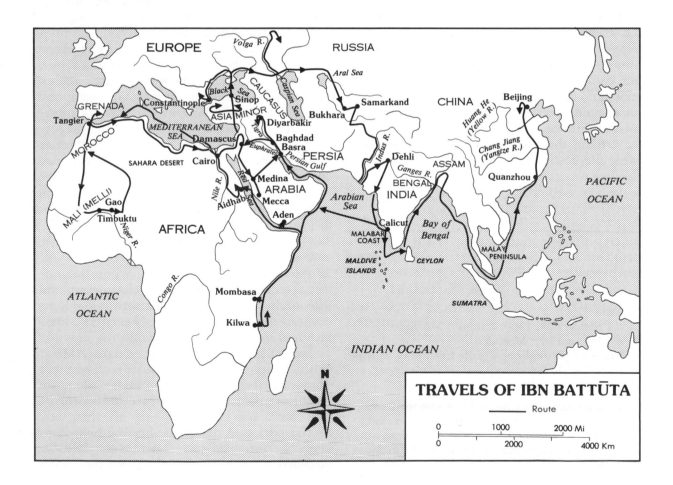

TRAVELS OF IBN BATTŪTA

——— Route

Istanbul, Turkey), a city he described in great detail. Ibn Battūta then made his way across the steppes (arid plains) of Russia, around the north side of the Caspian and Aral seas, and passed through the city of Bukhara before entering Afghanistan. He reached the border of India on September 12, 1333.

Upon his arrival in Delhi, Ibn Battūta found the sultan Mohammed bin Tughlak as benevolent as his reputation suggested. Ibn Battūta was given robes of honor, an annual salary, and an estate. Soon the sultan made him a judge over the city, a position he maintained for nine years. However, his comfortable situation became potentially lethal when he was arrested for his chance association with a sheik who conspired against the sultan. Ibn Battūta reported, "Then the Sultan commanded that four slaves were to watch over me in the audience hall and not to move from my side. Such an order usually means that the person under guard does not escape with his life." Although the sultan was also known to be capable of great cruelty, he showed mercy toward Ibn Battūta and reinstated him as a judge.

Soon thereafter, the sultan commissioned Ibn Battūta to lead an embassy on his behalf to the emperor of China. The traveler's first attempt was short-lived: soon after the expedition left Delhi in July 1342, it was attacked by rebel Indians, and Ibn Battūta barely managed to escape. The second attempt was no less hazardous. After journeying by land and sea from Delhi to Calicut, all of the expedition's ships were sunk by a fierce storm in the Arabian Sea. Ibn Battūta was the sole survivor; he happened to be in a mosque praying for the success of the expedition when the storm struck.

Ibn Battūta chose not to return to Delhi but sailed south from Calicut to the Maldive Islands in the Indian Ocean instead. After working there as a judge for eighteen months, he tried to return to India, but his ship was driven off course and he landed on Ceylon (present-day Sri Lanka). "The entire coast of the land of Ceylon is littered with the trunks of the cinnamon-tree, which come floating down the rivers from the mountains," Ibn Battūta observed. He saw other exotic items as well:

> On the forehead of the white elephant I saw seven rubies which were larger than hen's eggs, and at the palace of the sultan Airi Sakarvati I saw a spoon of precious stones which was as large as the palm of a hand filled with oil

of aloes. I wondered at this, but he said, "We have others which are far larger."

Ibn Battūta then sailed from Ceylon to India's Malabar Coast, but he was shipwrecked and robbed, so he returned to the Maldives by way of Calicut. He next decided to complete his twice-aborted trip to China. He sailed for forty-three days along the east coast of India until he reached Bengal and Assam, then turned southeast until he reached Sumatra (in what is now Indonesia). The ruler of that island equipped Ibn Battūta with a junk (a type of Chinese ship) for the seventy-one-day voyage across the South China Sea to Quanzhou (or, as he referred to it, Zayton), in China.

Like MARCO POLO, Ibn Battūta was fascinated by Quanzhou and the other cities he visited in China, including Beijing. But his descriptions of them lack intensity, perhaps due to his personal reactions to the country: "I did not like the land of China, in spite of the many beautiful things it may have possessed. On the contrary, I was greatly troubled at the idolatry that prevailed there. . . . When I happened to meet believers in China, it was as if I were meeting with my kith and kin."

From Quanzhou, he began his slow return to Egypt, passing through Sumatra, Calicut, Arabia, Persia, and Syria, where he witnessed the Black Death (the epidemic of bubonic plague) of 1348. From Cairo, he made a final pilgrimage to Mecca, then decided at long last to return to his home. He arrived in Morocco in November of 1349; he was forty-five years old and a veteran of twenty-four years of travel.

His keen appetite for travel had not yet been sated, however. The following year, he set out to visit a Muslim region not yet known to him: the kingdom of Granada, the last stronghold of Moorish Spain. In 1352 Ibn Battūta was sent by the sultan of Morocco to explore the interior of Africa, primarily to learn more about the little-known empire of Mali (probably Timbuktu), whose ruler had caused a great stir when he appeared in Cairo at the head of a vast and wealthy caravan making a pilgrimage to Mecca. Ibn Battūta's itinerary took him across the broad stretches of the Sahara Desert. He spent seven months in Timbuktu and one month in Gao (both now in Mali). It was an expedition Ibn Battūta had not desired, and he summed it up by saying he had "never known a more unpleasant route than this."

Ibn Battūta finally returned to Morocco for the last time in 1353. At the request of the sultan, Ibn Battūta described his extensive travels to the scribe Ibn Juzayy, who rendered Ibn Battūta's simple prose in an ornate style, adding fragments of poetry to the narrative. The result, Ibn Battūta's *Rihlah*, is a document of lasting historical and geographical significance. After journeys totaling some 75,000 miles, the "traveler of Islam," as he is often called, lived out his final years as a judge in a town in Morocco.

SUGGESTED READING: Daniel J. Boorstin, *The Discoverers* (Random House, 1983); Frank Debenham, *Discovery and Exploration* (Crescent Books, 1960); Ross E. Dunn, *The Adventures of Ibn Battūta: A Muslim Traveler of the 14th Century* (University of California Press, 1986); H. A. R. Gibb, ed., *The Travels of Ibn Battūta*, 3 vols. (Cambridge University Press, 1958–71).

• Idrīsī, al- (Idrīsī, ash-Sharīf al-)

Arab
b 1100; Ceuta, Morocco
d 1165 or 1166; Sicily
Wrote one of most important medieval works of descriptive geography

The Arab known as al-Idrīsī (whose full name is Abū 'Abd Allāh Muḥammad ibn Muḥammad ibn 'Abd Allāh ibn Idrīs al-Ḥammūdī al-Hasanī al-Idrīsī) spent most of his life working for a Christian—which may explain why little is known about the life of this remarkable geographer. After extensive travels across northern Africa, western Europe, and Asia Minor, al-Idrīsī was invited by Roger II, the Norman king of Sicily, to become the official court geographer in about 1145. Although his fellow Muslims would subsequently judge al-Idrīsī a renegade for entering the service of a Christian king, the forty-five-year-old traveler accepted the position and remained part of the king's court for the rest of his life. His geographical achievements during his twenty-year tenure at Palermo included a map of the world engraved on a silver plate measuring twelve feet by five feet, an extensive geographical key to the world map, and another world map divided into seventy sections by a grid of horizontal and vertical lines.

Al-Idrīsī's early life is unusually obscure for a person of his stature, but his name suggests a direct link to Mohammed, the prophet and originator of the Islamic religion. Al-Idrīsī was born in a Spanish enclave in Morocco, into a family descended from the Hammudid line, which had once ruled parts of Spain and North Africa. The Hammudids had fled to Morocco in 1057 when they lost their last foothold in Spain. They traced their lineage through the Idrisids of Morocco to al-Hasan ibn 'Ali, Mohammed's eldest grandson. Why a Muslim with such a heritage should be inclined to enter the service of a Christian king remains a puzzle, but world geography prospered as a result.

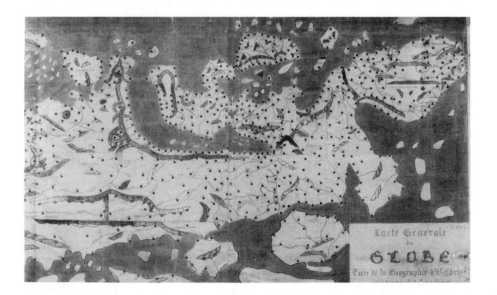

A map by al-Idrīsī. Bibliothèque Nationale, Paris.

Using clues found in his work and other evidence, historians have been able to piece together an outline of al-Idrīsī's early life. He is known to have lived in the Spanish city of Córdoba; in Marrakesh, Morocco; and in Qustanti-nah, Algeria. When he was about sixteen, he visited Asia Minor, though the reason for his journey is unknown. His accurate, detailed knowledge of North Africa and Spain suggests he spent a number of years traveling throughout these regions. Other journeys probably took him to Portugal, the Atlantic coast of France, and southern England.

Al-Idrīsī had garnered a substantial collection of firsthand geographical information by the time he entertained Roger II's invitation to come to Palermo to make a map of the world. Two possible reasons have been advanced to account for his acceptance of the king's offer. Some of al-Idrīsī's Hammudi relatives had already attained powerful and prestigious positions among the Muslims of Sicily, according to the Spanish-Arab traveler Ibn Jubayr. Al-Idrīsī may also have been swayed by the nature of Roger's appeal. According to a fourteenth-century Arab scholar, Roger told al-Idrīsī:

You are a member of the caliphal family [that descended from Mohammed]. For that reason, when you happen to be among Muslims, their kings will seek to kill you, whereas when you are with me you are assured the safety of your person.

Whatever his reason, he agreed to become the king's official court geographer and embarked on a major new course in his career.

Al-Idrīsī drew on several different resources as he began to draw his map and to compile his book on geography. Realizing the value of firsthand observation, he dispatched a number of people, including some who were skilled artists, to various countries to bring back eyewitness reports and sketches of geographical features. One expedition, for example, set out for extreme northern Europe in order to locate the tribes of Gog and Magog. The existence of these tribes had long been an article of faith, since both the Hebrew prophet Ezekiel, author of one of the books of the Bible, and the Muslim Koran warned of these barbarian cannibals who would invade from the north. Because no one before al-Idrīsī had discovered the precise location of Gog and Magog, the source of the coming invasion was unknown, making it all the more

threatening. Al-Idrīsī, confident that on-site observation was the key to good geography, sent a group of men to discover the legendary wall that held back the pagan forces of the Apocalypse.

He also made broad use of the work of earlier geographers and cartographers. The grid scheme employed on his map is similar to that on Chinese maps; neither makes allowance for the earth's curvature. Grid maps of China probably reached the Arabs in Sicily by way of the Arab colony at Guangzhou (Canton). Al-Idrīsī was also influenced by PTOLEMY's *Megiste*, or The Greatest, as the ancient Greek mathematician's influential work on geography and astronomy was known. This book had been translated into Arabic by the ninth century and was thus available for use by both Arab and European scholars.

Al-Idrīsī's reliance on Ptolemy is most apparent in his drawing of the regions beyond the Mediterranean basin and the Balkans. In fact, al-Idrīsī's map is not significantly better than one that a classical cartographer may have drawn from Ptolemy's description of the outlying areas of the earth. However, he was able to name some of the islands in the Indian Ocean, and he knew from Arabian sea captains that Africa did not extend as far to the east as Ptolemy thought, but was bounded by the open sea.

After al-Idrīsī had finished his research, he produced two maps of the world and one book on geography. The map that was engraved on a silver panel was destroyed by a plundering mob only a few years after it had been made. Copies of the second map have been preserved, however, and they show a grid covering regions north of the equator. The seventy sections of the grid are formed by seven horizontal lines that divide the map into climate zones of equal size and by ten equidistant vertical lines.

Because al-Idrīsī had not mastered some of the physical and mathematical aspects of geography, his map was not as accurate as it might have been. For example, even though he was obviously familiar with many of the places in the Baltic region, he was unable to outline the countries in that area properly. He also did not make use of important geographic advances made by other scientists of his day, nor was he sufficiently critical of earlier Greek and Arab sources.

Nevertheless, al-Idrīsī's monumental work of

descriptive geography establishes him as one of the greatest geographers of the medieval period. Often referred to as *The Book of Roger* in honor of the king who sponsored its author, its Arabic title means "The Pleasure Excursion of One Who Is Eager to Traverse the Regions of the World." Completed in 1154, shortly before Roger's death, it contains a wealth of vital geographical information, especially about the Mediterranean basin and the Balkans.

Geography and cartography did not consume all of al-Idrīsī's considerable talents. His *Book of Simple Drugs* lists common drugs of the day, naming each in as many as twelve different languages. He was also a dedicated student of Arabic literature and an accomplished poet, with some of his verses surviving to this day.

• Irala, Domingo Martínez de

Spanish
b 1487; Vergara
d 1557; Asunción, Paraguay
Explored South America

Domingo Martínez de Irala, the first governor of Paraguay, was also one of its initial European colonists. He first came to South America as a member of an ill-fated 1535 expedition to the Río de la Plata. He subsequently settled on the shore of the Paraguay River at a site that became the country's capital of Asunción. While there is some question as to whether he actually founded Asunción, Irala is credited with developing it into a powerful colonial center. Irala's style of colonization was unusual among explorers and settlers of his era. Not only did he befriend the natives of the region, but he also made efforts to adapt to their mode of life.

The quest for silver originally brought Irala to the continent to take part in the massive Spanish-German expedition led by Don Pedro de Mendoza. When the explorers reached the mouth of the Río de la Plata and built a settlement there (Buenos Aires) at the end of 1535, they experienced severe famine and attacks from the hostile native Indians. Of the more than 2,500 Spaniards originally with the expedition, nearly 2,000 died, most of hunger; the survivors fled from the disastrous settlement. Irala was among those who escaped north into the interior, stopping nearly 1,000 miles from

Buenos Aires at the point where the Paraguay and Pilcomayo rivers join. The fort built by the explorers in 1537 was dedicated in August on the Feast of the Assumption and named Asunción in honor of the holy day. As a colonization site, Asunción carried two important advantages over the first settlement—its land was fertile enough to provide food, and its native Indians were peaceful.

Well-organized and placid by nature, these Indians, the Guaraní, lived in small communities of six families, each surrounded by a wall of logs to guard against attack. Irala and his men waged no attacks on them, however. Unlike many of the aggressive colonists of the day who were determined to displace or even exterminate native tribes, Irala's group tried to live amicably among the Guaraní, and Irala even encouraged his men to intermarry with the Indian women, a trend that resulted in a large population of Spanish-Indian descendants known as **mestizos**. While the Spanish settlers clearly became dominant within the region, Irala made some unusual concessions to native sensibilities. Rather than force the Indians to learn Spanish, for example, he insisted that both the original colonists and the missionaries who followed learn the Guaraní language. The cooperation of the Indians ensured, Irala and his group undertook further colonization efforts.

Crediting Irala's leadership for the success of Asunción, as well as for much of the expansion in the region, the settlers elected him governor of Paraguay by acclamation. The king of Spain confirmed this appointment in 1539, after the governor he had sent to rule the territory was rejected by the colonists.

Using Asunción as a base of operations, Irala explored other areas of La Plata, a vast region that encompassed present-day Paraguay, Uruguay, Argentina, and portions of Bolivia and Chile. Returning south, Irala's men established settlements at Corrientes (in present-day Argentina), Santa Fe (in present-day Bolivia), and once again in Buenos Aires. To the northwest, they established a link with the Spanish settlers in Peru. In addition, they helped solidify the Spanish colonial holdings in Brazil. The eastern half of Brazilian territory had been granted to Portugal, and under Irala's direction a number of forts went up along the boundary line to protect against encroachment by the Portuguese.

These expansion initiatives, spanning nearly

two decades, steadily increased the size and importance of Asunción, which was to remain the administrative center of the region's Spanish colonies for roughly six more decades. An educational system took root in Asunción with the arrival of Jesuit missionaries, who established the first school in Paraguay in 1544. In addition to their thriving farming efforts, residents of the area raised cattle successfully after 1555, when livestock were brought in from Bolivia.

Such early Spanish successes in colonizing central South America were in large part due to the pioneering efforts of Irala. In his twenty-two years of work there as both explorer and administrator, he proved to be a resourceful and effective leader, noted especially for the unusual cooperation and consideration he extended to the native Indians of the region.

• Jansz (Janszoon), Willem

Dutch
b late 1500s; ?
d after 1629; ?
Explored northern Australian coast

A sea captain from Amsterdam, Willem Jansz is credited with being the first European to investigate the Australian mainland. Early in the seventeenth century, he explored miles of the continent's northern coast.

Jansz made the first of his many journeys to the East Indies in 1598 as a mate aboard the *Hollandia*, a vessel in the Dutch East India Company fleet. With him was Jan Lodewycksz van Roossengin, who would later accompany Jansz on his exploration of the Australian coast. Eventually Jansz was made skipper of the three-masted *Duyfken* (Dove) under Admiral Steven van der Hagen. When van der Hagen captured the island of Amboina in the Moluccas (or Spice Islands), he left Jansz there to make some exploratory journeys in the region. Van Roossengin came aboard as a commercial agent.

Jansz left the north coast of Java (in present-day Indonesia) on November 18, 1605. He sailed first to the Aru Islands, west of New Guinea, then to New Guinea near what is now False Cape. From there, Jansz sailed south by southeast into the Gulf of Carpentaria and reached the west side of what is now Australia's Cape

York Peninsula at today's Pennefather River. He then sailed south across the mouth of Albatross Bay, charted the coast as far south as Cape Keerweer, then returned to Albatross Bay.

When he went ashore near the mouth of the present-day Batavia River, Jansz encountered **aborigines**, who attacked and killed some of his men. He then continued north past Crab Island, then left the coast about 30 miles southwest of Cape York and sailed west past Prince of Wales Island and north of Banks, Mulgrave, and Jervis islands to the south coast of New Guinea. Amazingly, he covered 200 miles of Australian coastline without finding the Torres Strait. He mistook the western end of the strait for part of a long bay, and thought that the Cape York Peninsula and south coast of New Guinea all were part of a continuous coastline. Jansz's journal of the voyage was lost; but an entry on the area in the books of the Dutch East India Company reads "no good to be done here," so apparently Jansz was not impressed with what he saw.

On a subsequent voyage in 1618, after having sailed east from Africa's Cape of Good Hope with skipper Lenaert Jacobszoon aboard the *Mauritius*, Jansz found what he believed to be a large, inhabited island at 22° South latitude. It was probably the peninsula now called the North West Cape on the west side of Australia's Exmouth Gulf.

Jansz later served as a maritime commander in the Dutch wars against the Portuguese and the English. He retired to the Netherlands with the rank of admiral in 1629 after a long and distinguished career in the service of the Dutch East India Company.

• Jenkinson, Anthony

English
b ?
d 1611
Explored central Asia; advocated northeast sea route from England to Asia

Anthony Jenkinson was an English explorer who was motivated by a desire to find new markets for English goods. He directed his investigative energies toward the east: China and, in later years, India. Jenkinson hoped to establish a northeastern sea passage to these areas, enabling British merchant ships to avoid the long and perilous southern route around Africa to the East. Jenkinson did not succeed in finding the passage he sought, but he did help set in motion a pattern of exploration and development that would eventually lead to English domination of seaborne trade during the Elizabethan age.

In the mid-sixteenth century, Spain was both an example and a nemesis to English merchants. It had used its newfound mineral wealth as the basis for developing extensive trade links with other countries. Spanish merchants were the envy of traders everywhere, a situation reinforced by the Spanish fleet's rule of the seas. The challenge posed by the Spanish led to a revival of interest among the English in seeking a northern route to Asia, outside the realm of Spanish dominance.

Consequently, in 1557 Jenkinson embarked on a three-year expedition to inaugurate trade with China. He traveled first to Moscow, where he obtained letters of introduction from the Russian czar to rulers in the East. With these in hand, he set out for central Asia in 1558. He and his men sailed south from Moscow on the Volga River until they reached Astrakhan, where the Volga empties into the Caspian Sea. After crossing to the east coast of the Caspian, they disembarked and traveled east by camel caravan through Bukhara to establish trade with merchants from China and eastern Asia.

In the years following his return to England, Jenkinson worked to develop commercial relations with India. The sea voyage to India, however, was more hazardous than the journey he had made to Bukhara. Unpredictable weather, uncharted waters, and the guns of the Spanish fleet combined to challenge traders who might travel by sea from England to India. Jenkinson placed his faith in a northern sea route to the east, and in 1565 he asked Elizabeth I, queen of England, to fund another search for the northern route, telling her that he did not doubt the existence of such a passage. The queen denied his request, choosing to support a rival expedition, which ended in failure.

Jiménez de Quesada, Gonzalo

Spanish
b 1510?; Córdoba
d February 16, 1579; Bogotá, Colombia
Explored Colombia; founded city of Bogotá

A lawyer by profession, Gonzalo Jiménez de Quesada was unique among the Spanish **conquistadores** in that he pursued diplomacy over bloodshed in his conquests. In 1536 he led an extraordinary expedition through the jungle maze and rugged terrain of the Colombian interior, intending to reach Peru. Instead he discovered the Chibcha Indian empire, a legendary land of gold. Within three years he had not only explored much of present-day Colombia but had also taken control of the Chibcha region, founded present-day Bogotá, and averted war with other conquistadores who claimed the region.

Jiménez de Quesada was born about 1510 in Córdoba, Spain, and studied at the University of Salamanca. He had an established law practice in Granada by 1533, but in 1535 he left Spain for the New World to become magistrate of Santa Marta, a settlement on the Caribbean coast of present-day Colombia. In 1536 he was chosen by the governor of the province to lead an expedition whose purpose was twofold: to obtain more information on the geographical features of the province and to try to reach Peru via the Magdalena River.

Departing Santa Marta on April 5, 1536, with about 600 men, Jiménez de Quesada proceeded eastward, circling the Sierra Nevada de Santa Marta to avoid hostile Indians. Traveling along the flooded banks of the Magdalena River during the rainy season, the party survived attacks by crocodiles and other wild animals, plagues of insects, and intense heat. After reaching a prearranged point on the Magdalena, they waited for five ships that had been sent to join them. When these did not arrive (three had wrecked and two had returned to port), Jiménez de Quesada's strong will prevailed over pleas to turn back, and the expedition continued. Jiménez de Quesada and his men were finally met by three ships with supplies, but not before they had had to resort to eating snakes, lizards, and bats after their food had run out.

Pressing onward, they covered only about 1 mile a day, hacking their way through dense undergrowth and moving through snake-infested swamps. It took them eight months to reach the Indian village of Tora (present-day Barrancabermeja) on the Magdalena, only 300 miles from their starting point.

Hearing that beyond the mountains lived an advanced Indian civilization that mined gold and emeralds, Jiménez de Quesada decided to abandon the Magdalena River and penetrate farther inland (to the east). By March of 1537, he was in the uplands of present-day Colombia with only 166 men left. After subduing the Tunja and Cundinamarca Indians, Jiménez de Quesada and his men reached the plateau of Bogotá, the land of the Chibcha Indians, where they found gold, emeralds, and semiprecious stones. The Chibcha were friendly to the Spaniards and gave them gifts of gold hearts, each weighing two pounds. Jiménez de Quesada named the new land he had conquered New Granada and founded the city of Santa Fe de Bogotá (present-day Bogotá).

In 1539 two other conquistadores reached the plateau of Bogotá: NIKOLAUS FEDERMANN, who had come west from Venezuela, and SEBASTIÁN DE BENALCÁZAR, who had come north from Quito, Ecuador. Jiménez de Quesada managed to avoid a conquistadorial war through negotiation. The three expeditionary forces agreed to leave together to submit their various claims to the **Council of the Indies** in Spain. Disappointingly, the council awarded Jiménez de Quesada only an honorary position rather than a governorship, primarily because he was not adept at the kind of political maneuvering needed to support such a claim.

After traveling in France and Portugal from 1541 until 1545, he returned to Spain where he received the title of marshal of New Granada. In 1551 he went back to Bogotá, where he was respected as a far-sighted and humane leader by Spaniards and Indians alike.

Jiménez de Quesada made one last expedition in 1569 to search east of the Andes for **El Dorado**, the legendary city of gold. (He did not believe that the Chibcha empire he had already conquered was El Dorado, despite the fact that it was located in the area where the land of El Dorado was reputed to be.) Traveling across the mountains and **llanos** of New Granada, he got as far as the Orinoco River where modern Colombia and Venezuela meet. After three years of great suffering from disease and near starvation, those left in his expedition gave up and returned to Bogotá, unsuccessful in their quest.

Jiménez de Quesada died in Bogotá in 1579, after spending his last years writing an accurate account of his conquest of New Granada. An honest and gifted leader, he managed to explore and conquer a huge area of Colombia without the usual wide-scale bloodshed.

· Jolliet (Joliet), Louis

French-Canadian
b 1645; Beauport, Québec
d 1700; Gulf of St. Lawrence?
Explored upper Mississippi River

Born in Québec more than 100 years after the first French colonists arrived in Canada in 1541, Louis Jolliet was the first native North American of European heritage to make a mark exploring the continent. He traveled along the Mississippi River in 1673 on a five-month, 2,500-mile expedition that was accomplished with considerable skill, caution, and diplomacy toward the Indian tribes of the region. This expedition paved the way for the French domination of the Mississippi Valley, which lasted until Louis XV ceded the region to the English at the close of the French and Indian Wars, ninety years after the expedition.

Jolliet's parents, Jean and Marie, emigrated from France in the early part of the seventeenth century and settled near Québec, where their third child, Louis, was baptized on September 21, 1645. After Jean, a wheelwright and wagonmaker, died in 1651, Marie remarried and the family moved into Québec proper. Along with his two brothers, Adrien and Zacharie, Louis attended Jesuit school, distinguishing himself in mapmaking and music.

During Jolliet's childhood, New France (comprising regions lying along both sides of the length of the St. Lawrence River and into the eastern Great Lakes) was a wilderness. The French drive to settle the area had been slowed by governmental disinterest, the death of the French explorer SAMUEL DE CHAMPLAIN, and the fierce hostility of the Iroquois Confederation, which was responsible for the torture and deaths of a number of Catholic missionaries. Nevertheless, Jesuit "black robes" and rugged fur trappers ventured farther and farther west each year. In 1638 JEAN NICOLETT DE BELLEBORNE

A bronze plaque of Louis Jolliet. Chicago Historical Society.

(Marie Jolliet's brother-in-law) reached Lake Michigan, and by 1670, Jesuit missionaries were preaching to Indians in what is now eastern Wisconsin.

In 1662, Jolliet took minor religious orders, remaining at the Québec seminary while his older brother, Adrien, started a fur-trading business at Cap de la Madeleine on the St. Lawrence River. During this time Louis devoted himself to music—becoming accomplished on the harpsichord, flute, trumpet, and organ—and to the art of formal disputation. But by 1667 he had left the clergy (for reasons that remain unclear) and journeyed to France, where he is believed to have studied cartography.

During his absence a new governor, the Comte de Frontenac, and Jean Talon, his intendant (an administrative official), established themselves in New France. Talon in particular paid attention to rumors spread by fur traders, missionaries, and Indians about copper deposits near the Great Lakes and a "Big Water" still farther west that might lead to China. He commissioned several expeditions, one of which included Adrien Jolliet.

By October 1668 Louis had returned from France. At some point during his stay abroad, he had reached the decision to join Adrien in the fur business. To that end, he borrowed 587 **livres** from his bishop for guns, **wampum**, tobacco, and other equipment.

There are no records to indicate exactly how Louis spent the next two years. It is known that he and Adrien drew up a contract to trade with the Ottawa Indians in 1670 and that by March of that year Adrien had died. That summer Louis journeyed to Sault Ste. Marie, where he established a trading post and met Father JACQUES MARQUETTE.

In the summer of 1672, Intendant Talon summoned Louis to Québec. Had Adrien lived, he might have been the Jolliet to receive the Intendant's commission to explore westward in search of the great river reported by various Indian tribes. But Louis, by now an experienced fur trader, an ex-seminarian still favored by the Jesuits, and a talented mapmaker, was a strong replacement. As was customary for French explorers, he had to finance the trip himself, though he was granted exclusive right to trade with Indians along his route, giving him the chance to recoup his expenses. Jolliet carefully selected **voyageurs** to accompany him west, among them his younger brother, Zacharie. He also carried orders with him from the superior of Jesuit Missions on the Lakes that would add a final member to the company—the missionary and Indian linguist, Father Marquette.

Rendezvousing with Marquette in December 1672 at the Mission of St. Ignace near the Straits of Mackinac (joining Lakes Michigan and Huron), Jolliet spent the winter with him sketching a map of their proposed route and interviewing Indians about the body of water they knew as the Messipi. Then, on May 17, 1673, Jolliet, Marquette, and five fellow voyageurs set off in two birch-bark canoes loaded with food and equipment, including Jolliet's **astrolabe** and Marquette's traveling altar. They canoed around the northwest shore of Lake Michigan (averaging 30 miles a day) until they arrived at the mouth of the Fox River on Green Bay. There

Menomini Indians warned the party to turn back, reporting that the inhabitants of the Mississippi Valley were merciless savages and that the great river itself held horrible monsters and demons barring the way.

Undeterred, the party paddled up the treacherous Fox, and, with the help of two Mascouten Indian guides, **portaged** to a tributary of the Wisconsin River. On June 17, 1673, they reached the Mississippi. With prayers of thanks and rejoicing, they entered the river, which clearly flowed south.

The Frenchmen met no Indians on the river until they arrived at a friendly Illinois village 200 miles below the mouth of the Wisconsin. The rumored monsters turned out to be cliff paintings near present-day Grafton, Illinois, and the demons pure myth, perhaps created to explain the river's turbulence at its confluence with the powerful Missouri. After more than 1,000 miles on the Mississippi, the party stopped when it encountered hostile Quapaw Indians near the Arkansas River. Though Marquette was able to placate the Quapaws somewhat, Jolliet noted the Spanish trade goods they possessed. The presence of these Spanish goods supported Quapaw claims that the Mississippi emptied into the Gulf of Mexico—enemy territory for Frenchmen—so the expedition turned back.

The return voyage took the men to Lake Michigan by way of the Illinois River and then back to Green Bay in late September 1673. Their extremely successful expedition was marred by only one disaster, when Jolliet's canoe overturned on rapids just outside of Montreal. In the accident his two canoemen and an Omaha slave boy drowned; also, his journal and map—and, in fact, all tangible evidence supporting the findings of his expedition—were lost. A diary reputedly written by Father Marquette remains the chief, though sadly abbreviated, record of this first major exploration of the Mississippi River.

Despite his wish to settle along the Illinois River, Louis Jolliet never returned west, and further exploration of the Mississippi River would fall to RENÉ ROBERT CAVELIER, SIEUR DE LA SALLE. After the loss of his papers, Jolliet was ignored by the French authorities and plagued by legal battles over the proceeds of the trip. Instead of making further expeditions, in 1675 he married Claire-Françoise Bissot, who would bear him six children, and

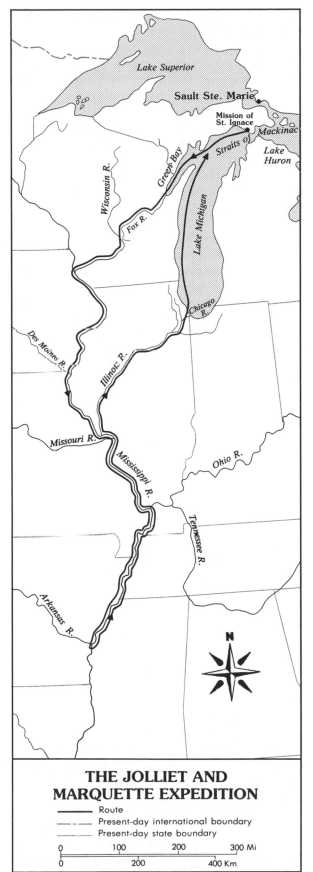

THE JOLLIET AND MARQUETTE EXPEDITION
— Route
--- Present-day international boundary
⋯ Present-day state boundary

0   100   200   300 Mi
0   200   400 Km

established himself in Québec as a codfish and seal-oil merchant.

Finally, in 1679 Governor Frontenac granted Jolliet lucrative fishing rights in the Mignan Isles. That same year Jolliet took three canoes up the Saguenay and Rupert rivers to gather information about British fortifications on Hudson Bay. So well did he manage this espionage mission that he was awarded Anticosti Island at the mouth of the St. Lawrence River; in a letter Frontenac described him as "clever, intelligent, and able to acquit himself successfully of any undertaking entrusted to him."

In his later years, Jolliet explored the coast of Labrador, producing a map and notes on the Eskimo language. When in Québec he played the organ in its Cathedral of Notre Dame. A trip to France in 1695 led to his being commissioned as royal **hydrographer**. By 1697 he had returned to Québec, where he produced maps of the St. Lawrence River and Cabot Strait and opened a school for pilots and mapmakers. At the close of the winter semester of 1700, Louis Jolliet set out for his land holdings in the north, only to disappear somewhere in the Gulf of St. Lawrence.

physique that he died soon after his return.

Kane's was the second American expedition funded by the American merchant and philanthropist Henry Grinnell with the aim of finding the lost party of Sir JOHN FRANKLIN (Kane had been ship's doctor on the first, De Haven's abortive 1850 expedition). His real object on this expedition, however, was to reach the North Pole by sailing through the ice barrier that he imagined surrounded an open polar sea. After reaching a record-high latitude in what is now Kane Basin, his ship, the *Advance*, was frozen in and became in need of rescue. After two winters, during which some short **sledge** trips were made, Kane and his rancorous crew were forced to abandon ship and head south on boats and on foot. After a three-month ordeal, during which the **Inuit** gave a great deal of assistance, the Kane party reached Upernavik, Greenland, on August 6, 1855.

In addition to making some important meteorological, magnetic, and tidal observations, Kane brought back the exciting—though incorrect—news that an open polar sea lay just out of reach to the north of Kane Basin. This exag-

---

• Kane, Elisha Kent

American
b February 3, 1820; Philadelphia, Pennsylvania
d February 16, 1857; Havana, Cuba
Explored Canadian Arctic; attempted to reach North Pole by sea

A doctor whose reputation as a physiologist was established even before he graduated from medical school, Elisha Kent Kane had an appetite for travel and adventure that took him far from the laboratory and the clinic. Even his work as a navy surgeon did not satisfy his longing to experience the exotic; on missions to Brazil, India, China, and West Africa, he always took extended leave from his medical assignment in order to explore. From the Asian island of Macao, for instance, he traveled to the Philippines, where he descended into the crater of a live volcano. But his expedition of 1853–55 to the northwest shores of Greenland (farther north than any non-Eskimo had previously been) was so trying on his surprisingly frail

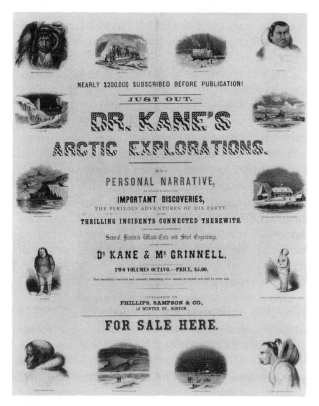

A promotion for Kane's narrative detailing his Arctic explorations. Library of Congress.

gerated account of a major break in the ice (he had seen some open water in Kennedy Channel) was to mislead explorers and geographers for some time.

Kane's contribution to Arctic geography may have been slight, but his published accounts more than made up for this in the eyes of an adoring American public. Kane's was the first written account that brought the romantic imagination to the cold, unfeeling North. In his eyes, icebergs became the embodiment of the sublime, while the Inuit became noble savages. His colorful tales turned him into a hero and helped inspire a generation of Arctic explorers, most notably his fellow American CHARLES FRANCIS HALL.

· Karlsefni, Thorfinn

Norse
b 980?; Skagafjord
d ?
Led first European attempt to found permanent settlement on North American mainland

Sometime shortly after the year 1000, Thorfinn Karlsefni proposed and led a colonizing expedition to the land that LEIF ERIKSON had discovered and named Vinland. Although the colonists failed to establish a permanent settlement, they inhabited the North American mainland for three years and thus are given credit for being the first Europeans to settle in North America.

A wealthy Icelandic merchant, Karlsefni plied his wares between Norway and Greenland. Sometime around 1008 he spent the Christmas season with the children of ERIK THE RED. Early in the next year, he married Gudrid, the widow of one of Erik's sons. Within the next few years, he proposed to settle Vinland, which Leif Erikson had discovered around 1001. Karlsefni assembled an expedition of three ships carrying approximately 160 men and women, including the pregnant Gudrid and Erik's daughter Freydis and her husband.

Retracing Erikson's journey, Thorfinn sailed first past Helluland (probably Baffin Island) and then past the coast of Markland (probably Labrador). At this point the two Norse sagas that tell Thorfinn's story differ. Whether or not he found Vinland and the houses built by Erikson's party is unclear. The first autumn the would-

be colonists settled on an island in a bay with strong currents, thought by some historians to be present-day Belle Isle at the entrance to the Gulf of St. Lawrence. There, Gudrid gave birth to Snorri, the first European child to be born in North America. The winter was more difficult than expected, and the cattle they had brought did not do well. The fishing was also poor.

The next year Karlsefni is said to have sailed south in search of better land, finding it at the mouth of a river that flowed into a small landlocked bay. There they found the grapes and self-sown wheat that characterized Vinland. And there too they were visited by natives of the region whom they called skraelings (barbarians, weaklings). The first encounters with them were peaceful trading sessions, but the next summer, the skraelings returned in a more warlike mood. According to the saga, the resulting battle seemed to be going in their favor until the pregnant Freydis bared her breasts in the frenzy of battle, slapped them with a sword, and shrieked at the top of her lungs, so shocking the skraelings that they retreated. This encounter convinced Karlsefni's party that the land was not hospitable to settlement. After another winter, they set sail to return to Greenland. Karlsefni and his family eventually returned to Iceland.

Although the records reveal little of the character of Thorfinn Karlsefni, it is not difficult to imagine some aspects of it. To take a pregnant wife and over 100 settlers to a land he had never seen, based only on the word of a trusted friend, reveals not only great faith but also great courage. To retreat from a land of hostile inhabitants also reveals a man of caution and wisdom. Though his settlement did not last, Thorfinn Karlsefni led a daring attempt to form a Norse settlement in the totally unknown lands of North America.

· Kelsey, Henry

English
b 1667?; East Greenwich?
d November 2, 1724; East Greenwich
Extended reach of Hudson's Bay Company to Saskatchewan River; discovered Canadian prairies

At a time when the Cree Indians were attempting to monopolize trade with the Hudson's Bay

Company, Henry Kelsey was quietly sent out to make contact with other Indian tribes west of Hudson Bay. If the Assiniboin and Gros Ventres could be persuaded to participate in the fur trade despite the efforts of the well-armed Cree, the Company would not only extend its reach but also prevent these other tribes from trading with the French to the south. That this desired result was largely achieved has been attributed—not without controversy—to Kelsey's genius at adopting Native American ways on his solo mission of 1690–92.

Even if Kelsey was a weapon in the struggle between English and French trading interests, his actions were benign and humane. He liked and respected the Indians and their way of life as much as they liked him. He spoke Cree and possibly Assiniboin, and unlike most Englishmen did not object to the crucial role traditionally played by Indian women in travel (including cohabitation). Kelsey entered the service of the Company in 1684 at the age of seventeen and immediately began working with PIERRE ESPRIT RADISSON and MÉDARD CHOUART, SIEUR DE GROSEILLIERS, the great French fur traders. Soon it became clear to the authorities that Kelsey was "never better pleased" than when traveling with Indians. From 1688 to 1690 he was on a mission with an Indian to make contact with the "northern Indians" (Eskimos) north of the Churchill River.

On his return to York Factory on the southwest shore of Hudson's Bay, Kelsey was sent on his great reconnaissance mission of 1690–92. His companion was the leader of a band of Assiniboin which had, despite the Cree, been trading at York. Unfortunately, his journal is very vague. He seems to have traveled up the Hayes River to the Fox, then through Cross Lake. He then proceeded to the Saskatchewan River and spent the next two years alone among the native people of the region, traveling as far southwest as present day Battleford, Saskatchewan, while trying to make peace between the Cree and Gros Ventres.

When he returned to York Factory in 1692, his report was sent to London, where he soon traveled to receive the praise of the British government for "keeping the Indians from warring one with another, that they may have the more time to look after their trade and bring larger quantities of Furrs and other Trade with them to the factory."

Kelsey then went back to serve the increas-

ingly profitable Company for nearly forty years, but his valuable accomplishment was kept from the public because it was viewed as a trade secret. When his journal was discovered in 1926, many believed it was nothing more than a romantic fabrication.

K'ien, Chang. See **Zhang Qian.**

• King, Clarence

American
b January 6, 1842; Newport, Rhode Island
d December 24, 1901; Phoenix, Arizona
Surveyed American West

Between 1867 and 1873 Clarence King made an exhaustive study of the mineral resources along the fortieth parallel from the Sierra Nevada to the eastern slopes of the Rocky Mountains. During the course of the survey, King made the only unique discovery of his career

Clarence King (far right), with three fellow geologists. The Bettmann Archive.

when he climbed Mount Shasta in northern California and, looking into its crater, observed three active ice glaciers.

From the age of seven, Clarence King had an interest in rocks. After earning a degree in science at Yale University in 1863, he traveled across the country by foot and horseback to California, where he worked for that state's geological survey for three years. In 1866 King returned to the East to propose to Congress his idea for a survey of the mineral resources of the areas along the fortieth parallel from the 120th meridian (near Reno, Nevada) to the 105th (near Denver, Colorado). His goal was to aid in the construction of the final leg of the transcontinental railroad.

King won the approval of Congress, and by July 1867 his handpicked party of scientists was on the slopes of the Sierra Nevada ready to begin work. The group spent close to six years working its way from west to east in a 100-mile band on either side of the fortieth parallel. Although they were not the first explorers of this territory, they endured many of the same hardships as others had, including heat so intense that they sought the shadow of a flagpole for shade, sudden mountain blizzards that completely obliterated their sense of direction, and hunger that reduced them to eating mules that had themselves died of starvation.

King himself had several near-fatal adventures. Once after he had set up his instruments on a mountain peak to determine its elevation, a bolt of lightning struck, wrecking the instruments and knocking him unconscious. Another time, he crawled into a cave after a bear in an attempt to shoot it and had to be pulled out by the ankles by an army sergeant.

King's report of the survey, the seven-volume *Systematic Geology*, is considered a masterpiece of the field. When Congress created the United States Geological Survey in 1878, King was asked to serve as its first director and agreed to do so only until a staff could be selected and the organization's work begun. He resigned in 1881, having before the age of forty completed his most important work—his great survey of the American West.

Kingsley, Mary Henrietta

English
b November 13, 1862; London
d June 3, 1900; Simonstown, South Africa
Traveled through western equatorial Africa; became first European to enter parts of Gabon

Mary Henrietta Kingsley's early years gave no intimation of the extensive travels she would undertake as an adult. "The whole of my childhood and youth was spent at home, in the house and garden," she once wrote. While her father, a physician, traveled widely as a medical attendant to affluent young noblemen on expeditions to distant places, Mary remained at home and cared for her invalid mother. However, when Mary Kingsley was thirty years old, both her parents died. She sailed for Africa eighteen months later. During the next eight years, she traveled extensively in western and equatorial Africa. As she studied African culture and collected zoological specimens for the British Mu-

Mary Henrietta Kingsley. Royal Geographical Society.

seum, she came to view the people of Africa not as children or an inferior race, as many Europeans did, but as fellow human beings of great promise. She argued powerfully for a responsible British policy toward Africa and its people:

> These negroes are a great world race—a race not passing off the stage of human affairs, but one that has an immense amount of history before it. Whatever we do in Africa, a thousand years hence there will be Africans to thrive or suffer for it.

From the time Mary was big enough to hold a broom, the domestic responsibilities of the Kingsley household fell on her shoulders, a role she accepted without complaint. Her itinerant father, a would-be ethnographer and dedicated naturalist at heart, was at home for only a few months at a time, and his long, amusing letters about adventures in exotic places were insufficient compensation for the hardships imposed upon his family by his absence. With her mother and Charles, her younger brother, Mary endured a hard life on meager means, but the family did manage to somehow scrape together $3,750 to spend on Charles's education. In 1886, the Kingsley family moved from Highgate to Cambridge, where he was attending university. Mary received no formal education except a German course that would later enable her to help her father with his research.

Although she bitterly resented "not being taught things," Mary's informal education was considerable. Her mother helped her learn to read, and Mary spent long hours in her father's library. Her tastes ran toward subjects ignored by many Victorian girls: travel, exploration and piracy, and—most of all—medicine and science. After the move to Cambridge, she began to make friends among the university's scientists and expanded her reading to include books on science from the university library. Her father took advantage of his daughter's interests to further his own ethnographic research, and she became his "underworker," as she later described her role. She was being too modest: her father had a reputation as an intellectual dilettante, and Mary's knowledge of early African religion and law almost certainly exceeded his.

In 1888, Mary's mother, whose health had always been fragile at best, began to require constant nursing, a situation that lasted until her death four years later. She died only several weeks after Mary's father had died from rheumatic fever, contracted on one of his overseas expeditions. After burying both of her parents, the thirty-year-old Kingsley took her first trip: a holiday excursion to the Canary Islands.

Not long after her return to England, Kingsley decided—not surprisingly, in retrospect— to go to West Africa to complete her father's research on African ethnography and perhaps to finish his uncompleted book on the subject. Years later, she reflected on this decision:

> When there were no more odd jobs to do at home, I, out of my life in books, found something to do that my father cared for, something for which I had been taught German, so that I could do for him odd jobs in it. It was the study of early religion and law, and for it I had to go to West Africa, and I went there, proceeding on the even tenor of my way, doing odd jobs, and trying to understand things, pursuing knowledge under difficulties with unbroken devotion.

Before she left England, Kingsley asked officials of the British Museum which natural-history pursuits a person who lacked formal training or an expansive budget might pursue in Africa. They suggested she collect specimens of beetles and fish, which she could do with a few pieces of inexpensive equipment.

In August 1893, Kingsley set sail on the cargo ship *Lagos*, an unlikely passenger sailing into a challenging new environment. It was with a "thrill of joy" that she first saw Freetown (in Sierra Leone), a name she knew well from the books she had read on exploration and piracy. She soon won the confidence of the region's sailors and traders, who taught her about navigation and told her where she might find the specimens she sought. In fact, Kingsley learned enough about navigation to later claim that she had piloted a 2,000-ton ship across the Forcados Bar of the Niger River on three separate occasions.

Although she wrote no chronological account of this first trip to Africa, incidental references in her writings indicate that she sailed as far south as St. Paul de Loanda (now in Angola) and explored the Congo (or Zaire) River as far as the Pallaballa Range above Matadi (now in Zaire). By the time she returned to England in January 1894, she had established her competence both as a traveler and a naturalist. On the strength of her fish and beetle collection, the British Museum agreed to equip her for further research.

Near the end of 1894, Kingsley sailed again for the coast of West Africa. Already, she was accepted as an "Old Coaster," a term applied to the region's courageous traders and adventurers who had proven their mettle by braving its considerable dangers, including malaria, yellow fever, and other tropical diseases that would often wipe out entire European settlements. To reduce the threat of disease, Kingsley made it a rule never to drink unboiled water. She was not adverse to risking solitary travel, however, and she set out to explore the Ogowe River (in present-day Gabon), which lay between the Niger and the Congo; she was intent on collecting fish for the British Museum and furthering her study of African culture.

Kingsley allayed the natural suspicions of the African people by traveling as a trader, an expedient that helped her financial situation as well. In her book *Travels in West Africa*, written after her second expedition, she describes how she dealt with people who had never seen a European before:

> I find I get on best by going among the unadulterated Africans in the guise of a trader; there is something reasonable about trade to all men, and you see the advantage of it is that, when you first appear among people who have never seen anything like you before, they naturally regard you as a devil; but when you want to buy or sell something with them, they recognize there is something reasonable and human about you, and then, if you show yourself an intelligent trader who knows the price of things, they treat you with respect. . . .

Kingsley traveled up the Ogowe in a canoe, rowed by native crewmen. The forest through which they passed was home to "a set of notoriously savage tribes chief among which are the Fans"—reportedly, a tribe of cannibals. Kingsley, however, grew to love both the forest and the Fans, whom she described as "a bright, energetic sort of African."

When she reached Kangwe, Kingsley spent several weeks at a Protestant mission station, then boarded a stern-wheel steamer for the journey upriver to Njole, where she hired a canoe and crew for the extremely dangerous trip through the rapids, whirlpools, and rock shoals in the river above Njole. She returned four days later, having survived what she called "a knockabout farce before King Death."

On July 22, 1895, Kingsley set out once again from Njole, this time on a week-long overland trek to the Rembwe River—in all likelihood, the most intense of her many adventures. During this brief journey, she came face-to-face with leopards (she hit one over the head with a water pot and freed another from a snare) and crocodiles (her canoe was marooned in a crocodile-infested lagoon, and she had to beat them off with her paddle), each time escaping unscathed. In one village where she was an overnight guest, she investigated the source of a particularly unpleasant smell and discovered a bag filled with the remains of a cannibal dinner: human ears, toes, and a hand. Nevertheless, the benefits of her solitary explorations outweighed the obvious hazards: "Unless you live alone among the natives, you never get to know them; if you do this you gradually get a light into the true state of their mind-forest." She recorded important details about many aspects of the culture, including religion, cannibalism, property laws, the place of women, and burial customs. She found her own religious beliefs and those of the Africans to be remarkably similar.

After she reached the Rembwe, Kingsley sailed to the island of Corisco off the coast of Gabon and collected shellfish. She then began her journey home, stopping long enough to become the first European woman to climb the Mungo Mah Lobeh (also known as Mount Cameroon), an active volcano and one of the highest peaks in Africa. Although her native guides deserted her midway through the climb, she continued alone and finally reached the mist-shrouded summit. "Verily I am no mountaineer, for there is in me no exultation, but only a deep disgust because the weather has robbed me of my main object in coming here, namely to get a good view," she later wrote.

Kingsley reached England in November 1895 and set to work on her book, *Travels in West Africa*. Her exceptional experiences and captivating writing style made it an instant success, as important for its novel view of the people of West Africa as for its wealth of scientific and cultural information. Soon she was in great demand as a lecturer, and she seized the opportunity to advocate her views about the proper British political role in Africa, a topic that became the subject of her second book, *West African Studies*.

By 1900, Kingsley had decided to make a third trip to Africa. She no longer enjoyed life in England, and besides, she "had caught the habit of thinking black." Instead of returning to West Africa, however, she responded to a desperate call for nurses in South Africa, where the Boer War was underway. She sailed to Cape Town and was assigned to Simonstown, the site of a hospital where Boer prisoners were dying of enteric fever in large numbers. Within two months, she caught the fever herself and died. She was buried at sea with full military honors.

SUGGESTED READING: Olwen Campbell, *Mary Kingsley: A Victorian in the Jungle* (Methuen, 1957); Katherine Frank, *A Voyage Out: The Life of Mary Kingsley* (Houghton Mifflin, 1986); Mary Kingsley, *Travels in West Africa* (Virago, 1982); Caroline Oliver, *Western Women in Colonial Africa* (Greenwood Press, 1982); Marion Tinling, *Women into the Unknown* (Greenwood Press, 1989).

· Kino (Chini; Chino; Chinus), Eusebio Francisco

Italian
b August 10, 1645?; Segno, near Trent
d March 15, 1711; Magdalena, Sonora province, Mexico
Explored Baja California, northern Mexico, southern Arizona (for Spain and Catholic Church)

Dedicating his life to "both Majesties"—the King of Spain and the Catholic Church—Father Eusebio Francisco Kino explored more than 50,000 square miles in northern Mexico and the southwestern United States. Many of the mission pueblos that he founded developed into modern towns, and he was the first to introduce animal husbandry and European fruits and cereals to the Indians of the region. Kino was not only a successful missionary and explorer but also a master geographer and cartographer. His maps are the earliest known that depict Baja California as a peninsula, not an island, and that show the Gila and Colorado rivers and southern Arizona.

It is generally accepted that Eusebio Francisco Kino was born on the day of his baptism, August 10, 1645, as it was the custom then to baptize a child on the day of birth. Raised in Segno, the northern Italian village of his birth, Kino was educated at the Jesuit College in nearby Trent. In 1663 he went to Hala, near

Innsbruck, Germany (now Austria), to continue his studies, but soon became critically ill from an unknown disease. This brush with death changed the direction of his life. He promised God that if he regained his health he would become a Jesuit missionary. After his recovery, he therefore entered the Jesuit novitiate in 1665; studied at universities in Innsbruck, Freiburg, and Ingolstadt; and was ordained in 1677. He wanted to follow in the footsteps of his patron, SAINT FRANCIS XAVIER, by getting a missionary post in the Orient; however, as the result of a lottery he ended up in New Spain (present-day Mexico) in 1681, and his passionate devotion to his vocation, coupled with his eagerness to explore this new land, soon overcame any disappointment.

On January 17, 1683, Kino left on his first expedition, commanded by Isidro de Atondo (or Otondo) y Antillón, to establish settlements and the Christian faith in Baja California. When they reached La Paz Bay along the Gulf of California, Kino met Indians for the first time and initiated the quiet diplomacy that would serve him well in future missionary journeys. He gave them glass beads and handkerchiefs and made it a point to learn their language. A colony was founded at La Paz but was soon abandoned due to lack of supplies.

Atondo, with Kino accompanying him, then established another colony farther north and called it San Bruno. From there Atondo and Kino made several trips inland, to the west, scaling a mountain that they called La Giganta (which is still called that today) and exploring a river they named Santo Tomás (the present-day La Purisíma). On New Year's Day 1685, they discovered a bay on the Pacific coast of Baja and called it Año Nuevo (modern Laguna de San Gregoris). Kino and Atondo thus became the first Europeans to cross California, at any point, to the Pacific Ocean. Unfortunately, drought and an epidemic of **scurvy** forced Atondo to abandon his colony. For the rest of his life, Kino would hope to return to California.

In 1687 Kino was sent to do missionary work in Pimería Alta, a part of the province of Sonora encompassing northwestern Mexico and present-day southwestern Arizona. During the next twenty-four years he would explore this vast area and establish a string of missions along what became known as the "rim of Christendom," extending the frontier of New Spain by peaceful means. Among the Indians he became known as "the Black Robe" and was welcomed wherever he traveled. The Church began to call him "the Apostle to the Pimas," a reference to the Upper Pima Indians who inhabited Pimería Alta.

Father Kino established the mission of Nuestra Señora de los Dolores in the San Miguel River valley in northwestern Sonora and made it his headquarters. From there he traveled into Arizona in 1691, establishing missions at Guevavi (just north of modern Nogales and the U.S.-Mexico border), Tumacácori (modern Tubac), and San Xavier del Bac (just south of modern Tucson). In 1693 he established missions along the Magdalena River valley in northwestern Sonora and made the first recorded journey to the lower Altar River, where he founded the mission village of Coborca. Then in 1697 he explored the San Pedro River valley from its beginnings near Cananea, Mexico, to somewhere near the site of the modern town of Benson, Arizona, christening the region's Indians and adding detail to his historical journal.

In 1698 and 1699 Father Kino made several important journeys. First he traveled north along the Santa Cruz River to the Gila River near modern Phoenix, establishing missions along both rivers. Next he went through Pápago Land in southwest Arizona and reached Casa Grande. Then he traveled along the Devil's Highway, considered by many the most difficult trail in the Southwest, and became the first European to traverse successfully the 200-mile-long trail through rocky canyons and desert-like plains where virtually no water is to be found. Skirting the Gila Bend Mountains and the "sterile plains" (what is now the Lechuguilla Desert), he reached the Gila River near the modern town of Wellton, Arizona. Turning upstream on the Gila, he made the first recorded exploration between the Gila Bend Mountains and Sierra la Estrella in the Maricopa Mountains.

Thinking that there might be a connection between the blue shells given to him by the Indian tribes in Arizona and the blue abalone shells he had found on the Pacific coast of Baja several years before, Father Kino set out late in 1699 to find a land passage to California. When he reached Wellton, he went down the Gila River to its convergence with the Colorado River near modern Yuma. Then he followed the Colorado to its discharge into the Gulf of California. On his return trip he at one point crossed the Colorado on a raft into California, confirming his theory that California could be reached by an overland route.

Father Kino made some fifty expeditions in all during his time in Pimería Alta, often only accompanied by a few Indians or another priest. He also became a successful cattle rancher and taught the Indians better farming and animal husbandry methods. He died on March 15, 1711, after dedicating a new chapel at the mission town of Magdalena in Sonora, Mexico.

Father Kino was a man of boundless energy and physical endurance with a genuine affection for the Indians among whom he worked. His expeditions, as detailed in his journals and on his maps, opened up a whole new area for further exploration and settlement. Unfortunately, all the records of his work were confined to Spanish archives for many years, unknown to the rest of the world. His accomplishments were eventually resurrected by the people of Arizona, who in 1965 dedicated a statue to him in the U.S. Capitol Rotunda in Washington, D.C., and today recognize him as the founder of their state. His remarkable journals have now been translated into English, and he is generally regarded as an explorer of the first rank. Oddly, after all his travels, the only place that bears his name today is Bahia de Kino, a bay along the northwestern coast of Mexico.

Kotzebue, Otto von

Russian
b December 30, 1787; Tallinn, Estonia
d February 15, 1846; Tallinn, Estonia
Explored Pacific Ocean and northwest coast of America for Russia; circumnavigated twice

Otto von Kotzebue went to sea at the tender age of fifteen and made a career of exploration, making several discoveries for Russia in the Pacific and along the coasts of Alaska and California. One of the finest writers of the literature of exploration by sea, he published accounts of his two major voyages.

The second son of the German poet and dramatist August Friedrich Ferdinand von Kotzebue, Otto von Kotzebue was born on December 30, 1787, in Revel (present-day Tallinn, Estonia). In 1803 he was a student at the St. Petersburg School for Cadets when his father asked that fifteen-year-old Otto and his younger brother, Martin, be allowed to participate in an expedition to be led by ADAM IVAN VON KRUSENSTERN. The boys were accepted, and Otto von Kotzebue served as a clerk on Krusenstern's three-year voyage around the world.

In 1815 Krusenstern recommended then-Lieutenant Kotzebue to command the **brig** *Rurik* on an expedition to find a Northwest Passage through the Bering Strait. (For a more complete discussion of the passage, see MARTIN FROBISHER.) With a crew of thirty-two, Kotzebue rounded Cape Horn and sailed up the South American coast, then sailed west to Easter Island, where he discovered and named Romanzof Island after the expedition's sponsor. Near Cook's Palliser Islands (now the Tuamotus) he found and named Krusenstern and Rurik islands, and subsequently Kutusov and Suvarov islands east of the Marshalls and the Gilbert Islands (present-day Kiribati).

Kotzebue spent the summers of 1816 and 1817 finding a safe anchorage and charting the northwest coast of Alaska in great detail. He was aided by members of the Russian-American Company and by Aleuts using one-seat kayaks. He located a sound north of the strait that he thought might lead to a Northwest Passage. It did not (the same sound bears his name today). Winters were spent in warmer climes, including the Marshall Islands and along the California coast, where several discoveries were made.

For all practical purposes, the expedition ended in July 1817. Spotting an apparently endless ice floe as he prepared to enter the Bering Strait, Kotzebue suffered an attack of angina that left him fainting and spitting up blood. He returned to St. Petersburg on August 3, 1818, by way of the Marshalls, Guam, and Africa's Cape of Good Hope.

From 1823 to 1826 Kotzebue commanded a second Pacific expedition, and again he circumnavigated the globe. His ship, the *Predpriyatiyen*, visited the Tuamotus, Tahiti, the Navigators Islands (now Samoa), the Marshalls, Kamchatka, and the northwest coast of America.

Kotzebue retired in 1830 due to ill health. He died in 1846.

Krusenstern, Adam Ivan (Johann) von (Krusenshtern, Ivan Fyodorovich)

Russian
b November 19, 1770; Haggud, Estonia
d August 24, 1846; Asz, near Tallinn, Estonia
Commanded first Russian circumnavigation

In the realm of nineteenth-century maritime exploration, Adam Ivan von Krusenstern helped put Russia on equal footing with Great Britain and France. In the process, he also established sea routes to expedite Russian trade.

Born on November 19, 1770, in Haggud (present-day Estonia) to a Baltic German family, Krusenstern served in the Russian navy during the Russo-Swedish War (1787–90). In 1793 he joined the British navy, serving in Africa, Asia, and North America. In 1798 he left the fleet to spend a year in Guangzhou (Canton), returning home by way of England in 1799.

During his travels Krusenstern developed a

Adam Ivan von Krusenstern. New York Public Library.

proposal to help improve trade between Russia's Baltic Sea ports and its colonies in America and Siberia. In 1801 the Russian emperor Alexander I became interested in the proposal and placed Krusenstern in charge of an expedition to the Pacific.

The British-built *Nadezhda* and *Neva* sailed August 7, 1803, from Kronstadt (now Kronshlot) on the Baltic Sea. After stops at Copenhagen, Falmouth, and Tenerife, they sailed to the Brazilian coast, with the expedition's naturalist studying phosphorescent marine plankton along the way. Krusenstern rounded South America's Cape Horn on March 3, 1804, and shortly after, the two ships were separated in the South Pacific. Krusenstern took the *Nadezhda* to the Marquesas, where he traded with the islanders on Nuku Hiva and witnessed secret funeral rituals at a *morai,* or burial site. After stopping in the Sandwich Islands (present-day Hawaii), the ship reached the Kamchatka Peninsula of Russia thirty-five days later.

Krusenstern's next destination was Japan, where he hoped to reestablish its relations with Russia. However, he and the Russian ambassador were met with hostility. This did not prevent Krusenstern from charting the Japanese coast and exploring Yeso (present-day Hokkaidō). Reaching Macao later in 1805, the *Nadezhda* and the *Neva* were reunited eighteen months after they had become separated. Krusenstern found the Chinese no more amiable than the Japanese, and the two ships barely escaped seizure there. Departing China in February 1806, the ships sailed west around the world, reaching Russia three years and twelve days after their departure. Krusenstern's voyage was considered a success for creating a maritime link among Kamchatka, Russia's North American colonies, and China. Krusenstern later published an account of the voyage and an *Atlas of the Pacific Ocean,* and in 1815 he attempted unsuccessfully to find the Northwest Passage.

When Krusenstern died on his estate, Asz, near Tallinn, on August 24, 1846, he held the rank of admiral. He had served as director of the Russian Naval Academy and as a member of the scientific committee of the Ministry of the Navy and the St. Petersburg Academy of Sciences.

La Condamine, Charles-Marie de

French
b January 27, 1701; Paris
d February 4, 1774; Paris
Explored Amazon Basin; measured earth's surface in Ecuadorean Andes

A restless spirit and inquisitive mind characterized Charles-Marie de La Condamine, who was a soldier, explorer, mathematician, and natural historian. He led the French Equatorial Expedition sent to the Ecuadorean Andes in 1735 to determine the exact length of a single degree of latitude at the equator, in order to settle the debate over the shape of the earth. When the measurements were completed, La Condamine decided to return to France via a journey down the Amazon River, a venture that became the first scientific exploration of the river. (For a map, see ALEXANDER VON HUMBOLDT.)

Charles-Marie de La Condamine was born in Paris into a wealthy, aristocratic family on January 27, 1701. He was educated at the Col-

Charles-Marie de La Condamine. New York Public Library.

lège Louis-le-Grand in Paris and entered the military upon graduation. He distinguished himself as a soldier during the French siege of Rosas (1719) against Spain. However, his restlessness and all-consuming curiosity led to dissatisfaction with the regimentation and limited scope of military life. He left the military and immersed himself in the study of mathematics, astronomy, cartography, and natural history, becoming part of the major scientific circles of Paris. He became friends with the famous philosopher and author Voltaire, who encouraged and supported La Condamine's ideas and explorations.

At the age of twenty-nine, La Condamine was elected to the prestigious Académie Royale des Sciences. In 1731 he went on his first expedition to the African coast of the Red Sea and to Constantinople (present-day Istanbul, Turkey), making mathematical and astronomical observations. The paper he presented on his findings firmly established his reputation as a scientist.

Greatly influenced by the philosophical, rational, and scientific spirit of the Enlightenment (or Age of Reason), which permeated much of eighteenth-century Europe, La Condamine became involved in the great debate over the shape of the earth. Was the earth elongated at the poles, as Jacques Cassini had proposed, or flattened at the poles and swollen at the equator, as Sir Isaac Newton had suggested? To find the answer, precise measurements were required at different geographical points. A degree of latitude had already been measured in France. Simultaneous expeditions to Lapland (led by Pierre Moreau de Maupertius) and to the equator were assembled to measure a degree of latitude at both locations in order to complete the calculations.

La Condamine was selected to lead the Equatorial Expedition of 1735, sponsored by the Académie Royale des Sciences. The king of Spain granted permission for the French expedition to enter South America, an extraordinary concession that made La Condamine's party the first Europeans other than the Spanish and Portuguese to openly explore the continent in 250 years.

Arriving at Portobelo, Panama, on November 29, 1735, the expedition traveled overland for 230 miles across the Isthmus of Panama and then by boat to Manta on the west coast of Ecuador. The group separated there. Most of the men proceeded down the coast to Guaya-

quil. Meanwhile, La Condamine, accompanied by Pedro Vicente Maldonado, the governor of the province of Esmeraldas, took the jungle route to Quito, the place chosen for the measurements. Traveling along the Esmeraldas River, they encountered blood-sucking flies and cockroaches the size of mice. Intrigued by the elastic material drawn from trees and called "caoutchouc," La Condamine had a bag made of it to protect his instruments; the new substance was natural latex, or rubber. Along the route he also discovered a metal referred to as "platina," which was later labeled a precious metal and named platinum.

After the groups reunited at Quito in early 1737 the expedition had to overcome incredible problems in obtaining the necessary measurements. The area chosen was mountainous, requiring them to climb steep volcanic mountains to complete the triangulations from the base line on the plain of Yaquí, northwest of Quito, northward to the town of Ibarra and southward to the town of Cuenca. The local people they encountered during the almost six years of the scientific investigation were highly suspicious of them, thinking their instruments were being used to find buried Inca treasure. Finally, after all their work, the scientists found out that the Lapland team had already returned to France with proof that Newton's theory was correct (La Condamine's own measurements would bear this out). The results of their years of work were thus rendered nearly inconsequential. But the hardships they had experienced had nevertheless taken a terrible toll on the members of the expedition. By the time La Condamine left on his momentous return voyage down the Amazon, two members of the expedition had gone mad, the medical doctor had been brutally murdered, and two others had died (one of malaria, one accidentally).

With Maldonado as his companion, La Condamine headed south, reaching Borja, some 200 miles from Cuenca, in June 1743. Traveling down the Marañón River (in present-day Peru) by canoe, the men reached the Amazon. The dramatic change in environment from the Quito area was recorded by La Condamine: "I found myself in a new world, separated from all human intercourse, on a freshwater sea, surrounded by a maze of lakes, rivers, and canals, and penetrating in every direction the gloom of an immense forest.. . ." On the journey down the Amazon he recorded its volume, depth, and speed of flow and produced a map that is so accurate that it could be used today to navigate the river. He also kept detailed notes on the Indian tribes he encountered along the river, remarking on their methods of fishing and of protecting themselves from insect bites. However, he expressed a negative attitude toward the Indian peoples as a whole, seeing little good in them.

After detouring up the Río Negro for several miles and discovering that it flowed from the northwest, La Condamine arrived in Pará (present-day Belém) on the coast of Brazil on September 19, 1743. While taking some measurements in Pará, he established that Marajó, located northwest of Pará, was a single island, not a series of islands as previously thought. Leaving Pará in December 1743, La Condamine sailed to Cayenne in French Guiana where he stayed for five months conducting experiments.

He finally returned to Paris on February 23, 1745, after ten years in South America during which time he had crossed the continent from the Pacific to the Atlantic Ocean, climbed the Andes, and explored the length of the Amazon River. He brought back a wealth of information not only about geographical features but also on the properties of rubber, Indian knowledge of insecticides and intoxicants, and the possibilities for the use of quinine and curare—to name just a few of his contributions. His observations would promote more thorough explorations of the Amazon.

He spent the rest of his life writing of his experiences; also, he became the "Don Quixote of inoculation" in his campaign for vaccination against smallpox. Since he had had smallpox in his youth, La Condamine felt very strongly about the need for vaccination and pursued the cause with his characteristic enthusiasm and optimism.

La Condamine married for the first time at age fifty-five and was elected to the prestigious Académie Française in 1760. By 1763 he was a complete cripple, almost deaf in one ear, and was forced to dictate his books and articles to his wife. He died in Paris on February 4, 1774, with the knowledge that he was recognized by the international scientific community as an outstanding scientist, naturalist, and explorer.

La Cosa, Juan de

Spanish
b 1460?; Puerto de Santa María, Cadiz
d February 28, 1510; near Cartagena, Colombia
Explored coasts of Venezuela and Colombia;
known as master cartographer

The famous *mappe-monde* (world map) of 1500, the first map to delineate the South American mainland and islands of the West Indies, was executed by Juan de La Cosa. Sailing with CHRISTOPHER COLUMBUS on his second voyage to the New World, then with ALONSO DE OJEDA to explore the northwestern coast of South America, and finally with RODRIGO DE BASTIDAS to explore the coast of modern Colombia, La Cosa developed complementary skills as a pilot, cartographer, and explorer. He then led an expedition to explore further the Gulf of Urabá area (in modern Colombia), penetrating as far north as the region of Darién in what is now Panama.

Much confusion surrounds the name of Juan de La Cosa because there were actually two men of that name born about the same time, both of Basque heritage and both having sailed with Columbus. One Juan de La Cosa was the owner and pilot of Columbus's flagship, the *Santa Maria*, during the 1492 voyage of discovery; he was disgraced when his ship ran aground. The more significant Juan de La Cosa, profiled here, was the famous cartographer and explorer of the **Spanish Main**, who was born about 1460 in Puerto de Santa María on the Gulf of Cadiz. He sailed with Columbus on the second voyage to the New World in 1493 as an able seaman on the *Niña*. Nothing is known of his life before he made the 1493 voyage. La Cosa credits Columbus with teaching him the principles of navigation, but there is no indication of where he learned the art of mapmaking.

By the time La Cosa sailed with Ojeda in 1499 he was already being described as a "great mariner." Skirting the coastlines of what are now British Guiana and Venezuela, La Cosa navigated the ships of the Ojeda expedition into the Gulf of Venezuela and Lake Maracaibo, then piloted them around the Guajira Peninsula as far as Cabo de la Vela in modern Colombia. This successful expedition, which immediately preceded La Cosa's important map of 1500, returned to Spain with pearls and slaves, making him a wealthy man.

Next he sailed with Rodrigo de Bastidas in

1501, again exploring the coast of Colombia and reaching Central America (what is now southeastern Panama) for the first time. As a result of his success on this voyage, La Cosa was granted broad rights in the Gulf of Urabá "and other islands of the Ocean Sea which have or will be discovered" by him. He was so highly regarded at this time that Queen Isabella of Spain told another adventurer, Cristobal Guerra, "In navigation, I command you to follow what appears best to Juan de La Cosa, for I know that he's a man who knows well what he is talking about when he gives advice."

With such royal favor, La Cosa left Spain in late September 1504 and reached the New World at Margarita Island off the coast of what is now Venezuela. After gathering pearls along what is known as the Pearl Coast (near modern Cumaná, Venezuela) and brazilwood on the islands of the Curaçao archipelago, he made for the Bay of Cartagena, where he found and aided the remnants of the Guerra expedition.

When he reached the Gulf of Urabá, La Cosa made several forays inland. On one he found a chest filled with gold masks and drums in an abandoned Indian hut. Captured Indians told him of more gold in the region of Darién (in present-day Colombia) on the other side of the Gulf. In pursuit of this gold, he and his party navigated the Atrato River in small boats and raided villages in Darién.

La Cosa was forced to rescue the remaining members of the Guerra party a second time near the Gulf of Urabá when their ships sprung leaks. He then had to abandon his own ships, which had been damaged by shipworms. The 200 survivors of both expeditions lived on the beach at Urabá for almost a year before sailing some patched-up boats to Santo Domingo (in what is now the Dominican Republic). While overall this expedition was a financial success, by the time he finally reached Seville on March 13, 1506, La Cosa had lost all but sixty men to starvation, disease, and Indian attacks.

Until his last expedition in 1509 La Cosa served as chief commander of the Spanish coasts. Then in November 1509 he left Hispaniola (the island now occupied by Haiti and the Dominican Republic) with Ojeda to establish a colony near present-day Cartagena, Colombia. Though La Cosa counseled against it, Ojeda killed many Indians in the area. The remaining Indians exacted a terrible revenge, killing the entire landing party, except Ojeda, who es-

caped. La Cosa died in agony, the result of wounds from poison darts, on February 28, 1510.

Juan de La Cosa's several voyages to the northwestern coast of South America and southern Central America, as well as his important map of 1500, added significantly to the knowledge of the New World. Of particular interest is the fact that he properly showed Cuba as an island on his map, in spite of having signed Columbus's statement to Ferdinand and Isabella that Cuba was a peninsula of the Asian mainland.

• Laing, Alexander Gordon

Scottish
b December 27, 1793; Edinburgh
d September 26, 1826; near Timbuktu
Explored Sahara, reaching Timbuktu

The first European known to reach Timbuktu (in what is now Mali), Alexander Gordon Laing had a brief but noteworthy career as an explorer

Alexander Gordon Laing. Hulton-Deutsch Collection.

of Africa. He journeyed across the Sahara Desert and suffered a near-fatal attack by the inhabitants on his way to Timbuktu. He also fell in love while in Africa, marrying the daughter of a British consul after a courtship of only a few weeks. However, Laing did not live long enough to enjoy either his marriage or the acclaim he would have received for his visit to Timbuktu. Shortly after his departure from the legendary city, he was murdered by his guide.

Educated at Edinburgh University, Laing received a British army commission to a West India infantry regiment while in his teens. Stationed in Sierra Leone, he was assigned to seek new interior trade routes. His primary interest, however, was in investigating the course of the Niger River. Although his request to conduct an expedition into interior Africa was denied, he was given command of a patrol near the source of the Niger River in 1822. When he became convinced that the Niger did not merge with the Nile River, he determined to discover the Niger's course. He also found the origin of the Rokel River before hostile natives barred him from exploring further.

Laing then served in the Ashanti War of 1823–24 and was selected to give a personal report on the conflict to Lord Bathurst, the secretary of state for war and colonies. Arriving in London in the summer of 1824, Laing used the opportunity to seek financing from Bathurst for exploration of the Niger River. The official agreed but directed him to travel south from Tripoli (in present-day Libya) to Timbuktu and then to pursue the course of the Niger from there.

Arriving in Tripoli in May 1825, Laing fell in love almost immediately with the daughter of Hanmer Warrington, the British consul there. Laing married Emma Warrington on July 14 and departed for Timbuktu only a few days later, accompanied by two officials from Tripoli. Traveling southwest by way of Ghadames and Ain Salah (in modern Algeria), he was forced to cross territory occupied by the violent Tuareg tribe, which attacked and nearly killed him in January 1826, shortly after he left Ain Salah. Proceeding heroically despite his injuries, Laing arrived in Timbuktu on August 25. He had completed an arduous desert journey of roughly 1,500 miles, the longest Saharan trek executed by a European to that time, and one of the longest ever made.

Laing spent five weeks in Timbuktu, a place known as the Queen of the Desert and normally forbidden to Christians. Europeans had long been fascinated by the city, glorified in literature and history as an exotic and opulent land, and Laing wrote letters stating that it lived up to his expectations. However, hatred of Christians apparently persisted there. A sheik who had befriended Laing finally implored him to leave, insisting that his life was at risk. Laing departed on September 24, 1826, and two days later was murdered by his own guide on the outskirts of the city.

Although he had been treated well during his stay, historians have speculated that Laing's presence was perceived as an omen of further interloping by Christians. When explorer RENÉ-AUGUSTE CAILLIÉ arrived in Timbuktu two years later masquerading as an Egyptian Arab, natives told him about Laing's visit and added that the traveler had been beaten to death because he was suspected of being a Christian spy.

Laing was buried near the site of his death, but the French exhumed his remains in 1910 and had him interred in Timbuktu. Since his journal was never recovered, Laing's expedition ultimately provided scant information about West Africa. The letters he sent to Tripoli in May, July, and September reveal little about his trip other than some of the places he visited, some brief impressions of Timbuktu, and his plan to abandon his pursuit of the Niger's course in favor of returning to Tripoli by way of West Africa. His account of his earlier, abortive exploration in Sulima, entitled *Travels in the Timannee, Kooranko and Soolima Countries in Western Africa*, was published in 1825.

• Lander, Richard Lemon

English
b February 8, 1804; Truro, Cornwall
d February 6, 1834; Fernando Póo (present-day Bioko)
Explored West Africa and traveled to mouth of Niger River

Richard Lemon Lander traced the course of the Niger River to its termination, a task many other explorers had attempted in vain. He began his first expedition as a servant but emerged as an explorer in his own right following the death of his employer and friend, HUGH CLAPPER-

TON, whose work he continued. It was on his second journey that he succeeded in traveling to the mouth of the Niger, after being captured and held for ransom by a native king. Lander never returned from his third trip to the Niger because he was fatally wounded in a battle with a tribe of the region.

The son of an innkeeper, Lander acquired a taste for travel during his years as a servant to wealthy gentlemen and noblemen. He spent time in continental Europe, the West Indies, and South Africa before applying for a job as servant to Clapperton on his second expedition to the Niger in 1825. From Badagri on the Bight of Benin they traveled northeast, crossing the Niger near Bussa and arriving at Kano in July 1826. While Lander stayed in Kano to recover from an illness, his employer proceeded west to Sokoto to make a second attempt to gain permission from Sultan Bello to follow the Niger's path southeast toward the Bight of Benin on the Gulf of Guinea. Lander rejoined Clapperton to find that this request had been denied, and they were still in Sokoto when Clapperton became ill. Lander took care of Clapperton until his death in April 1827 and had his mentor's journals published upon returning to England a year later.

Determined to complete the mission, Lander volunteered for another government-sponsored trip to the Niger. He departed in January 1830, this time accompanied by his younger brother, John. Lander was determined to follow the river directly to the sea, and he again landed at Badagri and headed north to Bussa. By September 1830 the brothers had purchased a canoe from the chief of Rabba and begun their journey down the Niger, where they were assaulted twice by native tribes. The first assailants retreated after realizing that the explorers did not intend to harm them; the second incident was far more serious. Marauding Ibo tribesmen captured the brothers near the town of Kiri, imprisoned them, and stole or destroyed all of their possessions. The Ibo king held the Landers for ransom, expecting to receive payment from one of the other Englishmen in the vicinity, but it was a slave trader from nearby Brass who redeemed the Landers in exchange for future compensation.

Richard Lander finished his voyage down the Niger as a slave working on a forty-paddle royal canoe while his brother remained in custody in Brass. Although he had assured the trader that any Englishman in the area would pay for his release, they met with refusal from the captain of the first English ship they encountered. Nevertheless, the two brothers were set free, and they returned to England that following June.

Lander was honored upon his return, receiving a newly established Royal Geographical Society award for his discovery. The brothers' account of their expedition, three volumes entitled *Journal of an Expedition to Explore the Course and Termination of the Niger*, was well received by the public when it was released in 1832.

Lander returned to Africa the same year and began his third and final expedition. Employed this time by a private firm, the Customs House at Liverpool, Lander was assigned to lead a trading expedition up the Niger. The expedition was beset with problems from the start, including insufficient provisions and difficulties with the crew, and Lander eventually decided to turn back. Lander and his crew were still approximately 100 miles from the river's mouth when native warriors at Angiama attacked, killing three crew members and wounding Lander. All Lander's journals and papers were lost in the assault, and the native warriors pursued him down the river for several hours before he escaped. Observing that his assailants had been armed with swords and muskets, Lander suspected that white men may have helped the tribesmen plan the attack.

Lander retreated to the nearby island of Fernando Póo (now Bioko), where he died a few days later from his injuries. A short time later, his brother John died from an illness he had contracted during his African expedition.

· La Pérouse (La Peyrouse), Jean François de Galaup, Comte de

French
b August 23, 1741; Chateau de Gua, Albi
d 1788?; Vanikoro Island
Explored Pacific; discovered La Pérouse Strait

Jean François de Galaup, Comte de La Pérouse, was sent to the Pacific in 1785 to discover any stones that may have been left unturned by the British explorer Captain JAMES COOK. Although word of his subsequent discoveries reached France by courier, La Pérouse never returned.

His fate was not learned until forty years after his mysterious disappearance.

La Pérouse was born in southern France in 1741, the oldest son of a merchant family that had attained nobility two centuries earlier. In 1756, at the age of fifteen, he joined the French navy to fight the British in the Seven Years' War. He served off the coast of North America, and in 1759 he was wounded and taken prisoner by Admiral Hawke.

La Pérouse made navy ensign in 1764 and continued his service in America and the Indian Ocean. He was given command of the *Adour* in 1767 and participated in the campaigns of Bengal, India, and China. While on Île de France (present-day Mauritius), he met and fell in love with Louise-Eléonore Broudou, a **creole** woman whom he married in 1783 after his family reluctantly gave their consent.

During the American Revolution, La Pérouse distinguished himself a number of times, including capturing a British raider and a **frigate** at Savannah, Georgia, in 1779 and capturing two British ships at Cape Breton, Nova Scotia, in 1781. In August 1782, as commander of the *Sceptre*, he became a hero when he attacked and captured two British forts on Hudson Bay.

In 1785 the French navy chose La Pérouse to command an ambitious expedition into the Pacific. He was to fill in any gaps in the exhaustive knowledge of the Pacific provided by Cook's three expeditions for the British. This would require exploration of the South Sandwich and South Georgia islands, as well as any islands between the Society Islands, New Zealand, Australia, and New Guinea. He also was to explore the coast of China and the Kamchatka Peninsula of northwest Russia, establish a French outpost for whaling and fur trading, and seek a Northwest Passage along the west coast of North America.

La Pérouse's two ships, the *Boussole* and the *Astrolabe*, left Brest, France, on August 1, 1785, with 114 officers and crew. After stops at Madeira, Tenerife (in the Canaries), and Brazil, they reached South America's Cape Horn on April 1, 1786. In February they were welcomed by the Spanish governor of Chile, and on April 9 they stopped briefly at Easter Island.

The warmer weather of spring in the Northern Hemisphere encouraged La Pérouse to turn north. He reached Maui, in the Sandwich Islands (present-day Hawaii), in May but spent only one day there before continuing northward. On June 23 the voyagers caught sight of Mount Saint Elias on Alaska's southeastern coast. They set up camp at a site La Pérouse called Port des Français (now Lituya Bay), where they felt that the native inhabitants "spent their nights looking for a favorable moment to rob us." In July the expedition lost a barge and two longboats—and the lives of

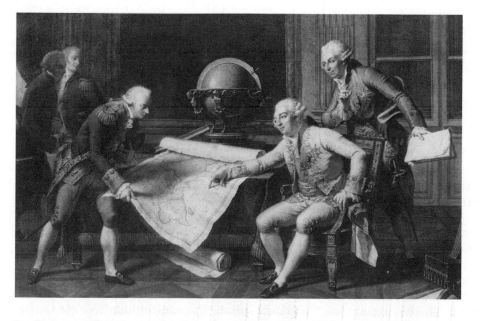

La Pérouse receiving instructions from King Louis XVI. N. Monsiau, Versailles. © Photo R.M.N., Paris.

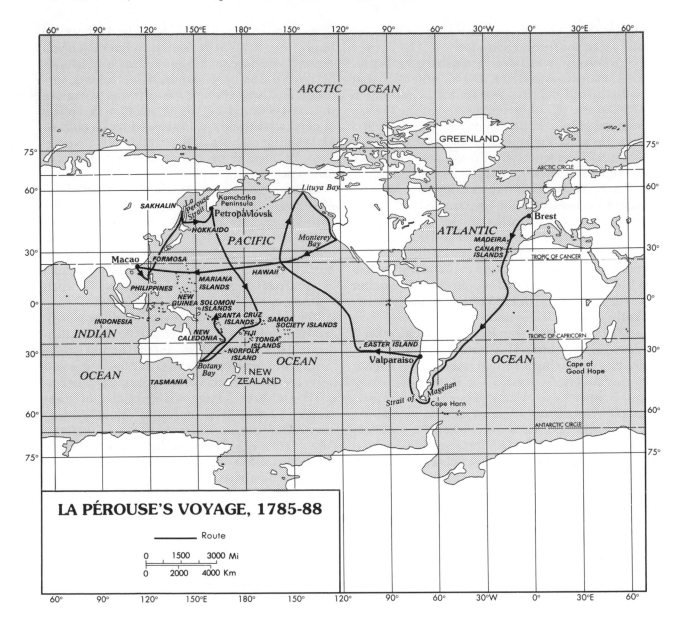

LA PÉROUSE'S VOYAGE, 1785-88

—— Route

0   1500   3000 Mi

0   2000   4000 Km

twenty-one men—to the turbulent waters in the narrow mouth of the bay. La Pérouse sailed south at the end of the month with a cargo of fur acquired through trade with the region's native inhabitants.

At Monterey Bay on the California coast, La Pérouse spent ten days studying the Spanish settlements as well as the area's wildlife. The expedition naturalists collected specimens of Monterey pine and discovered the California partridge. On September 24 the expedition sailed west, reaching Macao on the coast of China on January 2, 1787, after discovering

Necker Island (northwest of Hawaii) and touching in the Marianas. The *Astrolabe*'s naturalist disembarked at Macao, taking logs and maps with him back to France.

After a visit to the Philippines, La Pérouse headed for the northern coast of Asia, until then virtually unknown to European ships. He sailed between Formosa and the Ryukyus, reaching the Bay de Ternay on June 27 and Suffren Bay on July 4. At Oku-Yeso (now Sakhalin Island), north of Japan, the native people drew La Pérouse a map of their island, Asia's Tartary coast, and Yeso (present-day Hokkaidō, Japan). La

Pérouse then sailed as far north along the Tartary coast as De Kastri Bay, which he named for the minister of the navy. Turning south and sailing between Sakhalin and Hokkaidō, La Pérouse discovered the strait that bears his name today.

On September 6, 1787, La Pérouse reached Petropavlovsk on the Kamchatka Peninsula, where he received a letter from France promoting him to squadron commander and directing him to investigate a settlement in New South Wales (Australia). La Pérouse and his men spent nearly four weeks in Petropavlovsk, feasting and reveling with the Kamchatkans. Before he left, the commander sent the expedition's interpreter, Barthélemy de Lesseps, back to France with more of the records of the expedition.

The next stop was the Navigators Islands (now Samoa), where tragedy again struck the expedition. On December 9 the two ships anchored at Manua, where a thousand Samoans massacred twelve of the crew and wounded twenty others as they were refilling water barrels. From Samoa the ships sailed southeast, calling in the Fiji Islands and then at Norfolk Island.

On January 26, 1788, the *Boussole* and the *Astrolabe* reached Botany Bay (in present-day Australia), where La Pérouse got a cordial welcome from the British. There he put his most recent logs and papers aboard a British ship bound for Europe. In a letter dated February 25, 1788, La Pérouse described his plans to continue the expedition by exploring Tonga, New Caledonia, the Santa Cruz and Solomon islands, and the Louisiades near New Guinea, as well as the western coast of present-day Australia to Van Diemen's Land (now Tasmania). He intended to reach Île de France by December. On March 10, 1788, La Pérouse sailed from Botany Bay toward New Guinea, never to be seen or heard from again.

In 1791 the French sent Rear Admiral ANTOINE DE BRUNI, CHEVALIER D'ENTRECASTEAUX to find La Pérouse, but he was unsuccessful. Entrecasteaux abandoned the search on July 9, 1793, and died two weeks later.

In 1826 the British merchant captain Peter Dillon heard word that La Pérouse had reached the Santa Cruz Islands. Further investigations by the French explorer JULES DUMONT D'URVILLE in 1828 indicated that La Pérouse's ships had run aground near Vanikoro in the Santa Cruz Islands. La Pérouse's interpreter, de Lesseps,

identified wreckage found there as that of the *Boussole* and *Astrolabe*. Apparently the Melanesian islanders had killed some of La Pérouse's party, while others had survived and built a small boat from the timbers of the two wrecked ships. They may have sailed from Vanikoro, but their fate beyond that has never been determined.

• Larsen, Henry Asbjorn

Norwegian-Canadian
b September 30, 1899; Fredrikstad, Norway
d October 29, 1964; Vancouver, British
 Columbia, Canada
Navigated Northwest Passage

One of the great ice pilots of the century, Superintendent Henry Asbjorn Larsen of the Royal Canadian Mounted Police (RCMP) was the second to navigate the Northwest Passage, the first to do so in one season, the first to accomplish it west to east, and the first to accomplish it in both directions. His little ship, the 104-foot *St. Roch*, later became the first to circumnavigate North America when it sailed through the Panama Canal.

Larsen was born in a port at the mouth of Oslo Fjord in southern Norway, just 10 miles from the hometown of ROALD AMUNDSEN. As a boy of seven, he was thrilled when Amundsen returned triumphantly to Norway in 1906 from his pioneering voyage through the Northwest Passage. Just three years later, Larsen went off to sea in search of his own adventures. After a varied career at sea, he became a Canadian citizen in 1927 and in 1928 joined the RCMP. In 1928 he was assigned as first mate of the *St. Roch*, a new RCMP vessel specially designed for the Arctic. Within a year he was its skipper.

After a decade of patrolling the ice-clogged waters of the Canadian Arctic, in 1940 Larsen received the assignment he had been waiting for. Instead of returning to the Pacific after wintering in the Arctic—something he had done often enough—he was to continue on to the Atlantic.

But what Larsen thought he could do in ninety days ended up taking nearly 2½ years. He left Vancouver, British Columbia, on June 23, 1940, and after two winters frozen in pack ice, arrived in Halifax, Nova Scotia, on October

11, 1942. He took nearly the same route as Amundsen, only in the opposite direction. Hugging the continental coast to the tip of Boothia Peninsula, he then departed from Amundsen's route, cutting across Bellot Strait to take Prince Regent Inlet north to Lancaster Sound. When asked by reporters what the trying 7,500-mile voyage had been like, Larsen's response was, ''Routine.''

The *St. Roch* headed back to Vancouver on July 22, 1944. With ice conditions vastly improved, the trip took only eighty-six days—just about what Larsen had hoped for. This time he took WILLIAM PARRY's route through Viscount Melville Sound, then for the first time followed a passage through Prince of Wales Strait before the winter came, arriving in Vancouver on October 16, 1944.

After completing this circuit, Larsen continued to serve the Canadian Mounties. In 1950 he was made superintendent in charge of G Division, including the entire Northwest and Yukon territories, an area almost half the size of the United States. He retired in 1961. The *St. Roch* was retired to Vancouver in 1951, where it was preserved and put on display, being declared a National Historic Site in 1962.

La Salle in audience with King Louis XIV before his departure for New France. The Bettmann Archive.

La Salle, René Robert Cavelier, Sieur de

French
b November 22, 1643; Rouen, Normandy
d March 19, 1687; east Texas
Explored Mississippi River to its mouth

René Robert Cavelier, Sieur de La Salle, was a man with a vision. He wanted to extend the influence of the French Crown throughout North America. In pursuit of this goal, he became the first European to trace the Mississippi River to its mouth on the Gulf of Mexico, claiming the Mississippi and its valley for France. It was La Salle's tragedy, however, that his vision overreached the means available to achieve it. Thus, La Salle's dreams of a French empire were never realized, and the explorer eventually fell victim to the fatal consequences of his own haughty nature.

The son of a well-to-do Rouen merchant, La Salle was being educated for the Jesuit priesthood when he realized that he was more suited to a life of adventure. In 1666, therefore, he went to **New France**, where he settled west of Montréal. After farming the land for three years, he sold his holdings to become an explorer.

The Indians had told him of a beautiful river to the west, which they called the Ohio. From their description, La Salle theorized that this river might have its outlet in the rumored Vermilion Sea (Gulf of California) and thus might be a route to the Orient. In 1669 La Salle set out to find the Ohio. However, his movements for the next two years cannot be pinned down with any certainty. He may indeed have located the Ohio and explored part of its length, but the evidence is unreliable.

Wherever he had been, La Salle returned to Montréal in 1670 with a wealth of furs and dreams of further explorations in search of a route to Asia. In 1672 the Comte de Frontenac became governor-general of New France and put La Salle in command of Fort Frontenac, a trading post on Lake Ontario. While serving there, La Salle learned that LOUIS JOLLIET and JACQUES MARQUETTE had journeyed down the Mississippi River as far as what is now the Arkansas River and were convinced that the Mississippi discharged into the Gulf of Mexico. Though disappointed that his theory of a route to the Orient had been disproved, La Salle still had his dreams of founding a French empire in North America.

In 1677 Frontenac sent La Salle to France to present his ideas to the king. Louis XIV granted La Salle permission to explore the western part of New France and to build forts wherever he went. Since the French government could not afford to support such a venture, La Salle was responsible for raising the funds for his explorations. He was prepared to do this by trading for furs. When La Salle returned to New France in 1678, he was accompanied by Henri de Tonti, an Italian soldier of fortune who would remain his trusted friend and a fellow adventurer for the rest of La Salle's life.

Near the end of 1678, La Salle, Tonti, and Father LOUIS HENNEPIN, a Franciscan friar, established headquarters at Niagara, where they built a fort and a ship, *Le Griffon*, which was to transport the furs that would pay for an expedition through the Great Lakes. In August 1679

Le Griffon sailed into Lake Erie, becoming the first commercial vessel on that lake. La Salle's party sailed through Lake Erie, Lake Huron, and Lake Michigan. In the latter *Le Griffon* was loaded with furs accumulated by an advance group. Bearing this cargo, the ship headed back to the Niagara River without La Salle. It was never heard from again, leaving La Salle with no revenue to show for his efforts.

Unaware of their dwindling financial resources, La Salle and his group meanwhile proceeded to the southeast shore of Lake Michigan where they built Fort Miami (at the site of present-day St. Joseph, Michigan). Leaving the fort in December 1679, they began the arduous journey to the Mississippi. Traveling first down the St. Joseph River, they then carried their canoes overland to the Kankakee River, a tributary of the Illinois River, the latter of which would take them to the Mississippi. On the Illinois they built Fort Crèvecoeur (Heartbreak, near present-day Peoria, Illinois).

In February 1680 Father Hennepin and two others left the main party to explore the Illinois.

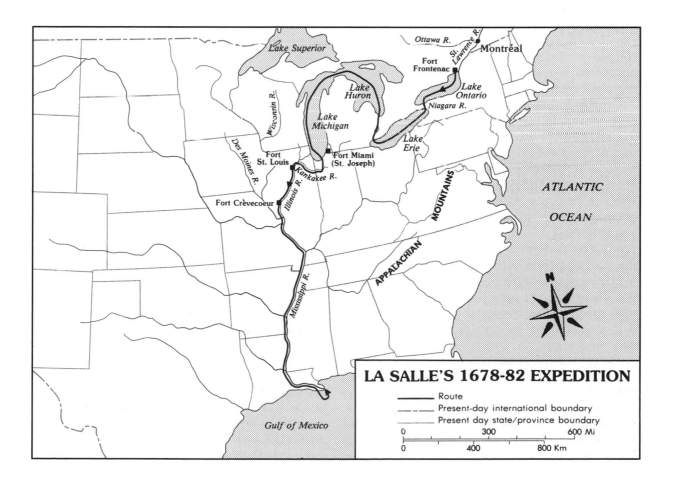

LA SALLE'S 1678-82 EXPEDITION

——	Route
– – –	Present-day international boundary
———	Present day state/province boundary

0   300   600 Mi

0   400   800 Km

Reaching the Mississippi they turned north but were eventually captured by Sioux Indians and never rejoined La Salle.

In desperate need of supplies and worried about *Le Griffon*, which had not been heard from, La Salle left Tonti in charge of Fort Crèvecoeur and returned to New France to raise funds. His overland journey of 1,000 miles through the melting ice and mud of late winter has been called the most difficult made by a European in North America to that time.

In Montréal, La Salle succeeded in raising money to continue the expedition. However, when he returned to Fort Crèvecoeur, he found the fort in ruins and strewn with the massacred bodies of his Indian allies. The dreaded Iroquois had made their way west. Tonti and the other white men were nowhere to be found. La Salle went down the Illinois to the Mississippi looking in vain for Tonti. Then he returned to Fort Miami to spend the winter, during which he formed an alliance with the enemies of the Iroquois. In spring of 1681 he went to Fort Frontenac to complete arrangements for a journey down the Mississippi. In the meantime, Tonti and the other survivors of the Crèvecoeur massacre who had been captured by Iroquois escaped and reached what is now Wisconsin. Helped by friendly Ottawa Indians, they were united with La Salle at Michilimackinac (in present-day Michigan) in June 1681.

On December 21, 1681, La Salle's party left Fort Miami for the Mississippi. They entered the river on February 6, 1682. On March 13, they arrived at the mouth of the Arkansas River, the southernmost point reached by Jolliet and Marquette in 1673. Hearing the war cries of Indians, they feared the worst. But when a party of Quapaw Indians paddled across the river towards them, La Salle held up the calumet (peace pipe). The Indians were delighted and invited the party to their village. In a scene that was to be repeated again and again, La Salle claimed the village for France in the presence of the unsuspecting Indians and then feasted and celebrated with those he considered to be new subjects of the king.

On April 6 the group reached the river's delta and split into three parties to explore the three main channels. They were reunited three days later at the Gulf of Mexico. On April 9, 1682, La Salle claimed the river and its valley for France and named the region Louisiana in honor of King Louis XIV.

La Salle's grand design for French control of North America entailed establishing two colonies: one on the Illinois River for the fur trade and one on the Gulf of Mexico. In 1683 Fort St. Louis was built on the Illinois, but the new governor of New France would not endorse the building of a city at the mouth of the Mississippi. So La Salle sailed for France to seek permission directly from the king. Having received the king's approval, La Salle left France in July 1684. But difficulties plagued his journey all the way to the New World. First there was conflict between La Salle and the naval officer who captained the ship. Then they were attacked by pirates and later shipwrecked. In the West Indies, La Salle was stricken with illness. And lastly, they seem to have sailed right past the mouth of the Mississippi without recognizing it. Some historians have suggested that this error may have been due not to geographic ignorance but rather to the fact that La Salle was under orders to find and raid Spanish mines in Mexico.

Whatever the reason, the colonists were put ashore at a point west of present-day Galveston, Texas, about 400 miles west of the mouth of the Mississippi. There La Salle established a temporary colony. After several attempts to reach the mouth of the Mississippi, La Salle left a small group on the gulf and tried to reach New France by an overland route. His men, weary and frightened by their leader's erratic behavior and his failure to communicate with them, became more and more dissatisfied. On March 19, 1687, somewhere in what is now east Texas, La Salle was murdered by some of his own men.

• Las Casas, Bartolomé de

Spanish
b 1474; Seville
d 1566; San Cristóbal, New Spain (Mexico)
Acted as advocate for American Indians; wrote accounts of conquests of Cuba and Peru

Father Bartolomé de Las Casas spent fifty years championing the rights of the native Indians of the Americas and became one of the most powerful men in the Spanish colonies. A prolific writer, he kept detailed records of events during PÁNFILO DE NARVÁEZ's conquests of Cuba

Las Casas bewailing the cruelty of the Spaniards.
Library of Congress.

and FRANCISCO PIZARRO's conquest of Peru, documenting and commenting on the Spanish mistreatment of the natives. At one time a wealthy slave owner, Las Casas went through an extraordinary enlightenment and devoted the rest of his life to defending the Indians against injustice.

Borne in Seville, Spain, in 1474, Las Casas attended the University of Salamanca. As a young man he saw his first Native American when CHRISTOPHER COLUMBUS brought back several from his first voyage of discovery. In 1502 Las Casas arrived in Cuba, where he built a large estate and purchased Indian slaves to work in the mines. In 1510 he took holy vows and served as chaplain during the Narváez expedition to survey and conquer Cuba. After witnessing the massacre of over 2,000 Indians, Las Casas left the expedition. Then, in 1514, while preparing a sermon, he had a "sudden illumination" that changed the direction of his life. He freed his slaves and vowed to work for "the justice of these Indian peoples, and to condemn the robbery, evil, and injustice committed against them."

Las Casas observed the failure of Spanish laws to protect the Incas during the brutal conquest of Cuzco, Peru, by Pizarro from 1532 to 1533. Appointed bishop of the province of Chiapas, New Spain (present-day Mexico), in 1544, he continued to pressure the king of Spain regarding Indian rights. The issue came to the forefront in August 1550 in Valladolid, Spain, in an event unique in the history of colonization: a debate between Las Casas, representing Indian rights, and Juan Ginés de Sepúlveda, representing the **conquistadores** and Spanish colonists. Though no concrete decision was made by the council hearing the debate, new laws favoring the Indians were passed subsequently, and the **Council of the Indies**, to which Las Casas was appointed, was formed to enforce them.

Las Casas was ahead of his time in promoting human rights. Although frequently called the "saintly fanatic," his forcefulness led to the official acknowledgment of the Indian as a person entitled to civil liberties. However, his use of colorful exaggeration in his description of Spanish conquests contributed to some occasionally unfair notions of Spanish brutality in the New World. Las Casas died in the episcopal palace at San Cristóbal, New Spain (present-day San Cristóbal de las Casas, Mexico), in 1566.

La Vérendrye, Pierre Gaultier de Varennes, Sieur de

French-Canadian
b November 17, 1685; Trois-Rivières, Québec
d December 6, 1749; Montréal, Québec
Explored Lake Winnipeg region and upper Missouri River

Opinions differ as to the true motives behind the explorations carried out by Pierre Gaultier de Varennes, Sieur de la Vérendrye. Some historians maintain that La Vérendrye was driven by curiosity and devotion to France to search for a waterway to the Orient. Others are equally certain that he was motivated primarily by the desire to monopolize the lucrative fur trade in central Canada. Without question, he and his sons engaged in both activities. As a family, they discovered and described Lake Winnipeg, Lake Winnipegosis, and Lake Manitoba and the rivers that run from the south and west into

A statue depicting La Vérendrye. National Archives of Canada.

Hudson Bay. In addition, they explored the upper reaches of the Missouri River.

La Vérendrye was born to a prominent family. His father was a military officer and a governor of Trois-Rivières, and his mother belonged to one of the noblest families of **New France**. La Vérendrye entered the French army as a youth and was severely wounded in Flanders in September 1709 during a battle of Queen Anne's War. Returning to New France, he married Marie-Anne Dandoneau du Sable, with whom he had six children. Between 1715 and 1727 he ran his family's fur business on the St. Maurice River and then at Nipigon and Kaministiquia, above Lake Superior. While there he heard from the local Indians of a large lake from which a river flowed west, ending in water that ebbed and flowed. La Vérendrye believed this lake to be the elusive and much sought Mer de l'Ouest, or Western Sea, and in 1730 he asked the French court for permission and financial support to explore this alleged route to the Pacific Ocean and thence to the

Orient. The court declined to give him money, but in the custom of the day, granted him a monopoly on the fur trade in the area of Lake Winnipeg. He in turn was expected to build forts, secure the area for French trade, woo the region's Indians away from trading with the English at Hudson Bay, and finance his search for the Western Sea with his profits.

On June 8, 1731, La Vérendrye, with a party that included his nephew (La Jemeraye) and three of his sons, set out from Montréal. By August they had reached the drainage divide that separates Lake Superior from the water route to Lake Winnipeg. La Vérendrye chose to spend the winter there, claiming that a threatened mutiny prevented him from going on. His detractors maintained that he stayed there to amass furs. He did, however, send a party on to Rainy Lake where they built the first of eight forts that La Vérendrye constructed as trading posts to purchase furs from Indians.

Over the next ten years La Vérendrye was beset by a series of disasters: some of his associates deserted him, his creditors would not send supplies, his nephew died, and a party returning to the east that included one of La Vérendrye's sons was massacred by Sioux. Despite all of this, the explorer managed to chart a vast area around Lake Winnipeg that was previously unknown to the French.

By 1733 he had learned that the river flowing north out of Lake Winnipeg (now called the Nelson River) emptied into Hudson Bay and not into the Western Sea as he had been previously misinformed. This setback caused him to lose interest in the search for a route to the Pacific. However, the French court at this time was becoming more interested in the Western Sea and was demanding that La Vérendrye fulfill the terms of his agreement. Fortunately, he picked up new intelligence about the sea. He was told that there was a nation on "the River of the West" who knew the way to the Western Sea. These were the Mandans living on the Missouri River, Indians whom MERIWETHER LEWIS and WILLIAM CLARK were to encounter some seventy years later on their exploration of the Louisiana Territory. La Vérendrye's haste in pursuing this information was increased when he learned that he was being prosecuted in New France for putting his fur trade before his commitment to explore.

In October 1738 La Vérendrye left Fort La Reine on the Assiniboine River with twenty men. The party traveled up the river until rapids and shallows made it impassable to canoes. Then, joined by a group of Assiniboin Indians, they struck out south across the prairie to look for the Mandan villages on the Missouri River. They reached the first one on December 3. In the exuberant hubbub that greeted them, the bag of gifts they had brought for the Mandans was snatched away. Without the means to proceed with the formality of gift-giving, nothing could be asked of the Mandans. La Vérendrye had planned to spend the winter there to learn more from them, but this plan was made impractical by the disappearance of his interpreter.

Leaving two men behind to learn the Mandan language, La Vérendrye returned to Fort La Reine on February 11, 1739. In September the two men who had stayed at the Mandan village returned to the fort telling of a group of western Indians who had appeared at the Mandan village and reported that they had seen white men living in brick houses (possibly California missionaries). They said they could take the Frenchmen to this place but would have to make a wide circuit to avoid warlike Indians.

La Vérendrye sent his son Pierre back to the Mandans to pursue this lead, but Pierre was unable to find guides and returned to the fort the next summer.

In the spring of 1742, Pierre and his younger brother, the Chevalier de la Vérendrye, left Fort La Reine with just two other Frenchmen to pursue the route west suggested three years earlier. For over a year, they were passed from one group of Indians to another, always thinking that they were getting closer to those who had seen the "lake that ebbs and flows." It is impossible to determine the precise route of their journey with the exception of two spots. On January 1, 1743, they saw in the distance a mountain range that has been identified as either the Bighorn Range of the Rocky Mountains (120 miles east of Yellowstone Park) or the Black Hills of South Dakota. Later that winter, after traveling east and southeast, they buried a plate of lead engraved with the coat of arms of the French king, which was dug up by a schoolgirl near Pierre, South Dakota, in 1913. The brothers returned to Fort La Reine on July 2, 1643.

In 1744, La Vérendrye returned to Montréal to once again request aid for his explorations. By this time, the governorship of New France had passed to someone who was not sympathetic to him. Instead of receiving financial support, he was commanded to stay on duty in the East. Another man was assigned to command the posts that La Vérendrye had built, manned, and supplied from his own pocket. Protests about the unfairness with which he was treated went unheeded until 1749, when he was given the Cross of St. Louis for his exploratory services to France, and a new governor granted him permission to return to the West.

The Vérendryes had concluded in the meantime that the Saskatchewan River was the most likely route to the Western Sea. At the river's great fork they questioned Indians about its outlet: "They were unanimous in replying that it came from very far, from a height of land where there were exceedingly high mountains, and that they had knowledge of a great lake on the other side of the mountains, whose water was undrinkable. . . . The heights can be reached only in the second year after leaving Montréal. . . ." La Vérendrye was making preparations for this arduous journey when he died. His sons were not allowed to continue his work.

Despite the controversy over his motives, Pierre Gaultier de Varennes, Sieur de la Vérendrye, and his sons can be credited with thoroughly exploring the continental crossroads at Lake Winnipeg. In doing so they established the routes taken through this region by the first two transcontinental expeditions almost two generations later. Whether they were greedy fortune hunters using the search for the Western Sea as a pretext for fur trading or dedicated explorers tied down by a burdensome method of financing expeditions, they deserve the credit for opening up central Canada for the French.

• Legazpi, Miguel López de

Spanish
b 1510; Guipúzcoa
d August 20, 1572; Philippines
Established Spanish rule in Philippines

Miguel López de Legazpi is often called the Conqueror of the Philippines. In the late sixteenth century, he established Spanish sovereignty in the Pacific island group and served as the colony's first governor-general.

Born in the Basque province of Guipúzcoa in northern Spain, Legazpi settled in Mexico.

He had long been a resident of the North American colony when, in 1564, Spain's King Phillip II asked him to establish a colony in the Philippines and to convert the Filipinos to Christianity. Spain had made no serious claims to the islands since FERDINAND MAGELLAN had claimed them for the king in 1521.

On November 21, 1564, Legazpi left the Mexican port of Navidad with five ships, 400 soldiers and sailors, and 6 Augustine monks, including his cousin, ANDRÉS DE URDANETA, who headed the mission.

Legazpi landed in the Philippines in February 1565. After spies sent by the prince of Cebu returned with tales of men who ate rocks (actually hard biscuits) and breathed smoke (from tobacco), the prince decided it was in his best interest to befriend the strangers. On April 27, Legazpi entered and took the town that now is Cebu City. Although the islanders at first resisted, eventually they gave in to his policies of persuasion and religious conversion, supplemented by force only when necessary. Over the next four years, Legazpi extended his rule to other islands in the group, including Panay. In 1570 he sent his grandson, Juan de Salcedo, to subdue the Muslim stronghold on Luzon. Salcedo landed near what is now Manila and secured a peace treaty that gave the Spaniards Batangas and Mindoro as well.

On June 24, 1571, Legazpi established a city council in Manila, made it the capital, and declared Spain the sovereign ruler of the *Islas Filipinas*. The colony was placed directly under the control of the Spanish viceroy in Mexico City, and Legazpi became its first governor-general. He established a system of military and civil administration there that helped unify the island communities. Legazpi died in the islands in 1572 at the age of sixty-two.

• Leichhardt, Friedrich Wilhelm Ludwig

German
b October 23, 1813; Trebatsch
d after April 3, 1848; Queensland, Australia
Explored northeastern Australia

A colorful figure in Australian exploration, Dr. Friedrich Wilhelm Ludwig Leichhardt made several forays into the continent's interior north

Friedrich Wilhelm Ludwig Leichhardt. Photo Researchers, Inc. Engraving from the *Illustrated London News*.

of Brisbane between 1843 and 1848, when he mysteriously disappeared into the bush.

Born in Prussia and educated as a naturalist at the universities of Berlin and Göttingen, Leichhardt arrived in Australia on February 14, 1842, after deserting the Prussian army. Despite a poor sense of direction, he planned to earn a name for himself by exploring the interior of his new homeland. After being turned down for a position with the surveyor general of New South Wales, Leichhardt lectured on natural history and made several plant-collecting trips, including an ambitious 480-mile walk from Newcastle to Moreton Bay, near Brisbane.

Most of Leichhardt's time was spent closer to civilization, however. During his first two years in Australia he was often seen around Sydney wearing a Malay coolie hat and carrying a sword instead of the more normal gun, for he was afraid of firearms.

In 1844 Leichhardt organized a privately sponsored expedition into the interior, hoping to establish an overland passage between Sydney and Port Essington in Arnhem Land, west of the Gulf of Carpentaria. Such a passage, it was believed, would make it possible to open an Indo-Australian trade route with Port Essington as a point of entry. With Leichhardt's small group was the ornithologist John Gilbert, an experienced bushman. The explorers sailed from Sydney to Brisbane, then left Moreton Bay on October 1 and headed north overland, staying within 10 miles of running water at all times, because each man carried only a quart flask.

Such inadequate equipment was just one of the expedition's many problems. Leichhardt frequently became lost in the bush, so the expedition moved slowly. Furthermore, he discovered early in the journey that most of the party's provisions had already been consumed. Still he pressed on, crossing the Great Dividing Range in mid-May 1845 and reaching the Mitchell River, east of the Gulf of Carpentaria, the following month. There **aborigines** killed Gilbert and wounded two others in the party.

From the Mitchell, Leichhardt headed for the gulf and followed the coastline. Stricken by **scurvy** and short on supplies, the group reached Port Essington on December 17, mostly due to the help of two aboriginal guides named Charley Fisher and Harry Brown. Although he had lost most of his botanical specimens along the way, Leichhardt had discovered "an excellent country, available, almost in its whole extent, for pastoral purposes," and so was given a hero's welcome as well as a rich reward of £1,500 upon his return to Sydney. The king of Prussia even pardoned him for his desertion from the army.

In 1846 Leichhardt prepared his *Journal of an Overland Expedition in Australia from Moreton Bay to Port Essington*, which was published the following year. He also developed a plan to cross the continent from Darling Downs to the Swan River following a roundabout route that would take him to the Barcoo River, then north to the Gulf of Carpentaria, then west to the coast and south to the Swan. He led an underequipped party of eight from Sydney in December and returned, defeated, six months later, having covered a mere 500 miles. Most of the members of the expedition suffered from malnutrition and malaria.

But Leichhardt was nothing if not determined. By March 1848 he had gathered another small party for a renewed attempt to reach the settlement at Swan River. The expedition left McPherson Station in Darling Downs and headed for the upper Barcoo. The seven explorers and nearly eighty pack animals were last seen on April 3, 1848, headed west on the Condamine River. Two camps found later on the Barcoo are believed to have belonged to Leichhardt's party. Beyond that, they left no trace. This unlikely explorer, who seems to have had more courage than common sense, is believed to have become lost in the Simpson Desert as he traveled west from the Barcoo River.

Ironically, Leichhardt was seen as a hero, despite his incompetence, during an era when many Australian explorers who made what are now acknowledged as major discoveries were considered failures merely because they did not find new grazing lands.

Leif Erikson. See **Erikson, Leif.**

Le Moyne, Pierre, Sieur d'Iberville. See **Iberville, Pierre Le Moyne, Sieur d'.**

León, Juan Ponce de. See **Ponce de León, Juan.**

Lewis, Meriwether

American
b August 18, 1774; Albemarle County, Virginia
d October 11, 1809; near Nashville, Tennessee
With William Clark, led major expedition exploring Missouri River and northwestern United States

As the head of the Lewis and Clark expedition (officially named the Corps of Discovery), Meriwether Lewis organized and brilliantly led an exploration of the Missouri River from its mouth near St. Louis on the Mississippi to its source in present-day Montana. From there the explorers crossed the Rocky Mountains and the Cascades and followed the Columbia River to the Pacific coast, where they wintered before retracing their steps across half a continent.

At the age of twenty, Meriwether Lewis enlisted in the army and served under General "Mad Anthony" Wayne in the campaign against the Indians of the Northwest Territory (what is now Ohio, Indiana, Illinois, Wisconsin, and Michigan). One of the officers with whom he served was WILLIAM CLARK, his future partner in exploring the West. Lewis was still in the army in 1801 when Thomas Jefferson, a former

Meriwether Lewis. The Bettmann Archive.

neighbor in Virginia, was elected president. Jefferson and Lewis had a mutual interest in the exploration of the vast interior of the American continent. In fact, in 1792, when Lewis was eighteen years old, he had written to Jefferson (then secretary of state) asking to be included should any such expedition take place. When Jefferson later became president, he wrote to ask Lewis to be his private secretary. Then after two years of faithful service in that capacity, Lewis was rewarded.

Early in 1803, several months before the Louisiana Purchase brought the Louisiana Territory under the control of the United States, Jefferson proposed to Congress an expedition that would trace the Missouri River to its source, cross the "Stony Mountains," and find the best water route to the Pacific Ocean for commercial purposes. Jefferson's real purposes were broader than commerce, but his proposal to Congress had to be couched in those terms to pass the test of constitutionality. Congress readily agreed and allocated $2,500 for the expedition.

Jefferson knew he wanted Lewis to lead this important expedition. Lewis had proven himself to be reliable, honest, and resourceful and had established a reputation as a courageous woodsman who knew how to survive in the wilderness. For his co-commander, Lewis was equally certain that he wanted William Clark, who accepted the position.

Jefferson's instructions to Lewis revealed more of his purpose than his message to Congress had. The expedition was to (1) establish precise geographical positions using astronomical observations so that a map could be made; (2) make a careful study of the Indians encountered; (3) study the "soil and face of the country"; (4) note any volcanic activity; and (5) keep statistics on the weather. In short, Jefferson wanted to know everything imaginable about the land and its inhabitants. In order to prepare Lewis for the intellectual demands of the expedition, Jefferson sent him to Philadelphia to study natural history with the best scientific minds of the times. Later he was given access to the most recent maps of the West.

The success of the Lewis and Clark expedition was due in no small part to the thorough grounding Jefferson had provided for Lewis and the careful preparation Lewis undertook on his own. Lewis purchased scientific equipment, arms, goods to trade with the Indians, and all of the supplies thought necessary to take an expedition through the wilderness for two years.

By spring of 1804 preparations for the expedition were complete, and the Louisiana Territory had been transferred from France to the United States as a result of the Louisiana Purchase. On May 14, the Corps of Discovery started up the Missouri River. The party was impressed with the beauty and fertility of the lower Missouri Valley. Although the journey was made difficult and hazardous by floating debris, unpredictable currents, and shifting sandbars, at least there were no serious hostile encounters with Indians. By September the explorers had reached what is now South Dakota, where the newly trained naturalist was thrilled by the vast herds of buffalo, deer, elk, and antelope. Lewis noted with interest the pronghorn antelope—new to science—and badgers, white-tailed jackrabbits, coyotes, and black-billed magpies. He was especially taken with small animals he

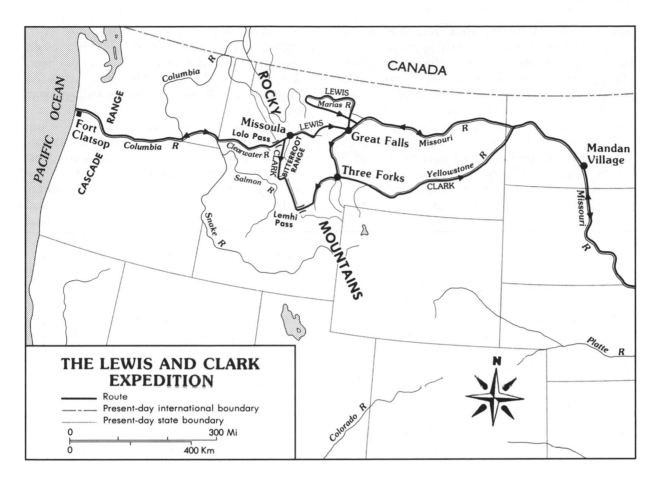

THE LEWIS AND CLARK
EXPEDITION
— Route
--- Present-day international boundary
--- Present-day state boundary
0   300 Mi
0   400 Km

called barking squirrels—animals which another member of the group named prairie dogs, the name that eventually prevailed.

Early in November the Corps built winter quarters in what is now west-central North Dakota near the Mandan villages that had been visited earlier by LA VÉRENDRYE. During the winter the men built six dugout canoes for faster travel on the journey westward. The explorers were visited at their winter quarters by the French-Canadian trapper Toussaint Charbonneau and his pregnant wife Sacajawea, a Shoshone who had been captured by the Minetaree Indians and sold by them to Charbonneau. Since Lewis and Clark hoped to meet up with the Shoshones further west and acquire horses from them, they immediately recognized the value of Sacajawea and welcomed the couple—and soon their newborn son—to the expedition.

On April 7, 1805, sixteen members of the party headed back down the Missouri with surplus supplies, presents for President Jefferson, animal and plant specimens, and dispatches about the first part of the journey. This was

the last time Lewis and Clark were heard of for eighteen months. Two days later, April 9, the rest of the party headed up river. In addition to Lewis and Clark, the expedition at this point consisted of twenty-six soldiers or river men (including JOHN COLTER); Clark's black slave, York; the hunter and explorer GEORGE DROUILLARD; and Charbonneau, Sacajawea, and their papoose, Jean-Baptiste Charbonneau.

From the Mandan village to Great Falls (in present-day Montana) the river trip was relatively uneventful. After encountering the Minetarees, they met no Indians until August 11. However, just below the Great Falls, the trip became more hazardous and uncomfortable as the river began to climb into the foothills of the Rockies. At the junction of the Missouri and a river Lewis named Marias after a cousin, there was confusion about which branch to follow. Amid disagreement they decided to follow the southern branch and were eventually rewarded with a view of the Great Falls. One entire month (June 16 to July 15) was spent in the area getting around 10 miles of rapids and making preparations to proceed. By then they were in Shoshone territory, but still no Indians appeared. Near the end of July, they reached what is now Three Forks, where the Missouri splits into three feeder streams. They named the streams Jefferson, Madison, and Gallatin and chose to follow the southwest branch, the Jefferson.

Lewis put Clark in charge of the river operations while he took a small party overland to try to find the Shoshones. On August 11 he scared a Shoshone warrior, who ran off. On August 12 he "met a large plain Indian road" that led him to the Lemhi Pass through the Rockies. Lewis recognized the Continental Divide (the drainage divide between rivers that flow east and those that flow west), crossed it, and came to a creek flowing west. Eventually an old woman and girl led them to a Shoshone camp. Three days later Clark, Charbonneau, and Sacajawea joined Lewis and his party there. Sacajawea expressed great joy at being among her people again and was overwhelmed when she recognized Chief Cameahwait as her brother.

The reunion did not last long, as the Shoshones were eager to travel east for the yearly buffalo hunt, and Lewis was equally eager to travel west to the Pacific before winter set in. Leaving the valley of the unnavigable Salmon River with one Shoshone guide and several horses, the party traveled into the Bitterroot Range of the Rocky Mountains. For one exhausting month they hacked their way through the wilderness, sometimes unable to proceed because of heavy snow. Finally they reached the villages of the peaceful Nez Percé Indians, where they became friendly with two chiefs who volunteered to take them to the sea. They began the journey down the Clearwater River on October 7, entered the Snake River on October 10, and reached the Columbia River on October 16.

On October 22 the explorers came to the Cascades, the second major mountain range that had to be crossed before they could reach the Pacific. Surmounting one more obstacle, they pushed on and by November 2 had reached tidewater. Following the tidal estuary, they finally caught sight of the Pacific Ocean on November 15. Rather than spend the winter there, they backtracked to a spot where the expedition's hunters could find elk. There they built Fort Clatsop near the site of present-day Astoria, Oregon.

Lewis had expected to find ships on the coast to take the party back east by sea, but when no ships had appeared by March 23, 1806, when the weather cleared, he gave the orders to head back to Missouri by land. The Corps retraced its route to the Bitterroot River valley, near modern-day Missoula, Montana, and there divided into two parties. While Clark took some men down the Yellowstone River, Lewis followed an Indian shortcut to the Missouri and explored the Marias River. During this time Lewis experienced the only violent encounter with Indians of the entire expedition. He and his men convinced a party of fierce Blackfoot Indians that the white men were on a peaceful mission, but during the night the Blackfoot Indians attempted to steal their guns, and in the resulting fray one Blackfoot was shot and another stabbed.

The two parties of the Corps were reunited on the Missouri River near the mouth of the Yellowstone on August 12. Two days later they left Sacajawea and her family at the Mandan villages, and on September 23, 1806, they arrived at St. Louis.

After the expedition Lewis resigned from the army, and Jefferson appointed him governor of Louisiana, which encompassed all of the territory north of the present state of Louisiana. He brought the same honesty and fairness to this task as he had to his other endeavors. In October 1809 he was on his way to Washington on business when he died at an inn in central Tennessee. Jefferson, who knew Lewis to suffer from what is now called manic depression, assumed he had committed suicide, but his family and the people at the inn believed it was murder. The evidence, according to modern historians, seems to favor Jefferson's explanation.

The success of the Lewis and Clark expedition is in large measure due to the qualities of character that Meriwether Lewis brought to the job. His attention to detail, his grasp of everything in his charge, and his thoroughness ensured not only that the expedition traveled its more than 7,500 previously unexplored miles safely (losing only one member, to a ruptured appendix) but also that the information it brought back was of the greatest possible use in opening up the West to settlement. Guided by the wise instructions of Thomas Jefferson, Lewis and Clark added immeasurably to the knowledge about the American West.

SUGGESTED READING: Ralph K. Andrist, *To the Pacific with Lewis and Clark* (American Heritage, 1967); John

Bakeless, *Lewis and Clark: Partners in Discovery* (William Morrow, 1966); Rhoda Blumberg, *The Incredible Journey of Lewis and Clark* (Lothrop, 1987); Richard H. Dillon, *Meriwether Lewis: A Biography* (Western Tanager, 1988).

• Linschoten, Jan Huyghen van

Dutch
b 1563; Haarlem
d February 8, 1611; Enkhuizen
Sailed around Cape of Good Hope to India;
searched for Northeast Passage

In 1583 Jan Huyghen van Linschoten sailed from Holland to the Portuguese settlement of Goa on the west coast of India, where he remained for about six years. By the time he returned to Holland, he was convinced that the already lucrative commercial relations with nations in the Far East could be enhanced further by finding a Northeast Passage from Europe to China and India. Linschoten's subsequent expeditions into the Arctic Ocean in search of such a passage, while unsuccessful, stimulated a number of later expeditions of similar purpose.

While Portuguese and Spanish explorers were the first Europeans to settle in the Far East, the Venetians and the Dutch were not far behind. Linschoten, after sailing around the Cape of Good Hope with a group of Portuguese traders, spent six years in India serving as bookkeeper to the Portuguese archbishop of Goa. During this time, he collected extensive information on trade between Goa and other ports under Portuguese control in the East. When he returned to Holland in 1589, he wrote two books describing the people and customs of India in great detail.

Linschoten's experiences in India spurred his interest in organizing an expedition to find a shorter route to Asia. Merchants from his hometown of Enkhuizen provided some of the capital, the Dutch government sent one ship, and merchants from Amsterdam sent two more. WILLEM BARENTS agreed to act as the expedition's chief pilot and commander of two of the fleet's four ships. In June 1594 the expedition set out "to sail into the North seas, to discover the kingdoms of Cathaia [Cathay] and China," as Linschoten described their mission. When the fleet reached one of the islands of Novaya

Zemlya, Barents sailed up its west coast while Linschoten continued east into the Kara Sea. Bad weather soon forced the ships to return to Holland, but Barents and Linschoten were not to be dissuaded. The following year, the two explorers took a fleet of seven ships outfitted with funds supplied by the Dutch government into the Kara Sea, but the ice pack foiled their journey to the East once again. Linschoten was not to make a third try to find a Northeast Passage (Barents did and died in the attempt), but the publication of his journal in 1601 inspired later Dutch and English explorers to search for alternative routes to the East.

Litke, Fyodor Petrovich. See **Lütke, Fyodor Petrovich.**

• Livingstone, David

Scottish
b March 19, 1813; Blantyre
d May 1, 1873; Ilala (now in Zambia), Africa
Explored Central Africa

The impact of David Livingstone on the exploration of Africa is difficult to overestimate, and it is equally difficult to assess. He was first and foremost a missionary doctor, dedicated to using modern medicine to alleviate the suffering of the African people and Christian truth to alleviate what he believed to be their spiritual ignorance. But Livingstone's religious motivations do not account for the fact that he, more than any other explorer, brought Africa to the attention of Europe. This fact is largely due to Livingstone's remarkable powers of observation. As his convictions and curiosity drove him ever deeper into the unknown regions of Central Africa, his keen eye missed nothing, and his tireless pen recorded almost everything. His writings contain endless descriptions of geography and native customs, medical practices and dietary conventions, birds and animals, trees and flowers—a total, in the three books he eventually published, of over 750,000 words. His journals and books are a comprehensive body of information about Africa that is still being explored by scholars today. The major impact of Livingstone's work has been contradictory. By opening up its interior to European influence, Livingstone paved the way for colonization and exploitation of Africa by the countries

David Livingstone. New York Public Library.

of Europe. At the same time, his belief in the ability of the native peoples of Africa to take their place in the modern world has been a factor in the development of African nationalism.

Livingstone's early life prepared him well for the rigors and demands he would face in Africa. His grandfather, an impoverished sheep farmer, had moved to Blantyre to find work in a cotton mill along the banks of the Clyde River. David's father was a clerk turned itinerant tea vendor who was "too conscientious ever to become rich," as his son later wrote. The seven members of the Livingstone family lived in a single room, ten feet by fourteen feet, in a three-story tenement. Because of the family's poverty, David began working fourteen hours a day in a cotton mill when he was only ten years old.

With his first wages, he bought a Latin grammar book, which he would prop up on the spinning jenny so he could memorize Latin sentences. His studies continued when the machines shut down. For two hours each night, he carried on his education with a schoolmaster, and then he studied at home until about midnight. On his rare holidays, David collected insects, plants, and fossils in the countryside surrounding Blantyre, an early sign of the intense interest in natural history that would make his explorations in Africa so valuable.

The Livingstones instilled in their children a deep Calvinist piety and a dedication to spreading Christianity. By the time David turned twenty, he had resolved to devote his life "to the alleviation of human misery." The rest of his life can only be understood in light of this controlling decision. Specifically, he wanted to become a doctor so that he could respond to a church appeal for medical missionaries to China. He continued to work at the mill part-time for two years while studying Greek, theology, and medicine in Glasgow.

Even then, he was a man of singular determination. One of his classmates recalls: "His face wore at all times the strongly marked lines of potent will. I never recollect of him relaxing into the abandon of youthful frolic or play. I would by no means imply sourness of temper. It was the strength of a resolute man of work."

In 1838, Livingstone was accepted into the London Missionary Society, and he moved to London to complete his medical studies and prepare for China. News of an opium war in China then thwarted his plans. But he soon became acquainted with Robert Moffat, a famous Scottish missionary in southern Africa, who shifted Livingstone's focus. Moffat later wrote:

> I observed that this young man was interested in my story. . . . By and by he asked me whether I thought he would do for Africa. I said I believed he would, if he would not go to an old station, but would advance to unoccupied ground, specifying the vast plain to the north, where I had sometimes seen, in the morning sun, the smoke of a thousand villages, where no missionary had ever been. At last Livingstone said, "What is the use of my waiting for the end of this abominable opium war? I will go at once to Africa." The Directors concurred, and Africa became his sphere.

In November 1840, Livingstone qualified as a doctor in Glasgow, spent one night at home—the last time he would see his father—and proceeded to London, where he was ordained a missionary on November 20. Eighteen days later, he set sail for southern Africa.

Livingstone landed at Cape Town on March 14, 1841. Although Africa had been circumnavigated and roughly mapped in the fifteenth century, it remained relatively unknown to Europeans. Africa had few natural harbors, and its dense forests, vast deserts, often inhospitable climate, and insect-borne diseases made exploration beyond its coasts difficult. Livingstone remained unfazed by these obstacles, however, and he immediately set out on the 700-mile, three-month journey by ox-drawn wagon to Kuruman, Moffat's mission on the Cape frontier. Beyond Kuruman lay the Kalahari Desert, which no European had ever crossed, and beyond that, the vast, unknown mysteries of Africa's interior.

At Kuruman, Moffat and his wife had built thatched houses, planted flower gardens and vegetable beds, and set up carpentry and blacksmith shops. It was a comfortable homestead—too much so, in fact, for a young man whose deepest ambition was "to preach beyond another man's lines." Within two months, Livingstone had set out toward the Kalahari.

Over the next several years, he made several trips north in search of sites for new mission stations, pushing farther into the Kalahari than had any European before him. His journals from this period reveal a strong missionary determi-

nation, a delight in geographical discovery, and a growing respect for the African people and their customs.

In 1844, Livingstone went to build a mission at Mabotsa, about 220 miles north of Kuruman. Along the way, he was nearly mauled to death by a lion that had already ben wounded by two bullets. In Livingston's words: The lion "caught my shoulder as he sprang, and we both came to the ground below together. Growling horribly close to my ear, he shook me as a terrier dog does a rat." Livingstone survived, but the damage was extensive: "Besides crunching the bone into splinters, he left eleven teeth wounds on the upper part of my arm." Livingstone returned to Kuruman, where the Moffats nursed him back to health. He never regained the full use of his left arm, however.

In 1845, Livingstone married Robert Moffat's daughter, Mary. Over the next several years, David and Mary Livingstone explored the region south of the Kalahari Desert; built the mission station at Mabotsa, as well as stations at Chonuane and Kolobeng (near what is now the

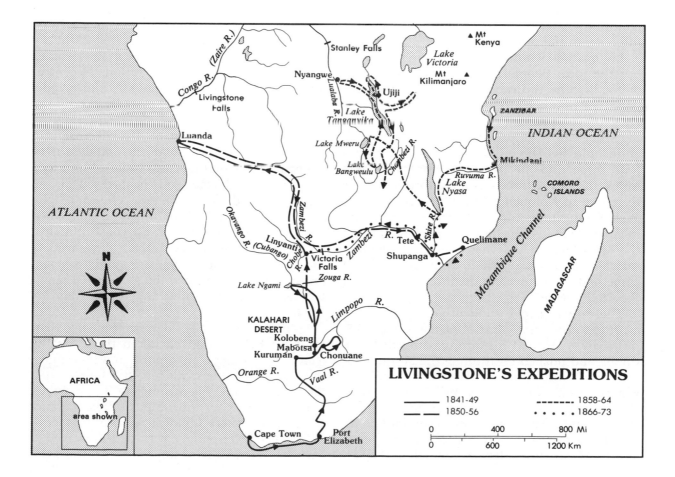

LIVINGSTONE'S EXPEDITIONS

——— 1841-49   - - - - - 1858-64
— — — 1850-56   · · · · · 1866-73

0   400   800 Mi
0   600   1200 Km

Botswana–South Africa border); and had three children. Soon, however, Livingstone became restless. He wanted to investigate the other side of the Kalahari Desert, where, according to the native people, Lake Ngami was located. And beyond the lake, he was told, lay the fertile land of the Makololo tribe, who were governed by the powerful ruler Sebituane. The prospect of new geographical discoveries—and new missions—drew Livingstone to the north.

Leaving his family in Kolobeng, he set out in June 1849 in the company of three big-game hunters and a support crew of about forty. The expedition circled the desert until it came to the Zouga, a river that the local people said flowed out of Lake Ngami, located to the northeast. Livingstone wrote, "It was on 1st August 1849 that we first reached the northeast end of Lake Ngami, and for the first time this fine-looking sheet of water was beheld by Europeans." This event had far-reaching consequences for Livingstone's future explorations. When the Royal Geographical Society in England received word of his find, they awarded him a gold medal and a monetary prize. More importantly, the society encouraged Livingstone to continue his work in Africa and advocated his interests to the public.

Livingstone wanted to press on to the north, but the local people refused to supply guides or food, so he returned to Kolobeng and prepared for another attempt to reach Sebituane. He was accompanied on his second attempt by his wife, who was pregnant with their fourth child, and his three children, who were ages four, three, and one. After two months and 600 miles, they were forced by an outbreak of fever to return to Kolobeng. Not to be denied, however, Livingstone and his family set out again in April 1851. When they reached the land of the Makololo, in the vast swampy regions of Africa's central watershed, Sebituane himself came 400 miles to meet them on the banks of the Chobe River.

There Livingstone suddenly decided to find a route to the west coast of Africa, some 1,800 miles away. He left his family camped by the Chobe and pushed on through the swamps for about 130 miles in search of another site for a Christian mission. He was then "rewarded by the discovery of the Zambesi, in the centre of the continent. This was a most important point, for that river was not previously known to exist at all." Meanwhile, Mary gave birth to the Liv-

ingstones' fourth child, a son, and David finally decided to send his family back to the safety of England. After a grueling 1,500-mile trek to Cape Town, Mary and the children set sail on April 23, 1852.

Livingstone then made his way back to the land of the Makololo, who always remained his favorite tribe of all the African people he met. There, two troubling events occurred in quick succession: he caught fever for the first time, and he discovered unmistakable evidence of an active Portuguese slave trade. Livingstone's resolve to find a route to the west coast was redoubled. If he could open the interior to civilization, he reasoned, Christianity could advance to save African souls, and commercial development could provide an alternative to the slave trade. But the task was daunting. The journey could well be his last, as Livingstone implicitly acknowledged when he wrote to Moffat, "I shall open up a path to the interior, or perish." Nevertheless, Livingstone was poised to make what has since been called "the greatest single contribution to African geography that has ever been made."

In November 1853, Livingstone and his small band of Makololo companions departed Linyanti and began paddling up the Zambezi. Along the way, Livingstone filled notebook after notebook with copious descriptions of central Africa's plants, animals, geology, and people. He discovered that the Kalahari Desert did not meet the Sahara, as many had thought. He traveled through the fringes of Africa's vast rain forests. Although fever, malaria, and dysentery (an acute intestinal disease) reduced him to a shadow of his former self, he pressed on. As supplies dwindled, local tribes refused to help, since Livingstone had nothing to trade. When his party approached the west coast of Africa, however, Portuguese and Arab slave traders came to their rescue. Livingstone and his Makololo companions reached the Atlantic Ocean at Luanda (in what is now Angola) on May 31, 1854.

Livingstone was offered passage back to Britain by a British ship anchored there, but he feared his African companions could not make their way back home alone. After he regained his health, he and his men began the year-long journey back. After a brief but refreshing stay at Linyanti, where Livingstone and his men—all twenty-seven safely returned—received a hero's welcome, Livingstone set off toward the east. Traveling with 114 Makololo volunteers down the Chobe and the Zambezi, he reached what he said was "the most wonderful sight I had witnessed in Africa": the majestic, thundering falls of Mosi-oa-tunya. The overwhelmed explorer named it Victoria Falls after the British queen—"the only English name I have affixed to any part of the country," he later wrote. Livingstone and his companions reached the coastal city of Quelimane (now in Mozambique) on May 20, 1856. While he waited for a ship to take him back to England—he had not seen his family in four years—he reflected on his successful crossing of the African continent and decided that he had not reached the main goal of his exploration, "the elevation of the inhabitants." Therefore, he concluded, "I view the end of the geographical feat as the beginning of the missionary enterprise."

Livingstone reached England on December 9, 1856. He was already a national hero, and the publication of his *Missionary Travels and Researches in South Africa*, along with his lectures throughout England in 1857, stirred the enthusiasm of the public even more. Honors poured in; Africa had become fashionable in England, as geographers, scientists, and businesspeople caught their first glimpses of the complex, mysterious continent. Livingstone, however, was already planning his return to Africa.

Because of his previous accomplishments, he received the backing of the British government for his plan to explore the Zambezi further. The British foreign office gave him this directive: "The main object of the Expedition is to extend the knowledge already attained of the geography and mineral and agricultural resources of Eastern and Central Africa." Livingstone had his own private agenda as well: to plant "an English colony in the Healthy highlands of Central Africa." Only then, he thought, could civilization and Christianity take root and eradicate the slave trade.

Livingstone's expedition departed Britain on March 12, 1858, for an estimated two-year exploration of the Zambezi. But it would be more than six years until he returned. Although this expedition was impressively equipped with a paddle steamer and abundant supplies and attended by ten Africans and six Europeans (including Livingstone's brother Charles), difficulties came early. As Livingstone started up the Zambezi, he found that even its deepest channel was too shallow for the steamboat. Furthermore, the expedition's British navigator refused to take orders from a missionary and had to be sent back to England; and many of the remaining Europeans were struck down by fever.

Livingstone sent word back to England that he needed a more suitable vessel. Meanwhile, he set up a base at Shupanga on the lower Zambezi to store supplies, and then decided to explore the Shire River, one of the Zambezi's tributaries. In July 1859, he sailed up the Shire and then crossed the Shire highlands to the region around Mount Zomba. There, in the pleasant climate and stunning beauty of the fertile and mineral-rich land, Livingstone found one of the things he had been looking for: a site for a European settlement.

After several more weeks of travel, he came upon Lake Nyasa (also known as Lake Malawi), the main geographical discovery of the Zambezi expedition. Livingstone's excitement was soon dashed, however, when he discovered that the southern end of the lake was a crossroads for several major slave-trading routes. By this time, Livingstone was also suffering from severe bleeding hemorrhoids, the medical condition that would eventually contribute to his death. After 1,400 difficult miles, Livingstone arrived back in Tete (now in Mozambique) on November 23, 1860.

Two months later, a new vessel arrived from England, but it too proved unsuitable. Meanwhile, Livingstone had become increasingly militant in his opposition to slavery, and in July 1861 he began to free all slaves he encountered. Before long, he had emancipated more than 100, for whom he set up a village complete with a school. He then returned to explore the region around Lake Nyasa further. He failed to circumnavigate the lake but collected valuable information on its geography and concerning the region's slave trade.

The remainder of the expedition was one tragedy after another. On April 27, 1862, Livingstone's wife, Mary, who this time had accompanied him to Africa, died at Shupanga on the Zambezi. "I feel willing to die," he wrote after he buried her there. The following January, he traveled by boat—the four-oared gig *Pioneer* and a steamboat, the *Lady Nyasa*, which had recently arrived from England—up the Zambezi to the Shire Valley. To his horror, he found that slave traders had wreaked terrible havoc upon this once idyllic region and its people.

Both the river and the earth were littered with dead bodies. Entire villages had been burned to the ground; once lively markets echoed with a deadly silence.

To add to Livingstone's general disillusionment, he received word in July that his expedition had been called back to Britain. He then tried to find a buyer for the *Lady Nyasa*, but the only people who were interested in the steamship were the Portuguese slave traders. So Livingstone and a small crew left Zanzibar in the *Lady Nyasa* on May 1, 1864, sailed 2,500 miles across the Indian Ocean, and left the ship in Bombay, India. He reached England on July 23 of the same year.

With the assistance of his brother Charles, Livingstone wrote his second book, *Narrative of an Expedition to the Zambesi and its Tributaries*, which sold 5,000 copies on the day it became available. His lectures, which once again drew international attention to the continent of Africa, featured fierce verbal attacks on Portuguese slave traders in Africa. While in England, Livingstone visited his five-year-old daughter, whom he had never seen before. But, within a year, he was eager to return to his beloved Africa.

Livingstone's final expedition was supported by the Royal Geographical Society and by private donors. His two main goals were, as usual, to push the frontiers of the Christian faith ever deeper into Africa and to eradicate the slave trade. But he had another goal as well: to find the sources of the Zambezi River, the Congo (or Zaire) River, and, above all, the Nile. He left England in mid-August, stopped in Bombay long enough to sell the *Lady Nyasa*, and arrived at Mikindani on the east coast of Africa on March 24, 1866. He was healthy and glad to be back:

> The mere animal pleasure of travelling in a wild unexplored country is very great. When on lands of a couple of thousand feet elevation, brisk exercise imparts elasticity to the muscles, the mind works well, the eye is clear, the step is firm, and a day's exertion always makes the evening's repose thoroughly enjoyable.

It was a feeling Livingstone would enjoy only briefly.

He assembled a group of fifty-seven men for the expedition, some of whom he had recruited in Bombay, and set out for Lake Nyasa and the unknown country beyond. Before long, familiar difficulties began to appear. Most of the pack animals died, the expedition ran out of food, Livingstone had trouble controlling his companions, and constant signs of the slave trade discouraged everyone. Livingstone had intended to journey north of Lake Nyasa, in order to avoid the Portuguese territory, but Ngoni raids forced him to take a more southerly route. He reached Lake Nyasa on August 8, 1866, and the Shire on September 15. There, all but eleven of his party deserted Livingstone, who responded, "They have been such inveterate thieves that I am not sorry to get rid of them." As they fled, the deserters took most of the supplies with them. Livingstone continued trekking northwest but was soon met by further tragedies. His poodle Chitane, his constant companion, drowned while attempting to cross a flooded river, and an escaped slave he had hired ran off with his medicine chest. This was no minor loss, since Livingstone had begun to suffer severe attacks of rheumatic fever.

Nevertheless, in January 1867, he reached the Chambezi River, part of the immense watershed of the Congo River. He thought the Chambezi might be the headwaters of the Nile, and he spent the rest of his life trying to confirm his suspicions. On April 1, Livingstone came upon the "surpassing beauty" of Lake Tanganyika and then promptly collapsed into unconsciousness. It was almost a month before he recovered sufficiently to travel again.

Instead of making his way to Ujiji, an Arab trading post on the east shore of the lake, Livingstone pressed on into the interior. By early November, he had discovered Lake Mweru, but his spirits were flagging: "I am so tired of exploration without a word from home or anywhere for two years, that I must go to Ujiji on Lake Tanganyika for letters before doing anything else." The rains soon began, however, and much of the region became impassable. After months of almost aimless wandering during the rainy season, he made another significant geographical find: Lake Bangweulu, a vast, marshy lake southeast of Lake Mweru. By now desperately ill with pneumonia, he was saved by Arab traders, who gave him medicine and carried him to Ujiji, which he reached on March 14, 1869.

Later that year, the indomitable explorer set out once again to find the source of the Nile. On March 29, 1871, Livingstone reached Nyangwe (now in Zaire), a village on the Lualaba River and the most northerly point of all his travels. This journey was by far his most difficult. He was constantly sick and hungry, was almost killed in an ambush, and in the end did not solve the puzzle of the Nile. By the time he returned to Ujiji on October 23, his sickness and failure were almost too much for him to bear: "I felt as if dying on my feet. Almost every step was in pain, the appetite failed, and a little bit of meat caused violent diarroea. . . . All the traders were returning successful; I alone had failed and experienced worry, thwarting, baffling, when almost in sight of the end toward which I strained." It would get worse. The Africans to whom he had entrusted his stores in his absence had sold them all and squandered the proceeds. Livingstone was destitute.

On November 10, 1871, HENRY MORTON STANLEY, a reporter for the *New York Herald* who had come to Africa to find the famous explorer, arrived in Ujiji. His greeting would become the most famous line in the history of exploration: "Doctor Livingstone, I presume." Stanley brought much-needed food, medicine, and companionship, and after Livingstone had recovered, the two men searched for an outlet to the Nile from the northern stretches of Lake Tanganyika and traveled to Unyanyembe, 200 miles to the east. Stanley pleaded with Livingstone to leave Africa with him, but Livingstone steadfastly refused. When Stanley left Tabora on March 14, 1872, he was the last non-African Livingstone ever saw.

Livingstone set out again to find the source of the Nile. He decided that he could solve the puzzle if he approached the Lualaba River from the south. Within a month, he was ill again, and his condition quickly became serious. By early 1873, Livingstone was approaching Lake Bangweulu in the middle of the rainy season: "Rain, rain, rain, as if it never tired on this watershed. . . . I must plod on." For the first time in his travels, he became lost, the result of accidental damage to his **chronometers** and a fault in his **sextant**. Because of his sickness, Livingstone often had to be carried by his companions. His bleeding worsened, and dysentery set in. In the predawn hours of May 1, 1873, in a village near Lake Bangweulu, Livingstone's companions found him dead, kneeling beside the bed in his hut.

Livingstone's heart and viscera were buried under a tree in the village. His body was then carried by African members of his party for nine months and 900 miles to the coast, where it was placed on a ship for transport to England. He was buried in Westminster Abbey on April 18, 1874.

Livingstone, by his own accounting, failed in many ways. He did not find the source of the Nile, end the slave trade, or establish permanent missions in Africa. But soon after his death, the slave trade diminished dramatically and Christian missions began to flourish, largely due to his pioneering work. More important, Livingstone's numerous contributions to the geographical knowledge of Africa are without equal, even today.

SUGGESTED READING: Elspeth Huxley, *Livingstone: His African Journeys* (Weidenfield and Nicolson, 1974); Tim Jeal, *Livingstone* (G. P. Putnam, 1973); David Livingstone, *Missionary Travels and Researches in South Africa* (Ayer, 1972); James I. Macnair, ed., *Livingstone's Travels* (J. M. Dent and Sons, 1955); Oliver Ransford, *David Livingstone: The Dark Continent* (St. Martin's, 1978); I. Schapera, *Livingstone's African Journal, 1853–1856* (Chatto & Windus, 1963).

• Lobo, Jerome (Jeronimo)

Portuguese
b 1593?; Lisbon
d January 29, 1678; ?
Explored East Africa

Father Jerome Lobo, a Jesuit priest of the seventeenth century, was one of the first Europeans to visit Lake Tana, the source of the Blue Nile. After exploring the Juba River and Malindi (now Kenya), he went to Abyssinia (now Ethiopia) to work as a missionary. There he spent eight years before being expelled by anti-Christian leaders who came to power. He later wrote two books about his experiences in Africa, and, despite challenges to his credibility long after his death, his claims were ultimately validated.

Entering the seminary at the age of sixteen, Lobo was ordained eleven years later and was first appointed to a teaching position at the college at Coimbra, Portugal. In 1622, he was sent to Goa, a Portuguese colony on the west coast of India, to complete his theological studies and prepare for a missionary assignment in Abyssinia. The same year, the Jesuits' Abyssinian missionary, Father Pero Páez, died, and Lobo was chosen to accompany the newly appointed

Bishop Alphonso Mendes to his new post. Since the emperor of the territory had been converted to Christianity, the Jesuits did not anticipate any animosity from the native people of Abyssinia. However, gaining access to the country could be perilous because of hostile Turks occupying areas along the Red Sea.

Lobo departed from India in 1624 and, unable to reach Abyssinia on his first attempt, traveled south instead, to the Juba River and Malindi. He arrived in Abyssinia the following year and, as expected, found its native people receptive to Catholic teachings. An avid explorer, Lobo traveled to Lake Tana, as Páez had done ten years earlier, and thus became the second European known to visit the source of the Blue Nile, the smaller of the river's two main tributaries. He also went southeast to the cataracts (falls or steep rapids) of the lake, known as Tisisat Falls, an experience he described poetically in a journal published later as *A Voyage to Abyssinia*.

Lobo's story was to come under attack more than 150 years later by the next European visitor to the cataracts, Scotsman JAMES BRUCE. Highly competitive and fiercely anti-Catholic, Bruce returned from his own treacherous journey and announced that Lobo could not have preceded him there because the priest's description of the falls was inaccurate. He disputed Lobo's assessment of the height of the falls and scoffed at Lobo's telling of sitting on a ledge underneath the precipice and peering through the cascading waters at rainbows in the gorge. According to Bruce, it was not physically possible to gain such a vantage. Subsequent explorers refuted Bruce's claims, however, citing a difference in seasons as explanation of the reported disparity in the size of the falls.

After seven productive years as a missionary in Abyssinia, Lobo suddenly found himself unwelcome in the country upon the death of its Catholic emperor, Susenyos, in 1632. The new leadership strenuously opposed Christianity, and by 1634 all Jesuit missionaries had been expelled. Lobo sailed back to Goa and then on to Madrid and the Vatican. He reported the situation in Abyssinia to the religious leaders of Spain and to the Pope, trying unsuccessfully to persuade them to intervene with the new government on behalf of the Jesuit mission.

Unable to continue his missionary work in Africa, Lobo returned to Goa, where he was appointed rector Jesuit provincial. He remained in the city for nearly twenty years before returning to Portugal. The rest of his life was spent primarily in writing about his experiences and observations in Africa. Although neither of his books was published in his native country, one was translated into English and published in London in 1669. The more extensive of Lobo's works was translated into French and published forty years after his death. In 1735 that book was translated into English and published by British author Samuel Johnson, who later published a book of his own set in Abyssinia. Johnson also became Lobo's most strenuous defender against the criticisms aired by Bruce more than a century after the priest's death.

Long, Stephen Harriman

American
b December 30, 1784; Hopkinton, New Hampshire
d September 4, 1864; Alton, Illinois
Explored American West

As a member of the United States Army Corps of Topographical Engineers, Stephen Harriman Long made three explorations of the North American interior. The most significant took place in 1820 when he led a party along the Platte River to the Rocky Mountains and then south to the Arkansas and Canadian rivers. Long's report of the expedition confirmed ZEBULON PIKE's earlier opinion that the Southwest was a Great American Desert unfit for human habitation, a conclusion that squelched interest in the area for at least thirty years.

A graduate of Dartmouth College, Long joined the army and taught mathematics at West Point for two years before transferring to the Corps of Topographical Engineers. His first expedition, in 1817, took him up the Mississippi River to the Falls of St. Anthony at what is now Minneapolis, Minnesota. Long's aim was to select appropriate sites for military installations as part of the government's attempt to subdue hostile Indians and to protect United States fur traders from the incursions of the British. As a result of Long's work, the government built Fort Snelling at the juncture of the Mississippi and Minnesota rivers. Long was also involved in the construction of Fort Smith on the Arkansas River.

In 1819, Secretary of War John C. Calhoun proposed to establish a military outpost near the juncture of the Missouri and Yellowstone rivers for the "protection of our northwestern frontier and the greater extension of our fur trade." The result of Calhoun's proposal was the Yellowstone Expedition. In the spring of 1819, 1,000 men under the command of General Henry Atkinson headed up the Missouri in five steamboats. A sixth steamboat carried Long in command of a group of scientific explorers and artists. It was the first time steamboats had been used on the Missouri and the first time scientific experts had been sent on an exploration of the West. The steamboats proved to be unsuitable for navigating the Missouri, and the military component of the expedition bogged down at Council Bluffs (in present-day Iowa), where all of the men became ill. After 100 men had died of **scurvy**, Congress, appalled at the escalating costs of the expedition, canceled the project. Long was ordered to change his direction entirely and move via the Platte River and the Great Plains to the Arkansas and the Red rivers in the Southwest. The Red River was considered strategically important, for it was assumed at the time to be the border between the United States and Spanish territory.

On June 6, 1820, Long and his party set out from Council Bluffs and traveled west along the Platte, where they encountered giant herds of buffalo and painted Pawnee Indians. On June 30, they caught sight of the Rockies and named the highest peak they could see Longs Peak. In mid-July they reached the point where the South Platte comes out of the mountains (just south of present-day Denver), and a few days later, on July 18, some of the party scaled Pikes Peak, becoming the first recorded ever to have done so.

The expedition followed the Arkansas River as far as the Royal Gorge but failed to reach the river's source. Long then divided his party into two groups. The first would descend the Arkansas, traveling east as far as the border of what is now Oklahoma. Long himself led the second group south until they reached a river they believed to be the Red. They showed no interest in ascending to the source of the river, instead turning east to follow it downstream. The journey was one of extreme hardship. At times Long and his party were forced to eat their own horses, and typically, the Indians they encountered were hostile. Finally they came to the end of the river, only to discover, to their mortification, that it flowed into the Arkansas and was thus not the Red River but the Canadian. (The Red River is roughly parallel to and just south of the Canadian and flows into the Mississippi.) To make matters worse, they found out that three deserters from the other group had taken most of the expedition's journals and scientific notebooks. Thus, Long's return was less than triumphant.

Despite the failings of his second expedition, Long was given another chance. In 1823 he was ordered to explore the area between the Mississippi and Missouri rivers. This expedition followed the Mississippi and then traveled up the Minnesota River to its headwaters, where Long's party marked the international boundary between the United States and Canada at the forty-ninth parallel. Long arrived back in Philadelphia on October 26, 1823, to the only triumphant return he ever had from a westward exploration.

Long's explorations were over, but his career of service was not. The rest of his life was spent in the army with the Topographical Engineers, where he distinguished himself as a surveyor of routes for new railroads and eventually became an authority in the new field of railroad engineering.

Although Long's exploration of the Southwest failed to locate the Red River (or to trace the Arkansas and Canadian to their sources) and despite the fact that many of the journals and notebooks were lost, the report and map resulting from his second expedition were the most significant produced since those of MERIWETHER LEWIS and WILLIAM CLARK. The report, supervised by Long, was actually written by Edwin James, chief geologist of the expedition, and his account of the plains and the Rocky Mountains was remarkable for the daring approach it took to describing geologic time. At a time when many scientists still felt constrained to calculate the age of the earth in the literal, biblical manner—making it less than 6,000 years old—James hypothesized that the formation of the Rockies and the plains had taken eons. Also contained in the report were complete descriptions of plants and animals of the plains, including a number of new animal species, such as the coyote, that were discovered and named on the expedition. To further enhance the report, Long added a seventeen-page supplement on Indian sign language that was

LOPES DE SEQUEIRA, DIOGO

the first attempt to record and understand this universal language of the plains Indians. Future explorers used his map and report as well as his personal advice in planning their travels. The report even served as the inspiration for literature when James Fenimore Cooper used it to supply most of the details for his Leatherstocking novel *The Prairie*.

In spite of the usefulness of Long's report, historians have continued to criticize him for the one passage that seemed to take hold of the American consciousness. He wrote:

> In regard to this extensive section of the country, I do not hesitate in giving the opinion, that it is almost wholly unfit for cultivation, and of course uninhabitable by a people depending upon agriculture for their subsistence. Although tracts of land considerably extensive are occasionally to be met with yet the scarcity of wood and water, almost uniformly prevalent, will prove an insuperable obstacle in the way of settling the country. . . .

It was this opinion that caused Long to be labeled the creator of the Great American Desert myth that dissuaded settlers from emigrating to the Great Plains for over thirty years. In fact it was Zebulon Pike who first voiced that myth in 1810, and Long's report had merely confirmed Pike's earlier claim, albeit emphatically. A good argument can be made that they were correct—the Southwest of the 1820s was not suitable for widespread settlement. As Pike and Long accurately noted, it was an area with little timber for building or fuel, with a scarcity of surface water, and with an abundance of sandy soil. Its winters were bitterly cold, vast herds of buffalo dominated the landscape, and hostile Indians guarded their hunting grounds fiercely. Given what he had seen, Long's estimation was fair and accurate.

• Lopes (Lopez) de Sequeira (Sequira; Siqueira), Diogo (Diego)

Portuguese
b ?
d 1520?
Led first European fleet to explore Malay Archipelago

The historical renown of the Portuguese explorer Diogo Lopes de Sequeira has certainly been eclipsed by that of his fellow countryman and explorer FERDINAND MAGELLAN. But Lopes de Sequeira was the first European navigator to sail the seas described centuries before by MARCO POLO. In fact, Magellan made his first voyage to the East as part of a fleet commanded by Sequeira, who set out from Portugal in the first decade of the sixteenth century to explore the Malay Archipelago. Magellan died nearby—in what is now the Philippines—in 1521, thus falling short of circumnavigating the globe by almost exactly the distance he had traveled a few years before with Lopes de Sequeira.

Little is known about Lopes de Sequeira's early life or precisely when he sailed from Portugal for the East. Magellan is known to have volunteered for service in India in 1504, to have been attached to a ship under the command of Lopes de Sequeira, and to have reached the coast of India in 1509. Upon their arrival, the Europeans encountered stiff resistance from the native people of Goa and Cochin, both located on the southwestern coast of India.

That same year, Lopes de Sequeira's fleet embarked from Calicut, rounded Ceylon (now Sri Lanka), crossed the Bay of Bengal, and landed somewhere on the northern part of the island of Sumatra (in what is now Indonesia). After negotiating a treaty with a local chief, Lopes de Sequeira sailed on to the Moluccas (also in present-day Indonesia), which he reached in September. He and his crew were astounded by what they found: a busy and thriving port city crowded with ships and traders from Arabia, Persia (now Iran), Bengal (India), Burma, Java (Indonesia), China, and what are now the Philippines. The arrival of the Europeans caused some initial consternation on the part of the Moluccans, but Lopes de Sequeira soon established friendly relations with the traders and arranged to purchase spices to load on his ships. The local Malay ruler was less graciously inclined toward the newcomers, however, and mounted a plot to kill Lopes de Sequeira and his men. The conspiracy would have succeeded had not a benevolent trader warned Lopes de Sequeira in time for him to sail to safety—although at the expense of leaving some of his men prisoners of the Malaysians.

The city of Ternate in the Moluccas marked the easternmost extent of Lopes de Sequeira's travels. His fleet arrived back in Portugal in

1512, marking the end of his contributions as an explorer.

López de Legazpi, Miguel. See **Legazpi, Miguel López de.**

• Lütke (Litke), Fyodor Petrovich

Russian
b September 17, 1797; Leningrad
d August 8, 1882; Leningrad
Circumnavigated twice; explored Arctic and Pacific oceans

Fyodor Petrovich Lütke led the *Senyavin* circumnavigation (1826–29), one of the most fruitful voyages of discovery in the Pacific in the nineteenth century. A career naval officer who first circumnavigated on the Kamchatka expedition (1817–19), Lütke charted the waters of the northern Pacific and the Bering Sea for Russia.

Born in 1797, Lütke attended the Russian school for naval cadets. At the age of twenty he accompanied Captain Vasily Mikhailovich Golovnin aboard the *Kamchatka* on a voyage to determine the position of several islands in the Bering Sea. From 1821 to 1824 he took the *Apollo* into Arctic waters, mapping the Murmansk Coast of Russia's Barents Sea and the western and southern coasts of Novaya Zemlya.

In 1825 Lütke became an **aide-de-camp** of Czar Nicholas I. The following year the Russian ruler put him in command of the *Senyavin* on a Pacific voyage of discovery. With a team of scientists aboard, the ship sailed from Kronstadt (now Kronshlot), on the Gulf of Finland, on September 1, 1826, and reached the Canary Islands by November. After a brief stop in Rio de Janeiro, Brazil, the *Senyavin* rounded South America's Cape Horn and stopped at Valparaíso, Chile, on March 26, 1827. After a three-week rest ashore, Lütke sailed north to Alaska's Sitka Island.

Lütke reached Unalaska, far to the west of Sitka, in the Aleutian Islands, in late August. Taking advantage of the mild weather, he sailed north into the Bering Sea, mapping St. Matthew Island, then charting the Asiatic coast as far as Petropavlovsk, which he reached on September 25.

In December he sailed south for the Carolines, where the expedition naturalists found the only known specimen of a bird they called the Caroline rail. Lütke spent most of his time in the Carolines on Ualan, where the islanders were hospitable. But he toured the **archipelago** and charted several other islands, including Ponape and Palau (now Belau), where the inhabitants seemed hostile, keeping Lütke from landing. He reached Guam on February 26, 1828, then in April visited the Bonin Islands near Japan, where a naturalist discovered another rare bird, the Bonin hawfinch.

In northern waters during the summer of 1828, Lütke mapped Ostrov Karaginsky (Karagin Island) and present-day Litke Strait, as well as what is now Senyavin Strait between the continent and Arakamchechen Island in the northern Bering Sea.

Lütke visited the Carolines again and then the Philippines before returning to Europe by way of Sumatra and Africa's Cape of Good Hope. He reached Kronstadt on September 16, 1829. During the course of the three-year circumnavigation, his scientists had discovered more than 300 species of birds, 700 insects, and 150 crustaceans and collected more than 300 mineral specimens, 4,000 plants, and the largest collection of algae species to date.

In 1835 Lütke was made rear admiral and published his *Voyage Around the World*. He was later one of the founders of the Russian Geographical Society (1845) and served as maritime governor of Revel (now Tallinn; 1850) and Kronstadt (1853). In 1855 he was promoted to admiral and named a member of the Council of State. He was also a corresponding member of the Paris Academy of Sciences and president of the St. Petersburg Academy of Sciences. Lütke died in 1882 in St. Petersburg (now Leningrad).

• Mackenzie, Alexander

Scottish
b 1764?; Stornoway, Outer Hebrides
d 1820; near Pitlochry, Perth
Explored western Canada; reached Pacific Ocean via land route over Canadian Rockies

Sir Alexander Mackenzie made two daring expeditions from his fur-trading post on Lake Athabasca in the northernmost reaches of

Alexander Mackenzie. New York Public Library.

on June 3, 1789. With four Canadian **voyageurs**, the wives of two of them, a German, a Chipewyan called English Chief, and the latter's extended family, Mackenzie left Lake Athabasca and traveled up the Peace River to the Slave River and then northwest to the Great Slave Lake. Reaching the lake on June 9, he found it still covered with ice, and it took the party until June 23 to pick their way north through breaks in the ice. Having reached the north shore of the lake, they then spent another six days searching the shore for what is now called the Mackenzie River.

Once on the river, they were pleased to discover that it ran west, and in some places southwest, for 300 miles. This, they felt, was a good sign that it would eventually reach the Pacific Ocean. Further evidence of their westward direction came on the morning of July 2, when a fog lifted and they were treated to the majestic sight of the snow-capped Rocky Mountains in the distance. However, instead of penetrating the mountains as Mackenzie had expected it to, the river soon turned north.

present-day Alberta province. In the first (1789), he followed the river that now bears his name to its outlet on the Arctic Ocean. In the second, he crossed the Rocky Mountains to reach the Pacific Ocean in 1793.

After emigrating to Canada, Mackenzie became involved in the fur trade in Montréal. Ambitious and adventurous, he eagerly accepted the job of running the North West Company's post at Lake Athabasca in what are now the Canadian provinces of Alberta and Saskatchewan. The departing director of the post was the American explorer PETER POND. Pond had developed the theory that the river flowing out of the Great Slave Lake (northwest of Lake Athabasca) was the same one that Captain Cook had described as flowing into the deep Alaskan bay now known as Cook Inlet. Mackenzie quickly became a supporter of Pond's theory and was eager to test it out. He hoped to discover the Northwest Passage to the Pacific that so many North American explorers had sought and failed to find (for a more complete discussion of the passage, see MARTIN FROBISHER).

After putting the trading post on firm financial footing, Mackenzie spent the winter of 1788–89 preparing for the journey, which began

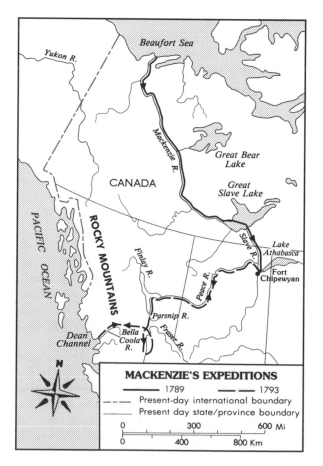

MACKENZIE'S EXPEDITIONS
―――― 1789 ―― ―― 1793
– – – Present-day international boundary
――― Present day state/province boundary

0   300   600 Mi
0   400   800 Km

Disappointed, Mackenzie and his party nonetheless continued on, eventually encountering Slave and Dog-Rib Indians, who, according to Mackenzie's journal, warned them of monsters and other dangers down the river and offered the chilling prediction "that it would require several winters to get to the sea, and that old age would come upon us before the period of our return." Still undaunted, they canoed on, and on July 10, entered the 100-mile-long Arctic delta of the Mackenzie, where "the river widens, and runs through various channels, formed by islands, some of which are without a tree." Mackenzie took a latitude reading at this point and was both surprised and disappointed to learn how far north he was. It took the party another two days to reach open water at a point now called Mackenzie Bay in the present-day Beaufort Sea. They then spent five dangerous days paddling their bark canoes between the shore and the ice field, exploring the bay.

Then the expedition turned homeward in a race to get back before winter set in. However, the approaching winter did not stop Mackenzie from contemplating a side trip to the Pacific when he was told by an Indian they met that across the mountains was a river that would take him to the "White Man's Lake." The Indian refused to guide him, however, and by doing so probably helped Mackenzie avoid mutiny on the part of English Chief, who was reluctant to be dragged even farther from home than he had been already.

The party returned to Fort Chipewyan on September 12, two days after the first snowstorm. In 102 days, they had traveled almost 3,000 miles, had mapped one of the world's great rivers, and had—nearly—given final rest to the idea of a navigable Northwest Passage to the Pacific. Reflecting his feelings about failing to reach the Pacific, Mackenzie named the river Disappointment, but the name was later changed to Mackenzie to honor the first man to explore its length.

Mackenzie was determined to try again to reach the Pacific, but he realized that if his explorations were to have any real value to science, he would have to learn more about determining exact geographic position and mapping. To that end, he took a leave of absence from the company and in 1791 traveled to England. There he studied astronomy, navigation, and geography at his own expense and bought the latest instruments for reckoning longitude and latitude. By fall of 1792 he was back at Lake Athabasca, making preparations for his next journey of discovery.

He spent the winter at a hastily built fort 200 miles up the Peace River to facilitate a head start in the spring. On May 9, 1793, in a large, extremely lightweight canoe built to his specifications, Mackenzie set out with ten people and 3,000 pounds of supplies. Besides Mackenzie's second-in-command, Alexander Mackay, the party included six French-Canadian voyageurs (two of whom had been on Mackenzie's previous trip) and two Indian interpreters and hunters.

By May 17, earlier than they had expected, they were in sight of the Rocky Mountains. But the next leg of their journey slowed them considerably as they found themselves in the Peace River canyon, a turbulent 22-mile run of falls and rapids, much of it between rocky cliffs. For six arduous days they first poled and towed the canoe up the river and then **portaged** an exhausting 9 miles up a steep mountain and across wooded hills before returning to a more peaceful stretch of the river. A week of easy paddling brought them to a fork in the river. Of the two alternatives, the river now called the Finlay seemed the more likely one to lead to the Pacific. But against his better judgment, Mackenzie chose the other river (the present-day Parsnip) because a Beaver Indian had previously told him that the Finlay led only deeper into impenetrable mountains, while the Parsnip would take him across the mountains to another river than would lead to the ocean.

Between June 1 and July 4, the party was surrounded by mountains and traveling up confusing rapid, shallow rivers. Heat, mosquitoes, and gnats plagued them. To add to their discouragement, it was becoming clear that no river paralleled the Mackenzie on the west side of the Rockies leading to Cook Inlet (contrary to what they had been told). The party traveled up the Parsnip to the Continental Divide and then crossed to the Fraser River. Eventually local Indians told them not only that the river canyon became nearly impassable but also that its route to the sea was a long one.

By June 22 Mackenzie had decided that the only practical route to the Pacific was overland rather than by river. But to reach the overland route he would have to backtrack up the Fraser, and he feared that his weary men would balk at this notion. To his surprise they agreed unanimously to the change in plans, and on July 4 the party left their surplus supplies at the junction of the Fraser and the Blackwater rivers and set out overland with heavy packs on their backs.

For fifteen days they marched toward the sea in a landscape that was totally new to them. They marveled at the warm moist coastal slope with its gigantic trees and native tribes who were dependent on salmon rather than game for their sustenance. They observed with wonder the Indians' large houses covered with carvings and paintings and their enormous seagoing canoes, hewn from cedar logs. Then on July 17 they arrived at a village on what is now called the Bella Coola River and were so warmly greeted by the inhabitants that they named the place Friendly Village. After a day of feasting, they continued toward the coast and on July 19 arrived at the mouth of the river, which emptied into a long narrow inlet of the sea, now called the Dean Channel (in present-day British Columbia).

These coastal Indians were decidedly unfriendly, however, and Mackenzie's men would just as soon have headed for home immediately. But their leader was not to be dissuaded from his purpose. He was determined to find a spot where they could stay long enough to take the daytime and nighttime readings necessary for establishing longitude and latitude exactly. After two days of being followed by anxious Indians, Mackenzie took the readings he required from a defendable rock ledge on the Dean Channel. Then he mixed some vermilion dye with melted grease and on a rock painted this proof of his feat: "Alexander Mackenzie, from Canada, by land, the twenty-second day of July, one thousand seven hundred and ninety-three." The same words are now chiseled into the same rock.

At last he was ready to head for home. The trip west had taken ten hard weeks; the return journey was made in four weeks. By August 24 they were back at the fort on the Peace River, and Alexander Mackenzie's exploring days were over. However, it was not until 1801, when his journals were finally published, that the world began to learn of his extraordinary accomplishments.

Alexander Mackenzie was a man of imagination and grit. By sheer force of his personality and leadership skills he was able to complete two of the most difficult explorations ever undertaken on the North American continent. Under the most discouraging, laborious, and dangerous circumstances, he had the faith and stamina to persist and the gift to impart his faith to those who journeyed with him. He is fittingly commemorated by a river, a mountain range, and a bay that bear his name.

SUGGESTED READING: Roy Daniells, *Alexander Mackenzie and the North West* (Oxford University Press, 1971); Alexander Mackenzie, *Voyages from Montreal on the River St. Lawrence Through the Continent of North America to the Frozen and Pacific Oceans in the Years 1789 and 1793* (Tuttle, 1971); James K. Smith, *Alexander Mackenzie, Explorer, the Hero Who Failed* (McGraw-Hill Ryerson, 1973).

• MacMillan, Donald Baxter

American
b November 10, 1874; Provincetown,
   Massachusetts
d November 10, 1970; Provincetown,
   Massachusetts
Explored Arctic by sledge and plane

An assistant in ROBERT PEARY's final expedition to the North Pole in 1908–1909, Rear Admiral Donald Baxter MacMillan of the U.S. Naval Reserve subsequently spent several of his thirty-one trips to the Arctic filling in gaps in the map of the Canadian Arctic left by Peary. From 1913 to 1917, for instance, he attempted to reach Peary's mythical Crocker Land, said to lie northwest of Ellesmere Island, only to discover that the reported sighting had been a mirage. But unlike Peary, MacMillan had serious scientific projects to pursue in the Arctic, ranging from anthropological fieldwork among the **Inuit** to studies of glacial movement and natural history. He proved, for example, that the polar regions had once sustained heavy tree growth when he discovered a coal deposit in the Sverdrup Islands, at 81° North latitude.

When MacMillan first met Peary in 1901, he was an instructor of Latin and physical training at Swarthmore Preparatory School. Peary asked MacMillan to tutor his son in outdoor skills at his summer camp at Casco Bay. Before that he had been the principal of a high school in Maine. He had also studied anthropology at Harvard.

After the Peary expedition, MacMillan spent three years in the Labrador region (1910–12). There he began the serious ethnological work that would lead to his appointment as professor of anthropology at Bowdoin College, his alma mater, in 1918. Like VILHJALMUR STEFANSSON, his interest in the people of the globe was always tightly connected to his passion for exploring the lands they inhabited. From 1913 to 1917 he led the expedition in search of the nonexistent Crocker Land northwest of Axel Heiberg Island.

In 1920 MacMillan visited Canada's Hudson Bay area to report on trading post possibilities and the next year explored southern Baffin Island in the *Bowdoin* for the first time. He had this sixty-ton engine-fitted **schooner** specially built to cope with Arctic conditions and used it regularly thereafter on his northern trips, often crewed by college students. In 1923 he returned to the far north to investigate tidal and meteorological conditions and other scientific features in northwestern Greenland. Then in 1925 (at the same time ROALD AMUNDSEN was preparing for his polar flight), MacMillan helped begin a new era in Arctic exploration when an expedition that he had organized with the U.S. Navy, and which was sponsored by the National Geographic Society, succeeded in flying across Ellesmere Island. This was the first of RICHARD BYRD's flights in Arctic conditions; FLOYD BENNETT was aboard as pilot and mechanic.

MacMillan's career in the Arctic continued for many years. His work added greatly to information on the polar region and aided a variety of practical projects, both civilian and military, as well as pioneering the use of aircraft, shortwave radio, and snowmobiles in Arctic exploration. MacMillan took his last trip in 1957 at the age of eighty-two.

· Magellan, Ferdinand (Fernando de) (Magallanes, Fernao de; Magalhães, Fernão de)

Portuguese
b 1480?; Sabrosa, Trás-os-Montes, or Ponta de Barca
d April 27, 1521; Mactan, Philippines
Circumnavigated (for Spain); reached East Indies by sailing west; discovered Strait of Magellan

Ferdinand Magellan is one of the most heroic—and important—figures of maritime explora-

tion. Credited with being the first to lead a circumnavigation of the globe, this dauntless navigator accomplished what CHRISTOPHER COLUMBUS had set out to do some thirty years earlier: he reached the East Indies by sailing west from Europe. In the course of doing so, he found a crucial passageway into the South Sea, which he named the Pacific Ocean, and revealed its vastness to the eyes of European civilization.

This historic voyage into the unknown was accomplished despite extreme hardships and against formidable odds. Its success is directly attributable to Magellan himself—to his skills both as a navigator and as a leader. Stern and self-disciplined, he led with a firm but even hand. While he demanded great sacrifices from his crew, he always asked even more of himself. In return, he was feared but respected by those who sailed for him and inspired the unwavering allegiance necessary for such a voyage of privation and endurance. Sadly, the constancy of character that made Magellan the ideal captain also contributed to his death when he stubbornly initiated a futile battle with native people of the Philippines.

Ferdinand Magellan. New York Public Library.

Magellan was born in Portugal around 1480 to Dom Ruy Magalhães and Donha Alda de Mesquita, a family of minor nobility. Dom Ruy was a trusted officer of Portugal's King John II. The youngest of three children, Ferdinand was raised in his family's rambling farmhouse, and at the age of seven he was sent to a monastery school at Vila Nova de Mura. At twelve he became an apprentice page at the court of John's queen Dona Leonor, where he studied advanced mathematics, geography, cartography, and navigation, in addition to skills such as hunting and etiquette.

In 1495 Magellan entered the service of John II's successor, King Manuel I (the Fortunate). Manual I found the young Magellan likable, tough, and ambitious and allowed him to go to sea to advance Portuguese trade and dominion in Eastern seas.

On March 25, 1505, Magellan sailed for India under Francisco de Almeida, first viceroy to the East. With twenty-two ships and nearly 2,000 men, it was the largest fleet ever to leave Portugal. At a skirmish at Cannanore, on India's Malabar Coast, Magellan received the first of several serious wounds incurred during his career.

After building a fort at Cannanore, the Portuguese sailed for the east coast of Africa, where they spent eighteen months destroying Arab settlements and replacing them with Portuguese outposts. During much of this time Magellan patrolled the coast. He returned to India's Malabar Coast in 1507, where he fought under Nuno Pereira. In February 1509 he was wounded again at the Battle of Dui, where nineteen Portuguese ships defeated 200 Muslim vessels in the Indian Ocean.

That August, after his recuperation, Magellan joined DIOGO LOPES DE SEQUEIRA on an ill-fated expedition to Malacca, on the Malay Peninsula. When they arrived in September, Magellan and his cousin, Francisco Serrano, got wind of a plot against the Portuguese by a local ruler, but no one believed them. As a result, the Portuguese lost sixty men in a battle during which Magellan fought bravely.

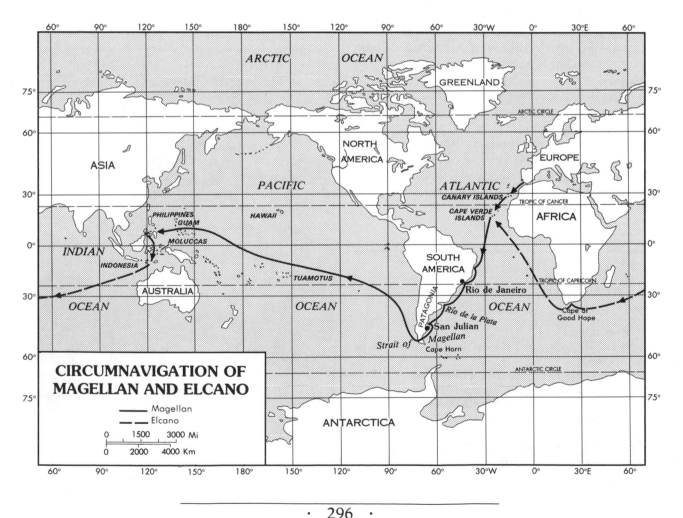

CIRCUMNAVIGATION OF
MAGELLAN AND ELCANO

——— Magellan
– – – Elcano

0   1500   3000 Mi
0   2000   4000 Km

In October the ships were attacked by a pirate junk, a type of Chinese ship, and Serrano was taken captive. Magellan boarded the junk unseen, liberating not only his cousin but the ship's pirate treasure as well. Unfortunately, the treasure was later lost when the junk, which was under tow, had to be cut loose in a storm. In yet another battle, this time at Calicut, India, Magellan was wounded again, and then became shipwrecked briefly off the shoals of Padua in the Arabian Sea.

When he returned to India in October 1510, Magellan's bravery was recognized by the new governor, AFONSO DE ALBUQUERQUE, who made him captain and gave him command of a **caravel**. The following month Albuquerque orchestrated a vicious attack on the Indian port of Goa. Although it is believed that Magellan took part in the attack, Albuquerque's account makes no mention of him, nor is Magellan listed as partaking of the spoils. Historians believe that Magellan had little taste for this wholesale slaughter and pillaging. It was probably about this time that his interests turned to exploration.

In the summer of 1511 Magellan accompanied Albuquerque on a successful voyage to capture Malacca. There Magellan obtained a thirteen-year-old Malay boy, who became known as Black Henry or Malacca Henry. Black Henry would remain with Magellan for the rest of the captain-general's life.

In December 1511 Albuquerque sent ships from Malacca to find the Moluccas, or Spice Islands. Serrano was a part of this voyage and eventually settled there, sending home tales of the endless riches to be had in the islands. Some historians believe Magellan may have taken part in the journey, as well, while others feel he spent the time patrolling Malacca, after falling out of Albuquerque's favor. Eventually it seems that he did undertake a voyage, possibly on his own, sailing as far as Luzon and Mindanao in what are now the Philippines.

Although Magellan was a brave and skilled seaman, he had a stubborn streak that worked to his disadvantage, and he lacked the finesse necessary to navigate the complicated politics of the Portuguese court and its foreign outposts. He returned to Portugal in 1512 only to lose his holdings to an unscrupulous moneylender.

In August 1513 the navigator went to battle once again, this time volunteering for duty at Azamor, Morocco. There, he received a wound that left him lame for life. Placed in charge of the prisoners and booty, he was later accused of stealing the spoils and trading with the Moors of the region. The charges were subsequently dropped, but Magellan never got over the insult. Three years later, he asked King Manuel for more money and a chance to mount an expedition to the Indies. When the king denied both, Magellan asked his leave to go elsewhere. Manuel is said to have replied, "Serve whom you will, clubfoot. It is a matter of indifference to us."

Furious, Magellan retired to Pôrto, a port in northern Portugal that was a haven for discontented seamen. There he met renowned navigator John of Lisbon, who told Magellan there was a pass through the Americas, and DUARTE BARBOSA, an old friend from the India campaigns. Barbosa had relatives in Spain who wanted to outfit an expedition to the Spice Islands and were willing to put Magellan in command.

Magellan left for Spain on October 12, 1517. There he married Barbosa's sister (some historians say cousin) Beatriz, as previously arranged. Eventually they would have two children. He was introduced around Seville and soon met with young king Charles I of Spain, who commissioned the proposed voyage on the spot.

Spain had much to gain by finding new lands for trade. The Moluccas, lying west of New Guinea, were thought to be a potentially valuable source of coconuts, palm oil, hemp, sandalwood, teak, camphor, quinine, dyes, pepper, spices, and other goods. The **Treaty of Tordesillas** (1494) had divided the globe between Spain and Portugal; Magellan hoped to prove that these valuable islands lay in Spain's half of the world. By sailing west, he intended to avoid Africa's Cape of Good Hope, controlled by the Portuguese. It was a bold, experimental proposal that defied the conventional geographic wisdom of the sixteenth century.

Magellan began his voyage with five ships and a crew of about 250 men, many of whom were political appointees and their servants rather than experienced seamen. Some of the crew were Spanish, but most of the officers and pilots were Portuguese, probably handpicked by Magellan. This division created a great deal of tension on board, as did the fact that the expedition's route and destination were kept secret.

The ships—the flagship *Trinidad*, the *San An-*

tonio, the *Concepción*, the *Victoria*, and the *Santiago*—were small and medium-sized merchant vessels. They were provisioned with 213,800 pounds of biscuits, 72,000 pounds of salt beef, and 57,000 pounds of salt pork, plus cheese, beans, chick-peas, onions, raisins, figs, rice, and various other stores. They also carried armament, repair supplies, and a cargo of 20,000 bells, 500 mirrors, knives, fishhooks, brass bracelets, copper, mercury, and cloth for trade. The expedition sailed from Sanlúcar de Barrameda on September 20, 1519.

Trouble started almost immediately. When the ships turned west from the West African coast, a group of rebels led by the Spaniard Juan de Cartagena, captain of the *San Antonio*, tried to provoke Magellan so as to create an act that would justify killing him. Characteristically, the captain-general stood his ground, however, relieving Cartagena of his command and making him a prisoner.

Unfavorable sailing conditions did not help his crew's mood. First they encountered terrible storms, then sat becalmed in the stillness of the **doldrums**. Finally, on December 8, they sighted the coast of Brazil, anchoring five days later at what is now Rio de Janeiro, which Magellan called Porto de Santa Lucia. There they reprovisioned and repaired the ships. Two weeks later, they sailed south along the South American coast.

On January 11, 1520, they reached what looked to be a passage to the west. Magellan sent Juan Serrano, a relative of his old friend and cousin Francisco Serrano, to investigate in the ship *Santiago*. The passage turned out to be a wide river, the present-day Río de la Plata, which empties into the Atlantic near what is now Montevideo, Uruguay. South of the river mouth, they sailed into waters no European had ever explored.

After nearly two months of sailing, Magellan decided to winter in Patagonia, at present-day San Julián, Argentina. The five ships anchored on March 31, and there the crew saw for the first time strange birds that walked upright (penguins), sea wolves (fur seals), and animals resembling camels (guanacos, a type of llama).

On Easter another of Magellan's Spanish captains, Gaspar de Quesada, led a revolt. He freed Cartagena and promised the mutineers they could return to the safety and comfort of Spain. Most of the true sailors on the expedition sided with Magellan, and with their help he put an

end to the mutiny. Quesada was condemned to death and executed, and Cartagena was marooned in Patagonia along with a French priest who had been part of the mutiny. These punishments were meted out with Magellan's usual resolve and demonstrated his belief in the need for discipline on so demanding a voyage.

Shortly after the mutiny, Magellan's party was visited by a very tall native inhabitant, whom Magellan named Juan Gigante (giant) for his size. Over the course of a week or so, several others visited as well. Magellan called them Patagonians, from the Spanish word *pata* (paw), which their feet resembled because they wore guanaco skins as shoes. His men captured two of these giants to take back to Europe, but they died during the voyage.

In May Magellan sent Serrano south to scout the coast. The *Santiago* ran aground near the mouth of the present-day Santa Cruz River, and the crew walked 60 miles back to camp.

Magellan spent five months at San Julián, three of them careening (cleaning and repairing) the ships. During this period, it became apparent that Portuguese merchants, hoping to sabotage the expedition, had cheated them by supplying only half the provisions specified. Magellan estimated that existing stores would last the crew only three months. Still, he said prophetically, "Even if they were to be reduced to eating the leather on the ship's yards, he would fulfill his promise to the Emperor."

In mid-October Magellan sailed south again. On October 21, after a storm, he saw that the coastline turned west. He sent the *San Antonio* to explore a body of water that ran southwest and gave its captain orders to return in three days. He never saw the vessel again (it sailed back to Spain). With his three remaining ships, Magellan then entered the important strait that now bears his name.

The passage was difficult. The ships had to navigate through large waves and around whirlpools, staying away from the cliffs rising alongside the strait. The land to the south appeared to be filled with fire, and Magellan consequently named it Tierra del Fuego (Land of Fire). On November 27, 1520, thirty-seven days after entering the strait, Magellan and all three of his ships reached open sea. (Depending on the season of the year and tidal conditions, subsequent navigators would make it through the treacherous strait in as little as sixteen days or as long as three months—if they did not give up entirely.) At the time of this passage, Magellan said, "We are about to stand into an ocean where no ship has ever sailed before. May the ocean always be as calm and benevolent as it is today. In this hope I name it the Pacific Ocean." The cape at the westernmost end of the strait he called Cape Desire.

And so Magellan entered the ocean he named the Pacific. Using crude navigational instruments, he headed on a west-northwest course; historians disagree about what his exact route was. With food supplies running short, the crew fished for bonita and albacore using hooks covered with rags meant to look like flying fish. By Christmas the vessels had reached 10° South, the latitude of the Spice Islands, but saw no signs of land. The penguin and seal meat they had taken aboard had rotted in the heat, and maggots had consumed what little remained. The crew members were reduced to eating sawdust and oxhide used to tie down the sails and to drinking saltwater mixed with fresh. They began to die of **scurvy**, a severe vitamin deficiency. Driven by hunger, they caught and sold rats among themselves.

The journey to the Moluccas that the captain-general had expected to last four weeks dragged on endlessly. On January 20, 1521, a disgusted Magellan threw his maps into the sea, saying, "With the pardon of the cartographers, the Moluccas are not to be found at their appointed place."

The next day, the crew sighted land, probably in what are now the northern Tuamotus. Magellan named the island San Pablo, in honor of Saint Paul, whose feast day it was. He and his crew spent a week at the otherwise uninhabited spot, catching rainwater in the ships' sails and funneling it into casks to take with them. When he sailed again, Magellan maintained his west-northwest course and sighted another uninhabited island. He referred to these first two islands as Las Desventuradas (the Unfortunate Islands). Sharks seemed to be the only fish found in these waters. The ships sailed on, crossing the equator on February 13.

On March 4 Magellan's flagship, the *Trinidad*, ran out of food. Two days later, Magellan again sighted land, probably present-day Rota in the Marianas. Finally, after four months on the open sea, he landed on what is now Guam. The Europeans called these islands the Ladrones (now the Marianas), Spanish for "thieves," because the native islanders, although friendly, stole everything they possibly could. In return, Magellan went ashore and gathered coconuts, yams, and rice to feed his crew. Although Magellan's enforcement of discipline could verge on cruelty, he could also act with compassion toward his crew. During this time, for example, he took special care of those of his crew who were ill and often visited the sick bay with special gruel to nurse them back to health.

From the Ladrones, Magellan sailed west-southwest, sighting Samar in what he called the Archipelago de San Lazaro (the present-day Philippines) on March 16 and anchoring off Humuno for a week. Two days after the Europeans' arrival, nine islanders from Zuluan arrived with provisions to exchange for trinkets. Although the islanders appeared to be poor and wore little clothing, they possessed bracelets and earrings of gold.

On March 28 Magellan removed the ships to an island called Mazagua. When they anchored, a large canoe came out to greet them. Magellan's servant, Black Henry, called out in Malay and was answered in his own tongue. From there, the Portuguese knew the way home. Magellan, who had sailed in the Indies earlier in his career, had effectively circled the world. Three days later, he and his crew celebrated Easter Mass on shore. Colambu, the raja of Mazagua, joined them.

After trading in the Philippines, Magellan's crew was eager to sail for the Spice Islands, but the captain-general had reasons for staying where he was. He hoped to find gold as well as a familiar landmark verifying that he had, in fact, circumnavigated the globe. Also, King Charles had promised Magellan that if he found a group of six or more islands, he could keep two of them.

Like most of those who sailed for Spain, the devoutly religious Magellan hoped to win converts to Christianity, and Colambu seemed open to the idea. In early April he took Magellan to meet his relative, the raja of the neighboring island of Cebu. At Cebu Magellan acquired provisions for his ships and built a stone chapel on the shore. By April 14 the chapel was complete, and Mass again was celebrated. Both Colambu and the raja of Cebu wanted to be baptized, perhaps because Magellan had told them that the Christian God would help them conquer their enemies.

Magellan also told the other chiefs of the region that they must obey the Christian king.

When one refused, Magellan attacked and burned his village, erecting a cross at the site. Magellan made the same demand of Cilapulapo, chief of Mactan, who refused to obey a stranger. Against the advice of Juan Serrano and the raja of Cebu, Magellan decided to punish Cilapulapo. On April 26, 1521, he sailed to Mactan at midnight with sixty of his crew and a thousand troops from Cebu.

Magellan landed with forty-nine of his men and burned some of the houses on Mactan. Defenders then appeared on both sides of the Europeans, armed with stones, arrows, and lances, and a battle raged all day. Despite the Europeans' crossbows, muskets, and armored headgear, the warriors of Mactan became progressively bolder. Just as Magellan ordered a retreat, an arrow pierced his leg. Acting with characteristic bravery and leadership, he stayed ashore to ensure that his troops reached the safety of their ship. He was then wounded again, this time in his sword arm. When a warrior wounded Magellan's already weakened right leg, the captain-general fell on his face and died. As ANTONIO PIGAFETTA, an Italian nobleman who sailed as a civilian observer and chronicled the expedition, wrote, "And so they slew our mirror, our light, our comfort and our true and only guide." Pigafetta also noted that, "but for him, not one of us in the boats would have been saved, for while he was fighting, the rest retired."

Upon Magellan's death, command of the expedition fell to Juan Serrano and Duarte Barbosa, both of whom were also killed a few days later at Cebu. The remaining voyagers elected João Lopes Carvalho as their leader. Carvalho burned one of the remaining ships, the *Concepción*, along with most of Magellan's records. Four months of piracy followed, as Carvalho raided any ship that passed, but apparently was incapable of finding the Moluccas. At Borneo, command was given to JUAN SEBASTIÁN DE ELCANO, who reached the Moluccas in November 1521 and continued on to Spain aboard the *Victoria* with forty-nine of the original crew and thirteen East Indians. The other remaining ship, the *Trinidad*, stayed in Tidore (in present-day Indonesia) for repairs.

Elcano sailed by way of Africa's Cape of Good Hope, reaching Spain on September 8, 1522, with a mere seventeen other European survivors and four East Indians. Among those survivors was Pigafetta, to whom the world owes its knowledge of Magellan's (and Elcano's) incredible voyage. He had kept a detailed journal throughout the three-year voyage, and upon his return, shared it with the king of Spain. It was published in French in 1523. Of Magellan, Pigafetta wrote,

> So noble a captain . . . he was more constant than any one else in adversity. He endured hunger better than all the others, and better than any man in the world did he understand sea charts and navigation. . . . The best proof of his genius is that he circumnavigated the world, none having preceded him.

The last remaining ship of the expedition, the *Trinidad*, left Tidore in April 1522 under the command of Gonzalo Gómez de Espinosa. He planned to return to Spain by recrossing the Pacific but did not succeed. Eventually Espinosa was forced to return to the Moluccas, where the Portuguese kept him prisoner until 1526.

The impact of Magellan's legacy is immeasurable. Although many historians rank his achievement second only to Columbus, Magellan's accomplishment was possibly even greater. His expedition was larger and lasted longer under more inhospitable conditions. He crossed a wider, more mysterious ocean. His crews were more unruly, and yet he managed them. And by linking Europe with Asia via the Pacific, he opened the door not only to a rich new world of trade possibilities, but—like Columbus—to a whole new world to be explored by the countries of Europe.

SUGGESTED READING: Ian Cameron, *Magellan and the First Circumnavigation of the World* (Saturday Review Press, 1973); F. H. H. Guillemard, *The Life of Ferdinand Magellan* (AMS Press, 1971); Hawthorne Daniel, *Ferdinand Magellan* (Doubleday, 1964); Charles McKew Parr, *Ferdinand Magellan, Circumnavigator*, orig. *So Noble a Captain* (Thomas Y. Crowell Company, 1964); Antonio Pigafetta, *Magellan's Voyage*, trans. by R. A. Skelton (Yale University Press, 1969); Seymour Gates Pond, *Ferdinand Magellan, Master Mariner* (Random House, 1957); Edouard Roditi, *Magellan of the Pacific* (McGraw-Hill, 1972); Katherine Elliott Wilkie, *Ferdinand Magellan: Noble Captain* (Houghton Mifflin, 1963).

Malaspina, Alejandro (Alessandro)

Italian
b November 2, 1754; Mulazzo, Parma
d April 9, 1810; Pontremoli, Parma
Circumnavigated; explored Pacific Ocean and North and South America for Spain

Alejandro Malaspina led one of the most important scientific voyages to leave Spanish shores and one of the first Spanish-sponsored expeditions since the Pacific voyage of PEDRO FERNANDEZ DE QUIRÓS in 1605.

Born in 1754 to a noble Italian family, Malaspina traveled to Cadiz, Spain, as a young man of twenty and entered the Spanish maritime service. He proved his valor during a variety of military confrontations. Already captain of a **frigate**, he was promoted to commander of the much larger vessel *Astrea*, in which he completed a global circumnavigation following a route somewhat similar to that of FERDINAND MAGELLAN. During the course of this voyage, he demonstrated both his navigational abilities and scientific interests.

In 1789 Spain launched an ambitious expedition under Malaspina's direction; the expedition had a twofold purpose. First, he wanted to perform a comprehensive survey of South America, developing hydrographic charts "for the most remote regions of America" and sea charts to facilitate navigation. Second, he wanted to assess the political and economic climate of the far-flung Spanish Empire.

On July 30, 1789, Malaspina sailed from Spain aboard the *Descubierta*, accompanied by the *Atrevida* under the command of José de Bustamante y Guerra. The expedition's first destination was Brazil, where surveyors mapped the coastline in great detail. They also surveyed the Río de la Plata, which empties into the Atlantic between present-day Buenos Aires, Argentina, and Montevideo, Uruguay. The expedition then continued south, exploring and mapping the coastlines of Argentina and Patagonia. Malaspina also visited the Malvinas (or the Falklands) in the South Atlantic and spent time in Tierra del Fuego before rounding Cape Horn into the Pacific.

Malaspina and his scientists then tackled the western shore of South America, sailing north along the Chilean coast to Guayaquil, Peru. Both coasts proved to be rich sources of scientific specimens, and the biologists on board were kept busy collecting samples and illustrating even more. After leaving the expedition, one of the botanists continued on to Bolivia, where he surveyed that inland country's plant life. Malaspina continued sailing north, visiting the Galápagos Islands, Panama, and Acapulco, Mexico. In addition to the biological data that his scientists were collecting, Malaspina gathered political and economic information from the Spanish colonies he visited along the way.

In 1791 Malaspina sailed as far north as southeastern Alaska, perhaps seeking the elusive Northwest Passage to Hudson Bay. The Malaspina Glacier, which flows for 50 miles from Mount St. Elias to the Gulf of Alaska, is named for him, although it was not recognized as a glacier until 1880. Located about 240 miles northwest of present-day Juneau, Malaspina Glacier covers about 1,500 square miles and is more than 1,000 feet thick.

In 1792 Malaspina sailed west across the Pacific to the Philippines. He spent the following year in the southwest Pacific, visiting New South Wales (in present-day Australia), New Zealand, and Tonga.

Some sources say Malaspina recrossed the Pacific in 1794, returning to Spain by way of Cape Horn. Others say his return journey took him west across the Indian Ocean and around Africa's Cape of Good Hope. If the latter was the case, he completed a second circumnavigation.

In any event, Malaspina returned to Spain on September 21, 1794. For his achievements, he was promoted to brigadier in 1795. But his glory would not last long. He brought back from his five-year voyage a conviction that Spain should free her colonies in the New World. Malaspina's liberal ideas were not well received at the Spanish court, and he was arrested, jailed, and stripped of his titles. After six years in jail, he was released on the condition that he not remain in Spain. He retired to his native Italy, where he died at Pontremoli in 1810.

As a result of Malaspina's fall from grace, much of his work was lost. What was not lost was forgotten for at least thirty years. In fact, most of the results of the voyage were kept secret until 1885. Nevertheless, the Malaspina expedition was significant for its scope and, ironically, because it helped consolidate Spanish commercial and political interests in the Pacific.

• Marchand, Jean-Baptiste

French
b November 22, 1863; Thoissey
d January 13, 1934; Paris
Explored Niger River, Sudan, and Ivory Coast

An explorer of the Niger River, the Sudan, and the Ivory Coast, Jean-Baptiste Marchand is best known for commanding France's 1898 attempt to block British expansion in the Sudan. A military officer by profession, he led what was known as the Marchand Mission in a bold effort to prevent the larger and more powerful British forces from controlling the White Nile. The so-called Fashoda Incident that resulted brought the two countries' long-standing territorial rivalry to the brink of war.

Marchand joined the military as a youth and served for four years before being sent for training as an officer. Commissioned a sublieutenant in 1887, he saw active duty in West Africa two years later, against forces of two of the region's native tribes. He was wounded several times and subsequently was made a **chevalier** of the

Jean-Baptiste Marchand. J.B. Culver Pictures.

Legion of Honor. The following year, he began a series of expeditions on the Niger to investigate its sources.

He explored the Western Sudan in 1892, and from 1893 to 1895 he traveled through the inland region of the Ivory Coast. While he was in Gabon, in the French Congo, orders came from the French government in 1896 for the mission in the Sudan.

France's action, prompted by the British occupation of Egypt, was aimed at breaking Britain's colonial stronghold in the Sudan by seizing control of the Nile River in order to reaffirm French claims of ownership. After several months of preparation, Marchand and his men set out from Brazzaville (in what is now the Congo) in January 1897, traveling east across Central Africa to the town of Fashoda (now Kodok) on the White Nile in the Sudan. After an arduous trek across the continent, Marchand and his troops arrived in Fashoda in July 1898, but their occupation of the town was short-lived. Far outnumbered by British forces under the command of H. H. Kitchener, Marchand's troops were forced to depart. The incident nearly escalated into full-scale combat—the closest the two nations ever came to waging war over territories in Africa—before France defused the situation by relinquishing its claims to the Nile.

While Marchand's campaign was unsuccessful, he was hailed as a hero upon his return to Paris. His courage in crossing the continent and facing the British troops earned him a promotion to commander of the Legion of Honor. He later served as a general in World War I and died in Paris in 1934.

• Marcos de Niza (Marcus de Nice)

French
b ?; Nice
d 1558; Mexico
Explored southwestern United States (for Spain)

Father Marcos de Niza was the chaplain during PEDRO DE ALVARADO's conquest of modern Guatemala and on his expedition to Quito, in present-day Ecuador. Then, under Spanish auspices, Marcos led an expedition to explore the territory north of the frontier of New Spain (present-day Mexico), taking him into modern New Mexico and Arizona. From this journey he brought back stories of the seven enchanted cities of Cíbola—stories that inspired a major expedition led by FRANCISCO VÁSQUEZ DE CORONADO to set out to find and conquer the cities.

Virtually nothing is known of Marcos de Niza's early life, not even his birthdate. His place of birth—Nice (Niza, in Spanish), France—is known because it is part of his name. It is not known when he arrived in New Spain as an ordained Franciscan friar, but he served as chaplain during Pedro de Alvarado's march through what are now Guatemala and El Salvador (1523–26). He then accompanied Alvarado on his expedition to Quito in 1533.

Because of such valuable experiences and his knowledge of the Gila River region in Arizona, which he acquired while doing missionary work among the Indians there, Marcos was chosen by the viceroy of New Spain, Antonio de Mendoza, to lead an expedition north of the Spanish territory's frontier. Its objectives were to explore the lands beyond the frontier, verify the reports of ÁLVAR NÚÑEZ CABEZA DE VACA, and assure the Indians—falsely, as things turned out—of Spain's peaceful intentions. Leaving Culiacán in New Galicia (the modern Mexican states of Sinaloa and Nayarit) on March 7, 1539, Marcos was accompanied by the slave Estéban, who had also been with Cabeza de Vaca on his remarkable odyssey.

There has been much controversy over the extent of the friar's journey and concerning exactly what he saw. His journal is full of exaggerations and fantastic accounts of camels, elephants, and unicorn-like animals. Nevertheless, his route has been fairly well plotted; places mentioned in his journal entries correlate to descriptions in other reliable sources. Thus, it is known that the party traveled along the coast of what is now western Mexico to the Yaqui River; then inland, up the Sonora River valley to its headwaters; and over a pass to the San Pedro River, which was then followed downstream into present-day Arizona.

Around this time Marcos heard from local Indians of a great country to the north with seven rich cities that they called Cíbola, and he no doubt imagined another Inca or Aztec empire. He thought these cities could be the seven enchanted cities that, according to legend, were founded by seven Portuguese bishops who had fled an Arab invasion of Iberia in the eighth century. The Indians said the people of these cities wore cotton clothing, had pots and jars made of gold, and even used little blades of gold to wipe the sweat off their bodies.

Determined to find these seven cities of Cíbola, Marcos headed northeast through the desolate area of present-day southeastern Arizona and into what is now New Mexico. Indians came from miles around to receive his blessing, and he became known as Sayota (meaning "man from heaven"). His expectations of finding a rich empire were heightened when he received gifts of turquoise and finely worked leather from Indians along the way, who also confirmed the stories of cities with four- and five-story buildings.

He sent Estéban ahead to scout, instructing him to send back white crosses that would vary from small to large depending upon the significance of what he found. After several trips, Estéban sent back a cross as tall as a man, and news that Cíbola was close. Excited, Marcos pushed onward, even after he heard of Estéban's death at the hands of the Zuñi Indians.

In late May 1539 Marcos climbed a mountain knoll and looked down on what he thought was Cíbola, writing in his journal: "[T]he houses are . . . all of stone, with their stories and flat roofs. As far as I could see from a height where I placed myself to observe, the settlement is larger than the city of Mexico." In all likelihood, he had seen the Hawikuh pueblo, one of a six-city confederacy of the Zuñi Indian nation. Fearful of entering the city given the fate of Estéban, he instead returned to Mexico City, arriving in late August 1539 with his fantastic account of Cíbola.

Whether he purposely exaggerated or his imagination, spurred by visions of Inca and Aztec riches, led him to see what he wanted to see, no one really knows. But as a result of his "discovery" a major expedition under Coronado was mounted in 1540 to conquer the reported cities, with Marcos serving as its guide. However, Coronado found something quite different when he reached his destination—a mere "collection of huts." Marcos was sent back to Mexico City in disgrace, where he was branded the "Lying Monk" by his contemporaries. An invalid for the last fifteen years of his life, he died in New Spain in 1558.

Though he did not discover Cíbola (there was no Cíbola to discover, in fact), Father Marcos explored areas of what are now eastern Arizona and western New Mexico previously unknown to the Spanish and, through the tales he told, provided the impetus for the remarkable journey of Coronado.

• Marquette, Jacques

French
b June 10, 1637; Laon
d May 18, 1675; territory of Illinois Indians
Explored Mississippi River

After arriving in North America in 1666, the Jesuit missionary Father Jacques Marquette traveled throughout the western Great Lakes area before being invited to accompany LOUIS JOLLIET on a voyage of discovery down the Mississippi River. When Jolliet's papers describing the expedition were lost in a canoe accident, Marquette's journal became the only surviving first-person narration of the historic journey. (For a map of their route, see JOLLIET.)

Jacques Marquette's longings to explore faraway lands came upon him early in life. In 1665, when he had been studying to become a Jesuit priest for eleven years, he wrote a letter to his spiritual superior urging "that your Paternity

Father Jacques Marquette. The Bettmann Archive.

order me to set out for foreign nations of which I have been thinking from my earliest boyhood." A year later, Marquette was granted his wish, and on September 20, 1666, he arrived in Québec.

After a year spent studying Montagnais and other Indian languages (he was eventually fluent in six), Father Marquette joined his Jesuit superior, Father Dablon, at the Ottawa mission near Sault Ste. Marie (in between Lake Superior and Lake Huron). A year later, he founded a new mission at Chequamegon Bay near the western end of Lake Superior. (It was here that Marquette first made contact with the peaceable and courteous Illinois Indians, with whom he was to spend his last days.) When the Huron Indians fled his mission after a quarrel with the more numerous Sioux, Father Marquette followed the Hurons east and set up a new mission on the north shore of the Straits of Mackinac (between Lake Michigan and Lake Huron).

To this mission on December 8, 1672, came Louis Jolliet, on the first stage of his exploration of the Mississippi River. He had been charged with determining whether the river flowed into the Gulf of Mexico or into the Pacific Ocean. At the behest of the Jesuits, Father Marquette was to go along as a chaplain and Christian emissary to the Indians.

During the winter, Marquette and Jolliet gathered information from the Indians about the proposed route. Not all of this information was encouraging—or reliable. The Green Bay Indians, for example, tried to discourage Marquette with talk of natives "who never show mercy to strangers, smashing their heads without any cause," of "horrible monsters, which devoured men and canoes together," and of heat "so excessive that it would inevitably cause . . . death." According to his journal, Marquette "thanked them for their good advice, but told them I could not follow it, because the salvation of souls was at stake and for this I would be willing to give my life."

Marquette, Jolliet, and five other men left the mission of St. Ignace on the shores of the Straits of Mackinac in May 1673. They paddled their birch-bark canoes to the tip of Green Bay (on the west shore of Lake Michigan), continued up the Fox River, made a short **portage** to the Wisconsin River, and entered the Mississippi on June 17, 1673. In his journal, Marquette records the many new forms of wildlife that impressed them: "monstrous fish [probably catfish], one of which struck our canoe so violently that I thought it was a great tree which was going to break our canoe into pieces," a monster swimming in the water with "the head of a tiger that was gray with a neck quite black [probably a lynx]," and wild cattle [bison] so large that when one of the party killed one "it took three men to move it, and they had difficulty."

The first Indians they encountered were the Illinois, and the explorers were relieved to be greeted in peace and friendship. An elder of the tribe, stark naked and standing with his hands lifted toward the sun, greeted them with the words, "How beautiful the sun is, O Frenchmen, when you come to visit us." The Illinois also outfitted the party with a calumet (peace pipe), which they used for the remainder of the journey when meeting other tribes for the first time. Marquette was so moved by the courtesy of the people of this village that he promised to return the next year to live with them and teach them.

As Marquette and Jolliet progressed down the river, it became obvious that it flowed south rather than west. Then one June day, while paddling through calm waters, they heard the tumultuous noise of great rapids ahead. They had reached the mouth of the Missouri and "floating islands of debris" were pouring from it into the Mississippi. The explorers immediately realized that this was probably the route west. Marquette reported, "One day I hope to discover the California Sea by following its course."

Despite their conviction that the Mississippi flowed south and the Missouri was probably the way to the west, Marquette and Jolliet continued on their predetermined route. Passing the mouth of the Ohio River, they eventually reached a point just north of the present-day Arkansas River; they had already paddled their canoes more than 2,500 miles in just four months. At this location the Indians told them that they were about ten days from the sea but that it was dangerous to proceed because further on they would find warlike tribes who possessed guns. Feeling that they had the answer to their question—that the Mississippi entered into the Gulf of Mexico—and unwilling to risk capture by the Spanish (the likely source of the mentioned guns) or by hostile Indians, the party turned north on July 17, 1673.

Paddling upstream against the strong current of the Mississippi made for a difficult jour-

ney. At the mouth of the Ohio, Marquette gave a letter written in Latin to a group of Indians who said they traded with Europeans. He may have been hoping to establish contact with the Jesuits and Franciscans who labored in Maryland. The letter eventually was passed from a Virginia trader to William Byrd of Virginia, to William Penn, and finally to Robert Harley in England. Two hundred and twenty years later it was discovered among the papers Harley had left behind.

Taking the advice of the Indians, Marquette and Jolliet followed an easier route back, going up the Illinois River, across a brief portage to the Chicago River, and thus to the tip of Lake Michigan. Marquette went to recuperate at Green Bay, and Jolliet, after doing some further exploring, joined him there for the winter.

In October 1674 Marquette set out to keep a previous promise to return to a Kaskaskia Indian village, but ill health required him to spend the winter at a spot that is now one of Chicago's suburbs. Continuing his journey in the spring, he reached the Kaskaskia village on the Illinois River during Holy Week and preached to a circle of 500 chiefs with 1,500 braves standing behind them. Realizing that he was dying, Marquette left to return north to the mission of St. Ignace, but his body, made frail by dysentery (an acute intestinal disorder), could no longer withstand the rigors of travel. He died at the mouth of a river that now bears his name.

Controversy and confusion surround the written record of Marquette and Jolliet's voyage down the Mississippi. Since Jolliet's papers were lost in a canoe accident, the only remaining narration is Marquette's journal. Some historians have claimed that Marquette was not its author and that the journal was written by Father Dablon from the recollections of Jolliet and the notes of Marquette. The controversy remains unresolved.

Whether or not he was the author of the journal attributed to him, Father Jacques Marquette was a dedicated missionary with an adventurous soul. These characteristics combine to explain his enthusiasm for his journey of exploration and discovery down the Mississippi. The journal of his journey manifests both elements of his nature.

Martínez, Estéban José

Spanish
b December 9, 1742; Seville
d October 28, 1798; Loreto, Baja California
Explored northwest coast of North America

In 1788, Spanish naval officer Estéban José Martínez commanded an expedition to the northwest coast of North America that took him as far north as present-day Unalaska Island in the eastern Aleutian Islands. There, Martínez acquired valuable information about a proposed Russian settlement of Nootka Sound, which precipitated the Spanish settlement of Nootka in 1789.

Having entered the Spanish naval academy at the age of thirteen, Martínez went to sea at sixteen and was eventually assigned to the naval command at San Blas, New Spain (present-day Mexico). In 1774, he served as second-in-command to JUAN JOSEF PÉREZ HERNÁNDEZ as part of the first Spanish expedition to the northwest coast of North America, which was initiated in response to rumors of Russian advances in the area.

From 1776 to 1788, Martínez commanded supply ships on routine voyages between San Blas and new Spanish settlements in California. In 1788, Spain once again became alarmed by rumors that Russia was expanding its holdings in the Aleutians. Martínez was put in charge of a two-ship expedition with orders to sail at least as far as 61° North latitude, to thoroughly investigate Russian settlements in the region, and to take formal possession of land for Spain wherever he could do so conveniently.

The two ships sailed on March 8, 1788, and by mid-May were near the entrance to Prince William Sound (in present-day Alaska). There Martínez began to exhibit erratic behavior, quarreling violently with some of his subordinates. (His men later attributed his actions to drunkenness.) After several days of indecisiveness, he proceeded to Unalaska Island in the eastern Aleutians, where he was cordially received on July 21 by the lone Russian at the outpost.

From the Russian at Unalaska, Martínez learned that Russia planned to settle Nootka Sound (on the west coast of present-day Vancouver Island) the next year in order to counter British fur-trading activity in the area. Before leaving Unalaska, he conducted a brief and surreptitious ceremony of possession, although he was aware that the Russians had preceded the Spanish there.

Upon his return to San Blas, he reported the information about the Russian plans and volunteered to lead an expedition to settle Nootka immediately. His offer was accepted, to the eventual detriment of Spanish interests in Nootka. Martínez's high-handed treatment of British ships and subjects in Nootka caused Britain to protest to Spain. The result was the Nootka Convention of 1790, which opened to all nations any territory that was not settled by Spain as of that year. Thus, Martínez's combative nature worked against the establishment of the Spanish supremacy in the Northwest that he sought.

Though numerous complaints were filed against Estéban José Martínez for his violent and overbearing treatment both of men under his command and of foreign nationals, his actions and explorations were predicated upon his desire to serve his country well; unfortunately his good intentions were undermined by his contempt for others and his unruly temper.

Martínez de Irala, Domingo. See **Irala, Domingo Martínez de.**

Maury, Matthew Fontaine

American
b January 14, 1806; Spotsylvania County, Virginia
d February 1, 1873; Lexington, Virginia
Collected, compiled, and published scientific data concerning world's oceans

All ocean charts issued by the U.S. Oceanographic Office today bear this imprint: "Founded upon the researches made in the early part of the nineteenth century by Matthew Fontaine Maury, while serving as a lieutenant in the U.S. Navy." That credit, while impressive testimony to Maury's impact on sea travel, does not do justice to the breadth of his influence. In addition to collecting data for wind and current charts of the world's oceans, Maury led the move to establish meteorology as a universal science, produced a profile of the Atlantic Ocean floor, wrote the first modern oceanographic textbook, and recommended the first set of traffic rules for the sea.

Matthew Fontaine Maury. Cook Collection/Valentine Museum, Richmond.

Nineteen-year-old Matthew Maury joined the American navy in 1825. By 1830, he had sailed around the world, and six years later he was promoted to lieutenant. An unfortunate stage-coach accident in 1839 left Maury lame and unable to continue active sea duty, but within three years he was put in charge of the navy's Depot of Charts and Instruments, the precursor of the U.S. Naval Observatory and Hydrographic Office. Maury developed special log-books to give to sea captains, who recorded data on ocean currents, depths, tides, winds, and temperatures for Maury's intensive study of the world's oceans. He studied and compiled this vast quantity of data and, in 1847, began publication of his revolutionary wind and current charts. Maury's findings resulted directly in the establishment of new, more efficient sea routes. As an example, the average passage from New York to San Francisco via Cape Horn dropped from 180 days to 153 days.

After a conference of the world's maritime nations in 1853—which Maury helped organize and which gave rise to the International Hydrographic Bureau—Maury's collection of oceanic data expanded to include reports from the majority of the sea captains of the world's maritime nations. Using this information, he was able to produce accurate charts of the Atlantic, Pa-

cific, and Indian oceans. Deep-sea soundings carried out under Maury's direction produced the first profile of the floor of the Atlantic Ocean, establishing the feasibility of laying a transoceanic telegraph cable.

Published in 1855, Maury's comprehensive study of the ocean, *Physical Geography of the Sea*, is regarded as the first textbook of modern oceanography. In the same year, his *Sailing Directions* described new sea routes that his studies had shown would be shorter and safer than established routes. He was also responsible for recommending that eastbound and westbound ships travel in separate lanes in order to avoid collisions. Maury's major oceanographic contributions, acclaimed throughout the world, largely ceased in 1861 with his decision to support the Confederacy in the Civil War. He died in Virginia in 1873.

Mawson, Douglas

Australian
b May 5, 1882; Bradford, Yorkshire, England
d October 14, 1958; Adelaide
Explored Antarctica

With a few notable exceptions, polar exploration until recently has been the work of adventurers with little or no interest in science. Sir Douglas Mawson was one of the most remarkable of the exceptions. A professor of geology and mineralogy, Mawson not only carried out the most systematic examination of Antarctica during the early twentieth century, but also—and unintentionally—pleased the public with his daring exploits and narrow escapes in the land of blizzards. Never doubting that his main mission was scientific, he turned down a chance to accompany ROBERT FALCON SCOTT to the pole (a lucky choice, as events proved) and instead organized and led the Australian Antarctic Expedition of 1911–14. Though the data collected on this and his other major expedition to Antarctica in 1929 were voluminous and his discoveries of new territory immense, the majority of Mawson's 123 books and articles concerns the geology of Australia.

Mawson moved with his family from England to Sydney, Australia, when he was only four. He attended the University of Sydney, where he specialized in chemistry, mining, and chemical geology. In 1903 he joined the first

Douglas Mawson. UPI/Bettmann.

geological survey of New Hebrides (present-day Vanuatu) and in 1905, after finishing his bachelor of science degree, was appointed lecturer in mineralogy and petrology (the study of rocks) at the University of Adelaide. There he received his doctorate in 1909 and was finally appointed professor of geology and mineralogy in 1920. But there were some serious interruptions along the way.

At Adelaide he began working with the geologist T. W. Edgeworth David, who was soon appointed scientific director of Sir ERNEST SHACKLETON's Antarctic Expedition of 1907–1909. On David's recommendation, Mawson was appointed its physicist. While Shackleton was occupied with his dash to the pole, Mawson, David, and Dr. Alistair Forbes MacKay in 1908 ascended Mount Erebus, an active volcano on James Ross Island. Later that year they **sledged** 1,300 miles on a round-trip to the South Magnetic Pole, arriving on January 16, 1909. During this expedition, they were the first to see, let alone study, the complex geological structure of Victoria Land.

With David's encouragement and the financial support of the Australian Association for the Advancement of Science, Mawson next organized the first careful scientific survey of Antarctica from Oates Coast to Queen Mary Coast. Using three land bases linked with a ship by radio (another Antarctic first), the maximum possible amount of ground was covered. Leaving Australia on December 2, 1911, the *Aurora* landed the first party on Macquarie Island, while Mawson continued on to discover the flat, windswept George V Coast, where winter camp was set up. From there, five parties spread out to examine and map the region, extending as far west as JULES DUMONT D'URVILLE's Adélie Coast, while the *Aurora* sailed west to drop the third landing party (under the command of Frank Wild) on unknown shores.

Mawson's party, with dogs pulling the sledges, headed east toward Oates Land across the deeply crevassed and glaciated surface. Whether it was because of lack of experience or the ferocious conditions, Lieutenant B. E. S. Ninnis lost control of his dogs and plunged into a seemingly bottomless crevasse. Gone with him was the bulk of the party's food, leaving Mawson, Dr. Xavier Mertz, and the rest of the dogs to struggle back to George V Coast on nearly nothing. As the dogs starved to death, their scrawny carcasses were eaten, but soon that meager source was consumed. Mertz died in his sleep soon after. Somehow Mawson continued on for another thirty-one days, hauling his sledge with its small store of food until he reached base. There he discovered that he had just missed the *Aurora*, which had left to relieve the party on the third land base 1,200 miles to the west.

Dazed and raw from exposure, Mawson then had to last another winter with the party the *Aurora* had left behind. When he recovered, he was ready to continue the survey. In all, close to 2,000 miles of coast was explored by ship and 4,000 miles of the interior by sledge by the time the *Aurora* returned to Australia.

After World War I, Mawson was recruited by the British to run a mission to Antarctica, mainly for the purpose of claiming rights to the land from the Ross Sea to Enderby Land. Flying on a de Havilland Gypsy Moth seaplane from the *Discovery* (Scott's former ship) from 1929 to 1931, Mawson covered much new territory and laid claim to Mac Robertson Land and Princess Elizabeth Land, segments of Australian Antarctic Territory. This was the basis for the large claim by Britain that it handed over to Australia in 1936. Though territorial expansion was his major purpose, Mawson as usual collected a great deal of scientific data, which he spent the rest of his life editing.

• McClintock (M'Clintock), Francis Leopold

Anglo-Irish
b July 8, 1819; Dundalk, County Louth, Ireland
d November 17, 1907; London, England
Explored Canadian Arctic

Though he charted hundreds of miles of Arctic territory in his eleven-year career as an explorer, Admiral Sir Francis Leopold McClintock was not motivated by the usual desires of explorers. He did not expect to gain riches, to open up new territories for exploitation or trade, or to solve any great geographical riddles; and in fact he did none of these things. His only goal, following orders from the British Admiralty, was to find the lost expedition led by Sir JOHN FRANKLIN—first, with the hope of saving lives; then, as the years passed, simply of learning what had happened to Franklin. There were many men engaged in the same pursuit in the decade after Franklin disappeared, but McClintock was the dominant figure and the leader of the party that first stumbled across the corpses of the lost explorers.

Sir Francis Leopold McClintock. National Portrait Gallery, London.

Though his first commanding officer in the Arctic, JAMES CLARK ROSS, pioneered the British navy's use of man-hauled **sledges** to travel over Arctic ice, McClintock perfected the technique (which involved setting up supply depots) and is often considered its originator. On his four voyages over ice (in 1849, 1851, 1853, and 1859), he personally covered over 3,000 miles, while as general coordinator of sledging operations he was responsible for the charting of enormous lengths of coastline. He also became adept at dog sledding, but a combination of navy philosophy and the difficulty of obtaining well-trained dogs on short notice prevented him from taking advantage of this superior method of travel.

McClintock entered the navy at the age of twelve, serving in a variety of warm-water posts until he joined Ross in 1848 aboard the *Enterprise*. In the spring of 1849, he and Ross sledged along the coast of Somerset Island (in the present-day Northwest Territories of Canada) in search of Franklin. While serving on the *Assistance* in 1851, McClintock sledged from Cornwallis Island to Melville Island. Then on an expedition under Captain Edward Belcher in 1852, McClintock commanded the steam tender (support ship) *Intrepid*. In the spring of 1853 he set a record for distance traveled by sledge when he journeyed from the southern portion of Melville Island to Prince Patrick Island (which he discovered) and beyond—more than 1,200 miles all told.

By the time McClintock returned in 1854, the British navy had given up the search for the Franklin party. But Franklin's widow, Lady Jane Franklin, insisted that no one had as yet looked in the one place Franklin would most likely be—off the coast of King William Land (now Island). (The Hudson's Bay Company agent JOHN RAE had heard from the **Inuit** that a party of white men had been seen in the area, thus confirming Lady Franklin's long-held suspicion.) McClintock was the obvious person to command the mission, which he undertook without pay since Lady Franklin was financing the bulk of the project.

After fitting out the steam-powered *Fox* for ice navigation, McClintock first went to Greenland in the summer of 1857 to obtain sled dogs and Inuit drivers. On the way to Lancaster Sound, the *Fox* became caught in the pack ice and could not escape until the next April, after drifting some 1,194 miles with the ice. Narrowly missing destruction upon its release from the pack, the ship then made its way through Barrow Strait, down Peel Sound, all the way to the entrance to Bellot Strait, where it settled in for the winter of 1858–59.

This location was an ideal position from which to conduct searches by sledge. McClintock spent the winter setting up depots for three search expeditions that would radiate outward. He also met some Inuit who had a number of European artifacts, obviously gleaned from a shipwreck.

In the spring each party went out with one man-hauled sledge and one sled pulled by dogs. Allen Young led a party around the southern coast of Prince of Wales Island, while McClintock took the southernmost route to the mouth of the Great Fish River (now the Back River). McClintock generously gave the most promising route around the north and west coast of King William Land to William Hobson. Hobson consequently became the first to find the only surviving written record of the Franklin expedition, in a cairn (stone pile) on Victory Point. He then saw a sledge loaded with a mountain of heavy, unnecessary items and cradling two skeletons. McClintock himself came across the same eerie scene a few days later, having already found another skeleton, stretched out face down on the south shore of King William Land.

McClintock had at long last eased the dread and anxiety of Franklin's widow. He had also completed the coastal survey of Boothia Peninsula begun by John Rae, thus fitting in the last piece of the North American coastal puzzle. After returning to London on September 23, 1859, he was knighted and given all the honors customarily due an Arctic hero. He continued to serve in the navy, returning to the Arctic in 1860 to conduct soundings for the first North Atlantic telegraph line. He achieved the rank of admiral in 1884 and died in London in 1907 at the age of eighty-eight.

McClure, Robert John Le Mesurier

Anglo-Irish
b January 28, 1807; Wexford, Ireland
d October 17, 1873; London, England
Explored Alaskan and Canadian Arctic; became first European to negotiate Northwest Passage from Pacific to Atlantic

One of several commanders sent by the British navy in 1850 to relieve Sir JOHN FRANKLIN's missing expedition, Vice Admiral Sir Robert John Le Mesurier McClure is judged by some historians to have been the first European to negotiate the Northwest Passage. He did it by sailing east from the Bering Strait, which separates Alaska and Siberia. As he had expected, this won him the applause of the British public, as well as a large cash prize voted by Parliament. However, since he abandoned his ship, the *Investigator*, on the north coast of Banks Island in Mercy Bay and then traveled with a rescue party by **sledge** to a vessel waiting in Melville Sound to the east, he did not actually traverse the Northwest Passage by ship. (For a more complete discussion of the passage, see MARTIN FROBISHER.) Still, his party did survive three winters in the Arctic (twenty-one months without outside human contact) and their sledging expeditions did establish the contours of the westernmost island in the Arctic **archipelago**, thus linking east and west in a continuous, if partially frozen, waterway.

Though McClure was an impetuous, sometimes brutal, person, he had the finest schooling England offered, having left the family estates in Ireland to attend Eton and Sandhurst (Great Britain's military academy). After a slow start in the navy, he was appointed mate aboard Captain GEORGE BACK's expedition to Hudson Bay (1836–37). He later held a succession of minor posts on ships from Canada to the West Indies. He returned to the Arctic aboard the *Investigator* in 1848 as part of Sir JAMES CLARK ROSS's mission to rescue the Franklin party.

On January 20, 1850, McClure left Plymouth as commander of the *Investigator*, rounded Cape Horn, then beat his commanding officer (Richard Collinson, on the *Enterprise*) to the Bering Strait by cutting through the Aleutians. This allowed him to make it all the way up the Prince of Wales Strait between Banks and Victoria islands (thereby discovering the Northwest Passage) before the ice from Melville Sound pushed him back that fall. The next summer he tried going up the west coast of Banks Island to reach WILLIAM EDWARD PARRY's westernmost point, but this time his ship became imprisoned in the ice for two winters. On April 6, 1853, a rescue party from Sir Edward Belcher's *Resolute* found the starving party, just as McClure had decided that its weakest members should attempt an overland escape, fearing they could not survive another winter on the ship. McClure's crew had to spend one more winter aboard the rescue vessel *Resolute* and arrived in England to a hero's welcome on September 28, 1854. After being knighted, McClure continued serving in the Pacific until his retirement in 1861.

McKenzie, Donald

Scottish
b June 16, 1783; near Inverness
d January 20, 1851; Mayville, New York
Explored Snake River region of American West

Like so many of the explorers of the American West, Donald McKenzie was a fur trader. Sent out by Montréal's North West Company to revive declining trade in the area east of the Columbia River, he made three important explorations of the Snake River region in the years between 1818 and 1821.

After ten years in the fur trade, McKenzie joined John Jacob Astor's Pacific Fur Company in 1811 and participated in a long and nearly disastrous overland journey west from St. Louis to the mouth of the Columbia River. Along the way, he recognized the potential of the Snake River as fur-trapping country, although the rest of the party disagreed with him. When Astor sold out to the North West Company, McKenzie revived his ideas about the Snake River region, and by 1816 he had been put in charge of reviving the fur trade east of the Columbia River.

McKenzie saw at once that the old system of setting up trading posts and waiting for the local Indians to bring in their pelts would not work in this region because the Indians here were not accustomed to trapping beaver and would rather spend their time otherwise. Instead, he developed a system of sending brigades of free-lance Canadian and American trappers into the field and supporting them with

provisions from the post—the first known use of this technique, which was to become standard in the Rocky Mountain fur trade.

After building Fort Nez Perce near the juncture of the Columbia and Snake rivers (in what is now southern Washington State), McKenzie began his explorations. Moving up the Snake River, he eventually turned south and east, reaching the area between the Snake and Green rivers, a region rich in beaver—and hostile Indians.

On his second expedition, he wanted to find out whether supplies could be brought to his men in the field via the Snake River. On his trip up the Snake, he became the first non-Indian ever to traverse Hells Canyon (on the modern Oregon-Idaho border). In the summer and fall of 1819, McKenzie sent trappers throughout the country between the Snake and Green rivers, as far south as Bear Lake in what is now eastern Utah.

Before leaving the area in 1821, McKenzie made one more trek into the Snake River country, but because of his reluctance to spend his time in the field keeping a journal, little is known of this trip. Throughout his years in the fur trade, Donald McKenzie developed a reputation as a fearless explorer and a bold trader who made invaluable contributions to the exploration of the Snake River region.

M'Clintock, Francis. See **McClintock, Francis.**

Mendaña de Nehra, Alvaro de

Spanish
b 1541
d 1595; Santa Cruz Islands
Discovered Solomon Islands, Marquesas, and
  Santa Cruz Islands

Alvaro de Mendaña de Nehra made two ambitious trans-Pacific voyages (1567–69 and 1595). Although he did not find the lands of gold and silver that he sought, nor the great unknown Southern Continent, he was the first European to discover islands in the present-day Solomon, Marquesas, and Santa Cruz groups. He was also the last European to see the Solomons for nearly two centuries.

Mendaña was twenty-six when his uncle, the viceroy of Peru, chose him to lead an expedition into the South Seas. From the **cosmographer** and historian Pedro Sarmiento de Gamboa, the viceroy had heard the Incan legend of Tupac Yupanqui, who was said to have crossed the sea and found islands rich with silver and gold off the coast of a large continent. Mendaña intended to seek out those legendary islands and to find this continent, which could only be *Terra Australis Incognita*, the great unknown Southern Continent that geographers had long believed to dominate the South Seas. (For a more complete discussion, see ALEXANDER DALRYMPLE.) He meant to establish a Spanish settlement there and to convert any infidels, or nonbelievers, to Catholicism.

Mendaña left Callao, the Spanish port near Lima, Peru, on November 19, 1567, with two ships—the *Capitana*, *Los Reyes* and the *Almiranta*, *Todos Santos*—and a crew of 150, including soldiers, Franciscan friars, and slaves. They carried enough provisions for about one-third of a journey that would take them 7,000 miles. Mendaña set sail on a west-southwest course that took him between what are now the Tuamotus and the Marquesas. Missing both groups, he changed his course slightly to the northwest; he did not see land until January 15, 1568, when he sighted what was probably Nui in the Ellice Islands (now Tuvalu), north of Fiji. There the Spaniards tried to land to replenish their tainted water supplies, but treacherous currents and hostile islanders in canoes drove them off.

In February, after nearly running aground on a line of reefs that probably were part of Ontong Java, the voyagers landed at a place Mendaña called Santa Isabel after the saint on whose feast day they had sailed. They had been at sea for eighty days. At first, they believed they had found a continent, but further exploration revealed that Santa Isabel was an island— one of the group that came to be known as the Solomons.

The Spaniards' first encounter with the Melanesian islanders was friendly. The islanders accepted Mendaña's gifts of beads and bells and helped themselves to much more, and their chief, Bilebanara, promised the Spaniards food. When the food did not arrive after a few days, however, Mendaña sent a party in search of supplies. The Spanish were instructed to try to trade rather than use force, but they encountered some hostility from inland villages, and a skirmish followed. Similar scenes were re-

played several times over the next six months, and relations with the islanders ranged from peaceful to belligerent.

In their first month on Santa Isabel, Mendaña's men built a small **brigantine** that could navigate the island's complex reefs safely. Using it, they first explored Santa Isabel, then what are now Guadalcanal, Malaita, and San Cristóbal. In August Mendaña called his crew together to vote on their next course of action. He wanted to search for the great continent that he believed was close at hand. A few men wanted to stay in the Solomons and look for gold. The majority, considering the short supply of food, wanted to sail for home.

The third group prevailed, and on August 15, 1568, Mendaña began the return journey across the Pacific. Taking advantage of the prevailing winds, the ships' pilots took a northeast course, which brought them within sight of isolated Wake Island in October. Soon after, a hurricane struck, and the two ships were separated. Exhausted and stricken by **scurvy**, Mendaña's crew reached Baja California in December. They met their consort some months later. After being repaired, the reunited vessels sailed southward, reaching Peru in July 1569.

Mendaña subsequently spent several years in Spain trying to convince the court to back a second expedition. Eventually they agreed, and in 1576 Mendaña set sail from Spain, only to be jailed in Panama by enemies of his uncle, the viceroy. Years later, when the Spanish had become unsettled by the exploits in the Pacific of the English **privateer** Sir FRANCIS DRAKE, Mendaña got another chance. In June 1595 he set sail for the Solomons with four ships and nearly 400 soldiers, sailors, women, and children with the intention of creating a new Spanish colony.

In late July the expedition reached islands that Mendaña called the Marquesas, where the islanders tried to take the Spanish ships for their own. In the fight that ensued, the soldiers killed 200 of the islanders. In September Mendaña reached what are now the Santa Cruz Islands (so named by Mendaña) and anchored at Ndeni. Dissension among the members of the expedition, which had been evident from the day the ships left Callao, by then made it virtually impossible to organize a permanent settlement. Fever was also rampant, and Mendaña died on Ndeni without seeing the Solomons again. (In fact, no European would see them again until PHILIP CARTERET rediscovered the islands in 1767, and they were not identified as Mendaña's islands until 1792.) The Spanish settlement on Ndeni subsequently failed, and the would-be settlers, including Mendaña's widow, sailed on to the present-day Philippines under the command of their chief pilot, PEDRO FERNANDEZ DE QUIRÓS.

· Nachtigal, Gustav

German
b February 23, 1834; Eichstedt
d April 19, 1885; Gulf of Guinea
Explored North Africa

Best known for his desert expeditions, Dr. Gustav Nachtigal undertook several journeys into the heart of Africa late in the nineteenth century to study unexplored regions of the Sahara and the Sudan. During his twenty-two-year stay on the continent, he volunteered his medical skills to combat a severe plague and completed a rigorous diplomatic mission that ultimately earned him access to areas traditionally forbid-

Gustav Nachtigal. New York Public Library.

den to outsiders. One of Germany's greatest geographers, he laid a solid foundation for further exploration and eventual colonization of Africa by Germany.

The son of a Prussian clergyman, Nachtigal might never have left Cologne, where he enjoyed his post as a military surgeon, if he had not become seriously ill at the age of twenty-eight. The victim of a lung ailment, he knew that his best chance for recovery lay in the therapeutic, arid climate of North Africa. He knew little about the continent when he arrived in Algeria in 1862, but after a brief recuperation he got acquainted with the territory on an expedition with the Tunisian army. This year-long journey through the desert, treating soldiers who were wounded in combat against bands of hostile nomads, gave Nachtigal a new sense of purpose. Enthralled with both the mystique of Africa and the excitement of exploration, he began to read avidly on both subjects and set about mastering the Arabic language.

When the 1864 campaign ended, he felt restless. The trip had given him his first taste of adventure, and the intensive study had unleashed his imagination. He became unwilling to resume the relatively tame medical work he had done previously in Tunis. By 1868, however, he found himself desperately needed in Tunis to fight a raging epidemic of typhus, a task he undertook without any financial compensation. That same year, fate delivered him another chance to be of service—an offer that promised both the travel and the excitement he craved.

The opportunity came from explorer FRIEDRICH GERHARD ROHLFS, who had been chosen by the German Colonial Office for a diplomatic mission in the Sudan and, for his own reasons, desperately wanted to avoid the assignment. Nachtigal agreed to go in Rohlfs's place to Bornu (in present-day Nigeria) to visit its Sultan Omar as the ambassador of King William I of Prussia. Laden with gifts that included life-size statues of the royal family, a large throne, and an arsenal of weapons, Nachtigal started out from the North African coast for Bornu, which lay nearly 2,000 miles away to the south.

Traveling east over the Tarhuna mountains, Nachtigal then proceeded south across the central Sahara and, after reaching Murzuch (now in southwest Libya), decided to make a side journey to Tibesti. Inhabited by the hostile Tibbu, this mountainous area southeast of Murzuch (which today lies near the border of Chad

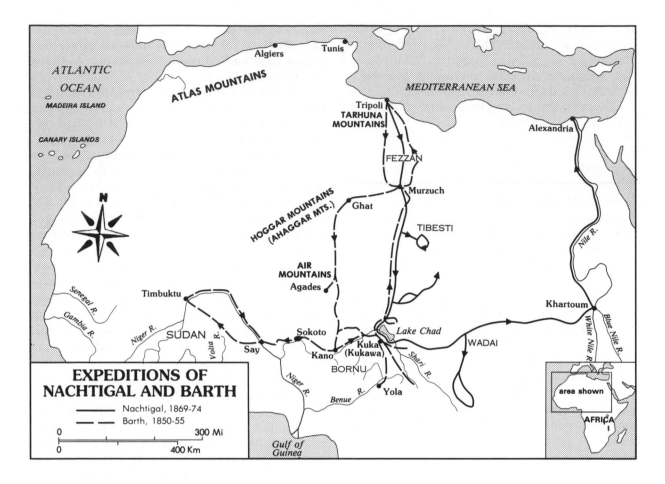

EXPEDITIONS OF
NACHTIGAL AND BARTH

—————— Nachtigal, 1869-74
- - - - - Barth, 1850-55

0   300 Mi
0   400 Km

and Libya) had never been visited by a European. Nachtigal, braving temperatures that exceeded 100 degrees Fahrenheit despite the altitude, reached the region's main town only to find the natives near starvation and begging for food. His generosity did not diminish their hatred of outsiders, however; the Tibbu jailed Nachtigal once his provisions were nearly gone. He managed to escape and flee across 500 miles of desert back to Murzuch. From there he made his way south to Kuka, capital of Bornu, for his audience with the sultan.

Nachtigal's diplomatic visit was a great success, and Omar's hospitality allowed the explorer to use Kuka as a base while he conducted a number of expeditions over a three-year period. One of his most notable journeys took him to the Wadai area to the south, where Eduard Vogel, also an explorer, had ventured seventeen years earlier, never to return. Nachtigal, posing as a Muslim sheriff, was able to discover the fate of his predecessor; he learned that Vogel, suspected of being a spy, had been assassinated on orders from the sultan.

Nachtigal's final expedition in 1874 took him east to Khartoum, where he was given a hero's welcome. He was later named consul general in Tunis, served as an adviser to other expeditions, and compiled his travel accounts into a three-volume publication. A meticulous notetaker, Nachtigal staggered his readers with the comprehensiveness of his facts and observations. His writings on Africa ranged from exact geological and meteorological data to reports on tribal social and economic systems to comments on sexual and political trends. German leaders of his day drew heavily on his understanding of Africa and its people in planning their successful campaign to colonize Togo and the Cameroons, and they used him to negotiate treaty agreements. Shortly after doing so, he died at sea off the Ivory Coast.

Nansen, Fridtjof

Norwegian
b October 10, 1861; Froen, near Oslo
d May 13, 1930; Lysaker, near Oslo
Explored Greenland and Arctic Ocean

A consummate zoologist and oceanographer, a writer and artist of lyric sensibility, and a winner of the Nobel Peace Prize, Fridtjof Nansen brought an uncommon combination of intelligence and grace to the harrowing world of Arctic exploration. He was the first to cross both the Greenland ice cap and the Arctic Ocean. Both expeditions rested on a simple, elegant conception regarding their methods of travel, and both involved a large, if carefully considered, amount of risk. Neither plan was considered sound or safe (or even sane) by established Arctic authorities of the day, but neither resulted in a single casualty.

As a youth, Nansen had instilled in him by his parents a great love of the outdoors. In 1880 he entered the University of Oslo to study zoology, largely because of the opportunity to do fieldwork. In 1883, the year after he was appointed curator of zoology at the Bergen museum, he read that Baron NILS ADOLF ERIK NORDENSKIÖLD had led an expedition into the depths of the Greenland ice sheet. The two Lapps accompanying him, who had gone the farthest into the interior, reported that the skiing was excellent. This led the robust young zoologist to the heady notion, which, he said, "struck me with all the speed of lightning," that he should be able to ski right across Greenland. He had become entranced by the massive ice cap on a zoological field trip to the Greenland coast in 1882 and was anxious to get back.

After his initial vision, it took him four years to plan the expedition in the detail he required, since at the same time he was doing pathbreaking work in histology (the study of tissue structures) and zoology. Though experts were skeptical of his plan to cross with a small party, which called for being dropped on Greenland's uninhabited east coast (thus allowing no retreat), enough of them were impressed by his capabilities that the necessary support was forthcoming. Nordenskiöld, by then retired from exploration, lent him his snow boots and admonished him in a fatherly way to "look after your feet."

Despite being an excellent skier and meticulous planner (he invented the Nansen cooker for this outing), Nansen was taking a great gamble. If, as Nordenskiöld still thought possible, the smooth-skiing plateau did not extend the full width of Greenland, Nansen and his five companions would be trapped without provisions for the winter. Nansen thought that having the prevailing easterly wind at his back was worth the risk. Even more important was eliminating the temptation of failure: "I have always," he later explained, "regarded the much-praised line of retreat as a trap for people who want to reach their goal."

After some difficulty landing on the coast, Nansen, OTTO SVERDRUP, and the other members of the party (all excellent skiers) reached the journey's highest point, roughly 9,000 feet above sea level, on September 14, 1888, a little over a month after they had left Greenland's east coast. In another ten days they reached the west coast, and on October 3 Nansen and Sverdrup arrived at Godthaab in an improvised boat. Everything but the initial landing had gone well, and Nansen and Sverdrup had been able to make up for the lost time by turning the skis and **sledges** into sailing rigs, with "square Viking-like sails showing dark against the white snowfield. . . ."

Nansen returned to Norway a hero, but Arctic experts outside Norway were still unprepared to accept his next, even more daring and origi-

Fridtjof Nansen. Bettmann/Hulton.

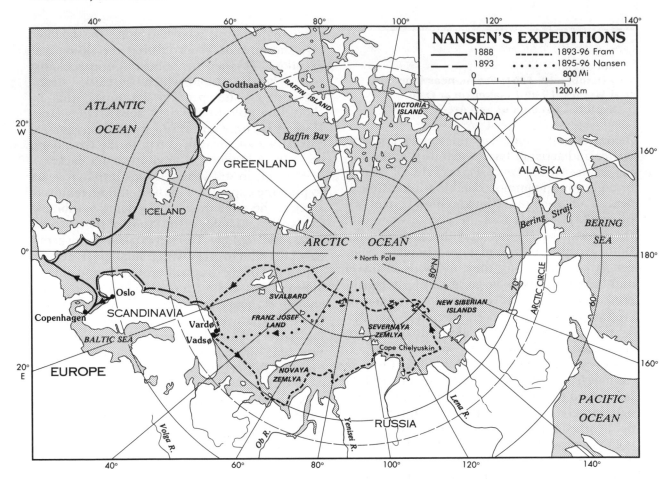

nal, plan. The American general Adolphus Greely, for instance, thought it "an illogical scheme of self-destruction." The idea once again had come suddenly to Nansen in 1884, after reading about the drift of wreckage from GEORGE WASHINGTON DE LONG's *Jeannette.* Two scientists, Carl Lytzen of Denmark and Henrich Mohn of Norway, speculated that the only way the wreckage could have reached the southwest coast of Greenland from north of Siberia was by drifting on the pack ice over the North Pole. Lytzen actually suggested that an explorer could plant his ship in the ice and follow the drift. Nansen's genius was to turn the theory into practice. He had the idea to construct a ship with such a rounded and shallow hull that the expanding ice that crushed De Long's ship would slip right under it. Then he had the good sense to find a shipbuilder, Colin Archer, who could do the job.

The result was the *Fram,* the first ship designed specifically for the Arctic. Aside from having the requisite shape (more like a bathtub than a normal seagoing vessel), the *Fram* was built like a rock. The bow, for instance, had three sections of oak timbers, altogether a yard thick, covered with iron sheeting and rails. Construction began in 1890 and was completed in October 1892.

On June 26, 1893—nine years after the original idea—Nansen and twelve others departed from Vadsø in northernmost Norway for the New Siberian Islands in the Russian Arctic, where the *Jeannette*'s wreckage had begun its long drift. On August 1, they took on dogs at Khabarova, and by September they were fighting their way through an ice-clogged channel along the coast of Cape Chelyuskin. After rounding the cape, they sailed northwest through the waters that Nordenskiöld had found impassable fifteen years earlier.

On September 20 the *Fram* ran into the solid ice pack. She was tethered to a floe and within a few days was frozen in, ready to begin what was to be a three-year drift. In mid-October the ice began squeezing the *Fram* to the surface of the pack, and two months later she had begun to drift northeast.

Using the ship as a floating scientific observatory, Nansen quickly made two fundamental discoveries. By early October he was getting very deep soundings and finding the Arctic Ocean warmer than expected. Eventually he took a sounding of 2,000 **fathoms**, completely overturning the theory that the polar basin was shallow and its waters cold, not to mention the theory that there was a large continent surrounding the North Pole.

Despite a rigorous schedule of scientific observations and unusually good relations among the crew (they avoided the strict naval hierarchy and all lived in the same room), Nansen was restless by the second winter. When it became clear that the *Fram* was going to drift south of the pole by several hundred miles, he decided on the apparently reckless course of leaving the ship to Sverdrup's command while he and Frederik Halmar Johansen took off on dogsleds for the North Pole.

The pair left the ship on March 14, 1895, and reached a record high latitude on April 18 (86°13' North) before beginning the trek back to land. Reaching Franz Josef Land, they were forced to spend a miserable winter in a walrus-hide hut before setting off again in May 1896. With incredible luck they ran into another explorer, Frederick Jackson, who had had no idea Nansen was anywhere near. Jackson had planned on exploring for land north of Franz Josef Land, but Nansen assured him he would be making better use of his time by saving the two filthy and exhausted Norwegians, since there was no land to be found.

Coincidentally, the *Fram* arrived in Norway only a few days after Nansen (who landed at Vardø on August 13, 1896), having reached a record high latitude (85°55' North) for a vessel (unbroken until the U.S. atomic submarine *Nautilus* went under the pole in 1958). This dual arrival created a great sensation, but Nansen's life was so full of important work and responsibilities that these adventures of his late twenties and early thirties seemed normal to him.

Nansen continued his scientific work, which kept him traveling throughout the Northern Hemisphere and resulted in many important oceanographic findings. His fame—and his abilities—gradually led him to a prominent role in public affairs. In 1906 he was appointed Norway's first minister in London, and during the First World War he played a key diplomatic role. But it was after the war that his most important work began. He was one of the leading figures in the League of Nations, taking on the enormous task of relocating the great numbers of political refugees resulting from the war and from the Russian Revolution. In 1921 he headed an international effort to bring famine relief to Russia and later did the same for Greece and Armenia. In 1922 he received the Nobel Peace Prize for this work, and after his death in 1930 the League of Nations established the Nansen International Office for Refugees to continue it. To Nansen, the time he spent in the Arctic working shoulder to shoulder with people he regarded and treated as equals, drifting through the beautiful Arctic night ("It is dreamland, painted in the imagination's most delicate tints . . ."), was a preparation for the hard task of encouraging peace.

Narváez, Pánfilo de

Spanish
b 1470?; Valladolid
d 1528; Gulf of Mexico
Explored Florida and Cuba

Pánfilo de Narváez was a ruthless and rather inept leader who made some serious blunders on his expeditions to Mexico and Florida early in the sixteenth century. Although he initially gained fame during the conquest of Cuba, he was subsequently humiliated when his superior forces were defeated by HERNÁN CORTÉS during an attempt to overthrow Cortés in New Spain (present-day Mexico). Several years later he received a grant to conquer and settle the unexplored regions of Florida and embarked on an expedition in 1528 from which he and most of his men never returned.

Pánfilo de Narváez was born in Valladolid, Spain, about 1470 and emigrated to Hispaniola (the island now occupied by Haiti and the Dominican Republic) in 1498 to seek his fortune as a soldier. In 1509 he accompanied Juan de Esquirel in the conquest of Jamaica. Then between 1511 and 1518 he commanded an expeditionary force with the objective of surveying and completing the conquest of Cuba. During this enterprise he gained a reputation not only for bravery but also for cruelty. According to the chronicle of Father BARTOLOMÉ DE LAS CASAS, the priest on part of the expedition, the cam-

Panfilo de Narvaez. Patrimonio Nacional, Madrid.

paign was a bloody slaughter during which Narváez personally killed 2,000 Indians.

In 1520 Narváez was sent by Diego Velásquez, the governor of Cuba, to supercede Cortés, who had flouted Velásquez's authority in New Spain. On April 23, 1520, Narváez landed at Vera Cruz and entered into negotiations with emissaries from Cortés while also pursuing secret talks with representatives of the captured Aztec emperor Montezuma II. However, Narváez's obstinacy and imperceptiveness gave the clever Cortés an opportunity to infiltrate his camp and engineer a surprise attack. Though outnumbered five to one, Cortés and his army defeated the Narváez forces and imprisoned Narváez for two years.

After regaining his freedom, Narváez went to Spain to lobby for permission to conquer new lands. In 1527 he was granted a royal charter to conquer and explore the area from the River of Palms (the present-day Rio Grande) in northeastern Mexico east to the unexplored regions of Florida. Armed with the title of Grand Constable and with too much confidence in his own ability, he sailed from Spain on June 27, 1527, with 600 men in five ships. By the time he landed in April of 1528 at the head of present-day Tampa Bay on the west coast of Florida, he had already lost a ship and several men during a hurricane and had been forced to leave 140 men at Hispaniola when they refused to continue.

At this point Narváez made a tactical error that would eventually cost him and most of his men their lives. Against the advice of ÁLVAR NÚÑEZ CABEZA DE VACA, the treasurer and high sheriff of the expedition, Narváez divided his force. While he marched inland with some 300 men, the remaining men were to sail the ships along the coastline and reestablish contact with the land force somewhere farther north. After a year of searching for the land force, the seagoing force gave up and headed west for Vera Cruz (in what is now Mexico).

Meanwhile, Narváez led his men toward the interior of Florida, making slow progress through swamps filled with poisonous snakes and alligators. From some captured Indians he learned of a place called Apalachen where there was supposedly an abundance of gold. For two weeks the men marched northwesterly, crossing the present-day Suwannee River and heading toward the Florida Panhandle. When they finally reached Apalachen, near present-day Tallahassee, they found forty thatched huts and fields of golden corn—but no gold. This failure to find great riches, plus a dwindling food supply, forced Narváez to head for the Gulf coast.

Narváez and his party finally reached a place called Aute where the modern Wakulla and St. Marks rivers converge near Apalachee Bay, where they realized they had missed the ships. (Recent archaeological finds place the site of Aute at the modern Saint Marks Wildlife Refuge.) Narváez named the place the Bay of Horses because they were forced to kill and eat all the remaining horses while there. Improvising, the men built barges in hopes of sailing to Pánuco on the northeastern coast of modern Mexico. They used iron from stirrups and crossbows to make nails, horsehide to cover the frames of the barges, and shirts for sails. They were constantly harassed by Indians, and several men died of disease and hunger during the sixteen days it took to build five barges. Finally, on September 22, 1528, the overloaded barges set sail with about 200 men on board.

Because no one knew how to navigate, they sailed close to the coastline and landed periodically to search for food. When they reached the mouth of the Mississippi River, the strong river current and gale-force winds carried them farther out to sea, and the barges became separated. Only two barges made it to what is now Galveston Island, Texas. Cabeza de Vaca, one of the survivors, reported that they had earlier lost sight of Narváez's barge; it is believed that Narváez drowned somewhere near the mouth of the Mississippi in 1528.

• Nearchus

Greek
b 360 B.C.?
d 312 B.C.
Opened up sea route from India to Arabian peninsula

Nearchus was one of the most outstanding geographers of ancient times. His detailed record of his journey from the Indus River (now in Pakistan) to the Euphrates River (in present-day Iraq) gave the Mediterranean world its first accurate knowledge of the sea route to India. In the second century A.D., the Greek historian Arrian included a summary of Nearchus's narrative in his book titled *Indica*.

ALEXANDER THE GREAT ruled Greece from 336 B.C. to 323 B.C. and conquered much of Europe, Africa, and Asia during that period. As Alexander and his armies marched across Asia, laying claim to the land and its people, they came upon the Indus River. To their surprise, they found crocodiles in the Indus. Knowing the Nile River also contained crocodiles, they concluded that perhaps the Indus was the source of the Nile, that Asia and Africa were linked in the south. To explore this possible river route, Alexander commissioned Nearchus to build a fleet of oared **galleys** and cargo ships. Reports of the Indus flowing into a "Great Sea" soon changed Alexander's mind about the Indus–

Nile link, but he remained intrigued by the possibility of a direct water route from India to the Mediterranean.

Alexander reluctantly decided to turn back from his conquests when his soldiers, who had been on the march for eight years, refused to continue east into an unknown land where elephants were said to live. But Alexander, ever the explorer, elected to investigate the coast between the Indus and the Euphrates on the return to Greece. By this time, Nearchus was standing by with his fleet in the Hydaspes (now the Jhelum) River, a tributary of the Indus. In 325 B.C., Alexander's forces and Nearchus's fleet joined and proceeded together down the Indus to the Indian Ocean. There Alexander and 12,000 of his troops embarked to march along a land route following the Arabian Sea and the Persian Gulf, while Nearchus and 5,000 men returned by a parallel sea route in a fleet of 150 ships.

Nearchus sailed along the south coast of Asia, into the Persian Gulf, to the mouth of the Euphrates. His log described with great precision the distance the fleet traveled each day, where it anchored, the configuration of the coastline, and the location of natural harbors. Subsequent explorers confirmed the reliability of his account. Under Alexander's orders, Nearchus then continued his exploration of the sea route between India and the Mediterranean by effectively circumnavigating the Arabian peninsula, a remarkable achievement for his day.

Nehra, Alvaro de Mendaña de. See **Mendaña de Nehra, Alvaro de.**

• Nicollet (Nicolet) de Belleborne (Bellesborne), Jean

French
b 1598?; Cherbourg
d October 27, 1642; Sillery, Québec
Explored Lake Michigan and Green Bay

Acting as a liaison between the government of **New France** and the Indians of the Great Lakes, Jean Nicollet de Belleborne lived among the Algonquins, the Nipissings, and the Hurons for many years. In 1634, on a mission for SAMUEL DE CHAMPLAIN, he became the first European to see Lake Michigan and Green Bay.

In 1618, at the age of twenty, Nicollet arrived in New France to become one of the young men sent by Champlain to live among the Indians and learn their languages and customs. For two years he lived with the Algonquins on Allumette Island high up the Ottawa River. There he learned both the Algonquin and Huron languages. Returning to Québec, he was sent out to live among the Nipissings near the lake of the same name, located between the Ottawa River and Georgian Bay of Lake Huron. The Nipissings were a vital link in the trading route between the French and the Indians to the west of the Nipissings as well as the tribes of Hudson Bay. Nicollet's task was to secure the loyalty of the Nipissings so that furs found their way to the French rather than to the English on Hudson Bay.

Nicollet spent nine years with the Nipissings. When the English captured Québec in 1629, he went farther west and worked against English attempts to get the Hurons to trade with them. In 1633, after Québec returned to French control, Nicollet asked for a job as clerk at Trois-Rivières (Three Rivers) on the St. Lawrence River. Champlain granted his wish but asked him to undertake one last mission.

On this mission Nicollet had two goals. The first was to establish relations with the Winnebagoes on the northwest side of Lake Michigan and to prevent them from trading with the Dutch from the Hudson River region. The second was to search for the fabled China Sea, which the Indians had told him was west of what is now Green Bay. Thus, before his departure, Nicollet acquired a ceremonial robe of "China damask, all strewn with flowers and birds of many colors" so he would be ready to greet the "mandarins of Cathay" in suitable style.

When Nicollet arrived at Green Bay—the first European to do so—he donned his damask robe and, appearing godlike to the Winnebagoes, convinced them to sign a peace treaty. He then made a vain attempt to find the China Sea, first traveling down the Fox River until he was only three days' journey from the Wisconsin River, a tributary of the Mississippi, and then journeying south toward the Illinois River.

Frustrated by his failure to find anything resembling the China Sea, he returned to Québec in 1635 and assumed his duties as clerk at Trois-Rivières. In 1642 he drowned while navigating rough waters between Québec and Trois-Rivières. Jesuit memoirs portray Nicollet as a man of exemplary character who was "equally and singularly loved" by both the French and the Indians.

Niza, Marcos de. See **Marcos de Niza.**

Nobile, Umberto

Italian
b January 21, 1885; Lauro, Avellino, near Naples
d July 29, 1978; Rome
Explored Arctic Ocean by air

General Umberto Nobile designed and piloted the first aircraft to cross the Arctic Ocean. A brilliant engineer specializing in **dirigible** design, he became director of the aeronautical factory in Rome in 1919 while still only thirty-four. In 1922 the new Fascist government created a military corps of aeronautical engineers, and Nobile was made a lieutenant colonel. In the summer of 1925, he received a telegram from the great Norwegian Arctic explorer ROALD AMUNDSEN. Amundsen and his American benefactor LINCOLN ELLSWORTH wanted to buy the semi-rigid dirigible N-1, which Nobile had designed, for a flight across the Arctic Ocean from Eurasia to North America. They also wanted to employ Nobile as pilot. The ensuing negotiations were difficult and protracted. Though they finally resulted in a working agreement, Amundsen never reconciled himself to the fact that on this last effort of his career he was more promoter than explorer. Despite his original conception and all the work he did preparing for the expedition, he was merely a passenger on the flight itself.

The *Norge* (renamed by Amundsen to honor his own country, Norway) left Svalbard on May 11, 1926, and arrived at the North Pole the next day. After dealing with fog and very dangerous icing of the craft, the party landed at Teller, Alaska, northwest of Nome, on May 14, following seventy hours of continuous and strenuous flight in covering the 3,400 miles. It was an effort for which all involved deserved credit. But when world attention naturally turned to Nobile, the pilot and designer of the *Norge*, Amundsen felt slighted.

The clashing of egos during this first hazardous crossing of what would eventually become

Nobile's dirigible *Italia*. National Archives.

a major commercial air route would have been comic were it not for the repercussions. Amundsen saw what the Italian dictator Benito Mussolini perceived—that all the attention focused on Nobile, resplendent in his Italian officer's uniform, would reflect glory on the Fascists. Amundsen found the wild patriotic demonstrations of the Italians profoundly disturbing, and he felt he had inadvertently furthered the Fascist cause.

Nobile, on the other hand, was humiliated by Amundsen's attempt to rein him in. He was not as interested in politics as in aeronautics, a field in which he was a genius. He therefore set out to achieve on his own an even more ambitious Arctic expedition. He planned three separate flights, one along the Siberian coast, one along the north coasts of Greenland and Canada, and one to the North Pole, where a landing would be made. Once again, Mussolini backed the plan, overriding the objections of Air Marshal Italo Balbo, who preferred to concentrate on developing the airplane. Even Pope Pius XI became excited about the prospect and personally presented Nobile with an oak cross to plant in the ice at the pole. But this time there was to be little glory for the Italians.

Nobile went to the old Arctic veterans FRITDJOF NANSEN and OTTO SVERDRUP for advice on supplies. He fitted the dirigible with **sledges**, tents, canvas boats, and all the other accoutrements of Arctic travel, then made the long trip from Milan, Italy, to Svalbard, north of Norway. When the dirigible *Italia* took off from Kings Bay on May 11, 1928, weather conditions forced an early return. But on May 15 the first flight, that toward Siberia, began in earnest. After flying north of Franz Josef Land, Nobile made it just short of his destination at Severnaya Zemlya, a distance of 2,500 miles.

After this great success, spirits were high for the trip to the pole. Departing on May 23, Nobile and his crew of fifteen reached the pole easily, but bad weather prevented a landing. On the return flight the wind worsened and ice accumulated on the craft, eventually flying from the propellers like shrapnel into the vulnerable soft sides of the vessel. Fog made accurate navigation impossible, and ice jammed part of the *Italia*'s steering gear as Nobile was attempting to determine his position. The helmsman managed to free it, but soon the ship began to sink rapidly. Nothing could be done to avert the fall, some 180 miles northeast of Svalbard.

The impact of the crash on the ice tore the gondola from the dirigible's hull, leaving its ten occupants stranded on the ice while the hull rebounded upward with six members of the crew dangling in the framework, never to be seen again. Of those on the ice, one mechanic had been killed immediately, but otherwise only Nobile and a technician were injured. Fortunately, a tent, a radio, and twenty-four days of provisions were found among the wreckage, enabling all but one to survive what would become a long wait for rescuers.

Aside from the eight members of the *Italia* who lost their lives, several would-be rescuers became lost due to bad weather during the resulting large-scale international relief operation by air and sea. Ironically, one was Nobile's former collaborator, Roald Amundsen. Despite his estrangement from Nobile, he had unhesitatingly responded to the call for help and flown to his death aboard a Latham biplane, which became lost over the Barents Sea. Nobile was rescued on June 24 by the Swedish Air Force. The remainder of the survivors were rescued on July 12 by the Soviet icebreaker *Krassin*, though the Swedish scientist Finn Malmgren had died in setting out over the ice to seek help for his fellow survivors.

Though Nobile probably could not have prevented the disaster, Air Marshal Balbo took the opportunity to destroy his rival by orchestrating an inquiry that found Nobile guilty of negligence. The Italian aeronaut was consequently stripped of his rank and his many honors. In need of a job, he went to the Soviet Union in 1932 to build dirigibles. After World War II, he was exonerated and allowed to return to Italy. Obviously influenced by his tenure with the Soviets, he was elected to the Italian Constituent Assembly in 1946 as a Communist. He died in Rome in 1978 at the age of ninety-three.

Nils Adolf Erik Nordenskiold. Swedish Institute.

• Nordenskiöld (Nordenskjöld), Nils Adolf Erik

Swedish-Finnish
b November 18, 1832; Helsinki, Finland
d August 12, 1901; Stockholm, Sweden
Explored Canadian and Norwegian Arctic;
**   navigated Northeast Passage**

A "practical geographer" in his own estimation, Baron Nils Adolf Erik Nordenskiöld stands out among Arctic explorers of the late nineteenth century for his success at opening up new trade routes, rather than simply charting inaccessible territories or racing to one of the poles for the sake of being first. By showing Russian and Scandinavian merchants that they could use the Siberian coastal waterway to connect the trade of the great rivers of northern Asia with northern Europe, Nordenskiöld revived the spirit of an earlier age, when trade was the primary motive of exploration. Like the Elizabethan discovery of the White Sea trade (see RICHARD CHANCELLOR), Nordenskiöld's work altered the life of an entire region. The climax of his career came when he navigated the Northeast Passage in 1878, thus extending the potential reach of Siberian products to the Pacific. This laid the foundation of the northern sea route of the Soviet Union, a fundamental link in today's world trade network.

In charting the Northeast Passage, Nordenskiöld became the first explorer since the search began in the sixteenth century to find a navigable northern connection between the Atlantic and the Pacific. For northern Europeans, the

original motive had been the same whether the goal was to sail over America or Eurasia: to find a route to the riches of the Orient that was not dominated by the southern European maritime powers, Spain and Portugal. Many lost their lives in the struggle to penetrate the icy waters above Eurasia (HUGH WILLOUGHBY and WILLEM BARENTS among them), but there were also positive spin-offs such as the lucrative whaling and fishing grounds discovered off Spitsbergen (now part of Svalbard) and the White Sea trade.

By the time Nordenskiöld took up the quest for a Northeast Passage, however, many considered it a waste of time. The Spanish and Portuguese had long ceased to dominate the southern trade routes. Cargo could be sent across North America efficiently by rail, and soon Asia would be traversed by rail as well (though the Trans-Siberian Railway was not completed until 1917). The Panama Canal was in the works (though it was not completed until 1914), and the Suez Canal had just opened. Moreover, even if a daring explorer could make it across the waters above Eurasia, the critics argued, the route would always be dangerous and inefficient.

None of these objections struck Nordenskiöld

as serious. Through patient study of fishing journals and historical accounts (in later life he became a distinguished historian of exploration), and through his own numerous preparatory voyages, he laid a solid foundation for his world-renowned voyage. So successful was he that the actual expedition was quite uneventful.

Nordenskiöld hypothesized that the Ob, Yenisei, and Lena rivers warmed the coastal waters north of Russia enough to provide a reasonably reliable, though narrow, passage in the summer. Previous explorers had erred by ranging too far from the mainland, often with the false hope of finding an open polar sea. By simply hugging the coast, Nordenskiöld was able to pass all the imagined obstacles with ease. Had the route already been charted, he could have made it all the way across Eurasia in one summer.

Nordenskiöld entered the field of exploration through his early work as a mineralogist. As a child, he explored mineral deposits all over Finland with his father, a mineralogist with the mining administration. In 1853, after graduat-

ing from the University of Helsingfors (Helsinki), he and his father traveled to the Ural Mountains of Russia, where they conducted metallurgical experiments. On his return to Finland, he drew on his wide travels to write a handbook on the country's mineral deposits.

His serious academic work in mineralogy won him two scientific positions, one with the state mining administration and one with the university. Together these gave him the financial means and time to pursue his doctorate. He was well on his way to becoming a settled scientist, rather than a restless explorer. Soon all that changed.

In the middle of the Crimean War—when the Russian autocracy that ruled Finland was nervous about Scandinavian patriotism—Nordenskiöld, whose family was Swedish in origin, voiced his anti-Russian sentiments. As a consequence, he was fired from both his posts in 1855. Then began a period of moves in and out of Finland and conflicts with the authorities that resulted (after he received his doctorate) in his eventual emigration to Sweden.

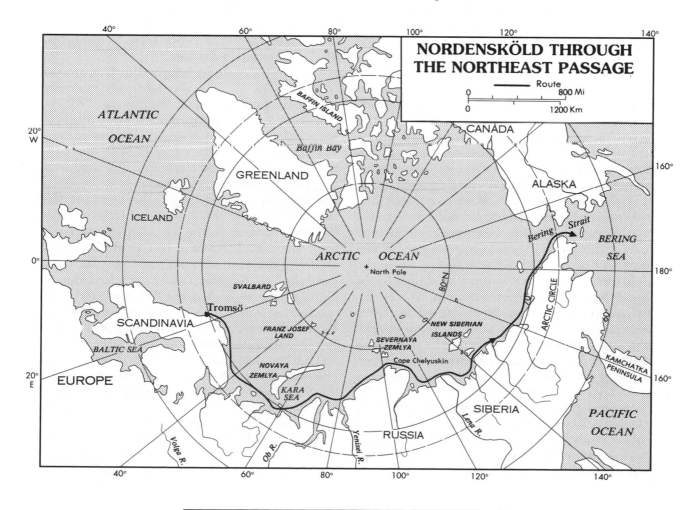

In 1858 he was invited by a Swedish geologist, Otto Torell, on a scientific expedition to Spitsbergen. This was a highly successful venture, yielding an impressive number of specimens illustrating the natural history of the region. It was the sort of work that would become Nordenskiöld's hallmark. In 1861, now chief of mineralogy at the Stockholm museum, he once again joined Torell in an expedition to Spitsbergen, where they set up bases to be used later in measuring the curvature of the earth. Torell had planned to make a dash for the North Pole by dogsled, but they arrived in northern Spitsbergen too late in the season to make the attempt.

In 1864 Nordenskiöld led another expedition to Spitsbergen, this one sponsored by the Swedish Academy of Science. Aside from the usual collection of specimens, the main task was to continue the work of measuring the arc of the meridian. By now completely dedicated to Arctic exploration, he led an expedition in 1868 financed by the Swedish government and the wealthy industrialist Oscar Dickson, who was to continue as Nordenskiöld's main supporter. Using the iron steamer Sofia supplied and manned by the navy, Nordenskiöld returned to Spitsbergen again, this time determined to investigate the Arctic Ocean closer to the North Pole than had been done previously. On September 18 the Sofia reached the highest latitude yet attained in the hemisphere, 81°42′ North.

On his return to Sweden, Nordenskiöld threw himself into the new politics created by the liberal reforms of 1865 and was elected to Parliament in 1869. But the next year he was off again, this time to Greenland. With a botanist and two native Greenlanders, he became the first to explore any significant distance into its interior ice sheet, making many important discoveries about the nature of the region.

In 1872 he planned to dash by **sledge** to the North Pole, but ice conditions prevented his two supply ships from returning south. Three vessels and their crews were frozen in instead of the one planned. With twice the number of people to feed and care for during the winter, the well-planned trip turned into a dangerous ordeal. When a storm scattered the party's reindeer, any remaining chance of reaching the pole vanished. Remarkably, all but two of the group survived, and Nordenskiöld took ten crew members on an impressive 150-mile trek by foot, surveying northeastern Spitsbergen.

At this time, Nordenskiöld was already a celebrated figure in Sweden and was recognized throughout the world as a great scientific explorer. Giving up his quest for the North Pole, he focused on his next ambition—to open the Northeast Passage. His first, decisive move was to take the Pröven along the Siberian coast all the way to the mouth of the Yenisei River in the Kara Sea (which he reached on August 13, 1875). From there he took a small rowboat upstream until a Russian fisherman took him and his five companions on a slow, 1,000-mile trip upriver to Yeniseisk in central Russia. In immediate human and economic terms, this voyage was more significant than the more famous voyage of the Vega through the Northeast Passage. Here was an exiled Finn—a liberal member of the Swedish Parliament and a distinguished scientist—rowing up the middle of Siberia in a small boat. The Russians, never mentioning his well-known anti-Russian sentiments, went out of their way to welcome this man who had opened the Siberian coast to European trade. Alexander Sibiryakov, a wealthy Russian merchant, became a loyal financial backer. He was so impressed by the new trade route that he immediately sent the Dawn from Yeniseisk to St. Petersburg, via Sweden.

When Nordenskiöld returned to Sweden on November 30, 1875, he wasted no time preparing for the final attack on the passage. Within two years, with the backing of Dickson, Sibiryakov, and the king of Sweden, the expedition was ready. Sibiryakov, eager to start the new trade, provided three ships to carry coal and supplies for the Vega, two stopping at the Yenisei with commercial cargo, the other at the Lena. On July 31, 1878, the four ships met in the strait leading to the Kara Sea to start the long, uneventful trip east. Nordenskiöld sailed briefly to the northeast of Cape Chelyuskin toward the New Siberian Islands, but ice stopped him. Otherwise he hugged the coast until he reached his wintering place close to the Bering Strait, which separates Siberia from Alaska. On July 20, 1879, the Vega was freed from the ice and sailed easily into the strait. A triumphal tour then ensued around Eurasia and through the Suez Canal, ending in Stockholm on April 24, 1880 (a date now known as Vega Day in Sweden).

Nordenskiöld made one more expedition to the ice sheet of Greenland in 1883, his tenth Arctic expedition, where with two Lapps he penetrated 140 miles inland. This journey demonstrated that ice probably covered all of interior Greenland, inspiring the young FRIDTJOF NANSEN to ski across it four years later.

Finally, Baron Nordenskiöld (who had been ennobled in 1880) retired to a life of scholarship, though he continued to advise explorers. He kept up the fight for Finnish independence until the day he died, no doubt realizing the irony that it was his opposition to the Russian autocracy that catapulted him into the career that made him famous.

SUGGESTED READING: L. P. Kirwan, *A History of Polar Exploration* (W. W. Norton, 1960); George Kish, *Northeast Passage: Adolf Erik Nordenskiöld, His Life and Times* (Nico Israel, 1973); L. H. Neatby, *Discovery in Russian and Siberian Waters* (Ohio University Press, 1973).

Novaes, Bartolomeu de. See **Dias, Bartolomeu.**

Nuñez de Balboa, Vasco. See **Balboa, Vasco Nuñez de.**

Odoric of Pordenone

**Italian
b 1286?; Villanova, near Pordenone, Friuli
d January 14, 1331; Udine
Traveled in Middle East, Asia, and Indonesia**

In about 1316, after Odoric of Pordenone took his vows to become a Franciscan friar, he was sent to Asia as a missionary. By the time he returned to Italy some fourteen years later, he had baptized more than 20,000 people and written descriptions of Asian life that would endure in the European imagination for several hundred years. Odoric's narrative, a compelling blend of accurate reporting and inventive exaggeration, was probably the basis for the fourteenth-century English work *The Voyage and Travels of Sir John Mandeville, Knight.*

Odoric's journey to the East first took him to a number of Franciscan residences in Asia Minor and Persia (now Turkey, Iraq, and Iran). After a stay in Hormuz, at the eastern end of the Persian Gulf, he boarded a ship bound for India. He landed near Bombay in about 1322 and proceeded to visit many parts of India. Odoric then sailed from India to southeast Asia on board a junk (a type of Chinese ship), passing

through Sumatra, Java, and Borneo on the way. He arrived in China only a decade after MARCO POLO had left.

Odoric's journals include colorful descriptions of his three-year stay in Beijing, his visit to the court of the Great Khan, and his extensive travels throughout Asia. Hangzhou, he wrote, "is the greatest city in the world. It is one hundred miles in circumference, and in this vast area there is not a single spot that is not inhabited." Odoric was the first European to describe the long fingernails of Chinese aristocrats, the ritual binding of girls' feet (to keep the feet from growing), and the methods of Chinese fishermen who used cormorants to catch fish.

When Odoric decided to return to Italy, he set out overland, traveling through the uncharted regions of central Asia. He was probably the first European to visit Lhasa, the capital and holy city of Tibet, which he described as "very beautiful: it is built of white stone and its streets are well paved. . . . No one in this city dares to spill the blood of man or animal, out of veneration for an idol which they worship." The people of Tibet, according to Odoric, lived in tents made of black felt. When Odoric reached Italy, another friar wrote down the story of his travels in simple Latin. Odoric died several months later, in 1331.

Ogden, Peter Skene

**Canadian
b 1794; Québec City, Québec
d September 27, 1854; Oregon City, Oregon
Explored American West**

Peter Skene Ogden spent most of his life in the fur trade, ranging over the North American continent. From 1824 to 1830 he led six expeditions in the American West. In the course of these travels, he thoroughly explored the Snake River area, became the first non-Indian to see the present-day Humboldt River in what is now Nevada, and reached as far south as the Gulf of California.

Ogden joined the North West Company at the age of fifteen or sixteen and for the next twelve years developed a reputation as a ruthless trader who would stop at nothing short of murder in the pursuit of his goals. His acts of violence and intimidation against agents of

Peter Skene Ogden. Oregon Historical Society.

the rival Hudson's Bay Company left him without a job when the two fur companies merged in 1821. But Ogden eventually convinced the Hudson's Bay Company that he would be as much of an asset to them as he had been a liability against them, and by 1823 he was posted to Spokane House in what is now eastern Washington State with instructions to lead a trapping expedition to the Snake River in the spring of 1824.

At that time, no firm boundary had been established between the United States and Canada in the Northwest. The Oregon Territory, as it was called, was open to both British and American trappers, but the British rightly anticipated a time when the United States would attempt to take over the area. It was therefore in the interest of Ogden's fur company—which was British—to take every beaver pelt it could, especially if it meant leaving nothing for future American trappers. Ogden's job was not only to trap every beaver in sight but to discover every possible source of beaver pelts to assure that Hudson's Bay Company trappers effec-

tively denuded the Oregon Territory's streams of beaver.

In the trapping season of 1824–25, Ogden explored the Snake and Bear river country thoroughly and got far enough south that one of his men, scaling a mountain, caught sight of the Great Salt Lake. (It had been seen by Americans the previous fall.)

Ogden's most significant expedition took place from 1828 to 1829, during which he discovered the Humboldt River (in what is now Nevada) and followed it from its source to the Humboldt Sinks, a series of marshy lakes where the river peters out. Ogden called it the Unknown River. Years later JOHN CHARLES FRÉMONT named the river after the great German explorer ALEXANDER VON HUMBOLDT (who never saw it), but by rights the honor should have gone to Ogden. Ironically, the river he found would soon become one of the important links on the trail that led Ogden's rivals, American settlers, to California.

In August 1828, JEDEDIAH SMITH and two of his men limped into Fort Vancouver, having narrowly avoided a massacre that befell the rest of their party on the Umpqua River. While Smith was still at the fort, Ogden returned there to learn firsthand of Smith's two expeditions across the Mojave Desert and into California. This gave Ogden the idea for his last and most intriguing exploration of the West, a journey that took him south, probably as far as the Gulf of California. Unfortunately, this expedition is the least understood of Ogden's travels because his journals, as well as nine of his men, were lost in a whirlpool of the Columbia River shortly before the end of the journey. Reconstructing the trip from his letters and later reports, historians have surmised that he and his experienced party of thirty traveled south from the Columbia River to the Humboldt Sinks, where they turned southeast and traveled through what Ogden called the Great Sandy Desert of the Great Salt Lake, probably the Great Basin of modern Nevada. The trek was arduous, and Ogden and his men were reduced to eating the flesh of horses that died on the trail and drinking the animals' blood to quench their thirst.

Eventually they came to the "South West branch of the Rio Collorado"—probably the point on the river where Jed Smith had encountered a band of Mojave Indians, somewhere around present-day Needles, California. Unlike Smith, Ogden and his men were prepared for the hostility of the Mojaves and quickly dispatched the Indians with guns and handmade spears. The party then proceeded down the Colorado to the Gulf of California, making Ogden the first non-Indian to travel the length of the American West from north to south.

Turning north, the explorers crossed the mountains near San Bernardino and eventually arrived in the San Joaquin Valley, which they followed north, keeping far enough from the coast to avoid detection by the Spanish, in whose territory they were trespassing.

Peter Ogden spent another twenty-four years in the fur trade, but none of his later travels equaled those made during the six years he had spent exploring the American West. It was a region that challenged the toughness of character he had been building throughout his life, and he found it a worthy, if not always welcome, opponent. At one point, when liquid mud was the only drink available to his men, Ogden wrote: "This is certainly a most horrid life, in a word I may say without exaggeration Man in this Country is deprived of every comfort that can tend to make existence desirable." Still he persisted in the face of many such hardships and in doing so added greatly to what was known at the time about the North American West.

· Ojeda, Alonso de

Spanish
b 1468?; Cuenca
d 1515?; Hispaniola
Explored coasts of Venezuela and Colombia

Ruthless and aggressive, Alonso de Ojeda enjoyed his role as **conquistador**, pillaging the lands he explored and treating the Indians he encountered with extreme cruelty. He was commander of a ship on CHRISTOPHER COLUMBUS's second voyage to the New World (1493–95), and explored the interior of Hispaniola (the island now occupied by Haiti and the Dominican Republic) in search of gold. Later he led several of his own expeditions to South America and founded San Sebastián (on the Gulf of Urabá, in present-day Colombia), which, though eventually abandoned, was the first Spanish settlement on South American soil.

Ojeda was born into a noble Spanish family sometime between 1466 and 1470 in the town of Cuenca. As a youth he was described as a hothead who was constantly brawling. After serving in the household of the duke of Medina Celi, he gained fame fighting in the effort to expel the Moors from Spain. As part of Columbus's second expedition, Ojeda proved his mettle by penetrating the interior of Hispaniola, fighting its Indians as well as its dense undergrowth and heat.

Upon returning from this voyage, he was commissioned by the Spanish Crown to search for more riches in the New World. When the expedition departed from Cadiz on May 16, 1499, it included the cartographer JUAN DE LA COSA and the financial representative AMERIGO VESPUCCI. The expedition's ships divided after passing the Cape Verde Islands, with Vespucci exploring to the southeast of South America while Ojeda sailed along its northwest coast. Traveling on this course, Ojeda passed the mouths of two large rivers (most likely the Essequibo in modern British Guiana and the Orinoco in Venezuela) and reached the Gulf of Paria. He made his first landfall on the island now known as Trinidad, encountering "Caribs or cannibals of gentle disposition." Proceeding north to the island that is now Curaçao, he skirted the modern Paraguaná Peninsula, which juts into the Caribbean Sea; entered the present-day Gulf of Venezuela; and sailed into what is now Lake Maracaibo. There he discovered people who fished for pearls and lived in houses built on pilings in the shallows of the lake. These dwellings inspired Ojeda to name the land Venezuela (Little Venice). Returning to the Gulf of Paria, he sailed around the modern Guajira Peninsula (in present-day Colombia) and then north to meet Vespucci at Hispaniola. The entire expedition returned to Spain with enough pearls and Indian slaves to make the voyage a financial success.

Ojeda was awarded the title of **adelantado** of Coquibacoa (the area around Lake Maracaibo) and in 1501 was granted a royal license to cut brazilwood in Hispaniola and nearby islands and to further exploit the pearl trade. His next expedition reached the Peninsula of Paria, Venezuela, in March 1502 and plied the coast trading with the Indians for pearls (the area became known as the Pearl Coast). Whenever provisions became short, Ojeda would attack Indian villages, enslave or massacre the entire population, and take everything he could find. When supply ships finally arrived from Jamaica, he was accused of not paying the royal fifth (one-fifth of all riches acquired were payable to the Crown). He was taken to Hispaniola, where he was convicted. He managed to return to Spain, where he cleared himself of the charges and had all rights restored on November 8, 1503.

Ojeda made a brief voyage in 1505 about which little is known, then undertook a major expedition in 1508 to establish a settlement in South America. He landed at the site of what is now Cartagena, Colombia, and attacked a Carib Indian village to get slaves to sell as a means of improving his dwindling finances. Against the advice of his lieutenant, Juan de La Cosa, he slaughtered or enslaved all the Indians of the village. Neighboring Caribs then took a terrible revenge, attacking the Spaniards with poisoned darts that caused a slow, agonizing death. Ojeda was the only one to escape since he was small enough to hide behind his shield (which took some 300 arrow hits).

In 1510 Ojeda established a settlement called San Sebastián, on the Gulf of Urabá. Indian attacks and food shortages forced him to leave and seek aid for the colony. Shipwrecked on Cuba, Ojeda eventually reached Hispaniola only to discover that his colonists had abandoned San Sebastián, leaving him in financial ruin. According to some accounts, he entered a Franciscan friary in Hispaniola and died there about 1515 in abject poverty.

Despite his great cruelty toward the Indians, Alonso de Ojeda did successfully explore the coastal area of Venezuela and part of Colombia, opening these areas for further exploration and colonization by Spain. Today the city of Ciudad Ojeda stands along the shore of Lake Maracaibo near the spot where Ojeda first encountered the pearl-fishers almost 500 years ago.

· Oñate, Juan de

Spanish
b 1549?; Mexico
d 1624; Spain
Explored and colonized American Southwest

Don Juan de Oñate was one of the richest men in New Spain (present-day Mexico) when he volunteered, at his own expense, to lead an expedition, the purpose of which was the "discovery, pacification, and conversion of the . . . provinces of New Mexico." Although his stated purpose was to explore and colonize, Oñate was also eager to search for the mythical land of Quivira that FRANCISCO VÁSQUEZ DE CORONADO had also sought. This legendary land of fabulous wealth, where gold was said to be moved by the wagonload and the king's canoes supposedly had golden oarlocks, was thought to be located in the northeast. However, neither Oñate nor Coronado found Quivira; they only found vast wilderness and poor Indians.

Though the exact date of Oñate's birth in New Spain is unknown, it has generally been accepted as about 1549. His father was one of the discoverers of the Zacatecas mines and a former governor of New Galicia (the modern Mexican states of Nayarit and Sinaloa). Oñate was very influential in New Spain and gained even more prestige when he married the great-granddaughter of the Aztec king Montezuma II. In all he did, Oñate combined a strong sense of duty with a great deal of ambition and personal pride. Determined to lead the New Mexico expedition, he waited a long time for approval from the lord viceroy of New Spain and King Philip II of Spain.

Finally, in the summer of 1597, Oñate's expedition left New Spain with 400 men (130 brought their wives and children), several Franciscan friars, and Indians to carry supplies. He also took with him articles to barter with the native Indians, four bells for a church, and many personal belongings—including a suit of armor, twelve saddles, and two state coaches.

The expedition moved slowly, hampered at first by heavy rains, then by five days of desert travel and extreme thirst. Eventually Oñate and his group found the Rio Grande. As the official log recorded, "We were exploring and feeling our way. . . . We suffered a great deal because of not knowing it." Following the Rio Grande north, Oñate entered New Mexico on April 30, 1598, and immediately claimed the land for Spain. Resuming the march upstream, the expedition went through a mountain pass which Oñate named El Paso del Norte (near present-day El Paso, Texas), crossed to the east bank of the Rio Grande, and continued north across a vast plain east of the mountains. Oñate and his party encountered many friendly Indian

pueblos along the way. On July 7 Oñate met with seven Indian chieftains who pledged obedience to the king of Spain.

On August 11, 1598, the expedition came to the junction of the Rio Chama and the Rio Grande. Here Oñate chose to establish his capital, calling it San Juan de los Caballeros. It was the first European settlement west of the Mississippi River. By early October he had left the capital with a small party to explore the wilderness in the west. Another expeditionary force that went to join him was massacred during an uprising at the pueblo of Acoma. When Oñate received the news, he immediately returned to the capital and received the priests' authorization to wage war on the Acoma Indians. He defeated the Acomas, but maintained an uneasy peace with several of the other Indian pueblos thereafter.

Oñate continued to explore, reaching present-day Kansas in 1601 in his search for Quivira and, turning west and south, the mouth of the Colorado River and the Gulf of California in 1605. By 1607, however, many of the colonists had become discontented, and secret reports discrediting Oñate had reached the lord viceroy of New Spain. In addition, no vast riches had been found. In 1609, Oñate was recalled to New Spain, demoted, and put on trial for various crimes. He was banished from New Mexico in 1614 after being found guilty of using inhumane severity in the war against the Acoma and sending false reports about conditions in the New Mexican capital. Oñate appealed the verdict to the **Council of the Indies** and lost his entire fortune over the next seven years pleading his case. The Council recommended clemency in 1622, but the king delayed his decision. At age seventy-five, Oñate went to Spain to appeal to the king directly. In 1624 the king pardoned him, restored his title of **adelantado**, and gave him the position of Inspector of Mines and Lodes in Spain. Impoverished, Oñate died in Spain in the same year—with his honor restored.

Oñate is remembered for opening up New Mexico for future settlement, for establishing the first permanent colony there, and for finding a more direct northerly route to New Mexico from New Spain. Today visitors to New Mexico can still see Oñate's name carved on the face of the huge sandstone mesa called El Morro (popularly called "Inscription Rock"). It was on his return from the Gulf of California that Oñate stopped there to carve "Pasó por aquí" [there passed by here] "Don Juan de Oñate . . . 1605."

Orellana, Francisco de

Spanish
b 1511?; Trujillo, Estremadura
d 1546; Amazon, Brazil
Explored Amazon River; crossed South America

According to his own account, Francisco de Orellana participated "in the conquest of Lima . . . and Cuzco and in the pursuit of the Inca . . ." when FRANCISCO PIZARRO conquered what is now Peru (1531–34). In 1541 he joined Gonzalo Pizarro on the first recorded expedition eastward across the Andes in search of the fabled **El Dorado** and the "Land of Cinnamon." Quite unintentionally, however, Orellana became the first European to cross South America via the Amazon River. As a result of his Amazon adventure, he was accused of treason and desertion by Gonzalo Pizarro; these charges have echoed throughout the ensuing centuries.

Orellana, a kinsman of Francisco Pizarro, was born in Trujillo, Spain, about 1511. Sometime during his youth (probably around 1527) he traveled to the New World in search of fame, fortune, and adventure. Though the exact location of his landing is not known, it more than likely was in present-day Panama, since the Pizarro family had some power there. When Francisco Pizarro left to conquer Peru in 1531, Orellana accompanied him and distinguished himself in the campaign against the Incas. During one battle he lost an eye.

Once Peru was under Pizarro's control, Orellana established residence in Portoviejo, on the coast of present-day Ecuador. He went to war again to help repulse Indian attacks at Cuzco and Lima and also fought on the side of Pizarro in the conquistadorial war against DIEGO DE ALMAGRO for control of Cuzco. In order to keep the other **conquistadores** from challenging his control, Pizarro dispatched them to explore and conquer new lands, and Orellana was commissioned to explore the province of Culata. After conquering Culata, he reestablished a destroyed Spanish settlement on the present-day site of Guayaquil, Ecuador, in 1537.

In 1541 Orellana joined Gonzalo Pizarro (Francisco's half brother) on an expedition to explore east of the Andes in search of the cinnamon forests (cinnamon was valued almost as much as gold) and the fabled El Dorado, or "gilded one." El Dorado was reputed to be a king who covered himself in gold dust daily, then washed it off in a lake as his subjects showered him with emeralds and gold objects. Driven by their insatiable thirst for riches, the conquistadores were ready to face any hardships in order to find this lake filled with gold.

Having missed the departure from Quito (Ecuador) of the main expeditionary force, Orellana and his small contingent endured near starvation and Indian attacks before they overtook Pizarro. Friar Gaspar de Carvajal, the official chronicler of the expedition, noted that Orellana "had still left only a sword and a shield" by the time he reached the main group. By Christmas 1541 the Spaniards had set up camp on the Coca River. They were exhausted and nearly starved and had lost all their Indian slaves to disease. They had found no great wealth and were reduced to living on "grass, nuts, and poisonous worms." At this point, Orellana was sent downstream with fifty-seven men in a small boat and ten canoes to search for food.

Sailing down the Coca into the Napo River, Orellana's party traveled 700 miles through uninhabited country where there was nothing edible available. Their provisions ran out, and they "were eating nothing but leather, belts and soles of shoes, cooked with certain herbs" when they arrived at an Indian village on January 9, 1542, and obtained food through trading and friendly overtures. It was at this point that Orellana decided to continue downstream to the Northern Ocean (the Atlantic), a decision that would excite controversy for centuries to come. Did he callously abandon Pizarro, as he was accused of doing, or did he and his men believe that to return upstream against the swift current would be impossible? Modern scholarship supports the latter reason, although surviving documents give conflicting evidence.

After persuading the Indians to help build

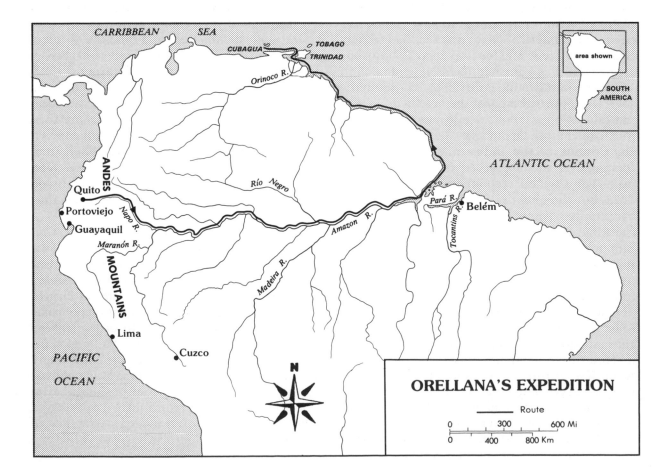

ORELLANA'S EXPEDITION

Route

0   300   600 Mi
0   400   800 Km

another boat, Orellana and his group resumed their journey on April 24 and by June 3 had reached another river, which Orellana named the Río Negro (a major branch of the Amazon). Orellana heard stories of a tribe of tall, white, women warriors to whom many Indian villages paid tribute. These women permitted no men in their villages, except once a year for mating purposes, and sent male children to be raised in their fathers' villages. Their leader reportedly ate from gold and silver bowls, and they wore garments made from llama wool. Carvajal not only records the legend of these women, but also reports that ten to twelve of them had been encountered during a battle with an Indian tribe. He describes them as being "very robust" and "doing as much fighting as ten men." Orellana called them Amazons, since they resembled the Amazons of Greek legend, who were supposedly a warrior tribe of women living north of the Black Sea.

The expedition continued the length of the Amazon, reaching the Atlantic on August 26, 1542, after fighting the bores (great tidal surges) at the river's mouth. "Without either pilot, compass, or anything useful for navigation," and with blankets for sails, Orellana's expedition struggled along the South American coast. The two boats were separated at one point but were able to reunite at the island of Cubagua.

Carvajal's account of this epic journey indicates that it covered over 3,000 miles down the Amazon and its tributaries through unknown territory. It was primarily a trip of survival rather than one of exploration. Most of the party's time was spent obtaining food, either from natural sources or from the Indians through trading or pillaging. The group also had to cope with extreme heat, swarms of biting insects, man-eating piranha fish, and giant capybura (huge aquatic rodents).

In May 1543 Orellana returned to Valladolid, Spain, where he tried to get royal backing to return to the Amazon region to explore and settle the area. In an order dated February 13, 1544, King Charles I of Spain made Orellana governor-general of the lands he had discovered (named New Andalucia), giving him permission to explore and colonize them. However, more than a year passed before Orellana acquired adequate financing and satisfied the royal inspectors. Then, with four ships and his young wife aboard, he left Sanlúcar on May 11, 1545—against the orders of the king's officials—and

arrived on the Brazilian coast just before Christmas 1545. He had already lost a ship and many men, and his expedition continued to suffer from shipwrecks and desertions. During a troubled attempt by the expedition to travel up the Amazon in 1546, Orellana—weak and frustrated—died.

Francisco de Orellana was the first European to successfully navigate the length of the Amazon, from its beginnings in the foothills of the Peruvian Andes to its mouth at present-day Belém, Brazil—an amazing accomplishment, however inadvertent. Though the river's mouth had been discovered in 1500, the river itself was known as the Marañón when Orellana traversed it. However, as a direct result of his stories of the Amazon women living in the vicinity of the continent's largest and most important river, it has been called the Amazon ever since his incredible journey.

• Palliser, John

Irish
b January 29, 1817; Comragh, Waterford
d August 18, 1887; Comragh, Waterford
Explored western Canada

A wealthy man who spent a large part of his time hunting, John Palliser turned his passion for sport into something useful when he volunteered to survey a large section of southwestern Canada for the British government. During various hunting trips, especially on the American plains, Palliser had learned the art of living off the land in a wilderness occupied primarily by Native Americans.

Palliser's published account of his adventures on the American prairies in 1847 and 1848, addressed to "my brother sportsmen of England, Ireland, and Scotland" (*Solitary Rambles*, 1853), was enormously popular, owing largely to its practical advice about what sorts of rifles to buy and how to shoot a buffalo. But its upbeat account of the daily slaughter of game on a hunting trip supported by Palliser's seemingly unlimited funds presents a disturbing contrast to the contemporary plight of poor Irish who were starving by the thousands.

Palliser next proposed investigating the potential for colonization of what was called the British West from Red River to the Canadian

Rockies and exploring the mountain passes to the west. His proposal was submitted to the Royal Geographical Society for its support in 1856. This was just seven years after the start of the great wave of migration to North America caused by the Irish famine, so Palliser's plan was responding to an urgent need. On the recommendation of both the Royal Geographical-Society and the Royal Society, the government agreed to fund an expedition under Palliser's leadership and added the territory between Lake Superior and the Red River to the area to be surveyed.

In addition to reporting on soil composition, general geography, and potential trade routes, the Palliser expedition was also to gather scientific data. Dr. James Hector was responsible for geology and natural history, as well as for the health of the party; Lieutenant Thomas Blakiston took the magnetic readings; Eugene Bourgeau made botanical collections; and John W. Sullivan worked in astronomy. The area to be surveyed extended from Lake Superior west across the southern prairies all the way to British Columbia, just north of the international border. Special attention was to be paid to finding a pass through the Rocky Mountains for a railway. This was not to be a harrowing journey through completely unknown and unpeopled land, but a thorough scientific survey of some of the most beautiful plains and spectacular mountains in North America.

Backed by the supplies and personnel of the Hudson's Bay Company, Palliser and company spent the summer of 1857 traveling from Sault Ste. Marie (in present-day Ontario) to Red River Settlement (now Winnipeg, Manitoba). From there they traveled along Canada's border with the United States until they were about a third of the way through Saskatchewan, then turned northwest as far as the bend in the South Saskatchewan River. They wintered at Fort Carlton, though Palliser himself traveled back overland to Montréal and New York to negotiate with the British colonial office for more time and money and to repair damaged scientific instruments.

In the spring and summer of 1858 the company divided to seek out additional passes through the Rockies besides the Athabasca Pass, which had been used for over a quarter of a century by fur traders. Palliser, now returned, explored North Kananaskis Pass and North Kootenay Pass before joining the rest of the party at Fort Edmonton, Alberta, for the winter. Hector explored the Kicking Horse Pass, which later became the route used by the Canadian Pacific Railway, and Vermilion Pass.

The next year, more time was spent surveying the southern plains and foothills east of the Rockies, and Palliser once again took the North Kootenay Pass through the Rockies. This time he pressed on to the Columbia River at Fort Colvile, where Hector joined him after having negotiated the Howse Pass and the Kootenay Valley. Together they traveled overland and downstream to Portland and then by steamboat to Victoria on Vancouver Island. The journey with horses and on foot had been difficult, and Palliser came to the mistaken conclusion that no railway could be affordably built through the Canadian Rockies. But his accurate charts of the region were the basis for all future work in the region, and his identification of a belt of fertile land beyond the most arid sections of the southern prairies was instrumental in forwarding plans for subsequent settlement.

Palliser continued his travels and in 1869, while hunting walrus, sailed 30 miles north of Novaya Zemlya in Siberia—a pioneering effort. He could have rounded Cape Zhelaniye and reached the Kara Sea if he had not earlier picked up the crew of a wrecked fishing vessel and consequently run out of supplies. He then headed south and passed into the Kara Sea through the Kara Strait. His final years were spent managing his Irish estates and performing public duties as a justice of the peace.

• Park, Mungo

Scottish
b September 10, 1771; Fowlshiels, Selkirkshire
d January 1806?; near Bussa, Nigeria
Explored Niger River

One of the first explorers sponsored by England's famed African Association, Doctor Mungo Park traced the northern reaches of the Niger River and settled an age-old question as to the direction of its flow. His first glimpse of the river, in July 1796, followed an arduous eleven-month journey during which he was robbed and imprisoned and also experienced near-fatal bouts of fever and starvation. Return-

Mungo Park. Library of Congress.

ing safely to England, he published a best-selling account of his adventures and earned international fame for his achievements.

The son of a farmer, Park was educated as a surgeon at Edinburgh University and in 1792 became a medical officer on an East India Company ship. While stationed in Sumatra, Park studied the island's animal and plant life, discovering eight new fish species that he later described in a London science journal. His work impressed English scientist JOSEPH BANKS, founder of the Association for Promoting the Discovery of the Interior Parts of Africa (also known as the African Association). Seeking an able traveler who possessed "good temper and conciliatory manner" to explore the Niger River, Banks chose the affable young Scot for the assignment.

Arriving on the west coast of Africa in July 1795, Park traveled only 200 miles inland before becoming ill, delaying the expedition by several months. He used his recuperation period, in the village of Pisania on the banks of the Gambia River, to study the local language and customs before proceeding north to the Senegal River.

Park had hoped to travel into the interior with a caravan, but the suspicious native tribes of the region refused to accompany him. He was consequently forced to cross the river basin with only two servants, making him easy prey for the robbers who took all his money and possessions on Christmas Day in the Senegalese kingdom of Kajaaga. After traveling on foot for several days through forests and swamps as well as mountain terrain, he was taken prisoner by Arab soldiers from the kingdom of Ludamar.

Park was held captive for several months by the Arabs, who had never before seen a white man, and regarded him with a mixture of hostility and fascination. Increasingly fearful that he would be murdered, Park escaped in early July and, despite the loss of all his possessions, chose to proceed toward the Niger rather than retreat to the west coast. He nearly died of thirst on the first day of his flight but was saved when a thunderstorm enabled him to suck the rainfall out of his clothing. Luck was on his side again when he encountered a group of refugees whom he was able to accompany to Ségou (in present-day Mali), a market town on the banks of the Niger River. Reaching his destination at the end of July, he caught his first glimpse of the river at daybreak and later described the experience as follows:

> [L]ooking forwards, I saw with infinite pleasure the object of my mission—the long-sought-for majestic Niger, glittering to the morning sun, as broad as the Thames at Westminster, and flowing slowly to the eastward. I hastened to the brink, and having drunk of the water, lifted up my fervent thanks in prayer to the Great Ruler of all things, for having thus far crowned my endeavors with success.

Hoping to meet with King Mansong, who ruled the territory, Park remained in Ségou for several days. Again the presence of a white stranger upset the local citizens, but in this case their discomfort worked to Park's advantage. Officials of the court gave the penniless explorer a large sum of money in return for his promise to leave the area. While his mission was officially completed, Park could not resist using some of his windfall to continue his investigation of the Niger. He traveled downstream for six days and reached the town of Silla before realizing that both the heavy tropical rains and the presence of hostile tribesmen nearby would make further travel too difficult and dangerous.

Park began his return trip in August, only to encounter many of the same troubles that had plagued him en route to the Niger. Suspicion and animosity persisted among many of the tribes of the region, and again he was robbed of nearly all his belongings except his hat, which concealed his journal notes. Park also suffered another bout of fever and was nursed back to health by the inhabitants of a small village on the Niger, mainly because they were awed by his ability to write. Joining a westward caravan in April, he reached Pisania two months later, this time by a more southerly route to the Gambia. The small group of European settlers on the Gambia, who had assumed Park to be dead, did not recognize the haggard, exhausted explorer. After proving his identity, however, he earned their congratulations on becoming the first explorer to return from the unknown interior territory.

Greater glory awaited Park in London, where he returned at Christmas and prepared a report on his expedition. Publication of *Travels in the Interior Districts of Africa* made him an instant celebrity as Europeans savored its blend of adventure, humor, and poignancy. Park earned a large sum of money from the book, which was translated into many languages, and looked forward to a lucrative career as a now-famous physician. But although he married in 1799 and set up a medical practice in Peeblesshire, Scotland, his enchantment with African exploration prevailed. After repeated requests, he finally won permission from the English government to lead another expedition to follow the Niger to the end of its course.

Park's insistence that the mystery of the Niger was far from solved proved to be correct. In fact, his discovery of the river's eastern flow had caused more confusion than it had eliminated. While he had ended speculation that the Niger was a tributary of the Nile, Park had not yet explored thoroughly enough to learn that the Niger turns sharply southward below Timbuktu. Therefore, he wrongly suspected the Niger of linking with the Congo (or Zaire) River to the east and hoped to prove this theory as he embarked up the Gambia River in April 1805.

Starting with an expedition of forty, Park sailed as far as Kaiaf before traveling overland to the Niger. Malaria and dysentery (an acute intestinal disease) were rampant among the crew during this rainy season, however, and only eleven remained when the party reached Bamako (in what is now Mali) and sighted the Niger in August. This number had dwindled to five by the time Park reached Sansanding, to the north of Ségou, and set sail down the river in the company of a guide and three servants.

What Europeans learned of Park's journey beyond this point was revealed in fragments of information provided by local tribes long after his disappearance. He apparently traveled the river past Timbuktu, where it curves sharply southward, and traveled more than half its remaining length before the rapids at Bussa (in present-day Nigeria) blocked his passage. Evidently he had previously incurred the wrath of many communities along the river by withholding the tolls they requested, and this may have accounted for a local tribe's attack on the expedition party at Bussa. According to one of his former servants, Park fell in the rapids and drowned while trying to flee his assailants.

· Parry, William Edward

English
b December 19, 1790; Bath
d July 8, 1855; Ems, Germany
Explored Canadian Arctic from Baffin Bay to Beaufort Sea and Norwegian Arctic north of Svalbard

Rear Admiral Sir William Edward Parry was the most successful Arctic explorer of the first half of the nineteenth century. By combining meticulous planning, keen observation, good humor, and good luck, Parry was able to chart a major portion of the **archipelago** that lies between the west coast of Greenland and the Beaufort Sea. He thus broke the barrier that had separated Europe from much of the Arctic since the great voyages of WILLIAM BAFFIN in the early seventeenth century. His expedition of 1819–20 marked the beginning of the modern era of Arctic exploration.

Parry got his sea legs early, joining the navy in 1803 at the age of thirteen. He immediately went to sea in the Channel Fleet, blockading the French coast of the English Channel, then to the North Sea and the Baltic, quickly working his way up the ranks. From 1810 to 1813 he received Arctic training as a lieutenant aboard

William Edward Parry. National Portrait Gallery, London.

the *Alexandria*, a **frigate** assigned to protect the whaling fleet off Spitsbergen (now part of Svalbard). During these years he became so accomplished as a navigator that a training manual he wrote for his squadron, *Nautical Astronomy by Night*, was published in 1816. This book impressed the second secretary of the navy, JOHN BARROW, who in 1818 put Parry (who had just returned from service in North America) in command of the *Alexander*. Parry's assignment was to accompany John Ross's *Isabella* on the navy's first effort after the Napoleonic Wars to use its fleet for the purpose of discovery.

This mission to the waters west of Greenland was notable only because it confirmed the authenticity of William Baffin's account of his voyage to the region more than two centuries earlier. Ross's mission had not been simply to rediscover Baffin Bay, but to probe the inlets on its western shore for channels that might lead west. The goal was actually the same as Baffin's had been—to find a Northwest Passage to the Pacific around North America—but John Barrow was convinced that the modern British navy should be able to succeed where the Elizabethans and Jacobeans had failed. (For a more complete discussion of the passage, see MARTIN FROBISHER.)

Ross's failure to find such a passage was such a disappointment to Barrow that when Parry pointed out to him that Ross may have been misled by a mountainous mirage into thinking that Lancaster Sound was a dead end, Barrow was quick to respond. He put Parry in charge of an expedition to return to Baffin Bay the following year.

The 375-ton vessel *Hecla* and the less seaworthy **brig** *Griper* were loaded with supplies to last three years and left England on May 11, 1819. Soon Parry was able to show that he was right about Ross's error. But he could not have been prepared for the thrill in store for him when he sailed through the wide channel of Lancaster Sound. After boldly charting a course directly through the pack ice in Davis Strait, Parry not only slipped past Ross's mirage in Lancaster Sound but kept sailing west, turning south into Prince Regent Inlet when ice blocked further progress temporarily, but again threading his way westward through the broken sea ice until he reached what is now Melville Island. Suddenly, the Admiralty's fantastically optimistic instructions to sail through the Bering Strait and on to Siberia did not seem so farfetched.

In fact, by reaching Melville Island, Parry had succeeded in passing through the major land obstacles in the way of a Northwest Passage and thus in charting the link between the Atlantic and Arctic oceans. Unfortunately, the sea so far north never clears of ice sufficiently to allow an open water passage, as Parry discovered. But this in itself was worth knowing. The mere feat of reaching the 110° West longitude mark was enough to win Parry accolades (and a £5,000 reward from the British Parliament).

On September 22 Parry decided to stop fighting the ice in Melville Sound. His crew sawed a long channel through the ice pack back to Melville Island to set up winter quarters at what came to be called Winter Harbour. During the many years of Arctic exploration a wide variety of methods for coping with the long, frigid winters had been tried, but none can compare in results with the Parry method. Rather than enforce a dour military discipline, Parry turned the *Hecla* into a "winter resort" headquarters, with music, theater, opera (Parry composed an operetta called *North-West Passage*), a newspaper, a school, and an exercise area. The scene

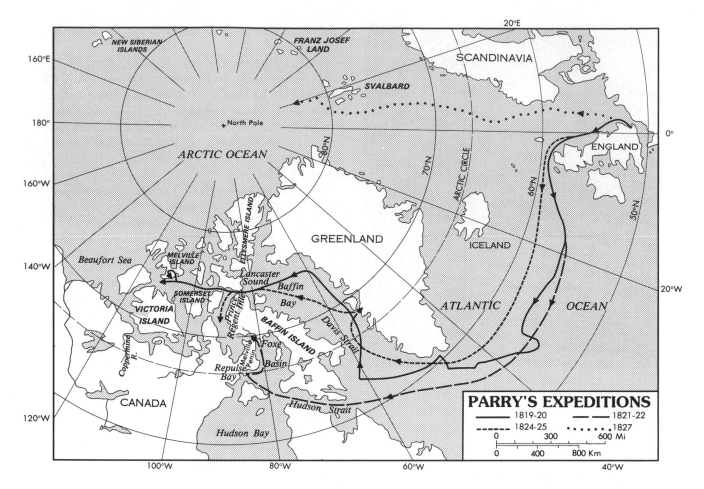

was closer to Parry's native Bath (a middle-class vacation spot and health spa) than to the frozen Arctic prison that it in fact was. Only one man died during this first wintering of Europeans in the islands north of America, from a disease unrelated to the conditions. The one case of **scurvy** among his crew was quickly cleared up the following summer.

It helped that his officers were all young and, apparently, good natured. Parry made a point of picking sailors who would get along, and he knew how to accomplish this: "Good wages, good feeling, and good treatment are not always to be had, poor fellows! and as we bear a tolerably good character in these respects, we have been quite overwhelmed with volunteers," wrote Parry. Self-congratulatory words, to be sure, but nevertheless characteristic of the tone set by Parry on his remarkable voyage to the rim of the Arctic Ocean.

In late spring, an expedition explored Melville Island to its north coast, using the rather lumbering cart methods that were to typify later naval efforts in the Arctic. When the ice

cleared in midsummer, Parry tried unsuccessfully to push farther west but gave up at Cape Dundas. His voyage home was smoothly executed, and on his return (Peterhead, Scotland, was reached October 29, 1820), Parry was feted and promoted to commander.

At this point, Parry believed that a Northwest Passage could be negotiated (if at all) only farther south, along the coast of the North American mainland. While JOHN FRANKLIN was exploring the coast from the mouth of the Coppermine River east toward Hudson Bay, Parry advised the Admiralty to try to reach the waters of Prince Regent Inlet (which he had explored from the north) from the south via Hudson Bay. In fact, such a link exists in Fury and Hecla Strait north of Melville Peninsula, but it has only been navigated in modern times by icebreakers, so Parry's next voyage was doomed to failure.

Both Parry and Barrow realized that the waters north of Hudson Bay, in Foxe Basin, had been iced over during every attempt to navigate them since the seventeenth century (see

LUKE FOXE), but they believed that the unusually favorable ice conditions warranted one more try. Still, Parry was "confident another Expedition will end in disappointment," especially when the results were compared to his first. But the important thing was to keep up the effort, not least because of "a fear of the Russians being beforehand with us" (that is, penetrating to the Atlantic from Alaska and claiming sovereignty over the route).

In May 1821 Parry set off with the *Fury* and the *Hecla*. Skillfully weaving through the ice fields of Frozen Strait, he arrived at Repulse Bay on August 22, well before winter. After confirming Christopher Middleton's report of 1742 that the bay had no outlet, he proceeded north up the coast of Melville Peninsula in search of one.

When winter came, Parry once again set up his seasonal quarters (off present-day Winter Island), this time with elaborate costumes for the theater and an unusual performance of Richard Sheridan's *The Rivals* in which every member of the crew played a part. The isolation was punctuated by visits from local **Inuits**, who set up a village of igloos near the ships. Parry took careful notes describing their customs and songs. He did not just listen to their songs, but sang back. "I thought some of them, especially Iligliuk, would have gone into fits with delight, when I introduced our names mingled with theirs, into a song we were singing," he wrote. Iligliuk was an intelligent woman whose knowledge of local geography and skill as an artist laid the foundations for Parry's efforts for the following two years when she sketched Melville Peninsula and the strait to its north, leading from Foxe Basin in the east to the waters at the bottom of Prince Regent Inlet in the west.

In the summer of 1822 Parry followed Iligliuk's map up the coast to the strait, which he named Fury and Hecla Strait after his ships. There he waited in vain for the ice to melt—not just for the rest of the summer, but for the bulk of the following summer as well. The time was not all wasted, however, since Parry and his crew explored the strait and much of Melville Peninsula by foot and boat. More significantly, Parry began the long process through which Europeans learned from the Inuits how to travel in the Arctic. His attempts at dogsledding were not very successful, but one of the young crew members, JAMES CLARK ROSS, would

eventually become famous for his mastery of the art.

On his return to England in October 1823, Parry found that his failure to find a passage had not dampened the navy's enthusiasm for Arctic work. The British public was also excited by his efforts, especially since Franklin had returned from his daring exploration of the open coastal waters east of the Coppermine River. Accordingly, Parry was sent in 1824 with the *Fury* and the *Hecla* to explore the southern sectors of Prince Regent Inlet.

As he had predicted, the results were once again disappointing. His old course through Davis Strait and Lancaster Sound was not so accommodating this time. It took two summers to penetrate Prince Regent Inlet, which he had so easily sailed into in 1819. Then, as the ships were heading down the inlet's west coast, they were squeezed ashore by the ice pack. This seriously damaged the *Fury*, making it impossible for her to survive another such grounding, which happened a month later, on August 21. All that could be done was to transfer the crew to the *Hecla* and return to England. The extra supplies were set ashore on Somerset Island, where they later saved the lives of the John Ross expedition of 1829–33. Bad luck or good, Parry always performed flawlessly. The navy recognized this and on his return made him **hydrographer** to the Admiralty (this put him in charge of mapping operations on a global scale).

Despite a worsening case of rheumatism, Parry made one more Arctic voyage. In the spring and summer of 1827, he became the first in a long line of intrepid, sometimes fanatical, explorers who tried to reach the North Pole. His method, which consisted of pulling heavy **boat-sledges** over the polar ice cap north of Spitsbergen, was completely inadequate. He could cover no more than 7 miles a day, and his progress was often negated by the southward drift of the ice pack. Still, he reached 82°45′ North latitude on July 23, a mark not surpassed until 1876. When Parry returned to England, he was knighted and honored with a doctorate from Oxford. He then held a succession of important civilian jobs until his death in 1855.

SUGGESTED READING: Pierre Berton, *The Arctic Grail* (Viking, 1988); Brendan Lehane, *The Northwest Passage* (Time-Life, 1981); Jeannette Mirsky, *To the Arctic*

(University of Chicago Press, 1970); Ann Parry, *Parry of the Arctic* (Chatto and Windus, 1963).

Pasha, Emin. See **Schnitzer, Eduard.**

• Payer, Julius von

Austrian
b September 1, 1842; Teplitz-Schönau
d August 30, 1915; Bled, Yugoslavia
Explored Russian Arctic; discovered Franz
  Josef Land

Despite centuries of effort by northern Europeans to explore the Arctic north of Eurasia, the basic geographic questions about the area had still not been answered when in 1871 a lieutenant in the Austro-Hungarian army, Julius von Payer, began making preparations for his voyage, which yielded the discovery of Franz Josef Land. Coming from Austria, Payer had an advantage his English and Dutch predecessors lacked—experience climbing the glaciated Alps, which he had used to good effect while on a German expedition to the east coast of Greenland in 1869 (where the tallest peak in Franz Josef Fjord was named after him).

Was there a continental landmass on the Antarctic scale north of Novaya Zemlya, or was there a frozen or open sea? If the sea was open, did the Gulf Stream cut a passageway through the ice barrier, or was there an impenetrable ring around it? These were the questions Payer and his naval counterpart, Lieutenant Karl Weyprecht, sought to address when they sailed from Tromsø, Norway, in June 1871 on a reconnaissance mission aboard the chartered Norwegian ship *Isborn*. Hoping to follow the Gulf Stream north, they were disappointed to find that from Spitsbergen (now part of Svalbard) to Novaya Zemlya there was no break in the ice. They then decided to come back to Novaya Zemlya with an expedition equipped for ice travel.

To that purpose, the 200-ton steamer *Tegethoff* left Germany on June 13, 1872, with a multinational crew of twenty-two, reaching Novaya Zemlya on August 3. On August 21 the ship became stuck in the ice off the north coast of Novaya Zemlya and drifted to the northwest all winter. Payer and his crew set themselves up to survive the winter in the hope of new

discoveries the following summer. This they accomplished, sighting from the ship the northernmost **archipelago** of Eurasia, which they named Franz Josef Land after their emperor, on August 30, 1873. A second winter then had to be spent on the ship.

After making several **sledge** trips around the region in the spring of 1874, stopping periodically to scale its peaks, Payer came to the mistaken conclusion that the sprinkling of small islands was actually two large landmasses. He was also tricked by the sharp outlines of Arctic fog into believing that another large land lay to the north (something FRIDTJOF NANSEN later disproved).

Having charted the new territory, there remained the difficult task of making it home. The ice-bound *Tegethoff* was abandoned on May 20, 1874, and the long journey by the ship's three boats began, first over ice, then on the open sea. Fortunately, a Russian fishing boat picked up the party on August 21, just south of Matochkin Shar.

After emblazoning his emperor's name on the map of the Arctic, Payer was able to retire in comfort. He took up painting and became widely admired for his depiction of Arctic scenes.

• Peary, Robert Edwin

American
b May 6, 1856; Cresson, Pennsylvania
d February 20, 1920; Washington, D.C.
Explored Arctic and Greenland; first to reach
  vicinity of North Pole

Still generating controversy seventy years after his death, Robert Edwin Peary (often referred to as a rear admiral, because Congress voted him a pension appropriate for that rank) was the first to present a plausible, if unverifiable, claim to have reached the North Pole. By devoting himself to Arctic exploration for a quarter of a century, Peary slowly built up the necessary inventory of technologies, strategies, and resources that allowed him to penetrate deep into the ice-covered Arctic Ocean. Though there was little of scientific value to gain from it, Peary's push to reach the North Pole captured the imagination of nearly everyone. For Americans in particular, it seemed to fill the gap left by the

Robert Edwin Peary.   Library of Congress.

disappearance of the frontier they had sought to conquer for so long. Many also believed it was a way for the ambitious young nation to win glory. President Theodore Roosevelt wrote the introduction to Peary's best-selling account of his voyage to the pole, proclaiming that "we, his fellow Americans, are his debtors."

Peary himself admitted that he was unaccountably obsessed with his quest. The best he could do in explaining it was to say that he had caught "Arctic fever" and was possessed, like an artist or an inventor, by an idea. Of course, he won the fame and wealth he had hoped to gain from it, but there were easier—and probably more satisfying—ways for a man of his talents and intelligence. When in 1909, at the age of fifty-three, he finally attained the pole, he experienced a major anticlimax: "It seems all so simple and commonplace." There was nothing particular to observe, only more polar ice, and he could not even be sure where the exact point lay.

Aside from a fascination for the Arctic shared by many of his era who read of the adventures of the famous Arctic explorers, two personal factors contributed to Peary's drive to live at the edge of the world. After a brilliant undergraduate career at Bowdoin College (a major

in civil engineering, he graduated second in his class), Peary spent two years living with his mother in Fryeburg, Maine, with nothing but odd jobs to keep him busy. The petty gossip and Victorian smugness of the small town drove him to desperation, and he jumped at the chance to work in Washington as a draftsman with the U.S. Coast and Geodetic Survey. He jumped again at the chance to go to Nicaragua in 1881 as a commissioned civil engineer with the navy.

Peary also had a need, which seems to have been encouraged by the literature he read as a young man, to find and tap the "restless wild essence of life," as he expressed it in an ode he wrote in college. There was a yearning for escape from the tired conventions of civilization, a need to return to a more elemental existence. The Arctic was one of the last places where "the poetry of the world" had not yet been spoiled by the "pressure of man's foot," where the "grand old primal elements" had not yet been mastered. But Peary never tried to melt into the Arctic scenery or identify with the **Inuit**, as the American explorer CHARLES FRANCIS HALL had done. His single-minded pursuit of the pole turned the raw Arctic into something he must master. As for the Inuit, though he admired and copied their skills, he always felt himself to be their moral and intellectual superior.

Peary's involvement with the Arctic cannot be separated from his literary career. He was as much a journalist as an explorer, and much of his living derived from book, magazine, and newspaper contracts. He was always the hero at the center of the adventure, but his spare writing style had the same kind of admirable economy as his expeditions, and his books were immensely popular. His journals were not so much records of scientific data as rough notes for his publications—a fact that got him into trouble when people wanted to see proof that he had reached the pole. Like a reporter with a scoop, he jealously guarded his plans and findings, refusing his assistants the right to publish competing accounts in order to heighten the financial potential of his own.

Peary's first brush with the Arctic came in 1886, after reading NILS ADOLF ERIK NORDENSKIÖLD's account of his trip to Greenland. Peary received leave from the navy in order to explore,

at his mother's expense, part of Greenland's west coast and succeeded in penetrating 100 miles inland with a young Danish companion (not as far as Nordenskiöld's Lapps had gone, though Peary boasted that he had gone farther than any other explorer). After returning to Nicaragua to head a survey of possible routes for an interoceanic canal in 1886, he came back to make a reconnaissance of northern Greenland in 1891 with his new wife, Josephine Diebitsch Peary. The privately financed, seven-person party included his servant and assistant for the remainder of his Arctic career, MATTHEW HENSON, and his future archrival, Dr. FREDERICK ALBERT COOK. After wintering on Inglefield Gulf in northwestern Greenland, Peary traveled 500 miles by dog **sledge** with a Norwegian companion, Eivind Astrup, to Independence Fjord on Greenland's northeast coast. This was the beginning of his work that would eventually prove that Greenland was an island (though in his eagerness to create a sensation, he dressed up his early findings to anticipate the desired result).

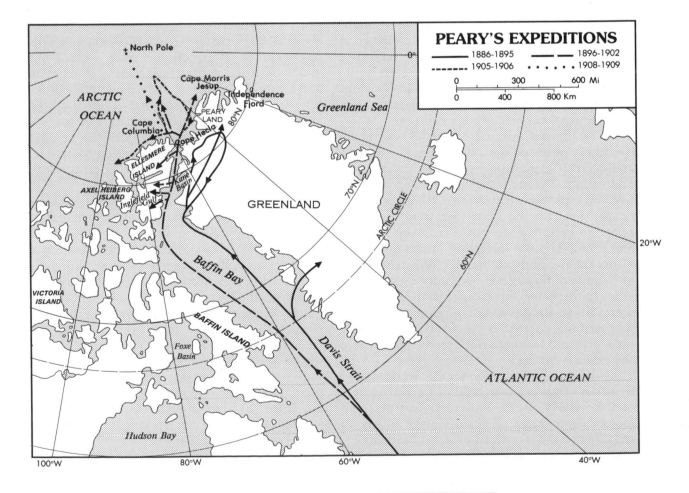

With this successful sledge trip, which doubled the distance FRIDTJOF NANSEN had covered to the south a few years earlier, Peary became instantly famous. A lecture tour provided finances for a new expedition, and the U.S. Navy rather reluctantly granted him another leave. He returned to Inglefield Gulf in 1893 to retrace much of his previous route and hopefully start north to the pole. However, when severe weather rendered the expedition a failure, he stayed the following year with Henson and Hugh Lee while the rest of the party returned home. On April 1, 1895, they returned to Independence Fjord but made no further progress. In order to provide some evidence of achievement, they brought back from the vicinity of Cape York south of Inglefield Gulf two large meteorites that had been used by the Inuit as a source of iron. Peary justified the removal of their property on the grounds that white traders like himself now supplied all the knives and metal they needed.

In the summers of 1896 and 1897 Peary returned to Greenland in order to remove a 100-ton meteorite, study Inuit culture, develop exploration techniques, and bring some unfortunate Inuits back to the United States for anthropological study. (They soon died.) Back home he stayed busy lecturing and cultivating rich supporters, the chief of whom, Morris K. Jesup, soon formed the Peary Arctic Club, which would support Peary's ventures for the next decade. An influential friend secured yet another long leave for him from the very reluctant navy.

On July 4, 1898, Peary set off on the *Windward* to try a new route (for him) to the pole, through Kane Basin north of Etah. While wintering there, he became so worried that OTTO SVERDRUP (who was wintering on his ship, the *Fram*, 40 miles to the south) would beat him to the pole that he traveled in the dead of the severe Arctic winter to Fort Conger, still farther north on Hall Basin on the east coast of Ellesmere Island. When he arrived, Henson pulled off Peary's boots to find that several frostbitten toes had come off with them. Peary then had to wait until the spring of 1900 to set off again, but this time he was successful in reaching the northernmost point of Greenland (named Cape Morris Jesup by him) on May 13. He was unable to proceed very far over the sea ice toward the pole, however. This expedition finally proved that Greenland was an island.

Peary stayed in the Arctic another two years, shaken by his failure to get near the pole and by some personal tragedies. He rallied in the spring of 1902 and tried another route: off Cape Hecla on northern Ellesmere Island. He succeeded in attaining a record northern latitude for the Western Hemisphere at 84°16′ on April 21, but was delayed by open water and slow supply sledges.

Discouraged only temporarily, Peary returned home and soon had raised sufficient funds to construct a ship modeled on Nansen's *Fram*, but with a pointed bow for penetrating the ice. The 184-foot-long steam vessel *Roosevelt* left New York on July 16, 1905, and reached the northeastern coast of Ellesmere Island at Cape Sheridan before winter. On February 9, the expedition's support parties left Point Moss west of Cape Hecla to set up supply depots on the sea ice to the north, and on March 6 the full expedition set off. After once again being delayed by the big lead (a channel of water through ice) above 84° North latitude, Peary, Henson, and some Inuit members of the party forged on alone to reach a record northernmost point at 87°6′ latitude on April 21, 1906. (Critics, however, have doubted he could have gotten this far.) With the condition of his dogs deteriorating and his supplies dwindling, Peary was forced to turn the small party back within 180 miles of their goal. Disappointed again, Peary struck off to explore the northern coast of Ellesmere Island before heading home. On this journey he made it to the northern tip of Axel Heiberg Island, where he reported sighting land still farther to the northwest. He named it Crocker Land, but it was later found to be nonexistent.

Peary's last attempt to reach the pole was a remarkable feat of planning and endurance, the culmination of almost a quarter of a century of experience. Clothes, sleeping quarters, sledges, food, dogs, methods of supply—all had been chosen and developed to the point of perfection. Using the same route as in 1906, with slight alterations to account for the big lead, the first supply party left Cape Columbia (the northernmost point of Ellesmere Island) on February 28, 1909. The second party left soon afterwards, and on March 1 Peary and Henson departed in the final group. After making excellent time, Peary and Henson and their four Inuit companions made the final dash of 133 nautical miles alone on April 2. It was still early in the season—early enough, Peary hoped, to beat the

At the pole.   Hulton-Deutsch Collection.

disturbance of the ice caused by the pull of the moon and warmer weather each spring. After five days of record-breaking marching, with very little sleep or rest, Peary, now fifty-two, reported reaching camp just 3 miles short of the pole, at 10 A.M., April 6, 1909. In the next thirty hours he crossed the area he believed to be the actual pole, then headed back to Cape Columbia. Despite Peary's exhaustion—he was a "dead weight," according to Henson—the party made remarkable time over the beaten path home, covering 70 miles in one day.

When Peary returned to New York, he learned that his former colleague, Frederick Cook, had claimed five days earlier to have beaten him to the pole on April 21, 1908. Though no one in Peary's party gave credence to this apparently fraudulent—and soon generally discredited—claim, Peary was never able to prove to everyone's satisfaction that he himself had not lied. For Peary, who had so long and so fervently desired this singular fame, it was doubly galling to have his recognition first delayed by a pretender, then diminished by doubters. To this day, scholars, navigators, and other Arc-tic experts look for irrefutable proof that he and Cook did or did not make it. Recent work still leaves doubts about both claims, but Peary is generally recognized as the first person ever to reach the North Pole.

SUGGESTED READING: Pauling K. Angell, *To the Top of the World: The Story of Peary and Henson* (Rand McNally, 1965); Wally Herbert, *The Noose of Laurels: Robert E. Peary and the Race to the North Pole* (Atheneum, 1989); William R. Hunt, *To Stand at the Pole: The Dr. Cook–Admiral Peary Controversy* (Stein & Day, 1982); John Edward Weems, *Peary: The Explorer and the Man* (Houghton Mifflin, 1967).

• Pérez Hernández, Juan Josef

Spanish
b 1725?; Majorca
d November 2, 1775; at sea off California coast
Explored northwest coast of North America

An officer in the Spanish navy, Juan Josef Pérez Hernández escorted one of the first groups of

Spanish colonists from Mexico to Alta California (present-day California) in 1769. Five years later, he led a maritime expedition up the northwest coast of North America, reaching as far north as the islands off the southern coast of present-day Alaska.

Little is known of Pérez's life before 1767, when he was assigned to the department of San Blas on the west coast of New Spain (present-day Mexico), the administrative headquarters for Spanish naval activity to the north. A few years later, alarmed at reports that the Russians were expanding east from the Aleutian Islands, the Spanish decided to solidify their claims to North America by pushing their colonizing efforts north of Baja (Lower) California to what was then called Alta (Upper) California. In 1769, Pérez commanded the packet boat that carried some of the first colonists to San Diego and Monterey. For the next several years, he traveled to these ports regularly with supplies for the colonists.

In 1774, the Spanish command decided to send an expedition to explore the coastline north of Alta California and at the same time to look for signs of Russian expansion. Although only an ensign, Pérez was the highest ranking officer in San Blas at the time and thus was put in command of the expedition. Second-in-command was ESTÉBAN JOSÉ MARTÍNEZ. Pérez was given sealed instructions to be read only after he was at sea that commanded him to sail as far as he pleased, beyond a minimum latitude of 60° North. On his return he was to keep as close to the shore as possible and to land whenever he could do so safely. He was not to establish any settlements but was to note likely sites for future colonies and was to take possession of them by a prescribed formula: A standard possession form was to be signed by Pérez, the chaplain, and two pilots; placed in a glass bottle stoppered with pitch; and then hidden in a cairn of stones at the foot of a large wooden cross. Pérez was also to avoid settlements or ships of other nations, to treat well any Indians he met, and to make a thorough study of their customs.

Pérez read these instructions in his ship, the *Santiago*, after leaving Monterey in June 1774. Sailing northwest until he reached latitude 50°, he then turned directly north and sighted land near the present Canada-Alaska border on July 18. The next day he anchored off the northernmost of the present-day Queen Charlotte Is-

lands, where three canoes of Haida Indians came to the ship to trade. Although the language barrier prevented Pérez from questioning the Haida about their customs, the observations he recorded in his journal were rich in detail and provided many clues about the ways of the Haida. Pérez was prevented from going ashore by a lack of wind and a current that was dragging the ship seaward.

After four days in the area, Pérez sailed farther north, reaching a latitude of 55° and catching sight of what is now Cape Muzon on Dall Island off the southeastern tip of Alaska. When strong winds and currents prevented him from sailing any farther north, Pérez decided to head back without fulfilling his instructions to reach latitude 60° and without completing the crucial task of taking formal possession at the northernmost point he had reached. He did note that he was in a maze of offshore islands and that they seemed well populated with Indians who were interested in trading. Fear of being carried onto reefs or into breakers by unfavorable winds kept Pérez from examining the coast carefully both in the north and on his southward voyage.

Proceeding south, the expedition sailed along the west coast of what is now Vancouver Island, which they thought was part of the mainland. On August 8, they dropped anchor at the mouth of a large bay, later named Nootka Sound. Local Indians came out to the ship to trade. One of them must have stolen some silver spoons from Martínez; four years later, when British Captain JAMES COOK entered the sound, Cook bought the spoons, which he took as proof that the Spanish had been there before him. Pérez reported that this bay was a potentially strategic spot for a Spanish settlement, which it later became.

After one failed attempt to land at Nootka, Pérez sailed on, eventually passing the present-day Strait of Juan de Fuca without taking note of it. While they were in the vicinity of the strait, the weather was clear enough for them to see a snow-capped mountain, which Pérez named Sierra Nevada de Santa Rosalia; today it is called Mount Olympus.

By this time the crew had begun to suffer from **scurvy**, the habitual curse of those who went too long without fresh food. Perpetual fog and the unknown dangers of an uncharted sea were beginning to wear on everyone's nerves as well, and Pérez proceeded south as quickly as possible.

Although the viceroy of Mexico was not

pleased with the results of the expedition, especially with Pérez's failure to land and take formal possession anywhere along the coast, he did recommend a reward for Pérez. The ensign was then assigned as second-in-command to another rigorous exploration of northern waters in 1775 (see BRUNO DE HEZETA), from which he returned broken in health. He was buried at sea in November 1775.

• Pigafetta, Antonio Francesco
(Antonio Lombardo)

Italian
b 1491?; Vicenza, near Venice
d 1534?; Malta
Participated in and chronicled Magellan's
circumnavigation

Antonio Pigafetta was one of the few men who successfully completed FERDINAND MAGELLAN's attempted circumnavigation of the globe. His detailed journal was the only written account of that historic and perilous three-year journey.

Born to a noble family in the Lombardy region of northern Italy, Pigafetta was well schooled and well traveled as a youth, with a flair for languages. When he arrived in Seville in the summer of 1519, he already had visited many of the capitals of Europe, knew the spice trade well, and had navigated both the North Atlantic and Mediterranean. Pigafetta's connections and credentials gained him passage as a civilian observer on Magellan's expedition to reach the Spice Islands (the Moluccas) by sailing west.

Pigafetta made himself useful on the voyage by preparing glossaries of the unfamiliar languages encountered and, when **scurvy** struck early in the journey, by writing farewell messages for the dying men, which he later had wandering friars deliver. Unlike many of the crew, he drank little and was more interested in converting natives to Christianity than in pillaging their villages.

An ardent admirer of Magellan, Pigafetta supported the captain during attempted mutinies and was at his side when Magellan was killed in the Philippines. Pigafetta himself escaped death twice in the Philippines: once, he slipped off a wet bulwark while fishing and nearly drowned; later, while defending Magel-

lan, he took a poisoned arrow in the face. He colorfully described these and other adventures and hardships of the historic journey in his journal.

Pigafetta and seventeen others returned to Seville on September 8, 1522, completing the first successful circumnavigation of the world in just under three years. Immediately he reported to King Charles I of Spain, and later to officials in Venice, Paris, Lisbon, and Rome. The French version of his account was published in 1523.

He turned over a copy of his journal to the Knights Hospitalers of St. John of Jerusalem when he joined the order in 1524. In 1530 he was sent to Rhodes, where he later died defending the island from the Turks.

• Pike, Zebulon Montgomery

American
b January 5, 1779; Trenton, New Jersey
d April 27, 1813; Toronto, Canada
Explored Rocky Mountains in central Colorado

A military man from his youth until his death, Zebulon Montgomery Pike carried out two major explorations in the line of duty. On his first expedition, undertaken in 1805, he followed the Mississippi River to a lake he mistakenly believed to be its source. The following year he led an expedition to the source of the Arkansas River and to the southern Rocky Mountains, where he attempted unsuccessfully to scale the peak that now bears his name.

While still a boy, Pike joined his father's army company as a cadet and became a commissioned first lieutenant at the age of twenty. For several years he served in the frontier army. In 1805, his commanding officer, General James Wilkinson, ordered him to take a group of twenty soldiers up the Mississippi River to its source. Their mission was twofold: to inform the Indians of that area that they were now subject to the United States government and to warn the numerous British fur traders of the north that they were in American territory.

Pike and his party traveled up the Mississippi in a keelboat. When winter came on, he left some men behind in a hastily built stockade, while he and the others continued on foot, dragging their supplies behind them on sleds. After

Zebulon Montgomery Pike.   Library of Congress.

reaching Cass Lake, which Pike mistakenly thought to be the source of the Mississippi, they returned to St. Louis on April 30, 1806.

Pike's second and final expedition, undertaken just a few months after the completion of his first, is still not wholly understood by historians. While the facts are obvious, the motives behind them are clouded. Again, Pike was given his orders by General Wilkinson, who at the time was both commanding general of the United States Army and governor of the Louisiana Territory. He was also, as it turns out, being paid by the Spanish, who had great interest in what the United States might be planning for the newly acquired territory. To complicate matters further, Wilkinson has been connected with Aaron Burr's vague schemes to establish an empire in the Southwest. History has cleared Pike of any complicity in Wilkinson's double-dealings. Whatever his superior's intentions may have been, Pike believed he was serving his country, as indeed he was.

Pike's orders for his second expedition were to locate the headwaters of both the Arkansas and the Red rivers. According to the United States (but not to Spain), the upper Red River

was the boundary between Louisiana and New Spain. Pike was also to bring back whatever information he could glean about New Spain that might be of use to the United States, though his written orders instructed him to honor scrupulously the boundaries between the United States and Mexican territory. In other words, he was to spy without giving the appearance of doing so, perhaps by getting conveniently "lost" inside Spanish territory.

To add to the confusion about exactly what was going on, Wilkinson seems to have let the Spanish know about Pike's route ahead of time, for a Spanish force of 600 men led by Don Facundo Melgares marched north from New Mexico and preceded Pike to Pawnee villages in what is now Kansas that were to be one of the first stops on his journey. Having warned the Pawnees not to deal with the Americans, the Spanish turned around and marched home, leaving a broad path for Pike to follow.

In the meantime, Pike had set out from St. Louis on July 15, 1806, first delivering some Osage Indian captives to their villages on what is now the western border of Missouri and then traveling north to separate Pawnee villages in what is now Nebraska. Following Melgares' orders, the Pawnees gave Pike a hostile reception, after which he turned south until he reached the Arkansas River and then turned west to follow it into the Rockies. On November 15, the party caught sight of a mountain that looked like "a small blue cloud." The peak was actually 120 miles away, and it was November 23 before the party got close to it. At this point it appeared to be only a day's march farther, and Pike determined to take three others with him to attempt to ascend the mountain. Clad only in summer uniforms (they had no others), the men set off to scale the summit. But they had misjudged the mountain's height and distance and the ruggedness of the intervening foothills. After 3½ bitterly cold days, including one snowstorm, they gave up. Pike referred to the peak as the Great Mountain, but today it bears his name as the famous Pikes Peak.

The party spent November and December exploring the Rockies in what is now Colorado, reaching as far north as the source of the South Platte River and as far south as the Sangre de Cristo Mountains. In January, Pike left some men in a small fort on a tributary of the Arkansas and with thirteen others made a difficult winter crossing of the Sangre de Cristos. When

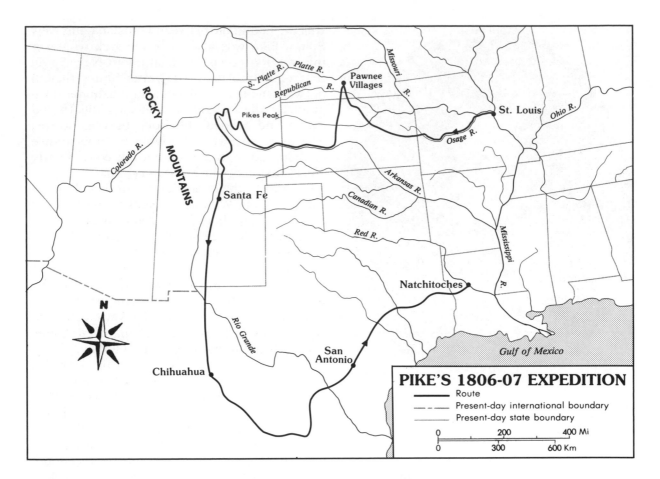

the bitter ordeal was over, six men were suffering from gangrene resulting from frostbite and had to be left behind with a promise that they would be rescued (which they were).

The others pushed on. Two weeks after leaving the Arkansas, they arrived at a branch of the Rio Grande. They were well into Spanish territory, west and north of the source of the Red River, and although Pike wrote that they "hailed [it] with fervency as the waters of the Red River," one of his men later allowed that everyone knew it was a branch of the Rio Grande. There they built a small log fort and a Dr. Robinson, a friend of Wilkinson's, set off down the river to Santa Fe to collect a trading debt. Reaching Santa Fe, he informed the Spanish of Pike's whereabouts, and by February 26 the Spanish had arrived to arrest Pike and his men. It is generally believed that Pike was being facetious when he greeted the Spanish troops with the remark, "What, is not this the Red River?"

Being captured by the Spanish seems to have been just what Pike had intended. He and his men were led to Santa Fe and then on to the governor in Chihuahua, giving Pike an excellent opportunity to observe much of the Spanish territory. His powers of observation were so great that when he returned to the United States he was able to give precise information on the number and type of Spanish troops he had seen as well as a detailed report on the Spanish military leaders who were his escorts. Pike's papers were confiscated, but otherwise he was treated royally and eventually escorted back to the United States. Pike died in 1813, a casualty of a battle near Toronto, Canada, during the War of 1812.

Prior to his death Pike published his report of the march to Santa Fe and south to Chihuahua, which has been called the most significant work to that time on northern Mexico. His ideas, though erroneous in part, were instrumental in shaping U.S. policy in the Southwest for the next forty years. First, he characterized the plains of the Southwest as a barren land with little water and no timber, basically unfit for habitation. He saw this as a benefit, containing

Americans in the land east of the Mississippi and thus preserving the union, which he felt would be endangered by a widely dispersed population. Second, he proposed that the best route from the Atlantic to Pacific lay across the Southwest from the Arkansas River to the Colorado, envisioning a sort of Southwest Passage. Third, and probably most important, he underscored the trade possibilities of Santa Fe and northern Mexico. These three themes put forth in Zebulon Pike's report were to dominate American thinking about the Southwest for many years after its publication.

Pineda, Alonso Alvarez de. See **Alvarez de Pineda, Alonso.**

• Pinzón, Martín Alonso

Spanish
b 1440?; Palos
d 1493; Palos
Explored Great Inagua Island; discovered Hispaniola

Martín Alonso Pinzón, head of a leading Spanish seafaring family, was commander of the *Pinta* during CHRISTOPHER COLUMBUS's historic voyage of discovery in 1492. It was the lookout on the *Pinta* who first sighted land; shortly thereafter, Pinzón, lured by tales of gold, broke away from Columbus to explore Babeque (present-day Great Inagua Island of the Bahamas) and subsequently discovered Hispaniola and the gold mines of Cibao.

Born about 1440 at Palos in the Andalusia region of Spain, Martín Alonso Pinzón entered the maritime trade with his younger brothers, VICENTE YÁÑEZ PINZÓN and Francisco Martín Pinzón. He traded in West Africa and the Mediterranean, gaining skill as a navigator, acquiring a wealth of information on sea routes and exotic places, and amassing a great fortune.

Controversy has surrounded Pinzón's involvement in the 1492 voyage, centering on the extent of his influence and control and the question of whether a transatlantic voyage was originally his idea. This issue stems primarily from the story that Pinzón had examined a map in the Vatican Library showing a transoceanic voyage to Japan long before Columbus received support for such a venture. Whatever the truth

Martín Alonso Pinzón.   Naval Museum, Madrid.

may be, Pinzón was without question an enthusiastic supporter of Columbus's expedition and helped acquire men, supplies, and financial backing for the undertaking.

When Columbus's fleet left Palos on August 3, 1492, Pinzón was commander of the *Pinta* with his brother Francisco as master, and his brother Vicente was in command of the *Niña*. Sighting land (most likely the Bahama Islands) on October 12, 1492, the elder Pinzón relayed the good news to Columbus, and a landing was made.

A month later, however, Pinzón deserted the two other ships to search for an island called Babeque, described by an Indian guide as a land where people gathered gold on the beaches. He failed to find any gold after a cursory search of the island he was led to, but he did subsequently discover present-day Hispaniola (the island now occupied by Haiti and the Dominican Republic). Sailing along its coast, he anchored at Puerto Blanco and penetrated the interior, where he became the first European to discover gold in the mountain ranges the Indians called Cibao.

When Pinzón heard of the shipwreck of the *Santa Maria* through the Indian "grapevine," he rejoined Columbus, who was by then on the

Niña in Hispaniola on January 16, 1493. Although Columbus forgave him for his disloyalty, Pinzón then tried to reach Spain before the Admiral in order to claim for himself all the glory for the discovery of the New World. Demoralized by his failure to arrive back first, he returned to his home in Palos in April 1493, where he died shortly thereafter from a combination of overexposure, exhaustion, and syphilis. Although made while Pinzón was being disloyal to Columbus, Pinzón's discovery of Hispaniola and its gold mines would prove significant, luring many explorers to the New World in search of their fortunes.

• Pinzón, Vicente Yáñez

Spanish
b 1463; Palos
d after 1523
Explored Central and South America

Vicente Yáñez Pinzón, a navigator who participated in the famed first voyage of CHRISTOPHER

Vicente Yáñez Pinzón. Naval Museum, Madrid.

COLUMBUS, went on to undertake several of his own expeditions to Brazil and Central America. The first and most notable took him to northeastern Brazil (this was possibly the first European exploration of that country) and on to the mouth of the Amazon River in 1500. In subsequent expeditions he explored the Yucatán peninsula, returned to Brazil, and traveled to Hispaniola (the island now occupied by Haiti and the Dominican Republic) and the Bahamas. Like his former commander, with whom he stayed on good terms, Pinzón also attempted to find a water route leading west to India.

Pinzón was one of three brothers from a wealthy family of shipowners who accompanied Columbus and helped finance his journey. Pinzón served as commander of the *Niña*, said to be the favorite ship of Columbus, and unlike his more rebellious older brother, MARTÍN ALONSO PINZÓN, remained loyal to his leader throughout the voyage. Having acquired a taste for adventure, he decided to launch his own discovery initiative after completing the 1492–93 mission with Columbus.

Setting sail from his hometown of Palos in late 1499, he reported reaching northeastern Brazil, at a cape he named Santa María de la Consolación, in January of 1500, placing Pinzón in Brazil months ahead of Portuguese explorer PEDRO ÁLVARES CABRAL. (This date of arrival has been contested by the Brazilian and Portuguese historians who recognize Cabral as the discoverer of Brazil. Some historians believe AMERIGO VESPUCCI preceded them both.) From this cape on the Brazilian coast near Recife, Pinzón was making his way northwest when he noticed that the water had changed color.

This observation, some thirty **leagues** from the coastline, led Pinzón to an important discovery. He tasted the water, found that it was fresh rather than salty, and decided to look for its source. Dubbing the body of water Mar Dulce, the Sweetwater Sea, he followed it until he reached the islands at the mouth of what is now known as the Amazon River. Fearful of its strong currents and tides, Pinzón did not linger near the great river. Before he left, however, he raided the Indian settlements on the banks of the river and took dozens of Indians as prisoners aboard his ship. Pinzón's aggression has been cited by historians as a possible reason for the hostility Indians displayed toward future explorers in the Amazon region. After stopping at Hispaniola and the Bahamas, and losing two of his four ships at sea, Pinzón arrived back in Palos in September of the same year.

In 1502, Pinzón returned to the coast of Brazil, this time to an area slightly north of his original landfall, known as Cape São Roque. The two-year journey also took him back to Hispaniola, where he encountered Columbus following the Italian explorer's rescue from Jamaica after his ships had become unseaworthy.

Pinzón's next expedition, in the company of Juan de Solís, took place in 1506. The two explorers traveled to the Central American coastal area visited by Columbus in his 1502–1504 voyage but took their expedition several steps further. They explored all of the Yucatán peninsula, to the north of the Panama-Nicaragua area sailed by Columbus, and proceeded south to Trujillo (in modern Honduras). Pinzón, credited by some historians with discovering Honduras, was appointed governor of the lands he had found; however, he never actually took formal possession of them.

In his final known voyage, beginning in 1508, Pinzón was commissioned by Spain to undertake yet another effort to find a body of water that would lead west to the Spice Islands (the Moluccas). Once more Pinzón set sail for the coast of Brazil, again accompanied by Solís. He aborted this mission the following year, reportedly because of difficulties with Solís, and returned to Spain. Very little is known about the remainder of his life.

· Pizarro, Francisco

Spanish
b 1475; Trujillo, Estremadura
d July 26, 1541; Lima, Peru
Explored, conquered, and colonized Peru and Ecuador

Francisco Pizarro was a clever, ruthless **conquistador** who, with an armored military force of fewer than 200 men, conquered the much larger army of the Inca empire, placing Peru directly under Spanish rule. His additional conquests and colonization efforts extended that control as far south as Chile, drastically affecting the future of South America and assuring Pizarro a permanent place in its history.

Pizarro was born in 1475, in Trujillo, in the province of Estremadura, Spain, the illegitimate son of an army captain and a farmer's daughter. Nothing is known of his early life except that as a young man he worked as a swineherd; also, he never learned to read. In 1502 he went to the West Indies in the fleet of Nicolás de Ovando, the new governor of Hispaniola (the island now occupied by Haiti and the Dominican Republic). In 1509 he was a member of ALONSO DE OJEDA's expedition to the Gulf of Urabá (on the coast of modern Colombia) and was placed in charge of the settlement there when Ojeda left to obtain needed supplies. Promoted to captain, Pizarro became part of VASCO NUNÉZ DE BALBOA's discovery expedition across Darién (in present-day Colombia) in 1513 and was reported to have been the second European to see the Pacific Ocean.

Pizarro next settled in Panama and established himself as a cattle breeder and trader in association with DIEGO DE ALMAGRO, a wandering adventurer, and Hernando de Luque, a priest with money and good relations with the governor of Panama, Pedro Arias de Ávila (known as Pedrarias). The business prospered and was expanded to embrace mining, agriculture, and slave trading with the Indians.

Pizarro obtained permission from Governor Pedrarias for his first expedition to Peru to search for a rich civilization rumored to exist there. With Luque supplying the necessary funds, Pizarro sailed south from Panama in 1524 with the main force, and Almagro followed with a support vessel. Absorbing heavy losses from starvation and battles with the Indians along the coast of present-day Colombia, the expedition came to an early and disappointing end, with no great riches or fabled cities having been discovered.

Early in 1526, however, another force was assembled and two ships set out to explore the coast of what is now Colombia. They found a little gold and, while Almagro returned to Panama for reinforcements, Pizarro sailed south and explored the area that is now Ecuador. There he found more indications of gold and signs of a highly developed civilization. When Almagro returned, he and Pizarro wanted to begin their conquest but felt their force was too small for such an undertaking. Almagro again returned to Panama for reinforcements while Pizarro awaited his return on the island of Gorgona. Instead of the requested reinforcements, the new governor of Darién sent two

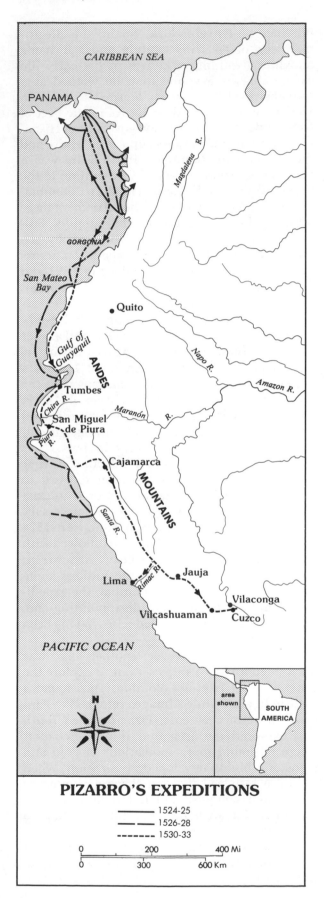

PIZARRO'S EXPEDITIONS

——————— 1524–25
—— —— —— 1526–28
- - - - - - - 1530–33

0   200   400 Mi
0   300   600 Km

ships to bring back any men who wished to return, thus ending another attempt to find and conquer the rich Indian civilization of northwestern South America.

However, a secret message from Almagro and Luque advised Pizarro to continue, and he promptly forced a decision that would ultimately affect the fate of a vast empire. He reportedly drew a line in the sand with his sword, pointed south and said: "Shipmates and friends! There lies the hard way, leading to Peru and wealth." Then he pointed north and said: "That way lies Panama and peace and rest, but also poverty. Take your choice." Pizarro then crossed the line to the southern side; thirteen men followed him.

The fourteen men waited seven months before Almagro returned with a ship and provisions; there was no additional manpower beyond the ship's crew. The small expeditionary party first sailed to the Gulf of Guayaquil, then to 9° South latitude. Enroute they made three landings, during which they acquired a nominal amount of gold and confirmed the existence of a highly developed Indian civilization; they then returned to Panama.

Pizarro then sailed to Spain to present the royal court with his information on the Inca Empire and to show them evidence of its nature, such as llamas, fine fabrics, and gold and silver trinkets. He sought the authority to conquer the civilization, which at that time extended over 2,000 miles from north to south, encompassing what are today Ecuador, Bolivia, Peru, and part of northern Chile. The presentation was convincing, and on July 26, 1529, Queen Isabella authorized Pizarro to discover and conquer this vast area. He was named captain general of Peru. Almagro (to his chagrin) was appointed only commandant of Tumbes (an Inca city in Peru), and Luque, protector of the Indians.

After returning to Panama with many new recruits—including his four half brothers—Pizarro set sail for Tumbes on December 27, 1530, beginning his third and most important expedition. Due to strong headwinds he was forced to land at San Mateo Bay on the Ecuadorean coast. This necessitated months of wearisome marching south along the coast, during which the Spaniards were hampered by food shortages, an epidemic of buboes (swollen glands), the necessity of fording rain-swollen rivers, and skirmishes with local Indians. When the expedition finally arrived at Tumbes, the city was in ruins as a result of civil war within the Inca Empire. Although the members of the party were despondent, their spirits were revived when the seasoned conqueror, SEBASTIÁN DE BENALCÁZAR, arrived by ship with thirty men; soon after, the adventurer HERNANDO DE SOTO arrived with supplies, horses, and 100 more volunteers from Nicaragua.

It was May 1532 before Pizarro left Tumbes. He proceeded to the Chira River, explored northwestern Peru, selected a site for the first Spanish settlement, and founded the town of San Miguel de Piura. Leaving 60 Spaniards behind as the town's first citizens, he set out to conquer the Inca empire with only 62 horsemen and 106 foot soldiers.

It was fortunate for Pizarro that his invasion came at a time when there was extreme contention between two factions of the Incas for control of the empire. This resulted from the sudden deaths between 1525 and 1527 of the established and respected ruler, Huayna-Capac; his probable heir, Ninan Cuyuchi; and most of the royal court, due to a violent epidemic (possibly smallpox brought by the Spaniards and rampant among the Incas). One son of the deceased emperor, Huascar, became ruler of the city of Cuzco, while another son, Atahualpa, took charge of the imperial army in the city of Quito. War subsequently erupted between the two brothers, and the Spanish invaders were able to capitalize on the situation.

Pizarro planned to attack the city of Cajamarca when he learned that Atahualpa was there with his army. This huge force was actually camped in tents among the hills outside the city, and Atahualpa was kept informed of the Spanish movements. As a result, when a reconnaissance party headed by Soto returned, it was accompanied by an envoy from Atahualpa bearing gold bracelets and other gifts. Pizarro, sensing an opportunity to avoid a major military confrontation, lured the Inca chief into the city for supposedly friendly discussions and then took him captive, using concealed troops to trap him. Atahualpa, in an effort to obtain his release and save his life, offered to fill a room with gold and silver as his ransom. This took considerable time to accomplish, but eventually the treasure was accumulated and turned over to Pizarro. Nevertheless, Atahualpa was

Detail of a painting depicting Pizarro's conquest of the Incas. Art Resource Center.

executed by Pizarro in July 1533, supposedly for a role in the murder of his brother Huascar.

Pizarro then started his march on Cuzco with 100 horsemen and 30 foot soldiers. Their route through the Andes would have been impassable except for the superb roads of the Incas; the Royal Inca Highway ran along the spine of the Andes from present-day Colombia to Cuzco and then on through modern Bolivia to Chile—a distance of more than 3,000 miles. The expedition traveled 750 miles along these roads and over secondary mountain ranges, fording wild river torrents and fighting the colder temperatures and thinner air of the higher altitudes. There were four battles enroute—at Jauja, Vilcashuaman, Vilaconga, and the pass above Cuzco. These proved without question the superiority of the mounted, armored Spaniards over the Inca warriors, no matter how vast the number of Incas. By the time Pizarro entered Cuzco, there was no resistance or fighting; the conquest of Peru was complete.

On January 6, 1535, Pizarro founded a new city on the Rímac River and named it the "City of the Kings" (later named Lima, through a corruption of the word Rímac). In order to keep the other conquistadores from getting restless and challenging his authority, Pizarro sent them on additional expeditions into the adjacent regions, including present-day Ecuador, Colombia, and Chile.

But Pizarro's ruthlessness and conniving finally caught up with him. On July 26, 1541, Pizarro was murdered in Lima by Almagro's illegitimate son, commonly known as "the Lad," who was avenging Almagro's earlier death at the hands of Pizarro's half brother, Hernando.

Although he explored much of northern South America, Pizarro is known primarily for his brutal conquest of the Incas, which filled the coffers of Spain with great treasures and made that country the major power of the time. More than anyone, Pizarro shaped the future of South America, solidifying the future role of Spain on the recently discovered continent.

SUGGESTED READING: John Hemming, *The Conquest of the Incas* (Macmillan, 1970); Paul Horgan, *Conquistadors in North American History* (Farrar, Straus & Co., 1963); Joachim G. Leithäuser, *Worlds Beyond the Horizon*, trans. by Hugh Merrick (Knopf, 1955); Albert Marrin, *Inca and Spaniard: Pizarro and the Conquest of Peru* (Atheneum, 1989).

Polo, Marco

Italian
b 1254?; Venice
d 1324; Venice
Explored Central Asia and Far East; wrote influential firsthand account of travels in Asia

Marco Polo was perhaps the most outstanding European traveler of the Middle Ages and certainly one of the greatest explorers of all time. As a teenager in the company of his father and uncle, both Venetian merchants, he crossed Asia Minor and Central Asia and entered Cathay (present-day China), reaching the court of Kublai Khan. The emperor befriended the Polos, and Marco served the khan as a courtier and diplomat, traveling throughout the Far East. After nearly a quarter of a century of such travel, he returned to Europe.

Ironically, the story of his travels might well have been lost had he not been captured by

Marco Polo. Bettmann/Hulton.

the Genoese, military and commercial rivals of his native Venice, and thrown into prison. There he dictated an account of his adventures to a fellow inmate named Rusticello, a writer of popular medieval romances. This book of Polo's observations and descriptions of the exotic East came to be called *Il milione*. The origin and meaning of this title are obscure. It has been taken as an indirect reference to Polo's frequent use of superlatives in his text. Some scholars think the title may have been a corruption of a family nickname, Aemilione, or "Big Emile." Originally written in Franco-Italian, the book became, in the context of its day (prior to the invention of the printing press), an instant best-seller. It was translated into Latin and dozens of other languages. Nevertheless, *Il milione*, known in English as *The Travels of Marco Polo*, was criticized as being nothing but a compilation of tall tales. No authenticated original copy is known to exist, and no two copies of the oldest existing manuscript versions are identical.

An illustrated page from a manuscript of Polo's account of his travels. Bodleian Library, Oxford.

Even today scholars debate what parts of the book were fabricated or embellished by medieval translators.

Indeed, Polo himself has had as many detractors as admirers. Some critics, for example, have been flabbergasted by his tendency to omit important details—for example, he never mentions the Great Wall of China or the ideographic script of the Far East. But whatever their criticisms, his place in history is well deserved. More than any other European of his time, he tore back the curtain of ignorance about Asia and fired the imagination of the European Renaissance explorers who would sail East in search of the rich lands he had described.

Polo was born in Venice in 1254. The exact date of his birth, like so many other facts about his life, is uncertain. His family was one of wealthy merchants, but little else is known about them. In the latter part of the thirteenth century, Venice was one of the wealthiest city-states of northern Italy. Its merchant families specialized in the Asian trade, and its ships sailed as far east as the Black Sea.

Some time in 1255, Marco's father Niccolò and uncle Maffeo left on a trading venture for Constantinople (the modern Turkish capital of Istanbul), where they remained for six years. In 1261 the Polo brothers converted much of their capital into jewelry, which was lighter and easier to hide than other commodities, and sailed to the port of Sudak (now in the Soviet Union) on the Black Sea. There they joined their brother, Marco the elder, a prominent trader in the Crimea. From Sudak, the Polos planned to open up trade with Russia, using Marco's local connections to pass Russian goods on to Constantinople and then to the West. Together, Niccolò and Maffeo journeyed up the Volga River to Sarai, the site of the court of Barka Khan, king of the western Mongols, a tribe of marauding nomads who had settled in Russia. Known as the Golden Horde, they were part of the great Mongol empire founded by Genghis Khan, whose armies had conquered most of China, Central Asia, and Russia in the first half of the thirteenth century. The khanates, or kingdoms, they established now paid fealty to the great Mongol Kublai Khan (the grandson of Genghis), who ruled from the city of Cambaluc (present-day Beijing).

Through shrewd trading and Barka Khan's support, the two brothers doubled their assets.

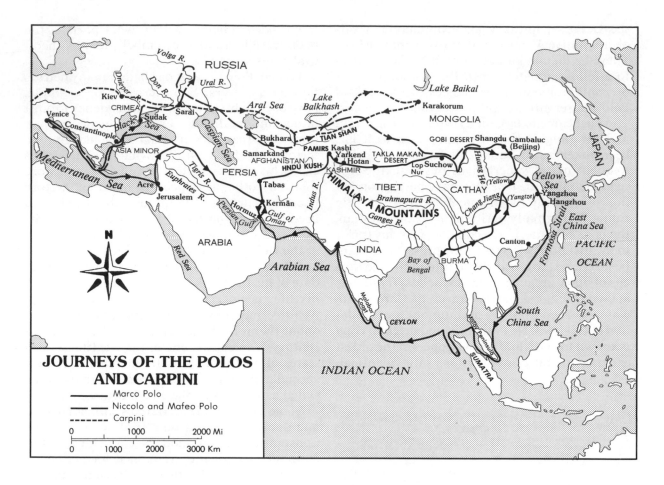

JOURNEYS OF THE POLOS
AND CARPINI
——— Marco Polo
— — — Niccolo and Mafeo Polo
- - - - - - Carpini

| 0 | | 1000 | | 2000 Mi |
| 0 | 1000 | 2000 | 3000 Km | |

But when war broke out between Barka Khan and a neighboring ruler, they were prevented from returning to the Crimea. Instead, the two Venetian merchants decided to head farther east. They journeyed to the court of Djagatai Khan at the city of Bukhara (in the modern Soviet republic of Uzbekistan). Bukhara was a major trading stop on the great Silk Road that carried merchant caravans bearing the treasures of the Orient. Business was good, and the Polos remained in the city for three years. Then, in the early months of 1265, they joined a caravan of Mongol envoys from western Iran, who told them that Kublai Khan was inviting foreign traders to his court at Cambaluc. Heading eastward through the great commercial city of Samarkand (also in present-day Uzbekistan), they crossed the Tian Shan mountains and skirted the edge of the Gobi Desert. Before the year's end they reached the imperial court of Shangdu, the summer residence of the khan (probably the site of Xanadu, the "stately pleasure dome" of the famous poem written more

than 500 years later by Samuel Taylor Coleridge).

The Polo brothers were well received, for the emperor of China was interested in foreigners and eager to learn more about the mysterious lands of the West. Kublai Khan asked the two Venetians to serve as his envoys to the pope, requesting that the Vatican send 100 intelligent men to his court, where they would debate the finer points of Christianity with the imperial philosophers. The khan also asked that they bring back oil from the lamp burning at Christ's sepulcher in Jerusalem. For their protection, he gave the Polos a golden tablet inscribed with the imperial seal to guarantee them good treatment and hospitality during their return journey through Mongol territory.

It took the Polo brothers three years to get back to Venice, which they reached in 1269. Niccolò's wife had died in the interim and son Marco was about fifteen years old by this time, which was his first chance to speak to his father. The travelers had been absent for fourteen years, but they were not destined to remain long in Venice.

Pope Clement IV had died in 1268, and political bickering had delayed the election of a new pontiff for two years. The Polos feared that they would lose initiative if they postponed their journey back to Cathay much longer. Thus they decided not to wait for an as yet unnamed pope to appoint emissaries to the court of Kublai Khan. Taking young Marco with them, they traveled to Jerusalem in 1271 to obtain the requested oil from the Holy Sepulcher. There they heard that a new pope, Gregory X, had been named. They were in luck, for the pontiff was an old friend named Teobaldo Visconti who had become acquainted with the Polos when he had served as papal legate (emissary) to the city of Acre in Palestine. Gregory X was eager to open diplomatic relations with Cathay. He named the Polos his official ambassadors, provided them with fine gifts to present to the emperor of Cathay, and ordered two friars to accompany the Venetians back to the Orient.

In 1271 the Polos left Palestine, crossing present-day Iraq and Iran to the city of Hormuz on the Persian Gulf. The journey over the freezing mountains and blistering deserts of Persia was mostly uneventful, except for sporadic, unsuccessful attacks by bandits. Nevertheless, the two friars, fearful of the unknown perils that lay ahead, declared they would go no farther and turned back.

In Hormuz the Polos had planned to take a ship to India, but instead they opted to continue their journey by land. Heading north to the city of Kermān (in what is now central Iran), they trekked across the rim of the Dasht-e-Lūt desert until they reached Tabas (on Iran's present-day border with Afghanistan). There they rested and were no doubt entertained by the townspeople, who regaled them with legends of the "Old Man of the Mountains," the head of a heretical Muslim sect who was said to be specially favored by Allah and to rule a mythical kingdom as bountiful as paradise itself. The Old Man, they said, drugged his followers with hashish and was protected from his enemies by special guards known as hash-shashin, or "hemp-eaters." At his command, it was said, they killed without mercy. Historically, there was some basis for these tales, for medieval Muslim rulers did train corps of elite killers, which, in the West, became known as assassins.

Crossing into Afghanistan, the travelers paused in Badakhshān, the country's northernmost region, where they rested for as long as a year, possibly to recover from malaria. Some scholars suggest that during this period, Marco explored lands to the south, possibly journeying across the Hindu Kush to Pakistan, perhaps even reaching Kashmir. In any event, the travelers recovered their health and continued east to the Pamir Mountains. Traversing peaks between 13,000 and 15,000 feet above sea level, they marveled at the mountains, the steepest ever seen by Western eyes, which would one day be known as "the rooftop of the world." There Marco first saw the long-horned mountain sheep that were later named for him, the *Ovis poli*.

Now the travelers began their descent, reaching Kashi in Chinese Turkistan (now part of Xinjiang Province in China). To the east lay the great Takla Makan desert, which Marco would later describe as a vast wasteland that "looks as if it had never been traversed by man or beast." Passing through the Silk Road cities of Yarkend (present-day Soche) and Hotan, the Polos pushed on to the oasis of Lop Nur, where they paused to rest before crossing the fear-inspiring Gobi Desert. In *Il milione* Marco writes that they saw neither "beast nor bird" in that empty ocean of sand, for there was absolutely nothing there to eat. He writes too of mirages that played tricks with men's minds and of phantoms and evil spirits that tempted hapless travelers and lured them to their deaths.

After a monthlong trek, the Polos reached the city of Suchow (present-day Jiuquan), at the edge of the Great Wall that separated Cathay from its barbarian neighbors. In those days the wall ran from Suchow all the way to present-day Beijing, but much to the puzzlement of generations of scholars, Marco never mentions it in his writings. The Polos then continued eastward through unknown regions that Marco says contained the land of Prester John, the mythical king who, according to Western tradition, ruled a wealthy Christian kingdom somewhere in the East (for a more complete discussion, see PÊRO DA COVILHÃ). Marco's statements that Prester John did indeed exist would prompt later generations of explorers to search for his kingdom from the shores of Africa to the wastelands of Central Asia, without, of course, any success.

As the Polos continued eastward following

the Huang He (Yellow River), they were met by emissaries of the emperor, who escorted them to Kublai Khan's summer court at Shangdu in 1274 or 1275. *Il milione* is never specific about dates, and modern scholars dispute the year, but they generally agree that the Venetians remained in China for sixteen or seventeen years.

It is difficult to glean exact biographical data from the writings of Marco Polo, for he was not attempting to give a detailed personal account of his travels. Initially, *Il milione* may have been intended as a straightforward, factual report to aid other Western merchants in the East. Rusticello doubtlessly embellished Polo's account to make it more exciting, yet he omitted the details of the author's life and a chronology of his explorations.

Polo was about twenty years old when he arrived in Cathay, a seasoned traveler and accomplished linguist who soon attracted the attention of the emperor, a man who delighted in stories of exotic lands. This much can be surmised from *Il milione*. Beyond these few facts, the personality of Marco Polo has been the subject of unending speculation—among screenwriters and novelists, as well as scholars—but an accurate picture of his character has been lost to history. Some critics see him as a humorless, matter-of-fact man with little insight or personality. Others chastise him for reporting legends as though they were established facts—and he did indeed relate stories about places that he had not actually seen. Nevertheless, he must have been a man of intelligence and charm, for he soon became one of Kublai Khan's most prominent **courtiers**.

Little is known of the activities of Niccolò and Maffeo during those years in China, except that they remained close to the imperial court, engaged in commerce, and became very rich. The Mongol khans were invaders who had usurped the throne of China, and they may have preferred to promote foreigners rather than ethnic Chinese to prominent posts. The exact nature of Marco's duties is unknown, except that he was allowed to roam throughout the realm in the khan's service. Some editions of *Il milione* suggest that he became governor of the city of Yangzhou in the modern province of Jiangsu, but the text's wording is ambiguous. In any event, he traveled from the Formosa Straits to the present-day countries of Burma, Laos, and Vietnam, and even to India. Some historians believe that he may have served in some high capacity regarding the government's monopoly on salt.

Despite the lack of personal information, Polo left detailed observations of much of what he saw. His medieval readers must have been enthralled by his descriptions of Kublai Khan's immense wealth—his huge palaces and hunting estates, the costly apparel worn by his retinue, and his legendary generosity. Polo describes how Kublai Khan fed famine victims whose crops had failed with grain from the imperial warehouses, how he opened his treasury to the poor, and how he was revered by his people as a god.

Polo also writes of the exotic customs of Cathay. For example, the court issued and honored paper money, a notion medieval Europeans would have thought absurd. Readers of *Il milione* must also have been titillated by Polo's descriptions of everyday life. Of a region that he considered to be part of Tibet but is now thought to have been in western China, Polo writes: ". . . men do not mind if foreigners, or anyone else for that matter, make love to their wives, daughters, sisters, or other female relatives. In fact they are very pleased because they think their gods and idols will be glad and shower them with wealth." Elsewhere in the book, he tells how tribes in Burma required a woman who has just given birth to relinquish the care of her child to her husband, who then climbs into bed with the infant while she goes about her work.

Polo also discusses the great technical achievements of the Chinese. He describes the Grand Canal, which today stretches for nearly a thousand miles from Hangzhou, a port city on the East China Sea some 100 miles below Shanghai, to Tianjin, less than 100 miles south of Beijing. Marco believed that the canal had been built on the orders of Kublai Khan, who had indeed restored and extended the waterway, but it was actually begun some 600 years before the Polos first saw it. Polo was also amazed by the heavy traffic on the Chang Jiang (Yangtze River) and Huang He. Of the Chang Jiang he wrote: ". . . the total volume of traffic exceeds all the rivers of the Christians put together and their seas into the bargain."

Although he marveled at the achievements of Cathay, Polo also describes some of its failures, such as its ill-fated military expedition to conquer Japan (a kingdom previously unknown to Europe) in 1281. The Mongol fleet was destroyed by a typhoon, the kamikaze or "divine wind" of Japanese legend. Kublai Khan, he reports, had the unlucky commanders of the expedition put to death.

Among the last of Polo's extensive travels on behalf of the emperor was a visit to India. Little is known about the trip except that Marco made some of it by ship. The chapters in *Il milione* regarding India are vague. Polo describes at length the customs and beliefs of the subcontinent's various kingdoms, although it remains unclear what region he actually visited. He talks a great deal about Saint Thomas the Apostle, who supposedly preached Christianity in India, and, according to Marco, was accidentally killed (while saying his prayers) by an arrow shot from the bow of a pagan peacock hunter. *Il milione* also contains many details about Hindu and Buddhist religious practices, indicating that Marco may have been a man of some religious and philosophical depth. He writes, for example, with great respect for India's Brahmin (Hindu priest) merchants, calling them the most honest in the world.

Polo's efforts at ethnography enthralled his readers even while feeding criticism that he was too willing to report gossip as fact. Nevertheless, much of what he wrote was confirmed by later generations of explorers. And while he certainly did not visit all the places he described, such as Japan and Java, he nevertheless went to regions so remote that they were not visited again by Western travelers for hundreds of years.

Polo returned to Cambaluc from India around 1290 to find his father and uncle eager to return to Italy. Although the Polos had acquired wealth and prestige in Asia, they must have grown homesick as the years passed and voiced an increasing desire to return to Europe. More importantly, Kublai Khan was by then in his seventies. His death might result in a new regime that could prove less favorable to the Europeans, who doubtlessly had made many enemies as well as friends at court. At first hesitant to let them leave, the aged khan at last acquiesced to their request. It was decided that they would accompany a Mongol princess who was to sail to Persia to marry Kublai Khan's vassal, the Arghun Khan. As experienced sea travelers with firsthand knowledge of the mysterious lands to the west, the Polos were considered ideal escorts. They joined a fleet of fourteen ships containing approximately 600 sailors, soldiers, and courtiers and set sail sometime around 1292.

Marco Polo does not describe the voyage home in detail. The fleet stopped in what is now Vietnam, as well as several islands around the Malay Peninsula. It spent five months on Sumatra (in what is now Indonesia) to wait out the monsoon season before sailing on to the island of Ceylon (now Sri Lanka). From there, the Chinese fleet hugged the Indian coast. While it is not clear how much time the Polos spent ashore, Marco describes the wealth of India at some length, from the pearl-diving industry of Ceylon to the rich merchant cities of India's Malabar Coast. His accounts would inspire later generations of explorers to risk any dangers to tap India's immense resources. However, that wealth would be inaccessible to direct trade from Europe for another 200 years, until VASCO DA GAMA's voyage around the horn of Africa made it possible.

Making its way westward along the coast of modern Pakistan, the expedition sailed through the Gulf of Oman to Hormuz. There they debarked and proceeded overland to the khanate of Khorāsān, where the princess was handed over to the son of the Arghun Khan, since the elder khan had died during his would-be bride's long voyage. (The princess is reported to have been pleased by this turn of events.) It was there that the Polos heard that the great Kublai Khan had also died. Eventually (exactly when is unclear) they left Khorāsān to return to Europe. But the Polos' official protection ended once they left the lands that pledged loyalty to the Mongol Khans. Entering regions of Christian influence in what is now Turkey, they were attacked by bandits and robbed, losing much of their hard-earned wealth.

Finally, in 1295 the travelers reached Constantinople and sailed for Venice. They had been away from home for twenty-four years. According to legend, the Polos were so bedraggled from their travels that their own family at first refused to believe that the three men who arrived in Venice were indeed their long-lost relatives. But the Polos astounded everyone by producing precious stones and jewels stitched into the lining of their garments, proving that they indeed had returned from rich, exotic lands.

This story is probably apocryphal, as undoubtedly are many of the details about the rest of Marco Polo's life. Some facts can be reconstructed from various contemporary documents. In 1296 or 1298 (accounts differ) he was captured during a battle at sea with the forces of Genoa and thrown into prison. There he met Rusticello of Pisa, who had been taken prisoner a decade earlier, and the two agreed to work on the book. In 1299 Genoa and Venice ended their war, and the prisoners were freed. Polo returned to his native city, where he continued to trade, married, and had a large family. He seems to have been a prosperous citizen, but he became the source of some amusement to his fellow Venetians, most of whom did not believe his exotic tales. He died in 1324 at the age of seventy.

Il milione continued to be a fantastic literary success, a book read as much for Rusticello's embellishments as for Marco Polo's observations. In some versions, medieval monks who transcribed the book excised portions that they considered heretical, for Polo's descriptions of many places, peoples, and events often clashed with the orthodox views of the time.

Through the centuries the reputation of Marco Polo has gone through as many revisions as *Il milione*. Despite criticism of his book, the gigantic accomplishment represented by his travels throughout the Far East—however inaccurate some of his accounts of those travels may have been—is undeniable. Indeed, it is a pity that he did not write more, for, as Polo himself is said to have declared on his deathbed: "I did not write half of what I saw."

SUGGESTED READING: Henry H. Hart, *Marco Polo, Venetian Adventurer* (University of Oklahoma Press, 1967); Marco Polo, *The Travels of Marco Polo* (Orion Press, N.D.); Teresa Waugh, *The Travels of Marco Polo, A Modern Translation* (Sidgwick & Jackson, Ltd., 1984).

Juan Ponce de Leon. The Bettmann Archive.

· Ponce de León, Juan

Spanish
b 1460?; San Tervás de Campos, León
d July 1521; Havana, Cuba
Discovered Florida and Bahama Channel;
    explored and colonized Puerto Rico

The exploits of Juan Ponce de León have become a basis for legend and romance in American history. His discovery of Florida in 1513 has been continually associated with a search for a mythical fountain of youth, giving rise to numerous literary works, including Eugene O'Neill's play, *The Fountain*. The real Ponce de León, however, was a highly regarded discoverer, explorer, colonizer, and administrator, recognized for his discoveries of Florida and the Bahama Channel; his exploration, colonization, and subsequent governing of Puerto Rico; and his attempt to establish the first settlement in Florida. Described by his contemporaries as a man of valor and sober judgment and an experienced and practical navigator, Ponce de León is also remembered for his belief in peaceful conquest and colonization. Throughout his life he showed a degree of kindness and friendship to the Indians that was unusual among Spanish explorers of the time.

Ponce de León was born about 1460 into a poor but noble family living in the village of San Tervás de Campos in the province of León, Spain. He was given a basic military education and became a page to the prince of Castile, who would later become King Ferdinand of Castile and Aragon. His career as an explorer began when he accompanied CHRISTOPHER COLUMBUS on the latter's second voyage to the New World in 1493. Then in 1502 he joined Nicolás de Ovando on his expedition to Hispaniola (the island now occupied by Haiti and the Dominican Republic). Ponce de León would spend most of the rest of his life in the New World, faring well politically, financially, and militarily.

First, he became the governor of the Province of Higüey (in present-day Haiti) and proceeded to develop the area peacefully, gaining great personal wealth in the process. In 1508 Ponce de León explored the island of Borinquén as a result of an invitation by its Indian inhabitants. There he started a settlement and renamed the island San Juan de Puerto Rico. When word of his strong administrative capabilities reached King Ferdinand, he was made **adelantado** of Puerto Rico in 1509. Relieved of the governorship in 1511 due to political intrigue, Ponce de León immediately applied for a royal grant to settle the islands of Bimini (north of Cuba) where a miraculous fountain of youth was rumored to exist. While there is no historical evidence that he specifically set out to find the fountain, the route he chose may have been influenced by the legends.

Upon receiving approval, Ponce de León left Puerto Rico on March 3, 1513, with three ships, sailing northwest. He sighted the mainland of Florida on March 27, landed on April 2 just north of what is now the city of St. Augustine, and remained ashore until April 8. He named the new land Tierra La Florida (Land of Flowers) in honor of its discovery on Easter Sunday, called Pascua Florida in Spanish.

At sea again, Ponce de León sailed south along the east coast of Florida and discovered the Bahama Channel, which proved to be of inestimable value since it provided a new sea route from the West Indies to Spain. Continuing his voyage, he next traced the contours of the Florida peninsula, skirting the Florida Keys (which he named the Martyrs) and sailing north along the west coast, perhaps as far as Pensacola Bay, before returning south. He continued sailing along the southwest coast, stopping at some islands that he named the Tortugas (now called the Dry Tortugas) for the nesting turtles found

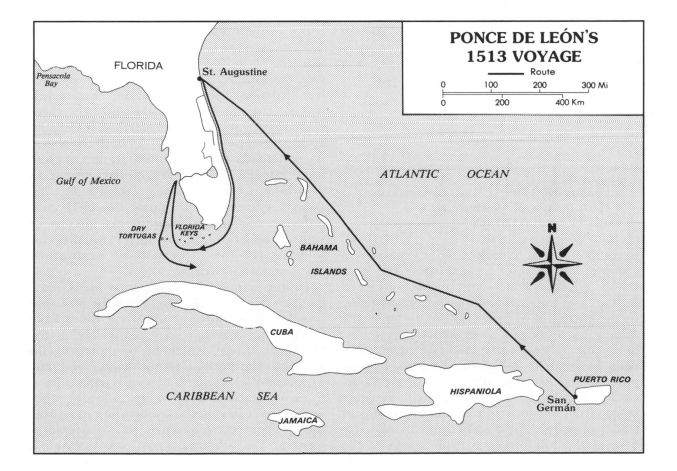

there. He returned to Puerto Rico on September 21, 1513.

Returning triumphant to Spain in 1514, Ponce de León was knighted, given a personal coat of arms, finally granted a royal patent to colonize "the islands of Bimini and Florida," and officially named the Adelantado Don Juan Ponce de León, Governor of the Island of Bimini and Florida.

His second expedition, intended to colonize Florida, was not started until February 20, 1521, when he sailed from Puerto Rico with 200 men. They landed on the west coast of Florida, either near the mouth of the Caloosahatchee River or on Sanibel Island, where they attempted to establish a settlement. During an attack by hostile Indians, Ponce de León was critically wounded, and the settlement was abandoned. The expedition sailed as far as Havana, Cuba, where Ponce de León died in July 1521.

An outstanding explorer and colonizer, Juan Ponce de León was also a skillful administrator whose kindness improved the quality of life for the Indians of Haiti and Puerto Rico. Today, Puerto Ricans reserve a special place of honor for him, and many places in Puerto Rico (as well as in Florida) proudly bear his name. Ponce de León's epitaph provides a tribute to the man and his accomplishments: "This narrow grave contains the remains of a man who was a lion by name and much more so by his deeds."

• Pond, Peter

American
b January 18, 1740; Milford, Connecticut
d 1807; Boston, Massachusetts?
Explored central Canada

A competitive and resourceful member of a group of Montréal fur traders (the North West Company), Peter Pond kept pushing northward in search of untapped sources of beaver pelts. In the spring of 1778 he set out to find Lake Athabasca, a body of water known to Indians. In reaching it he became the first man of European heritage to make the arduous 13-mile **portage** that connects the basin of the Churchill-Saskatchewan river system with the Mackenzie River basin. While remaining a diligent trader afterward, he also became an avid student of the Northwest, drawing maps of the

region that greatly influenced the travels of subsequent explorers.

Pond entered the fur trade in 1765 and spent several years based in Detroit, trading on and near the upper Mississippi River. Later he moved farther north and established himself on the North Saskatchewan River. When the North West Company's archrival, the Hudson's Bay Company, established a competing post on the Saskatchewan above Pond's post (thus drawing the Indians who previously traded with him), Pond decided he needed to head for uncharted territory. Earlier explorers had tried and failed to reach the rumored Lake Athabasca (in what is now northern Alberta and Saskatchewan). In the spring of 1787 Pond undertook the journey. He canoed up the Churchill River to Île-à-la-Crosse Lake, headed northwest for Methye Lake, and from there made an exceedingly difficult 13-mile portage to the Clearwater River. The Clearwater then took him to the Athabasca River, by which he finally reached the lake.

Pond spent much of the next ten years trading very successfully out of the post that he built 30 miles up the Athabasca River. But he also spent time acquiring information about the territory to the north and west of Athabasca. In 1785 he constructed a map from what he had learned. While this map was not totally accurate (he grossly underestimated the distance from Athabasca to the Arctic, for example), it was an attempt to synthesize all of the then-current information about northwest Canada. Pond gave copies of the map to both the governor of Canada and the United States Congress in an attempt to win financial backing for an expedition to find a route to the Pacific. The latter map came into the possession of Thomas Jefferson and helped prompt his interest in transcontinental exploration, eventually culminating in the expedition of MERIWETHER LEWIS and WILLIAM CLARK.

Failing to interest either country in his ideas, Pond returned to Lake Athabasca. He probably traveled as far north as the Great Slave Lake in 1787 and may have reached its outlet (the Mackenzie River, which he predicted would flow into the Pacific). In the winter of 1786–87, the suspicious death of a rival caused Pond to leave Athabasca and the fur trade altogether without ever having the opportunity to test his theory about the Mackenzie. But his replacement at the Athabasca post was ALEXANDER

MACKENZIE, who did go down the river that now bears his name and learned that it empties into the Arctic Ocean, not the Pacific. Although Pond's theory was proved wrong, his work in the region was fundamental to Mackenzie's journey of discovery.

• Powell, John Wesley

American
b March 24, 1834; Mount Morris, New York
d September 23, 1902; Brooklin, Maine
Explored length of Colorado River and Grand
    Canyon by boat

During the summer of 1869, Major John Wesley Powell led nine men in four small wooden boats on a 1,000-mile expedition down the unexplored length of the Green and Colorado rivers and through the Grand Canyon of the Colorado; Powell and his party were the first to journey through the Grand Canyon by boat. Powell's feat—which he repeated in 1871—is the extent of what most history books record about him. The full measure of Powell's influence on the development of the West, however, includes his work as a scientist and government official in addition to his journeys of exploration.

John Wesley Powell was born in March 1834 in Mount Morris, New York. His parents, Joseph and Mary Powell, were English immigrants. Joseph had been first a farmer and then a tailor in England. He was a devout Methodist and had been licensed as a lay preacher. In America, the Powells moved frequently—always further west—as Joseph sought good farmland and opportunities to minister. With each move, he would settle his family on their new farm and then leave them to run it while he traveled for weeks at a time preaching. John Wesley's early years thus were spent on a succession of farms in Ohio and Wisconsin. While young, he became fascinated with natural science and spent his free time collecting specimens of rocks, fossils, animals, and plants. He received little formal education, however, and was largely self-taught.

Shortly before he turned sixteen, Powell left home after his father refused his repeated requests to allow him to attend school to study science. He attended a one-room school for one year, working on a nearby farm to pay the tuition. During the next ten years, he supported himself—and his own further studies—by teaching in a succession of one-room schools, testifying to the success of his own self-education. Each summer he embarked on long collecting trips by boat, hunting specimens along the banks of the Mississippi River. He also spent three semesters studying at the Illinois Institute and one semester at Oberlin College, but in both places he found that he was already more knowledgeable than most of his professors.

Early in 1860, Powell joined the Union Army. Already knowing a great deal about surveying and mapmaking, he quickly made himself an expert on military engineering in order to qualify for a commission. During the Civil War, at the Battle of Shiloh, Powell was struck in the right arm by a rifle ball. Two days later, April 8, 1862, the arm was amputated above the elbow, creating a handicap in light of which his later achievements would seem all the more remarkable.

At war's end, Powell moved to Illinois, where

John Wesley Powell, late in life. New York Public Library.

he became a professor of natural science, first at Illinois Wesleyan University and then at Illinois State University. He taught botany, cellular histology, comparative anatomy, physiology, zoology, natural philosophy, geology, and mineralogy. A few years later he became the curator of the newly created Illinois State Natural History Museum. Under the museum's sponsorship he organized in 1867 his first scientific expedition to the Rocky Mountains and the vast drainage area of the Colorado River. Accompanied by his wife Emma, Powell and his party of fifteen scientists and students collected plant, animal, and mineral specimens as they made their way through the varied terrain west of Denver. They also made an arduous ascent to the summit of Pikes Peak; Emma Powell became the first woman to have climbed it successfully. She did so wearing a plain dress over the obligatory petticoats of the day.

The success of this first expedition enabled Powell to gain financial support from a variety of sources, including (again) his museum, his university, the Chicago Academy of Sciences, and some personal friends. He returned in the summer of 1868 with a much larger party of scientists, including experts in zoology, botany, paleontology, entomology, and ornithology. After a summer of exploration in northern Colorado, Powell and some members of his group went into winter camp on the White River, the winter home of a large tribe of Ute Indians. In addition to conducting extensive surveys of the courses of the White, the Yampa, and the Grand rivers, Powell spent the winter studying the Utes' language and customs. This new interest of Powell's in ethnology, particularly of the Indian tribes of the Rocky Mountains, was thereafter as great as his interest in topography and geology.

On May 24, 1869, Powell and nine companions set out on the boat trip that would bring him national attention. Powell was the only scientist on this trip; his companions were the hardiest mountain and river men he could find. They traveled in four heavily laden, specially built wooden boats propelled by long oars. Powell directed their efforts himself, sitting in a chair lashed to the deck of the lead boat, his right sleeve dangling empty at his side. As they traveled, Powell made constant scientific observations, taking compass readings and calculating distances, altitudes, longitudes, latitudes, river flow rates and volumes, and water temperatures.

The dangerous tasks of running perilous rapids and portaging around impassable falls took their toll. Early in the trip, one boat was lost, along with nearly half of the expedition's food, supplies, and equipment. One member of the expedition quit after only a few days. By the midpoint of the trip, the food supply was down to a bag of dried apples, some coffee, a bag of wormy flour, and some rotting bacon. There was also little game to hunt at the bottom of the deep canyon.

Powell's party was in danger at nearly every moment, never knowing what was around the next bend in the uncharted river. The major wrote in his journal, "We are three quarters of a mile in the depths of the earth, and the great river shrinks into insignificance, as it dashes its angry waves against the walls and cliffs that rise to the world above. . . . They are but ripples and we but pigmies running up and down the sands or lost among the boulders."

Often at night the party was forced to make camp on narrow ledges or sand bars. "We find a few sticks which have lodged in the rocks," Powell wrote. "It is raining hard and we have no shelter, but kindle a fire and have supper. We sit on the rocks all night, wrapped in our ponchos." All three boats were leaking badly from the constant battering against the rocks.

Three more members gave up and left the expedition near the lower end of the Grand Canyon. They successfully climbed to the canyon rim but were killed by Indians as they attempted to hike out of the wilderness. Finally, on August 30, Powell and his remaining companions arrived nearly drowned and starved at the mouth of the Virgin River in Arizona, the end of their voyage.

Major Powell had originally planned to take from six to nine months to complete his trip down the Colorado. Because of the loss of food and equipment and the lack of game, the trip had been completed in approximately three months. The observations that Powell had been able to make were limited, and most of his notes and specimens had been lost on the river when the boats capsized or loads had to be lightened.

Powell immediately began making plans for a larger, better supported expedition. With funds appropriated by Congress, he spent most of 1870 seeking supply routes to the river and caching supplies at intervals along the way. He also spent time with the Indian tribes of the region, studying their languages and cultures, and collecting specimens, many of which he shipped back to Washington.

On May 22, 1871, Powell set off again down the Colorado. This expedition spent 4½ months on the river, covering about half its length, stopping finally at the foot of Glen Canyon (today the site of Lake Powell). They returned in August 1872 and continued the survey, finishing at the mouth of the Kanab River.

Powell's written accounts of his adventures on the Colorado, as well as his public lectures, gained him national fame. His scientific publications earned him respect from the scientific community and attention and support from the government. His observations in the Grand Canyon shook up the geology of the day and in the process created a new science: physiography. He argued that the river had not, as believed, carved down thousands of feet through the mountains. Rather, over more than 60 million years, the land had been thrust up, and the river sliced through the folds as they rose.

For paleontologists he had unearthed many previously unknown fossils. For ethnologists Powell's two expeditions had produced Indian artifacts and located prehistoric village sites. For sociologists and historians he had provided Indian vocabularies and detailed information on Indian culture and traditions. Finally, for the U.S. government he had produced the first accurate topographical and hydrological surveys of this part of the country.

Powell continued to study the Colorado River region. In 1878, he published his *Report on the Lands of the Arid Region of the United States*, which criticized public land policy in the west at the time. Believing that his knowledge should become the basis for constructive action, Powell was largely responsible for writing the bill through which Congress, in 1879, created the U.S. Geological Survey to gather data and conduct research in geochemistry, geology, geophysics, hydrology, topology, and other sciences. He became one of the survey's first commissioners and director of its Bureau of Ethnology, devoted to collecting information on the fast-disappearing Indian tribes. He held this post for the rest of his life, as well as becoming the active director of the U.S. Geological

Powell, on horseback, c. 1895. The Bettmann Archive.

Society itself from 1881 to 1894. Powell died at "Haven," his summer home in Maine, in September 1902.

A gifted naturalist who became an intrepid explorer, John Wesley Powell was also a productive scientist. His efforts had an immeasurable effect on the economic, political, and social development of the vast segment of the American continent that he helped disclose through his remarkable river expeditions.

SUGGESTED READING: William Culp Darrah, *Powell of the Colorado* (Princeton University Press, 1951); John Wesley Powell, *The Exploration of the Colorado River and Its Canyons* (Doubleday, 1961); Wallace Stegner, *Beyond the Hundredth Meridian: John Wesley Powell and the Second Opening of the West* (Houghton Mifflin, 1954); John Upton Terrell, *The Man Who Rediscovered America: A Biography of John Wesley Powell* (Weybright & Talley, 1969).

Przhevalski (Prjevalski), Nikolai Mikhaylovich

Russian
b April 6, 1839; Smolensk
d November 1, 1888; Przhevalsk (formerly Karakol)
Explored east central Asia; made important natural history discoveries

Between 1870 and 1888 Nikolai Przhevalski undertook what has been called the Race for the

Nikolai Przhevalski.   New York Public Library.

Holy City of Lhasa, the capital of Tibet and at that time the residence of the spiritual leader of Tibetan Buddhism, the Dalai Lama. Tibetan anxiety over the intentions of foreign explorers foiled Przhevalski's repeated efforts to reach Lhasa. Yet his skill as an explorer and naturalist added vast chapters to the once slim catalog of European knowledge concerning east central Asia's geography, as well as its distinctive plant and animal life. Among his major zoological discoveries were two previously unknown species: a wild camel and a wild horse now called Przhevalski's horse.

In 1869 Przhevalski made his way to Irkutsk, a city in eastern Siberia on Lake Baikal. The following year, he and three companions set out toward Lhasa, traveling southeast through Mongolia and the Gobi Desert to Kalgan (now Zhangjiakou), about 100 miles from Beijing. Al-

though forced to turn back by the harsh winter, he acquired a reputation of being tough. On one occasion, he held his own against a group of a hundred bandits. When some members of his Mongol caravan once refused to continue, Przhevalski threatened to shoot them. He seemed impervious to ambushes, and the word spread among local people that he was a saint on the way to see the Dalai Lama.

Przhevalski's second attempt to reach Lhasa began in 1876 at Kuldja (now Yining), on the western border of Xinjiang Province. He headed directly for the holy city but again met with failure. By 1879, when he undertook his third expedition, Przhevalski had become one of the foremost scientific explorers of his day. This time he traveled from Russian Turkistan, across the mountains called the Altun Shan, around the eastern edge of the swamps and valleys of the Tsaidam depression, to within 170 miles of his goal. There he was met by Tibetan officials who, suspecting that Przhevalski was the spearhead of a Russian plot to capture the Dalai Lama, forced him to turn back.

Przhevalski's efforts were not without value, however, for he returned with many detailed scientific descriptions and plant samples. For example, he noted a contrast between the unusually large number of herbivorous animals and the poor vegetation. Northern Tibet had no trees, he reported, and only three types of bushes and several varieties of grass. But this vegetation sustained immense herds of yak, antelope, and ass. He also described the elevated salt marshes and clay flats at Tsaidam, which were swept by persistent and terrible winds, and the weary desolation and utter loneliness he felt while traveling through the barren lands.

In 1883, Przhevalski, by then a major general in the Russian army, began his fourth and final expedition, attempting to reach Lhasa by way of the rugged mountain regions that lie between Mongolia and Tibet. Along the way, he visited Issyk-Kul, one of the world's largest mountain lakes. He died there from drinking typhoid-infected water and was buried on the shore of the lake. He was forty-nine at the time of his death and, in his travels, had covered more than 20,000 miles through the wilds of central Asia, primarily in China and Mongolia. In recognition of the magnitude of his numerous accomplishments as an explorer, a town near the site of his death was named after him.

Ptolemy (Claudius Ptolemaeus)

Greek
b A.D. 90; Alexandria, Egypt
d A.D. 168
Developed an influential world map; refined grid system used on maps

Ptolemy was the source of many revolutionary ideas in the fields of geography, astronomy, and mathematics. His detailed description of the universe with the earth at its center governed the thinking of astronomers for over a thousand years. Unfortunately for the history of thought, the influence of an idea is not always determined by its validity. Not until 1543, when the Polish astronomer Nicolaus Copernicus proposed a sun-centered universe, was Ptolemy's geocentric theory laid to rest. Ptolemy's work in geography was equally influential, although it too suffered from a series of erroneous assumptions and observations. Nevertheless, Ptolemy was a first-rate mathematician, and he made important advances in geometry and optics. His major contribution to world exploration was the development of a world map that showed vast areas of unknown land yet to be investigated.

Ptolemy's geographical innovations drew on the earlier work of both ERATOSTHENES and HIPPARCHUS. In fact, one of Ptolemy's books, the *Almagest,* is the major source of what is known about the work of Hipparchus. Ptolemy's *Guide to Geography,* which he divided into eight books, became a standard geographical reference work, a status it retained for hundreds of years. In his *Guide,* Ptolemy adapted and refined the grid system developed by Hipparchus. Hipparchus had divided the sphere of the earth into 360 longitudinal segments (degrees); Ptolemy divided each degree segment further, into minutes and seconds. His improved grid system remains the basis for all modern cartography. Ptolemy may or may not have been the first to use the terms "latitude" and "longitude" (some scholars think Hipparchus should receive the credit), but he certainly brought the terms into popular usage. His listing of the latitude and longitude of 8,000 locations in Europe, Africa, and Asia helped bring this about.

Ptolemy also established the custom of orienting maps with north at the top. This convention may have developed because the best-known areas of the world were to the north of the less well-known areas. He devised a way to project the most populated quarter of the spherical earth onto a flat surface by means of a technique modern cartographers call a modified spherical projection. The essential weakness displayed by Ptolemy's maps and geographical descriptions was a lack of accurate facts. He mentioned nothing about the climate, natural resources, or inhabitants of the areas he described, and his treatment of rivers and mountains was so limited that the information was of little value.

Ptolemy's lack of data led to what has been called one of the most influential miscalculations of history. More than 300 years earlier, the Greek astronomer Eratosthenes had calculated the circumference of the earth. He had assumed that each degree of longitude at the equator was equal to about 70 to 80 miles on the surface of the earth (the correct figure is 69) and had arrived at a remarkably accurate estimate of the earth's circumference. Ptolemy, for reasons that remain unclear, calculated that each of the 360 degrees of longitude covered only 50 miles, making the circumference of the earth only 18,000 miles—far less than its actual circumference of about 25,000 miles. Furthermore, Ptolemy's maps portrayed the continent of Asia as stretching over 180 degrees of longitude, rather than its actual 130 degrees. The net effect of these two miscalculations was to reduce the extent of the space devoted to the unknown parts of the earth. In particular, Ptolemy's maps showed that the distance from the eastern end of Asia to the western end of Europe was relatively small, which is one reason CHRISTOPHER COLUMBUS, who lived more than 1,300 years after Ptolemy, believed he could reach Asia by traveling west from Europe. Ptolemy's maps also suggested that the Indian Ocean was bounded by a continent to its south (which eventually came to be referred to as *Terra Australis Incognita;* for a more complete discussion, see ALEXANDER DALRYMPLE). The existence of this continent was not disproved until Captain JAMES COOK returned from his second voyage to the Southern Hemisphere in 1775.

Ptolemy's conception of an unmoving earth at the center of the universe was one of his most influential theories. It held sway for so many centuries partly because of the common-sense evidence he presented in its defense, and partly because people found the idea of a universe with human life at its center so attractive. The earth was fixed at the center of the universe, argued Ptolemy; why else would all falling objects drop toward the center of the earth? Moreover, he continued, if the earth were rotating once each day, an object thrown upwards would not return to the same spot on the surface. But since it does, the earth must not be rotating. Around this fixed earth, according to Ptolemy, orbited the Moon, Mercury, Venus, the Sun, Mars, Jupiter, and Saturn, in that order. Ptolemy's system was accepted scientific wisdom until the time of Copernicus.

In spite of some conceptual shortcomings, Ptolemy gave substantial impetus to the cause of world exploration. A thousand years earlier, the Greek epic poet Homer had thought that the known world was surrounded by uninhabited ocean; in his understanding, the days of discovery had passed. But Ptolemy's maps suggested vast unknown lands in other parts of the world, lands that called out to people with courage and daring to discover their secrets.

• Purchas, Samuel

English
b 1577?; Thaxted, Essex
d 1626; London
Compiled writings on early British exploration

The length of the title of Samuel Purchas's second collection of travel and discovery writings gives an immediate indication of its scope. It took four volumes in 1625, and twenty in the 1905–1907 edition, to publish *Hakluytus Posthumus or Purchas his Pilgrimes; Contayning a History of the World, in Sea Voyages and Lande Travells, by Englishmen and Others.* The influence of *Purchas his Pilgrimes,* as the anthology was usually called, was as extensive as its title was long: his collected tales were read with enthusiasm throughout England, and they challenged the English to test their mettle against the hazards of exploring little-known regions of the world. In many cases, his volumes are the only source of reliable information on early English exploration and geographical history.

Purchas was a clergyman by profession, but he displayed a lifelong preoccupation with the

discoveries being made in new lands around the world. Rather than taking to the high seas or overland trails himself, Purchas began to gather the stories of those who had. He did not blaze a new literary trail in writing a travel encyclopedia; rather, he continued in the spirit of the noted English chronicler RICHARD HAKLUYT. In fact, the two men probably knew each other. Hakluyt's letters and books, published as England was becoming a colonial nation, encouraged the continued exploration and colonization of the New World. His book *The Principal Navigations, Voyages and Discoveries of the English Nation* is one of the primary sources of information on early English voyages to North America.

In 1613 Purchas published his first collection of travel writings, titled *Purchas his Pilgrimage: Relations of the World and the Religions Observed in All Ages and Places Discovered,* a work whose contents displayed both his zeal for exploration and his professional interests as a clergyman. It was eagerly received by the reading public and remained popular for many years. Almost two centuries later, *Purchas his Pilgrimage* was the favorite reading of Samuel Taylor Coleridge, the renowned English poet and theologian. Purchas's second collection, *Purchas his Pilgrimes,* contains some of Hakluyt's unpublished manuscripts, procured by Purchas after the geographer's death in 1616.

Qian, Zhang. See **Zhang Qian.**

Quadra, Juan Francisco de la Bodega y. See **Bodega y Quadra, Juan Francisco de la.**

Quesada, Gonzalo Jiménez de. See **Jiménez de Quesada, Gonzalo.**

• Quirós, Pedro Fernandez (Fernandeo) de

Portuguese
b 1565; Evarol
d 1614; Panama
Discovered Vanuatu for Spain; explored Marquesas and Santa Cruz Islands with Mendaña

In a brief span of twenty years, navigator Pedro Fernandez de Quirós went from hero to outcast.

His death marked the end of Spanish maritime exploration until the late eighteenth century.

Born in the Portuguese province of Evarol, Quirós spent most of his life in the service of Spain. At the age of about thirty, he was appointed chief pilot on ALVARO DE MENDAÑA DE NEHRA's second voyage from Peru to establish a Roman Catholic colony in the South Seas (1595). After Mendaña died in the Santa Cruz Islands, Quirós, in order to escape growing hostilities with the islanders, led the would-be settlers to safety in the Philippines. The successful completion of the three-month voyage in rotting boats through uncharted seas made Quirós a hero.

After his return to Peru, Quirós continued to Spain and then to Rome with a new vision: He was divinely chosen to discover *Terra Australis Incognita*, the great unknown Southern Continent, and to establish there a settlement where all lived in Christian brotherhood in the land of the Holy Spirit. (For a more complete discussion of *Terra Australis Incognita*, see ALEXANDER DALRYMPLE.) He even received the blessing of Pope Clement VIII for his mission. While religious conversion fueled much Spanish exploration, Quirós's zeal was extreme, even for his time. In the prow of each of his ships he put a statue of Saint Peter, the founder of the Church.

On December 21, 1605, he left Peru with three ships. Less than five months later, he sighted a large, mountainous land mass, which he christened Austrialia del Espíritu Santo after Phillip III, a prince of the house of Austria. It was an island in Vanuatu (formerly New Hebrides) that is still known as Espíritu Santo.

It is known that Quirós's seemingly endless religious ceremonies and strict, puritanical restrictions alienated his crew and that his attempts to build a city on Espíritu Santo sparked hostility from the native islanders. Either fact may have contributed to the unknown cause for Quirós's sailing for Peru after only three weeks on the island, without offering a word of explanation to his second in command, LUIS VAEZ DE TORRES.

Quirós reached Acapulco on November 23, 1606, and seven months later Torres led the remainder of the expedition from Espíritu Santo to the Philippines. However, the decision makers in New Spain and in Madrid who once called Quirós a visionary now ignored his pleas for a new expedition, calling him a fraud and a nuisance. The navigator sank into poverty and spent his time writing papers in an effort to clear his name.

Finally, in October 1614 Spanish officials in Madrid gave him a letter authorizing a new expedition. At the same time, they told officials in Peru to ignore the letter and not to dispatch ships. It did not matter; Quirós died at Panama on his way to Peru. For a combination of reasons, the Spanish would not mount another voyage of discovery for nearly 200 years.

Radisson, Pierre Esprit

French
b 1636; Paris?
d 1710; England
Opened up Hudson Bay to fur trade

Wherever he went, Pierre Esprit Radisson attracted adventure—and misfortune. He and his brother-in-law, MÉDARD CHOUART, SIEUR DE GROSEILLIERS, were the first Europeans to travel deep into the forests near Hudson Bay. Above all else, they established the viability of Hudson Bay as an outlet for fur trading. When their native France would not heed their advice to exploit this route, they brought the British in, adding one more nail to the coffin of French aspirations in North America.

Arriving in **New France** around 1651, Radisson encountered his first misfortune soon thereafter when, at the age of fifteen, hunting near Trois-Rivières, Québec, he was captured and adopted by Iroquois. Eventually he escaped and made his way to Fort Orange (present-day Albany, New York), where he served as an interpreter until he was able to make his way back to Trois-Rivières.

In 1653 his widowed half sister married Groseilliers, and in his brother-in-law Radisson found the perfect partner, the careful organizer to counterpoint his own flair for the dramatic. It is not clear whether Radisson accompanied Groseilliers on a fur-trading journey west from 1654 to 1656, but it is definite that the two journeyed west together in 1659, possibly reaching the upper Mississippi River. They also at this time made contact with some of the western Indians, who up to that point had been kept from the fur traders by the Hurons and other eastern Indians, who acted as middlemen.

During the long winter nights around Indian

campfires in the area north of Lake Superior they heard tales from the Cree, Sioux, and Hurons of ponds between Lake Superior and Hudson Bay that were rich in beaver. The two partners at once recognized the advantage of being able to ship fur out of Hudson Bay by sea rather than having to bring it back to Québec by an overland route.

Returning to Québec with a rich supply of valuable furs, the key to where more could be found, and a plan for bringing them out of the interior more easily, Radisson and Groseilliers expected a hero's welcome. Instead, their furs were confiscated and they were fined because they had departed from Québec without a license from the governor to trade. Aware that their furs had somewhat bolstered the faltering economy of Québec, Radisson and his partner were incensed by their treatment and decided to take their business, and their ideas, elsewhere.

After several years of miscellaneous trading activities in New England and what is now eastern Canada, they went to Boston in 1664, where they met up with Colonel George Cartwright, a commissioner of King Charles II of England. To Cartwright they proposed a journey to Hudson Bay in the interest of the British. Cartwright took them to London, where on October 25, 1666, they explained their plan to Charles II himself. The king, always interested in schemes to bring money into the royal coffers, promised them a ship to make a trading voyage to Hudson Bay. Under the patronage of the adventurous Prince Rupert, a group of merchants outfitted the expedition, which left England in June 1668 with Radisson on one ship and Groseilliers on another. Just west of Ireland a storm forced Radisson's ship to turn back, and he spent the next two years in London while Groseilliers completed the voyage.

The two partners were reunited when Groseilliers returned to London after a successful trading venture in Hudson Bay. The journey had proven the partners' theory that a profitable fur-trading business could be conducted out of Hudson Bay, and Charles II was pleased to grant a royal charter to the Hudson's Bay Company giving it all proprietary rights to the sea and land of the Hudson Bay and its drainage system.

Radisson made several voyages to Hudson Bay for the company. Then in 1674, feeling unappreciated by the English, he and Groseilliers switched their loyalties back to France and did their best to undermine the English in Hudson Bay. On one memorable occasion in 1683 Radisson so bamboozled a group of inexperienced Englishmen in Hudson Bay that he managed to return to Québec not only with his own furs but with theirs as well. Once again, his own countrymen refused to appreciate Radisson's accomplishments: they levied a 25 percent tax on the furs. Again enraged by his ill-treatment, Radisson went back to the English. His loyalty never wavered again, but he was ill-served by the company that owed its existence to him and his partner Groseilliers. In the later years his power steadily eroded until he was finally reduced to begging for a job in the London warehouse. Hudson's Bay Company records show that in 1710 it paid a niggardly six pounds for Radisson's funeral expenses.

Pierre Esprit Radisson left behind a legacy in the form of his *Voyages*, a chronicle of his adventures full of descriptive details that are quite vivid—but not entirely accurate. Perhaps his greatest legacy, however, was the Hudson's Bay Company, which still exists today.

• Rae, John

Scottish
b September 30, 1813; Hall of Clestrain, Orkney Islands
d July 22, 1893; London, England
Explored central Arctic coast of Canada

As the British navy and Lady Jane Franklin were sending ship after ship and spending more than half a million pounds on one of the biggest rescue operations in history, John Rae happened to uncover the fate of the missing Sir JOHN FRANKLIN and his crew while on an overland survey of Boothia Peninsula in 1854. Using the highly developed survival skills he had learned from Native Americans, Rae and his four companions from the Hudson's Bay Company showed the navy what efficient Arctic travel was all about. Ironically, on the same trip Rae also discovered the strait that separates King William Island from Boothia Peninsula (now called Rae Strait)—the last unknown link in the Northwest Passage. Had Franklin known of it, he might have avoided entrapment in the ice pack in M'Clintock Channel and become the first to sail around North America from the Atlantic to the Pacific.

Rae became involved in Arctic work when he joined the Hudson's Bay Company in 1833, first as ship's surgeon, then as the company's resident surgeon at Moose Factory south of James Bay. While attending to ailing traders throughout the territory, Rae developed his skills as a hunter and learned the native modes of travel by snowshoe, dogsled, and canoe. He learned to travel light and to live off the land, to build igloos, and to fend off **scurvy** by consuming berries and fresh game (all skills the British navy was very slow to learn). On his first mission of exploration in 1846, he charted 700 miles of previously unknown coast from Melville Peninsula to Boothia.

The navy then invited him to join Sir John Richardson in an overland search for Franklin along the north coast of the Canadian mainland between the Mackenzie and Coppermine rivers. This expedition (1848–49) turned up nothing, but Rae performed so well that the government put him in charge of another search party. This second expedition, for which Rae conducted a preliminary survey with two other men in the spring of 1851, surveyed the southern coast of Victoria Island, then proceeded up Victoria Strait. It was after this that Rae made his famous survey of Boothia, during which he heard accounts of the Franklin tragedy from local Pelly Bay **Inuits**. From them he purchased some silver spoons and other identifiable relics—the first compelling proof of Franklin's fate, which he reported to England in 1854.

After the Boothia trip, Rae continued an active life of exploring. At the same time, he took on increasing responsibilities in the government and business, while never neglecting his scientific studies. Aside from the hundreds of miles of new coastline that he charted, he is said to have walked over 23,000 miles in the Arctic, often at record-breaking paces. Never widely celebrated as an Arctic explorer (possibly because naval historians have belittled his achievements and also because of his own modesty), he ranks with ROALD AMUNDSEN, at least in terms of technique, as one of the greatest Arctic explorers.

• Raleigh (Ralegh), Walter

English
b 1554?; Hayes Barton, Devon
d October 29, 1618; London
Organized first English settlement in North America; explored Orinoco River in South America

Sir Walter Raleigh is perhaps best known for the chivalrous act of spreading his cloak over a mud puddle so that Queen Elizabeth I could avoid soiling her shoes. But chivalry was only one aspect of this knight's personality. He was also the driving force behind two early British settlements at Roanoke in what is now North Carolina. Although the Roanoke colony did not endure, it was the first organized attempt by the British to colonize North America. Later,

Sir Walter Raleigh. New York Public Library.

Raleigh also explored the Orinoco River in South America in search of the fabled land of **El Dorado** and its golden treasures.

The younger half brother of Sir HUMPHREY GILBERT, Raleigh was cut from the same cloth. A smooth talker and far-ranging thinker, he was, again like Gilbert, a favorite of Queen Elizabeth I. When Gilbert was lost at sea on a return voyage from North America, Raleigh took over his brother's plans to establish a British colony there. With unusual patience and forethought for a man of action, Raleigh first sent out an expedition to explore the North American coast and to select a site for settlement. Led by Philip Amadas and Arthur Barlowe, the expedition left Plymouth in April 1584 and eventually landed on a barrier island near what is now Nags Head, North Carolina, where they claimed the land for England. After a peaceful encounter with the Roanoke Indians, the expedition turned back to England, arriving in September 1584.

For his role in claiming part of North America for Great Britain, Queen Elizabeth rewarded Raleigh with a knighthood and graciously allowed him to call the new territory Virginia in her honor. (Being unmarried, Elizabeth was called the Virgin Queen.) The name Virginia was applied at this time to all of the English holdings along the Atlantic coast south of Cape Breton (now part of Nova Scotia).

Throughout the winter of 1584–85, Raleigh was busy preparing a colonizing expedition for the next spring. His main concern was to finance the expedition, and to raise money he did some **privateering**. (Raiding the ships of other nations was an acceptable method of making money in the sixteenth century, provided one was careful not to prey on the ships of any valued ally.) Still, Raleigh needed more money. The queen would grant him financial aid only if he would stay at home. She was not about to lose him to a watery grave as she had Gilbert.

So Raleigh appointed a commander in chief for the voyage (Sir Richard Grenville) and a governor (Ralph Lane) to head the colony once established. He also began a tradition in English exploration that lasted at least 300 years by sending along a scientist to study the new land and its peoples and to make maps. He also sent an artist to make drawings of the new land and its people, animals, and plants. It is a tribute to Raleigh's organizational skills that an expedition involving 500 people was ready to leave England within seven months of the re-turn of the Amadas-Barlowe reconnaissance voyage.

The ships set sail on April 9, 1585, with about 250 sailors and 108 colonists aboard. The rest of the 500 were soldiers, specialists, and others not expected to stay in the colony. On July 3, they arrived at Roanoke Island. While most of the colonists remained on board, Grenville led a group on an exploration of Pamlico Sound, the body of water separating the barrier islands from the mainland at this point on the coast. Later, after Grenville left to return to England, Governor Lane also did some exploring, getting near the headwaters of the Chowan and Roanoke rivers.

In the meantime the Indians of Roanoke Island had invited the English to establish a colony there. When they did so, however, the rest of the area's Indians became uncomfortable with the presence of strangers, and after a while relations turned decidedly uncordial. Friction among colonists, steadily decreasing supplies, and fear of Indian attack began to take their toll on the colony. So when Sir FRANCIS DRAKE paid a call in June 1586, the entire group of 103 surviving colonists hastily decided to go back to England with him. So great was their eagerness to flee that they left behind three men who had gone off exploring.

When the first group of colonists returned home unexpectedly, Raleigh immediately made plans to send another group, and in spring of 1587, 117 settlers arrived in Roanoke, comprising fourteen families and 78 single men. They were led by John White, who had been on the first expedition, and their plan was to start a brand new settlement in Chesapeake Bay, possibly near the mouth of the James River (site of the first permanent English settlement some twenty years later). For unknown reasons, the ship's captain refused to go farther than Roanoke, and so this second group ended up in the same troubled spot as its predecessors.

These colonists made attempts to better relations with the local Indians, and for a time all seemed to be going well. On August 18, 1587, Governor White's daughter gave birth to a daughter (Virginia Dare), the first English child born in North America. Later in August, when it was time for the ships to sail back to England, the colonists implored White to return on one of them to keep Raleigh interested in the colony and to encourage him to send relief supply ships.

White accepted their mission, but it was three years before he was able to return to Roanoke. In 1588, the Spanish armada attacked England, and this crisis—which ultimately ended in the armada's defeat and the ascendancy of England over Spain—absorbed all of England's attention and resources.

When White finally managed to get back to Roanoke in 1590, he found no trace of the colonists. He did find one word carved on a tree. The word was "Croatoan," the name the Indians used for present-day Hatteras Island. White took this as a sign that the colonists had moved to the relatively safe island where the Indians were friendly, but when he tried to reach Croatoan, bad weather drove his ship farther and farther into the Atlantic until the decision was made to return to England.

None of the Roanoke colonists was ever seen again. However, there remains among the Lumbee Indians of present-day Robeson County, North Carolina, a strong oral tradition that the Roanoke colonists intermarried and mixed with their tribe. If this is true, then some of the Lumbees must be descendants of the lost colony of Roanoke.

Raleigh's two attempts to establish English settlements in North America came to naught, and soon he had even greater worries. In 1588 he had married secretly, aware that Queen Elizabeth would not be happy about his attachment to another woman. The secret was revealed in 1592 when a son was born to Raleigh's wife. For a time the queen imprisoned both husband and wife in the Tower of London. Even when he was released, Raleigh was no longer welcomed at court. However, he now had much greater freedom to quench his thirst for first-hand adventure. Thus, in 1595 he set off for South America in search of the gold of the fabled kingdom of El Dorado. Anchoring his ship off the island of Trinidad, he entered the swamps and jungle of the Orinoco River (in present-day Venezuela). The expedition failed to find gold, but Raleigh returned to England with tall tales about headless men with eyes in their shoulders and mouths in the middle of their breasts.

In 1603, Queen Elizabeth died and was succeeded by James I, and Raleigh's popularity at court declined even more. A Catholic, James wanted peace with Catholic Spain, and Raleigh's anti-Spanish sentiments were not appreciated. He was imprisoned in the Tower of London for conspiring against the king and remained there for thirteen years under sentence of death. In 1616, he made a bid to regain his freedom by promising to undertake another expedition to South America and to bring back gold, without raiding Spanish mines. James freed him to attempt to do so, but warned that the death sentence would be imposed if any piracy occurred.

Again Raleigh went up the Orinoco River, but the only gold to be found was in Spanish mines; Raleigh's son was mortally wounded at a scuffle at one of these mines. When Raleigh returned to England empty-handed, the king used the incident at the mine as an excuse for ordering the death sentence; Raleigh was executed in 1618.

Sir Walter Raleigh was a man of vision who dreamed of populating both North and South America with English colonists. Whether through ill fortune or his own failures, none of his visions came to fruition.

· Rapôso de Tavares, Antonio

Portuguese
b 1598?; province of Alentejo
d ?
Explored from Atlantic coast of Brazil to Andes in Peru

Honored by Brazilians as an explorer, pioneer, and patriot, Antonio Rapôso de Tavares was the greatest **bandeirante** among the Paulistas (inhabitants of São Paulo) during the **bandeira** movement of the early seventeenth century in Brazil. He led several bandeiras into modern Paraguay, Argentina, Bolivia, Uruguay, and Peru, as well as into unexplored areas of southern and western Brazil. During his most important journey, Rapôso de Tavares traversed South America from the Atlantic coast of Brazil to the Andes in Peru, then traveled down the Amazon to present-day Belém, exploring a vast area between the Tropic of Capricorn and the equator. Bandeiras such as this not only brought new slave labor and wealth to the Brazilian economy but also extended Portuguese power.

Antonio Rapôso de Tavares was born about 1598 in the province of Alentejo, Portugal. He arrived in São Vicente (in what is now Brazil) with his father in 1618; nothing is known about his first twenty or so years. Moving to São Paulo in 1622, he led his first major slave-hunting bandeira in 1627. Heading south into the Paraná River valley, he raided villages of Indians who had been converted by the Jesuits; these were located between the lower Paraná and Uruguay rivers in present-day Argentina. Successful there, he pushed into the Guaíra region between the Paranapanema and Iguaçu rivers in southern Brazil, ousting the Spanish, enslaving the Indians, and claiming the land for Portugal.

While the Spanish focused their attention on the riches of Peru, Rapôso de Tavares and other bandeirantes penetrated past the Spanish-Portuguese boundary established by the **Treaty of Tordesillas** and claimed the lands for Portugal. On his next bandeira (1636–38) Rapôso de Tavares traveled north to the Itatí Indian region along the Taquari River in the modern state of Mato Grosso, Brazil.

The Portuguese monarchy was restored in 1641 after years of Spanish rule, and the bandeira movement became more politically and geographically oriented. Thus, when Rapôso de Tavares left in May 1648 on what would be called the "greatest bandeira by the greatest bandeirante," his primary mission was to gather geographical information that would help establish boundaries with the Spanish domains and to open a route to Peru, as well as to search for gold or silver mines. The capture of Indians to serve as slaves became a secondary goal. Leaving São Paulo with 200 Portuguese and more than 1,000 Indians, Rapôso de Tavares traveled downstream on the Tietê River to the Paraná River. Then he went overland to Corumbá where he waited until the end of the rainy season.

In April or May of 1649 the bandeira traversed the swampy regions of the upper Paraguay River and crossed into the Chaco region of Paraguay. From this point until they embarked on the Río Grande in Bolivia, the men faced great hardship through famine, fever, and Indian attacks. The expedition skirted the eastern slopes of the Andes to Potosí and explored the little-known jungle rivers near Santa Cruz de la Sierra in modern Bolivia. Navigating the Grande to the Mamoré to the Madeira rivers, Rapôso de Tavares reached the Amazon. Though his exact route from this point is uncertain, he did penetrate to Quito (in what is now Ecuador). Legend has it that he waded into the Pacific with his sword held high in triumph, but there is no historical evidence to support the claim that he reached the Pacific.

From Quito the bandeira traveled down the tributaries of the upper Amazon, into the Amazon itself, and detoured to explore the Río Negro before continuing down the Amazon to present-day Belém, Brazil. By the time Rapôso de Tavares returned to São Paulo in 1652, he was so disfigured from his arduous journey that reportedly neither family nor friends recognized him.

Though the exploits of Rapôso de Tavares are well documented, the man himself is an enigma. The date and place of his death, for example, remain unknown. He nevertheless became an epic hero of Brazil as the result of this great bandeira that covered over 7,000 miles through vast and virtually unknown areas. According to Portuguese historian Jaime Cortesão, the major accomplishment of his great journey was its geopolitical and geographic scope, establishing Portuguese rule in uncharted regions of Brazil and extending Portuguese power into new territories, ultimately fostering the foundation of the Brazilian state.

· Rasmussen, Knud Johan Victor

Danish
b June 7, 1879; Jakobshavn, Greenland
d December 21, 1933; Gentofte
Explored Greenland and Canadian Arctic; studied entire range of Inuit cultures

Driven by an intense curiosity about his **Inuit** heritage, the Danish ethnologist and explorer Knud Rasmussen traveled the breadth of the Arctic in the Western Hemisphere, from eastern Greenland to the Bering Strait. Although he came on the scene too late to make any major geographic discoveries, he did make some minor corrections, especially to the deeply flawed map of northern Greenland that ROBERT PEARY had drawn. As Rasmussen explained his own relation to Peary and other previous explorers, "The role we were to play would be comparable to that of the little polar fox, which everywhere on the Arctic coast follows the footsteps of the big ice-bear, hoping that something good may be left for it." His hopes were well justified, since his brilliant ethnological fieldwork, made possible by his fluency in the Inuit language,

Knud Rasmussen.   UPI/Bettmann.

laid the foundation for the modern understanding of Inuit culture. Basing himself in a trading station he set up on the northwest coast of Greenland, which he called Thule (the ancient Greek word for the far north), he led a series of seven scientific missions known as the Thule Expeditions. Beginning with a study of the northwestern Greenland Eskimos (known to Europeans as Arctic Highlanders, or Polar Inuit) and their environment, Rasmussen gradually broadened the scope of his studies to all of the Inuit peoples.

Rasmussen was born in a small settlement on Disko Bay in western Greenland. This was an Inuit settlement that was undergoing conversion to Christianity, and Knud's father was a Danish missionary there. Since his mother was part Inuit, however, he grew up bilingual, learning the customs of both cultures. His studies at Copenhagen University gave him the culture of a European, but he retained a longing to understand his maternal heritage. As a young boy, he had heard a great deal about the Polar Inuit, the tribe that was least contaminated by

European culture and was said to live "with the North Wind himself." He decided when he was twelve that he would go there someday, but it was not until he was twenty-three that he accompanied the Danish expedition led by Mylius-Erichsen to the far north (1902–1904). This followed a trip to Iceland in 1900 as a correspondent for the *Christian Daily* and to Swedish Lapland in 1901 to collect materials for his own book on the Lapps (which did not appear until 1908). Feeling that he was responding to some kind of ancestral call that he "never succeeded in slinking away from," he returned repeatedly to visit the Polar Inuit of Greenland's Cape York district. This led ultimately to his "reception into the tribe as one of their own, as a friend and fellow-hunter."

In 1910 Rasmussen and Peter Freuchen established the trading station at Thule on Wolstenholme Fjord north of Cape York and began their efforts to modernize and westernize the native people of the region. (The station was also to serve as a permanent base for continuing exploration and research in northern Greenland.) Peary had already done much to alter the native economy by introducing guns and raw materials not native to the area, such as steel and lumber. Rasmussen wanted to continue the process without destroying the native traditions, hoping to achieve a kind of harmony that he desired for himself as well.

In 1912 Rasmussen led the first Thule Expedition. Along with Freuchen, two Inuit, and fifty-four dogs, he crossed the Greenland ice sheet from Clements Markham Glacier on the west coast to Denmark Fjord on the northeast coast, a 504-mile journey. From the base of the fjord the party traveled 72 miles to the sea. The immediate purpose was to find the missing Einar Mikkelsen group, but in the process they made discoveries in the Denmark Fjord region and proved that Peary's "channel," which supposedly separated the northern land area now known as Peary Land from Greenland proper, was not a fjord but a lowland. The next three Thule Expeditions continued research on Greenland, studying its ice cap, the geography of the north coast, and the mythology of the Polar Inuit. Rasmussen led the Second Thule Expedition in 1917 on a thorough investigation of the major inlets of the north coast. He was not part of the Third Expedition of 1919, which laid down a food depot for Amundsen at Cape Columbia, but he was back leading the fourth in 1920 to the east coast, collecting Inuit stories in the settlement of Angmagssalik.

The great Fifth Thule Expedition (1921–24), again led by Rasmussen, was a large undertaking with several different stages and kinds of activities, but the overarching purpose was to gain a general understanding of Inuit ethnology and migration across the whole of North America. In the beginning stages, two Danish anthropologists, Therkel Mathiassen, who specialized in archaeology, and Kaj Birket-Smith, an ethnographer, studied the region around Danish Island, north of Southampton Island in Hudson Bay. Their work was fundamental in showing that the Thule culture differed from that of the earlier so-called Dorset culture. Other members of the expedition took valuable film footage of the Inuit in their last phase before being overwhelmed by European civilization.

Rasmussen's own work on this expedition tied all of the other results together with a sweeping survey of the North American Arctic coast. He departed Danish Island on March 11, 1923, and arrived at Kotzebue, Alaska, on August 21, 1924, studying all the existing Inuit peoples along the way. Traveling overland with only two Inuit companions and living off the land, Rasmussen closed the era of premechanized exploration with the most impressive exhibition of Inuit traveling technique that observers from the south had ever witnessed. So efficient had he become at **sledge** traveling and hunting, that he was able to use the same dog team all the way, a distance of more than 1,800 miles. Nothing like it had ever been attempted before.

In doing so, he proved the ease with which the Inuit originally could have migrated from Asia, collecting along the way evidence that all the current Inuit populations descended from one great wave of people, which he called the Thule culture. Anthropologists and archaeologists have confirmed his findings, showing that the Thule Inuit replaced the earlier Dorset culture around A.D. 1000.

On the next two Thule Expeditions, Rasmussen carried out cartographic, ethnographic, and archaeological work in southeastern Greenland. On the last expedition, a bout of food poisoning led to influenza and then pneumonia, and he died while on his way back to Copenhagen.

Rasmussen's body of work as an ethnographer was uniquely valuable because of his rare fluency in the difficult Inuit language, while his work as organizer of the Fifth Thule Expedition produced an unsurpassed wealth of factual and theoretical material that took scientists decades to digest. His published volumes include *Greenland by the Polar Sea* (1919) and *Across Arctic America* (1928).

Ricci, Matteo

Italian
b October 6, 1552; Macerata
d May 11, 1610; Beijing, China
Traveled and lived in China; created influential world map

During a time when China was closed to nearly all outsiders, Matteo Ricci was a notable exception. But why did the Chinese allow him to

Mateo Ricci. Bibliothèque Nationale, Paris.

travel freely in their country? Why did the emperor Wan-li summon Ricci to the imperial city of Beijing and allow him to spend the last nine years of his life there? One factor may have been his intellectual abilities. By all accounts, he was a brilliant man whose scholarly interests extended to a wide variety of fields: mathematics, rhetoric, theology, geography, and hydraulics. But the key to Ricci's success may have been his determination to meet the Chinese on their own terms. He dedicated his life to mastering the Chinese language and learning about its land and people. He could memorize at a single reading a list of 400 written Chinese characters, then later recite them either forward or backward. He drafted maps of China, woodcut copies of which were eagerly sought by many of the Chinese themselves. In many ways, Ricci became the avenue through which China and the West began to learn about each other.

The son of an Italian pharmacist, Matteo Ricci was sent by his father to Rome to study law but within several years had joined the Society of Jesus (the Jesuits). After studying mathematics for a short time, Ricci volunteered to work at Jesuit missions in the Far East and was sent to Goa, a Portuguese settlement on the west coast of India. There he taught rhetoric for four years before being selected to prepare for mission work in China. He went to Macao to study Chinese, and his superiors took the unusual step of ordering that none of his other tasks interfere with his language study. Much was at stake: thirty years of continual effort by many different Christian groups had yielded not even a single permanent Christian settlement in China. As a result, the missionary strategy of the Jesuits had changed from trying to impose Western customs on the Chinese to infiltrating Chinese culture by adapting to it.

Ricci's intense preparation was assisted by a stroke of luck. In 1583, following a change of local governors, Ricci and a fellow Jesuit received permission to settle in Zhaoqing, then capital of Guangdong Province. They built a small mission house there, part of which became a museum of Europe. They furnished it with items made in Europe: glass prisms, chiming clocks, solar spheres, and a collection of books with maps of European towns and drawings of their buildings. All of this was intended to introduce the museum's Chinese visitors to the culture of Europe.

On the wall of the reception room in the mission house hung an oval-shaped world map— a map that startled the Chinese people who saw it. The Chinese, Ricci wrote later, were almost wholly ignorant of the outside world. In the late sixteenth century their maps of the world showed the fifteen Chinese provinces surrounded by the sea and a few small slivers of foreign land. The sea and the foreign land together, however, were smaller than one Chinese province. Naturally, the map on the mission wall, with its more accurate proportions, came as a surprise, if not a shock. The mandarins (high officials of the empire) asked Ricci to make a Chinese version of his world map for them.

Ricci agreed to draw a new world map, but, ever aware of the delicacy of his position, he made some revisions. He placed China in the center of his new map and employed a projection that would exaggerate the size of the map's central regions. The result was a huge success among the mandarins, and Ricci received so many requests for copies that he decided to revise it thoroughly and draw a new, larger map. Into this revision Ricci incorporated the most recent discoveries made by explorers, as well as information from Chinese sources.

Ricci's new map has been called a landmark of cartography. It measured six feet by twelve feet and was printed on fine paper and silk. The map was supplemented by extensive geographical annotations: it was a map and a gazetteer (geographical dictionary) combined. The map's influence was so widespread that it served as a sort of geographical ambassador between China and the Western nations. The annals of the Ming dynasty record that a hand-painted copy of the map reached the emperor himself. Copies of the Ricci map sent to the West introduced Europe to the geography of their vast neighbor to the east.

Ricci's work was not limited to geography. Influential mandarins asked him to teach them mathematics, and they also requested his expert technical opinion on matters ranging from hydraulics to the manufacture of clocks. Ricci's place in Chinese society gave him unprecedented freedom to advance his mission work as well. In 1601 the emperor Wan-li called Ricci to the imperial city of Beijing, where he remained until he died in 1610.

• Richthofen, Ferdinand Paul Wilhelm, Freiherr von

German
b May 5, 1833; near Brzeg, Poland (formerly Karlsruhe, near Brieg, Prussia)
d October 6, 1905; Poland
Explored, and wrote about geography of, China

Ferdinand Richthofen is generally considered to have contributed more than any other single individual to the knowledge of China's geography. His five-volume *China, the Results of My Travels and the Studies Based Thereon* presented geographical data gathered on a long series of journeys to all parts of the country. Some of Richthofen's other writings dealt with the tasks, methods, and future of geography in the nineteenth century. He also worked to develop the branch of geology called geomorphology, which is concerned with the relief of the land.

Richthofen's early efforts focused on the geology of Transylvania (in what is now Romania) and of the Dolomite Alps. His work attracted the attention of the organizers of an 1860 German economic mission to the Far East, who invited Richthofen to serve as their geologist. In this capacity, he visited Ceylon (now Sri Lanka), Japan, Formosa (now Taiwan), the Celebes, Java (in present-day Indonesia), and the Philippines and crossed the Malay Peninsula from Bangkok to Moulmein, Burma (now Myanmar).

Starting in 1863 Richthofen spent time studying the geology of California. Some of his investigations led to the discovery of new gold fields there. He then returned to the Orient and made a series of seven expeditions that covered almost every region of China. In 1867 the first of these expeditions followed the course of the Chang Jiang (Yangtze River), then explored the region south of the river on the return trip to Beijing. His subsequent trips investigated the entire eastern coast of China from the Liaodong Peninsula southwest to Guangzhou (Canton).

Richthofen also explored the interior regions of China, traveling overland between Beijing and Guangzhou and exploring the provinces of Shanxi, Shaanxi, and Sichuan. His trips into these regions came only a few years after the expeditions of the French explorer Francis Garnier, and their routes almost met at several points. For his part, Richthofen, through his skill as both a geographer and a geologist, substantially improved the general maps of China.

• Rivera, Juan Maria de

Spanish
b 1700s
d 1700s
Explored southwestern United States

A veteran Spanish frontier fighter, Juan Maria de Rivera made the first recorded journeys into the mountainous regions of present-day Colorado and Utah. Between 1761 and 1765 he led three expeditions north from Taos to the southern Rocky Mountains, getting as far as the Gunnison River in southwestern Colorado and to southeastern Utah via the Colorado River.

There is no information on Juan Maria de Rivera's life before he gained attention fighting in the Spanish war against the Ute Indians, who had attacked settlements in the northern frontier of New Spain (present-day Mexico). He then burst upon the stage of history for a few years, made his mark as an explorer, and disappeared.

During his first two expeditions Rivera explored for gold, silver, and precious stones and conducted Jesuit missionaries to the frontiers of New Spain. On the initial journey, in 1761, he headed northwest from Taos and followed the San Juan Piedra River into modern Colorado, passing the San Juan Mountains on the western side of the Continental Divide. Near the modern town of Durango, he discovered silver ore and named the surrounding La Plata (Silver) Mountains.

On his second journey Rivera took a group of soldiers, traders, and missionaries along the Taos–San Juan Piedra–Durango route, skirting west of the La Plata Mountains. After following down the Dolores River to its convergence with the San Miguel River, the party forded the San Miguel and climbed to the Uncompahgre Plateau.

In 1765 Rivera was sent by Governor Cachupín of New Mexico on a trading and prospecting expedition into the lands of the Ute. This time he rounded the San Juan Mountains and followed the Uncompahgre River valley until he reached the junction of the Uncompahgre and Gunnison rivers at the modern town of Delta, Colorado. There he carved a cross, his name, and the year on a poplar tree. He established a brisk trade with the Indians in the Gunnison area and returned to New Mexico. Though his journal of the expedition is lost, most historians agree that on the return trip he traveled down the Gunnison to the Colorado River in southeastern Utah, and finally down the Dolores River. His subsequent life and date of death are unknown.

Juan Maria de Rivera opened several important trade routes into the southwestern United States from Mexico. In addition, his journals—which were later lost—provided Father SILVESTRE VÉLEZ DE ESCALANTE with important geographical information for his expedition ten years later. Baron ALEXANDER VON HUMBOLDT also used geographical data gathered by Rivera (as well as that of other early explorers in the area) in charting his famous map of 1811.

Roggeveen, Jacob

Dutch
b February 1, 1659; Middelburg, Zeeland
d 1729
Discovered and named Easter Island

Jacob Roggeveen led the last great Dutch voyage of discovery into the Pacific (1721–22), marking the end of the Dutch search for *Terra Australis Incognita*. Although Roggeveen did not find that great unknown Southern Continent, he was the first European to discover Easter Island and what is now Samoa.

The son of an enterprising businessman, Roggeveen worked for the Dutch East India Company and eventually rose to councillor of the Council of Justice in Batavia (now Jakarta, Indonesia). In 1696 Roggeveen's father, a friend of the Dutch explorer ABEL TASMAN, proposed to the rival Dutch West India Company an expedition to find the elusive Southern Continent. The elder Roggeveen died before the project could take shape, but he willed the rights to the expedition to his son.

By 1721 Roggeveen had retired from the Dutch East India Company with a handsome fortune. Nevertheless, at the age of sixty-two, he approached the Dutch West India Company and renewed the application for the voyage. At the time, company officials were aware of the English navigator WILLIAM DAMPIER's account of the voyage of Captain Edward Davis, who claimed to have found a "low, sandy island," beyond which lay the great Southern Continent. Eager to find these lands, the company approved Roggeveen's request and outfitted him with three ships.

Roggeveen and his crew sailed from Texel Island on August 21, 1721. Off the Canary Islands they repelled an attack by five pirate ships. After crossing the Atlantic, they touched briefly at the present-day Falkland Islands, then sailed for Le Maire Strait and Cape Horn. During the three-week passage to the Pacific, the frigid, foul weather convinced Roggeveen that a large land mass existed in the polar region, but he believed it was part of *Terra Australis Incognita* (for a more complete discussion, see ALEXANDER DALRYMPLE).

Roggeveen was so taken by his next stop, the Juan Fernández Islands, off Chile, that he planned to establish a settlement there on his return voyage. From these islands he sailed west at about 28° South, looking for the sandy island Dampier had mentioned.

On April 5, 1722, Roggeveen came upon an island he named Paasch Eyland (Easter Island) in honor of the day. It was a fertile spot that showed many signs of life. The Dutch quickly established friendly relations with the island's native inhabitants, despite their tendency to take whatever possessions of the Dutch they fancied—even the hats from the sailors' heads.

The Dutch marveled at these people, who wore very little, if anything, and were covered with tattoos. Their earlobes were pierced and distorted by ornaments that were often three inches long. In his log, Roggeveen observed that if the islanders' earlobes got in the way of what they were doing, they simply looped them over the top of their ears.

When Roggeveen and his men went ashore, one of the Polynesians tried to grab a Dutchman's musket. A small skirmish ensued, and ten islanders were killed. But the remaining islanders remained cordial, bringing Roggeveen and his crew bananas, potatoes, sugarcane, and poultry.

Roggeveen and his men saw the Polynesians bowing down in front of huge stone figures that "caused us to be filled with wonder." Some were thirty feet high and all were "made into the semblance of a human figure." They appeared to be robed and to carry great baskets on their heads. Roggeveen noted that the figures seemed to be made of clay covered with flat stones or flint. Anthropologists today still debate the meaning and origin of the stone figures.

Not being low or sandy, Easter Island did not fit Dampier's description, so after a week Roggeveen sailed on. In mid-May he hit the fringes of the northern Tuamotus, where he stayed at present-day Takapoto, Makatéa, and perhaps other islands. At Makatéa, members of Roggeveen's crew fired on a crowd of islanders standing on the beach. Although the Dutch thought they had successfully made peace afterward, the next day a group of islanders ambushed them and stoned ten of the sailors to death. In the Tuamotus Roggeveen lost one ship and nearly lost the other two to the perilous maze of reefs surrounding the islands.

After a month he held a council. His crew was discouraged by their inability to find *Terra Australis Incognita* and was concerned about whether their wages would be paid. Instead of returning to the Juan Fernández Islands, Roggeveen decided to continue sailing west for Dutch outposts at Java (in present-day Indonesia).

His new course took him past Bora-Bora and other Leeward Islands of the Society group (where he may have landed), then to Samoa. By then, **scurvy** among the crew was so bad that Roggeveen did not dare stay. He continued sailing north of the Solomons and New Guinea and sighted Java in September 1722.

When Roggeveen reached Batavia, the Dutch East India Company seized his ships and sent him and his crew back to the Netherlands, virtually as prisoners. Eventually the two rival companies went to court, and restitution was made to Roggeveen and his crew.

Despite Roggeveen's discoveries, his sponsors considered the voyage a commercial failure, and he received no credit. A cape at the eastern tip of Easter Island today bears Roggeveen's name, testament to his most enduring and significant discovery.

Rohlfs, Friedrich Gerhard

German
b April 14, 1831; Vegesack, near Bremen
d June 2, 1896; Rüngsdorf, near Bad Godesberg
Explored North Africa

Gerhard Rohlfs, the first European to cross Africa from the Mediterranean to the Gulf of Guinea, is credited with gathering a wealth of information about previously unknown regions of the continent. Fascinated by the land and people of Africa, Rohlfs aborted promising careers in the military, medical, and diplomatic fields to undertake treacherous journeys through the northern interior. His major expeditions took him to many areas never before traveled by a European, notably the Oases of Kufra in modern Libya. While his lack of technical training limited the scientific value of his work, his detailed sketches and writings are highly regarded for the light they shed on the mysteries of the terrain and culture of North Africa.

Restless even as a youth, Rohlfs abandoned both medical school and the Austrian army before going to Africa in the service of the French Foreign Legion. He spent five years in Algeria, absorbing the native customs and language, and

Gerhard Rohlfs. The Bettmann Archive.

after his discharge in 1861 he traveled to Morocco. There his fluency in Arabic, coupled with his medical training, earned him the prestigious post of physician general to the army of the sultan of Morocco. Despite the respect he commanded, unusual in a land where foreigners were deeply mistrusted, Rohlfs soon grew impatient. He left the post in 1862 to set out for the unknown African interior. Disguised as an Arab he headed south, crossing Morocco's Atlas Mountains and continuing to the Oases of Tafilalt, where he was savagely attacked by a band of robbers.

The near-fatal incident did not deter him, however. He was determined to learn what lay in the interior, and the prospect of further danger only heightened his enthusiasm. So Rohlfs headed on, first east to Ghadames in a failed effort to reach Timbuktu, and then south through the Sahara, crossing the continent from the Mediterranean to the Gulf of Guinea in the process.

Following the latter expedition, which lasted from 1865 to 1867, Rohlfs went to Tripoli, from which he intended to proceed east to the Libyan Desert. The German Colonial Office in Berlin had other plans for Rohlfs, however. Impressed by his accomplishments, the Colonial Office chose him for a diplomatic mission to Bornu (in present-day Nigeria), to the south, to visit Sultan Omar on behalf of King William I of Prussia. Rohlfs, eager to explore the desert oases to the east of Tripoli, was enraged by the commission. In the face of his furious protests, the Colonial Office relented and allowed Rohlfs to suggest a suitable replacement ambassador for the Bornu mission. After persuading physician and explorer GUSTAV NACHTIGAL to accept the assignment, Rohlfs was free to launch his own expedition.

Kufra, Rohlfs's principal destination, lay southeast of Tripoli with hundreds of miles of desert separating the two. Kufra was home to the Senussi, a people who harbored a deep hatred of Christians. Rohlfs was so determined to be the first foreigner to reach the Oases of Kufra that he undertook three grueling expeditions through areas where rain had not fallen

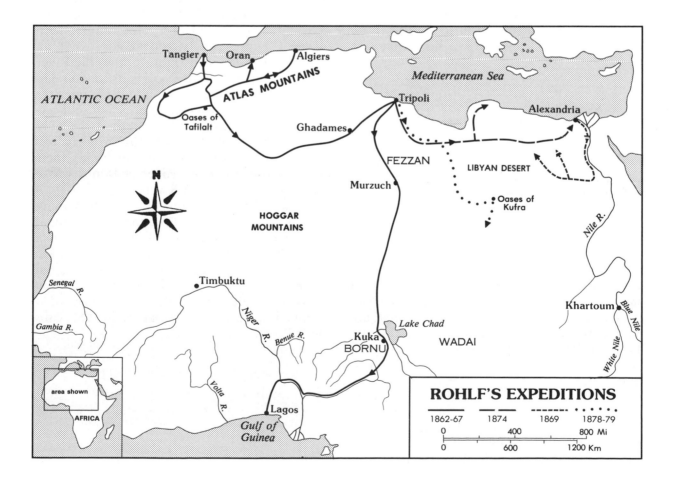

ROHLF'S EXPEDITIONS

| 1862-67 | 1874 | 1869 | 1878-79 |

0 400 800 Mi
0 600 1200 Km

for a decade. His attempts spanned ten years and were finally rewarded in 1879 when the seemingly endless Libyan Desert gave way to the lakes, mosques, and castles of the Oases of Kufra. His visit was brief because of the intense hostility he encountered, and he later wrote in his journal that while the entire venture had aged him greatly, it had been worthwhile. He nevertheless stated: "For thousands I could not be persuaded to relive such days as I have experienced in Kufra. . . ." For forty years he held the distinction of being the only European to have visited there.

From Kufra, Rohlfs started south on an expedition to Wadai (in modern Chad) in the employ of the German government. But this journey had barely begun when he was ambushed by Suaya Arabs and robbed of all his equipment, forcing him to abandon the project. Rohlfs's remaining days in Africa, before his return to Germany, were spent uneventfully as German consul in Zanzibar.

Rohlfs explored Africa for nearly twenty years, considerably longer than any other German up to that time. His observations added substantially to the existing body of knowledge on Africa and greatly influenced the perception of the continent, especially in his native Germany.

• Rondón, Cândido Mariano da Silva

Brazilian
b May 5, 1865; Cuiabá, Mato Grosso
d January 19, 1958; Rio de Janeiro
Explored northwest Brazil; discovered and explored River of Doubt

Between 1906 and 1909, Brigadier General Cândido Mariano da Silva Rondón explored 193,000 square miles of northwestern Brazil, charted the course of fifteen rivers, and discovered and named the River of Doubt (Rio da Dúvida). Then, in 1913, he mapped that river during the famous Roosevelt-Rondón Scientific Expedition.

Cândido Rondón was born on May 5, 1865, in Cuiabá, Brazil (in the state of Mato Grosso), and was raised by his uncle after being orphaned at the age of one. As a young man he enlisted in the army and graduated from mili-

tary school in 1890. After teaching mathematics at the school for a short time and then serving with the army corps of engineers, he was selected in 1906 by the Brazilian government to map a river system in an unknown region of the state of Mato Grosso and to supervise the construction of telegraph lines in the area.

During the next four years Rondón led expeditions deep into the Brazilian jungle and mapped the courses of the Sepotuba and Juruena rivers, among others. On May 3, 1909, he left on a journey that would take him down the Jiparaná River and into the Madeira River. By the time his party reached the Madeira after several months of difficult travel, they were near starvation and additionally weakened by fatigue, illness, and overexposure. Undaunted, Rondón pressed onward and discovered a new river running northwest between the Jiparaná and Juruena rivers and named it the River of Doubt, since the river was at that time unexplored and its nature a matter of conjecture.

During the course of his explorations, he became an expert on the vegetation, animals, and Indians of the Brazilian interior, as well as its physical geography. The new information Rondón had acquired led to a joint venture with former U.S. president THEODORE ROOSEVELT, an adventurer in his own right, to map the River of Doubt. The resultant Roosevelt-Rondón Scientific Expedition started in late 1913 and, after months of harrowing experiences and soul-trying hardships, reached the mouth of the river on April 26, 1914. The exploration party collected valuable scientific data, including their determination that the River of Doubt was a branch of the Aripuanã River.

Rondón devoted the rest of his life to helping the Indians of Brazil, directing the National Service for the Protection of Indians until 1940. For his humanitarian efforts and his promotion of inter-American harmony he was nominated for the 1952 Nobel Peace Prize. In recognition of his contributions, the Brazilian government renamed the territory of Guaporé in 1956, calling it Rondônia.

• Roosevelt, Theodore

American
b October 27, 1858; New York, New York
d January 6, 1919; Oyster Bay, New York
Explored River of Doubt in Brazil

Theodore Roosevelt was not only governor of New York (1898–1900), twenty-sixth president of the United States (1901–1909), heroic leader of the Rough Riders, and recipient of the 1906 Nobel Peace Prize for mediating an end to the Russo-Japanese War—but also a respected historian and author, an avid conservationist, and an explorer. He was an outspoken advocate for ethics in politics who possessed an almost encyclopedic knowledge of American history. Having lived in the wilds of the Dakota Territory in the 1880s and gone to Africa on a hunt in 1910, Roosevelt culminated his adventurous life on an expedition in 1913–14 that mapped the 400-mile-long River of Doubt in western Brazil.

Born in New York City on October 27, 1858, Roosevelt showed an early interest in natural history. He graduated Phi Beta Kappa from Harvard University in 1880, became a freelance historian and author, and entered politics in 1898. As a child he had overcome asthma and defective eyesight by teaching himself to ride, shoot, and box. But, by the time of the Brazilian expedition, he was blind in one eye, due to a boxing accident.

After serving two terms as U.S. president, Roosevelt went on a lecture tour to Argentina and Brazil in 1913. In conjunction with the tour, an expedition to map the River of Doubt was organized. By arrangement with the Brazilian government, CÂNDIDO RONDÓN, who had previously explored the river, joined the group, thus forming the Roosevelt-Rondón Scientific Expedition. After traveling by canoe, auto-van, mule train, and foot from Tapirapoan to the Utianiti Falls on the Rio Papagaio, and across the land of the Nãmbiquaras of western Brazil, the expedition began the descent of the River of Doubt on February 27, 1914. Battling fire ants, flies, termites, torrential downpours, terrible heat, torturous rapids, and illness, the expedition made its way to the mouth of the river on April 26. During the journey two members of the group were killed in a whirlpool, and Roosevelt and his son, Kermit, almost drowned. Besides near drowning, Roosevelt also had along the way suffered from fever, dysentery, an ulcerated leg, and heart problems—but his spirit remained indomitable.

The mapping expedition was a great success, and Rondón renamed the river Rio Roosevelt. In addition, the expedition collected over 2,500 specimens of birds and about 500 mammal specimens, many of them new to science.

• Ross, James Clark

English
b April 15, 1800; London
d April 3, 1862; Aylesbury, Dorset
Discovered North Magnetic Pole and parts of
**   Antarctica; explored Canadian Arctic**

Rear Admiral Sir James Clark Ross was the protégé of WILLIAM EDWARD PARRY and his heir as the premier polar explorer in the British navy. Like Parry, and unlike many (if not most) Arctic explorers, Ross had a well-balanced character to match his sound judgment. When he was at the peak of his career in the 1840s, he turned down the chance to lead what was ex-

Sir James Clark Ross. National Maritime Museum, Greenwich.

pected to be the navy's final assault on the Northwest Passage so that he could enjoy some hard-earned domestic tranquility with his new wife. Many have since wondered whether he could have averted the disaster that befell the large expedition led by the aging Sir JOHN FRANKLIN. Such speculation is as much due to Franklin's recklessness as to Ross's supreme competence, which culminated in his great Antarctic mission (1839–43).

Ross's early career fell under the influence of Parry and of Sir John Ross, his uncle and a skilled, if often unlucky, Arctic explorer. From the time he joined the navy in 1812 until 1817, young Ross served under his uncle in three different ships, covering northern waters from the North to the White seas. In 1818 he joined his uncle and Parry on the mission that rediscovered Baffin Bay, but missed the entrance to the Northwest Passage (for a more complete discussion, see MARTIN FROBISHER). Then, in 1819, he boarded the *Hecla* with the first expedition to the Arctic led by Parry and thereafter served on every one of Parry's expeditions.

In the 1821–23 exploration of the Melville Peninsula (in the present-day Northwest Territories of Canada) he was aboard the *Fury*. There he witnessed the first attempt of Europeans to learn the **Inuit** art of dog sledging, a skill he would eventually master himself. In 1824 he again served on the *Fury* and was on board when it was wrecked in Prince Regent Inlet. Two years after returning home, he was again with Parry on the failed mission to reach the North Pole from Spitsbergen (now part of Svalbard) by **boat-sledge**.

After returning from this grueling venture, he was promoted to commander on November 8, 1827. By then he was an accomplished sailor of icy waters, an expert in magnetism, a money-making whaler, and an avid student of natural history—well on his way toward filling Parry's shoes. It was at this point that Ross agreed to accompany his uncle on a privately financed attempt to take up the search for the Northwest Passage at the point in Prince Regent Inlet where the ice had forced Parry to turn back four years earlier.

Sir John Ross was trying to gain back the respect he had lost when he missed the opening to the passage in 1818. Though he had not been able to interest the British Admiralty in the project, public interest in Arctic exploration was running so high that one donor, Sir Felix

Booth, contributed £18,000 toward a private venture, a very large sum of money in those days. As it turned out, Ross once again missed the strait (later named Bellot Strait) connecting the Prince Regent Inlet to what would later be called Franklin Strait, but he more than satisfied the public's taste for romance and adventure. And thanks largely to the presence of James Ross, the expedition accomplished some serious science and exploration.

Trapped in the ice at Lord Mayor Bay at the base of Boothia Peninsula for three years (1829–33) in an old steam **packet** named the *Victory*, then for another in a makeshift shelter on Somerset Island, the Ross expedition set a record for Arctic survival by Europeans. Meeting with good luck initially, the *Victory* made it farther in the summer of 1829 than Parry had gone in two summers, passing southwards through Prince Regent Inlet into the Gulf of Boothia. The warm weather was the main reason for such rapid progress. Unfortunately, the freakish warmth led to such deep penetration into the gulf that the ship became imprisoned in the ice.

John Ross did not have the same enlivening influence on his men that Parry had had, but James broke the boredom by making long trips by **sledge**, taking magnetic and celestial observations, and collecting specimens. Most crucially, he used his knowledge of local dialect and custom to begin communications with the Inuits who approached the ship in January 1830. The good relations that ensued turned out to be essential to the survival of the party, since the Inuits provided not only good company, but fresh game and clothing suitable for Arctic winters. Like the Inuits Parry had met in 1822, these were excellent geographers. They drew a map of the southern part of the Gulf of Boothia showing (correctly) that there was no local outlet which might serve as a link to the Northwest Passage.

In the spring of 1830, James Ross began exploring by dog sledge, once again with the indispensable help—and dog power—provided by the Eskimos. He made several trips around Boothia Peninsula with Eskimo guides. That May, he crossed to the west coast and proceeded across the strait later named after him. He then explored the west coast of the strait (which he called King William Land; now Island) north to Cape Felix and then southwest to Victory Point, but low supplies prevented him from continuing farther. At Cape Felix he witnessed the massive pressure of the ice flowing down from the northwest—the ice that would soon engulf the Franklin expedition. At Victory Point he was close to the point where Franklin's ships were subsequently entrapped.

During these travels, Ross had made enough magnetic observations to calculate the position of the North Magnetic Pole. He reached the exact spot the next year, on May 31, 1831, thus satisfying a long-held ambition. This discovery had, in fact, more scientific significance than the discovery of a Northwest Passage, so Ross believed he had made good on Booth's investment.

As the ice did not give up the *Victory* in 1832, there was nothing to do but abandon the ship and return by sledge to Parry's old camp at Fury Point, then by boat to Baffin Bay. Ice again forced them to winter at Fury Point (1832–33). (This long agony ranks with that suffered by WILLEM BARENTS and his crew in the Barents Sea more than two centuries earlier.) By the time the Rosses and their crew, scrawny and weatherbeaten, rowed out of Prince Regent Inlet, to be picked up by Ross's old ship, the *Isabella* (by then a whaler), in the summer of 1833, they had been presumed dead. On returning to heroes' welcomes in England, the Rosses received many awards and honors. James was made a post captain, and John was knighted, having finally vindicated himself in the eyes of the public.

But for James there was still a great deal of work ahead. In 1836 he returned to the Arctic in command of the *Cove* on a mission to save some frozen-in whalers in Davis Strait. Then in April 1839 he was appointed to command an expedition to the South Magnetic Pole. The *Erebus* and *Terror* set off from England the following September. Reacting to the concurrent attempts by the Frenchman JULES DUMONT D'URVILLE and the American CHARLES WILKES, Ross changed his original course to head straight through the ice belt that encircles Antarctica. After a trying voyage through the ice pack, which damaged both ships badly, he discovered and named Victoria Land on January 10, 1841. Soon after came the Ross Sea and Barrier (now Ice Shelf), and the two great volcanoes that he named after his ships.

On this voyage Ross demonstrated his consummate skill as a commander of a scientific expedition in the most difficult of sailing conditions. Not only did he keep his crew healthy for four years (he was wise enough to winter each year either on Van Diemen's Land, now Tasmania, or in Australia), but he maintained a rigorous program of observations on magnetism, deep-sea temperatures, aquatic life, and ocean floor depths (though the latter were somewhat flawed). Among many other important findings, Ross established (through the use of a deep-sea clam) that life-forms thrived on the ocean floor, no matter how deep.

On his return to England in September 1843, Ross was knighted and received many other honors. He married the same year and settled in Aylesbury, Buckinghamshire, far from the sea. He interrupted his life of farming and study only once, when in 1848 he was persuaded to command the *Enterprise* and *Investigator* on an expedition in search of the lost Franklin party—the expedition he had turned down. After wintering at Port Leopold, Somerset Island, he searched the north coast of the island for his respected friend (Franklin had been his host in Van Diemen's Land), then followed its western coast southward, unknowingly retracing Franklin's route along Peel Sound. Others in his party searched Prince Regent Inlet to no avail. Everyone was disappointed, but it was the example of the Rosses' four-year survival in the same waters that encouraged the massive search and relief effort of the next decade. After returning to England in the fall, Ross lived the rest of his days on land. He died peacefully at the age of sixty-two.

Rubruck, William of. See **William of Rubruck.**

Saint Brendan. See **Brendan, Saint.**

Saint Francis Xavier. See **Xavier, Saint Francis.**

• Schiltberger, Johann (Hans)

German
b 1380; near Lohhof, Bavaria
d 1440?
Traveled throughout Asia as captive of Turks and Mongols

Hans Schiltberger, a young German nobleman of the Middle Ages, had the misfortune of conducting his explorations involuntarily. While serving King Sigismund of Hungary in his crusade against the Turks, Schiltberger was taken prisoner by the Ottoman sultan Bajazet. For the next thirty-two years, Schiltberger was passed from one master to another in Asia, some of whom permitted him to travel freely. After he escaped and returned home to Bavaria, he wrote an account of his adventures in the distant Orient. His narrative, published posthumously about 1460 as the *Reisebuch* (Travel Book), was one of the first German contributions to the expanding field of geography.

Schiltberger, the son of a German nobleman, was only fifteen years old when he was captured on September 28, 1396, during the battle at Nicopolis, where a cavalry unit commanded by the duke of Burgundy was crushed by the Turks. Ten thousand captured German soldiers were beheaded the following day; only those under the age of twenty were spared, and they were enslaved. Bajazet took Schiltberger and the other young slaves to Constantinople (now Istanbul, Turkey). In his book, Schiltberger writes:

> I was taken to the palace of the Turkish king; there for six years I was obliged to run on my feet with the others, wherever he went, it being the custom that the lords have people to run before them. After six years I deserved to be allowed to ride, and I rode with him, so that I was twelve years with him.

These experiences as the sultan's footman and outrider gave Schiltberger an extensive and detailed knowledge of Asia Minor and Egypt. During this time, he made one brave attempt to escape the clutches of his Turkish captors, but to no avail.

When the Turks were defeated by the Mongols at Ankara on July 20, 1402, a great battle Schiltberger describes in some detail, he became a prisoner of the Mongol khan Timur (Tamerlane). His descriptions of the khan's hideous brutality corroborate those of others unlucky enough to become familiar with Timur's tactics. For example, after Timur had conquered one town and occupied it with a garrison, he departed for home. Along the way, he received word that the townspeople had succeeded in a revolt and had executed his troops. Enraged, Timur reversed his march and stormed back to the scene of rebellion. In his book, Schiltberger describes how the angry khan assembled the citizens and presided over the killing of all the men in the town. He then marched the 7,000 women and children to a plain outside the city, where he had most of the young children killed. After setting fire to the town, Timur took the women and remaining children back to his own city.

Fortunately for Schiltberger, he did not incur the wrath of the khan. In fact, Timur took Schiltberger to Samarkand (now in the Soviet Union, near Tashkent), where the German's resulting status has been compared to that of MARCO POLO in Cathay (present-day China). Although Schiltberger was not allowed to return home, his book reveals that he went on extensive journeys throughout Armenia, Georgia, the middle Volga, and southeastern Russia. After Timur died in 1405, Schiltberger was turned over to the khan's son, Shah Rokh, who lived in the kingdom of Herāt, at Khorāsān. Schiltberger lived in Khorāsān until a young Tartar prince residing at the court was called back to Siberia to rule his home region. Schiltberger was ordered by Shah Rokh to accompany the prince, and he consequently began a long journey to Tobolsk and Tomsk in Siberia. He also visited Mecca (in present-day Saudi Arabia) under his new master, and his account of the Muslim religion and the life of the Prophet Mohammed is remarkably clear and accurate. Upon his return to Caffa (now Feodosiya) on the Black Sea, Schiltberger and four other German prisoners escaped from their masters and boarded a European vessel bound for Constantinople. From there, they returned to Munich by crossing east central Europe on a route running north of the Carpathian Mountains.

Schiltberger's chronicle of his wanderings remains an important account of medieval Asian history and topography. Other explorers had traversed Asia before him; but his perspective is unique, for he saw the Eastern lands not as an Occidental explorer honored in the courts of Oriental rulers, but from the point of view of a slave. His account, like that of Marco Polo, was read widely during the late Middle Ages by Europeans with geographical interest. These narratives offered the West a glimpse of the mysteries of the vast lands to the east, in anticipation of the age of discovery that was soon to follow.

Schnitzer, Eduard (Emin Pasha)

German
b 1840; Opole, Poland (formerly Oppeln, Prussia)
d October 1892; Kinema, Congo
Explored East Africa; served as governor of Equatoria for British

Originally enlisted as a medical officer on an expedition into the heart of Africa, Eduard Schnitzer remained there for more than a decade as governor of the Egyptian province of Equatoria (in present-day Sudan). While he was unable to eradicate slave trading in the region, his goal, he helped to develop the area and to upgrade its standard of living. Threatened by a large-scale revolt by Mahdist Arabs in 1883, he appealed to Europe for help and thereby became the object of a rivalry between English and German rescue expeditions. Schnitzer remained committed to his work, however, and returned to the interior after reluctantly allowing himself to be rescued.

Raised by a widowed mother, Schnitzer was enthralled by natural history as a youth but chose to study medicine. After graduating, he left Berlin in 1864 and went to Turkey, where he became a tutor and later moved with a family he worked for to western Albania. He then roamed around Europe for several years and in 1874 traveled to Egypt, where he practiced medicine in Alexandria to earn money for a trip south to Khartoum (in present-day Sudan). Schnitzer arrived there in 1875 to find that his medical services were needed on an expedition in Equatoria.

Schnitzer went south to Lado to meet the mission's leader, British colonel Charles Gordon. (It was at this time that Schnitzer took the name Emin, meaning "faithful one," and the title of Pasha.) Gordon intended to explore the region, combat its rampant disease, and protect its natives from the thievery and slave trading of the Egyptians. Once the British forces had restored some order, Gordon left in late 1875, while Schnitzer remained as Equatoria's surgeon general. In addition to serving in this post, Schnitzer explored extensively, paid diplomatic visits to local tribal rulers, and collected botanical specimens to send to Europe. Gordon returned in 1878 and, since illness had forced two previous governors to resign, named Schnitzer to the post.

The native people of Equatoria came to respect their slight, well-dressed leader, who ruled them like a strict father and developed towns, roads, and an active farming enterprise. However, he met with resistance from Egyptians residing there, many of whom were civil servants exiled to the region as punishment for dishonesty. Although their efforts to oust Schnitzer failed, his administration fell prey to a revolution led by a self-proclaimed messiah called Mahdi. Forced to retreat even further south in Equatoria after Lado came under siege in 1883, Schnitzer petitioned for help. It was 1886, however, before word of his plight reached the outside world.

Spurred by public demand, both the British and German authorities mounted rescue campaigns. Explorer HENRY MORTON STANLEY, leader of Great Britain's expedition, located the deposed governor at Lake Albert (in present-day Uganda) in 1888. However, Schnitzer wanted help protecting his province, not escaping from it. Another year elapsed before he grudgingly traveled to Africa's east coast with Stanley, who bitterly resented his ingratitude. Schnitzer also alienated the British public, first by refusing to travel to England and then by accepting Germany's commission to return to the interior in 1890 to claim territory on its behalf. Traveling west via Lake Victoria, he got as far as the village of Kinema, near the Congo River, when he was beheaded by Arab soldiers on the orders of the district chief.

Schomburgk, Robert Hermann

English
b 1804; Freiburg, Germany
d 1865; Berlin, Germany
Explored interior of British Guiana

The naturalist and explorer Sir Robert Hermann Schomburgk investigated the wild and relatively unknown interior of British Guiana between 1835 and 1837. Then, in 1841, he explored, surveyed, and established boundaries in the territories disputed by British Guiana, Brazil, and Venezuela. One result of this expedition was the establishment of the Schomburgk

Robert Herman Schomburgk. Bettmann/Hulton.

the mountain of Roraima in southern British Guiana.

Schomburgk returned to England in 1839 and recommended further development of British Guiana. Returning to Guiana in 1841 as boundary commissioner, he surveyed and marked its boundaries with Brazil and Venezuela. In accomplishing this, he traveled overland to the mouth of the Rio Branco in Brazil, ascended that river into Guiana above the modern city of Boa Vista, and surveyed the Orinoco River delta in Venezuela. While surveying the Waini River he discovered a natural channel connecting it with the Barima River. His survey was completed as he traveled down the Cuyuni River in Venezuela to its confluence with the Essequibo in British Guiana.

Robert Hermann Schomburgk was knighted in 1844 for his contributions in opening up the interior of British Guiana and providing essential data for Britain's border disputes with Brazil and Venezuela. He served as British consul at Santo Domingo (in what is now the Dominican Republic) in 1848 and at Bangkok from 1857 to 1864. He died in Berlin in 1865.

Line, which formalized the boundary between Venezuela and Guiana.

As a youth Schomburgk showed a great interest in natural history. In a letter he noted that, "My love for botany and natural history, and an ardent desire to travel, led me, in 1830, to the West Indies." There, in 1831, he surveyed the coast of Anegada, one of the British Virgin Islands, in order to help navigators avoid dangerous shoals and reefs surrounding the island.

In 1835 Schomburgk was commissioned by the Royal Geographical Society to explore the interior of British Guiana and collect botanical and geological specimens. In pursuit of this objective, he began the ascent of the Essequibo River late in February 1836 with a party of twenty-two. The upper river was blocked by a large cataract (a waterfall or steep rapids), however, and he was forced to turn back. Next he explored the upper reaches of the Courantyne River in eastern British Guiana until his progress was again blocked by waterfalls. Then he turned his attention to the Berbice River where he had to cope with stampeding hogs, swarms of attacking ants, and a scarcity of fresh food. Finally, he returned to and completed his survey of the Courantyne by going overland around the falls. While exploring the Rupununi River in 1838, he became the first European to see

Schouten, Willem (William) Corneliszoon (Cornelisz)

Dutch
b 1567?; Hoorn, Holland
d 1625
Discovered Le Maire Strait; named Cape Horn; explored South Pacific

Navigator Willem Corneliszoon Schouten piloted Jacob Le Maire's ship, *Eendracht*, on a voyage to find new trading lands that were not already under the control of the Dutch East India Company. In doing so, he discovered a new route into the Pacific and charted numerous islands, including the north coast of New Guinea.

In 1615, when businessman Isaac Le Maire, Jacob's father, proposed a private expedition to the South Seas, Schouten was a well-known navigator who had already made three voyages to the East Indies. Schouten's brother Jan skippered the ship that accompanied the *Eendracht*, the *Hoorn*, which later was destroyed by fire while beached at Patagonia.

Confident of thwarting the explorers' plans,

the Dutch East India Company forbade the two ships to enter the Pacific Ocean via Africa's Cape of Good Hope or through the Strait of Magellan near the southern tip of South America. Schouten nevertheless sailed in May 1615, crossed the Atlantic, and reached Port Desire, Patagonia, in December. After the loss of the *Hoorn*, the voyage resumed in January. South of the Strait of Magellan, Schouten found another passage (which became Le Maire Strait) that led him to the Pacific without rounding the cape he named Hoorn (now Horn), after his birthplace in northwest Holland.

Schouten sailed west, eventually through what probably were the present-day Tuamotus, Fiji, and Samoa. He found and named the Hoorn Islands, Alofi and Futuna (now the Futuna Islands), southwest of the Wallis Islands. When Jacob Le Maire suggested that they sail west to look for the great Southern Continent, Schouten countered that the waters below what is now New Guinea were unknown and dangerous. Instead they sailed along and charted the north coast of New Guinea, discovering and naming the Schouten Islands just off its northwest coast.

Shortly after the explorers reached Java (in present-day Indonesia), officials from the Dutch East India Company threw Schouten, Le Maire, and several other members of the expedition in jail, not believing that Schouten had found a new passage into the Pacific. They were shipped back to Holland with Joris van Spilbergen, who was completing a circumnavigation. Le Maire died en route, but Schouten lived to tell the tale of their discoveries. His account of the voyage was published in Amsterdam in 1619. That same year, Le Maire's journal was published along with Spilbergen's.

· Schweinfurth, Georg August

German
b December 29, 1836; Riga, Latvia, Soviet Union
d September 19, 1925; Berlin
Explored East and Central Africa

Credited with the discovery of Africa's Uele River, Georg August Schweinfurth explored extensively in the upper Nile River region and crossed huge sections of uncharted desert territory to the north. A trained scientist, he studied

Georg August Schweinfurth. The Bettmann Archive.

the geology, botany, and other natural history of the East African interior. He also created valuable maps that helped locate the region's bodies of water and included valuable information about little-known tribes of the interior. His detailed accounts and analyses contributed significantly to Europe's understanding of the lands and people of Africa.

Educated at the universities of Munich, Heidelberg, and Berlin, Schweinfurth originally specialized in the field of botany. As he examined samples of Africa's vegetation while he was still in school, he became intrigued with the idea of traveling to the continent. He completed his formal education in 1862 and departed for Egypt the same year. During his initial expedition of three years, he traveled up the Nile as far south as Khartoum in the Sudan and explored the coast of the Red Sea. On the basis of the botanical specimens he brought back to Germany, he received a grant from the Humboldt-Stiftung of Berlin for additional scientific study in the East African interior.

Returning to Khartoum in January 1869 by way of the Red Sea and its coastal city of Suakin, he set sail up the White Nile to the Bahr al-

Ghazal, a region of the upper Nile basin. From its headwaters, he crossed the Nile-Congo watershed until he came to an unknown westward-flowing river in March 1870. Schweinfurth at first assumed his discovery, the Uele River, to be a tributary of the Niger River, which in reality lay far to the northwest. It proved instead to be a tributary of the Ubangi River to the south. His location of the Uele—which flowed in the opposite direction of the headwaters of the Nile—was significant in helping establish the western limits of the extensive Nile River system.

During this two-year expedition, Schweinfurth made a thorough study of the botany and geology of the Sudan. He also investigated several tribes about whom little or nothing was known to that point. These included the Bongo, Mangbetu, Pygmy, and Naim-Naim peoples, the latter of whom were said to be cannibals who sharpened their teeth into points. His report on the short-statured Pygmies of the Congo was not the first, since the explorer PAUL BELLONI DU CHAILLU had noted a similar encounter in 1863. However, Schweinfurth's was considered the first authoritative report on the diminutive people.

Schweinfurth returned to Germany in 1871 and published a two-volume book about his travels entitled *The Heart of Africa*, a comprehensive and scientifically based account that was valued for its wealth of data. Shortly after its publication in 1873, he went back to Africa and took part in an expedition in northern Central Africa. Schweinfurth traveled this time in the company of fellow German FRIEDRICH GERHARD ROHLFS, an experienced explorer of Morocco and the western Sahara who was married to Schweinfurth's niece. Rohlfs was a former foreign legionnaire who was determined to visit the Oases of Kufra. This entailed crossing a vast, unexplored expanse of the Libyan Desert, including territory where rain had not fallen in ten years. After their camels had gone without water for more than two weeks, the explorers were forced to turn back.

In 1875, Schweinfurth traveled to Cairo, where he was to make his home for more than a decade. He conducted two minor desert expeditions but concentrated primarily on the botany, geology, and archaeology of Egypt. He also served as a consultant to its government on exploration-related matters and assisted in the founding of Egypt's geographical society. Of-

fered the position of leader of the famous British-sponsored Kilimanjaro Expedition in 1885, he declined the honor, citing his numerous responsibilities in Egypt and observing that his own series of rigorous expeditions had already taken their toll on his health. The explorer was to live another forty years, however. He retired to Germany in 1888, where he continued to write, primarily scientific publications, and remained involved in African studies and developments until his death in 1925 at the age of eighty-nine.

· Scoresby, William

English
b October 5, 1789; Cropton, Yorkshire
d March 21, 1857; Torquay
Explored Norwegian Arctic and East Greenland
  as whaling captain and scientist

A man with interests ranging from marine biology to theology, the British whaling captain William Scoresby made his mark in the history of exploration when he noticed an unusual warming of the Arctic Ocean off the coast of Greenland in 1817. His correspondence with the president of the Royal Geographical Society, Sir JOSEPH BANKS, regarding this possible climate shift led directly to intense efforts by the British navy to locate an open Northwest Passage (for a more complete discussion, see MARTIN FROBISHER). Though the navy never directly made use of Scoresby's considerable navigational skills, all of the naval officers sent to the Arctic benefited from his brilliant observations on every aspect of the Arctic, many of which were published in 1820 in *An Account of the Arctic Regions and Northern Whale Fishery*. This book also made a deep impression on Herman Melville, who referred to it frequently in *Moby-Dick*.

For a man who later became a minister of the Church of England with a doctorate in divinity from the University of Cambridge, Scoresby had an unusual background. His father was a prosperous whaler who expertly began training his son in the business when the boy was only eleven. When the younger Scoresby was seventeen, he took a ship as chief mate under his father to a record-high latitude (81°30' North, east of Svalbard). The next year he began studying natural philosophy and chemistry at the University of Edinburgh but gave it up to join the navy, which put him directly into battle. After more adventures at sea, he returned briefly to his studies, but when he turned twenty-one, his father put him in command of a whaling ship. It was this continual mixture of study and hard experience that made Scoresby a particularly valuable observer of the Arctic.

After writing his first book, Scoresby captained three whaling voyages that brought in enormous profits. In 1822 he and his father explored over 800 miles of East Greenland coast in two ships. But when his first wife died in 1823, the loss moved the younger Scoresby to study for the ministry, to which he devoted the rest of his life. He held several posts in the church, but nevertheless continued to write voluminously on various scientific topics connected with navigation and the Arctic until his death in 1857.

Robert Falcon Scott. Royal Geographical Society.

• Scott, Robert Falcon

English
b June 6, 1868; Devonport, Devonshire
d March 29?, 1912; Ross Ice Shelf, Antarctica
Explored Antarctica; became second person to reach South Pole

After leading a successful three-year scientific expedition to Antarctica at the beginning of the twentieth century, Captain Robert Falcon Scott decided in 1909 to join the race to become the first to attain the South Pole. He succeeded in reaching the pole, only to find that a rival explorer had done so first, preceding his party by a month. Crestfallen, his team trudged back toward their base camp until stalled by worsening conditions. Tragically, his party became the first to die of exposure in Antarctica. The heroic and romantic dimensions of Scott's failure and death, however, captured the imagination and sympathy of the world, and especially his compatriots.

When Scott was chosen in 1900 to lead the first British expedition to explore the interior of Antarctica, he was a little-known lieutenant in the British navy with no experience in polar exploration. The son of a brewer, he had caught the attention of the president of the Royal Geographical Society, Sir Clements Markham, thir-

teen years earlier when, as an eighteen-year-old midshipman, he had won a sailing race. Markham subsequently dined with the victor and was so impressed by his "intelligence, information, and the charm of his manner" that he immediately began thinking of Scott in the role of commander of some future, as-yet-unplanned, Antarctic expedition. Markham was a Victorian romantic who believed that Scott's personal qualities as a British officer were sufficient qualification for any task. Markham was also clever enough to realize—correctly, as things turned out—that this articulate, dashing young officer would capture the hearts of the British public.

Antarctica, a once-lush landmass, now lies beneath an ice sheet that is 8,800 feet thick at the pole. Its climate is frigid, its weather the most severe in the world. But in 1900 very little was known about the interior of this uninhabited and inhospitable continent. The scientific questions to be answered by Scott's proposed expedition were therefore important. The scientists of the Royal Society wanted the celebrated geologist, J. W. Gregory, to lead the land party, rather than Markham's inexperienced and relatively uneducated officer. But Markham, the moving force behind the expedition, believed the navy should predominate, so Professor Gregory resigned. Scientific work was still on the agenda, however, and a great deal of valuable data was collected.

On August 6, 1901, Scott's ship, the *Discovery*, set sail, and by January it was at the edge of the floating glacier called the Ross Ice Shelf (discovered by and named after JAMES CLARK ROSS). After using a passenger balloon to survey the land, Scott set up base on James Ross Island. In the spring, he sent **sledge** parties out in three directions. Scott, Dr. Edward Wilson, and ERNEST SHACKLETON explored the ice shelf 380 miles toward the pole, reaching a latitude of 82°17′ South on December 30, 1902, fifty-nine days after leaving base camp. Their return trip was a nightmare despite the depots of supplies that had been set up along the way. As the dogs starved, they were killed and fed to the remaining dogs. Shackleton and Scott came down with **scurvy**, while Wilson suffered from snow blindness. (Scott's parties were to have recurring problems with scurvy, a disease that had been all but eliminated on other contemporary Arctic expeditions through the careful management of diet.) "Misfortunes never come singly," Scott wrote in his diary on December 21, still 300 miles from base. On February 3, 1903, the three finally made it back to camp. Shackleton was so ill that he had to be sent back to England earlier than planned on a relief ship.

The next spring Scott set out once again on a grueling 360-mile trip up Ferrar Glacier, to the polar plateau 9,000 feet above sea level. There were no dogs this time, but in fifty days of traveling Scott's team averaged 14½ miles a day with each member of the party pulling sledges attached to harnesses. To Scott the experience was glorious, even if antiquated by the standards of contemporary Norwegian explorers:

> To my mind no journey ever made with dogs can approach the height of the fine conception which is realized when a party of men go forth to face hardships, dangers, and difficulties with their own unaided efforts. . . . Surely in this case the conquest is more nobly and splendidly won.

Indeed, Scott had significant accomplishments to be proud of. Braving temperatures and conditions worse than anything found in the Arctic, he became the first human to see the South Polar ice cap on this expedition. In February 1904, after blasting out of the ice, the *Discovery* returned to England, arriving triumphantly on November 7, 1904.

Even though Scott had done an admirable job organizing the expedition, it fell far short of contemporary standards of polar exploration. Ill-advisedly, Scott had rejected the advice of the great Norwegian Arctic authority and explorer FRIDTJOF NANSEN to learn a modified version of the age-old **Inuit** technique of driving Greenland dogs. Although he attempted to use Siberian dogs in his own fashion, it was a terrible failure. Much later, Markham was to claim that Scott had rejected Nansen's recommendations because they required killing dogs as a sledge load lightened (after food was consumed), then feeding them to the other dogs. Despite his good intentions, however, Scott's treatment of animals (both dogs and ponies) was actually less humane, since he generally allowed them to starve before killing them.

After five more years of service in the British navy, Scott decided in 1909 to try for the South Pole. This time, his expedition was to be financed privately; it took him nearly two years to raise the required £40,000, to which the British government was to add another £20,000. Finally, his new ship the *Terra Nova* departed England in June 1910, reaching James Ross Island on January 22, 1911. But while stopping en route in Australia, Scott had received some bad news. The great Norwegian explorer ROALD AMUNDSEN was also on his way to conquer the South Pole. Amundsen had made a name for himself by successfully navigating the Northwest Passage from 1903 to 1906, accomplishing with a small crew what the whole British navy had not been able to do in several centuries of attempts. (For a more complete discussion of the passage, see MARTIN FROBISHER.) Now a new race was on, but it was not really a race between equals.

Scott may have panicked; he certainly hurried. At any rate, with his sledging techniques

The *Terra Nova* in ice pack, 1910. The Bettmann Archive.

no better than before, he and three others set off for the pole in late September with extensive support parties powered by dogs, ponies, and motorized sledges. He soon made a serious mistake. Separating from his last supply party at the top of the Beardmore Glacier (which Shackleton had discovered in 1908) on January 4, 1912, Scott suddenly decided to add Lieutenant H. R. Bowers for the final stretch of the polar assault. (For a map of their route, see ROALD AMUNDSEN.) Aside from requiring supplies that had not been allowed for, Bowers was a short-legged man with no skis. The party was already exhausted by fighting blizzard conditions, and now their progress was further hampered by Bowers. Nevertheless, the courageous party persevered, making tedious progress in the face of horrific conditions. Finally, on January 16, 1912, they reached their goal, only to find a black flag marking Amundsen's earlier success. Scott wrote in his diary: "Great God this is

an awful place and terrible enough for us to have labored to it without the reward of priority."

Thoroughly demoralized, the Scott party began the 800-mile trek back to their base. The first member died on February 16, the second a month later after wandering into a blizzard alone. Eleven miles short of One Ton depot (only 150 miles from their base), another blizzard descended on the three survivors. Scott was to amaze and move the world by remaining stoically in his tent, writing a volley of brave and eloquent diary entries to his family and the public while starving and freezing to death. His last words were: "We shall stick it out to the end, but we are getting weaker, of course, and the end cannot be far. It seems a pity, but I do not think I can write anymore."

Sequeira, Diogo Lopes de. See **Lopes de Sequeira, Diogo.**

• Serra, Junípero

Spanish
b November 24, 1713; Petra, Majorca
d August 28, 1784; Carmel, California
Explored and settled California

A Franciscan missionary, Father Junípero Serra traveled overland from Baja (Lower) California to present-day San Diego to establish the first mission in present-day California. In all, he established nine missions between San Diego and San Francisco that formed the heart of the Spanish settlement of Alta (Upper) California.

Baptized Miguel José, Serra took the name Junípero when he finished his probation as a Franciscan in 1731. In 1749, though well embarked on a distinguished teaching and preaching career in Spain, Serra requested permission to join a group of Franciscans heading for missionary work in New Spain (present-day Mexico). After nine years among the Indians of Sierra Gorda and several more years in Mexico City, Serra was appointed president of the Franciscan missions in Baja California in 1767. He was soon thereafter requested to take on a new assignment.

The visitor general to New Spain, José de Gálvez, was determined to extend the Spanish empire in America, in part because of persis-

Father Juniper Serra. The Bettman Archive.

two land and two sea expeditions set out for Alta California. Serra was in the second and larger land expedition, commanded by Don Gaspar de Portola. The struggle across the arid landscape of Baja California was made even more difficult for Serra by severe pains in one of his legs. He had suffered from these pains periodically since coming to New Spain, but now the leg swelled to the point he could barely walk on it. When Portola threatened to send Serra back, the priest asked one of the mule handlers to do for him what he would do for a mule with sore legs. The handler made a poultice of herbs and tallow, and within a few days, Serra's leg was improving. Nonetheless, when the overland expedition reached San Diego, Serra was left behind with **scurvy**-ridden sailors who needed tending, while Portola proceeded north to look for Monterey Bay. On Sunday, July 16, 1769, Serra founded the mission of San Diego de Alcala.

In the spring of 1770, a ship that had been sent back to Mexico for supplies arrived at San Diego, and Serra was finally able to sail to Monterey. There, on June 3, he founded the mission of Carmel that was to be his headquarters for the rest of his life. During the next fourteen years, Serra worked tirelessly to establish the mission system of California, founding San Antonio (south of Monterey) and San Gabriel (near present-day Los Angeles) in 1771, San Luis Obispo in 1772, San Francisco (Mission Dolores) and San Juan Capistrano in 1776, Santa Clara in 1777, and San Buenaventura (now Ventura) in 1782. In spite of recurring leg pains, he made frequent visits to his missions, where he was always welcomed with great affection, both by his fellow Franciscans and by local Indians.

Serra was an ardent foe of prejudice and a strong supporter of fair treatment of the Indians to whom he ministered. He was also aware of the need to minister not only to their souls but to their material needs as well. By the end of 1783, seven months before Serra's death, 6,000 Indians had been converted to Christianity, nearly 30,000 head of livestock had been introduced to Alta California, and the yearly harvest of the missions produced about 30,000 bushels of grain and vegetables. In addition, Serra and the other friars had taught the Indians various arts and crafts, from sewing to blacksmithing, and mission workshops produced many of the material goods needed in California.

Strong-willed and determined, Father Serra

tent rumors that the Russians were expanding eastward from the Aleutian Islands. Gálvez's plan to combat any possible encroachment by Russia on the Pacific coast of North America was to establish a chain of missions at intervals of one-day's ride from the border of Baja California to Monterey, which had been discovered by Sebastian Vizcaino in 1602. Missions in Alta California, Gálvez reasoned, would lead to Spanish settlements that would discourage any attempts by Russia or any other foreign power to establish its own colonies. The logical choice for president of the new system of missions was the head of Baja California's missions, Father Junípero Serra.

Gálvez's plan became a reality in 1769, when

frequently came into conflict with the Spanish civil authorities with whom he had to share the governing of California. But no one ever doubted his loyalty to Spain. His dedication was fundamental in establishing a strong Spanish presence in Alta California. More important to Serra, however, was his dedication to the souls he served, who in turn honored, respected, and loved the frail but iron-willed Franciscan.

· Shackleton, Ernest Henry

Anglo-Irish
b February 15, 1874; Kilkee, County Kildare
d January 5, 1922; South Georgia, Scotia Sea
Explored Antarctica

Known affectionately as "the Boss" by the members of his expeditions, Sir Ernest Henry Shackleton had an uncanny ability to take advantage of his luck without ever taking it for granted. Though he engaged in some of the most dangerous exploits of modern exploration and had his share of bad luck, his work left no one dead or injured—a remarkable achievement in the history of British polar exploration. His wise decision in 1909 to turn back just 97 miles from the South Pole was the kind of action that won him both a loyal following and a knighthood. He had faced incredible odds to get that far, but he knew that to go farther would be courting disaster.

Shackleton was born in County Kildare, Ireland, the son of an English doctor and an Irish mother. He was a poor student but did attend college in England before joining the merchant marine. A large and vital man who craved adventure, his various tours of duty kept him interested for a time. He served, for instance, on a ship that took soldiers to the Boer War, and coauthored a book on his experiences. Then, in 1901, he joined the Royal Naval Reserve as a sublieutenant. It was in this capacity that he applied to accompany ROBERT FALCON SCOTT to Antarctica.

But what could have been a sure road to fame and fortune led to humiliating disappointment. One of three chosen to accompany Scott on his long southward **sledge** journey over the Ross Ice Shelf, Shackleton came down with a serious case of **scurvy** and became a hindrance to the party. He then had to be sent home early

on a relief ship. Though the public believed he had pulled through heroically, he nevertheless rankled when Scott told the world in his popular book that "at the end of each march he is panting, dizzy, and exhausted."

Still, with his charm, imagination, and lilting Irish brogue, he was soon in demand on the lecture circuit. In 1904 he became secretary of the Royal Scottish Geographical Society, where his energetic leadership caused a stir. Convinced of his popularity, he ran for a seat in Parliament in 1906 as a Liberal-Unionist candidate in Dundee, Scotland, and carried its working-class districts. His campaign, though unsuccessful, caught the eye of a Glasgow industrialist, William Beardmore, who offered him a job. It was not long before he had convinced Beardmore to sponsor his expedition to Antarctica.

After Shackleton announced his plans to use Scott's base on James Ross Island to reach both the geographic and magnetic poles, Scott asked him to find his own base, since he too had plans for returning. Shackleton agreed, and in August 1907, he sailed on the *Nimrod* for a point to the east of James Ross Island. But when the *Nimrod* reached the Ross Ice Shelf in January

Shackleton (right) in camp. Royal Geographical Society.

1908, ice conditions forced him to stick to his original plan.

While one party under Professor T. W. Edgeworth David made a remarkable journey to the South Magnetic Pole, Shackleton headed out across the ice shelf in the Antarctic spring of 1908, having previously laid out supply depots. The journey to the geographic pole and back would be 1,730 miles. Though he was innovative enough to bring an automobile, which helped move supplies across the frozen McMurdo Sound, he, like Scott, failed to procure Greenland dogs for hauling the sledges. Instead, he decided to use ponies, which inevitably failed to make it very far. This meant man-hauling the sledges in the classic British fashion. This time Shackleton was in top shape, as were his three companions.

After crossing the ice shelf, the party came across the great glacier, which they named after Beardmore, that cuts through the mountains to the polar plateau. Ascending this slick, rapidly rising surface full of dangerous crevasses, the last pony was lost when it stepped through a snow bridge over a chasm. By Christmas the four had made it to the 9,500-foot-high polar plateau. On January 9, 1909, they had reached their goal, the South Magnetic Pole, at 88°23′ South latitude, at an altitude of 11,600 feet. They turned around and were back at base on February 28.

Shackleton's next Antarctic venture was an even more ambitious attempt to explore the Weddell Sea and then cross over the continent to Victoria Land, where a supply party would meet them. But World War I broke out just as his *Endurance* and *Aurora* were ready to set sail. Shackleton offered the ships to the government, but he was instructed to proceed with his mission. When the *Endurance* reached Coats Land on the Antarctic shore of the Weddell Sea in January 1915, it was beset in the ice, drifted for nine months, and was finally crushed a thousand miles from any source of help. Shackleton subsequently led the marooned party to Elephant Island by sledge and boat and then, with only a small crew, navigated 800 miles across the rough South Atlantic to South Georgia on a twenty-two-foot boat. There help was finally found. It was one of the most remarkable rescues of maritime history, made possible only by Shackleton's masterful leadership. The gripping story is told in Shackleton's book *South*.

A variety of missions and business schemes kept Shackleton busy until he returned once more to Antarctica aboard the *Quest* in 1921. This time the object was to explore Enderby Land, but Shackleton's heart gave out before he could cross the Antarctic Circle. His memorial service in the spring of 1922 was an occasion of national mourning.

Sharif al-Idrīsī, ash-. See **Idrīsī, al-**.

· Sheldon, May French

American
b May 10, 1847; Pittsburgh, Pennsylvania
d 1936; London, England
Explored East Africa

Before the middle of the nineteenth century, women explorers who traveled alone or led their own expeditions were rare or unheard of. That situation changed quickly as women in Europe and in America began to make successful forays as independent travelers. May French Sheldon led an expedition into East Africa in 1891 hoping to prove that African tribes would accept white people who approached them in a friendly way. Although she knew her journey was a "thorough innovation of accepted priorities"— most expeditions at that time were harsh military expeditions led by men—her project was successful. In recognition of her accomplishments, she became one of the first women elected a Fellow to the Royal Geographical Society.

Although born and raised in America, Sheldon married an American banker and publisher who lived in London, where she herself owned a publishing company. She was one of HENRY MORTON STANLEY's most enthusiastic admirers and was inspired by his exploits to visit Africa. Stanley and others tried to dissuade her—the jungle was no place for a woman, they said— but she would not be denied. She appealed for help to the sultan of Zanzibar, who supplied her with porters and letters commanding all she met to give her safe passage.

When she set out, her retinue included over 100 porters, headmen, guides, and servants. In addition to a huge quantity of supplies and provisions, they carried a wicker palanquin (an enclosed litter borne on poles) large enough for her to sleep and ride in. She had with her an elaborate silk dress to wear whenever she met a chief. Although she wore expensive tailored suits, Sheldon quickly earned a reputation as a tough campaigner. Her crew called her "Bebe Bwana," Swahili for Lady Boss. On one occasion they refused to continue, thinking she did not know the way. In response, Sheldon took aim at a vulture flying overhead and brought it down, demonstrating that she was a sure shot. She then offered to shoot any man who did not follow her.

On her trek through what is now Tanzania, Sheldon viewed Africa's highest mountain: "I saw more than I can ever hope to recount of the grandeur of Kilimanjaro." Her caravan visited thirty-five different tribes, most of whom she found friendly and happy: "They live to enjoy, and enjoy to live, and are as idyllic in their native ways as any people I ever encountered." She also visited Lake Chala, circumnavigating it in a copper pontoon left behind by a previous visitor. Although intent on exploring the land of the Masai, her guides and carriers adamantly refused to enter the territory of these fearful warriors. Faced with a wholesale mutiny, Sheldon turned back.

Sheldon's expedition confirmed the ability of women explorers to meet their male counterparts on the most challenging ground Africa had to offer. She was one of the first white travelers to approach the African people and their culture in a sympathetic way. After her return to London, Sheldon chronicled her explorations in her book *Sultan to Sultan*.

• Simpson, Thomas

Scottish
b July 2, 1808; Dingwall, Ross-shire
d June 14, 1840; Territory of Dakota Sioux, near Red River Settlement
Charted Arctic coast of Canada

Highly energetic, well-educated, and ambitious to a fault, Thomas Simpson was the driving force behind the expedition of 1837–39 that charted the last unknown stretches of the navigable waterway along the Arctic shore of North America from what is now Point Barrow, Alaska, to Canada's Boothia Peninsula. By traveling west from the Mackenzie River to Point Barrow and east from the mouth of the Coppermine River to Chantrey Inlet, Simpson and his superior, Peter Warren Dease, completed the coastal survey begun by JOHN FRANKLIN. This kept alive the old quest for the Northwest Passage, making it conceivable that the shrinking area of unknown waters north of what is now Simpson Strait would link the coastal waterway with the route from Baffin Bay. The Hudson's Bay Company, which sponsored Simpson's effort, had thus returned to one of the missions for which it was originally chartered: to discover the Northwest Passage. Simpson's work on this expedition also complemented that of GEORGE BACK: Simpson located the mouth of the Great Fish (now Back) River, which Back had navigated.

A distinguished graduate of King's College, University of Aberdeen, Simpson came to the rough work of exploration through his uncle, Sir George Simpson, the governor-in-chief of the Hudson's Bay Company. Soon the romantic young Simpson was inflamed by the explorer's passion, and on both the eastern and western legs of his expedition, he energetically pushed ahead when Dease could go no further.

Simpson reached Point Barrow by foot on August 4, 1837, returned with Dease to winter at Great Bear Lake, and the following June started down the Coppermine to complete the eastern half of the survey. Bad weather prevented their progress beyond Franklin's easternmost point (Turnagain Point), and it was not until the following summer (after wintering again at Great Bear Lake) that they succeeded in reaching Boothia Peninsula. After traveling through the strait south of King William Island (soon to be named after Simpson), they found a cache of goods left by George Back in Chantrey Inlet and then proceeded to Boothia.

Time did not allow a thorough exploration of this area, but Simpson was convinced that he was on the verge of discovering the passageway to the Gulf of Boothia, and hence the key to the Northwest Passage (for a more complete discussion of the Northwest Passage, see MARTIN FROBISHER). When it received word of Simpson's achievement and his plan for further exploration of this area (without the slow-moving Dease), the British government thoroughly approved of all that Simpson had accomplished and planned. Unfortunately, before he could hear of this, Simpson died of gunshot wounds to the head while traveling through the Sioux country, on his way to New York. His companions claimed he went mad and shot himself and two others, but the truth was never satisfactorily determined.

• Sinclair, James

Canadian
b 1806; Oxford House post, north of Lake Winnipeg
d March 26, 1856; Oregon Territory
Explored southern Canadian Rocky Mountains

A highly successful fur trader and merchant, James Sinclair led a party of Canadian settlers across the little-known southern Canadian Rockies and into the Oregon Territory in 1841. He crossed the Rockies two more times, in 1850 and 1854, before settling in the Oregon Territory, only to be killed two years later in an Indian uprising.

The son of a Hudson's Bay Company official and a part-Cree mother, Sinclair was born at Oxford House in Rupert's Land (the territory around Hudson Bay held by the Hudson's Bay Company) but was sent to Scotland at the age of eight for his education. He returned to Rupert's Land in 1826 and in 1827 established his home at the Red River Settlement (south of Lake Winnipeg). There he became a highly successful private trader with loose ties to the Hudson's Bay Company monopoly.

By 1841, the monopoly was increasingly disturbed by the number of independent traders engaging in illegal fur trading in its territory. Company officials responded to this threat with various plans to reduce the population around Red River. One scheme involved hiring Sinclair to lead a party of twenty-three families across the Rockies and into the Oregon Territory. By this move the company hoped not only to reduce the number of free traders at Red River but also to establish a strong British presence in Oregon, which at the time was occupied jointly by the United States and Britain.

On June 5, 1841, Sinclair left Red River at the head of a party of 121 men, women, and children. Most of the emigrants were the descendants of mixed marriages between French-Canadians and Indians, the group of people who most commonly engaged in illegal free trading. These were hardy people, well equipped to survive under difficult circumstances, and the trip provided few serious problems for them.

Two weeks before Sinclair's departure, George Simpson, governor of Hudson's Bay Company territories, had set off on his own transcontinental trek, after ordering Sinclair to follow the same route. However, at Edmonton House, Sinclair met Mackipictoon (or Maskepetoon), a Cree Indian, who, insulted that he had not been chosen to guide Simpson's party, told Sinclair there were passes through the Rockies that white men had not yet found. He offered to lead Sinclair's group through one of them. Disobeying Simpson's order, Sinclair agreed. Mackipictoon took the party across the mountains at what became known as White Man Pass and then guided them through an eerily narrow canyon where 1,000-foot walls of rock nearly blotted out daylight. This was Red Rock Gorge (now Sinclair Canyon, Kootenay National Park, British Columbia).

After guiding the group to the safety of a Hudson's Bay Company fort, Mackipictoon left them to return east, and Sinclair led his party down the Columbia River, arriving at Fort Vancouver on October 13. By ignoring Simpson's orders, Sinclair had discovered a much simpler and easier route through the Rockies than any previously known to non-Indians.

Sinclair returned to Red River, where he helped lead a movement by native-born people to convince the Hudson's Bay Company to allow them to engage in free trade, unrestricted by the company's monopoly. Although the movement achieved some success, Sinclair was still dissatisfied with the lack of economic opportunity at Red River and decided to take his family to the Oregon Territory. In 1849 he became a citizen of the United States at St. Paul, Minnesota, and then returned to Red River to lead his family west. In 1850 spring floods prevented a group migration, but Sinclair traveled west alone to scout the Rockies. He crossed the mountains again and spent two years in Oregon and California, returning to Red River in 1852 by way of the Isthmus of Panama, Cuba, and New York.

After secretly reconciling with the Hudson's Bay Company against the free-traders, Sinclair accepted a job with the company to take charge of its trading post at Fort Walla Walla in what is now the state of Washington, then a part of the Oregon Territory. As the company's secret agent, he again led a party of emigrants, including his wife and family, from Red River to the Oregon Territory. Twenty-eight families and

250 head of cattle left Red River in May 1854 to travel across the plains. Going up the Bow and Kananaskis rivers (in present-day Alberta), they crossed the Rockies by a different route from Sinclair's previous crossing and after great difficulty came to Canal Flats (near the headwaters of the Columbia River). Although supposedly a better route than those taken in Sinclair's earlier crossings, it was very hard on the cattle. The party eventually reached Walla Walla on December 24. Sinclair was killed in an attempt to save a party of American settlers under attack by Indians at the Cascades on the Columbia River in March 1856.

A shrewd trader and—for a time—a courageous leader of the natives of Rupert's Land against the Hudson's Bay Company monopoly, James Sinclair was also an active explorer who became the first man to lead large parties of emigrants through the southern Canadian Rockies. His accomplishments are memorialized in the name of Sinclair Canyon, through which the Banff-Windermere Highway now runs.

• Sintra, Pedro de (Cintra, Pêro da)

Portuguese
b 1445?
d ?
Explored West Africa

One of the last seafarers dispatched by Prince Henry the Navigator to explore the western coastline of Africa, Pedro de Sintra is credited with discovering the mountains of what is now Sierra Leone and giving the range and the country their name. He also explored some 250 miles south along the coast of present-day Liberia. Sintra's two expeditions opened up a substantial portion of the coast to the Portuguese.

Sintra was a young squire in Prince Henry's service when he was chosen in 1460 to sail a **caravel** as far as possible down the coast of West Africa. For more than four decades, the prince had sent his most able navigators on similar missions in an effort to find unknown lands with commercial possibilities. On his first voyage Sintra traveled as far as present-day Guinea, and, on his return, the prince was pleased enough with the explorer's work to begin equipping Sintra for a second, more extensive trip down the coast. Preparing Sintra for this second expedition, however, was one of the last activities of Henry's life. He died in 1460, bringing a spectacular era of discovery to a close.

While his successor, King Alfonso V, did not share his Uncle Henry's enthusiasm for exploration, he nevertheless allowed Sintra to proceed with the planned voyage the following year. With two caravels, Sintra sailed past the Gambia River to the Bissagos Islands, off the coast of Guinea. Exploring the interior of one of the two islands, he tried unsuccessfully to communicate with its native inhabitants before resuming his expedition. Beyond this point the coastline was unknown, and after following it for approximately 250 miles, Sintra reached a lofty headland that he named Cape Sagres, after the home of Prince Henry. Continuing south, he found the hilly coastal terrain giving way to a massive range of mountains. Because the rocky peaks seemed to roar as thunder reverberated through them, he called the mountains Sierra Leona, meaning "mountains of the lioness." At the end of the range, about 8 miles offshore, he found a trio of small islands that he dubbed the Selvagens.

Thirty miles past Sierra Leona, he found a river that he named Rio Roxo because of the reddish tint it took on from soil runoff, as well as a small island he called Ilha Roxo. By July 1462 Sintra reached a gulf he called Santa Maria das Neves (St. Mary of the Snows) and a small island nearby that he called Ilha dos Blancos. Another 25 miles south he found and named Cabo de Santa Anna, commemorating the feast of Saint Anne, and 60 miles beyond this point he reached a river he named Rio das Palmes for the palm trees growing on its banks.

After covering an estimated 600 miles of unexplored coastline, he reached a small headland and then, a short distance away, a wooded area he named Bosque de Santa Maria (St. Mary's Grove). There native people in canoes approached the ship, and Sintra decided to take an African back to Portugal with him. When Sintra returned and presented the West African tribesman to the court, the Portuguese excitedly tried to communicate with their exotic guest. After repeated attempts failed, they presented him with new clothes and gifts and later returned him to West Africa.

Siqueira, Diogo Lopes de. See **Lopes de Sequeira, Diogo.**

Smith, Jedediah Strong

American
b June 24, 1798; Bainbridge, New York
d May 27, 1831; near Cimarron River
Led first American overland expedition to California

A fur trapper by profession, Jedediah Strong Smith set out from the Great Salt Lake in August 1826 to look for new trapping grounds. Although he soon found himself outside of beaver country, he persisted in his journey, eventually crossing the Mojave Desert to reach what is now southern California. His return trip by way of the searing Great Basin of present-day Nevada ranks as one of the most grueling explorations ever made on the North American continent. He soon made an even longer round-trip trek to California (1827–29) that solidified his reputation as an important explorer of the American West.

Born in upstate New York, Jed Smith became

Jedediah Strong Smith. Denver Public Library.

a clerk on a Lake Erie freighter at the age of thirteen. Intrigued by stories he heard from traders returning from the West, Smith migrated to St. Louis, where he joined WILLIAM HENRY ASHLEY's Rocky Mountain Fur Company in 1822.

By fall of 1823 he was considered a seasoned mountain man and natural leader and was given his first expedition to lead west. After traveling through the South Dakota badlands and reaching the Black Hills, Smith had an encounter with a grizzly bear that not only marked him for life but also highlighted his powers of physical and mental endurance. Springing from a thicket, the grizzly took Smith's head in his mouth, laying bare Smith's skull from just over his left eye to his right ear. Miraculously, Smith remained conscious. Bleeding profusely and with one ear hanging loose, he directed one of his men to sew up his wounds and reattach his ear with a needle and thread. After ten days of recuperation, Smith led his men west. Early in 1824 they came upon South Pass, a 20-mile-wide cut through the Rocky Mountains that was later to become the gateway through which thousands of settlers journeyed into Oregon and California. Smith's party was the second to come upon the pass, rediscovering it twelve years after ROBERT STUART had first passed through it in 1812.

In the spring of 1826, Smith and two others bought out Ashley. Later that year, Smith and his two partners divided up the work to be done. While the other two traded for furs in the Rocky Mountains, Smith was to take a party southwest to search for new trapping territory. In August 1826, he left the vicinity of the Great Salt Lake with fifteen men. For over a month they wandered south over the Wasatch Mountains near the eastern rim of the Great Basin of modern Nevada, traveling farther and farther into what Smith called a "country of starvation." The landscape of reddish sandy soil and isolated clumps of sagebrush made it obvious that they had passed beyond beaver territory. Still they pushed on, eventually crossing the Colorado River and following its east bank into the Black Mountains of what is now northwestern Arizona. By this time the shortage of food and water had put the men in imminent danger. Suddenly, they passed from the mountains into a valley filled with willow and mesquite. There they encountered friendly Mojave Indians who gave them supplies and pointed out a westward trail that the Indians used for reaching the ocean. Smith realized that there was no hope of finding beaver ahead, but he feared to travel back the same way he had come. Instead, he and his men, resupplied by the Indians, headed west across the Mojave Desert, following a river that frequently disappeared underground for miles at a time.

After fifteen days in the blazing sun, enduring constant hunger and thirst, they arrived at Mission San Gabriel near present-day Los Angeles. It was mid-November. At this point Smith's problems became political. He was an alien without a passport in Mexican territory, and he had a hard time convincing the authorities that he was a simple fur trader and not a spy. After three American sea captains intervened on his behalf, Smith was released on the condition that he leave Mexican territory the same way he had come in. Smith agreed and then completely disregarded the conditions.

He spent the winter with his party in the San Joaquin Valley trapping beaver, and in May 1827 tried to lead his expedition east over the Sierra Nevada only to find that the way was still blocked by snow. Taking his party back to a sheltered spot, he left eleven members there and took two with him on another attempt to cross the mountains. This time they did it, but it took eight days and cost them two horses and a mule. However, crossing the mountains was only the beginning of their ordeal. They were now face to face with the Great Basin, a desolate desert that stretched ahead of them for hundreds of miles. There was nowhere to go but forward, so on they went. On June 25 one of the men, Robert Evans, collapsed, and the other two had no choice but to leave him. However, 3 miles further on they found water, and Smith carried some back to Evans, enabling him to revive and move on. On July 3, 1827, the three reached Bear Lake, the site of the 1827 trappers rendezvous (an annual meeting of mountain men and their suppliers). An epic journey lasting one year had come to an end.

However, for Smith the expedition was not completed. There were eleven men waiting for him to return and lead them east, and after less than ten days at the rendezvous, Smith set out to rescue those men, taking with him a party of eighteen men and two Indian women. Not wanting to cross the Great Basin again, Smith led the party south on much the same route as the previous year with much the same

difficulties of hunger and thirst. This time, however, there was no oasis in the land of the Mojaves before the brutal desert crossing; in the short span of a year, the Mojaves had turned hostile, perhaps because they had been attacked and defeated by a band of trappers from the east, perhaps for other reasons. In any case, they attacked Smith's group while it was attempting to ferry the Colorado River, killing ten men and taking the two squaws prisoner. Smith and the eight other men still in the middle of the river on a raft escaped—but with few supplies, little ammunition, and the Mojave Desert crossing still ahead of them.

The next several months saw history repeat itself. Again the Mojave was difficult to cross; again Smith was detained in California for being an alien without a passport, and again a sea captain came to his rescue, convincing the authorities to release Smith on the condition that he leave California immediately. Smith agreed once more to the condition with no intention of keeping his promise.

Picking up the remaining members of both expeditions, he headed north to spend the winter in the Sacramento River valley. The next summer (1828) Smith and his party traveled north, generally along the coast toward the Columbia River, looking for an eastward route that would take them north of the Great Basin. After a hostile encounter with some Kelawatset Indians, Smith took two men on a scouting expedition up the Umpqua River. The Indians took the opportunity to retaliate, killing fifteen of the sixteen men left at the camp. The wounded survivor made his way to Fort Vancouver on the Columbia River, where he met up with Smith and the other two. The four spent the winter there, treated royally by their rivals in the fur trade, the men of England's Hudson's Bay Company. Before leaving Smith had ample opportunity to take notice of the excellent possibilities for agricultural and commercial settlement in the Northwest. Upon his return he made a complete intelligence report to the United States secretary of war, which pointed out that settlers with loaded wagons and even dairy cows could be brought easily through the South Pass of the Rockies and all the way to the Pacific.

Smith returned east to the Rockies in 1829 and retired from the fur trade in 1830. He settled in St. Louis, intent on drawing maps that would show his accomplishments. But before turning to that task, he decided to make one last trading expedition. With a party of eighty-three, he set out for Santa Fe, but close to the Cimarron River (near the border of present-day Oklahoma, Colorado, and Kansas), while looking for water alone, Smith was taken by surprise and killed by Comanches.

A bold explorer, Jedediah Strong Smith went where no other Americans had gone before. He was the first American to make an overland journey to California and the first to cross the Great Basin of Nevada. Even more important than his journeys were his reports of the places he saw, including his vision of the westward expansion of the United States, which began soon after his death.

• Smith, John

English
b 1580; Willoughby, Lincolnshire
d June 21, 1631; London
Explored and mapped Chesapeake Bay and
    New England coast

A member of England's first permanent settlement in America, at Jamestown, Virginia, in 1607, John Smith almost singlehandedly saved the colony from starvation in its first difficult years. During this time he also managed to explore Chesapeake Bay, making a map that served sailors and colonists for over 100 years. Later in his life, he mapped the coast of New England and gave the region its name.

As a young man, Smith spent several years as a soldier and adventurer in Europe. His last engagement there was against the Turks; he later told numerous tales of adventure, including the time he was taken prisoner and sent to Constantinople as a gift to the Pasha's wife, who fell in love with him. Small wonder that he was not content with humdrum English domestic life when he returned in 1604.

Seeking further adventure, Smith signed on with the Virginia Company of London and claimed to have been actively involved in promoting and organizing its Jamestown venture. When the settlers arrived in Jamestown in April 1607, their most pressing need was food. Smith soon took on the task of trading for corn with the local Indians, a task which he performed successfully and sometimes aggressively in the face of Indian reluctance. On one such excursion

John Smith. UPI/Bettmann.

he was captured by Chief Opechancanough of the Pamunkey tribe and managed to save his life only by showing the chief a compass and entertaining him in broken Algonquin with tales of the sun and stars. Opechancanough eventually took Smith to his brother, Chief Powhatan. As Smith later told the story, Powhatan debated with his counselors and then decided to kill Smith. But the chief's beloved twelve-year-old daughter, Pocahontas, placed her head on top of Smith's to prevent the warriors from clubbing him to death. He was then returned unharmed to Jamestown; the settlement's relations with Powhatan remained uneasy.

In January 1608 new settlers arrived in Jamestown; the same month a fire that started through carelessness burned down much of the settlement. In the spring Smith organized the rebuilding of the village and the planting of crops and then escaped the burden of managing a colony full of shirkers and schemers by going exploring. In the summer of 1608 he made two separate excursions around Chesapeake Bay. In the first, he encountered Indians on the eastern shore of the bay and then traveled a distance up the Potomac and Rappahannock rivers, where the Indians were more suspicious and potentially hostile. On his second expedition, he went to the head of Chesapeake Bay and discovered the mouth of the Susquehanna River, where he met the Susquehanna Iroquois, who offered him trade goods that they had gotten from the French farther north. Smith's summer explorations resulted in a map of the bay region that was considered valuable by mariners and colonists for more than 100 years.

Smith returned to Jamestown to find that he had been officially chosen the new leader of the colony. For the next year, he continued to be the colony's primary problem-solver, repeatedly pressuring food out of the Indians, who were becoming more wary as more settlers arrived. When seven ships with nearly 300 new settlers arrived from England in August 1609, Smith was overwhelmed by the prospect of feeding them all. Fortunately, responsibility was to be lifted from him, as a new governor was expected from England soon. But an ironic form of relief for Smith arrived even sooner. A quantity of gunpowder accidentally discharged in Smith's canoe, and he was burned severely enough to warrant his immediate return to England in October 1609.

Smith returned to North America in 1614 at the behest of a group of London merchants who wanted him to map the coast of an area called North Virginia (present-day New England). He summered on Monhegan Island (off the coast of Maine). From Monhegan, Smith mapped the coast as far south as Cape Cod. IIis map included a harbor called Patuxet, which Prince Charles insisted on renaming Plymouth, being convinced that it would be easier to attract English settlers to places with English rather than Indian names. This Plymouth was soon to become the home of the Pilgrims.

Smith returned to England, where, in 1616, he published *A Description of New England*, which gave a name to the region and proclaimed its desirability as a location for a colony. The Pilgrims relied on Smith's map and book but had no interest in inviting him to join the colony. The later years of Smith's life were spent in writing numerous books, the last of which was *Advertisements for the Unexperienced Planters of New England, or Anywhere*, a work that contains valuable and sometimes amusing advice based on his personal experiences.

John Smith was not only a daring and courageous explorer, willing to go anywhere and do anything, he was also a knowledgeable, responsible, and resourceful leader. The Jamestown colony, filled as it was with those who did not want to pull their own weight, would not have survived its first two years without him, and, without the use of his map and book, the Pilgrims would probably have had an even more difficult time settling in the New World than they did. John Smith therefore deserves much credit for the establishment and survival of the first two permanent English colonies in America.

· Smith, William

English
b 1800?; Blyth, Northumberland
d ?
Discovered South Shetland Islands and tip of Graham Land on Antarctic Peninsula

Like all sea captains who sailed past South America's Cape Horn on their way between the Atlantic and the Pacific, William Smith worried about being driven by northerly winds into the perilous pack ice south of Drake Passage. Unlike all who sailed before him, however, he was driven almost 500 miles south of Cape Horn by severe weather into a bevy of previously unknown islands. Coming at a time when the commercial world was looking for new sealing grounds and the world at large was becoming fascinated by the polar regions, Smith's landfall became widely known. On a subsequent voyage to the region, he penetrated even farther to the south, sighting a mainland. Though there are other claimants, today most historians credit him with discovering continental Antarctica.

Smith was on the *Williams* when he first sighted what later became known as the South Shetland Islands on February 18, 1819. He had been hired by an English engineer to bring machinery from Chile to the Río de la Plata in Argentina via Cape Horn. When he reported his find, no one believed him, but eventually he was able to return and plant the British flag in October 1819.

By this time word of Smith's discovery of islands richly populated by seals was getting around, and soon the British navy was organizing a serious survey of the area. Smith was commissioned to serve as pilot and master of the *Williams* on an expedition commanded by Edward Bransfield. Fitted out with a year's supplies, they set sail on December 20, 1819, arrived in the islands in January 1820, and sighted the Antarctic continent on the thirtieth of that month. Their resulting chart of the South Shetland Islands, the tip of Graham Land on the Antarctic Peninsula, and several outlying islands was sent to the British Admiralty in December 1821, and a year later the Admiralty published its official map of the region.

Even after Smith discovered this strategically important area, the British did nothing to establish their sovereignty over the islands or the peninsula. Other powers soon began exploring and fishing there, setting up rival claims, some of which have still not been resolved. As for Smith, his accidental discovery gave history its only chance to record his activities. He remains otherwise obscure.

• Solander, Daniel Carl

Swedish
b February 19, 1736; Piteå, Nordland
d May 13, 1782; London, England
Assisted as naturalist on James Cook's first
circumnavigation

Doctor Daniel Carl Solander was part of the first team of naturalists to catalog the flora and fauna of Tierra del Fuego, Tahiti, Australia, and the Great Barrier Reef as members of the first expedition of Captain JAMES COOK (1768–71).

Little is written about Solander until 1750, when he entered the University of Uppsala to pursue theology but became instead a top student of Linnaeus (Carl von Linné), the botanist who established the modern system of naming and classifying all plant and animal life. Like all of Linnaeus's students, he was encouraged to travel and to search for unknown species. To this purpose, Solander made botanical trips to Lapland, Russia, and the Canary Islands.

In 1760 Linnaeus sent his protégé to London to lecture on his new classification system. While in London, Solander joined the staff of the British Museum, where he became assistant curator in 1766. Two years later, the naturalist JOSEPH BANKS hired Solander, who already had

established his own reputation as a botanist, to assist on a major expedition to the South Pacific and around the world.

From 1768 until 1771 Solander and Banks traveled with Captain James Cook on board the *Endeavour* as the ship explored the South Pacific. In Tahiti they studied not only plants and animals, but Polynesian culture as well, and Solander learned to speak the native language reasonably well. Over the course of the journey the naturalists collected more than 1,000 plants, 500 fish, 500 bird skins, and countless insects, shells, coral, rocks, artifacts, cloth, and carvings. Banks and Solander were well received upon their return to England and even were interviewed by King George III.

Solander joined Banks again the following year on the latter's yearlong expedition to the Hebrides and Iceland. When the journey ended, he returned to London and, in 1773, was named curator of the natural history department of the British Museum. He died in London in 1782.

• Soto, Hernando de

Spanish
b 1496–1501; Jerez de los Caballeros, Badajoz
d May 21, 1542; near Natchez, Mississippi
Explored southeastern United States;
discovered Mississippi River

The Marquis Don Hernando de Soto played a major role during the sixteenth-century conquests of present-day Nicaragua and Peru and led the first extensive exploration of what is now the southeastern United States. On the latter, his party traveled through parts of modern Florida, Georgia, North Carolina, South Carolina, Tennessee, Alabama, Mississippi, Louisiana, and Arkansas, thus becoming the first Europeans to cross the Appalachian Mountains and to discover the Mississippi River and many of its inland tributaries.

Hernando de Soto was born into a family of minor nobility in the town of Jerez de los Caballeros in the Spanish province of Badajoz; his birthdate has variously been given between 1496 and 1501. Nothing is known of his youth, but he probably arrived in the New World in 1514 with the new governor of Panama, Pedro Arias de Ávila (known as Pedrarias). For the next several years he developed his skills as a

Hernando de Soto. The Bettmann Archive.

soldier under the tutelage of Pedrarias. He distinguished himself as a soldier and leader during the conquest of what is now Nicaragua under Francisco Fernández de Córdoba in 1524 and became one of the leading citizens of the newly founded colony.

Seeking greater independence and power, Soto joined FRANCISCO PIZARRO's Peruvian expedition of 1531–34 against the Incas. The 100 men and twenty-five horses he brought to Puná Island on December 1, 1531, were welcomed by Pizarro, who was greatly outnumbered by the Inca forces. A key figure during the ensuing conquest, Soto, on a reconnaissance mission to locate passes through the Andes, was the first Spaniard to see the wonders of the advanced Inca civilization. After crossing the mountains on the Marañón River watershed, he reached the village of Caxias along the Inca highway. There he saw indications of great wealth. He also became the first Spaniard to meet the Inca emperor, Atahualpa, and was reportedly opposed to his subsequent execution.

When Soto returned to Spain in 1536 after

his successful exploits in Peru, he was a wealthy and much admired man. He was described by those around him as a gentleman—kind, generous, and charming. The king of Spain rewarded him with the Knighthood of Santiago and marquisate, making him the Marquis Don Hernando de Soto. He also married a daughter of Pedrarias, Isabella de Bobadilla.

However, Soto still wanted independent power and kept petitioning the king for a governorship, preferably in either present-day Ecuador or Guatemala. In 1537 he was granted the right to conquer and colonize the ill-defined territory of La Florida (the name applied to all territory north of Cuba) and to select territory running 200 **leagues** along its coast, over which he would become governor. He was also made the governor of Cuba. Soto had more men volunteer for the Florida expedition than he needed, partially because of his prestige, and partially because of their expectation of finding great riches, as Pizarro had in Peru and HERNÁN CORTÉS had in Mexico.

Soto set sail on April 7, 1538, from Sanlúcar de Barrameda, Spain, with 650 men and women, 12 priests, and about 250 horses. After a supply stop at Cuba, the expedition sailed from Havana on May 18, 1539, and landed on May 30 on the southeast side of present-day Tampa Bay at a place now called Shaw's Point, near the modern town of Bradenton. (Some historians have proposed that Charlotte Harbor was the actual landing place, but no conclusive evidence has been found to substantiate this.) After establishing a camp at a Timucuan Indian village on Terra Ceia Island, Soto prepared to journey inland.

Information about Soto's three-year trek through what is now the southeastern United States comes from four primary sources: the journal of a "gentleman from Elvas," first printed in 1557; the diary of Rodrigo Rangel, Soto's secretary; the official 1544 report to the **Council of the Indies** by Hernández de Biedma, quartermaster of the expedition; and the reminiscence of Gonzalo Silvestre, a member of the expedition, published in Garcilasco de la Vega's *La Florida del Inca* in 1605. In addition, Soto's route was reconstructed in the twentieth century by the United States DeSoto Commission (1935–39).

Traveling north-northwest from Tampa Bay, the expedition crossed the modern Withlacoochee, Santa Fe, and Suwannee rivers, suffering

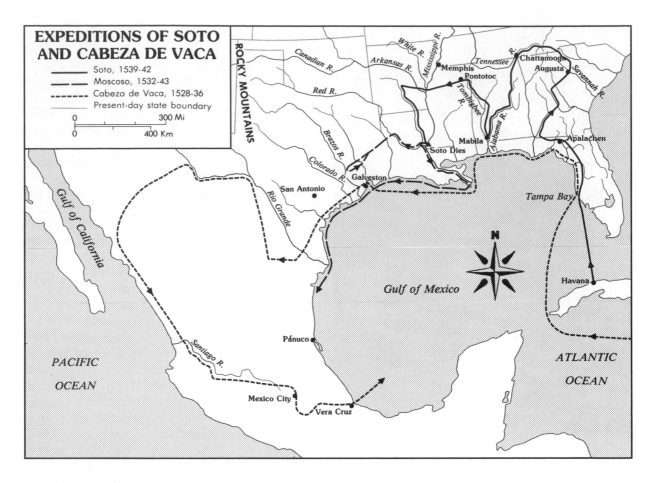

EXPEDITIONS OF SOTO AND CABEZA DE VACA

———— Soto, 1539-42
—— — Moscoso, 1532-43
---- Cabeza de Vaca, 1528-36
—— Present-day state boundary

0 — 300 Mi
0 — 400 Km

from the heat "under a grievous sun" the first few days, then from heavy rain that stopped their movement for two days and made crossing the swollen rivers difficult. During an attack on some hostile Indians, they came upon Juan Ortiz, a survivor of the ill-fated PÁNFILO DE NARVÁEZ Florida expedition of 1528; he joined the Soto expedition as an interpreter.

They reached Apalachee Indian country once they crossed the present-day Aucilla River, and Soto decided to winter at the village of Apalachen (near present-day Tallahassee), which was the same village where Narváez had spent some time. Soto has been criticized for his cruel treatment of the Indians there and elsewhere on his journey. His men would often terrorize villages, shackling captives to use as slaves and setting vicious dogs on escapees. As a result, to avoid such treatment, other Indians tended to tell him what he wanted to hear, namely, that a land of gold existed not far away. Thus, a report from an Indian prisoner about the wealthy land of Cofitachequi ruled by a queen "in the direction of the sun's rising" prompted Soto to head

first northwest and then to the east, after he broke camp on March 3, 1540.

Reaching the present-day Flint River near modern Bainbridge, Georgia, the explorers followed it to the Ocmulgee River; they then forded the Ocmulgee and marched along its eastern bank. A little north of modern Macon, they turned east, crossed the Oconee River, and arrived on April 30 opposite Cofitachequi, at or near modern Silver Bluff on the Savannah River, just below modern Augusta. The "Lady of Cofitachequi," as the Indian queen was called, sent canoes to ferry Soto and some of his men to the town and gave them freshwater pearls—but no gold.

Another report of gold toward the north, in the region of the Chiaha Indians, sent Soto in that direction, following a route between the Savannah and the Saluda rivers in modern South Carolina. He and his party reached what is now the Little Tennessee River at the present site of Franklin, North Carolina, and headed west to cross the Appalachian mountains, becoming the first Europeans to do so. When they reached what is now the Tennessee River above Chattanooga, they traveled downstream along its south bank until they reached the Chiaha Indian settlement on present-day Burns Island on June 6. There they found plenty of food, but again, no gold.

Soto then heard of a great Indian chief, named Cosa, in the south, so he marched the expedition in that direction. Crossing and re-crossing the Tennessee River, he continued south into modern Alabama, crossing the Sand mountains to reach the Coosa River. He met with Chief Cosa just north of modern Childersburg, Alabama, and was taken to meet another chief, Tuscaloosa of the Choctaw nation, at a village along the present-day Alabama River. Still moving south after trading with these Indians, Soto crossed into Mobile Indian territory in present-day Monroe county and had a bloody battle with the Indians at Mabila (possibly near modern Choctaw Bluff, Alabama). As a result of the battle, much of the Spaniards' equipment was destroyed and their clothes were in tatters. They were forced to make clothing out of animal skins and to fashion tools from various natural materials.

Soto and his party decided to head north again, crossing what is now the Black Warrior River and then following the Tombigbee River into modern Mississippi. They wintered near present-day Pontotoc, Mississippi. On March 4, 1541, however, they had to fight a surprise attack by the Chickasaw Indians in which twelve of Soto's men and fifty horses died.

Soto left his winter camp in April 1541 and headed west, hoping to find a path to the South Sea (Pacific Ocean). He discovered the Mississippi River on May 8 and directed the building of four barges to carry the expedition across the river. They crossed south of modern Memphis, Tennessee, and spent several months traversing present-day Arkansas from the delta between what are now the White and Arkansas rivers to some point above modern Pine Bluff. They then went west as far as present-day Hot Springs. Having waded through swamps, climbed hills, and forded the Arkansas twice, all under severe drought conditions, the expedition settled in for the winter at the Tula Indian village of Utiangue near modern Camden or Calion, Arkansas.

After a bitterly cold winter with heavy snowfall, the Soto expedition began traveling again on March 6, 1542, by which time only 300 sol-diers and forty horses were left. Soto chose to move south along the present-day Ouachita River, trying to reach the Mississippi River to find an outlet to the sea. Marching on the river bank, the group moved from modern Arkansas into Louisiana, where it was forced to stop for four days due to an unusual spring snowstorm. Soto then came down with a serious fever and died on May 21, 1542, near modern Natchez, Mississippi. Members of the expedition weighted their leader's body with sand and lowered it into the Mississippi in an effort to keep local Indians from learning of Soto's death.

Soto's successor as leader of the expedition was Luis de Moscoso. He first led the party west, attempting to reach New Spain (present-day Mexico) by land, perhaps getting as far as the Brazos River in Texas. Failing to find a route, he turned back and spent the winter of 1542–43 near Natchez. The remaining members of the expedition then built seven boats and embarked down the Mississippi on July 2, 1543. Entering the Gulf of Mexico, the remnants of the Soto expedition reached settlements in New Spain in September.

The tremendous accomplishments of the Soto expedition were not recognized at the time; they were simply glossed over, since no great land of wealth had been discovered. However, history has shown that this was one of the most important journeys of exploration in the New World. Soto and his party traversed over 4,000 miles of wilderness, compiling detailed information on an extensive area of the southeastern United States and the first descriptions of the life and customs of the southern Indian tribes. When he died, a "disappointed, disillusioned, and financially-ruined man," by one account, Hernando de Soto could not have foreseen that the land he explored would become part of a major new nation. Nor could he have foreseen the importance of his own accomplishments being reaffirmed by the reenactment of his landing conducted each year near Bradenton, Florida, more than 450 years after he went ashore there.

SUGGESTED READING: Miguel Albornoz, *Hernando de Soto, Knight of the Americas*, trans. by Bruce Boeglin (Franklin Watts, 1986); Theodore Maynard, *De Soto and the Conquistadors* (AMS, 1969); John R. Swanton, *The United States DeSoto Expedition Final Report* (Smithsonian Institution Press, 1985); Buckingham Smith, trans., *Narratives of de Soto in the Conquest of Florida, as told by a gentleman of Elvas* (Palmetto Books, 1968); Garcilaso de la Vega, *The Florida of the Incas; a History of Adelantado, Hernando de Soto,* trans. and ed. by John Grier Varner and Jeanette Johnson Varner (University of Texas Press, 1951).

• Speke, John Hanning

English
b May 4, 1827; Jordans, Somerset
d September 15, 1864; Bath
Explored East Central Africa; discovered source of White Nile

Credited with solving the mystery of the Nile, John Hanning Speke traced the origin of the river to what is now known as Lake Victoria, locating the cataracts (a waterfall or steep rapids) that fed its northward course in 1862. He found and named the lake on his second trip to Africa's interior (1856–58) and returned two years later to seek the location where the Nile emerges from the lake. (For a map of his expeditions, see RICHARD FRANCIS BURTON.) His resulting claims met with strenuous challenges, most notably from his companion and leader on his first two expeditions, Richard Francis Burton. Tragically, Speke accidentally shot himself to death the day before he was to respond to Burton's criticisms in a public forum in England. The controversy over his work continued for years after his death before subsequent exploration affirmed that Lake Victoria was indeed the river's origin.

Born to an affluent family, Speke left home at age seventeen to join the British Indian Army. He served in the Punjab campaign as well as in the Second Sikh War, spending considerable time exploring and hunting in the Himalaya Mountains during his leaves. While on an extended leave in 1854, he traveled to Aden, on the east coast of Africa. There he met Burton, whom he joined on an expedition to Somaliland (now Somalia). Speke suffered near-fatal injuries during an attack by Somali inhabitants in 1855, but the incident did not deter him from returning to Africa with Burton the following year after briefly serving in the Crimean War.

Speke and Burton embarked on their second expedition together in December 1856, this time heading for the eastern interior. Their mission, sponsored by the Royal Geographical Society, was to search for the origin of the White Nile

John Hanning Speke. Mansell Collection, London.

(the larger of the river's two major tributaries) and for an unexplored body of water known as the Sea of Ujiji (now Lake Tanganyika). The expedition team, of which Speke was second in command, traveled west from coastal Zanzibar to Kazeh (now Tabora, Tanzania) and arrived at the lake early in 1858. Speke was unable to see his first major discovery, however, because trachoma, a tropical eye disease, had temporarily blinded him. Burton, meanwhile, had become seriously ill with malaria and was forced to remain in the area while Speke, somewhat recovered, proceeded to investigate the lakes of the region. He learned that the Sea of Ujiji included two other lakes as well: one to the southeast, Lake Nyasa (also called Lake Malawi), and another, much larger lake to the northeast. Speke sensed that the latter body of water fed the Nile River.

Speke arrived on July 30 at the southern shore of the lake then known as Ukerewe, and he dubbed the lake Victoria Nyanza in honor of Britain's queen. With his vision largely restored, Speke had his first full view of the lake on August 3 but found no evidence that the

Nile emerged there. While he did not explore the lake, he questioned both local tribes and German missionaries in the area who contended that a large river began on the lake's north side. Rejoining Burton, Speke recounted his experience and was met with ridicule from his colleague, who doubted that the Nile flowed from Lake Victoria and chided Speke for accepting hearsay so readily. Nevertheless, Speke was convinced that Lake Victoria held the key to the Nile's origin and became determined to establish a connection between the two bodies of water.

Speke then beat Burton back to England, where he presented his theory to the Royal Geographical Society. While officials there would not accept the theory outright, they agreed to finance an additional trip in order to determine the Nile's origin with certainty. Accompanied this time by an army acquaintance, JAMES AUGUSTUS GRANT, Speke departed for East Africa in April 1860. Again heading west, Speke arrived in Tabora in 1861 and proceeded north around the western perimeter of Lake Victoria. The following year, on July 27, he reached the falls to the north of the lake where the White Nile emerged. He described the spectacle in the following journal entry:

> It was a sight that attracted one to it for hours—the roar of the waters, the thousands of passenger-fish, leaping at the falls with all their might . . . made, in all, with the pretty nature of the country—small hills, grassy topped with trees in the folds, and gardens on the lower slopes—as interesting a picture as one could wish to see. The expedition had now performed its function. I saw that old father Nile without any doubt rises in the Victoria Nyanza and, as I had foretold, that lake is the great source of the holy river. . . .

Speke named the cataracts Ripon Falls in honor of the Royal Geographical Society president, the Second Earl of Ripon. (He later notified the Society of his discovery by sending a telegram stating: "The Nile is settled.")

Although he had hoped to sail the length of the Nile on his return home, Speke was barred from making the trip by hostile tribes of the area. Instead, he rejoined Grant, who had been detained in the Bantu region of Karagwe (west of Lake Victoria) because of an infected leg, and the two traveled north toward Gondokoro in August, following the Nile by land as closely as possible. They encountered more difficulties with the inhabitants while in the Bunyoro region; the native ruler there delayed their passage briefly. By February 1863 they reached Gondokoro (where they ran into fellow explorer SAMUEL WHITE BAKER), and they proceeded from there to Africa's northern coast. They then returned to England, where they were greeted as heroes.

While many were convinced that Speke had conclusively proven Lake Victoria to be the source of the Nile, others remained skeptical. Speke's biggest detractor was Burton, who insisted that Speke had not followed the Nile's entire course to Gondokoro and therefore could not prove that it was the Nile that emerged from Lake Victoria. Speke and Burton had not been on good terms since their expedition to the interior lake region, and Burton's skepticism has been attributed to envy that his less-experienced subordinate made the more important discovery of that previous journey. In an effort to settle the issue, the two rivals were invited to debate each other on September 16, 1864, at a meeting of the British Association for the Advancement of Science at Bath. Known as the Nile Duel, the highly publicized meeting was to be attended by hundreds of England's leading geographers and scientists. The day before the debate was to take place, however, Speke accidentally shot himself to death while hunting on his uncle's nearby estate.

The controversy continued, fed by unfounded rumors that Speke had deliberately shot himself because he was unprepared to debate Burton. Grant assumed the role of expedition spokesman and, although he had not actually been present at the discovery of the Nile's source, upheld the position of his friend and colleague. Speke's discovery was later confirmed in expeditions by three prominent explorers.

• Stanley, Henry Morton

Welsh-American
b January 28, 1841; Denbigh
d May 10, 1904; London
Explored East and Central Africa and Congo

Considered by many to be the leading explorer and colonizer of Africa, Henry Morton Stanley remains best known for the first of his many exploration-related achievements—locating the

Sir Henry Morton Stanley. Bettmann/Hulton.

The details of Stanley's early life bear an eerie resemblance to those in a novel by Dickens. This is not entirely a coincidence. As recent historians have pointed out, his own *Autobiography*, taken as factual for years, contains a number of elaborate and deliberate fictions. His reasons for lying can only be guessed at. The facts of his early years are themselves wretched and dramatic enough, and perhaps help explain the psychological reasons he might have had for embellishing and obscuring his own past.

Christened John Rowlands, Stanley was born in North Wales to an unwed, impoverished mother and abandoned to a workhouse school at the age of four. A good but strong-willed student, he ran away from school when he was fifteen (he claimed his flight followed a fight with the school's sadistic headmaster). He then spent a year trying to find a home with a series of relatives, all of whom proved unwilling or unable to take him in permanently. Finally, the disillusioned youth took a job as a cabin boy on a ship sailing from Liverpool to New Orleans.

On his arrival in Louisiana he found both a job and an adoptive home with a cotton merchant named Henry Hope Stanley, whose name he took. His rebellious nature led to conflicts in his new home, however, and he ran away several times. Eventually his adoptive father sent him to work on a farm in Arkansas. The *Autobiography* claims that the elder Stanley died without a will in 1861, leaving the younger Stanley penniless. (In fact, Henry Hope Stanley lived until 1878.) When the Civil War erupted that year, the younger Stanley joined the Confederate Army and was captured at Shiloh in 1862. He later enlisted in the Union Army to avoid a federal prison term, but a severe case of dysentery (an acute intestinal disorder) soon earned him a release. Still determined to find a place with his family of birth, he returned to Wales in the summer of 1862 to see his mother. When, according to his own account, she shut the door in his face, he returned to the United States, where he soon earned his citizenship and embarked on a long and successful career.

After serving briefly in the United States Navy, he took a job as a reporter with the *New York Herald*. Ideally suited to a job that involved travel and adventure, the drifter knew immediately that he had found his professional niche. Stanley's talent and dedication won him increasingly important assignments, including

missing British missionary DAVID LIVINGSTONE in Central Africa. In a series of expeditions that spanned two decades, he circumnavigated Lake Tanganyika and Lake Victoria, settled the remaining questions regarding the source of the Nile River, and aided both Belgium and England in developing African colonies. Stanley was the first European to travel the entire length of the Congo (or Zaire) River, the first to visit Mount Ruwenzori, and the third (after Livingstone and VERNEY LOVETT CAMERON) to cross Africa. A journalist, he detailed his travels in books and news stories and was often labeled a self-serving adventurer who was more interested in sensationalism than in serious investigation. Whatever his motives, Stanley's discoveries, writings, diplomatic efforts, rescue operations, and missionary endeavors have earned him a prominent place in the history of exploration.

coverage of the military campaign against the Indians of the American West and the British expedition in Abyssinia (modern Ethiopia). He was on assignment in Madrid in late 1869 when his publisher, James Gordon Bennett, summoned him to Paris and gave him the journalistic opportunity of a lifetime.

Stanley, however, did not see it in that light. Finding the missionary and explorer David Livingstone, who had vanished into the African interior two years earlier, loomed as an impossible task that would cost him his hard-won reputation if he failed. His search was not to begin for about a year, following several assignments in the Middle East, and privately Stanley hoped Livingstone would show up during the interim. However, in January 1871, a reluctant Stanley was forced to begin the journey that would bring him worldwide fame and a brief but important friendship.

The Stanley expedition consisted of nearly 200 people, most of whom departed from coastal Zanzibar in March 1871. To cover more territory, the party divided into five groups,

with Stanley heading south to Bagamoyo, on the east coast of Africa, and then west to Tabora (both in present-day Tanzania). His destination was Ujiji, a caravan station Livingstone had reportedly planned to visit, which lay farther west on the eastern shore of Lake Tanganyika. The pace of the expedition was slow, owing to Stanley's unfamiliarity with the mountains, swamps, and forests of the interior and also to disputes with hostile native tribes and rebellious subordinates. Moreover, he had been warned in Zanzibar to anticipate another complication—namely, that the obsessed Livingstone might not want to be found. Therefore, when Stanley learned from eastbound travelers that Livingstone had recently returned to Ujiji, the would-be rescuer redoubled his efforts. Fearing that Livingstone would hide if he learned of the search party, Stanley accelerated his pace by bullying his group into forced marches. Taking the weary Livingstone by surprise amid a group of Arabs, the jubilant reporter was later to charm *Herald* readers with his account of the November 10 meeting:

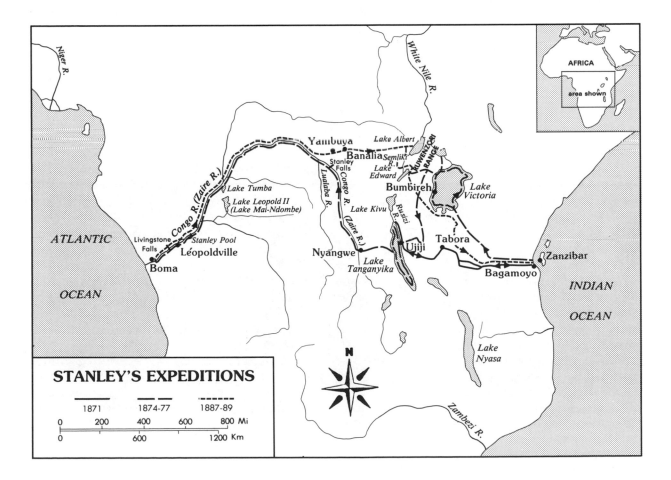

STANLEY'S EXPEDITIONS

| 1871 | 1874-77 | 1887-89 |

I would have run to him, only I was a coward in the presence of such a job,—would have embraced him, only, he being an Englishman, I did not know how he would receive me; so I did what cowardice and false pride suggested was the best thing—walked deliberately to him, took off my hat, and said:

"Dr. Livingstone, I presume?"

"Yes," said he, with a kind smile. . . .

Despite his precarious health and his liking for Stanley, the elderly explorer refused to leave Africa until he had determined whether the Lualaba River (in what is now Zaire) joined the Nile or the Congo. Stanley spent four months with Livingstone, exploring Lake Tanganyika and trying in vain to coax his ailing friend back to civilization in order to recuperate. But Livingstone's influence on Stanley was stronger. The great explorer was never to leave Africa, and his death a year later brought Stanley back to the African interior to complete the work of the man who had made him famous.

After a triumphant trip to England and a news assignment in West Africa, where he had learned of Livingstone's death, Stanley launched an expedition inland from Bagamoyo in 1874. This time sponsored by the London *Daily Telegraph* as well as his own paper, he had mapped out a series of explorations and wanted to complete them quickly. Not only was he eager to return to Alice Pike, the woman he had become engaged to in London, but he was racing to complete his work before Englishman Verney Lovett Cameron, who was on a similar course.

Along the caravan route to Tabora he struck northward at Mpwapwa and took an untried shortcut to Lake Victoria. He reached the lake in January 1875 and, while circumnavigating it, met with King Mtesa of Buganda and laid the groundwork for a Christian mission there. Blocked from reaching Lake Albert (in present-day Zaire) by Mtesa warriors, and narrowly escaping death at their hands, Stanley proceeded south to Lake Tanganyika, arriving in May and sailing around its entire perimeter. His exploration of these two bodies of water strengthened the theory that the White Nile began at Lake Victoria and confirmed that Lake Tanganyika was not linked to the Nile system. He then turned west toward the Lualaba River, reaching it in October 1876 and setting off downriver

"Dr. Livingstone, I presume?" Culver Pictures.

in January. The Lualaba led into the Congo, and, braving tribal attacks and perilous rapids, Stanley followed it to the Atlantic Ocean, arriving in August. He thus became the third person to have crossed Africa. Livingstone had completed his journey in 1856, and Cameron had done so in late 1875, also traveling east to west. Nevertheless, Stanley defeated his rival in their competing searches for the origin of the Lualaba. After sailing south from coastal Cabinda to Cape Town, Stanley began cabling the story of his trip to the sponsoring newspapers. One of his avid readers was King Leopold II of Belgium, who was to give Stanley his next commission.

Agents of the king met Stanley in Marseilles, France, in late 1877 to seek his services in colonizing the Congo region. Loyal to his native country, he would not accept the commission until he had offered to colonize the Congo on behalf of the British. His offer was rejected. Despite his celebrity status as an adventurer and storyteller, Great Britain did not consider Stanley a credible explorer and scorned his Congo proposal. He therefore returned to the Congo in 1879 and spent five years creating the large Belgian Congo Free State (now Zaire) in the African interior. In addition to negotiating settlement treaties with the region's native chiefs, he explored extensively, discovering Lake Tumba and Lake Leopold II (now Lake Mai-Ndombe) in 1883. The region also came to include the Stanley Falls and Stanley Pool, both part of the Congo River system, and the town of Stanleyville (now Kisangani) on the river's north shore. His relentless push to settle the area earned him the nickname "Bula Matari," meaning Rock Breaker, among his overworked subordinates. But the world at large called him the "Congo King."

It was the British public that chose Stanley for his final great mission in Africa. Stanley was resting in Europe when word came in 1886 that the appointed governor of the Egyptian Province of Equatoria, EDUARD SCHNITZER (also known as Emin Pasha), was under siege. Under public pressure, Britain engaged Stanley to rescue the German explorer, whose homeland countered by hiring Dr. Carl Peters to lead a rival mission for the same purpose. Arriving in Africa in 1887, Stanley located Schnitzer at Lake Albert the following year and again found himself trying to persuade a reluctant victim to be rescued instead of staying to finish his work. This episode ended in anger rather than gratitude, as Schnitzer returned to civilization only briefly for formality's sake. However, the trip enabled Stanley to explore the Mount Ruwenzori and the Semliki River, clarifying the White Nile's link to Lake Albert and Lake Edward, and to negotiate settlement treaties for England in its East African Protectorate.

While his first expedition had cost Stanley his former fiancée, he finally married at age forty-nine, shortly after his return from his Schnitzer mission. Settling happily in England with Dorothy Tennant, whose father was a member of Parliament, he resumed his British citizenship in 1892. He served in Parliament from 1895 to 1900 and during that time went to South Africa for a brief visit, his last on the continent. Stanley was knighted in 1899, five years before his death from a stroke at age sixty-three.

SUGGESTED READING: Ian Anstruther, *I Presume: Stanley's Triumph and Disaster* (Bles, 1973); John Bierman, *Dark Safari: The Life Behind the Legend of Henry Morton Stanley* (Knopf, 1990); Byron Farwell, *The Man Who Presumed: A Biography of Henry M. Stanley* (Greenwood Press, 1974); Richard S. Hall, *Stanley: An Adventurer Explored* (Houghton, 1975); Roger Jones, *The Rescue of Emin Pasha: The Story of Henry M. Stanley and the Emin Pasha Relief Expedition, 1887–1889* (Allison & Busby, 1972); Henry Morton Stanley, *Through the Dark Continent*, vols. 1–2 (Dover, 1988).

• Stark, Freya

English
b January 31, 1893; Paris, France
living
Explored and wrote about Middle East

Dame Freya Stark, an inveterate traveler whose collected works comprise eight volumes of letters, fourteen travel books, and a three-volume autobiography, displays both her passion for travel and her lyrical writing style in this description of the day she "discovered the Desert."

And then the wonder happened! Camels appeared on our left hand: first a few here and there, then more and more, till the whole herd came browsing along, five hundred or more. . . . I can't tell you what a wonderful sight it was: as if one were suddenly in the very morn-

Freya Stark. Bettmann/Hulton.

ing of the world among the people of Abraham or Jacob. The great gentle creatures came browsing and moving and pausing, rolling gently over the landscape like a brown wave just a little browner than the desert that carried it. . . . I stood in a kind of ecstasy among them. It seemed as if they were not so much moving as flowing along, with something indescribably fresh and peaceful and free about it all, as if the struggle of all these thousands of years had never been, since first they started wandering. I never imagined that my first sight of the desert would come with such a shock of beauty and enslave me right away.

Already a traveler at the age of four, Stark developed a taste for wandering through rough places, through worlds that few had seen—and certainly none with her unique vision. Unlike explorers who sought conquest or commerce or converts, Stark sought only to observe beauty with her own eyes and to craft words that fit her vision.

Freya Stark was born to a family constantly on the move: first to Devon to visit one grandmother, then to Genoa, Italy, to visit another. Her parents were both painters, but neither was happy with the marriage. So her mother moved Freya and her sister to Italy, where they were raised by governesses. Freya soon became self-reliant, perhaps even wild at times, but then began to read—Dumas, Milton, Plato—and to teach herself Latin. A near-fatal accident in an Italian carpet factory owned by a close friend of her mother put her in the hospital for four months and left her with a slight, but permanent, disfiguration. At age fifteen she returned to London and by age twenty-one had completed a degree in history at a university in London. Her language skills were strong: she spoke fluent Italian and adequate French and German. When World War I began, she went to Italy to train as a nurse but caught typhoid fever and nearly died. When she was well enough to travel, she returned to London.

Ever since Stark had received a copy of *The Arabian Nights* for her ninth birthday, she had dreamed of exploring the enchanting land of Arabia. Deciding that her opportunity had arrived to "travel single-mindedly for fun," she learned Arabic and set out for the East in November 1927. Her health was poor, but she said she would rather die than live like an invalid and proceeded to travel as though she feared neither fate. She made her way across Lebanon to Damascus, Syria, then wandered south into the land of the bedouin, the nomadic camel-owning tribes of the Arabian desert, eventually arriving in Egypt.

The winter of 1927 found Stark in Baghdad, Iraq, resolved to write a travel article by combining her travel notes with a history of the fortresses of the "Assassins." These were a violent band of outlaws whose leader had controlled them with "hashasin," the Arabic word for hashish and the source of the English word "assassin." This group had built a series of castles from Aleppo (in present-day Syria) to the Persian (now Iranian) border in the thirteenth century. Stark spent part of the winter learning Persian, then embarked alone on an expedition to the castle at Alamut, where the Assassins were headquartered until their defeat by the Mongols in 1256. She was the first European woman to travel in these areas, and her presence aroused great curiosity. In addition to tropical heat, Stark battled malaria and dysentery. Nevertheless, her trip was so successful that the Royal Geographical Society in Britain encouraged her to return to map the area, which she did in 1931, also discovering a previously unknown Assassin castle. The article she had wanted to write eventually became a book, *The Valley of the Assassins*, which was published in 1934.

Once Stark had established what was to be her lifelong rhythm of traveling and writing, the trips and the books came quickly. She spent the 1930s continuing her exploration of the Near East and southern Arabia, until, as the decade ended and war began, she made herself available to Aden (then a British colony, now southern Yemen) as an information officer. In 1941 she returned to Baghdad and became involved in the politics of the region. She traveled to the United States in 1943 to speak about British policy on Palestine and then in 1945 to India to help devise a plan for involving Indian women in voluntary service. By 1949 she had written ten travel books.

In the early 1950s, Stark turned her attention to the classical civilization brought by the Greeks to Asia Minor. She read classical history and traveled extensively in Turkey, which yielded yet another sequence of books. Her interest in the classical world expanded to include the Asian frontier of ancient Rome, which she began to investigate at the age of sixty-four. It was the subject of her last major book, *Rome on the Euphrates*. Not even the age of seventy proved an obstacle to the wandering Stark, for she had discovered the pleasure of taking her young friends and godchildren on her journeys. In 1970, by then seventy-seven, Stark set out for yet another, more distant goal: the Himalayas. Crossing the range in November of that year, she wrote, "[N]othing I can ever tell you will describe the awe and majesty of this approach, the last terrestrial footsteps to infinity."

Vilhjalmur Stefansson. National Archives of Canada.

• Stefansson, Vilhjalmur

Canadian-American
b November 3, 1879; Arnes, Manitoba
d August 26, 1962; Hanover, New Hampshire
Explored Arctic

Vilhjalmur Stefansson explored the Arctic widely, discovering the last major unknown landmasses in the Canadian Arctic Islands (including Borden, Brock, Meighen, and Lougheed islands). He is best known, however, for his unorthodox methods and his personal view of

Arctic lands. Stefansson insisted that Europeans in the Arctic should learn to live off the land instead of bringing in supplies and adapt to the actual environment instead of trying to create an artificial one. He raised eyebrows by proclaiming that the Arctic is a "friendly" place, but his prophecies proclaiming the economic value of the northern regions are now generally accepted.

Stefansson was the son of Icelanders who emigrated first to Canada and then to the United States. His independent nature revealed itself early. He was expelled from the University of North Dakota after two years—allegedly for nonattendance, but by his own account for stirring up trouble. Afraid that other schools would not want him if his record were known, he entered the University of Iowa as a first-year student and then passed tests to fulfill most of his course requirements.

After graduating from college, Stefansson attended Harvard Divinity School on a scholarship from a religious group—awarded despite his insistence that he would study religion only as folklore. After a year he transferred to the department of anthropology, where he completed his studies.

It was by pure chance that Stefansson embarked on his first Arctic expedition. He was on his way to Africa when he was invited to join the Anglo-American Polar Expedition, which was to study Victoria Island in the Canadian Arctic.

Although the expedition never reached Victoria Island, Stefansson gained much valuable experience and knowledge about the Arctic. In 1906 he first traveled overland via Toronto, Winnipeg, and Edmonton before boarding riverboats to head down the Mackenzie River system to Herschel Island, studying the Indians who lived along the river. When he finally reached Herschel Island, he learned that the expedition's ship, which was to take them to Victoria Island, was trapped in ice. When the ice melted, the ship sank, ending the expedition short of its goal. Stefansson readily decided to spend six months in the winter of 1906–1907 living with an **Inuit** family on the Yukon Arctic coast, learning their customs and languages. His lifelong love affair with the Arctic had begun.

After returning to the United States in the fall of 1907, Stefansson and the zoologist Rudolph M. Anderson planned another expedition to Victoria Island, this one sponsored by the American Museum of Natural History and the Geological Survey of Canada. They intended to prove Stefansson's theory that explorers could find plenty of food in the Arctic. The two scientists did not make elaborate arrangements for supplies. They simply "disappeared over the ice to the north," living off the land from 1908 to 1912. Along Coronation Gulf they made studies of people they called Copper Eskimos due to their copper implements. Also known as Blond Eskimos, they exhibited some European features, and it was theorized that these people were descendants of the Norse who occupied Greenland in medieval times and then mysteriously disappeared.

Again from 1913 to 1918, Stefansson tested his theories about surviving in the wild. He led a two-party expedition sponsored by the Canadian government, a northern party headed by himself and a southern party headed by Ander-

son. Leaving most of the northern party aboard its vessel, the *Karluk*, which had frozen in off Arctic Alaska, he and two companions, with one **sledge** and six dogs, headed north over the Arctic Ocean ice. They traveled some 500 miles and mapped large areas of unexplored territory, including the previously unknown Borden, Meighen, and Lougheed islands lying north of Axel Heiberg and Prince Patrick islands. In 1918 Stefansson set up a station on ice drifting in the Beaufort Sea. (Such floating stations later became an accepted method of studying Arctic conditions.)

Meanwhile, the southern party, under Anderson, carried out detailed scientific observations, particularly in the Coronation Gulf area of the western Canadian Arctic. During this time, the ill-fated *Karluk* drifted westward with the ice pack and eventually sank north of Siberia. Its captain, R. A. Bartlett, led the remaining members of the northern party over the sea ice to Wrangel Island. He then pushed on to Siberia and Alaska to bring aid to the survivors. Throughout this period—and subsequently—the expedition was plagued by bitter internal dissension, with the level of rancor particularly high between Anderson and Stefansson.

Stefansson vigorously pursued his interests in the Arctic for the rest of his life, though he increasingly became regarded as a writer and a promoter rather than as a scientist. In an ill-considered, unauthorized venture in the early 1920s he tried to set up a Canadian colony on Wrangel Island. The colonists died tragically, and in 1924 the Soviets took over the island. Stefansson later served as a consultant to Pan American Airways as it set up transpolar routes and worked with the U.S. military on its Arctic policies during World War II. He also continued to advocate an all-meat diet—such as what he ate during his own Arctic travels—and participated in several lengthy medical experiments to prove its healthfulness.

Stefansson finished his career at Dartmouth College in the Department of Northern Studies. He was a prolific writer. Among his best-known works are *My Life with the Eskimo*, *The Friendly Arctic*, and *Discovery: The Autobiography of Vilhjalmur Stefansson*. He died in New Hampshire at the age of eighty-two.

STUART, JOHN MCDOUALL

Stuart, John McDouall

Scottish
b September 7, 1815; Dysart, Fifeshire
d June 5, 1866; London, England
Explored southern Australia and traversed continent

The first to reach the center of the continent, John McDouall Stuart also was one of the first to cross Australia from south to north. The trail he blazed for the overland telegraph from Adelaide to present-day Darwin unified the continent and linked it with the rest of the world.

The son of an army officer, Stuart was born in Scotland in 1815 and moved to South Australia in 1838. He worked as a surveyor for the colonial government and in 1844 joined the explorer CHARLES STURT on an unsuccessful expedition to reach the center of the continent.

In 1858 Stuart struck out on his own, exploring the lands of South Australia between Lake Torrens and Streaky Bay. The next year he made two surveys of pastureland west of Lake Eyre. On the second journey, he experienced periods of near blindness, which would plague him on future expeditions.

In 1860 the South Australian Parliament offered a £2,000 reward to the first individual who could establish an overland route for a telegraph. Stuart took up the challenge and, along with two companions, left Chambers Creek on March 2 and headed north. By April 22 he had reached the geographical center of the continent approximately 125 miles north of Alice Springs. There he named a nearby hill Central Mount Sturt "after the Father of Australian Exploration, for whom we gave three hearty cheers and one more for Mrs. Sturt and family," he wrote. The hill was later renamed Central Mount Stuart after its discoverer.

The three explorers continued northward for another 175 miles, until they reached Attack (Tennant) Creek. Weakened by **scurvy** and a shortage of food, and under attack by local **aborigines**, they turned back. Once again, Stuart was nearly blind for a good portion of the journey. He reached the safety of Chambers Creek, below Lake Eyre, on September 1. Shortly afterward, the parliament gave him money for a second attempt at crossing the continent.

When Stuart left Mount Margaret Station, a farm west of Lake Eyre, on January 11, 1861, he took with him thirteen men and forty-nine horses. By April 25 he reached Attack Creek. From there, only 300 miles south of the Gulf of Carpentaria, he made several attempts to reach the gulf or the Victoria River but was held back by the thick scrub, "as great a barrier as an inland sea or wall." He advanced 100 miles past his last turning point but on July 12, short of food and fresh water, again turned his expedition around.

Stuart reached Adelaide in September, three months after the death of ROBERT O'HARA BURKE, the first person to make the south-to-north crossing. In October, fully reprovisioned, Stuart made a third attempt at the crossing. This time he was successful. In July 1862, nine months after leaving Adelaide, he reached the Indian Ocean at the mouth of the Adelaide River on Van Diemen Gulf in Arnhem Land. The tide was out, and Stuart waded in a muddy tidal flat riddled with crab holes. He washed his feet and face in the sea, "as I promised the late Governor Sir Richard Macdonnell I would." He then stripped the branches from a small tree and raised the Union Jack with his name sewn across the center.

The trek had taken its physical toll, and Stuart started back almost immediately after reaching the coast. He suffered from night blindness and scurvy and could eat only boiled flour. He wrote, "I completely lost the use of my limbs and had to be carried about like an infant" on a litter slung between two horses. The expedition returned home in December "leading a string of limping, emaciated horses." The South Australian Great Northern Exploring Expedition, as it was called, had been a success.

Unlike Burke, who was censured posthumously for his imprudent leadership, Stuart returned home a hero. For his feat he received £3,000 and a land grant of 1,000 acres of grazing land rent-free for seven years. He also earned the gold medal of England's Royal Geographical Society. However, he was not to enjoy his success very much. He never fully regained his health and lost his memory and ability to speak. He went to England in April 1864 and died there, near poverty, two years later.

The overland telegraph was erected less than nine years after Stuart blazed its path. From Darwin, a line was run across the sea, linking Australia with Java (now in Indonesia), Asia, and, finally, Europe. The railroad line that today runs from Adelaide to Alice Springs and the paved road that continues on to the northern coast also trace the path blazed by Stuart.

• Stuart, Robert

Scottish-American
b February 19, 1785; Callander, Perth, Scotland
d October 29, 1848; Chicago, Illinois
Explored American West; discovered South
  Pass

A partner in John Jacob Astor's Pacific Fur Company, Robert Stuart made a journey east from Astoria on the Columbia River to St. Louis from 1812 to 1813. During the course of his travels, he discovered South Pass, a 20-mile-wide opening in the Rockies that would later become the main entryway for settlers to the West coast.

Stuart emigrated to Montréal in 1807 and joined the North West Company. In 1810, following the example of his uncle, David Stuart, he became a partner in a new fur-trading venture being formed by businessman John Jacob Astor. Astor's plan was to establish a series of fixed posts along the route of MERIWETHER LEWIS and WILLIAM CLARK with a combined headquarters and supply post at the mouth of the Columbia River. In 1810, WILSON PRICE HUNT led an overland expedition to the mouth of the Columbia, while several other partners, including Robert Stuart, traveled by ship around Cape Horn to the coast of present-day Oregon. Stuart's group arrived first, and after a trading post, named Astoria, had been built, Stuart led a band of trappers into the valley of the Willamette River.

Near the end of June 1812, Stuart was given the important task of carrying dispatches back to Astor in New York. Setting out with a small group, Stuart followed Hunt's outward route into what is now southwestern Idaho. There they met a lone Indian who told them of a route across the Rocky Mountains that was shorter than the one Hunt had followed. After accepting numerous gifts intended to induce him to guide them to the pass, the Indian disappeared.

Stuart and his group rode east, through dry country of "sage brush and its detested relations." They were following the route that would later become the Oregon Trail. Still headed toward the pass that the Indian had

told them about, they were on the Bear River when a group of Crow Indians began to menace them. Although the Crows did not attack outright, they did relieve the party of its horses. Trying to evade the Crows, Stuart and his party turned east from the Bear River and wandered uncertainly in the mountains. Eventually they happened onto the Greys River, which they rightly assumed would bring them to the Snake. When they reached the Snake they built rafts and headed downstream, hoping to find Snake Indians willing to sell them horses. Failing to do so, they abandoned the rafts and turned east, heading toward Teton Pass in what is now western Wyoming. On the way they found fresh signs of Blackfoot Indians, and though there was plenty of game about they dared not fire their rifles for fear of attracting members of that violent tribe. But by the time the Blackfoot Indians had disappeared, the game had as well. After three days without a meal, one member of the party suggested that they should draw lots to see which of them should be killed to make a meal for the others. Stuart cocked his rifle at the offender, who fell to his knees and asked the forgiveness of the whole party, promising never to broach the subject of cannibalism again. The next day, a lone buffalo appeared providentially, and they slaughtered it for a feast.

The party then struck out southeast, moving parallel to the Wind River Range. At this point the men were only about 100 miles from where they had left the Bear River a month earlier, having traveled over 400 miles in a useless U-shape. They had, however, at last approached the pass they had been told of, and on October 22, Stuart's party made the first known crossing by non-Indians of South Pass. It would be another twelve years before JEDEDIAH SMITH would rediscover the important pass and put it on the map for good.

Having crossed the Rockies, Stuart and his party came upon the Sweetwater River, the western tributary of the North Platte River. They built a cabin near present-day Casper, Wyoming, in which to wait out the winter. On December 12, after a group of seemingly friendly Arapaho Indians discovered the cabin, the cautious Stuart moved the group closer to the Nebraska border. In spring they proceeded on foot and by canoe to St. Louis, where they were welcomed by cheering crowds in a reception that rivaled the one given Lewis and Clark at the end of their epic journey seven years earlier.

On May 16 Stuart left St. Louis on horseback, and he arrived in New York City about June 23. There he presented John Jacob Astor with the dispatches from the Oregon Territory as well as the report of his journey east. Stuart was clearly aware of the significance of his accomplishment, and he rightly predicted that wagons would be able to reach the West along the trail that he had followed east. However, his insights were to remain hidden from the public for some time to come. Stuart's journal became the private property of Astor, and Astor, being a businessman, was not in the habit of sharing trade secrets. Even so, news of Stuart's accomplishments—including reference to a pass across the Rockies—appeared in several newspapers, from St. Louis to Washington, D.C. But Astor largely succeeded in keeping Stuart's discoveries to himself. Had he not, the American westward migration might have begun many years earlier than it did.

Robert Stuart spent many more years in the fur trade, but none of his future exploits rivaled this first one for sheer adventure or significance. A cool-headed and clear-thinking leader, he brought his party through a difficult journey and perceived the importance of his discovery.

Charles Sturt. The Granger Collection.

Sturt, Charles

**English
b April 28, 1795; Bengal, India
d June 16, 1869; Cheltenham
Discovered Darling River and Lake
Alexandrina; explored South Australia and
New South Wales**

Lauded as the father of Australian exploration, Charles Sturt was one of the first to explore Australia's interior. He is best known for solving the mysteries surrounding the continent's largest river system. His efforts on the Darling, Murrumbidgee, and Murray rivers, along with other explorations, opened up untold miles of new lands.

The son of a judge in Bengal under the British East India Company, Sturt was born in India in 1795 and educated at Harrow. He entered the army under the patronage of the prince regent and attained the rank of captain, serving in Spain and Canada before taking garrison duty in Ireland. In 1826 he was sent to New South Wales with the Thirty-Ninth Regiment to guard convicts. Sturt liked the wild new country immediately and developed a strong interest in its geography. He also became friends with several explorers.

Sturt was appointed military secretary under Governor Sir Ralph Darling, who sent him on several forays into unknown country. Sturt took careful notes, and his accurate charts and descriptions added immensely to existing knowledge of the continent.

In 1828 Sturt took part in his first major expedition, joining HAMILTON HUME to explore the lands beyond the Macquarie River. The party left Sydney in November, crossing the Blue Mountains to the Macquarie Marshes, which John Oxley had discovered a decade before. In the heat of the summer, the marshes were significantly drier than they were when Oxley encountered them, and Sturt pressed on. Eventually he came to the wide Darling River, near the present-day town of Burke. Although the river's saltiness led him to believe in a great inland sea, he did correctly determine that the Bogan, Castlereagh, and Macquarie rivers all flowed into the Darling.

In November 1829 Sturt left on another expedition, this one to follow the Murrumbidgee River either to its mouth or to the Darling. Of the landscape he found west of Sydney he wrote, "Neither bird nor beast inhabited these lonely and inhospitable regions, over which the silence of the grave seemed to reign. We had not, for days past, seen a blade of grass." He reached the Murrumbidgee in the last days of December. Within a week he assembled a twenty-seven-foot whaleboat and started downriver on January 7, 1830.

The ride was a wild one, made dangerous by rapids and floating trees. On the second day out, the explorers lost the small boat that carried many of their provisions in twelve feet of water. After a week, Sturt noted that the river took a sudden turn to the south, "narrowed and started an ominous twisting." The party soon came to a junction with "a broad and noble river." Not recognizing it as the waterway Hume had named after his father in 1824, Sturt called it the Murray River after Sir George Murray, secretary of state for the colonies. The river flowed northwest, and Sturt assumed it would lead to his inland sea.

A week later, on January 21, some 600 armed **aborigines** appeared alongside the river chanting war songs. The current carried the boat out of reach, but the warriors followed. Sturt was afraid he might have to take action when a second tribe appeared and drove off the first. Anthropologists later explained that Sturt's rescuers believed him to be the god-hero who, according to legend, had led their tribe to the mouth of the river.

Downstream Sturt discovered that the Darling flowed into the Murray. In early February the expedition reached the estuary between the Murray and the Gulf of St. Vincent; Sturt named it Lake Alexandrina. The Murray then flowed to the open ocean.

The downstream trip took thirty-three days. With no boat waiting in the gulf, Sturt decided to sail up current and made it back to the Murrumbidgee in a month. At the Murrumbidgee, the explorers had to pull the boat against a flooded river for three weeks, and the exertion temporarily blinded Sturt. On May 25, 1830, he returned to Sydney a hero, having opened up 2,000 miles of navigable waterway and

paved the way for the settlement of Adelaide on the Gulf of St. Vincent. The first settlers arrived there in 1836, three years after Sturt published his account of the journey.

Sturt then took sick leave in England, married Charlotte Greene, and left military service. But he returned to Australia in 1834 and, after two failed attempts at farming and livestock, took a post in the South Australian Survey Department in 1839.

In 1844 Sturt set out on his last major expedition—an attempt to reach the center of the continent. His team of sixteen men, including JOHN MC DOUALL STUART, left Adelaide on August 10, following the Murray and Darling rivers. The expedition spent six months trapped by drought at Depot Glen, where temperatures reached 119 degrees Fahrenheit in the shade, and they dug an underground room to stay cool. In July they moved on as far as the Simpson Desert, and Sturt became the first nonaborigine to set foot in this vast wasteland. Beaten in their attempt to reach the continent's midpoint, the party returned to Adelaide in January 1846. Two men had died of **scurvy**, and Sturt was never to regain his own health. The shock of seeing him arrive home in his weakened condition is said to have turned his wife's hair gray overnight.

In 1849 Sturt published further accounts of his explorations. He also was named colonial secretary, a post he held until his retirement in 1851. He spent his last years in England and was only days away from being knighted when he died in 1869.

- Sverdrup, Otto Neumann

Norwegian
b October 31, 1854; Bindal, Helgeland
d November 26, 1930; Oslo
Explored Greenland and northern Canadian
  Arctic

Otto Sverdrup was the chief assistant of fellow Norwegian explorer FRIDTJOF NANSEN on his two famous expeditions and, as captain of the ingeniously designed *Fram*, commanded an expedition to the Canadian Arctic from 1898 to 1902. In this single expedition, conducted with matter-of-fact confidence and expertise, Sverdrup charted an enormous amount of new territory in Canada's northernmost Arctic islands.

Sverdrup was born on a coastal farm 100 miles south of the Arctic Circle. Nansen was obviously impressed by this background: "Accustomed from childhood to wandering in the forest and on the mountains, on all kinds of errands and in all sorts of weather, Otto learned early to look after himself and to stand on his own legs." Growing up on a fjord also put the sea in his blood, and at the age of seventeen Sverdrup began life as a sailor, continuing to hone his skills over the next fifteen years, ultimately gaining his captain's papers. In 1885, he returned to his father's farm, where, as Nansen put it, "he spent his time at all sorts of work, in the forest, on the river, floating timber, in the smithy, and fishing at sea where as boat's captain he is unsurpassed." He was also an excellent skier.

All of this provided an ideal background for an Arctic explorer, of course, but it hardly gave Sverdrup the kind of stature that would attract influential supporters in big cities where new expeditions were being planned. In 1888, however, while rooming with Nansen's brother, Alexander, in Namsos, Sverdrup learned that Fridtjof was looking for skiers who could accompany him across the Greenland ice cap. Alexander saw that Sverdrup could ski with agility and strength, and the hitherto obscure farmer was chosen to take part in the famous explorer's planned trek. Sverdrup proved himself beyond anyone's expectations in this first crossing of Greenland, which marked the first time Europeans had actually discovered territory in the Arctic, rather than simply mapping land frequently traveled by **Inuits**. Sverdrup's strength, endurance, and calmness under pressure became clear to Nansen during the difficult landing on the east coast of Greenland, after the *Jason* had dropped them on the pack ice 12 miles from shore. His ingenuity revealed itself when he rigged up an ice boat created from the **sledges**. With tent-canvas sails, it fairly flew across the ice of the flat plateau, cutting six days off the traveling time.

As soon as Nansen arranged financing for his next famous voyage, in 1890, Sverdrup was recruited to captain the *Fram* and supervise its construction. The plan for this voyage was to plant the *Fram* in the pack ice north of Siberia and allow it to follow the drift over the North Pole to Greenland. This required a vessel with a shallow, rounded hull that would allow the expanding ice to slip right under it, rather than

crush it. The *Fram*, which looked more like a bathtub than a ship, departed from Vadsø, Norway, on June 26, 1893. Nansen conceived of and directed the project, but it was Sverdrup who guided the ship on its unprecedented three-year voyage. While Nansen made his spectacular sledge trip to the north from the *Fram* (1895–96), Sverdrup stayed with the ship. Extracting the *Fram* from the ice at the end of the voyage so that it could return to Norway before supplies ran out was no mean feat. It took twenty-eight days of blasting and cutting ice to navigate the 180 miles to open sea. According to the modern editor of Sverdrup's narrative, this "at once made him a living legend among mariners."

Sverdrup obviously knew how to handle the *Fram*, and Nansen had no trouble obtaining financial backing for a second voyage of discovery, this time with Sverdrup in command from beginning to end. The plan was to sail up the west coast of Greenland and through Robeson Channel to the frozen Arctic Ocean. Then the party was to explore the north coast of Greenland, past the point reached by the Adolphus Greely expedition in 1882.

To ROBERT PEARY, this seemed like an encroachment on what he had decided was his route to the North Pole. The stated aim of Sverdrup's mission was to discover whether there were any islands north of Greenland, but it is likely that, had circumstances permitted, Sverdrup would have attempted to make the pole. Sverdrup, as part of Nansen's party, had already stolen Peary's glory when he beat him across the Greenland ice cap. (Peary made it in 1895, but had tried first in 1886.) Commanding the formidable *Fram*, Sverdrup must have seemed invincible to Peary.

The American explorer made it clear that he did not like meeting Sverdrup at Cape Sabine on the east coast of Ellesmere Island—just two hours south of his wintering place—during the first winter of both expeditions (1898–99). He wrote in his diary of "the introduction of a disturbing factor in the appropriation by another of my plan and field of work," and shared nothing of his plans during this meeting with Sverdrup. Sverdrup, in contrast, played the gentleman and offered Peary a cup of coffee, which was refused. Sverdrup later claimed to have "rejoiced at having shaken hands with the bold explorer, even though his visit had been so short that we hardly had time to pull off our mittens."

As it turned out, the *Fram* was unable to penetrate the ice far enough to the north in order to carry out the original plan. It was built to ride on top of the ice, not to cut through it. Sverdrup then decided to explore to the west. Using the *Fram*, with its five years' worth of supplies, as a base, the party spent the next three years exploring Jones Sound, the southern and western coasts of Ellesmere Island, and what are now called the Sverdrup Islands to the west. Sverdrup claimed these islands for Norway, but after twenty-eight years of dispute Norway finally relinquished its claims to Canada. The Canadian government then paid Sverdrup $67,000 for all the original documents relating to his expedition, which also yielded fifty-three cases of geological, botanical, and zoological specimens. In 1903 Sverdrup received the Patron's Medal of England's Royal Geographical Society for his efforts on this expedition, which he chronicled in his two-volume work *New Land*, published in 1904.

Sverdrup did not quit the sea after his return to Norway in the fall of 1902. He commanded ships through ice for both the Imperial Russian and Soviet governments in the following years. In 1914 and 1920 he commanded rescue operations in the Kara Sea and in 1921 commanded the icebreaker *Lenin* as it escorted a convoy of freighters across the Kara Sea to the mouth of the Yenisei River. This was the route opened up by NILS ADOLF ERIK NORDENSKIÖLD in 1875, but only now was it being used by the Soviets as they attempted to thwart a blockade imposed on the young Bolshevik government by the Allied powers.

Sverdrup was not the last to use the *Fram*. ROALD AMUNDSEN took it to the South Pole in 1910, returning in 1912, and then on an abortive voyage in 1914. The *Fram* then was allowed to rot in harbor for two years until Sverdrup began a long fight to preserve it. He died in 1930, five years before the ship was finally put on display at Fram House near Oslo.

Tasman, Abel Janszoon

Dutch
b 1603; Lutjegast, Groningen
d 1659; Jakarta, Indonesia
Discovered Tasmania, New Zealand, and Fiji Islands

On two great voyages of discovery, the seventeenth-century Dutch navigator Abel Janszoon Tasman proved that Australia was not part of *Terra Australis Incognita*, a continent the size of Eurasia that at the time was believed to exist somewhere in the South Sea. He also became the first European to discover Tasmania, New Zealand, and the Fiji Islands. Yet his sponsors considered both expeditions failures, because neither led to lucrative new trading posts, nor did Tasman accomplish any of what he was sent to do.

A native of Holland, Tasman arrived in Batavia (present-day Jakarta, Indonesia) around 1632, where he obtained a job as a skipper for the powerful Dutch East India Company. From 1633 until 1638 he took part in trading voyages throughout present-day Indonesia and to Japan, Formosa (now Taiwan), and Cambodia, interrupted only by a brief trip back to the Netherlands in 1637. In 1639 he voyaged to the northern Pacific with Mathijs Quast.

Apparently Tasman distinguished himself in his maritime career, for in 1642 Anton van Diemen, the governor-general of Batavia, chose him to command a major expedition into the southern and eastern Pacific Ocean. Dutch explorers had discovered discontinuous stretches of a large land mass south of Indonesia. Tasman was to explore the known parts of this Great South Land, as it was called (present-day Australia), search for *Terra Australis Incognita* (for a more complete discussion, see ALEXANDER DALRYMPLE), and seek a passage between the Indian and Pacific oceans that would give the Dutch a shortcut to the riches of Chile. Van Diemen wanted Tasman to do no less than chart "the remaining unknown part of the terrestrial globe." If Tasman could find new sources of pepper, spices, and other goods, and establish trade relations with the people he encountered, so much the better.

Tasman and the **hydrographer** Frans Jacobszoon Visscher left Batavia on August 14, 1642, with two ships, the *Heemskerk* and the *Zeehaan*, a crew of some 110 men, provisions for eighteen

Abel Janszoon Tasman, with wife and daughter. National Library of Australia.

months, and miscellaneous cargo to trade along the way. They sailed first for Île de France (present-day Mauritius), in the Indian Ocean east of Madagascar, where they obtained fresh water and firewood. Theoretically, his west-to-east course increased Tasman's chances of finding a new route to Chile.

Tasman had two major options concerning his course. He could sail east at the latitude of Mauritius across the Indian Ocean to Eendrachtsland (that part on the western coast of the Great South Land discovered in 1616 by DIRCK HARTOG), or he could take an eastward heading at a much more southerly latitude—52° to 54° South—to seek *Terra Australis Incognita*. He intended to do the latter, but the weather in the southern latitudes at that time of year proved too severe. Instead, Tasman followed a course that Visscher suggested, which was to sail east at 44° South.

In late November, Tasman saw "the first land

we had met with in the South Sea." It was an island with mountains, two of which the English explorer MATTHEW FLINDERS would later name Mount Heemskerk and Mount Zeehaan in Tasman's honor. For a week Tasman's two ships circled the large island, which he christened Van Diemen's Land (now Tasmania), finally anchoring on December 1, 1642.

When a landing party went ashore, they found a wild island where abundant greens and fruit trees grew naturally, rather than in cultivated rows. Tasman reported that they saw no other human beings, "although we surmise some were not far away and were with watching eyes observing our goings-on." The Dutch sailors heard sounds and saw smoke from fires in the distance.

Later a party tried to land to claim the island for the Dutch East India Company. But the surf was too rough for their small landing boat, so Tasman sent the ship's carpenter swimming to

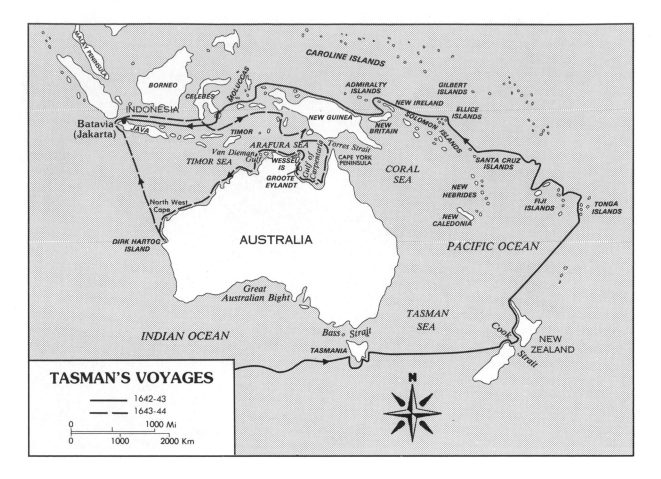

TASMAN'S VOYAGES

— 1642-43
--- 1643-44

| 0 | | | 1000 Mi |
| 0 | 1000 | | 2000 Km |

shore with an appropriately inscribed pole. However, since the island had yielded neither riches nor spices, Tasman did not want to waste much time on it. (Neither did his Dutch financiers. The island was not visited again until the Frenchman Marion du Fresne anchored there 130 years later.) Tasman's two ships sailed on December 4, continuing their eastward course.

Nine days later, Tasman sighted land again after crossing the sea that today bears his name. He had come upon what is now South Island, New Zealand. He believed—wrongly—that this body of land, which he called Staaten Land, was connected to parts of the Great South Land (what is now Australia) that had been explored in 1616 by Jacob Le Maire. He mistook the strait dividing New Zealand's two main islands for a bay. When a party went ashore, hostile Maori tribesmen killed four of the Dutch sailors, so Tasman left quickly. He named the anchorage Murderers Bay.

Tasman sailed north then northeast off the west coast of Staaten Land. His course took

him to Tongatapu and Nomuka in the present-day Tonga (or Friendly Islands) group, where he was able to replenish his supplies of food and water. On these islands, he traded nails for coconuts, a transaction that would displease his employers. A northwest course from the Tongas took Tasman to another group of islands, mostly uninhabited. This was Fiji, a region that Tasman was the first European to discover. As he continued his voyage, he sighted the Ontong Java atoll (formerly Lord Howe Islands) north of the Solomon Islands, then sailed along the north coast of New Guinea. He arrived back in Batavia on June 15, 1643.

By effectively circumnavigating what is now Australia without seeing it, Tasman proved that it was not part of *Terra Australis Incognita*, which was postulated as being much larger in order to balance the mass of the northern continents. But his superiors considered his voyage a failure. Less than a year later, however, they sent Tasman and Visscher on another voyage—this one to determine whether New Guinea was attached to the Great South Land. Not having found the Torres Strait south of New Guinea, the Dutch believed that what is now Australia's Cape York Peninsula was connected to New Guinea.

On February 29, 1644, Tasman set sail with three ships. When he reached New Guinea, he missed the Torres Strait again and sailed down the western side of the Cape York Peninsula approximately to the present-day Gilbert River. He then followed the coastline of the Gulf of Carpentaria. The gulf's reefs and shoals kept him far enough from shore that he mistook islands in the modern Wellesley and Sir Edward Pellew groups for capes. Throughout the voyage he made similar misidentifications and missed several bays. Although no journal of the voyage survived, his mistakes were reflected in a map produced in Batavia after Tasman's return. Still, he navigated what he estimated to be 8,000 miles of dangerous and uncharted waters between the Cape York Peninsula and the North West Cape and south to Dirk Hartog Island— a greater distance than any explorer before him. He charted areas on the northern coast of Australia that Dutch eyes had not yet seen, particularly from the Gilbert River to what are now Groote Eylandt, the Wessel Islands, the west side of the Cobourg Peninsula, and Van Diemen Gulf.

When Tasman returned to Batavia in August 1644, he once again faced a displeased and disappointed employer. Trade possibilities in the regions he had explored were unlikely, a company report said, for the only people Tasman had seen were "naked, beach-roving wretches, destitute even of rice . . . miserably poor, and in many places of very bad disposition." And, his superiors complained, Tasman should have explored the interior.

After 1644 Tasman made no more voyages of discovery, but he did stay in the employ of the Dutch East India Company. In fact, he was given the rank of commander and made a member of the Council of Justice of Batavia, so apparently his accomplishments were perceived to outweigh his failures. Still, the company remained silent about his voyages and never published an account of them. (An account of his first journey was published privately after Tasman's death.) The Dutch generally thought it was to their advantage to let the rest of the world believe that there was nothing of value in the southwestern Pacific. They still hoped that riches could be found in the Great South

Land and did not want to stir undue curiosity about the area until they were in a position to control it.

Tasman continued to sail in a commercial capacity for the company, and in 1647 he commanded a trading fleet on a voyage to Siam (present-day Thailand). Upon his return, he led an attack against the Spanish in the Philippines (1648–49). When two of his sailors disobeyed his orders, Tasman tried to hang them. The company suspended him briefly over the incident, but he continued to work for them until his retirement in 1653.

After retiring, Tasman remained in Batavia until his death in 1659. It would be another hundred years before anyone else would mount a serious search for the nonexistent *Terra Australis Incognita*. The waters Tasman had explored, with their mazelike coral reefs, were deemed too dangerous and the commercial potential of the lands they surrounded too insignificant to make such a voyage worthwhile.

SUGGESTED READING: J. C. Beaglehole, *The Exploration of the Pacific* (A&C Black Ltd., 1934); Charles R. Boxer, *The Dutch Seaborne Empire 1600–1800* (Alfred A. Knopf, 1965); Roderick Cameron, *Australia History and Horizons* (Columbia University Press, 1971); C. M. H. Clark, *A History of Australia*, vol. 1 (Cambridge University Press, 1961); Andrew Sharp, *The Discovery of Australia* (Clarendon Press, 1963); Andrew Sharp, *The Voyages of Abel Janszoon Tasman* (Cambridge University Press, 1968).

Tavares, Antonio Rapôso de. See **Rapôso de Tavares, Antonio.**

· Teixeira, Pedro de

Portuguese
b 1570–93; Castanheira
d June 4, 1640; São Luis do Maranhão, Brazil
Explored Amazon

Captain Pedro de Teixeira initially came to Brazil to help expel the English, Dutch, and French, who were encroaching on Spanish and Portuguese territories in South America. Then, in 1637, he led a remarkable transcontinental expedition on the Amazon River from Pará (present-day Belém, Brazil) to Quito (in modern Ecuador) and then back to Pará. This was the first all-Portuguese expedition to navigate the Amazon, as well as the first of any kind to travel the length of the Amazon upstream. The most important result of the journey, however, was that Teixeira established Portuguese sovereignty in the lands along the Amazon.

Pedro de Teixeira was born into a noble family in the town of Castanheira, Portugal. His exact date of birth is unknown, but it has been placed as early as 1570 and as late as 1593. Nothing is known of his early life in Portugal; he came to Brazil sometime in the early 1600s as part of a Portuguese military contingent.

During the years 1615 and 1616 Teixeira helped evict the French from the coastal town of São Luis do Maranhão and accompanied Francisco Caldira de Castelo Branco when he founded the port of Fort Presépio on the Pará River delta. In 1618 he was named governor of the territory of Pará; however, he was superceded by Benito Maciel in 1622. During the next five years he led several military raids against the English and Dutch, destroying their settlements along the Xingu River. He also went on a slaving expedition up the Amazon to the Tapajós River and on a journey with Luis Aranha de Vasconcelos to map the lower Amazon River. Teixeira next commanded a major expedition up the Amazon in 1629, with 120 Portuguese and 1,600 Indians in 98 canoes. They captured English, Dutch, and Irish settlements in the territory around Manacapuru. As a result of all these expeditions, Teixeira gained considerable knowledge of the lower Amazon and many of its tributaries, as well as the region's Indian tribes.

Having disposed of all foreign rivals by the 1630s, the Portuguese in Brazil turned their attention to solidifying and expanding their influence in Spanish-dominated South America. Though Spain and Portugal were politically united under one monarch at this time (a situation that would change in 1641 with the restoration of the Portuguese monarchy in the person of King John IV), the Portuguese remained intensely nationalistic. Therefore, the surprising arrival in Pará of two Spanish friars from Peru was fortuitous, albeit alarming, and Teixeira was chosen to lead an expedition up the Amazon under the pretext of escorting these priests back to Quito. However, he had sealed orders from the governor of Maranhão province detailing the real purpose of the venture. He was instructed to "carefully note the river until Quito, to verify the best places at which the river could be fortified," to establish good will with the Indians, to found a Portuguese settlement, and to mark the boundaries between the domains of Spain and Portugal, as determined by the **Treaty of Tordesillas** in 1494.

Accordingly, Teixeira set out from Pará on October 28, 1637, with 47 canoes carrying 70 soldiers and almost 2,000 Indian and Negro slaves, making this the largest expedition ever to attempt to navigate the length of the Amazon. Although the expedition encountered few difficulties during the journey upstream, its progress was slow due to the opposing force of the current, the need to send scouting parties ahead to determine which fork of the river to take, and the time required to collect food. Since the Indians along the Amazon could not feed so large a group, the expeditionary force had to provide its own food by stopping frequently to hunt, fish, and gather fruits. As a result, it took Teixeira's expedition eight months to reach the first Spanish settlement along the Amazon.

The major problem faced by Teixeira was keeping the Indians and Negro slaves rowing, since they became increasingly disgruntled as well as exhausted from rowing against the strong river current. Using a mix of persuasion and diplomacy, he convinced them to keep rowing by telling them that they were almost at their destination. To reinforce this illusion, he would send small parties ahead as if to announce their arrival; in actuality, these were scouting parties.

When the expedition reached the upper Amazon, in the territory occupied by the Omagua Indians between the Napo and Juruá rivers, Teixeira left some of his force to construct a camp and await his return. Pushing ahead, the remainder of the expedition reached the Napo River and entered the region of the Quijos Indians. At this point Teixeira sent an advance party of eight canoes to find the best river route to Quito. Initially, they chose the Quijos River, thinking it to be the shortest route; however, they had to abandon the river because of its very swift current. They then were forced to complete the journey to Quito on foot, scaling the Andes mountains, and arriving in the city in 1638.

The people of Quito gave a huge welcome to the Teixeira expedition, holding parties and bullfights in their honor. The Spanish authorities, however, were quick to realize the significant implications of Teixeira's journey. After much debate over what course of action to take, the officials decided to encourage Teixeira to return to Pará at his earliest convenience.

In order to determine the extent of Portuguese influence in the Amazon, the officials wanted to send a Spaniard with the return expedition in order to carefully observe, record, and map the Amazon for future Spanish ventures. Father CRISTÓBAL DE ACUÑA, brother of the governor of Quito, was chosen for this job. His detailed journal of the expedition from Quito to Pará is the major source of information about the return journey. Teixeira also agreed to take a contingent of Spanish soldiers to some undetermined point where they would establish a fortress to protect Peru from possible invasion by the English or the Dutch.

The expedition departed Quito on February 16, 1639, and followed the Napo River until it reached the Amazon. Arriving at the place where he had left the contingent on the voyage upstream, Teixeira discovered that these men had fought many battles with an unfriendly tribe of Omagua Indians. Taking decisive action, Teixeira attacked and slaughtered the Indians, then founded a town that he called Franciscana in honor of the Franciscan friars who were responsible for the journey. During the dedication of the settlement on August 16, 1639, Teixeira claimed the surrounding lands for Portugal, and none of the Spaniards objected. Somewhere in the vicinity of the settlement he also put a carved log in the ground as a mark of delineation between Portuguese and Spanish domains. Historians are not sure of the exact location of either the marker or the town, though both are believed to be near the modern town of Tabatinga, located close to the present Brazil-Peru border.

When they reached the mouth of the Río Negro, the expedition stopped for a while. Many of the men wanted to hunt slaves on the Río Negro, but Father Acuña objected on the basis of moral concerns and his desire to reach Pará as soon as possible. Though tempted by slave hunting, Teixeira supported Acuña, and the men proceeded down the Amazon without further incident. Passing the mouth of the Madeira River, they landed on the large island now called Tupinambarana. There they encountered the Tupinambá Indians, who told them stories of a land peopled by dwarfs. The expedition finally reached Pará on December 12, 1639.

Pedro de Teixeira was honored for his accomplishments: he won a military promotion and on February 28, 1640, was named governor of the province of Pará. A few months later, on June 4, 1640, he died in São Luis do Maranhão. Little has come down through history about the nature of the man, except that he was extremely patriotic and favored Portuguese control of the entire Amazon region long before his historic journey. Even Father Acuña's detailed journal says very little about Teixeira; however, the journal does refer to him at the start of the journey as "a person whom Heaven has undoubtedly chosen on this occasion, on account of his prudence."

As a result of his round-trip, transcontinental journey, Pedro de Teixeira established Portuguese control over the entire Amazon River region. Wisely, the Portuguese had acted upon the idea that whoever controlled the Amazon would also control a large part of South America. Thus, when King John IV ascended the throne of Portugal on April 3, 1641, the Amazon had already been secured by Teixeira, despite the fact that most of it had been previously granted to Spain under the Treaty of Tordesillas.

SUGGESTED READING: John Hemming, *Red Gold: The Conquest of the Brazilian Indians* (Harvard University Press, 1978); Clements R. Markham, trans. and ed., *Expeditions into the Valley of the Amazons* (Hakluyt Society, 1859); Anthony Smith, *Explorers of the Amazon* (Viking, 1990).

• Thesiger, Wilfred Patrick

English
b June 1910; Addis Ababa, Ethiopia
living
Lived and traveled among remote tribal
peoples, mainly in Arabia and Africa

Wilfred Thesiger's mode of discovery was governed by a concern rarely found among explorers who came before him. Thesiger once wrote:

While I was with the Arabs I wished only to live as they lived, and now that I have left them I would gladly think that nothing in their lives was altered by my coming. Regretfully, however, I realize that the maps I made helped others with more material aims to visit and corrupt a people whose spirit once lit the desert like a flame.

For almost fifty years of the twentieth century, Thesiger lived among tribal people in remote and often dangerous parts of the world—in the vast deserts of Africa and Arabia, in the marshes of Iraq and the swamps of the upper Nile, in India's Karakoram Range and the Hindu Kush of Pakistan. Thesiger's writings reveal the depth of understanding underlying what he called a "strange compulsion" to wander the great deserts of the East, living as the native people of these areas lived.

His early life certainly set the stage for his unusual adventures. The oldest son of a British minister stationed in Addis Ababa (in present-day Ethiopia), Thesiger traveled with his family in the deserts and Abyssinian (now Ethiopian) highlands of Africa and in India. After schooling at Eton and Oxford in England, he returned to Abyssinia and explored the Awash River and the Aussa region to the north. From 1935 to 1939 he served in the Sudanese political service, during which time he explored the area from Khartoum west to the Darfur mountain region and northwest to Tibesti (now in Chad). Thesiger spent the years of World War II in Ethiopia, Syria, and North Africa, assisting in the Allied defense of those regions.

After the war, Thesiger began a series of treks across the "Empty Quarter": the desert region in the southern Arabian peninsula never before penetrated by Europeans. He was employed by the Desert Locust Service, an organization whose workers added substantially to the sparse knowledge about Arabia. Along the way, he became friends with the bedouin, the camel-herding nomads who made the desert their home, and developed a great respect for their way of life. Thesiger spent most of his time from 1951 to 1958 living in and exploring Iraqi marshes in the region northwest of Basra, around the confluence of the Tigris and Euphrates rivers. From 1968 to 1976 he spent nine months each year in Kenya, mainly on safari. He has written extensively about his travels; his books include *The Last Nomad: One Man's Forty Year Adventure in the World's Most Remote Deserts, Mountains and Marshes*, *Arabian Sands*, and *The Marsh Arabs*.

· Thompson, David

English
b April 30, 1770; London
d February 10, 1857; Longeuil, near Montréal, Canada
Explored Canadian West and Columbia River from source to mouth

After surveying and mapping over 9,000 square miles in Canada east of the Rocky Mountains, David Thompson turned his attention farther west. In 1807 he crossed the Rockies through Saskatchewan Pass and followed the Columbia River to its source in Lakes Windermere and Columbia. Between 1807 and 1811, he traveled every inch of the river, mapping it from its source to its mouth on the Pacific Ocean.

Thompson's father, a Welshman, died when David was only two. Left impoverished, he was educated in a charity school, where he showed a special aptitude for mathematics. He was apprenticed to the Hudson's Bay Company of fur traders in 1784 and worked for the company until 1797. During that time he traveled and surveyed many of the rivers that emptied into the west side of Hudson Bay. Unfortunately for the Hudson's Bay Company, its leaders failed to recognize the importance of Thompson's work. They wanted him to spend less time exploring and more time engaged in the fur trade.

So Thompson left the Hudson's Bay Company to join its rival, the North West Company. One of his first journeys for his new employers was a trip from the Assiniboine River (in present-day Manitoba) to the Mandan villages on the Missouri River, a trip similar to that made by LA VÉRENDRYE in 1738. Around the same time he explored the headwaters of the Mississippi River in what is now northern Minnesota. This work established that the designated boundary between the United States and Canada was based on a geographic impossibility. The boundary line was supposed to run west from the northwest angle of Lake of the Woods until it intersected the Mississippi. But Thompson's survey showed that the source of the Mississippi was probably south of Lake of the Woods and that a line running west of the lake would therefore never intersect the Mississippi.

In the early 1800s, Thompson turned his attention to the foothills of the Rocky Mountains and explored the upper waters of the North and South Saskatchewan and Athabasca rivers

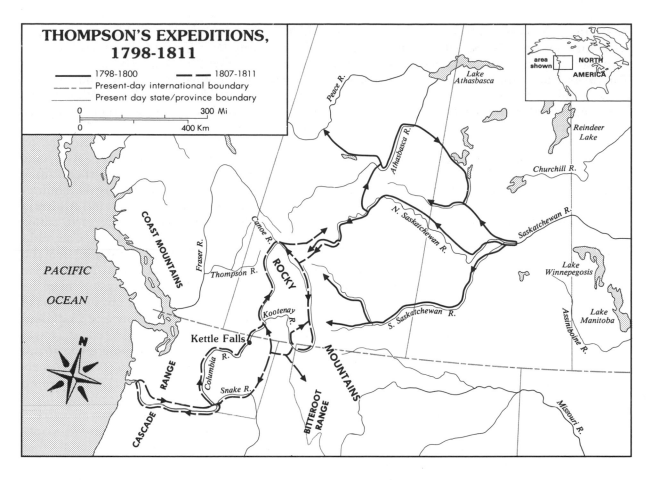

THOMPSON'S EXPEDITIONS,
1798-1811

——— 1798-1800   ——— 1807-1811
—·—·— Present-day international boundary
——— Present day state/province boundary

0 ——————— 300 Mi
0 ——————— 400 Km

of western Canada. The North West Company was most interested in finding a feasible route across the mountains to the Pacific coast. Such a route would enable them to bring trade goods by ship to the Pacific shore and take the goods overland to trading posts in the mountains, thus avoiding the long and expensive overland journey from the East. Although ALEXANDER MACKENZIE had not been able to discover a navigable river on the Pacific side of the Rockies in 1793, Thompson hoped that by searching south of Mackenzie's crossing he would succeed where Mackenzie had failed.

While trading in the eastern foothills of the Rockies, Thompson became acquainted with a branch of the Blackfoot Indians called the Piegans. In the winter of 1800 he was trading with some of them when he learned that a group of Kootenay Indians from west of the mountains was camped in the eastern foothills. The Piegans did not want Thompson trading (especially guns) with their traditional enemy and discouraged him from making contact with the Kootenays. Nonetheless, Thompson, eager for information

concerning the west side of the Rockies, secretly sought out the Kootenays and had two of his trappers return with them to their homes to reconnoiter the area west of the Rockies.

Thompson was unable to use the information his scouts brought back for several years because a costly trade war kept his attention focused on business. However, in 1807 he was ordered by the North West Company to seek out business with the Indians on the western slopes of the mountains. With a large party that included his Métis wife and three children, Thompson made his way to Saskatchewan Pass, where he was forced to wait out a group of Piegans who were stationed there to prevent his crossing. When the Piegans eventually went off to join a war party, Thompson crossed the mountains. Soon after reaching the summit, he came across a river flowing north, which he named the Kootenay. It was actually the Columbia, which had been named by ROBERT GRAY when he discovered its mouth in 1792, but Thompson did not recognize it as the Columbia because he expected the Columbia to flow south.

(Actually, it flows north before making a horse-shoe turn around the Selkirk Mountains and turning south.) Later, when it became clear that Thompson had actually happened upon the upper Columbia, the name Kootenay was given to the principal tributary of the Columbia.

After arriving at the river, the party stopped and built canoes and then paddled upstream to what is now Lake Windermere. Near the lake, Thompson built a fort, where his party later survived a siege by the angry Piegans. In the spring of 1808 the explorer continued south (upstream) and located the source of the Columbia in what is now Columbia Lake. From there he followed the Columbia's principal tributary (now the Kootenay) into what is now Idaho and eventually established trading posts in Idaho and western Montana.

From 1807 to 1810 Thompson explored various rivers west of the Rockies, including parts of the Columbia, and established several trading posts to gain the allegiance of the Indians and ensure that they brought their furs to him rather than his competitors. In 1809 he met a rival from the Hudson's Bay Company who had been exploring the upper Columbia. This indication of increasing competition caused Thompson to give up a planned journey along the Columbia to its mouth in order to once again give greater attention to the fur business. However, events were soon to compel him to complete the task he had begun of charting the length of the Columbia River.

In the spring of 1810, Thompson received word that John Jacob Astor's Pacific Fur Company intended to establish a post on the Pacific coast at the mouth of the Columbia River. Thompson was ordered to descend the Columbia to its mouth. It is still not clear whether his goal was to get to the mouth before the Astorians in order to claim the territory for the North West Company or whether the company simply wanted him to find a viable route through the mountains to the coast. In any case, Thompson seems to have been more concerned with consolidating his business in the interior for he did not begin his descent of the river until July 3, 1811.

He had spent the winter and spring of 1810–11 at the juncture of the Columbia and Canoe rivers, where the Columbia makes its big bend and turns south (in present-day British Columbia). In the spring, he decided to canoe down the Kootenay and then make his way overland to the Columbia at Kettle Falls in what is now northeastern Washington. (It is not clear whether he did this because he thought the stretches of the Columbia he did not know might be difficult to navigate or whether he simply wanted to visit his posts along the Kootenay.) He left Kettle Falls on July 3 and arrived at the sea on July 15 to discover that the Astorians had already established their post there. After a convivial week spent with his rivals, Thompson set out again, traveling overland to Kettle Falls and then returning to the river to canoe north and explore the parts of the Columbia he had not yet seen. Thus, he completed the survey of the river he had begun in 1807. He was the river's non-Indian discoverer from its source in the Rockies down as far as the Snake River. West of the Snake, Lewis and Clark had preceded him.

In the spring of 1812, Thompson retired from the fur trade, but his exploration of North America was not quite finished. In 1817 he accepted a position as surveyor and astronomer for a joint United States–Canada commission to determine the boundary between the two countries, a thankless task he worked on for another ten years.

David Thompson was a tireless and curious traveler. Wherever he went—and he covered more than 50,000 miles all told—he made careful surveys and maps of his route and the surrounding regions. So significant were his numerous accomplishments that one authority in the field of surveying, J. B. Tyrell, has called Thompson "the greatest practical land geographer that the world has produced."

• Thomson, Joseph

Scottish
b February 14, 1858; Penpont, Dumfriesshire
d August 2, 1895; London
Explored Africa

Joseph Thomson was the first European to venture into several areas of East Africa, most notably the hostile Masai territory of Kenya, and to reach Lake Nyasa (also Lake Malawi) from the north. A geologist and naturalist, he gathered extensive information about the conti-

Joseph Thomson. Culver Pictures.

nent's terrain and wildlife, and he subsequently had both a waterfall in Kenya and an animal species he identified in East Africa—"Thomson's gazelle"—named for him. He is also credited with providing the first written accounts of many East African territories in which he traveled. Late in his career, Thomson further distinguished himself through his work as a treaty negotiator for trading and mining ventures in present-day Nigeria and Zambia.

Fascinated with the natural sciences as a youth, Thomson became the student and protégé of scientist Archibald Geikie, who recommended him for his first expedition in 1879. He was hired as the geologist for this journey to Central Africa, sponsored by the Royal Geographical Society, but he took command of the expedition six months later upon the death of its leader, Alexander Keith Johnston. Traveling through what is now southern Tanzania, the group reached northern Lake Nyasa and proceeded north to Lake Tanganyika. Thomson then attempted to penetrate the Congo (now Zaire) to the west but was forced to retreat by

the region's warlike tribe. He discovered Lake Rukwa before returning to the eastern coast of Africa by way of the city of Tabora (in present-day Tanzania) in 1880.

In the same year, Thomson published a two-volume account of the expedition, entitled *To the Central African Lakes and Back*, in England. This book, based on his meticulous journal observations and technical information he had collected, was highly valued for the insight it provided into the geography and physical properties of East African lands and lake systems. These scientific achievements led to Thomson's next assignment in 1881, from Sultan Barghash of Tanzania. He was engaged to search for coal around the Ruvuma River and its tributaries, a mission that proved unsuccessful.

On his return to England, Thomson received a second commission from the Royal Geographical Society in 1882. His assignment, to locate the shortest route between Tanzania and Uganda, entailed crossing western Kenya through the land of the militant Masai tribe. Starting at coastal Mombasa, near the border of Kenya and Tanzania, he traveled northeast and passed Mount Kilimanjaro. He discovered Lake Baringo on this journey and arrived at Lake Victoria in December of 1882. The trip across Masai territory and back, which Thomson survived unarmed, earned him the distinction of being the first European to gain entry to the country of the Masai. This expedition was considered the most significant of Thomson's accomplishments because it opened up the potential for establishing commercial routes through an area previously untraveled by outsiders. As a result, he was honored with the Founder's Medal of the Royal Geographical Society upon his return to England in 1883. He described the expedition in a book entitled *Through Masailand*, published two years later.

Having gained a reputation as an able diplomat, Thomson then traveled to West Africa in 1885 to serve as a treaty negotiator in Nigeria. He secured trading agreements in Sokoto and Gwandu on behalf of Britain's Royal Niger Company and then traveled farther to the northwest to explore the Atlas Mountains. He also visited Morocco in 1888 as an independent traveler, and he published *Travels in the Atlas and Southern Morocco* the following year.

In 1890, Thomson was again employed as a treaty negotiator, this time in the south of the continent. Hired by Cecil Rhodes of the British South Africa Company, he spent two years in what is now northeastern Zambia negotiating agreements for mining and trading.

While his career was considered extremely promising and his expertise was much in demand, Thomson could not withstand the physical strain of exploration. His health failing, he returned to England, where he died at the age of thirty-seven.

• Tinné, Alexine (Alexandrine-Pieternella-Francoise)

Dutch
b October 17, 1835; The Hague
d August 1, 1869; near Ghāt, Libya
Investigated course of Nile River; explored
Central Africa and Sahara Desert

No less an authority on the rigors of exploration than DAVID LIVINGSTONE made this pronouncement regarding the courage of Alexine Tinné:

> The work of Speke and Grant is deserving of the highest commendation. . . . Mr. Baker also showed courage and perseverance worthy of an Englishman in following out the hints given by Speke and Grant. But none rises higher in

Alexine Tinne. Library of Congress.

my estimation than the Dutch lady, Miss Tinné, who, after the severest domestic afflictions, nobly persevered in the teeth of every difficulty.

Born the richest heiress in the Netherlands, Alexine Tinné visited Egypt for the first time at the age of nineteen, and soon the exploration of Africa became her passion. Her aunt and mother died of fever and exhaustion resulting from an expedition into the Nile swamps, yet Tinné would not be dissuaded, even though she was "without any other motive than her passion for unknown things and without any other protection than her courage," in the words of a contemporary writer. After several expeditions to explore the course of the Nile, she attempted to cross the Sahara Desert, the first European woman to do so.

One day when she was ten years old, Tinné, who like other children of wealthy court families was raised by governesses and taught by tutors, was found sprawled on the floor in the royal library, fascinated by a very large book. Her uncle noted that the book was on one of her favorite subjects: geography. A voracious reader, Tinné also displayed an unusual ability to grasp facts, particularly those of a scientific nature. Although her life was a flurry of social activities, the geographical interests of the young heiress were further stimulated by the family's extended travel holidays each summer.

In 1855, after the traumatic collapse of a romance with a count from Saxony, Tinné set out with her mother on a grand European tour, which they extended to include a visit to Egypt. Although they led an active social life in Alexandria and Cairo, Tinné had more adventurous designs: she began to learn Arabic and engaged a *dahabeah* (a type of Egyptian boat) ninety feet in length and with a crew of fourteen for a voyage up the Nile River to Aswan. There she and her mother left the boat to travel east by camel to Al-Quseir on the Red Sea. The entire trip lasted ten weeks, and by the time they returned to Cairo Tinné had resolved to make a second voyage the following winter. She planned to go upriver to Khartoum, Sudan, but was advised that such a trip was impossible without a steamer. None was available, so she had their furniture, food, champagne, and livestock loaded onto an even bigger *dahabeah*, hired a larger crew, and after a big party, set off.

The trip upriver to Aswan included stops at Asyūt and Luxor, where Tinné tried without success to make arrangements for a tour of the surrounding desert by camel caravan. Cataracts (waterfalls or steep rapids) in the river forced them to change into a smaller boat at Aswan. After another week, they came to Abu Simbel, the massive temple built in honor of Ramses II. Tinné tried again to persuade the local bedouins to take her party on a desert tour, but once more they refused. Disappointed, her party turned back, arriving in Cairo in March 1857.

In 1860, after she had visited Lebanon, Turkey, Italy, Austria, and the Netherlands, Tinné returned to Cairo with renewed determination to make an even longer trip up the Nile. By January 1862, she had assembled her largest expeditionary force to date: three boats, provisions for a year, five pet dogs, and her mother's sister, "Aunt Addy." When the expedition disembarked at Korosko for a long-awaited tour of the desert, 102 camels were needed just to carry the luggage and the dogs. After twelve weeks on the Nile, they reached Khartoum.

On May 11, Tinné and her entourage left Khartoum, and within a week came to the trading station at Jebel Dinka. There Tinné hired a new steamer for a year, taking it upriver to Lake No, where she decided to continue up the Bahr al-Jebel, a tributary of the White Nile. The expedition made its way slowly up the narrowing stream for 150 miles, spent some time at the Holy Cross mission station, and finally reached Rejaf (in southern Sudan), where the river became too treacherous to navigate safely. By then, one of her crew had drowned, her aunt was desperate to return home, and Tinné herself had fallen ill. She decided to return to Khartoum to reassess her plans.

After recovering, Tinné began to assemble provisions and crew for an even more adventurous expedition. She wanted to sail up another tributary of the White Nile, the Bahr al-Ghazal, and then to make her way to the central highlands of Africa, perhaps even as far as the equator. In February, she set out once again, this time with her mother and aunt, six servants, a botanist, an ornithologist, and seventy-one soldiers accompanying her in one steamer and seven smaller boats, which also carried ammunition and provisions for six months. The trip lasted for eleven trying months; the storms, floods, and hostilities endured by her party were only a prelude to a more profound tragedy: Tinné's mother and aunt, two of the family's longtime maids, and the botanist all died of fever.

Nevertheless, Tinné explored unknown territory and brought back an important botanical collection. Her book *Plantae Tinneanae* illustrates some of these plants and chronicles the expedition.

Tinné lived for some time in Cairo, and then moved to Algiers in 1867 preliminary to exploring the Algerian desert. In January 1869, she began a trip across the Sahara Desert. Along the way, she was murdered by a band of roving Tuareg bandits. Her name today appears on a monument to African explorers at Juba in the Sudan.

· Torres, Luis Vaez de

Portuguese
b ?
d 1613
Discovered Torres Strait while sailing for Spain

Luis Vaez de Torres solved one of the major geographical puzzles of the seventeenth century. He sailed through the strait lying between what are now New Guinea and Australia, thus proving that the land mass was in fact an island and not a peninsula of the mysterious Great South Land referred to as *Terra Australis Incognita*. Ironically, he seemed unaware of the significance of his discovery.

Little is known about Torres's life before or after his voyage with PEDRO FERNANDEZ DE QUIRÓS, a fellow Portuguese also sailing in the service of Spain. In December 1605 Torres was commander of the *San Pedrico*, one of three ships that left Callao, Peru, under Quirós. The purpose of the expedition was to establish a Spanish colony in the South Seas.

After months of sailing, stopping at various islands, the ships reached the island the Spanish named Espíritu Santo, in the present-day New Hebrides. But the islanders there were unfriendly, and Quirós's crew became restless. Three weeks later, Quirós sailed off suddenly, without any explanation; Torres searched for him for weeks unsuccessfully.

Taking matters into his own hands, Torres sailed on to Manila. En route he encountered the present-day Louisiades east of New Guinea, and it took him thirty-four days to navigate its maze of reefs and shoals. When he reached the eastern tip of New Guinea, he attempted to sail north of it, as others had before him, but the monsoon winds forced him to sail southwest, along the island's south side and through the strait that now bears his name.

Historians disagree about which of several channels in the strait Torres might have used; but if, as some believed, he took the southernmost route, he could have been the first European to see Australia's Cape York Peninsula. If he did in fact see the geographical equivalent of the theoretical Southern Continent *Terra Australis Incognita*, he must have been unaware of it, for after his voyage, Spain abandoned its search for the still-undiscovered continent. (For a more complete discussion of *Terra Australis Incognita*, see ALEXANDER DALRYMPLE.)

Torres reached Manila in the summer of 1607 and on July 12 wrote a letter to the king of Spain detailing his journey. In December 1613 the king received another account of the voyage from Diego de Prado y Tovar, an officer who usually is credited as being the codiscoverer of what is now called Torres Strait.

Although notes on a 1622 Dutch map mention Torres's route, the Dutch would not rediscover the strait for some fifty years. Torres, who fell into obscurity after the voyage, did not get credit for his discovery until the capture of Manila in 1762, when the English obtained documents from his important voyage.

• Tristão, Nuño (Tristam, Nunes)

Portuguese
b ?
d 1447; Gambia, West Africa
Explored West Africa; discovered Arguin Island and Cape Blanc

Credited with the discovery of the island of Arguin and nearby Cape Blanc on the west coast of Africa, Nuño Tristão later earned notoriety as one of the first Europeans to get involved in African slave trading. Commissioned by Prince Henry the Navigator in the second phase of the prince's large-scale exploration efforts, Tristão navigated a substantial portion of the continent's western coastline in a series of expeditions during the 1440s. His last and longest voyage, from which he never returned, took him to the Gambia River.

Tristão, a young knight, was among the first adventurers engaged by the court to revive the country's exploration effort, which had ceased in 1437 after Prince Henry's brother had died in a failed attempt to conquer Tangier, Morocco. Commanding one of two vessels dispatched in 1441, Tristão was sailing down the coast of Africa when he encountered the second ship, commanded by Antâo Gonçalves, loading a cargo of sealskins at Río de Oro. There the two mariners decided to capture native people of the area to take back to Portugal on Gonçalves's ship. In their raid on a site they named Porto de Cavaleiro, three members of a local tribe werc killed and ten were captured, including a high-ranking leader and two wealthy youths from the tribe. Gonçalves then sailed back to Portugal with the captives; Tristão continued south, reaching a headland at the northern border of what is now Mauritania and naming it Cape Blanc for its white sands. He then realized his provisions were running low and headed for home.

Praised by Prince Henry for both his discoveries and his part in capturing the natives, Tristão was sent out again in 1442. This time he sailed past Cape Blanc and came upon the island of Arguin. Continuing south, he reached the mouth of a large river (the present-day Senegal) and sailed on until the sands gave way to a stretch of green coastline lined with people signaling to the ship. But high waves prevented him from landing there and again his supplies were running out; Tristão changed course and returned to Portugal.

The discoveries he reported to the Prince spurred tremendous interest among Portuguese merchants, adventurers, and slave traders. Tristão followed his expedition with a series of slave raids on the West African coast during the next few years. Meanwhile, the three prominent tribesmen captured originally had pleaded to be released, promising that each of them would be exchanged for five less important villagers. When the prince consented and had them returned home, the freed captives promptly disappeared with no exchanges forthcoming. As a direct result, the Portuguese thereafter felt justified in raiding West African communities to capture slaves.

Soon after Tristão had discovered the island of Arguin, it had become an active slave-trading station, the first to be operated by Europeans. As the practice spread, many of the native tribes of West Africa became increasingly resentful that their slaves were being stolen rather than bought. By the time Tristão set out on his third voyage, they were ready for reprisal.

Sailing past the Senegal River to the green section of the coast seen on his earlier voyage, Tristão passed the westernmost point of the continent, recently identified by another explorer as Cape Verde (Green). When the ship reached the mouth of the Gambia River in 1446, Tristão and most of his crew decided to row upstream to investigate it. Suddenly surrounded by canoes, Tristão and his men were assaulted by a volley of poison-tipped arrows. Some of the crew died before they could return to the mouth of the river, but Tristão was said to be among those who later died aboard the ship within the first day of their return voyage. Tristão's death was partially responsible for a policy made 10 years later forbidding the Portuguese from stealing slaves, though trading for them would persist in the region for more than 400 years.

• Urdaneta, Andrés de

Spanish
b 1498; Villafranca de Oria, Guipúzcoa
d June 3, 1568
Charted route from East Indies to Mexico

Andrés de Urdaneta, an accomplished seaman and an Augustine friar, was the first navigator to sail and chart the return route from the East Indies to New Spain (present-day Mexico). Known as Urdaneta's Passage, it changed the face of Pacific navigation. It became the route of the treasure-laden Manila **galleon** that traveled regularly between Manila and Acapulco.

Urdaneta was born in 1498 in the province of Guipúzcoa. As a youth, he joined fellow Basque navigator JUAN SEBASTIÁN DE ELCANO and Francisco García Jofre de Loaysa on an expedition to claim the Moluccas for Spain in 1525. By the time the Spaniards reached the islands, they had lost five of seven ships and two-thirds of the crew, as well as both of the expedition's leaders. Urdaneta and the other survivors held out in Tidore (in what is now Indonesia) against the Portuguese for years. Eventually they surrendered and were sent back to Lisbon and then Spain.

In 1538 Urdaneta sailed with Pedro de Alvaro to Mexico, where he fought in the Mixtón War. He served the government there and gained a reputation as a geographer. He joined the Order of Saint Augustine in 1552, and in 1557 he was ordained a priest.

In 1559, at the request of Spain's King Phillip II, Urdaneta was a pilot on an expedition to the Philippines under MIGUEL LÓPEZ DE LEGAZPI. Shortly after the fleet of five ships left Mexico on November 21, 1564, the *San Lucas*, the smallest ship, disappeared. It visited the Marshall and Caroline islands, and returned by sailing to latitude 40° North and letting what is now known as the Japan Current carry it east to America. Unfortunately, the new course was not charted.

Urdaneta continued with the other ships to the Philippines. After helping Legazpi win the native Filipinos over to Spanish rule (and Christianity), Urdaneta left the islands on June 1, 1565, aboard the *San Pedro*. He crossed the Pacific in a wide arc, sailing as far north as 42° North to catch the prevailing **westerlies**, reaching California on September 18, 1565, then sailing south to Acapulco—a total distance of more than 11,000 miles.

The eastward journey was twice as long as the westward, but it opened up new trade possibilities. For nearly 300 years Spanish ships carrying cargo between Manila and Acapulco would use this route, beginning the annual six-month-long eastward journey sometime between May and September to take advantage of the favorable winds and currents.

Vaca, Álvar Núñez Cabeza de. See **Cabeza de Vaca, Álvar Núñez.**

Vaez de Torres, Luis. See **Torres, Luis Vaez de.**

• Vancouver, George

English
b June 22, 1757; King's Lynn, Norfolk
d May 10, 1798; Petersham, Surrey
Surveyed Pacific coast of North America

A veteran of Captain JAMES COOK's second and third voyages, George Vancouver was later put in command of a major maritime expedition to the Pacific coast of North America. Between 1792 and 1794, he and his crew completed one of the most difficult surveys ever undertaken, charting every bay, cape, and channel along the Pacific coast from just north of San Francisco, California, to Cook Inlet (in present-day Alaska).

After joining the Royal Navy at the age of thirteen, Vancouver was brought to the attention of Captain James Cook, who was then preparing a voyage of discovery to search for a postulated but undiscovered southern continent. The voyage with Cook lasted three years, during which time Vancouver received instruction from the noted astronomer William Wales, who was aboard. In 1776, Cook again chose Vancouver to accompany him, this time on a voyage to search for the Pacific outlet to the fabled Northwest Passage, alleged to connect Hudson Bay with the Pacific Ocean (for a more complete discussion of the passage, see MARTIN FROBISHER). In March 1778 Vancouver and some of his shipmates became the first Europeans to land on the coast of what is now British Columbia (at Nootka, Vancouver Island). Later in the voyage, Vancouver narrowly escaped death during an altercation at the Sandwich (now the Hawaiian) Islands, just one day before Cook was himself killed by islanders there. The expedition returned to England in October 1780. Over the next nine years, Vancouver worked primarily in the Caribbean and was promoted to first lieutenant.

At this time Britain was greatly interested in the commercial possibilities of the Pacific Northwest. Sea otter skins taken by some of Cook's men to China had brought a good price, and Britain was increasingly unwilling to accept Spain's claim to exclusive control of all of the Pacific coast as far north as Prince William Sound (in present-day Alaska). Britain was also interested in finding out once and for all if a Northwest Passage existed. Cook had shown that there was no passage north of latitude 55° North, but the possibility of a passage south of that point had not yet been ruled out. Accordingly, Britain decided to send an expedition to survey the Pacific coast of North America, with Vancouver as second-in-command. However, before it could get started, word reached London that several British trading ships had been seized by the Spanish in Nootka Sound (on the west coast of present-day Vancouver Island). Such an action in peacetime enraged the Brit-

ish, who protested vehemently to Spain. Unprepared to go to war over the issue, Spain signed the Nootka Sound Convention on October 28, 1790. The convention stipulated that Spain would make restitution to British citizens whose property had been seized and, more importantly, that Spain renounced its claim to exclusive ownership of the Pacific coast.

Britain's expedition to the northwest coast of North America was revived, and this time Vancouver was given its command. In addition to surveying the coast, he now had two additional goals: to receive from the Spanish at Nootka any land or buildings to be restored to British citizens and to spend his winters in the Sandwich Islands completing the survey begun by Cook.

Vancouver's ship, the *Discovery*, sailed from Falmouth on April 1, 1791, accompanied by a small tender, the *Chatham*. The ships sailed south and east around Africa's Cape of Good Hope and on to New Holland (now Australia), New Zealand, Tahiti, and the Sandwich Islands before reaching the Pacific coast of North America, at latitude 39°27' North (about 110 miles north of what is now San Francisco), on April 17, 1792.

From there Vancouver sailed north and began his survey, proceeding quickly and without difficulty along the coasts of what are now Oregon and Washington. He has been criticized for failing to explore the Columbia River, which the American Captain ROBERT GRAY would enter early in May of the same year, but there is some evidence that Vancouver noted the river and intended to leave its exploration for later in his survey. (When he learned that Gray had penetrated the Columbia, Vancouver sent his second-in-command, Lieutenant Broughton, to explore the river. Broughton traveled 100 miles up the Columbia and compiled the first map of the river, but this effort was not sufficient to establish a British claim to the Columbia in the face of Gray's earlier presence there.)

By April 29, Vancouver had reached the Strait of Juan de Fuca (between present-day Washington and Vancouver Island), to which he had been ordered to pay particular attention. There the survey became a much more complicated matter. Vancouver was determined to trace every inlet to its head to make certain that it was not the beginning of the much sought after Northwest Passage, and the *Chatham* had been sent along in the expectation that it could

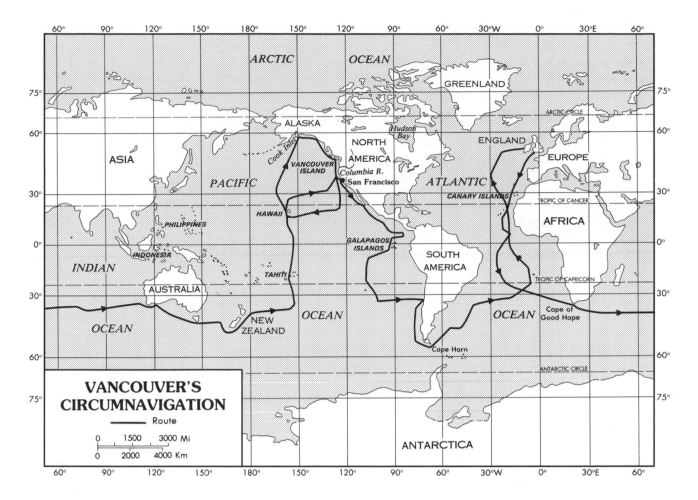

VANCOUVER'S CIRCUMNAVIGATION

——— Route

0   1500   3000 Mi

0   2000   4000 Km

penetrate waters too narrow for the *Discovery* to attempt. However, Vancouver soon learned that even the *Chatham* was not safe among the numerous small inlets of Puget Sound, and from there northward he was forced to use both ships' small boats, making the surveying a more difficult and dangerous task than had been expected.

Near the end of June, Vancouver met up with two Spanish surveying ships and was disappointed to learn that they had preceded him in exploring the Strait of Juan de Fuca and the Strait of Georgia (between present-day Vancouver Island and the Canadian mainland). However, he was pleased to learn that they had not been in Puget Sound. He continued up the east coast of what is now Vancouver Island, sailing between it and the mainland and eventually coming out in Queen Charlotte Strait, proving once and for all that the large land mass was indeed an island. After rounding the top of the island he headed down the west coast and arrived at Nootka Sound, where the Spanish commander JUAN FRANCISCO DE LA BODEGA Y

QUADRA was waiting for him to complete the property transfer stipulated by the Nootka Sound Convention.

Although the two became close friends, they were unable to come to a mutual understanding of the provisions of the convention and decided to await more specific instructions from their respective governments. Vancouver and his men were entertained royally by Bodega y Quadra and then sailed south to San Francisco and Monterey, where they were likewise regaled by the Spanish governor of California before setting off for their winter task of surveying in the Sandwich Islands.

In May 1793 Vancouver was back on the northwest coast working his way north again. In June he explored Dean Channel, and by a remarkable coincidence just missed meeting AL-EXANDER MACKENZIE, who ended his historic overland journey across the Rockies at that point near the end of July. By September Vancouver had reached latitude 56° North. He then sailed south again to California, hoping his friend Bodega y Quadra would be there with official

Vancouver's *Discovery*, on the rocks in Queen Charlotte's Sound. Library of Congress.

word as to how the Nootka Sound Convention was to be interpreted. But Bodega was not there. Instead Vancouver met with a chilly reception from the new governor and soon departed to sail south to latitude 30° North, the southernmost limit of his survey. That winter he completed his survey of the Sandwich Islands.

In the spring of 1794, Vancouver decided to head north to Cook Inlet near the sixtieth parallel, the northernmost extreme of his survey. From there he proceeded south, completing his survey on August 19 in a bay off Baranof Island that he appropriately named Port Conclusion. After celebrating with "such an additional allowance of grog as was fully sufficient to answer every purpose of festivity on the occasion," the expedition headed home by way of Cape Horn, arriving in the Thames on October 20, 1795. Less than three years later, George Vancouver died at the age of forty while preparing his journals for publication.

In under five years, Vancouver had sailed approximately 65,000 miles, with the small boat excursions adding another 10,000 miles to that total. He had completed the most extensive scientific survey ever attempted by a single expedition, and he had proved that there was no Northwest Passage south of the Arctic Ocean. Vancouver left his mark on the Pacific Northwest in the form of several hundred place names that he gave to its physical features, including Puget Sound, named after the lieutenant of the *Discovery;* Mount Rainier, named after an offi-

cer he had known in the Caribbean; and, of course, Vancouver Island, which he originally named Quadra and Vancouver's Island in honor of his great Spanish friend.

van Linschoten, Jan Huyghen. See **Linschoten, Jan Huyghen van.**

Varennes, Pierre Gaultier de, Sieur de La Vérendrye. See **La Vérendrye, Pierre Gaultier de Varennes, Sieur de.**

- Varthema, Ludovico (Lodovico) di

Italian
b 1465?; Bologna
d 1517; Rome
Explored Middle East, India, and Southeast Asia

The first European to reach India by way of the Red Sea and return by the Cape of Good Hope, Ludovico di Varthema also traveled extensively in Egypt and visited Persia, Burma, and Sumatra. In addition, Varthema infiltrated the holy Islamic lands of the Middle East, which were forbidden to Christians. Knighted for his service to the Portuguese navy in India, he returned to his native Italy to publish an account of his travels.

Love of adventure, rather than an interest in fame or profit, prompted Varthema to leave his home, wife, and child in 1502 and sail for Egypt. He visited Cairo and Damascus, Syria, studying Arabic as he traveled in order to pose as a Muslim. He then joined a military garrison in Damascus and, as a soldier, took part in a pilgrimage to the Islamic lands in the spring of 1503. He visited Mecca and Medina, both barred to Christians, during this two-month journey and is the first European to give an account of these holy lands.

Varthema then departed for India by way of the Red Sea, but he was arrested on the coast of Yemen on charges of being a Christian spy. Imprisoned by the sultan of San'a, he escaped with the help of one of the sultan's wives who had become infatuated with him. He explored southwestern Arabia before heading to Persia (now Iran), where he befriended a merchant in Shīrāz who agreed to accompany him to India. Sailing around India's coast, they visited Calicut and Ceylon (present-day Sri Lanka) and went on to Burma (now Myanmar), Sumatra, Java, and other islands of Southeast Asia.

Returning to India, Varthema abandoned his Persian companion to join a Portuguese garrison in combat against the natives. For his services, he was knighted by the viceroy, Francisco de Almeida, before departing from India in late 1507. Varthema traveled home via the east coast of Africa and the Cape of Good Hope, also stopping at Lisbon to be honored at the palace of Manuel I for his service on behalf of the Portuguese.

He reached Italy in late 1508 and within two years published a highly successful account of his travels. He is believed to have died in Rome in 1517.

Vásquez de Coronado, Francisco. See **Coronado, Francisco Vásquez de.**

Vélez de Escalante, Silvestre. See **Escalante, Silvestre Vélez de.**

Verrazano, Giovanni da

Italian
b 1485?; near Val di Greve, Chianti?
d 1528?; Guadeloupe?
Explored Atlantic coast of North America (for France)

Under French auspices, the Italian navigator Giovanni da Verrazano set sail in late 1524 or early 1525 in hopes of finding a northern strait to China and the spice-rich lands of the East. He explored the Atlantic coast of North America from Cape Fear, North Carolina, to Maine—and perhaps as far north as Newfoundland—discovering present-day Narragansett Bay, Block Island, New York Bay, and the mouth of the Hudson River in the process. The detailed accounts of his voyage give the first documented geographical description of a major area of North American coastline, as well as important information on the appearances and customs of the Indian tribes he encountered. His expedition also established France's right to claim territory in North America.

Though the exact place and date of his birth is not known with certainty, it is generally ac-

Giovanni da Verrazano. Library of Congress.

cepted that Giovanni da Verrazano was born at Castello Verrazano, home of the wealthy and aristocratic Verrazano family, near Val di Greve in the province of Chianti, Italy. Throughout his life Verrazano was referred to as a Florentine, probably because his ancestral home was only 30 miles from Florence, a powerful center of business, art, and politics during the Renaissance. He was well-educated, excelling in mathematics. About 1506–1507 he moved to Dieppe, France, to pursue a maritime career.

At this time the French were receptive to Italian influence, and King Francis I had surrounded himself with Italian intellectuals and artists. Verrazano seized the opportunity to make a name for himself in France. Entering the French service, he made several voyages to the Levant (countries on the Mediterranean from Greece to Egypt) and became a successful **corsair** capturing Spanish treasure ships.

In 1524 Verrazano was commissioned by Francis I to lead an expedition to the New World, with the twofold purpose of discovering a northern passage to China and finding land for future French settlement. He was to investigate the vast unexplored area between Florida (claimed by Spain) and Newfoundland (claimed by England). Accordingly, the expeditionary fleet of four ships departed some time in late 1524 or early 1525, financed by a syndicate of Florentine bankers and merchants of Lyons. On board Verrazano's flagship, *La Dauphine*, was his brother Girolomo, a mapmaker who would produce the world map of 1529 showing Verrazano's route of exploration and discoveries. There is no record of the other men who sailed with the brothers; in his official letter of discovery to the king, written at the end of the voyage, Verrazano simply refers to the crew as "la turba maritima" (the maritime mob). Only his flagship made the entire voyage; two ships wrecked soon after departure, and a fourth returned to France loaded with captured treasure.

On or about March 1, 1525, Verrazano made landfall at or near present-day Cape Fear, North Carolina. He sailed south for another 50 miles looking for a harbor but turned back toward Cape Fear because he did not want to encounter the Spanish. Continuing on a north-northeasterly course, Verrazano sighted what was most likely present-day Chesapeake Bay and mistook it for "a strait to penetrate to the Eastern Ocean [Pacific]." Calling it the Verrazano Sea, he made no effort to sail across it, pursuing his coastal

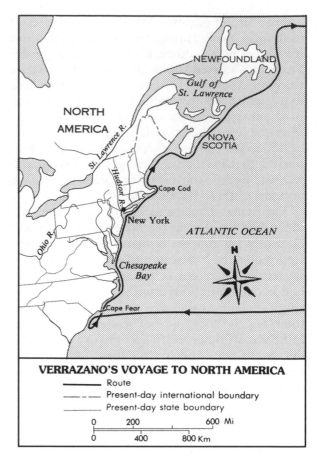

VERRAZANO'S VOYAGE TO NORTH AMERICA
— Route
— · — Present-day international boundary
— Present-day state boundary

exploration instead. This geographical error, however, appeared on maps for over a century, showing the New World in the shape of an hourglass with the Verrazano Sea at the narrowest part.

Enjoying mild spring weather in a usually turbulent area of the coast, Verrazano sailed along the shores of present-day Delaware and New Jersey, discovering what is now New York Bay on April 17, 1525. He described the steep hills surrounding it, and he chose to anchor in the narrows of the bay, which today bear his name. (This entrance to New York Harbor is now spanned by the Verrazano-Narrows Bridge, linking Brooklyn and Staten Island.) He further described the upper bay as a "pleasant lake" and named it Santa Margarita in honor of the king's sister. He called all the land that he explored Francesca, after King Francis I.

After discovering present-day Block Island, Rhode Island, Verrazano sailed into Narragansett Bay to avoid bad weather. He permitted a local Indian to guide the ship to a sheltered anchorage (present-day Newport Harbor) and remained in the area for about two weeks. Search parties sent about 30 miles inland noted the fertile soil and forests of oak and walnut that they found. Verrazano traded with the Wampanoug Indians and found them to be the "goodliest people, and of the fairest conditions that we have found in this our voyage." The women in particular were "very handsome and well favored" and "as well mannered . . . as any woman of good education."

Starting north again on May 5 or 6, the expedition sailed through present-day Vineyard Sound and Nantucket Sound, and rounded Cape Cod. It reached the coast of Maine at or near present-day Casco Bay and found the Abnaki Indians, whom Verrazano described as "crude" with "evil manners." He consequently named this area the Land of Bad People. He became quite poetic, however, in describing the natural beauty of Maine, counting thirty-two islands that were "small and pleasant to the view" surrounded by the "turquoise sea." He might have gone as far north as Newfoundland before returning to Dieppe on July 8, 1525.

Optimistic about what these newly discovered lands had to offer, Verrazano tried to organize a second expedition. However, France was at war, and his financial backers saw no immediate wealth to be gained. He finally made an expedition in 1527, but only to the Brazilian coast in order to obtain brazilwood.

In the spring of 1528 he received support for a voyage to find a passage to Asia south of the North American regions he had explored during his 1525 expedition. The only information available about this voyage is from the story Girolomo Verrazano told upon his return to France. According to his account, the expedition reached the coast of Florida, then changed course and followed the chain of the Lesser Antilles. The ships anchored off one of the islands (probably Guadeloupe) and Verrazano took a small boat to the shore, not realizing that the local Indians were cannibals. As told by Girolomo and repeated in poems and narratives ever since, Verrazano was killed and eaten by these Caribs—within view of his horrified brother—sometime in 1528.

Though he failed to find the northern passage to China, Giovanni da Verrazano provided valuable geographic data about the eastern coast of North America and its inhabitants. His great-

est wish had been to colonize the lands he explored. In his letter of discovery to the king he summarized his feelings about North America when he said, "We greatly regretted having to leave this region, which seemed so delightful and which we supposed must also contain great riches."

Vespucci, Amerigo (Vespucius, Americus)

Italian
b March 9, 1451?; Florence
d February 22, 1512; Seville, Spain
Explored coast of South America (for Spain and Portugal)

Amerigo Vespucci, whose name was given to an entire hemisphere, has been portrayed by historians as a scoundrel who robbed CHRISTOPHER COLUMBUS of the honor of having his new world named after him. From the hostile verbal attacks of Father BARTOLOMÉ DE LAS CASAS in his own time, to the vituperative words of Ralph Waldo Emerson in 1856—that "Amerigo Vespucci . . . managed in this lying world to supplant Columbus and baptize half the earth with his own dishonest name"—Vespucci has been persona non grata. Scholars of the nineteenth and twentieth centuries (most notably Alberto Magnaghi and Germán Arciniegas) have reexamined the "Vespucci Question" and put the man and his accomplishments into a more positive, balanced perspective. In their interpretations of history, Vespucci emerges as a businessman who was more interested in ideas than in voyages of conquest, more attuned to poetry and music than to the quest for fame and fortune. He was a friend of Columbus and his family and a trusted confidant of the powerful Medici family of Italy, the monarchs of Spain and Portugal, and the great navigators of his day. On his voyages he explored South America, discovered Guanabara Bay and the mouth of the Río de la Plata, and was the first to realize that the new lands Columbus had discovered were not a part of Asia but rather a new continent.

Vespucci was born in Florence, Italy, on March 9, 1451, into a wealthy banking and commercial family. During his youth he developed the intellectual ambitions and avid curiosity that would dictate the course of his life. He

Amerigo Vespucci, as portrayed in the dome of the United States Capital Building. Architect of the Capitol.

rini letter states that Vespucci made a total of four voyages and that the first one reached new lands somewhere in Central America in 1497, which is one year earlier than Columbus's discovery of Venezuela. The authenticity of this letter has been challenged, and many authorities now believe that it was either altered, or completely fabricated, by supporters of Vespucci. However, the de Medici letters, which describe only two voyages, are considered authentic. Vespucci's expedition with ALONSO DE OJEDA from 1499 to 1500 and his expedition of 1501–1502 are also supported by evidence in addition to the de Medici letters.

Vespucci was the commercial representative on the Ojeda expedition, which left Cadiz on May 16, 1499, under the auspices of the Spanish Crown. Apparently, Vespucci had considerable authority of his own, since Ojeda named him one of the pilots and he separated from Ojeda after they passed the Cape Verde Islands in order to explore on his own. He explored to Cape Santo Agostinho at the shoulder of Brazil, entering a wide gulf (thought to be the Amazon estu-

collected maps and books and developed a particular interest in **cosmography** and astronomy. His business career began when he became a member of Lorenzo de Medici's embassy to France (1479–80). Around 1492 Vespucci left Florence for good and went to Seville, Spain, where in 1495 he became the director of a ship brokerage firm that provided supplies for the Spanish voyages of exploration. Evidence suggests that Vespucci met Columbus there in 1496, after the latter's second voyage to the New World.

Controversy exists about this period of Vespucci's life as to when he made his first voyage and how many voyages he actually made. The only existing firsthand documentation is a letter from Vespucci to Piero Soderini, a Florentine official, dated 1504, and three private letters from Vespucci to the Medici family. The Sode-

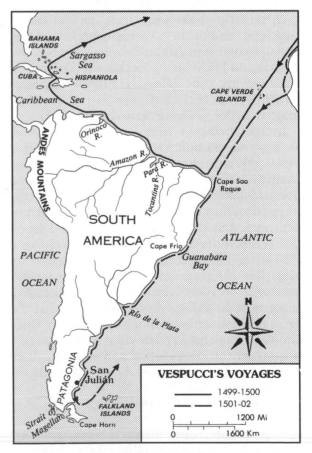

ary), which he named Santa Maria. He sighted the mouth of the Orinoco and penetrated two other large rivers (the one flowing from the south was probably the Pará). Low provisions, worm-eaten ship hulls, and unfavorable winds forced him to sail to the island of Hispaniola (the island now occupied by Haiti and the Dominican Republic) to rejoin Ojeda. The members of Vespucci's expedition may have been the first Europeans not only to touch Brazil but also to cross the equator in the waters of the New World.

Vespucci's next expedition, under the auspices of King Manuel I of Portugal, left Lisbon on May 13, 1501. At the Cape Verde Islands he encountered PEDRO ÁLVARES CABRAL, who was returning to Lisbon from India. Vespucci realized that the land of Brazil, which Cabral had discovered on the outbound leg of his voyage, was the same land that Vespucci had explored on the Ojeda expedition. He was interested in returning to this land to determine if Columbus's claim that the new lands were a part of Asia was valid.

Vespucci made landfall in Brazil at 5° South latitude, naming the place Cape São Roque. He then followed the coast of South America for about 2,400 miles in a southwesterly direction, passing Cape Frio and discovering Guanabara Bay (on which Rio de Janeiro is now situated) and the Río de la Plata (located between present-day Uruguay and Argentina). While some historians think Vespucci went no farther than Cape Frio, others accept his account that he reached latitude 49° South in Patagonia, naming the area Porto de San Giuliano (present-day San Julián, Argentina).

When Vespucci returned to Lisbon on July 22, 1502, he brought back the most important discovery of his expedition—that the discovered lands west of the Atlantic were not part of Asia but rather a separate land mass, a fourth continent, a New World. He showed that the accepted cosmography of PTOLEMY was inadequate, and he identified constellations not visible in the Northern Hemisphere. He called this land mass *Mundus Novus* (New World); and his written account of this New World proved so popular that it went through more than twenty editions in several languages before 1508. It was the popularity of Vespucci's discovery that prompted the German cartographer, Martin Waldseemüller, to call this New World (present-day South America only) "the land of Amerigo,

or America, after Amerigo, its discoverer, a man of great ability" in his geography book of 1507. In spite of much disagreement, the name America prevailed, and in 1538 Gerhardus Mercator became the first to designate both North America and South America on a world map.

Vespucci thus had no direct part in naming the New World. Significantly, Columbus never felt that Vespucci had stolen any of his acclaim. In a letter to his son Diego, Columbus said of Vespucci, "It has always been his wish to please me; he is a man of good will; fortune has been unkind to him as to others; his labors have not brought him the rewards he in justice should have."

In 1505 Vespucci became a Spanish subject, got married, and settled permanently in Seville. King Ferdinand II, acting for his daughter Joanna, queen of Castile, appointed Vespucci the first pilot major, an office created as part of the Casa de Contratación (an agency that governed trade with the New World). As pilot major he trained pilots and tested their proficiency, collected data on navigation, and prepared and updated the official map of the newly discovered lands. Vespucci died in Seville on February 22, 1512. His life and work will undoubtedly always be best remembered for the two continents named for him.

· Vial, Pedro (Pierre)

French
b 1746–55?; Lyons, France
d 1814; Santa Fe, New Mexico
Explored southwestern United States;
    established Santa Fe Trail

For 200 years the only way to reach Santa Fe, New Mexico, was through Chihuahua (in Mexico) until Pedro Vial's 1786–87 expedition established a new route from San Antonio, Texas. He then increased the accessibility of Santa Fe further by traveling from there to New Orleans, Louisiana, then back to San Antonio. Later, from 1792 to 1793, he established the famous Santa Fe Trail from St. Louis, Missouri, to Santa Fe.

The exact birthdate of Pedro Vial is unknown, but existing records indicate that he was born between 1746 and 1755 in Lyons, France. Information on his early life is also lacking, although he left some personal remarks indicating that he was on the Missouri River during the American Revolution. He lived among the Indians of Natchitoches (modern Louisiana) for several years, but by 1786 he was in the service of Spain.

Pedro Vial's first expedition for Spain was to open an overland trail from San Antonio to Santa Fe. Leaving on October 26, 1786, and accompanied by only one other person, Vial took the most direct route and reached Santa Fe on May 26, 1787. He had traveled through almost 1,200 miles of uncharted wilderness and encountered at least five different tribes of Indians along the way. On June 24, 1788, Vial left on his second trailblazing journey which took him east from Santa Fe to New Orleans, then west to San Antonio and back to Santa Fe.

Pedro Vial set out on his most famous journey—from Santa Fe to St. Louis—on May 21, 1792. He had been commissioned by the governor of New Mexico to attempt to open communications between New Mexico and the territory of Illinois, then a dependency of Louisiana. After a month of difficult travel through the northwestern tip of modern Oklahoma and southwestern Kansas, Vial and his two companions were captured by Indians of the Kansas tribe who beat and threatened them. After six weeks, one Indian who spoke French recognized Vial and obtained their release. They resumed the journey on September 11, traveling along the Kansas and Missouri rivers in a **pirogue** with a French trader. Vial arrived at St. Louis on October 3, 1792. He had established the Santa Fe Trail, which would prove to be a crucial contribution to the opening of the American West.

Five years after returning to Santa Fe, Vial left the service of Spain and went to live with Comanche Indians near St. Louis. By 1805, however, he was operating under Spanish orders again, mounting several other journeys, none of which had great historical significance. He died in Santa Fe in 1814.

von Drygalski, Erich Dagobert. See **Drygalski, Erich Dagobert von.**

von Kotzebue, Otto. See **Kotzebue, Otto von.**

von Krusenstern, Adam Ivan. See **Krusenstern, Adam Ivan von.**

von Payer, Julius. See **Payer, Julius von.**

von Richtofen, Ferdinand Paul Wilhelm, Freiherr. See **Richthofen, Ferdinand Paul Wilhelm, Freiherr von.**

• Walker, Joseph Reddeford

American
b December 13, 1798; Virginia?
d October 27, 1876; Contra Costa County, California
Blazed practical overland route to California

As a contemporary put it, Joseph Reddeford Walker was a man whose "chief delight" was "to explore unknown regions." His most lasting contribution to the exploration of America was a year-long trek from the Green River in what is now western Wyoming across the rugged Sierra Nevada to the Pacific Coast. On the return trip, Walker discovered a pass through the Si-

Joseph R. Walker. Joslyn Art Museum, Omaha.

erra Nevada, which later bore his name and became the main highway for emigration to California.

Raised in Tennessee, Joseph Walker moved to Independence, Missouri, in 1819. He later took part in the expedition that surveyed and mapped what was to become the Santa Fe Trail between Missouri and what is now New Mexico. In 1831 he met Captain BENJAMIN BONNEVILLE and signed on with him as field commander of a party of 110 men that Bonneville was taking west to trap furs. After trapping in the Salmon and Snake river valleys with disappointing results, the party headed for the 1833 trappers rendezvous (an annual meeting of mountain men and their suppliers) on the Green River. There, at Bonneville's behest, Walker began to recruit men for a westward expedition. As with many of Bonneville's actions, the ultimate purpose of the expedition was never clear. It may have been simply to search for new beaver territory, or it may have been to search for an easy route to the Pacific coast.

With a party of around fifty, Walker left the Green River on August 20, 1833, abundantly supplied with horses. For a month the men traversed barren plains before reaching the present-day Humboldt River in what is now north-central Nevada. They followed the river to a series of marshy lakes called the Humboldt Sinks and then proceeded southwest to the Sierra Nevada. For three grueling weeks they fought their way across the mountains, suffering from severe cold and hunger. After reaching the crest of the mountains, they were rewarded with the breathtaking sight of what is now called Yosemite Valley. Soon they began to descend the Sierra Nevada and found themselves in the interior of California. New experiences dazzled them: giant redwoods, a meteor shower, the rumbling of what was probably an earthquake but which Walker interpreted as the roar of the ocean (still 70 miles distant), and finally the ocean itself, where they observed whales stranded on the shore. Traveling south to the territorial capital at Monterey, they were well received by the Mexican government. After a month or so of feasting and entertainment, they headed back in January 1834, confirmed boosters of the delights of California.

Walker was determined to find an easier route back through the mountains, and so the party followed the range south until coming to a pass, later named for Walker, where they could cross at the relatively low altitude of 5,200 feet (the mountains themselves ranged well above 10,000 feet). There were still difficult times ahead, however, and in the Nevada badlands, they were forced to quench their thirst with the blood of horses who had died on the trail. Nonetheless, Walker appeared at the 1834 trappers rendezvous with his entire party intact, a tribute to his leadership skill and his organizational abilities.

As one of his contemporaries noted, Joseph Walker did not follow trails, he blazed them. And the trail that he blazed between the Rocky Mountains and California became the most important route of emigration to the West Coast soon after it was discovered. Walker personally led some of the emigrants into what he felt was the Promised Land, and he eventually settled there himself, still vigorous, at the age of sixty-nine.

Walker's achievements are perhaps best appreciated in contrast to those of a slightly earlier traveler to California, JEDEDIAH SMITH. Whereas Smith lost some twenty-six men on his two expeditions and twice followed a route that proved to be of little future use, Walker was a model of efficiency and careful leadership, losing not one man and opening up a route that would serve emigrants for years to come.

· Wallace, Alfred Russel

English
b January 8, 1823; Usk, Monmouthshire, South Wales
d November 7, 1913; Broadstone, Dorset
Explored Amazon River basin and Malay Archipelago

Alfred Russel Wallace, like CHARLES DARWIN, is recognized as one of the outstanding naturalists of the nineteenth century. His accomplishments included important contributions to natural-history exploration, evolutionary biology, zoogeography (the study of the distribution of animals), and scientific writing. A self-educated man who developed an interest in natural history early in life, from 1848 to 1852 Wallace explored along various rivers of the Amazon basin in Brazil, where he collected specimens

Alfred Russel Wallace. Collection Viollet.

of insects, butterflies, and birds and began to formulate his theories on evolution. In 1854, he explored the Malay Archipelago (present-day Indonesia and Malaysia), again collecting specimens and expanding his ideas on evolution and natural selection.

Alfred Russel Wallace was born at Usk in South Wales on January 8, 1823, into an impoverished family of nine children. Forced to drop out of school at fourteen, he supported himself as an apprentice surveyor in his brother William's business from 1837 to 1843. It was during this time that he first became interested in the natural world. During this period Wallace once visited London, where he spent time at the Hall of Science, a workmen's club for advanced teachers. There he became acquainted with Robert Owen's philosophies of secularism and socialism, which he would follow for most of his life. A voracious reader, especially of travel books, biographies, and classics, Wallace was particularly influenced by Darwin's journal of

the voyage of the *Beagle*, the personal accounts of ALEXANDER VON HUMBOLDT's explorations, and Robert Chambers's controversial book on evolution, *Vestiges of the Natural History of Creation*.

When the surveying business declined in 1844, Wallace turned to teaching to make a living and qualified to serve as a schoolmaster in Leicester. There he met and became close friends with HENRY WALTER BATES. They went on beetle-collecting expeditions together in nearby Charnwood Forest and avidly discussed all aspects of nature. After his brother William's death in 1845, Wallace returned to the surveying business for a while but continued to correspond with Bates. The publication of W. H. Edwards's *A Voyage up the River Amazon* in 1847 inspired Wallace to propose an expedition to the Amazon river basin, where he and Bates could explore and support themselves by collecting specimens to sell to museums.

On May 28, 1848, Wallace and Bates arrived at Pará (present-day Belém), Brazil, located near the mouth of the Amazon River. Together they explored the region around Pará and journeyed along the Tocantins and Río Negro. (While exploring the Tocantins, Wallace lost part of his hand near the wrist as the result of an accidental gunshot.) During these early explorations, Wallace was fascinated by the saúba ants, a species that built earthen mounds thirty or more feet in length, ten feet in width, and three to four feet high. He also collected many specimens of birds, such as toucans and herons, while exploring Mexiana Island near Marajó on the equator.

By 1849 the two friends had separated temporarily in order to explore different areas. Wallace journeyed up the narrow channels that connect the Pará River and the Amazon, then continued up the Amazon with stops at Santarém and Óbidos. He was reunited with Bates on January 22, 1850, at Barra do Rio Negro (present-day Manaus). After a joint exploration of the area, the friends separated again, with Wallace continuing north along the Río Negro. They would not meet again on this expedition.

After passing the mouth of the Casiquiare, Wallace hiked to the town of Yavita, Venezuela, near Orinoco, where he discovered forty new species of butterflies. He also penetrated as far west as Micúru on the Uaupés River. During his explorations he carefully observed and noted the geographical distribution of specific plants and animals and became the first scientist to determine species habitat areas in South America.

Due to illness, Wallace decided to return to England in 1852. The journey was a disaster. First, he suffered a malaria attack. Then he was forced to abandon ship 700 miles from Bermuda because of a fire on board. After drifting for ten days in an open boat, he was rescued and eventually reached England. However, all his specimens and notes from the previous four years were lost, thus preventing him from publishing his detailed scientific findings. He nevertheless managed to publish two books about the expedition in 1853: *Travels on the Amazon and Río Negro* and *Palm Trees of the Amazon*.

Undaunted by the problems that plagued the end of his South American expedition, Wallace left for the Malay Archipelago of Southeast Asia in 1854. He spent the next eight years exploring the areas encompassed by Celebes (now Sulawesi) in the north, Timor in the south, the Aru Islands in the east, and Malacca and Malaya in the west. He traveled more than 14,000 miles all told and collected about 127,000 specimens before returning to England in 1862. His book describing these travels, *The Malay Archipelago*, published in 1869, earned him international acclaim. On this expedition he also gathered enough evidence to support his theory on the organic evolution of the species through natural selection.

When Wallace sent his essay "On the tendency of varieties to depart indefinitely from the original type" to fellow naturalist Charles Darwin (the two knew each other's work), the latter recognized that the material was almost identical to ideas in his unpublished 1842 manuscript. To avoid the issue of which man was first in defining the principle of natural selection, both men published their articles simultaneously in 1858 and both were generally credited with the discovery of the mechanism of natural selection. At the time, Darwin thought that Wallace might question his claim to the honor, but he found Wallace to be a man of "generous and noble disposition."

While his interest in natural history never waned, Wallace became involved in many other activities. His interest in socialism led to his election as the first president of the Land Nationalization Society in 1881. He was an outspoken advocate of women's rights, and he also got involved in the debate over the need for vaccination. Never one to avoid controversy,

Wallace, at age eighty-four, challenged the astronomer Percival Lowell's idea that intelligent life existed on Mars. An ironic change in viewpoint, however, resulted from his belief in evolution. A secularist and religious skeptic for most of his life, he eventually came to believe in God as a way to explain the things he had observed in nature.

Wallace was elected a fellow of the Royal Society in 1893. He also received many other honors and awards, including the first Darwin-Wallace Medal of the Linnaean Society, which he was awarded in 1908. By the time he died at Broadstone in Dorset on November 7, 1913, he was widely recognized as one of the greatest scientific men of his age.

• Wallis, Samuel

English
b 1728; Fentonwood, Cornwall
d January 21, 1795; London
Circumnavigated; explored Tahiti (first European to do so)

British naval officer Samuel Wallis is best known as commander of the *Dolphin* on its second voyage to the Pacific (1766–68). Of his many discoveries and explorations, perhaps the most significant was the month he spent on Otaheite (now Tahiti), the largest of the Society Islands.

Born in Cornwall in 1728, Wallis received a commission in the Royal Navy at the age of twenty. In 1755, on the eve of the Seven Years' War between England and France, he was made lieutenant commander and two years later attained the rank of captain. Wallis served in the Channel fleet and, as a commander, took part in the capture of Louisbourg, Canada, in 1758.

When JOHN BYRON brought the *Dolphin* back to England in 1766 after an unsuccessful voyage, Wallis was put in command of this fast, copper-sheathed **frigate** and directed to search for *Terra Australis Incognita*, the long-postulated but ultimately nonexistent Southern Continent (for a more complete discussion, see ALEXANDER DALRYMPLE). The *Dolphin* and the barely seaworthy *Swallow* left Plymouth on August 22, 1766. In December they reached the Strait of Magellan at the tip of South America. (For a map of their route, see LOUIS-ANTOINE DE BOUGAINVILLE.)

The two ships spent four harrowing months

navigating the dangerous strait in hostile weather. Wallis said the terrible passage was "more chaos than Nature." In April 1767, just as the expedition reached the open Pacific, a gust of wind caught the *Dolphin* and pulled her far ahead of her consort. The *Swallow* went her own way, and the two vessels never met again.

The difficult passage had taken its toll on the crew. Despite good provisions, many had **scurvy**, and Wallis kept his eye out for land. In early June he reached two South Pacific islands, which he claimed for Great Britain and named Whitsun Island and Queen Charlotte's Island. Neither provided a good anchorage, however, so he continued on his way.

In mid-June he reached a safe harbor and anchored there. A fog covered the bay. In the morning the mist lifted to reveal hundreds of wooden canoes occupied by the native people of the island. Relations with the islanders were touch and go for a week or so. At first, they were friendly and curious, and many islanders boarded the *Dolphin*. When a goat butted one of them, however, they all jumped overboard. Some started to stone the boat, and the British answered with gunfire. Eventually, the two groups made peace. Wallis, who was ill, sent Second Lieutenant Tobias Furneaux ashore with the British flag. He claimed the island and called it King George the Third's Island. The islanders called it Otaheite.

Once good relations had been established with the Tahitians, they remained cordial. The two groups traded with each other—pigs and produce for iron cooking pots. The islanders liked to trade for nails—much to the detriment of the *Dolphin*. Eventually Wallis would have to confine his crew to the ship before they completely disassembled the vessel.

When he had recovered, Wallis went ashore, where he was greeted enthusiastically by a woman named Obarea, whom he took to be a queen. He sent Furneaux and the first mate to explore the island, which they found to be "pleasant and populous."

When, on July 26, Wallis and his men took leave of the island, many of the Tahitian women had tears in their eyes. They may have been left with more than memories of the Englishmen. Historians have long debated whether it was Wallis's or Louis-Antoine de Bougainville's expedition (1766–69) that introduced venereal disease to this tropical paradise.

Sailing west, Wallis encountered several small islands, which he named for various figures in the Royal Navy. He traversed the Tonga Islands and, because his ship was in need of repair, charted a course to Batavia (present-day Jakarta, Indonesia). Near a small **archipelago**, some islanders tried unsuccessfully to capture the *Dolphin*; the ship's crew named these the Wallis Islands.

Before reaching Batavia, Wallis spent parts of September and October on Tinian in the Northern Marianas. After a stop at Batavia, the *Dolphin* was refitted in Cape Town, South Africa, and reached The Downs, England, on May 19, 1768, by way of St. Helena in the South Atlantic. Wallis had suffered no losses.

Although Wallis was unsuccessful in locating the great Southern Continent, his discovery of Tahiti was important. In fact, it was Wallis who recommended the island as the ideal vantage point from which to observe the forthcoming transit of Venus across the sun, a mission for which the Admiralty chose Captain JAMES COOK as commander.

After Wallis's return to England, he served as captain of the *Torbay* and of the *Queen* until 1772, when he resigned from active service. He served as commissioner of the navy from 1782 until his death in London on January 21, 1795.

- Wegener, Alfred Lothar

German
b November 1, 1880; Berlin
d November 1930; Greenland
Explored Greenland; postulated theory of continental drift

A geophysicist who revolutionized the study of geology, Alfred Lothar Wegener entered the world of exploration through another of his fields, meteorology. His work on the thermodynamics of the atmosphere took him to the Greenland ice field on four different expeditions (1906–1908, 1912–13, 1929, and 1930).

Wegener was one of a group of brilliant scientists and intellectuals who flourished in Germany's Weimar Republic before the rise of the Nazis. Although his doctorate was in astronomy, he was fascinated by thermodynamics. In 1906 he signed on as meteorologist and physicist for a Danish expedition led by Mylius-Erichsen, which was charged with exploring the

Alfred Lothar Wegener. Roger-Viollet.

continental drift, postulating that magnetic and tidal forces had drawn apart the seven continents from a single original landmass. Though the theory was at first severely criticized, after Wegener's death it transformed the field of geology.

In 1919 Wegener succeeded his father-in-law as director of meteorological research at the Marine Observatory at Hamburg. Five years later, he was appointed professor of both geophysics and meteorology at the University of Graz.

Wegener's 1929 Greenland expedition was a reconnaissance for a major undertaking the following year. On his final expedition of 1930, he used echo-sounding (seismic) equipment and sledges mounted with airplane engines and propellers to measure the depth of the ice. This time he gained the inland ice from the west coast near Disko Bay. That autumn he established a research station (Eismitte) on the ice cap of central Greenland, while a large staff of scientists on both coasts compiled voluminous amounts of data. The fifty-year-old Wegener died of exhaustion in November 1930 while returning from the ice cap station to the west coast.

northeast coast of Greenland as far as ROBERT PEARY's northernmost point. On March 13, 1908, Wegener and three companions discovered, some 24 miles from the coast, an ice-free area or nunatak, which he named Dronning Louise Land. The party spent two winters in the Arctic, during which time the commander of the expedition died due to the severe cold. The results of the team's explorations, however, were notable for exposing the gross inaccuracies of Peary's earlier charts of the region.

In 1912 Wegener joined another Danish expedition, led by Johan Koch, which crossed Greenland at its widest point. The party wintered on the ascent to Wegener's Dronning Louise Land and, after Koch recovered from a broken leg, made the 700-mile trip to the west coast at about 77° North latitude, using ponies rather than dogs to pull the **sledges**. They reached an altitude of 9,800 feet on their straight-line course toward Upernavik.

When Wegener returned to Germany, he published *The Origin of Continents and Oceans* (1915), which expanded on a lecture he had given in 1912. In it, he described his theory of

Wentworth, William Charles

Australian
b October 26, 1790; Norfolk Island
d March 20, 1872; Winborne, Dorset, England
Explored Australia's Blue Mountains

One of Australia's first great "native sons," William Wentworth is known primarily as a writer, a publisher, and a patriot who made several outstanding contributions to Australian government and society. Often called the Great Native, Wentworth was also an explorer whose words captured the drama of the first crossing of the Blue Mountains.

Records concerning Wentworth's actual date and place of birth are unclear. It is known that he was born to Dr. D'Arcy Wentworth, an Irish surgeon, and Catherine Crowley, a convict transported to Norfolk Island, a penal colony off New South Wales. Thanks largely to his father's status, Wentworth was educated at Greenwich, England. He returned to Australia in 1810.

William Charles Wentworth. Hulton-Deutsch Collection.

By 1813, Wentworth had become one of Australia's largest landowners, with more than 2,750 acres in New South Wales. That year, in a search for fertile lands for grazing, he joined GREGORY BLAXLAND in an attempt to cross the Blue Mountains, which had until that time been nearly impenetrable. The explorers determined that it was possible to reach the other side of the barrier by sticking to the ridges instead of the valleys.

In 1816 Wentworth returned to England to study law and the British constitution, with the intention of drafting such a document for Australia—"a new Britannia in another world." In 1819 he published two volumes on Australia. Based on a glimpse of a green valley Wentworth and Blaxland had seen, the books described the almost limitless pastureland beyond the Blue Mountains of the Great Dividing Range, which

was wrongly said to be ideal for raising sheep for the expanding wool industry.

Returning to Sydney in 1824, Wentworth practiced law and became prominent in the emancipation movement for greater self-government. In 1835 he started the newspaper *The Australian*, which put forth his views. In later years he became steadily more conservative, but he is recognized as one of the major authors of Australia's constitution. In 1852 he founded the University of Sydney, and his Vaucluse House is now a state museum.

For many years, Wentworth traveled between England and Australia, finally settling in England in 1862. After his death there in 1872, his body was sent to Sydney, where he was buried.

· Wheeler, George Montague

American
b October 9, 1842; Hopkinton, Massachusetts
d May 3, 1905; New York, New York
Surveyed American West

A member of the United States Army Corps of Engineers between 1871 and 1879, George Montague Wheeler conducted geographical surveys of United States territories west of the 100th meridian of longitude. During the course of his surveys, his teams crossed and recrossed 175,000 square miles of the American West, from the Mexican border to Oregon and from the Sierra Nevada to eastern Colorado.

Wheeler graduated from West Point in 1866. Three years later, while making a survey of southeastern Nevada and western Utah to find a more direct route for moving troops from the north to Arizona, Wheeler proposed a general survey of the West, which was to become his life's work. At the time there were already three western survey expeditions in the field led by civilians (Ferdinand Hayden, CLARENCE KING, and JOHN WESLEY POWELL). But Wheeler argued that these expeditions were primarily interested in the geology of the region whereas the army needed maps that stressed such human features as mines, farms, villages, roads, railroads, and dams.

Wheeler's argument was persuasive, and he was sent into the field in 1871 to survey the territory south of the Central Pacific Railroad, embracing parts of eastern Nevada and Arizona. After splitting into several teams that fanned out to cover the area, Wheeler's men later converged on Death Valley for a particularly arduous portion of the survey conducted in stifling heat. Soon afterward, Wheeler led his men on an exploration of the Colorado River, traveling upstream on flat-bottomed boats, which they frequently had to tow. Although Powell had already made the downstream journey, Wheeler asserted it had not been adequate for army purposes. Unfortunately, Wheeler's difficult journey up the Colorado accomplished little because his men spent much of their time struggling to stay alive.

In his report for 1871, Wheeler acknowledged that the "day of the path-finder has sensibly ended" and proposed a plan for accurate surveys of broad regions of the West, which he began to implement in his survey of 1873. By this time his work was overlapping that of the civilian surveyors, who resented Wheeler and sought to discredit his work in every way imaginable. A congressional hearing in 1874 allowed Wheeler to continue his work, but by 1878 it was clear that he was duplicating the efforts of others. Congress therefore refused to vote funds for his project and instead created the United States Geological Survey in 1879 to consolidate all survey work under one agency.

George Wheeler's detractors picture him as an incompetent surveyor, intent on carving out a niche for the army at a time when it was losing control of its traditional responsibility for surveying and mapmaking to civilians. His supporters, however, maintain that had Wheeler been allowed to complete his work, which was of high caliber from 1873 on, the country would have had a good, useful, and complete map of the West.

Edward Whymper. Hulton-Deutsch Collection.

• Whymper, Edward

English
b April 27, 1840; London
d September 16, 1911; Chamonix, France
Explored Andes, Alps, and Rockies; first to reach summits of Matterhorn and Chimborazo

Edward Whymper was a famous mountaineer and explorer who studied the effects of altitude on plant and animal life. The first person to reach the summit of the formidable Matterhorn in Switzerland and the summits of Chimborazo in Ecuador, he also explored the Andes of South America, mountain ranges in France and Greenland, and the Great Divide of the Rocky Mountains in the United States and Canada.

Born on April 27, 1840, in London, Whymper showed an early aptitude for art and a love of nature. In 1860, while making sketches of Alpine peaks for a London publisher, he became fascinated with the mountains. From 1861 to 1865 he made several ascents in the French and Swiss Alps, culminating in his reaching the summit of the Matterhorn on his seventh attempt. He thus became the first person to conquer this almost vertical spike towering above Zermatt, Switzerland. His victory was overshadowed by tragedy, however, when four members of the party died in the descent.

He also made two expeditions to the glacial mountains of Greenland (1867 and 1872), collecting rare fossils and shrub specimens. Then, in 1879, in an effort to discover the cause of mountain sickness, Whymper traveled to Chimborazo in the Andes, hoping to figure out why climbers in South America seemed to get sick at lower altitudes than did climbers in Europe.

He began his ascent of Chimborazo on December 26, 1879, and discovered that the mountain had two summits, rather than one as previously thought. He also found glaciers, which had not been known to exist on Chimborazo. By the second encampment on the ascent, all members of Whymper's party were suffering from the fever and headaches of mountain sickness. After becoming more accustomed to the altitude, they resumed the climb and reached the lower, western summit (approximately 20,000 feet) on January 5, 1880, crawling on their hands and knees at times to keep from sinking too deeply into the snow. They then crossed a plateau and climbed to the higher, eastern summit (20,561 feet), becoming the first to conquer both summits.

On February 14, 1880, Whymper climbed to the edge of the cone of Cotopoxi in the Andean range, the highest active volcano in the world. After scaling other peaks in the Ecuadorean Andes and collecting data on the effects of altitude, he returned to England in late 1880. Much later, between 1901 and 1905 (while he was in his sixties), he explored the Rocky Mountains, concentrating on the Great Divide. He died in Chamonix, France, on September 16, 1911.

Edward Whymper not only added to the knowledge about the height and formation of some of the greatest mountain ranges in the world but also collected botanical and insect specimens that aided scientific understanding of life at high altitudes. In addition, he determined that the primary cause of mountain sickness was changes in air pressure, which could be regulated by climbing gradually.

Wilkes, Charles

American
b April 3, 1798; New York, New York
d February 7, 1877; Washington, D.C.
Commanded first American circumnavigation

Often called the American Captain Cook, naval officer Charles Wilkes commanded the U.S. South Seas Exploring Expedition (1838–42) into the Pacific and Antarctic waters, traveling some 80,000 miles in all and crossing the Pacific three times. The first and last major U.S. government–sponsored voyage in the age of sail, it was also one of the first three, nearly simultaneous, expeditions to reach and explore the Antarctic continent, as well as the first American circumnavigation. It mapped 800 miles of the Oregon coast, surveyed 280 islands, and was responsible for the creation of 180 navigational charts. It also yielded thousands of scientific specimens and added immeasurably to the knowledge of biology, **hydrography**, geology, ethnography, and other disciplines.

Wilkes was born in New York City on April 3, 1798, to John Deponthieu Wilkes, a well-to-do businessman, and his wife, Mary Seton Wilkes, sister of the first Roman Catholic American saint, Elizabeth Seton. As a youth, Charles Wilkes spent his days looking out the windows

Charles Wilkes. U.S. Naval Academy Museum.

of his father's countinghouse, watching merchant ships in New York Harbor. He soon developed a desire to go to sea.

In 1815 Wilkes's father arranged for the young man to join the merchant marine. Despite the harsh treatment he received there, he joined the navy as a midshipman three years later. He served first in Boston, then in the Baltic and Mediterranean seas, and in 1821 was sent on a cruise of South America. On April 26, 1828, Wilkes married Jane Jeffrey Renwick. Two days after his wedding, he was promoted to lieutenant commander.

Wilkes developed a strong interest in astronomy and surveying and became an authority on hydrographic science. When the United States, ripe for expansion and eager to take its place in the scientific world beside the French and the British, first proposed a major sea expedition in 1828, Wilkes expressed an interest in participating. In the meantime, he took charge of the Department of Instruments and Charts in 1833. Four years later, the expedition had become a reality, and he was asked to take a

post in its astronomical department. On March 20, 1838, after several predecessors had come and gone, he received orders to command what was called the South Seas Exploring Expedition; President Martin Van Buren approved the appointment on April 20.

On August 18, 1838, six ships—the *Vincennes*, the *Porpoise*, the *Peacock*, the *Sea Gull*, the *Flying Fish*, and the *Relief*—left Norfolk, Virginia, bound for Rio de Janeiro, Brazil, carrying twelve civilian naturalists and draftsmen and a full complement of naval officers. The vessels were old and ill-prepared for a journey that would take them through treacherous seas and icy waters. In fact, only three would return home, among them the *Vincennes*, a 780-ton **sloop** upon which Wilkes spent most of the expedition.

After stops in Madeira and the Cape Verde Islands, the vessels moored in Rio on November 24 and six weeks later sailed south for Tierra del Fuego. There Wilkes established a base camp at Orange Harbor near Cape Horn, at the southern tip of the continent. It was mid-

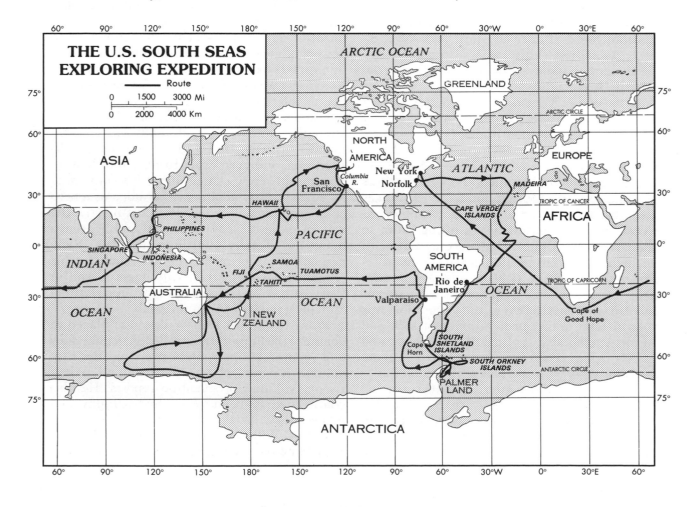

February—the middle of the nesting season—and the naturalists found all manner of species to observe there, including Magellan penguins, sheathbills, geese, plovers, leopard seals, and Magellan wolves.

On February 25, 1839, Wilkes took the *Porpoise* and the *Sea Gull* to explore the Antarctic waters between the South Orkney Islands and what is now known as Palmer Land on the Antarctic continent. He then headed toward the South Shetland Islands and beyond, sailing at a latitude of 69° South until, like others before him, he faced an impenetrable wall of ice at approximately 100° West.

Next, the expedition sailed up the South American coast to Valparaíso, Chile. There Wilkes noted that the village he had visited some eighteen years earlier had become a bustling, cosmopolitan town. The expedition's naturalists gathered specimens in the Andes before the now-reduced flotilla (the *Sea Gull* had disappeared off Cape Horn, and the *Relief* had been disabled and sent home) left for Australia via the Tuamotus, Tahiti, Samoa, and other islands. Evidence of the impact of European visits greeted them everywhere, it seemed. Christian missionaries had been at work on several islands, including Tahiti, where, in response to missionary influence, the islanders were now fully clothed.

At the end of November 1839 Wilkes arrived in Sydney, Australia, primed for a second foray into the southernmost latitudes. Putting his naturalists ashore to investigate Australia and New Zealand, Wilkes sailed south from Sydney in late December and sighted the first icebergs on January 10, 1840. On January 19, Wilkes saw what he believed to be land, but other explorers were to contest his resulting claim to being the first to sight the Antarctic continent. Regardless, a great portion of the continent today bears his name (Wilkes Land). Ten days later, after navigating through severe storms and treacherous icebergs, the expedition was able to land and collect samples of rock and basalt. Facing a wall of ice, the *Vincennes* and its exhausted crew turned back to New Zealand to rendezvous with the rest of the squadron.

Wilkes spent the winter of 1840 surveying Fiji. He departed the islands in early August, shortly after two of his men were killed and others wounded in an unprovoked attack by the islanders. In September he reached Oahu in the Sandwich Islands (present-day Hawaii). The *Vincennes* explored the **archipelago**, while the other ships were sent their separate ways to continue mapping and charting throughout the South Pacific. A team remaining on Oahu spent three weeks studying the double crater of Mauna Loa and Kilauea volcanoes.

After rejoining in April 1841, the remaining ships of the expedition set out together for the northwest coast of North America. For most of the summer the expedition surveyed Puget Sound and more than 100 miles of the Columbia River. A land team explored the Oregon coast while the ships sailed south to San Francisco. In November the expedition headed west for home, via Hawaii, Manila, and Singapore.

Wilkes reached New York City on August 9, 1842. In three years and ten months the expedition had traveled more than 80,000 miles and charted more than 300 Pacific islands, 800 miles of Oregon rivers and coast, and 1,600 miles of Antarctic coastline. As had been originally hoped, the successful completion of this ambitious mission confirmed the ability of the young American republic to mount a seagoing expedition comparable in scope to the great scientific explorations of the major maritime powers of the day, Great Britain (most notably by JAMES COOK) and France (by JULES DUMONT D'URVILLE). Much of the credit for success was due to the maritime skills, scientific sensibilities, and sheer willpower of Wilkes. Despite his strengths, however, he had liabilities as a commander, as well. He could be impetuous, self-righteous, and even cruel to his subordinates. Some of his crew chafed under his command. As a result, instead of being heralded as a hero on his return, Wilkes faced a court-martial (he was eventually acquitted) and public reprimand for illegally punishing his crew. Nicknamed "the Stormy Petrel" as much for his temperament as for his willingness to sail in foul weather, Wilkes may have inspired Herman Melville's fanatical Captain Ahab.

From 1845 until 1861 Wilkes was placed in charge of the Exploring Expedition's collections and reports. He personally prepared the five-volume account of the journey and edited twenty volumes of scientific reports. He also contributed to volumes on hydrography and meteorology.

In 1844 Wilkes was made a commander, and in 1848 he received the Founder's Medal of the

London-based Royal Geographical Society. After the death of Jane Renwick Wilkes in 1848, he married Mary Lynch Bolton in 1854.

Wilkes's temper surfaced again during the Civil War, when, as commander of the U.S.S. *San Jacinto*, he created an international incident by seizing two Confederate commissioners from the British mail steamer *Trent* in 1861, violating neutrality agreements and touching off what became known as the *Trent* affair. In 1862 he commanded the Union's James River flotilla. In September of that year he was promoted from commodore to acting rear admiral and placed in command of the West India squadron. Acting in that capacity in the Caribbean, he again violated neutrality agreements. After another court-martial (this time he was found guilty), he was removed from active duty in 1864.

Wilkes retired from the navy in 1866 as a rear admiral. In 1871, at the age of seventy-three, he began writing his autobiography. He died on February 7, 1877, in Washington, D.C., and is buried in Arlington National Cemetery.

George Hubert Wilkins. UPI/Bettmann.

· Wilkins, George Hubert

Australian
b October 31, 1888; Mount Bryan East, South
Australia
d November 30, 1958; Framingham,
Massachusetts
Explored Arctic and Antarctica by plane,
submarine, and on foot

A pioneer in many fields, an adventurer with boundless energy and determination, yet an unassuming man who did not seek publicity, Sir George Hubert Wilkins deserves to be better known. He was the first person to fly over the Arctic Ocean by airplane, the first to fly over Antarctica, and the first to explore under the Arctic polar ice cap with a submarine. He was also a versatile photographer and cinematographer who covered front-line battles in the Balkans and France as well as Arctic expeditions. As a scientist, he was a respected field researcher in geology and botany, while in meteorology he pioneered the notion that a worldwide network of stations could be used to accurately predict the weather.

The common strand in all of this was vigorous and intelligent outdoor activity. Raised on a sheep and cattle station in the remote South Australian outback, Wilkins developed the restless energy and skills of a pioneer at an early age. From the **aborigines**, who continued to live off the land outside the fences that the white settlers had erected, he learned to approach nature with cunning. From them, rather than from textbooks, he learned the basics of natural science.

After a broad technical and musical education in Adelaide, he became involved in cinematography and worked for a carnival. He left Australia in 1908 after he was offered a job in England as a cinematographer for the Gaumont Company. He first stowed away to Algiers. After being kidnapped by Arab gun smugglers, he managed to escape and make his way to London. Once there, he worked as a reporter and a cameraman, covering events all over Europe. From 1912 to 1913 he covered the conflict in the Balkan states, often barely escaping death. He joined VILHJALMUR STEFANSSON as a correspondent and photographer for the Canadian Arctic Expedition (1913–17). On this trip he learned Arctic survival skills that would later serve him well.

When in 1916 he learned that the First World

War had broken out, Wilkins left the Stefansson expedition and joined the Royal Australian Flying Corps (having learned to fly in England) as a photographer. His subsequent work won him much acclaim and the rank of captain. After his discharge, he remained active as a photographer and continued to pursue his passion for flying. His plans to participate in a major airplane expedition to the Arctic collapsed when the principal organizer was unable to obtain financial backing. Then in 1920 he was made second-in-command of the British Imperial Antarctic Expedition. This was followed by a stint as a naturalist with Sir ERNEST SHACKLETON's Antarctic *Quest* expedition. In 1923 the British Museum chose him—despite his lack of formal education—to head a biological survey of northern Australia, which resulted in his fine illustrated book, *Undiscovered Australia.*

After a great deal of preparatory work—including a reconnaissance flight over the Beaufort Sea in 1926 and a longer one in 1927 that involved three emergency landings—Wilkins and his pilot, Carl Ben Eielson, flew from Point Barrow, Alaska, to Svalbard on April 15, 1928, the first transarctic plane flight. Using a Lockheed Vega skiplane, they made the 2,500-mile trip in twenty hours, covering over a thousand miles never previously seen by humans. Wilkins was knighted for his achievement.

On November 16, 1928, Wilkins and Eielson made the first flight over Antarctica, covering 1,200 miles round-trip along the coast of the Antarctic Peninsula (Graham Land), thus beating the American explorer RICHARD BYRD's first flight by two months. Wilkins made several important geographical discoveries on two separate expeditions in 1928 and 1929. Wilkins's claim that Graham Land was an island rather than a peninsula, which initially was controversial, was later proved to be incorrect when it was found that he had mistaken glaciers for frozen sea channels. Between his two trips he found time in 1929 to participate in the three-week round-the-world flight of the **dirigible** *Graf Zeppelin.*

In 1931 Wilkins gathered a team to explore under the Arctic polar ice cap with the submarine *Nautilus,* which he named after the fictional Jules Verne creation. The U.S. Navy had planned to scrap it to satisfy a postwar arms treaty, so Wilkins was able to purchase it for one dollar. His hope was that the submarine could be used to explore the still largely unknown polar basin, surfacing occasionally to make radio contact and weather observations. As it turned out, however, the vessel was so hampered by mechanical problems that it could make only a few short dives under the ice before turning back. But the principle had proved workable, and Wilkins lived to see the nuclear-powered submarine *Nautilus* of the U.S. Navy reach the North Pole in 1958.

Throughout the 1930s, Wilkins took part in LINCOLN ELLSWORTH's four expeditions to the Antarctic, commanding the base ship while Ells-

Wilkins (left), with Carl B. Eielson beside their Lockheed-Vega monoplane. UPI/ Bettmann.

worth explored by air. He planned no more exploring trips on his own but remained active working for the U.S. government in many capacities. In all he spent twenty-six winters and five summers in the Arctic and eight summers in the Antarctic. After he died in 1958, the nuclear-powered submarine *Skate* took his ashes to the North Pole and, after an official navy funeral, scattered them to the winds.

- William of Rubruck (Rubrouck)
(Willem van Ruysbroeck;
Wilhelmus Rubruquis)

French
b 1215?
d 1295?
Wrote detailed account of trip across Asia to Mongol empire

Fewer than six years after the papal emissary GIOVANNI DE PLANO CARPINI returned from his embassy to the Mongol emperor Kuyuk—the first recorded European expedition to the Mongols—another Franciscan friar, William of Rubruck, set out on a similar mission for King Louis IX of France. Rubruck's journey was not more successful than Carpini's, nor was it more remarkable, but Rubruck had a keen eye and a talented pen. IIis descriptions of the Mongol people and their customs are regarded by many as the finest written by any medieval Christian traveler. Rubruck also made crucial geographic and historical discoveries. He was the first European to assert with conviction that the Caspian was an inland sea and not an ocean gulf. And he was the first traveler to unravel the tangled legend of Prester John and the lost Asian Christians.

In the middle of the thirteenth century, King Louis IX, like Pope Innocent IV, was searching for an effective means of driving the Saracens (nomadic peoples of the Arabian deserts) out of Palestine and the Holy Land. After the Mongol invasion of eastern Europe, the king thought perhaps he could make an alliance with the Mongols, who could then strike the Saracens from inland while the Christian crusaders attacked by sea from Cyprus. While King Louis was waiting at Acre in Palestine for French reinforcements for his crusade, one of his envoys, Andrew of Longjumeau, returned from an un-

successful mission to Mongolia. William of Rubruck immediately volunteered to embark on a new embassy on behalf of the beleaguered king. Like many Franciscan friars of the time, William was an educated man with a good command of languages and thought his chances of success might increase if he approached the Mongols not as an official ambassador, but as a private citizen and missionary. The king agreed, and William and his small party departed from Constantinople (now Istanbul, Turkey) on May 7, 1253.

William and his companions sailed across the Black Sea to the Crimean town of Sudak (now in the Soviet Union). There they met Mongols who gave them oxen and carts for their long trek across the steppes (arid plains of Europe and Asia) to the camp of Batu, the Mongol conqueror of eastern Europe, whose son Sartach was rumored to be a Christian sympathizer. Batu, however, ordered William and his one fellow Franciscan companion to continue under escort to the court of the Great Khan at Karakorum, some 5,000 miles farther east in central Mongolia. The two Franciscans then set out on horseback along the Mongol courier roads that stretched across Asia, riding north of the Caspian and Aral seas and eventually onto the great Mongolian plains. Their 3½-month journey was full of hardships and adversities. William later wrote: "There was no end to hunger and thirst, cold and exhaustion."

Finally, on January 3, 1254, William was given an audience with the Great Khan, who treated him with respect and gave him a letter to King Louis, inviting the king to send official ambassadors so the khan might learn whether the French wanted peace or war. William remained with the khan until July, when he was ordered to begin his return journey. By September 16, William had reached Batu's camp, from which he took a northerly route back, passing through Derbent on the Caspian Sea and near Mount Ararat. He reached Tripoli (now in Lebanon) on August 15, 1255.

William's mission was a modest political success, but the lengthy narrative of his experiences in Mongolia reveal him as a significant early explorer of Asia. He was the first to discover that Prester John, the legendary king of a group of Christians in Asia, was in all probability the leader of a partially Mongolized Turkish people, who called him King John. (For a more complete discussion of Prester John, see PÊRO DA

COVILHĀ.) John's brother ruled, among other tribes, a group of Mongol Christians—hence the rumors about the Asian Christians. William also reconstructed King John's role in the rise of Genghis Khan, which was confirmed by later historians.

William made important geographical notations, such as his description of the Volga River and the Caspian Sea, in which he displays the careful observation that made his narrative so valuable.

> Thus we came to the [Volga], a very large river. It is four times as wide as the Seine and very deep, and comes from Greater Bulgaria far in the north, flows south and runs out into a lake or a sea. . . . Isidorus calls it the Caspian Sea. . . . Andrew [of Longjumeau] traveled along two of its shores, the south and the east. I traveled along the other two, the north when journeying from Batu to Mangu Khan and again on the way back, and the west when returning from Batu to Syria. It is possible to travel round the sea in four months, and what Isidorus says of it, that it is an arm of the ocean, is not true. For it is never in contact with the ocean, and is surrounded everywhere by the mainland.

William also described in detail the large portable tents used by the Mongols, and he was the first European traveler to refer to the "incarnate **lamas**," the itinerant clerics of Tibetan Buddhism. He had an ear for languages as well. He noted small villages in the Crimea that had their own languages, and he made the first Western reference to Chinese writing. His landmark chronicle has been published in English as *The Journey of William of Rubruck to the Eastern Parts of the World, 1253–1255.*

Sir Hugh Willoughby. Bettmann/Hulton.

• Willoughby, Hugh

English
b ?; Nottinghamshire
d 1554; Murmansk coast, Soviet Union
Attempted Northeast Passage; discovered
   Novaya Zemlya

Sir Hugh Willoughby was knighted for his role in the violent land campaign against the Scots in 1544, not for anything he did at sea. But when court politics caused him to lose his position as captain of a castle on the Scottish border, his mariner friends convinced him to try his luck as a navigator. With only his ability as a commander to recommend him and apparently little navigational or nautical experience, he does not seem to have been a good choice to lead an Arctic marine expedition.

Nevertheless, in May 1553 a fleet of three ships left London under his command, with the ambitious goal of reaching Cathay (now China) by sailing north of Europe, the first attempt at the Northwest Passage. SEBASTIAN CABOT organized the venture for the newly formed Company of Merchant Adventurers (soon to be called the English Muscovy Company) in 1553. He no doubt believed all would go well as long as Willoughby kept the men in order while the pilot-general, RICHARD CHANCELLOR, kept the ships going in the right direction. Unfortunately, the ships were separated in a storm, and Willoughby took the *Bona Esperanza* and the *Bona Confidentia* on a series of wild zigzags to the coast of Novaya Zemlya, which was afterwards named Willoughby's Land. By the time a leak in the *Bona Confidentia* forced him to turn back in mid-September, the ice pack had trapped Willoughby and his crew for the winter at the mouth of the Arzina River, on the Murmansk coast of what is now the Soviet Union.

Although they had plenty of food, they were unprepared for the cold.

In 1554 some Russian fishermen found them frozen to death on board the ships. Willoughby's journal indicates that he had sent his men in vain to find help and that some survived until January 1554. The ships and bodies were sent back to England by the new Muscovy Company's agents in Russia.

Meanwhile, Chancellor had also failed to reach Cathay but had penetrated the White Sea to the site of present-day Archangelsk, from which he traveled overland to Moscow. There he established the flourishing trade of the Muscovy Company.

· Wills, William John

Australian
b 1834; Ballarat, Victoria
d June 30, 1861; Cooper's Creek, Queensland
Chronicled tragic Great Northern Exploration Expedition

William John Wills accompanied ROBERT O'HARA BURKE on one of the most tragic journeys in Australian history. His field notes from the Great Northern Exploration Expedition of 1860–61 paint a picture of bravery against a brutal background of inhospitable terrain, extreme weather, and bad judgment.

Born the son of a surgeon in Ballarat, a town northwest of Melbourne, Wills was trained as a surveyor. It was as a surveyor and astronomical observer that he was chosen to join an expedition to cross Australia from Melbourne in the south to the Gulf of Carpentaria in the north. Wills also had some experience in the outback (Australia's rural region). When Burke's original second-in-command resigned early in the journey, the post fell to Wills.

One of the best-equipped and most expensive undertakings of its kind, the expedition left Melbourne on August 21, 1861. (For a map of the party's route, see BURKE.) Wills took meticulous field notes and accompanied Burke as the exploring party became smaller and smaller. Only four actually made the crossing to the gulf—Burke, Wills, Charles Gray, and John King.

The return journey was a nightmare, with few supplies and several weeks of rain. Gray contracted dysentery (an acute intestinal disor-

der) and died two weeks later. "Poor Gray must have suffered very much," Wills writes, "when we thought him shamming." At one point Burke had even thrashed Gray for feigning illness.

Near starvation, the three remaining travelers were forced to kill and eat their horse and camels, then survived only due to the generosity of local **aborigines**. Bad decisions on Burke's part kept the explorers in the wilderness longer than necessary. But, although Wills was intelligent, he was much younger than the forty-year-old Burke and lacked the force of character necessary to assert himself. It proved to be his downfall.

"I may live four or five days if the weather continues to warm . . . my legs and arms are nearly skin and bones," Wills wrote near the end. His writing then trails off into an illegible scrawl. Burke died two days before Wills, on June 28, 1861. King was rescued in September 1861.

To the Victorian society of nineteenth-century Australia, Wills and Burke were heroes—all the more so, since they died in the course of their tragic quest. Although they died largely due to Burke's poor judgment, they did manage to cross the continent successfully, a milestone in the history of Australian exploration.

· Wyeth, Nathaniel Jarvis

American
b January 29, 1802; Cambridge, Massachusetts
d August 31, 1856; Cambridge, Massachusetts
Led first American settlers to Oregon

Nathaniel Jarvis Wyeth was a successful Yankee businessman who sought to establish himself in trade in the Oregon Territory. Although his business failed and he discovered no new lands, he helped establish the region's first permanent American settlement.

Wyeth's interest in Oregon was stirred up by Hall J. Kelley, an idealistic teacher who fervently believed that the United States should encourage settlement of the Northwest. When Kelley failed to follow through with a plan of his own to take settlers to Oregon, Wyeth organized an expedition. He hoped to keep expenses down by sending supplies on a ship around Cape Horn, while he led an expedition overland. The ship would then take furs and dried salmon back to Boston in what would become, Wyeth hoped, a profitable and ongoing commercial venture.

In March 1832 Wyeth and his group left Boston to begin their long journey. In Independence, Missouri, they met up with some experienced mountain men who led them to the Green River rendezvous, where fur trappers met to trade for needed supplies. While at the gathering, Wyeth contracted with the Rocky Mountain Fur Company to bring in the supplies for its rendezvous the next year.

Continuing west, Wyeth and a reduced party reached Fort Vancouver near the mouth of the Columbia River on October 29, 1832. There he received the disheartening news that his ship had been wrecked at sea. He was left with nothing to do but head east and prepare to bring out another expedition the following year.

Wyeth set out from Boston again in 1834, having once more sent a ship by way of Cape Horn. This time his expedition included two naturalists and a Methodist missionary. Wyeth's first major disappointment on this trip came when the Rocky Mountain Fur Company refused to honor its contract to buy the trade goods Wyeth had carted across two-thirds of a continent. Attempting to recoup his losses through fur trading, Wyeth built Fort Hall at the juncture of the Snake and Portneuf rivers, later a famous stopping place for settlers on their way west.

Arriving at Fort Vancouver on the Oregon coast, Wyeth experienced another disappointment. His ship had been delayed for three months for repairs after being hit by lightning and had arrived too late for the salmon season. Throughout the fall of 1834 and winter of 1835, Wyeth tried to establish himself in the fur trade, although he was constantly undermined by the well-established Hudson's Bay Company outpost there.

While on the Oregon coast, Wyeth became the first person to chart the Willamette River (a southern tributary of the Columbia) using instruments. But discouraged by the outcome of his business ventures in the Northwest, Wyeth in 1836 headed back east to the profitable ice business he had left to follow what he had thought was his destiny. He left behind him, however, the Methodist mission of Jason Lee and several other members of his party to form the first permanent settlement of Americans in the Pacific territory below the Columbia River.

Xavier, Saint Francis

Spanish
b April 7, 1506; Navarre
d December 3, 1552; Shangchuan Island, China
Traveled as Christian missionary to India, Malay archipelago, and Japan

In the European quest to bring Christianity to the people of the East, the members of the Society of Jesus (the Jesuits) saw themselves as "the light horse of the Church." Saint Francis Xavier, one of the founding members of this band of devoted Catholic clergy, became one of the most remarkable figures in Europe's early involvement with Asia. Shuttling incessantly about the continent, Xavier established the style and scope of the Jesuit presence in Asia for all time. This "Apostle of the Indies" is universally regarded as the greatest Roman Catholic missionary in the modern history of the Christian church. He established the policy of adapting to the customs and culture of the local people, a strategy refined and broadened by later Jesuits, including the remarkable MATTEO RICCI. Xavier's grand reconnaissance of Asia furnished Europeans with their first reports of the newly discovered land of Japan.

One of the younger sons of a Basque nobleman, Francis Xavier received training for an ecclesiastical rather than a political career. At the age of nineteen, he traveled to the University of Paris, where Europe's finest theological faculty was located. There he met fellow Basque Ignatius of Loyola, who had undertaken theological training after a number of years in the military. Ignatius wanted Xavier to join him in establishing a religious order based on the ideals of poverty, celibacy, and the imitation of Christ and whose members would be devoted to missionary work. At first, Xavier resisted Ignatius's appeal, but finally he joined Ignatius and five other students in forming the Society of Jesus in 1534.

Once their studies were completed, the seven Jesuits converged on Venice, where Xavier was ordained a priest. They then proceeded to Rome in the hope of a papal assignment to some distant land. When the Portuguese king John III asked for priests for his new lands in Asia, Xavier was one of those chosen. He left Rome, stopping in Lisbon before sailing for the East Indies.

On May 6, 1542, Xavier arrived in Goa on

India's west coast, the main Portuguese outpost in the Far East. It was also the center of the Catholic church in the region: the diocese of Goa stretched from China to the southern tip of Africa. Xavier spent several years on the southeastern coast of India among the Paravas, a group of simple pearl fishers. There he developed the approach that would govern his interaction with people throughout Asia for the next ten years. After translating a catechism into the local Tamil language with the help of interpreters, Xavier traveled almost without pause from village to village. Like many Jesuit missionaries who would follow him, Xavier also wrote detailed descriptions of the people and places he visited. These notes were collected by the Jesuits and used by later priests to familiarize themselves with the geography and customs of a region. Over time, the Jesuits compiled an impressive catalog of geographical information, which was later used by both cartographers and historians.

After a few months with the Macuans, who lived on the southwestern coast of India, Xavier was attracted to the Malay archipelago. He sailed first to the Portuguese commercial center of Malacca, then continued to the Spice Islands (now the Moluccas), the center of the spice trade. For two years, Xavier traveled among the islands of the Banda Sea, living with the Malays and the savage headhunters who made these islands their home. Xavier also met a man quite unlike these simple island people: Anjiro, a native of Japan whose intellectual abilities and sophistication led Xavier to believe that the future of Christianity in the Far East depended on a successful mission to Japan.

Xavier returned to Goa for a short time, then set sail for Japan, which had become known to the Western world only five years before. On August 15, 1549, Xavier, Anjiro, and several companions disembarked at the Japanese port city of Kagoshima. Xavier's enthusiasm for Japan and its people was unbridled; his first letter from Japan pronounced the Japanese "the best people yet discovered." During the two years Xavier remained in Japan, his letters gave Europeans their first glimpse into a culture whose sophistication rivaled that of their own.

Xavier returned to India in late 1551, convinced that the Japanese would respond to Christianity more readily if they saw the people of China converted, since the Japanese looked to China for wisdom. He dispensed with his administrative duties at Goa in short order, then set out for China. At Shangchuan, an island off the coast of a China closed to foreigners, Xavier died of fever on December 3, 1552. He was canonized by the Roman Catholic church in 1622 for his contributions as an early missionary to Asia.

• Xuan Zang (Hsüan-tsang; Hsüan-chuang; Huien-tsiang)

Chinese
b 602; Ch'en-lu (now Kaifeng, in Henan Province)
d 664
Undertook sixteen-year trip from China to India and back

Xuan Zang did not endure the rigors of his long, seventh-century journey to India in order to write his *Records of the Western Regions of the Great T'ang Dynasty*. He went because, as a student of Buddhist philosophy, he was troubled by the contradictory teachings he found in Buddhist holy books. He thought that if he could locate original Buddhist texts, and perhaps even visit some holy places, he could resolve the discrepancies. So the twenty-eight-year-old monk set out for India, the birthplace of Buddhism. By the time he returned sixteen years later with 520 cases of Buddhist scriptures, Xuan Zang had traveled through much of central Asia. (For a map of his route, see ZHANG QIAN.) The T'ang emperor then called him to the Chinese capital to give a detailed report on the climate, resources, agriculture, and culture of the places he had visited. Xuan Zang's written narrative of his journey of more than 40,000 miles—the *Records*—proved an important resource for later scholars interested in the geography and history of early China and India.

Xuan Zang was introduced to the teachings of Buddha by one of his older brothers, who was a Buddhist monk. It quickly became apparent that Xuan Zang was a young man with exceptional promise. Shortly after he also became a monk, he and thirteen other monks were selected by royal mandate from among several hundred candidates to be fully supported while they pursued their studies. Xuan Zang worked diligently, traveling throughout China to study under the most celebrated Buddhist scholars.

Although he mastered even the most difficult texts with apparent ease, he became increasingly troubled. Every scholar interpreted the holy texts in a different way, and Xuan Zang was at a loss to determine which interpretation was correct. The only way to resolve his dilemma, he decided, was to travel to the birthplace of Buddhism—India.

Xuan Zang departed for India from the Chinese city of Liang-zhou, an important center for merchants and traders. At the start, he was accompanied by two companions, but one soon deserted and the other proved too frail for the difficult journey. So Xuan Zang continued alone, intent on reaching his distant goal. A biography written by a disciple, Hui-li, includes this description of the young wayfarer:

> His coloring was delicate, his eyes brilliant. His bearing was grave and majestic, and his features seemed to radiate charm and brightness. . . . His voice was pure and penetrating in quality and his words were brilliant in their nobility, elegance, and harmony, so that his hearers never grew weary of listening to him.

Xuan Zang's resources were put to the test on more than one occasion. When seized by river pirates who wanted to sacrifice him to the goddess they worshiped, he protested that he was on a holy pilgrimage, but to no avail. As he was preparing for his death, a fierce storm arose, and the terrified pirates, seeing it as an omen, begged Xuan Zang's forgiveness and sent him on his way. Another time, as he passed through Turpan (now in Xinjiang Province), the khan was so impressed with the young monk that he asked Xuan Zang to stay to become leader of the Buddhist church in Turpan. Xuan Zang declined, but the khan insisted, so Xuan Zang resorted to a hunger strike to emphasize his will to continue his journey. The khan not only relented, but he subsequently became Xuan Zang's greatest benefactor. He gave the monk enough gold and silver to support him for twenty years, and provided him with letters and gifts to help ensure safe passage to his destination.

Not all the obstacles Xuan Zang met were human: he also crossed the vast deserts of central Asia and the rugged mountains of northwest India. But in 633, four years after he left China, he finally reached Buddhism's homeland. While there, he visited all the sites in India made holy by their association with the Buddha. He trav-

eled up and down the east and west coasts of the subcontinent. True to his mission, however, Xuan Zang spent most of his time at Nalanda, where he studied Sanskrit and Buddhist philosophy. In all his wanderings, Xuan Zang was a relentless collector—of Buddhist images and holy books and of descriptions of people he met and places through which he traveled.

Though Xuan Zang's fame spread throughout India, he resisted the effort by Indian monks to convince him to remain in the birthplace of the Buddha. He rejected their contention that China was a land of barbarians, pointing to China's effective laws, virtuous rulers, loyal subjects, and advances in astronomy, music, and engineering. Xuan Zang, at first acting as a sort of ambassador for his native land to the people of India, effectively became an ambassador for India upon his return to China in 645. There he began to translate the Sanskrit texts he brought from India and to enlighten the people of China about their neighbors to the west. He also composed his *Records*, the account of his travels. Some scholars believe that his cross-cultural efforts caused the beginning of political relations between India and China. Whatever his role in that development, the Buddhist texts and the invaluable geographical information he gathered on his hazardous journey ensured his standing as one of the most famous Buddhist monks in history, as well as one of the most accomplished Asian travelers of the Middle Ages.

• Yermak, Timofeyevich

Russian
b ?
d August 6, 1584; Siberia
Led early Russian attempt to annex Siberia

The story of Timofeyevich Yermak is the story of an outlaw who became a Russian folk hero. Yermak's early history is obscure, but he probably grew up among the renegade Free Cossacks who lived in the Crimea and along the banks of the Don and Volga rivers. He became an adventurer, the first in a series of explorers and conquerors who carried the Russian flag ever deeper into the heart of northern Asia. By the time these explorers reached the Pacific, the once-small nation of Russia had laid claim to one-fourth of Asia and added 10 percent of the world's land to the Russian Empire.

Yermak's exploits began when the Stroganov family, rulers of what at that time was Russia's easternmost province, called on him to lead a force across the Ural Mountains to subdue the Siberians, who were making raids on land controlled by the Stroganovs. The request was both more and less than it appeared to be: the Stroganovs wanted to be rid of the troublesome Yermak, and they assumed he would never return. The Urals had long been accepted as the eastern frontier of Europe. Only a handful of fur traders had crossed this "Iron Wall" into the unknown, and they had returned with frightening tales about cannibals. Yermak, however, was not put off; the mission appealed to his recklessness, and the prospect of seizing furs from the Siberians provided added incentive. So, accompanied by 540 cossacks (Russian cavalrymen) and 300 Stroganov soldiers, Yermak set off for Siberia in July 1579.

It took the expedition ten long months to cross the rugged Urals. Finally, they reached the Tobol River, where they built rafts to take them farther into Siberia. It took another year of hard, slow travel before Yermak and his party reached the heart of Siberia, which was then ruled by Kuchum, a Tartar warlord who led a people that had terrorized what is now eastern Russia for 200 years. As Yermak advanced, Kuchum's opposition increased. The crucial final battle pitted Yermak's small force against 10,000 cavalry under the command of Kuchum's nephew. The combat went on for five days, much of it hand to hand, but in the end the cossacks' superior firepower won out. Siber, the capital of Siberia, belonged to Yermak.

Yermak soon realized that he alone could not hold on to Siberia and its vast wealth of furs. He was in a difficult spot, but his ingenuity and craftiness did not desert him. Although Russians regarded Yermak as an outlaw, he appealed to Czar Ivan IV (the Terrible) of Russia to send soldiers, telling him Siberia was his to rule. Five hundred troops soon arrived, but so did the winter, and they suffered greatly from disease and starvation.

The following summer, Yermak and some of his soldiers moved south along the Irtysh River, trying to put down an endless series of revolts against their rule. One day in August 1584, Kuchum's forces ambushed the cossacks. Yermak, protected by a coat of chain mail given to him by the czar, tried to fight his way back to the cossack boats. But he fell into the Irtysh and drowned, dragged under by the weight of his armor.

• Younghusband, Francis Edward

English
b May 31, 1863; Murree, northern India
d July 31, 1942; Lytchett, Dorset
Explored continental Asia; led British military expedition that opened Tibet to outside world

On the surface, Sir Francis Younghusband was the archetypal Victorian hero—a courageous soldier, explorer, and diplomat. While still in his twenties he made several dangerous explorations of central Asia. Later, as head of a controversial British military force sent to open up "The Forbidden Land" of Tibet, his dogged persistence and tactful diplomacy earned him a knighthood. But perhaps Younghusband's greatest achievements lay in his efforts to ad-

Sir Francis Younghusband. Hulton-Deutsch Collection.

vance the fellowship of humanity. Gifted with an unusual capacity to understand and get along with people of different nations and cultures, Younghusband was also a mystic with a deep religious sense who founded the World Congress of Faiths.

Younghusband was born in 1863 in Murree, a hill station on British India's northern frontier, to a family with strong military traditions that traced its ancestors back to the days when the Saxons ruled England. His father was Major General J. W. Younghusband; his mother, Clara Jane Shaw, the sister of Robert Shaw, a noted explorer of Asia. All three of their sons would have distinguished military careers.

Educated in England, Younghusband graduated from Sandhurst, Britain's West Point, in 1882. He was commissioned a subaltern (an officer ranking below captain) in the first Royal Dragoon Guards and sent to India. In 1886, at the age of twenty-three, he took leave of his regiment to make an extensive exploration of Manchuria. In 1887 he made a dangerous, solitary, 1,200-mile journey from China westward across the Gobi Desert and over the Tian Shan mountains of Chinese Turkistan. Turning south, he crossed the Himalayas through areas that had yet to be mapped. In 1888 he went to England to lecture before the Royal Geographical Society. The following year, he was back in the northwestern Himalaya and Pamir mountains, under orders to explore the passes and to note any Russian activity in the region.

Younghusband's travels would make him a key player in the "Great Game," a contemporary euphemism for the rivalry between two clashing empires. Both Russia and Britain viewed Tibet as a key buffer state between the borders of their respective empires. Both vied to be the first to form an alliance with Lhasa, the capital city isolated for centuries by Tibet's indomitable mountains. But the **lamas** who governed Tibet from the Potala, the Dalai Lama's palace in Lhasa, shunned all diplomatic overtures.

In 1903 Lord Curzon, the British viceroy of India, seeking to head off any Russian designs upon Tibet, decided to send a military force to Lhasa to demand an alliance. In May he appointed Younghusband to lead the expedition. As head of 1,200 British, Ghurka (Nepalese in the service of Britain), and Indian soldiers (and their 10,000 bearers and hangers-on), Younghusband was to try to form an alliance and win Lhasa's assurance that it would not open itself up to Russian influence.

In December, Younghusband's well-armed force crossed the frontier. By Christmas, the British were 60 miles into Tibet. Between skirmishes, the hostile lamas warned them to leave the country, but the British continued their slow winter march. Then, on March 31, 1904, they met a Tibetan army of 1,500 on the plains of Guru. The Tibetans, armed with swords and muskets, carried pictures of the Dalai Lama, which they were told would make them invincible in battle. They had never seen anything like the British army's Maxim machine guns before. The slaughter was so appalling that British soldiers later said they simply could not keep firing. Some 700 Tibetans were killed. Then, to the Tibetans' amazement, the British tried to save the wounded.

Over the next few months the fighting continued, but gradually Lhasa realized resistance was futile. On August 4, Younghusband's command became the first Western army to enter Lhasa. The Tibetans, still hesitant to accept demands but eager for the British to leave, insisted they wanted nothing to do with Russia. Finally a treaty was concluded requiring Tibet to refrain from making foreign alliances without London's permission, to pay Britain a war indemnity, and to allow a British trade representative in Lhasa. In September the British headed back to India.

In London the government faced a storm of international protest and toned down the terms of the treaty. Nevertheless, Younghusband was rewarded with a knighthood. But for him, perhaps the greatest event of the expedition was a spiritual awakening that came upon him as he took one last look at the Potala. "Never again," he wrote later, "could I think evil, or ever again be at enmity with any man."

Younghusband devoted the rest of his life to geography and religion. As president of the Royal Geographical Society, he sponsored early attempts to climb Mount Everest. As a religious thinker and author, he came to believe that all the great religions of the world are one with Christianity, and spent his last years advancing the ideals of the World Congress of Faiths. He died in 1942 at the age of seventy-nine.

Zang, Xuan. See **Xuan Zang.**

Zarco, João Gonçalves

Portuguese
b ?; Matozinhos
d ?; Funchal, Madeira
Discovered and settled island of Madeira

One of Prince Henry the Navigator's earliest explorers, João Gonçalves Zarco laid the groundwork for Portugal's large-scale exploration efforts of the fifteenth and sixteenth centuries. He rediscovered two near-forgotten islands off the coast of North Africa, one of which—Madeira—he later colonized; and he explored stretches of coastline to the south in a subsequent expedition. His settlement of Madeira gave Portugal a thriving colony less than 400 miles northwest of the coast of Africa.

Initially a squire, Zarco distinguished himself in the Battle of Ceuta before offering his services to the court in 1418. Prince Henry the Navigator, eager to claim new territory, dispatched him with orders to try to reach Guinea on Africa's west coast. Zarco and a military acquaintance, Tristão Vaz Teixeira, sailed southwest on the Atlantic Ocean, where their first discovery took place by accident. Seeking refuge in a severe storm, they landed on a small island that they named Porto Santo, meaning "holy haven." After a three-day visit, they returned to Portugal with the news that they had found an unclaimed island with fresh water and fertile soil.

On instructions from an elated Prince Henry, who envisioned a supply base for African exploration, the two men returned to the island to start a colony. Accompanying them was court-appointed governor Bartolomeu Perestrello, later to become the father-in-law of Christopher Columbus. Perestrello's pregnant rabbit would eventually prove to be the undoing of the settlement. For two years, the rapidly breeding animals multiplied, eventually eating every crop the colonists planted and forcing even the governor to abandon the island temporarily. Zarco then received approval to continue exploring and, around 1424, set sail for an island he had sighted near Porto Santo.

Madeira—the word means "wood" or "timber"—was named by Zarco for its forests. The island (known much earlier to the Romans) held such promise as a colony that Zarco returned with his wife and three children to make a home there, also bringing convicts he had recruited

as settlers. After early problems, including a fire that swept the island, the new colony flourished under Zarco's leadership. He established the capital city of Funchal and apportioned tracts of land to its settlers, who raised crops successfully enough to export them for profit. Two decades later, when Madeira had become a prosperous settlement with several towns and villages, Zarco took part in another voyage of discovery, commanding one of fourteen **caravels** that sailed down the coast of Africa to Cape Verde.

Zeno, Antonio

Italian
b ?
d ?
Explored Faeroe Islands, Orkney Islands, and North America?

The story told about Antonio Zeno and his brother (or father?) Nicolo is simple enough. The trouble is that it is very likely untrue. The story takes place in the fourteenth century, before the Age of Discovery, and tells of a Venetian nobleman, Nicolo Zeno, traveling to an island called Frisland (in the Faeroe Group?) in the northeast Atlantic, where he served under a chief named Zichmni (Prince Henry Sinclair, Earl of Orkney?), and from there to Engroneland (Greenland?). It also tells of two fishermen discovering the remains, apparently, of a Norse colony in Estotiland and Drogeo (parts of North America?). More remarkably, it tells how Antonio came to Frisland and then sailed with Zichmni in a fleet to the "new world" discovered by the fishermen. By some interpretations, this has been taken to mean that a Venetian had been to America a century before Columbus.

The story—which is plausible—was written up by Antonio on his return to Venice. But he did not circulate the manuscript, and certainly he did not print it—since printing had not yet been invented. The problem is that when it was published in 1558 by Nicolo's great-great-great-grandson, also called Nicolo Zeno, the original text had been mutilated and replaced, we are told, by a reconstruction based on surviving letters of the Zenos. Nicolo the editor provided the quaint story that when he was a boy he found Antonio's manuscript in a trunk and tore it to shreds for the fun of it. The editor also provided a map, which he said was copied from the original.

When it was published, this text gained wide acceptance, and the map was incorporated into the important world map of Gerardus Mercator in 1569, and again into the map of Abraham Ortelius in 1570. MARTIN FROBISHER, JOHN DAVIS, and WILLIAM BAFFIN all used it in their travels to what is now Baffin Bay, and all were confused by it.

Still, it continued to be accepted as a genuine, if misguided, map constructed in the fourteenth century. Then in the late nineteenth century, scholars began to notice that much of the Zeno map had been copied from earlier printed maps. The best that could then be said of Zeno the editor was that he dressed up his manuscript map with modern information. But most scholars were inclined to believe the worst—that the whole production was a fraud, perpetuated in order to bring some credit for discovery to the Venetians and particularly to the Zenos.

However, the new information says nothing about the Zeno story itself, nor does it prove that the map was wholly fabricated. The chief value of the story may well be that it reminds us of the possibility—even probability—that travelers, merchants, fishermen, and prospective settlers journeyed to many places that were only later "discovered" by professional explorers.

· Zhang Qian (Chang Ch'ien; Chang K'ien)

Chinese
b ?
d 107 B.C.
Explored lands to west of China and helped open trade with these lands

Zhang Qian, a diplomat turned explorer, made possible the first Chinese trade relations with western states. In 138 B.C. he was dispatched by the Han emperor Wu-di to persuade the Yue-

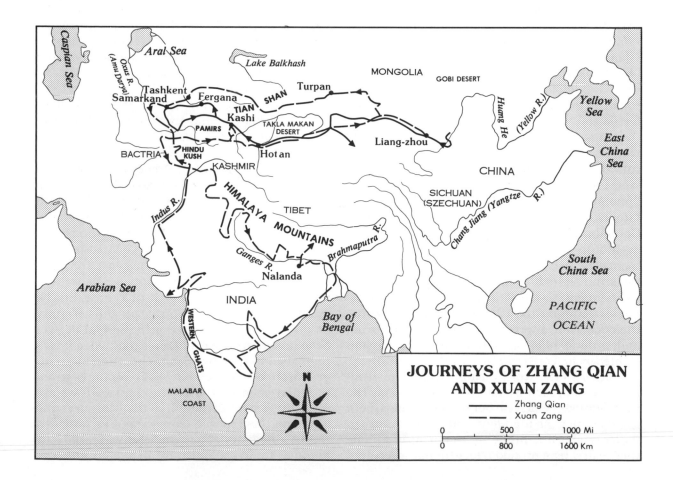

JOURNEYS OF ZHANG QIAN AND XUAN ZANG

——— Zhang Qian
— — — Xuan Zang

chi, an Iranian tribe, to become allies in the war with the Huns. Zhang Qian spent most of the next twelve years in Hun prisons. He failed to convince the Yue-chi to join the Han cause, but he returned to China bearing valuable information about the previously unknown lands to the west. Based on his report, Wu-di sent him on a second reconnaissance mission, which led to the opening of the famous Silk Road.

Before 140 B.C., China knew virtually nothing about the lands that lay to the west. Wu-di, determined to enlarge the Chinese sphere of influence, sent out a number of exploratory diplomatic missions to make contacts with western states. One of these was that led by Zhang Qian to enlist the Yue-chi in a war against the Huns, who held land to the west of the Hans. Zhang Qian set out with over a hundred troops, but he was promptly captured by the Huns and imprisoned for ten years. He finally escaped and made his way to Fergana (southeast of Tashkent in the present-day Soviet Union). With the help of friendly Ta-yuan people, he located the Yue-chi. He discovered, however, that the Yue-chi had conquered a new land since being driven out of their original homeland by the Huns and had no desire to return and avenge their earlier defeat.

His mission thwarted, Zhang Qian tried to return to China by way of Tibet, only to be captured again by the Huns. When the Hun ruler died several months later, Zhang Qian took advantage of the confusion surrounding the ensuing fight over the throne and escaped. He arrived in China in 126 B.C., accompanied by only two of his original party. In his report to the emperor, Zhang Qian described the unknown western lands he had visited, including Fergana, Syria, Babylonia, and Bactria. Zhang Qian also suggested a different strategy for forging links with the west: bypassing the Huns and the Tibetans to establish direct contact with western states. He cited an existing trade route between Sichuan (on the upper Chang Jiang, also known as the Yangtze River) and India as proof that such an approach was possible.

About ten years later, the emperor sent Zhang Qian back to the west to explore this possibility. Zhang's second expedition was more productive, if less adventurous, and he and his agents investigated potential routes between China and Fergana. Zhang Qian's subsequent report to the emperor resulted in the opening, in 105 B.C., of the Silk Road, the primary trade link

between northern China and Europe for hundreds of years.

· Zheng He (Cheng Ho)

Chinese
b 1371; Yunnan Province
d 1433?
**Commanded sea expeditions throughout
southern Asia, Middle East, and East Africa**

In the early fifteenth century, Yung He, the third emperor of the Ming dynasty, decided to send an imperial naval expedition to display his greatness to the people of the surrounding seas. He chose Zheng He, one of his most distinguished court eunuchs, to command the fleet. This initial expedition was soon followed by another. In fact, between 1405 and 1423, Zheng He led seven expeditions, some of which involved as many as 37,000 men and 317 ships. Unlike some of his European counterparts, the Ming ruler did not intend for Zheng He to conquer new territory, collect slaves, or spread religion. His designs were more subtle by far: when a neighboring state saw firsthand the power and sophistication of the Ming dynasty and received gifts made by its finest craftsmen, it would gladly offer tribute appropriate to China's status as the one and only center of civilization. Many states did exactly that, as the results of Zheng He's seven expeditions attest.

Zheng He was born a Muslim in the southern province of Yunnan, the last Mongol stronghold in China. When Chinese forces conquered Yunnan, he was sent to the imperial capital, where he served as a court eunuch. In this strategic position as a trusted assistant and adviser to the emperor, Zheng He was able to distinguish himself. During this time, Emperor Yung He was building Beijing into a grand imperial capital with the Forbidden City at its center, and he had set his sights on conquering the Mongol Empire to the north. When he decided to proclaim the glory of the Ming dynasty on foreign shores, he chose Zheng He for the task.

Zheng He's fleet was built to reflect the glory of the emperor it represented. The largest of the several hundred ships in the fleet had nine masts and measured roughly 450 feet long, the smallest had five masts and measured 180 feet long, and many were multistoried. It was a beautifully designed and well-built fleet, unlike anything the people of the western seas had ever seen and the largest maritime enterprise in Chinese history. Zheng He had compasses and other navigational instruments at his disposal, as well as navigational charts marked with compass bearings.

Supported by two successive emperors, Zheng He's seven expeditions explored the area from Java to the mouth of the Persian Gulf, and down the east coast of Africa. One expedition visited thirty-six states scattered across the Indian Ocean. Another established relations with twenty realms and sultanates, from Java in the east to Mecca, and along the African coast. Unfortunately, Zheng He's accounts of his extensive voyages were destroyed, presumably to foil the designs of another eunuch who sought to emulate his enviable success.

GLOSSARY OF TERMS

aborigine The term aborigine refers in its general sense to one of the native inhabitants of a region. In its more specific sense, aborigine refers to the native inhabitants of Australia. Considered part of the Australasian race, these dark-skinned people exhibit numerous regional variations in anatomical features and hair color and are divided into approximately 500 different tribal groups. They are seminomadic hunter-gatherers with a well-developed trading economy.

Aborigine society was gradually eroded after Europeans arrived in Australia. Aborigines were killed in clashes with the newcomers and driven into the bush (backcountry). Many more died as the result of epidemics of European diseases, to which they had no immunities. Prior to the arrival of the Europeans the aborigines of Australia are estimated to have numbered about 300,000; their current population is 125–130,000.

adelantado In sixteenth-century Spanish America, an adelantado was an appointed official of the crown who was in complete charge of military and civilian affairs, both judicial and administrative. The office was later replaced by that of alcalde (mayor or magistrate).

ague Ague refers to a fever, like that associated with malaria, characterized by periods of sweating, chills, and shaking and accompanied by malaise, pains in the bones and joints, and various other symptoms.

aide-de-camp A subordinate military or naval officer, an aide-de-camp acts as a secretary and confidential assistant to a superior officer at the rank of general or admiral.

archipelago An archipelago is either a large group or chain of islands or any large body of water interspersed by many islands (such as the Aegean Sea).

arquebus/arquebusier (also **harquebus/harquebusier**) An arquebus was a heavy, portable long gun operated by a matchlock or wheel-lock mechanism, dating from about 1400. A soldier armed with an arquebus was known as an arquebusier.

astrolabe First used by Greek astronomers as early as the third century B.C., an astrolabe was an instrument used to measure the altitude of the sun and stars. It originally consisted of a wooden disk suspended by a ring, with degrees of a circle marked around the disk's edge and a pointer that pivoted on a center pin. The sun or a star was sighted along the pointer, and the altitude of the celestial body was then read from the graduated scale around the rim. In the late fifteenth century Martin Behaim, a German geographer, adapted the astrolabe for navigational use by the addition of tables of the sun's declination, making it possible to determine latitude. The astrolabe remained the principal instrument used by navigators until it was superseded by the **sextant** in the eighteenth century. Later astrolabes were often made of metal and had a second disk, the rete, which indicated the positions of the principal stars. With this feature, the time of day could also be determined.

bandeira/bandeirante Meaning "flag," "banner," or "faction" in Portuguese, the term bandeira refers to a seventeenth-century Portuguese raiding expedition into the Brazilian interior, undertaken primarily to locate Indians to take as slaves but also to look for gold and silver. Bandeirantes (the members of such expeditions) were usually mamelucos (people of mixed Indian and Portuguese ancestry) from São Paulo.

The effects of the bandeiras were twofold: the expansion of the Brazilian frontier and the near extermination of Brazil's native Indian tribes. Comprising anywhere from fifty to several thousand members, bandeiras often lasted years and were characterized by raiding, trading activities, the founding of settlements, road building, and farming.

The prime targets of bandeira slave raids were the Indian mission villages established by the Jesuits. The Jesuits and the Indians fought back—and also moved their villages to more remote regions, farther south and west—but the bandeirantes nevertheless captured thousands of Indians, massacred many others, and exposed Indian communities to European diseases to which they had no immunities (for example, smallpox, influenza, and measles). After the middle of the seventeenth century, the bandeiras focused on obtaining gold and other precious metals and stones, rather than slaves.

boat-sledge Used in arctic expeditions, a boat-sledge is a boat mounted on the runners of a **sledge**, allowing for travel over both open water and solid ice. It was most often used in the spring when breaks (also called leads) in the ice were frequently encountered.

brig The brig was a small, fast sailing vessel used from about 1700 until 1860. Brigs were employed primarily as merchant ships and as military reconnaissance vessels. They had two masts and were **square-rigged**. This setup required large crews to handle the sails, so the brig was eventually replaced by **schooners**, which were fore-and-aft rigged (that is, with triangular sails running along the length of the ship) and were more easily handled by a smaller crew. A transition vessel was the **brigantine**.

brigantine A brigantine was a two-masted sailing ship, **square-rigged** on the foremast and fore-and-aft rigged (that is, with triangular sails running along the length of the ship) with square upper sails on the mainmast. It was the transition vessel between the two-masted square-rigged **brig** used between about 1700 and 1860 and the fore-and-aft-rigged **schooners** that came later.

buccaneer A buccaneer was a pirate, especially one who preyed on Spanish colonies and ships in the West Indies and along the American coast during the seventeenth century.

caravel The caravel originated in the fourteenth century as a small merchant ship and was then developed into a larger oceangoing vessel by the Portuguese in the fifteenth century. It was commonly used for exploration in the fifteenth and sixteenth centuries; both the *Niña* and the *Pinta* of CHRISTOPHER COLUMBUS were caravels. The earliest caravels were **lateen-rigged** on two masts. A third mast was added later, using a combination of lateen and square sails, the latter of which were preferred by navigators like Columbus for long voyages.

chevalier   The lowest title of rank in the old French nobility, chevalier refers to a member of certain orders of knighthood or merit, such as the Legion of Honor.

chronometer   First devised in 1659 and perfected by JOHN HARRISON in 1762, a chronometer is an exceptionally precise clock set to Greenwich Mean Time, the recognized international time standard. Used in conjunction with a **sextant**, the chronometer made it possible for the first time to determine longitude as well as latitude at sea. To minimize the effect of a ship's motion, the chronometer is hung in gimbals to keep it in a horizontal position. It also has devices to overcome the effects of temperature changes and to regulate the power of the mainspring as it unwinds. The chronometer was the forerunner of accurate pocket watches.

conquistador   Spanish for "conqueror," the term conquistador refers to the Spanish (and sometimes to Portuguese) leaders who were responsible for the European conquest of the New World, Mexico and Peru, in particular, during the sixteenth century. Since the conquistadores were mostly commoners in their native countries, they sought fame and fortune in the new lands overseas. The conquistadores were rugged adventurers, capable of enduring intense hardships. They were also fierce and ruthless fighters, often perpetrating severe cruelties and injustices upon the native Indians. Some of the most famous conquistadores were VASCO NUÑEZ DE BALBOA, HERNÁN CORTÉS, FRANCISCO PIZARRO, HERNANDO DE SOTO, and FRANCISCO VÁSQUEZ DE CORONADO.

corsair   The term corsair refers either to a fast ship used for piracy, especially along the Barbary Coast of Africa, or to a person who sailed on such a ship. Corsairs sometimes operated with official sanction.

cosmography/cosmographer   Cosmography refers to the study of the constitution of nature; it is no longer practiced as a science. A cosmographer, one who studied this science, attempted to describe and map the main features of the universe, incorporating elements of astronomy, geography, and geology.

Council of the Indies   From its founding in 1524 by Holy Roman Emperor Charles V (King Charles I of Spain) until its dissolution in 1834, the Council of the Indies was the supreme governing body of Spain's empire in America and the Philippines. Consisting of a president and four to ten members, the council had legislative, executive, and judicial power over the colonies. It framed the laws of the Indies, codified in 1681; nominated all high colonial officials to the king; approved all important acts and expenditures by colonial officials; controlled taxation; acted as a court of last resort in civil and criminal cases appealed from colonial courts; censored all literature in the empire; and even supervised ecclesiastical matters of the Roman Catholic Church in the colonies, including the nomination of bishops and archbishops. After 1790 it served in only an advisory capacity.

coureur de bois   Literally "woods runner" in French, the term coureur de bois referred to a French or French-Indian fur trapper, especially one who operated in Canada.

courtier   A courtier is an attendant at the court of a king or other royalty.

creole   The term creole has different meanings depending on the geographical context. Creole can variously refer to a person of European, usually Spanish, ancestry born in the West Indies or Spanish America; a person descended from or culturally related to the original French settlers of the southern United States, especially Louisiana, or from the Spanish and Portuguese settlers of the Gulf states; a person of mixed European and Negro ancestry who speaks a creole dialect; or, most specifically, one of the indigenous people of Haiti. The term also refers to the French, or sometimes Spanish, dialect spoken by these people.

dirigible   A dirigible is a lighter-than-air craft. Like a hot air balloon, it uses a lighter-than-air gas (usually hydrogen or helium) in its huge cigar-shaped body to rise from the ground and stay aloft. Unlike a balloon, a dirigible has an engine to move it through the air and equipment for steering. The term comes from the Latin *dirigere*, meaning "to direct." Dirigibles were introduced in the mid-1800s as the first manned aircraft capable of having a prolonged flight and being steered. They were used through the 1930s by the military and by passenger services. The use of dirigibles gradually decreased due to their vulnerability to stormy weather, the increasing development and use of airplanes in the 1930s and 1940s, and a succession of disasters (the best known was the explosion of the *Hindenburg* over Lakewood, New Jersey, in 1936). Dirigibles (usually nonrigid blimps) are still used today for transport of bulky cargo (such as rocket launch craft), oceanographic research, surveillance, and advertising.

doldrums   The doldrums is a belt of calm or light and variable winds in equatorial regions, mainly over the oceans. Within this belt, the northeast and southeast **trade winds** meet, producing a slow uplift of air that causes sudden thunderstorms and gusty winds, creating one of the rainiest regions of the world. This zone is known by meteorologists as the Intertropical Convergence Zone (ITCZ). Sailors began calling this zone the doldrums (meaning a state of listlessness) because their sailing ships were often stranded there for weeks at a time due to the lack of wind.

El Dorado   Literally meaning the "gilded one" or "gilded man," El Dorado was the name given first to a person, then to a city, and finally to a region. All were legendary and centered on the presence of vast amounts of gold in an unspecified region of central South America. These rumors motivated a considerable amount of the exploration of South America during the sixteenth century, including the expeditions of SEBASTIÁN DE BENALCÁZAR, NIKOLAUS FEDERMANN, FRANCISCO DE ORELLANA, FRANCISCO PIZARRO, and WALTER RALEIGH.

The legend of El Dorado probably stemmed from an actual ceremony of an Indian tribe that inhabited what is now Colombia. This tribe is said to have anointed its new chiefs by covering their bodies with gold dust. The gilded chief was then either floated onto or plunged into a lake while his people threw offerings of emeralds and gold into the water surrounding him.

Accounts of this ceremony quickly became known to the early European explorers of South America, mutating and gaining force as they were passed on. The lure of El Dorado and its vast wealth became a dominant factor in the early exploration of South America.

encomendero   A Spanish soldier or colonist who was granted a tract of land or a village in the American colonies, along with domain over its Indian inhabitants, was known as an encomendero. Under this early sixteenth-century system, encomenderos were theoretically to provide protection and instruction in the Christian faith to the Indians in return for rights to goods and labor, but in practice encomenderos often abused and enslaved the Indians. The leading reformer working against this system was the missionary BARTOLOMÉ DE LAS CASAS. In 1542 laws were passed abolishing the system, but they went unenforced, and encomenderos endured for some time.

fathom   A fathom is a unit of length equivalent to six feet (1.8 meters) used chiefly in measuring marine depths. Navigators mark a rope in fathoms and drop it into the water to determine the depth. The measure originated as the distance from the middle fingertip of one hand to the middle fingertip of the other hand on a man of average height holding his arms fully extended. The word comes from the Danish *faedn*, meaning "outstretched arms."

frigate   The term frigate first applied to the small oared **galley** of the fourteenth century used for reconnaissance and for carrying dispatches. In the seventeenth century it referred to a small sailing warship. Around 1750 a new type of sailing warship was introduced. These frigates were three-masted and **square-rigged** and had two decks. Since the main artillery was mounted on the upper deck only, these ships were faster and more maneuverable than larger ships with two or three gun decks. This made them ideal for conducting raids and escorting merchant fleets. Steam frigates came into use in the late nineteenth century. Today the term frigate applies to a naval class of antisubmarine escort vessels.

galleon   The term galleon refers loosely to a large sailing ship of the fifteenth and sixteenth centuries used as a fighting or merchant ship, especially by England and Spain. Galleons were the first ships to carry heavy artillery, revolutionizing naval warfare, which had previously relied on boarding and hand-to-hand combat. A galleon had three or four masts and was **square-rigged** on the foremast and mainmast and generally **lateen-rigged** on one or two aftermasts. The early versions of galleons had sterncastles, structures at the rear of a ship rising as many as four decks high and housing elaborate living quarters; and forecastles, somewhat smaller structures that bulged out over the ships' bows. Around 1550 the sterncastle was reduced to two or three decks, each shorter than the one below, and the lofty forecastle was pulled well back from the bow; the term galleon usually refers to this form of ship, which became the standard vessel of European navies in the late 1500s.

galley   Used on the Nile as early as 3000 B.C., the galley was a ship used for both war and commerce; it flourished for over 4,000 years, especially in the Mediterranean. A light, slender, shallow vessel, the galley was propelled primarily by banks of oars but was also equipped with sails for cruising. The earliest galleys had only one bank (or row) of oars on each side. Around 700 B.C. the Phoenicians developed a galley with a second row of oars. The Greeks then added a third bank around 500 B.C., creating a ship which by the first century B.C. had become the backbone of Roman naval power.

   The galley remained the standard European battle vessel until the late sixteenth century, when it was replaced by the sail-driven, more heavily armed **galleon**.

hydrographer/hydrography   A hydrographer is a scientist involved with the measurement, description, and mapping of oceans, lakes, rivers, and other surface waters of the earth; the hydrographer is especially concerned with acquiring and organizing information useful for the navigation of such waters.

Inuit   The term Inuit refers to the native people of the world's Arctic regions. Commonly referred to as Eskimos, these are a racially distinct people sharing a common language and a rich culture. Their ways of life are dictated by and adapted to the harsh realities of the Arctic, particularly its frigid climate. The Inuit live in various small dwellings made of animal skins, earth, or, in the case of what is known as the igloo, blocks of snow and ice. Their effective methods of fishing and of hunting—particularly of caribou, seals, walrus, and whales— provide nearly all of their clothing and food. They travel over water in small umiaks and kayaks, Inuit boats made of animal skins. They travel over land with the aid of sleds pulled by teams of dogs.

Inuit culture has its own family and social organization, as well as its own art, music, dance, and religion. This rich and distinctive culture developed independently and has changed or been threatened as the result of contact with Western cultures, initiated by European explorers of the Arctic in the sixteenth century and continuing to this day. Significantly, many of the early failures of Arctic explorers can be attributed to their inability to learn from and adapt Inuit methods of dress, transport, and survival. The successes of explorers such as ROBERT EDWIN PEARY and ROALD ENGELBREGT GRAVNING AMUNDSEN were in large part due to their appropriation of Inuit ways and use of Inuit guides.

lama   A lama is a priest or monk of high rank in Lamaism (the Buddhism of Tibet and Mongolia).

lateen-rigged   The lateen-rigged vessel, used as early as the second century A.D. in the Mediterranean, was the first fore-and-aft-rigged sailing vessel (meaning it was rigged with triangular sails running along the length of the ship). The front edge of the sail was attached to a long yard (crossbar) that was mounted at its middle to the top of the mast. The yard ran diagonally so that it extended forward nearly down to the deck and to the rear far above the mast. The sail could take the wind on either side of the mast, giving a ship great maneuverability, which made it especially useful in coastal sailing. Its disadvantage as compared to the **square-rigged** ship was that it could not catch as much wind and was therefore not as fast before the wind on open seas. Both the **brigantine** and the **galleon** used a combination of these two common types of rigging.

league   This unit of distance has varied in definition through history and in different countries. In English-speaking countries, a statute league is usually estimated today at roughly 3 miles (4.8 kilometers). A nautical league is equivalent to 3 nautical miles, or approximately 3.45 land miles (5.52 kilometers).

livre   This former French currency was issued in coin form, first in gold, then in silver, and finally in copper. It was discontinued in 1794.

llanos   Meaning "plains" in Spanish, llanos refers to vast grassy plains—especially those of Colombia and Venezuela, which are drained by the Orinoco River and its tributaries.

mesa   Rising from a surrounding plateau, a mesa (literally "table" in Spanish) is a flat-topped elevation with steep walls, common in arid and semiarid regions of the southwestern United States and Mexico.

mestizo   In general terms, a mestizo is a person of racially mixed ancestry. In Latin America, the term refers to someone of mixed American Indian and European (usually Spanish or Portuguese) ancestry; in the Philippines, to someone of mixed native and foreign ancestry.

mizzenmast   The third mast from the front on a sailing ship is called the mizzenmast. A mizzen is a sail on this mast.

New France   The name originally assigned to all of the territories explored and claimed by France in the New World, New France gradually came to refer more specifically to the French-settled area of the St. Lawrence River valley centered on Québec. This distinguished it from the Atlantic coastal possessions, called Acadia, and from the Mississippi Valley area, later known as Louisiana.

In 1524, GIOVANNI DA VERRAZANO explored the coasts of North America from present-day Cape Fear, North Carolina, to present-day Cape Breton, Nova Scotia. The name New France first appears on a map prepared by his brother in 1529. From 1534 to 1542 JACQUES CARTIER explored the St. Lawrence River region to present-day Montréal, trading for furs with the Indians and claiming the land for France in the name of King Francis I.

Actual settlement in North America was postponed, however, due to religious wars occurring in France. Then in 1603 SAMUEL DE CHAMPLAIN sailed into the St. Lawrence; and in 1608 he founded Québec, which attracted few settlers. France's Cardinal Richelieu founded the Company of New France in 1627 and agreed to bring 200 to 300 settlers a year to New France in exchange for a monopoly on the fur trade in the colony. However, war with England began then. Québec was surrendered to the English in 1629 but restored to France in 1632 by the Treaty of St. Germain.

Colonization of North America by the French remained slow, as the Company of New France never really recovered from its initial difficulties. It nevertheless controlled New France until 1663, when King Louis XIV canceled its charter and assumed direct control. The region prospered under his reign. In 1666 the Iroquois were defeated, making it possible to develop and settle New France; 3,000 settlers were sent to North America from France in the 1660s. This was an active period of exploration by LOUIS JOLLIET, RENÉ ROBERT CAVELIER, SIEUR DE LA SALLE, LOUIS HENNEPIN, DANIEL GREYSOLON, SIEUR DULHUT, JACQUES MARQUETTE, and others, during which French boundaries expanded to cover the Great Lakes and the Mississippi Valley. Then in 1689 a long period of rivalry with England began that would run through four wars, starting with the War of the Grand Alliance (known in the colonies as King William's War) and ending in 1763 with the Seven Years' War (also known as the French and Indian War). Acadia was eventually ceded to Britain by the Treaty of Utrecht in 1713, and New France was ceded by the Treaty of Paris in 1763. French authority over Louisiana ended in 1803 with the Louisiana Purchase, thus ending all of France's claims in the New World.

packet   Packets were small, speedy vessels used during the nineteenth century to carry mail, freight, and passengers on regular schedules along fixed routes; this was an important new concept in shipping. The first vessels were sailing ships, which were later replaced by steam vessels.

pinnace   The term pinnace refers to a light sailing ship formerly used in attendance on a larger merchant or war vessel or to any of several kinds of ships' boats used for a variety of tasks, especially that of sailing in waters unnavigable to a larger ship.

pirogue   A pirogue was most often a canoe made from a hollowed tree trunk.

portage   Portage refers to the transporting of boats and supplies overland between two navigable waterways or around an unnavigable portion of a river. As a noun, the term refers to the route used for such transport.

privateer   Privateer refers to a privately owned and manned ship commissioned by a government to capture or attack enemy vessels in time of war; to the commander or crew member of such a ship; or, as a verb, to the act of operating a privateer.

pueblo   Spanish for "people" or "nation," the term pueblo most commonly refers to a communal dwelling of certain Indian tribes of the southwestern United States, built up to five stories high of stone or adobe, sometimes into the sides of cliffs. It can also refer to the tribes inhabiting such dwellings, to an Indian village community, or to any small town or village in Spanish America.

quadrant Used from medieval times in astronomy, navigation, and surveying to measure the altitude of the sun and stars, a typical quadrant consisted of a flat plate cut from wood or brass shaped like a quarter-circle, with a scale marked on its curved edge, two sights attached to one of the sides, and a plumb bob hanging from its apex. After using the instrument to determine the altitude of a given celestial body, a navigator could consult a star chart to find out his latitude. Arabic and medieval European astronomers developed sophisticated variants, some from which time could be calculated directly. The seaman's reflecting quadrant was invented in 1730 by JOHN HADLEY and was the precursor of the modern **sextant**.

schooner Used extensively in the eighteenth and nineteenth centuries, a schooner was a sailing vessel with two or more fore-and-aft-rigged masts (masts having triangular sails running along the length of the ship), enabling it to run closer to the wind. This made it faster, more maneuverable, and more easily handled by a smaller crew than were comparable **square-rigged** ships, such as the **brig**.

scurvy A disease now known to be caused by lack of vitamin C in the diet, scurvy is characterized by bleeding from the gums, under the skin, around the bones, and in the joints, and also by extreme weakness. Wounds do not heal properly, and the bones become more brittle; anemia may be present in chronic cases. Epidemics of scurvy were once common among sailors on long sea voyages due to the virtual absence of fresh fruits (particularly citrus) and vegetables in their diets. The consequent disease and death among crews effectively limited the length of sea voyages.

Captain JAMES COOK was the first to beat the problem by his recognition of the need for an appropriate diet for his sailors, including cress, sauerkraut, and a kind of orange extract. Cook was awarded one of the highest honors of England's Royal Society, the gold Copley Medal, for a paper he prepared detailing his work against scurvy. Beginning in 1795, lime juice was issued to all British naval vessels to aid in the prevention of scurvy; hence the term "limey" to denote a British sailor. During the winter of 1535–36 French explorer JACQUES CARTIER and his crew had been introduced to a Huron Indian cure for scurvy that consisted of an infusion of bark and needles from the white cedar tree.

sea dog Usually meaning a sailor, especially an old or experienced one, sea dog sometimes referred specifically to a pirate or privateer.

sextant A sextant is an optical instrument used in navigation since the mid-eighteenth century to obtain measurements of the altitude of celestial bodies. These measurements, in combination with the precise time as determined by a **chronometer** and data in navigation almanacs, can yield the latitude and longitude of a ship's position at sea. The **quadrant** was the precursor of the sextant.

The early sextant had a metal-frame arc of one-sixth of a circle (60°), from which the instrument derives its name. Arcs of modern sextants vary, but they are all commonly known as sextants. The device consists of this arc (marked off in degrees), a movable radial arm that pivots from the center of the circle, a small telescope that is lined up with the horizon, and two mirrors, one stationary and the other moving in conjunction with the radial arm. When the mirrored reflection of a celestial body is lined up on the horizon as seen through the telescope, its altitude can be determined on the graduated scale of the arc.

shallop   A shallop was an open boat, fitted with oars, sails, or both, used for sailing or rowing in shallow water. The term shallop most commonly refers to a two-masted vessel of the seventeenth and eighteenth centuries.

sledge   Used primarily for transporting goods and people over ice and snow, a sledge is a vehicle mounted on parallel runners (instead of wheels) and drawn by dogs, reindeer, horses, or other draft animals. The earliest sledges were made from logs that were tied together and dragged along the ground. Runners were added later to allow the sledge to move with less resistance. Sledges have been a primary means of transport in both Arctic and Antarctic exploration.

sloop   A sloop is a small vessel with one mast and fore-and-aft rigging (triangular sails running along the length of the ship). It has a mainsail, jib, and sometimes one or more headsails. Sloops today are mainly used for recreational purposes.

Spanish Main   This name was given to parts of the Spanish colonial empire in the Western Hemisphere from the 1500s to the 1700s, particularly the area from the mouth of the Orinoco River on the northern coast of South America west to the Isthmus of Panama. It later came to include the Caribbean coast of Central America, and even the Caribbean Sea itself, which was part of the route of the Spanish treasure **galleons**. These galleons were regularly plundered by English, Dutch, and French **buccaneers**, and the Spanish Main consequently came to be associated with piracy.

square-rigged   Square-rigged ships have rectangular sails suspended from yards (crossbars hanging from masts) at right angles to the length of the ship. A square-rigged ship, intended primarily for sailing before the wind (that is, with the wind coming from directly behind a ship), could catch more wind and move faster on the high seas than could fore-and-aft-rigged vessels (which had triangular sails running along the length of the ship). However, square-rigged vessels required larger crews, since men had to climb up and out onto the yards to adjust the sails; on fore-and-aft-rigged ships the sails could be hoisted or lowered from the deck. Square-rigged ships were also not as maneuverable as fore-and-aft-rigged ships, which could be tacked (steered into or across the wind). One type of square-rigged ship was the **brig**, while the **brigantine** and the **galleon** used a combination of square and fore-and-aft rigging.

topsail   The sail, or pair of sails, set above the lowest sail on a mast of a ship is known as the topsail.

trade winds   The trade winds (or trades) are nearly constant easterly winds that occupy most of the earth's tropic and subtropic latitudes, blowing toward the equator from the northeast in the Northern Hemisphere and from the southeast in the Southern Hemisphere. Created by temperature differences between the polar regions and the low latitudes, the trades originate in the subtropical high-pressure regions at about 30° North and South and blow towards the equator where they die out in the **doldrums**. Because these winds have such consistent direction and velocity, mariners in the days of sailing ships named them trade winds, which meant course, or track, winds. Ships of this era depended greatly on the trades.

Treaty of Tordesillas   This historic treaty was created to settle conflicts between Spain and Portugal resulting from their "discoveries" of new lands late in the fifteenth century. After CHRISTOPHER COLUMBUS, sailing for Spain in 1492, reached the islands now known as the West Indies, the Spanish attempted to secure the rights to a trading monopoly in the western Atlantic from Pope Alexander VI (a Spaniard). In response, the pope declared a north-south line of demarcation 100 leagues west of the Azores. Spain was given the rights to so-called new (meaning non-Christian) lands to the west of the line; Portugal was granted "new" lands lying to the east of the line, in the area of its most significant explorations until that time, particularly those of BARTOLOMEU DIAS and VASCO DA GAMA.

Portuguese king John II was dissatisfied with the declaration, however, and demanded to renegotiate its terms directly with Spain. To that end, ambassadors of each country met in the town of Tordesillas, in northwestern Spain, in 1494. There they agreed to move the demarcation line to a point 370 leagues west of the Azores. Still to the east of Columbus's landfall, this dividing line gave Portuguese navigators more "room" to the west in order to round the bulge of West Africa more easily on their route around Cape Horn to the East.

This westward shift of the line soon gave Portugal its entrée to the Americas. In 1500, Portuguese navigator PEDRO ÁLVARES CABRAL landed in what is now eastern Brazil at a point lying east of the line specified in the treaty, giving Portugal a legitimate beachhead on the newly discovered continent. Over the next 200 years, Portuguese explorers ventured west, gradually extending the boundaries of their colony beyond the specified boundary line to the limits of the modern border of Brazil.

vizier   A vizier is a high officer (often a minister of state) in certain Muslim governments, especially in the old Turkish Empire.

voyageur   French for "traveler," the term voyageur referred to an expert woodsman, boatman, and guide, especially one employed by fur companies to transport furs and supplies between remote stations in the United States and Canadian Northwest.

wampum   Also called peag, seawan, or sewan, wampum consisted of cylindrical beads made from polished shells, pierced and strung, which were formerly used by North American Indians as currency and jewelry and for ceremonial and sometimes spiritual purposes.

westerlies   The prevailing westerlies are belts of wind that lie between the latitudes of 30° and 60° in both the Northern and Southern hemispheres. Separated by the tropical easterlies (**trade winds**), both belts blow generally eastward. More storms occur in the westerlies than in any of the other wind belts.

LIST OF EXPLORERS BY NATIONALITY

AMERICAN

Akeley, Delia Denning
Akeley, Mary Lee Jobe
Ashley, William Henry
Bartram, John
Bennett, Floyd
Bingham, Hiram
Bonneville, Benjamin Louis Eulalie de
Boone, Daniel
Boyd, Louise Arner
Byrd, Richard Evelyn
Chaillé-Long, Charles
Clark, William
Colter, John
Cook, Frederick Albert
De Long, George Washington
Ellsworth, Lincoln
Frémont, John Charles
Gray, Robert
Hall, Charles Francis
Henson, Matthew Alexander
Hunt, Wilson Price
Kane, Elisha Kent
King, Clarence
Lewis, Meriwether
Long, Stephen Harriman
MacMillan, Donald Baxter
Maury, Matthew Fontaine
Peary, Robert Edwin
Pike, Zebulon Montgomery
Pond, Peter
Powell, John Wesley
Roosevelt, Theodore
Sheldon, May French
Smith, Jedediah Strong
Walker, Joseph Reddeford
Wheeler, George Montague
Wilkes, Charles
Wyeth, Nathaniel Jarvis

ANGLO-IRISH

McClintock, Francis Leopold
McClure, Robert John Le Mesurier
Shackleton, Ernest Henry

ARAB

Ibn Battūta
Idrīsī, al-

AUSTRALIAN

Giles, Ernest
Hume, Hamilton
Mawson, Douglas
Wentworth, William Charles
Wilkins, George Hubert
Wills, William John

LIST OF EXPLORERS BY NATIONALITY

AUSTRIAN

Payer, Julius von

BELGIAN

Hennepin, Louis

BRAZILIAN

Rondón, Cândido Mariano

CANADIAN

Fraser, Simon
Hind, Henry Youle
Ogden, Peter Skene
Sinclair, James

CANADIAN-AMERICAN

Stefansson, Vilhjalmur

CARTHAGINIAN

Hanno

CHINESE

Xuan Zang
Zhang Qian
Zheng He

DANISH

Bering, Vitus Jonassen
Rasmussen, Knud Johan Victor

DUTCH

Barents, Willem
Hartog, Dirck
Jansz, Willem
Linschoten, Jan Huyghen van
Roggeveen, Jacob
Schouten, Willem Corneliszoon
Tasman, Abel Janszoon
Tinné, Alexine

ENGLISH

Anson, George
Back, George
Baffin, William
Baker, Samuel White
Banks, Joseph
Barrow, John
Bates, Henry Walter
Bell, Gertrude Margaret Lowthian
Blaxland, Gregory
Bligh, William
Burton, Richard Francis
Bylot, Robert
Byron, John
Cameron, Verney Lovett
Carteret, Philip
Cavendish, Thomas
Chancellor, Richard
Cook, James
Dampier, William Cecil
Darwin, Charles Robert
Davis, John
Denham, Dixon
Doughty, Charles Montagu
Drake, Francis
Everest, George
Eyre, Edward John
Fawcett, Percy Harrison
Fitzroy, Robert
Flinders, Matthew
Foxe, Luke
Franklin, John
Frobisher, Martin
Fuchs, Vivian Ernest
Gilbert, Humphrey
Hadley, John
Hakluyt, Richard
Hargraves, Edward Hammond
Harrison, John
Hearne, Samuel
Herbert, Walter William
Hudson, Henry
Jenkinson, Anthony
Kelsey, Henry
Kingsley, Mary Henrietta
Lander, Richard Lemon
Parry, William Edward
Purchas, Samuel
Raleigh, Walter
Ross, James Clark
Schomburgk, Robert Hermann
Scoresby, William
Scott, Robert Falcon

Smith, John
Smith, William
Speke, John Hanning
Stark, Freya
Sturt, Charles
Thesiger, Wilfred Patrick
Thompson, David
Vancouver, George
Wallace, Alfred Russel
Wallis, Samuel
Whymper, Edward
Willoughby, Hugh
Younghusband, Francis Edward

FRENCH

Audubon, John James
Baudin, Nicolas
Bethencourt, Jean de
Bougainville, Louis-Antoine de
Brulé, Etienne
Caillié, René-Auguste
Cartier, Jacques
Champlain, Samuel de
Charcot, Jean-Baptiste-Étienne-Auguste
Charlevoix, Pierre François Xavier de
Cousteau, Jacques-Yves
David-Neel, Alexandra
Dulhut, Daniel Greysolon, Sieur
Dumont d'Urville, Jules-Sébastien-César
Duveyrier, Henri
Entrecasteaux, Antoine Raymond Joseph de
    Bruni, Chevalier d'
Foucauld, Charles-Eugene de
Groseilliers, Médard Chouart, Sieur de
La Condamine, Charles-Marie de
La Pérouse, Jean François de Galaup, Comte de
La Salle, René Robert Cavelier, Sieur de
Marchand, Jean-Baptiste
Marcos de Niza
Marquette, Jacques
Nicollet de Belleborne, Jean
Radisson, Pierre Esprit
William of Rubruck

FRENCH-AMERICAN

Du Chaillu, Paul Belloni

FRENCH-CANADIAN

Drouillard, George
Iberville, Pierre Le Moyne, Sieur d'

Jolliet, Louis
La Vérendrye, Pierre Gaultier de Varennes,
    Sieur de

GERMAN

Barth, Heinrich
Drygalski, Erich Dagobert von
Federmann, Nikolaus
Forster, Johann Georg Adam
Forster, Johann Reinhold
Hornemann, Friedrich Konrad
Humboldt, Alexander von
Leichhardt, Friedrich Wilhelm Ludwig
Nachtigal, Gustav
Richthofen, Ferdinand Paul Wilhelm, Freiherr
    von
Rohlfs, Friedrich Gerhard
Schiltberger, Johann
Schnitzer, Eduard
Schweinfurth, Georg August
Wegener, Alfred Lothar

GREEK

Alexander the Great
Eratosthenes
Herodotus of Halicarnassus
Hipparchus
Nearchus
Ptolemy

IRISH

Brendan, Saint
Burke, Robert O'Hara
Houghton, Daniel
Palliser, John

ITALIAN

Abruzzi, Luigi Amedeo, Duke of the
Cabot, John
Cabot, Sebastian
Cadamosto, Alvise da
Carpini, Giovanni de Plano
Columbus, Christopher
Conti, Nicolò de
Goes, Bento de
Kino, Eusebio Francisco
Malaspina, Alejandro
Nobile, Umberto

LIST OF EXPLORERS BY NATIONALITY

Odoric of Pordenone
Pigafetta, Antonio Francesco
Polo, Marco
Ricci, Matteo
Varthema, Ludovico di
Verrazano, Giovanni da
Vespucci, Amerigo
Zeno, Antonio

ITALIAN-FRENCH

Brazza, Pierre-Paul-François-Camille
   Savorgnan de

NEW ZEALANDER

Hillary, Edmund Percival

NORSE

Erikson, Leif
Erik the Red
Herjolfsson, Bjarni
Karlsefni, Thorfinn

NORWEGIAN

Amundsen, Roald Engelbregt Gravning
Borchgrevink, Carstens Egeberg
Heyerdahl, Thor
Nansen, Fridtjof
Sverdrup, Otto Neumann

NORWEGIAN-CANADIAN

Larsen, Henry Asbjorn

PORTUGUESE

Albuquerque, Afonso de
Alvares, Francisco
Barbosa, Duarte
Cabral, Pedro Álvares
Cabrillo, Juan Rodriguez
Cão, Diogo
Covilhã, Pêro da
Dias, Bartolomeu
Eannes, Gil
Gama, Vasco da
Lobo, Jerome
Lopes de Sequeira, Diogo

Magellan, Ferdinand
Quirós, Pedro Fernandez de
Rapôso de Tavares, Antonio
Sintra, Pedro de
Teixeira, Pedro de
Torres, Luis Vaez de
Tristão, Nuño
Zarco, João Gonçalves

RUSSIAN

Bellingshausen, Fabian Gottlieb von
Chirikov, Aleksei
Dezhnev, Semyon Ivanov
Kotzebue, Otto von
Krusenstern, Adam Ivan von
Lütke, Fyodor Petrovich
Przhevalski, Nikolai Mikhaylovich
Yermak, Timofeyevich

SCOTTISH

Bruce, James
Campbell, Robert
Clapperton, Hugh
Dalrymple, Alexander
Grant, James Augustus
Laing, Alexander Gordon
Livingstone, David
Mackenzie, Alexander
McKenzie, Donald
Park, Mungo
Rae, John
Simpson, Thomas
Stuart, John McDouall
Thomson, Joseph

SCOTTISH-AMERICAN

Stuart, Robert

SPANISH

Acuña, Cristóbal de
Alaminos, Antón de
Almagro, Diego de
Alvarado, Pedro de
Alvarez de Pineda, Alonso
Anza, Juan Bautista de
Balboa, Vasco Nuñez de
Bastidas, Rodrigo de
Benalcázar, Sebastián de

Bodega y Quadra, Juan Francisco de la
Cabeza de Vaca, Álvar Núñez
Coronado, Francisco Vásquez de
Cortés, Hernán
Elcano, Juan Sebastián de
Escalante, Silvestre Vélez de
Garcés, Francisco Tomas Hermenegildo
Hezeta, Bruno de
Irala, Domingo Martínez de
Jiménez de Quesada, Gonzalo
La Cosa, Juan de
Las Casas, Bartolomé de
Legazpi, Miguel López de
Martínez, Estéban José
Mendaña de Nehra, Alvaro de
Narváez, Pánfilo de
Ojeda, Alonso de
Oñate, Juan de
Orellana, Francisco de
Pérez Hernández, Juan Josef
Pinzón, Martín Alonso
Pinzón, Vicente Yáñez
Pizarro, Francisco
Ponce de León, Juan
Rivera, Juan Maria de
Serra, Junípero
Soto, Hernando de

Urdaneta, Andrés de
Vial, Pedro
Xavier, Saint Francis

SWEDISH

Andrée, Salomon August
Hedin, Sven Anders
Solander, Daniel Carl

SWEDISH-FINNISH

Nordenskiöld, Nils Adolf Erik

SWISS

Burckhardt, Johann Ludwig

WELSH

Button, Thomas

WELSH-AMERICAN

Stanley, Henry Morton

LIST OF EXPLORERS BY AREA OF EXPLORATION

Profiled explorers are listed alphabetically below under the major regions of their explorations. Within those broad regions, specific areas explored are listed after an individual's name. Where no specific locations are given, it is either because the exact location is vague or unknown or because the individual's explorations within the region were so wide-ranging as to make a more specific designation arbitrary. Present-day place names have been used in this listing; question marks indicate cases where there is doubt concerning the specific area explored. For a more thorough understanding of the regions explored by any of the profiled explorers, readers are encouraged to consult the appropriate biographical profile.

AFRICA

Akeley, Delia Denning: Kenya; Zaire

Akeley, Mary Lee Jobe: Central Africa

Alvares, Francisco: Ethiopia

Baker, Samuel White: source of the White Nile; Sudan

Barth, Heinrich: North and Central Africa; Timbuktu

Brazza, Pierre-Paul-François-Camille Savorgnan de: Central Africa

Bruce, James: source of the Blue Nile

Burckhardt, Johann Ludwig: East Africa

Burton, Richard Francis: East and West Africa; Lake Tanganyika

Cadamosto, Alvise da: coastal West Africa

Caillié, René-Auguste: North Africa; Sahara Desert; Timbuktu

Cameron, Verney Lovett: Central Africa

Cão, Diogo: coastal West Africa

Chaillé-Long, Charles: Egypt; Uganda; Zaire

Clapperton, Hugh: Lake Chad; Niger River; West Africa

Covilhã, Pêro da: Ethiopia

Denham, Dixon: Lake Chad; West Africa

Dias, Bartolomeu: Cape of Good Hope; coastal West Africa

Du Chaillu, Paul Belloni: Central Africa

Duveyrier, Henri: Sahara Desert

Eannes, Gil: Cape Bojador

Foucauld, Charles-Eugene de: Algeria; Morocco

Grant, James Augustus: East Central Africa; Lake Victoria; source of the White Nile

Hanno: coastal West Africa

Herodotus of Halicarnassus: Egypt; North Africa; source of the Nile

Hornemann, Friedrich Konrad: North Africa

Houghton, Daniel: Niger River

Ibn Battūta: Egypt; Timbuktu

Kingsley, Mary Henrietta: Ogowe River; West Africa

Laing, Alexander Gordon: West Africa

Lander, Richard Lemon: Niger River; West Africa

LIST OF EXPLORERS BY AREA OF EXPLORATION

Livingstone, David: Central Africa; southern Africa

Lobo, Jerome: East Africa

Marchand, Jean-Baptiste: Ivory Coast; Niger River; Sudan

Nachtigal, Gustav: Sahara Desert; Sudan

Park, Mungo: Niger River

Rohlfs, Friedrich Gerhard: North Africa

Schnitzer, Eduard: East Africa

Schweinfurth, Georg August: East and Central Africa

Sheldon, May French: East Africa

Sintra, Pedro de: coastal West Africa

Speke, John Hanning: East Central Africa; Lake Victoria; source of the White Nile

Stanley, Henry Morton: Central Africa

Thomson, Joseph

Tinné, Alexine: Central Africa; Nile River; Sahara Desert

Tristão, Nuño: coastal West Africa

Zarco, João Gonçalves: coastal West Africa; Madeira

ANTARCTIC

Amundsen, Roald Engelbregt Gravning: South Pole

Bellingshausen, Fabian Gottlieb von

Borchgrevink, Carstens Egeberg

Byrd, Richard Evelyn: South Pole

Charcot, Jean-Baptiste-Étienne-Auguste: Graham Land; Palmer Archipelago

Drygalski, Erich Dagobert von

Dumont d'Urville, Jules-Sébastien-César: Adélie Coast

Ellsworth, Lincoln

Fuchs, Vivian Ernest: South Pole

Hillary, Edmund Percival: South Pole

Mawson, Douglas

Ross, James Clark: Ross Ice Shelf; Victoria Land

Scott, Robert Falcon: South Pole

Shackleton, Ernest Henry

Smith, William: Graham Land; South Shetland Islands

Wilkins, George Hubert

ARCTIC

Abruzzi, Luigi Amedeo, Duke of the

Amundsen, Roald Engelbregt Gravning: Northwest Passage

Andrée, Salomon August

Back, George: Canadian Arctic

Baffin, William: Greenland; Northwest Passage

Barents, Willem: Northeast Passage

Bennett, Floyd: North Pole

Bering, Vitus Jonassen: Alaska; Siberia

Boyd, Louise Arner: Greenland

Button, Thomas: Hudson Bay; Northwest Passage

Bylot, Robert: Hudson Bay; Northwest Passage

Byrd, Richard Evelyn: North Pole

Chancellor, Richard: Northeast Passage; Russia

Chirikov, Aleksei: Alaska; Siberia

Cook, Frederick Albert: Greenland

Davis, John: Baffin Island; Greenland; Northwest Passage

De Long, George Washington: Alaskan and Russian Arctic

Dezhnev, Semyon Ivanov: Bering Strait; Siberia

Drygalski, Erich Dagobert von: Greenland

Ellsworth, Lincoln

Erik the Red: Greenland

Foxe, Luke: Hudson Bay; Northwest Passage

Franklin, John: Northwest Passage

Frobisher, Martin: Greenland; Northwest Passage

Hall, Charles Francis: Canadian Arctic

Henson, Matthew Alexander: Greenland; North Pole

Herbert, Walter William: Arctic Ocean; North Pole

Kane, Elisha Kent: Canadian Arctic

Larsen, Henry Asbjorn: Northwest Passage

Linschoten, Jan Huyghen van: Northeast Passage

MacMillan, Donald Baxter: Baffin Island; Ellesmere Island

McClintock, Francis Leopold: Canadian Arctic

McClure, Robert John Le Mesurier: Northwest Passage

Nansen, Fridtjof: Arctic Ocean; Greenland

Nobile, Umberto: North Pole

Nordenskiöld, Nils Adolf Erik: Greenland; Northeast Passage

Parry, William Edward: Canadian and Norwegian Arctic; Northwest Passage

Payer, Julius von: Franz Josef Land

Peary, Robert Edwin: Greenland; North Pole

Rae, John: Canadian Arctic

Rasmussen, Knud Johan Victor: Canadian Arctic; Greenland

Ross, James Clark: Canadian Arctic; Northwest Passage

Scoresby, William: Greenland; Norwegian Arctic

Simpson, Thomas: Canadian Arctic; Northwest Passage

Stefansson, Vilhjalmur

Sverdrup, Otto Neumann: Canadian Arctic; Greenland

Wegener, Alfred Lothar: Greenland

Wilkins, George Hubert

Willoughby, Hugh: Northeast Passage; Novaya Zemlya

ASIA

Albuquerque, Afonso de: Malabar Coast; Malay Peninsula; Persian Gulf

Alexander the Great

Barbosa, Duarte: India; Philippine Islands; Sumatra

Carpini, Giovanni de Plano: Central Asia

Conti, Nicolò de: Southern Asia

Covilhã, Pêro da: India

David-Neel, Alexandra: Tibet; Western China

Everest, George: India

Gama, Vasco da: Malabar Coast

Goes, Bento de: China; India

Hedin, Sven Anders: Central Asia

Ibn Battūta: China; India

Jenkinson, Anthony: Central Asia

Linschoten, Jan Huyghen van: India

Lopes de Sequeira, Diogo: Indonesia

Nearchus: Arabian Sea; India; Persian Gulf

Odoric of Pordenone

Polo, Marco

Przhevalski, Nikolai Mikhaylovich: Central Asia

Ricci, Matteo: China

Richthofen, Ferdinand Paul Wilhelm, Freiherr von: China

Schiltberger, Johann

Varthema, Ludovico di: India; Southeast Asia

Wallace, Alfred Russel: Malay Archipelago

William of Rubruck: Central Asia

Xavier, Saint Francis: India; Japan; Malay Archipelago

Xuan Zang: Central Asia; India

Yermak, Timofeyevich: Siberia

Younghusband, Francis Edward: India, Tibet

Zhang Qian: Central Asia

Zheng He

AUSTRALIA

Baudin, Nicolas: coastal Australia

Blaxland, Gregory: Blue Mountains

Burke, Robert O'Hara

Dampier, William Cecil: Northwest Coast

Entrecasteaux, Antoine Raymond Joseph de Bruni, Chevalier d': coastal Australia

Eyre, Edward John: southern Australia

Flinders, Matthew: coastal Australia

Giles, Ernest

Hargraves, Edward Hammond: New South Wales

Hartog, Dirck: West Coast

Hume, Hamilton: New South Wales; Victoria

Jansz, Willem: North and West coasts

Leichhardt, Friedrich Wilhelm Ludwig: northeastern Australia

Stuart, John McDouall

Sturt, Charles: New South Wales; Simpson Desert; Victoria

Tasman, Abel Janszoon: north coast; Tasmania

Wentworth, William Charles: Blue Mountains

Wills, William John

CENTRAL AMERICA, MEXICO, AND THE WEST INDIES

Alaminos, Antón de: Gulf of Mexico

Alvarado, Pedro de: El Salvador; Guatemala; Mexico

Alvarez de Pineda, Alonso: Gulf of Mexico

Balboa, Vasco Nuñez de: Panama

Bastidas, Rodrigo de: Panama

Cabrillo, Juan Rodriguez: Central America; Mexico

Columbus, Christopher: coastal Central and South America; West Indies

Cortés, Hernán: Mexico

Humboldt, Alexander von: Mexico

La Cosa, Juan de: Panama

Las Casas, Bartolomé de: Mexico

Narváez, Pánfilo de: Cuba; Mexico

Ojeda, Alonso de: Hispaniola

Pinzón, Martín Alonzo: West Indies

Pinzón, Vicente Yáñez: West Indies; Yucatán Peninsula

Ponce de León, Juan: West Indies

CIRCUMNAVIGATORS

Anson, George

Banks, Joseph

Bougainville, Louis-Antoine de

Byron, John

Carteret, Philip

Cavendish, Thomas

Cook, James
Dampier, William Cecil
Drake, Francis
Elcano, Juan Sebastián de
Entrecasteaux, Antoine Raymond Joseph de Bruni, Chevalier d'
Forster, Johann Georg Adam
Forster, Johann Reinhold
Kotzebue, Otto von
Krusenstern, Adam Ivan von
Lütke, Fyodor Petrovich
Magellan, Ferdinand
Malaspina, Alejandro
Pigafetta, Antonio Francesco
Solander, Daniel Carl
Wallis, Samuel
Wilkes, Charles

MIDDLE EAST

Alexander the Great
Bell, Gertrude Margaret Lowthian
Burckhardt, Johann Ludwig: Arabian Peninsula
Burton, Richard Francis: Mecca; Medina
Covilhã, Pêro da: Mecca; Medina
Doughty, Charles Montagu: Arabia
Herodotus of Halicarnassus
Ibn Battūta
Schiltberger, Johann: Mecca
Stark, Freya
Thesiger, Wilfred Patrick: Arabia, Iraq
Varthema, Ludovico di: Mecca; Medina

MISCELLANEOUS

Bethencourt, Jean de: Canary Islands
Brendan, Saint: Atlantic Ocean?
Cousteau, Jacques-Yves: oceans of the world
Herodotus of Halicarnassus: Mediterranean and Balkan Europe
Heyerdahl, Thor: Atlantic Ocean
Idrīsī, al-: Asia Minor; Europe; North Africa
Zeno, Antonio: Atlantic Ocean?

NORTH AMERICA

Akeley, Mary Lee Jobe: northwestern Canada
Anza, Juan Bautista de: California; southwestern United States
Ashley, William Henry: Green River
Audubon, John James: United States
Bartram, John: eastern United States

Bodega y Quadra, Juan Francisco de la: northwest Pacific Coast
Bonneville, Benjamin Louis Eulalie de: Rocky Mountains
Boone, Daniel: Kentucky
Brulé, Etienne: eastern United States and Canada; Great Lakes
Cabeza de Vaca, Álvar Núñez: northern Mexico; southern United States
Cabot, John: Newfoundland?
Cabot, Sebastian: eastern coastal Canada; Hudson Bay
Cabrillo, Juan Rodriguez: California
Campbell, Robert: Northwest Territories; Yukon
Cartier, Jacques: Gulf of St. Lawrence; St. Lawrence River
Champlain, Samuel de: eastern Canada
Charlevoix, Pierre François Xavier de: Great Lakes; Mississippi River
Clark, William: Missouri River; northwestern United States
Colter, John: Idaho; Montana; Wyoming
Coronado, Francisco Vásquez de: southwestern United States
Drake, Francis: coastal California
Drouillard, George: Rocky Mountains
Dulhut, Daniel Greysolon, Sieur: upper Great Lakes
Erikson, Leif: Newfoundland?
Escalante, Silvestre Vélez de: southwestern United States
Fraser, Simon: western Canada
Frémont, John Charles: western United States
Garcés, Francisco Tomas Hermenegildo: southwestern United States
Gilbert, Humphrey: Newfoundland
Gray, Robert: Columbia River; northwest Pacific Coast
Groseilliers, Médard Chouart, Sieur de: Hudson Bay
Hearne, Samuel: Coppermine River; northwestern Canada
Hennepin, Louis: Niagara Falls; upper Mississippi River
Herjolfsson, Bjarni: Newfoundland?
Hezeta, Bruno de: Columbia River; northwest Pacific Coast
Hind, Henry Youle: Labrador; Manitoba; Saskatchewan
Hudson, Henry: Hudson Bay; Hudson River
Hunt, Wilson Price: western United States
Iberville, Pierre Le Moyne, Sieur d': Hudson Bay; lower Mississippi River

Jolliet, Louis: upper Mississippi River
Karlsefni, Thorfinn: Newfoundland?
Kelsey, Henry: Manitoba; Saskatchewan
King, Clarence: western United States
Kino, Eusebio Francisco: California; southwestern United States
La Salle, René Robert Cavelier, Sieur de: Great Lakes; Mississippi River
La Vérendrye, Pierre Gaultier de Varennes, Sieur de: Central Canada; North Central United States
Lewis, Meriwether: Missouri River; northwestern United States
Long, Stephen Harriman: western United States
Mackenzie, Alexander: Mackenzie River; western Canada
Malaspina, Alejandro: Pacific Coast
Marcos de Niza: Arizona; New Mexico
Marquette, Jacques: Mississippi River
Martínez, Estéban José: northwest Pacific Coast
McKenzie, Donald: Snake River
Narváez, Pánfilo de: Florida
Nicollet de Belleborne, Jean: Lake Michigan
Ogden, Peter Skene: western United States
Oñate, Juan de: southwestern United States
Palliser, John: southwestern Canada
Pérez Hernández, Juan Josef: northwest Pacific Coast
Pike, Zebulon Montgomery: southwestern United States
Ponce de León, Juan: Florida
Pond, Peter: Canada
Powell, John Wesley: Colorado River
Radisson, Pierre Esprit: Hudson Bay
Raleigh, Walter: North Carolina
Rivera, Juan Maria de: southwestern United States
Serra, Junípero: California
Sinclair, James: Oregon Territory; western Canada
Smith, Jedediah Strong: western United States
Smith, John: New England; Virginia
Soto, Hernando de: Mississippi River; southwestern United States
Stuart, Robert: western United States
Thompson, David: Columbia River; western Canada
Vancouver, George: northwest Pacific Coast
Verrazano, Giovanni da: Atlantic Coast
Vial, Pedro: southwestern United States
Walker, Joseph Reddeford: California; Nevada; Utah

Wheeler, George Montague: western United States
Wyeth, Nathaniel Jarvis: Oregon

PACIFIC

Banks, Joseph: South Pacific; Tahiti
Bligh, William: Australia; South Pacific; Tahiti
Bougainville, Louis-Antoine de: Tahiti
Carteret, Philip: South Pacific
Cook, James
Dalrymple, Alexander: South Pacific
Dampier, William Cecil: South Pacific
Darwin, Charles Robert: Galápagos Islands
Dumont d'Urville, Jules-Sébastien-César: South Pacific
Fitzroy, Robert
Forster, Johann Georg Adam: South Pacific; Tahiti
Forster, Johann Reinhold: South Pacific; Tahiti
Heyerdahl, Thor: Easter Island; Polynesia
La Pérouse, Jean François de Galaup, Comte de
Legazpi, Miguel López de: Philippine Islands
Mendaña de Nehra, Alvaro de: Marquesas; Santa Cruz Islands; Solomon Islands
Quirós, Pedro Fernandez de: Espíritu Santo
Roggeveen, Jacob: Easter Island; Tuamotu Islands
Schouten, Willem Corneliszoon: Cape Horn; Hoorn Islands; New Guinea
Solander, Daniel Carl: South Pacific; Tahiti
Tasman, Abel Janszoon: Fiji; New Zealand; Tonga
Torres, Luis Vaez de: New Hebrides; Torres Strait
Urdaneta, Andrés de: Moluccas; Philippine Islands
Wallis, Samuel: Tahiti

SOUTH AMERICA

Acuña, Cristóbal de: Amazon River
Almagro, Diego de: Chile; Peru
Alvarado, Pedro de: Ecuador
Bastidas, Rodrigo de: Colombia
Bates, Henry Walter: upper Amazon River Basin
Benalcázar, Sebastián de: Colombia; Ecuador; Peru
Bingham, Hiram: Machu Picchu; Vitcos
Cabeza de Vaca, Álvar Núñez: Central South America

LIST OF EXPLORERS BY AREA OF EXPLORATION

Cabot, Sebastian: Río de la Plata
Cabral, Pedro Álvares: coastal Brazil
Darwin, Charles Robert
Fawcett, Percy Harrison: Bolivia; Brazil; Paraguay
Federmann, Nikolaus: Colombia; Venezuela
Humboldt, Alexander von
Irala, Domingo Martínez de: Central South America
Jiménez de Quesada, Gonzalo: Colombia
La Condamine, Charles-Marie de: Amazon River; Ecuador
La Cosa, Juan de: Colombia
Las Casas, Bartolomé de: Peru
Malaspina, Alejandro: Atlantic and Pacific coasts

Ojeda, Alonso de: Colombia; Venezuela
Orellana, Francisco de: Amazon River
Pinzón, Vicente Yáñez: Brazil
Pizarro, Francisco: Ecuador; Peru
Raleigh, Walter: Orinoco River
Rapôso de Tavares, Antonio
Rondón, Cândido Mariano da Silva: Brazil
Roosevelt, Theodore: Brazil
Schomburgk, Robert Hermann: Guiana
Teixeira, Pedro de: Amazon River
Vespucci, Amerigo: Brazilian Coast
Wallace, Alfred Russel: upper Amazon River Basin
Whymper, Edward: Andes Mountains

BIBLIOGRAPHY

GENERAL WORKS

Albion, Robert J., ed. *Exploration and Discovery.* New York: Macmillan, 1965.

Armstrong, Richard. *The History of Seafaring.* Vol. 2, *The Discoverers.* New York: Frederick A. Praeger, 1969.

Baker, J. N. L. *A History of Geographical Discovery and Exploration.* rev. ed. New York: Cooper Square, 1967.

Bettex, Albert. *The Discovery of the World.* New York: Simon & Schuster, 1960.

Boorstin, Daniel J. *The Discoverers.* New York: Random House, 1983.

Boxer, Charles R. *The Dutch Seaborne Empire, 1600–1800.* New York: Alfred A. Knopf, 1965.

———. *The Portuguese Seaborne Empire, 1415–1825.* London: Hutchinson, 1969.

Brendon, John Adams. *Great Navigators & Discoverers.* London: George G. Harrap, 1929. Reprint. Salem, N.H.: Ayer, 1977.

Burrage, Henry S., ed. *Early English and French Voyages Chiefly from Hakluyt 1534–1608.* New York: Barnes & Noble, 1959.

Cameron, Ian. *Lodestone and Evening Star: The Epic Voyages of Discovery, 1493 B.C.–1896 A.D.* New York: E. P. Dutton, 1965.

———. *To the Farthest Ends of the Earth: 150 Years of World Exploration by the Royal Geographical Society.* New York: E. P. Dutton, 1980.

Cary, M., and E. H. Warmington. *The Ancient Explorers.* London: Methuen, 1929.

Clark, William Ronald. *Explorers of the World.* Garden City, N.Y.: Natural History Press, 1964.

Connell, Evan S. *A Long Desire.* New York: Holt, Rinehart and Winston, 1979.

Crone, G. R. *The Explorers: Great Adventurers Tell Their Own Stories of Discovery.* New York: Thomas Y. Crowell, 1962.

David, Richard, comp. *Hakluyt's Voyages.* London: Chatto & Windus, 1981.

Debenham, Frank. *Discovery and Exploration: An Atlas-History of Man's Journeys into the Unknown.* New York: Crescent Books, 1960.

Delpar, Helen, ed. *The Discoverers: An Encyclopedia of Explorers and Exploration.* New York: McGraw-Hill, 1980.

Divine, David. *The Opening of the World: The Great Age of Maritime Exploration.* New York: G. P. Putnam's Sons, 1973.

Dos Passos, John. *The Portugal Story: Three Centuries of Exploration and Discovery.* Garden City, N.Y.: Doubleday, 1969.

Downs, Robert B. *In Search of New Horizons: Epic Tales of Travel and Exploration.* Chicago: ALA, 1978.

Finger, Charles. *Valiant Vagabonds.* New York: Appleton-Century, 1936. Reprint. Salem, N.H.: Ayer, 1977.

BIBLIOGRAPHY

Fleischer, Suri, and Arleen Keylin. *Exploration and Discovery: As Reported by the New York Times.* Salem, N.H.: Ayer, 1976.

Gersi, Douchan. *Explorer.* Los Angeles: Jeremy P. Tarcher, 1987.

The Glorious Age of Exploration. Garden City, N.Y.: Doubleday, 1973.

Grosvenor, Melville Bell, ed. *Great Adventures with National Geographic: Exploring Land, Sea, and Sky.* Washington, D.C.: National Geographic Society, 1963.

Gvodzdetsky, N. A. *Soviet Geographical Explorations and Discoveries: In the U.S.S.R., Antarctica and World Oceans.* Woodstock, N.Y.: Beekman, 1975.

Hakluyt, Richard. *The Principal Navigations, Voyages, Traffiques and Discoveries of the English Nation.* Edited by John Masefield. 10 vols. New York: E. P. Dutton, 1927.

Hale, J. R. *Age of Exploration.* New York: Time-Life Books, 1966.

Hamalian, Leo, ed. *Ladies on the Loose: Women Travellers of the Eighteenth and Nineteenth Centuries.* New York: Dodd, Mead, 1981.

Hampden, John, ed. *New Worlds Ahead: Firsthand Accounts of English Voyages.* New York: Farrar, 1968.

Hart, Henry H. *Sea Road to the Indies.* New York: Macmillan, 1950. Reprint. Westport, Conn.: Greenwood, 1971.

Heawood, Edward. *A History of Geographical Discovery in the Seventeenth and Eighteenth Centuries.* New York: Macmillan, 1912. Reprint. New York: Octagon Books, 1965.

Herrmann, Paul. *Conquest by Man.* Translated by Michael Bullock. New York: Harper & Bros., 1954.

———. *The Great Age of Discovery.* Translated by Arnold J. Pomerans. New York: Harper & Bros., 1958. Reprint. Westport, Conn.: Greenwood, 1974.

Humble, Richard. *The Explorers.* Alexandria, Va.: Time-Life Books, 1978.

Jackson, Donald Dale. *The Explorers.* Alexandria, Va.: Time-Life Books, 1983.

Keay, John. *Explorers Extraordinary.* Los Angeles: Jeremy P. Tarcher, 1986.

Key, Charles E. *The Story of Twentieth-Century Exploration.* New York: Alfred A. Knopf, 1938.

Knight, Frank. *Stories of Famous Explorers by Land.* Philadelphia: Westminster Press, 1965.

Lacey, Peter, ed. *Great Adventures That Changed Our World: The World's Great Explorers, Their Triumphs and Tragedies.* Pleasantville, N.Y.: Reader's Digest Association, 1978.

Langnas, I. A. *Dictionary of Discoveries.* New York: Philosophical Library, 1959.

Lansing, Marion. *Great Moments in Exploration.* New York: Doubleday, Doran, 1936.

Leithäuser, Joachim G. *Worlds Beyond the Horizon.* Translated by Hugh Merrick. New York: Alfred A. Knopf, 1955.

Ley, Charles David, ed. *Portuguese Voyages, 1498–1663.* London: E. P. Dutton, 1947.

Lucas, Mary Seymour. *Vast Horizons.* Toronto: Macmillan of Canada, 1943.

Mackay, David. *In the Wake of Cook: Exploration, Science & Empire 1780–1801.* New York: St. Martin's, 1985.

Mallery, Richard D., ed. *Masterworks of Travel and Exploration: Digests of Thirteen Great Classics.* Garden City, NY: Doubleday, 1948. Reprint. Freeport, N.Y.: Books for Libraries, 1970.

Mitchell, J. L. *Earth Conquerors: Lives and Achievements of the Great Explorers.* New York: Simon & Schuster, 1934.

Neider, Charles. *Man Against Nature: Tales of Adventure and Exploration.* New York: Harper & Bros., 1954.

Newby, Eric. *The World Atlas of Exploration.* New York: Crescent Books, 1985.

Newton, Arthur Percival, ed. *The Great Age of Discovery.* London: University of London Press, 1932. Reprint. New York: B. Franklin, 1970.

———. *Travel and Travellers of the Middle Ages.* New York: Alfred A. Knopf, 1950.

Olds, Elizabeth Flagg. *Women of the Four Winds.* Boston: Houghton Mifflin, 1985.

Outhwaite, Leonard. *Unrolling the Map: The Story of Exploration.* rev. ed. New York: John Day, 1972.

Parry, John Horace. *The Age of Reconnaissance: Discovery, Exploration and Settlement, 1450–1650.* rev. ed. Berkeley: University of California Press, 1982.

———. *The Discovery of the Sea.* New York: Dial Press, 1974. Reprint. Berkeley: University of California Press, 1981.

———. *The European Reconnaissance: Selected Documents.* New York: Harper Torchbooks, 1968.

———. *The Spanish Seaborne Empire.* London: Hutchinson, 1966.

———. *Trade and Dominion.* London: Weidenfeld & Nicolson, 1971.

Penrose, Boies. *Travel and Discovery in the Renaissance, 1420–1620.* Cambridge: Harvard University Press, 1952. Reprint. New York: Atheneum, 1962.

Pohl, Frederick J. *Atlantic Crossings Before Columbus.* New York: W. W. Norton, 1961.

Pond, Seymour G. *The History & Romance of Exploration, Told with Pictures.* New York: Cooper Square, 1966.

Prestage, Edgar. *The Portuguese Pioneers.* New York: Macmillan, 1933. Reprint. New York: Barnes & Noble, 1967.

Reid, Alan. *Discovery and Exploration: A Concise History.* London: Gentry Books, 1980.

Rittenhouse, Mignon. *Seven Women Explorers.* Philadelphia: J. B. Lippincott, 1964.

Riverain, Jean. *Concise Encyclopedia of Explorations.* Chicago: Follett, 1969.

Roberts, David. *Great Exploration Hoaxes.* San Francisco: Sierra Club Books, 1982.

Roberts, Gail. *Atlas of Discovery.* New York: Crown, 1973.

Ronan, Colin A. *The Astronomers.* New York: Hill & Wang, 1964.

———. *Discovering the Universe.* New York: Basic Books, 1971.

Rowse, Alfred Leslie. *The Expansion of Elizabethan England.* New York: Macmillan, 1955.

Schurz, William L. *The Manila Galleon.* New York: E. P. Dutton, 1939. Reprint. New York: E. P. Dutton, 1959.

Skelton, R. A. *Explorer's Maps: Chapters in the Cartographic Record of Geographical Discovery.* New York: Spring Books, 1958.

Stefansson, Vilhjalmur, ed. *Great Adventures and Explorations: From the Earliest Times to the Present, as Told by the Explorers Themselves.* rev. ed. New York: Dial Press, 1949. Reprint. New York: Telegraph Books, 1985.

Sykes, Sir Percy. *A History of Exploration from the Earliest Times to the Present Day.* 3d ed. London: Routledge and Kegan Paul, 1949. Reprint. Westport, Conn.: Greenwood, 1976.

Thomas, Lowell. *Untold Story of Exploration.* Garden City, N.Y.: Doubleday, 1935.

Thomson, J. O. *History of Ancient Geography.* Cambridge: Cambridge University Press, 1948.

Tinling, Marion. *Women into the Unknown: A Sourcebook on Women Explorers and Travelers.* New York: Greenwood, 1989.

Williams, Neville. *The Sea Dogs: Privateers, Plunder and Piracy in the Elizabethan Age.* New York: Macmillan, 1975.

Williamson, James A. *The Age of Drake.* 5th ed. New York: Meridian Books, 1965.

Wood, H. J. *Exploration and Discovery.* London: Hutchinson, 1951.

Wright, Helen, and Samuel Rapport. *The Great Explorers.* New York: Harper & Bros., 1957.

Wright, Louis B. *Gold, Glory, and the Gospel: The Adventurous Lives and Times of the Renaissance Explorers.* New York: Atheneum, 1970.

WORKS BY REGION OF EXPLORATION

Africa

Axelson, Eric Victor. *Congo to Cape.* New York: Harper & Row, 1973.

———. *Portugal and the Scramble for Africa, 1875–1891.* Johannesburg: Witwatersrand University Press, 1967.

———, ed. *South African Explorers.* New York: Oxford University Press, 1954.

Birmingham, David. *The Portuguese Conquest of Angola.* London: Oxford University Press, 1965.

Bovill, Edward William. *The Golden Trade of the Moors.* New York: Oxford University Press, 1958.

———. *The Niger Explored.* London: Oxford University Press, 1968.

Duffy, James. *Portuguese Africa.* Cambridge: Harvard University Press, 1968.

Exploring Africa and Asia. Garden City, NY: Doubleday, 1973.

BIBLIOGRAPHY

Forbath, Peter. *The River Congo*. New York: Harper & Row, 1977.

Gardner, Brian. *The Quest for Timbuctoo*. New York: Harcourt, Brace, & World, 1969.

Hallett, Robin. *The Penetration of Africa to 1815*. New York: Frederick A. Praeger, 1965.

———, ed. *Records of the African Association, 1788–1821*. London: Thomas Nelson and Sons, 1964.

Hammond, Richard James. *Portugal and Africa, 1815–1910: A Study in Uneconomic Imperialism*. Stanford: Stanford University Press, 1966.

Hibbert, Christopher. *Africa Explored*. New York: W. W. Norton, 1983.

Howard, C., and J. H. Plumb, eds. *West African Explorers*. New York: Oxford University Press, 1952.

Lloyd, Christopher. *The Search for the Niger*. Newton Abbot: Readers Union, 1974.

Miller, C. *The Lunatic Express*. New York: Macmillan, 1971.

Moorehead, Alan. *The Blue Nile*. rev. ed. New York: Vintage Books, 1983.

———. *The White Nile*. rev. ed. New York: Harper & Row, 1971.

Moorhouse, Geoffrey. *The Fearful Void*. Philadelphia: J. B. Lippincott, 1974.

Mountfield, David. *A History of African Exploration*. Northbrook, Ill.: Domus Books, 1976.

Oliver, Caroline. *Western Women in Colonial Africa*. Westport, Conn.: Greenwood, 1982.

Oliver, Roland Anthony, and Caroline Oliver. *Africa in the Days of Exploration*. Englewood Cliffs, N.J.: Prentice-Hall, 1965.

Perham, Margery, and Jack Simmons, comps. *African Discovery: An Anthology of Exploration*. 2d ed. London: Faber & Faber, 1957.

Porch, Douglas. *The Conquest of the Sahara*. New York: Alfred A. Knopf, 1984.

Richards, Charles Anthony Langdon, and James Place, eds. *East African Explorers*. New York: Oxford University Press, 1959.

Robinson, Ronald, John Gallacher, and Alice Denny. *Africa and the Victorians: The Climax of Imperialism in the Dark Continent*. New York: St. Martins, 1961. Reprint. Garden City, N.Y.: Doubleday, 1968.

Rotberg, Robert I., ed. *Africa and Its Explorers: Motives, Methods, and Impact*. Cambridge: Harvard University Press, 1970.

Severin, Timothy. *The African Adventure*. New York: E. P. Dutton, 1973.

Silverberg, Robert. *The Realm of Prester John*. Garden City, N.Y.: Doubleday, 1972.

Welland, James. *The Great Sahara*. New York: E. P. Dutton, 1965.

West, Richard. *Congo*. New York: Holt, Rinehart and Winston, 1972.

Arctic, Northwest Passage, Antarctic

Andrist, Ralph K. *Heroes of Polar Exploration*. New York: American Heritage, 1962.

Barrow, John. *A Chronological History of Voyages into the Arctic Regions*. 1818. Reprint. Newton Abbot: David & Charles Reprints, 1971.

Berton, Pierre. *The Arctic Grail: The Quest for the North West Passage and the North Pole, 1818–1909*. New York: Viking, 1988.

Bertrand, Kenneth J. *Americans in Antarctica, 1775–1948*. New York: American Geographical Society, 1971.

Bowman, Gerald. *Men of Antarctica*. New York: Fleet, 1958.

Burpee, Lawrence J. *The Search for the Western Sea: The Story of the Exploration of Northwestern America*. rev. ed. Toronto: Macmillan of Canada, 1935.

Cantwell, Robert. *The Hidden Northwest*. Philadelphia: J. B. Lippincott, 1972.

Caswell, John E. *Arctic Frontiers*. Norman: University of Oklahoma Press, 1956.

Chapman, Walker. *The Loneliest Continent*. Boston: New York Graphic Society, 1964.

Cooke, Alan, and Clive Holland. *The Exploration of Northern Canada, 500–1920*. Toronto: Arctic History Press, 1978.

Cooper, Paul Fenimore. *Island of the Lost*. New York: Putnam, 1961.

Crouse, Nellis M. *In Quest of a Western Ocean*. London: J. M. Dent, 1928.

———. *The Search for the North Pole*. New York: Richard R. Smith, 1947.

———. *The Search for the North-West Passage*. New York: Columbia University Press, 1934.

Davies, K. G. *The North Atlantic World in the Seventeenth Century*. Minneapolis: University of Minnesota Press, 1974.

Day, Alan Edwin. *Search for the Northwest Passage: An Annotated Bibliography*. New York: Garland, 1986.

Debenham, Frank. *Antarctica: The Story of a Continent*. New York: Macmillan, 1961.

Dodge, E. S. *Northwest by Sea*. New York: Oxford University Press, 1961.

Euller, John. *Arctic World*. New York: Abelard-Schuman, 1958.

Fedorov, Y. *Polar Diaries*. Chicago: Imported Publications, 1983.

Freuchen, Peter. *Book of Arctic Exploration*. New York: Coward-McCann, 1962.

Friis, Herman R., and Shelby G. Bale, eds. *United States Polar Exploration*. Athens: Ohio University Press, 1970.

Giaver, John. *The White Desert: The Official Account of the Norwegian-British-Swedish Antarctic Expedition*. New York: E. P. Dutton, 1954.

Golder, Frank Alfred. *Russian Expansion on the Pacific, 1641–1850*. Cleveland: Arthur H. Clark, 1914. Reprint. Gloucester, Mass.: Peter Smith, 1960.

Greely, A. W. *Handbook of Polar Discoveries*. T. Fisher Unwin, 1910.

Herbert, Wally. *Across the Top of the World*. London: Longmans, 1969.

Hobbs, William Herbert. *Explorers of the Antarctic*. New York: House of Field, 1941.

Hunt, William R. *To Stand at the Pole*. New York: Stein and Day, 1981.

Jones, Gwyn. *A History of the Vikings*. New York: Oxford University Press, 1968.

————. *The Norse Atlantic Saga: Being the Norse Voyages of Discovery and Settlement to Iceland, Greenland, America*. London: Oxford University Press, 1964.

Jones, Lawrence F., and George Lonn. *Pathfinders of the North*. Toronto: Pitt, 1969.

Keating, Bern. *The Northwest Passage: From the Mathew to the Manhattan: 1497 to 1969*. Chicago: Rand McNally, 1970.

Kirwan, Lawrence Park. *A History of Polar Exploration*. New York: W. W. Norton, 1959.

Lamb, Harold. *New Found World*. New York: Doubleday, 1955.

Land, Barbara. *The New Explorers: Women in Antarctica*. New York: Dodd, Mead, 1981.

The Last Frontiers. Garden City, N.Y.: Doubleday, 1973.

Laut, Agnes. *The Adventurers of England on Hudson Bay*. Toronto: University of Toronto Press, 1964.

Leacock, Stephen. *Adventurers of the Far North*. Toronto: University of Toronto Press, 1964.

Lehane, Brendan. *The Northwest Passage*. Alexandria, Va.: Time-Life Books, 1981.

Ley, Willy. *The Poles*. New York: Time, 1962.

Markham, Clements. *The Lands of Silence*. Cambridge: Cambridge University Press, 1921.

Mickleburgh, Edwin. *Beyond the Frozen Sea: Visions of Antarctica*. New York: St. Martin's, 1987.

Mirsky, Jeannette. *To the Arctic! The Story of Northern Exploration from Earliest Times to the Present*. Chicago: University of Chicago Press, 1970.

Mountfield, David. *A History of Polar Exploration*. New York: Dial, 1974.

Mowat, Farley. *Canada North*. Boston: Little, Brown, 1968.

————, ed. *Ordeal By Ice*. Boston: Little, Brown, 1961.

————, ed. *The Polar Passion: The Quest for the North Pole, with Selections from Arctic Journals*. Boston: Little, Brown, 1968.

Neatby, Leslie Hilda. *Conquest of the Last Frontier*. Athens: Ohio University Press, 1966.

————. *Discovery in Russian and Siberian Waters*. Athens: Ohio University Press, 1973.

————. *In Quest of the North-West Passage*. New York: Thomas Y. Crowell, 1958.

————. *Search for Franklin*. Edmonton: M. G. Hurtig, 1970.

Neider, Charles, ed. *Antarctica: Authentic Accounts of Life and Exploration in the World's Highest, Driest, Windiest, Coldest and Most Remote Continent*. New York: Random House, 1972.

Oleson, Trvggvi J. *Early Voyages and Northern Approaches, 1000–1632*. New York: Oxford University Press, 1964.

Orlob, Helen. *The Northeast Passage: Black Water, White Ice*. New York: Thomas Nelson, 1977.

BIBLIOGRAPHY

Ortzen, Len. *Famous Arctic Adventures*. London: Barker, 1972.

Rasky, Frank. *The North Pole or Bust: Explorers of the North*. Toronto: McGraw-Hill Ryerson Ltd., 1977.

Ross, Frank Xavier. *Frozen Frontier: The Story of the Arctic*. New York: Thomas Y. Crowell, 1961.

Sauer, Carl O. *Northern Mists*. Berkeley: University of California Press, 1968.

Smith, William D. *Northwest Passage*. New York: American Heritage, 1970.

Speck, Gordon. *Northwest Explorations*. 2d ed. Portland, Oreg.: Binford-Metropolitan, 1970.

Stefansson, Vilhjalmur. *Greenland*. New York: Doubleday, Doran, 1942.

———. *Northwest to Fortune*. New York: Duell, Sloan and Pearce, 1958.

———. *Unsolved Mysteries of the Arctic*. New York: Macmillan, 1939.

Sullivan, Walter. *Quest for a Continent*. New York: McGraw-Hill, 1957.

Thomson, George Malcolm. *The Search for the North-West Passage*. New York: Macmillan, 1975.

Victor, Paul-Emile. *Man and the Conquest of the Poles*. New York: Simon & Schuster, 1964.

Weems, John Edward. *Race for the Pole*. New York: Henry Holt, 1960.

Wilkinson, Doug. *Arctic Fever*. Toronto: Clarke, Irwin, 1971.

Williams, Glyndwr. *The British Search for the North-west Passage in the Eighteenth Century*. London: Longmans, Green, 1962.

Zaslow, Morris. *A Century of Canada's Arctic Islands, 1800–1980*. Ottawa: Royal Society of Canada, 1981.

———. *The Opening of the Canadian North*. Toronto: McClelland and Stewart, 1971.

Asia

Bidwell, Robin. *Travelers in Arabia*. London: Hamlyn, 1976.

Bishop, Peter. *The Myth of Shangri-la: Tibet, Travel Writing and the Western Creation of Sacred Landscape*. Berkeley: University of California Press, 1989.

Dunne, George H. *Generation of Giants: The Story of the Jesuits in China in the Last Decades of the Ming Dynasty*. Notre Dame, Ind.: University of Notre Dame Press, 1962.

Exploring Africa and Asia. Garden City, N.Y.: Doubleday, 1973.

Freeth, Zahra, and Victor Winstone. *Explorers of Arabia*. New York: Holmes and Meier, 1978.

Hopkirk, Peter. *Trespassers on the Roof of the World: The Secret Exploration of Tibet*. Los Angeles: Jeremy P. Tarcher, 1982.

Keay, John. *When Men and Mountains Meet: The Explorers of the Western Himalayas, 1820–75*. Hamden, Conn.: Shoe String, 1981.

Lach, Donald. *Asia in the Making of Europe*. Chicago: University of Chicago Press, 1965.

Landström, Björn. *The Quest for India*. Garden City, N.Y.: Doubleday, 1964.

Lattimore, Owen. *The Desert Road to Turkestan*. London: Methuen, 1928.

Lattimore, Owen, and Eleanor Lattimore. *Silks, Spices and Empire: Asia Seen Through the Eyes of Its Discoverers*. New York: Delacorte, 1968.

Macgregor, John. *Tibet—A Chronicle of Exploration*. New York: Frederick A. Praeger, 1970.

Mason, Kenneth. *Abode of Snow: A History of Himalayan Exploration and Mountaineering*. New York: E. P. Dutton, 1955.

Miller, Luree. *On Top of the World: Five Women Explorers in Tibet*. Seattle: Mountaineers, 1984.

Mirsky, Jeannette, ed. *The Great Chinese Travelers: An Anthology*. New York: Pantheon Books, 1964.

Severin, Timothy. *The Oriental Adventure: Explorers of the East*. Boston: Little, Brown.

Warner, Langdon. *The Long Old Road in China*. New York: Doubleday, Page, 1926.

Australia

Cameron, Roderick. *Australia: History and Horizons*. New York: Columbia University Press, 1971.

Carter, Jeff. *In the Steps of the Explorers*. Sydney: Angus and Robertson, 1970.

Carter, Paul. *The Road to Botany Bay: An Exploration of Landscape and History*. New York: Alfred A. Knopf, 1987.

Feeken, Erwin H. J., G. E. E. Feeken, and O. H. K. Spate. *The Discovery and Exploration of Australia.* London: Thomas Nelson and Sons, 1971.

Moorehead, Alan. *Cooper's Creek.* New York: Harper & Row, 1963. Reprint. New York: Atlantic Monthly, 1987.

————. *The Fatal Impact: An Account of the Invasion of the South Pacific, 1767–1840.* New York: Penguin Books, 1968.

Scott, Ernest, ed. *Australian Discovery.* 2 vols. New York: E. P. Dutton, 1929. Reprint. New York: Johnson Reprint, 1966.

Sharp, Andrew. *The Discovery of Australia.* New York: Oxford University Press, 1963.

Shaw, Alan George Lewers. *The Story of Australia.* 2d ed. Mystic, Conn.: Lawrence Verry, 1966.

Maritime and the Pacific

Allen, Oliver E. *The Pacific Navigators.* Alexandria, Va.: Time-Life Books, 1980.

Beaglehole, John C. *The Exploration of the Pacific.* 3d ed. Palo Alto, Calif.: Stanford University Press, 1966.

————. *The Life of Captain James Cook.* Stanford: Stanford University Press, 1974.

————, ed. *The Journals of Captain James Cook on His Voyages of Discovery.* 3 vols. Cambridge: Hakluyt Society, 1955–67.

Brosse, Jacques. *Great Voyages of Discovery: Circumnavigators and Scientists, 1764–1843.* Translated by Stanley Hochman. New York: Facts on File, 1983.

Cameron, Ian. *Magellan and the First Circumnavigators of the World.* New York: Saturday Review Press, 1973.

Day, Arthur Grove. *Adventurers of the Pacific.* New York: Meredith Press, 1969.

————. *Explorers of the Pacific.* New York: Duell, Sloan and Pearce, 1966.

Dodge, Ernest S. *Beyond the Capes: Pacific Exploration from Captain Cook to the* Challenger, *1776–1877.* Boston: Little, Brown, 1971.

Dos Passos, John. *Easter Island.* Garden City, N.Y.: Doubleday, 1971.

Dousset, Roselene, and Etienne Taillemite. *The Great Book of the Pacific.* Translated by Andrew Mouravieff-Apostal and Edita Lausanne. Secaucus, N.J.: Chartwell Books, 1979.

Dunmore, John. *French Explorers in the Pacific.* Oxford: Oxford University Press, 1965.

Friis, Herman R., ed. *The Pacific Basin: A History of Its Geographical Exploration.* New York: American Geographical Society, 1967.

Gilbert, William Napier John, and Julian Holland. *Pacific Voyages.* Garden City, N.Y.: Doubleday, 1971.

Golder, F. A. *Russian Expansion on the Pacific, 1641–1850.* Cleveland: Arthur H. Clark, 1914. Reprint. Gloucester, Mass.: Peter Smith, 1960.

Kemp, P. K., and Christopher Lloyd. *The Brethren of the Coast.* London: Heinemann, 1960.

Kirker, James. *Adventures to China: Americans in the Southern Oceans, 1792–1812.* New York: Oxford University Press, 1970.

Moorehead, Alan. *The Fatal Impact: An Account of the Invasion of the South Pacific, 1767–1840.* New York: Penguin Books, 1968.

Oliver, Douglas L. *The Pacific Islands.* Cambridge: Harvard University Press, 1962.

Scammell, G. V. *The World Encompassed: The First European Maritime Enterprises c. 800–1650.* Berkeley and Los Angeles: University of California Press, 1981.

Schurz, W. L. *The Manila Galleon.* New York: E. P. Dutton, 1939. Reprint. New York: E. P. Dutton, 1959.

Sharp, Andrew. *Ancient Voyages in the Pacific.* London: Polynesian Society, 1957.

————. *The Discovery of the Pacific Islands.* Oxford: Oxford University Press, 1960.

Silverberg, Robert. *The Longest Voyage: Circumnavigators in the Age of Discovery.* New York: Bobbs-Merrill, 1972.

Smith, Bernard. *European Vision and the South Pacific, 1768–1850.* Oxford: Clarendon, 1960.

Van Loon, Hendrik Willem. *The Golden Book of the Dutch Navigators.* New York: Century, 1916. Reprint. Salem, N.H.: Ayer, 1977.

Ward, Ralph T. *Pirates in History.* Baltimore: York Press, 1974.

Withey, Lynne. *Voyages of Discovery: Captain Cook and the Exploration of the Pacific.* New York: William Morrow, 1987.

North America

Adamson, Hans Christian. *Lands of New World Neighbors.* New York: Whittlesey House, 1941.

BIBLIOGRAPHY

Andrews, Kenneth R. *The Spanish Caribbean: Trade and Plunder, 1530–1630.* New Haven: Yale University Press, 1978.

Bakeless, John Edwin. *The Eyes of Discovery: The Pageant of North America as seen by the First Explorers.* Philadelphia: J. B. Lippincott, 1950. Reprint. New York: Dover, 1961.

Bartlett, Richard A. *Great Surveys of the American West.* Norman: University of Oklahoma Press, 1962.

Batman, Richard. *The Outer Coast.* San Diego: Harcourt Brace Jovanovich, 1985.

Becker, Robert E., Henry R. Wagner, and Charles L. Camp, eds. *The Plains and Rockies: A Critical Bibliography of Exploration, Adventure and Travel in the American West, 1800–1865.* 4th ed. San Francisco: John Howell Books, 1982.

Berry, Don. *A Majority of Scoundrels.* New York: Harper, 1961.

Beston, Henry. *The St. Lawrence.* New York: Farrar & Rinehart, 1942.

Billington, Ray Allen. *The Far Western Frontier 1830–60.* New York: Harper & Row, 1956.

——. *Westward Expansion: A History of the American Frontier.* 2d ed. New York: Macmillan, 1960.

Blegen, Theodore C., ed. *Five Fur Traders of the Northwest.* St. Paul: Minnesota Historical Society, 1965.

Bolton, Herbert E. *The Spanish Borderlands: A Chronicle of Old Florida and the Southwest.* New Haven: Yale University Press, 1921.

——. *Spanish Exploration in the Southwest, 1542–1706.* New York: Scribner's, 1916.

Bourne, Edward Gaylord. *Spain in America, 1450–1580.* New York: Barnes & Noble, 1962.

Brebner, John Bartlet. *The Explorers of North America, 1492–1806.* 2d ed. Magnolia, MA: Peter Smith, 1965.

Bry, Theodore de. *Discovering the New World.* Edited by Michael Alexander. New York: Harper & Row, 1976.

Burpee, Lawrence J. *The Discovery of Canada.* Ottawa: Graphic, 1929. Reprint. Salem, N.H.: Books for Libraries, 1976.

——. *The Search for the Western Sea: The Story of the Exploration of Northwestern America.* rev. ed. Toronto: Macmillan of Canada, 1935.

Campbell, Marjorie Wilkins. *The North West Company.* Toronto: Macmillan of Canada, 1957.

Carse, Robert. *The River Men.* New York: Charles Scribner's Sons, 1969.

Carter, Hodding W. *Doomed Road to Empire: The Spanish Trail of Conquest.* New York: McGraw-Hill, 1963.

The Conquest of North America. Garden City, N.Y.: Doubleday, 1973.

Cook, Warren L. *Flood Tide of Empire.* New Haven: Yale University Press, 1973.

Cooke, Alan, and Clive Holland. *The Exploration of Northern Canada, 500–1920.* Toronto: Arctic History Press, 1978.

Corney, Peter. *Early Voyages in the North Pacific, 1815–1818.* Fairfield, Wash.: Ye Galleon Press, 1965.

Craner, Verner W. *The Southern Frontier, 1760–1782.* Ann Arbor: University of Michigan Press, 1956.

Crone, G. R. *The Discovery of America.* New York: Weybright and Talley, 1969.

Crouse, Nellis M. *In Quest of a Western Ocean.* London: J. M. Dent, 1928.

Cumming, William P., S. E. Hillier, David Beers Quinn, and G. Williams. *The Exploration of North America, 1630–1776.* New York: G. P. Putnam's Sons, 1974.

Cumming, William P., R. A. Skelton, and David Beers Quinn. *The Discovery of North America.* New York: American Heritage Press, 1972.

Cutter, Donald C. *The California Coast.* Norman: University of Oklahoma Press, 1969.

Descola, Jean. *The Conquistadors.* Translated by Malcolm Barnes. London: Allen & Unwin, 1954.

DeVoto, Bernard. *The Course of Empire.* Boston: Houghton Mifflin, 1952.

Discoverers of the New World. New York: American Heritage, 1960.

Dreppard, Carl. *Pioneer America: Its First Three Centuries.* Garden City, N.Y.: Doubleday, 1949.

Driver, H. E., ed. *The Americas on the Eve of Discovery.* Englewood Cliffs, N.J.: Prentice-Hall, 1964.

Duffus, R. L. *The Santa Fe Trail.* New York: Longmans, Green, 1930.

Eccles, W. J. *The Canadian Frontier, 1534–1760.* New York: Holt, Rinehart and Winston, 1969.

Elliott, J. H. *The Old World and the New, 1492–1650.* Cambridge: Cambridge University Press, 1970.

Faulk, O. B. *Land of Many Frontiers: A History of the American Southwest.* New York: Oxford University Press, 1968.

Gerhard, Peter. *The North Frontier of New Spain.* Princeton: Princeton University Press, 1982.

Gibson, Charles. *Spain in America.* New York: Harper & Row, 1966.

Gilbert, Bil. *The Trailblazers.* New York: Time-Life Books, 1973.

Gilbert, E. W. *The Exploration of Western America, 1800–1850.* Cambridge: Cambridge University Press, 1933.

Goetzmann, William H. *Army Exploration in the American West, 1803–1863.* New Haven: Yale University Press, 1959.

———. *Exploration and Empire: The Explorer and the Scientist in the Winning of the American West.* New York: Vintage Books, 1966.

———. *Exploring the American West, 1803–1879.* Washington, D.C.: Division of Publications, National Park Service, U.S. Department of the Interior, 1982.

———. *New Lands, New Men: America and the Second Great Age of Discovery.* New York: Viking, 1986.

Golding, Morton J. *The Mystery of the Vikings in America.* Philadelphia: J. B. Lippincott, 1973.

Gough, Barry M. *Distant Dominion: Britain and the Northwest Coast of North America, 1579–1809.* Vancouver: University of British Columbia Press, 1980.

Hafen, LeRoy, ed. *Mountain Men and Fur Traders.* Lincoln: University of Nebraska Press, 1982.

Hafen, LeRoy, and Ann W. Hafen. *The Old Spanish Trail.* Glendale, Calif.: Arthur H. Clark Co., 1954.

Hammer, Trudy J. *The St. Lawrence.* New York: Franklin Watts, 1984.

Hamskere, Cyril. *The British in the Caribbean.* Cambridge: Harvard University Press, 1972.

Hannon, Leslie F. *The Discoverers.* Toronto: McClelland & Stewart, 1971.

Haring, C. H. *The Spanish Empire in America.* New York: Harcourt Brace Jovanovich, 1963.

Helps, Sir Arthur. *The Spanish Conquest in America.* rev. ed. New York: AMS Press, 1966.

Hodge, Frederick Webb, and Theodore H. Lewis, eds. *Spanish Explorers in the Southern United States, 1528–1543.* New York: Barnes & Noble, 1965. Reprint. Austin: Texas State Historical Association, 1984.

Hoffman, Bernard G. *Cabot to Cartier: Sources for a Historical Ethnography of Northeastern North America, 1497–1550.* Toronto: University of Toronto Press, 1961.

Horgan, Paul. *Conquistadors in North American History.* New York: Farrar, Straus and Giroux, 1963.

Johnson, Adrian. *America Explored: A Cartographical History of the Exploration of North America.* New York: Viking/Studio Books, 1974.

Jones, Gwyn. *A History of the Vikings.* New York: Oxford University Press, 1968.

———. *The Norse Atlantic Saga: Being the Norse Voyages of Discovery and Settlement to Iceland, Greenland, America.* London: Oxford University Press, 1964.

Karamanski, Theodore J. *Fur Trade and Exploration: Opening the Far Northwest, 1821–1852.* Norman: University of Oklahoma Press, 1983.

Kendrick, Sir Thomas Downing. *A History of the Vikings.* New York: Barnes & Noble, 1968.

Kirkpatrick, Frederick A. *The Spanish Conquistadors.* 3d ed. Gloucester, Mass.: Peter Smith, 1963.

LaFeber, Walter. *The New Empire: An Interpretation of American Expansion, 1860–1898.* Ithaca, N.Y.: Cornell University Press, 1963.

Lang, James. *Conquest and Commerce: Spain and England in the Americas.* New York: Academic Press, 1975.

Lavender, David. *The Rockies.* New York: Harper & Row, 1968.

———. *The Way to the Western Sea.* New York: Harper & Row, 1988.

———. *Westward Vision: The Oregon Trail.* New York: McGraw-Hill, 1963.

Leach, Douglas E. *The Northern Colonial Frontier, 1607–1763.* New York: Holt, Rinehart and Winston, 1966.

BIBLIOGRAPHY

Logan, Donald F. *The Vikings in History*. New York: Barnes & Noble, 1983.

Masselman, George. *The Cradle of Colonialism*. New Haven: Yale University Press, 1963.

Meredith, Roberts, and E. Brooks Smith, eds. *Exploring the Great River: Early Voyagers on the Mississippi from DeSoto to LaSalle*. Boston: Little, Brown, 1969.

Milanich, Jerald T., and Susan Milbrath, eds. *First Encounters: Spanish Explorations in the Caribbean and the United States, 1492–1570*. Gainesville: University of Florida Press, 1989.

Mirsky, Jeannette. *The Westward Crossings: Balboa, Mackenzie, Lewis and Clark*. New York: Alfred A. Knopf, 1946. Reprint. Philadelphia: Richard West, 1978.

Morison, Samuel Eliot. *The European Discovery of America: The Northern Voyages, A.D. 500–1600*. New York: Oxford University Press, 1971.

———. *The Great Explorers: The European Discovery of America*. New York: Oxford University Press, 1978.

———. *Portuguese Voyages to America in the Fifteenth Century*. Cambridge: Harvard University Press, 1940.

Muller, Gerhard F. *Voyages from Asia to America*. Amsterdam: N. Israel, 1967.

Newman, Peter C. *Caesars of the Wilderness*. New York: Viking, 1987.

———. *Company of Adventurers*. New York: Viking, 1985.

Norman, Charles. *Discoverers of America*. New York: Thomas Y. Crowell Co., 1968.

Parkman, Francis. *France and England in America*. New York: The Library of America, 1983.

Pethick, Derek. *First Approaches to the Northwest Coast*. Vancouver: J. J. Douglas, 1976.

Phillips, Fred M. *Desert People and Mountain Men: Exploration of the Great Basin, 1824–1865*. Bishop, Calif.: Chalfant Press, 1977.

Prescott, William H. *The Complete and Unexpurgated History of the Conquest of Mexico and History of the Conquest of Peru*. New York: Random House, 1936.

Quinn, David Beers. *England and the Discovery of America, 1481–1620*. New York: Alfred A. Knopf, 1973.

———. *North America from Earliest Discovery to First Settlements: The Norse Voyages to 1612*. New York: Harper & Row, 1977.

———, ed. *North American Discovery circa 1000–1612*. Columbia: University of South Carolina Press, 1971.

Rasky, Frank. *The Taming of the Canadian West*. Toronto: McClelland & Stewart, 1967.

Rawling, Gerald. *The Pathfinders*. New York: Macmillan, 1964.

Rich, E. E. *The Fur Trade and the Northwest to 1857*. Toronto: McClelland & Stewart, 1967.

Sauer, Carl O. *The Early Spanish Main*. Berkeley: University of California Press, 1966.

———. *Sixteenth-Century North America: The Land and the Peoples as Seen by the Europeans*. Berkeley: University of California Press, 1971.

Savage, Henry, Jr. *Discovering America, Seventeen Hundred to Eighteen Seventy-Five*. New York: Harper & Row, 1979.

Severin, Timothy. *Explorers of the Mississippi*. New York: Alfred A. Knopf, 1967.

Sherwood, Morgan B. *Exploration of Alaska, 1865–1900*. New Haven: Yale University Press, 1965.

Smith, I. Norman. *The Unbelievable Land*. Ottawa: Queen's Printer, 1965.

Snell, Tee Loftin. *The Wild Shores: America's Beginnings*. Washington, D.C.: National Geographic Society, 1974.

Steensel, Maja Van. *People of Light and Dark*. Ottawa: Queen's Printer, 1966.

Stewart, George. *The California Trail*. New York: McGraw-Hill, 1962.

Terrell, John Upton. *Furs by Astor*. New York: William Morrow, 1963.

Todorov, Tzvetan. *The Conquest of America: The Question of the Other*. Translated by Richard Howard. New York: Harper & Row, 1984.

Townsend, John K. *Across the Rockies to the Columbia*. Lincoln: University of Nebraska Press, 1978.

Toye, William. *The St. Lawrence*. Toronto: Oxford University Press, 1959.

Trappers and Mountain Men. New York: American Heritage, 1961.

Viola, Herman J. *Exploring the West*. Washington, D.C.: Smithsonian Books, 1987.

Weddle, Robert S. *Spanish Sea: The Gulf of Mexico in North American Discovery, 1500–1685.* College Station: Texas A&M University Press, 1985.

Winsor, Justin. *Cartier to Frontenac: Geographical Discovery in the Interior of North America, 1534–1700.* New York: Cooper Square, 1970.

Wood, Peter. *The Spanish Main.* Alexandria, Va.: Time-Life Books, 1979.

Wright, Louis B., and Elaine W. Fowler, eds. *The Moving Frontier: North America Seen Through the Eyes of Its Pioneer Discoverers.* New York: Delacorte, 1972.

———. *West and By North: North America Seen Through the Eyes of Its Seafaring Discoverers.* New York: Delacorte, 1971.

South America

Arciniegas, Germán. *Germans in the Conquest of America: A 16th Century Venture.* Translated by Angel Flores. New York: Macmillan, 1943.

Boxer, Charles R. *The Golden Age of Brazil, 1695–1750.* Berkeley and Los Angeles: University of California Press, 1962.

Crone, G. R. *The Discovery of America.* New York: Weybright and Talley, 1969.

Cutright, Paul Russell. *The Great Naturalists Explore South America.* New York: Macmillan, 1940.

Descola, Jean. *The Conquistadors.* Translated by Malcolm Barnes. London: Allen & Unwin, 1954. Reprint. Fairfield, N.J.: Augustus M. Kelley, 1970.

Driver, H. E., ed. *The Americas on the Eve of Discovery.* Englewood Cliffs, N.J.: Prentice-Hall, 1964.

Goodman, Edward J. *The Explorers of South America.* New York: Macmillan, 1972.

Hanson, Earl Parker, ed. *South from the Spanish Main: South America Seen Through the Eyes of Its Discoverers.* New York: Delacorte, 1967.

Haskins, Caryl P. *The Amazon.* New York: Doubleday, 1943.

Hemming, John. *The Conquest of the Incas.* London: Macmillan, 1970.

———. *Red Gold: The Conquest of the Brazilian Indians.* Cambridge: Harvard University Press, 1978.

Kelly, Brian, and Mark London. *Amazon.* San Diego: Harcourt Brace Jovanovich, 1983.

Kirkpatrick, Frederick A. *The Spanish Conquistadors.* 3d ed. Gloucester, Mass.: Peter Smith, 1962.

Lang, James. *Conquest and Commerce: Spain and England in the Americas.* New York: Academic Press, 1975.

Lockhart, James. *The Men of Cajamarca: A Social and Biographical Study of the First Conquerors of Peru.* Austin: University of Texas Press, 1972.

Markham, Sir Clements. *The Conquest of New Granada.* London: Elder, 1912.

———, ed. *Early Spanish Voyages to the Strait of Magellan.* London: Hakluyt Society, 1911.

Morison, Samuel Eliot. *The European Discovery of America: The Southern Voyages, 1492–1616.* New York: Oxford University Press, 1974.

———. *Portuguese Voyages to America in the Fifteenth Century.* Cambridge: Harvard University Press, 1940.

Morse, Richard M., ed. *The Bandeirantes: The Historical Role of the Brazilian Pathfinders.* New York: Alfred A. Knopf, 1965.

Pocock, H. R. S. *The Conquest of Chile.* New York: Stein and Day, 1967.

Prescott, William H. *The History of the Conquest of Peru.* abdg. ed. New York: New American Library, 1961.

Severin, Timothy. *The Golden Antilles.* New York: Alfred A. Knopf, 1970.

Smith, Anthony. *Explorers of the Amazon.* New York: Viking, 1990.

Vigneras, Louis-André. *The Discovery of South America and the Andalusian Voyages.* Chicago: University of Chicago Press, 1976.

Von Hagen, Victor W. *The Golden Man: A Quest for El Dorado.* Lexington, Mass.: D. C. Heath, 1974.

———. *Realm of the Incas.* rev. ed. New York: New American Library, 1961.

———. *South America Called Them.* New York: Alfred A. Knopf, 1945.

BIBLIOGRAPHY

SPECIFIC WORKS

For the following explorers, additional works may be found in the suggested reading lists following their profiles:

Amundsen	Darwin	Magellan
Balboa	Drake	Nordenskiöld
Barth	Frémont	Parry
Bering	Frobisher	Peary
Burton	Gama	Pizarro
Cabot, J.	Hedin	Polo
Cartier	Hudson	Powell
Champlain	Humboldt	Soto
Clark	Ibn Battūta	Stanley
Columbus	Kingsley	Tasman
Cook, J.	Lewis	Teixeira
Coronado	Livingstone	
Cortés	Mackenzie	

Akeley, D. D.

Akeley, Delia. *J. T., Jr: the Biography of an African Monkey.* New York: Macmillan, 1928.

———. *Jungle Portraits.* New York: Macmillan, 1930.

Alexander the Great

Fox, Robin L. *The Search for Alexander.* Boston: Little, Brown, 1980.

Lamb, Harold. *Alexander of Macedon: The Journey to World's End.* Garden City, N.Y.: Doubleday, 1946.

Selincourt, Aubrey de. *The Campaigns of Alexander.* New York: Penguin, 1976.

Alvarado

Kelly, John E. *Pedro de Alvarado, Conquistador.* Port Washington, NY: Kennikat Press, 1971.

Amundsen

Partridge, Bellamy. *Amundsen.* London: Robert Hale, 1933.

Andrée

Adams-Ray, Edward, trans. *Andrée's Story: The Complete Record of His Polar Flight, 1897.* rev. ed. New York: Viking, 1960.

Putnam, George Palmer. *Andrée: The Record of a Tragic Adventure.* New York: Brewer & Warren, 1939.

Anza

Bolton, Herbert E. *Anza's California Expeditions.* 5 vols. New York: Russell & Russell, 1966.

———. *Outpost of Empire: The Story of the Founding of San Francisco.* New York: Alfred A. Knopf, 1931.

Teggart, Frederick J., ed. *The Anza Expedition of 1775–1776: Diary of Pedro Font.* Berkeley: University of California Press, 1913.

Ashley

Dale, Harrison C. *The Ashley-Smith Explorations and the Discovery of a Central Route to the Pacific, 1822–1829.* Glendale, Calif.: Arthur H. Clark, 1941.

Morgan, Dale L. *The West of William Ashley.* Denver: Old West, 1964.

Audubon

Audubon, John J. *Delineations of American Scenery and Character.* Reprint. Salem, N.H.: Ayer, 1970.

Ford, Alice, ed. *Audubon, By Himself.* Garden City, N.Y.: Doubleday, 1969.

Back

Back, George. *Narrative of the Arctic Land Expedition to the North of the Great Fish River, and along the Shores of the Arctic Ocean, in the Years 1833, 1834, and 1835.* Reprint. Edmonton: M. G. Hurtig, 1970.

Baffin

Markham, Clements R. *Voyages of William Baffin.* London: Hakluyt Society, 1881.

Baker

Hall, Richard. *Lovers on the Nile: The Incredible African Journeys of Sam and Florence Baker.* New York: Random House, 1980.

Middleton, Dorothy. *Baker of the Nile.* London: Falcon Press, 1949.

Banks

Beaglehole, J. C. *The* Endeavour *Journal of Joseph Banks.* 2 vols. Sydney: Angus & Robertson, 1962.

Carter, Harold B. *Sir Joseph Banks, 1743–1820.* Detroit: Omnigraphics, 1987.

Barbosa

Barbosa, Duarte. *The Book of Duarte Barbosa.* 2 vols. Translated by M. L. Dames. London: Hakluyt Society, 1921.

Barrow

Lloyd, Christopher. *Mr. Barrow of the Admiralty: A Life of Sir John Barrow, 1764–1848.* London: Collins, 1970.

Bartram

Cruickshank, Helen Gere, ed. *John and William Bartram's America.* Greenwich, Conn.: Devin-Adair, 1957.

Bates

Bates, Henry Walter. *The Naturalist on the River Amazon.* abdg. ed. Berkeley and Los Angeles: University of California Press, 1962.

Bell

Winstone, H. V. F. *Gertrude Bell.* New York: Quartet Books, 1978.

Bellingshausen

Bellingshausen, Fabian Gottlieb von. *The Voyage of Captain Bellingshausen to the Antarctic Seas, 1819–1821.* 2 vols. Cambridge: Hakluyt Society, 1945.

Bennett

Clarke, Basil. *Polar Flight.* London: Ian Allen, 1964.

Bingham

Bingham, Alfred M. *Portrait of an Explorer: Hiram Bingham, Discoverer of Machu Picchu.* Ames: Iowa State University Press, 1989.

Bingham, Hiram. *Lost City of the Incas.* 1948. Reprint. New York: Greenwood, 1981.

Bligh

Kennedy, Gavin. *Captain Bligh: The Man and His Mutinies.* London: Duckworth, 1989.

Mansir, A. Richard. *The Journal of Bounty's Launch.* Montrose, Calif.: Kittiwake, 1989.

McKinney, Sam. *Bligh: A True Account of the Mutiny Aboard His Majesty's Ship Bounty.* Blue Ridge Summit, Pa.: International Marine Publishing, 1989.

Nordhoff, Charles, and James Norman Hall. *Men Against the Sea.* Boston: Little, Brown, 1934.

———. *Mutiny on the Bounty.* Boston: Little, Brown, 1932.

———. *Pitcairn's Island.* Boston: Little, Brown, 1934.

Bonneville

Irving, Washington. *The Adventures of Captain Bonneville.* Boston: Twayne, 1977.

Boone

Bakeless, John. *Daniel Boone.* New York: William Morrow, 1939.

Elliot, Lawrence. *The Long Hunter: A New Life of Daniel Boone.* New York: Reader's Digest Press, 1976.

Flint, Timothy. *The Life and Adventures of Daniel Boone.* Cincinnati: U. P. James, 1958.

Bougainville

Hammond, David, ed. *News from New Cythera: A Report of Bougainville's Voyage 1766–69.* Minneapolis: University of Minnesota Press, 1970.

Thiery, Maurice. *Bougainville: Soldier and Sailor.* London: Grayson & Grayson, 1932.

Brendan

Ashe, Geoffrey. *Land to the West: St. Brendan's Voyage to America.* New York: Collins, 1962.

Severin, Timothy. *The Brendan Voyage.* New York: McGraw-Hill, 1978.

Bruce

Reid, James Macarthur. *Traveller Extraordinary, the Life of James Bruce of Kinnaird.* New York: W. W. Norton, 1968.

Burckhardt

Sim, Katharine. *Desert Traveller: The Life of Jean Louis Burckhardt.* London: Victor Gollancz, 1969.

Burke

Colwell, M. *The Journey of Burke and Wills.* Sydney and New York: P. Hamlyn, 1971.

BIBLIOGRAPHY

Byrd

Bernard, Raymond. *Hollow Earth.* New York: Citadel Press, 1976.

Byrd, Richard Evelyn. *Alone.* Reprint. Washington, D.C.: Island, 1984.

————. *Discovery: The Story of the Second Byrd Antarctic Expedition.* Reprint. Detroit: Gale, 1971.

————. *Little America.* New York: G. P. Putnam, 1930.

Hoyt, Edwin P. *The Last Explorer: The Adventures of Admiral Byrd.* New York: John Day, 1968.

Montague, Richard. *The First Flights over Wide Waters and Desolate Ice.* New York: Random House, 1971.

Rose, Lisle A. *Assault on Eternity: Richard E. Byrd and the Exploration of Antarctica.* Annapolis, Md.: Naval Institute Press, 1980.

Byron

Shankland, Peter. *Byron of the* Wager. New York: Coward, McCann & Geoghegan, 1975.

Cabeza de Vaca

Bishop, Morris. *The Odyssey of Cabeza de Vaca.* New York: Century, 1933.

Cabeza de Vaca, Álvar Núñez. *Adventures in the Unknown Interior of America.* Edited and translated by Cyclone Covey. Albuquerque: University of New Mexico Press, 1966.

Cabot, J.

Williamson, James A. *The Voyage of the Cabots and the English Discovery of North America.* London: Argonaut Press, 1929.

Cabot, S.

Beazley, Raymond. *John and Sebastian Cabot.* London: T. Fisher Unwin, 1898. Reprint. New York: Burt Franklin, 1964.

Kurtz, Henry. *John and Sebastian Cabot.* New York: Franklin Watts, 1973.

Williamson, James A. *The Cabot Voyages and Bristol Discovery Under Henry VII.* London: Hakluyt Society, 1962.

————. *The Voyage of the Cabots and the English Discovery of North America.* London: Argonaut Press, 1929.

Cabral

Greenlee, William Brooks. *The Voyage of Pedro Álvares Cabral to Brazil and India, from Contemporary Documents and Narratives.* London: Hakluyt Society, 1938.

Cabrillo

Kelsey, Harry. *Juan Rodriguez Cabrillo.* San Marino, Calif.: Huntington Library, 1986.

Cameron

Foran, William Robert. *African Odyssey: The Life of Verney Lovett Cameron.* London: Hutchinson, 1937.

Campbell

Wilson, Clifford. *Campbell of the Yukon.* Toronto: Macmillan of Canada, 1970.

Carteret

Wallis, Helen, ed. *Carteret's Voyage Around the World, 1766–1769.* London: Hakluyt Society, 1965.

Champlain

Bishop, Morris. *Champlain.* London: Macdonald, 1949.

Chirikov

Fisher, Raymond H. *Bering's Voyages: Whither and Why.* Seattle: University of Washington Press, 1978.

Müller, Gerhard Friedrich. *Bering's Voyages: The Reports from Russia.* Translated by Carol Urness. Fairbanks: University of Alaska Press, 1986.

Colter

Harris, Burton. *John Colter: His Years in the Rockies.* Basin, Wyo., Bighorn Book Co., 1977.

Cook, F.

Cook, Frederick Albert. *My Attainment of the Pole.* New York: Polar, 1911.

————. *Return from the Pole.* Edited by Frederick J. Pohl. New York: Pellegrini & Cudahy, 1951.

Freeman, Andrew A. *The Case for Doctor Cook.* New York: Coward-McCann, 1961.

Hunt, William R. *To Stand at the Pole: The Dr. Cook–Admiral Peary North Pole Controversy.* New York: Stein & Day, 1982.

Wright, Theon. *The Big Nail: The Story of the Cook–Peary Feud.* New York: John Day, 1970.

Cook, J.

Cook, Captain James. *Seventy North to Fifty South.* Edited by Paul W. Dale. Englewood Cliffs, N.J.: Prentice-Hall, 1969.

Fisher, Robin, and Hugh Johnston, eds. *Captain James Cook and His Times.* Seattle: University of Washington Press, 1979.

Vandercook, John W. *Great Sailor: A Life of the Discoverer James Cook.* New York: Dial, 1950.

Cousteau

Cousteau, Jacques-Yves, Frédéric Dumas, and James Dugan. *Silent World.* New York: Harper & Row, 1953.

Dugan, James. *Man Under the Sea.* New York: Harper & Row, 1956.

David-Neel

David-Neel, Alexandra. *My Journey to Lhasa.* Boston: Beacon Press, 1986.

Foster, Barbara M. *Forbidden Journey.* New York: Harper & Row, 1987.

Middleton, Ruth. *Alexandra David-Neel: Portrait of an Adventurer.* Boston: Shambhala, 1989.

Dezhnev

Fisher, Raymond. *The Voyage of Semen Dezhnev in 1648: Bering's Precursor.* London: Hakluyt Society, 1981.

Doughty

Doughty, Charles M. *Travels in Arabia Deserta.* 2 vols. London: Jonathan Cape, 1921.

Tabacknick, Stephen E. *Exploration in Doughty's Arabia Deserta.* Athens: University of Georgia Press, 1987.

Drake

Aker, Raymond. *Report of Findings Relating to Sir Francis Drake.* Palo Alto, Calif.: Drake Navigators Guild, 1976.

Heizer, Robert Fleming. *Francis Drake and the California Indians, 1579.* Berkeley: University of California Press, 1947.

Escalante

Bolton, Herbert E. *Pageant in the Wilderness.* Reprint. Salt Lake City: Utah Historical Society, 1972.

Briggs, Walter. *Without Noise of Arms: The 1776 Dominguez–Escalante Search for a Route from Santa Fe to Monterey.* Flagstaff, Ariz.: Northland Press, 1976.

Eyre

Eyre, John Edward. *Journals of Expeditions of Discovery into Central Australia and Overland from Adelaid to King George's Sound, 1840–41.* 2 vols. London: Boone, 1845.

Fawcett

Fawcett, Percy Harrison. *Lost Trails, Lost Cities.* Edited by Brian Fawcett. New York: Funk & Wagnall's, 1953.

Fleming, Peter. *Brazilian Adventure.* New York: Scribner's, 1960.

Fitzroy

Eisely, Loren. *Darwin's Century.* Garden City, N.Y.: Doubleday, 1958.

Moorehead, Alan. *Darwin and the* Beagle. New York: Harper & Row, 1969.

Flinders

Flinders, Matthew. *Narrative of His Voyage in the Schooner* Francis, *1798.* Edited by Geoffrey Rawson. London: Golden Cockerel Press, 1946.

Forster, J. R.

Forster, Johann Reinhold. *The* Resolution *Journal of Johann Reinhold Forster.* Edited by Michael Hoare. London: Hakluyt Society, 1982.

Foxe

Foxe, Luke. *North-West Fox or Fox from the North-West Passage.* London: B. Alsop and

BIBLIOGRAPHY

T. Fawcet, 1635. Reprint. New York: Johnson Reprint, 1965.

Franklin

Beattie, Owen, and John Geiger. *Frozen in Time: The Fate of the Franklin Expedition.* London: Bloomsbury, 1987.

Franklin, Sir John. *Narrative of a Journey to the Shores of the Polar Sea in the Years 1819–20–21–22.* Edited by Louis Melzack. 1819. Reprint. Edmonton: M. G. Hurtig, 1969.

———. *Narrative of a Second Expedition to the Shores of the Polar Sea in the Years 1825, 1826, and 1827.* Edited by Leslie H. Neatby. London: John Murray, 1828. Reprint. Edmonton: M. G. Hurtig, 1971.

Nanton, Paul. *Arctic Breakthrough: Franklin's Expeditions, 1819–1847.* Toronto: Clarke Irwin, 1970.

Owen, Ruderic. *The Fate of Franklin.* London: Hutchinson, 1978.

Sutherland, Patricia D. *The Franklin Era in Canadian Arctic History, 1845–1859.* Ottawa: National Museums of Canada, 1985.

Fraser

Fraser, Simon. *Simon Fraser: Letters and Journals, 1806–1808.* Edited by W. Kaye Lamb. Toronto: Macmillan of Canada, 1960.

Hutchinson, Bruce. *The Fraser.* New York: Rinehart, 1950.

Frémont

Eyre, Alice. *The Famous Frémonts and Their America.* Boston: Christopher Publishing House, 1961.

Gudde, Erwin G., and Elizabeth K. Gudde, eds. *Exploring with Frémont: The Private Diaries of Charles Preuss.* Norman: University of Oklahoma Press, 1958.

Frobisher

Stefansson, Vilhjalmur. *The Three Voyages of Martin Frobisher.* 2 vols. London: Argonaut, 1938.

Fuchs

Fuchs, Sir Vivian. *Of Ice and Men: The Story of the British Antarctic Survey, 1943–73.* Owestry, England: Anthony Nelson, 1982.

Fuchs, Sir Vivian, and Sir Edward Hillary. *The Crossing of Antarctica.* Boston: Little, Brown, 1958.

Garcés

Garcés, Francisco. *A Record of Travels in Arizona and New Mexico, 1775–1776.* Edited by John Galvin. San Francisco: John Howell Books, 1967.

Gilbert

Chidsey, Donald B. *Sir Humphrey Gilbert.* London: Hamish Hamilton, 1932.

Gilbert, Sir Humphrey. *The Voyages and Colonising Enterprises of Sir Humphrey Gilbert.* 2 vols. Edited by David Beers Quinn. London: Hakluyt Society, 1940.

Giles

Dutton, Geoffrey P. H. *Australia's Last Explorer: Ernest Giles.* London: Barnes & Noble, 1970.

Groseilliers

Nute, Grace Lee. *Caesars of the Wilderness: Médard Chouart, Sieur des Groseilliers and Pierre Esprit Radisson, 1618–1710.* New York: Appleton-Century, 1943. Reprint. St. Paul: Minnesota Historical Society, 1978.

Hakluyt

Blacker, Irwin R., ed. *Hakluyt's Voyages.* New York: Viking, 1965. Parks, George Bruner. *Richard Hakluyt and the English Voyages,* 2d ed. New York: Frederick Ungar, 1961.

Young, Delbert A. *According to Hakluyt.* Toronto: Clarke, Irwin, 1973.

Hall

Hall, Charles Francis. *Life with the Esquimaux.* Edited by George Swinton. Reprint. Edmonton: M. G. Hurtig, 1970.

Loomis, Chauncey. *Weird and Tragic Shores: The Story of Charles Francis Hall, Explorer.* New York: Alfred A. Knopf, 1971.

Hanno

Warmington, B. H. *Carthage.* New York: Frederick Praeger, 1966

Hearne

Hearne, Samuel. *A Journey to the Northern Ocean*. Edited by Richard Glover. Toronto: Macmillan of Canada, 1958.

Speck, Gordon. *Samuel Hearne and the Northwest Passage*. Caldwell, Idaho: Caxton Printers, 1963.

Henson

Angell, Pauling K. *To the Top of the World: The Story of Peary and Henson*. Chicago: Rand, McNally, 1965.

Henson, Matthew A. *A Black Explorer at the North Pole*. New York: Frederick A. Stokes, 1912. Reprint. New York: Arno Press, 1969.

Robinson, Bradley. *Dark Companion*. New York: Medill McBride, 1948.

Herbert

Herbert, Wally. *Across the Top of the World*. London: Longmans, Green, 1969.

Herodotus

Herodotus. *The Histories*. Translated by Aubrey de Selincourt. New York: Penguin, 1954.

Selincourt, Aubrey de. *The World of Herodotus*. Boston: Little, Brown, 1962.

Heyerdahl

Heyerdahl, Thor. *Early Man and the Ocean*. Garden City, N.Y.: Doubleday, 1979.

———. *Fatuttiva: Back to Nature on a Pacific Island*. New York: New American Library, 1976.

———. *Kon-Tiki: Across the Ocean by Raft*. New York: Garden City Books, 1950.

———. *The Ra Expeditions*. New York: New American Library, 1972.

Jacoby, Arnold. *Señor Kon Tiki*. Chicago: Rand McNally, 1967.

Hillary

Fuchs, Sir Vivian, and Sir Edmund Hillary. *The Crossing of Antarctica*. Boston: Little, Brown, 1958.

Hillary, Sir Edmund. *High in the Thin Cold Air*. Garden City, N.Y.: Doubleday, 1962.

———. *Nothing Venture, Nothing Win*. New York: G. P. Putnam, 1975.

Hind

Morton, W. L. *Henry Youle Hind*. Toronto: University of Toronto Press, 1980.

Hudson

Gerson, Noel Bertram. *Passage to the West: The Great Voyages of Henry Hudson*. New York: Messner, 1963.

Jolliet

Steck, Francis Borgia. *The Jolliet–Marquette Expedition, 1673*. Glendale, Calif.: Arthur H. Clark, 1928.

Kane

Corner, George. *Doctor Kane of the Arctic Seas*. Philadelphia: Temple University Press, 1972.

Elder, William. *Biography of Elisha Kent Kane*. Philadelphia: Childs & Peterson, 1958.

Mirsky, Jeannette. *Elisha Kent Kane and the Seafaring Frontiers*. Boston: Little, Brown, 1954.

Villarejo, Oscar M. *Dr. Kane's Voyages to the Polar Lands*. Philadelphia: University of Pennsylvania Press, 1965.

Kelsey

Kelsey, Henry. *The Kelsey Papers*. Edited by Arthur G. Doughty and Chester Martin. Ottawa: King's Printer, 1929.

Kingsley

Gwynne, Stephen. *The Life of Mary Kingsley*. London: Macmillan, 1932.

Kino

Kino, Eusebio Francisco. *Kino's Historical Memoir of Pimeria Alta, 1683–1711*. Translated by Herbert E. Bolton. Berkeley: University of California Press, 1948.

Lander

Hallett, Robin, ed. *The Niger Journal of Richard and John Lander*. New York: Frederick Praeger, 1965.

BIBLIOGRAPHY

La Pérouse

Allen, E. W. *The Vanishing Frenchman: The Mysterious Disappearance of La Pérouse*. Rutland, Vt.: Charles E. Tuttle, 1959.

Dunmore, John. *Pacific Explorer: The Life of Jean François de la Pérouse, 1741–1788*. Annapolis, Md.: Naval Institute Press, 1985.

La Pérouse, Jean François. *The First French Expedition to California: Lapérouse in 1786*. Edited and translated by Charles N. Rudkin. Los Angeles: Glen Dawson, 1959.

Rawson, Geoffrey. *Pandora's Last Voyage*. London: Longmans, 1963.

Larsen

Farrar, F. S. *Arctic Assignment: The Story of the St. Rock*. Toronto: Macmillan of Canada, 1974.

La Salle

Parkman, Francis. *La Salle and the Discovery of the Great West*. Boston: Little, Brown, 1942.

Terrell, John Upton. *La Salle: The Life and Times of an Explorer*. New York: Weybright and Talley, 1968.

Las Casas

Las Casas, Bartolomé de. *The Devastation of the Indies, a Brief Account*. Translated by Hera Briffault. New York: Seabury, 1974.

Leichhardt

Aurosseau, M. *Letters of F. W. Ludwig Leichhardt*. Cambridge: Cambridge University Press, 1970.

Mackenzie

Mackenzie, Alexander. *The Journals and Letters of Sir Alexander Mackenzie*. Edited by W. Kaye Lamb. Toronto: Macmillan of Canada, 1970.

MacMillan

Allen, Everett S. *Arctic Odyssey*. New York: Dodd, Mead, 1962.

MacMillan, Donald B. *Four Years in the White North*. Boston: Hale, Cushman, & Flint, 1933.

Magellan

Nowell, Charles E., ed. *Magellan's Voyage Around the World: Three Contemporary Accounts*. Evanston, Ill.: Northwest University Press, 1962.

Syme, Ronald. *Magellan, First Around the World*. New York: William Morrow, 1953.

Welch, Ronald. *Ferdinand Magellan*. New York: Criterion Books, 1956.

Zweig, Stefan. *The Story of Magellan*. Reprint. Philadelphia: Century Bookbindery, 1983.

Marcos de Niza

Hallenbeck, Cleve. *The Journey of Fray Marcos de Niza*. New York: Greenwood, 1949.

Maury

Lewis, Charles Lee. *Matthew Fontaine Maury, the Pathfinder of the Seas*. Annapolis, Md.: U.S. Naval Institute, 1927.

Maury, Matthew Fontaine. *Physical Geography of the Sea*. New York: Harper & Bros., 1855.

Williams, Francis Leigh. *Matthew Fontaine Maury: Scientist of the Sea*. New Brunswick, N.J.: Rutgers University Press, 1963.

McClintock

Markham, Clements. *The Life of Admiral Sir Leopold McClintock*. London: John Murray, 1909.

McClintock, F. L. *The Voyage of the "Fox" in the Arctic Seas: A Narrative of the Fate of Sir John Franklin and His Companions*. Reprint. Edmonton: M. G. Hurtig, 1972.

McClure

M'Clure, Robert Le Mesurier. *The Discovery of the North-West Passage*. Edmonton: M. G. Hurtig, 1969.

Osborn, Sherard. *The Discovery of the Northwest Passage by Captain Robert Le Mesurier M'Clure*. Edited by William C. Wonders. Reprint. Edmonton: M. G. Hurtig, 1969.

Mendaña de Nehra

Amherst, Lord of Hackney, and Basil Thompson. *The Voyage of Mendaña to the Solomon Islands in 1568*. London: Hakluyt Society, 1901.

Jack-Hinton, Colin. *A Search for the Islands of Solomon, 1567–1838*. Cambridge: Cambridge University Press, 1907.

Markham, Sir Clements. *The Voyages of Pedro Fernandez de Quirós.* London: Hakluyt Society, 1904.

Nansen

Hall, Anna Gertrude. *Nansen.* New York: Viking, 1940.

Hoyer, Liv Nansen. *Nansen: A Family Portrait.* Translated by Maurice Michael. Toronto: Longmans, Green, 1957.

Lewis, Lorna. *Nansen.* London: Thomas Nelson, 1937.

Nansen, Fridtjof. *Farthest North.* 2 vols. New York: Harper & Bros., 1898.

Särensen, J. *The Saga of Fridtjof Nansen.* New York: American-Scandinavian Society, 1932.

Shackleton, Edward. *Nansen the Explorer.* London: H. F. & G. Witherby, 1959.

Twiley, Charles. *Nansen of Norway.* London: Methuen, 1933.

Whitehouse, J. Howard. *Nansen: A Book of Homage.* London: Hodder & Stoughton, 1930.

Nobile

Nobile, Umberto. *My Polar Flight.* London: Muller, 1961.

Orellana

Carvajal, Gaspar de. *The Discovery of the Amazon According to the Account of Friar Gaspar de Carvajal, and Other Documents.* Edited by H. C. Heaton. New York: American Geographical Society, 1934.

Palliser

Spry, Irene M. *The Palliser Expedition.* Toronto: Macmillan of Canada, 1963.

Park

Lupton, Kenneth. *Mungo Park: The African Traveler.* New York: Oxford, 1979.

Park, Mungo. *The Travels of Mungo Park.* New York: E. P. Dutton, 1907.

Peary

Goodsell, John. *On Polar Trails: The Peary Expedition to the North Pole 1908–1909.* Austin, Tex.: Eakin, 1983.

Hobbs, William Herbert. *Peary.* New York: Macmillan, 1936.

MacMillan, Donald B. *How Peary Reached the Pole.* Boston: Houghton Mifflin, 1934.

Rawlins, Dennis. *Peary at the Pole: Fact or Fiction?* Washington: Robert Luce, 1973.

Wright, Theon. *The Big Nail: The Story of the Cook–Peary Feud.* New York: John Day, 1970.

Pigafetta

Paige, Paula Spurlin, trans. *The Voyage of Magellan: The Journal of Antonio Pigafetta.* Englewood Cliffs, N.J.: Prentice-Hall, 1969.

Pike

Pike, Zebulon Montgomery. *The Journals of Zebulon Montgomery Pike, with Letters and Related Documents.* Edited by Donald Jackson. 2 vols. Norman: University of Oklahoma Press, 1966.

Van Every, Dale. *The Final Challenge.* New York: William Morrow, 1964.

Ponce de León

Jerome, Father. *Juan Ponce de León.* Meinrad, Ind.: Abbey Press, 1962.

Przhevalski

Rayfield, Donald. *The Dream of Lhasa: The Life of Nikolay Przhevalsky (1839–88), Explorer of Central Asia.* Athens: Ohio University Press, 1976.

Ptolemy

Grasshoff, Gerd. *The History of Ptolemy's Star Catalogs.* New York: Springer-Verlag, 1990.

Purchas

Purchas, Samuel. *Purchas his Pilgrimes.* 20 vols. Glasgow: James MacLehose and Co., 1905–1907.

Quirós

Markham, Sir Clements. *The Voyages of Pedro Fernandez de Quirós.* London: Hakluyt Society, 1904.

BIBLIOGRAPHY

Radisson

Adams, Arthur T., ed. *The Exploration of Pierre Esprit Radisson.* Minneapolis: Ross & Haines, 1961.

Nute, Grace Lee. *Caesars of the Wilderness: Medard Chouart, Sieur des Groseilliers and Pierre Esprit Radisson, 1618–1710.* New York: Appleton-Century, 1943. Reprint. St. Paul: Minnesota Historical Society, 1978.

Radisson, Pierre Esprit. *Voyages of Peter Esprit Radisson.* New York: Burt Franklin, 1967.

Rae

Rich, E. E., and Alice M. Johnson, eds. *John Rae's Correspondence with the Hudson's Bay Company on Arctic Exploration, 1844–1855.* London: Hudson's Bay Record Society, 1953.

Richards, R. L. *Dr. John Rae.* Whitby, England: Caedmon of Whitby, 1985.

Raleigh

Buckmaster, Henrietta. *Walter Raleigh: Man of Two Worlds.* New York: Random House, 1964.

Lacey, Robert. *Sir Walter Raleigh.* New York: Atheneum, 1973.

Ross, Williamson, H. *Sir Walter Raleigh.* Reprint. New York: Greenwood, 1978.

Wallace, Willard M. *Sir Walter Raleigh.* Princeton: Princeton University Press, 1959.

Rasmussen

Freuchen, Peter. *I Sailed With Rasmussen.* New York: Viking, 1961.

Ricci

Ricci, Matteo. *China in the Sixteenth Century, in the Journals of Matteo Ricci, 1583–1610.* Translated by Louis J. Gallagher and S. J. Gallagher. New York: Random House, 1953.

Roggeveen

Roggeveen, Jacob. *The Journal of Jacob Roggeveen.* Edited by A. Sharp. Oxford: Clarendon University Press, 1970.

Rondón

Zahm, John A. *Through South America's Southland.* New York: Appleton, 1916.

Roosevelt

Roosevelt, Theodore. *Through the Brazilian Wilderness.* New York: Scribner's, 1914.

Ross

Dodge, Ernest. *The Polar Rosses: John and James Clark Ross and Their Explorations.* London: Faber & Faber, 1973.

Schnitzer

Manning, Olivia. *The Remarkable Expedition.* Garden City, N.Y.: Doubleday, 1985.

Smith, Iain R. *The Emin Pasha Relief Expedition.* Oxford: Clarendon, 1972.

Scoresby

Scoresby, William. *The Polar Ice.* Reprint. Whitby, England: Caedmon of Whitby, 1980.

———. *Remarks in the Probability of Reaching the North Pole.* Reprint. Whitby, England: Caedmon of Whitby, 1980.

Stamp, Tom, and Cordelia Stamp. *William Scoresby, Arctic Scientist.* Whitby, England: Caedmon of Whitby, 1976.

Scott

Huntford, Roland. *Scott and Amundsen.* New York: Atheneum, 1984.

Scott, Robert Falcon. *The Voyage of the* Discovery. 2 vols. Reprint. New York: Greenwood, 1969.

Wilson, Edward. *Diary of the* Discovery *Expedition to the Antarctic Regions, 1901–1904.* Edited by Ann Savours. London: Batsford, 1967.

———. *Diary of the "Terra Nova" Expedition to the Antarctic: 1910–1912.* Edited by H. R. King. New York: Humanities, 1972.

Serra

Ainsworth, Katherine, and Edward M. Ainsworth. *In the Shade of the Juniper Tree.* Garden City, N.Y.: Doubleday, 1970.

Geiger, Maynard. *The Life and Times of Fray Junípero Serra.* 2 vols. Washington, D.C.: Academy of American Franciscan History, 1959.

Tibesar, Antonine. *Writings of Junípero Serra.* 4 vols. Washington, D.C.: Academy of American Franciscan History, 1955.

Wise, Winifred E. *Fray Junípero Serra and the California Conquest.* New York: Scribner's, 1967.

Shackleton

Shackleton, Sir Ernest. *South: The Story of Shackleton's Last Expedition, 1914–1917.* London: William Heinemann, 1919.

Simpson

Simpson, Alexander. *The Life and Travels of Thomas Simpson, the Arctic Discoverer.* London: Richard Bentley, 1845. Reprint. Toronto: Baxter, 1963.

Sinclair

Lent, D. Geneva. *West of the Mountains: James Sinclair and the Hudson's Bay Company.* Seattle: University of Washington Press, 1963.

Smith, J. S.

Dale, Harrison C. *The Ashley–Smith Explorations and the Discovery of a Central Route to the Pacific, 1822–1829.* Glendale, Calif.: Arthur H. Clark, 1941.

Morgan, Dale L. *Jedediah Smith and the Opening of the West.* New York: Bobbs-Merrill, 1953.

Smith, J.

Barbour, Philip L. *The Three Worlds of Captain John Smith.* Boston: Houghton Mifflin, 1964.

Soto

Bourne, Edward G., ed. *Narratives of the Career of Hernando de Soto.* 2 vols. New York: Allerton, 1922.

Stark

Stark, Freya. *The Valley of the Assassins and Other Persian Travels.* Los Angeles: Jeremy P. Tarcher, 1983.

Stefansson

Berry, Erick. *Mr. Arctic: An Account of Vilhjalmur Stefansson.* New York: David McKay, 1966.

Diubaldo, Richard J. *Stefansson and the Canadian Arctic.* Montreal: McGill-Queens University Press, 1978.

Gregor, Alexander. *Vilhjalmur Stefansson and the Arctic.* Agincourt, Ontario: Book Society of Canada, 1978.

Hanson, Earl Parker. *Stefansson, Prophet of the North.* New York: Harper & Bros., 1941.

Le Bourdais, D. M. *Stefansson, Ambassador of the North.* Toronto: Harvest House, 1962.

Noice, Harold. *With Stefansson in the Arctic.* Toronto: Ryerson, 1943.

Stefansson, Vilhjalmur. *Discovery: The Autobiography of Vilhjalmur Stefansson.* New York: McGraw-Hill, 1964.

———. *The Friendly Arctic.* New York: Macmillan, 1943.

———. *My Life With the Eskimo.* New York: Macmillan, 1913.

Stuart

Mudie, Ian Mayleston. *The Heroic Journey of John McDouall Stuart.* Sydney: Angus & Robertson, 1968.

Sturt

Sturt, Charles. *Journal of the Central Australian Expedition, 1844–5.* London: Caliban Books, 1984.

Sverdrup

Fairley, T. C. ed. *Sverdrup's Arctic Adventures.* Toronto: Longmans, 1959.

Thesiger

Thesiger, Wilfred. *Arabian Sands.* London: Collins, 1983.

———. *The Last Nomad.* New York: E. P. Dutton, 1980.

———. *The Marsh Arabs.* London: Allen Lane, 1964.

Thompson

Holbrook, Stewart. *The Columbia.* New York: Rinehart, 1956.

Hopwood, Victor G., ed. *David Thompson: Travels in Western North America.* Toronto: Macmillan of Canada, 1971.

Thompson, David. *David Thompson's Narrative 1784–1812.* Edited by Richard Glover. Toronto: Champlain Society, 1962.

BIBLIOGRAPHY

Thomson

Rotberg, Robert J. *Joseph Thomson and the Exploration of Africa*. London: Oxford University Press, 1971.

Tinné

Gladstone, Penelope. *Travels of Alexine: Alexine Tinné, 1835–1869*. London: John Murray, 1970.

Torres

Markham, Sir Clements. *The Voyages of Pedro Fernandez de Quirós*. London: Hakluyt Society, 1904.

Vancouver

Anderson, Bern. *Surveyor of the Sea*. Toronto: University of Toronto Press, 1960.

Godwin, George. *Vancouver, a Life*. New York: D. Appleton, 1931.

Marshall, James Stirrat, and Carrie Marshall. *Vancouver's Voyage*. Vancouver: Mitchell, 1967.

Syme, Ronald. *Vancouver: Explorer of the Pacific Coast*. New York: William Morrow, 1970.

Verrazano

Murphy, Henry Cruse. *The Voyage of Verrazano: A Chapter in the Early History of Maritime Discovery in America*. Reprint. New York: Books for Libraries, 1970.

Wroth, Lawrence Counselman. *The Voyages of Giovanni da Verrazano, 1524–1528*. New Haven: Yale University Press, 1970.

Vespucci

Pohl, Frederick J. *Amerigo Vespucci: Pilot Major*. New York: Columbia University Press, 1944. Reprint. New York: Octagon, 1966.

Vespucci, Amerigo. *El Nuevo Mundo*. Eng. ed. Edited by Roberto Levillier. Buenos Aires: Editorial Nova, 1951.

———. *Letters of Amerigo Vespucci and Other Documents Illustrative of His Career*. Edited by Clements R. Markham. London: B. Franklin, 1894.

Vial

Loomis, Noel M., and Abraham P. Nasatir. *Pedro Vial and the Roads to Santa Fe*. Norman: University of Oklahoma Press, 1967.

Walker

Gilbert, Bil. *Westering Man: The Life of Joseph Walker, Master of the Frontier*. New York: Atheneum, 1983.

Wallace

Wallace, Alfred Russel. *A Narrative of Travels on the Amazon and Río Negro*. rev. ed. London: Ward & Locke, 1911.

Wallis

Carrington, Hugh, ed. *The Discovery of Tahiti: A Journal of the Second Voyage of H.M.S. "Dolphin" Round the World by George Robertson, 1766–1768*. London: Hakluyt Society, 1948.

Whymper

Whymper, Edward. *Scrambles Amongst the Alps*. 2d ed. London: John Murray, 1892.

———. *Travels Amongst the Great Andes of the Equator*. London: John Murray, 1892.

Wilkes

Hashell, Daniel. C. *The United States Exploring Expedition, 1838–1842, and Its Publications, 1844–1874*. New York: New York Public Library. Reprint. New York: Greenwood, 1968.

Jaffe, David. *The Stormy Petrel on the Whale*. Lanham, Md.: University Press of America, 1982.

Morgan, William J., et al., eds. *Autobiography of Rear Admiral Charles Wilkes, U.S. Navy, 1798–1877*. Washington, D.C.: Naval History Division, Department of the Navy, 1978.

Poesch, Jesse. *Titian Ramsey Peale, 1799–1885, and His Journals of the Wilkes Expedition*. Philadelphia: American Philosophical Society, 1975.

Stanton, William. *The Great United States Exploring Expedition of 1838–1842*. Berkeley and Los Angeles: University of California Press, 1975.

Tyler, David B. *The Wilkes Expedition. The First United States Exploration (1838–1842).* Philadelphia: American Philosophical Society, 1968.

Viola, Herman J., and Carolyn Margolis, eds. *Magnificent Voyagers: The U.S. Exploring Expedition, 1838–1842.* Washington, D.C.: Smithsonian Institution Press, 1985.

Wilkins

Grierson, John. *Sir Hubert Wilkins.* London: Robert Hale, 1960.

Thomas, Lowell. *Sir Hubert Wilkins.* New York: McGraw-Hill, 1961.

Wilkins, Sir Hubert. *Flying the Arctic.* New York: G. P. Putnam, 1928.

Wills

Colwell, M. *The Journey of Burke and Wills.* Sydney and New York: P. Hamlyn, 1971.

Xuan Zang

Waley, Arthur. *The Real Tripitaka.* New York: Macmillan, 1952.

Younghusband

Morris, Jan. *Farewell the Trumpets: An Imperial Retreat.* London: Penguin, 1979.

Seaver, George. *Francis Younghusband: Explorer and Mystic.* London: John Murray, 1952.

Younghusband, Sir Francis. *The Epic of Mount Everest.* New York: Longmans, Green, 1927.

INDEX

INDEX

INDEX

INDEX